The Art of the 20th Century

Protagonists, Movements and Themes of Art
from 1900 to the Present Day

The book has been published
thanks to the collaboration
and the contribution of

UniCredit Group

The Art of the 20th Century

2000 and Beyond
Contemporary Tendencies

SKIRA

Editorial Realisation

Design
Marcello Francone

Editorial Coordination
Emma Cavazzini

Copy Editor
Timothy Stroud

Layout
Serena Parini

Translation
Scriptum, Rome

Iconographic Research
Alessandra Mion

First published in Italy in 2009 by
Skira Editore S.p.A.
Palazzo Casati Stampa
via Torino 61
20123 Milano
Italy
www.skira.net

Printed and bound in Italy.
First edition

ISBN: 978-88-572-0128-3

Distributed in North America by Rizzoli International Publications, Inc., 300 Park Avenue South, New York, NY 10010, USA.
Distributed elsewhere in the world by Thames and Hudson Ltd., 181A High Holborn, London WC1V 7QX, United Kingdom.

The dossiers on the artists are the work of the following young scholars:

Leo Lecci (*L.L.*)
Domenico Quaranta (*D.Q.*)
Federica Tammarazio (*F.T.*)
Paola Valenti (*P.V.*)

The Unicredit & Art Project team are warmly thanked for their participation in the creation of the series

The Art of the 20th Century

2000 and Beyond

Contemporary Tendencies

Guide for Readers

The series *Art of the Twentieth Century*, whose roughly 2000 pages and as many illustrations provide a broad and complex overview of the movements, artists, works, and cultural phenomena characterizing the last century and the first decade of the new millennium, now reaches completion with *Contemporary Tendencies: 2000 and Beyond*. This final volume presents the multiform manifestations of art today and a selection of those artists who have made significant progress since the second half of the 1990s, gaining recognition or confirming their specific qualities in the early years of the twenty-first century.

The decision to dispense with a narrative text of art-historical and critical nature reconstructing the events, explorations and innovations of individual artists and groups was prompted by the fact that the contemporary scene is not only still in a fluid, inchoate state, but also in no way susceptible of systematic analysis and critical interpretation due to the lack of sufficient historical distance and detachment from the various creative experiences that have characterized the last few years. It was therefore decided to adopt a topical approach organized in thematic nuclei that are discussed at a theoretical and methodological level in individual essays. Each essay is then associated with those artists who are crucially engaged in the specific areas being examined. There are thus two parallel levels of reading: one of a broad and structured nature, the other offering a more detailed examination of the individual artistic experiences exemplifying the themes in question.

Essays

The series of essays opens with Lea Vergine's study of the changing geography of contemporary art: the shifting of the productive axis toward previously neglected areas of the world, the figures of the curator and the critic, female creativity, and Body Art. Nicolas Bourriaud then offers a richly detailed analysis of the themes and problems emerging in the post-medium era, with particular reference to installations, video and the media; Angela Vettese addresses the questions of identity, gender and vision of the self; and Klaus Honnef presents a rereading of the critical aspects of contemporary art and society.

These studies of a general character are followed by a number of specific analyses. Gabriella Belli examines the types and "poetics" of museums for and of contemporary art, Luca Molinari the increasingly close relations between architectural invention and the role of the contemporary arts, Paco Barragán the world-wide phenomenon of exhibitions and fairs of contemporary art, Walter Guadagnini the related subject of the art market and the role of foundations as new collectors, and Marco Scotini the relations between art and politics.

The series of essays ends with three addressing particular techniques of artistic expression. Filippo Maggia provides a stimulating overview of contemporary photography, Domenico Quaranta examines issues connected with the use of new media in contemporary art, and Valerio Terraroli suggests some possible links between the vocabulary of the decorative arts and contemporary artistic production.

Artists

The goal of presenting an emblematic and significant range of the artists emerging and establishing their positions over the last few years involved a selection process that gradually winnowed the candidates down to a "short list" of about one hundred names. While efforts were made to maintain a sort of balance between male and female, European and non-European, continuity and new forms of expression, the artists chosen were divided into macro thematic areas and have been presented within them in alphabetical order.

The areas identified regard themes connected with the following: the vision of time and the sense of memory; issues raised by the anthropology of globalization and the new definitions of gender; the relations between mankind and the environment; the new perception of space and architecture; artistic creativity as political commitment; the use of the body as a means of expression; developments determined by multimedia technology and the digital era.

The individual dossier for each artist comprises a biographical note, a summary of his or her artistic approach, and an analysis of the works presented in the illustrations.

Critical apparatus

The critical apparatus of the fifth volume consists of a concise bibliography in alphabetical order for the approximately one hundred artists featured in the different sections and an index of the names of the artists and works referred to in the essays and dossiers. The index is both a key tool of reference and a rich source of information, including not only the artists – together with biographical details and a chronological list of the works mentioned in the volume – but also historical and cultural figures, movements, groups, associations, exhibitions and magazines.

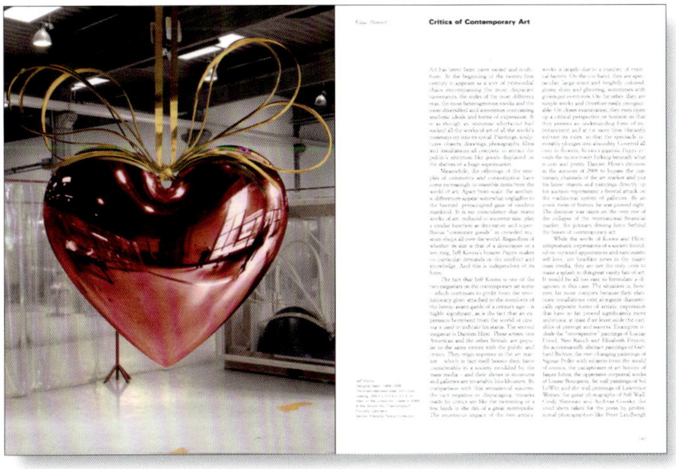

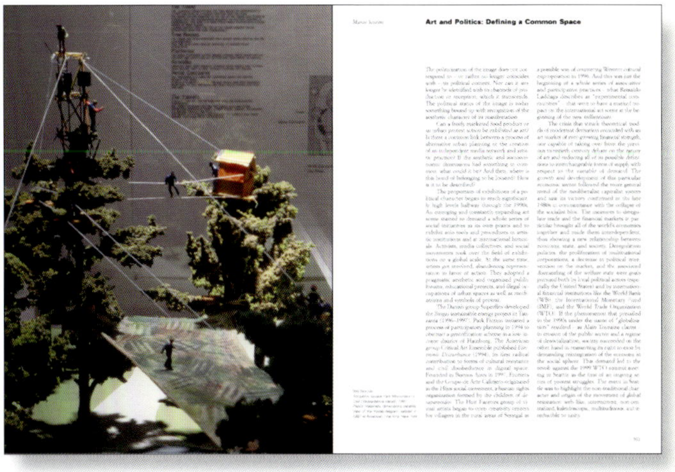

The essays

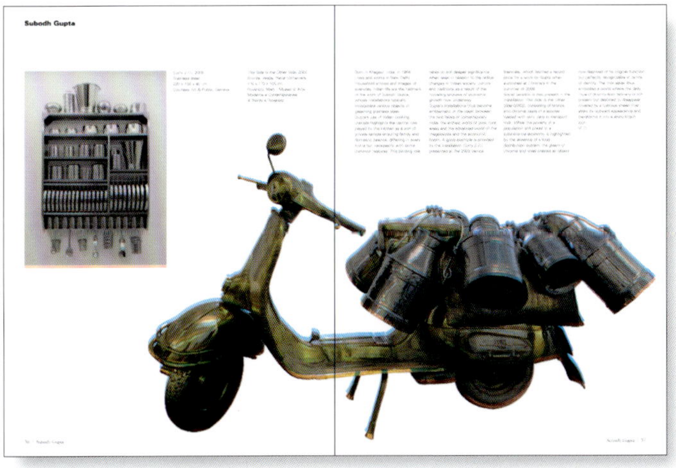

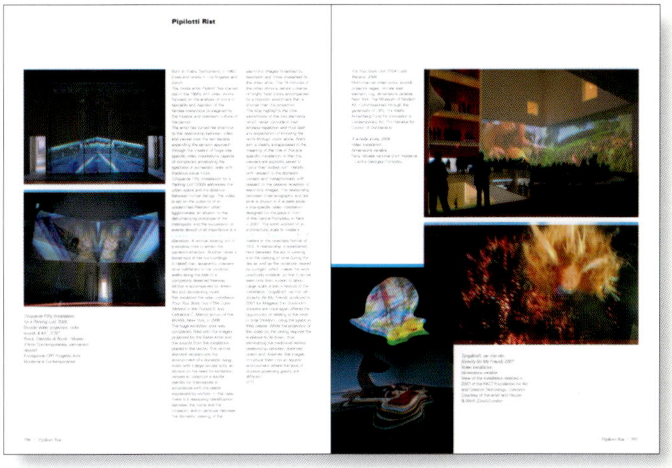

The entries

Scientific Committee

Gabriella Belli
Carlo Bertelli
Germano Celant
Ester Coen
Ida Gianelli
Valerio Terraroli, *editor of the work*

Contents

11 New Mutant Geographies in Art
Lea Vergine

29 Installation, Video, Actions: the Ascent of the Precarious in the Postmodern Era
Nicolas Bourriaud

Eija-Liisa Athila, Ai Weiwei, Darren Almond, Sophie Calle, Tacita Dean, Tracey Emin, Subodh Gupta, Emily Jacir, Rafael Lozano-Hemmer, Julie Mehretu, Mariko Mori, Nunzio, Wolfgang Tillmans, Francesco Vezzoli, Yang Fudong, Zhang Huan

81 Poetics of Identity: Notes on the Question of Gender, the Other, and the Self as Seen by the Self
Angela Vettese

Claude Closky, Martin Creed, Jimmie Durham, Jan Fabre, Damien Hirst, Jeff Koons, Takashi Murakami, Ernesto Neto, Adrian Paci, Richard Prince, Yinka Shonibare, Andreas Slominski, Simon Starling, Sam Taylor-Wood, Rirkrit Tiravanija, Rosemarie Trockel, Cesare Viel

141 Critics of Contemporary Art
Klaus Honnef

151 The Contemporary Museum: of Architecture and Meaning
Gabriella Belli

Doug Aitken, Pawel Althamer, Cecily Brown, Maurizio Cattelan, Wim Delvoye, Thomas Demand, Mark Dion, Giovanni Frangi, Liam Gillick, Dominique Gonzalez-Foerster, Sarah Lucas, Ron Mueck, Julian Opie, Gabriel Orozco, Paola Pivi, Neo Rauch, Tobias Rehberger, Gregor Schneider, Nedko Solakov, Luc Tuymans, Kara Walker, Matthias Weischer

217 New Frontiers Between Arts and Architecture. Projects, Experiences and Research at the Start of the Millennium
Luca Molinari

Banksy, Massimo Bartolini, Monica Bonvicini, Pedro Cabrita Reis, Gianni Caravaggio, Olafur Eliasson, Elmgreen & Dragset, Urs Fischer, Fischli & Weiss, Jeppe Hein, Thomas Hirschhorn, Carsten Höller, Huang Yong Ping, Eva Marisaldi, Lucy + Jorge Orta, Jorge Pardo, Tomas Saraceno, Arcangelo Sassolino, Rachel Whiteread

275 Neo-modernity, Neo-biennalism, Neo-fairism
Paco Barragán

293 The Art Market and New Forms of Art Collecting
Walter Guadagnini

301 Art and Politics: Defining a Common Space
Marco Scotini

Allora & Calzadilla, Atelier Van Lieshout, Regina José Galindo, William Kentridge, Shirin Neshat, Doris Salcedo, Santiago Sierra, Sislej Xhafa

333 Contemporary Photography, 2000–2009
Filippo Maggia

Ghada Amer, Matthew Barney, Vanessa Beecroft, John Currin, Marlene Dumas, Kiki Smith, Jeff Wall

359 Art and the New Media in the Post-Medium Era
Domenico Quaranta

Cory Arcangel, Cao Fei, Roberto Cuoghi, Douglas Gordon, Loris Gréaud, Pierre Huyghe, Eduardo Kac, Eva and Franco Mattes (0100101110101101.ORG), Steve McQueen, Carsten Nicolai, Philippe Parreno, Pipilotti Rist, Piotr Uklanski, Nico Vascellari

405 Contemporary Art and Decorative Arts: Technical Proofs of Connection
Valerio Terraroli

Appendix

413 Bibliography

417 Index of Names, Artists and Works of Art

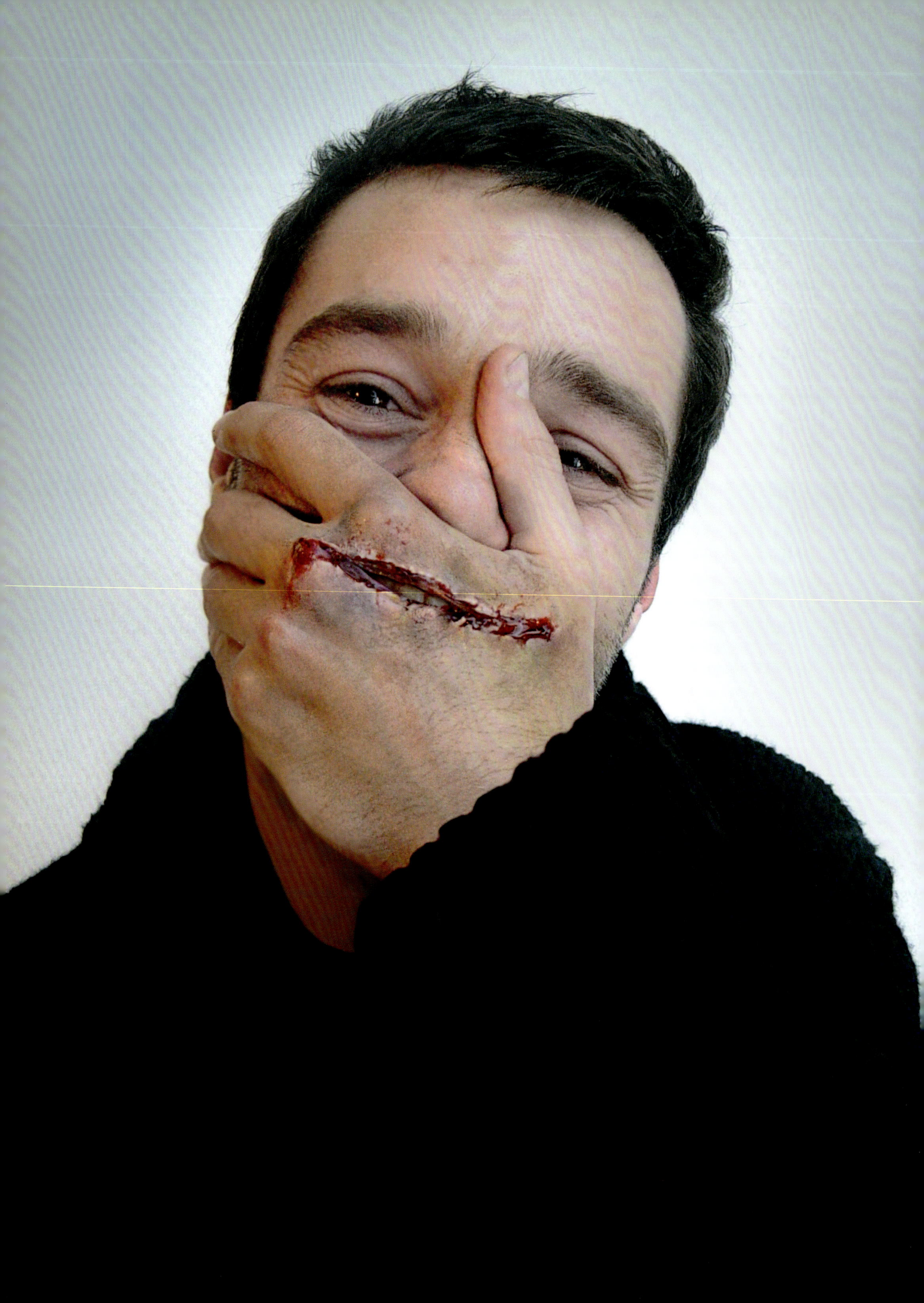

Lea Vergine

New Mutant Geographies in Art

"Some madmen tell the truth. Whoever tells the truth deserves to be followed. Therefore some people who deserve to be followed are madmen."
Antoine Arnauld

Artists are supported in their work by an irrationality that constitutes another sort of rule, a different and divergent view of the real world. They display self-worship, compensatory fantasies, compulsions, disturbing eccentricities. What is the origin of all this? I believe it originates in their pursuit of the idea of love. Because this is what art is: a shadow or an echo of love, an attempt to embody it. Artists toy with a quiet sort of madness that makes them bite the edges of things. And so they (and we) get round the knotty parts and go off on tangents of the theme, which is essentially always the same, namely the fear and strain of living.

Hence the impertinently "insignificant" inventions, the crazy gambles, and the sarcastic reversals: all speculations of a rhetorical cast – paradoxes, dilemmas, sophisms, and tautologies. Sometimes the impression is that artists are asking themselves once again what is the point of art and deciding that it is to find yourself. They meet their defeated selves and love them and save them and then lose them. This finding of the self with the self, concealed through the game of dream and art, often seems to have the same meaning as death. Artists feel death as something that idealizes or *romanticizes* life. Sometimes they are sadistic in the light and the darkness, the rapture and the blackness; sometimes they use cold and ruthless fury; sometimes they move under the cloak of irony, which is worn by self-pity and bears witness, as we know, to secret wounds.

We all do what we can, depending on how we manage to keep our balance, which is always very unsteady. Because the artist is a social error, already a figure of contrast and opposition. We are all discarded and have to start putting the pieces back together again every morning, whatever is left. This human characteristic is transferred into art, which is as always nothing other than the mirror of our fears and desires.

Any account of what has happened or been happening in the last ten years or so will point to a series of phenomena: the explosion of Chinese art in China and the West; the roles of antithetical (but now increasingly less so) figures like the critic and the curator; the undue confusion of art *tout court* and fashion; the increasingly massive presence of women artists and their great success on the market; the shift from *historical* performance (Body Art), with its use of the body as language, to forms of group representation, gaining in theatricality what is lost in confessional intimacy.

There has also been a rekindling of interest in figures from previous decades, reaching its peak for names like Francis Bacon, Louise Bourgeois, Gerhard Richter, Anselm Kiefer, Jan Fabre, and the Italian Giuseppe Penone.

"My way of drawing is like an obsession, sometimes maniacal and possessed. And series of works are needed to make this obsession clear. The oeuvre needs time to become obsessional. ... Obsession is a metaphor. So it will always evolve."
(Jan Fabre)[1]

Louise Bourgeois, whose fame began in 1982, is now unanimously regarded as a "classic," but one that appeals to the young and the very young. (She was born in 1911 and is still alive.) Devoid of any recognizable formal identity, scornfully indifferent to all social approval (success came very slowly), fashions, trends, and commercial considerations, extraneous to any aesthetic or moral imperative, her sculptures also have the highly exciting quality of natural indifference to the laughable. Like an ascetic, Bourgeois goes beyond the norms of worldly guarantees. She is of course not perfect, but perhaps the very essence of the artist lies in imperfection. Her charms include a gift for indirect, enigmatic assertion, playing with fire, getting the sparks flying, using whimsicality, riddles, and witticisms to disarm: all symptoms of python-like cunning to confuse those who must nearly always be transformed into accomplices. All of her paintings, drawings, installations, and sculptures seek to exorcise fear and death. Every work is imbued with compassion but there is no trace of

Roberto Cuoghi
Senza titolo, 2003
Color print, 18 x 13 cm
Courtesy Galleria Massimo De Carlo, Milan

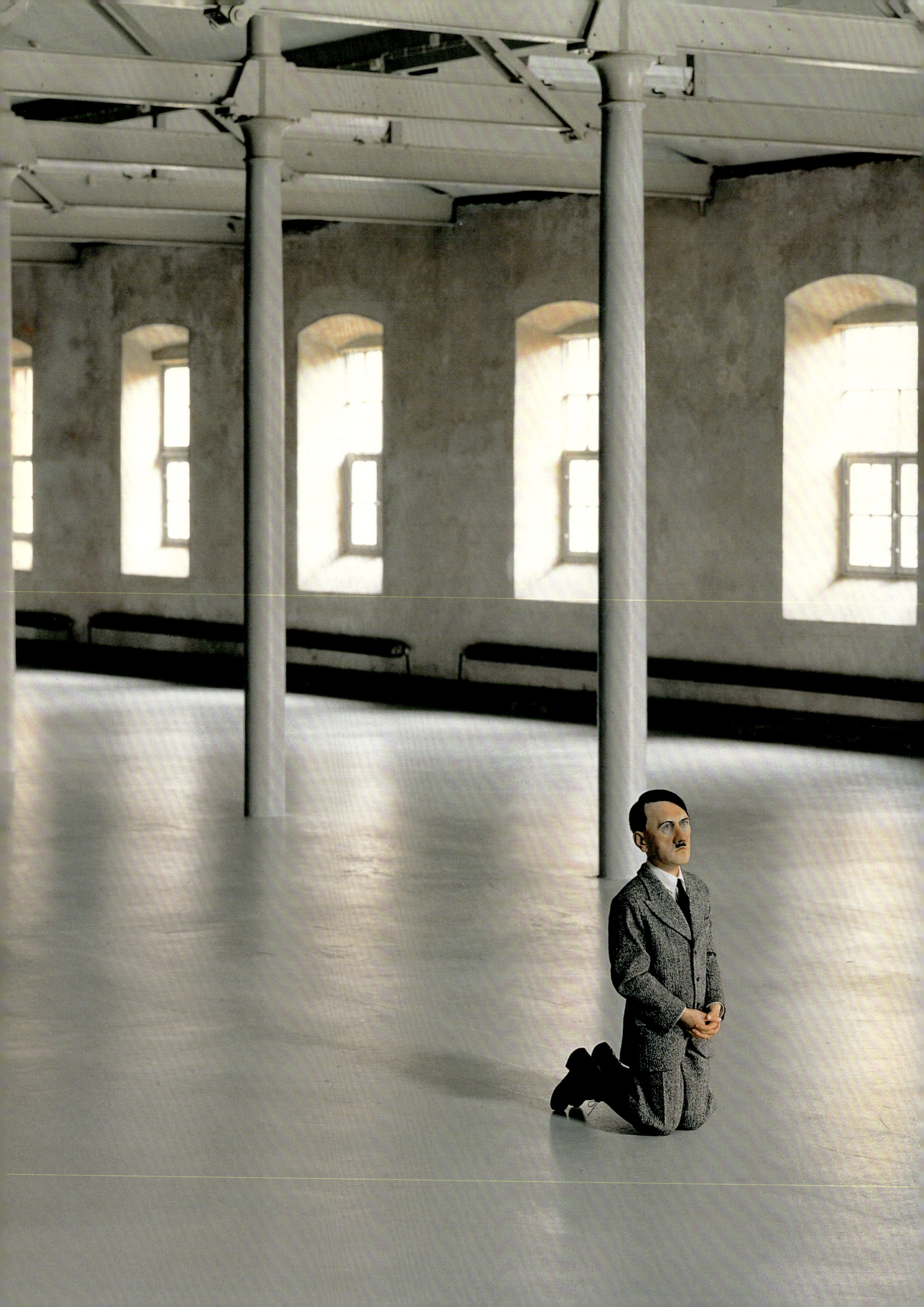

Maurizio Cattelan
Him, 2001
Resin, polyester, wax, hair, wool suit, 101 x 41 x 53 cm
Installation at Färgfabriken, Center for Contemporary Art and Architecture, Stockholm
Venice, François Pinault Collection

Paola Pivi
100 Cinesi, 1998
Performance, site-specific
Courtesy Galleria Massimo De Carlo, Milan

pietas or of abandonment unmarked by delirium. She works with exaggeration and excess. Exaggeration turns the frightening into the grotesque, as with *Spider*. The materials (wood, bronze, marble, rubber, cloth, glass, bones) take on metaphorical meanings and become wild, chaotic, and unbearable. The aim is to obtain a moment of irreparable angst capable of leaving the viewer dazed and wondering. This is the artist's intent and this has helped to make her a sort of revelation over the last decade.

"My sculpture allows me to re-experience the fear, to give it physicality so I am able to hack away at it. Fear becomes a manageable reality. Sculpture allows me to re-experience the past, to see the past in its objective, realistic proportion.
Fear is a passive state. The goal is to be active and take control. To move is from the passive to the active. If the past is not negated in the present, you do not live. You go through the emotions like a zombie, and life passes you by.
Since the fears of the past were connected with the functions of the body, they reappear through the body. For me, sculpture is the body. My body is my sculpture."
(Louise Bourgeois)[2]

"My childhood has never lost its magic, it has never lost its mystery, and it has never lost its drama. All my work in the past 50 years, all my subjects, have found their inspiration in my childhood."
(Louise Bourgeois)[3]

"My works are a reconstruction of past events. The past has become tangible in them; but at the same time they are created in order to forget the past, to defeat it, to relive it and to make it possible for the past to be forgotten. It means in short that the past, although I am intensely interested in it, is in fact sometimes far from being pleasant." (Louise Bourgeois)[4]

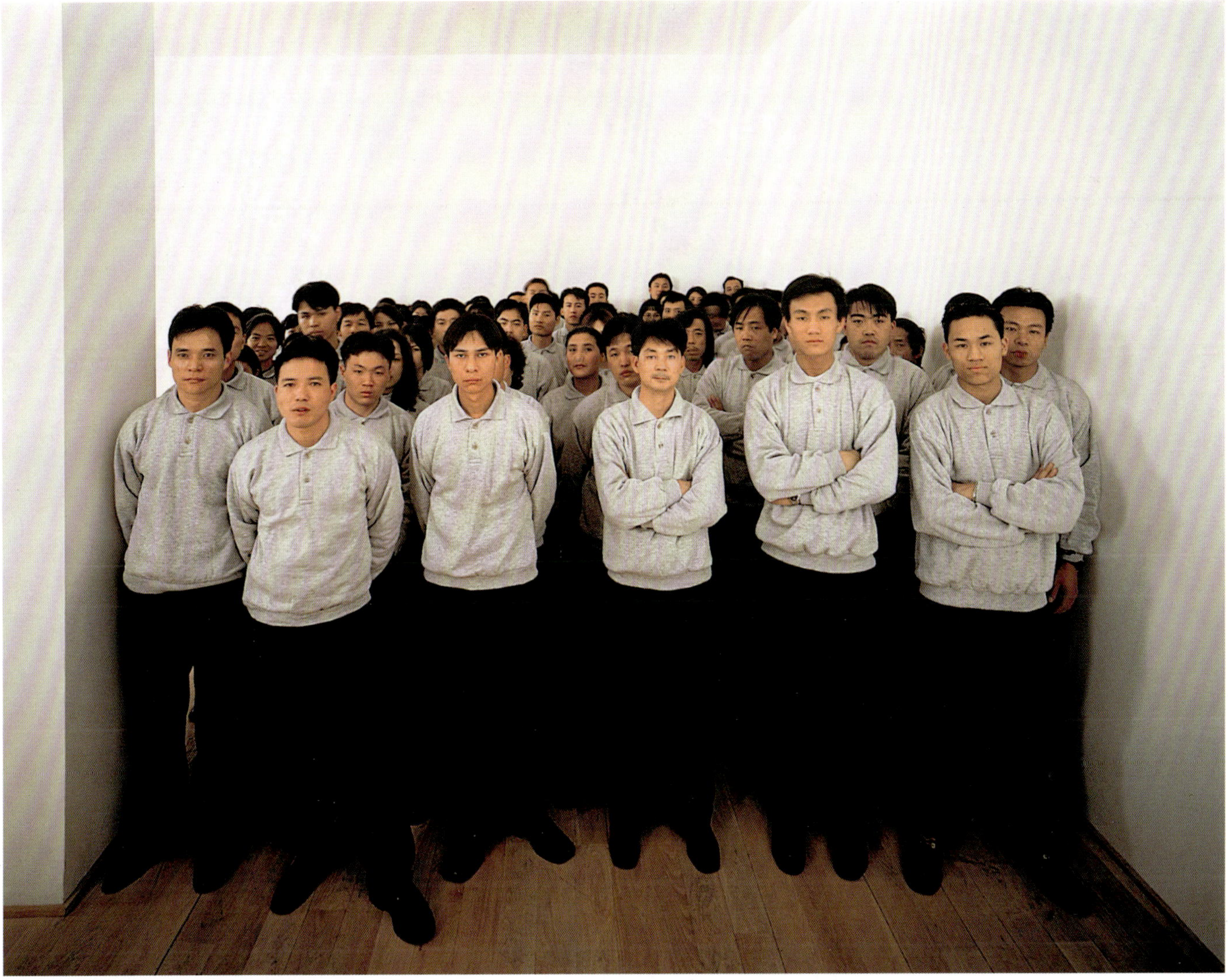

"The subject of pain is the business I am in. To give meaning and shape to frustration and suffering. What happens to my body has to be given a formal abstract shape. So, you might say, pain is the ransom of formalism. The existence of pain cannot be denied. I propose no remedies ox excuses.... I know I can't do anything to eliminate or suppress them. I can't make them disappear; they're here to stay. The *Cells* represent different types of pain: the physical, the emotional and psychological, and the mental and intellectual. Each *Cell* deals with fear. Fear is pain. Often it is not perceived as pain, because it is always disguising itself." (Louise Bourgeois)[5]

Then we have artists who started out in the early 1970s with Body Art and have gone on to diversify and expand the subject matter of their previous work. Among these, attention should be drawn at least to Urs Lüthi, Joan Jonas and Marina Abramovich.

Art is the Better Life is the title encompassing Lüthi's cycles of production all the way up to the casts, bronzes, and videos of the last few years. It tells us that even when plunged into the depths of despair, it is somehow impossible to be utterly and irrevocably devoid of hope. Irony and self-irony mitigate the bleakness of this condition. Consider the almost agonizing comic quality of the sequences of actions (housework, gymnastics for the overweight, etc.) shown on monitors scattered through the rooms of museums to display the uselessness of our compulsions, physical decline, a man observing and listening to himself and, in himself, all the rest of us. Lüthi covers his insistent investigation into how we can or must survive in the world today with a layer of "philosophical" sorrow while retaining the ecstatic attitude that makes him today – as it did yesterday – a true innovator in his grotesque fantasies of disguise. Another example of recent years is Joan Jonas.

"My first major prop was the mirror. The idea of a prop had a clear relationship to sculpture. Nevertheless, the prop in my work is usually not a piece of sculpture in itself but exists as a part of the whole ... From the beginning I thought of the sets as my sculpture, even if performance is most often my starting point...." (Joan Jonas)[6]

In *The Hand Reverts To Its Own Movement* (2007), a tribute to Aby Warburg, she orchestrates a long series of musical items (Satie, Jason Moran, and Hungarian songs), sounds and noises (executed by a group of pupils), and actors playing the part of shadows: disconnected fragments from which various reverberations spring, interchangeable images. There is a certain something that interacts, an element of "playing with" things. And then there is the artist, dressed in white, moving through the space with the gracefulness and bravado of a clown from the *commedia dell'arte*, painting child-like circles with a brush on silk panels; pantomime and theatrical action as process and not as finished work; a stage in her journey through the universe of folly, like bewilderment and

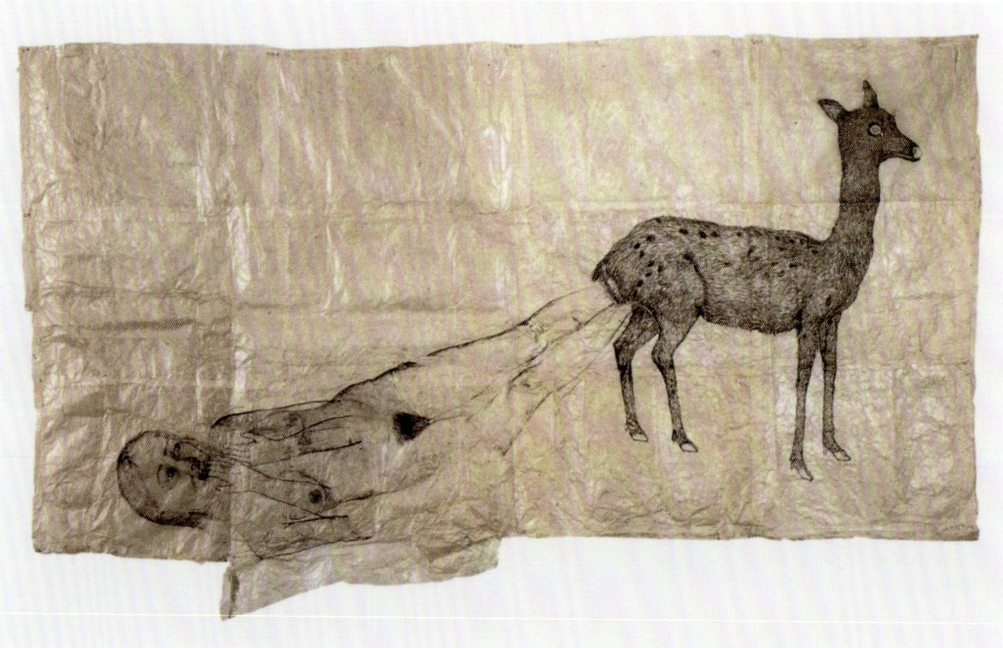

Kiki Smith
Born, 2001
Ink on paper, 750 x 1780 mm
Courtesy Barbara Gross Galerie, Munich

Zhang Huan
My Rome, 2005
Performance, Musei Capitolini, Rome
Courtesy of the artist

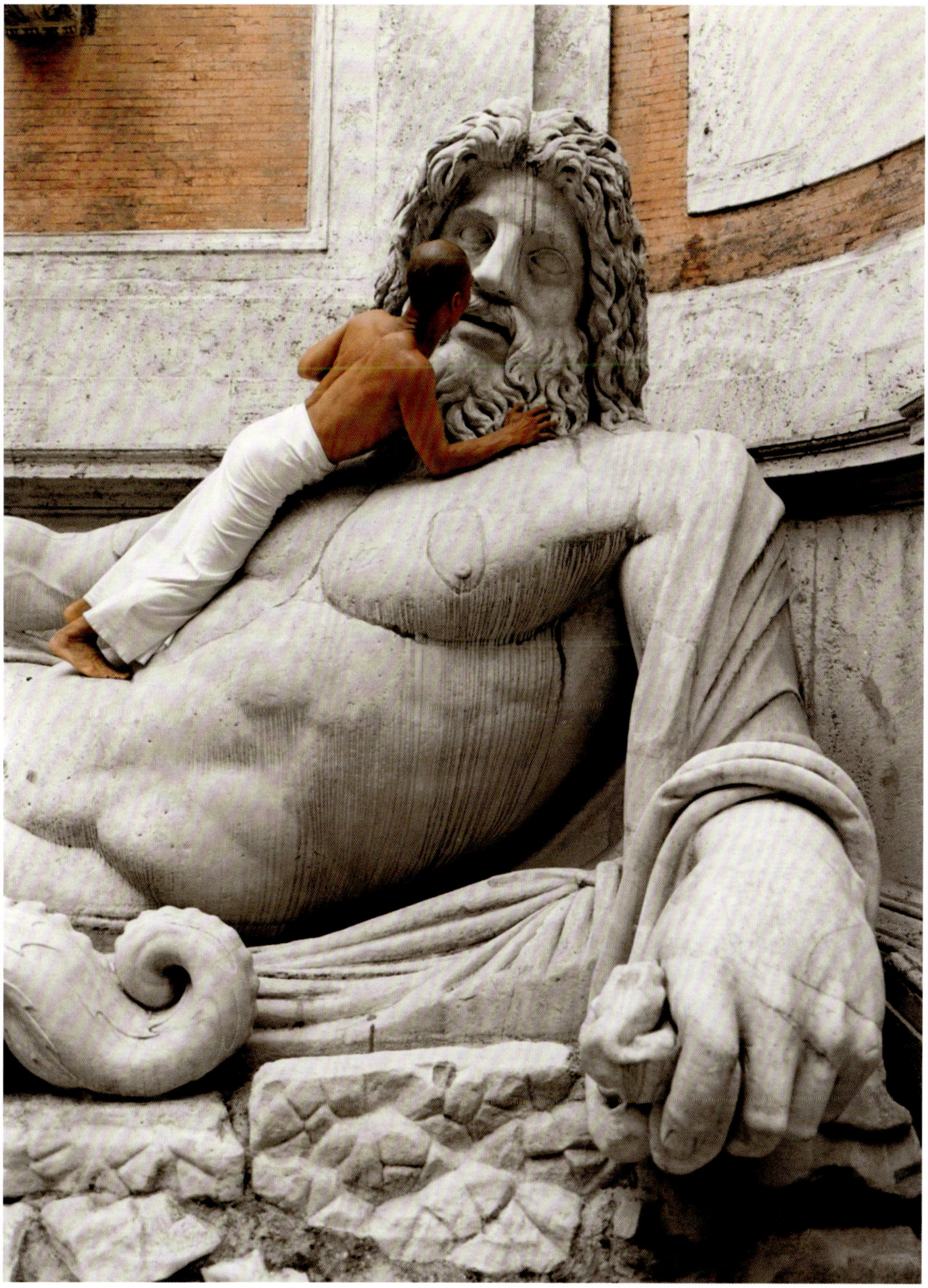

embrace. What Carmelo Bene might have called "disenchanted enchantment, a (dis)-concerto." This is what I meant when I spoke about performance losing the exquisitely diary-like components of previous years and turning them into group theatricality.

Marina Abramovich invites spectators to wear prosthetic devices designed to concentrate and strengthen the fields of energy around and within the person. With gestures of the utmost elegance, she situates imaginary forms in an arbitrary space. Energy lies buried but miraculously active in a certain area. Abramovich involves the public in a relationship of calculated flimsiness that is nevertheless always developed in minute detail: a sort of formal acupuncture.

Those leading us by the hand through the maze of the contemporary world, or rather thrusting the cruelty and injustice of life in our faces, are above all women, female rather than male artists. To summarize roughly, men philosophize while women embrace the role of the kamikaze. We refer to a generation now aged around fifty that attached great importance to the issue of women's rights. It is about thirty years since feminist protest and politics first exploded. Women

Santiago Sierra
250 cm Line Tattooed on Six Paid Persons, 1999
Performance at the Espacio Aglutinador, Havana, Cuba

Mona Hatoum
Hair Necklace, 1995
Hair, leather bust, and wooden base, 27 x 21 x 16 cm
Courtesy of the artist

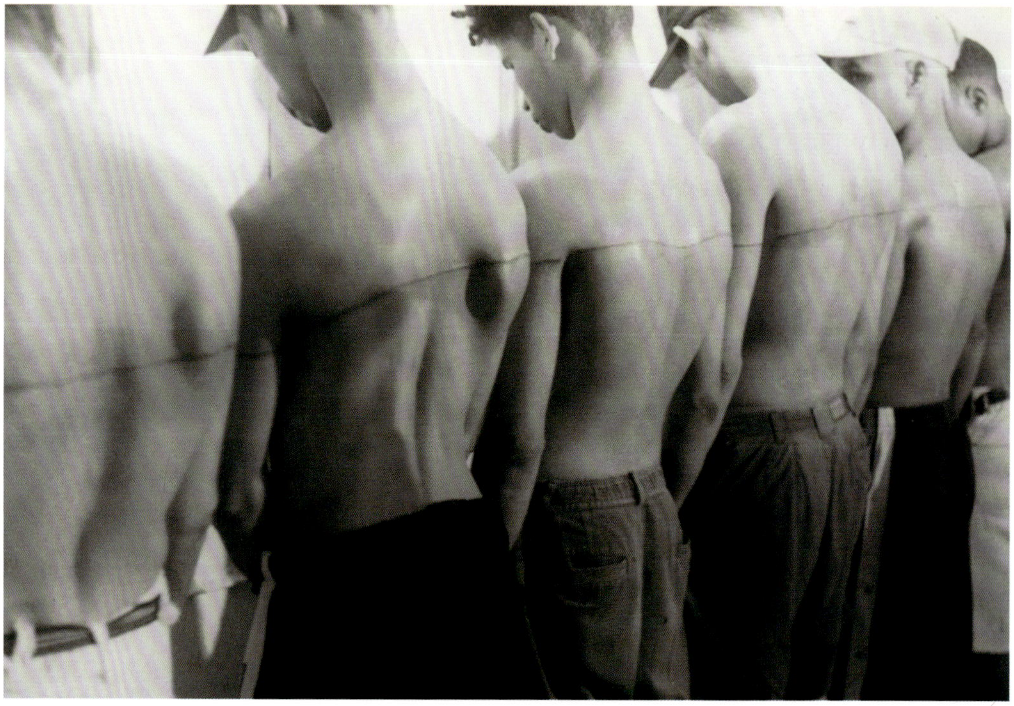

artists have tried to see the connections between these issues and social reality, especially the slices of the contemporary world undergoing the quickest change, thus giving rise to phenomena like the interest in the environment, multiethnicity, cultures of marginalization, and finally political terrorism. Calling into question their historical condition, women have overturned ideologies, conventions, and behavior patterns that are probably millennial. The decline of the American myth, the collapse of values, efficiency, and productivity, and the weakening of the ideal mortar that held an enormous community like the United States together, all this was first brought to attention by women artists some 20 years ago. They are the ones who first showed that the crushing effect of politics on culture had become the most worrying new element of the last few decades. The famous melting pot of races, languages, and lifestyles united by the fact of being American had given way to division and separation. A critical vision of the horror of the world arrived from women in art such as Jenny Holzer, Barbara Kruger, Annette Lemieux, Cady Noland, Cindy Sherman, Regina José Galindo, Tania Bruguera, Kiki Smith, Marzia Migliora, Janieta Eyre, and Francesca Woodman.

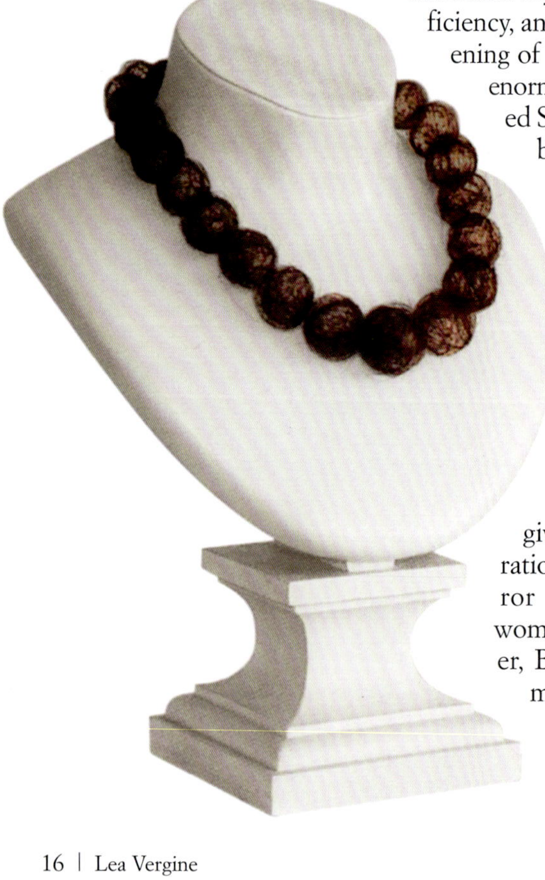

Allogenic – from the Greek *allogénes*, of another race – by natural condition, women artists have produced audacious and transparently painful emblems underscored with a ferocity that is nearly always connected with innocence. Consider the works of Mona Hatoum and Shirin Neshat.

The relations between art and fashion are generally translated into parodies or buffoonery in which the art mocks itself in a funfair setting with a huge and dangerous error in perspective. In the mega-shows held even in museums, the clothes are often placed on one side and the works of artists on the other, but even when they are mixed together, paintings and sculptures take on the appearance of merchandise on display and every possibility of aesthetic communication is immediately adulterated. The hypocrisy and ignorance of those who dish up things to wear and thought-provoking objects together result in writing and debate about contamination, multimediality, and the crossing of boundaries. In actual fact, it is only confusion and ideological fraud. While the introduction of clothes into museums (places for the preservation of ideas and inventions) is not necessarily scandalous in itself, the spectacle becomes embarrassing and disheartening when fashion designers are accorded the same status as artists in ridiculous farragoes. Shall we try to recall the difference between a couturier and a creator? The creator or artist is someone who originally invents a work, writes a text or composes a score. Creating is producing out of nothing and always has to do with something extraordinary and breathtaking, not with the blending of shapes and colors, no matter how tasteful. A tailor is someone of skill and talent who gives shape to new models. A designer is someone who produces clothes industrially on criteria taking up-to-date aesthetic trends into account. All the great couturiers of the last two centuries at least have been proud of their status, which has never interfered with the arts. The only correct relationship between art and fashion is that the makers of fashion buy the works of artists.

Another topical issue of recent years regards the "figure" of the critic and the curator or, as is claimed, the curator who acts as critic. The curator is not asked for insight into what is exhibited but essentially and exclusively to gather together material for exhibition. The idea of the curator, a figure of American derivation, being called upon to produce critical analyses is not only something unheard of but also, I would say, quite inconceivable. The curator is ultimately someone who invents nothing but possesses the managerial skills and contacts needed to organize an exhibition, which is something that all good gallery owners have always done. The major exhibitions organized by curators over the last few years, biennials above all, present no guiding idea. They are only required to favor some artists at the expense of others, a requisite linked to the predominant role of the collector in the art system today. It is the collector that decides the fate of art and represents the dominant class, which no longer feels the need to assert any specific quality or superiority but finds it quite sufficient to dominate. It is the collector that determines the taste of the market, the museums, art magazines, and galleries. Often transformed into obliging employees, small businessmen, and would-be tycoons, the critics jostling for position can be divided roughly into two groups: one forming strategic alliances at the service of American collectors and the other ready to switch sides at the drop of a hat in order to make a mark, no matter how short-lived.

There is constant conflict between those ready to shoulder the responsibility of freedom and those who shirk it out of fear, those who challenge the rules of general consensus and those who accept a regime of self-censorship that inculcates fear of one's own thoughts and frantic efforts to avoid any risk of non-unanimity. As Hans Magnus Enzensberger wrote, "Everyone has to pay for privileges: the client for recommendations, the politician for votes, the gangster for protection. The favorite, in order to remain such, must favor others in turn."

A curator is therefore not a critic but someone who practically lives on airplanes, setting off in search of new items and putting them on display, a far cry from those who study works of art in order to situate

Adrian Paci
Turn on, 2004
Video still, color, 3'33''
Courtesy francesca kaufmann

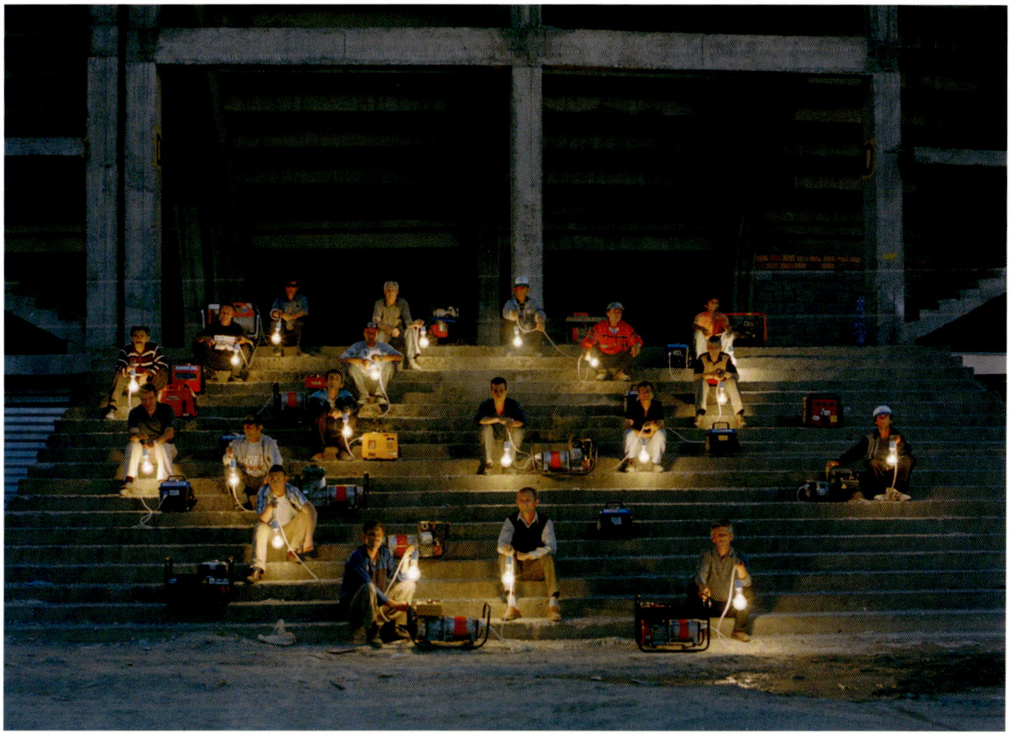

Hu Jieming
Raft of the Medusa No. 2 Liberty Leading the People, 2002
Color photograph, 200 x 300 cm
Courtesy of the artist and ShanghART Gallery, Shanghai

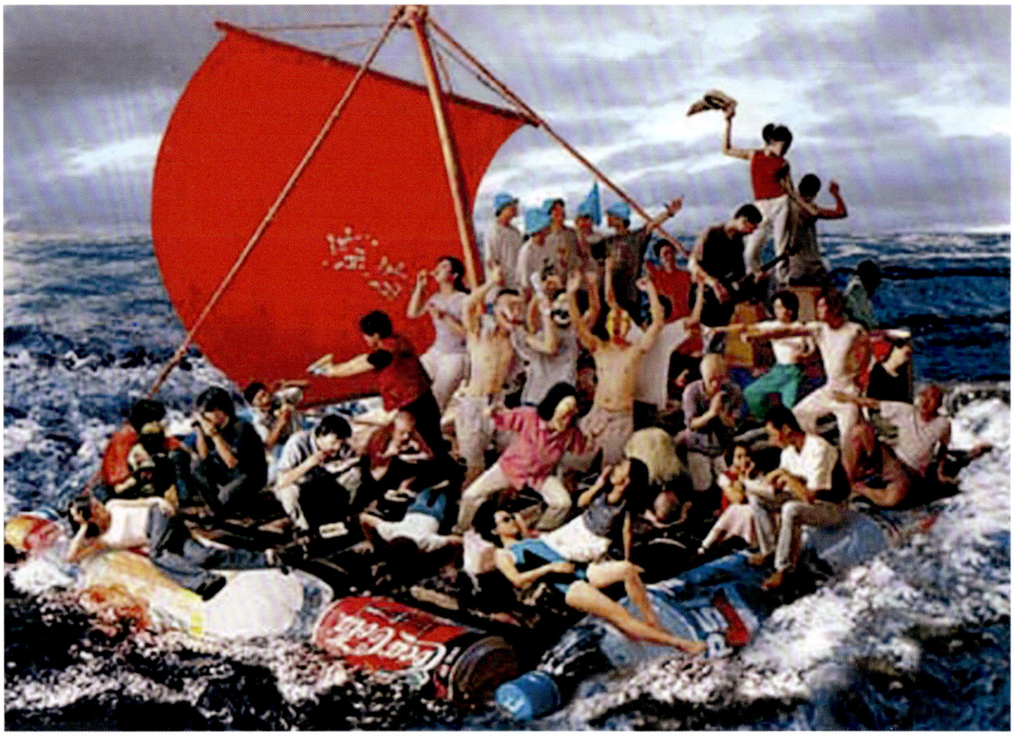

them in their historical, ideological, and philosophical context. The only exception was the late and greatly lamented Harald Szeemann, a scholar with a grounding in various disciplines, a gnostic oscillating between flagellation and libertinism, who gazed upon the sybaritic patristics and became the critic-creator of the finest and most challenging shows of the 1970s and 1980s.

Now that it has been and is consumed everywhere and has just *gone out of fashion*, we can try to formulate a hypothesis about contemporary Chinese art and draw attention to the certainly extraordinary works of Zhang Huan, Wang Qingsong, Chien-Chi-Chang, Yang Fudong, Li Wei, Chen Zhen, Lin Tianmiao, and Liu Zheng. Young and not so young, female and male, skilled above all in the use of photography and video, they are not artists amenable to Eastern conventions, to spectacular or ceremonious rhetoric. Nor do they focus exclusively on Western themes. Theirs is instead a vision in which the lineaments of a Taoist civilization encounter the horrors of today and clash with the scars in the social fabric of the China of the twenty-first century. Behind this there is always the sophisticated manner of high tradition (Tartar emperors and Tibetan magic). Above all, the 30-year-olds focus on splinters of this world and the one beyond, cause astonishment, engender bewilderment, and do so not only with imperturbable detachment but also with unsuspected freshness and nonchalance. Consider the works of Cui Xiuwen, Hu Jieming, and Shi Xinning. The Chinese world is in fact one that can often be read as a vision: fragments of a life that is no longer such because it is dead. In their accumulation of images and emblems from the lost world behind them as well as hybrid forms, they are perhaps inventing something that is more than a *mannerism*.

Let us briefly recapitulate the stages of the phenomenon of China. Four months before the tragic repression of Tiananmen Square in Beijing, the first *Avant-Garde China* exhibition opened with all the official trappings in 1989. In the 1990s, London exhibited the works of Yu Youhan, Li Shan, and Wang Guangyi as "political pop," the work of Liu Xiaodong as "rogue cynicism," the work of Zhang Xiaogang as "wounded romantic spirit," and the work of Wang Jianwei as "emotional bondage."

The floodgates burst definitively when Harald Szeemann presented 19 Chinese artists at the Venice Biennale in 1999 and still others at the 2001 Biennale. A great blossoming of catalogues began in the West, and London, Berlin, Cologne, Lucerne, and Milan were established as the most accredited centers of the market from 2004 on. In conclusion, what does the art arriving from China represent today? It neither reveals the mystery of the Orient nor presents itself as the prototype of a new conception of art. It sometimes exhibits elegant ruins and traces of bygone splendors or some archaic anguish. It attacks the divide between the desires of individuals and the schizoid strategy of social conventions. In this sense, the violence it also conveys – suffice it to recall the corporeal ferocity of Ma Liuming, Zhu Ming, Liu Jin, Li Wei, Huang Yan, Chen Lingyang, Liu Zheng, and Song Yongping – is paradoxically transformed into soft and gentle communication of a mysterious and almost angelic nature.

"When I was in Beijing, I worked almost exclusively underground; I didn't have any freedom in my creations. When I moved to New York, nonprofit public organizations began sponsoring my performances. It is the contrast between heaven and hell. Contemporary art is an important part of the mainstream. As a contemporary artist, I should have felt like a fish swimming in water with ease and comfort. However, this was not so. Too much 'freedom' makes a person 'nervous'.
Every place has its advantages. Problems and pressures in China are concrete. They are a visible reality. ... Every second one can feel that society has advanced to such a degree that it only creates worry and fear in people. Everyone is extremely skeptical. Homeless people and insane people are everywhere on New York streets. White-collar workers and powerful people look like mannequins. We live in a sick time.
I live here as a Henanese in New York, with my own culture and personality.

Yasumasa Morimura
A Requiem; Dream of Universe, Albert 2, 2007
Gelatin silver print, 120 x 96 cm
Courtesy of the artist

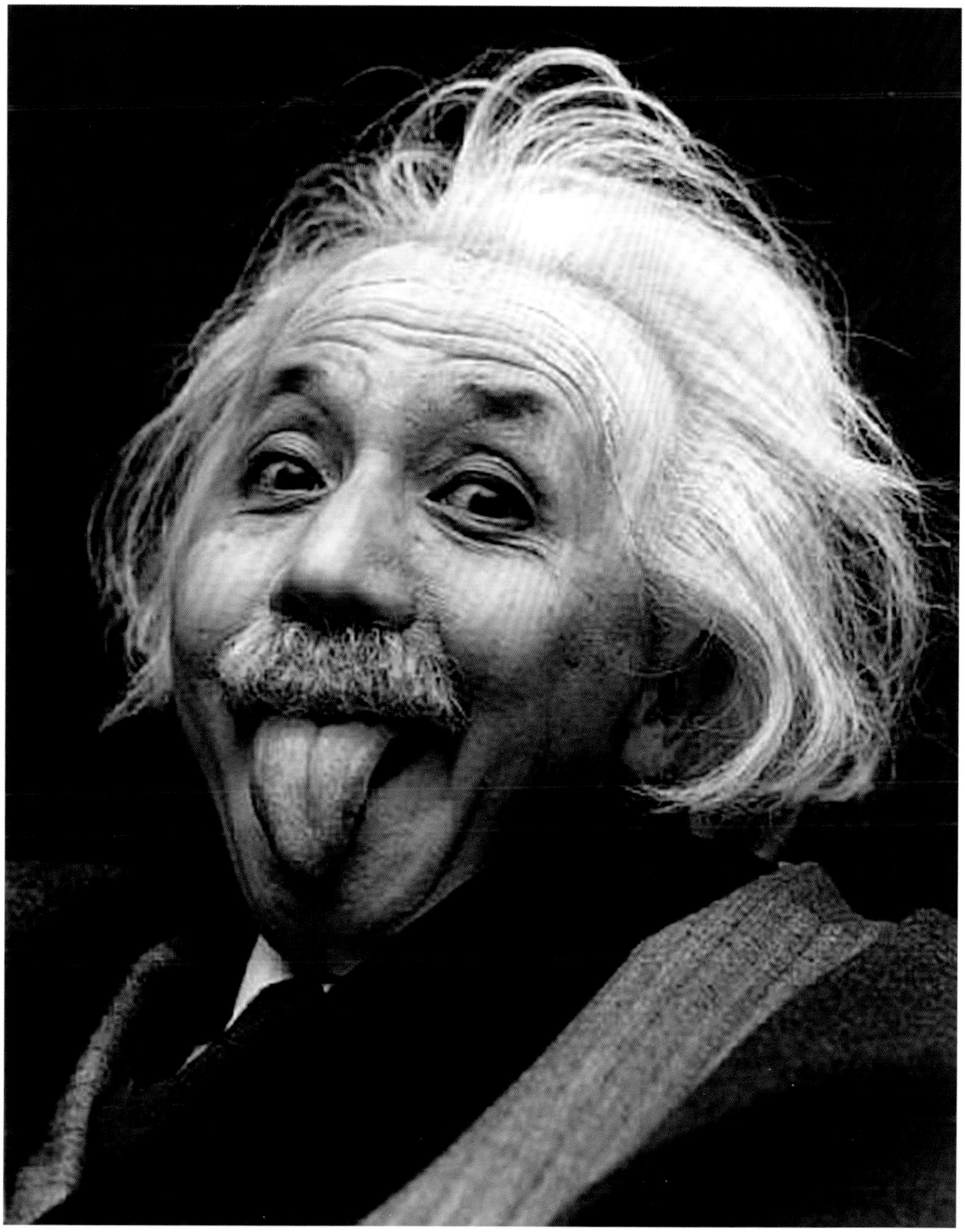

Identification is an issue that no one can avoid. When Westerners discuss contemporary art in China, they talk about 'China' first and 'art' later. This, to some degree, may say something about the status of contemporary Chinese art in the world. Besides keeping a distinctive style, artists are also representatives of a culture. I bring my body to art because I realize that the body is the most direct way of interacting with society. The body is the evidence of identification, and the solid self is the most essential part of a work of art. My mind determines the state of my body and its meaning. My body is the medium of my art." (Zhang Huan)[7]

There are some artists that have taken up an eccentric and provocative position in the Western figurative tradition. Belonging only in a manner of speaking to the tradition of visual art, they manifestly stray beyond its boundaries with boldness and a measure of gentle insolence, and prove to be only peripherally linked to the movements with which they are associated (ranging from Body Art to performance, Video Art, and so on). Yasumasa Morimura, for example, reaches the peak of the concepts of disguise and camouflage in his photographic portraits. Somewhere between Hoffmann's princess, Cardinal Pirelli, Dante Rossetti, and Jeremy Irons imitating Madame Butterfly, the Japanese artist displays inexhaustible verve in presenting the Western female par excellence without forgoing elements either of harmonious Eastern madness or of Pre-Raphaelite decadentism. His linguistic challenges are nearly always astonishing for their precision and relevance: Hitler, Stalin, Mao, Einstein, Gilbert& George, all results of a sarcastic and spine-chilling character.

Matthew Barney, a creature who combines elements of an indecipherable and ambiguous nature with something great and romantic, began a series of films entitled the *Cremaster Cycle* (the cremaster being the muscle that controls the position and temperature of the testicles) more than 15 years ago. A sort of humanoid disguised with ar-

Marzia Migliora
Bianca e il suo contrario / Bianca and her Opposite, 2007
Lambda print, 80 x 80 cm
Courtesy Lia Rumma, Milan-Naples

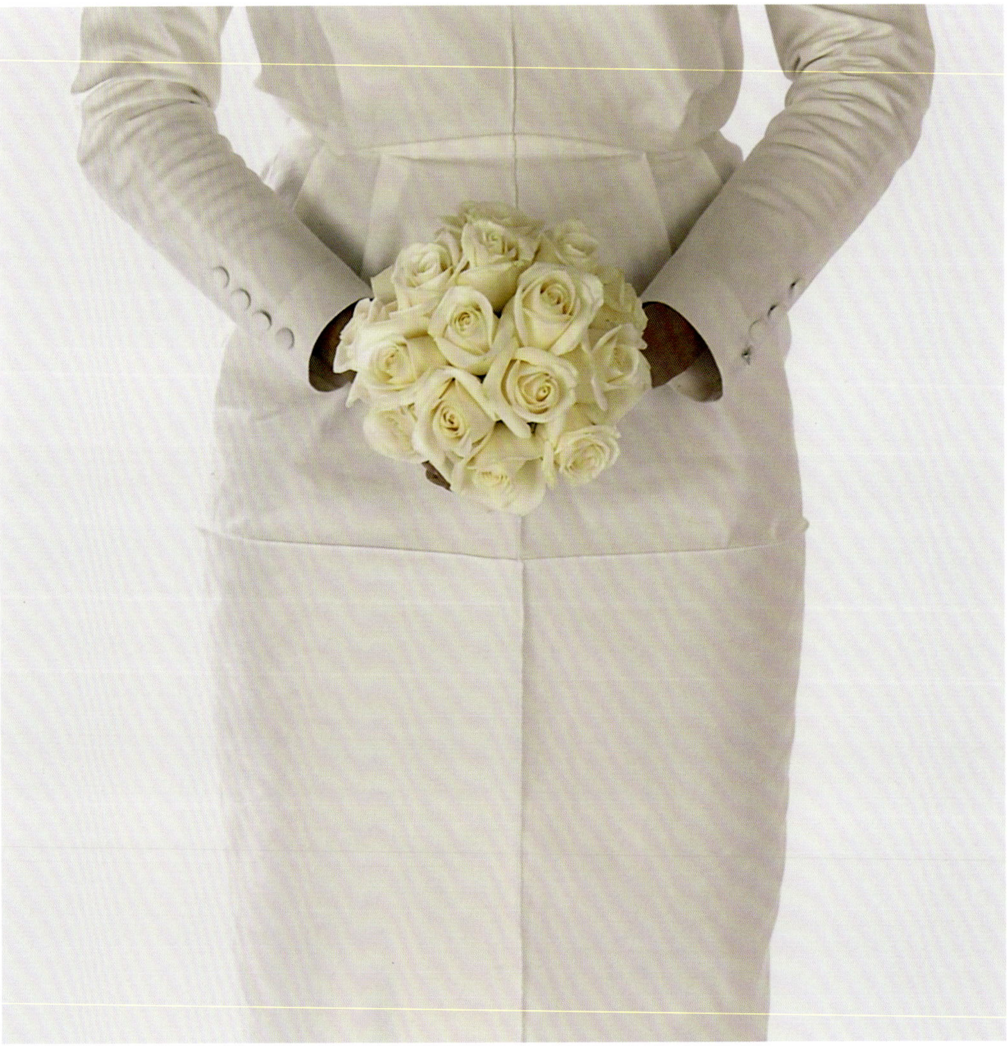

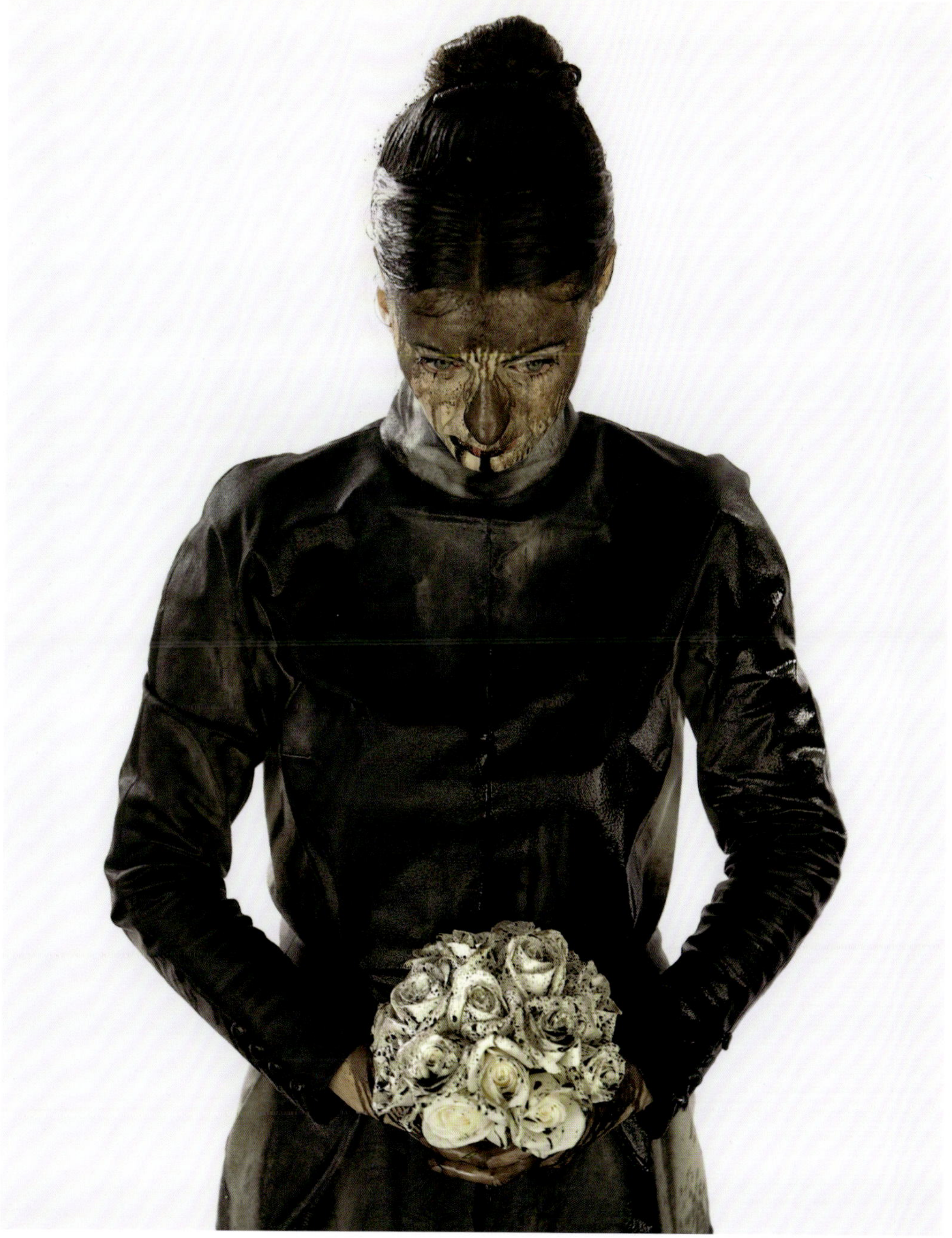

Marzia Migliora
Bianca e il suo contrario / Bianca and her Opposite, 2007
Lambda print, 70 x 100 cm
Courtesy Lia Rumma, Milan-Naples

tificial limbs, the fruit of an angelic or animal union, Barney is the Narrator, probably the Great Liar. The cycle talks about changing identity in a way that we could call present-day Gothic, certainly a bizarre and majestically infantile genre. It deftly and ironically mixes medical and sporting equipment, science fiction, dance, fairytale, myth, transsexuality, disguise, Houdini, and Bob Wilson, and serves up a dish spiced with artifice, ornament, and rhetorical illumination where the gestures have all the rigor of ceremony. A rococo background, a touch of Watteau, and a hint of Greenaway: the bewildered viewer is gripped by a sort intellectual dread. Francesco Vezzoli instead embroiders. By hand, with needle and thread, weaving patterns on cloth like Arachne, but without being turned into a spider by Minerva. He imagines himself being elevated to the Olympus of female stars that he illustrates in his many videos and films (from Gloria Swanson to Franca Valeri, from Joan Crawford to Marianne Faithfull).

The fetish of the self-portrait as star serves the function of suggesting the painful and difficult entanglement in the relationship between the two sexes. It is pervaded by a longing for self-loss and rediscovery in appearances, a desire to reunite what is separated in a single result of fascination and death. Misinterpreted due to the glamorous, *Vogue*-like aspects of her work, Vanessa Beecroft has refined her talent by focusing on socio-political

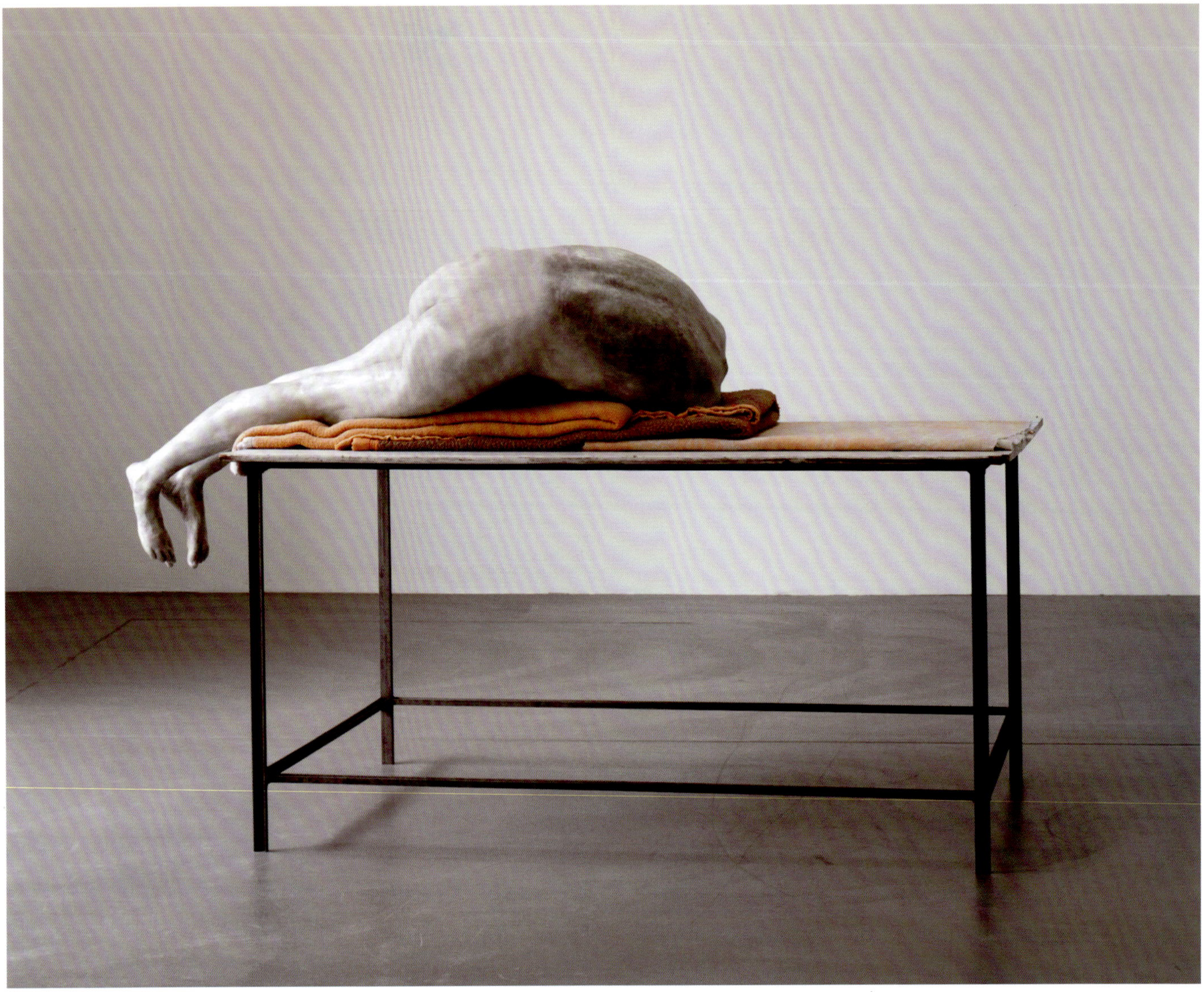

Berlinde de Bruyckere
Aanéén, 2003–2004
Wax, epoxy resin, wooden board and iron, blankets, 132 x 205 x 124 cm
Collection Antoin de Galbert
Courtesy Galleria Continua
San Gimignano/Beijing/Le Moulin;
Hauser & Wirth, Zürich-London

Francesco Vezzoli
Jean Cocteau Embroidered Tears on the Mask of Berenice, 2002
Black and white laser print on canvas with metallic embroidery, 125 x 65 cm
Private collection

themes such as the drama of immigration. She thinks in terms of figures, which are invented in a feverishly visual way. In a certain sense, this is theater, since no matter what the references, citations, and meaning may be, Beecroft's actions appear before us with figures, images and bodies together. Sometimes also allegorical, they are above all of visions of shattering immediacy: rage, consecration, anointment, investiture. The theatrical dimension develops in scenes and the compact discourse as a system of symptoms, sometimes frozen by the narration and perfected in a highly controlled alternation of palpitations and vibrations that betray memories of Carpaccio or Veronese here and there.

Edoardo Sanguineti wrote as follows in 1964: "The avant-garde rises up … against aesthetic commercialization and ends up falling into it. At the superstructural level, it has its avowed enemy in the museum, which ultimately devours it with the utmost tranquility, as in the worst folk tales. … The entrance of the avant-garde into the antiseptic rooms of the museum is parallel and complementary to its entrance into the filthy stalls of the market. The museum and the market are contiguous and communicating, being indeed the two façades of one and the same social building: price and value come to coincide." Consideration of figures like Jeff Koons and in many respects Damien Hirst will show that this foretold what was to happen just half a century later.

What has long been noted is the interest of artists in political dynamics. Environmental disasters, wars, religious conflict, and the drama (or indeed tragedy) of migration have never been such a presence in their production as in the last ten years. What are the works of Mona Hatoum, Adrian Paci, Shirin Neshat, Tania Bruguera, Regina José Galindo, Santiago Sierra, Berlinde de Bruyckere, Sisley Xhafa, Maurizio Cattelan, Anri Sala, Paola Pivi, Kimsooja, and Monica Bonvicini if not an act of political protest?

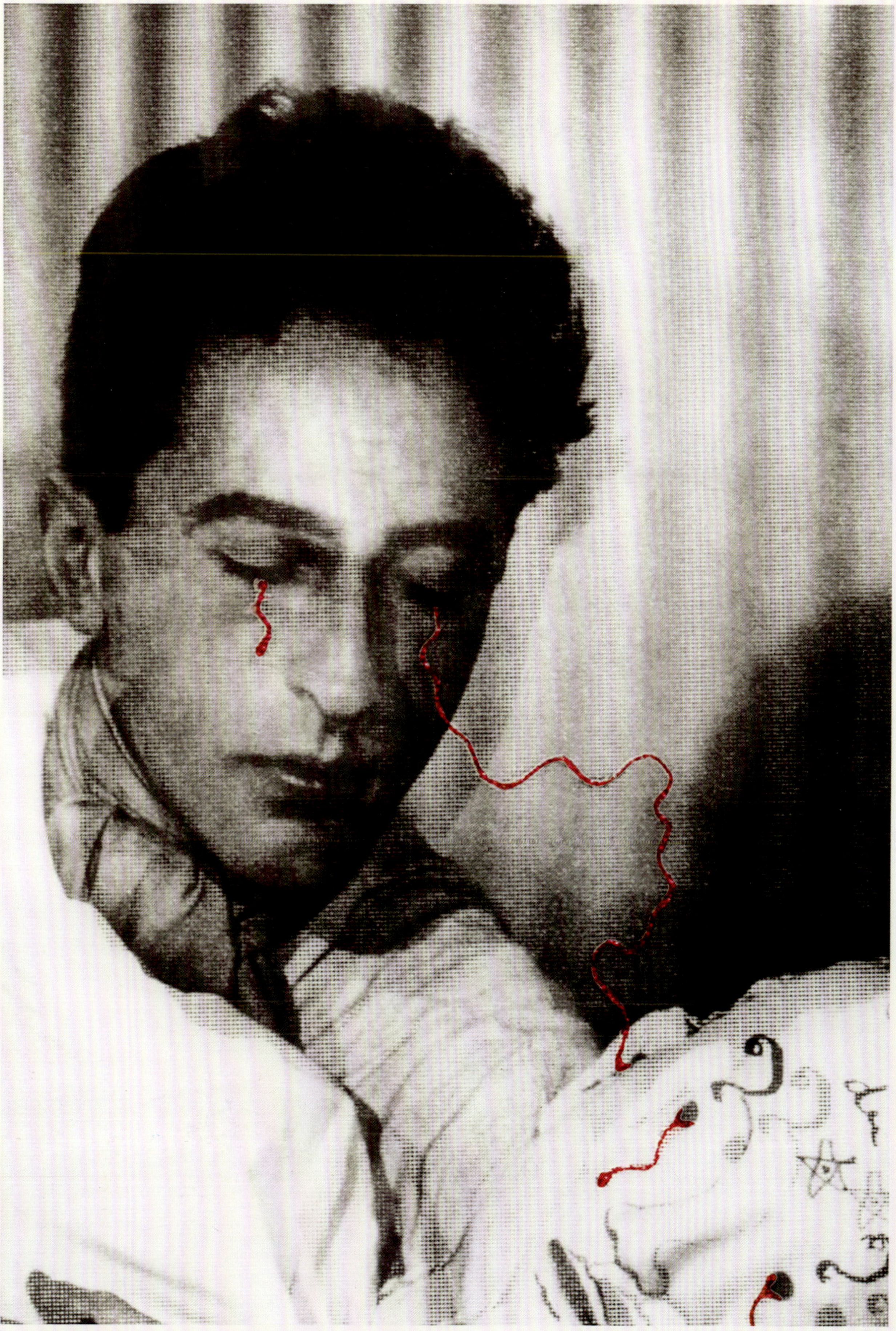

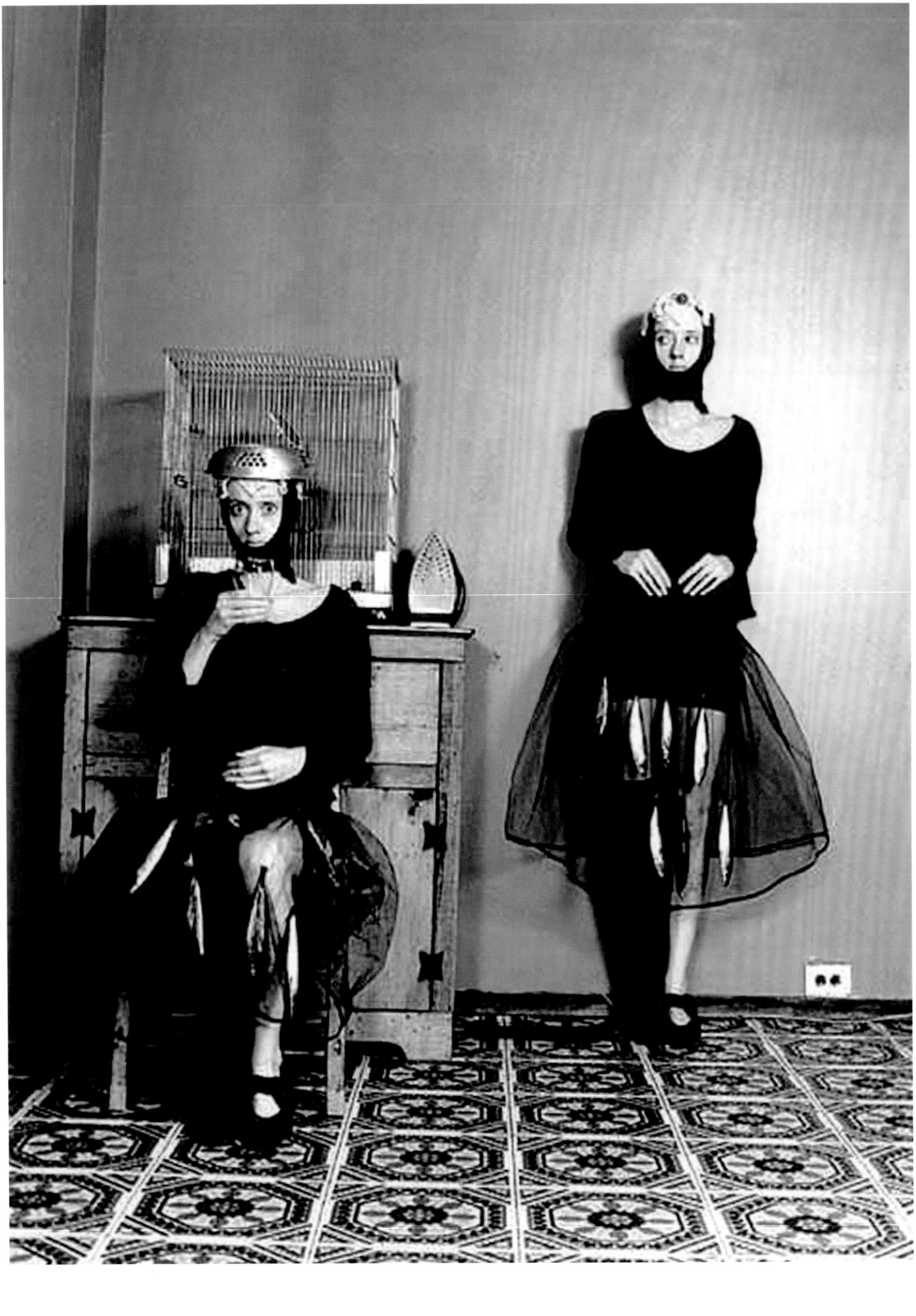

Janieta Eyre
Two Laundresses by the River Thames, 1998
Black and white photograph, 100 x 76 cm
Courtesy of the artist

Chen Zhen
Un village sans frontières, 2000
Wooden chair, colored candles, 77 x 41 x 42 cm
Courtesy Galleria Continua, San Gimignano/Beijing/Le Moulin

"Work is the selling of time, intelligence and strength of the worker in exchange for remuneration and a favour on the part of the contracted person. This isn't my thing: the work is what it is. Socially it is conceived in this way and my particular vision of the question is of little importance. The vision that must always prevail is what ties us to the rest, in such a way that the spectator knows what you are talking about and not left without knowing what to think, in the case that one deals with a particular vision." ... "The use of the word 'art' is embarrassing enough and very often it seems shameful to me to say that I am an artist. It's as if to say that you are more or better than the others, you are a poor soul and I am an artist. Art is commonly understood as work that becomes exalted via the skills of the worker, who, in consequence, will be defined as an 'artist', on a superior or superlative level with respect to the common worker." (Santiago Sierra)[8]

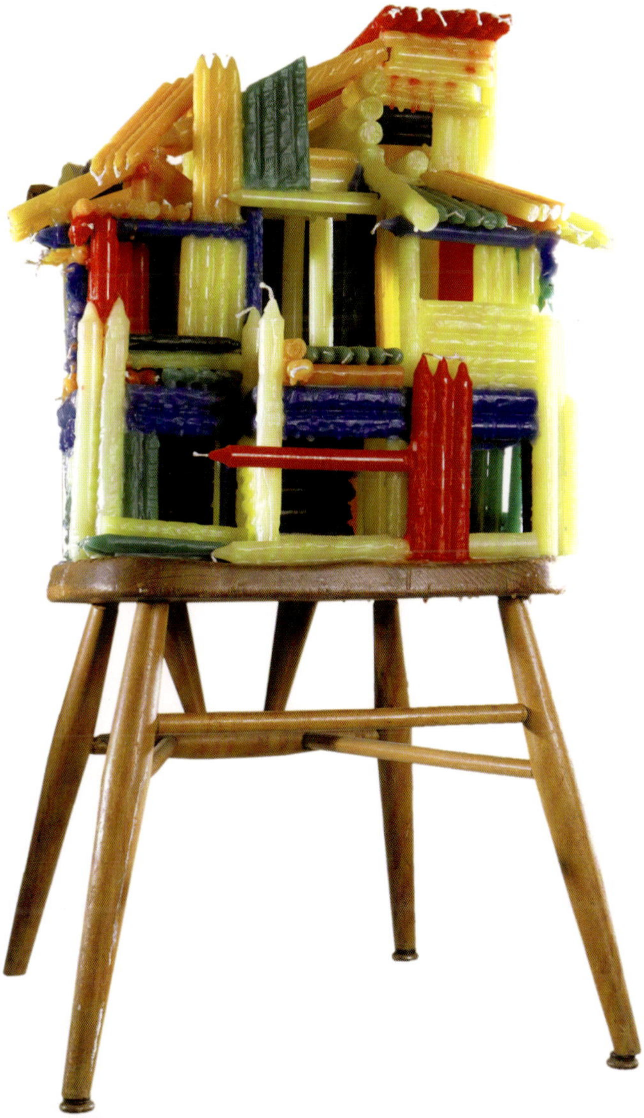

In my work, there aren't vertical forms; they are all heavy, dark horizontal, parallel to the floor or dug underground. All the repertory materials, whether these are cars, benches or plates, are always used in their function as containers of the human body or the goods that the body produces. There are abundant references to the objectified body, to the body that belongs only to someone else, to those who benefit from it. There is neither will nor value of its own merit, nor time wasted in my works. In as much as black is a strong, energetic color that absorbs all other colors, it the color of mourning in the Catholic culture, it is the only color used together with aseptic white and that ends at itself. Energy and physical force always appear to be associated with the negation of life and its transformation into work. So you live and you earn with your work." (Santiago Sierra)[9]

"For me, artists' practices are similar to that of Buddhist monks' in the sense that they both try to liberate and to go beyond themselves. ... the self, the body, the spirit, and the "Other" can be perused in many ways. Artists deal with different types of desires depending on their social and cultural context. Desire can be visualized in a physical form that satisfies the sense of possession; it can also be a purely psychological and metaphorical state that deals with desire as another subject. ... Finally, artists cannot help but ask themselves: 'What is the origin of my desire, and what is the role desire plays in my work?'" (Kimsooja)[10]

"I just want to offer different points of view and angles to look at my work. It's a trick maybe, to find a personality. And I have to find ways to get by." (Maurizio Cattelan)[11]

There is of course an enormous difference with respect to the uprising of 1968, which in any case addressed the problems and contradictions of making art. There is now nothing like the systematic attack on cultural structures launched in that period and no trace of any attempt to connect the role and function of galleries, museums, and universities with real moments in the proletarian struggle.

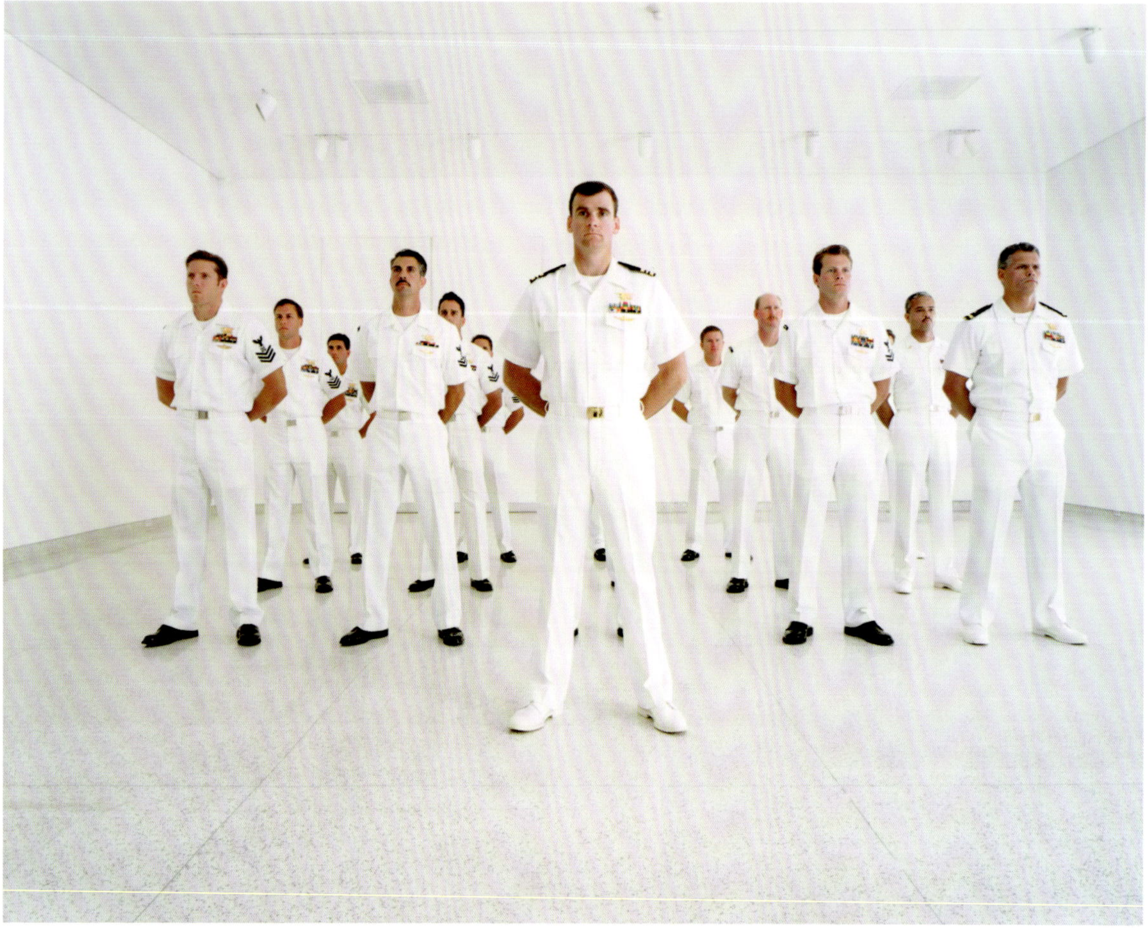

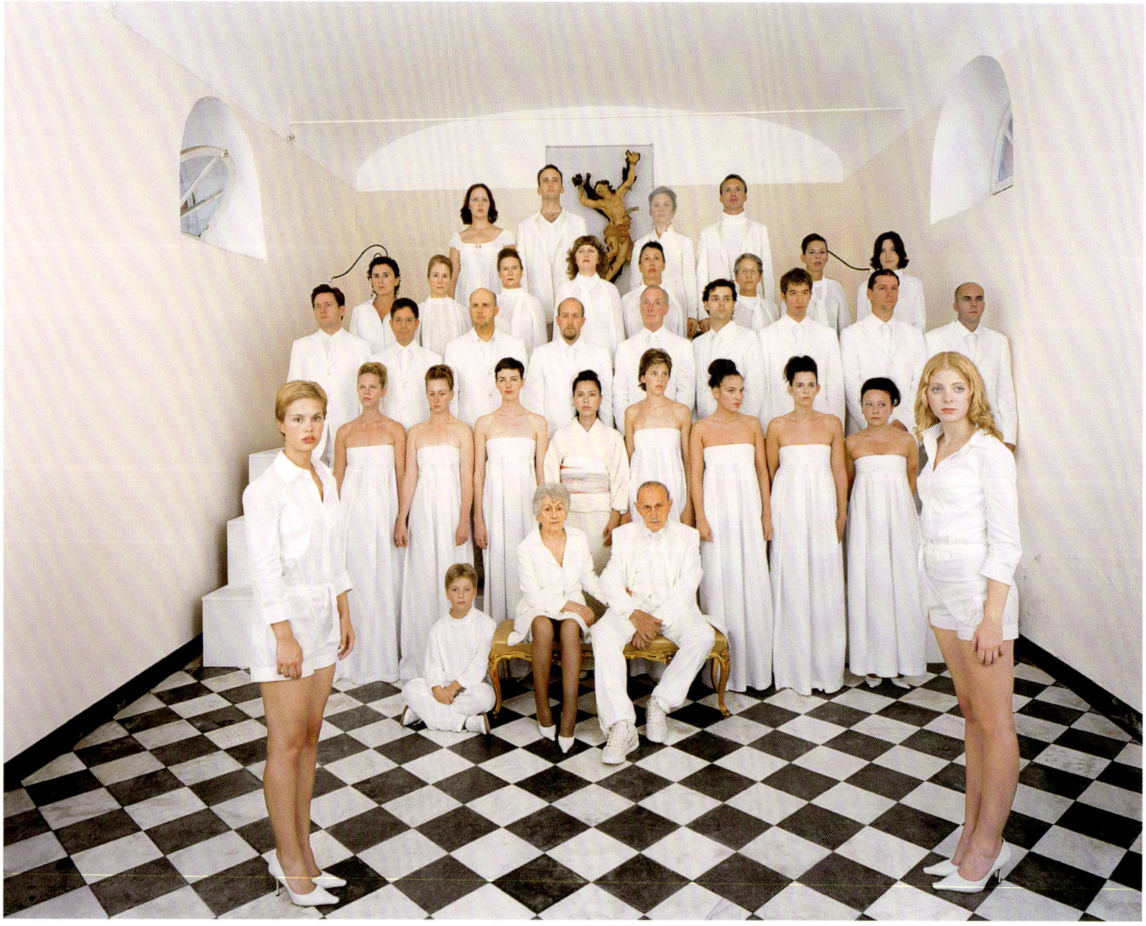

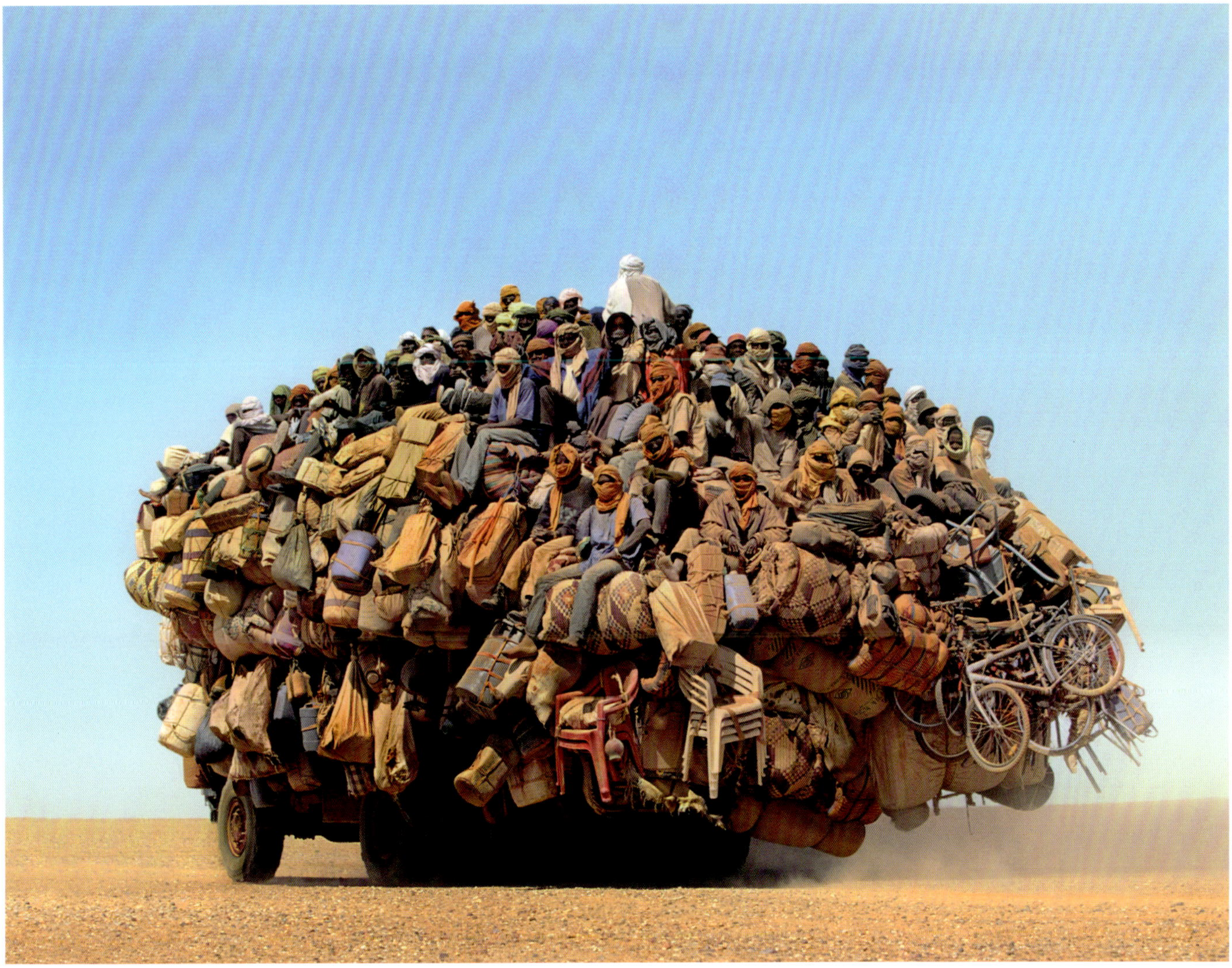

Vanessa Beecroft
VB39 / U.S. Navy Seal, June 5, 1999
San Diego, Museum of Contemporary Art

Vanessa Beecroft
VBGDW, Special Project, September 14, 2000
Portofino, cappella di San Sebastiano

Brigitte Niedermair
Let's Get Married, 2008
Color photograph, 145 x 190 cm
Installation for Museion at the Torre Eurac in Bolzano, May 2009
Courtesy of the artist and Galleria Galica, Milan

[1] S. Hertmans, *There's no Getting Used to Art (These are the drops of the lonesome heart)*, in *Jan Fabre. Gaude succurrere vitae*, exhibition catalogue (Ghent, S.M.A.K. Stedelijk Museum Voor Aktuele Kunst, 12 October 2002–2 February 2003; Bergamo, Galleria d'Arte Moderna e Contemporanea, 16 April–13 June 2003; Barcelona, Fundació Joan Miró, 19 July–2 November 2003; Lyons, Musée d'Art Contemporain, October 2004–January 2005), Imschoot, Ghent 2003.

[2] *Louise Bourgeois. Blue Days and Pink Days*, exhibition catalogue (ed. by) J. Gorovoy, P. Tatabatai Asbaghi (Milan, Fondazione Prada, 15 May–6 July 1997), Milan 1997, p. 271.

[3] *Ibid.*

[4] *Ibid.*, p. 273.

[5] *Ibid.*, p. 274.

[6] J. Jonas, *Space Movement Time*, in *Joan Jonas*, exhibition catalogue (ed. by) A. Daneri, C. Natalicchio (Como, Spazio San Francesco, 2-21 July 2007) (Milan: Charta, 2007), p. 22.

[7] Zhang Huan, *A Piece of Nothing*, in *Zhang Huan. Altered States*, exhibition catalogue (ed. by) M. Chiu (New York, Asia Society-Museum New York, 6 September–20 January 2008) (Milan: Charta, 2007), pp. 73–74.

[8] *Santiago Sierra*, exhibition catalogue (ed. by) F. Cavallucci, C. Jiménez (Trento, Galleria Civica di Arte Contemporanea, 8 October 2005–15 January 2006) (Cinisello Balsamo: Silvana Editoriale, 2005), pp. 85, 87.

[9] *Ibid.*, p. 96.

[10] N. Bourriaud, *Interview between Bourriaud and Kimsooja*, in *Kimsooja. Conditions of Humanity*, exhibition catalogue (Lyons, Musée d'Art Contemporain, 5 February –20 April 2003; Düsseldorf, Museum Kunst und Palast, 14 February–23 May 2004; Milan PAC Padiglione d'Arte Contemporanea, 24 June–19 September 2004) (Milan: 5 Continents, 2004), pp. 56–57.

[11] "We Are to Many", Hans Ulrich Obrist interview with Maurizio Cattelan, in *Work. Art in Progress*, January-March 2004, p. 39.

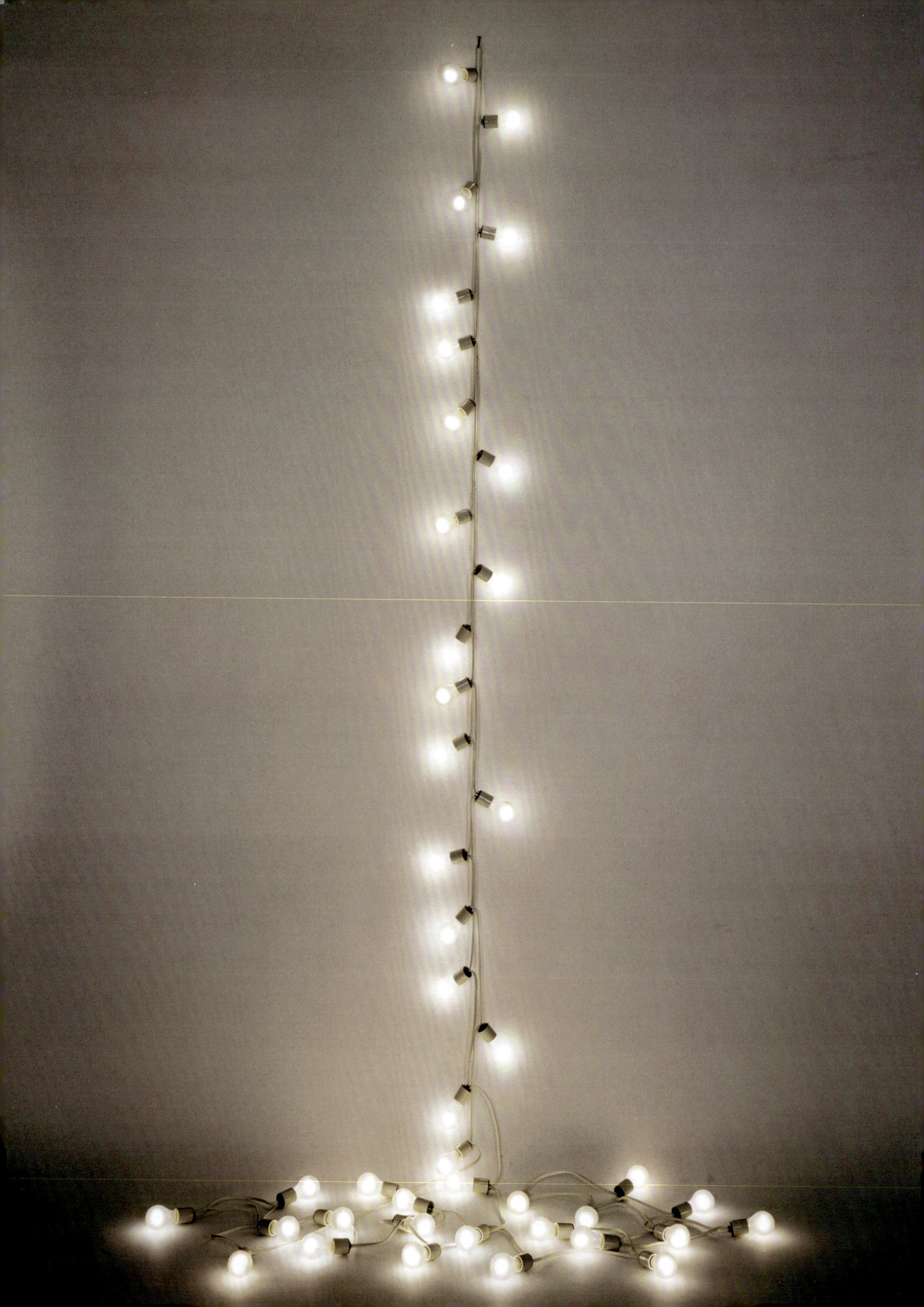

Nicolas Bourriaud

Installation, Video, Actions: the Ascent of the Precarious in the Postmodern Era

The watershed of the twenty-first century is dominated by the slow dismantling of traditional cultural hierarchies. It was in the 1980s that the various structural levels of the forms and practices of culture consumption gradually began to crumble and then decompose. The concepts of avant-garde and kitsch, the two fundamental opposites for modernist theorists of art like Theodor W. Adorno and Clement Greenberg, thus dissolved into a new configuration where "low" and "high" culture, the ephemeral and the lasting, developed in a wholly unprecedented shape. For Baudelaire, modernity meant "plunging into the unknown so as to find the new." *Plunging*? The figure of speech now proves obsolete in the panorama of globalized chaos where culture and entertainment, artwork and product, art and fashion, pop and highbrow music, airport literature and experimental novels, serious content and frivolity are all mixed indiscriminately within the framework of authentic cultural inflation fostered by the development of the Internet. The disruption of the hierarchy of the cultural levels thus takes place under the auspices of digital technology, a genuine hub for the redistribution of forms and utterances, but is also due to the pressures of the process of commodification in a now worldwide market economy. At the same time, the phenomenon in question is far from being completely negative, as the coded landscape of references within which artists and the public developed in the past led to the adoption of rigid attitudes and stances, such as the dichotomy of academic and avant-garde art. The chaotic turmoil of worldwide culture in the period between 1990 and 2010 has instead seen the appearance of hybrid figures and a new sort of artist: the "semionaut," an inventor of trajectories between signs, a cultural nomad connecting one world with another, a form with a narrative, a technology of today with a legend of yesterday. The semionautic artist proceeds like a search engine, setting off in pursuit of signs and surfing over gigantic masses of information in a cultural context characterized by hyperproduction and the multiplication of expressive formats as well as the expansion of the field of art in both geographic and disciplinary terms. A portable computer with an Internet connection can thus be considered the totemic instrument at this turn of the century. A producer of human relations and commercial space, a generator of communitarian utopias, and a means of contact for terrorist groups like Al-Qaeda, the Internet encapsulates all the upheavals of the age. In art it has fostered the development of the video thanks to image-processing software and the spread of a communication format like YouTube, as well as the emergence of new formal strategies based on the notion of the link and the practice of browsing. With its pop-ups and hypertext links, the surface of the screen has also permitted the development of new spaces and new modalities of visual thought, which were fully established by the mid-1990s.

A horizontal movement: globalization

The key year of this movement of cultural globalization was 1989, marked by the exhibition 'Les Magiciens de la Terre' – organized in Paris by Jean-Hubert Martin as the self-proclaimed "first world-wide exhibition of contemporary art" – but also the third Havana Biennial, intentionally conceived as an act of resistance against Western dominion and hence largely overlooked both in Europe and in the United States at the very moment when the fall of the Berlin Wall ushered in a new political era. This period could be described as characterized by the "horizontalization" of ideas and forms. In other words, the end of the division of the world into two juxtaposed systems opened up the way for the accelerated globalization of art, a process of geographic expansion at the expense of the vertical and historical dimension. This geographic expansion was very soon to disrupt the panorama of artistic practices and the conception of the art exhi-

Félix González-Torres
Untitled (Petit Palais), 1992
Porcelain sockets, light bulbs, electrical wire, length 1889.8 cm
Philadelphia, The Philadelphia Museum of Art, Gift of Peter Norton Family Foundation

bition radically. From the 1990s on, any show devoted exclusively to Western, heterosexual, white, male artists became inadequate by definition with respect to a multicultural and egalitarian vision of art and the world. Combined with the development of cultural studies and the post-colonialist school of thought, the fall of the Berlin Wall created an intellectual climate conducive to a rethinking of the Western artistic creed. In an article entitled *Post-'68* (*Flash Art*, January 1994), the American critic Laura Cottingham outlined the aesthetic legacy bequeathed to contemporary art by the Black Power movement and the battles of feminists and homosexuals. Artists like Zoe Leonard, Lyle Ashton Harris, and Steve McQueen can thus deliberately adopt minority viewpoints (Black, gay, lesbian) in revisiting the history of forms. Non-Western ritual practices, like the ones that made their entrance into art with 'Les Magiciens de la Terre,' became in turn legitimate formal models. The fireworks of Cai Guo-Qiang and the culinary performances of Rirkrit Tiravanija, based respectively on elements of Chinese and Thai culture, broaden the field of performance to include non-Western practices.

This expansion proved, however, to be not only cultural but also sociopolitical in nature. The most important and widely discussed item at the opening of the 1993 Whitney Biennial in New York was in fact not the work of an artist but a document created by a member of the public: videotape footage filmed by a passerby of policemen administering a lengthy beating to the African-American Rodney King in the middle of the street. The corpus delicti thus made its entrance into the world of contemporary art, marking on the one hand the birth of an urban Big Brother armed with video camera and on the other the repoliticization of art through more sector-specific battles, especially at the side of sexual, cultural, and ethnic minorities. Here lies one of the reasons for the star status conferred on the person and critical thinking of Michel Foucault, whose writings on sexuality and the microphysics of power constitute a primary source of inspiration for the artists and theorists of the 1990s. The artistic community proved largely receptive to his stringent analysis of the normative discourse and supposedly "subjective" utterances through which bodies and behaviors are controlled by the power structure permeating the institutions. Foucault's philosophy, which describes human life in terms of "truth games" that must be constantly called into question, was perfectly suited to contemporary art, whose criteria had suddenly been made obsolete by the massive influx of non-Western figures onto the art scene. In this way, the set of aesthetic values presiding over contemporary art became both precarious and prey to a whole variety of heterogeneous influences. No discipline or medium could now aspire to even a minimal degree of symbolic "authority."

A militant and precarious iconography

At the beginning of the 1990s, the militants of the Act Up association popularized the "Zap," a sudden and spectacular form of demonstration that consists, for example, in interrupting the speech of a homophobic politician or covering up a monument temporarily on the occasion of a media event. The new forms of political discourse that emerged in this period were sometimes born in the field of contemporary art. Félix González-Torres, an American artist of Cuban origin who died of AIDS in 1996, exemplifies this politics of form that turned the art of the 1990s upside down. With images of subtle and allusive abstraction (the photograph of sheets with the imprints of two bodies, a pair of curtains, the gravestone of a celebrated lesbian couple, the Minimalist drawings that prove to be the temperature curve of an AIDS victim), González-Torres completely revitalized the role of activism in art while creating works of astonishing formal harmony at the same time. He is not out to prove anything. His works are very far from propaganda art, but undermine forms from within, making them swing at the same time toward a Foucaultian ethics of homosexuality and an aesthetic of democracy and sharing. This is shown by a series of sculptures whose form borrows from the vocabulary of Minimalism (corner pieces or spreads), consisting of heaps of identical candies that visitors are invited to consume on the spot. Gradually threatened in its integrity, the work is thus defined as a structure in need of constant replenishment. The same applies to the series of stacks of again iden-

Steve McQueen
Once Upon a Time, 2002
Sequence of 116 color images based on slides, projected from a PC hard drive onto a screen with integrated soundtrack, 70'
Courtesy Marian Goodman Gallery, New York

Pages 32–33
Thomas Hirschhorn
The Green Coffin, 2006 (partial view)
Wood, spray paint, polyurethane, synthetic resin and ceramic hands, watches, tape, prints, cardboard, fabric, chess and chessboard, plastic shellfish, plaster sculptures, photocopies, bags,
3.59 x 11.29 x 4.36 m
Courtesy Galleria Alfonso Artiaco, Naples

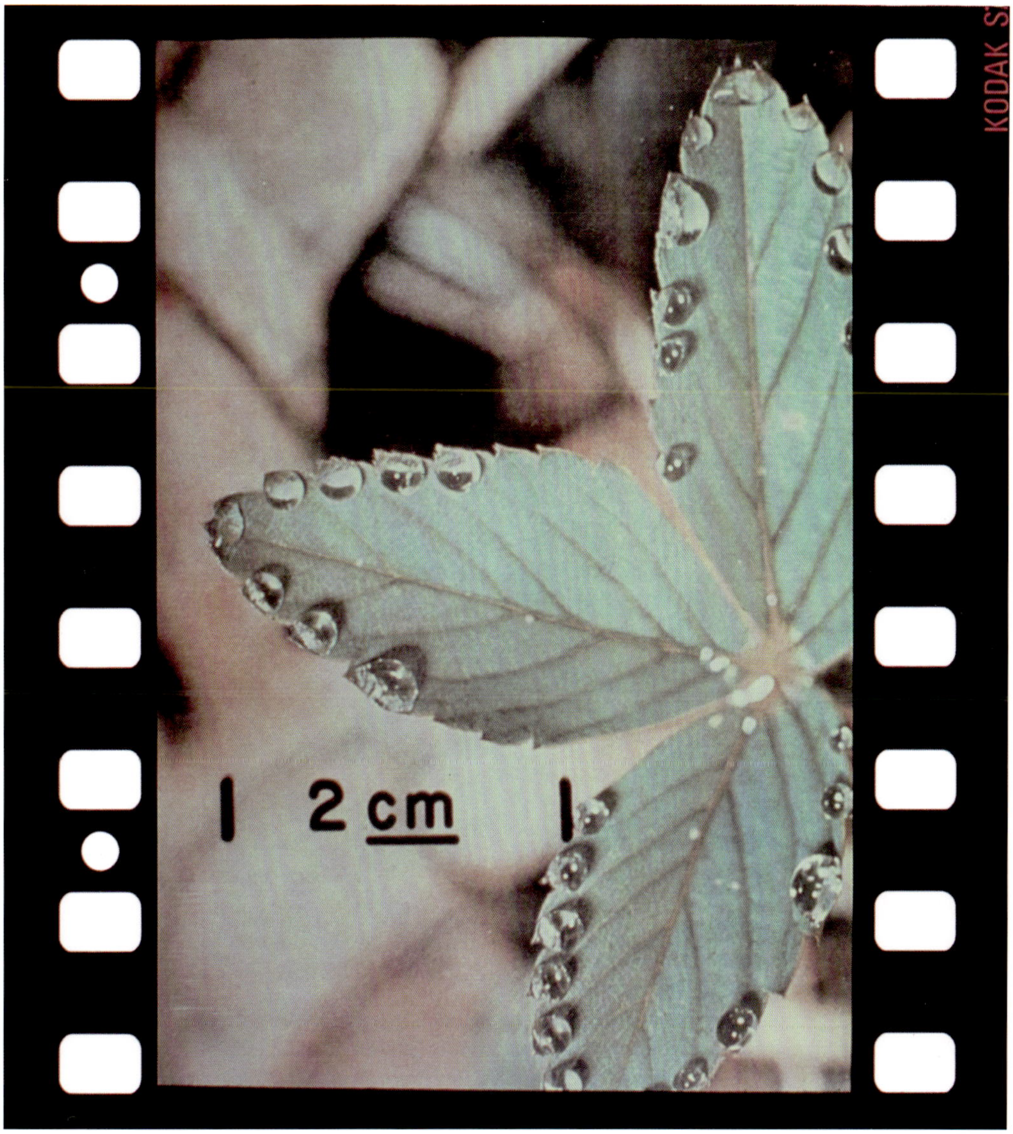

tical posters that viewers are allowed to take until there are none left and the work itself is no more. At the 'Post-Human' exhibition organized by Jeffrey Deitch in 1993, González-Torres presented a typically Minimalist white square on which a go-go dancer in blue hot pants performed every day.

The same subtlety runs through the work of David Hammons, characterized by a direct relationship with the street (or more precisely with the symbolic space of the sidewalk), waste materials, and symbols of the African-American imagination. With these two leading artists, the iconography of politics moves toward an aesthetic fragility that reflects the themes of social precariousness and the marginalization of ethnic minorities while also embodying the rejection of any preordained cultural hierarchy, even of a formal nature.

The historical forms of political militancy, especially public demonstrations and banners, became material for artists. When Philippe Parreno organized one with children yelling "No more reality" in 1991, his work raised the question of the banners images can march under and role they play in constructing the narrative of "reality" today. He later identified "social time" as the Gordian knot of his problem and the figure of the revolutionary intellectual "implanted" in a factory (like Robert Linhart, a historic leader of the French far left) as the model of artistic action. Thomas Hirschhorn's more direct approach involves accumulating handbills, documents, and news cuttings in installations of cardboard and aluminum whose informal appearance recalls the flows and networks of the globalized economy just as much as the temporary shelters of illegal immigrants. For

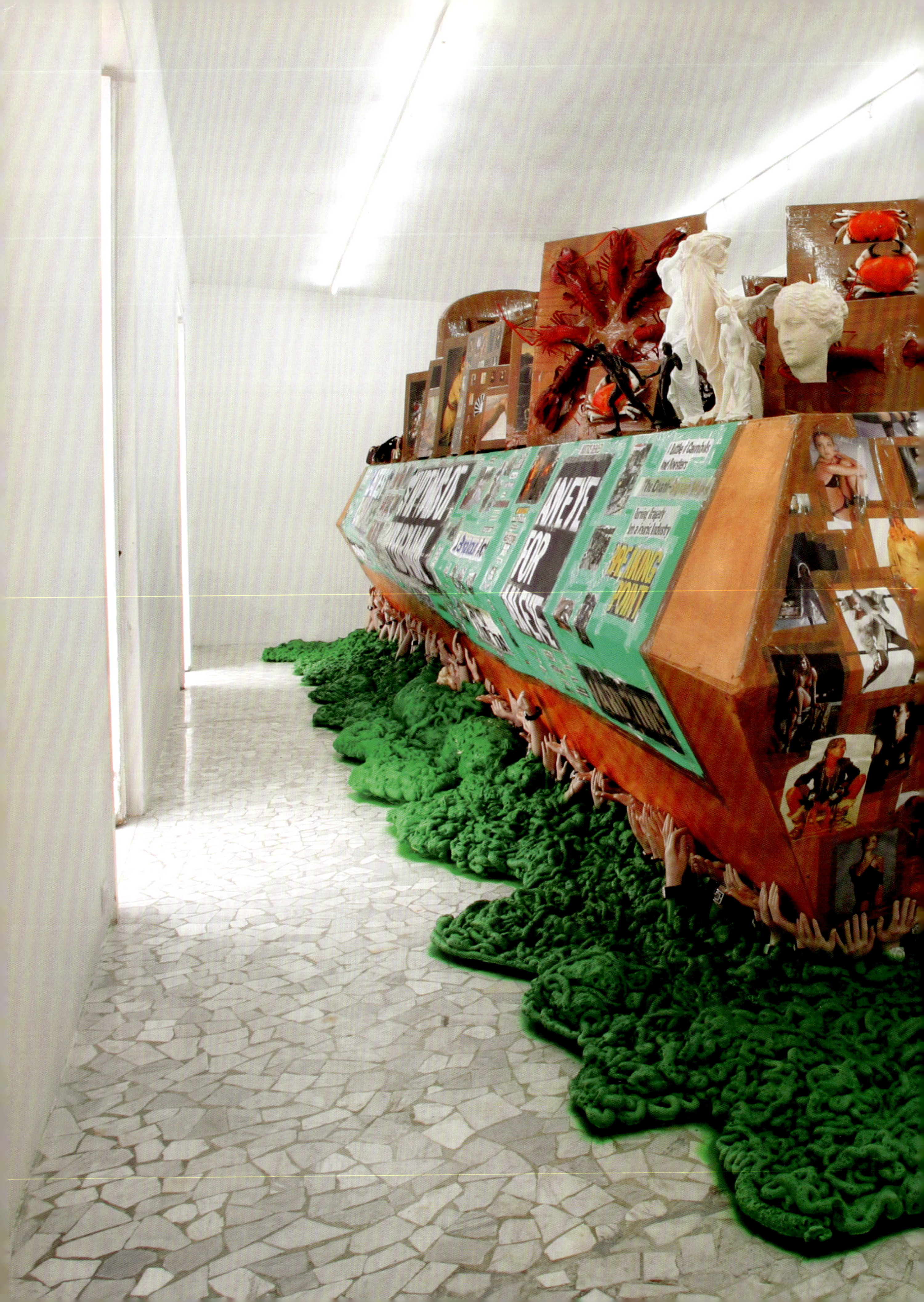
FOR
POINT

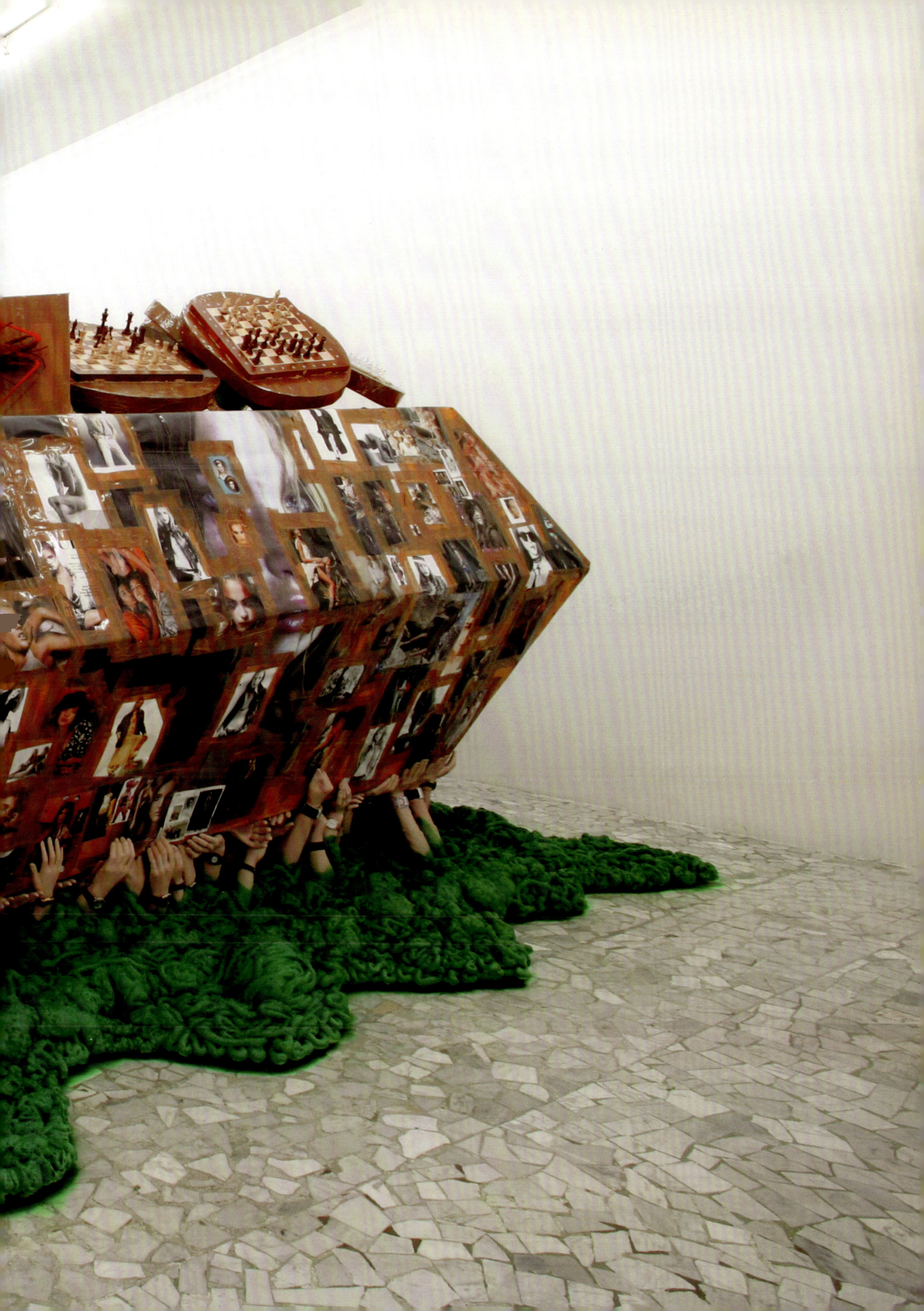

many artists and critics of the early 1990s, the point was to free artistic activities from the shackles of their specific history and develop them in the present-day social context. Since history now seems to be written in terms of the stock market and the economy, art should also establish itself on this terrain. Criticism of spectacle and the various forms of alienation in general gave rise to works calling into question the traditional distinction between an active artist and a passive viewer. The death of Guy Debord in 1994 and the re-publication of issues of the *Situationist International* magazine prompted artists to develop not only urban projects and ideas for "impassioning everyday life" but also and above all an analysis of the contemporary world and a method – the "construction of situations" – that became the basis of an authentic formal vocabulary.

The relational sphere

The lightning-fast development of the Internet, reflecting a need for social bonds and contact jeopardized by the post-industrial society, prompted artists to explore the new field of the interhuman sphere. The society of consumption gave way to the society of communication, the former generating Pop Art and the latter an art taking the sphere of human relations as its starting point. The roots of relational art are embedded not only in the widespread use of interactive technologies but also in the emergence of the tertiary sector and the industry of services. Contact with others became a concrete object just as much as a consumer product in our everyday life. Artists thus began to invent models of sociality or communication aimed at criticizing the reification of human relations emerging in more or less intangible terms over the flows of energy that connect human beings with one another. This new aesthetic was presented at the 1993 Venice Biennale, where Rirkrit Tiravanija's installation consisted of a metal gondola full of boiling water that visitors could use to make themselves a bowl of freeze-dried Chinese soup to drink sitting at one of the numerous camping tables scattered all around. The Italian Maurizio Cattelan rented his assigned space to a cosmetic company (*Lavorare è un brutto mestiere*, 1993). Carsten Höller ironically exhibited a car equipped for hunting children and Philippe Parreno a group of marionettes representing a demonstration of artists beneath a blanket of artificial snow. Christine Hill gave visitors massages and polished their shoes at the Unfair in Cologne the same year in accordance with her view of art as a practice called upon to generate relations between people and mend the tears in the social fabric.

The interview became an art form, as in the videos of Kutlug Ataman (*Küba*, 2004) and the early works of Dominique Gonzalez-Foerster, where the indirect and poetic viewpoint is less sociological. The latter gives form to the biographies of people that interest her, like the actress Maria de Medeiros (1990). In *The Daughter of a Taoist* (1993), Gonzalez-Foerster uses the biography of Esther Schipper, the owner of the gallery showing her work in Germany, as material for a work that takes shape as an allusive ensemble of heterogeneous images, objects, signs, and colors. The artist also set up a sort of "surgery" in one show for visitors to draw maps from memory of the places where they spent their childhood. Working on intimacy, narration, travel, and urban space, Gonzalez-Foerster operates in the sphere of human relations but always connects them with the dimension of fiction. Filmed as a long tracking shot on the river running through Kyoto with a telephone conversation between two Japanese adolescents who recently met at a party as its soundtrack, the video *Riyo* (2001) is characterized by this dual thrust.

Taking cognizance in both political and sociological terms of the failure of revolutionary ideologies and the triumph of the corporate culture, Liam Gillick develops an authentication tertiary aesthetic whose minimal forms are linked to the world of enterprise and reflect the parallel unfolding of stories. Examples include a work devoted to a Sony vice president (*Ibuka*, 1996) and some series on subjects like a major convention center and the efforts of a group of workers in the 1970s to reopen the disused factory in which they had worked for a long time (*Texte court sur la possibilité de créer une économie de l'équivalence*, 2005). The primary questioned addressed by Gillick's work can be summarized as how capitalism is translated into the grammar of everyday life. He explores the ways in which human relations and professional activities are shaped by ideology and brings to light the hidden links between the modernist iconography and the transformations of the world economy. His complex and discursive work seeks to identify a way out of postmodernism without relapsing into nostalgia for modernism or ceasing to exercise critical analysis.

This relational trend led in the 1990s to revaluation of the work of certain artists. One of these is Franz West, who exhibited about a hundred functional sculptures consisting of garden swing chairs for use by visitors at Documenta in 1992. He then saw his *Passtücke*, sculptural works designed for public use, transformed into icons by a new generation of artists whose reconsideration of the theme of human relations in art led them to accord primacy to concepts and ideas previously lacking any systematic theorization. The same thing happened to Nan Goldin, who had been photographing her friends in the shady universe of the New York underground for over 20 years, to the Brazilians Helio Oiticica and Lygia Clark, who see sculpture and installation as a way of connecting human beings, and the Americans Tom Marioni and Gordon Matta-Clark, who had used the exhibition space as a place of conviviality since the 1970s. This relational trend also gave rise to fierce criticism as it gathered momentum. After the English translation of my book in 2002, Claire Bishop gave an overview of its content while attacking its effect on the world of art, which she saw as the introduction of a sort of apolitical and pseudo-unifying utopianism. As she wrote, "Such work seems to derive from a creative misreading of post-structuralist theory: rather than the interpretations of a work of art being open to continual reassessment, the work of art itself is argued to be in perpetual flux. There are many problems with this idea, not least of which is the difficulty of discerning a work whose identity is willfully unstable." Now, the "unstable identity" of the work of art, which she appears to deplore, is in fact the heart of the problem addressed by these artists, whose objective is precisely to free art from its specification in disciplinary terms (the modern theme of experimentation on the medium) and place it in the middle of an endless web of formats and circuits. Philippe Parreno insists, for example, on the recognition of the process within which every image takes shape: pre-production, production, postproduction. No form can in fact escape reification except by constituting first of all an account of its own advent and its positioning in a broader context. Placing the work of art at the center of the interhuman sphere – the approach of artists as different from one another in formal terms as Pierre Huyghe, Rirkrit Tiravanija, Liam Gillick, and Dominique Gonzalez-Foerster – makes it possible to interfere with the mechanisms of commodification. Far from seeking to reduce art to its immaterial dimension, as certain critics frightened by the demand for "formal instability" have assumed all too hastily, these artists simply regard the object as a link in a more complex chain.

The theme of precariousness

The sociologist Zygmunt Bauman describes ours as an age of "liquid modernity" in which the "object-crushing industry takes over positions of strength in the economy." In a society of widespread disposability, what is durable becomes an exception. As we know, Hannah Arendt regarded culture and the ephemeral as mutually incompatible: art is what withstands and survives the process of consumption. It was in the early 1990s that the iconography of precariousness started to become omnipresent in art exhibitions. The immigrant and the urban wanderer became recurrent elements along with subjects like waste recovery and recycling. The Mexican Gabriel Orozco, for example, produced a series of urban photographs of "spontaneous sculptures" created by chance, discarded objects transformed by time and endowed with unusual forms, random assemblages of bicycles or other residual forms found on the sidewalk. *Yielding Stone* (1992) is a ball of plasticine sphere rolled through the city streets to pick up litter from the ground. Francis Alÿs, another artist resident in Mexico City, uses his walks as the starting point for work that combines painting, drawing, photography, film, and action. "My paintings, my images," he explains, "are nothing but attempts to illustrate the situations that I confront, cause or 'perform' at the level of public space, space that is mostly urban and ephemeral. ... I have tried to create painted images that could become the equiv-

Santiago Sierra
68 People Paid to Block a Museum Entrance, 2000
Performance at the Museum of Contemporary Art, Pusan, Korea
Courtesy prometeogallery di Ida Pisani, Milan/Lucca

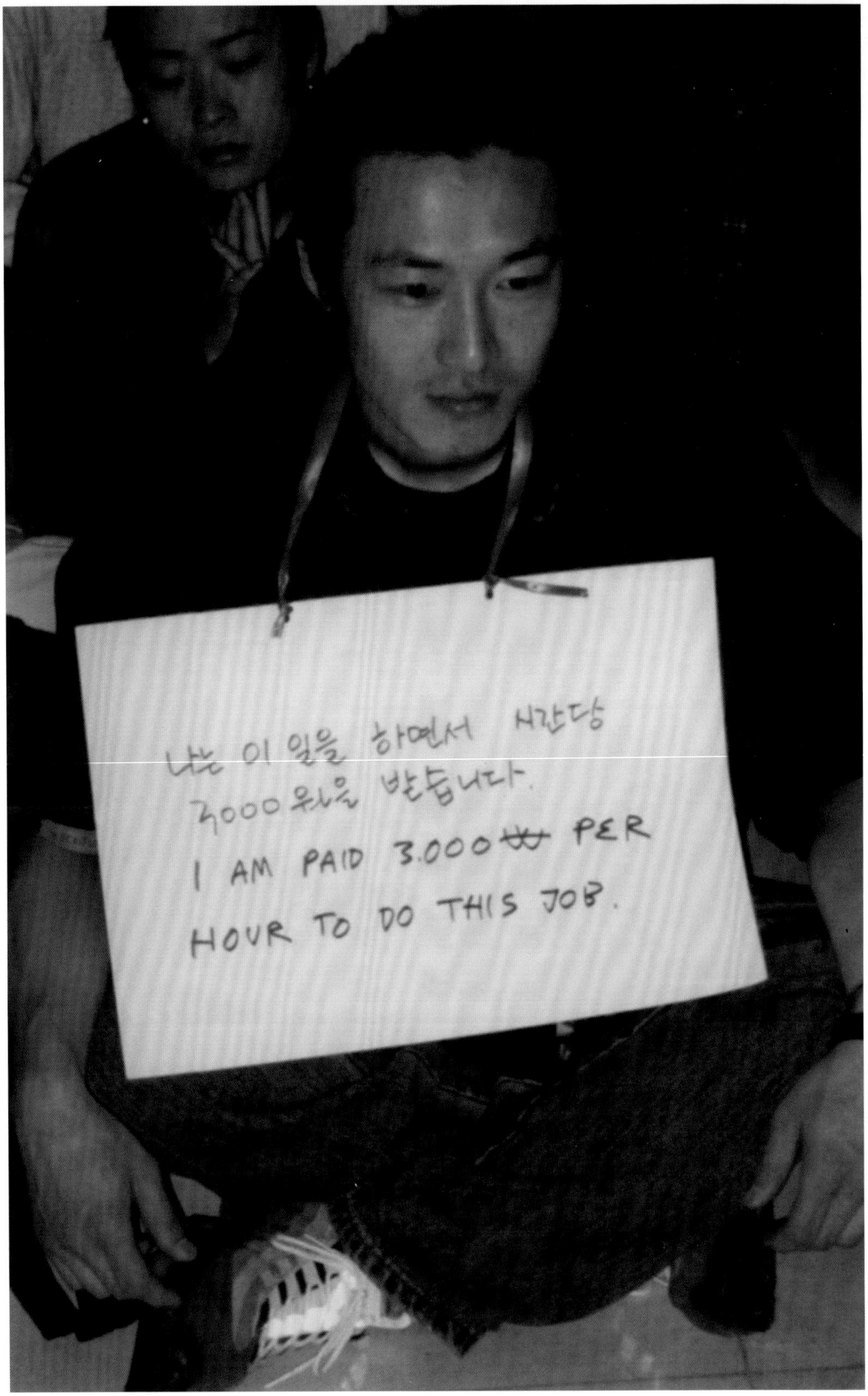

alents of action or memories but without representing the action itself in any literal way." The image thus becomes a simple *fixative*, its real value depending on a mental process. The creator of a photographic style that captures this aura of instability, Wolfgang Tillmans has endeavored since the early 1990s to subvert the imagery of fashion with his raw vision of the techno generation. The artist has no hesitation in presenting blurred, off-center snapshots, an authentic manifesto of carelessness whose spontaneity is carefully studied.

There is another form of composition that reflects this insistence on precariousness, namely *scatter*, a concept borrowed from the formal vocabulary of the sculpture of the 1960s. It denotes a structure in which the elements are scattered at random on the ground. This form of structural composition was taken up again in the 1990s and transformed into an emblematic visual parameter, far removed from the showcase aesthetic characterizing the previous decade. Expanding the scatter strategy into three dimensions, Jason Rhoades transformed art galleries into Formula 1 racing pits crammed with details and apparently heterogeneous elements recalling the suburban American culture of junk fairs. The Native American Jimmie Durham, George Adeagbo from Benin, Pascale Marthine Tayou from Cameroon, and other artists adopt this visual format but also connect it with compositional structures inspired by their own culture of origin. So chaotic in appearance as to preclude any idea of formal unity, these installations are based on the model of the network: heterogeneous elements held together by means of a subject, theme, topic or trajectory. In the era of immediate cultural consumption, they openly challenge the viewer's capacity for interpretation and analysis. How can such teeming complexity be read and understood?

Time-specific

In *A Voyage on the North Sea. The Post-Medium Condition* (1999), Rosalind Krauss reflects on the work of Marcel Broodthaers and criticizes the most recent developments in art for their abandonment of work on the medium and apparent dispersal in countless different directions. As she writes, "Television and video seem Hydra-headed, existing in endlessly diverse forms, spaces and temporalities for which no single instance seems to provide a formal unity for the whole. This is what Sam Weber has called television's 'constitutive heterogeneity.'" The artists of this generation do indeed move readily from one discipline or medium to another without establishing even the slightest hierarchy between an ephemeral action and a sculpture, a video, an installation, and an action. But the "unity" that Krauss fails to perceive is now developed through the exhibition itself, what Philippe Parreno calls a "film without a camera," the new basic unit of an artistic practice that explores the "time-specific" aspect of the work of art in terms of its form of temporal manifestation just as the artists of the 1960s worked on the site-specific dimension of art. The exhibition thus becomes a process capable of combining spatial objects and temporally circumscribed events through the juxtaposition of expressive formats and media. The characteristic "constitutive heterogeneity" of the television channel becomes in fact a dominant medium. Each artist broadcasts on his or her specific wavelength, which must be picked up in its continuity so as to reconstitute the "unity" jeopardized by the heterogeneity of the means employed.

As a child, Philippe Parreno and his schoolmates played football while delivering a running commentary on the action at the same time just like the TV sports commentators. Action and comment combine in his work in real time. How does form adapt to "prerecording"? It is this "staggering" with respect to the real world that determines the force of the image and constitutes the primary focus of Parreno's work. In the video *Ou* (1997), the figure of a young woman taking off a t-shirt decorated with a Disney character, a biographical reference to the artist's first sexual experience, turns into a search engine of the conditions of its manifestation as a work of art. A long credit sequence lists the books, films, and discussions leading up to the creation of this 30-second video. Investigating the autonomy of the individual and the group within social systems, Parreno's work occupies the in-between space that separates the image from its caption, labor from its product, production from con-

Tacita Dean
Diamond Ring, 2002
16 mm film
Courtesy Marian Goodman Gallery, New York/Paris and Frith Street Gallery, London and Fondazione Nicola Trussardi, Milan

sumption. Carsten Höller's works are also situated in a productive interval, the "space of doubt" that separates our free will from the neuronal or physiological forces that shape us. Mostly offering a physical or mental experience, sometimes of a panic-inducing nature, the artist transforms each of his exhibitions into a kind of laboratory where visitors are exposed to sensations that call their representation of the world into question, like wearing glasses that turn things upside down, walking through a space where

every object has a perfectly symmetrical double, being subjected to the frenetic flashing of a wall of light bulbs inspired by battery systems for poultry breeding, and so on. Höller installed a gigantic slide in the Tate Modern in 2007, thus showing his interest in intelligently combining the worlds of art and popular entertainment.

What would happen if the artists in a group show were allocated time rather than space? Taking this question as their starting point, Philippe Parreno and Hans-Ulrich Obrist organized *Il Tempo del Postino* (Postman Time) in Manchester in July 2007. Midway between art exhibition and theater production, this hybrid event involved Matthew Barney, Pierre Huyghe, Liam Gillick, Douglas Gordon, Anri Sala, Doug Aitken, Tino Sehgal, Olafur Eliasson, Trisha Donnelly, Dominique Gonzalez-Foerster, Rirkrit Tiravanija, Koo Jeong-A, Tacita Dean, and Carsten Höller. Time, its formal treatment, and its political implications constitute the primary focus of this generation of artists from Pierre Huyghe's "*partitions de temps*" of the 1990s up to the exploration of the experience of duration at the Lyons Biennial in 2005 (*L'Expérience de la durée*).

The cinematographic model

In their evolution into the temporal dimension, artists readily borrow the methods of filmmaking, for which time is the primary raw material. Moreover, a certain nostalgia for the story, increased need for communication with the public, and the power of the cinematographic imagination, the contemporary world's greatest producer of collective myths, lead to practices resembling a sort of "film director's art." According to Pierre Huyghe, "While the story may have been developed through cinema in a certain period, it no longer does so, or at least not exclusively. But if cinema did once make stories, it is interesting to analyze how it did so and how these stories were transmitted, how they were produced and disseminated." Cinema has preserved a direct relationship with fiction, one that modern art has abandoned in favor of self-analysis. Art and cinemas therefore try to find in one another what they lack or have lost.

The art exhibition thus evolved toward the form of a movie set. The tone was set in 1990 by a group show entitled *Les Ateliers du Paradise*, during which the three artists Pierre Joseph, Philippe Parreno, and Philippe Perrin literally lived inside a gallery laid out as a set, inviting numerous guests, dividing their use of time into sequences, and creating works and events on the spot. The art gallery thus became a "photogenic space" (an expression used by Gonzalez-Foerster, Joseph, Joisten, and Parreno in connection with the *Ozone* show of 1989) in which visitors were required to create their own sequences. As Eric Troncy wrote in 1994, "Pollock's *all-over* changes here into *all around*. The work is now all around and the spectator in the middle, no longer beholding the spectacle of the painting but immersed in the pictorial scene, sharing this space." The Thai artist Rirkrit Tiravanija includes the mention "lots of people" in his titles to indicate that the visitors are integral part of the work; the forms the artist presents to the public only become works of art when utilized and "inhabited" by their visitors/users.

The opening thus came to constitute the crucial moment of this evolution of the show into film, the moment of contact with the public, the link between exhibition and spectacle. It became normal to encounter living works of art and real people at inaugurations or set times. Damien Hirst placed twin sisters beneath two identical dot paintings in 1993. Meyer Vaisman presented a street musician with a monkey, Félix González-Torres couples dancing in a bare structure made up of small lamps, and Carsten Höller a girl wearing red contact lenses (*Jenny Happy*, 1994). Pierre Joseph filled his shows with "living characters for reactivation" in the shape of bit players dressed up as super heroes, lepers or fairies, replaced the following day with photographs taken of the scene. Vanessa Beecroft's installations instead present groups of young women with the same look (red or platinum blond wigs and similar underwear) who simply pose motionless in the middle of the visitors/voyeurs. In short, human beings became a support for artistic practice, just like models in a fashion parade or actors directed by a filmmaker. In offering the public objects to handle, actors, and models, the art exhibition posed the issue of the coexistence of human beings, objects, and forms.

Tino Sehgal also works on this ambiguity in staging situations played by actors that sometimes come in contact with the public and sometimes transform them into the audience of theatrical pieces made up of citations, a silent setting or discourse (as in *This is Propaganda*, 2002, where one of the actors shouts out the title of the work). Sehgal's works cannot be reproduced in any way. The only trace of their existence is the transfer of money from the collector's account to the artist's. There is no contract, no photography, no script. In this "economy of experience," transferred in the field of artistic practice, it is the recollection that takes the place of the product. Sehgal also involved the collectors in one of his works (*Those Thoughts*), organizing a dinner in the couple's home. When the main course was served, one of them stood up and left the room, followed a few minutes later by the other. They then returned but exchanged their places at table...

Luigi Pirandello wrote that the reversible relationship between reality and appearance is the only path of artistic access to the real world. Through tools at the disposal of the public, such as events, processes, objects, and images, Pierre Huyghe presents compositions aimed at interpreting life instead of being sub-

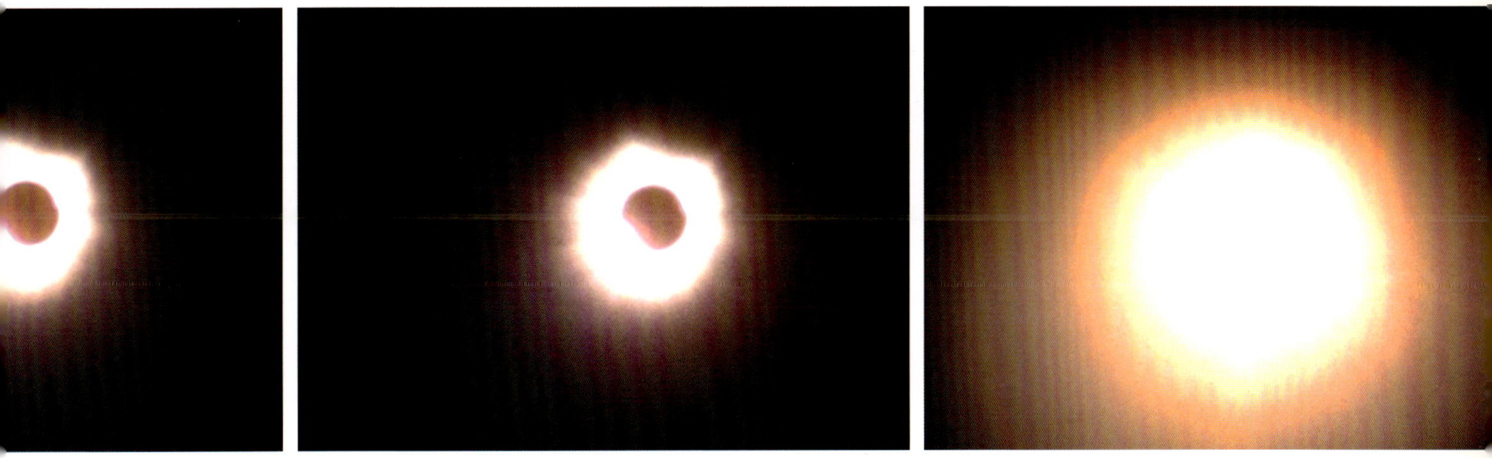

jected to its formatting. From the large billboards erected over a public construction site in Paris to display photographs of the work taking place in real time (*Barbés/Rochechouart*, 1994) to *A Journey That Wasn't* (2005), a lavish musical about the artist's trip to the Arctic Ocean, Huyghe asserts the artwork as a space of activity, a form wholly shaped by human interaction and economic, political, and social phenomena.

This polyphonic approach recalls the use of the reverse shot in cinema: how to develop tools capable of comparing heterogeneous words, of addressing reality not live but in montage? Huyghe's ethic of translation is marked by the rejection of any form of ventriloquism.

The idea is to speak not *for* but *with* another, to include the other and the elsewhere in the shot.

In addition to the model of the film set, the Hollywood method of production itself became a point of reference for art. "I was really fascinated by Hollywood and Hollywood Boulevard. I started using masks I'd bought on Hollywood Boulevard." Thus Paul McCarthy, whose trash performances survive in the form of videos projected in their settings. The artist makes his appearance dressed as a horror-film chef or Pinocchio and uses ketchup, food, and paint in an obscene and cathartic orgy. *Bossy Burger* (1991) and *Heidi* (1992, with Mike Kelley) plunge American culture into a pop nightmare where Beckettian and Disney characters rub shoulders. "There are times when my work has been compared to the Viennese Actionist school, but I always thought there was this whole connection with Pop. The ketchup, the hamburger, and also the movie world." (McCarthy quoted in *Double Trouble: The Patchett Collection*, Spain, p. 182).

On the occasion of the 2001 Venice Biennale, Maurizio Cattelan hired an airplane and flew collectors and personalities from the art world down to the outskirts of Palermo to inaugurate his latest work. Upon their arrival, the guests were taken by bus to a public rubbish dump where they found three tables covered with white cloths and an army of waiters in livery awaiting them in the blazing sun. Above them, halfway up the slope of a barren hillside, was a life-size reproduction of the famous Hollywood sign. Closely allied to the silent humor of Jacques Tati or American slapstick comedy, Cattelan's art consists in creating brutal, insolent short-circuits of this kind. The objects he exhibits are necessarily realistic and on a large-scale if possible, since their purpose is to shock the viewer. Described as the result of "*quelque chose de mécanique plaquée sur du vivant*" (tacking something mechanical onto something living) by Henri Bergson, laughter is always accompanied by a certain anxiety, as happens with the work *Him*, a hyper-realistic sculpture that the visitor initially sees from behind and interprets as a child kneeling down, perhaps in prayer, but then discovers on seeing of its face to be a portrayal of Adolf Hitler. As Cattelan explains, "My mother always told me that you can't really clean the floor unless you see where the dirt is first." This bad boy of the art world presents intensely disquieting and brutally upsetting situations like scenes in a film with all the appearance of reality.

Art "in socius"

Just as the site-specific artwork gave way to the time-specific, art *in socius* supplanted art *in situ*. Artists made use of structures and formats found in the real world, no longer representing things but rather making use of them. One example is Jens Haaning's *Untitled* (*De Appel – De Gelderse Roos*, 2000), which consists of a live video link between an art gallery and a psychiatric hospital. This cannot be regarded as a demagogic prototype of interchange, since the connection is one-way only and transforms an exhibition space into a human zoo or spectacle. The artist's work often addresses the immigrant community, as concretely materialized through the installation of loudspeakers in the street transmitting jokes in Turkish (*Turkish Jokes*, 1994) and Arabic (*Arabic Jokes*, 1996), thus excluding the "natives" and bringing together in laughter those who know the language. Jens Haaning's works demand our participation, not in theoretical terms (as was implied in the idea of participation in the happenings of the 1950s) but simply in order to test the concrete hypothesis they embody. When he set up a travel agency in the Galerie Chouakri in Berlin, it issued real tickets. When he opened a supermarket of imported goods in Freiburg, visitors were really able to compare the prices and buy the products

(*Superdiscount*, 1998). Far removed from an aesthetic of "reconstruction" (like the one pursued by the Belgian Guillaume Bijl with his transformation of exhibition spaces into *trompe-l'oeil* images), Haaning sets up structures whose effective functioning is the actual object of his artistic practice, above and beyond any observation on the nature of art or the museum.

Immigrant communities and the economic pressure exerted by global capitalism on the proletariat of the entire world constitute the primary subject matter also for the artist Santiago Sierra, whose black-and-white photographs document acts of violent exploitation. *Remunerated for a Period of 360 Consecutive Hours* (2000) involved the artist paying someone to spend 360 consecutive hours behind a wall erected in the exhibition venue.

Still more cynical is *Línea de 160 cm tatuada sobre 4 personas* (2000), for which the artist hired four drug-addicted prostitutes in Madrid to have a horizontal line tattooed on their backs in exchange of enough money to buy a dose of heroin. A merciless critic of the reality of capitalism, Santiago Sierra closely resembles Andy Warhol in the way he addresses the everyday spectacle of "economic horror" with apparent indifference.

Matthieu Laurette also played with forms of reality when he attempted to set up a real offshore bank with funds from a double ticket office installed in the entrance to a show (*Offshore*, 1999). Martin Creed works instead with the material aspects of institutional spaces. *On/Off* (2001) consisted of the lights in the exhibition room being switched on and off, and *Work No. 850* (2008) of someone running at top speed across the vast hall of Tate Britain in London every 30 seconds. Presented at Manifesta 3 in Ljubljana, *Film* (2000) by the Polish artist Pawel Althamer adopts the completely different visual strategy of the dissolving of the work of art in urban space. Althamer created an ordinary situation that, as such, was perfectly able to escape most people's notice. A homeless person sitting on a bench, two adolescents, a policeman, a young couple, a boy with a skateboard, and a street musician performed the same ordinary gestures within a subtly choreographed framework for 30 minutes every day and then moved away all together. Equally furtive was the project initiated by the Italian Roberto Cuoghi in 2000, undergoing a process to transformation designed to make him increasingly like his father in terms of clothing, physical appearance, and everyday habits. Like the performances of Tino Sehgal, this work is wholly undocumented apart from some photographs of no artistic value whatsoever.

Docufiction and prosopopoeia

Documentary or fiction: the relationship between the art of the period 1990–2010 and cinema lies in these two approaches, which are not necessarily mutually exclusive. As Jean-Luc Godard once put it, "*Le documentaire, c'est ce qui arrive à l'autre. La fiction, c'est ce qui m'arrive à moi.*" (The documentary is what happens to others. Fiction is what happens to me.) In moving from "me" to "us" the work of art ends up incorporating one into the other, using the imagination as a tool to discover reality. This is how Pierre Huyghe and Philippe Parreno describe their joint project the *Anna Sanders Magazine*: "Anna Sanders is the main character of a film which is still being written and also the title of a magazine in which the character is presented. The character is never actually seen but gradually discovered through the graphics, articles, images, and advertising ... Other characters will also appear in the same way and give their names to future issues. All together these magazines will tell a story...the *story of a feeling.*" The two artists later took this experiment still further by purchasing the character Ann Lee from a Japanese Manga catalogue: "This character, this cultural product, is now no longer bound for fiction. We have deviated it from its path. Our project today is to make a film of imagination rather than fiction.

The character Ann Lee now belongs to us but is still an empty sign with no author. ... The project is therefore to see how this sign can become a story and how the character can be a tool to grasp reality." Ann Lee starred between 2000 and 2003 in stories by Melik Ohanian, Liam Gillick, François Curlet, Dominique Gonzalez-Foerster, Pierre Joseph, M/M, Richard Phillips, Joe Scanlan, Rirkrit Tiravanija, and Anna-Léna Vaney before being officially "terminated" by the copyright holders.

It was by exiting from the mechanism of fiction that Ann Lee took on her status as a graphic sign and "work force"....

Prosopopoeia, a rhetorical device whereby an inanimate object is given a voice, has become a key motif in a world dominated by goods, a world in which articles of consumption and technological products have taken on an affective dimension. One example is provided by Douglas Gordon's series of works in which the time of art and the time of real life overlap. Taking Alfred Hitchcock's film *Psycho* as material, he slowed down the images to make the duration of the projection and the action coincide (*24-Hour Psycho*, 1993). Application of the same procedure to John Ford's *The Searchers* resulted in a five-year film. The anthropomorphous dimension thus given to cinematographic works can also be detected in *List of Names*, a work in progress since 1990, which involves him keeping a careful list of the names of all the people he meets.

While Gordon works on movies, Michael Elmgreen & Ingar Dragset take over celebrated works of art and turn them into remote-controlled theatrical characters for the time of a performance (*Drama Queens*, 2007). Jeff Koons's *Rabbit* and Alberto Giacometti's *Walking Man* are among the works given voices and involved in a plot that, with the international explosion of the art market, highlighted their status as star merchandise, exploiting their aesthetic characteristics in witty dialogues. With the Ann Lee project, Douglas Gordon's *détournement* of cinema, and the theater of Elmgreen & Dragset, artists became ventriloquists of social and cultural production.

The Viatorisation of forms

Simon Starling goes in search of the traceability of things, analyzing the social and economic constituent elements of our environment. For the project entitled *Flaga, 1972–2000* (2002), the artist drove a 1974 Fiat 126 from Turin, the company headquarters, to the Polish city of Cieszyn, where some of the 126 models put onto the market were produced at the time. He subsequently removed the engine and hung the dismantled bodywork, now repainted in the red and white colors of the Polish flag, on the wall like an abstract sculpture. Starling thus models relations of trade and export, using the physical journey from one city to the other as an artistic medium in its own right. *Shedboatshed* involved demolishing a boatshed to make a boat that the artist then sailed on the Rhine. In Spain he crossed a desert area on a hydrogen-powered bicycle and then used the water produced by its engine to paint a watercolor of a cactus (*Tabernas Desert Run*). Form becomes dynamic here, with each static work constituting nothing more than a point on a line of flight.

The Japanese artist Shimabuku draws errant lines on the earth's surface related to an initial subject that is no more than a pretext for movement. The project *Cucumber Journey* (2000) involved a trip by barge along the eighteenth-century canal between London and Birmingham for the purpose of making pickles: "The vegetables and small cucumbers I had bought fresh in London were already in brine when I reached Birmingham. ... During the journey people gave me recipes for pickles. I watched the foam, the birds, the leaves undulating on the water, and the cucumbers slowly turning into pickles."

Joachim Koester, Gerard Byrne, and Tacita Dean employ similar methods but add the dimension of historical investigation. Koester retraced a Swedish scientist's expedition to the North Pole (*Message from Andrée*, 2005) by displaying period documents around a practically monochromatic 16 mm film with dark stains and scratches, an authentic-fake document made by putting together photographs found 32 years later but severely damaged by the cold. Tacita Dean's work consists mainly of films made during her wanderings, including *Diamond Ring*, an eclipse of the sun shot in Madagascar in 2002, and *Pie* (2003), images of migratory birds perched in a tree, which are characterized by a poetry of starkness that prompts meditation. She deliberately uses obsolete materials, like 16 mm film and annotated archival photos, which allude to the early days of cinema. Gerard Byrne instead devotes his energies mostly to reenactments based on documents of recent history. He thus used an actor to play the part of Jean-Paul Sartre in a video – *Homme à femmes (Michel Debraine)*, 2004 – based on an interview in a French newspaper in which the philosopher talked about his somewhat misogynistic relationship with women. In *Case Study (Loch Ness)*, made between 2001 and 2008, Byrne uses a vast range of information, including photographs, documents, and specimens, to explore the mythology of the celebrated Scottish monster.

The artists who emerged in the period 1990–2000 use the interhuman and relational dimension, filmmaking procedures, attention to the time-specific dimension of artworks, and the use of forms and structures existing in the social realm to develop dynamic forms of composition. Generally regarding the work of art as a link in a chain, they "viatorize" forms in the sense that they set them in motion in time and space and envision movement as a method of composition in its own right, thus productively disrupting the respective values of the ephemeral act and the durable object in contemporary aesthetics. One of the stylistic keynotes of the art of the period 1990–2000 thus lies in this act of screen-based translation, which consists in producing hypertexts in real space-time.

Eija-Liisa Ahtila

Born in Hämeenlinna, Finland, in 1959. Lives and works in Helsinki. It was in the early 1990s, after work of a post-conceptual nature with painting, photography, installation and performance, that Eija Liisa Athila discovered video as the medium best suited to the creation of what she calls her "human dramas". The artist uses the camera to penetrate the nooks and crannies of the psyche and explore the hidden feelings and emotions that govern interpersonal relationships. The main characters in her works are above all young women, often filmed in their homes – the places she sees as best reflecting their fragility – and followed along the inner paths that can lead them to redemption, freedom, separation, discovery, mourning and madness.
Understood as both a physical and a mental space, it is precisely the home that constitutes the subject of the three-screen installation *The House*, presented in Kassel at Documenta in 2002. The home of the main character Elisa begins to fill up with sounds and voices that become increasingly insistent until she loses track of her spatiotemporal coordinates and is forced to barricade all the points of access in a desperate attempt to defend her world. The home returns as the metaphor of a mental condition in *The Wind*, a video triptych presented in New York at the MoMA in 2006, where a woman in an evident state of emotional disturbance "invites" a strong wind to enter her house and sweep everything away.
Athila's interest in borderline situations and the great and small dramas of life is reflected in *Lahja (The Present)* (2001), an installation made up of five monitors showing five brief stories in pairs. Presented two years earlier at the Venice Biennale, *Consolation Service* (1999) shows a young married couple in the painful process of separating and starting new relationships.
Athila uses cinematographic format, multiple projections or monitors as required to set up and present her works. Continuity with the artist's investigations of the 1980s emerges in her close attention to the relationship with space, as reflected in the meticulous planning of the position to be occupied by the spectator so as to ensure the best possible experience of her video installations. A conceptual approach also underlies the investigation of image structure and vocabulary, which leads Athila to use and often combine a documentary approach with elements borrowed from advertising and video clips.
(*P.V.*)

The House, 2002
Three-screen DVD installation, 16:9, aspect ratio 1:1.85, stereo surround
Courtesy Marian Goodman Gallery, New York/Paris

Lahja (The Present), 2001
Five-channel video installation with sound, variable dimensions
San Francisco, San Francisco Museum of Modern Art, Purchase through a gift of Chara Schreyer

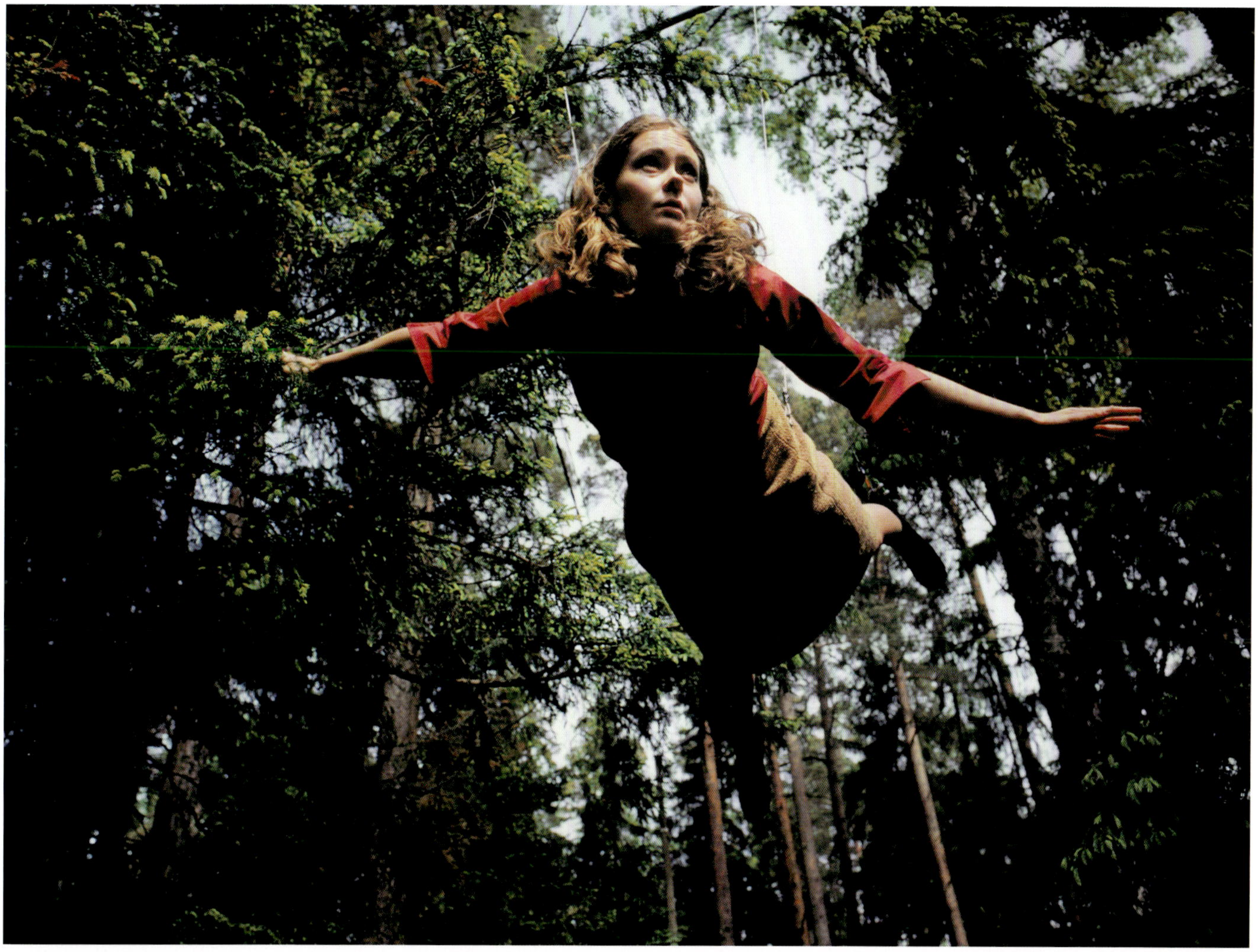

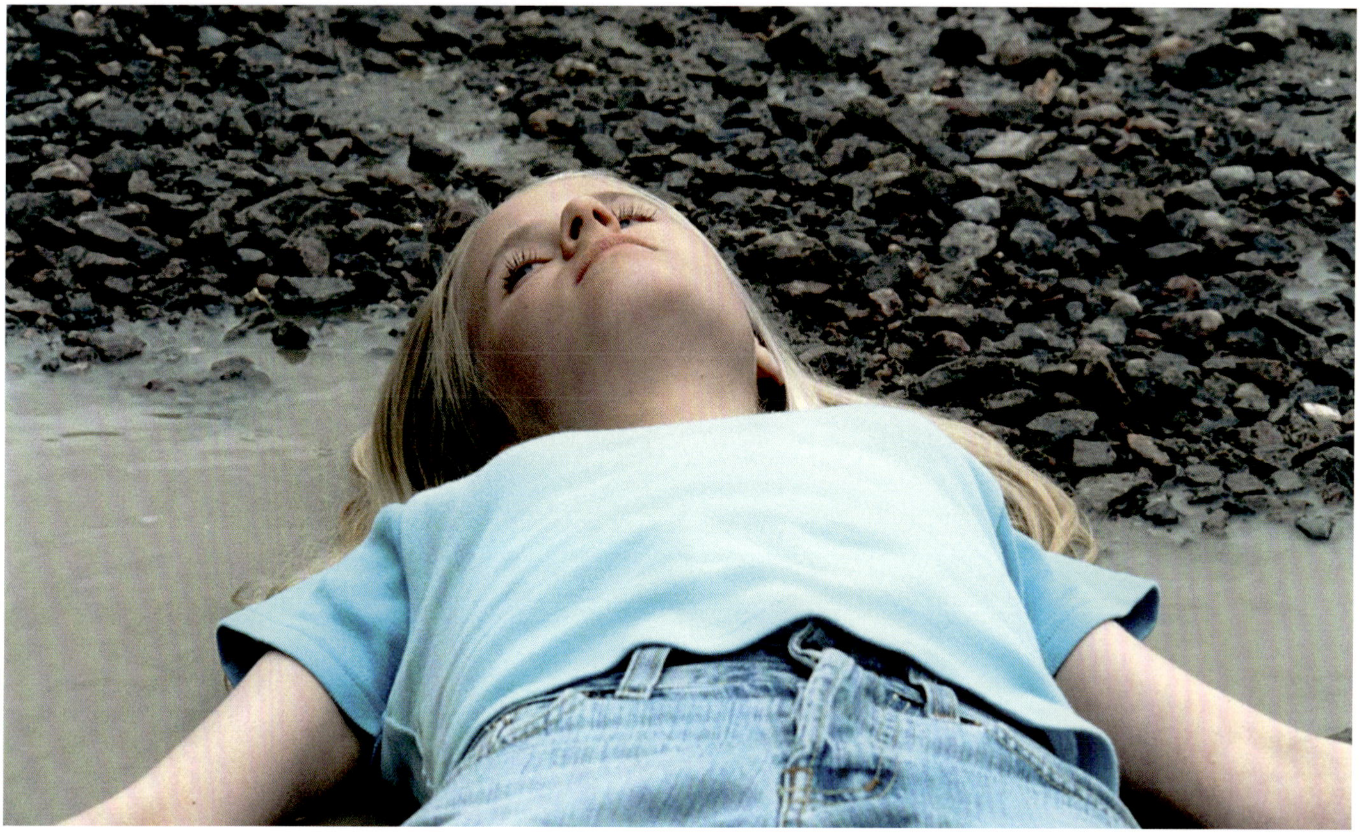

Ai Weiwei

Born in Beijing in 1957. Lives and works in Beijing.
There is certainly nothing new about the idea of the artist as creator of his or her environment, which was championed by many members of the historical avant-garde movements, above all those calling for direct action in the world outside the contexts traditionally linked to the production and use of artworks. One century later, however, it regains present-day relevance and proves perfectly fitting for the work of Ai Weiwei, a leading figure on the Chinese art scene for over 25 years now, who sees his work precisely as a way of working directly on the system of interpersonal social and cultural relationships defining the physiognomy of our age. It is this view that underlies his use of the extraordinary international showcase of Documenta to invite 1001 Chinese citizens to Kassel in 2007. In this way, he not only asserted his interest in cultural interchange but also generated an extraordinary switch in perspective by taking a large group of his countrymen to observe a major European artistic event from the inside and thus reversing the West's atavistic habit of looking down on the East from the height of its presumed cultural supremacy. Significantly entitled *Fairytale*, this project also involved transporting 1001 Qing dynasty chairs to Germany as an ideal offering from each of the Chinese guests to Documenta's "tired" visitors.
The chairs were then sold as works of art at the end of the event, thus introducing a further shift in meaning, as often happen in Ai's work, where traditional Chinese objects are frequently decontextualized and defamiliarized (*Han Dynasty Urn with Coca-Cola Logo*, 1994). This holds also for *Template* (2007), the other work presented at Documenta, an enormous structure halfway between sculpture and architecture that is characterized once again by a marked degree of social commitment. Shaped like a Chinese temple, the work was constructed with doors and windows from old demolished houses, thus bringing together tradition and innovation, loss and recovery. The play of opposites is in any case another constant in the work of Ai Weiwei, who moves freely between past and present. Suffice it to recall his collaboration as a non-professional architect with Herzog & de Meuron within the framework of the project for the construction of the Beijing Olympic stadium, a work in which tradition and modernity emblematically coexist.
(*L.L.*)

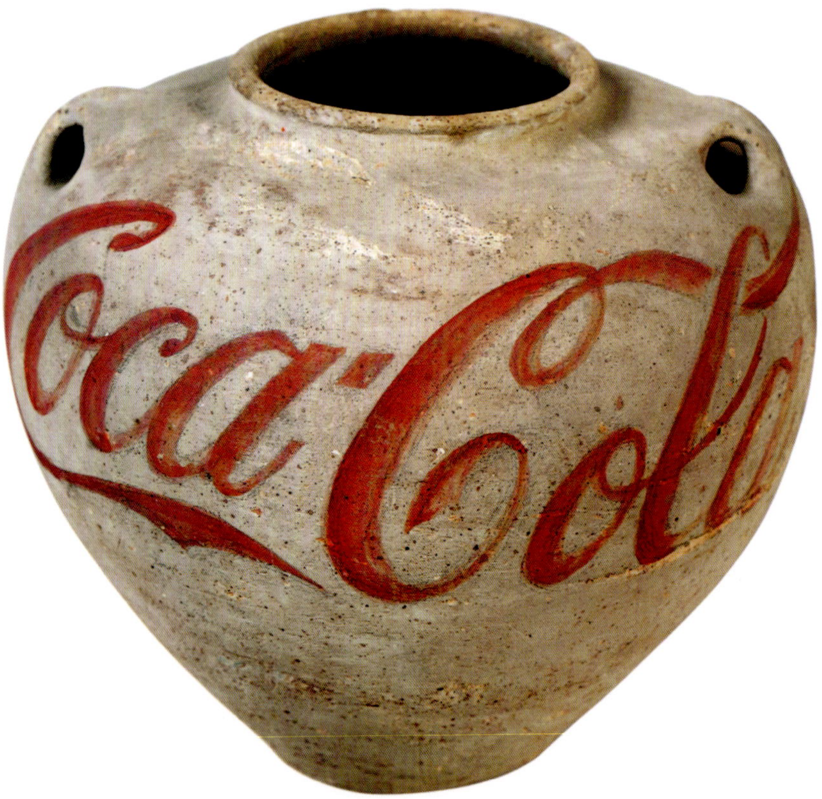

Han Dynasty Urn with Coca-Cola Logo, 1994
Han dynasty terracotta, red painting
25.5 x 28 x 28 cm
Courtesy Mary Boone Gallery, New York

Template (Before Collapsing), 2007
1001 wooden doors and windows from destroyed Ming and Qing dynasty houses, wooden base,
7.18 x 1.20 x 8.50 m
Installation at *Documenta 12*, Kassel, 2007
Courtesy Mary Boone Gallery, New York

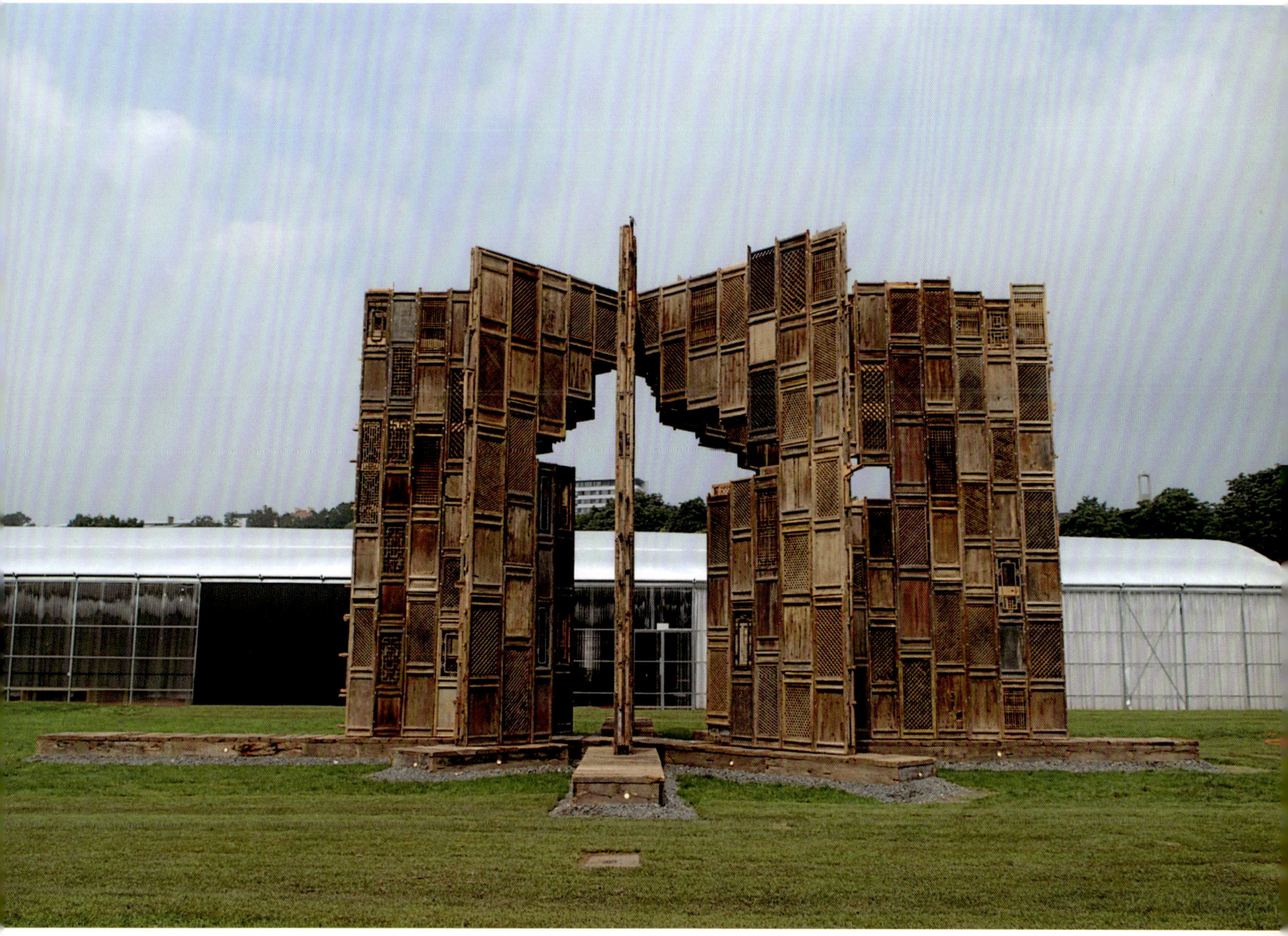

Darren Almond

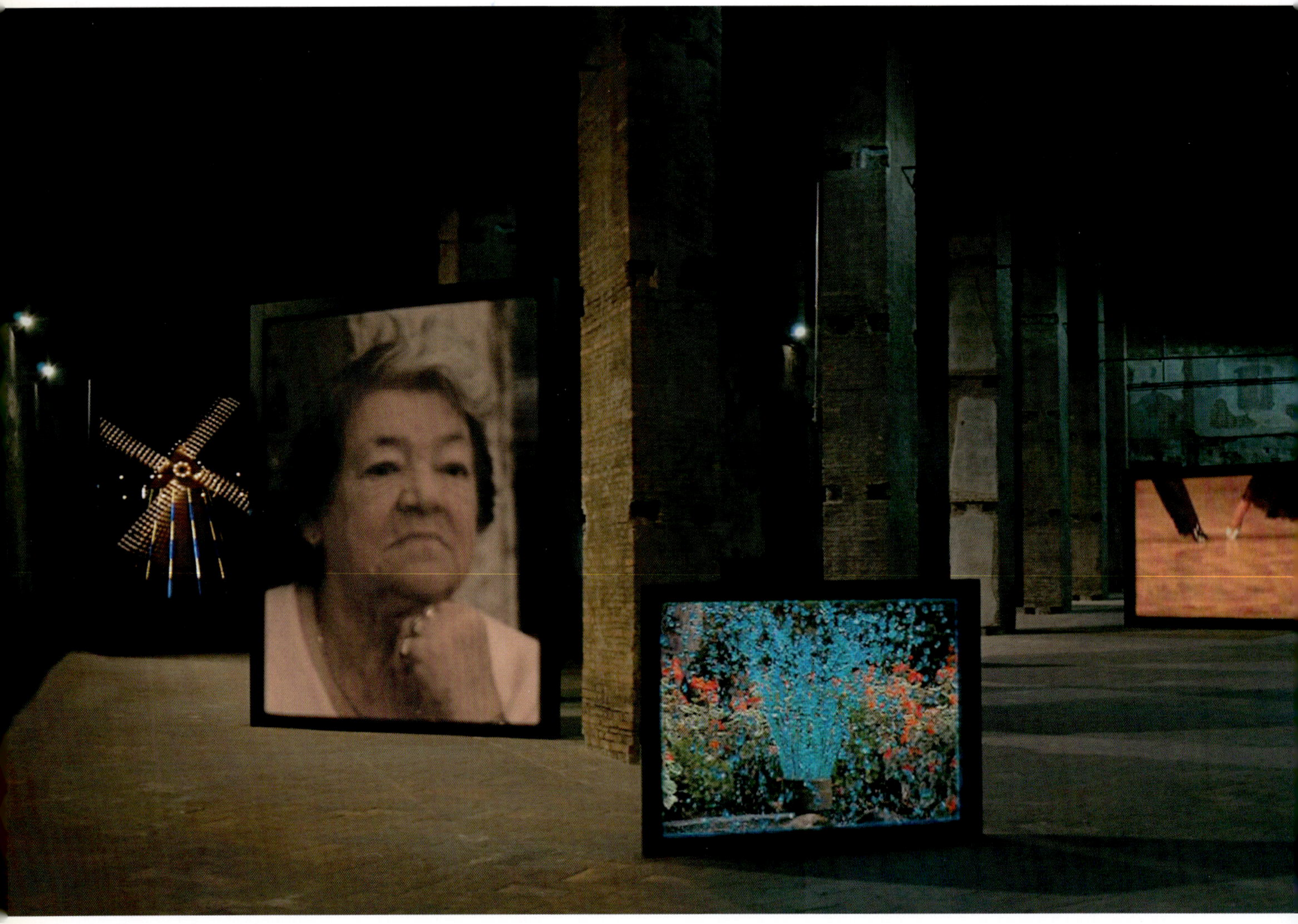

Born in Wigan, UK, in 1971. Lives and works in London.
Darren Almond's work is based on a sensory and emotive approach to the passing of time, understood as a fluid entity of human life.
The artist thus focuses on memory, using the emotional force of recollections and the rationalizing action of temporal distance to speak about the human condition.
Almond took part in the 2005 Turner Prize by invitation with the environmental video installation *If I Had You*, produced in 2003 by the Trussardi Foundation, Milan, as a twofold journey in the past and present of the life of the artist's family. The video tells the story of his grandmother's return to the town of Blackpool, where she spent her honeymoon, in sound and images. The artist accompanies her as she revisits the scenes of that romantic trip, gathering biographical information but also investigating the origin of his own existence.
The images of the town, a traditional holiday resort known for its Ferris wheel, are transformed into the woman's photographic diary and come to occupy a dimension outside of any chronological order, concentrating within themselves the stereotype of a timeless present and a distant past.
An operation on time also lies at the heart of *Tide* (2008), an installation of 600 digital clocks on a wall synchronized to mark the passing of the minutes in unison with a simultaneous beep.
An allusion to the inexorable flow of time and mankind's obsessive attempts to place it under control through mechanization, *Tide* confronts the viewer with the utmost iconic elaboration of invisibility. Simultaneous movement becomes a cadence of eternity, infinite repetition strives for perfection, the oppressive and intrusive sound is the analogue of a force over which man has no control.
(*F.T.*)

If I Had You, 2003
Video installation in Palazzo della Ragione, Milan
Produced by Fondazione Nicola Trussardi, Milan
Courtesy Jay Jopling / White Cube, London, Matthew Marks Gallery, New York and Gallerie Max Hetzler, Berlin

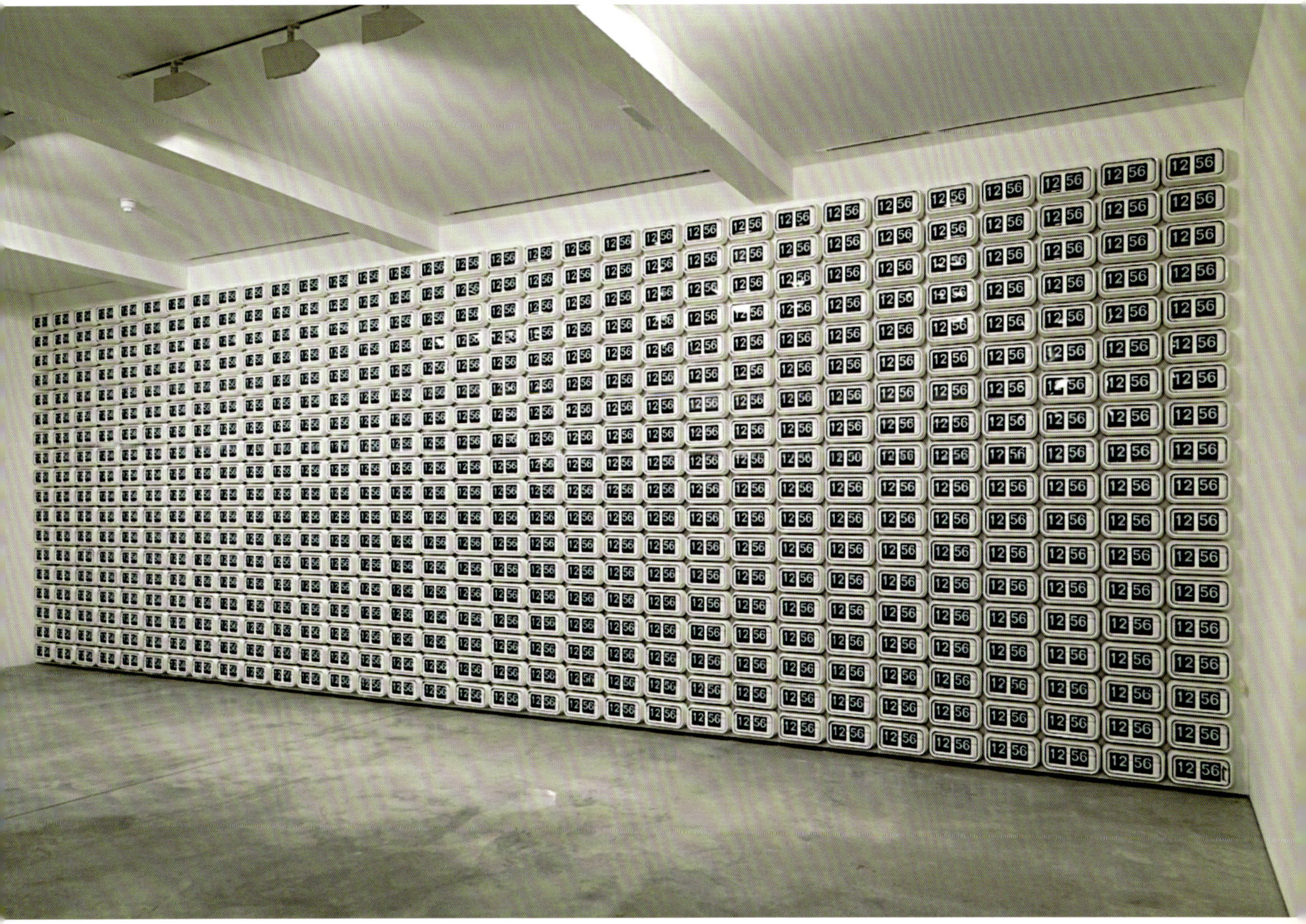

Tide, 2008
600 digital wall clocks, Perspex, electro-mechanics, steel, vinyl, computerized electronic control system and components
Each clock, 31.2 x 18.2 x 14.2 cm
Courtesy Parasol Unit Foundation for Contemporary Art, London

Sophie Calle

Born in Paris in 1953. Lives and works in Paris.
"Maria was an artist, but the work she did had nothing to do with creating objects commonly defined as art. Some people called her a photographer, others referred to her as a conceptualist, still others considered her a writer, but none of these descriptions was accurate, and in the end I don't think she can be pigeonholed in any way."
This is how Paul Auster presents Sophie Calle, the true identity of the character named Maria, in *Leviathan* (1992), one of his most enthralling novels.
As an artist, Sophie Calle has so many features in common with the characters created by Auster that the writer's decision to create her literary "double" is hardly surprising. Suffice it to recall the key stages in her career.
On returning to Paris after a long absence in 1979, she began to follow strangers so as to rediscover her city through their unwitting guidance. This practice of stalking people led her the next year all the way to Venice, where she kept constant track of the man she had followed there for two whole weeks, taking photographs of him and initiating a sort of seduction of which he was to remain wholly unaware (*Suite vénitienne*, 1983).
She then got a job as a chambermaid in a Venetian hotel so as to gain access to the guests' rooms and appropriate details of their lives by photographing their belongings (*L'Hotel*, 1983).
She found the address book of a man named Pierre by chance, made contact with the people listed there in order to obtain information about him from them, and published the results of her extraordinary "investigation" every day in *Libération* (*L'Homme au Carnet*, 1983).
The relationship between Paul Auster and Sophie Calle does not end, however, with the similarities between the artist's work and the behavior of his literary characters. Six years after the publication of *Leviathan*, the artist asked Auster to "direct" her for a year by writing a part specially for her that she undertook to perform in every detail. The writer declined to take on such a responsibility but did agree to guide her life in New York for a week by giving her a series of orders that she was to obey scrupulously. The instructions written by Auster and the documentation collected by Calle were gathered together in the book *Double Game*, published in English and French in 1998.
The tendency to blur and ultimately eliminate the boundaries between art and life that characterizes all of Sophie Calle's work reached its climax in the *Douleur exquise* project of 1999 (which gave rise to a book of the same name).
Using her customary combination of writing and photography, the artist documented every day of the period leading up to the moment when her lover would phone and tell her he had decided to break off their relationship and the following period, during which she would try to cope with and overcome her grief at their sudden separation.
Biography and art were interwoven once again when Calle asked numerous women of different ages and professions to read and comment on a laconic e-mail message with which a man ended an affair. Together with video and audio material, the photographs of the women reading the message and their observations make up the series *Take Care of Yourself*, presented at the Venice Biennale in 2007.
The difficulty of locating Calle's work within the sphere of any precise movement or even general area of art has led critics to fall back on adjectives, describing it as conceptual and sentimental, detached and intimate, cold and emotional at the same time. It is precisely this use of opposites that makes it possible to identify paradox as the scarlet thread running through the artist's works, where chance plays the leading part in games with pre-established rules, loved ones prove to be strangers, strangers become life-long companions, and a private matter loses its unique and unrepeatable character by being opened up to a range of variants through the involvement of the public. Sophie Calle is not looking for spectators but people capable of interacting with her story through their personal experience, sharing her rituals and playing her game.
(*L.L.*)

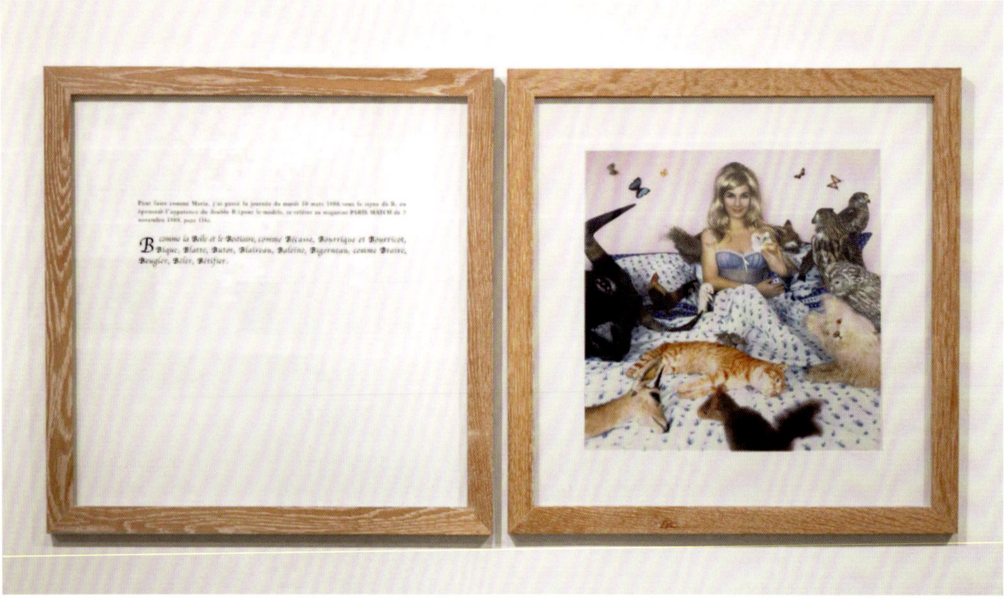

Des journées entières sous le signe du B, du C, du W. BB, 1998
Color photograph, text, frame, 67 x 67 cm each
Courtesy Jean-Baptiste Mondino

Prenez soin de vous, 2007
Letters, photographs, video performance, notes, newspaper cutouts, music scores, poems, and other materials
View of the installation at the French Pavilion, LII Esposizione Internazionale d'Arte, Biennale di Venezia 2007

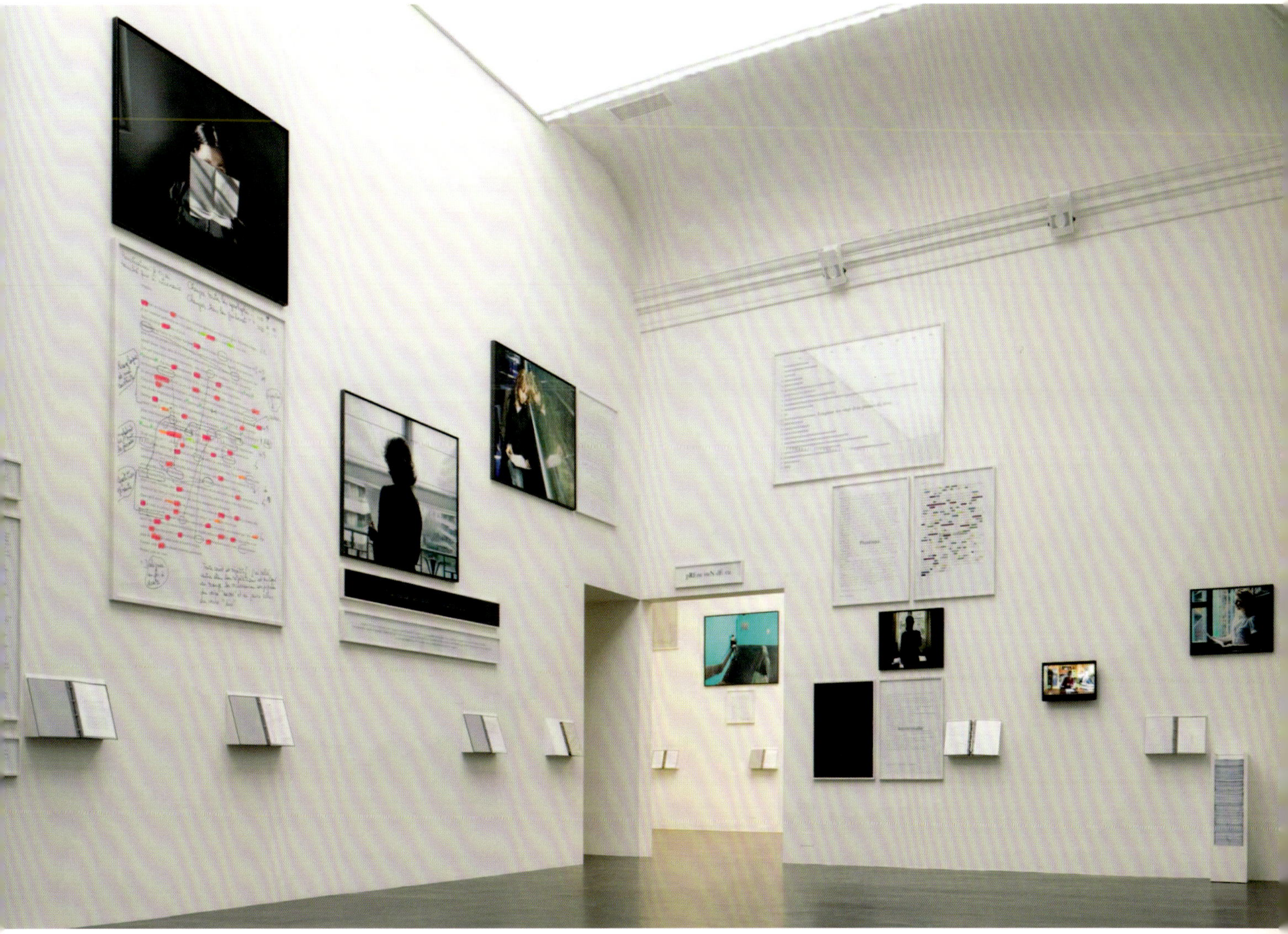

Tacita Dean

Born in Canterbury, UK, in 1965. Lives and works in Berlin.
Tacita Dean's work develops around two linchpins: the enchantment that can spring from observing our surroundings, especially what is destined to change or vanish quickly, and the closely related faculty of memory. Her photographs, drawings and above all her 16 mm films nearly always tell stories in which loss, failure, and disappearance play a fundamental part. Nominated for the Turner Prize in 1998, her 14-minute film *Disappearance at Sea* was devoted to Donald Crowhurst, a bankrupt businessman who lost his life in 1968 in a crazy bid to redeem himself by sailing around the world single-handed. Continued the following year in *Disappearance at Sea II*, Crowhurst's story became a trilogy in 1999, when the artist traveled to the Caribbean to document the remains of the trimaran used by the would-be solo mariner in his reckless enterprise (*Teignmouth Electron*, 2000). It was on this trip that Dean came across a futuristic structure suddenly transformed by the unforeseeable fate of its designer and owner into a contemporary ruin called the "bubble house" by locals. The deep impression it made on her is documented in a series of extraordinary photographs and a short film (*Bubble House*, 1999). The relentless passing of time and its effects on things and people remained constant themes in Dean's work, also after her definitive move to Berlin in 2000. In the 44-minute film *Fernsehturm* (2001), shot entirely in the revolving restaurant at the top of the television tower on the Alexanderplatz, an anamorphic lens is used to obtain a wide-angle effect similar to the old cinemascope taking in a broad section of the room and its windows. At the same time, the camera captures the way the restaurant's motion transforms the external space and the changes taking place inside as the sun goes down. When night falls, however, the windows become mirrors that reflect only images of what happen in the restaurant, thus turning a tourist attraction into a place of social relations. Significantly enough, the artist's attention has often focused on architecture in the German capital in an effort to document the radical changes underway in the political and social structure through changes in the urban environment.
Intense reflection on the passing of time has also led Dean to address the question of fast technological evolution. In *Kodak* (2006), shot in a company plant at Chalon-sur-Saône in France where the units producing movie film were about to be closed down, the artist made her customary use of precisely this celluloid medium to document its imminent disappearance in elegiac tones.
(*P.V.*)

Fernsehturm, 2001
Anamorphic 16 mm film, color, sound, 44'
Courtesy of the artist and Frith Street Gallery, London with Marian Goodman Gallery, Paris/New York

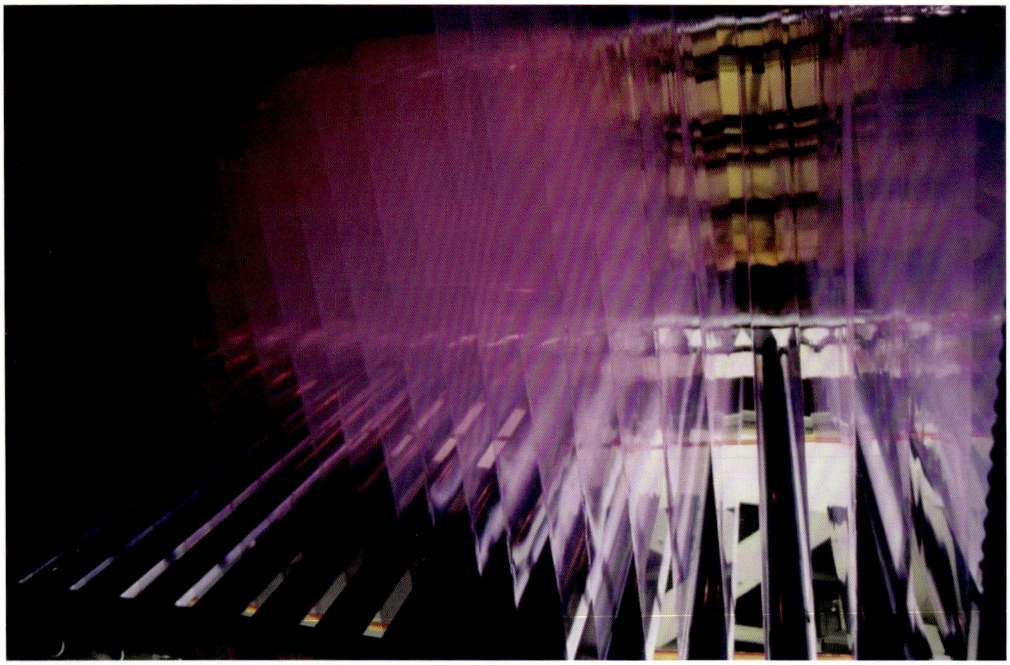

Kodak, 2006
16 mm film, color, optical sound, 60'
Courtesy of the artist and Frith Street Gallery, London with Marian Goodman Gallery, Paris/New York

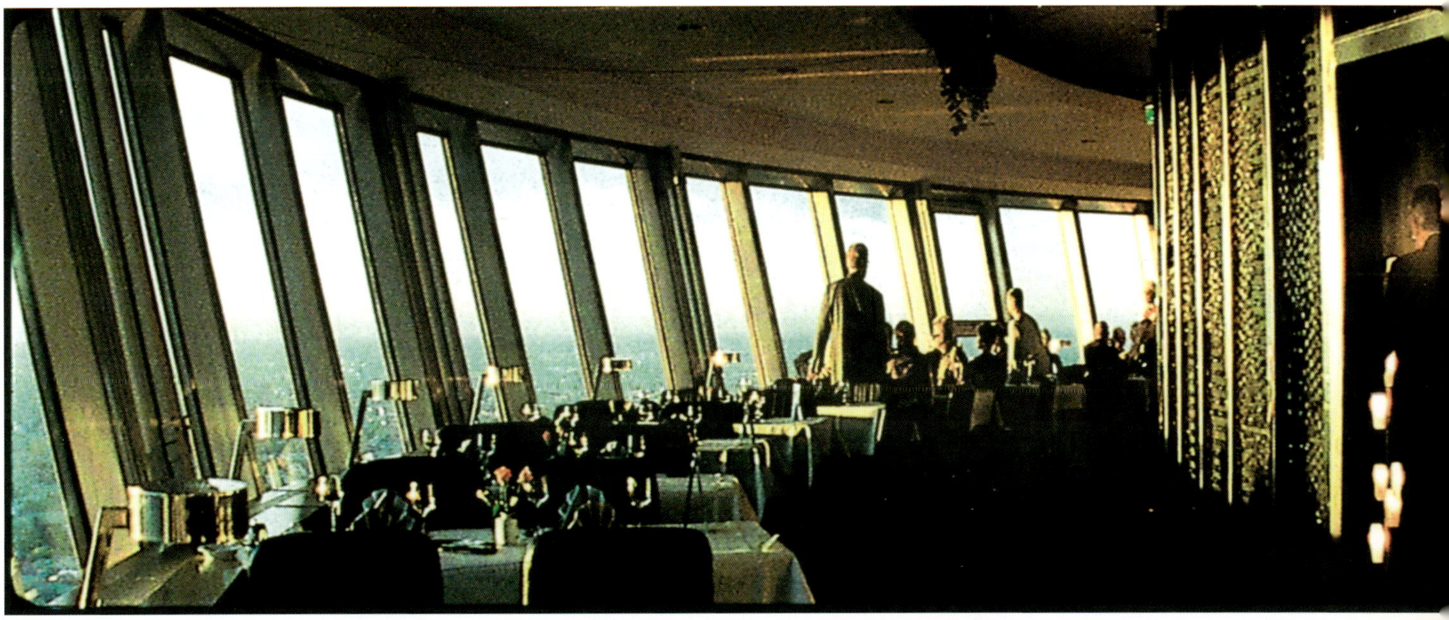

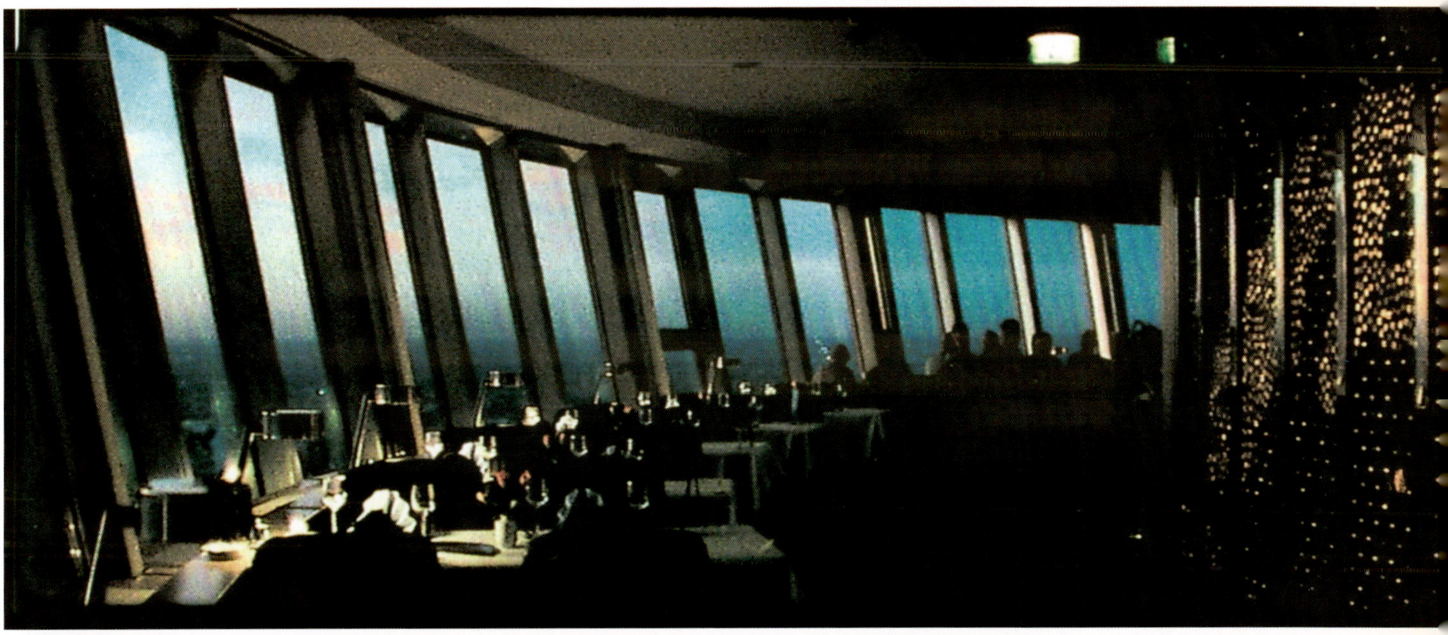

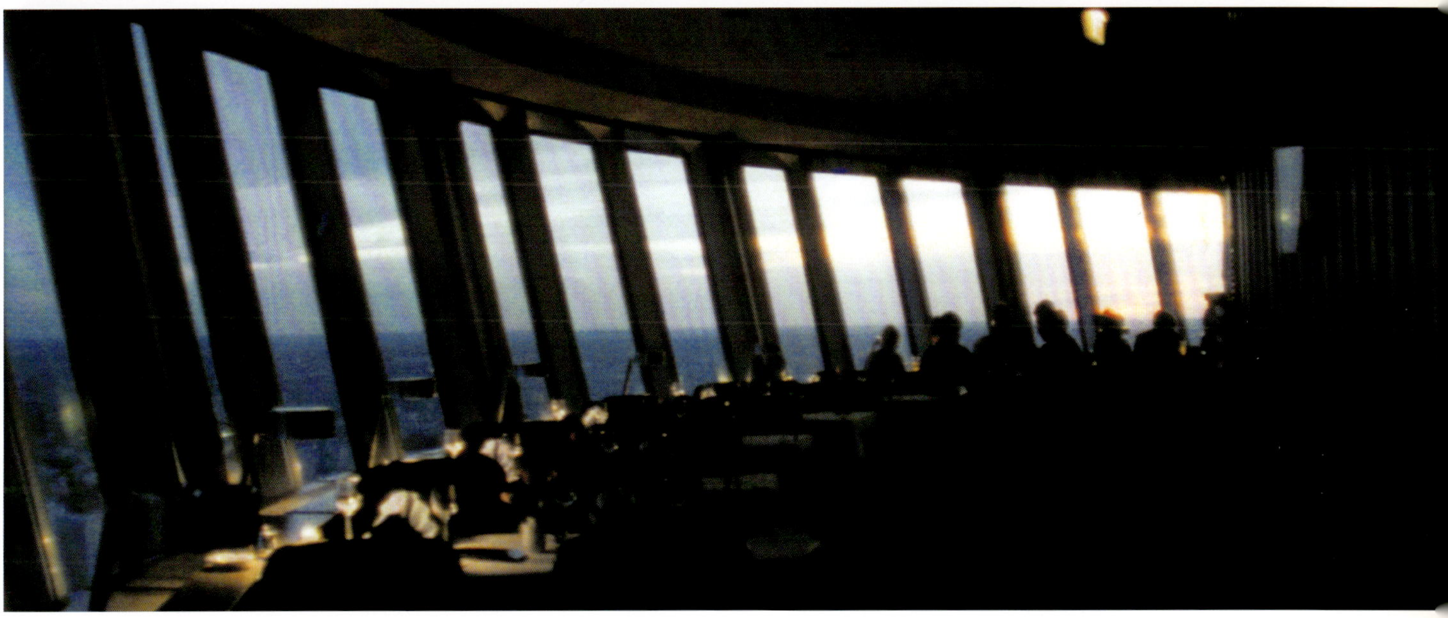

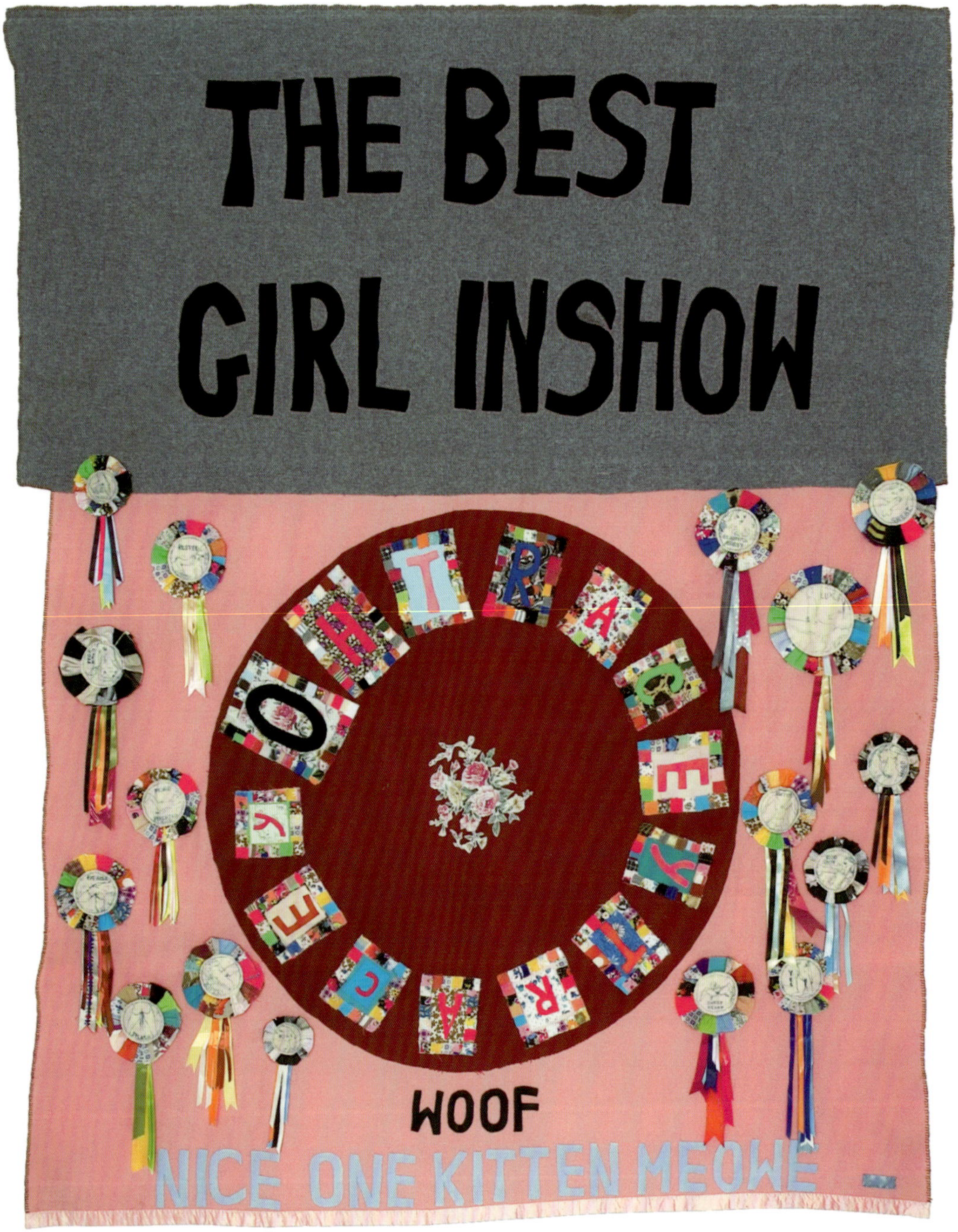

Woof, The Best Girl Inshow, 2005
Woolen cover with paperwork, embroideries, and ink drawings
210 x 120 cm
Courtesy Galleria Lorcan O'Neill, Rome

My Bed, 1998
Mattress, pillows, linens, objects,
79 x 211 x 234 cm
London, The Saatchi Collection

Born in London in 1963. Lives and works in London.
Like much of recent British art, Tracey Emin's work is concerned with individual and social identity. Strictly autobiographical in character, it is shot through with reflections on solitude, the instability of affective relations, the ambivalent and contradictory relationship with sex, and death. Regardless of the medium used – performance, installation, video, drawing, neon or needlework – the artist always draws upon her own life for "revelations" that force the spectator into the often awkward role of a voyeur. It is precisely the greater or lesser readiness of each viewer to perform this role that determines the contrasting reactions of the public and critics to Emin's works. Often accused of excessive self-indulgence in making public a private life that is nothing special in itself, the artist replies that the exceptional nature of her work lies precisely in the fact of addressing themes and experiences that are widely shared and comprehensible to everyone but about which nobody talks for reasons of convention, social taboo and a misplaced sense of propriety. Already a member of the Charles Saatchi stable, Emin took part in the exhibition *Sensation* at the Royal Academy in 1997 with *Everyone I Have Ever Slept With, 1963–1995*, a tent inside which all her lovers were remembered in different ways (later destroyed in a warehouse fire together with many works by other Young British Artists). The following year she created an unmade bed bearing obvious traces of recent sexual intercourse (*My Bed*) and presented it in 1999 at the annual Turner Prize exhibition, but failed to win the prestigious award. Both works, which are among the best known and most controversial produced by the artist, are born out of an irrepressible urge to confess and accentuated narcissism that takes to extremes the desire to make art and life coincide.
(*L.L.*)

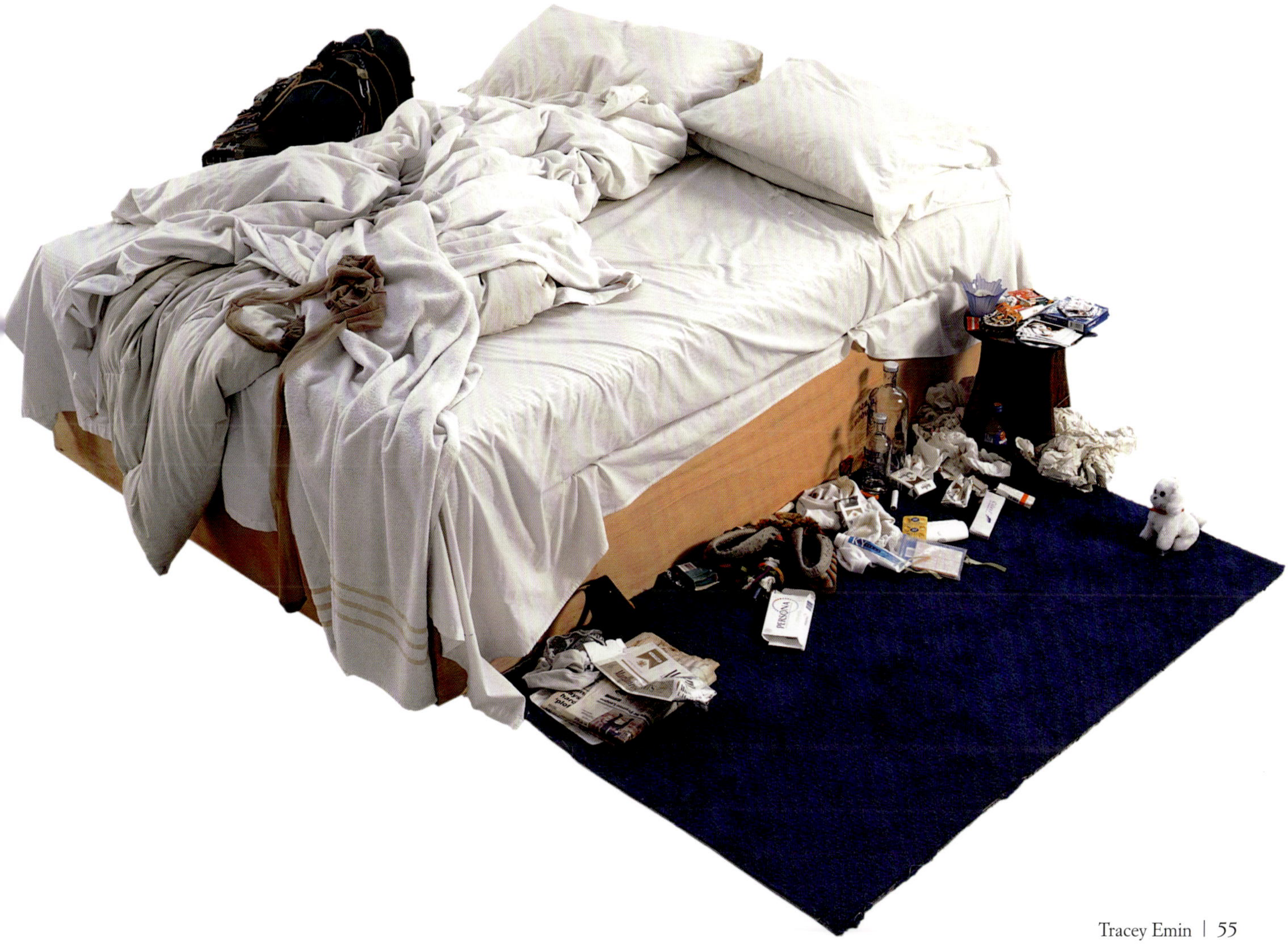

Subodh Gupta

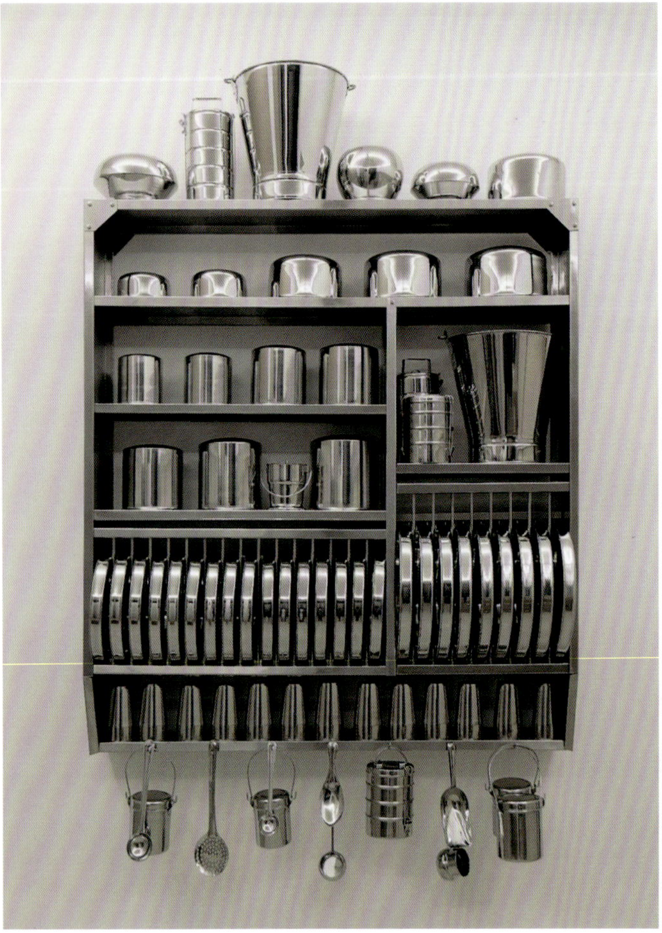

Curry 2 (1), 2005
Stainless steel,
220 x 138 x 40 cm
Courtesy Art & Public, Geneva

This Side Is the Other Side, 2002
Bronze, Vespa, metal containers,
170 x 170 x 105 cm
Rovereto, Mart – Museo di Arte
Moderna e Contemporanea
di Trento e Rovereto

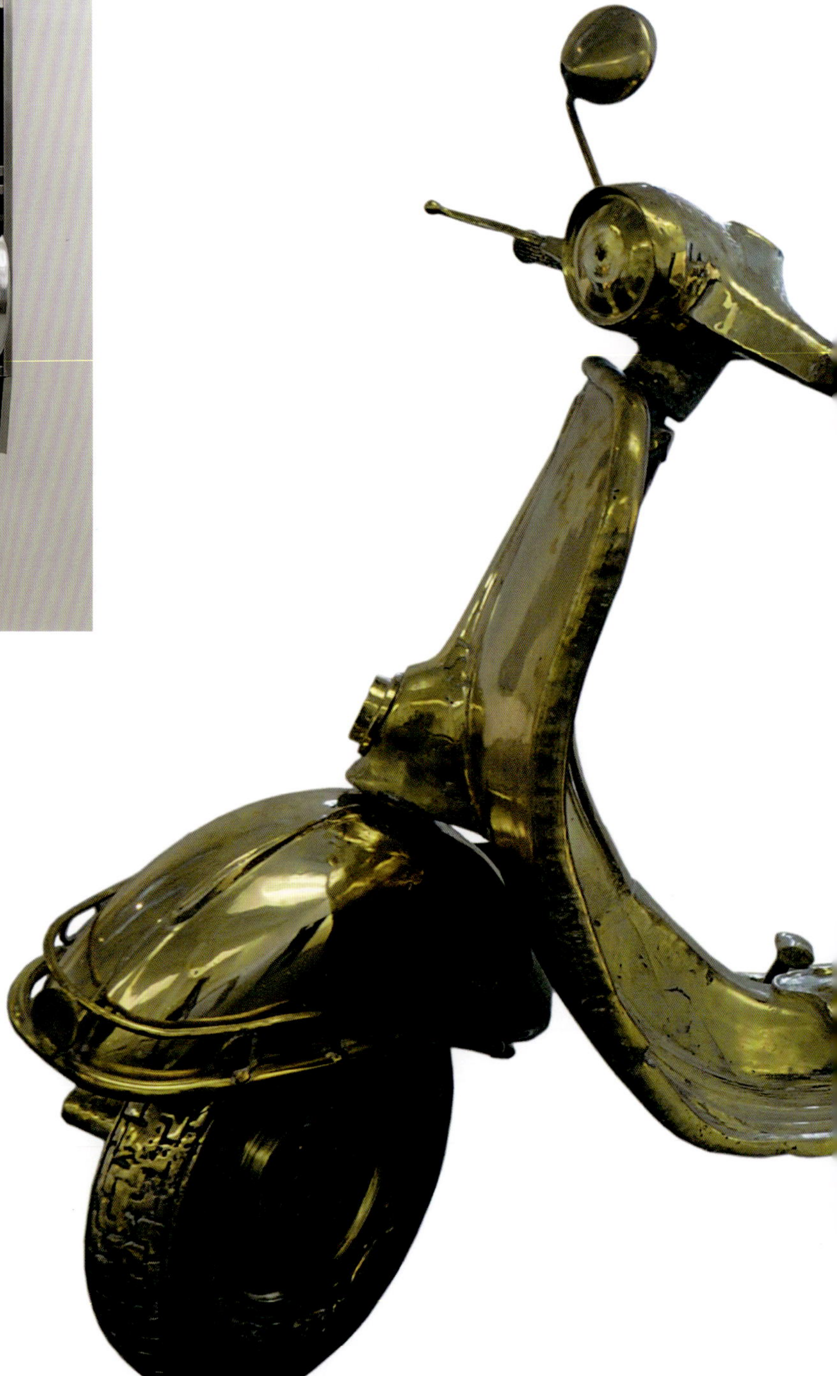

Born in Khagaul, India, in 1964. Lives and works in New Delhi.
Household articles and images of everyday Indian life are the hallmark of the work of Subodh Gupta, whose installations typically incorporate various objects of gleaming stainless steel.
Gupta's use of Indian cooking utensils highlights the central role played by the kitchen as a sort of private temple ensuring family and domestic balance, differing in every home but necessarily with some common features. This binding role takes on still deeper significance when seen in relation to the radical changes in Indian society, culture and traditions as a result of the rocketing process of economic growth now underway.
Gupta's installations thus become emblematic of the clash between the two faces of contemporary India, the archaic world of poor, rural areas and the advanced world of the megalopolis and the economic boom. A good example is provided by the installation *Curry 2 (1)*, presented at the 2005 Venice Biennale, which fetched a record price for a work by Gupta when auctioned at Christie's in the summer of 2008.
Social paradox is also present in the installation *This Side Is the Other Side* (2002), consisting of bronze and chrome casts of a scooter loaded with jerry cans to transport milk. While the poverty of a population still yoked to a subsistence economy is highlighted by the absence of a food distribution system, the gleam of chrome and steel creates an object now deprived of its original function but perfectly recognizable in terms of identity. The milk seller thus embodies a world where the daily ritual of door-to-door delivery is still present but destined to disappear, covered by a lustrous sheen that alters its outward appearance and transforms it into a shiny kitsch icon.
(F.T.)

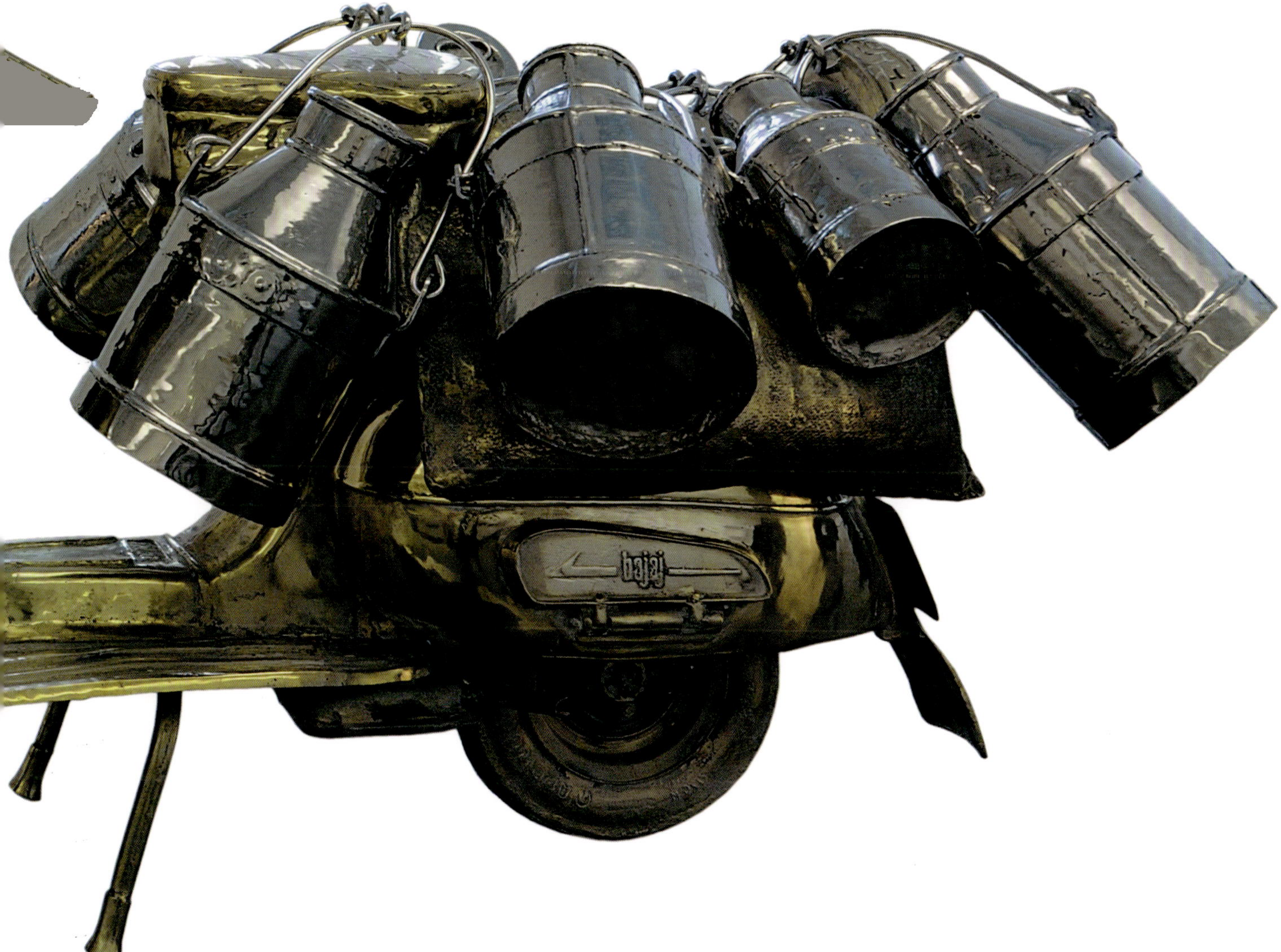

Emily Jacir

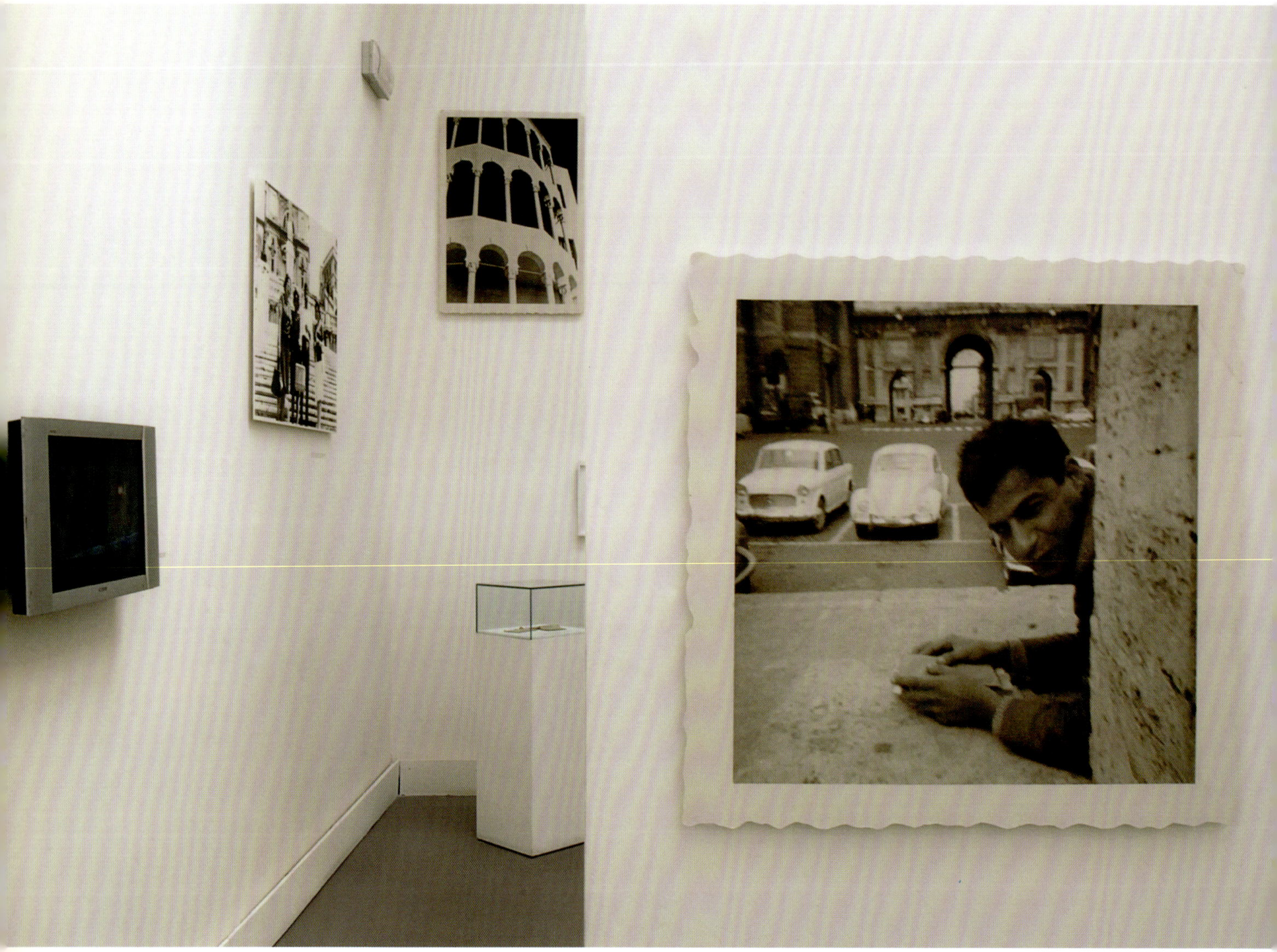

Born in Bethlehem, Palestinian Territories, in 1970. Lives and works in New York and Ramallah. Invited to take part in the 2007 Venice Biennale, the Palestinian artist Emily Jacir won the Golden Lion for the under-40 category with a work harnessing different media to examine exile as a condition of the individual and an entire people. *Material for a Film*, an ongoing installation conceived between 2004 and 2005 and subsequently exhibited on the occasion of the Hugo Boss Prize award ceremony in November 2008, is based on the personal history of the Palestinian intellectual Wael Zuaiter, who was assassinated in Rome in 1972 by the Israeli secret service. By collecting and cataloguing Zuaiter's personal effects, the Palestinian artist built up an archive of photographs, books, letters, and personal belongings so as to create a portrait of the deceased and an account of his life through direct contact with family, friends, and the places of his past. The title, *Material for a Film*, derives from a project developed by the Italian directors Elio Petri and Ugo Pirro, who published a collection of writings and poems about Zuaiter and his death in the late 1970s as a preliminary to the shooting of a documentary, which was never made because of Petri's death. Jacir had already investigated the subject of exile and the defense of personal identity in 2001 with the installation *Memorial to 418 Palestinian Villages That Were Destroyed, Depopulated and Occupied by Israel in 1948*. In this case, she examines the role of inhabited space and the change in its nature. The loss of the domestic universe is represented by the precariousness of the surrogate home used by the refugees, namely a tent of the kind distributed by the Red Cross and humanitarian organizations. The artist wrote the names of the 418 Palestinian villages occupied and evacuated by Israel in 1948 on the walls of fabric, entrusting the historical memory of the obliteration of territorial and human identities to the temporary shelter. (*F.T.*)

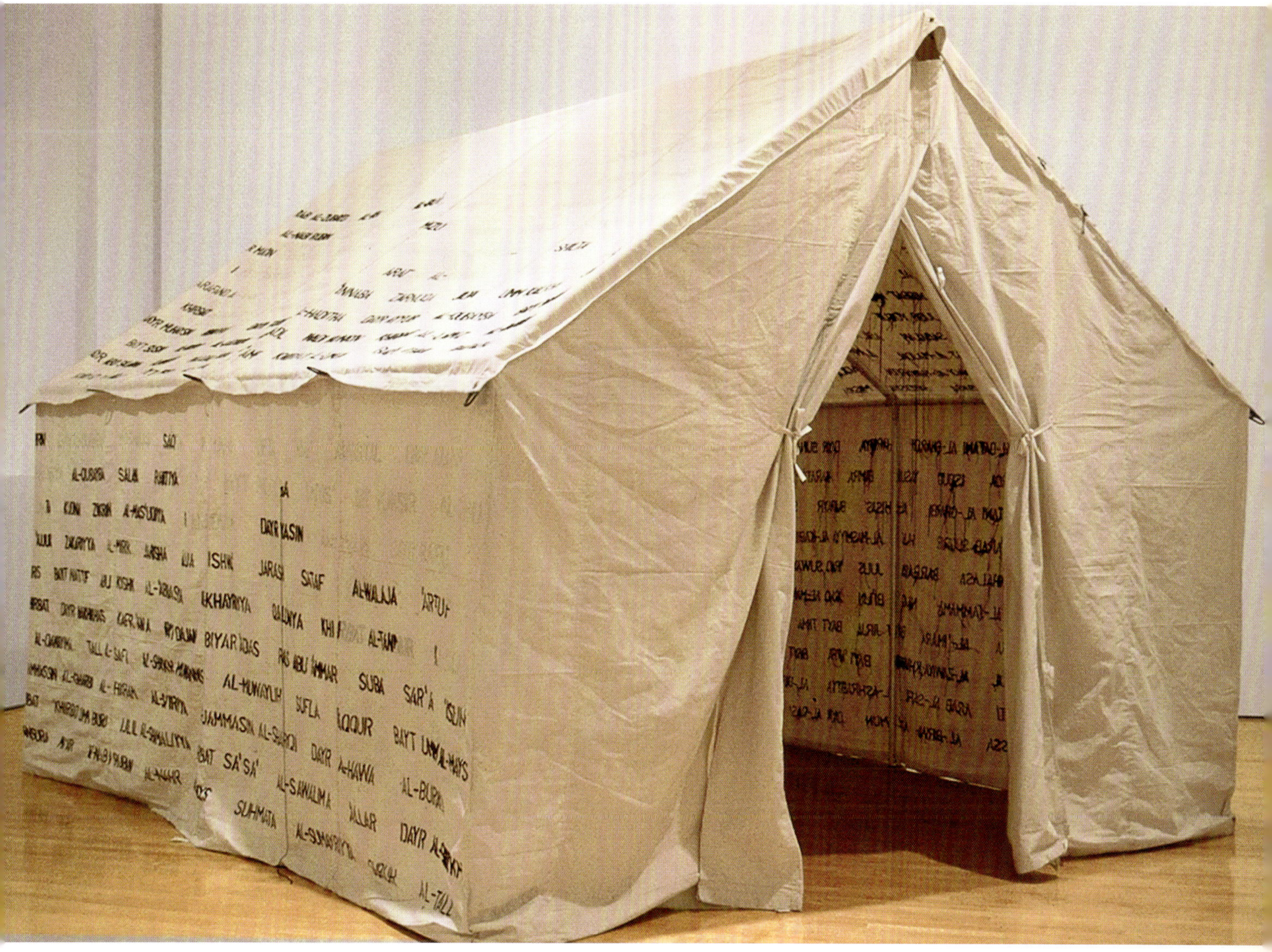

Material for a Film, 2004–2007
Film project: 120 photos with differing formats, letters, various objects, video, audio snippets, telephone recordings
View of the installation at the Italian Pavilion, LII Esposizione Internazionale d'Arte, Biennale di Venezia 2007

Memorial to 418 Palestinian Villages That Were Destroyed, Depopulated and Occupied by Israel in 1948, 2001
Refugee tent and embroidery thread
Courtesy of the artist

Rafael Lozano-Hemmer

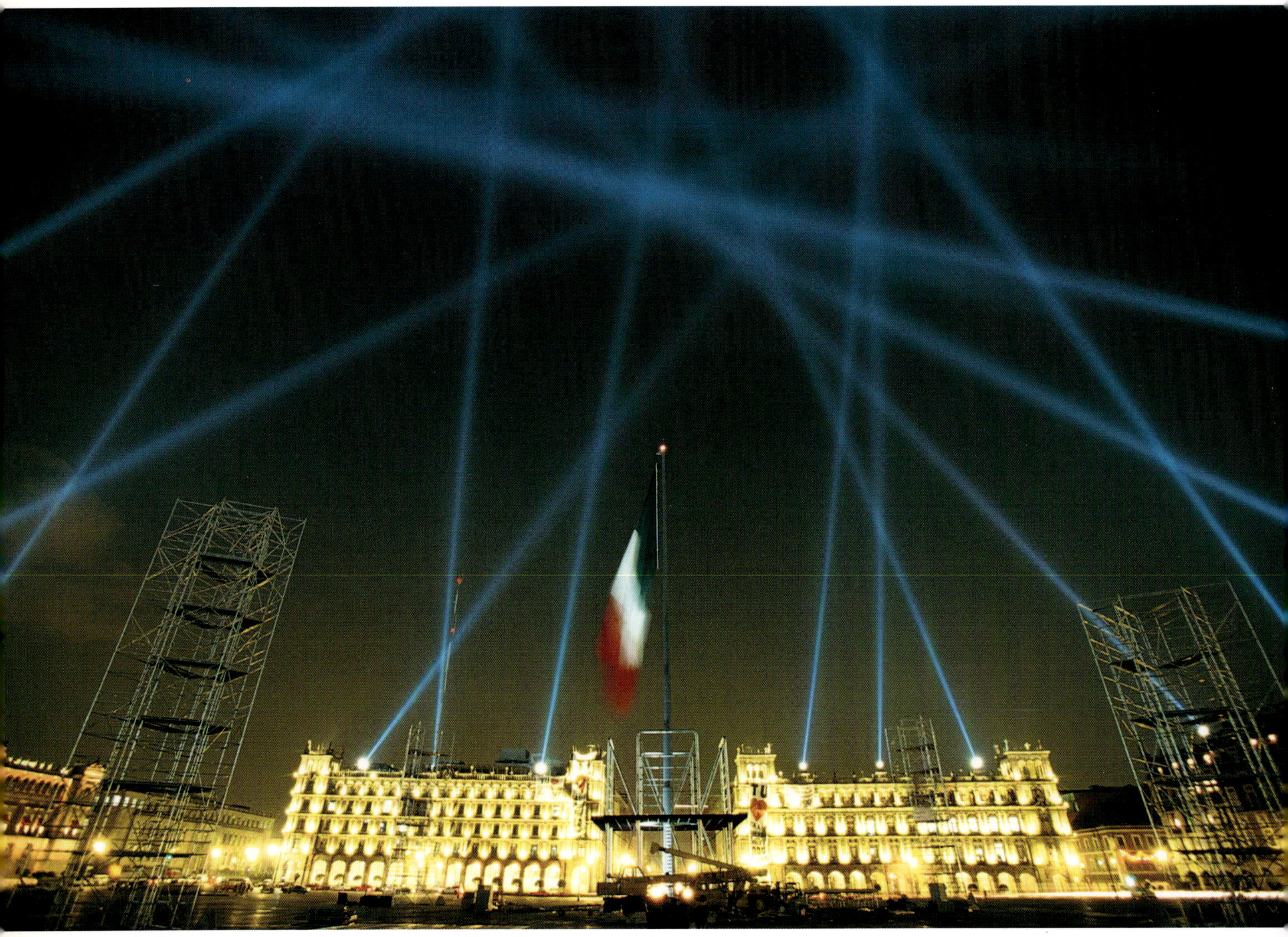

Born in Mexico City in 1967. Lives and works in Montreal, Canada.
Mexico City, 1999. Dozens of shafts of light, visible within a radius of 15 kilometers, moved in the sky over the metropolis to form new celestial edifices towering above the earthly city, one of the biggest and most chaotic in the world. The searchlights were controlled from the site alzado.net, which enabled anyone from any part of the world to redesign the skies of Mexico City. The project attracted something like 800,000 people and the numbers swelled to over 2,000,000 when the experiment was repeated at Artium in the Basque Country (2002), Lyons (2003), and Dublin (2004).
Vectorial Elevation is one of the most famous and ambitious projects developed by Rafael Lozano-Hemmer since he started out in the early 1990s. The Mexican artist's educational background in the sciences enables him to take over new technologies like motion tracking, video surveillance, robotics, cellular phones, and the Internet and put them to uses that are often very different from those for which they were created, in an effort to regain possession of urban space.
The focus of attention shifts in his public projects from technology to the social dynamics that it can generate. In *Amodal Suspension* (2003), commissioned for the opening of the Yamaguchi Center of Art and Media, the same spotlights were employed to convey messages sent in by the public via e-mail or SMS. The messages were translated into a sort of luminous Morse code and then back into text on being "captured" by the intended recipient. The installation *Pulse Room* (2006) used a sensor to record the pulse of the public and convert it into the flashing of 300 light bulbs. *Under Scan*, produced in 2006 and repeated in 2008 by the Tate Gallery in Trafalgar Square, is an installation in which the shadows cast by spectators on the pavement due to a powerful overhead lighting system turn into "video portraits" that come to life and interact with the public.
This focus on dialogue with the viewer continues also in the more private dimension of art-gallery works, as exemplified by *Microphones* (2008), an intriguing installation of vintage microphones connected with a system making it possible to record and reproduce the observer's voice. When the observer speaks into one of the microphones, this records his or her voice and then uses one of those previously recorded to answer with a time lag that makes it sound like an echo from the past.
Lozano-Hemmer became the first Mexican artist to represent his country at the Venice Biennale in 2007.
(D.Q.)

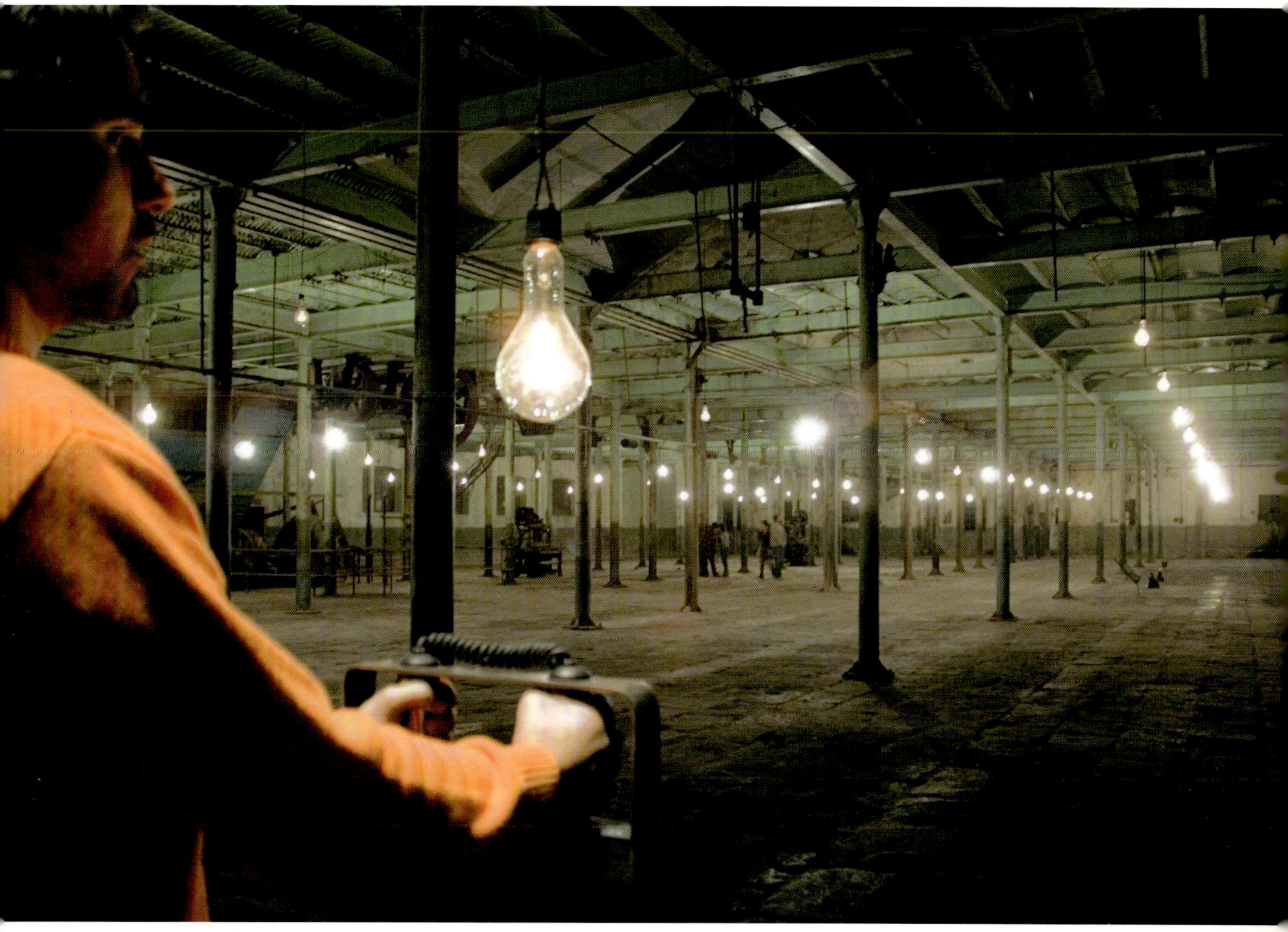

Vectorial Elevation, 1999–2000
View of the installation realized in 2002 at ARTIUM – Centro-Museo Vasco de Arte Contemporáneo, Vitoria-Gasteiz, Spain

Pulse Room, 2006
View of the installation realized in 2006 in Puebla, Mexico

Julie Mehretu

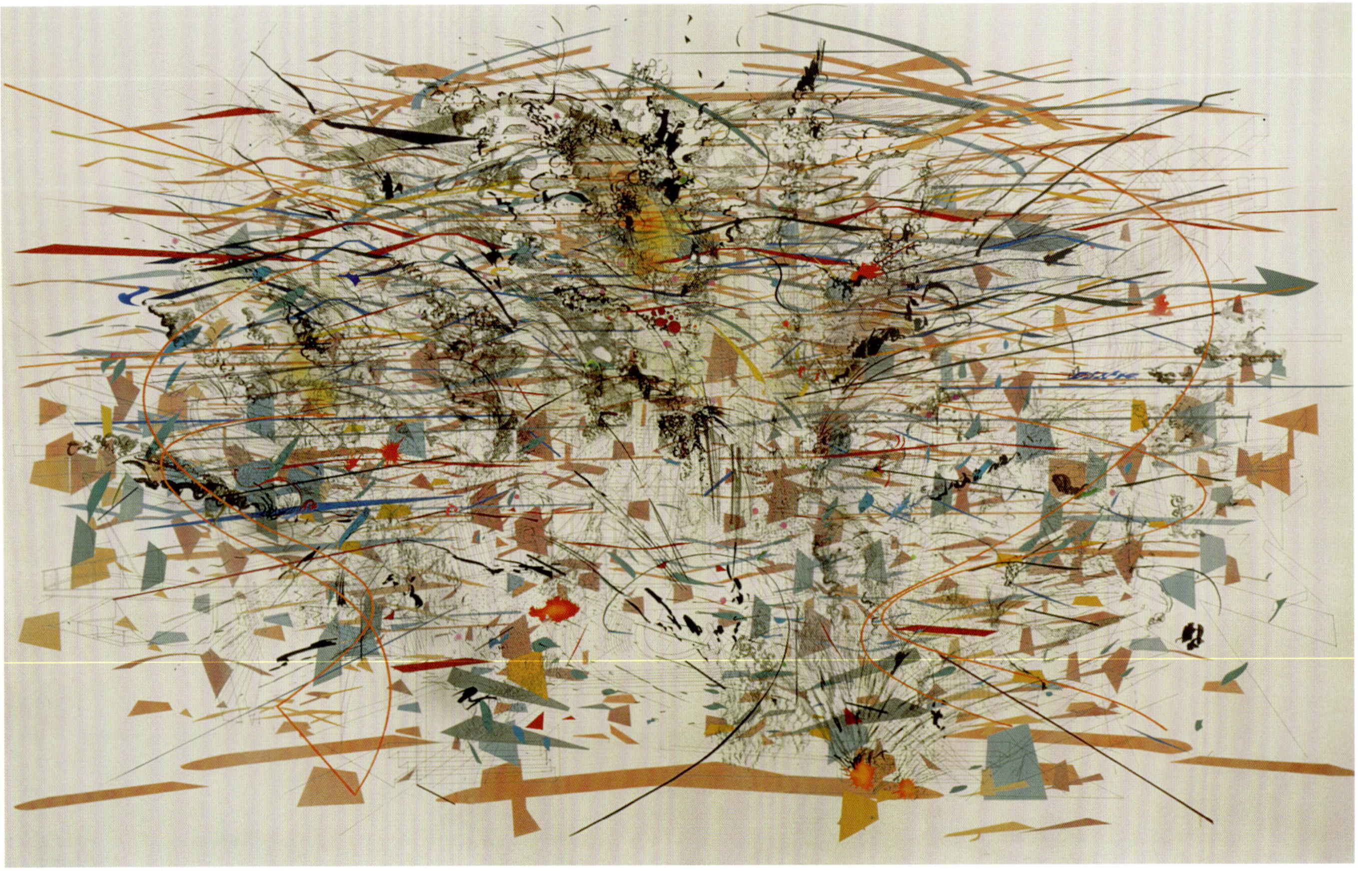

Renegade Delirium, 2002
Acrylic on canvas, 229 x 366 cm
Courtesy Jay Jopling / White Cube, London

Born in Addis Abeba, Ethiopia, in 1970. Lives and works in New York. Julie Mehretu's paintings are images of complexity. African by birth but educated primarily in the West, the artist uses pen and acrylic paints to cover large canvases with overlapping maps, diagrams, and plans of airports, stadiums, and ancient buildings, as well as abstract forms in synthetic colors dominated by entropic dynamics. Defining her paintings as "story maps of no location", the artist emphasizes the imaginary nature of her visions, which draw upon memory and layers of symbols more than reality. Formal concerns are accompanied by the desire to address "the multifaceted layers of place, space, and time that impact the formation of personal and communal identity". Current events, politics, and globalization enter into these complex abstract visions, intersecting with purely formal concerns and creating extraordinary visual metaphors of the overabundance of information and of a society that is the unstable product of various and never resolved tensions. As she points out, "I work with source material that I am interested in conceptually, politically, or even just visually. I pull from all of this material, project it, trace it, break it up, recontextualize it, layer one on the other, and envelop it into the DNA of the painting. It then becomes the context, the history, the point of departure. It becomes the place of the painting." Also in formal terms, the references seem to build up in Mehretu's paintings to the point of precluding any facile genealogy: from Art Informel to Futurism, from Geometric Abstraction to Action Painting and the abstract patterns of African fabrics.
(*D.Q.*)

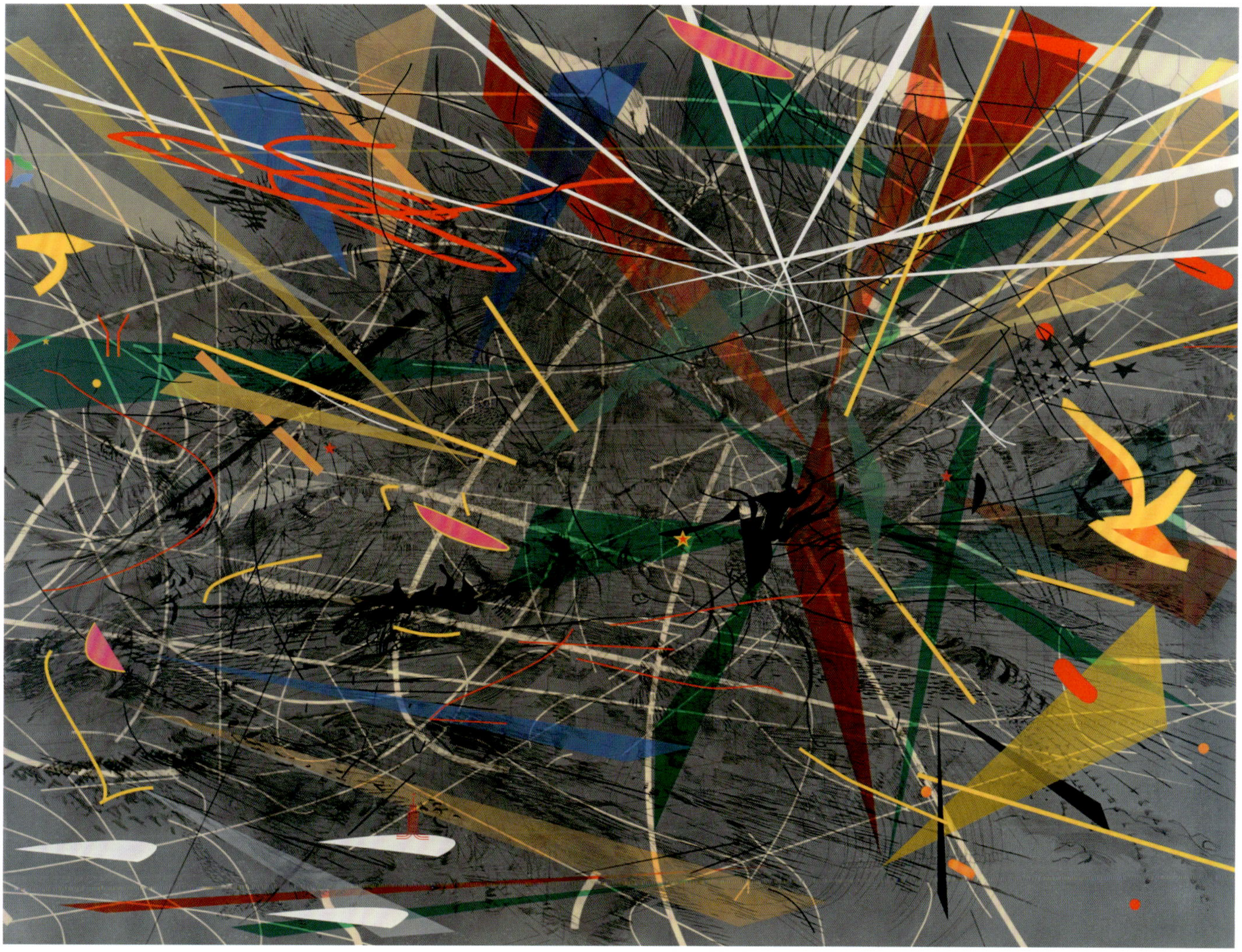

Grey Space (Distractor), 2006
Ink and acrylic on canvas,
183 x 244 cm
Courtesy The Project Gallery,
New York

Mariko Mori

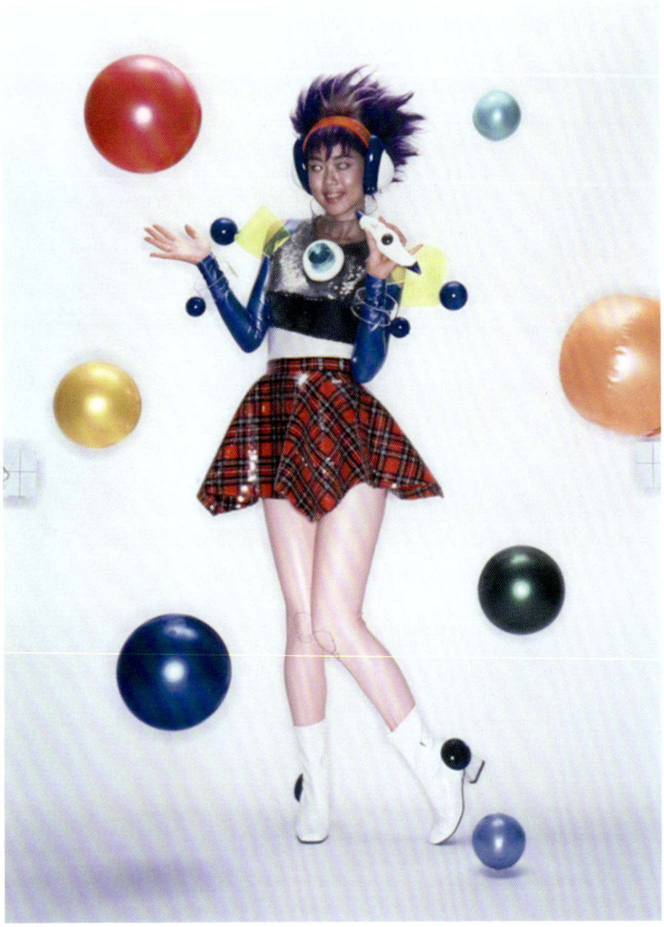

Birth of a Star, 1995
Duratrans print, acrylic, light box, CD, 183 x 122 cm
Courtesy of the artist and Deitch Projects, New York

Wave UFO, 2003
Aluminum, magnesium, carbon fiber, Technogel, and fiberglass, 4.90 x 11.30 x 5.20 m
Courtesy of the artist and Deitch Projects, New York

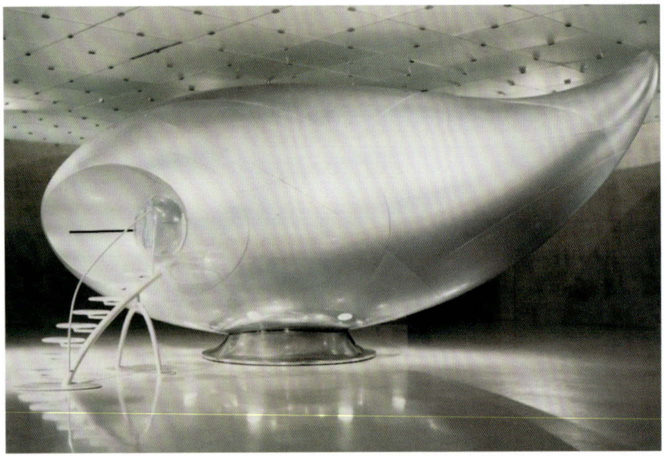

Born in Tokyo in 1967. Lives and works in New York.
The daughter of a rich Japanese businessman, Mariko Mori studied fashion design and worked as a model before taking up art in the early 1990s. Her initial works are distinguished by the creation of a fantastic world combining Japanese spirituality, the Manga culture, technology, and science fiction, in which the artist herself is the absolute protagonist. Transferred onto aluminum or presented by means of sophisticated light boxes, her first photographic prints involved complex operations of pre-production and post-production. The artist created her own costumes, had herself photographed, and then made large-scale use of digital technology to develop the scenario of futuristic machinery, likeable Buddhas and cyber-chic geishas. In *Birth of a Star* (1995), for example, Mori appears as a sexy postmodern divinity in an empty space, dressed as a teenager in the midst of hanging colored spheres. She hovers in *Pure Land* (1997–1998) above an expanse of water, light and elegant, surrounded by strange 3D sprites holding musical instruments.
While appropriating elements of the New Age aesthetic and kitsch, Mariko Mori steered clear of critique and ingenuous acceptance alike. She gave the impression of taking the bizarre spiritual world she creates very seriously indeed.
Once used, her costumes were sealed away for 25 years inside large Plexiglas capsules.
After a serious breakdown that she describes as verging on "mental death", Mori radically altered her approach, abandoning self-representation almost completely to create complex installations combining tradition and technology. As she explains, "I'm not interested in using ancient things; rather I want to connect them with contemporary life through the technology we have now. On the surface it appears high tech but looking into it one feels the genesis of traditional matters." Inspired by the Yumedono (Pavilion of Dreams) of Horyu-ji, Japan's oldest temple, *Dream Temple* (1999) marked the turning point as an attempt to create a modern space for meditation. On entering the innermost part of the temple, made out of ultramodern dichroic glass and standing on a bed of salt, spectators are plunged one at a time by means of advanced virtual reality technology into a flow of images of life such as atoms, planets, a human fetus, and a fertilized egg.
Held in 2003 at Deitch Projects, her New York gallery, the solo show *Oneness* consisted of two installations. The first, which gave the show its title, is a sculpture of six aliens in a circle. Disquieting and irresistible at the same time, these aliens of semi-transparent Technogel seem to have been made purely to be embraced. When this happens, their eyes light up and their hearts begin to beat. *Oneness* is at the same time a reference to the Buddhist concept of the world as a single organism and an allegory of connection, a theme taken up by *Connected World*, the other work on show. This is a series of circular, opalescent prints derived from the studies for the video shown within the framework of *Wave UFO*, the large-scale public project launched at the same time as the show.
On entering a futuristic spaceship barefoot three at a time, the spectators lie down on a Technogel couch and are hooked up to electrodes that record their brainwaves and show them on a screen.
Mori's most recent works continue in the same direction as hi-tech altars of a new form of mysticism that combines the latest advances in physics with Eastern and Western traditions.
(*D.Q.*)

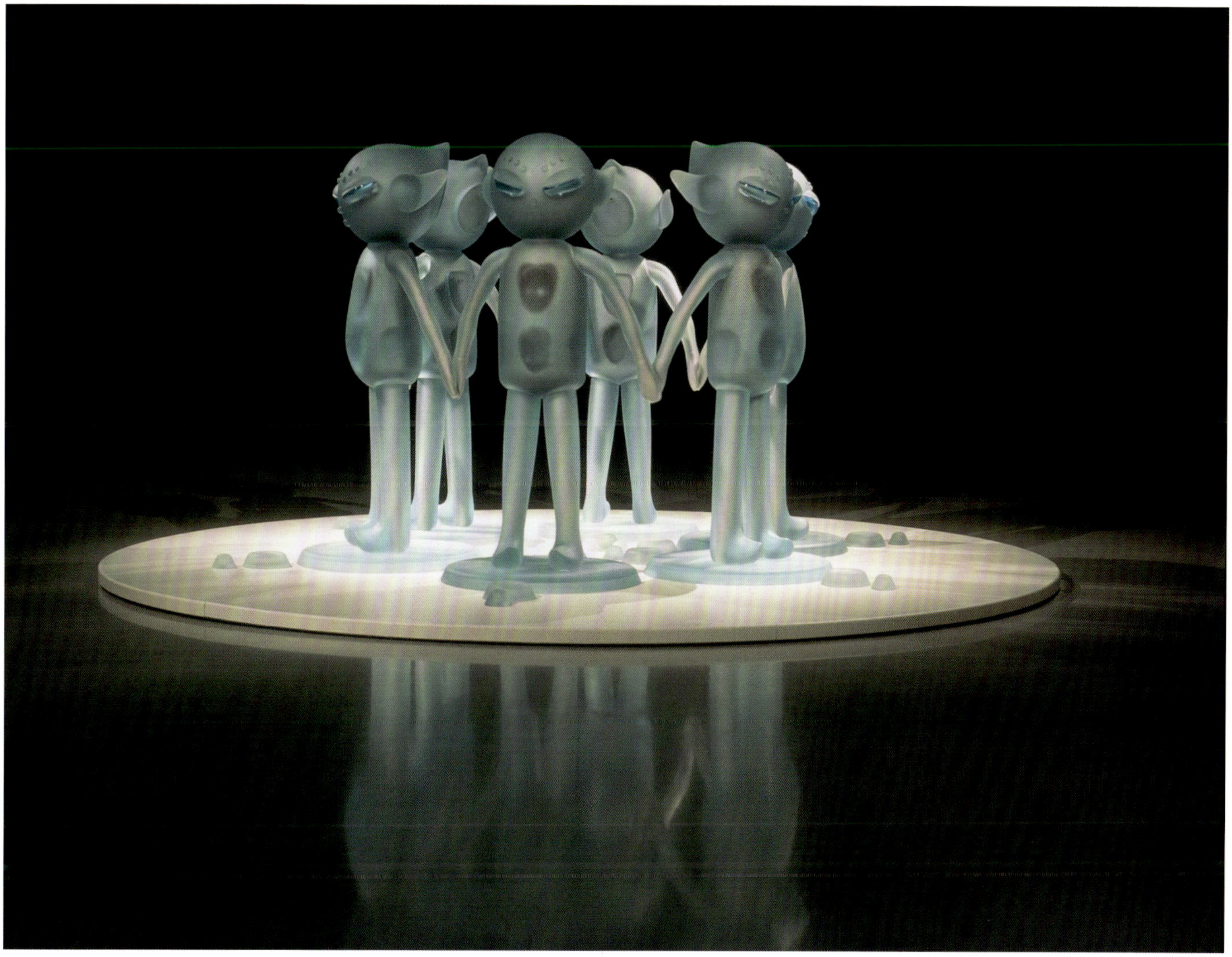

Oneness, 2003
Technogel, acrylic, cast aluminum, magnesium, 135 x 75.6 x 37.4 cm
Courtesy of the artist and Deitch Projects, New York

Pure Land, 1997–1998
Color photograph under glass
5 panels, 305 x 610 x 2.2 cm
Courtesy of the artist and Deitch Projects, New York

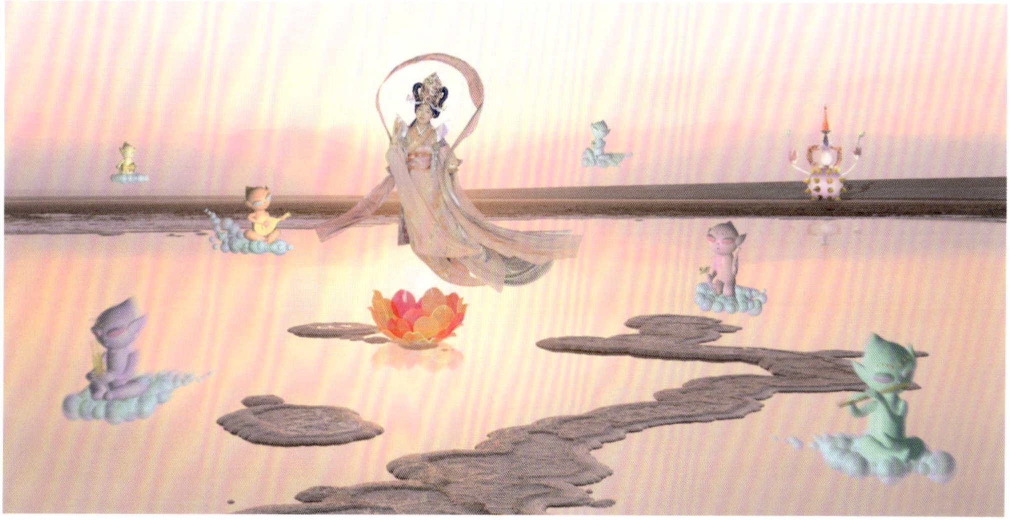

Nunzio

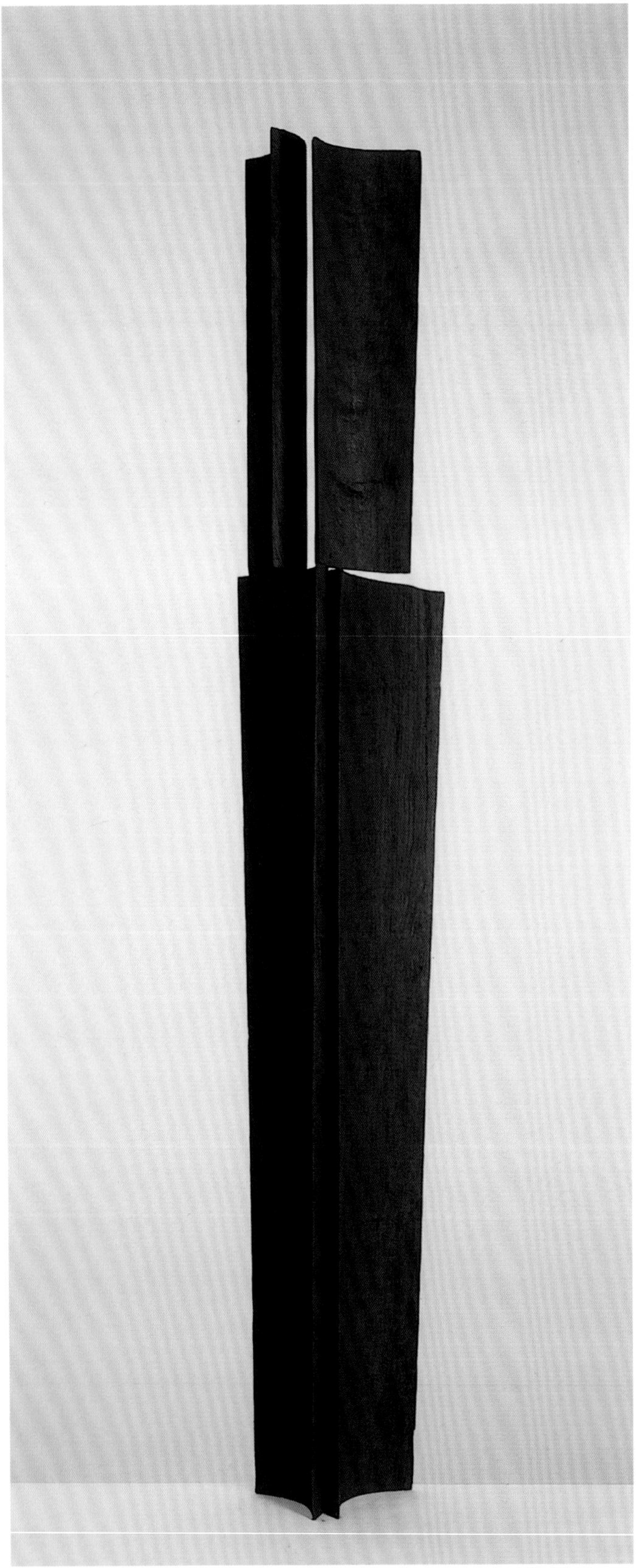

Nunzio Di Stefano, born in Cagnano Amiterno (Italy) in 1954. Lives and works in Rome and Turin.
It was a complex artistic trajectory that led Nunzio, a leading Italian sculptor since the 1980s, to the discovery of energy as a subject of great conceptual attraction that introduced the dualism of art and science, a theme of sensory, aesthetic and philosophical speculation, into his work. Good examples of this are provided by the charred wood of *Rovescio (Combustione)* (1999–2003) and *Senza titolo* (2003).
Though belonging to a much later generation, he recognizes the value of the Arte Povera aesthetic of the natural and archetypal as well as the glacial perfection of the work of Bruce Nauman, while managing to steer clear of stereotypes at the same time. His sculpture focuses once again on the question of form and hence of style, which becomes a link between tradition and innovation enabling him to negotiate the reefs of Conceptual Art and Arte Povera *tout court*.
Like the sculptors of the past, Nunzio sees matter as a shapeless element from which sophisticated processes of manipulation can draw vital energy, new forms and new beauty.
Fire is one of the elements most used by the artist to generate a process whereby matter in its virginal state undergoes successive alterations to attain a new natural condition and create a new form. Fire and heat work together with the sculptor's hands, acting respectively on the surface and in the depths of the material. While lampblack colors the rhythmic sequences of stelae poised in space or hanging in delicate balance on walls, fire reduces the thickness of the material, violating its consistency and torturing its wounded body with indelible burns and scars.
The work *Teorema* (2006) could be described as marking an authentic step beyond the Italian post-war tradition, superseding both the ideological pressures of Arte Povera and the existentialism of Alberto Burri's gestural art. Wholly rejecting any conceptualistic temptation, Nunzio rediscovers a possible synthesis of form and content in the transformation of matter, which appears once again to attain its full meaning precisely in this synthesis. (*P.V.*)

Senza titolo, 2003
Combusted wood, 245 x 35 x 32 cm
UniCredit Group Collection

Teorema, 2006
Combusted wood,
dimensions variable
Rome, collection of the artist

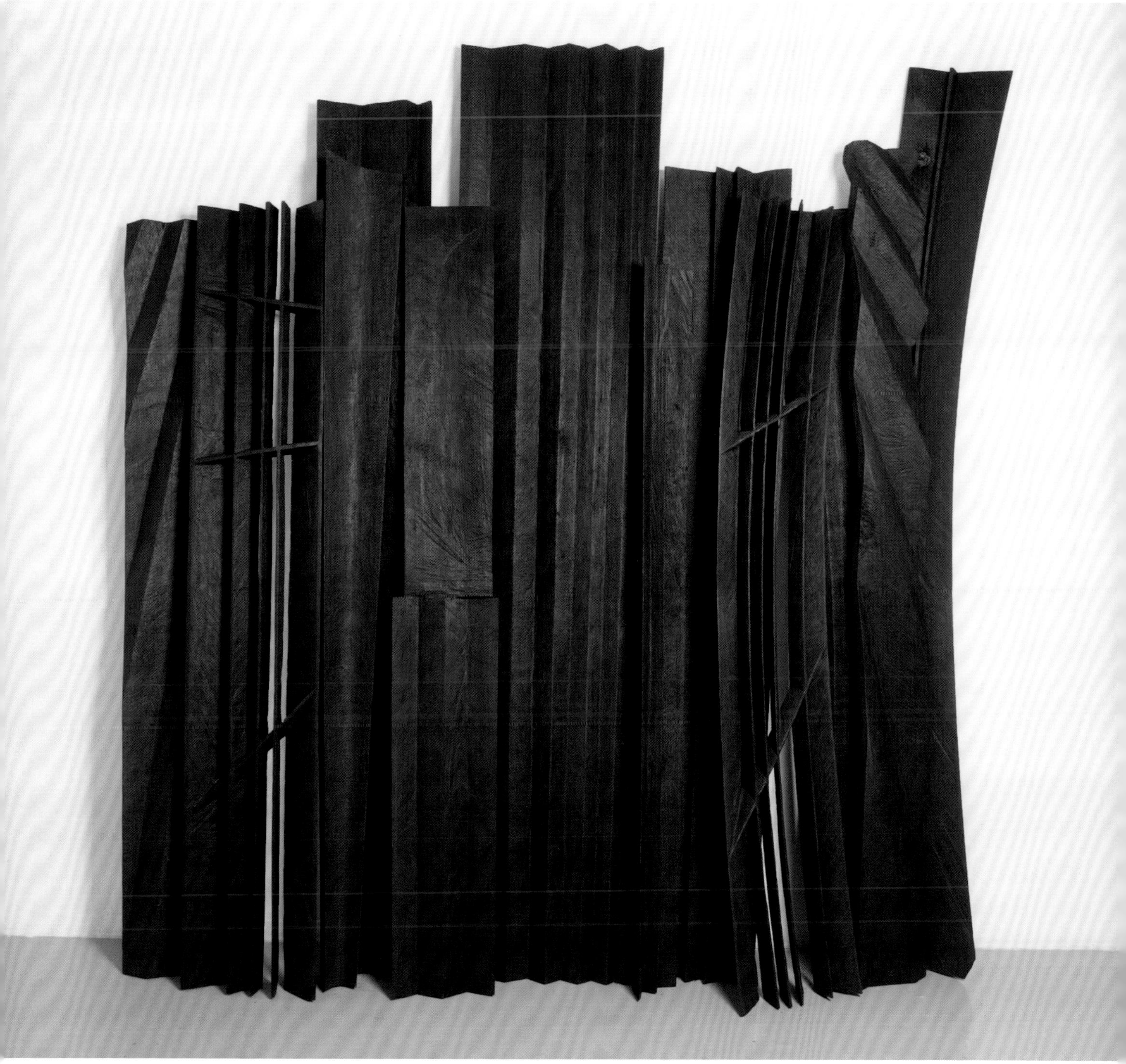

Wolfgang Tillmans

Born in Remscheid, Germany, in 1968. Lives and works in London and Berlin.
Wolfgang Tillmans uses photography as a transversal tool capable of encompassing some specific qualities of other artistic media as regards both language and thematic content. He thus moves with great naturalness through the "pictorial" genres of portraiture, still life and landscape into experimentation and abstraction. Frequent use is made of cuts and compositional approaches that endow his subjects with an almost sculptural or three-dimensional monumental character. He sometimes gives his photos the snapshot quality of stills taken from videos or films.
The choice of format is constantly varied and the relations between the individual images are arranged in relation to their exhibition setting in much the same way as an installation.
Underpinning this many-sided use of photography (as a medium) and photographs (as physical objects) is the deep conceptual coherence of the artist's endeavor to sample the real world around us in images and present it in an overall view based on no hierarchical criterion whatsoever, be it political, social, moral or aesthetic.
This "democratic vision" is also reflected in the way Tillmans arranges his photographs on the walls of galleries and museums or the pages of magazines and his art books. What may appear a free and haphazard layout at first sight is actually the result of a painstaking examination of distributive relationships aimed at creating a context in which the viewer's attention, instead of lingering over the individual works, can roam freely through a constellation of images, simply allowing itself to be guided by their communicative strength. For this reason, his installations never comply with any chronological or thematic criteria. Recent works are placed alongside older ones, everyday subjects and portraits of friends coexist with abstract compositions, and the end result – or indeed the very value of the work – derives precisely from the play of interlocking elements, the unexpected juxtapositions, and the combinations of form, color and even technique. Tillmans uses digital and analogical prints, matte and glossy surfaces and photocopies with ostentatious indifference to show that the value of the work lies exclusively in the images and not in their supports. Taking this operative approach to extremes, the artist embarked in 2005 on the *Truth Study Center* project, a work in progress that combines his own photographs with images and articles cut out of newspapers and magazines to create panels then exhibited in display cases so as to test the presumed veracity of the statements circulated by politicians, scientists and sociologists in the mass media. It is indeed the problem of the relationship between truth and fiction that Tillmans addresses in what could be called ethical terms. As he puts it, "Even though I know that the camera lies, I still hold on to the idea of a photographical truth."
It should be noted that Tillmans sees this "truth" as inherent in the medium and not in the subjects photographed. He thus resolves the supposed dichotomy of reality and abstraction by assuming from the outset that abstract works are nothing other than objects that represent themselves: "The paper on which the picture is printed is for me an object, there is no separating the picture from that which carries it." The results include series such as *Freischwimmer* and *Paper Drop*. While the first involves photographic experiments carried out without a camera by working on the emulsified paper with an optical pen and subjecting it to chemical processes, the second focuses on paper, which is folded to form a drop that takes on different shapes in relation to the light and space within the composition. The formal rigor that distinguishes the artist's abstract works, and especially those of the *Paper Drop* series, is also to be found both in the still lives, orchestrated in terms of the relations of form and color between their various constituent elements, and in the landscapes, which focus above all on the rhythms of the horizontal and vertical elements of the city skyline. On closer examination, the manifestly intimate and hence apparently informal portraits of friends also reveal great attention to the compositional structure and scenic layout of the image.
(*L.L.*)

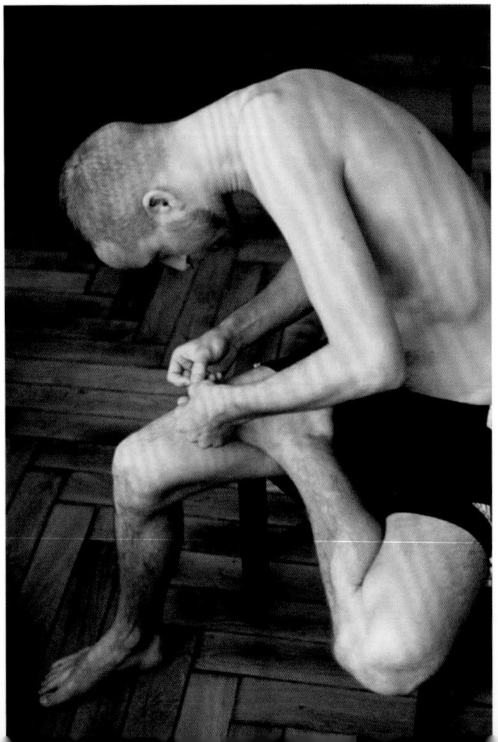

Anders Pulling Splinter from His Foot, 2004
Black and white photograph
40 x 30 cm
Courtesy Galerie Daniel Buchholz, Cologne

Page 70
Irm Hermann, 2000
Ink-jet print, 199 x 135 cm
New York, Solomon R. Guggenheim Museum

Page 71
Freischwimmer 40, 2004
Color photograph, 40 x 30 cm
Courtesy of the artist

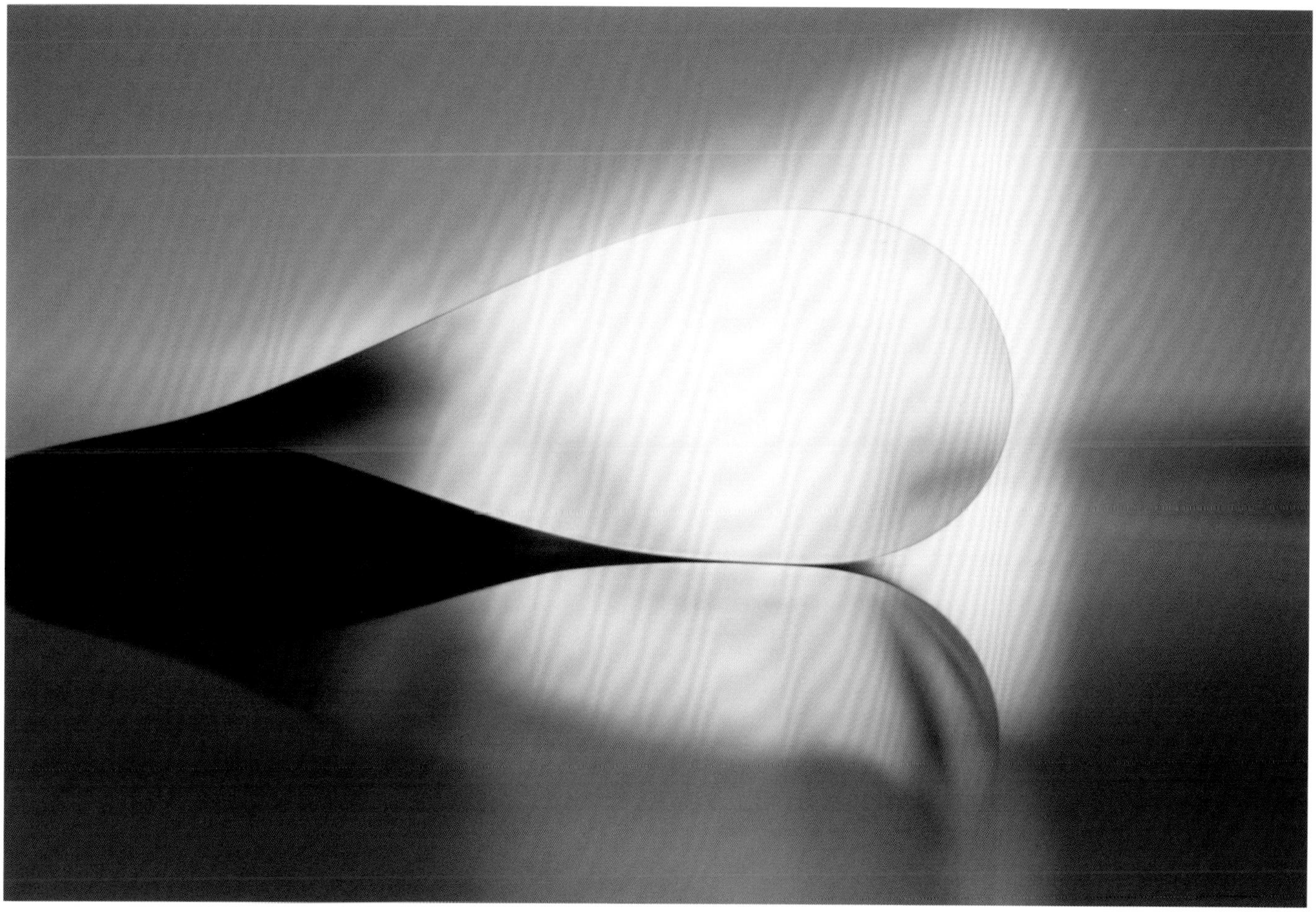

Paper Drop (Window), 2006
Color photograph, 30 x 40 cm
Courtesy neugerriemschneider,
Berlin

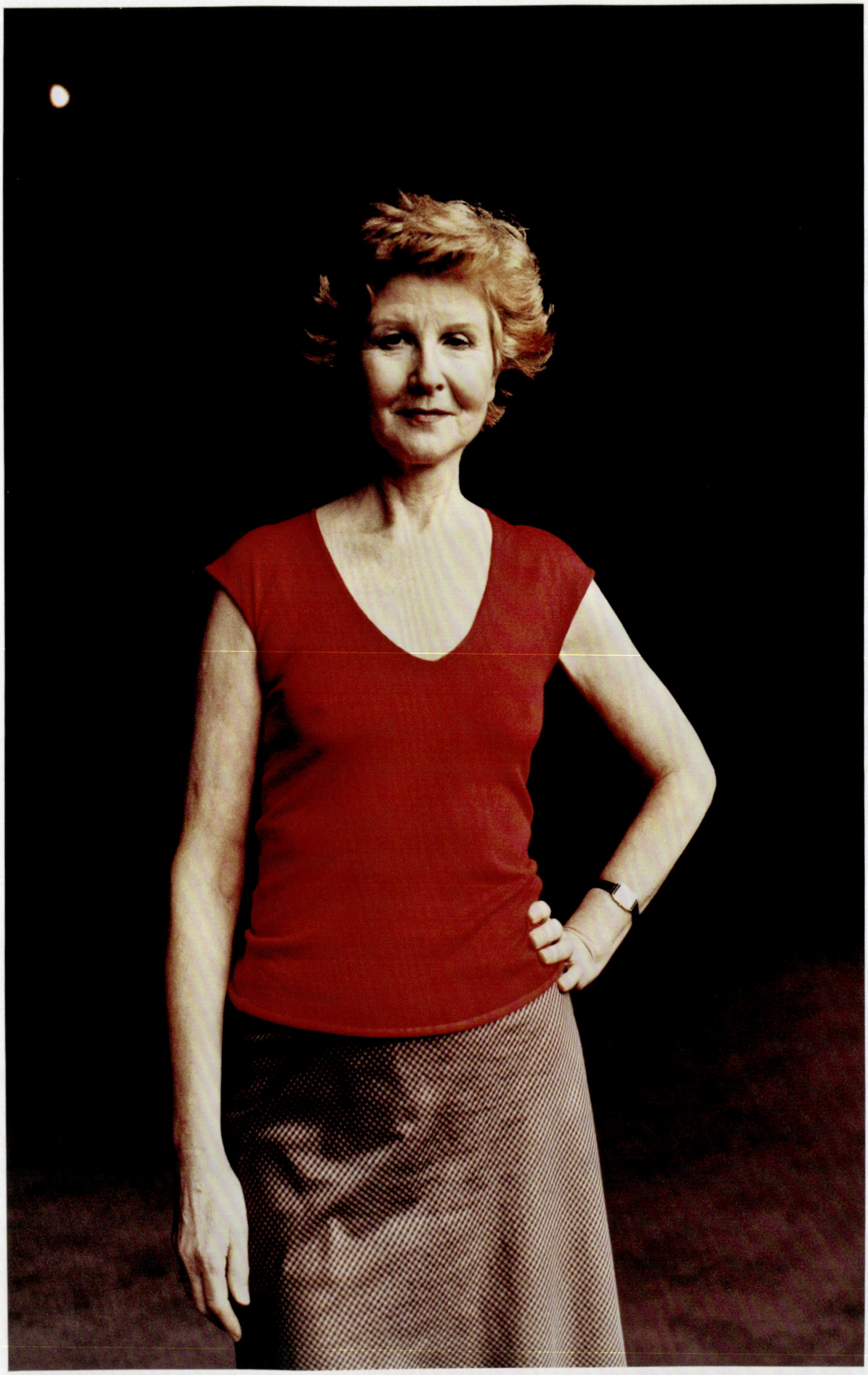

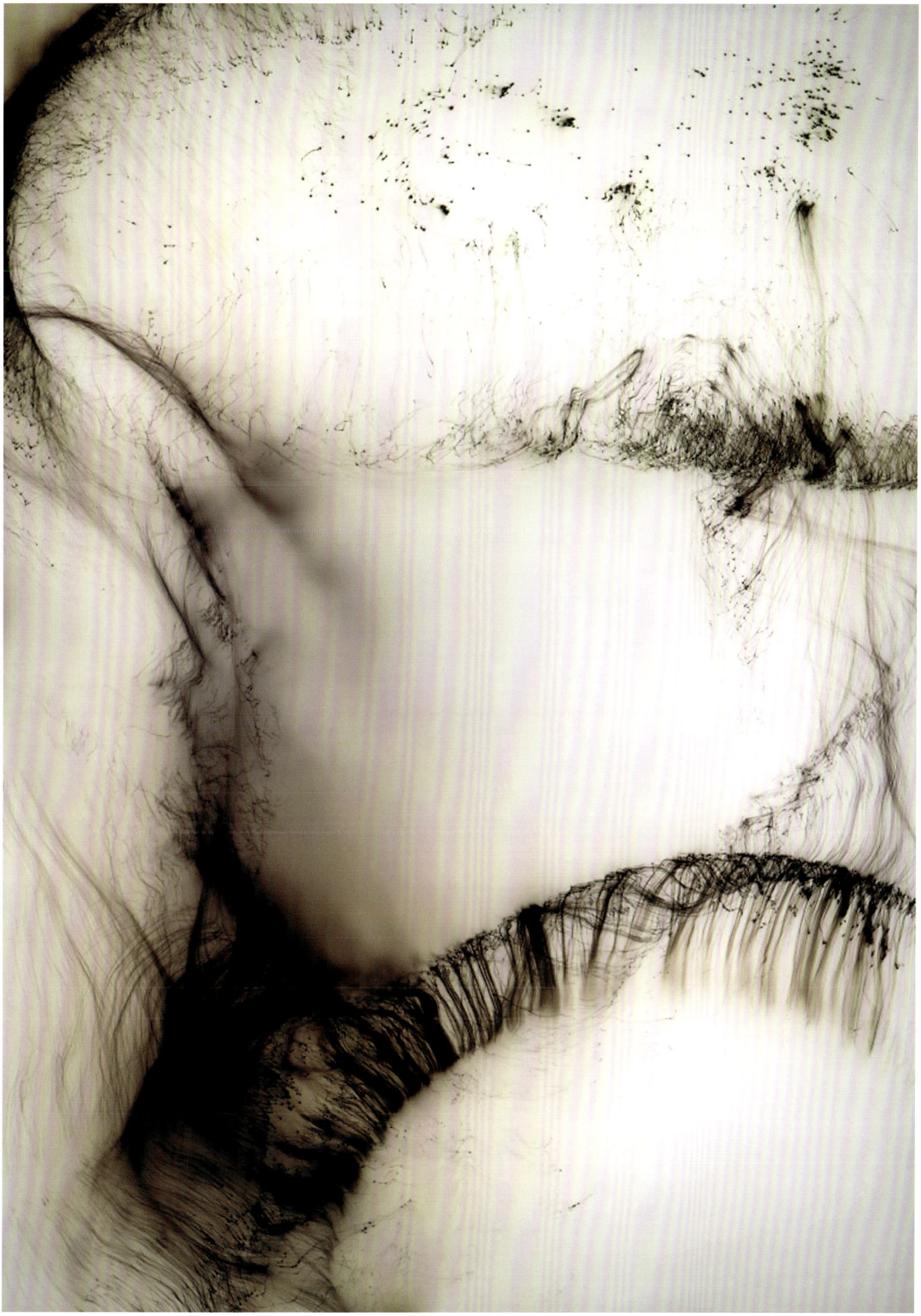

Francesco Vezzoli

Born in Brescia, Italy, in 1971. Lives and works in Milan.
Francesco Vezzoli's operations are closely related to Pop Art and its most famous representative, Andy Warhol. The work of the artist from Brescia combines love and death but also beauty and kitsch as well as high and low culture in the perspective of "base materialism," which Bataille identified as the refusal to mythicize and fetishize matter and Vezzoli develops in the sphere of cliché and bad taste. Lurex tears, decadence, and the embroidered faces of film stars constitute an iconographic choice developed by the artist from the starting point of his personal rejection of the gigantism of the British artistic environment with which he was in contact as a student. His response thus involves intimate, small-scale operations, with petit point embroidery as a way of refusing and getting away from the redundancy of so much of Young British Art.
Vezzoli focuses primarily on the investigation of image and the role of fame in contemporary society. His early works are portraits of Italian film stars of the period from the 1940s to the 1970s, above all Silvana Mangano. By streaking the actress's face with Lurex tears, Vezzoli enters into her private sphere and transforms the icon into a figure of emotional substance, thus bringing her into the universe of ordinary people.
The artist also creates a link between the woman's real life and his own artistic activity. For both, the practice of needlepoint constitutes a way to metabolize existential anguish, the difficulty for one to express his creative needs and the other the unhappiness of her emotional and family life.
Pain thus becomes an expression of the fall from the divine to the earthly universe, a reversal of the path repeatedly traveled by man in the mythological narratives, from Hercules to Gilgamesh. This comes about here through the work of needlepoint. In the existential experience of Silvana Mangano, this patient and constant activity, a proof of moral strength, represents the objectification of her state of mind and also becomes the tragic metaphor that links the technique with the myth.
The action of embroidering is in fact a reference to an archaic society in which female activity was connected to the creation of fabrics and objects for use in the transitional phases of human existence, like the wedding dress and the burial shroud. Embroidery also creates a bridge between the divine and mythological universe of ancient times, as represented by the tale of Arachne, and the mythicized sphere of the contemporary era, exemplified in this case by film stars.
Stardom is indeed a key element for Vezzoli. He identifies and underscores the decline of his subjects, highlighting the fleeting nature of youth and beauty, and essentially the ephemeral condition of the movie universe. He thus detects a lack of substance in the world of cinema and television, which he emphasizes by staging a series of situations that are very lifelike but lack one crucial element, namely real existence in the world. This is the starting point for Vezzoli's creation of trailers for films never made and pilot episodes for nonexistent TV series, all based on the story-building power of the image in the system of contemporary communication.
One example is his *Trailer for a Remake of Gore Vidal's 'Caligula'* (2005). Vezzoli involved Gore Vidal and a cast of artists, some of international renown and others who have gradually and inexorably dropped out of the limelight, in the production of a trailer for the remake of the film made by Vidal in the 1970s. The video is based on perfect imitation of the cinematographic language. As a climax builds up, emphasized by the choice of terms like sensuality, sexuality and perversity, the characters are presented in a context reminiscent of Pier Paolo Pasolini's *120 Days of Sodoma* and Ken Russell's *The Devils*. Sexual perversion becomes the interpretive key to a Roman world wholly extraneous to the canons of time and history, based rather on the clichés of pornographic film production and a certain brand of extremely kitsch architecture. Caligula, the leading character, is constantly mentioned by the co-stars but never seen until the end of the video, when the actress Courtney Love, in a scene of emptiness and silence contrasting with the previous splendors, dashes the audience's expectations with the statement, "I am Caligula."
Vezzoli develops a critique with ambiguous overtones, pointing out the capacity of cinema to confer reality on any scenario, even the most absurd, with respect to the narration of events that actually happened. The artist offers no ethical judgment on this power,

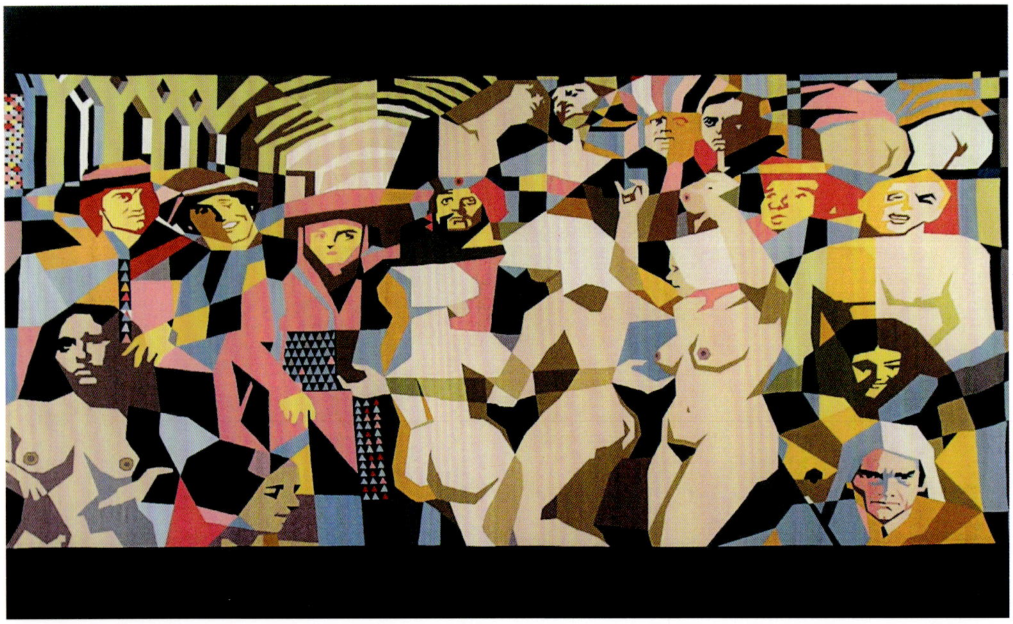

La fine di Canterbury, 2005
Wool Gobelin tapestry,
410 x 700 cm
Courtesy Fondazione Prada, Milan

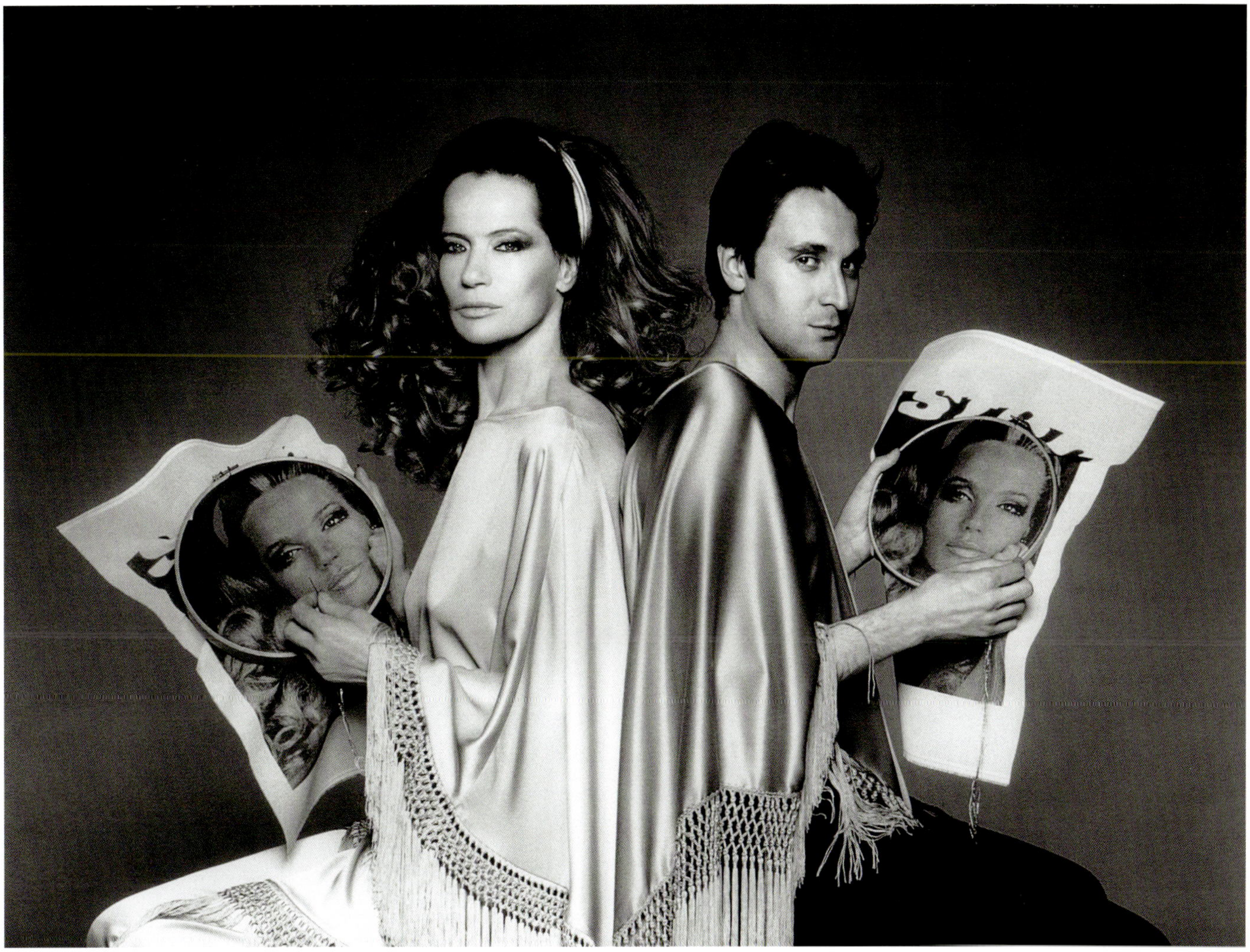

Self-portrait with Vera, 2001
Black and white digital print
on aluminum, 100 x 125 cm
Verona, Galleria d'Arte Moderna
Palazzo Forti, collezione AGI

Democrazy, 2007
Two video projections, color, sound, 1'
Unicredit Group Collection,
Long-term loan
MAXXI_MAXXI Museo nazionale delle
arti del XXI secolo, Rome

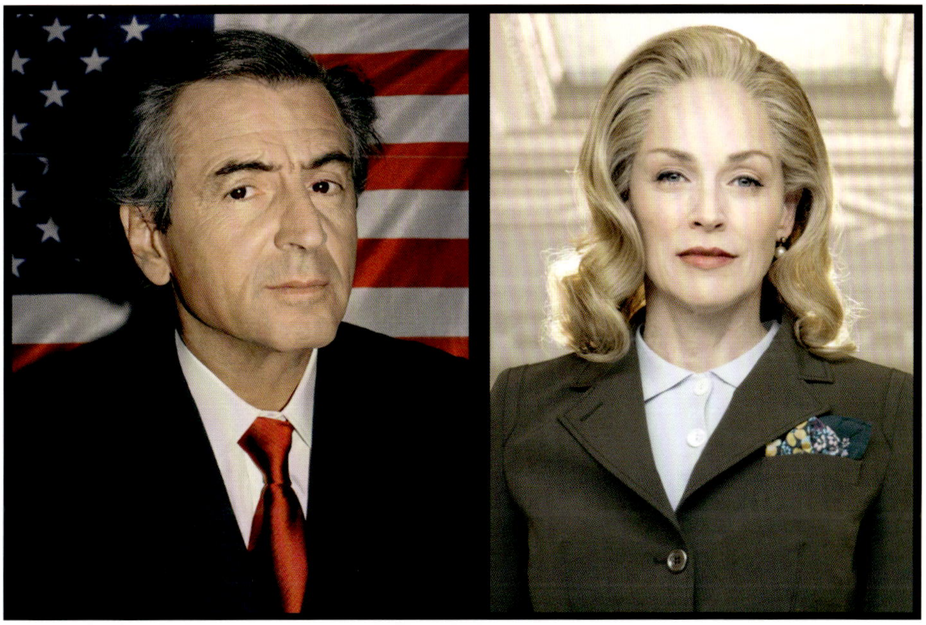

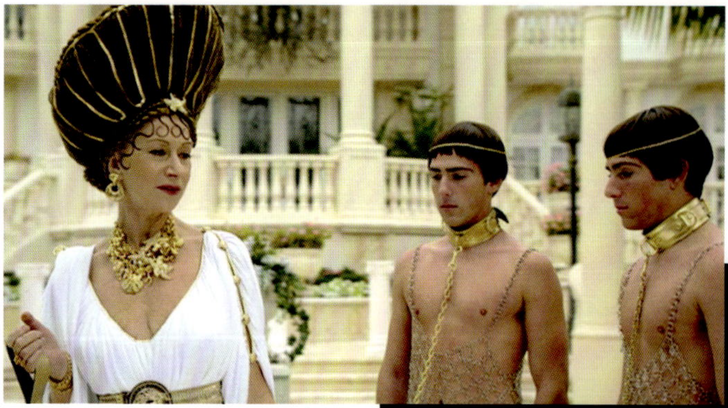

Trailer for a Remake of Gore Vidal's 'Caligula', 2005
Video projection, color, sound, 5'
Rivoli, Castello di Rivoli – Museo d'Arte Contemporanea, gift of the artist

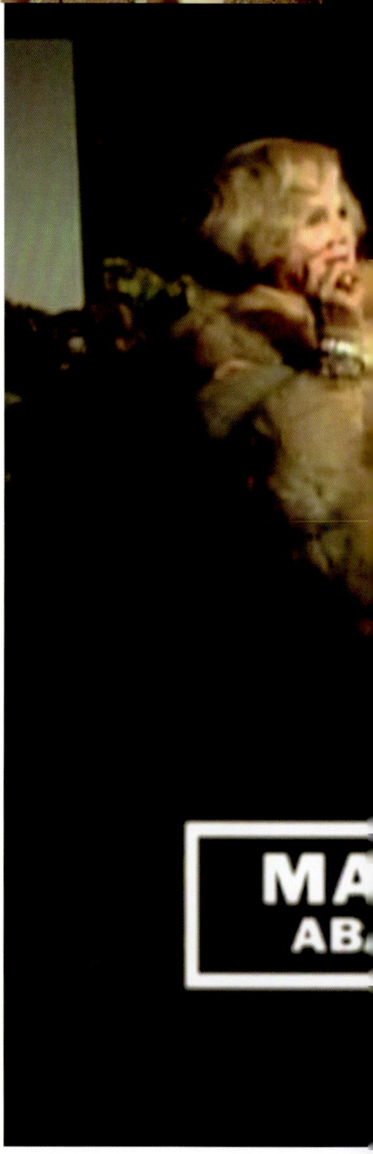

being interested rather in sounding its limits.
The ultimate sense of an illusory practice of this nature obviously becomes still clearer when it develops in the direction of visual actions of a markedly communicative character. One example is *Democrazy*, staged in the Italian Pavilion at the 52nd Venice Biennale as the presentation of two candidates for the presidency of the United States, played by the actress Sharon Stone and the philosopher Bernard-Henri Lévy. In response to the interest aroused in the media by the electoral campaigns of Obama, Clinton and McCain, Vezzoli undertook to offer a realistic picture of the electoral mechanisms of American democracy.
Here too, realism is the foundation underpinning the entire operation, which necessarily hinges on the credibility of the protagonists and construction of the film.
In particular, Vezzoli took the same approach to the public as occurred in real life, involving the agencies Public Strategies, which ran the Bush campaign in 2004, and Squier Knapp Dunn, Clinton's media advisors in 1996. As suggested by the play on words in its title, the work highlights ambivalence and duplicity but also standardization, and the two leading characters, Patrick and Patricia Hill, are identical apart from gender, a clear metaphor of the lack of any real political choice in the contemporary world.
Ephemerality is also a keynote of *Comizi di Non Amore*, a pilot episode for a nonexistent show produced by the Prada Foundation. The video involves numerous figures from the worlds of television and cinema, including the showgirl Ela Weber and the actresses Catherine Deneuve, Antonella Lualdi, Marianne Faithfull, Terry Schiavo, and Jeanne Moreau. Vezzoli's many points of reference here obviously include Pasolini, the brilliant creator of *Comizi d'amore*, a documentary investigation of the geography of sex and love in Italy halfway through the 1960s, but also the Buñuel of *Belle de jour* and the Truffaut of *Jules et Jim*. Love and death, the extreme coordinates of Vezzoli's work, are represented here through their greatest icons in postwar European cinema.
Involving a game where the public plays an active part in the final selection of the couples, Vezzoli's work becomes a rereading of certain TV shows of the 1980s and indeed of numerous contemporary programs of very similar character offered by Italy's various channels.
Vezzoli also focuses the medium of cinema on himself with a more than sarcastic attitude to the ambiguities of his life. Drawing inspiration from the narrative module of the sensationalistic documentaries on film stars in fashion in the United States, the artist created *Marlene Redux: A True Hollywood Story*, the trailer of a film on his life commissioned by the collector Pinault in 2006.
The (true) story plays on the negation of its own definition. Vezzoli depicts himself as a man of ambivalent and scabrous sexuality, behavioral difficulties, and creative incapacity. Transposing criticism and gossip into the video, Vezzoli offers the viewer a container of information about himself that intimately reflects not his life but rather what the typical audience of such shows wants to be told.
(*F.T.*)

Marlene Redux: A True Hollywood Story, 2006
Video projection, 15′ circa
Venice, François Pinault Collection

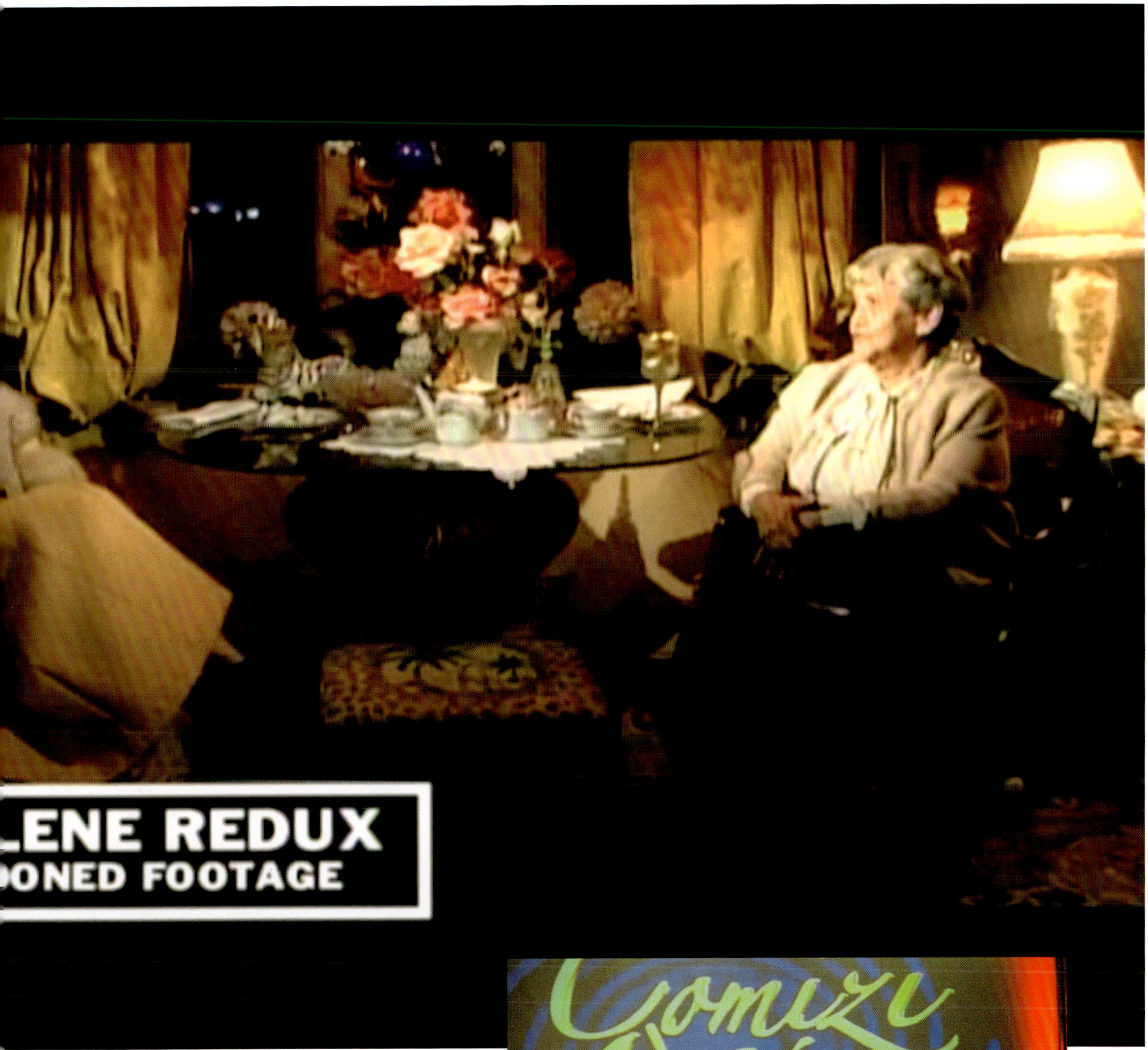

Comizi di Non Amore, 2004
DVD film, stereo sound, 63′50″
Courtesy Fondazione Prada, Milan

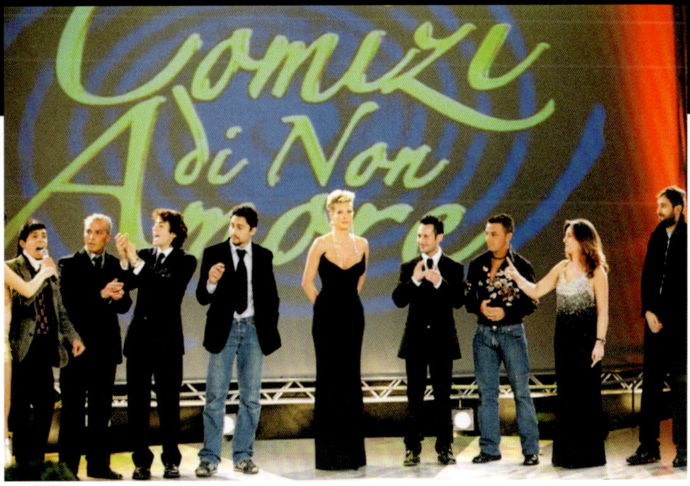

Yang Fudong

Born in Beijing in 1971. Lives and works in Shanghai.
The Chinese artist Yang Fudong uses video, photography and installation in work that focuses on the relationship between mankind and the contemporary world, understood as a situation of conflict, and constant rethinking of human action and individuality through a narrative approach closely akin to experimental cinema.
The link between the predominance of the metaphor of nature in the artist's video iconography and traditional Chinese painting was pointed out by Marcella Beccaria, curator of the show held at the Castello di Rivoli in 2006 within the framework of the exhibition *New Generations*. The main character of *The Revival of the Snake*, the video installation presented by the Chinese artist on that occasion, is a man in uniform, ambiguously identifiable as a deserter and a prisoner.
The narration concentrates on the man's last few days of life as he seeks to survive the hardship of winter on his own, far away from his unit. Solitude becomes a metaphor here of autonomy and freedom of choice in an autocratic country where individual liberty is subject to severe constraints and limitations. The ending of the video bears witness to the failure of the principle of self-determination as the essential condition for survival.
The human condition in the world is also addressed in the video *Robber South* (2001), where the situation verging on absurdity is an obvious parody of the American dream.
It shows the day in the life of a man who succeeds between dawn and dusk in changing from an almost penniless vendor into a *lingdao* or white-collar worker, his new status reflected in the possession of luxury goods. An important part is played in this attack on the social system by the iconography of the city, which is always filmed with the camera looking up. The metropolis of Shanghai is now a dead space, an urban representation of the problems of the consumer society.
(*F.T.*)

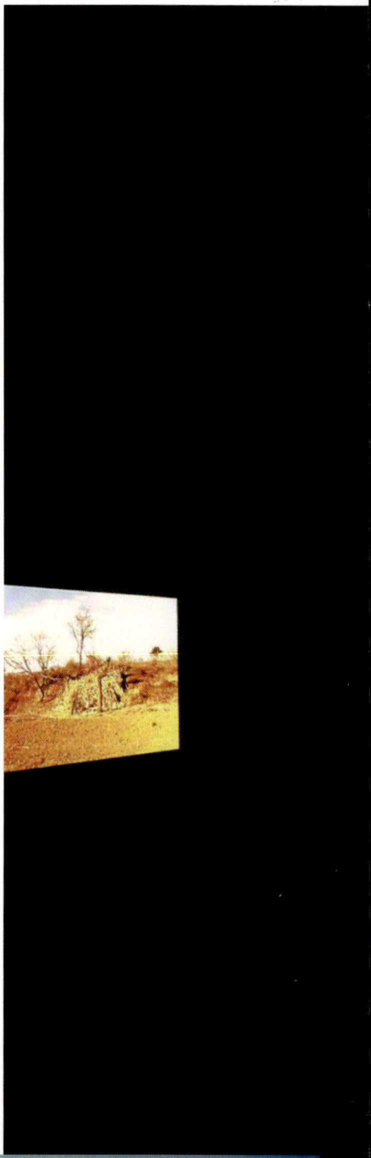

The Revival of the Snake, 2005
Ten-channel video installation, 2 projections, 8 plasma monitors, color, sound, 8'
Rivoli, Castello di Rivoli – Museo d'Arte Contemporanea, permanent deposit Fondazione CRT Progetto Arte Moderna e Contemporanea

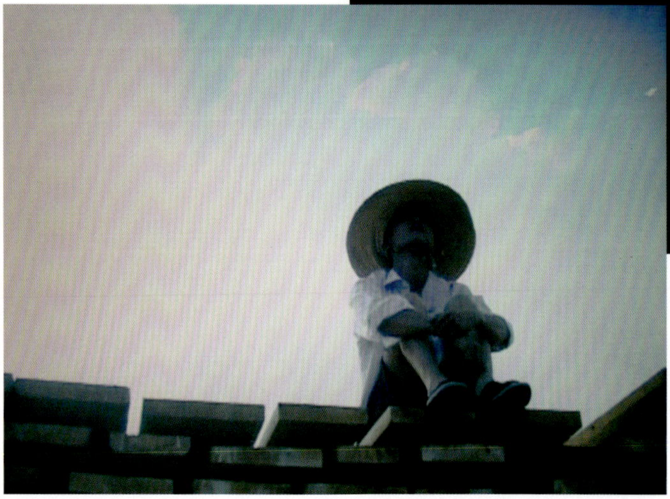

Robber South, 2001
Video, 18'
Naples, Maurizio Morra Greco Collection
Courtesy Raucci/Santamaria, Naples

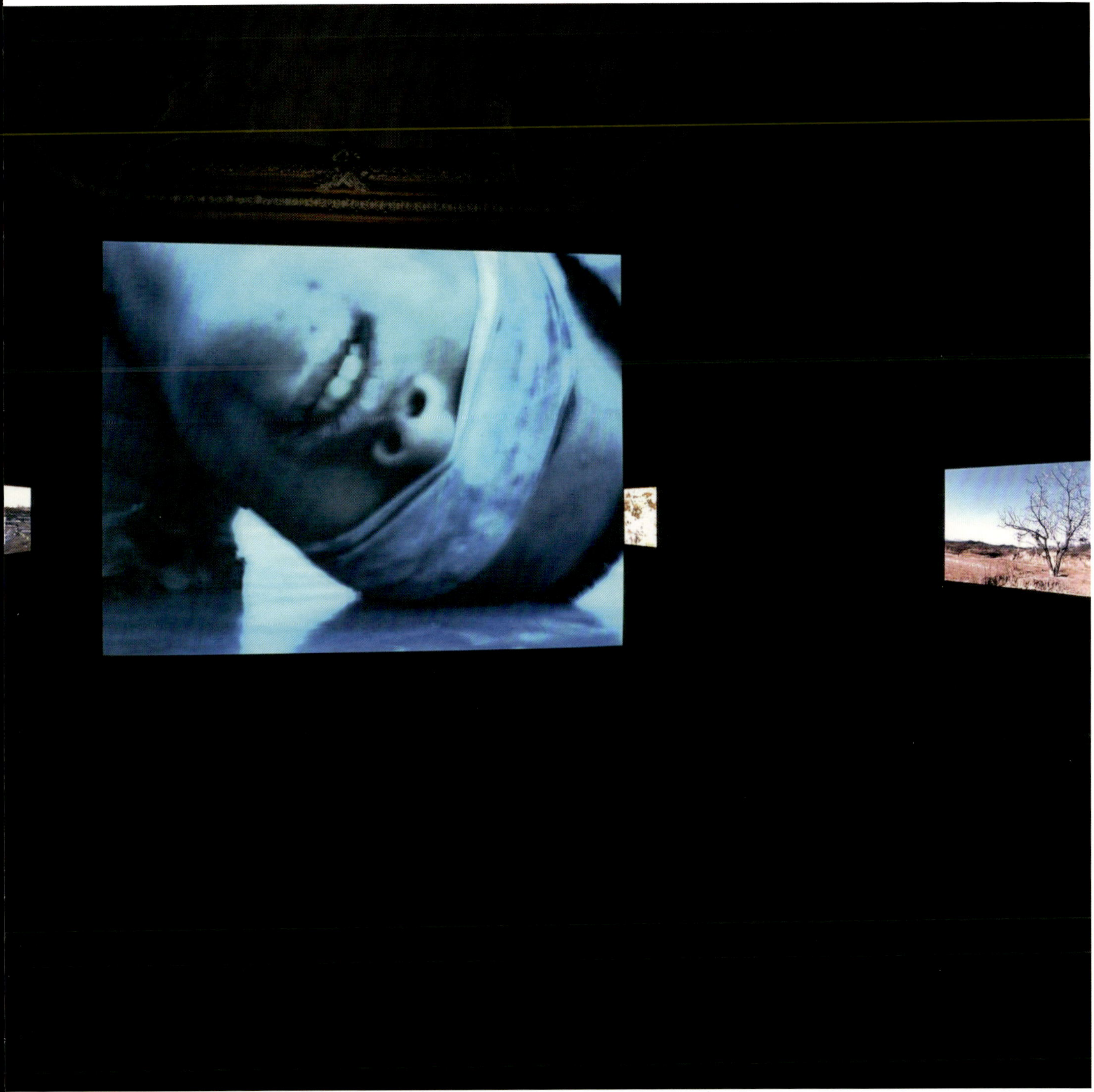

Zhang Huan

To Raise the Water Level In A Fish Pond, 1997
Color photograph, 127 x 178 cm
Courtesy F2 Gallery, Beijing

Born in An Yang City, China, in 1965. Lives and works in New York and Shanghai.
The project *To Raise the Water Level In A Fish Pond* reflects on human identity, the social condition, and relations with the iconographic tradition of Chinese painting. Zhang Huan's work involved a group of 40 newcomers to Beijing of peasant background, who were asked to enter a fishpond simultaneously and thus alter the level of the water. The city's new inhabitants left a tangible sign in the environment by changing their position in the water, thus modifying its geography in an ephemeral and reversible way. Initially arranged in a straight line dividing the pond in two, the men then moved freely until the volume of their bodies raised the level of the water by one meter, in accordance with the original plan of the performance. The symbolism of traditional Chinese iconography is the key to interpreting the images created by Zhang Huan, who uses the allegorical meaning of water, as a reference to the source of life, and the fish, as a reference to male fertility, to construct an ideal symbolic representation of the generating elements of creation.
The photograph of the performance shown in the exhibition *Inside Out* of 1998 (P.S. 1, New York; the Museum of Modern Art, San Francisco) brought Zhang Huan's work to attention at international level.
The relationship between form and symbolic meaning is also the focal point of the installation *Berlin Buddha* (2007), in which the artist created a completely hollow sculptural effigy of the divinity in aluminum and molded an identical figure of compacted ash from joss sticks inside it. The relationship between the two Buddhas begins with their separation, an operation that led to the gradual disintegration of the ash sculpture in the course of the exhibition.
The relationship between human and divine thus occupies a central position in the work of Zhang Huan. The meaning of the object simulacrum is always related to the spiritual universe, with which it maintains constant dialogue.
(*F.T.*)

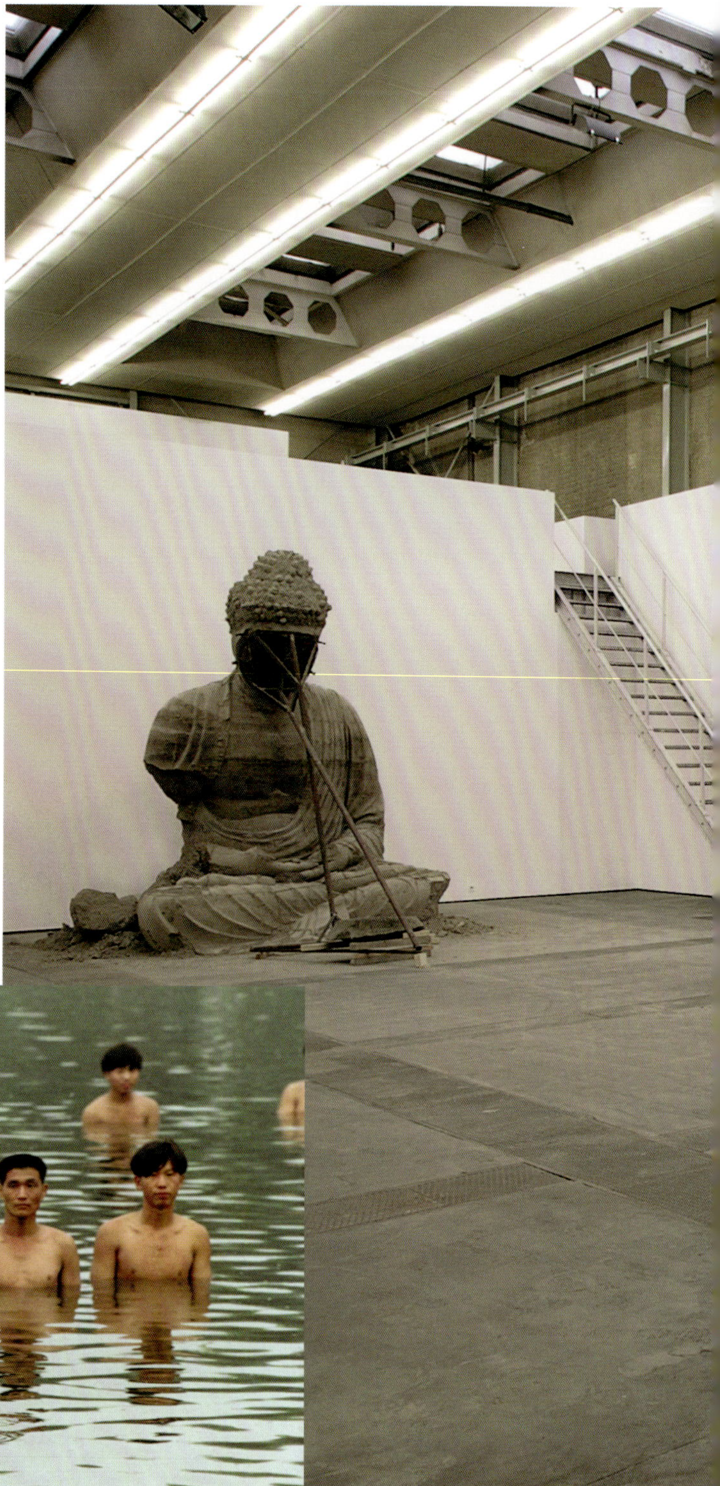

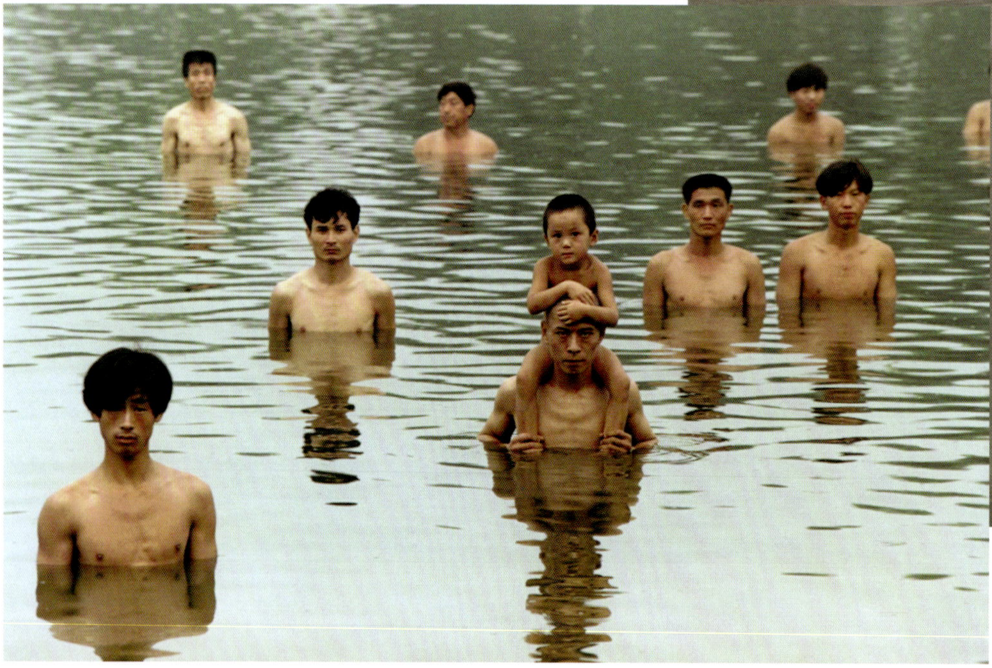

Berlin Buddha, 2007
Incense ash, iron, and aluminum
370 x 480 x 290 cm
Switzerland, private collection

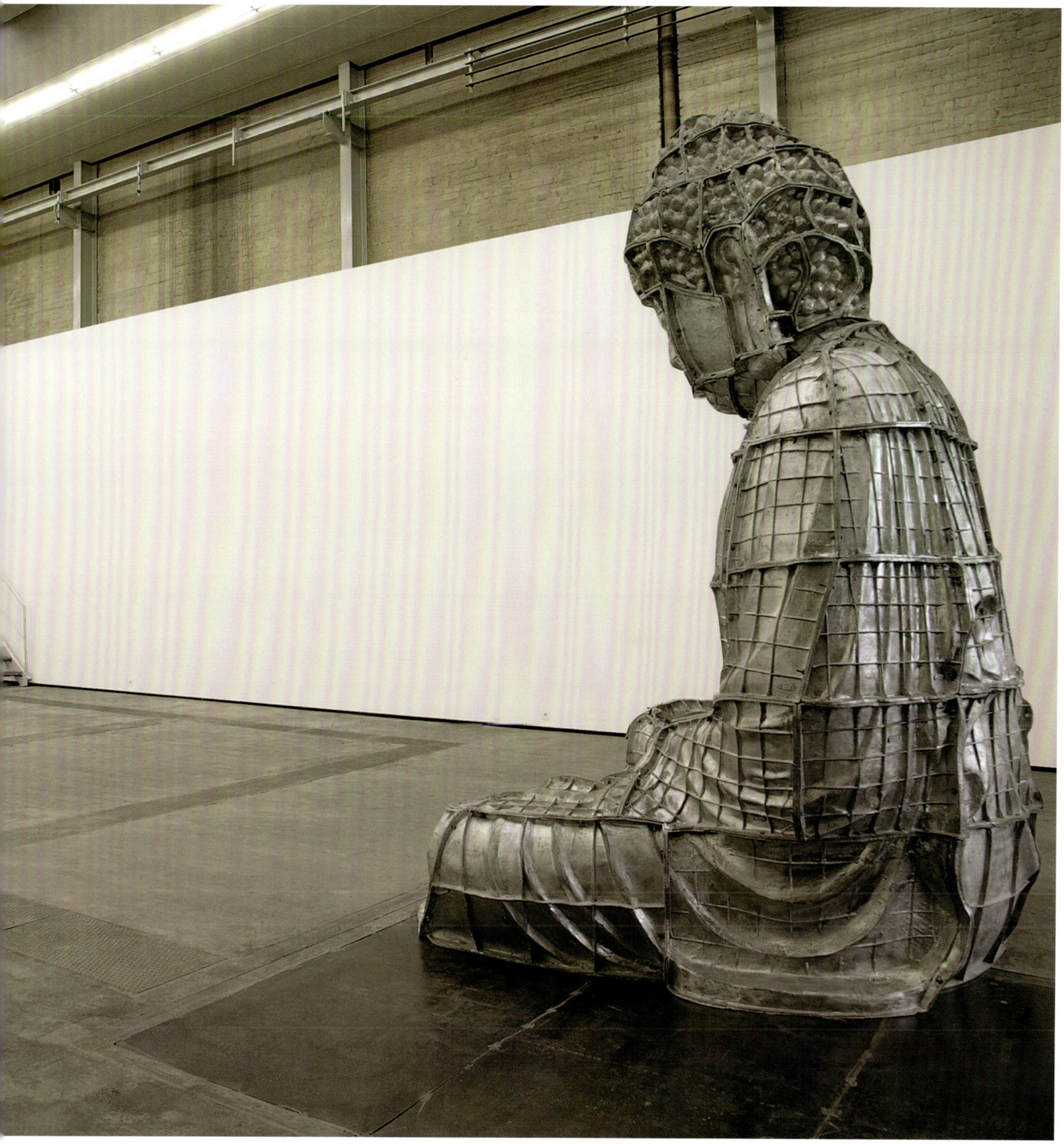

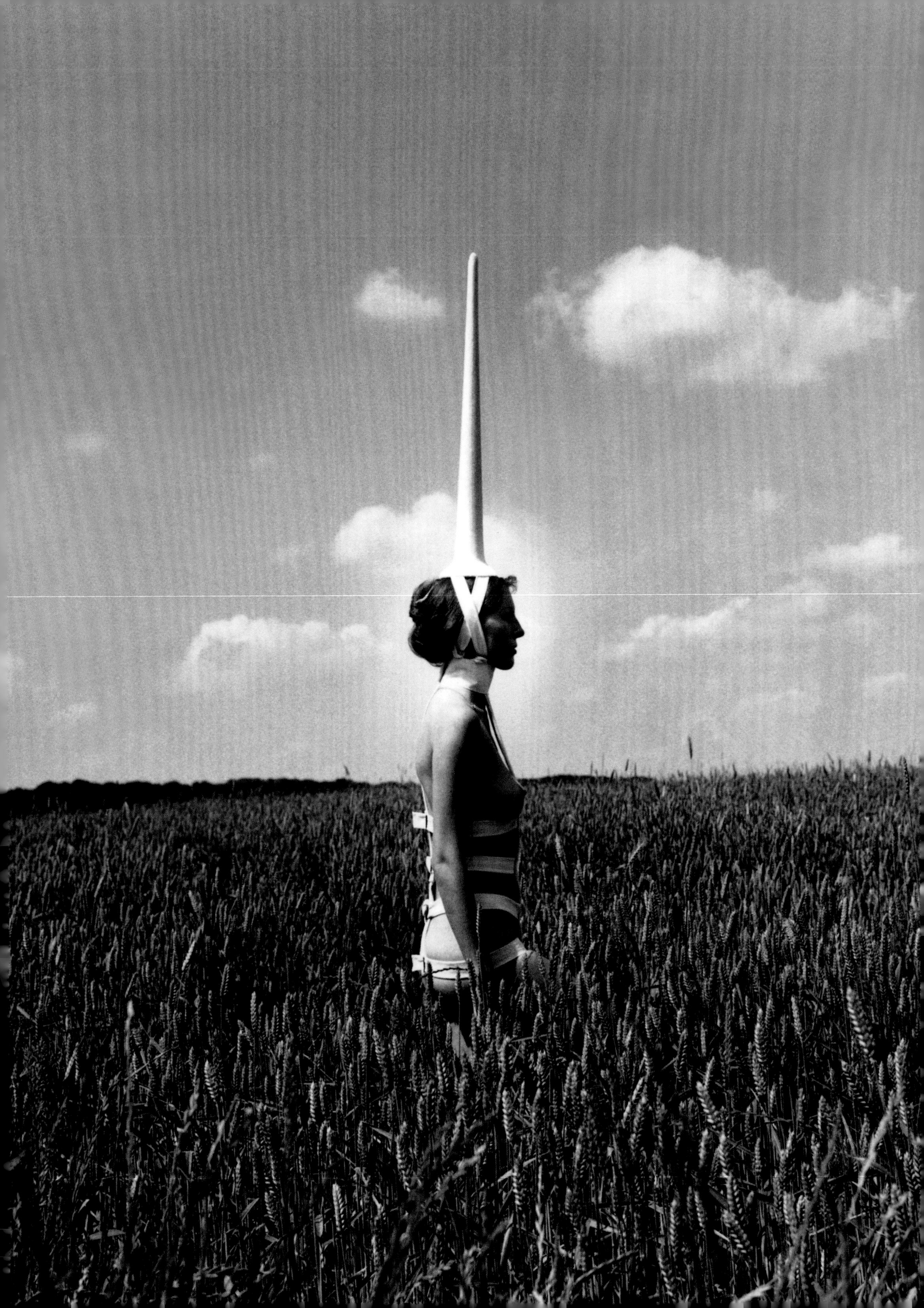

Angela Vettese

Poetics of Identity: Notes on the Question of Gender, the Other, and the Self as Seen by the Self

Rebecca Horn
Unicorn, 1970–1972
Black and white photograph,
40 x 30 cm
Private collection

Who am I? And who are you? Shifts around the idea of the self in twentieth-century art and modernity

It was not until the late Renaissance that artists began to respond to this question with lifelike portraits and self-portraits, granting individuality to the individual. This search for the truth about our appearance, developing also symbolically from the exterior into a probing of the interior, came in the early twentieth century to prefer ambiguous attire and lent itself to games like those in which Marcel Duchamp delighted. In the photographs he had taken by Man Ray during the age of Dada, he would present himself to his public in the male version or with a tonsured head, with a beard of shaving foam transforming him into a faun, wearing a hat, makeup, a pair of gloves, with a new name – Rrose Sélavy – changing him into his female alter ego. Identity was transformed from an opportunity for investigation into a problematic riddle.

One sign of the new importance attached to this issue is the drafting of documents that define the person and accord it priority with respect to the indistinct social mass, like the American Constitution and the Declaration of Human Rights. The whirlwind of technological innovations that was to bestow such reality on the birth of a subject as intrusive, self-referential, and widespread as the one that is today our daily bread was, however, unthinkable at the beginning of the contemporary era. The customs that had for centuries or millennia regulated relations between people, things, and places – the entire framework of habits that converged to make the relationships of you and me, you and us, mankind and the Earth less fraught with anxiety – were turned upside-down.

A world dominated by commercial or industrial enterprise appeared increasingly inclined to make a value of equality within the context of a colossal transformation of the individual into a consumer whose freedom to desire and buy had to be ensured.

The races set off on the path toward mutual tolerance that reached a symbolic milestone when Barack Obama, a man with African and Islamic roots on one side of his mixed parentage, was elected president of the United States in 2008.

Geography began to be written with radio stations, satellite photographs, and computer networks. We can find out what is happening on the other side of the globe and talk to the rest of the world or even go elsewhere with the greatest of ease. It is, however, also due to this new closeness that the clashes between civilizations have become more violent and migration has developed in waves of unprecedented scale and continuity.

In the so-called West, but not only there, constant exposure to the physical presence of others – from polygamists and polytheists to Blacks and Chinese – has accelerated the collapse of the most deeply rooted ethical axioms, such as the condemnation of homosexuality, of any refusal to form a couple and have children, of choices whereby individuals do not make themselves directly useful to the community.

Above and beyond the possession of goods and even before any possibility of an alternative between having and being for the people of today, it is the challenge of arduous adaptation – including the requisite changes in self-model – that faces women, migrants, homosexuals, those who travel for work and have lost any sense of belonging to a specific place in the overlapping of time zones, young people with no job prospects, adult parents deprived of the moral freedom to feel old and who are therefore "youthful" by obligation, and many other groups of individuals "deviating" from the canons of the past.

In the meantime, superseding any moral stance, technology has changed our bodily way of perceiving. Telescopes, electron microscopes, ultrasonography, radiography, and other technological devices developed above all in the medical and military sphere have given our eyes access to the great and the small. They can enter the body, see things repeatedly thanks to recording, capture images with photography and modify them with computer programs. Gertrude Stein already sensed at the beginning of the twentieth century what it meant for Picasso to belong to a generation able to look out from an airplane. Gustav Klimt called in a biologist to teach him and a group of acolytes about the form of the cells and the microscopic parts of living beings. Nor should it be forgotten that also with respect to ourselves, the body we perceive is at least partly unprecedented. Medicine and nutrition have increased the average height, resistance to infection, and life expectancy.

Finally, the sense of being a "person" has altered with demographic growth. The human population has increased steadily since 1710, when the industrial revolution first began. The new masses have clustered together far away from the land, from places where they could produce or find the minimum amount of food needed to live. They have gathered on the outskirts of cities, metropolises, and megalopolises, where they wait ideally to find a paid job. Nature has begun to present itself as a source of fear rather than food, of dread, distrust, menace, and fear that the pollution, abandonment, and violence to which we subject it will provoke its fatal vengeance.

This upheaval has had a number of salient consequences in the visual arts. A rebellion against the bourgeois way of life began back in the 1940s among young writers like Allen Ginsberg and Jack Kerouac, who met up in American colleges, as well as figures like Jean-Paul Sartre, Simone de Beauvoir and the existentialists of postwar Europe. The "Irascible Eighteen" reinvented painting as a physical practice at the Cedar Bar in New York: from Pollock's dance of the body to Klein's brutality of gesture and the discipline of Barnett Newman, something capable of involving the individual as a whole and not only the intellect. Something similar happened in Europe with Art Informel. On the other side of the Atlantic, Jean Fautrier, Jean Dubuffet, Antoni Tàpies, Lucio Fontana, and Alberto Burri also addressed the canvas like a field to be plowed, sown, and watered, to be dug into with the whole of the body.

In order to arrive, however, at any firm views in art about the nature of the person and its powers and limitations such as to involve physicality, it was necessary to develop practices presenting the body itself as part of the work and not only as a tool. After a Futurist and Dadaist debut, the 1950s saw a revival of happenings and performances, which were not only acts of protest but also assertions of difference, any difference, in the everyday ethos and in relationships such as male/female, black/white, central/peripheral, dominant/dominated.

The practice of taking oneself to the place of creative action spread all over the planet in just a few years. While this marked the adoption of a stance as regards vocabulary, its deeper aspect regarded not so much the canons of art as those of identity.

The resulting works focused increasingly on two points, albeit not necessarily on both within the context of a single event: on the one hand, the artist's body as place of sacrifice, mythic center, and sphere of radical experiences on the borderline of common sense, decency, and even survival; on the other, participation of the public, called upon to act as coauthor and not only spectator or witness, as though the work could not be called complete unless it succeeded in creating a sort of cohesive community in its development. A few examples of early operations aimed in this direction will help to clarify these remarks.

The body became painting. It was in Paris in June 1958 that Yves Klein showed the living body as paintbrush, using girls daubed with blue on the parts connected with procreation – belly, breast, and thighs (never the head) – in order to paint. Entitled *Anthropométries*, as though they were measurements of man or humanity in its essence, the works were created before a small gathering of witnesses in Robert Godet's apartment.

The artwork became elastic and ephemeral. It was in New York in October 1959 that Allan Kaprow held his first coordinated action, the famous *18 Happenings in 6 Parts*, at the Reuben Art Gallery with the participation of artists who were themselves authors of performative events. These included Dick Higgins, a leading member of the Fluxus movement from 1962 on, and Robert Rauschenberg, who had taken part in 1952 in what is considered the seminal moment par excellence of happening and performance, namely the event staged by John Cage and Merce Cunningham at Black Mountain College in North Carolina. Kaprow later insisted also in written texts on the ephemeral nature of the happening, evanescent to the point of repeating the evanescence of life itself. It should be recalled that *Fluids* involved making a building out of blocks of ice in a scorching desert; the only lasting construction was in fact the relationship between the people taking part in the event. In the case of Kaprow, and indeed much of the performance art that focused to an even greater extent on its author, we are obviously faced with a new ver-

Shigeko Kubota
Vagina Painting, performance at the Cinemateque, New York, July 4, 1965, during the *Perpetual Fluxus Festival*

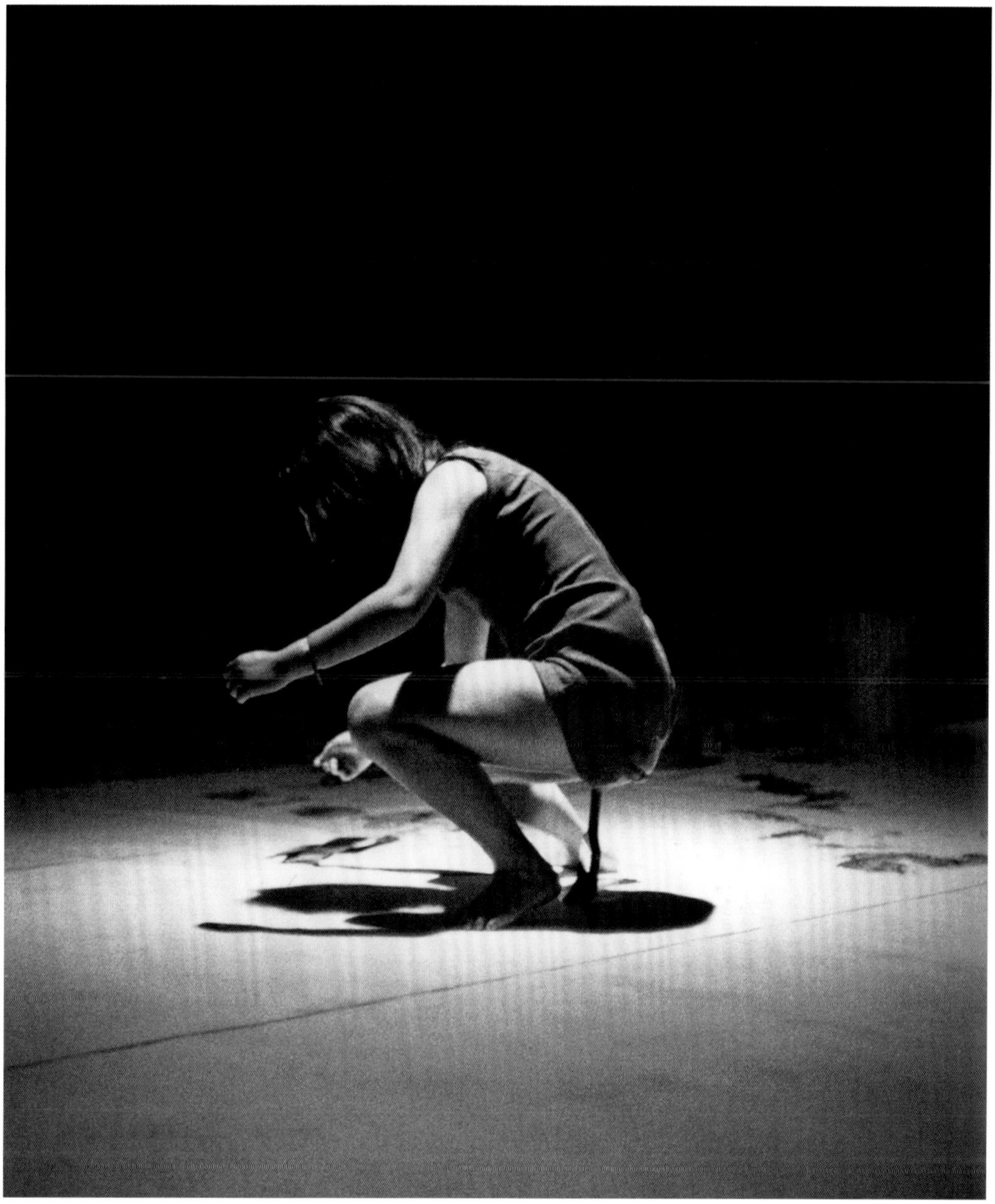

sion of the Romantic idea of the circular relationship of art and life.[1]

Momentary impulses became actions and objects. It was in Nice in 1961 that Arman destroyed a table and chair in an action entitled *Colère* and Niki de Saint Phalle shot at a board to which glass objects, paint-filled balls, and smoke bombs were attached. Aggressiveness became the nucleus around which the underground art scene revolved in Vienna. Otto Muehl and Günther Brus urinated into one another's mouths at the university theater and Rudolf Schwarzkogler mutilated his genitals in actions continuing the investigations into the extent, the nature, and the fear of the self born in Austria at the beginning of the twentieth century, from the psychoanalysis of Freud and Jung to the painting of Klimt, Kokoschka, and Schiele, and the literature of Schnitzler and Bernard.

Women approach the banquet of art: from feminism to femininity, from commitment for women to political involvement for the weak

When reproduction ceased to be a necessity, non-rural societies dispensed with their traditional homophobia. Lesbian artists like Hannah Höch, Claude Cahun, and Roni Horn, bisexuals like Nan Goldin, and male homosexuals like Félix González-Torres, Gilbert & George, and Luigi Ontani were able to thematize their position and make it a focal point of their works.

There has been a rise in the number of women artists and their degree of acceptance, as shown for example by the *Kunstkompass* rankings of the magazine *Capital*.[2]

What the artist Carolee Schneemann predicted in 1979 seems to have come true: "By the year 2000 no young woman artist will

Bruce Nauman
From Hand to Mouth, 1967
Wax on canvas,
71.1 x 25.7 x 10.2 cm
Washington, D.C., Hirshhorn Museum and Sculpture Garden

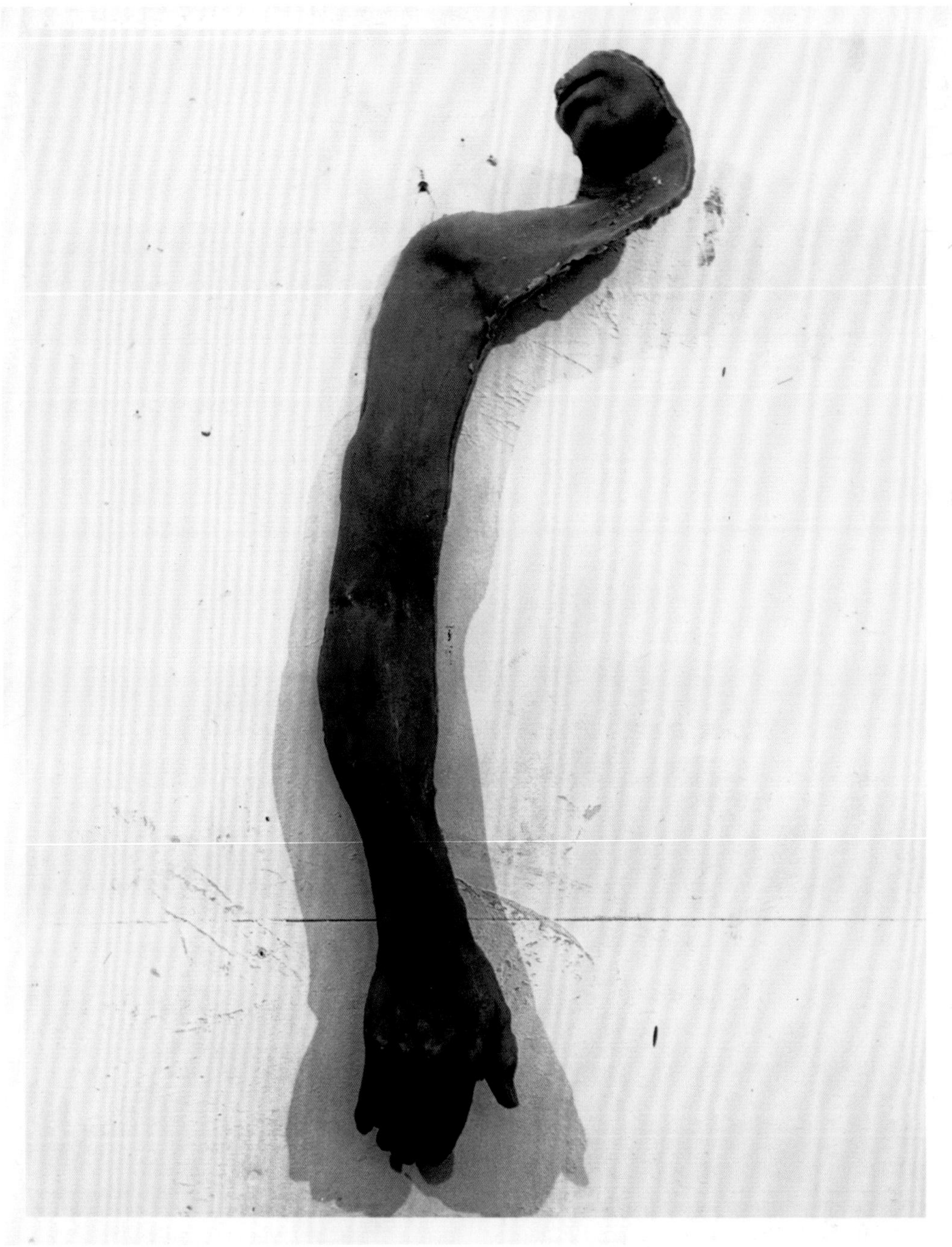

meet the determined resistance and constant undermining which I endured as a student. Her Studio and Istory courses will usually be taught by women; she will never feel like a provisional guest at the banquet of life.... Nor will she go into the 'art world' gracing or disgracing a pervading stud club of artists, historians, teachers, museum directors, magazine editors, gallery dealers – all male, or committed to masculine preserves."[3]

Given the above, it might be thought that the rocketing growth of women's studies in universities, especially in the USA, since the 1980s and the more or less explicit battles fought by women artists of the 1960s to obtain space in exhibitions and museums have achieved their objective. As Rosalind Krauss wrote in the opening chapter of her collection of essays entitled *Bachelors*, "art made by women needs no special pleading."[4] Undermining years of consolidation of the gender culture and – above all in universities – of a conception of female art as irreducible to the grammar of male art, the Columbia University scholar believes there is no longer any need of particular allowances for women artists as women. This was in any case the attitude of Walter Gropius with his students at the Bauhaus back around 1920. The German architect had just embarked on a utopian project in which male and female sensibilities were equally involved. The school he directed was the first in the world to be multidisciplinary and open also to women, two points that were not in truth entirely unrelated. With a contradictory residue of discrimination, women were channeled above all into the creative sphere closest to handicrafts.

While it is true that women artists did exist in the first part of the twentieth century, major figures like Annie Albers, Sophie Taüber Arp, and Sonia Delaunay already bore the surnames of more famous husbands. Olga Rozanova, Alexandra Exter, Gabriele Münter, Varvara Stepanova, Liubov Popova, Natalia Goncharova, and Katarzyna Kobro are personalities without whom the historical avant-garde movements would have developed very differently, and the Surrealists may have appreciated the work of the Mexican Frida Kahlo more than that of her husband Diego Rivera.

In any case, the Surrealist group admitted women who had been their models, like Meret Oppenheim, or wives of Max Ernst, like Leonora Carrington, Dorothea Tanning and the gallery owner Peggy Guggenheim. Even in the 1930s and 1940s, Georgia O'Keeffe was launched by her husband Alfred Stieglitz, Kay Sage was granted artistic status only as the widow of Yves Tanguy, and Lee Krasner never really succeeded in freeing herself from the burden of her relationship with Jackson Pollock. The male attitude was ambiguous in the best of cases as protective toward something/someone not truly regarded as an equal. This subordinate position continued also during the period of American Abstract Expressionism, when Joan Mitchell and Helen Frankenthaler enjoyed the support of the critic Clement Greenberg but not therefore the same popularity as their male colleagues.

The progress in terms of the female identity was, however, unquestionably fast. In 1772 the artists of the Royal Academy even had themselves portrayed without their vice president, Angelica Kauffmann, who attended their meetings only in the form of an effigy.[5] Moreover, emancipation did not bring only privileges. The disappearance of the protective network of fathers, brothers, and husbands, possessive though it may have been, meant greater vulnerability to acts of violence and rape, and being regarded as solely to blame. This contradictory combination of freedom and danger also had the further result of contributing to the growth of fundamentalism in all of the major religions, which advocated female segregation and repressed any non-orthodox forms of eroticism.

According to Roselee Goldberg, the greatest historian of performance art, it was the impetus of female demands that made this the medium most used in the new search for identity.[6] While the dates of actions by women artists do not go all the way back to 1952 and Black Mountain College, they did start very early and were curiously linked to a number of Japanese figures.

The Japanese Gutai group organized an event whose title could be translated as *Art Show on Stage* in Tokyo and Osaka in May 1957. Among other things, Atsuko Tanaka

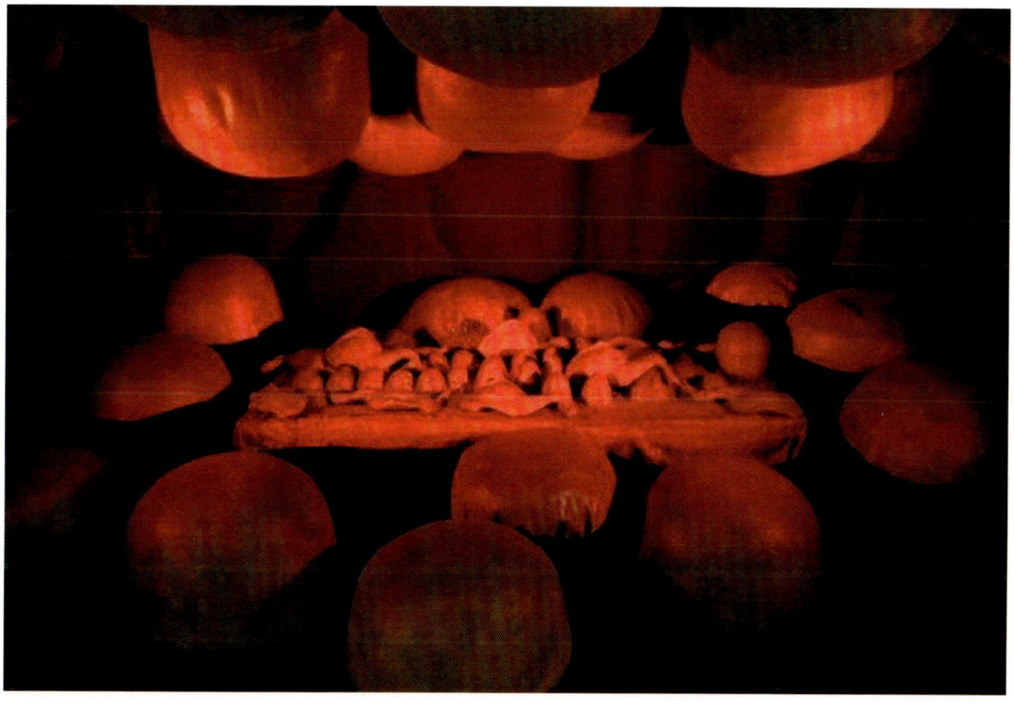

Louise Bourgeois
The Destruction of the Father, 1974
Plaster, latex, wood, fabric and red light, dimensions variable
Courtesy Cheim & Read, New York, Galerie Karsten Greve, Paris, Hauser & Wirth, Zürich/London

Yoko Ono
Cut Piece, 1965
Performance at the Carnegie Recital Hall, New York, March 21, 1965

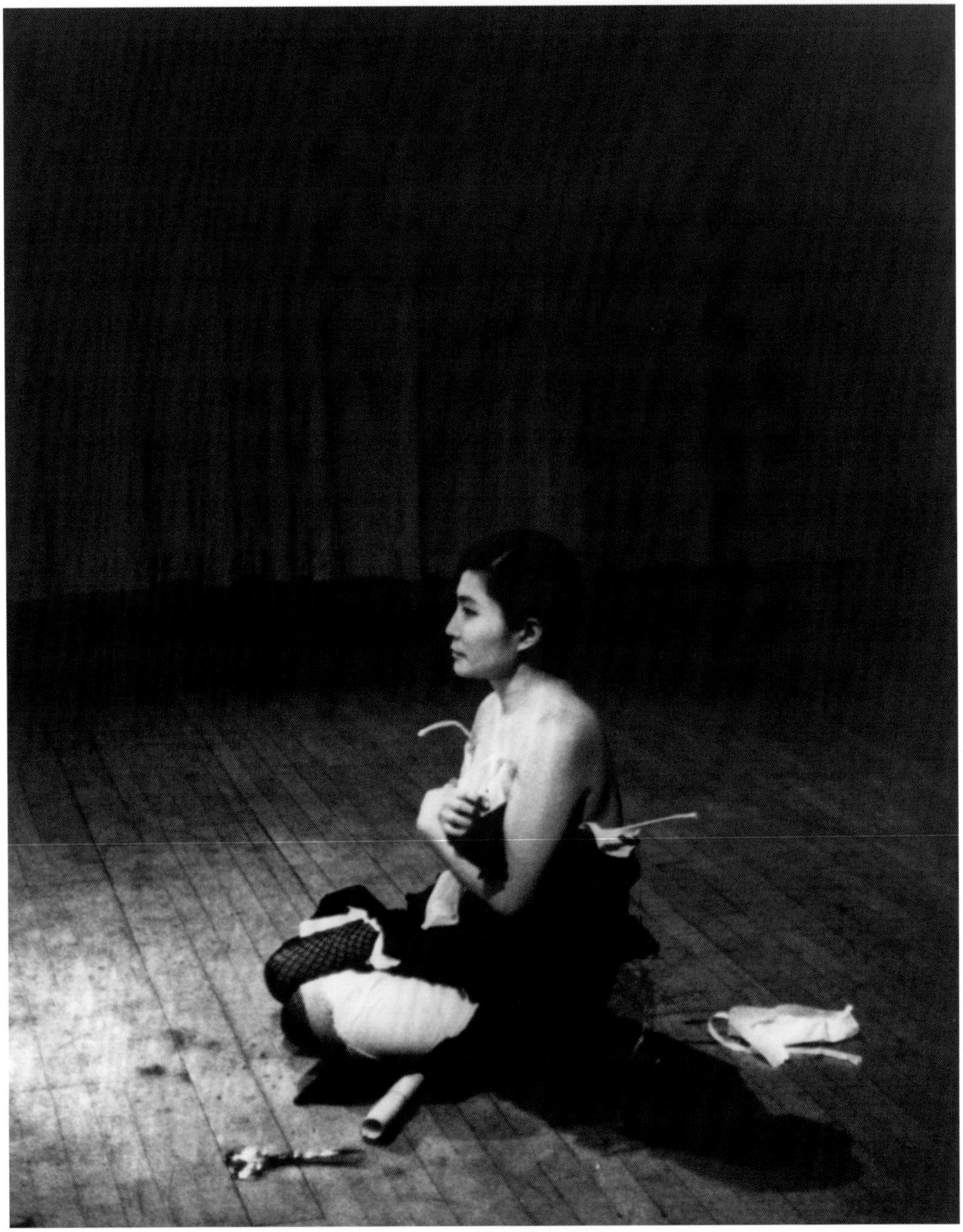

appeared in a dress of light bulbs and the stage was filled with balloons. In 1965 we find Shigeko Kubota crouched on the stage of the Cinémathèque on East 4th Street painting with a brush held in her vagina: any reference to sexuality and the discrimination of "uterine" women with respect to "rational" men was purely intentional. Yoko Ono (1933) started out as a musician and invented a concert "for strawberries and violin" with David Tudor entitled *A Grapefruit* and held at Carnegie Hall, New York, as early as 1961. This action then gave the title to a book of recipes for artistic events that in fact present themselves as poetic utterances the reading of which is sufficient in itself. In *Cut Piece* (first staged in Kyoto in 1964) the spectators were invited to cut off pieces of the artist's dress with scissors. Her loft was a meeting point for the visual arts and music with figures like Yvonne Rainer, Ornette Coleman, Jonas Mekas, and Ay-O. Her aim was to use weapons close to Zen and hence totally non-violent in a battle for the end of all abuse of power, from the exploitation of nature to attacks on the dignity of women. Yayoi Kusama, another Japanese expatriate, transformed the Castellnar Gallery, New York, into a maze of mirrors. The floor was covered with countless polka-dotted phallic protrusions. Her body lay in the middle of this, overwhelmed by disorientation, the obsessive ubiquity of the phallus, and the attempt perpetrated by her mother, the society of her homeland, and the political context to restrain her exuberance. The political side of these actions became clear above all with her "Anti-War Naked Happenings" of 1968, in which groups of naked youngsters painted with dots appeared as provocative living statues in key sites of New York like Central Park, Wall Street, and the Brooklyn Bridge.[7]

The 1960s saw the emergence of other leading figures, who were now also organizing themselves in the ranks of an explicit feminist movement.

Carolee Schneemann's performances *Eye Body* (1963) and *Meat Joy* (1964), constituting the first joyful celebration of the female body in all its carnality, were followed in 1975 by *Interior Scroll*, an event during which she read out a series of remarks by male critics on her work from a piece of rolled-up paper extracted from her vagina. Operations of this type, focusing on the genital organs, the "bad girl" stereotype, and bacchanalian rites, were important as assertions of opposition to the model of the selfless woman, happy to accept the violence of an unwanted but socially indispensable marriage.[8]

The Guerrilla Girls printed posters combining the image of the frightening female predator with statistics documenting the still negligible presence of women in the official world of art. This combination of aggressive and defensive action also appears in the work of the Austrian artist Valie Export, who presented herself to spectators in trousers with the crotch cut out pointing a rifle (*Action Pants: Genital Panic*, 1969). The Cuban Ana Mendieta acted out the rape actually inflicted on a classmate at college. Anyone looking for her in the rooms was liable to find her stretched out on a table, bleeding and too exhausted to react. Attracted by the combination of Catholicism and African Yoruba rituals, the artist also showed herself covered in mud, embedded into the landscape like an imprint (*Siluetas*, 1976), or bound to a tree as though part of the trunk-phallus and Earth-uterus at the same time (*Tree of Life*, 1977).

The Womanhouse in Los Angeles was a sort of alternative center of key importance for exploration of the female dimension. In her performance *Waiting* (1971) the artist Faith Wilding sat in a long skirt on a chair rocking back and forth and chanted a litany of anticipated acts ("Waiting to get married, Waiting for my child to come, Waiting to grow old, Waiting to die...") and surrender with no possibility of resistance, and perhaps even no desire for it. Some women wanted to be "good" to the point of offering themselves up in an act of self-sacrifice and blackmail at the same time, by no means devoid of eucharistic "partake of me and I will save you" allusions. Meret Oppenheim had herself served up on a dish, as did the Brazilian Lygia Clarck some years later in the performance *Baba Antropofagica* (1973). The latter, together with a group including Lygia Pape and Hélio Oiticica, also presented in her action a personal interpretation of the Brazilian libertarian movement in terms of anthropophagy, which involves placing oneself completely at the disposal of others.[9]

Nor is humor lacking in this rich gallery of performances. In *Light my Fire Sweetie?* (1975), for example, the African-American artist Adrian Piper took upon herself the stereotype of the self-assured colored man with a big moustache and a fine cigar walking along the street and asking girls for a light. In this swaggering posture we see the problem of race emerging alongside gender as aggravating circumstance, just like the rhetoric of hot-blooded, irrational blackness that worked until the 1990s to prevent all black women (and not only women) from enjoying any political power not linked to the assertion of claims.

The vocabulary of performance is often connected with the use of illness as a way of talking about oneself. It was in 1968 that the German artist Rebecca Horn embarked on a series of performances involving prosthetic devices that restricted her movements and altered her body. Her *Arm Extensions* (1968) were a pair of abnormally long sleeves attached to straps binding her body. The *Unicorn* hat of 1970 was a sort of aerial made of fabric highlighting her ability to plug into nature. These and subsequent works were also prompted by a lung infection that kept her in hospital for months. Close proximity with the threat of death was channeled into a way of conceiving the artwork as something that saves, protects, increases or decreases the power of physicality and ultimately of the entire person. The performance artist Hannah Wilke was later to transform her mortal illness into an event available to the public, eroding the taboo that requires the body – especially if female – to conceal its slow deterioration from the eyes of the healthy. It is no coincidence that the writer Susan Sontag also expressed herself in the same terms in her autobiographical book on cancer entitled *Illness as Metaphor.*

Magdalena Abakanowicz
Abakan Red I, 1970–1973
Linen fabric, Sisal, metal wire,
300 x 300 x 100 cm circa
Zurich, Museum für Gestaltung, Kunstgewerbesammlung

Women artists have seldom collaborated with men in their work. It is in this that we find one of the most distinctive peculiarities of Marina Abramovich, whose performances with her partner Ulay gave concise and effective expression to the collusive relationship of the couple and the way in which this manifests itself in life-threatening bonds. In *Relation in Space* (1976) the naked bodies of the two lovers run into one another, colliding and striking each other violently until one falls or they are forced to pull apart. The action is repeated countless times to the point of complete physical exhaustion. The drive for meeting generates exhaustion.

The 1980s led to a move away from pure performance and a focus above all on sculptural objects and settings. The female issue was still touched upon by many women artists but in varied ways and no longer bound up primarily with the practice of performance art. One vantage point to observe this evolution in the 1990s was the Venice Biennale. It was in 1990 that the American pavilion hosted a large-scale installation of marble tiles and poems displayed on panels of a thousand lights by Jenny Holzer, in 1993 that the protest developed for decades by Louise Bourgeois ultimately against the disturbing memory of her father received its first major recapitulation, and in 1997 that Ann Hamilton condemned war as unjustified masculine carnage, with blood red powder running down the walls and also appearing outside, like a sin impossible to hide.

The Caribbean American artist Janine Antoni exhibited six self-portraits in soap, which she washed away with her own hands, and six identical self-portraits in chocolate, which she nibbled, in the Aperto section of the 1993 Biennale. Recalling female obsessions like excessive cleaning and bulimia, the artist revealed new ways in which female anxiety, far from having disappeared, was beginning to manifest itself. The Anglo-Palestinian Mona Hatoum showed a video at the 1995 Biennale recalling violent performances that had investigated the body, such as the cuts Gina Pane inflicted on herself with razor blades in the 1970s. A view of her own personal endoscopy, projected on the floor like the progressive excavation of a hole in the ground, was made available to the public. Here too, a new female obsession emerged, namely the terror of feeding a hidden cancer instead of an evident child.

The "liberated" female identity is not, however, the only one to have won, as the new decade has also displayed a significant relapse. The French group Tiqqun expresses it as follows: "The Girl is currently the most luxurious of the goods circulating on the market of perishable commodities, the key merchandise of the fifth industrial revolution, serving to sell all the rest."[10] One of her main characteristics is a constant recalling of childhood that involves and consoles anyone in contact with her: "The Girl loves to talk emotionally about her childhood in order to suggest that she is not yet out of it and has remained essentially naïve. Like all whores, she dreams of *purity*. But unlike them, she insists on being believed, and being believed sincerely."[11] A similar model of girl is presented to some extent in various works by the artist Mariko Mori (1967) and in general by the *kawaii* (cuteness) movement, which is particularly active in Japan, in forms of expression that are not exceptionally artistic but highly pervasive as regards mentality. This widespread social phenomenon, recognizable for example in the success of the Hello Kitty range of products (bags, purses, skirts, etc., all infantile in character) was born when the *shojo bunka* or girl culture – *shojo* being a term that indicates the halfway stage in the female condition between puberty and marriage – met the Euro-American culture of ludic disengagement. The next stage was the *shojo manga*, where a crossing with the tradition of Western comics triggered an unexpressed but volcanic sexuality, at the end of the twentieth century. We are therefore faced with a new type of nymph, one sacred to the world of merchandise and communication precisely in virtue of the seductive appeal that feminist artists sought to jettison in the 1960s and 1970s. Her childish frills fuel a potentially pedophile desire in the viewer and present themselves as an effective means of escape from the anxiety of competition and responsibility that characterizes the adult world. This context makes the work of many women artists, also far away from Japan, more readily comprehensible.

Nathalie Djurberg makes animated films with grotesque plasticine figures, often involved in exaggerations of the erotic relationship and gender imbalance. The emotions of the characters with their accentuated characteristics (breasts, lips, movements) are born out of needs connected with the requisite of approval and self-esteem. The part of the "baddie" is not infrequently assigned to a sexy witch, as happens with the aging stepmothers of fairytales. Miwa Yana-

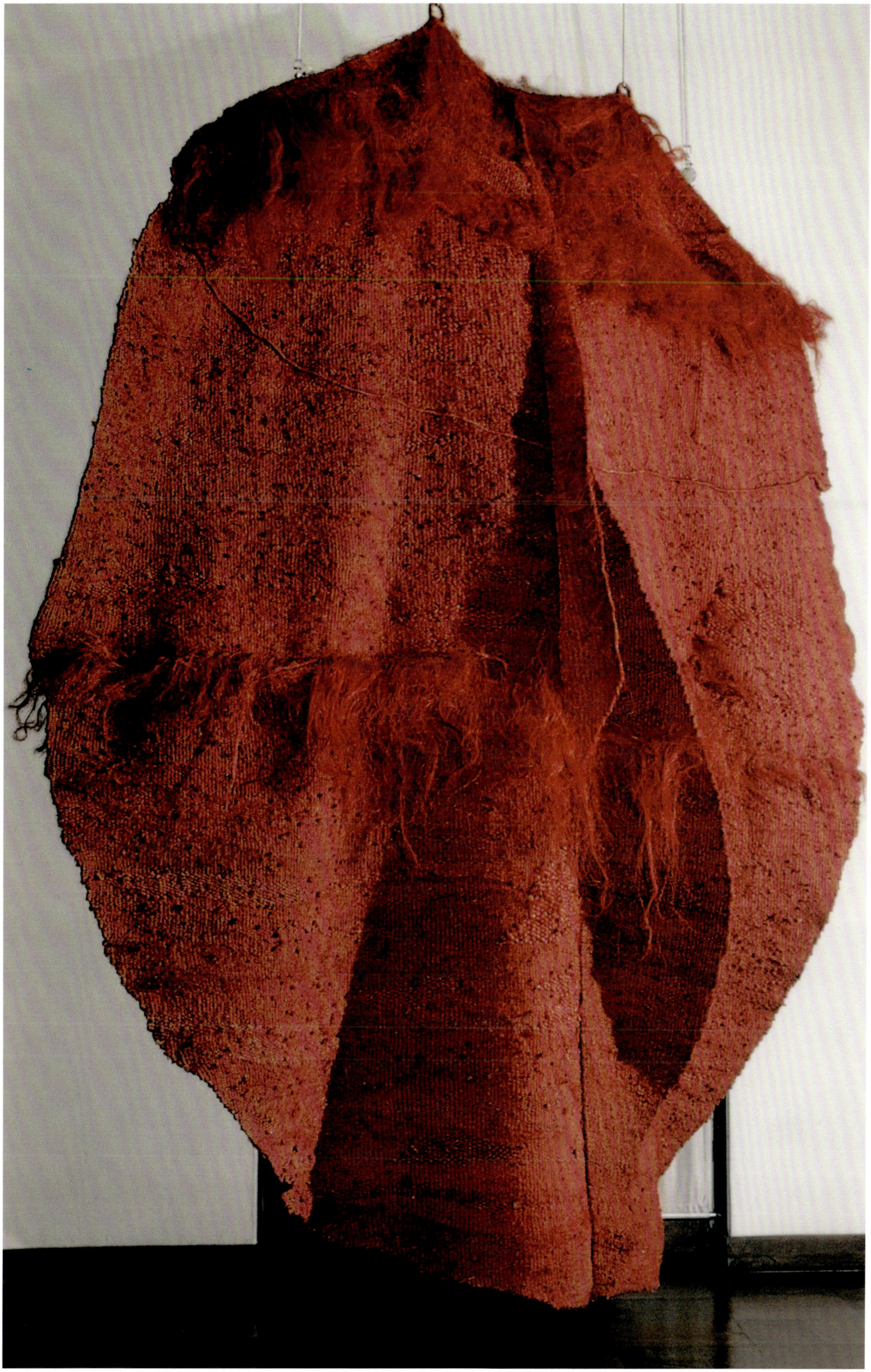

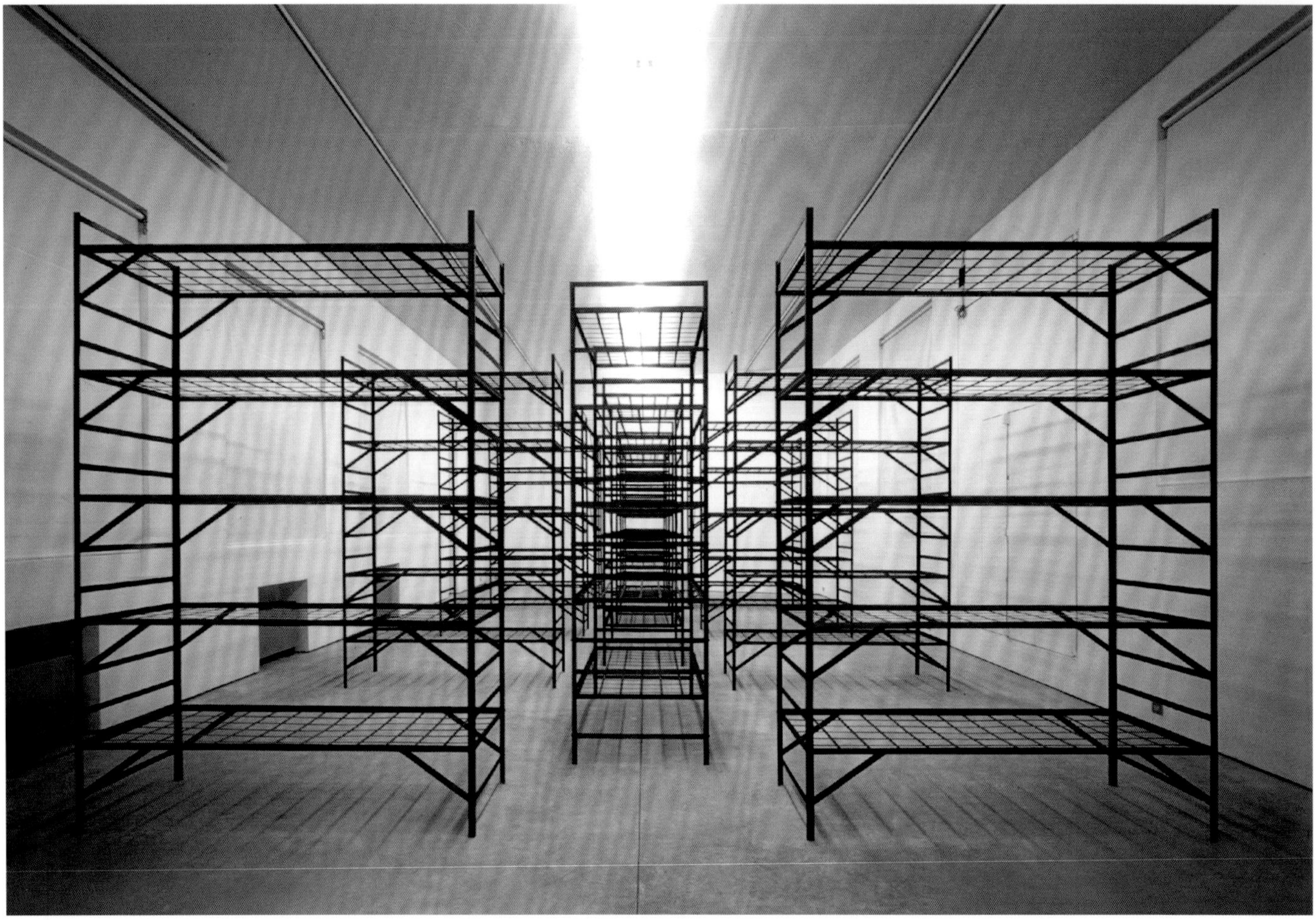

Mona Hatoum
Quarters, 1996
Twelve iron structures,
275.5 x 80.8 x 183 cm each
View of the installation at the galleria Viafarini, Milan

gi creates photographs and films constructed as sets for tales: girls exhausted after erotic encounters defended (or forced?) by a horrible old witch sitting beside the bed like a custodian or allusions to narrative constructions like *Sleeping Beauty* (the *Fairy Tale* series of 2004). Lisa Yuskavage paints girls from the lower-middle classes interested only in boys and their bodies: criticism of a stereotype or self-criticism? Girls are shown in the act of measuring each other's enormous bosoms, rivals and accomplices in seduction. It is not greater self-assurance but the possibility of having plastic surgery that this second generation derives from the freedom won by their mothers. They play dolls with themselves in pursuit of an impossible perfection. The persistent and obsessive relationship with corporality manifests itself in the work of many young female artists, however, as something in which women are beginning to recognize their own ability to defend themselves and to frighten rather than just be frightened.

Representation of the body can sometimes also be serene. Vanessa Beecroft indicates the great Renaissance paintings of mythological scenes with their numerous nude female figures as the model for her performances. Born out of problems with anorexia, her painting with living bodies has gone beyond an obsessive focus on beauty to arrive at political engagement, taking the artist away from an interest in herself to an interest in Blacks, child victims of discrimination, and the poor peoples of Africa, who have taken on the leading role in her *tableaux vivants*. Unless of course the commitment to the children of Darfur and the poor areas of the world developed in the late 2000s is in fact a reparatory type of transition on the artist's part from a phase of seduction and narcissism to one of maternal feelings and solidarity.

There are flights toward fairytale in the work of artists like Saskia Olde Wolbers, whose psychedelic videos sweep us away in a kaleidoscope of color and movement, and Liliana Moro, with her stories of animals cast in metal and lost in labyrinths but not therefore unhappy. Having started out with disturbing autobiographical sculptures, Kiki Smith turned in the 2000s to an art of magic and pantheistic sensibilities with carved and cast images of bird divinities and drawings placed in softly colored settings with many levels and layers of interpretation (as in the solo show of 2005 at the Fondazione Querini Stampalia in Venice) that become hymns to life and to woman as the vessel of rebirth.

Nature, the idea of the mother, and rebirth are firm points of anchorage for Cristina Iglesias, whose art pays tribute to her capacity for life no matter what the conditions. A small but characteristic example of her *modus operandi* is provided by the work set in the house of Federico García Lorca in Granada (2007), where the door of an upstairs room opens halfway as though something were pushing to get out. And what emerges is in fact a huge, dark tree of bronze that, like a concretion of life refusing to surrender to (the poet's) destiny, continues to resist and assert its existence in the world. Woman presents herself as a guarantee of endurance and future.

Though censored and blacked out by the Catholic church, which authorized its projection in a consecrated building but then detected unacceptable homoerotic elements, the video that Pipilotti Rist showed on the ceiling of San Stae in Venice during the 2005 Biennale also transmits a feeling of serenity. Occupying the entire space with the bodies of two women floating in complete harmony, this moving fresco recalled the iconography of the earthly paradise but with the original sin and Eve's sense of guilt both transcended.

What prevents us from describing the practices of the 2000s as "feminist" is the constant doubt that the problem has reverted to (or finally become) the definition of what being "female" means. Sylvie Fleurie is not afraid to expose her compulsive mania for shopping, for which she in any case feels no guilt. She can wish for a Cadillac painted with nail polish, dozens of Hermes handbags, and rooms with pink plush upholstery. Sophie Calle instead displays her life in an almost cruel way: an image of her recently deceased mother combined with a sort of poem describing and dedicated to their relationship (2007). Two women locked in unavoidable conflict that is resolved only through reversal of the role of care: we take care of our dying loved ones as though they were children, and this so very female action tends to dissolve all tension. A primary and very deep relationship in which the male, understood as a potential antagonist, no longer has any place. Iceland and the frozen wastes in which Roni Horn photographs rarefied atmospheres speak about the indefiniteness of things, people, places, and desires in terms of a typical and inevitable characteristic of female feeling. Tacita Dean seeks self-certainty in her videos through investigation of the old and abandoned, the structure that was once something and is now dilapidated or even no longer standing. A bulb-shaped house, an outlandish and incomprehensible work of architecture, becomes a place to make a film. An unsuccessful search for Robert Smithson's *Spiral Jetty* becomes one of the ways in which woman lives through trying and often failing, with the sole benefit of self-esteem derived from tenacity. The self-timer photograph of the lesbian artist Catherine Opie with her masculine physique breast-feeding a beautiful blond baby is a precise declaration: the stereotype of the mother and child can and must be revised (*Self Portrait/Nursing*, 2004). An apparently unsuitable and yet equally loving mother appears in the fiberglass sculpture *Big Mother* (2005) by the Australian artist Patricia Piccinini (1965). The life size woman is a sort of primate with blue plastic bags and diapers for the baby she is tenderly nursing. The same delicate and shocking scene is addressed by Margi Geerlinks in the *Mothers* (2000) series of photographs, one of which shows an elderly woman breast-feeding a child. The mother photographed by Rineke Dijkstra (1959), holding a baby in both arms while her exhausted body, clad in hospital underwear with a tattoo clearly visible, speaks of the joy in giving life, something addressed in the feminist era only by Mary Kelly's *Post-Partum Document* (1975), and then with elements of conflict.

Beyond gender: the assertion of hybrid geographic identities in the age of complex geographies

The search for female identity and the specific discourse on gender cannot be understood, however, if they are divorced from the process whereby identities that are also male are created. There would certainly not have been a whole tradition of female art and the redefinition of gender through politics, above all in women artists from other parts of the world, if these peripheral areas had not succeeded in winning a central role. We shall take as the starting point of a still strongly ongoing discussion *Les Magiciens de la Terre*, curated by Jean-Hubert Martin and held at the Centre Pompidou and other venues in Paris, the first exhibition to present a truly global array of artists, coinciding with – or rather just preceding – the fall of the Berlin

Matthew Barney
Cremaster 4: The Laughton Candidate, 1994
Color photograph, 49.5 x 45 cm
New York, private collection
Courtesy Gladstone Gallery, New York

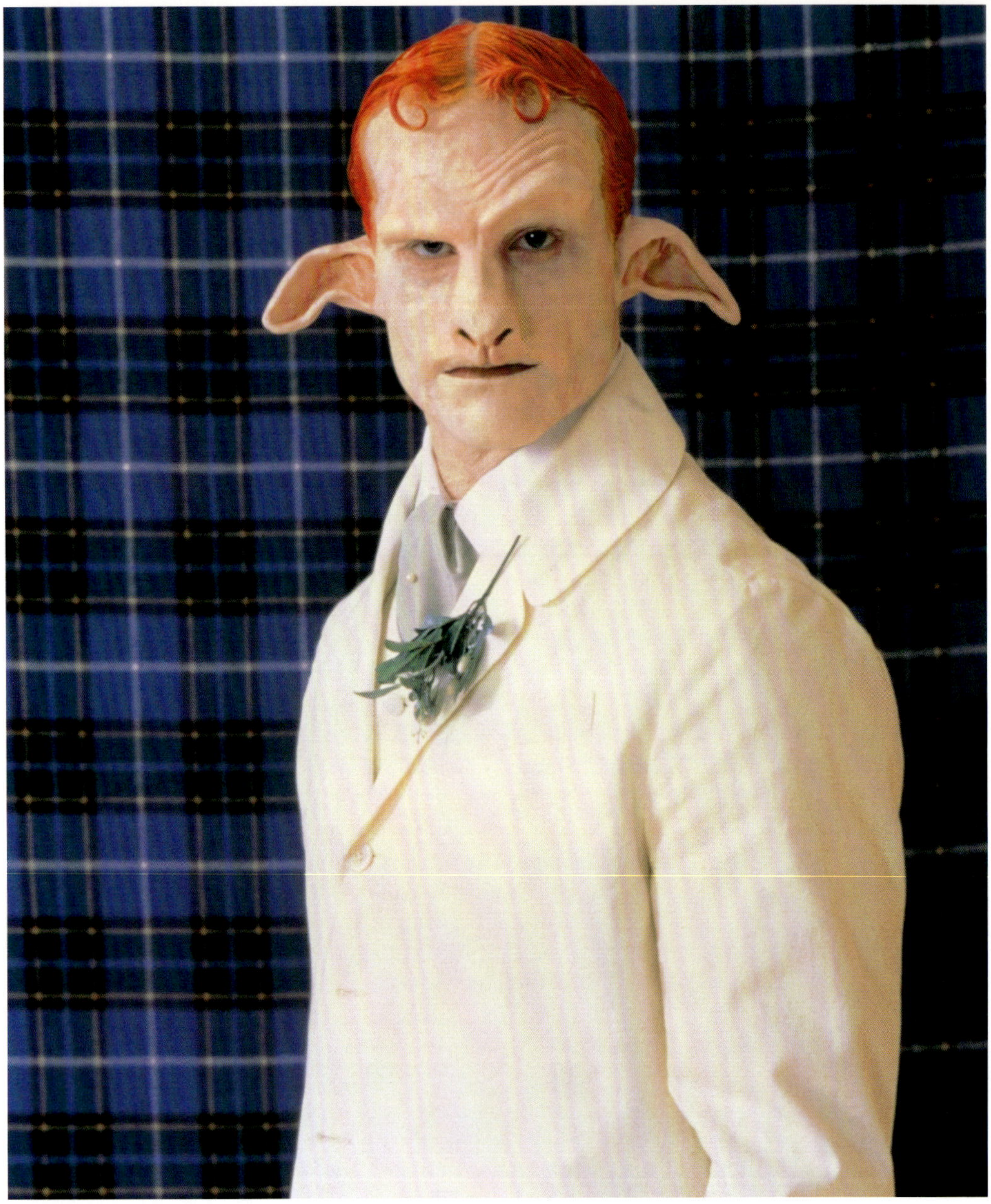

Wall, the protests in Tiananmen Square, Beijing, the end of apartheid in South Africa, and the start of the twentieth century's most massive wave of migration. This symbolic watershed can be taken as the beginning of debate on African, African-American, Indian, Asian and, generally speaking, non-white and non-Christian art.

Marjetica Potrč has worked in the "informal city" of urban slum areas. One of her best-known works was the installation of chemical WCs in a shantytown district of Caracas with no access to the municipal water grid and no facilities, including toilets (*Caracas Houses Project*, 2003). Her interest is in creating adaptive structures, an aspect assumed as one of the features of the female tradition implicit in taking care. The same viewpoint informs the work of Maria Papadimitriou, who creates tents in accordance with specific local traditions, such as the Mongolian, where recordings of folk tales in English, Turkish, Italian, and so on recall the universality of the theme of the home as a place of memory and not just subsistence. Andrea Zittel also focuses great attention on nomadism. In addition to designing small trailers for imaginary travels, she has set up a firm for the industrial production of units containing everything necessary for survival, which can be opened and closed like large trunks (*A-Z Living Units*). The effort to resist appears particularly strong where racial differences are added to those of gender. The banner of protest has been taken up by female artists who live in conditions of hardship, not only because they are women but also because they belong to globally marginalized peoples. In the silhouettes by the African-American artist Kara Walker (1969), often life-size cut-outs of black cardboard shown on a white wall in the glare of spotlights so that the viewer's shadow becomes part of the work, we see girls from the era of slavery mixed up with people of our day. The connecting element is always violence on a large or small scale, complicit or orgiastic behavior. Here too, however, the women are no longer only victims. Nor are they in the works of Renée Green (1959), another African-American artist, who constructs settings in which, for example, the drapery and upholstery are in the style of eighteenth or nineteenth-century France. Closer examination then reveals scenes in which the slave, male or more often female, assumes ambiguous positions. The prostitutes' cribs to which some of her other installations allude bring to mind a state of imprisonment, through the elements of coercion and routine, but also a protected place.

The part of the world in which blood and references to sacrificial suffering appear most often is Latin America. One work by the Guatemalan artist Regina José Galindo (1974) is a video recording of an operation she underwent to reconstruct her hymen, a surgical procedure made important and often practiced illegally and unhygienically in countries where the social pressure to preserve virginity until marriage is still very strong. *Himenoplastia* (2004) won her a major award at the Venice Biennale of 2005. A video by Teresa Margolles shows her washing in water used to clean the corpses of slain women, often sentenced to death in an atmosphere of inhumanity and corruption. Tania Bruguera's performances with her face superimposed on the blood and bones of sacrificial animals refers precisely to a continuing state of conflict and a female sensibility that seeks to ritualize rather than suppress the fact of violent death.

The Indian artist Nalini Malani combines the environmental use of video with dramatic content in works like *Unity in Diversity* (2003), where she animates a nineteenth-century painting of a group of Indian women, all with different clothing and musical instruments, presented as an allegory of unity between peoples of different religions, languages, and customs. A video on the destiny of Kashmir by the photographer and video artist Shilpa Gupta shows 18 soldiers in just 5 minutes. The panorama moves from tall chinaar trees to clusters of houses that prove on closer observation to be huts, all against the background of an inherent state of tension. Eternally torn apart by nationalist movements, India is intent on disintegration and Kashmir yearns for independence. While women cannot be soldiers, they can be eyewitnesses. Sonia Khurana opts for wordless video portraits of the women of her home-

Roni Horn
Clownpout (4), 2002–2003
Photographic drawing, 55 x 60 cm
Courtesy of the artist and Hauser & Wirth Zürich/London

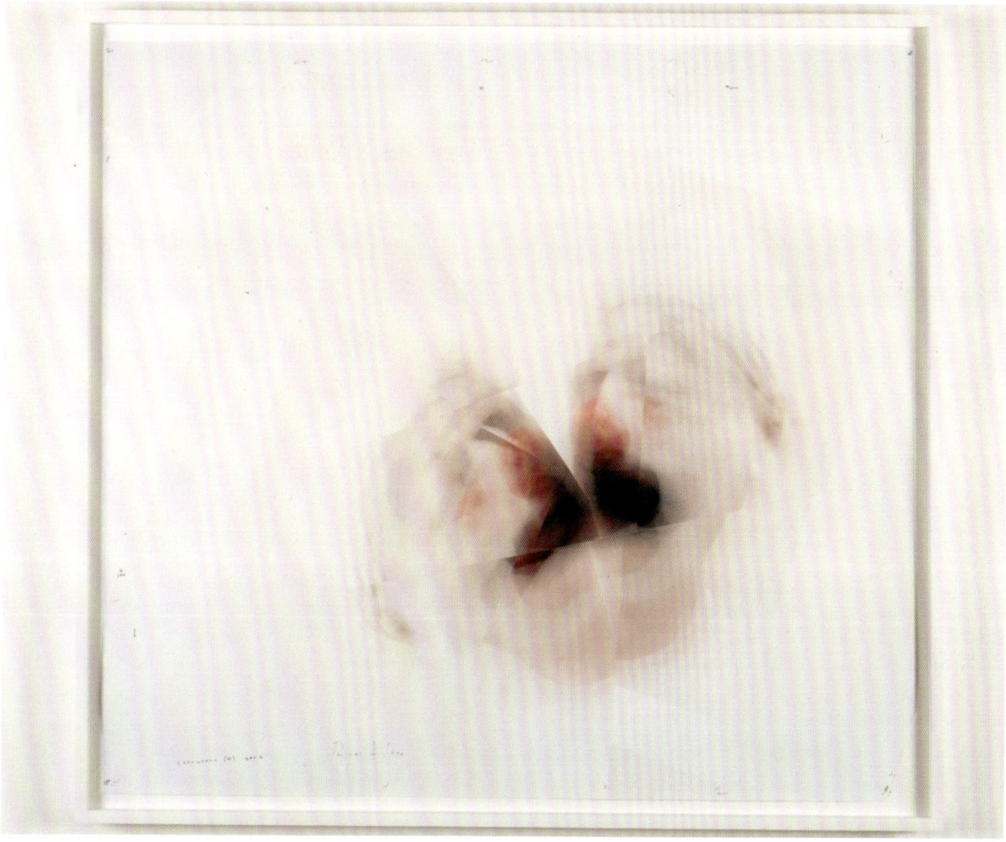

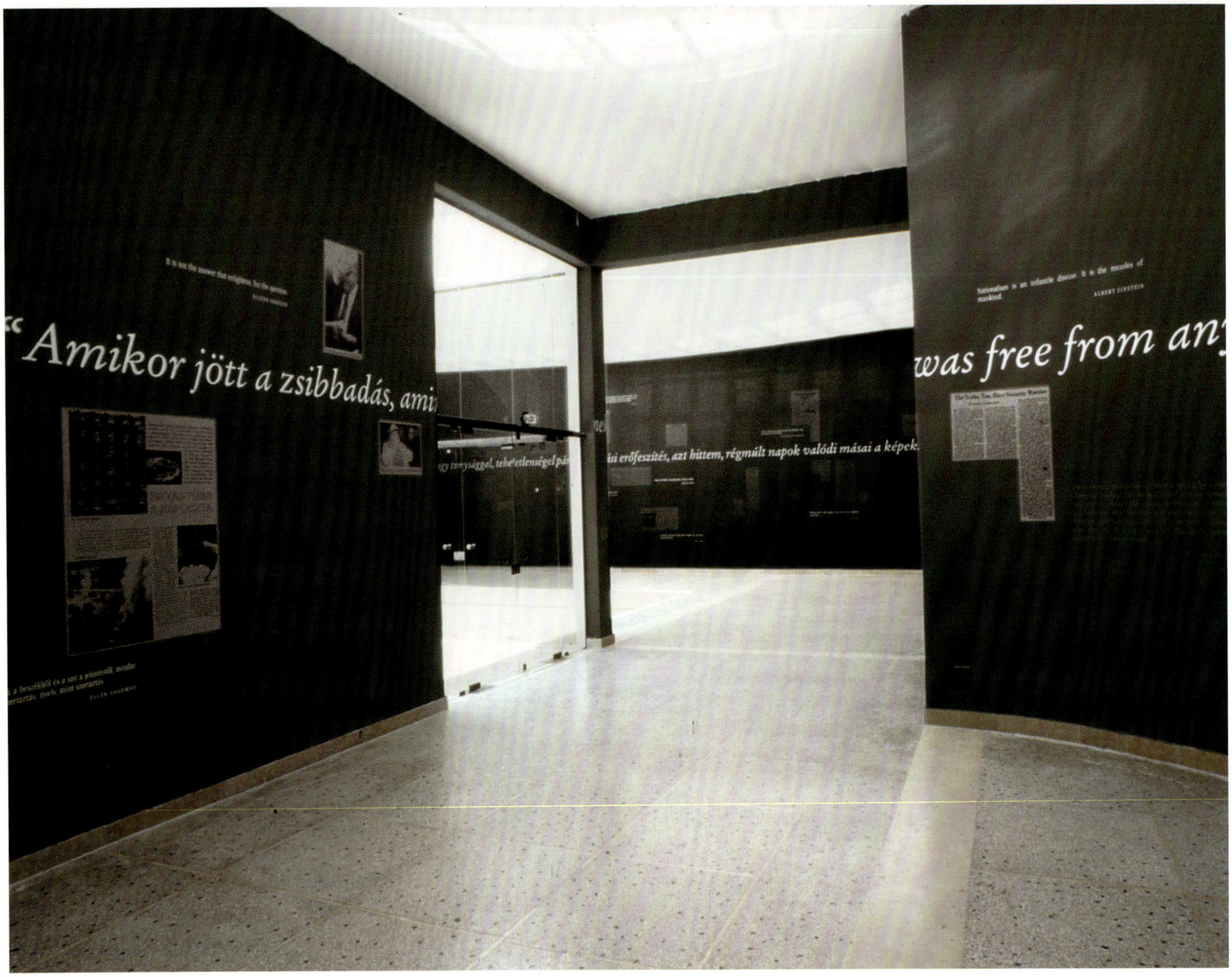

Joseph Kosuth
Zeno at the Edge of the Known World
View of the installation at the Hungarian Pavilion, XLV Esposizione Internazionale d'Arte, Biennale di Venezia 1993

land, whose faces contrast with the fertile fullness of Bollywood actresses.[12] The video *Mona's Song* (2004) features a eunuch who earns a living by exhibiting his physical disfigurement. Runa Islam, a British artist of Bangladeshi origin, shows Indian immigrants, rickshaw drivers, rose sellers, children and adults, people who live a hand-to-mouth existence both in their homeland and as immigrants but strive nevertheless to maintain their dignity. *Shibboleth*, the crack made in the floor of Tate Modern by the Columbian artist Doris Salcedo,[13] tells us once again that in postcolonial areas it is impossible to separate women's liberation from the efforts of a people to regain its identity and dignity. Berni Searle addresses the theme of dual survival: of herself and of her offspring, understood also as material and moral culture. The video *Snow White* (2001) shows her crouched on the ground making bread in an attitude of self-sacrifice and frantic haste, performing a ritual sequence of gestures that are picked out and stylized by a spotlight to emphasize the circle and hence the metaphor of the family, the community, the race.

Nor should we forget some steps toward redemption on a larger scale. African painters like Cheri Samba and Frédéric Bruly Bouabré, featured in the ground-breaking exhibition at the Pompidou, highlight the need to find a way to communicate with the world of colonizers (Samba) or to ensure that the original culture does not remain in the state of a solely oral and hence fragile tradition (Bouabré).[14]

The most important question regards the authenticity of autochthonous artistic traditions in the various parts of the world, which is called into question above all by the fact of colonial penetration. This can be direct, through political domination, as in the case of India and much of Africa, but also indirect, through cultural influence and domination channeled through products and lifestyles, as in vast areas of Asia and South America. At the same time, however, doubt as to the existence of an autochthonous art in a certain country can also involve cultures apparently rooted in what Harold Bloom describes as the Western canon.

Yinka Shonibare's installations feature dummies dressed in Western clothing of the colonial age that is, however, hybridized by the use of batik, a material regarded as typical of Africa even though it was in fact produced in the Netherlands and exported there.

These and other works seek to resolve the dilemma of authenticity and imitation while evading the myth of a native art. This has its equal and opposite counterpart in the dilemma of distinguishing between an original element of a place and a tasteless copy of the presumed original. This doubt undermining the very idea of authenticity arises in fact not only for countries and cultures weakened by a history of defeat but also for those that proved victorious, at least on paper, but now find themselves invaded and overwhelmed by the conquered peoples. In the words of Homi K. Bhabha, "The Western metropole must confront its postcolonial history, told by its postwar migrants and refugees, as an indigenous or native narrative internal to its national identity."[15] The reaction is often violent. The centennial edition of the Venice Biennale curated by Jean Clair included no Africans at all. What appears a more serious matter, however, is the inclusion/exploitation of many "other" artists, including women, in exhibitions, essays, series of publications, and collections so as to transform the marginal figures into a sort of requisite "dash of salt." If the male and above all female non-western artists generally present a high level of education and are in particular well versed in the history of recent art, this is perceived as a lack of depth. Critics would often prefer works allowing them to develop ethnographic and anthropological interpretations to ones totally focused on artistic themes. The warning note sounded by Salah Hassan in the mid-1990s still retains all its validity. As he pointed out, the recent interest of Western institutions in African art and non-western representation in general made no deep difference to the sense of superiority with which they viewed the cultural production of all those labeled as "others" for reasons of convenience. Nor did this attention represent a drastic change in Western strategies for hegemony, which continued to view the cultural practices generated outside its immediate spheres of influence with deep distrust.[16] In actual fact, recognition of the artistic dignity of these subjects presents the same difficulty as recognition of their civil rights.[17]

There is a video made in 2007 by the Albanian artist Adrian Paci that captures this state of inclusion/exclusion in all its metaphorical impact. It shows a group of refugees seemingly boarding an airplane. Everything appears to be in place and departure imminent. But then the camera moves back and we find that, absurdly enough, the steps lead nowhere. The travelers are left waiting in a state of suspension that verges on the ridiculous. To quote Salah Hassan again, "What we are witnessing is not the ultimate recognition of the plurality of history, but a return of Western grand narratives in the guise of asserting 'cultural difference,' evidenced in the ideology of neoconservatism and reactionary Western practice."[18]

At the root of these complications and sometimes contradictions between a critical theory of art that would welcome migrants and women and a dominant culture that would rather relegate them to the harmless sidelines is the hybrid position that is now peculiar to any potential Other. We no longer have the former-Soviet artist, the uneducated Nigerian, the Chinese artist unable to read anything but ideograms. The never-ending diaspora characterizing the start of the twenty-first century has practically seen the end of people with defined identities that decide to transplant themselves and enter into contact with an elsewhere, as was the case with the Italians and the Irish who arrived in New York in the late nineteenth and early twentieth centuries. As Franco La Cecla explains, "There is a logic of center and periphery or colonizers and colonized that is never linear.... The Indio in odd sneakers and the Aborigine with an alarm clock around his neck are not necessarily 'victims' of Western bad taste with cultures devastated by the invasion of the West. Very often what happens is more complex. These are ways of appropriating what is alien in order to turn it round, to 'personalize' its attempt to contaminate us."[19] This is something perfectly understood by women's fashion, which has – in the case of Antonio Marras, who also designs the Kenzo collections – been offering a mixture of Sardinian folklore and Japanese tradition since the 1990s.

Many authors have put forward interesting interpretive formulas. Arjun Appadurai has spoken of "multiscapes" (landscapes overlapping and intersecting in the same city) and the "global production of localism"[20] and Saskia Sassen has suggested the existence of a new form of localism that has nothing to do with an original past but is rather a third element, a direct consequence of globalization.[21]

The construction of identity and changes in perception of the self: between individual and collective, natural body and modified body

There are two more points to be recalled in this overview of the problem of identity, both of which engendered by the massive injection of technology into recent artistic practices. First of all, importance attaches to the idea of the author and the constant alternation between an individual *I* and a collective *we*. Secondly, attention should be drawn to the way the self changes shape in relation to changes in the means of observation.

As regards the first of these two points, it is a fact that some schools in the twentieth century promoted collective practices: from the Bauhaus in the 1920s and '30s to Black Mountain College in the 1940s and '50s, and Buffalo State University in the 1970s. And it was in the latter, in 1973, that Gerald O'Grady introduced the first program dedicated to the new digital media and hence to the group practices implicit in their use.[22] We are turning increasingly into multiple subjects, perhaps even before being male or female.

The second point regards change in our perceptual functions. The accentuation of altered states of consciousness, the ecstatic condition triggered both by mystical or ideal visions and more prosaically by drugs, was a constant of the culture emphasizing the subject and its ways of being. The investigation of individual identity could not but insist on these themes. Arnulf Rainer took photographs of himself with a self-timer in the 1960s and 1970s when he felt he had nearly lost control under the influence of alcohol and drugs. In the 1990s, the photographic self-portrait of Charles Ray (*Yes*, 1990) shows him high on LSD. The focus in other cases is on the perception (and hence the subjectivity) of the viewer. Lucio Fontana attached great importance to the disorienting effect on those entering his first environment (*Ambiente spaziale a luce nera*, 1949),[23] and the same sensation is involved in many of those subsequently created in Italy and other countries in the 1960s and 1970s: from Gianni Colombo's *Spazi elastici*, where the perceiving subject is constantly subjected to unexpected changes in orthogonal relations, through the countless shapes taken by the labyrinth in environmental art and all the way to the disorientation caused by walls of light in the "paintings" of James Turrell. Perhaps the most significant development in all this came with some works by Bruce Nauman, from sound pathways in which acoustic confusion is sometimes replaced by comprehensible language to long, narrow corridors where the spectator practically becomes a guinea pig to test anxiety-generating capacity. Much of the Process Art of the 1960s and '70s focused in fact on the alteration of mental states and the sense of personal identity, also in the presence of minimal stimuli and apparently slight prompts for disorientation. This is demonstrated also by the work of artists who opted in the 1990s for an apparently simple form of painting, from the murals of the American artist Sue Williams, which suggest and conceal scenes of rape, to the environments of the Dutch artist Lily van der Stokker, which resort to depressive infantilism, and the paintings of the Americans Elizabeth Peyton and Karen Kilimnik with their agonizing pursuit of beauty.[24]

Perceptual disorientation often took on an unprecedentedly spectacular form in the 1990s with ever-increasing involvement of the spectator. Consider the *Upside Down Mushroom Room* (2000) by the German Carsten Höller, where members of the public make their way through a maze in complete darkness, holding onto a rail so as not to lose balance, only to find themselves with huge red-dotted mushrooms spinning above their heads in a room where the ceiling and floor seem to have changed places and the spatial dimensions are distorted.

Who am I? The question is therefore still so completely open as to take us all the way back to the doubts expressed by the Greek skeptics. If the senses deceive, I cannot even be sure of what I perceive, the concepts it generates, and the memories it creates.

In any case, it is within this elastic subject that we will be required to live in the future.[25] Even more than politics and religion and their repercussions on ethical requirements, in our view it will be the constant redefinition of the duration, form, and characteristics of life deriving from the second scientific revolution to tell us who we are going to become. And perhaps we will become less dramatically self-referential people and create works less focused on the ego, which has been practically the sole protagonist for one hundred years now. As Italo Calvino wrote in his *Six Memos for the Next Millennium*, "Think what it would be to have a work conceived from outside the self, a work that would let us escape the limited perspective of the individual ego."[26]

[1] See A. Kaprow, *Essay on the Blurring of Art and Life* (Berkeley: University of California Press, 1993).
[2] See A. Vettese, *Invertir en arte* (Valencia: Universidad de Valencia, Ed. Piramide, 2002), pp. 232–37.
[3] In B. McPherson (ed.), *Carolee Schneemann. More than Meat Joy. Complete Performances Works and Selected Writings* (New York: Br New Platz, Documentext, 1979, p. 198. L.G. Mark, P. Schimmel (eds.), *Ecstasy. In and About Altered States*, exh. cat. (Los Angeles, Museum of Contemporary Art, 2005–2006) (Los Angeles-Boston: Museum of Contemporary Art-MIT Press, 2005).
[4] R. Krauss, *Bachelors* (Boston: MIT Press, 2000), p. 50.
[5] See the painting by Johann Zoffany, *The Academicians of the Royal Academy*, 1771–72, oil on canvas, 101.1 × 147.5 cm.
[6] R. Goldberg, *Performance: Live Art Since 1960* (New York: Harry N. Abrams, 1998), pp. 129–31. On the subject of female performance, see also L. Vergine, *Body Art e storie simili. Il corpo come linguaggio* (Milan: Skira, 2000); T. Warr, A. Jones, *The Artist's Body* (London: Phaidon Press, 2000); F. Naldi, *I'll be Your Mirror. Travestimenti fotografici* (Rome: Castelvecchi, 2003); L. Lippard, 'The Pains and Pleasures of Rebirth: Women's Body Art,' in *Art in America*, May-June 1976, pp. 73–81; L.C. Jones, 'Transgressive Femininity: Art and Gender in the 1960s and 70s', in *Abject Art, Repulsion and Desire in American Art*. exh. cat. (New York, Whitney Museum of American Art, June–August 1993), New York 1993; E. De Cecco, G. Romano, *Contemporanee* (Milan: Postmediabooks, 2002); A. Wagner, 'Performance, Video and the Rhetoric of Presence,' in *October*, 91, winter 2000; U. Grosenick (ed.), *Le donne e l'arte nel XX e nel XXI secolo*, Italian translation, Taschen, Cologne 2008 (original edition 2005); M. Reilly, L. Nochlin (eds.), *Global Feminism – New Directions in Contemporary Art* (with essays by N'Gone Fall, Geeta Kapur, Michiko Kasahara, Joan Kee, Virginia Pérez-Ratton, Elizabeth Lebovici, and Charlotta Kotik) (London-New York: Merrell, 2007); A. Vettese, 'Dal corpo chiuso al corpo diffuso,' in F. Poli (ed.), *Arte contemporanea. Le ricerche internazionali dalla fine degli anni '50 a oggi* (Milan: Electa, 2003), pp. 190–221.
[7] On the immense vitality of performance art of Japanese origin, see Shinichiro Osaki, 'Body and Place. Action in Postwar Art in Japan,' in P. Schimmel (ed.), *Out of Actions. Between Performance and the Object, 1949–1979* (London: Thames and Hudson, 1998), pp. 121–58; L.G. Mark, P. Schimmel, *op. cit.*
[8] See L. Cottingham, *How Many Bad Feminists Does it Take to Change a Light Bulb* (New York: After Words, 1994).
[9] See G. Brett, 'Life Strategies: Overview and Selection Buenos Aires-London-Rio de Janeiro-Santiago de Chile, 1960–1980,' in P. Schimmel, *op. cit.*, pp. 197–227; C. Basualdo, *Tropicalia. A Revolution in Brazilian Culture (1967–1972)*, exh. cat. (touring exhibition), 2005.
[10] Tiqqun, *Premiers matériaux pour une théorie de la Jeune-Fille*.
[11] *Tiqqun*, Paris, no. 1, 1999, p. 39.
[12] For an overview of the art scene in India, see I. Bonacossa, F. Manacorda, *Subcontingent. Il subcontinente indiano nell'arte contemporanea* (Milan: Electa, 2006).
[13] The title refers to the biblical account in the Book of Judges of a battle between the Gileadites and Ephraimites, the word *shibboleth* being used as a particular expression or term that distinguishes a community and serves to identify the enemy.
[14] R.F. Thomson, 'Frédéric Bruly Bouabré,' in *Robert Lehman Lectures in Contemporary Arts*, Dia Foundation, K. Kelly and B. Funke (eds.) (New York: Dia Art Foundation, 2004), pp. 77–84.
[15] H.K. Bhabha, *The Location of Culture*.
[16] S. Hassan, 'The Modernist Experience in African Art,' in O. Oguibe, O. Enwezor, *Reading the Contemporary* (London: InIVA, 1999), pp. 215–35, p. 217.
[17] See Etienne Balibar, "What is a Politics of the Rights of Man?" in *Masses, Classes and Ideas* (New York: Routledge, 1994), 205–26.
[18] S. Hassan, 'The Modernist Experience in African Art,' in O. Oguibe, O. Enwezor, *op. cit.*, pp. 215–35, p. 217.
[19] F. La Cecla, *Jet Lag e altri disturbi da viaggio* (Milan: Bollati Boringhieri, 2002), p. 62.
[20] A. Appaduraj, *Modernity at Large* (Minneapolis: University of Minnesota Press, 1996). Co-published with Oxford University Press, India.
[21] S. Sassen, *Cities in a World Economy* (Thousand Oaks [Cal]: Pine Forge Press, 2006) updated 3rd ed., original 1994; Series: Sociology for a new century.
[22] J.H. Reiss, *Utopia Post Utopia - Configurations of nature and Culture in recent Sculpture and Photography* (Boston [Mass]: MIT Press, 1988).
[23] See his remarks in C. Lonzi, *Autoritratto* (Bari: De Donato, 1969), p. 95.
[24] C.H. Butler, *Afterimage. Drawing Through Process* (Boston [Mass]: MIT Press, 1999).
[25] For the idea of a possible cyberman of the future, see D.J. Haraway, 'A Cyborg Manifesto: Science, Technology and Socialit-Feminism in the Late Twentieth Century' (1985), now in *Art and Technology* (London: Routledge, 1991), pp. 149–81; J. Deitch, *Post Human*, exh. cat. (Pully Lausanne and Castello di Rivoli, 1992), Turin 1992; T. Macrì, *Il corpo postorganico* (Genoa: Costa & Noland, 1996); F. Alfano Miglietti, *Identità Mutanti* (Genoa: Costa & Noland, 1997).
[26] I. Calvino, *Lezioni americane. Sei proposte per il prossimo millennio* (Milan: Mondadori, 2007), p. 135.

Claude Closky

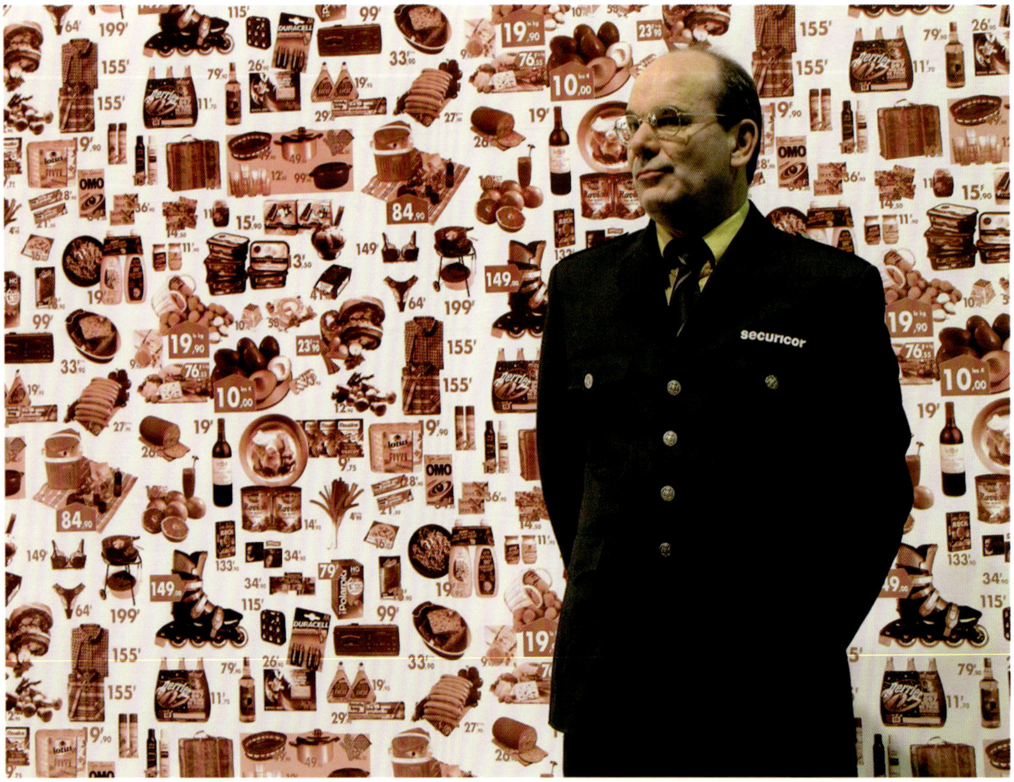

Sans titre (Supermarché), 1996–1999
View of the installation realized in 2003 at the Banque Générale du Luxembourg
Courtesy Mudam – Fondation d'Art Moderne Grand-Duc Jean, Luxembourg

Journal, 2005
Video installation, stereo sound, 24′
View of the installation realized in 2005 at the GEM – Museum voor actuele kunst, The Hague
Courtesy Galerie Laurent Godin, Paris

Born in Paris in 1963. Lives and works in Paris.
The work of Claude Closky could be described as a never-ending exploration, sometimes ironic and sometimes very serious, of the codes of our visual culture. Given the disproportionate enrichment of this culture brought about by the evolution of the media over the last 20 years, the mission Closky has set himself may appear impossible and indeed is so in some respects. At the same time, however, it should be stated that his approach of systematic organization and classification has both the seriousness of the great encyclopedists and the playfulness of authors like Perec, Queneau, and Borges, whose love of systems is always fuelled by awareness of their pointlessness. The artist observes advertising and delights in the abstract drawing of diagrams, numerical displays, and the infinite riches of the Internet. It is no coincidence that the book is a form that has featured frequently in his work ever since the late 1980s. *Magazines* (1998), for example, is a volume of over 300 pages made up of retouched advertisements, collages, drawings, Magritte-like observations on the relationship between words and things, lists and catalogues (including one of articles in order of price from 1 franc to 1000), and bizarre sets of instructions (such as all the ways to fold a cardboard box). Closky belongs to the generation of artists who rediscovered in the 1990s the work of figures from the 1970s, from Wegman to Baldessari and Broodthaers. As a post-conceptualist, he moves readily over a range of very different media including video, drawing, multimedia installation, and websites. His work is simultaneously insatiable and sober, light-hearted and obsessive. The best way to experience the complexity of this figure is his site *sittes.net*, which presents a collection of sketches that often verge on slapstick but always cast light on some particular aspect of communication. Commissioned by the Dia Center for the Arts, New York, in 1997, *Do You Want Love or Lust?* is an interminable questionnaire that uses questions culled from popular magazines about the tastes, habits, and tendencies of the public but never arrives at a response or a profile. *Television* (2004) is an installation that presents the visitor with 19 monitors, a remote control, and a range of 10,000 television channels, each of which shows a low-resolution animated film downloaded from the Internet to the accompaniment of background noise, thus commenting on the real poverty beneath the apparent richness of the Net. Total communication and the overabundance of information turn paradoxically into the absence of both.
(*D.Q.*)

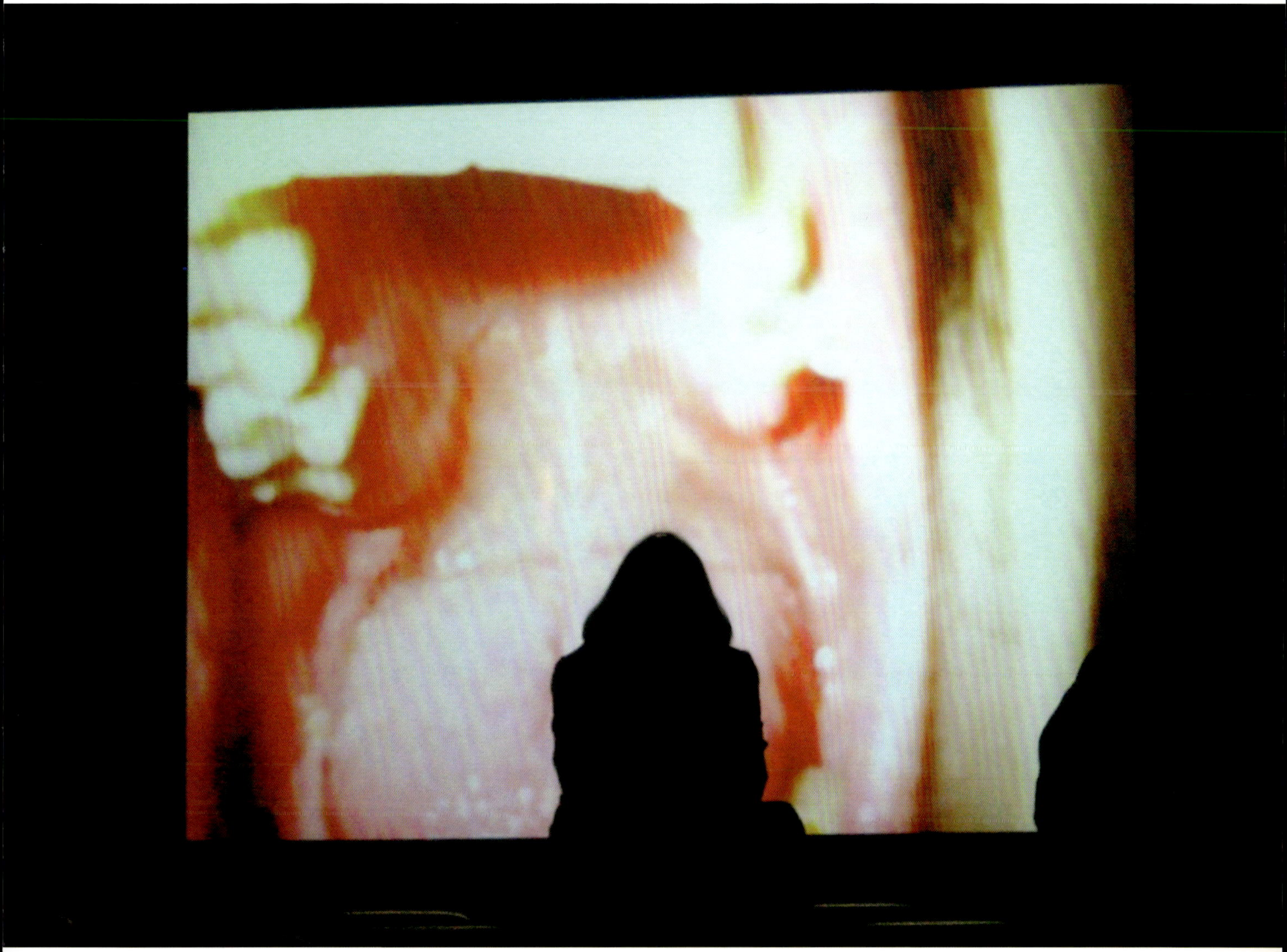

Martin Creed

Born in Wakefield, UK, in 1968. Lives and works in Glasgow.
Martin Creed focuses on the interaction between the work of art and the expectations it arouses in the viewer. Although the titles always use numeration to suggest a sequence of action, this is not in fact rigorously maintained, as the English artist deliberately chooses not to use decimals precisely because of their intrinsic sequential value.
At the same time, the propositions used as titles announce the content of the works in ordinary, straightforward language that is deliberately chosen as an ironic comment on the role of definition and the relations between Conceptual Art and the Post-Human sphere.
Work No. 227: The Lights Going On and Off, the environmental installation for which Creed won the Turner Prize in 2001, consisted of a pair of lights intermittently switched on and off in a completely empty room. An ironic comment on the redundancy of the art system and the power of placement in a museum to confer status, Creed's installation is striking by virtue of the practically minimal intervention on the part of the artist and the definitive absence of any observable visual element. In addition to being empty, the room at Creed's disposal is also poorly lit because of the low voltage of the lights and their intermittent functioning. Absence alternates with darkness in a neutral space that the viewer is free to interpret as a metaphor of the human condition, of birth or death. The repeated, rhythmic element evident in the alternating light in *Work No. 227* is present also in *Work No. 180: Largo, Larghetto, Adagio, Andante, Moderato, Allegro, Presto, Prestissimo*, which consists of seven metronomes set at the different tempos stated in the title. The proximity of the instruments actually makes it impossible to recognize the differences of rhythm and cadence, as the room is filled with non-cyclical sounds overlapping so as to preclude temporal identification.
The artist's investigation of the tautological proposition in relation

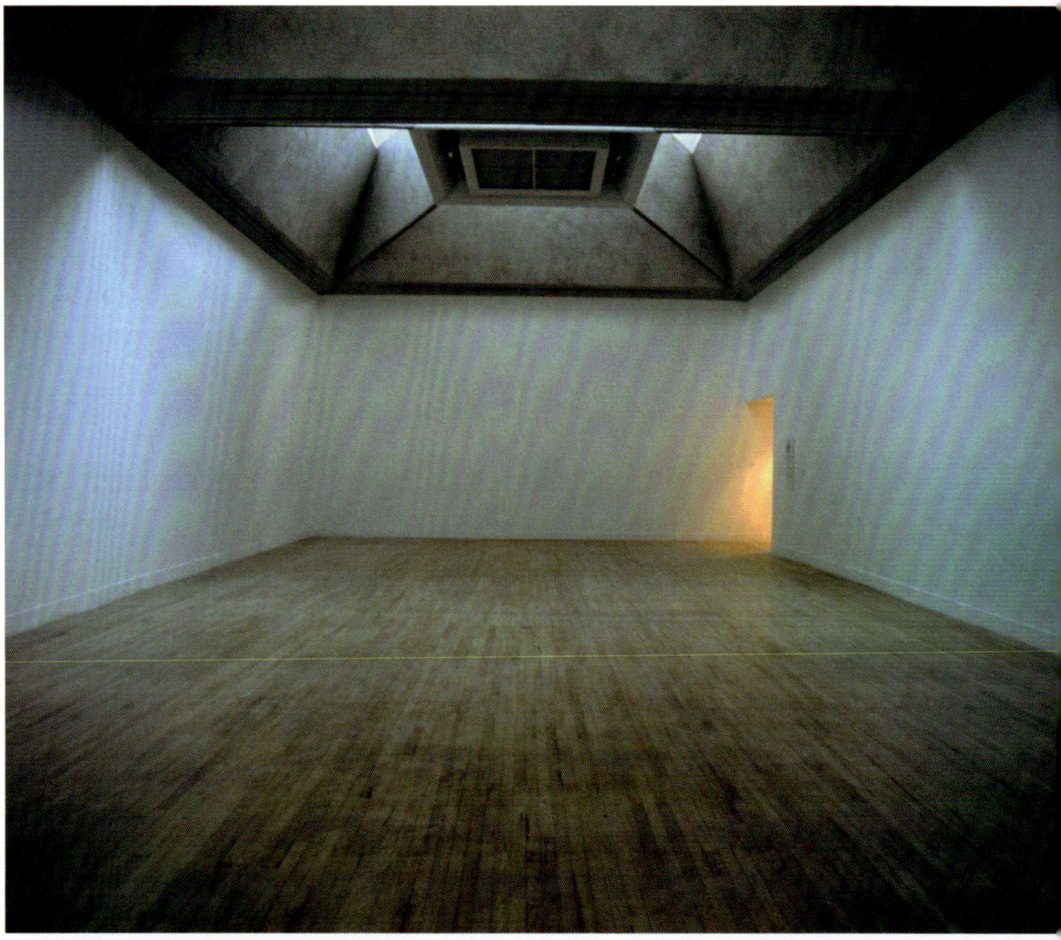

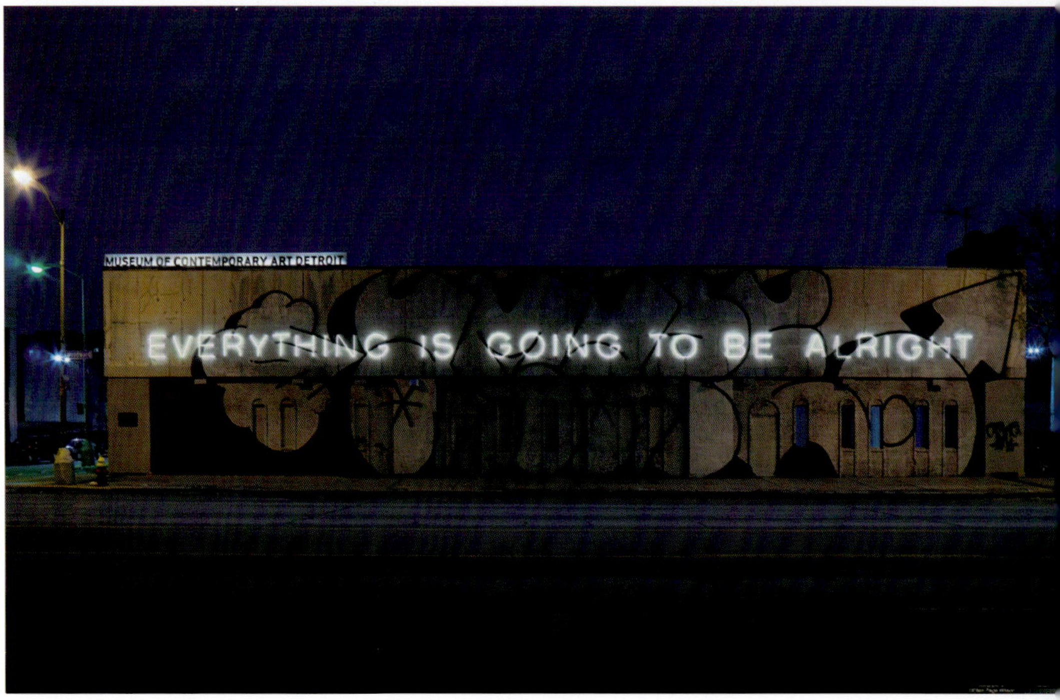

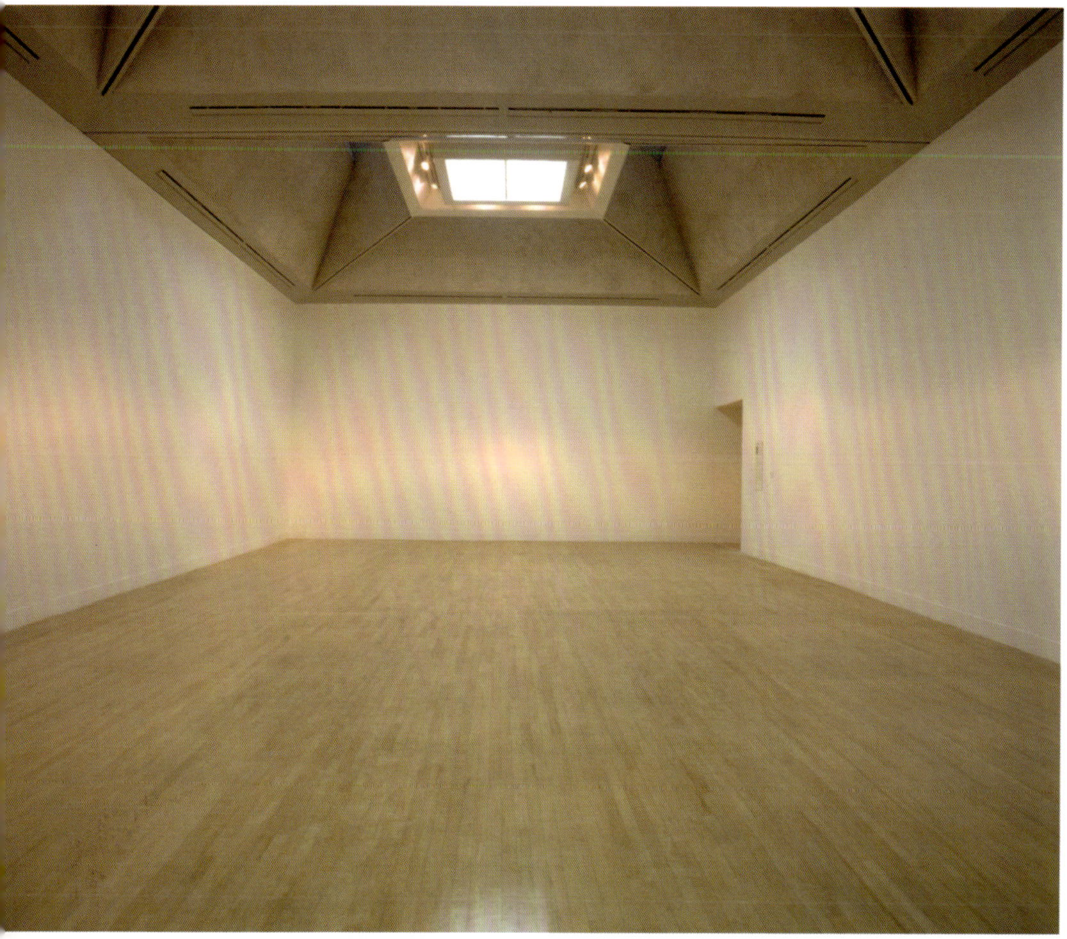

Work No. 227: The Lights Going On and Off, 2000
Lighting system, 5 seconds on, 5 seconds off, dimensions variable
View of the installation realized in 2001 at Tate Britain, London

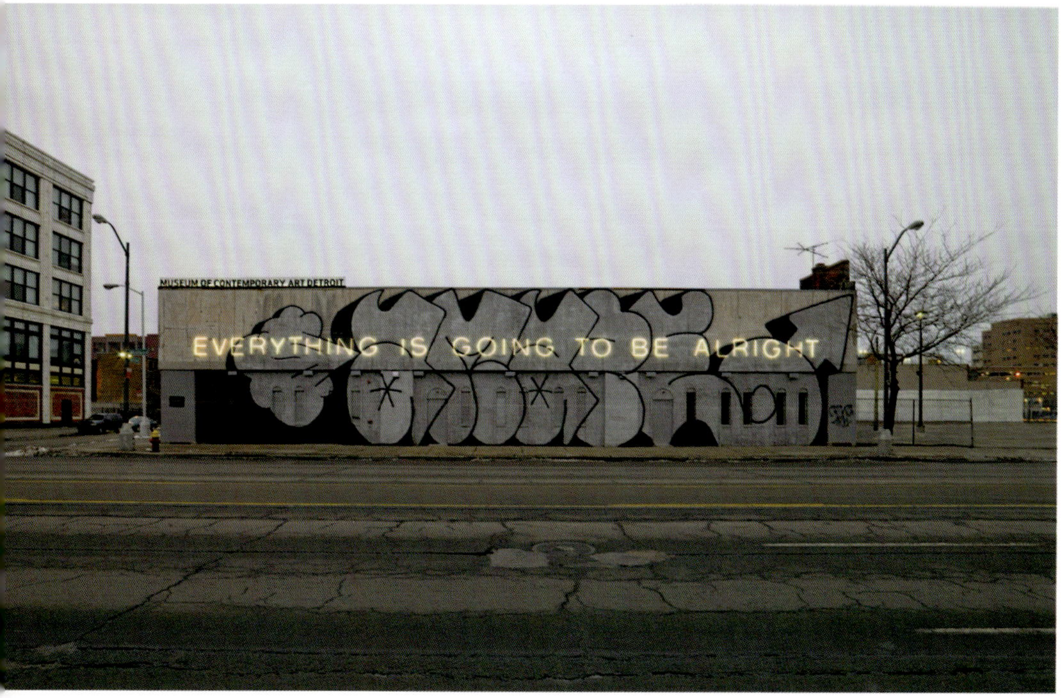

Work No. 790: Everything Is Going To Be Alright, 2007
Luminescent neon tubes, 81.28 x 251 x 20.32 cm
View of the installation at the Museum of Contemporary Art, Detroit

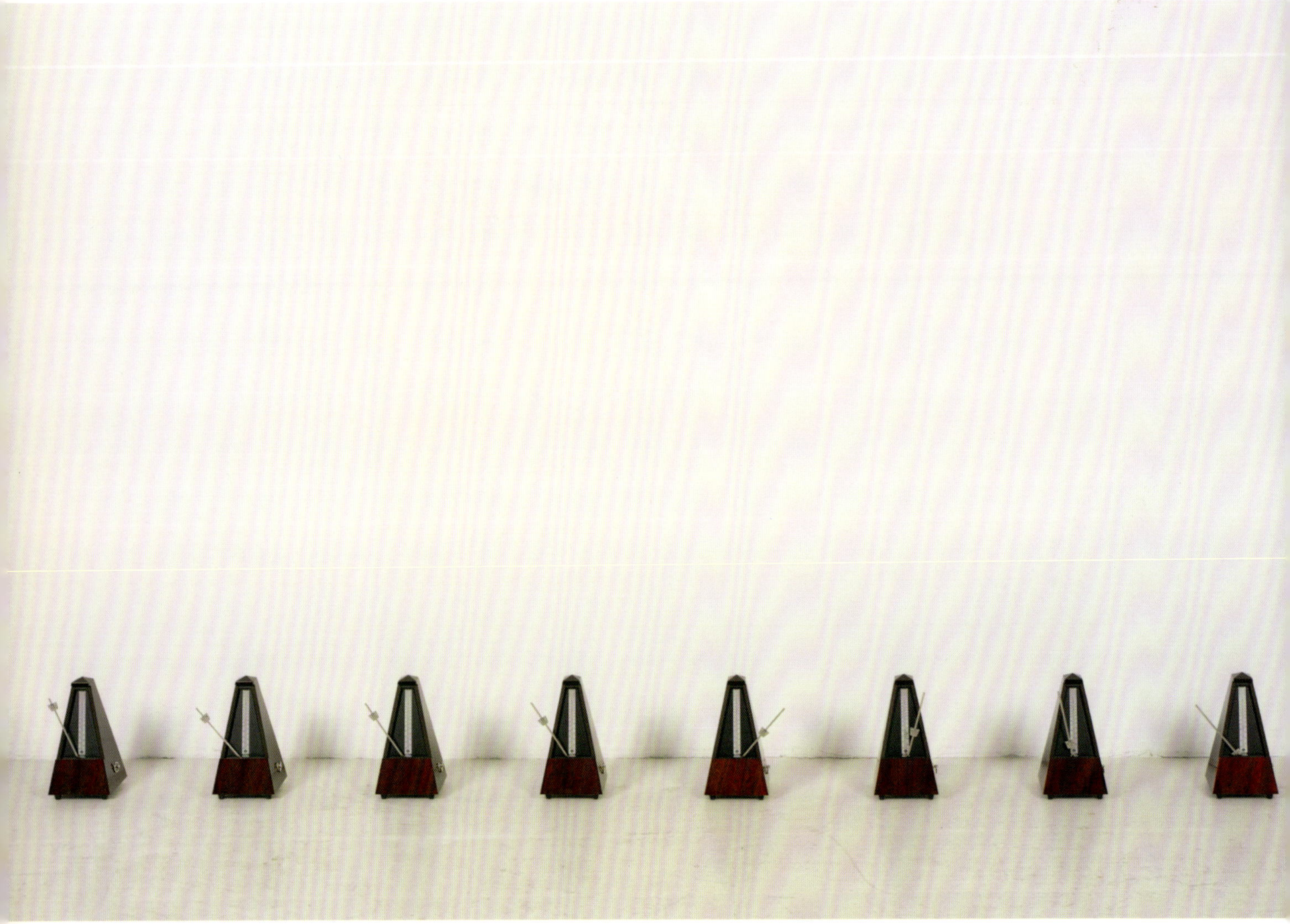

to the content of the artwork becomes irreverent criticism in *Work No. 790: Everything Is Going To Be Alright*, a neon installation presented in its first version in Times Square, New York, which deconstructs the idea of art providing consolation. The artist's aim in asserting that everything will be all right is actually to generate anxiety in the reader/viewer and prompt a search for what it is that could make things go wrong.
The apprehensions and uneasiness aroused by Creed's neon writing are actually groundless because nothing else happens.
This underlying ironic stance informs the artist's examination of the relationship between the artwork, the exhibition venue and the visitor. His recent works have thus turned the concept of vision and a mediated approach to the artistic object upside down by staging a timed race through the rooms of the museum reminiscent of the scene in Godard's film *Bande à part* when the three main characters run through the Louvre. Creed's humor draws on various elements to attain an enactment of the artistic object that negates its physicality. The installation *Work No. 360: Half the Air in a Given Space* (2004) thus consists of a completely transparent glass structure half filled with inflated balloons, playing on the presence and the quantity of the air in the inflatable elements and the room so as to materialize the situation described in the title and deconstruct it at the same time. The concepts of open and closed, and the claustrophobic feeling of being outnumbered and threatened by the almost pulsating presence of the shiny inflated objects transforms Creed's room into an anxiety-generating place that is only apparently habitable and knowable in spatial terms.
(F.T.)

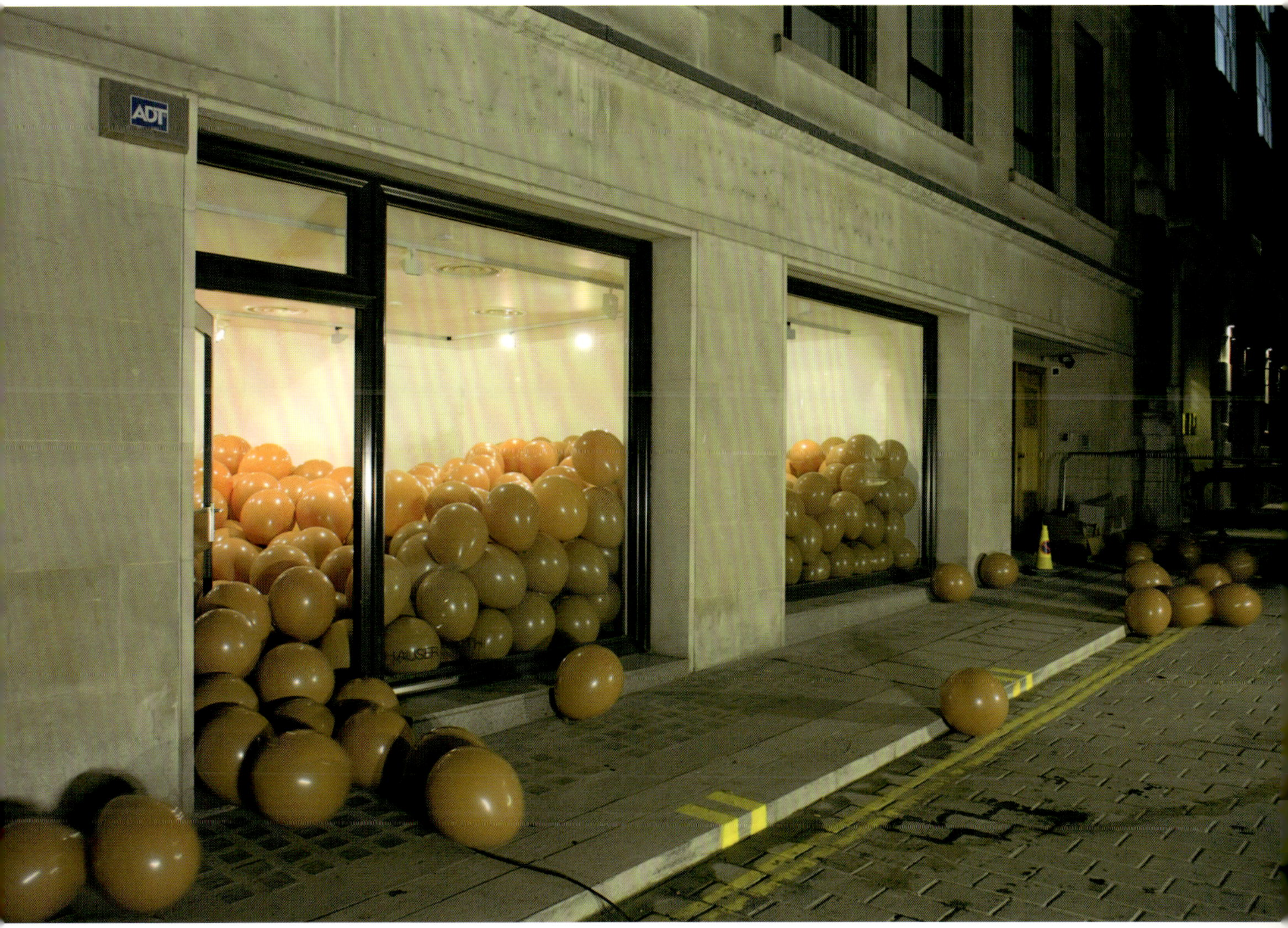

Work No. 180: Largo, Larghetto, Adagio, Andante, Moderato, Allegro, Presto, Prestissimo, 1995–2004
Eight metronomes, dimensions variable
Courtesy of the artist and Hauser & Wirth, Zürich/London

Work No. 360: Half the Air in a Given Space, 2004
Brown balloons, ø 40 cm, dimensions variable
Courtesy of the artist and Hauser & Wirth, Zürich/London

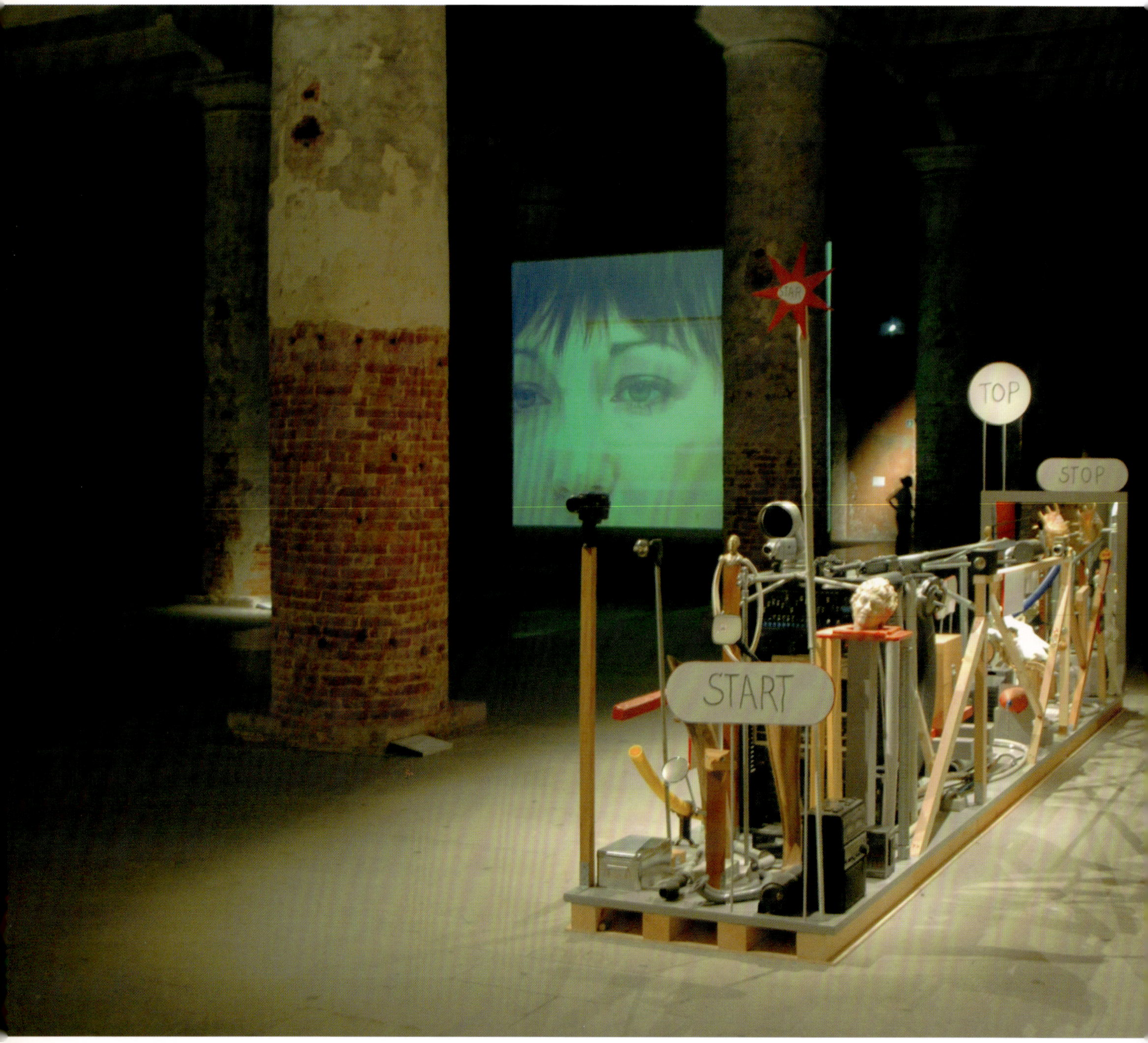

Something (Perhaps a Fugue or an Elegy), 2005
Mixed media assemblage,
180 x 160 x 700 cm
View of the installation,
LI Esposizione Internazionale d'Arte,
Biennale di Venezia 2005

The Flower of the Death of Loneliness, 2000
Mirror, wooden frame, stone,
90 x 90 x 25 cm
London, The Saatchi Collection

Jimmie Durham

Born in Arkansas, USA, in 1940. Lives and works in Rome.
A visual artist but also an essayist and political activist in the American Indian Movement, Jimmie Durham is one of the leading figures in Postcolonial Art, which became a focal point of art-critical debate with the renowned exhibition *Les Magiciens de la Terre*, organized by Jean Hubert-Martin at Centre Georges Pompidou, Paris, in 1989. Since then, moving gradually away from the forms of theater and performance developed in previous years, Durham has focused above all on sculptural works, mostly created with the technique of assemblage and conceived as installations, in a reconsideration and reappraisal of his own original Cherokee culture through forms of contamination with models and spaces belonging to other cultural contexts, and especially the Western world. The artist's primary aim is to deconstruct the stereotypes and prejudices of the West, endemically convinced of its cultural supremacy, with respect to lifestyles, customs, rituals, and forms of expression of peoples located outside its area of influence. While Durham frequently uses the weapon of irony to this end, he prefers by his own admission to do so in a way that is dialectical rather than aggressive or decidedly hostile, creating hybrid forms that are corrosive and amusing at the same time. Examples include his "fake Indian artifacts" and enigmatic "totems" assembled out of objects that evidently have no connection with one another but are presented so as to arouse curiosity and induce the Western public to venture complex and abstruse interpretations on the strength of its cultural dogmas and anthropological notions. One particularly significant example of this procedure is the work *Something (Perhaps a Fugue or an Elegy)*, presented by Durham at the Venice Biennale of 2005 and consisting of a platform covered in heterogeneous objects: tape recorders, synthesizers, heads of cherubs, cameras, quotations from the Portuguese Nobel laureate José Saramago, film cameras, animals skulls with electrical aerials and pipes instead of horns, television sets and various notices. Found objects from different ages and civilizations coexist in the incongruous layers of possible meanings and create a play of cross-references, not least due to the inclusion of numerous mirrors. In an interview with Achille Bonito Oliva in 2006, Durham connected his creative use of different materials with the concept of "*bricolage*" developed by Claude Lévi-Strauss with reference to primitive cultures, and expressed in particular his appreciation of situations in which objects are ready to move beyond themselves and their old limits. This is what happens, for example, in the work *The Flower of the Death of Loneliness* (2000), where a mirror smashed by a strange stone to which the artist has given the appearance of a deeply disturbing face reflects its distorted image in such way that the painted eyes seem to stare at the spectator from every possible angle. A stone, in this case black and of volcanic origin, also plays the leading role in the later work *Deposition* (2006). Durham regards stone as an inherently meaningful element, being a natural phenomenon, building material, and metaphorical object all at the same time. In *Deposition* the artist imagines his black stone hurled into the air in a volcanic eruption, landing on an array of glasses, smashing them, and then finding a precarious perch on top of a stepladder, ready to fly again. Implicit in this piece and

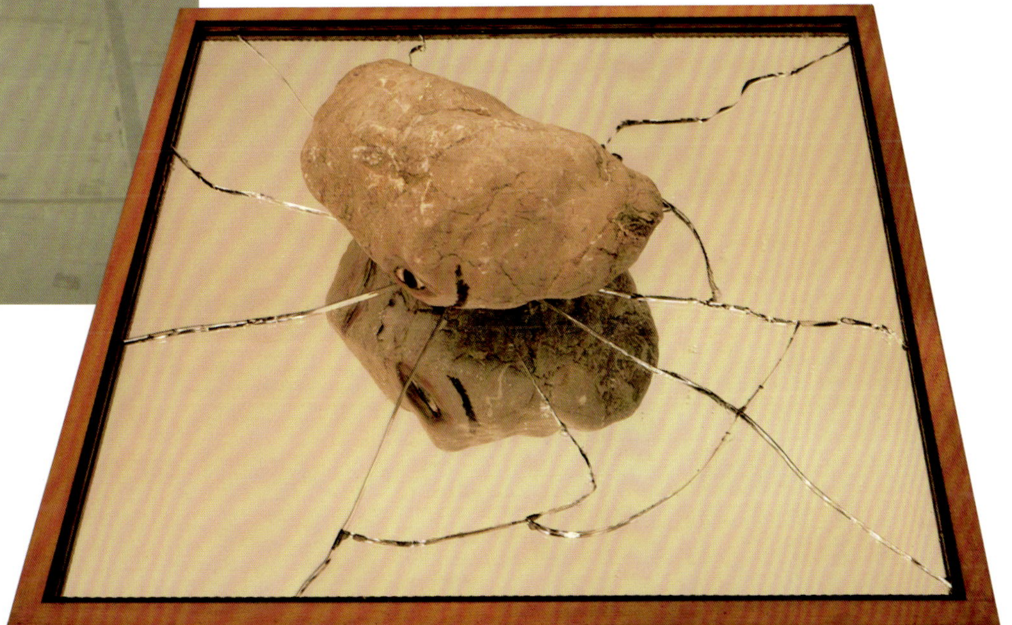

Deposition, 2006
Glasses, metal stepladder, obsidian, fabric, 140 x 387 x 97 cm
Courtesy RAM – radioartemobile

central in all of Durham's work, the idea of the stone as matter and the transformation of objects reappears in the installation *The Petrified Forest* (2003), where an office with computer, fax, shelves, chairs and desks was completely covered in heaps of cement. While critics intent on probing the possible meanings of this work have even suggested the tragedy of September 11 as one of the possible – and all too obvious – references, Durham himself offers only the laconic observation that cement is a strange sort of stone, being initially liquid before it hardens and sets. Recently repeated at the MADRE in Naples within the framework of a solo show, *The Petrified Forest* was placed alongside a similar work specially created for the occasion and again featuring cement, this time in the form of partially plastered blocks of reinforced concrete with rusty iron rods sticking out of them, either straight up or bending downward, to suggest the idea of a forest, possibly exposed to some mysterious fall of acid rain.
Once again, however, it is perhaps our Western culture and latent sense of guilt for our irresponsible use of the planet's resources and lack of respect for nature that lead us to this interpretation. The strange objects may simply be some of the possible forms this "liquid stone" can take.
(*L.L.*)

The Petrified Forest, 2003
Assembly of office furniture in metal and mixed media, 380 x 280 cm
Naples, Maurizio Morra Greco Collection
Courtesy Franco Soffiantino Arte Contemporanea, Turin

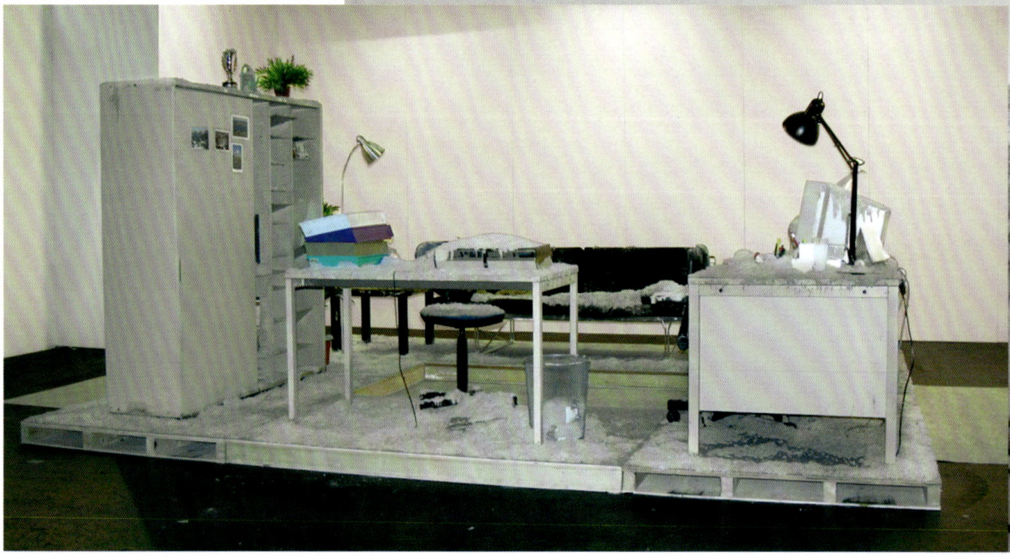

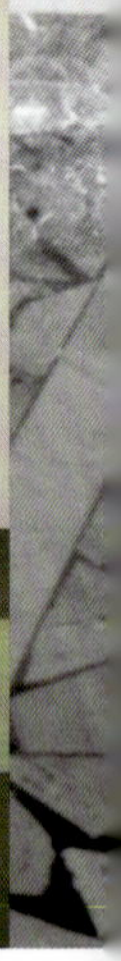

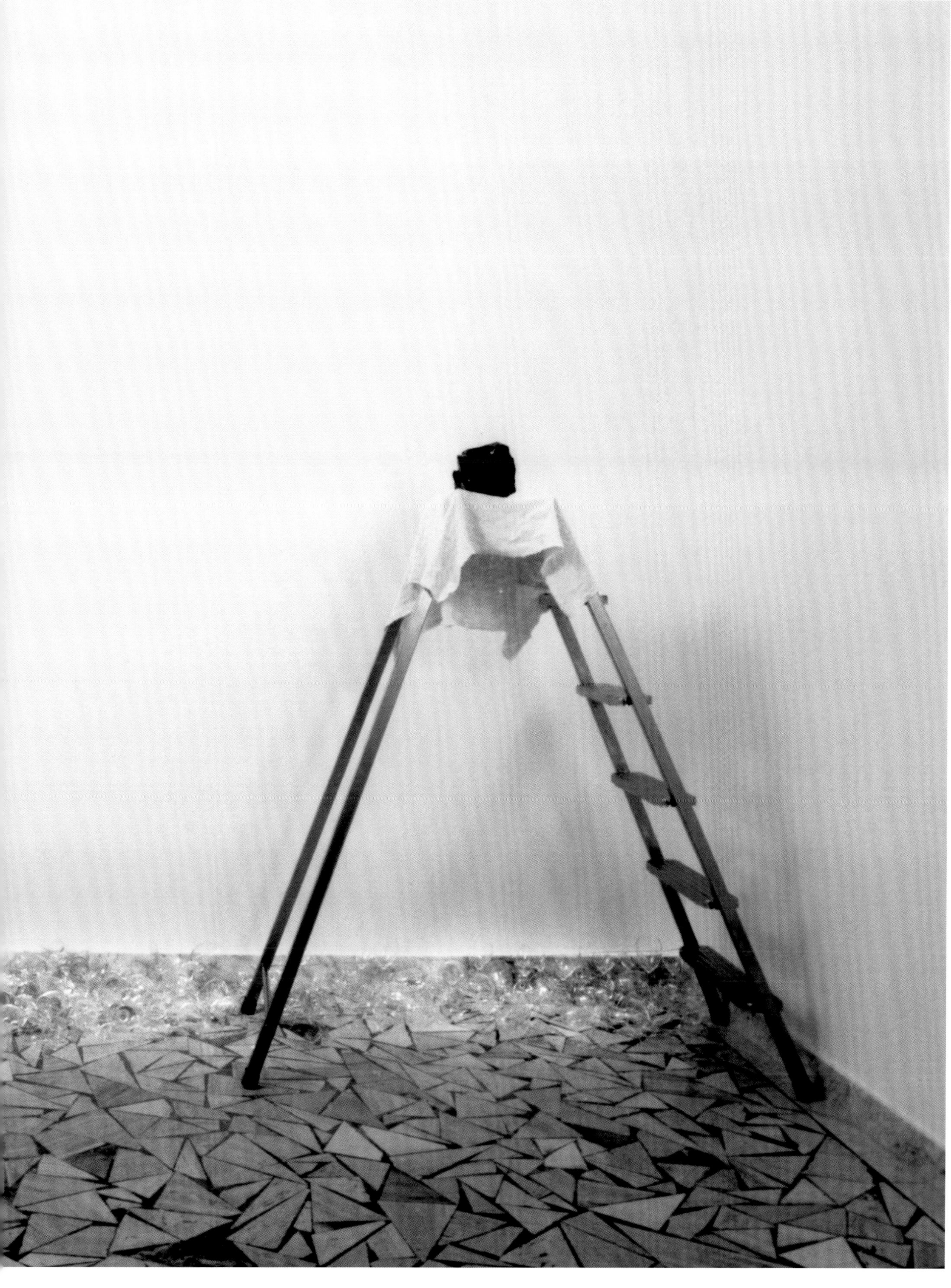

Jan Fabre

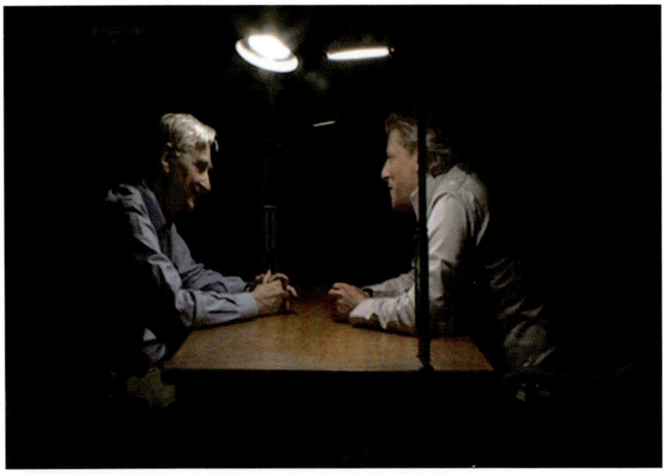

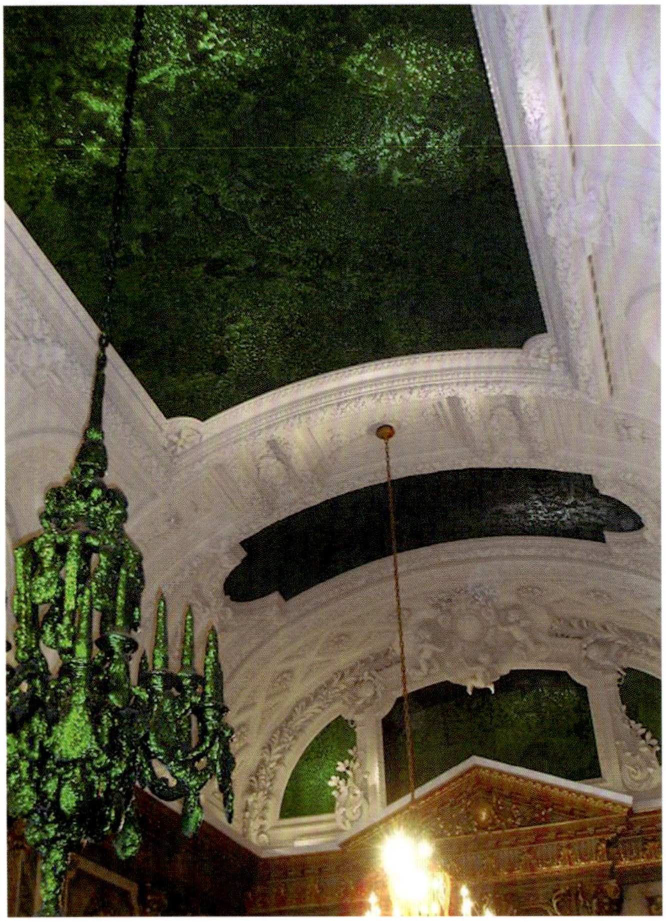

Born in Antwerp, Belgium, in 1958. Lives and works in Antwerp.
The constant point of reference in Fabre's work is the tradition of Flemish sixstieth- and seventieth-century painting, especially Bosch, Vermeer, and Rembrandt, combined with a rigorous scientific interest in human environments understood as objects to be investigated by means of tools drawn from study of the animal kingdom.
At the same time, this interest in zoology and especially entomology points to links of continuity with the activities of the artist's grandfather, the celebrated naturalist Jean-Henri Fabre. This was the background to *Heaven of Delight* (2002), a permanent installation commissioned by Queen Paula of Belgium for the Salle des Glaces in the Palais Royal in Brussels. Taking up the interior design developed for Leopold II but never completed, the project involved covering the ceiling decorations and central chandelier with iridescent green carapaces of over one million scarab beetles. Fabre conceived the space of the Salle des Glaces as a visual synthesis of a series of frescoes on historical subjects and a Renaissance *Wunderkammer*. The references are many and varied. While drawing inspiration from the triptych of *The Garden of Earthly Delights* (1504) by Hieronymus Bosch, the central panel of which is a metaphorical representation of a world torn between sin and pleasure, Fabre chose the beetle at the same time as an allusion to his country's colonial history. "Cockroach" was in fact a disparaging term used for the Tutsi, the ethnic minority elevated to become the dominant class by the colonizers in the Belgian Congo because of their closer physical resemblance to the standards of European physiognomy. Fabre also draws upon the meaning of scarab as a symbol of rebirth in Egyptian religious iconography and the emblem of the God Ra.
The role of scientific knowledge is the ironically dominant element in *Is the Brain the Most Sexy Part of the Body?* (2007), where Fabre departs from the analytical language of medical science to put forward an aesthetic characterization of the organ of knowledge. The video shows the artist confront the natural scientist and ecologist Edward O. Wilson in a sort of police interrogation where the solution to the mystery involves investigation into the meaning of the values of existence.
(*F.T.*)

Is the Brain the Most Sexy Part of the Body?, 2007
Film (HDV), 15', produced by Jan Fabre, Pascale Pollier-Green, Ann Van de Velde, Chantal Pollier

Heaven of Delight, 2002
Beetle wing cases fixed onto the ceiling and chandelier
Brussels, Palais Royal, Salle des Glaces

A Medieval Punishment for a Contemporary Artist (Landscape with Self-portrait), 2007
Chalk, ink, soil, and wood, dimensions variable
Detail of the installation realized in 2008 at the Spazio Oberdan, Milan

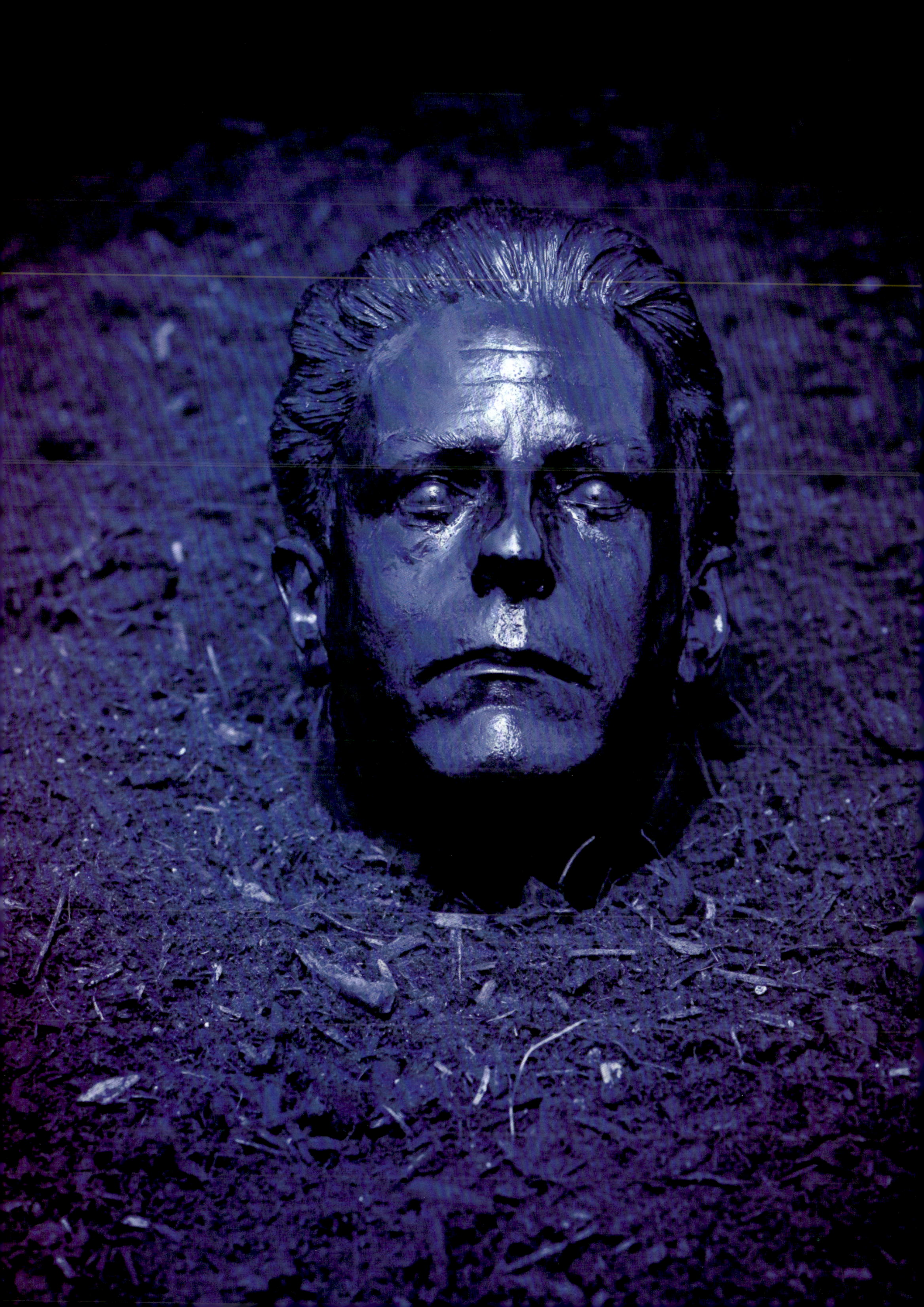

Damien Hirst

Born in Bristol, UK, in 1965. Lives and works in Devon.
With his sensational and subversive works, Damien Hirst has brought himself to the attention of critics and the general public as one of the most interesting and controversial artists on the international scene over the last two decades. While his debut on the London scene came during his studies at Goldsmiths College, which he attended, like many other artists then lumped together under the equally vague and popular label of Young British Art (YBA), in the second half of the 1980s, his extraordinary rise in the Who's Who of world art began in 1991 with the presentation of *The Physical Impossibility of Death in the Mind of Someone Living* amid general outcry. The work consists of an evidently Minimalist structure of three adjoining glass cubes of identical size with white steel edges, each containing a section of the body of a gigantic white shark kept in a solution of formaldehyde and silicon. The dead animal is thus presented to the morbid and, at the same time, subtly romantic contemplation of the spectators, who are almost overwhelmed by the majesty of the creature displayed in a situation that recalls its previous aquatic life, its strength and its ferocity.
It was a work of the same kind but, if possible, still more disturbing and radical that Hirst presented at the Royal Academy of London in the celebrated exhibition *Sensation* of 1998. Having now found favor with the collector Charles Saatchi, the artist featured dissection once again in *Some Comfort Gained from the Acceptance of the Inherent Lies in Everything*, a work using the customary showcases set at regular intervals to present two cows, each sliced vertically into six pieces, the segments being rearranged with a head at either end to create the image of a hybrid animal in the mind of any spectator seeking to reassemble the parts mentally. Most critics saw the work as a protest against experiments in genetic manipulation and cloning, thus paving the way for interpretations stressing Hirst's interest in vital contemporary

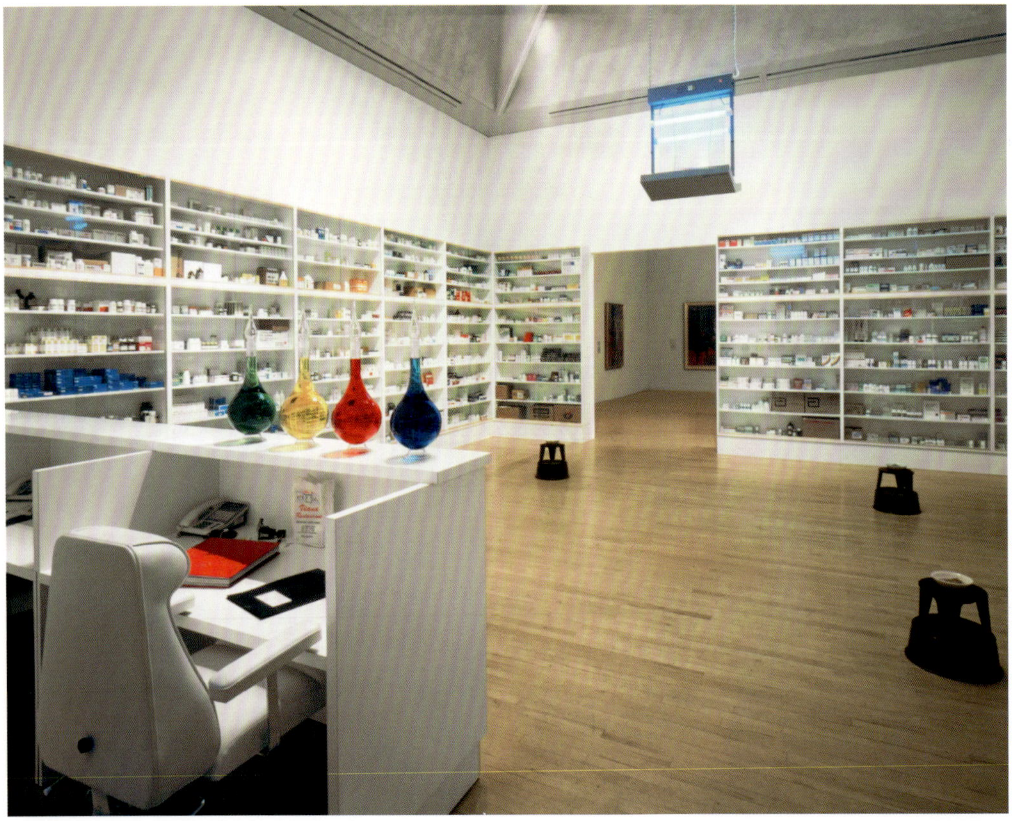

Pharmacy, 1992
Pharmacy furnishings, glass vases, plastic stools, medicine cartons, site-specific
London, Tate Britain

Some Comfort Gained from the Acceptance of the Inherent Lies in Everything, 1996
Glass, steel, formaldehyde solution and two cows contained in twelve tanks, 200 x 90.2 x 30.5 cm each tank
Venice, François Pinault Collection

Infinity, 2001
Glass and stainless steel cabinet with resin, metal, and plaster pills, 236.2 x 469.9 x 10.2 cm
Venice, François Pinault Collection

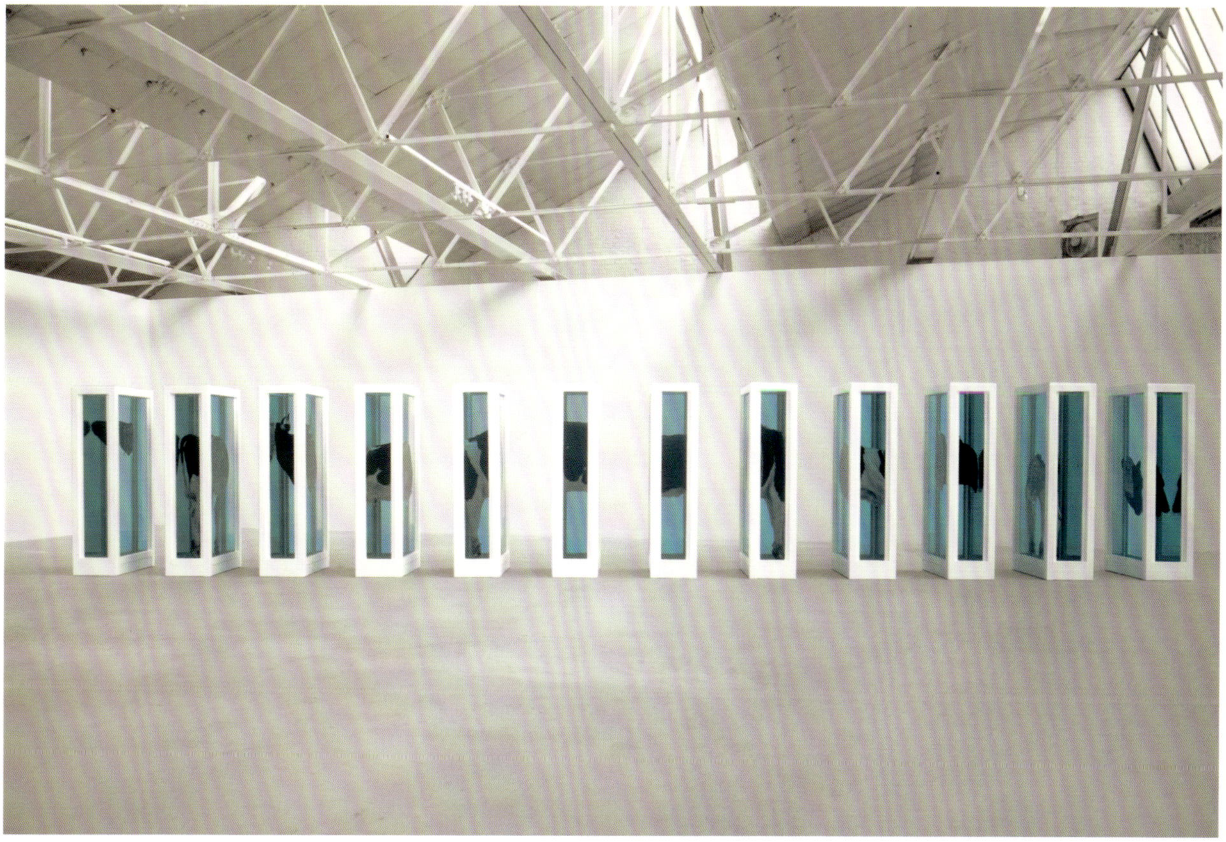

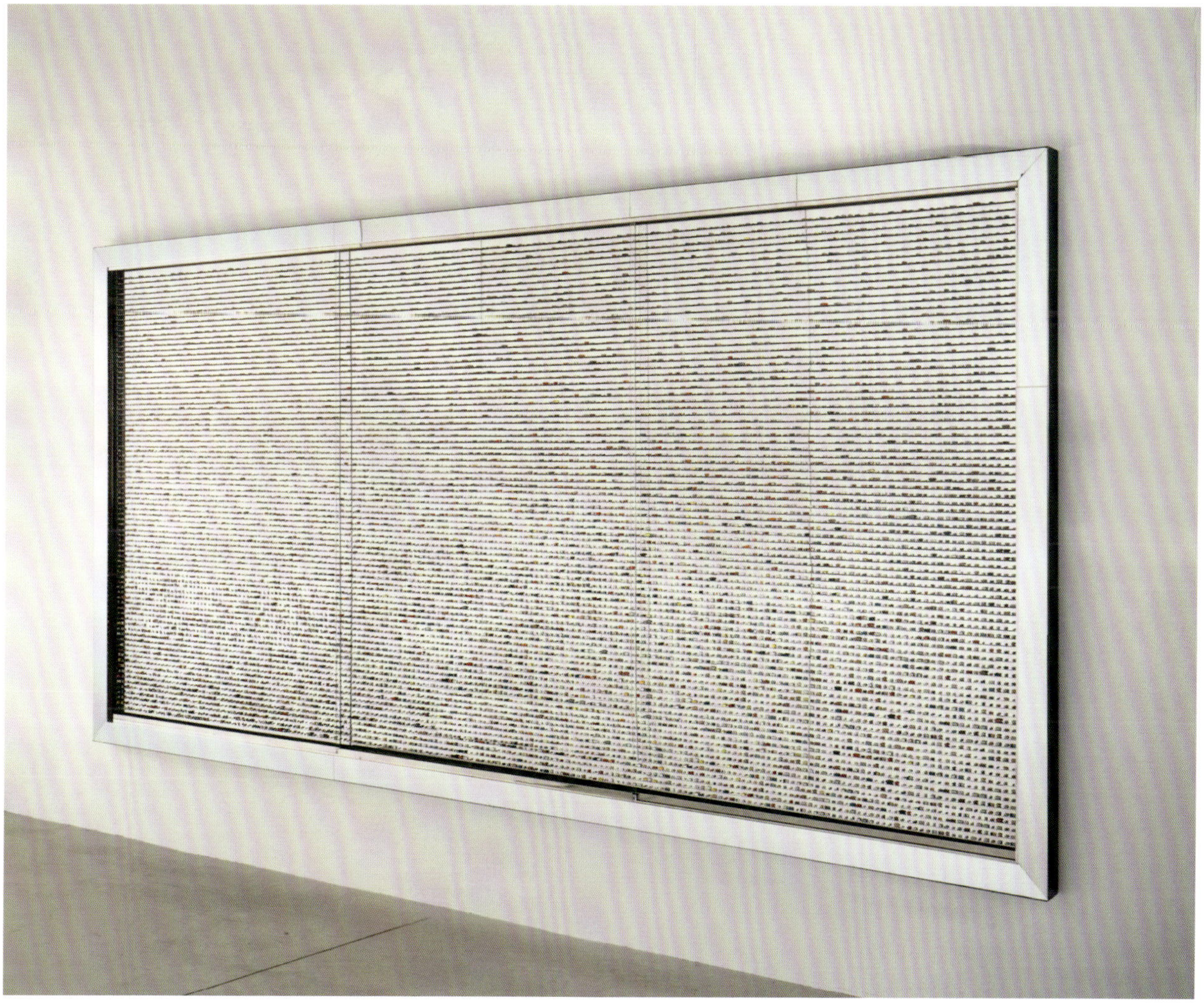

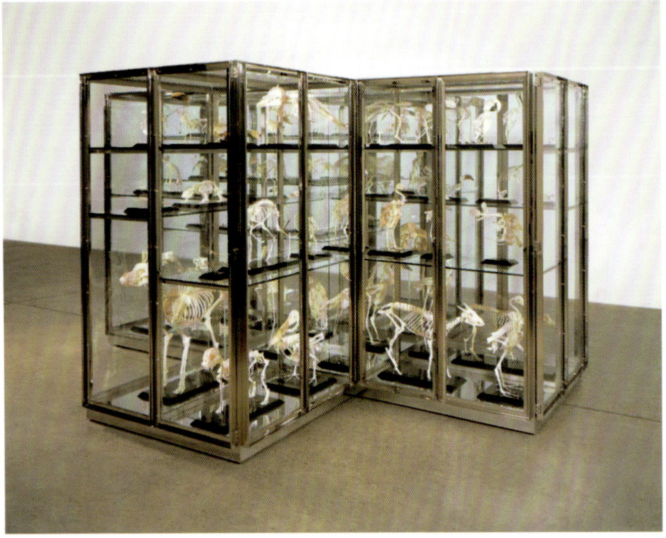

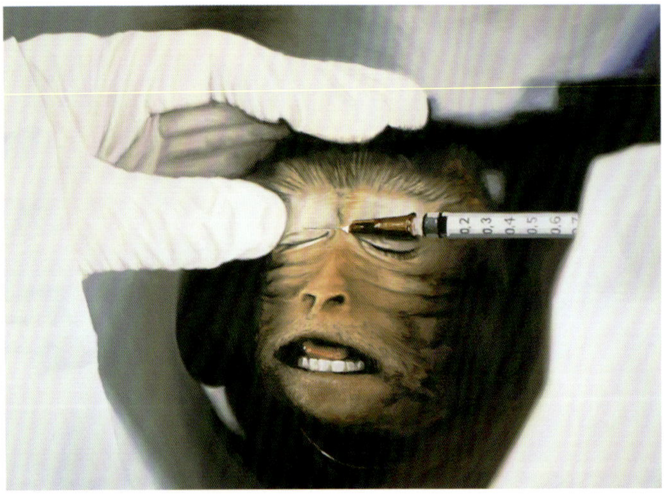

Where Are We Going? Where Do We Come From? Is There a Reason?, 2000–2004
Glass and stainless steel cabinet with animal skeletons,
204 x 365 x 365 cm
Venice, François Pinault Collection

Vivisection, 2004
Oil on canvas, 38.1 x 53.3 cm
Venice, François Pinault Collection

For the Love of God, 2007
Platinum, diamonds, and human teeth, 17.1 x 12.7 x 19.1 cm
Courtesy Jay Jopling / White Cube, London

issues of ethics and science. The artist's decision to exhibit his sliced animals in transparent cases similar to those used in laboratories and natural science museums provided support for these views, as did the semi-scientific interest in the existential and philosophical problems connected with evolutionary theories that he displayed with the animal skeletons in vitrines of the series *Where Are We Going? Where Do We Come From? Is There a Reason?* (2000–2004). Unquestionably well aware of the interest aroused by the system of mass communications with TV talk shows, thematic programs, popular magazines, sensational news reports, calls from religious figures and answers from scientists in the vague area between ethics and science, Hirst has shrewdly made this one of his primary areas of operations.
His works serve not so much to address the problem as to meet the now widespread public need for its presentation in spectacular form.
In a subtler but no less effective way, Hirst's works featuring pharmaceutical products also establish dialogue with the public's present interest in scientific and medical research. The artist thus responds to the fears aroused in human beings at the thought of aging, physical and mental breakdown, disease and death with countless boxes of pills in glass cabinets or expanses of colored tablets laid out like precious stones on mirror shelves in elegant display cases (*Infinity*, 2001). Rather than a protest against the excessive power of the pharmaceutical industry and the problem of the abuse of medicines, these works seem to address the human need to toy at least mentally with the idea of immortality and readiness to swallow the deceitful promises of those offering every sort of panacea (*Fragile Truth*, 1997–1998). This issue is even more explicit in a series of recent works that have not failed to arouse the customary outcry, not least because of their practically blasphemous content. Hirst has in fact addressed the theme of human salvation replacing the Eucharistic wafer with a marble paracetamol tablet, clearly suggesting that the hope in Christ advocated by the Church would be better placed in medicine.
The relationship with religion in Hirst's work is not, however, just another opportunity for the artist to raise the stakes – heightening the sensationalistic effect of his works with the certainty of making the biggest possible splash in the art system and the mass media – but also tied up with some interesting reflections of a philosophical nature.
Although Hirst devotes himself primarily to sculpture and is in every sense one of the contemporary artists whose objects and installations have done most to revitalize the discipline in terms of form and content, great interest also attaches to his paintings.
The themes addressed on canvas are the same ones examined in his showcases, including ethical boundaries and the social repercussions of scientific research (*Vivisection*, 2004), illness (*Biopsy Paintings*, 2007) and celebration of the wonder of life as inspired by the birth of a son (*Birth Paintings*, 2007).
The central role played by the duality of life and death and the striving for ideal immortality in Hirst's work as a whole can also be seen in *For the Love of God* (2007), the celebrated platinum cast of a human skull studded with 8,601 diamonds of the greatest purity, which ensured the artist's definitive elevation to the Olympus of world art. The skull, the symbol of death par excellence, "rises again" through its transformation into a work of art and becomes not only the most expensive object produced by a contemporary artist but also the tool through which its creator has ensured himself a reputation that promises to be at least virtually everlasting.
(*L.L.*)

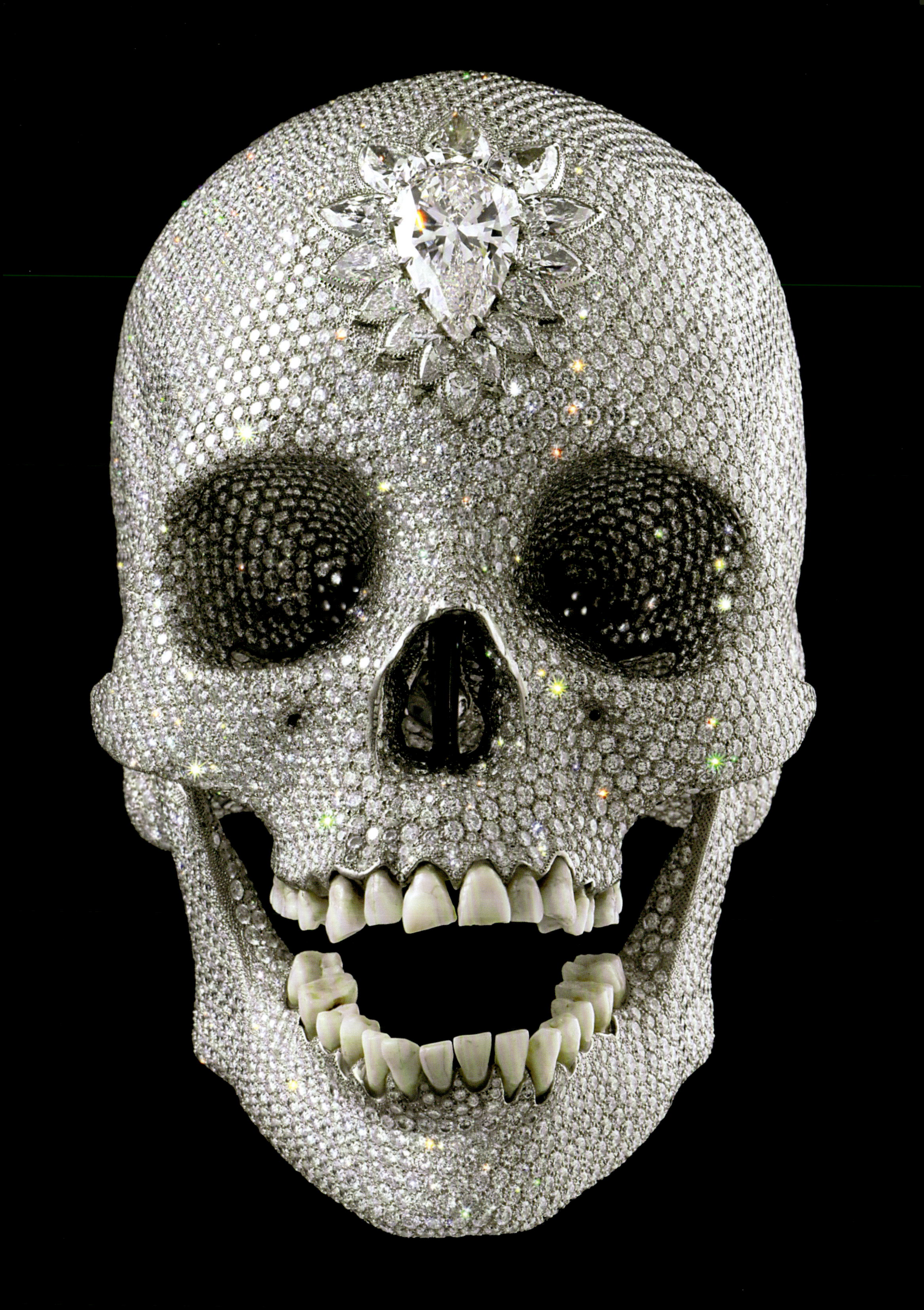

Jeff Koons

Couple, 2001
Oil on canvas, 259.1 x 350.5 cm
Santa Monica, The Broad Art Foundation

Hair, 1999
Oil on canvas, 274.3 x 201.3 cm
Private collection

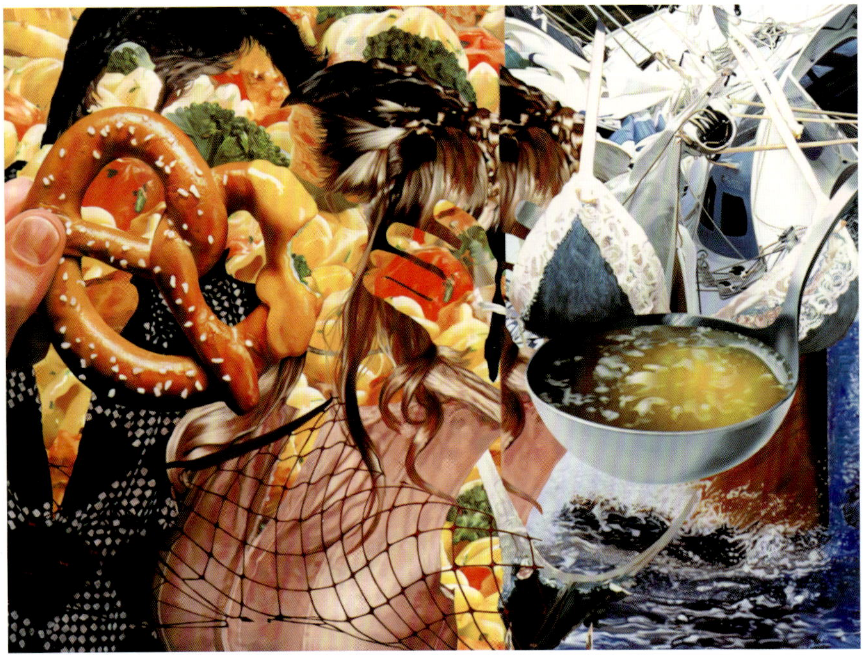

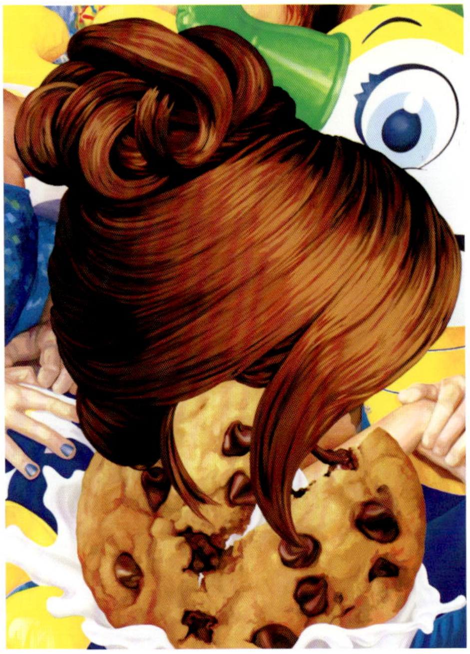

Born in York, Pennsylvania, in 1955. Lives and works in New York. "In this century there was Picasso and Duchamp. Now I'm taking us out of the twentieth century." Quoted by Calvin Tomkins in *The New Yorker*, this immodest claim by Jeff Koons probably contains a grain of truth. If the works of the *Banality* series, presented to a shocked public in 1988, and works like *Rabbit* (1986), a monumental copy of an inflatable bunny in polished steel, made him the undisputed icon of the 1980s, a hedonistic decade to which the sculptures and paintings of *Made in Heaven*, presented for the first time at the 1990 Venice Biennale, seemed to confine him irrevocably, Koons displayed a resilience shared by few of his colleagues with *Celebration*. Developed at enormous cost during the 1990s, this series consists of monumental sculptures in colored steel and hyper-realistic paintings devoted to joyous, colorful subjects from the world of childhood, including toys, flowers, hearts, slices of pie, party hats, twisted balloons, and ribbons. It is no coincidence that this sort of huge, unending birthday party should be dedicated to his son Ludwig, placed in the care of his first wife Ilona Staller after a hard-fought legal battle. We are still within the "readymade" horizon of *Banality*. Koons does not appropriate everyday reality, as Duchamp did. He does not draw inspiration from popular culture and mass media images so as to present them in the sophisticated and basically "discriminatory" language of contemporary art, as Pop Art did. He recreates these objects, often on a monumental scale, with the aid of the most skilled craftsmen and professionals in the conviction that, as he explained to Arthur C. Danto, the bourgeois admiration for craftsmanship is nothing to be ashamed of, no matter what the world of the art may decree. This declared desire to rescue "people" from the sense of guilt generated by their instinctive love of kitsch paved the way for and stimulated the globalization of taste, thus making Koons an indispensable point of reference for the art of the new millennium. The shaped mirrors and sensual paintings of *Easyfun* (1999–2001), the cuteness of *Puppy* (1992) and its monumental follow-up *Split Rocker* (2000), works covered entirely in flowers kept alive by a complex internal irrigation system, have only confirmed this position. The artist's more recent activities include the launching of two new series. *Popeye* (2003) is largely inspired by the iconography of colorful inflatable animals for the swimming pool such as seals, dogs, caterpillars, lobsters, and dolphins. The sculptures of the series in brightly colored aluminum introduce the new dimension of lightness, prompting the artist to have them hung from the ceiling on long chains. The paintings of the series differ from previous works by virtue of their extraordinary precision and complexity as highly detailed transcriptions of computer-generated images. Koons superimposes heterogeneous designs, experiments with the filters of post-production programs and 3D rendering in creations that succeed in combining immediate appeal and staggering complexity in both iconographic and stylistic terms. Benday dots are superimposed on simulated woodcuts, faux Art-Informel brushstrokes, and hyper-realistic images in overabundant and confused patchwork. This was continued in the *Hulk Elvis* series presented at the Gagosian Gallery in 2007, an aggressive, visceral, "very-high testosterone body of work", inaugurating an aesthetic of information overload in which every aesthetic and cultural input arrives with the same energy, and leaves the same void. The artist's claim to immediacy – his avowed desire to speak to a taste that has not been corrupted by great art (Danto) and leave it to the viewer to endow the work with content – is only partially refuted in these most recent works, bursting with references and citations. What Dan Cameron said about his work remains true: "If all you want is a good time, he won't let you down.
But underneath the primitive thirst for delight and pleasure in his works, I think he is deeply engaged in some philosophical questions. Both Marxists and kids can enjoy it."
(*D.Q.*)

Puppy, 1992
Stainless steel, soil, geotextile fabric, internal irrigation system, and flower plants, 1234.4 x 650.2 cm
New York, Rockefeller Center

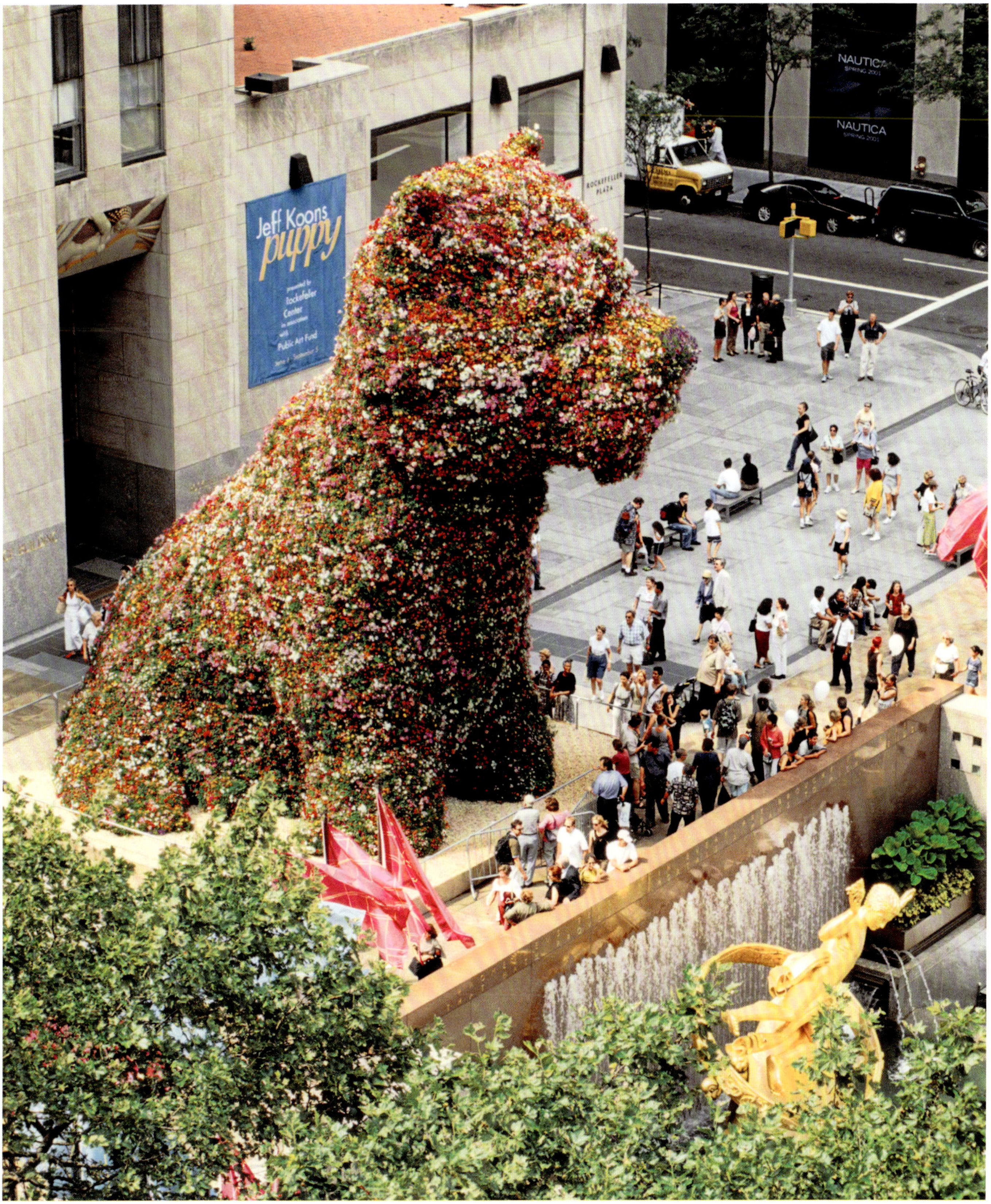

Takashi Murakami

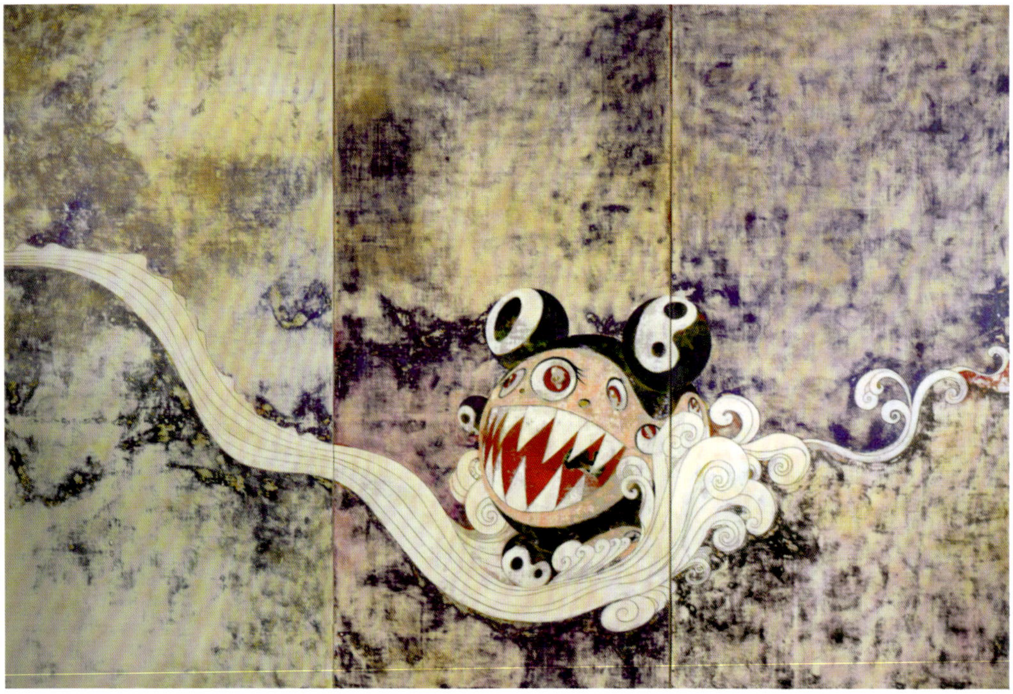

727, 1996
Acrylic on canvas mounted on board, 300 x 450 x 7 cm
Courtesy Tomio Koyama Gallery, Tokyo / Blum & Poe, Los Angeles

Born in Tokyo in 1963. Lives and works in New York and Tokyo. Takashi Murakami is the artist who has gone furthest in the dialogue between high and low, avant-garde and kitsch, that has characterized the twentieth century from Dada to Pop Art, followed by Jeff Koons and the other Appropriationists of the 1980s. He has managed in less than 15 years to create a production system that has conquered not only the world's greatest museums but also the wardrobes of modern women and the shelves of their children. Only a Japanese born in the 1960s and reaching maturity in the 1990s could have attempted such a feat. The cultural output developed by Japan over the last 30 years, above all through animated films and comics, has become incredibly popular in the West, producing a language that is as universal as it is deeply rooted in the long tradition and the psychopathology of a country that emerged from World War II in ruins. One of Murakami's merits, this time in his role as intellectual and exhibition curator, lies indeed in having highlighted these links and enabled the West to understand a phenomenon that it had previously confined itself to absorbing passively. Organized by Murakami in Tokyo in 2000 and then taken on tour through cities like Los Angeles and Minneapolis in the United States, the exhibition *Superflat* examined the Japanese figurative culture from the painting of the Edo period up to Manga and anime, identifying its primary element of continuity in two-dimensionality, the absence of depth and any obligatory viewpoint. This idea of flatness stems also, however, from the absence in Japanese culture of any distinction whatsoever between high and low culture, art and illustration, artistic expression and popular tradition. When Murakami founded the Hiropon Factory in Japan in 1996, he obviously paid tribute to Warhol but equally obviously adopted the model of the studios of the creators of Manga characters, whom he considers his equals.
While *Superflat* provided the stylistic key required for any understanding of the contemporary Japanese figurative culture, *Little Boy* (inaugurated in New York at the Japan Society in 2005) attempted a psychological analysis of the same. As the title suggests, the tragedy of Hiroshima and Nakasaki was the primary point of reference. According to Murakami, it was Japanese popular culture rather than art in the postwar period that undertook the onerous task of getting to grips with this horror and burying its ghosts beneath a delight in joyous color, an obsession with cuteness (*kawaii*) exemplified by the omnipresent icon of Hello Kitty, the accentuation of character traits, and an obsession with sex, which became the other face of *kawaii*.
Little Boy also offers the key to understanding the ambiguous fascination felt by the West and especially the United States for the work of this artist, who returns constantly to the trauma of the A-Bomb in his brightly colored, "superflat", skull-shaped atomic mushroom clouds. The sinister, sensual, aggressive joy of his works transmits a feeling of happiness tinged with dread to the observer. His obsession with surfaces of dazzling color that seem to have nothing to hide (described as "eye candy" by Jerry Saltz) reveals an underlying ambiguity that attracts and repels at the same time. The tragedy is not seen but shows through in the sharp smile of Mr DOB, the breathtaking legs of Miss Ko2, the enormous breasts of Hiropon, and the eyes and flowers sprouting everywhere.
Murakami developed his approach to contemporary art and vocabulary very quickly in the early 1990s. After completing his studies at the Tokyo National University of Fine Arts and Music with a doctorate on Nihonga art, a traditional style of figuration born in the nineteenth century out of the encounter between Japanese and Western culture, he went to New York in 1989. It was his exposure there to the work of Jeff Koons that prompted him to develop a new idea of art and the artist. Having returned to Japan, he took an interest in the *otaku* culture of kids devoted obsessively and almost pathologically to Manga, anime or videogames. He abandoned Nihonga between 1993 and 1995 for the flat hues of acrylic paints and began to create his own world of characters inspired by the Manga culture. The atomic mushroom cloud and Mr DOB appeared on canvases with a monochrome background, which the latter soon left behind him to soar in the air in the shape of a huge balloon.
The founding of the Hiropon Factory, followed in 2001 by Kaikai Kiki Co. Ltd., marked his definitive transformation into a trademark

affixed indiscriminately to paintings, sculptures, and every type of gadget. The dozens of specialists employed at the Kaikai Kiki actually work on Murakami projects, which the artist outlines on paper and then designs in detail by means of vectorial graphics software.
This detail is by no means unimportant. As Pamela Lee noted in *Artforum* (2007), it means that every single project can be reproduced on very different scales and adapted to meet all the requirements of a world market that is itself "infinitely scalable". Finally, the manual translation of the sketch into object (painting, sculpture or installation) raises it above the more commercial level of his output by ensuring its uniqueness and value. The large-scale resin statues of *Miss Ko2* (1997), *Hiropon* (1997), and *My Lonesome Cowboy* (1998) appeared in the late 1990s. The tempering of eroticism with cuteness in the first gave way to blatant sensuality in the later works, with enormous sexual organs discharging their respective secretions in the air, as developed also in painted form on the large panels associated with the sculptures (*Cream*, 1998, and *Spring Liquid*, 1998). The childlike and joyful side of the artist's work reappears in works like *DOB in the Strange Forest* (1999), a huge sculpture that shows DOB surrounded and almost threatened by a strange species of mutant mushrooms with eyes all over them, the sculptural versions of *Kaikai* and *Kiki* (2000), two small white and pink savages featured in the animated film that Murakami has been making since 2007, and *Second Mission Project ko² (ga-walk type)* (1999), where the sexy maid Ko2 becomes a monumental automaton capable of turning into a jet. As regards painting, the precise and impeccable translation of Murakami's vectorial sketches by assistants creates images of explosive and psychedelic imaginativeness, an artificial, metamorphic world in which concepts like "abstraction", "figuration", and "decoration" no longer have any meaning, as Western traditions like Surrealism and Expressionism meld with the Manga aesthetic in a now unmistakable mixture (*PO+KU Surrealism*, 1998–1999, and *Homage to Francis Bacon*, 2002).
Murakami was commissioned in 2003 to redesign the Louis Vuitton logo, design a limited edition of bags, and organize an image campaign including an anime commercial entitled *Superflat Monogram*. The operation proved a great success and the commercial dimension took on such importance in the artist's work as to prompt the curators of his recent retrospective at the MoCA in Los Angeles (significantly entitled *© Murakami*, 2007) to include a real shop inside the exhibition selling visitors a selection of the countless consumer goods produced by his Factory: from Vuitton bags to T-shirts, cups, and miniatures for children.
The point of this decision was to highlight the central philosophical importance of this intermingling in the artist's work.
The commission for Louis Vuitton was accompanied by new works like the maladjusted cyborg *Inochi* (2004) and some sculptures on a monumental scale, including *Tongari-kun* (2003–2004) and *Oval Buddha* (2007), which combine references to Buddhist religious sculpture with Murakami's now familiar but always surprising imagination.
(*D.Q.*)

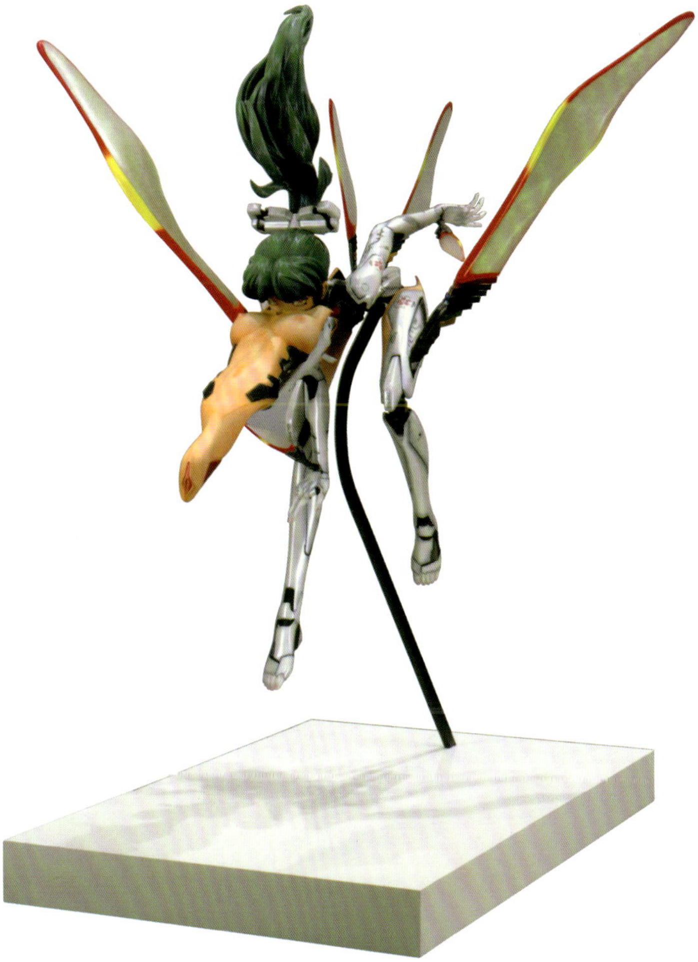

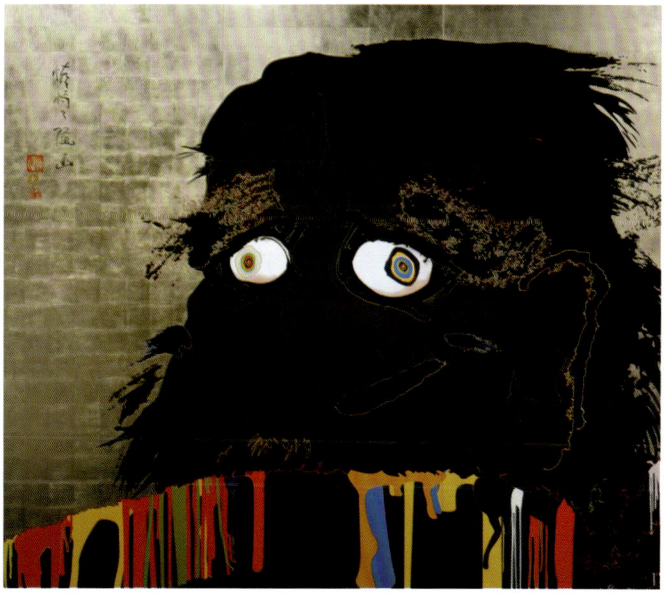

Second Mission Project ko² (ga-walk type), 1999
Painting in oil, acrylic, artificial resins, fiberglass, and iron,
224.4 x 176.9 x 131.5 cm
Courtesy Blum & Poe, Los Angeles

That I May Time Transcend, that a Universe My Heart May Unfold, 2007
Acrylic and silver gold foil on canvas mounted on board,
243 x 282 x 5 cm (3 panels)
Courtesy Gagosian Gallery, New York

Ernesto Neto

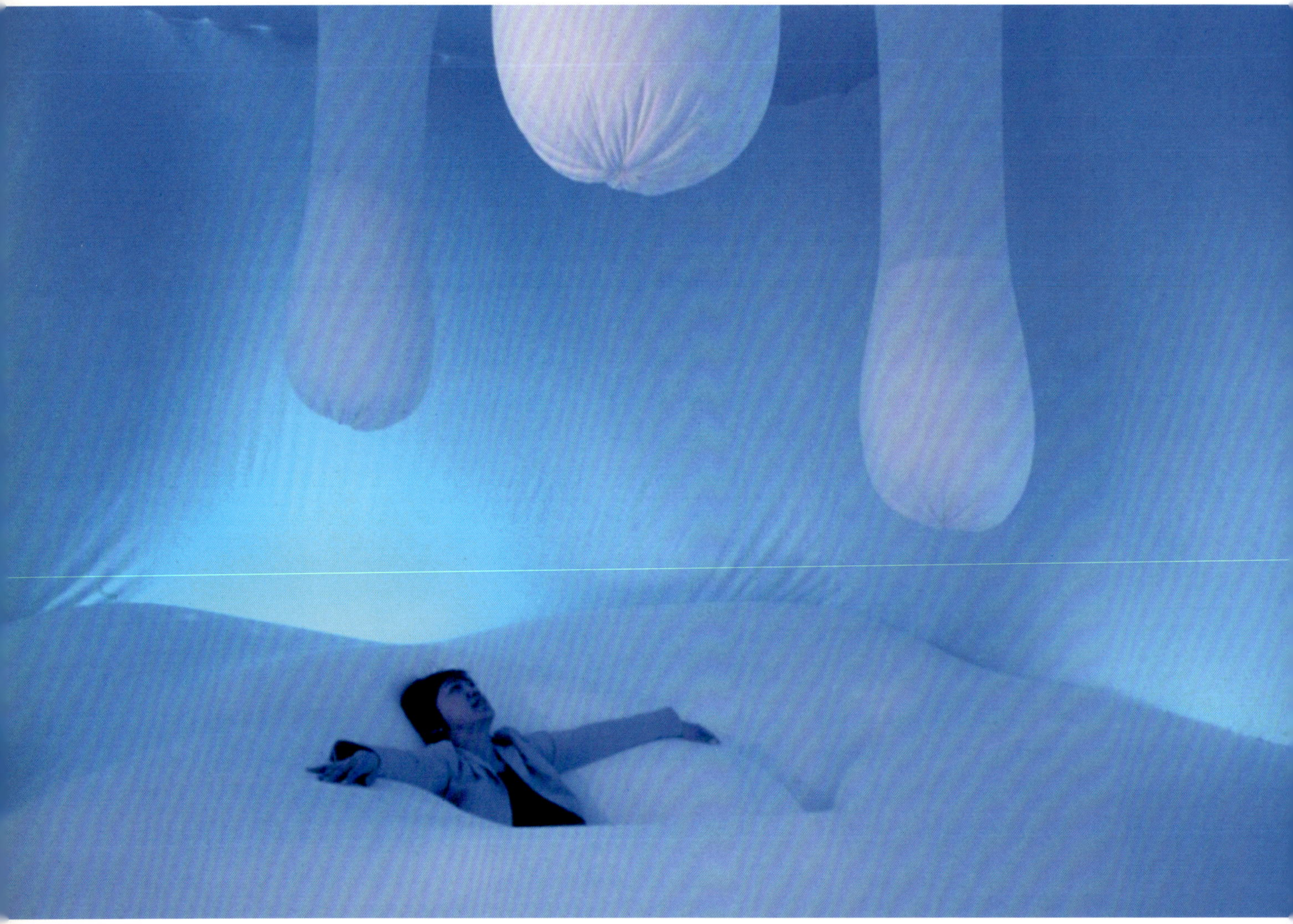

Born in Rio de Janeiro in 1964. Lives and works in Rio de Janeiro. In 2001 Ernesto Neto created a monumental installation at the Arsenale in Venice entitled *Ô bicho!* One of the first works brought to Italy by the Brazilian artist, it was also emblematic of his recent investigations. The title alludes both to the literal meaning of the term *bicho*, which is "animal", but also to a typical Brazilian expression indicating that an event or situation is highly improbable and hence very appropriate for a sort of illicit lottery based on animals and numbers. Like many of Neto's works, *Ô bicho!* consists of large receptacles made of Lycra hanging from the ceiling almost to the ground, weighed down and colored by the spices they contain. Neto returned to this subject in 2008 for his first solo show in Italy, which took place in the entrance hall of the MACRO in Rome. *While Nothing Happens* is in fact a reworking of the motifs of *Ô bicho!*: a large-scale installation that establishes direct dialogue between the rigidity and neutrality of the museum's architectural space and the ductile, organic shape of the elements hanging from the ceiling. Neto also highlights the characteristic role of the place housing the installation as a passageway, an area where – as the title says – nothing usually happens.
Here too, the long protuberances are filled with cloves, cumin, curcuma, pepper, and ginger, spices with pungent aromas that serve to immerse the visitor in a complex, all-enveloping experience.
Ernesto Neto focuses on phenomena that establish a relationship between space, memory, culture, and perception in the exhibition space. Hence the importance of sensory elements such as the aromas or others of an evocative and oneiric character, like the transparent, elastic material of which his structures are made. In *Walking in Venus Blue Cave* (2001), the blue of the room is so intense as to simulate the light inside an aquarium and the liquid character of the setting alludes to the conformation of Venus, the blue planet. The artist uses light, chromatic variations, and biomorphic elements to make visitors feel they have been swallowed up in the metaphorical belly of a whale and lose their ability to perceive the outside world.
(*F.T.*)

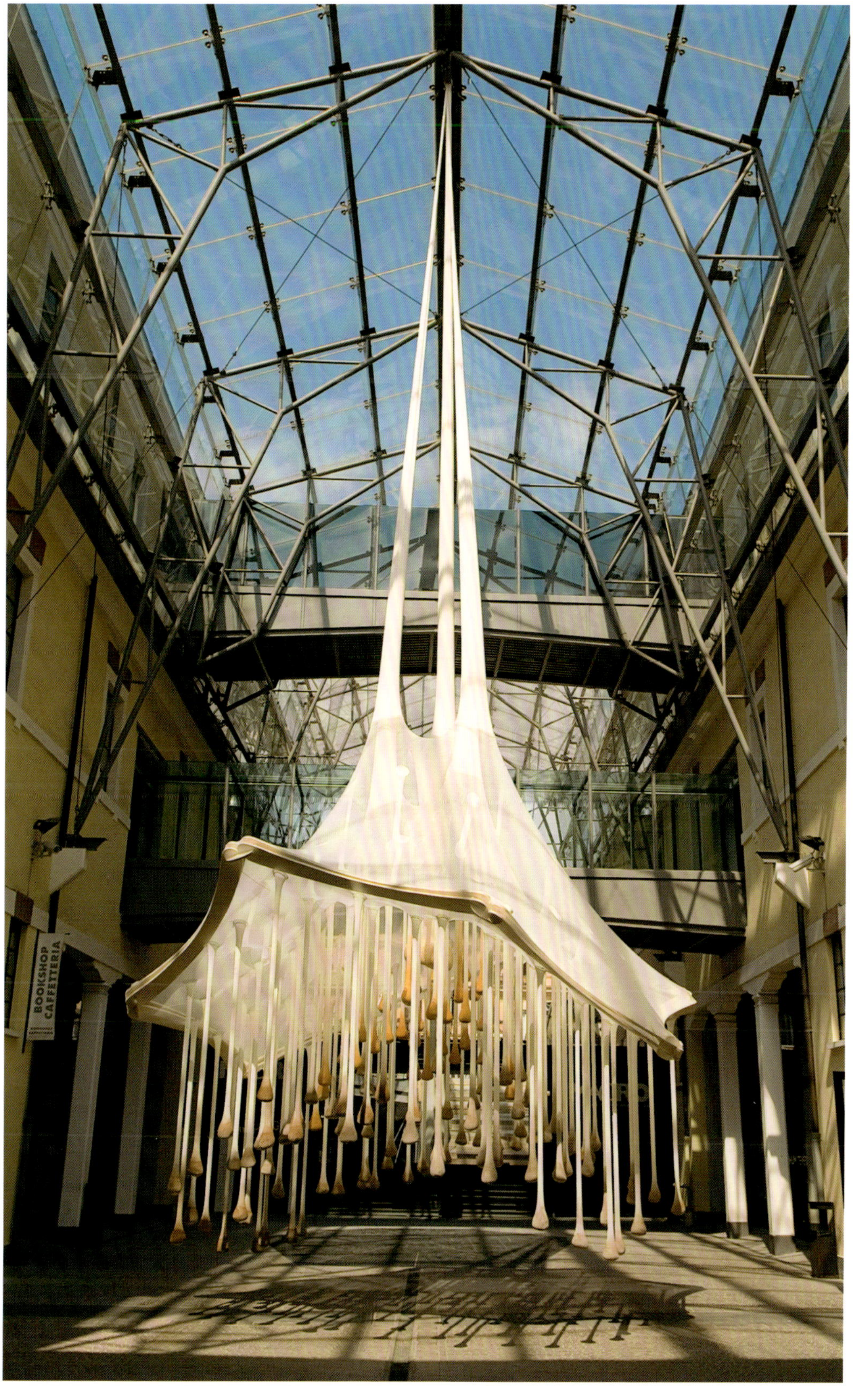

Walking in Venus Blue Cave, 2001
Tulle, polystyrene foam, buttons, incandescent lights,
396 x 777 x 812 cm
View of the installation realized in 2001 at the Tanya Bonakdar Gallery, New York
Courtesy of the artist and Tanya Bonakdar Gallery, New York

While Nothing Happens, 2008
Tulle and polyamide stockings, wood, spices, 400 x 760 cm
View of the installation realized in 2008 at the MACRO – Museo d'Arte Contemporanea di Roma, Rome
Courtesy of the artist and Tanya Bonakdar Gallery, New York; Galeria Fortes Vilaça, São Paulo

Adrian Paci

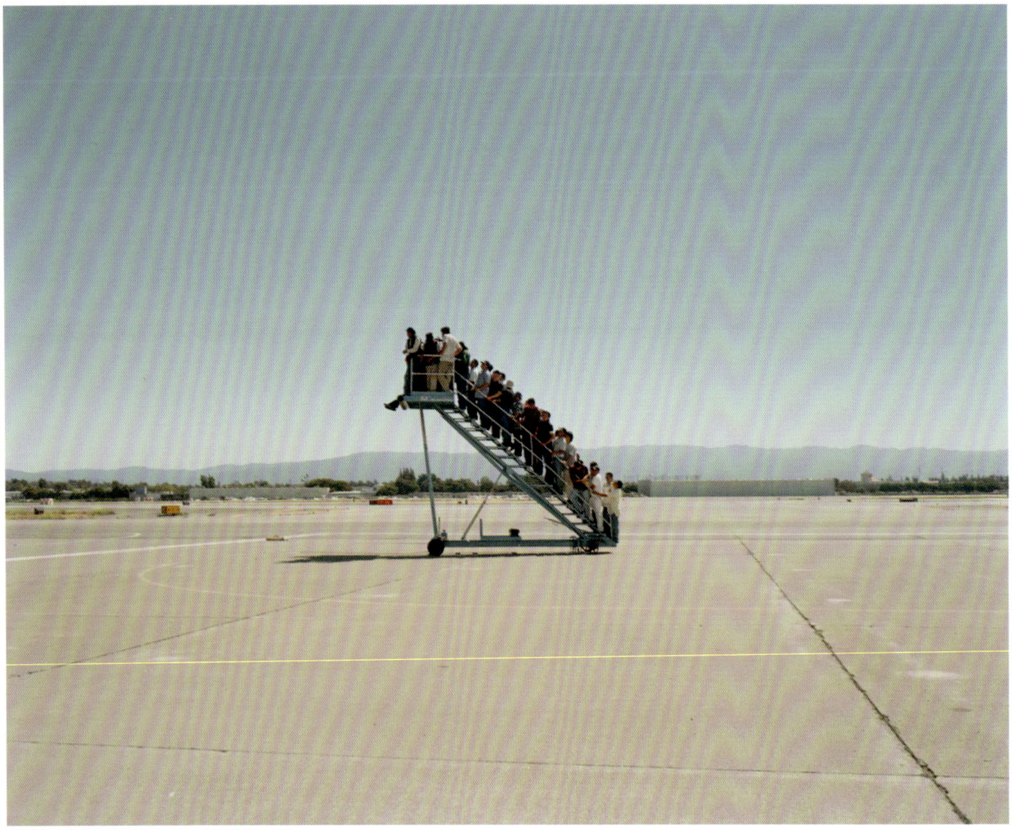

Centro di Permanenza Temporanea, 2007
Color video projection in 16:9, 5′30″
Courtesy francesca kaufmann

Back Home, 2001
Digital photo print, 105 x 125 cm
Courtesy francesca kaufmann

Born in Shkoder, Albania, in 1969. Lives and works in Milan.
Men and women of various nationalities move in a line towards the steps of an airplane. The first to arrive begin to go up with the others close behind them. Nobody speaks and they all look straight ahead. When the steps are completely full, the camera gradually moves back and we discover that there is no airplane for these passengers. As "illegal" immigrants with no documents and often no identity, they have ended up in the dismal camps (*centri di permanenza temporanea*, known also by the acronym CPT) that await all those who risk and often lose their lives trying to enter Italy. Once transferred to these centers, the immigrants lose all freedom of movement. It is precisely this restrictive measure, one of a whole range of procedures designed to deprive refugees of their socio-political identity, that provided the initial stimulus for Adrian Paci's video installation *Centro di Permanenza Temporanea* (2007). Even though this Albanian artist's status as a long-term resident in Milan is completely above board, he is familiar with immigrant status through direct experience. Whether videos, video installations, paintings, sculptures or photographs, his works always address the condition of distance, uprooting, loss of identity, and the struggle to make a "role" for yourself in a country radically different from your native land. One result is the poetic and nostalgic portraits of the series *Back Home* (2001), photographs of individuals or family groups posed – or rather about to pose, thus giving the images the deceptive quality of snapshots – in front of their homes, in their courtyards, in their living rooms, and even by the fireside, the symbol par excellence of domestic intimacy. Closer examination soon shows, however, that these are not real places but backdrops painted with an abundance of detail and great attention to perspective in a sophisticated range of grays. Like ghosts, these domestic settings dwell in the memories of all immigrants and remain with them forever, no matter where they might be.
(*L.L.*)

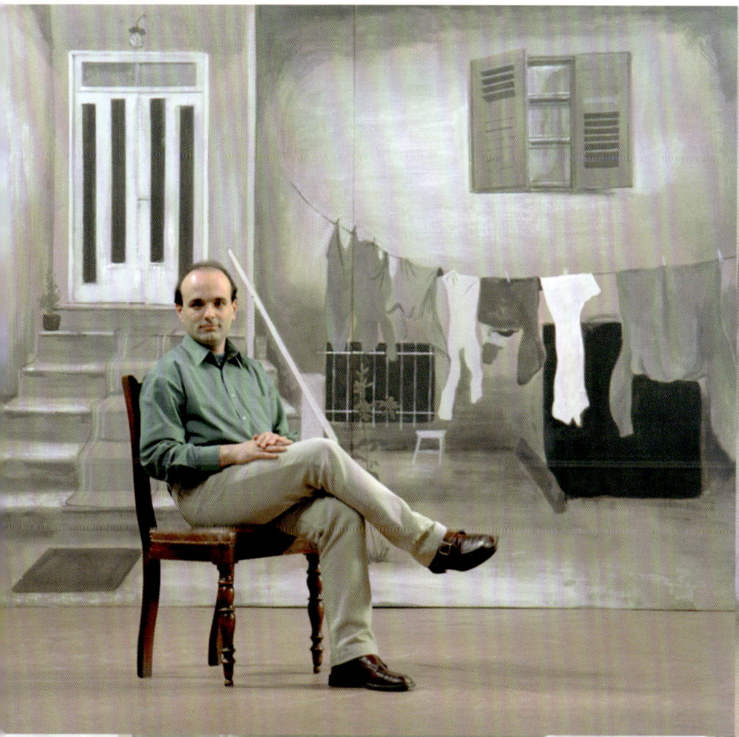
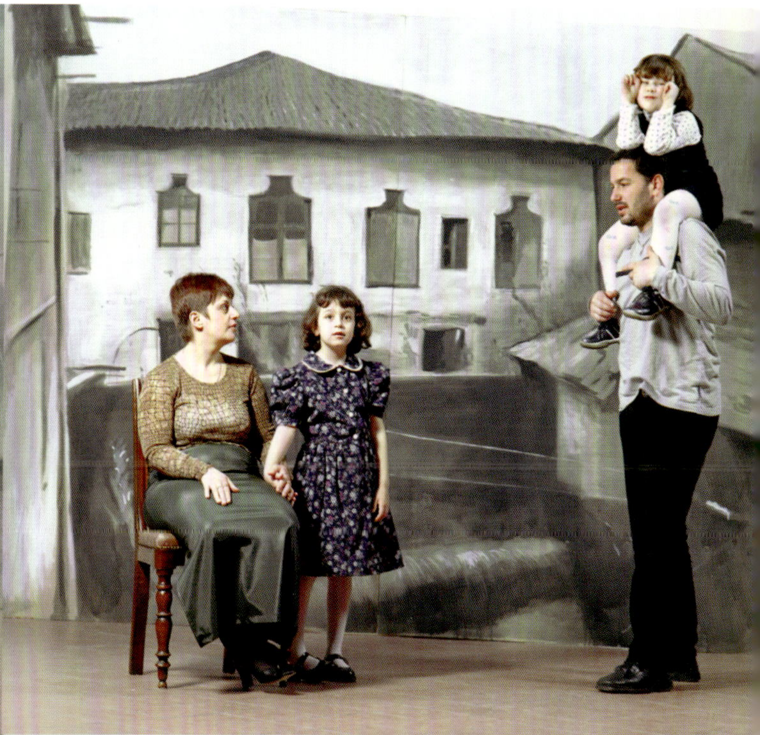
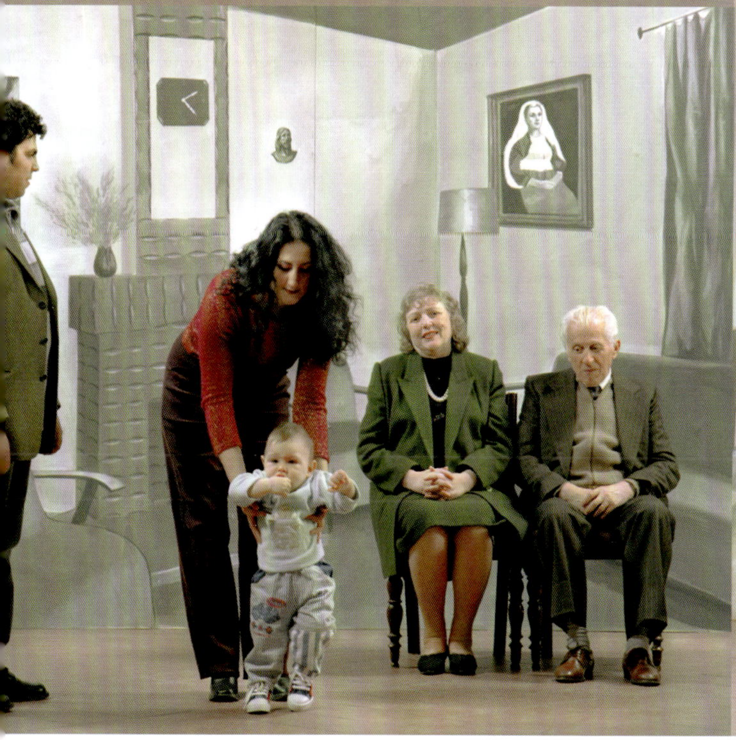
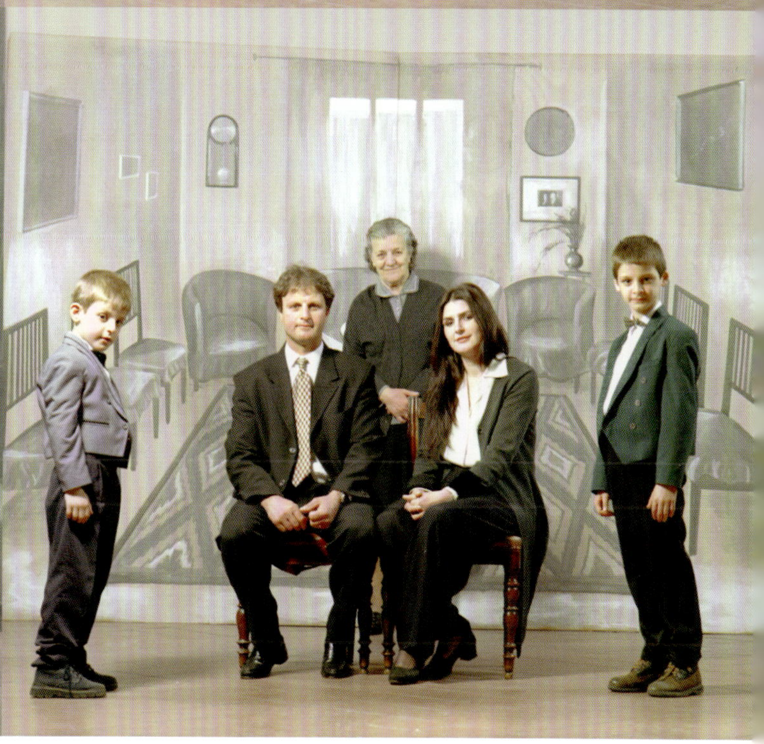

Richard Prince

Born in Panama in 1949. Lives and works in New York.
It was in the 1970s, when he was working for *Time-Life* magazine, that Richard Prince began to cut advertisements out of popular glossies, photograph them again, and exhibit them as his own works. This singular form of ready-made has come over the years to constitute the trademark of an artist made famous above all by his "appropriation" of the images of cowboys, horses and vast prairies at sunset used by the Marlboro multinational in its advertising campaigns. Some critics have seen this operation as an attack on the system of copyright and others as challenging the corporation's power to take over images of the Far West that rightfully belong to every American citizen. Whatever the intention might be, it is certain that these "heroic" endeavors have won Prince great acclaim not only from critics – as shown, for example, by the decision of Daniel Birnbaum and Francesco Bonami to devote an entire room to his cowboys at the 2003 Venice Biennale within the framework of the exhibition *Ritardi e Rivoluzioni* – but also on the art market, where one of his rephotographed "Marlboro Man" works recently sold for over three million dollars. Richard Prince is not only a simple photographer of photographs, however, but also a skillful manipulator of already existing images, which he painstakingly assembles in collages or collects in series of photos connected by subtle and unexpected links of form or content (*Untitled – Four Women Looking in the Same Direction*, 1977–1979; *Untitled [Publicity]*, 2003). At the same time, he is also a painter, producing canvases that again appropriate subjects already mediated by the dominant image culture of the United States: celebrities from the pages of glossy magazines, members of gangs from crime reports, and pornographic film stars from posters. The nurses recently added to Prince's iconography come from the covers of pulp romance novels popular in the 1940s and 1950s (*Nurse in Love*, 2003). Prince's art of appropriation is still finding new ready-made objects today, one example being the monograms, drawings and one-liners about sexual identity, race, poverty, and other subjects featured on the clothes and accessories of the Louis Vuitton spring-summer collection in 2008.
(*L.L.*)

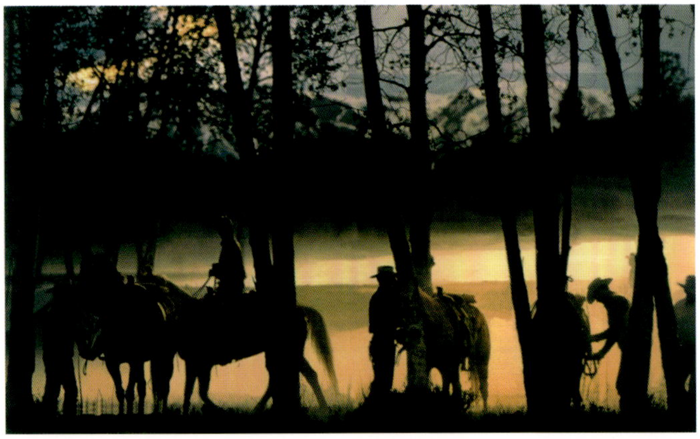

Untitled (Cowboy), 2000
Color photograph, 50.8 x 76.2 cm
Courtesy Gladstone Gallery, New York

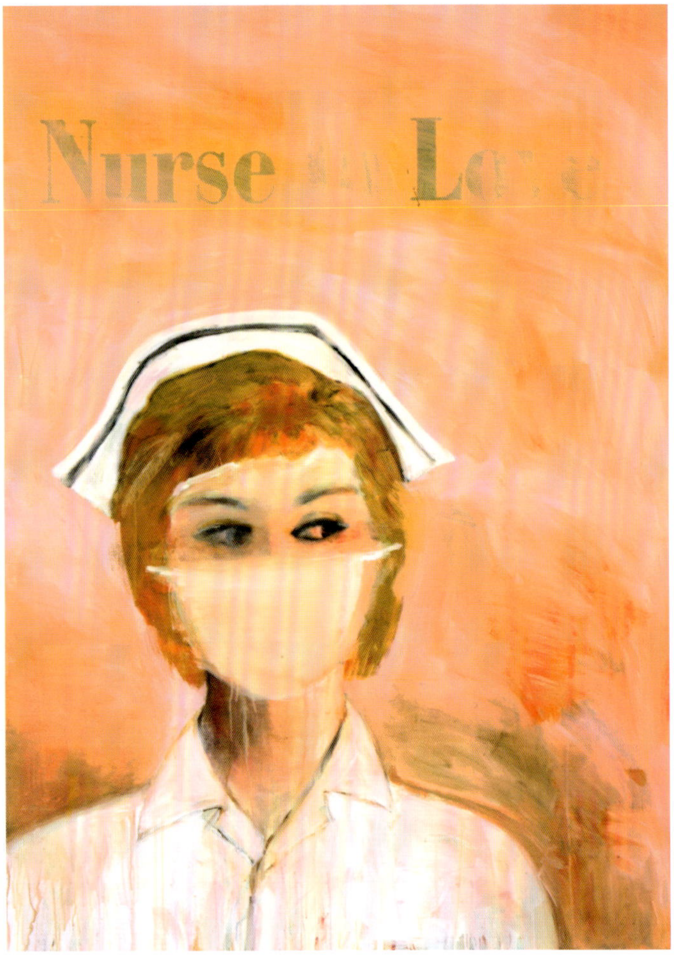

Nurse in Love, 2003
Ink-jet and acrylic on canvas, 175.3 x 124.5 cm
Courtesy Gladstone Gallery, New York

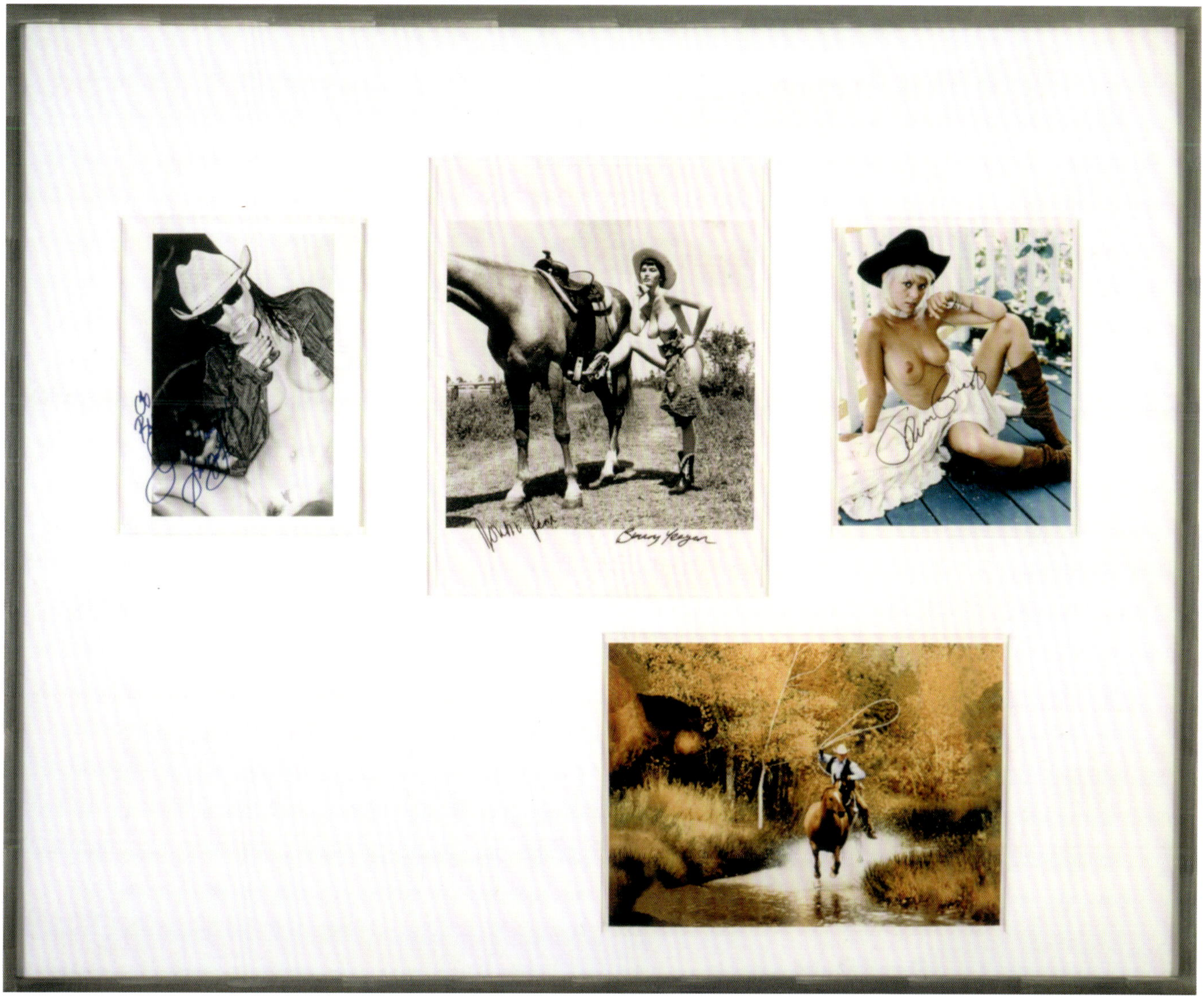

Untitled (Publicity), 2003
3 publicity color photographs and
1 Richard Prince color photograph,
83.8 x 104.1 cm
Courtesy Gladstone Gallery,
New York

Yinka Shonibare

The Swing (after Fragonard), 2001
Cotton fabric printed with "Dutch wax," mannequin, swing, artificial foliage, 330 x 350 x 220 cm
Courtesy of the artist; Stephen Friedman Gallery, London and James Cohan Gallery, New York

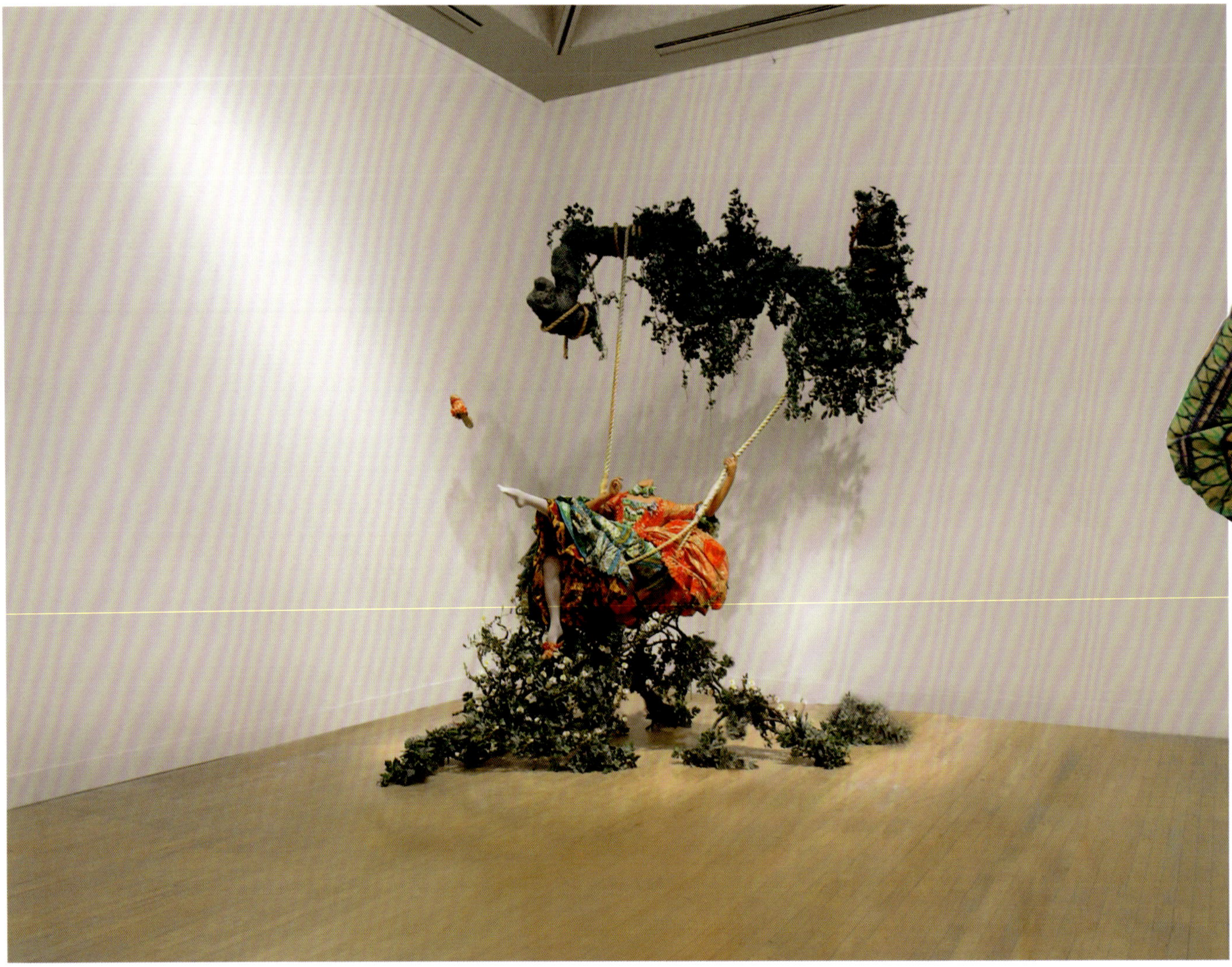

Born in London in 1962. Lives and works in London.
The mask is the key element of the work of Yinka Shonibare, an artist of Nigerian origin who was born and brought up in London.
The starting point is the idea of multiculturalism, sometimes cumbersome but above all explicit, which the artist translates into three-dimensional representations and films of events, situations and scenes of great renown. The transposition obviously includes the addition of details absent in the original or the insertion of elements capable of turning the sense upside down. The colonial question in particular is addressed in three-dimensional installations with headless dummies dressed in traditional African fabrics.
The mixture of Western culture and African tradition is the *modus operandi* at the root of *The Swing (after Fragonard)*, an installation based on the work of the same name painted by the French painter Jean-Honoré Fragonard in 1767 and now part of the Wallace Collection in London. Like the figure in the painting, Shonibare's young lady loses her shoe kicking up her voluminous Rococo-style skirts but made of batik fabrics, an evident ironic comment on the difficulty of the cultural coexistence of Africa and the West.
Batik is in fact a metaphor of colonial action. Identified as African, it was instead produced in Indonesia and introduced into Africa by the British only in the nineteenth century. Origin, authenticity, and identity are thus recurrent themes in the works of Shonibare, one of the finalists for the Turner Prize – awarded to Jeremy Deller – in 2004. Exhibited in the African pavilion at the 2007 Venice Biennale, the installation *How to Blow Up Two Heads at Once* shows two headless men aiming Victorian pistols at where their respective foreheads would be. Racism, the consequences of colonialism, and the question of African civil wars are present beneath the disguise of theatrical settings in which the physical protagonists have no characteristics that make them recognizable but communicate through highly colorful, fake British uniforms.
(*F.T.*)

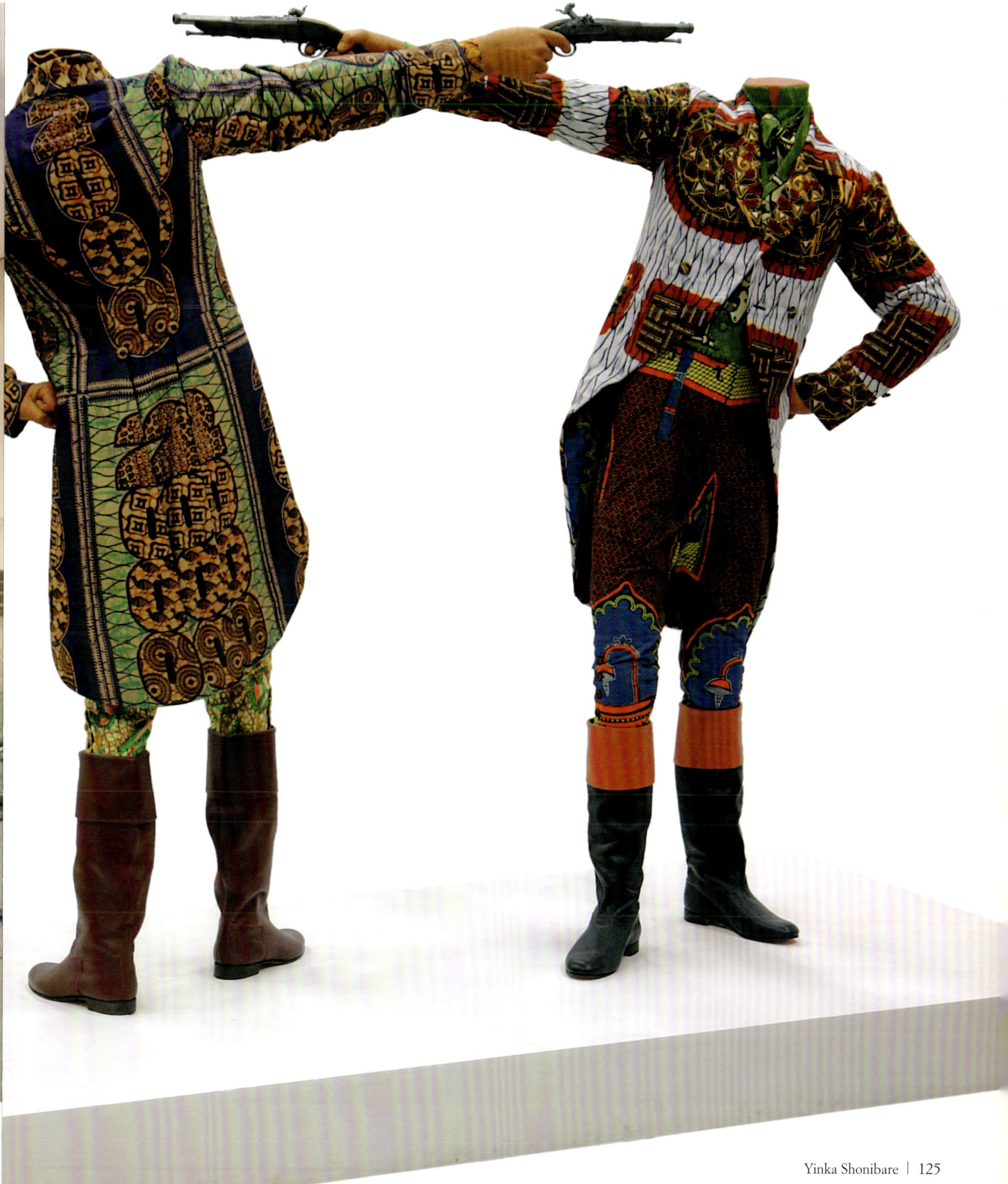

How to Blow Up Two Heads at Once, 2006
2 mannequins, African fabrics, leather shoes, 2 revolvers, 175 x 245 x 122 cm
View of the installation at the African Pavilion, LII Esposizione Internazionale d'Arte, Biennale di Venezia 2007

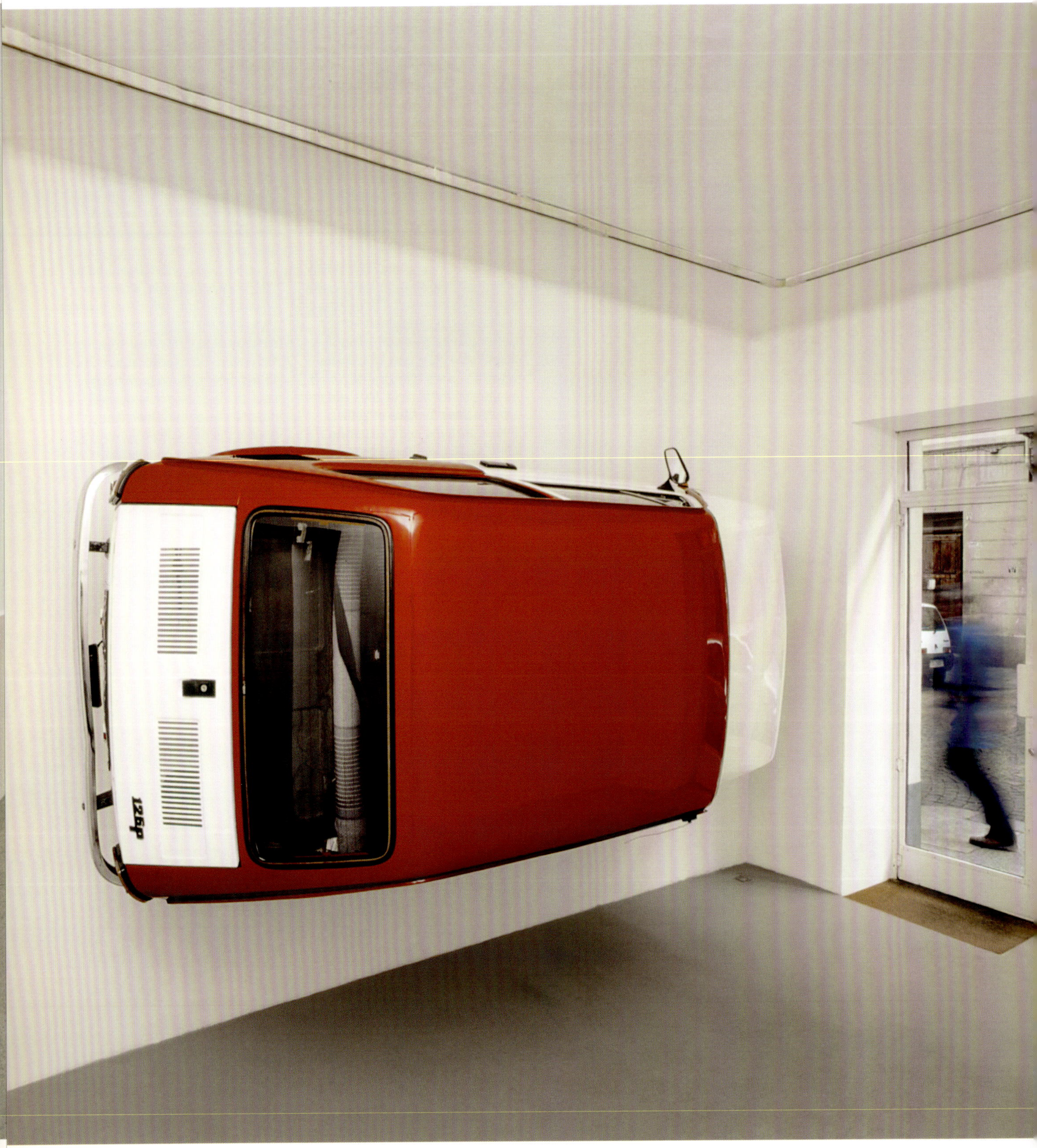
126p

Simon Starling

FLAGA (1972–2000), 2002
1974 Fiat 126, elaborated using auto body parts made and mounted in Poland after a journey of 1290 km from Turin to Cieszyn,
133 x 305 x 115 cm
Partial view of the installation at the Galleria Franco Noero, Turin
Courtesy Fondazione Sandretto Re Rebaudengo Collection, Turin

Tabernas Desert Run, 2004
Electric bicycle with various materials, glass showcase, wooden structure
View of the installation realized in 2005 at Tate Britain, London for the Turner Prize

Born in Epsom, UK, in 1967. Lives and works in Glasgow and Berlin. Simon Starling's work focuses on the element of process through the creation of documents and objects bearing witness to projects and experiences. The relationship between the artist's actions and the consequences deriving from them comes in his installations and photographs to create a circular path comprising the environment, mankind and the impact of production and technology on the world.
A finalist for the Turner Prize in 2005, Starling presented the installation *Tabernas Desert Run*, featuring the hydrogen-powered bicycle on which he had crossed the desert in the Spanish region of Andalusia. The vehicle produces no discharge harmful to the environment, only pure water, which the artist used to paint a picture of an Opuntia cactus. Starling thus highlights the difference between the resources that man and nature are capable of producing and harnessing, above all in extreme conditions.
The artist's work displays an evident focus on biological and technological cycles of production and a particular interest in highlighting the difference between human production and natural evolution in response to vital requirements.
The metaphor of travel – a recurrent element in his work – instead refers to the pathway, mutation and contamination. In addition to the recent crossing of the Andalusian desert, the English artist drove a Fiat 126 in 2002 all the way from Turin, the home of the automobile company and location of the factory in which the vehicle was manufactured until 1979, to the urban agglomerate of Cieszyn in Poland, where it was still in production in 2000. On arriving in Poland, Starling replaced the boot, bonnet and doors so that the bodywork was made up of red and white parts, colors shared by the Italian and Polish flags.
At the end of the journey, the artist exhibited the 126 mounted vertically on the wall, just like a flag.
(*F.T.*)

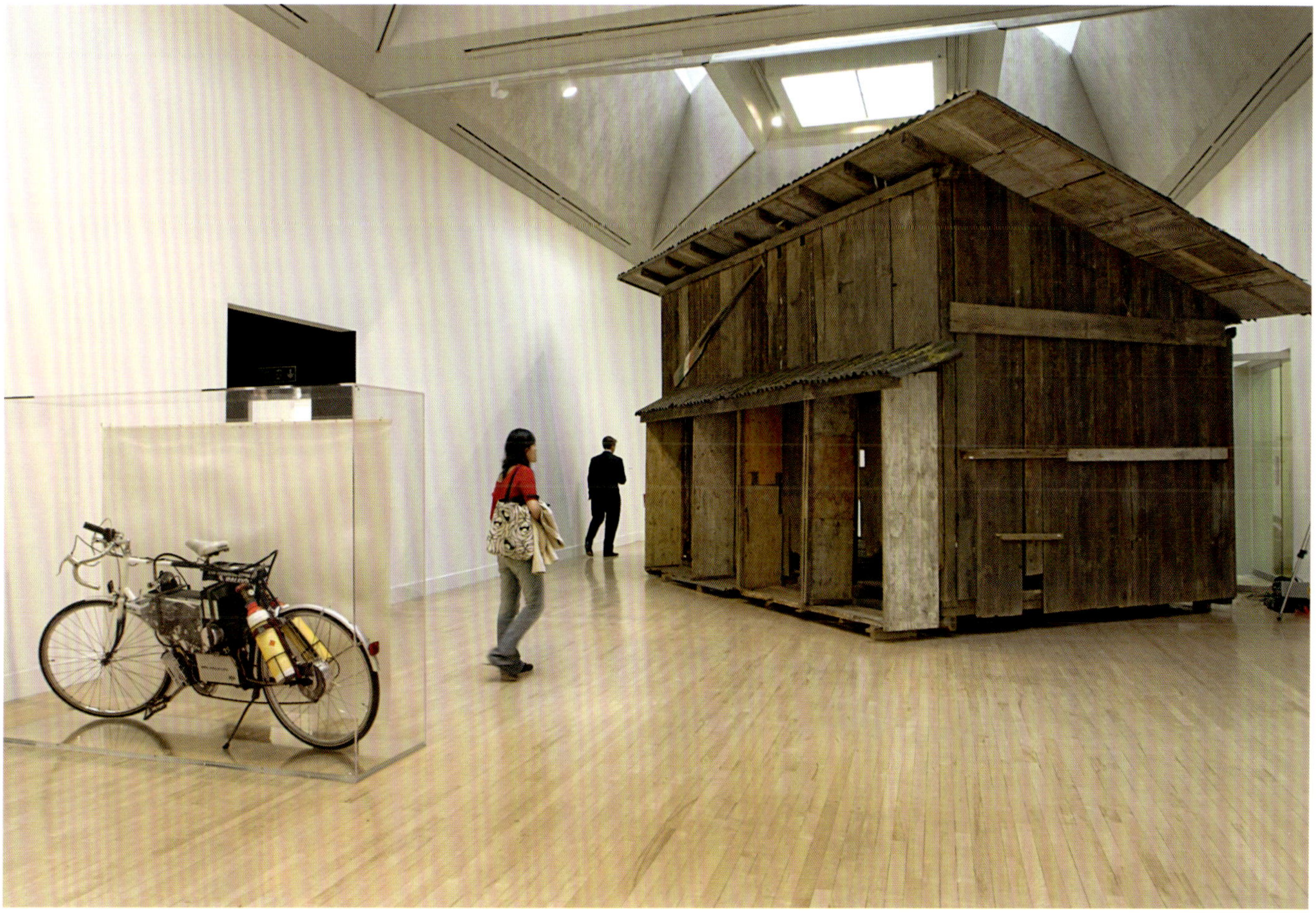

Sam Taylor-Wood

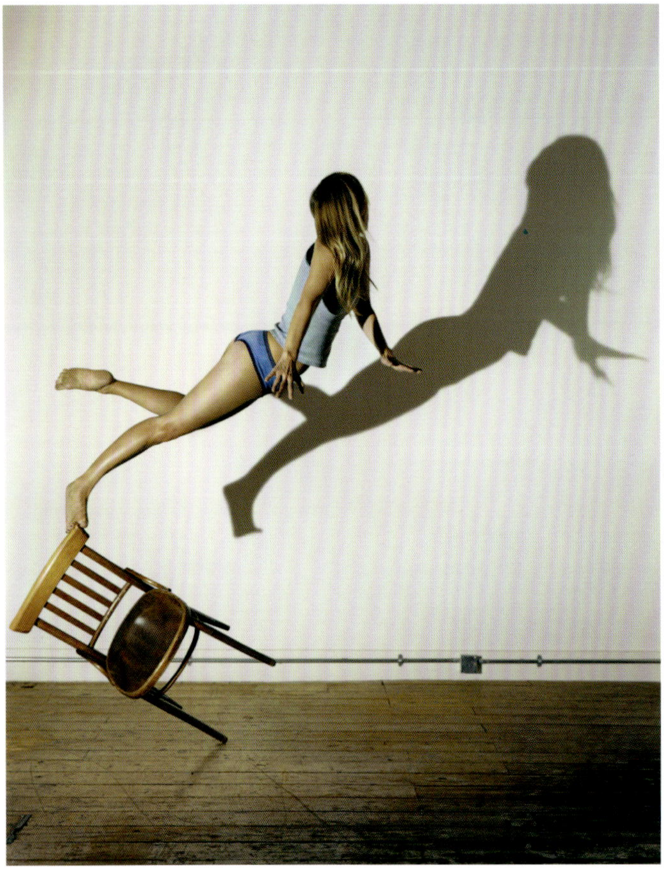

Bram Stoker's Chair VII, 2005
Color print, 121.9 x 96.5 cm
Courtesy White Cube, London

Ghosts X, 2008
Color print, 109.2 x 141 cm
Courtesy White Cube, London

Born in London in 1967. Lives and works in London.
Sam Taylor-Wood held a solo show entitled *Yes I No* in 2008 at the White Cube, Mason's Yard, in London. This included a series of photographs entitled *Ghosts* inspired by *Wuthering Heights*, the novel by Emily Brontë. In an article published on the occasion, the artist explained how she had looked in the area of the Yorkshire moors, traditionally regarded as the novel's source of inspiration, for the possibility of salvation and redemption denied to its characters. These recent photographs make it possible to distinguish a recurrent feature in the artist's works, a sort of scarlet thread connecting the photographs, videos, and installations that make up her oeuvre, namely the tendency to sketch out a story and leave it hanging, replacing the narration with exploration of the feelings and frames of mind that accompany the experiences addressed by the artist. In order to go beyond the narrative dimension, Taylor-Wood makes great use of devices serving to distance her images more or less evidently from reality, constantly reminding spectators that what they are observing is not a fragment of life but a representation with an allegorical or metaphorical purpose with respect to which they are called upon to play an active part by opening up the field of possible interpretations. The "both personal and social interest in deconstructing the scenario" frequently leads her to draw upon the history of art, above all the Renaissance, for elements of iconography and composition to present afresh in a contemporary light (*Soliloquy*, 1998). The artist also processes her photographs digitally and creates 360-degree dioramas of shots taken at regular intervals of five seconds (*Five Revolutionary Seconds*, 1995–1997). She works a great deal on the pre-production and post-production of her photographs and videos precisely in order to create particular effects of disorientation, as in the series of self-portraits entitled *Self-Portrait Suspended* and *Bram Stoker's Chair* (2004–2005), inspired by the idea of the liberation of female sexuality from the constrictions imposed by Victorian society. These called for her to hold long and exhausting poses hanging in mid-air from ropes and wires, which were then eliminated by computer processing. In the same way, the chair magically supporting her in her acrobatic "flight" has no shadow, just like Dracula.
(*L.L.*)

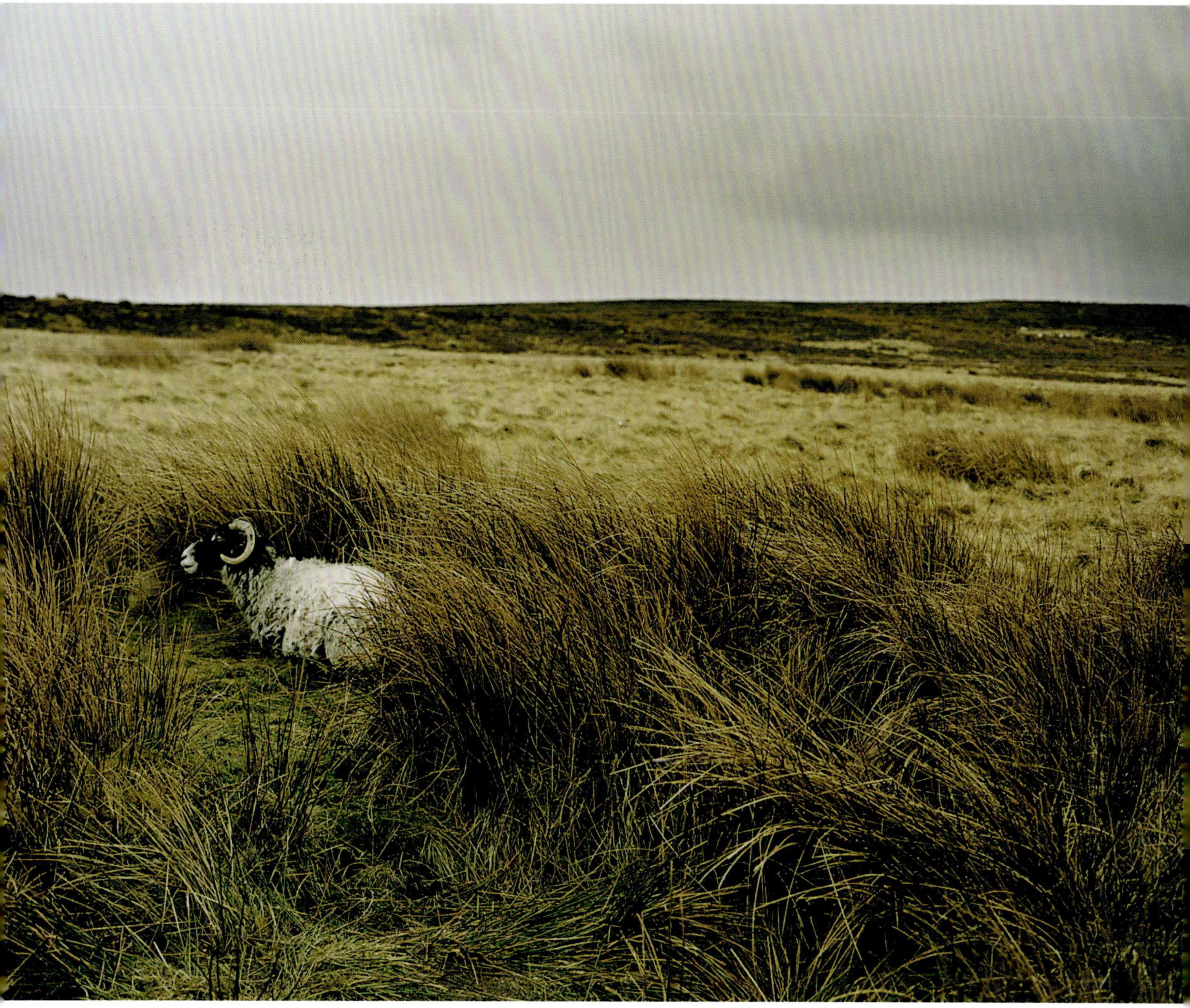

Rirkrit Tiravanija

Untitled 2002 (He Promised), 2002
Chromed stainless steel, TV
2.95 x 11.99 x 6 m
New York, Solomon R. Guggenheim Museum, Purchased with funds contributed by the International Director's Council and Executive Committee Members

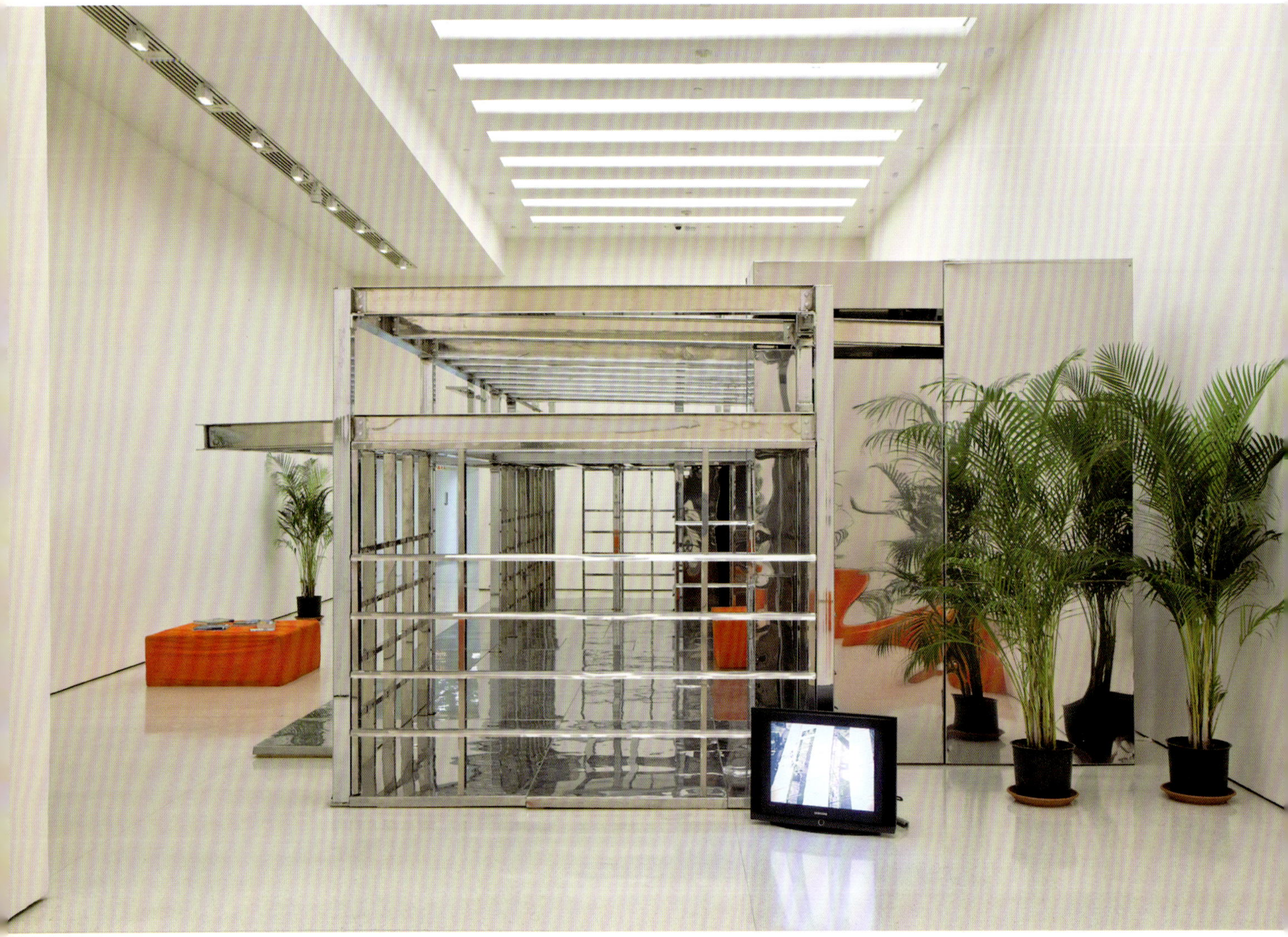

Born in Buenos Aires in 1961. Lives in New York, Berlin, and Bangkok. Rirkrit Tiravanija's work is based on the idea of cultural contamination and the unbalancing of relations that can be caused by enrichment of an expressive, cultural, and material context with elements from outside.
It is possible to recognize in his output a number of common but heterogeneously developed macro-themes. For example, food becomes a processual artistic approach to geopolitical differences and an attempt to break free of the traditional behavior expected in exhibition spaces. One of the artist's best-known actions, namely *Live and Eat, Eat and Die*, staged at the Randolph Street Gallery, Chicago, in 1993, thus consisted of setting up a kitchen and cooking for the visitors.
Untitled 2002 (He Promised), Tiravanija's winning entry for the 2004 Hugo Boss Prize, again addressed the subjects of contamination and interaction. The artist created a structure of polished steel and chrome based on the house built for Rudolf M. Schindler in West Hollywood (1921–1922), the original architectural plans of which provided for the cohabitation of a number of families and shared communal areas. Tiravanija expanded Schindler's idea so as to address contamination with his installation, which accommodated a range of public and private actions and activities including barbecues, DJ sets, film shows, and Thai massage sessions, the aim being to cross the threshold of the artistic context and offer the visitors, through their participation, a space of lived experience.
Set up during the exhibition *Luna Park. Arte Fantastica* in the grounds of Villa Manin (in Udine, Italy) in 2005, *Teahouse* was also experiential in character, consisting once again of an architectural construction in polished steel accessible to the public. The interior of this was designed, drawing inspiration from to the Eastern tea ritual, as a place to serve the visitors coffee, thus reflecting on the contamination of the different rituals of the East and the West in terms of the two beverages and their roots in two different cultures.
The issue of the social role of the television image was instead the focal point of the installation *Untitled*, created in 2005 and closely connected to the critical approach expressed in the project of the same name presented at the Hugo Boss Prize. This time Tiravanija devised a self-built, low-power TV station.

Untitled, 2005
TV antenna, DVD player, TV, cables, dimensions variable
Courtesy Galerie Chantal Crousel, Paris

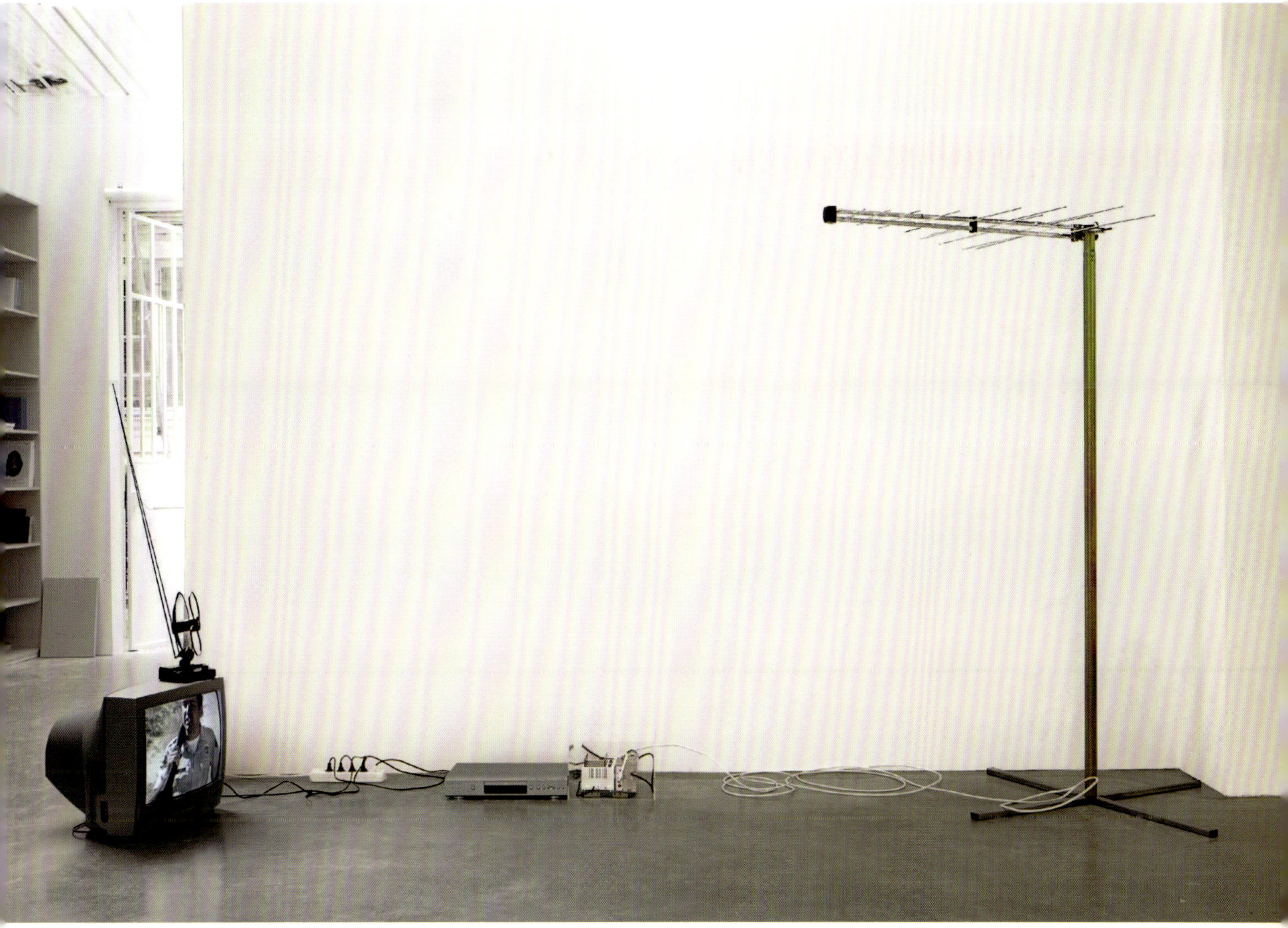

Freedom of thought is instead the starting point of the artist's most recent installation, *Foster, You're Dead*. Presented in 2008, the work highlights the great importance attached in Tiravanija's art to the development of a personal vision, a refusal to be conditioned by mass standardization, and the role of architectural design. The project was developed in collaboration with the New York architect Neil Logan as a reappraisal of the role and the *modus vivendi* of mankind in an historical period strongly characterized by the need to possess a place of safety and protection, such as an atomic shelter.

Drawing inspiration from the science-fiction story *Foster, You're Dead*, written by Philip K. Dick in 1955, and placing it physically inside the scene, Tiravanija and Logan reconstructed the interior of an American home of the late 1950s. The space is divided into two areas, namely an entrance with two tables, on which pieces of jigsaw puzzles depicting atomic mushroom clouds are scattered, and an adjacent room with an encased seat, in front of which a video shows a child reading Dick's story.
The lack of human presence manifests itself here in the interrupted, incomplete state of things, the replacement of physicality with an electronic image, and the depersonalization of the space through the absence of any sign of life. As with the main character of Dick's story, the fear of death and an awareness that there is no way out become omnipresent and obsessive elements that haunt the domestic space and are materialized in repeated images constructed, like the puzzle, by the human mind.
(*F.T.*)

Teahouse, 2005
Steel
View of the installation realized in 2005 at the Centro d'Arte Contemporanea Villa Manin, Codroipo
Courtesy Galerie neugerriemschneider, Berlin

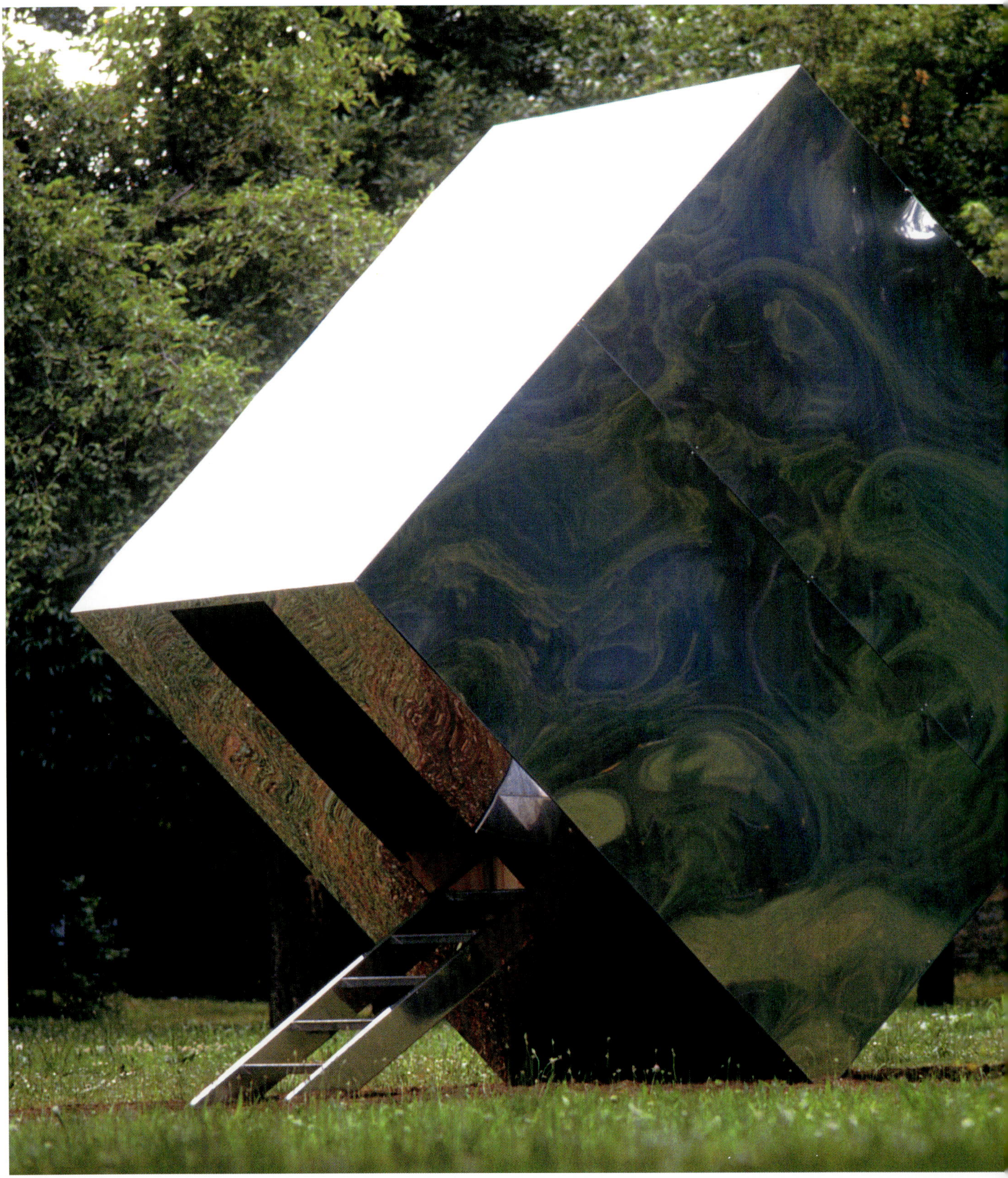

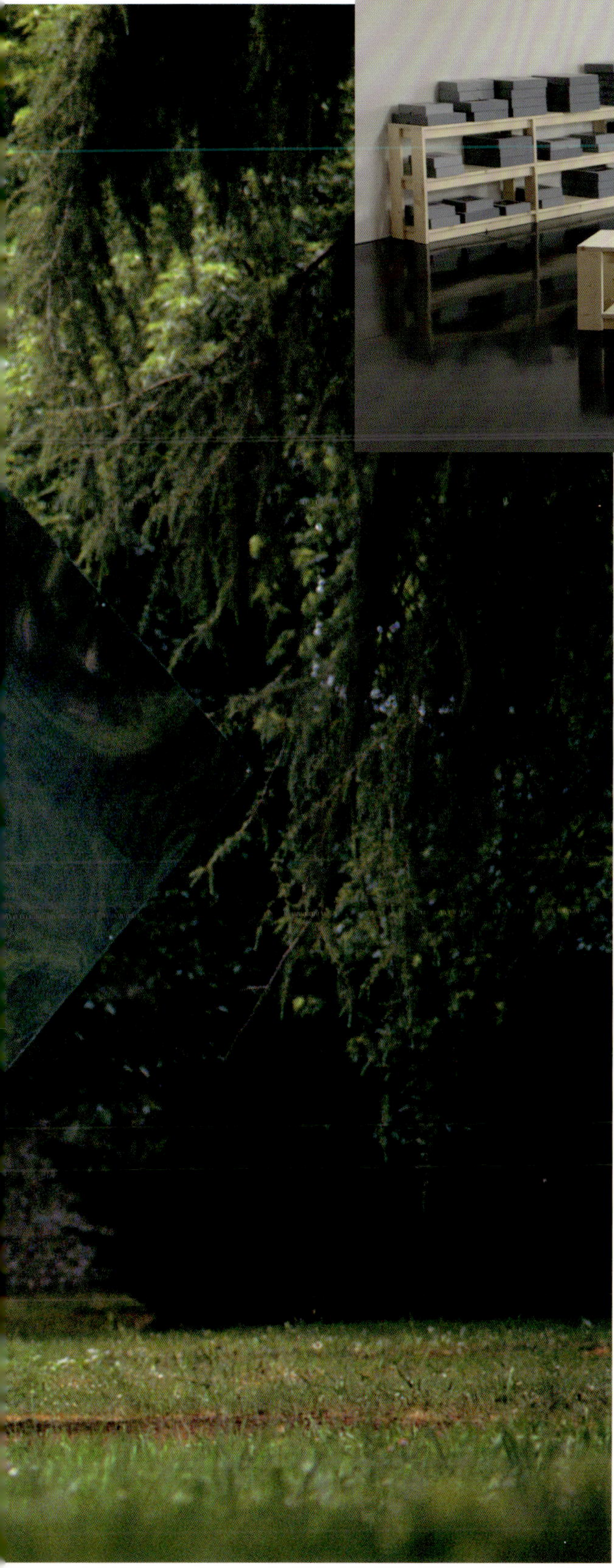

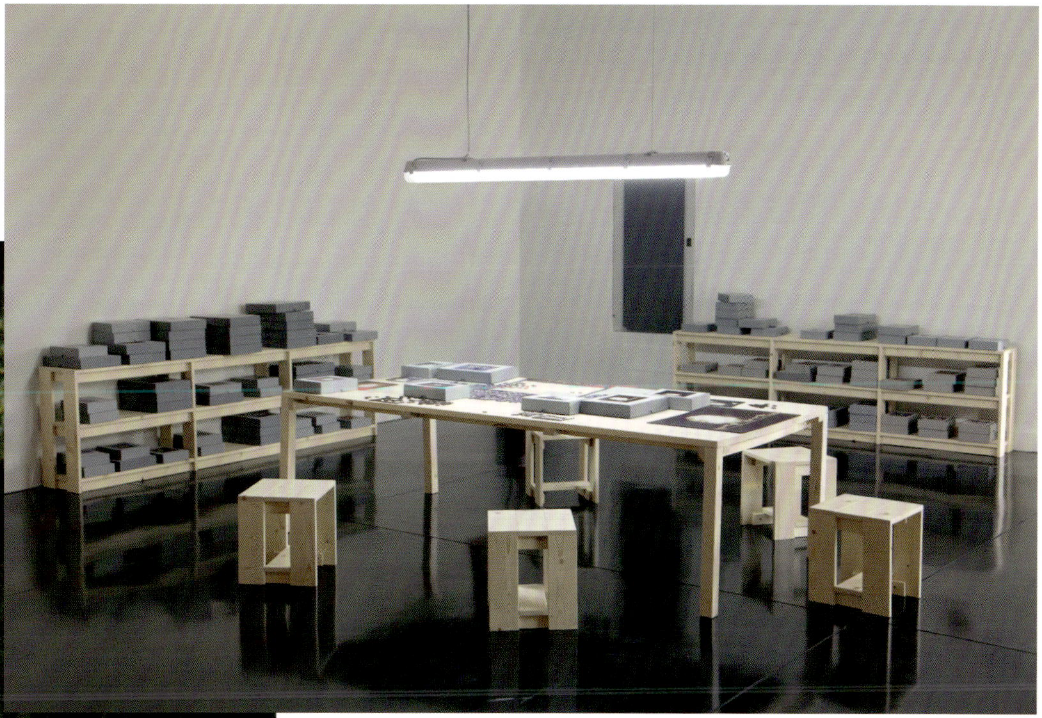

Foster, You're Dead, 2000
Wood furniture and mixed media, dimensions variable
View of the installation realized in 2009 at the MACRO – Museo d'Arte Contemporanea di Roma, Rome

Rosemarie Trockel

Born in Schwerte, Germany, in 1952. Lives and works in Cologne. Famous above all for the *Strickbilder* or "knitted pictures" of the early 1980s and the later woolen objects transformed into sculptures (*The Mystery of Malpica*, 1992), Rosemarie Trockel is actually a multifaceted artist who uses sculpture, video, installation, drawing, and other media to address issues connected with the social and political role of women. While her work is diversified also in the choice of subject matter, it is possible to find one constant feature: nothing is what it appears to be. The knitted works instinctively associated by the public with patient housewives and knitting needles are actually produced by industrial machinery on the basis of computer-generated patterns. In the same way, the blocks and slabs of lacquered metal fitted with black electrical hotplates of different sizes are not simple sculptures but ideal "Minimalist cookers" that the artist, playing with the stereotype of the "woman slaving over a hot stove", uses polemically to "invade" the male-dominated territory of Donald Judd, Robert Morris, and company (*Untitled*, 2000). The same ironic and challenging attitude underlies Trockel's recent combination of the rigorous standards of "virile" Minimalist sculpture with the female love of gardening at the Münster Skulptur Projekte in 2007. In a work of topiary that she insisted on having placed next to a sculpture by Judd, two hedges of yew were "sculpted" like wood, stone or metal to form two enormous monoliths (7 meters long, 4 high, and 3 wide) with just enough space between them to provide a view of Lake Aa.

Another constant element, intimately bound up with the artist's ironclad determination to refute any form of preconceived idea, is the idea of metamorphosis, transformation, and the flow of life. This has featured in her work from the "dance" of poisonous insects in the video *Parade* (1993) to the recent anthological exhibition *Menopause*, presented at the Ludwig Museum, Cologne, in 2005 and the MAXXI, Rome, in the spring of 2006.

The title of the show is in itself an explicit reference to the transition from one biological condition to another, the crucial moment in the life of every woman that inevitably marks a "before" and an "after", and regards not only the possibility of giving birth but also the need to find new creative fertility (*Atlas*, 2001).

(*P.V.*)

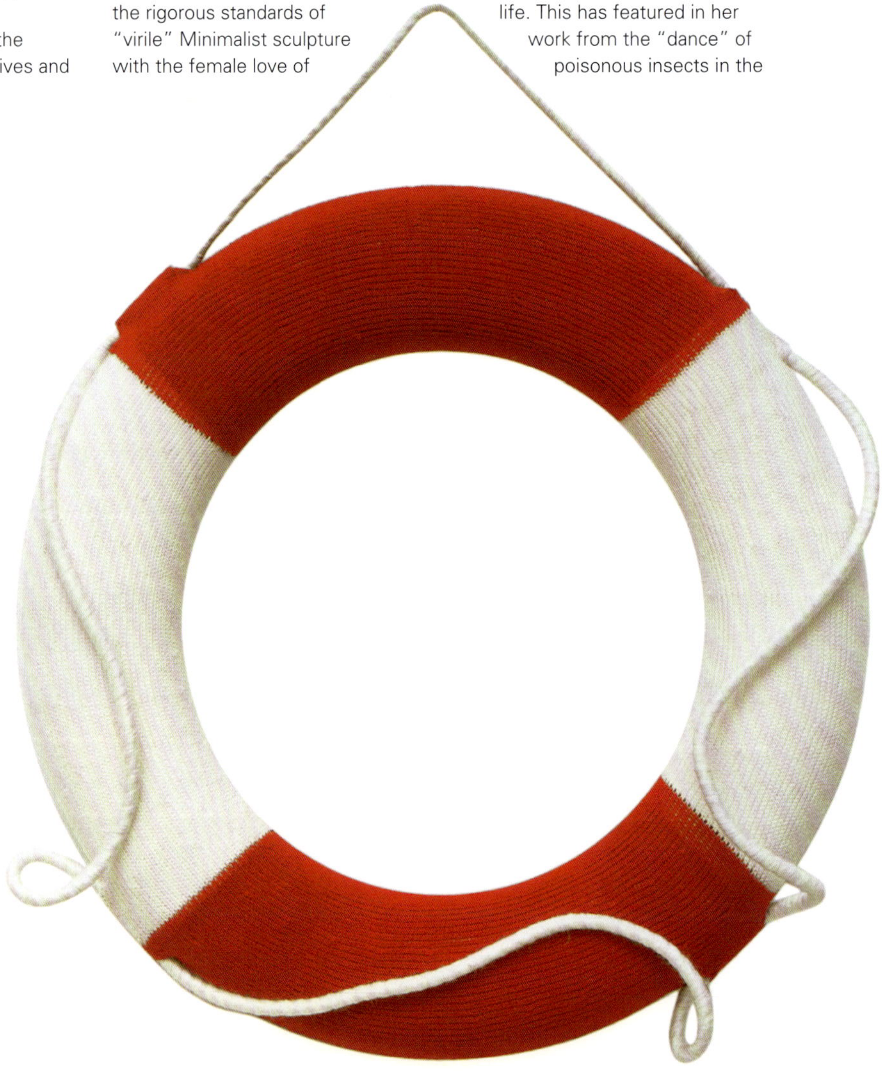

The Mystery of Malpica, 1992
Life belt covered in wool knit,
ø 80 cm
Courtesy Le Case d'Arte, Milan

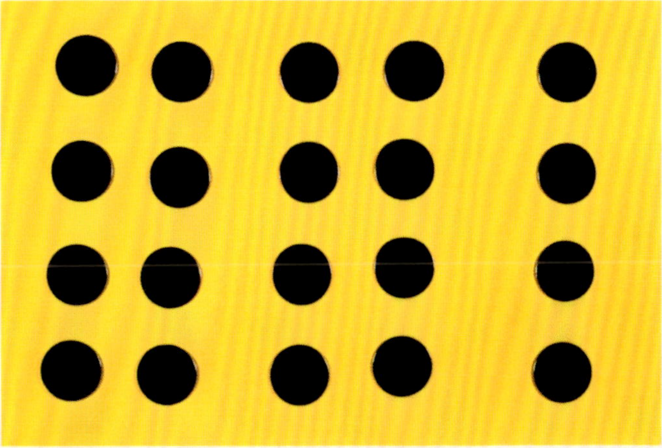

Untitled, 2000
Powder paint on aluminum,
20 electric hotplates,
172 x 260 x 11.3 cm
Courtesy MAXXI_Museo nazionale delle arti del XXI secolo, Rome

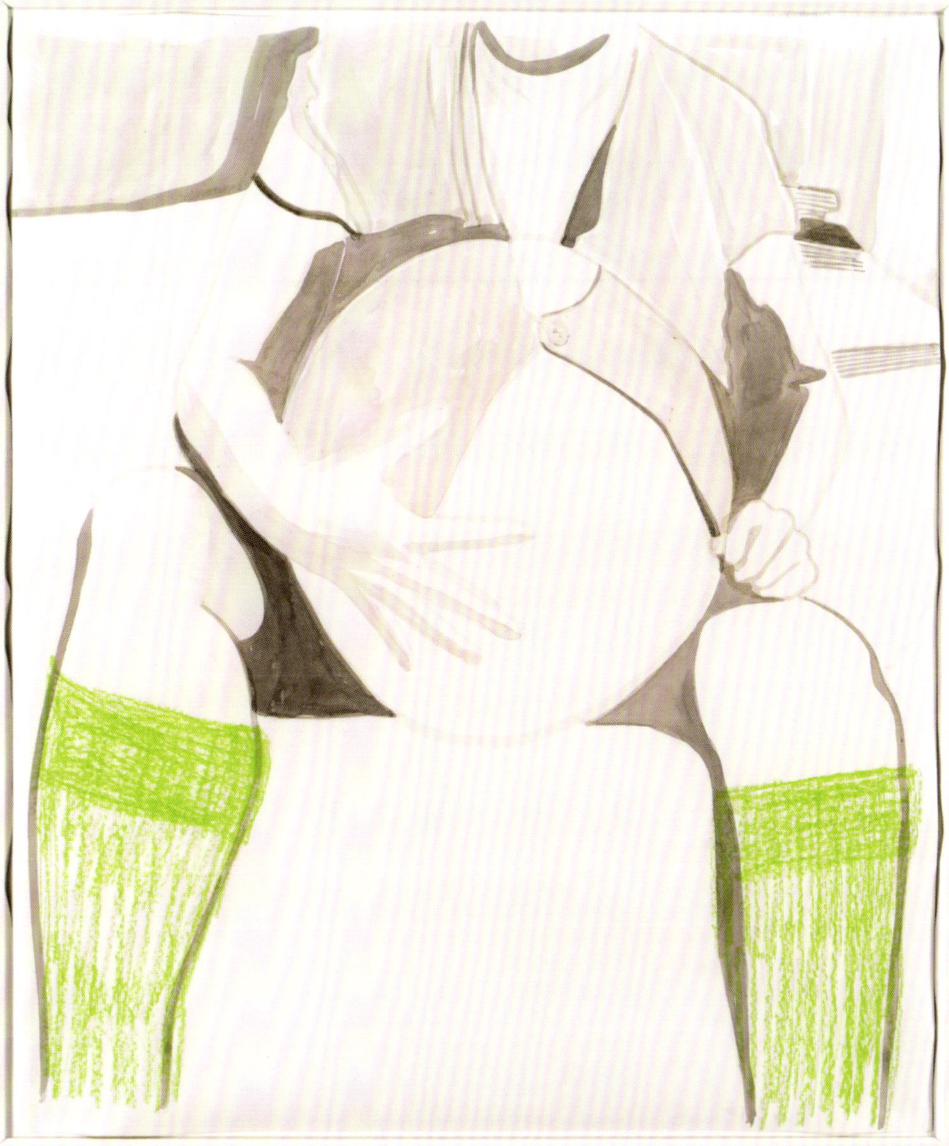

Atlas, 2001
Acrylic and pastel on paper,
57.15 x 49.53 cm
Minneapolis, Walker Art Center,
Miriam and Erwin Kelen Acquisition Fund for Drawings

Cesare Viel

Lost in Meditation, 1999–2001
Photograph (from performance, installation with audio), 86 x 120 cm
Genoa, Sergio Bertola Collection

Mi gioco fino in fondo, 2008
Rug of pure Himalayan wool, hand-woven, 180 x 295 cm
Genoa, Galleria Pinksummer

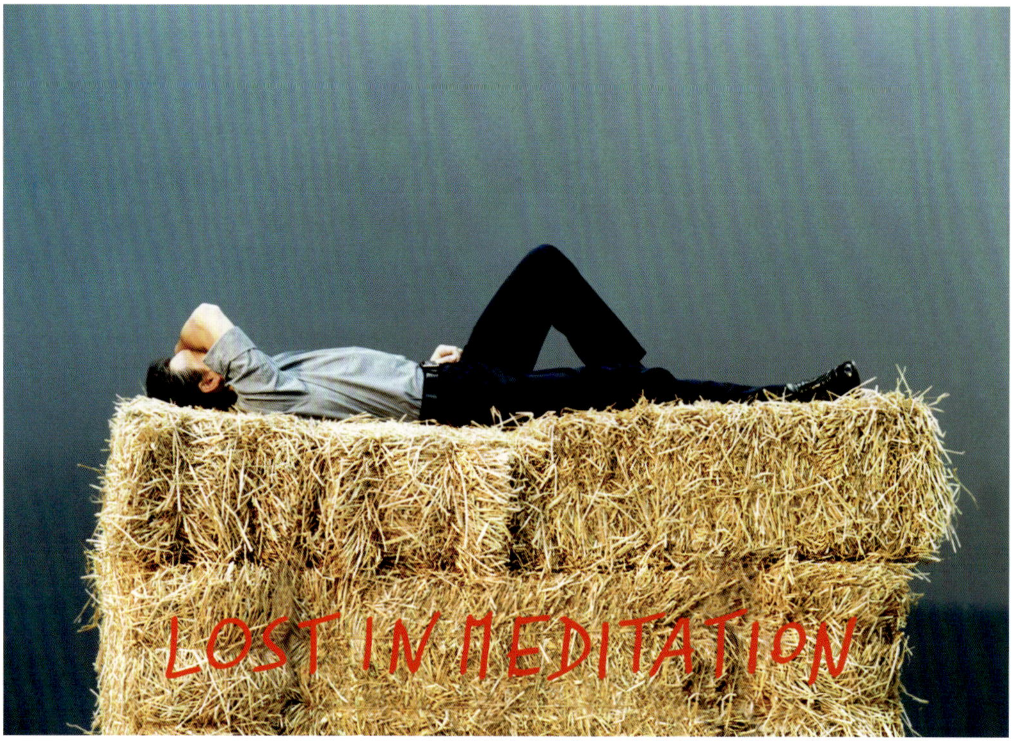

Born in Chivasso, Italy, in 1964. Lives and works in Genoa.
Cesare Viel adopts a constantly "subjective" approach in that it is precisely his view of the world, others, and himself that orients and determines his work as a whole, be it writing, drawing (a medium he finds most congenial), performance, installation, video or photography.
Writing has always been the artist's faithful companion. In the conceptual works of the early 1990s his elegant hand set the flow of his thoughts down on paper, presenting the viewer/reader with reflections on our way of being, communicating, and listening, not infrequently becoming an almost tautological tool to probe the problems of language itself (*Noi gestiamo il disordine quotidiano del pensiero*, 1990; *Scrivi la tua frase sulla molteplicità*, 1992).
The practice of writing has since developed in a range of directions, combining with images and drawings, turning into vocal recitation and song, and becoming action within the framework of performances. At the same time, the subjects addressed have broadened and diversified, albeit without any loosening of their ties with the artist's personal experience and emotional and existential dimension: the journey, real or metaphorical, as a condition of defamiliarization, discovery of oneself and others or stimulus for the invention of stories about anonymous fragments of everyday life (*Viaggiatori/Viaggiatrici*, 1994; *Short Stories*, 1995); the diary as a way of traversing personal and collective time and "repositioning" present-day events so as to preserve them from the manipulation typical of the system of global communications (*Diario contemporaneo*, work in progress, since 2003); interpretation of the exhibition space as an inner place that is open and modifiable (*Una stanza per sé*, 1997); encounters with poets and writers – including Ingeborg Bachmann, Emily Dickinson, Virginia Woolf, Cesare Pavese, Dino Campana and Paul Auster – as an opportunity to approach their work from different angles or assume their identity in actions and performances (*To the Lighthouse. Cesare Viel as Virginia Woolf*, 2004–2005).
Viel has assumed different identities on various occasions or allowed other people – frequently women – to alter and multiply their own. He has also developed a continuous osmosis of experiences, memories and emotions with the public, as in the performance *Lost in Meditation* (1999–2001), where the artist lies for a long time on a heap of hay, thus prompting spectators to free their thoughts and relive a childhood game. It is in fact important for Viel that the action should be susceptible of repetition by the public, which makes it possible for works born as performance to eliminate the bodily presence of the artist and turn into installations. This is what happens, for example, in *Mi gioco fino in fondo* (2008), where the rug on which Viel improvised dedications to the public at the opening of his recent anthological exhibition at the Museo d'Arte Contemporanea di Villa Croce, Genoa, remains to invite spectators – once again through the written word – to undertake the journey of self-discovery into the depths of their being.
(*P.V.*)

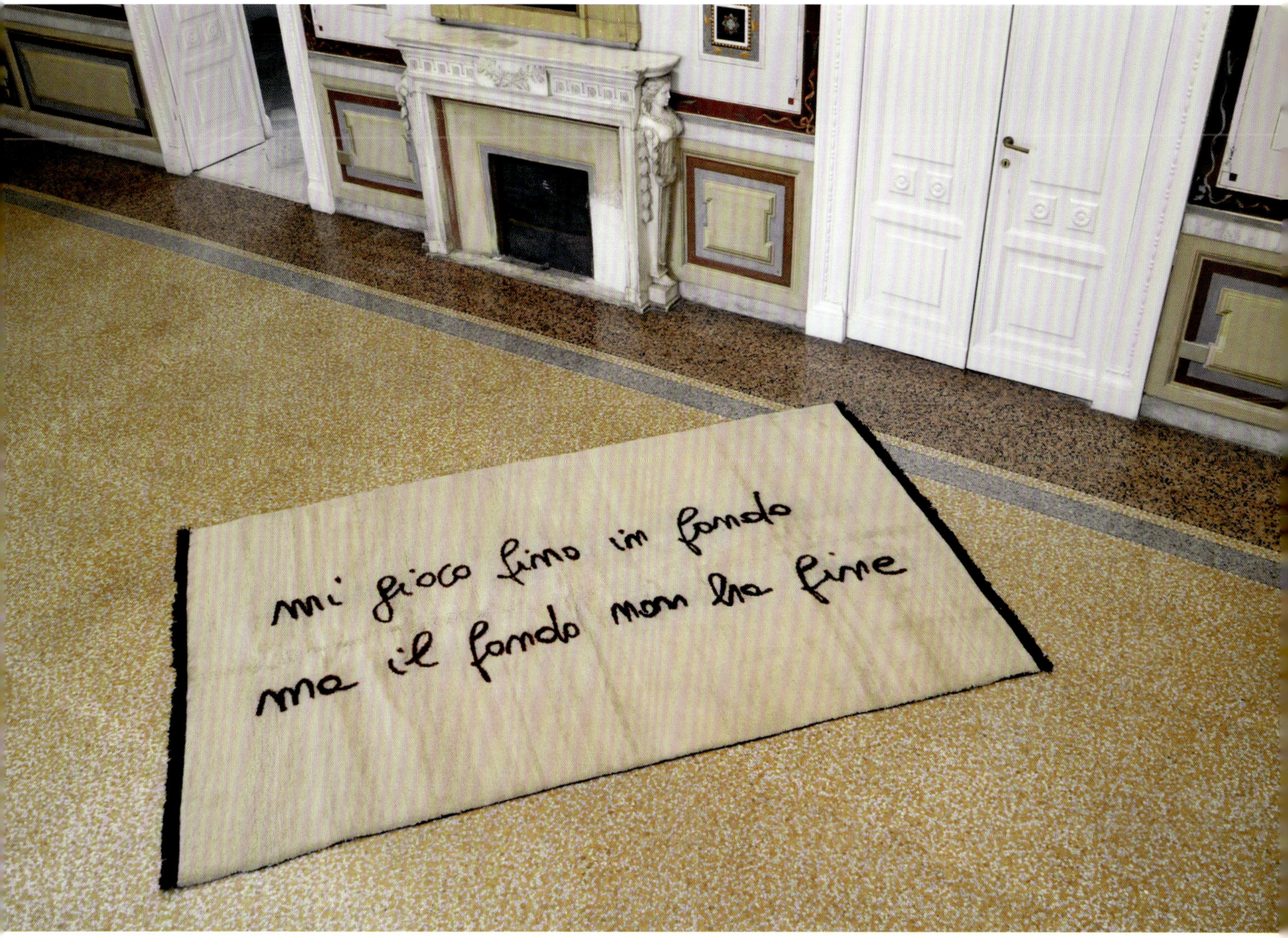
mi gioco fino in fondo
ma il fondo non ha fine

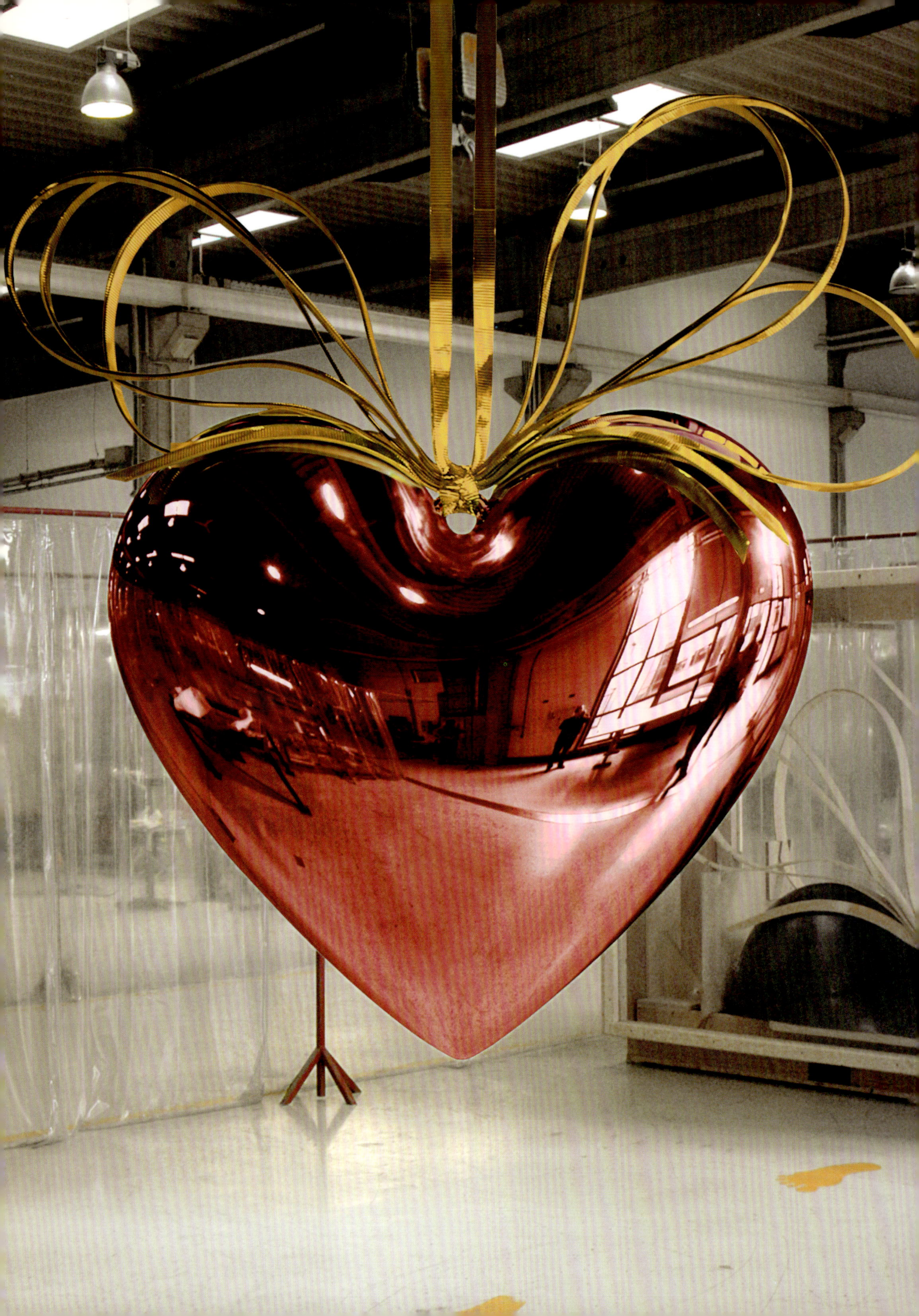

Klaus Honnef

Critics of Contemporary Art

Art has never been more varied and multiform. At the beginning of the twenty-first century it appears as a sort of primordial chaos encompassing the most disparate movements, the styles of the most different eras, the most heterogeneous media and the most diversified and sometimes contrasting aesthetic ideals and forms of expression. It is as though an immense whirlwind had sucked all the works of art of all the world's museums up into its spiral. Paintings, sculptures, objects, drawings, photographs, films and installations all compete to attract the public's attention like goods displayed on the shelves of a huge supermarket.

Meanwhile, the offerings of the temples of commerce and consumption have come increasingly to resemble items from the world of art. Apart from scale, the aesthetic differences appear somewhat negligible to the hurried, preoccupied gaze of modern mankind. It is no coincidence that many works of art, reduced to souvenir size, play a similar function as decorative and superfluous "consumer goods" in crowded museum shops all over the world. Regardless of whether its size is that of a skyscraper or a key ring, Jeff Koons's bizarre *Puppy* makes no particular demands on the intellect and knowledge. And this is independent of its form.

The fact that Jeff Koons is one of the two megastars on the contemporary art scene – which continues to profit from the revolutionary glory attached to the members of the heroic avant-garde of a century ago – is highly significant, as is the fact that an expression borrowed from the world of cinema is used to indicate his status. The second megastar is Damien Hirst. These artists, one American and the other British, are popular to the same extent with the public and critics. They reign supreme in the art market – which in fact itself boosts their fame considerably in a society moulded by the mass media – and their shows in museums and galleries are invariably blockbusters. By comparison with this sensational success, the rare negative or disparaging remarks made by critics are like the twittering of a few birds in the din of a great metropolis. The enormous impact of the two artists' works is largely due to a number of external factors. On the one hand, they are spectacular, large-sized and brightly colored, glossy, shiny and glittering, sometimes with grotesque overtones. On the other, they are simple works and therefore easily recognizable. On closer examination, they even open up a critical perspective or horizon in that they present an undemanding form of entertainment and at the same time blatantly subvert its rules, so that the spectacle inevitably plunges into absurdity. Covered all over in flowers, Koons's gigantic *Puppy* reveals the monstrosity lurking beneath what is cute and pretty. Damien Hirst's decision in the autumn of 2008 to bypass the customary channels of the art market and put his latest objects and paintings directly up for auction represented a frontal attack on the traditional system of galleries. By an ironic twist of history, he was proved right. The decision was taken on the very eve of the collapse of the international financial market, the primary driving force behind the boom of contemporary art.

While the works of Koons and Hirst, symptomatic expressions of a society founded on outward appearances and narcissistic self-love, are headline news in the major mass media, they are not the only ones to make a splash in this great vanity fair of art. It would be all too easy to formulate a diagnosis in this case. The situation is, however, far more complex because their elaborate installations exist alongside diametrically opposite forms of artistic expression that have so far proved significantly more ambitious, at least if we leave aside the variables of prestige and success. Examples include the "retrospective" paintings of Lucian Freud, Neo Rauch and Elizabeth Peyton, the accentuatedly abstract paintings of Gerhard Richter, the ever-changing paintings of Sigmar Polke with subjects from the world of comics, the paraphrases of art history of Jasper Johns, the oppressive corporeal works of Louise Bourgeois, the wall paintings of Sol LeWitt and the wall printings of Lawrence Weiner, the great photographs of Jeff Wall, Cindy Sherman and Andreas Gursky, the vivid shots taken for the press by professional photographers like Peter Lindbergh

Jeff Koons
Hanging Heart, 1994–2006
Chromed stainless steel with color coating, 269.2 x 215.9 x 101.6 cm
View of the production made in 2006 at the Arnold AG, Friedrichsdorf Foundry, Germany
Venice, François Pinault Collection

and David LaChapelle, not forgetting the video-dossals of Nam June Paik and Bill Viola, the gripping installations of Doug Aitken and Monica Bonvicini, the cinematographic works of David Lynch, Wim Wenders and Julian Schnabel, and the art films of Sharon Lockhart and Douglas Gordon. These are just some of the many celebrated artists whose position appears both emblematic and in need of clarification in the context of the now disappearing wake left by avant-garde art.

What is it that these artists have in common, apart from the fact that their works, together with those of many others not listed here, were produced in the period spanning the two centuries? In actual fact, the only thing they share is a concept, the concept of art.

No concept has assumed such an absolute sense in this new century as art, even though the word is often used in English and other languages in relation to activities and areas that have more to do with skills, as in references to the "art" of cooking or wine-making. In the context of a gentle transition of modern art to a subsequent and as yet indeterminate phase, the concept of art even seems to have been elevated above the historical dimension. Art now seems to have no need of any basis whatsoever in order to distinguish itself as such from other social and cultural phenomena. Art is solely and simply art and its concept seems impervious to all change.

On the other hand, opinions on what is to be considered a work of art appear to differ completely in concrete terms, and these divergences prove to be connected in particular with differences in social class and generation. Not to mention the idiocies fuelled by the various cultural horizons and traditions coexisting at the global level. The formation of aesthetic judgment has also undergone a process of differentiation and individualization in step with the value horizon of the pluralistic societies.

In a paradoxical phenomenon of reversal, however, it can be noted that the once clear-cut differences have gradually blurred and opinions have converged so that the relations between them are like a sort of elaborate "glissando" of subtle nuances, which nevertheless leaves intact the possibility of drawing conclusions about the origins and social positions of their advocates. At the same time, through the law of communicating vessels, there has been a marked increase in the number of solemn declarations calling for a more serious attitude in the field of art.

The more open-ended the concept of art appears, the more it eludes normative definition and the more impregnable its realm proves. The works of art appearing on the markets of Moscow, Shanghai and Dubai are not essentially different in terms of type and aesthetics from those to be seen in New York, London, Basel or Berlin. With the due exceptions, it can be said that it is always the same works and the same artists that dominate the market and the public and private museums of the five continents. It is always the same superstars and megastars that hog the limelight on the art scene. While the names sometimes change, the objects and phenomena declared "works of art" are so similar – despite a superficial veneer of variety and multiformity – as to be mistaken for one another. The first conclusion to be drawn from this is that the market welcomes this phenomenon gladly because it is symptomatic of the internationalization of the contemporary artistic vocabulary, in which an important need of modernity is finally met. Together with technological and scientific know-how, the conception of art typical of the western hemisphere has in fact also imposed itself in the eastern. Nor is this process in any way impeded by the fact that the eastern cultures have in the meantime overtaken their models by improving their application of technological and scientific instruments in pursuit of their interests in worldwide competition.

Just as the non-European industrial and post-industrial cultures have appropriated the tools and results of the West, a burning desire for success has led their aspiring artists to sever the umbilical cord connecting them to their cultural roots and accept the dominant models of Western contemporary art. In the light of this situation, it is hardly surprising that success has also come to some artists attempting an ambitious reconciliation of the now vanished traditions of the individual cultures as well as artists who, like the Kabakovs, have adopted the strategy of combining different cultural contents but in such way that the contradictions appear to be preserved.

The habit of reviling art as something purely arbitrary – a field where "anything goes" – is now fairly widespread among critics of contemporary culture. The basis of this view is the idea that everything boils down to declaring a given phenomenon a work of art, be it a rubbish dump, a con-

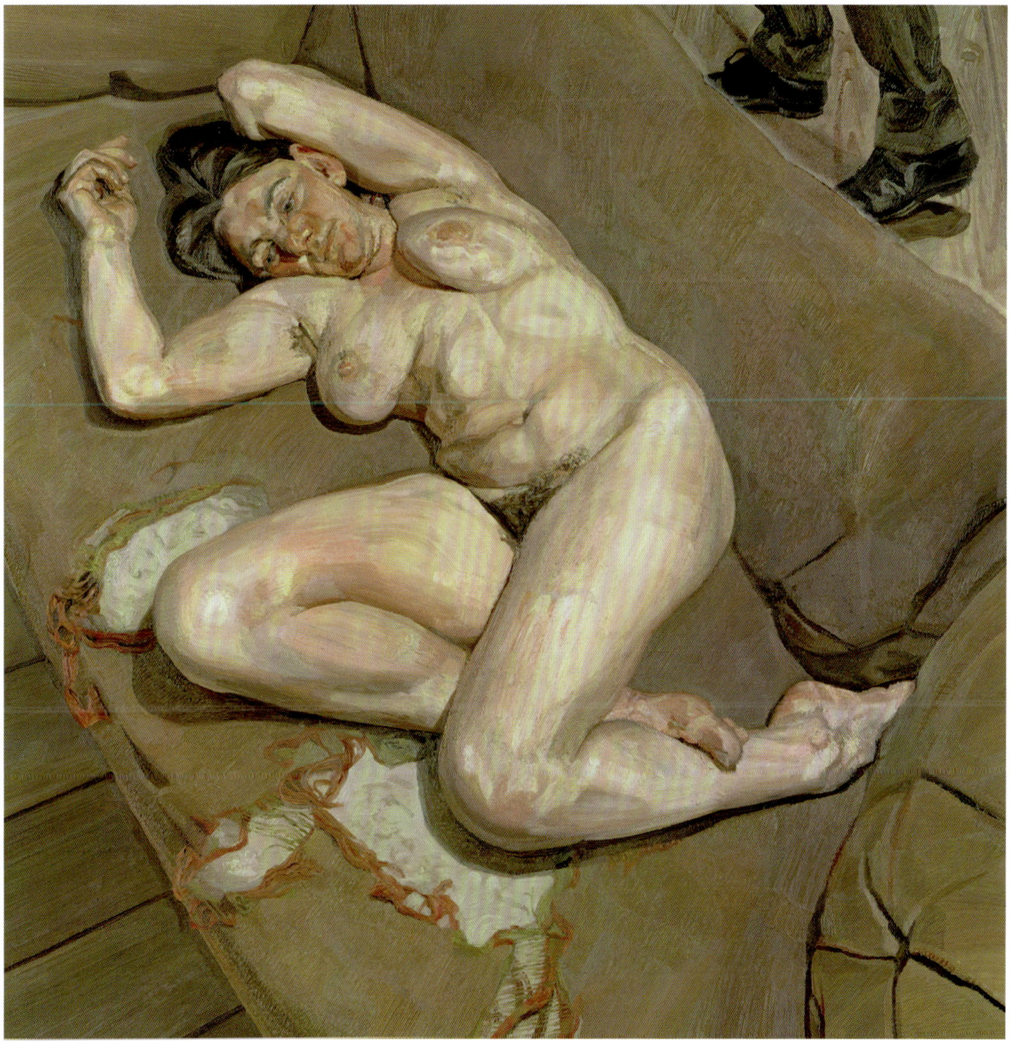

Lucian Freud
Naked Portrait with Reflection, 1980
Oil on canvas, 90.3 x 90.3 cm
Private collection

sumer article, a tawdry trinket, a fashion, a comic strip, a film, a bad painting or a reworked painting.

Ever since Marcel Duchamp placed a urinal on the pedestal of art in 1913, the traditional criteria of aesthetic judgment have given way to new and ever-changing parameters, mostly driven and indeed strengthened by the metaphysics of progress. The necessary sounding board was found in a constantly expanding conception of the museum, even though in negative terms the new position of the museum was confirmed and consolidated also by the most extreme and challenging manifestations of avant-garde art. As an institution concentrating within itself the ideals of bourgeois culture, the museum ended up gathering together the "works of art" of the history of the "West" and subjecting them to the egalitarian imperative in force in the unified and uniform realm of "art". And it did so regardless of the fact that these works had already been endorsed by history. When the avant-garde artists discovered "primitive" art for their own use and consumption, the rooms of this new museum also came to house the works of African, Asian and South American cultures, but in such a way as to reduce their existence to an inventory of pure forms or objects of aesthetically oriented observation. The visionary André Malraux gave the new institution its definitive conceptual structure with his "imaginary museum". For as long as the museum successfully performed the role of the primary channel of information and mediation in the field of art, it also supplied the context within which the requirements of aesthetic quality were defined and value judgments were formulated in both affirmative and negative terms. In this sense, the museum of modern art performed an exemplary function and one of extraordinary influence for a long time, vigorously putting into practice Ad Reinhardt's dictum: "Art is art. Everything else is everything else."

This situation underwent radical change in 1968. Contrary to what one might suppose, the cause is not to be found in the stu-

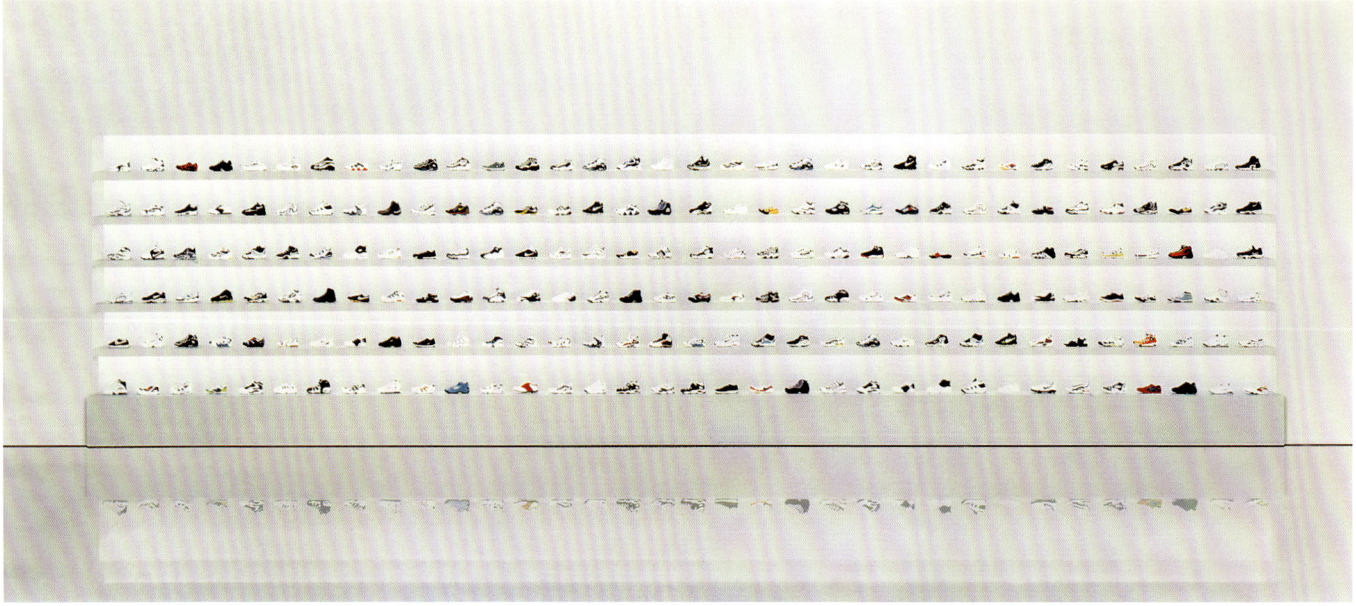

Andreas Gursky
Untitled V, 1997
Color Coupler print, 185.5 x 442.6 cm
Venice, François Pinault Collection

dent revolt that spread on both sides of the Atlantic but in the organization of the first art market by the "progressive galleries" of Cologne, an event that sprang from explicitly commercial aims and assumptions but made a considerable contribution to increasing the popularity of contemporary art. The success of this forum in achieving its objectives lay in offering a free, open market with absolutely no restrictions on access, whereas the European art market had previously been characterized by great discretion and the fact that all the transactions took place behind closed doors.

The adoption of the term "progressive" for these galleries also served to indicate the direction in which they were headed. The aim was not to give greater visibility to the mainstream expressions of contemporary art that, from Art Informel to Geometric Constructivism, were plunging ever deeper into monotonous conformism without ever having been truly popular. On the contrary, attention was focused on the most advanced trends in contemporary art, such as Pop Art, Op Art, monochromatic painting and Minimalism; in short, forms of expression that traditional aesthetic thinking still refused to recognize as works of art on the grounds that they were too banal and too closely connected with decorative functions.

The extremely elitist world of art mobilized all the resources at its disposal against the admittance of hitherto completely overlooked phenomena to its preserve (which also suggested the possibility of a new genealogical structure of modern art). The ramparts of an all-out defense of consolidated aesthetic conceptions were manned by the old guard of art historians, who had always been horrified by any intrusion of the contemporary scene into the artistic precincts, together with advocates of the absolute autonomy of art. The latter included such influential critics as Clement Greenberg and Robert Rosenblum, who saw the work as something emerging in total independence from the lowland of society to soar in the pure empyrean. They all drew, however, from the same source, namely German idealism and romanticism.

Pop Art was the lever that turned the world of art completely upside down. The offspring of the mass media and advertising, its iconography served the purposes of sales or entertainment in everyday life. Its message was easy to grasp and assimilate. Together with the iconographic repertoire, it incorporated all the mechanisms, affectation and glamour of the commercial world, including the star system.

The leading figures in Pop Art came from the world of advertising, comics and caricature. While some had studied art, the role of third-generation Abstract Expressionists brought them no success. Andy Warhol, the most emblematic representative of Pop Art, had been a celebrity on Madison Avenue, the headquarters of the great advertising agencies in Manhattan, before becoming the megastar of the industry of contemporary art that was to change its face radically. As early as 1939, the year when Nazi Germany triggered the outbreak of World War II, Clement Greenberg described Pop Art's primary source of inspiration as kitsch in a well-known essay: "popular, commercial art and literature with their chromeotypes, magazine covers, illustrations, slick ads and pulp fiction, comics, Tin Pan Alley music, tap dancing, Hollywood movies, etc., etc."[1] On the occasion of a symposium organized by the New York Museum of Modern Art in September 1962, the majority of the influential American and British critics attending denied the phenomenon of Pop Art any artistic quality whatsoever. Nearly all of them agreed that Pop artists did no more than copy their models from the universe of consumer goods, advertising, comics and newspapers. The objections raised by the young curator Henry Geldzahler, the only supporter of Pop Art at the symposium, who drew attention to the artists' creative handling of the visual vocabulary of advertising, were considered irrelevant. Dore Ashton retorted caustically that you would need a magnifying glass to see this.

The defenders of *pure* art were right. It is sometimes the opponents of change rather than its supporters that are more farsighted in discerning the breadth and implication of the processes underway. Close contact with the symbols and images of a mass culture of consumption resulted in the lasting contamination – or fertilization, depending on one's point of view – of an art whose conceptual foundations were informed by the humanistic philosophy of Immanuel Kant. In order to define the essence of an aesthetic judgment, the philosopher had introduced a rigorous distinction between aesthetic and sensual pleasure, or rather between "disinterested pleasure" as the only adequate criterion of aesthetic value and the "interest of the senses", to be more precise. The latter would be connected with what is "pleasant" and confined to the category of pleasurability as satisfaction of the senses. Closer examination shows that Pop Art took deeply altered social conditions as its starting point for a return to forms of artistic expression that the avant-garde had radically rejected.

Eighty years after the publication of Greenberg's memorable essay, this alleged kitsch has triumphed over "art as art" all down the line. In the polyphonic catalogue of criticism, there is now not a single discipline that does not figure in some respects as an object or indeed an integral part of contemporary art. With the triumph of the popular and industrial figurative vocabulary over the elaborate parameters of a rigidly self-referential artistic language, all effectiveness was lost even by the conceptual tools of an approach that drew exclusively on art as understood in the museum sense and saw the artwork as something extraneous to determinacy and hence transcendentally free.[2]

The conceptual tools developed by the art historian Erwin Panofsky – who distinguishes between art that is commercial and non-commercial, challenging and unchallenging, hermetic-elitist and commonplace-conceited – prove more useful with a view to an objective judgment on the results of contemporary art after the eclipse of the avant-garde. Panofsky points out how the contemporary variants of consolidated pictorial styles like Realism, Surrealism and Expressionism are also far cruder and fancier today than their original models and compete with the visual language of the mass media – photography, cinema, television and the Internet – to win the distracted attention of contemporary mankind, with results similar to those achieved by their competitors. Moreover, it is through the media that an art tending toward the spectacular seeks to make a public impact.

The phenomenon of Pop Art obviously paved the way for art fairs. It expanded the realm of art to include the popular world of the visual language of the mass media and can even be described as having "democratized" art, if this is understood as making it more accessible. In any case, it rescued the object of art from the arcane, elite environment of transactions behind closed doors. After the first event in Cologne, it was clear that the idea of a temporary art fair had all the requisites to ensure great and lasting success.

The museum began to lose ground in terms of its aesthetic function on being exposed to the fierce competition of the art fairs, biennials, spectacular auctions, exhibitions and countless other events of a predominantly entertainment-oriented character that have come increasingly to characterize the public image of Western art.

The museum itself has accelerated this process by abandoning its traditional detachment from the art scene and beginning to follow the market trends, evidently in order to avoid charges of being out of touch with a vital, pulsating art scene and acting as a "museal" repository of works. The museums of private collectors and museums of "contemporary art" – whose numbers have rocketed over the last decade – necessarily undermine the identity of the museum as an institution endowed with a paradigmatic and exemplary function. Every step taken to keep up with the artistic fads of the moment has

Douglas Gordon
A Divided Self I and II, 1996
Video installation
Turin, Sandretto Re Rebaudengo Collection

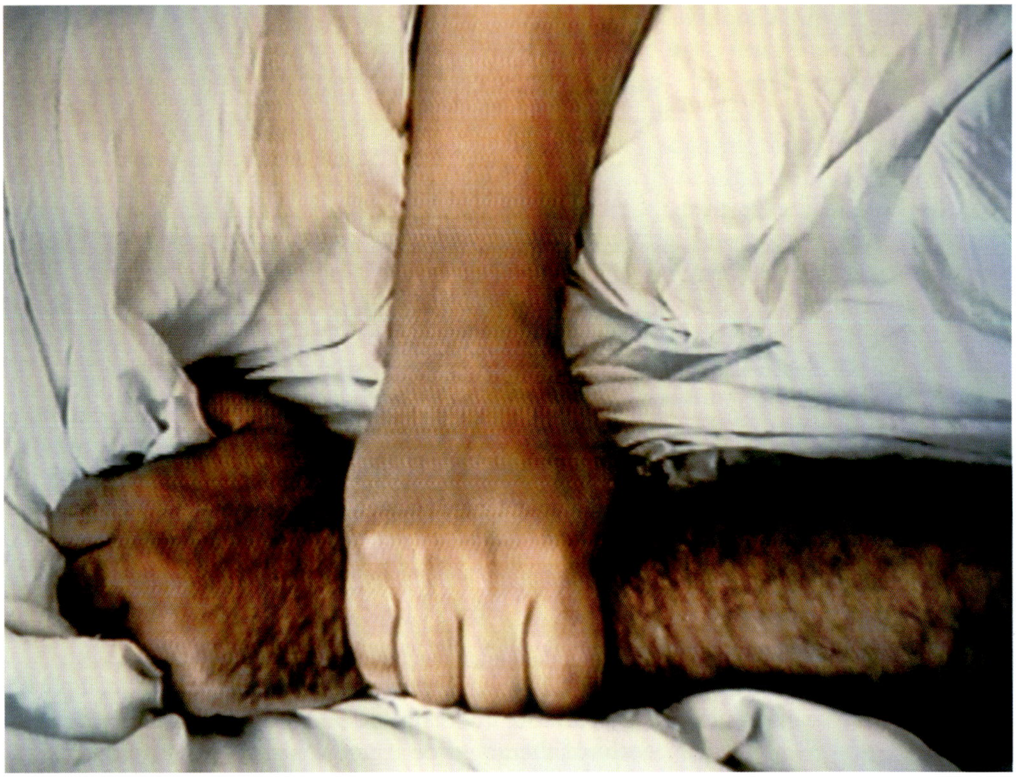

the advent of photography put an end to the previously unchallenged supremacy of painting and drawing in the field of images. As a result, after playing for time by fighting a useless rearguard action against the technical and electronic tools of image creation, art schools have abandoned an approach oriented towards teaching skills of execution to focus on developing the imaginative potential of the individual. This has helped to blur the distinction between the professional artist and the amateur. Generally speaking, there is good reason to believe that everything embraced by the art system can be called art and everything it expels or rejects can be branded as inartistic. This does not mean, however, that the latter cannot legitimately hope to find a welcome some day in the world of art.

If we recognize that the canons of aesthetic judgment now lack any binding character in our pluralistic society and leave aside the question of the market for a moment, the question arises of what objective requirements a work must satisfy today if it is to aspire legitimately to the status of art. The critic Jörg Heiser, who writes for a London-based art magazine with great influence over public opinion, has listed a few requisites in his book *Plötzlich diese Übersicht*: "conceptual clarity, critical potential, aesthetic quality, ease of approach and the ability to operate with a view to the demolition of privileges".[5] This list is sufficiently vague to prove more or less immune to unforeseen and unexpected changes of direction in artistic trends. It bears out the diagnosis formulated above, namely the pluralistic broadening of aesthetic criteria. Moreover, the elements listed are sufficiently elastic and variable to face historical transformations in step with an "extensive" and constantly extensible concept of art. Finally, they do not fail to regard also works of the Renaissance and the Baroque, which application of the criterion of self-referentiality of autonomous art would instead totally exclude from the realm of art as lacking the complete independence from any functional objective upon which it is grounded. Under the lens of these perceptual filters, the criteria of aesthetic appraisal dissolve into a kaleidoscopic variety of views and opinions organized solely by the guiding principle of subjective interests.

This vast and pluralistic range of aesthetic criteria does not include only stances and expectations deriving from the conceptual nature of modern art. On the contrary, the gradual relativization of their claims to validity has led to the resurfacing of views that seemed to have been long consigned to the archives of art history.

Examples include the idea that the work of art must arouse emotions in the viewer or that it must be capable of influencing the behavior of the individual or the community. This depends to a great extent on the fact that commercial visual media like photography and cinema have attained the status of art. Both photography and cinema preserve and cultivate a traditional concept of the image, one swept aside by the avant-garde and the ideology of "arte as art". If they were living in the contemporary era, Titian, Bernini, Rubens and Rembrandt would perhaps opt for filmmaking instead of painting or sculpture.

The range of criteria of aesthetic appraisal is riddled with contradictions. The requirement of complex, attractive composition stands alongside the need for simplicity, clarity and readability. The interest in a experience of cultural growth coexists with a desire for entertainment and amusement, which means the need to meet demands of a hedonistic or narcissistic nature. All this stems from a need for socialization that obviously manifests itself against the background of the growing isolation of the individual in society. None of these elements can be called groundless or illegitimate. The only ones to acquire competence in the field of aesthetic appraisal will, however, be those able to draw upon a deep and vast understanding of the different criteria – just like the "connoisseurs" of "classical" art or the film freaks who develop their knowledge by seeing movies over and over.

Anne-Marie Bonnet summed up the situation as follows after guiding future art historians through the maze of modern art: "The structures, strategies and intentions of the works and practices are so complex that any single form of approach, be it formal or contentual in nature, is bound to fail."[6] Apart from the author's view that even what it is known and familiar should appear new and different in the work of art, there is nothing else to add.

[1] Clement Greenberg, 'Avant-Garde and Kitsch', in *Partisan Review*, 6, 5 (1939), pp. 34–49.
[2] Thomas McEvilley, *Art and Discomfort*, Schirmer/Mosel, London 1993.
[3] Marc Chlimcher, cited in Eileen Kinsella, "Are You Looking at Prices or Art? Experts discuss how market appreciation is affecting art appreciation", in *ARTnews*, May 2007, p. 133.
[4] Judith Lembke, "Im Gespräch: Anne T., ehemalige Derivatebrokerin und Buchautorin: Investmentbänker sind verlogene Selbstdarsteller", *Frankfurter Allgemeine Zeitung*, 7 March 2009, no. 56, p. 20.
[5] Jörg Heiser, *Plötzlich diese Übersicht. Was gute zeitgenössische Kunst ausmacht*, Claassen, Berlin 2007, p. 344.
[6] Anne-Marie Bonnet, *Kunst der Moderne. Kunst der Gegenwart. Herausforderung und Chance*, Deubner Verlag, Cologne 2004, p. 151. See also Klaus Honnef, *Kunstkritik heute. Texte zwischen Wertung und Werbung*, vol. 18 in the series *Schriften zur Kunstkritik*, directed by Walter Vitt, aica, Internationaler Kunstkritikerverband – Sektion Deutschland, Nördlingen, Cologne 2008.

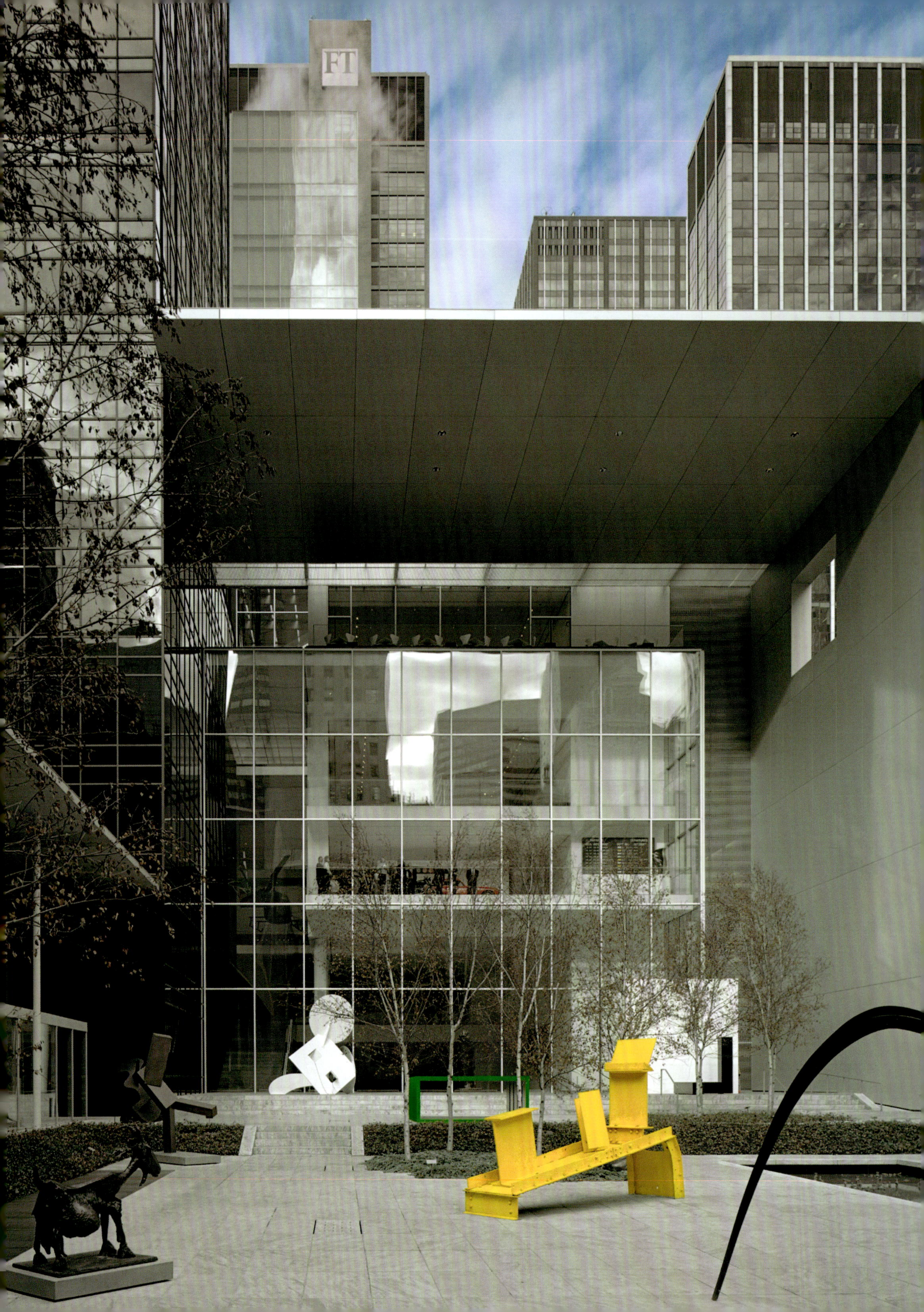
FT

Gabriella Belli

The Contemporary Museum: of Architecture and Meaning

Important examples from the twentieth century

The history of twentieth-century museum architecture came to a close in 1997 with the spectacular opening of Frank O. Gehry's Bilbao Guggenheim, a brilliant product of the fascinating development of contemporary museum design that began with Frank Lloyd Wright in 1943 and his first plans for the New York Guggenheim, inaugurated in 1959. The great spiral created by Wright to display the Solomon R. Guggenheim collection of non-figurative art was in fact the first indication of the radical shift in postwar architecture and museum design that was to prompt all museums to consider the meaning of their cultural mission, thus opening a continuing debate about the relationship between works of art and architecture.

Wright's spiral ramp, a form derived from his organic conception of architecture, fosters a completely new experiential process inside the museum for visitors, drawn into a continuous visual and emotional flow enabling them to relate uninterruptedly to the work of art in a very different way from the past and discover an unprecedented dimension of the space-time of aesthetic utilization. No architect had ever before forced his way so audaciously into the *hortus conclusus* of the museum, the undisputed preserve of museologists and museographers from the very outset. Frank Lloyd Wright's prodigious work of abstract sculpture on Fifth Avenue thus stated that architecture was no longer – and above all had no intention of being – ancillary with respect to the works of art but was instead determined to assert its autonomous critical and interpretive capacity.

Far from appearing intimidated by the works of the twentieth century's greatest artistic talents hanging on its walls, this wonderful container embedded in the orthogonal grid of Manhattan's streets seems indeed to overshadow them with its architecture, a situation that prompted James Johnson Sweeney, then director of the New York Museum of Modern Art, to describe it in 1960 as excellent Wright but a bad museum. Having been opened for no more than a year, the museum was already a subject of discussion. The renowned spiral ramp attached to the side walls of the building and overhanging the great hall flooded with natural light from the transparent domed roof was in fact severely criticized not only because it necessitated flow in a single direction, holding the public within the centrifugal force of its helical form, but also because it meant that the visitors could only observe the works of art from a non-canonical viewpoint, never frontal and always off-center. We have no way of knowing how aware Wright was of the disorienting effect his building had on the relationship between the visitor and the work of art or whether this was indeed what he had tried to obtain with his design. What is certain is that the architecture of this building, with its manifest contradictions, or rather its intrusion into the field of the formulation of critical judgment, marks the problematic beginning of the more recent history of the contemporary museum.

In point of fact, Wright's building presents and highlights a new complexity of the museum, coinciding with the epochal change to which Western society as a whole was subjected in the years immediately after World War II. Intense debate on the identity of the museum not only led to the development of new functions and promotion of its more intimate, educational vocation, but also raised the crucial question of architecture, which was now called upon for help of a non-sporadic nature in offering the best possible response to the needs of the new mass society and the ever-increasing interest in museums manifested during the postwar period in Europe and above all the United States.

Secular cathedrals of the contemporary city but also an expression of a strongly expanding economy of affluence, museums proliferated in all fields of knowledge, from the humanistic to the technological sciences, and developed new cultural models. Architecture played an increasingly important role in all this. The development of museum sciences in the second half of the twentieth century not only kept pace with that of architecture but was also in many cases influenced by it.

In this connection, it should be noted that Wright's Guggenheim Museum was not the only potential model on the threshold of the fateful 1950s. Among the others ex-

Yoshio Taniguchi
Museum of Modern Art of New York and the Sculpture Garden with the new exhibition building in the background to the west, realized in 2004

Stephan Braunfels Architekten
Pinakothek der Moderne, Munich,
north view, 2004

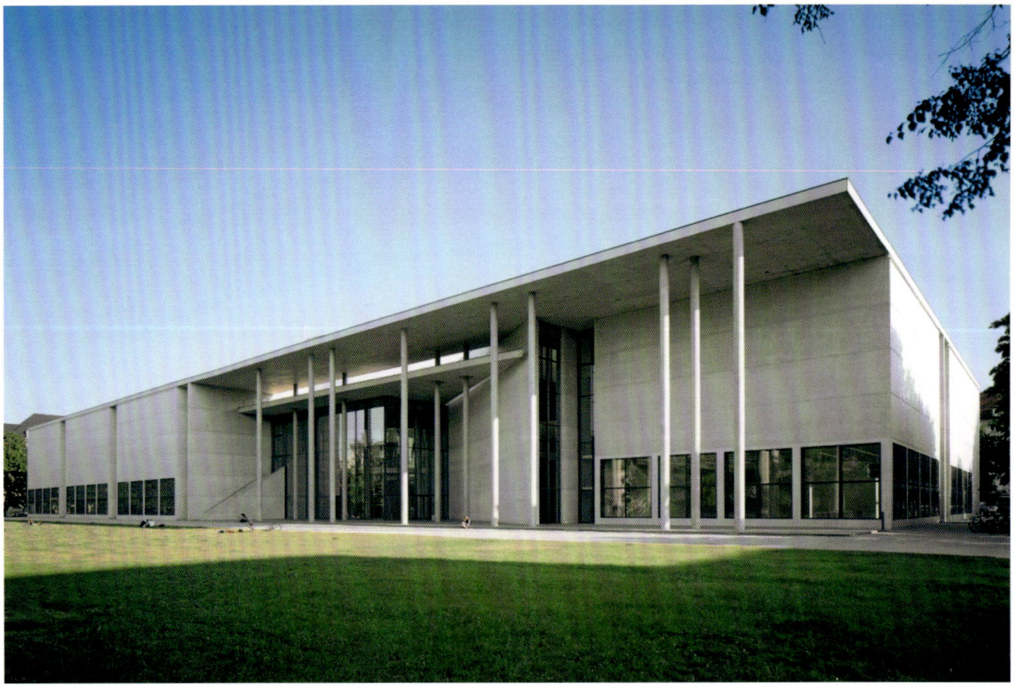

emplifying completely different architectural approaches, the most interesting case is perhaps the Louisiana Museum of Modern Art at Humlebæk, near Copenhagen, not least because it too was inaugurated in 1959. As is known, this authentic home of art and culture has made its geographic location overlooking the water and its peculiar architectural setting in a mansion built by Alexander Brun in 1855 key elements of an identity that has never once been betrayed in the phases of modernization and expansion that have accompanied the museum's history and the growth of its collections since 1958. A paradigmatic example of a virtuous relationship between architecture, art, and nature, the Louisiana Museum of Modern Art constituted for decades an alternative to Wright's *emblematic gesture*, a model capable of reconciling the demands of contemporaneity with those of history and of preserving the identity of the place, an indispensable value for any museum seeking to perform as well as possible not only its public, social, and educational role but also and above all its symbolic function as a point of convergence between the cultural demands of the community to which it belongs and those of the global community, which takes advantage of and identifies with it to an equal degree. The architecture of the Louisiana Museum, interpreted by Jørgen Bo and Wilhelm Wohlert in 1958 as continuity in change, has indeed managed to combine the museum's primary function as a home of art and artistic experience with the need for suitable spaces to perform its educational mission and to accommodate the public in general, and all this with no invasive artificial structures to endanger the integrity of the natural environment. The lightweight building of glass and wood that links the old mansion, now used as the main entrance, with the other exhibition spaces thus took shape from the very outset as the highest expression of the "*genius loci*" and highpoint of the entire structure in a felicitous relationship with a natural setting deftly integrated with the routes for visitors.

The New York Guggenheim opened the series of *emblematic buildings* that enjoyed great success in the last few decades of the twentieth century, not only for their ability to emerge as bold and increasingly daring urban landmarks, but also due to the effect of curiosity and wonder aroused in the public, stimulated by an interest in the museum that is often unconnected with its content. The sober volumes of the Louisiana Museum are instead associated with the idea of the museum as "white box", a model that is not self-referential and asks for architecture capable of serving its mission, hence the design of spaces as free as possible from interference (except of context, as in the case of the Louisiana's natural setting), capable of accommodating the work of art in all its integrity and establishing its relationship with the public. This could be described as architecture with a light touch, coexisting with the manifold expressions of modern and contemporary art but nevertheless asserting its own specific value in the relationship with the works. A historic example is provided in this connection by the Kimbell Art Museum in Fort Worth, Texas, designed by Louis Kahn and opened in 1972 as a masterly lesson in equilibrium and neutral elegance. Rigorously conceived in harmony with the site and consisting of a parallel array of vaulted buildings, the museum still amazes today by virtue of the monumental sobriety of its elevations and simple façades, a perfect place to accommodate the superb collection of ancient and modern art on display there.

Halfway through the 1970s, between the white box and Wright's emblematic building, the unflaggingly intense debate on the mission of the contemporary museum led to the birth of a new model of cultural aggregation and a corresponding new form of architectural experimentation, as exemplified by the opening of the Centre Pompidou in 1977. In its new role as a center of social life within increasingly multiethnic cities and communities, the museum experimented with a multidisciplinary cultural model that made unprecedented demands on architecture in order to contain the complexity of the languages of the visual arts, new media requiring different spaces and forms of presentation with respect to traditional works, and the new performative arts, which have played a part in defining the image of the contemporary museum ever since.

Designed by Renzo Piano and Richard Rogers, the Centre national d'art et de culture Georges Pompidou uses sophisticated technology and innovative transparency in its interpretation of the new utopia of the social function of the museum, a place where ideas travel and differences are gauged in a jumble of events, meetings, and shows; a place, in short, of cultural appropriation but also of sociality experienced through the many manifestations of art. Thirty years after its opening, the Pompidou has lost none of its impact and still constitutes today – in many variants and with many variables – a model of reference for contemporary museum design that is still unsurpassed in many respects. While the building cannot be considered any less emblematic than Wright's Guggenheim Museum – suffice it to recall the idea of escalators to connect the floors and the then completely innovative use of glass and industrial structures with a low aesthetic profile but extraordinary effectiveness in practical and expressive terms – there is no doubt whatsoever that the architecture made an unprecedented attempt to correspond to the cultural mission of the new institution. In accordance with the innovative quality of the project, Piano and Rogers made a great effort to produce a design capable of accommodating the whole variety of activities requiring adequate space in the new museum in the best possible way. It can therefore be stated that the multidisciplinary model of the Centre Pompidou also saw the birth of a new approach to museum architecture, no longer called upon exclusively to protect and display

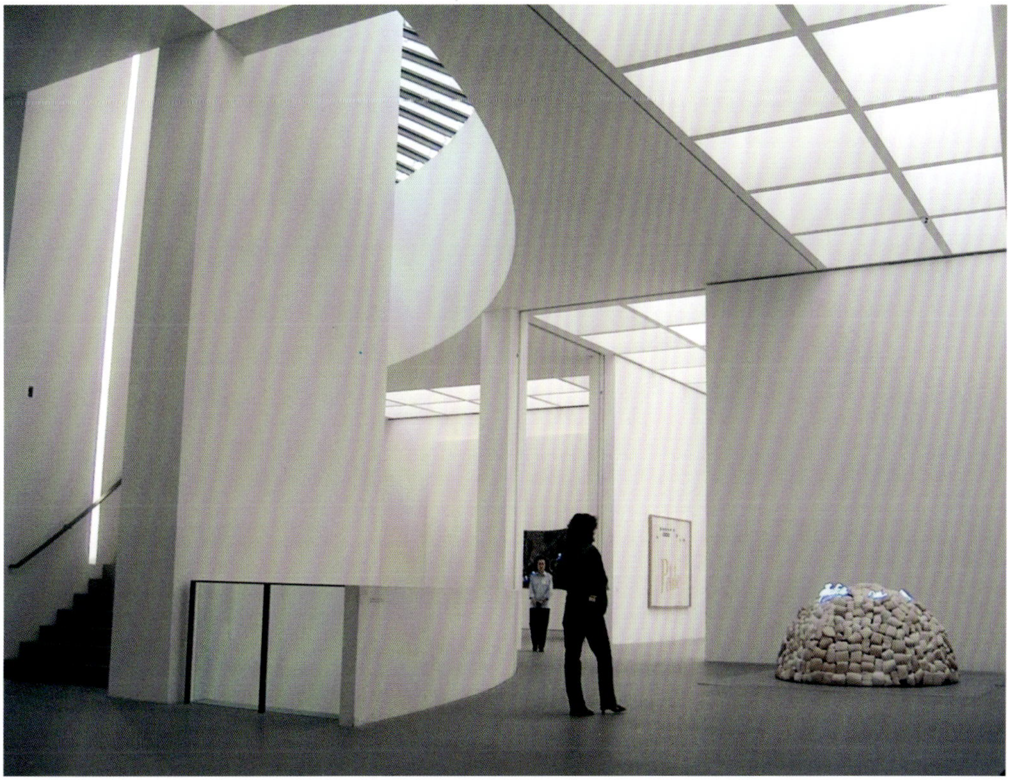

Stephan Braunfels Architekten
Pinakothek der Moderne, Munich, view of Room 24 with works by Arnulf Rainer, 2007

Jean Nouvel
Musée du quai Branly, Paris, east view, 2007

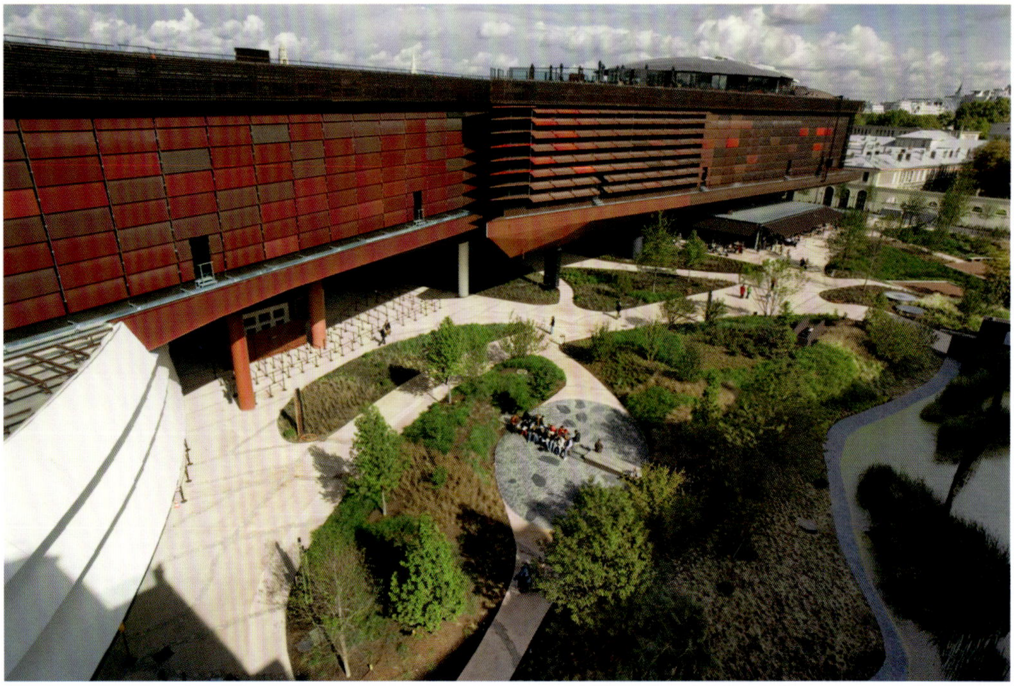

art, but also to represent and respond to multicultural social demands, and hence capable of rethinking the organization of spaces and functions in accordance with new principles of "democratic" management of scientific and exhibition-related activities and fostering real "occupation" by users of all the different parts of the museum all through the day. This constituted a miracle of cultural massification back in the 1970s.

Contemporary Narcissus

When the silvery titanium shapes of Frank O. Gehry's building in Bilbao came into the spotlight twenty years after the Pompidou experiment, some thought it was time to write the obituary of the contemporary museum but millions of travelers prepared to get to grips with what was publicized as the outermost frontier of art and architecture. Hitherto unsurpassed for the eccentricity and aloofness of its forms, this new Narcissus of contemporaneity stands in the center of a pool whose waters reflect its metallic beauty, lifting its titanium petals (smooth perpendicular or off-centered walls) like a newly opened flower to the sky over Bilbao, which has received gratifying economic returns every day since its birth.

One of the most spectral (but at the same time spectacular) creations of contemporary architecture, with armor that hides its inner life from sight and shapes that are no longer terrestrial but more like science fiction, is it not perhaps more beautiful than the Winged Victory of Samothrace? The Futurist aesthetic would certainly have approved of the beauty – "glistening like knives in the sunlight" – of Gehry's museum. It would have definitely fired Marinetti's imagination and still more justified his vehement attack on the traditionalist culture of museums and his call for courage, daring, and rebellion, for happy incendiaries with scorched fingers to "set fire to the libraries and divert the courses of canals to flood the museums." It should not, however, be believed that the building's claims to high-tech status end with the fantastically intersecting planes of its outer surfaces. The interior is equally surprising with its sequence of solids and voids and above all the particular organization of the spaces, which corresponds to a clear critical function developed through the fragmentation of viewpoints and routes, which spread out from the great hall – 50 meters high with a floor area of 650 m^2 and a floor-to-ceiling wall of glass looking onto the terraces over the water – in every direction and always return to the center, with no set route for visitors. Fragmentation thus encapsulates the spirit of the 1990s, an exciting time when the museum asserted its importance as an institution and above all as a cultural industry. Once again, architecture supported the drive for modernization of the museum sciences and became a symbol, an icon, a product of cultural consumption in the broadest sense.

The third path, midway between the white cube and emblematic architecture

It was London's Tate Modern that marked the year 2000 with the opening of its new showcase in the old Bankside power station on the Thames, suitably restored and refurbished by the Swiss architects Jacques Herzog and Pierre de Meuron. With a particular predilection for structures of industrial archeology, often possessing sterling architectural characteristics, vast spaces, and an interesting functional organization of interiors, the renovation of old buildings constitutes the third path of contemporary museum design. While developed also in the United States in recent years, this has been tried and tested with significant results above all in old Europe, which is richer in ancient, historical buildings and equally significant disused industrial structures.

At the international level, it was above all postwar Italy that attained primacy in the conversion of buildings of great historical and artistic importance into museums, starting with Carlo Scarpa's renowned project for the Castelvecchio Museum in Verona. Begun in 1957, developed in successive stages, and completed in 1974, it is still unsurpassed today as an operation capable of displaying extraordinary respect for the historical remains while developing at the same time a brilliant and unprecedented fusion of ancient and contemporary architecture. From the masterly placement of the equestrian statue of Cangrande della Scala in a heraldic position against the backdrop of the medieval walls to the choice of materials and their sophisticated handling, the citation of a great deal of the figurative culture of the twentieth century, and the careful selection of the plants in the grounds, everything in the 14th-century castle – opened to the public as a museum in 1964 – bears witness to Carlo Scarpa's exceptional achievement. Opening up really new perspectives in contemporary museum architecture – as well as other fields – and presenting innovative approaches to the dialogue between ancient and modern, his work offers a wealth of ideas and stimuli.

Ningura Napurrula
Interior view of room painted by the Australian artist, Musée du quai Branly, Paris

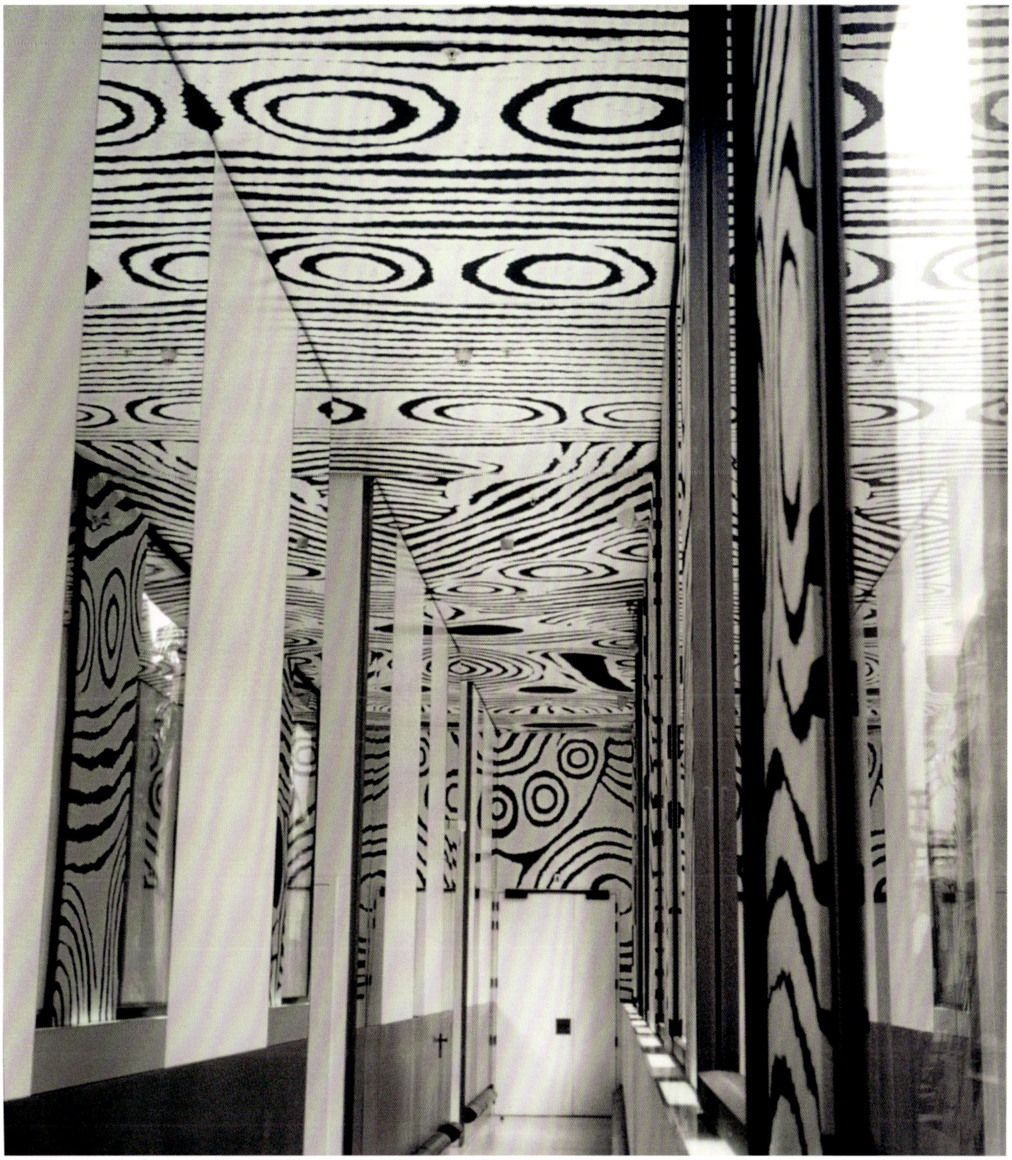

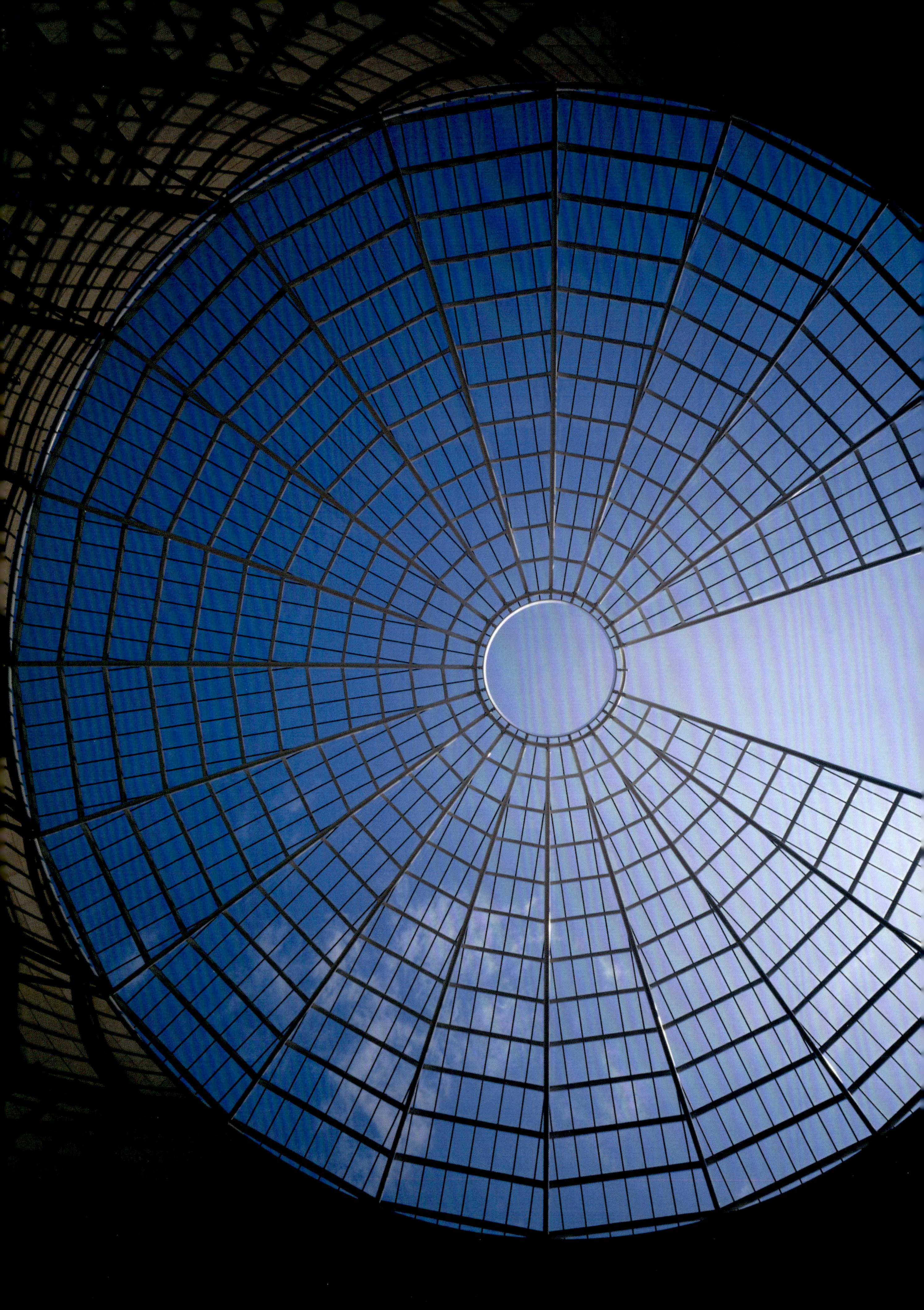

Mario Botta
Dome covering of Mart – Museo di Arte Moderna e Contemporanea di Trento e Rovereto, 2002

Above all, however, it encouraged contemporary architecture to address the challenge of the comparison between past and present with ever-greater pride. There can indeed be no doubt that his ideas about the reutilization of ancient buildings also played their part in enabling Europe to experiment successfully with this new approach to the museum by salvaging important but long abandoned and dilapidated historical structures and giving them a role in the cultural life of the city in completely renovated and more glorious attire.

Another example, and one of great appeal still today, is the famous Gare d'Orsay in Paris. Built in an eclectic style by the architect Victor Laloux and inaugurated in 1900 to coincide with the Exposition Universelle, this disused railway station, renovated by Gae Aulenti, opened its doors to the public nearly 90 years later, in 1986, as the Musée d'Orsay, the home par excellence of French Impressionism.

In Italy, the European country where museums are most frequently housed in ancient buildings, attention can be drawn to at least another three interesting examples. First, the Castello di Rivoli, which was built on the remains of an ancient medieval castle by various architects, including the renowned Filippo Juvarra (1718), as a royal residence for the House of Savoy. Renovated by Andrea Bruno, who remained faithful to Juvarra's design while developing his own sober interpretation of the spaces connecting the different parts of the huge complex, it has served since 1984 to house the Museo d'Arte Contemporanea. Second, the disused bakery in Bologna, renovated to plans drawn up by Aldo Rossi but completed after his death by the Milanese firm of ARA Associati Architettura, which reopened to the public as the MAMbo in 2007. Third, the MAXXI (national museum and center for documentation and promotion of the contemporary arts, scheduled for inauguration in the autumn of 2009), which Zaha Hadid created by combining the old Montello barracks in the Flaminio district of Rome with a new building of surprising formal effectiveness that can be classified by virtue of its sensational structural composition as one of the third millennium's first works of emblematic architecture. Conceived as an authentic piece of the city, the new building lends itself to an active and dynamic presentation of art thanks to a highly structured sequence of horizontal and vertical routes for visitors that unmistakably recall the inventions of Giovanni Battista Piranesi. Refusing to be confined to the simple function of connecting elements, these pathways become authentic places for use in their own right and lead visitors uninterruptedly through the space of the museum. Their fluid, visionary quality will not only generate a dynamic relationship between visitor, work of art, and architecture, but also offer a place for the formulation of critical judgments. In this sense, it could perhaps be claimed that Zaha Hadid's design develops the museum concept of Wright's Guggenheim, resolving

Mario Botta
Covered square of Mart – Museo di Arte Moderna e Contemporanea di Trento e Rovereto, 2002

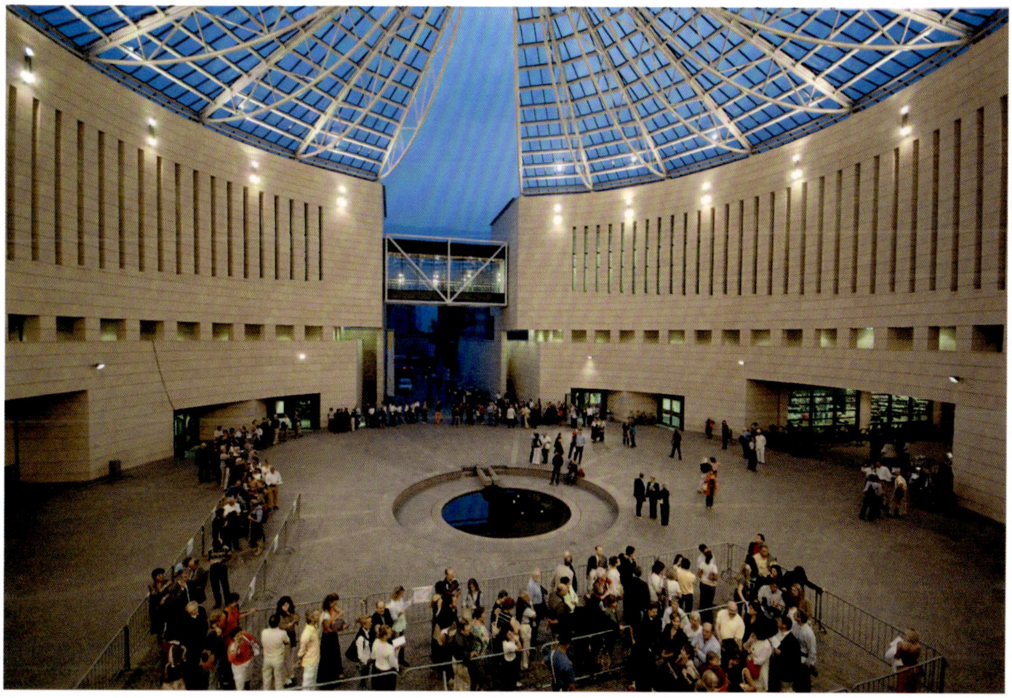

all the ambiguities of the spiral ramp in an explosion of vision. Unlike the building in New York, the MAXXI introduces the never-before experienced dimension of an authentic street of art, one that opens up to the city in both metaphorical and concrete terms through the outlets of the visitors' routes, which interact with the spaces outside. The creation of a new piazza and a pedestrian thoroughfare connecting the block of buildings in the Flaminio district will also lead to enhancement of the old military barracks. Facing onto the new piazza and endowed with new service functions, it will acquire a new identity of its own as simultaneously complementary and autonomous with respect to the life of the museum.

While the conversion of old industrial buildings is not frequent practice in the United States – the country of new museum building par excellence – there are some interesting cases. One is the project for contemporary art and the support of young artists developed by Art and Urban Resources Inc., which started exhibiting works in abandoned spaces on the outskirts of New York as early as 1971 and found permanent premises in a disused school in Long Island City (Queens) in 1976. Renovated in 1997, the P.S.1 Contemporary Art Center became an affiliate of the MoMA in 2000.

Still more interest attaches to the Dia Art Foundation, which undertook an effective and sensitive action of preservation and protection of historical heritage in the town of Beacon, 40 miles north of New York, in 2003 with the restoration of the carton making and printing plant of the National Biscuit Company (Nabisco), a characteristic example of early twentieth-century American industrial architecture built in 1929 with the large-scale use of steel, concrete, and glass. Carried out by the artist Robert Irwin and the OpenOffice firm of architects, the restoration began in 1999, when National Paper donated the building to the Dia Foundation. The magnificent structure, which preserves all the positive features of its industrial origin, including high ceilings, vast spaces, and large windows admitting natural light, now houses the Dia's superb collection of masterpieces of international contemporary art from the early 1960s to the present day.

An understated opening for the twenty-first century

It was thus with the conversion of an old power station into space for contemporary art that Tate Modern inaugurated the twenty-first century with a choice of approach that immediately ruled out any possibility of architecture prevailing over the museum's mission, functions, and cultural leadership in the art system. It was not a new building but Sir Giles Gilbert Scott's disused power station that struck the Tate Gallery's management as the ideal place not only to provide more space for its huge collection, but also to interpret a new and rigorous function of

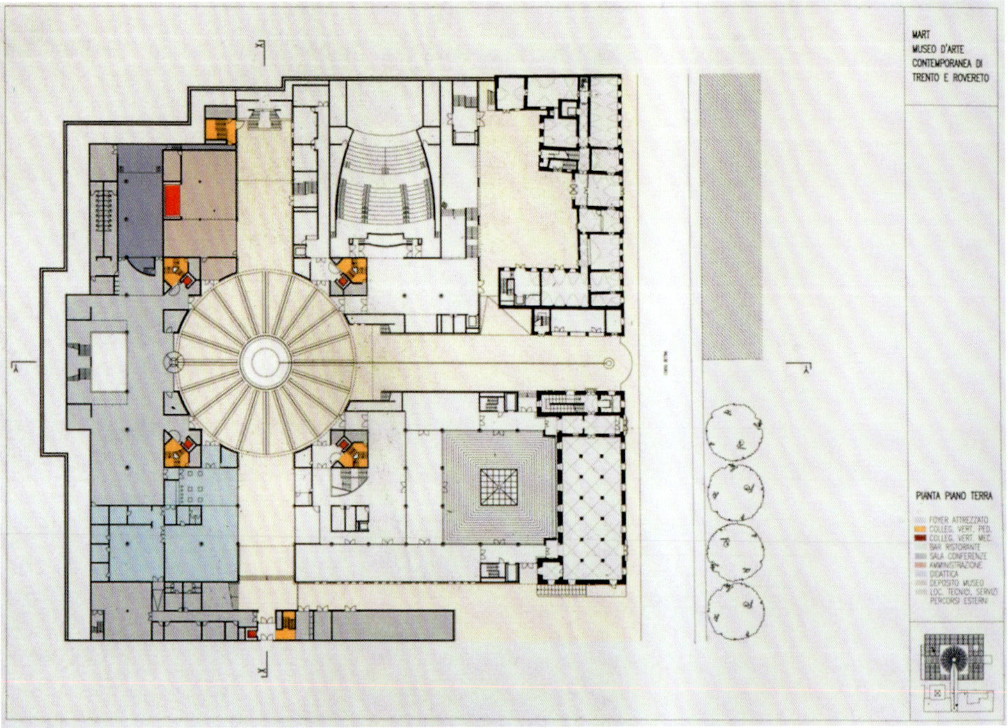

Mario Botta
Ground floor plan of Mart – Museo di Arte Moderna e Contemporanea di Trento e Rovereto, 2002

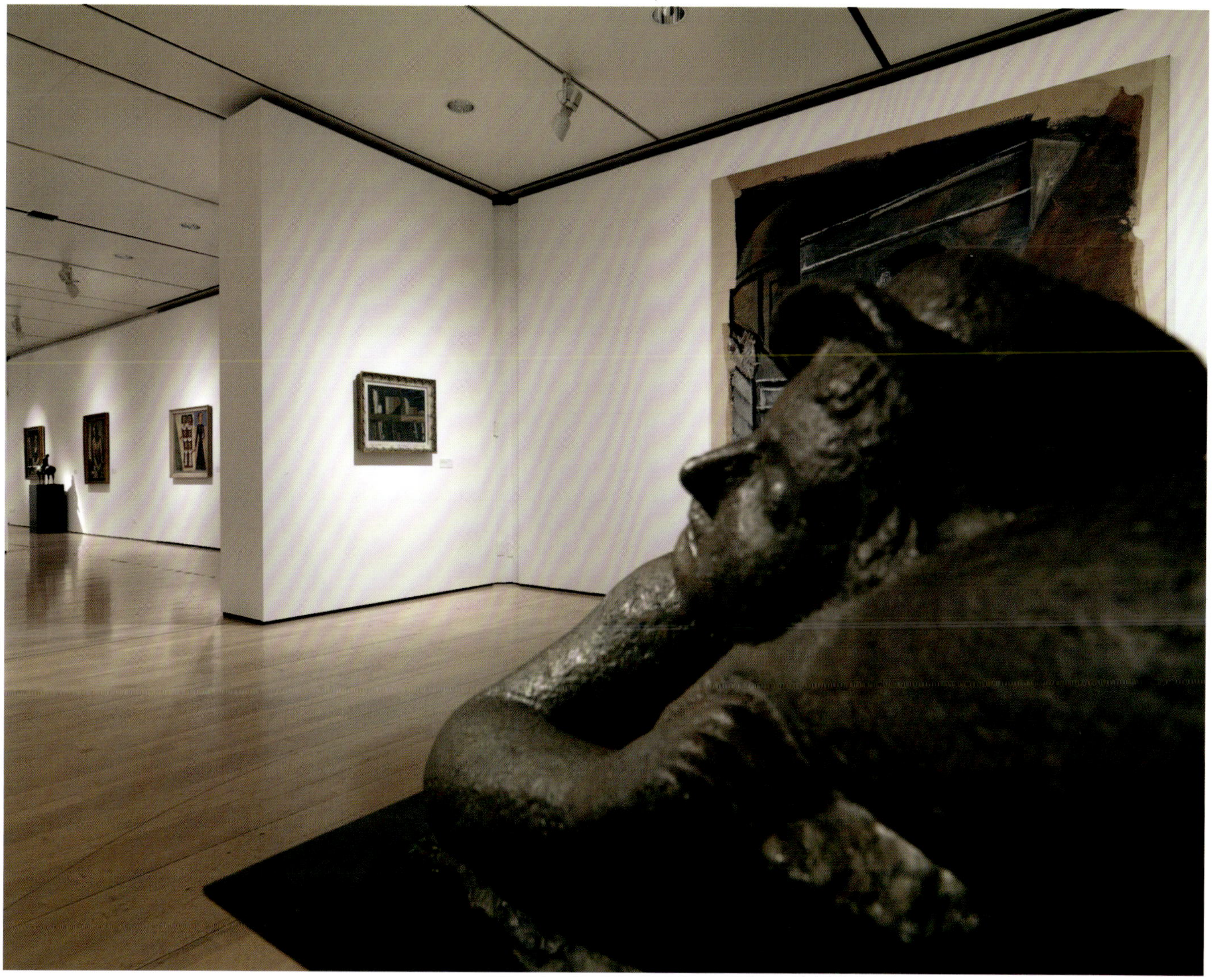

Dressing of the "Mario Sironi" and "Arturo Martini" rooms at Mart – Museo di Arte Moderna e Contemporanea di Trento e Rovereto

architecture in the field of the contemporary art at the dawn of the twenty-first century. Funding from the National Lottery enabled Herzog & de Meuron – who emerged as winners from a short list of competitors comprising Tadao Ando, Rem Koolhaas, and David Chipperfield – to embark on a project envisaging exemplary balance between restoration of the historical building – with renovation of the original spaces of greatest architectural importance, like the Turbine Hall and the gigantic chimney – and the creation of new areas to house the collection, temporary exhibitions, public facilities, and offices. The latter are located partly in the old building, with appreciable use of natural light from above particularly in the case of the exhibition areas, but also in the new transparent glass box running its entire length and offering hauntingly beautiful views of the city and the river.

The most difficult task for the architects engaged in restoring to public use this singular edifice, a milestone in the city's economic history and today a symbol of this precious legacy, was to ensure the capacity of the original structure – endowed with legitimate architectural ambitions but by no means exemplary as regards the solutions adopted at the time for the performance of its specific functions – not only to provide optimal support for the museum's mission, but also to make a strong communicative impression on the public, who are often attracted more easily by the spectacular nature of the architectural container than the primary functions carried out inside it.

In this sense, it is easy to understand why the architects chose to retain the huge Turbine Hall on the entrance level, which has led to new social use of the space as a sort of plaza capable of accommodating massive flows of visitors and hence to ensure large-scale participation in the museum's new activities in the fields of music, drama, and performance.

The great success of Tate Modern rests on the creation of a sharply defined identity

– underpinned by the need to expand the museum's physical spaces while revitalizing its social and educational function – combined with an intransigent (to say the least) attitude as regards the supporting role of the architecture. Almost ten years after its inauguration, it can now boast a public of over four million visitors a year, a somewhat embarrassing figure for those who thought it impossible in the twenty-first century to dispense with the spectacular museum building constituting a new economic powerhouse and all-devouring presence in the urban space. One truly outstanding example of buildings that have rejected the blandishments of architecture is Schaulager. Once again the work of Jacques Herzog and Pierre de Meuron, this was built for the precise purpose of offering conditions of the highest quality, not only for the preservation of artwork but also for study and research into modern and contemporary art. Erected in the vicinity of Basel and inaugurated in 2003, Schaulager has significantly been described as "not a museum, not a traditional warehouse ... a place to see and think about art differently." As with the design for the Tate Modern, the two Swiss architects focused in their formal and structural thinking on the mission of the place and the specific functions required by the client. The commission was not for a museum in the traditional sense of the term but rather a place of excellence for preservation, study, and research, a sort of great archives equipped with all the most sophisticated technologies for the control, safety and documentation of works belonging to the vast Emanuel Hoffmann Stiftung and housed here when not on display in the Basel Kunstmuseum or exhibitions in the Basel Museum für Gegenwartskunst. Open to scholars, museum curators, specialists, and researchers, Schaulager is the result of determination to create a new model of museum design that is highly advanced as regards both the preservation and the study of art. The works continue to live here – albeit on standby – in architecture that offers the greatest care as regards both their display in the "warehouse" areas and the large spaces for study and research, which are sometimes opened to the public for exhibitions (especially of new acquisitions). Above and beyond the rules around which the art system is organized in museums, standards of excellence operate here in a new approach to knowledge and the formulation of art-historical and critical judgments.

The first few years of the twenty-first century thus offer no small number of examples of how the focus of the debate on the sense and meaning of the museum has shifted to the social and educational impact of culture and detached itself from the "star system" of art, fashion, and indiscriminate massification. The latter options were generated in the last two decades of the twentieth century by an artificially distorted economic system that transferred determination of the work's value wholesale from the cultural sphere to the financial, with unsatisfactory – to say the least – results for which the only term of comparison now, as the first decade of the third millennium draws to a close, is the collapse of the world financial markets.

In 2002, two years after birth of the Tate Modern model, another museum of strategic importance for the contemporary art system opened in Munich. Strengthening the cultural line with respect to the spectacular and financial approach to art, the new Pinakothek der Moderne houses, preserves, and promotes the collections of no fewer than four of the city's institutions, namely the Staatsgalerie Moderner Kunst, the Neue Sammlung, and the Graphische Sammlung and the Architektursammlung from the Technischen Universität. As heated debate on the museum of contemporary art had stretched on in Munich for nearly four decades without arriving at any concrete result, the fine collection of twentieth-century art built up through major bequests and donations was exhibited in the Haus der Kunst, while the collections of design, architecture, and graphic arts were housed in something that could hardly be called a museum and seldom on show to the public. The plans were drawn up by the architect Stephan Braunfels and the work was carried out between 1996 and 2002. It was thanks to the support received by the local authorities from the private sector in the final phases that the museum was able to open just ten years after planning started in 1992. The riches of Munich's museum system are well known and the project developed by Braunfels, which aligns one of the building's main façades with the museum district and its two major art galleries, shows a positive response to this influence. The presence of four different collections laying claim to autonomy inside the museum posed an interesting architectural problem that was solved by dividing the interior in such a way as to avoid impairing the overall unity of the space, which is clearly evident to the visitor on first sight of the compact, rectangular exterior with a monumental cylinder rising in the center above the great

Tadao Ando Architect & Associates
Staircase of the Chichu Art Museum,
Naoshima, Japan, 2004

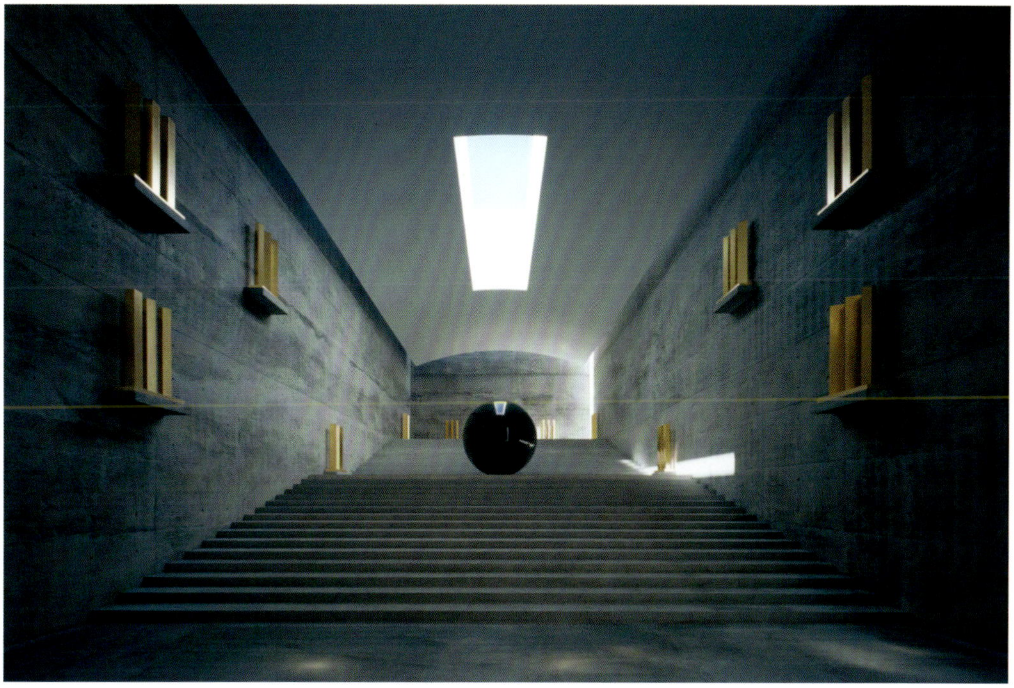

rotunda from which all the visitors' routes branch out. The series of outer walls is cadenced at frequent intervals by slender columns that support the functional canopy of the projecting roof, and a rhythmic array of large windows provides light for the interiors. Inside the museum, the elementary geometric forms of the circle, triangle, and rectangle play an important role in the architectural composition proper as regards the structural layout of the different floors and sections. All of these are equally affected by a singular full-height wall running diagonally lengthwise through the rectangular building. Receiving natural light from a great glass dome, the rotunda in the center constitutes the point of reference and orientation for visitors, the starting point for the flights of stairs leading to the areas in which the fine collections are exhibited in large rooms of regular, standard shape, all receiving light from above. Greater irregularity is to be found in the arrangement of the rooms in the basement, which house one of the world's finest collections of design and provide access to what Gottfried Knapp has described as a sort of ring-shaped crypt. Reflecting the circular layout of the rotunda, this demonstrates the importance attached in the overall design to the focus on this architectural element, which comes indeed to constitute the symbolic fulcrum of the entire building, clearly in accordance with an approach to museum design focusing on the care and preservation of materials, study and research, and educational activities.

Equal importance attaches to the plaza, covered for three-quarters by a transparent dome, of the Museo d'Arte Moderna e Contemporanea di Trento e Rovereto, designed by Mario Botta in collaboration with the engineer Giulio Andreolli. The place par excellence for social participation, the plaza is given a key role in the spatial organization of the architectural complex, comprising the museum as well as the annex of the municipal library and the new auditorium, which all stand along its circular perimeter with their sober masonry of Palladian stone from Vicenza. Opened in December 2002, six years after the laying of the first stone (1996) and twelve after the first plans were drawn up in 1989–1990, the MART was born in 1987 through the merger of two institutions long active in the region of Trentino, namely the contemporary art section of the Castello del Buonconsiglio in Trento, housed in the Palazzo delle Albere (Trento) and opened in 1981, and the Galleria Museo Fortunato Depero, founded in Rovereto by the Futurist artist in 1957–1960. The museum has displayed close attention to its relationship with the local area from the very outset as well as great readiness to establish contacts with the cultural world at the international level. A place representing the history and values of its community, the MART has interpreted its mission by addressing the cultures of modern and contemporary art in transversal and multidisciplinary terms, thus keeping faith with an idea of the museum as a place of coexistence for the arts, conceived and designed for the active preservation of artworks as well as promotion, discussion, research, verification, and knowledge of the plurality of forms of expression and experiences of our time as reflected in the multiform centers of the contemporary artistic scene. Born out of a long and arduous process of public discussion aimed at obtaining support from the entire community, the new building has ensured the best possible handling of the museum's functions and programmatic aims, making it possible to perform a proactive and experimental task as a laboratory and meeting place for new generations and new problems.

The MART is located in Rovereto, a small town in the north of Italy with a rich history that has preserved much of its ancient architecture practically intact, including the fine eighteenth-century mansions on Corso Bettini. It is from an opening right in the middle of this avenue lined with stately buildings – among which a particular role is played by the ancient theater and the university – that the architects built a street providing access to the MART. This leads into a large circular plaza that is unquestionably the most strongly symbolic element of the museum, which contrasts markedly in size with the town's sober, restrained architecture to offer the visitor a sensational "out of scale" experience.

Laid out internally on four levels, including a basement housing the archives and a specialized library, the MART is, so to speak, "self-effacing" with respect to the work of art. As designed by Mario Botta, the architectural element lays no claim whatsoever to a leading role in the areas assigned to scholarly studies, shows, and the permanent collection, but instead plays a key part in the spatial organization and aesthetic definition of areas for services, reception, educational activities, and connections between the different floors. Examples include the internal gallery running the length of the museum on the side overlooking the plaza, where vertical slits provide light and offer views of the city, and the transparent walkway connecting the two ample galleries on the second floor (more than 4000 m^2 housing the permanent collections and major events), which offers a view of the high mountains on the horizon of the valley in which the museum is situated. In the exhibition rooms, the use of the white cube – a standard square module measuring 7.8 × 7.8 meters (and multiples) – responds exclu-

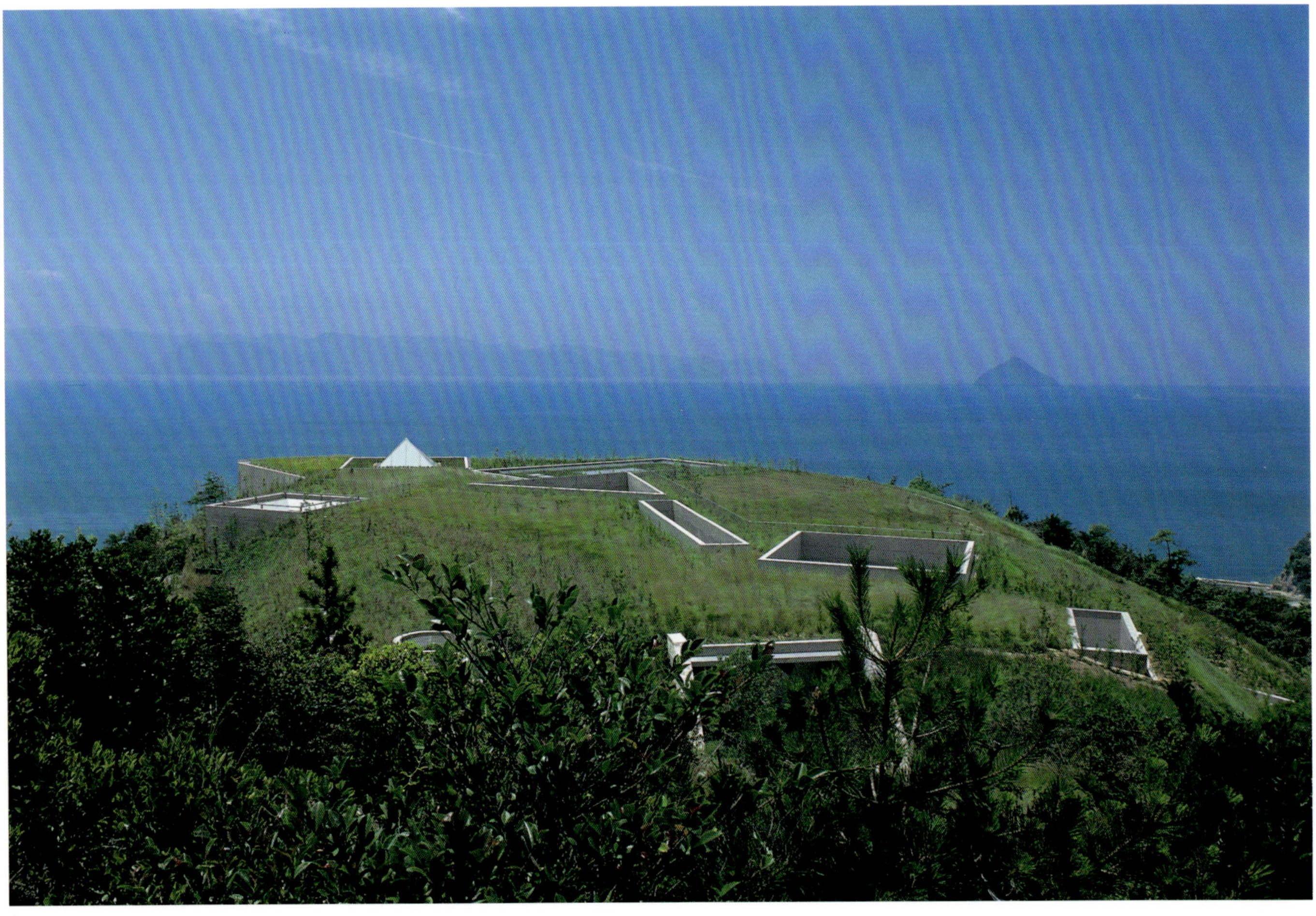

Tadao Ando Architect & Associates
Full view of the Chichu Art Museum of Naoshima, Japan, 2004

Renzo Piano Building Workshop
Exterior view of the Zentrum Paul Klee, Berne, 2005

Renzo Piano Building Workshop
Plans of the Zentrum Paul Klee, Berne, 2005

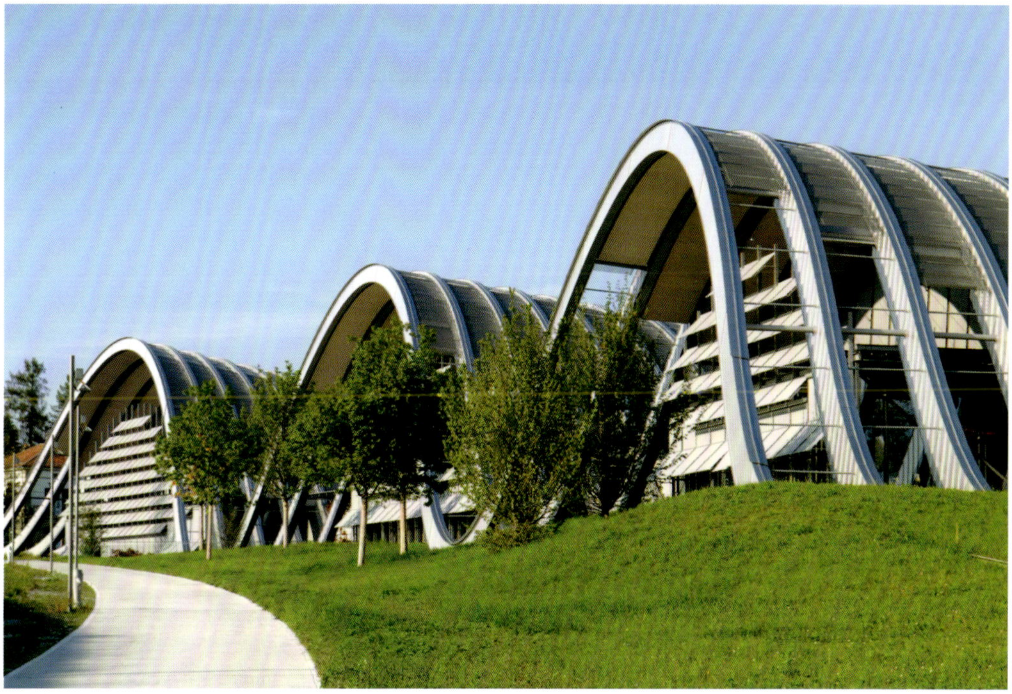

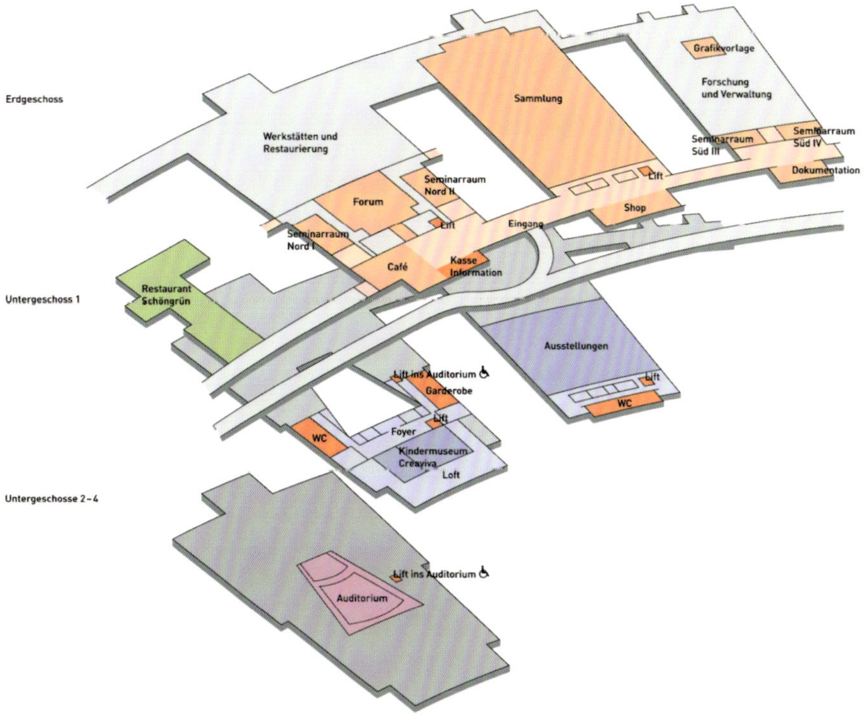

sively to the need to establish a dialogue between the spectator and the work of art, to foster understanding, and to further the formulation of critical ideas in the peace and quiet of a space designed with no superstructures or interference. The choice of natural light – which enters on the second floor through skylights designed to offer the optimal degree of intensity for preservation of the museum's precious collection – enhances the presentation of the works in relation to the "mood" of the day without freezing them in an artificial atmosphere. Thus alone can every painting and sculpture display the variability of its shapes, colors, chiaroscuro, and three-dimensional impact. It is this light that brings to life and transfigures everything in the museum.

Light is a constant problem in the design of the contemporary museum, which is moving increasingly away from the dramatic or spectacular presentation of the work of art through artificial lighting and toward an ideal attaching new importance to the value of natural light, above all in the display of permanent collections.

There are many architects who believe that the experience of art must be combined with the ability of the architectural space to react to the stimuli of the different hours of the day, the climate, the seasons, and even the exposure of the building. One of the most sophisticated examples is unquestionably the Beyeler Foundation in Riehen (Basel), designed by Renzo Piano and inaugurated in 1997, a perfect mechanism as regards lighting, which interacts almost simultaneously with changes in atmospheric conditions so as to ensure the best possible view of the works of art in a continuous, virtuous relationship with external light and space. Renzo Piano is perhaps the architect who has shown the most skill in the use of these principles in museum design, choosing to resolve the problem through the greatest possible synthesis and harmony between natural and artificial elements.

From the Beyeler in Riehen to the Zentrum Paul Klee in Bern (2005) and the new Eli Broad Building of the Los Angeles County Museum of Art (2008), Renzo Piano has developed his conviction that "a museum should attempt to interpret the quality of the collection and define its relationship with the outside world. This means taking an active, but not an aggressive role." Focusing particular attention on the relationship between inside and outside, he has attached central importance in his projects to the problem of presenting the work of art to its best possible advantage, not only in its relations with the visitor and the interior of the museum, but also in the more general context of the site, the territory, the surroundings, and the city. One interesting example is the new wing of the Los Angeles County Museum, a block with a travertine facing developed on three levels connected by means of escalators, designed by Piano in harmony with the nature of the place, the climate, the light, and even the vocation for ephemerality that – as he remarks – seem to be the most striking characteristic of this megalopolis, which is inclined toward constant upheaval and suspicious of the stability of the tectonic masses of architecture.

Between the East and the West

It was with the Zentrum Paul Klee in Bern that Renzo Piano explored a new frontier of museum design. As a museum devoted to a single artist, the project presented various difficulties, calling upon the architect to avoid any betrayal of the spirit of his own times while capturing the painter's personality and the voice of his works. In such cases, it seems that the architecture cannot confine itself to interpretation but must encapsulate within itself the sign of the artist's creation, the result of a life dedicated to art, as reflected here in an oeuvre of over 10,000 works. In this connection, however, it should be noted that Klee's cultural nomadism – which prompted him to experiment constantly with new spheres of creation and go beyond the limits set by the discipline of art so as to channel a whole variety of experiences into his work – steered the client, namely the Maurice E. and Martha Müller Foundation, toward a project capable of performing its mission of preserving and presenting the artist's works while constituting a place of cultural debate, open to the manifold needs of the contemporary world, as well as a place for the community to spend its free time. In seeking therefore to develop a multifunctional structure rather than one focusing rigidly and exclusively on the celebration of Klee's work, Renzo Piano thus had the opportunity to operate on two levels, combining the preservation of historical memory with purposes of social participation and culture in more general terms.

The result is an architectural complex perfectly integrated into the topography of its site. The shapes and volumes ideally reflect the natural scenery surrounding the city of Bern and especially the area where the museum is located, the rise and fall of gentle hills providing inspiration for the Zentrum's three superb waves of steel and glass, an authentic sculpture in the landscape, sloping down to disappear below ground and then soaring full of energy to heights of up to 19 meters, symbolic forms that unquestionably suggest the magical alchemy of Klee's work.

Situated close to an expressway, which is set at a lower level and practically invisible from the inside, the museum has its main façade precisely on that side, thus demonstrating the building's capacity to contain and interact – not as a barrier or obstacle but in perfect continuity – with the *topoi* of the urban and rural landscape, from the expressway to the green meadows and hills delimiting the opposite side.

The three wings stretching out along the terrain with a markedly undulating profile, each approximately 150 meters in length, are joined by the Museumstrasse accommodating the information center, bookshop, cafeteria, library, and other facilities. While the Hügel Nord houses a forum and

Zaha Hadid Architects
Atrium of the MAXXI_Museo nazionale delle arti del XXI secolo, Rome, 2009
Courtesy MAXXI_Museo nazionale delle arti del XXI secolo, Rome

rooms for seminars with an auditorium and the Creaviva children's museum in the basement, the collection of over 10,000 works is stored in the Hügel Mitte. For reasons of preservation, an alternating selection of no more than 200 is on show at any time. Very delicate and in many cases on paper supports, Klee's works require rigorous standards of display with indirect lighting so as to protect the precious surfaces from the deterioration that natural or artificial light would inevitably cause without perfect control. Interest attaches to the presence in the upper section of this great structure of about 1750 m² housing the permanent collection of a concealed system for the positioning of any dividing walls required in the exhibition area. A room for temporary shows, initially designed to exhibit work by great masters of the twentieth century, is located on the lower level. Smaller than the other two wings of the museum, the Hügel Sud houses the administrative offices and some rooms for seminars, research, and documentation regarding Klee's work. The most striking thing about the complex in Bern is the balance between architecture and environment, a sort of micro-ecosystem of two and a half hectares in which the crops follow the rhythm of the seasons and the choice of plants is in keeping with the climatic and geographic conditions. The buildings blend into the geological profile of their site with great humility and the sophisticated technology meets high standards of sustainable development in both environmental and economic terms.

The Zentrum Paul Klee thus opens up new horizons for contemporary museum design in terms that it would not be mistaken to describe as ethical, in that architecture is called upon to play a precise role in the social organization of communities, taking into account the ever-greater need to balance the museum's primary cultural interests with the equally important requirements of its social, economic, and environmental sphere of reference. This expansion of the mission of the museum and its architecture into areas of such importance today in the political debate of the international community corresponds to an inevitable evolution of the very concept of culture, and hence of the museum. This must necessarily regard as an active principle of its activities its capacity for significant impact in urban contexts, first and foremost as a model for environmentally sustainable architectural design, but also as a place in which the cultural mission can live and find justification in close connection with the priorities – and indeed emerging issues – of the new global society.

Far removed from the social mission of art that drove the idea of the museum in the 1970s, the ethical function of contemporary museum design is today no longer focused exclusively on the endorsement of culture as a tool of social development, an objective partly achieved with the massification of the art system and the extraordinary development of the museum circuits in the 1980s and 1990s. The target is now equilibrium in the social sector, the primary aim in this respect being the presentation of a cultural model grounded on the categories of equity, ecology and economy, understood as indispensable values of the individual and collective moral responsibility.

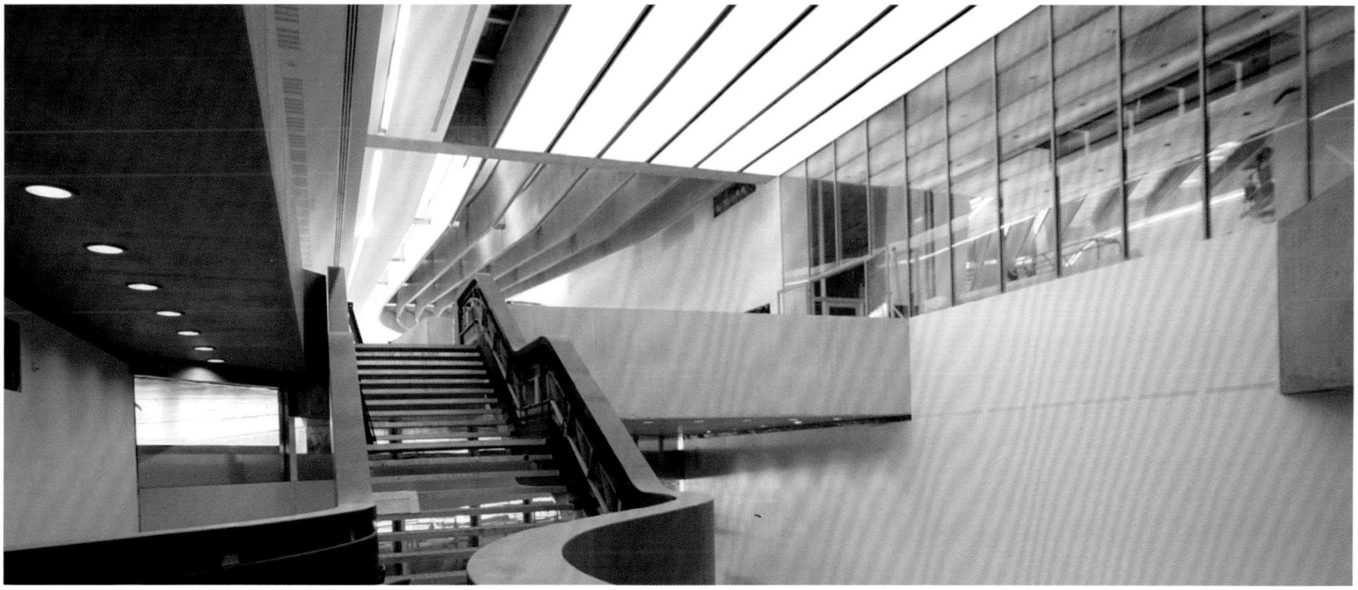

This precise responsibility is taken as a point of reference on the other side of the world also in the cultural mission of the 21st Century Museum of Contemporary Art in Kanazawa, Japan, with its the three programmatic Cs: consciousness, collective intelligence, and coexistence. Designed by Kazuyo Sejima and Ryue Nishizawa of the SANAA firm of architects and inaugurated in 2004, the museum was planned in close collaboration with the curator and hence taking its specific cultural mission very much into account.

The building is a fully transparent cylindrical structure with completely separate spaces for its activities. The unifying element is the glass cylinder of the external perimeter, which also inspired the graphic symbolism of the museum logo designed by Taku Satoh. Making visible the performance of the various functions inside the museum, above all shows, music, and performance, in both symbolic and concrete terms, the architectural decision to opt for transparency is also a precise ethical indication of the transparency of cultural and artistic processes.

The Western sensitivity to problems bound up with the design philosophy of buildings with high cultural potential – including the museum as place and the dualities of nature and artifice, reason and spirit, ethics and worldliness – unquestionably finds important stimuli and points of reference in contemporary Eastern architecture. Through the natural convergence of opposites, the dichotomies that have obstructed the concept of a totality of being in the West for centuries take shape in the East as new critical perspectives for architecture.

In addressing at the philosophical level the complex relationship between nature and artifice, inside and outside, architecture and landscape, Western museum design has therefore unquestionably drawn inspiration from Eastern culture and the example of a great deal of Eastern architecture. It is above all in Japan that architects have succeeded in channeling into the spaces devoted to culture and art, but also habitation in general, the best part of a philosophy that is highly mystical by definition and capable of understanding and reuniting the duality of the elements constituting the essence of mankind's rational and spiritual life better than its Western counterparts.

This clearly has a marked bearing on the design of museums, homes of the spirit par excellence, places where visitors are led toward meditation and the attainment of an increasingly enlightened awareness and understanding of things in their process of being and becoming. Some of the most interesting contemporary museums built in Japan provide true confirmation of the importance attached by the East to uniting opposites and lending balance and harmony to the relationship between the work of art and the space containing and surrounding it. It is no coincidence that the architectural model providing the most inspiration for new museums in the 1990s was the white cube, an element of the utmost austerity eliminating all interference and making possible the utmost concentration of eye and mind on the work of art in accordance with the most orthodox principles of Zen meditation. Some buildings by Tadao Ando – an architect whose work is developed with great skill at the point of intersection between the Eastern and Western cultures and nourished equally by both these great civilizations – stand out in the context of this fairly general approach. One is the Benesse House on the island of Naoshima, completed in 1992 and constituting Japan's first site-specific museum of contemporary art, which is based on a model widely adopted over the same period also in Europe, as in Hans Hollein's design for the Museum für Moderne Kunst in Frankfurt (1991).

The peculiarity of the Benesse House lies in the fact that it was the collection and the artist that determined the value of the project and the sense of the design project for perhaps the first time in the history of Japanese museums – which began as long ago as 1877 with a pavilion for the National Exhibition of Industry in Tokyo and continued through the early twentieth century with the use of ancient and illustrious historical buildings whose symbolic importance somewhat outweighed their suitability for the preservation and conservation of the items housed there.

Gradually enriched with permanent works of art created in perfect harmony not only with the museum but also with more symbolically characterized houses, temples, and sanctuaries scattered all over the island (the Art House Project), the Benesse House today presents site-specific works of exceptional interest and quality. Located once again on the island of Naoshima, the Chichu Art Museum (2004) – an underground complex housing masterpieces by Monet, Walter De Maria, and James Turrell – is another product of the extraordinary sensitivity of

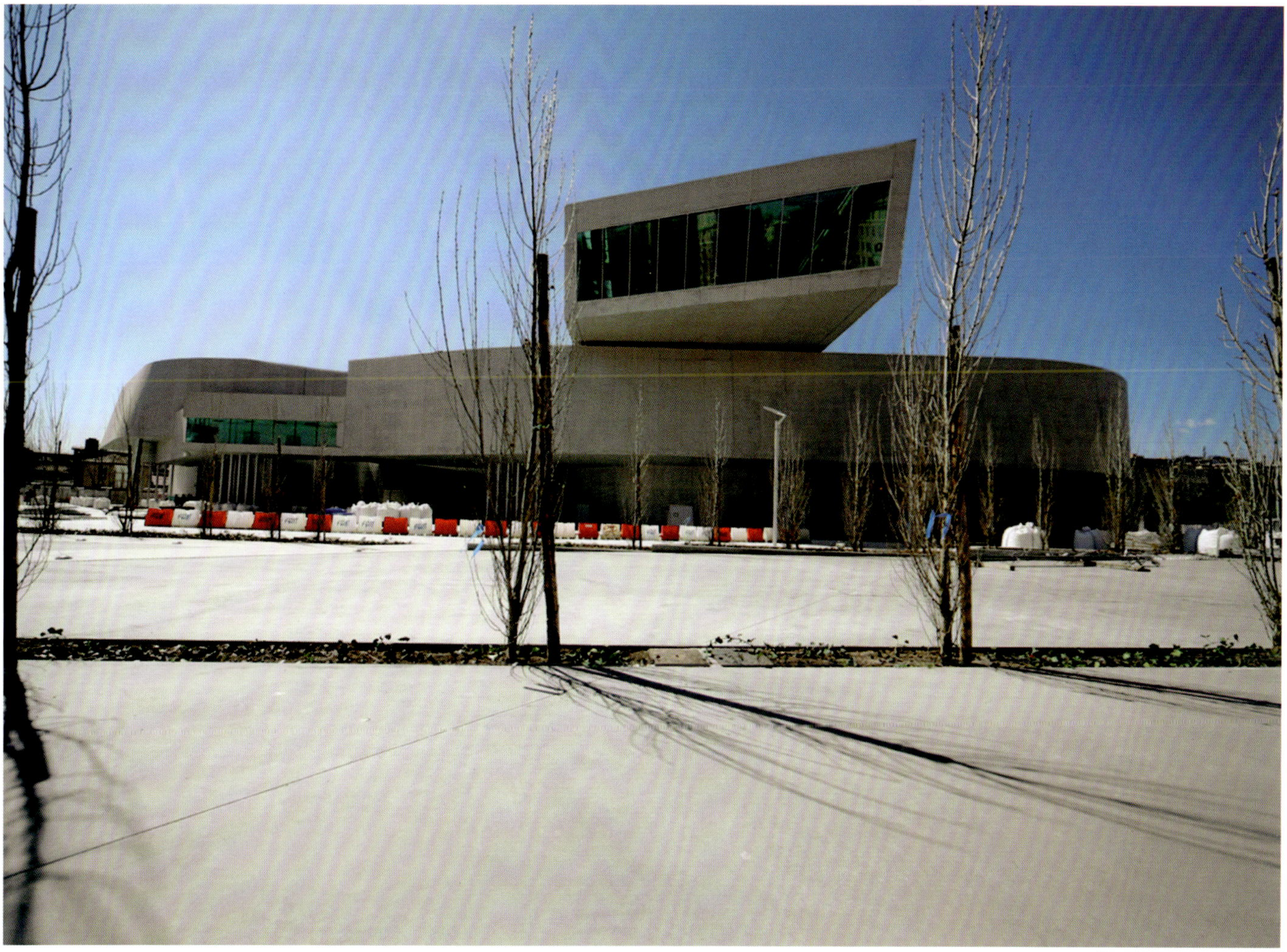

Zaha Hadid Architects
Exterior view of the MAXXI_Museo nazionale delle arti del XXI secolo, Rome, 2009
Courtesy MAXXI_Museo nazionale delle arti del XXI secolo, Rome

Tadao Ando and his firm Architects & Associates.

The museum is a paradigmatic work of architecture by virtue not only of its design but also the particular quality of the building, which represents and in some way makes explicitly universal the tormented condition and suffering of contemporary human beings in silent dialogue with themselves. As Tadao Ando wrote in the presentation of the project of this Japanese museum: "Darkness rather than light, below ground rather than above – the Chichu Art Museum is the most direct expression of this feeling rooted deep inside me."

The Chichu Museum is a work of singular beauty carved in the depths of the earth, a mysterious place that seems to withdraw before the unspoiled beauty of the natural countryside of this outermost strip of the island overlooking the Pacific Ocean. Created as an impenetrable sunken court, like other already known works by Tadao Ando, it is made still more amazing by the geometric simplification of the architectural devices adopted, which unite light and shadow, solid and void, depth and elevation, in the tranquility of silent spaces. Taken here as a paradigm for its perfect blending of nature and artifice, the museum is a model of particular interest that has arisen from a solution worked out between the East and the West.

The function and mission of the museum and its architecture appear to coincide finally in the formulation of a new Utopia, which, to the synthesis of the humanistic sciences and technologies, spirit and reason, the East and the West, now seems to want to add the ethical parameter of sustainable development. It can now be stated that the attention of the museum world is being drawn to a new humanistic thought, at the centre of which, in addition to purely disciplinary questions on the subjects of art and architecture, a complex debate has been opened, one that can no longer be postponed. It is a debate on social development founded on justness, ecology and economics, one that may stimulate the only adequate responses to the new cultural and civil needs related to the living, knowing and doing of the multiethnic and multicultural society that inhabits our planet.

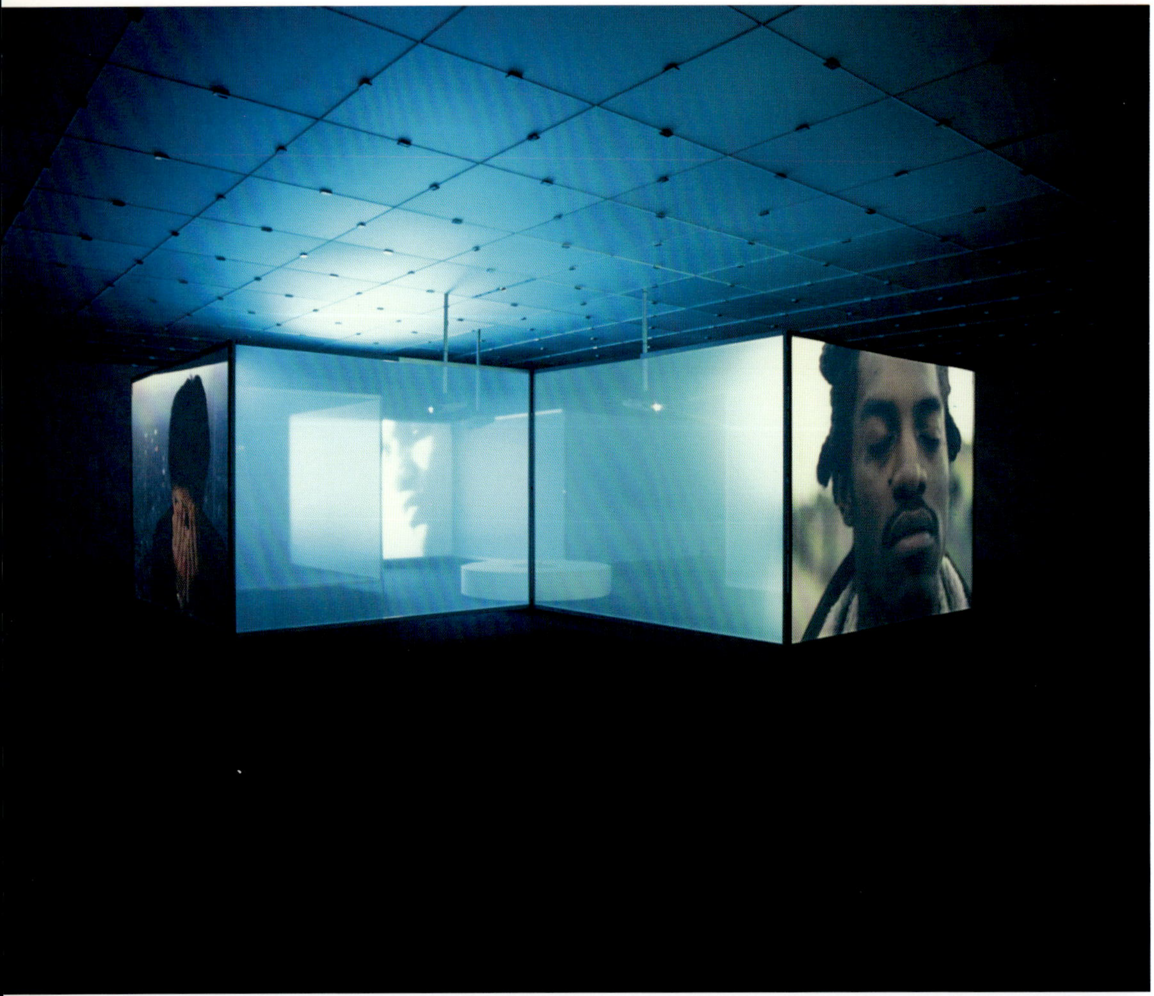

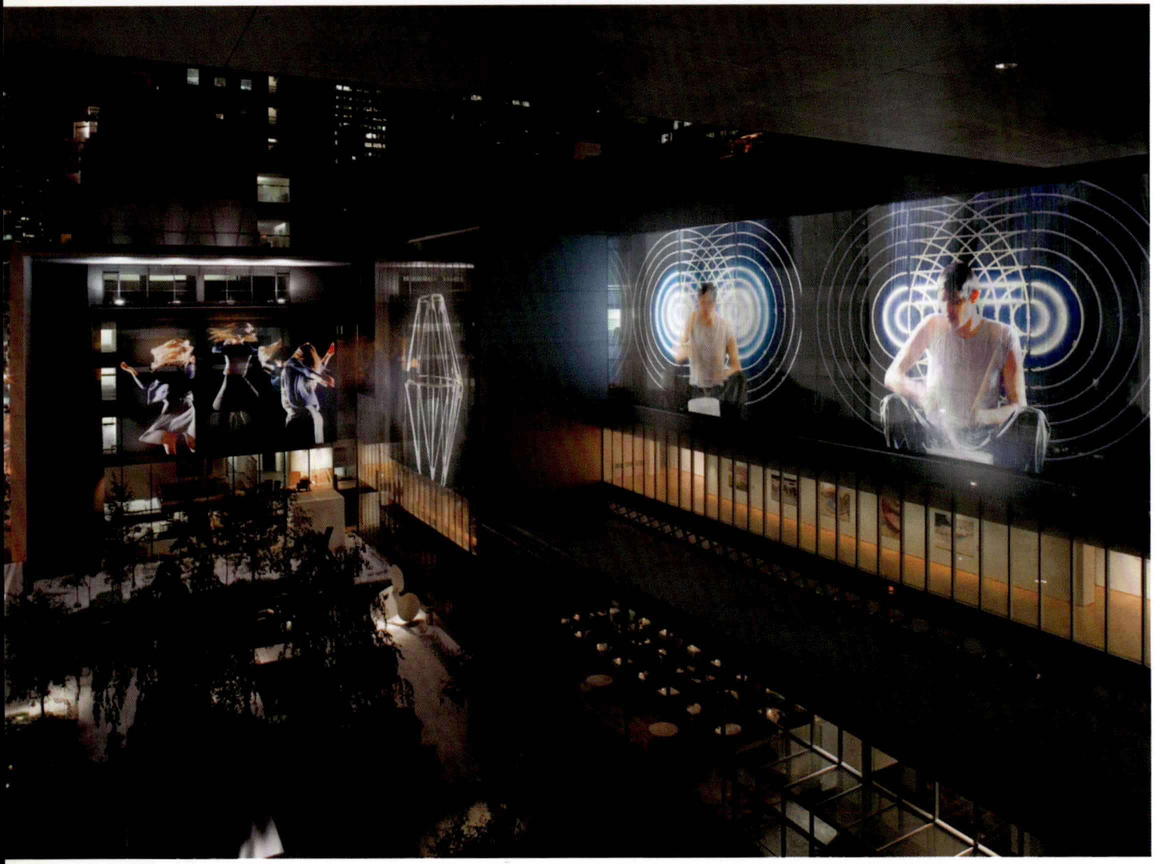

Doug Aitken

Born in Redondo Beach, California, in 1968. Lives and works in New York and Los Angeles.
Advances in projection technology and the example of Bill Viola led many artists working with video in the late 1990s to develop an architectural and environmental approach, using more than one screen to present their narratives and creating "full-immersion" situations in which the video is not just a story but a fragmented, complex, hypertextual experience involving all the senses. One of these is the Californian artist Doug Aitken, whose professional expertise in handling the camera and developing a strong relationship between image and sound clearly reflects his initial experience as a director of musical video clips.
Aitken appears to focus primarily on enabling the video to represent time in line with our current perception of this dimension, in a high-tech present in which time is no longer linear but made up of shifts and synchronies more similar to a closely interwoven mesh than a straight line. As he explains, "Film and video structure our experience in a linear way simply because they are moving images on a strip of emulsion or tape. They create a story out of everything because it's inherent to the medium and to the structure of montage. But, of course, we experience time in a much more complex way.
The question for me is, 'how can I break through this idea, which is reinforced constantly? How can I make time somehow collapse and expand?'"
At the same time, his videos address a series of themes that recur as point and counterpoint from one work to the next.
Produced by attaching the camera to a small rocket launched into the sky, *Inflection* (1992) introduces an obsession with speed, technology, and the contrast between the open spaces of nature and the urban environment. In *Monsoon* (1995), shot in the jungle of Guyana just before the rains, action gives way to expectation and the exploration of a place that will be completely transformed in the space of few hours with the arrival of a cataclysmic monsoon. *Diamond Sea* (1997) ventures into the diamond mines of Namibia located in the world's oldest desert, an area off-limits to visitors for decades. Underlying the apparently documentary approach is the artist's real interest in a place outside space and time, a sort of parallel world that he explores in a sort of dream-like state. The only inhabitants of this immense empty space are the diamond-extracting machines, which appear to work in complete autonomy. As Aitken explains, "I want non-decisive moments, inactions, what has happened before or what is to come."
The narrative flow in *Diamond Sea* is broken up into different projections spread over the exhibition space in such a way as to suggest a pathway. The same strategy is adopted in *Cathouse* (1997), the first of a number of works involving a delimited architectural context. Here we have a claustrophobic sort of house fitted with monitors, each of which presents a character (a woman, a man, and a child) engaged in a repetitive action of almost autistic nature. This deft handling of space paved the way for *Electric Earth* (1999), the eight-screen installation that brought Aitken success and the Golden Lion award at the Venice Biennale with the story of a man living out the "electric" rhythm of the city through dance. This heralded a steady increase in the architectural and narrative complexity of Aitken's works, from *New Ocean* (2001), the monumental installation presented on different floors at the Serpentine Gallery in London to *Sleepwalkers* (2007), an six-screen projection staged at night on the outer walls of the MoMA in New York and constituting the artist's first public project. The installation requires spectators to move around the museum's perimeter in order to follow the interwoven stories of five characters (played by stars like Donald Sutherland and Tilda Swinton) beginning their day, "captur[ing] the multiple facets of a living city as if seen through a cut diamond." At the same time, Aitken also began to work with other media, in particular on a number of interesting installations in which sound takes over from image in the construction of space. (*D.Q.*)

Interiors, 2002
Video installation/environment
Three-channel, screen, dimensions variable, produced in collaboration with Fabric Workshop and Museum, Philadelphia
View of the installation realized in 2003 at the Kunsthaus Bregenz, Breganze
Courtesy 303 Gallery, New York

Sleepwalkers, 2007
Six-channel video installation, dimensions variable
View of the installation realized in 2007 at the Museum of Modern Art, New York
Courtesy 303 Gallery, New York; Galerie Eva Presenhuber, Zurich; Victoria-Miro Gallery, London; Regen Projects, Los Angeles

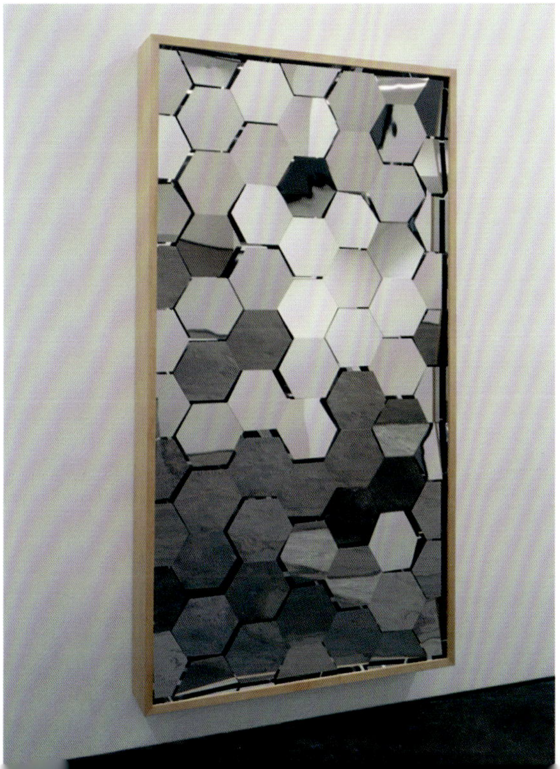

The Moment Is the Moment, 2004
Automated stainless steel mirrors, Baltic birch, electrical motors, 195 x 105 x 20 cm
Courtesy 303 Gallery, New York

Pawel Althamer

Born in Warsaw in 1967. Lives and works in Warsaw.
Pawel Althamer's videos and sculptures address the subject of the portrait, its present role, and its expressive forms. All of his work essentially involves the image of the human figure, based on himself and members of his family, but completely divorced from the context and status of official or bourgeois portrait painting.
The characters created by Althamer have a disturbing nature and convey a sense of disorientation and malaise through the elements that characterize their portraits, such as nudity and accessories of an enigmatic nature.
Althamer's universe is unquestionably anthropocentric and represents a journey into his lived experience and future, temporal spaces in which memory and clairvoyance are confused.
The artist portrays himself as a child and but at the same time with his face as an old man in an impracticable coexistence of images and facets of the self.
Balloon, a monumental project carried out in Milan in 2007, is an example of the ways in which the artist displays himself to the world in an ambiguous attitude of egocentricity and reticence.
It involved a huge self-portrait floating completely naked face downward in the sky over the city. The nudity is archaic in character and the position of the legs and the arms, parallel and close to the body, recalls the static posture of the early Greek *kouroi*. The result is thus a figure that displays its individuality outwardly but also eliminates it through a formal pose derived from public statuary.
Different aims are pursued with *Weronika*, an almost life-size portrait of the artist's daughter, a child with her hair neatly arranged in two braids holding a fishing rod with a feather on the end of the line. The sculpture is made of animal hide, hemp, and other perishable materials, which helps to suggest the existence of a form of life differing from the human not only in its physical characteristics but also in its moral qualities, thus arousing feelings midway between disgust and compassion in the viewer.
(*F.T.*)

Weronika, 2001
Hay, hemp, animal gut, wax, hair, glass, wood, feather,
110 x 40 x 25 cm
Switzerland, Lithops Collection
View of the installation realized in 2007 at the Arena Civica of Milan
Courtesy Fondazione Nicola Trussardi, Milan

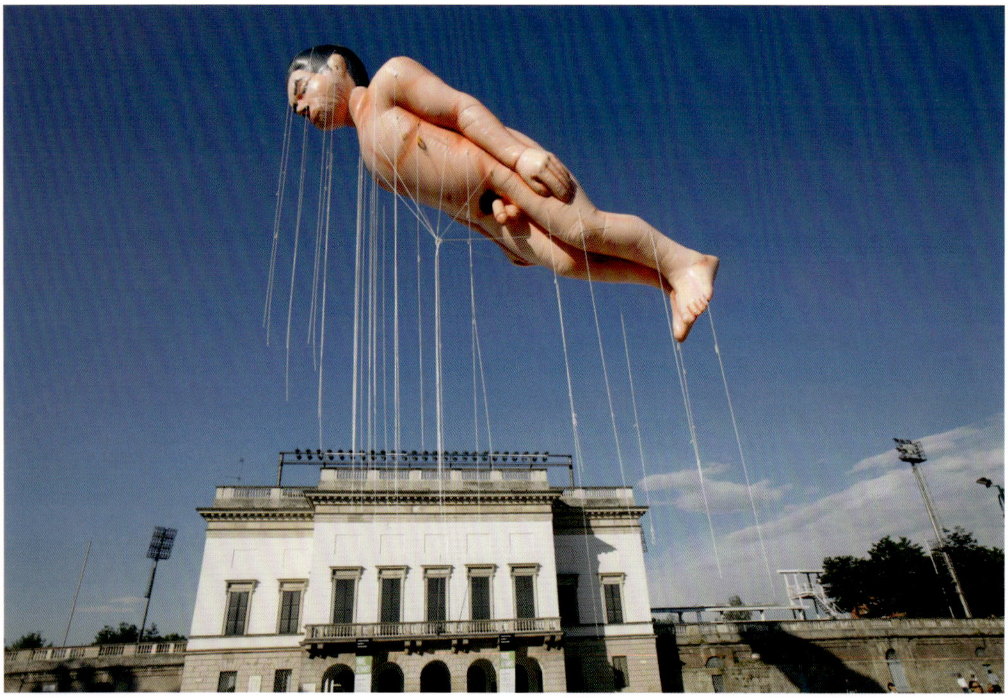

Balloon, 2007
Nylon, polyester, acrylic, ropes, helium, 2100 x 671 x 366 cm
View of the installation realized in 2007 at the Arena Civica of Milan
Courtesy of the artist; Foksal Gallery Foundation, Warsaw; Galerie Neugerriemschneider, Berlin; Fondazione Nicola Trussardi, Milan

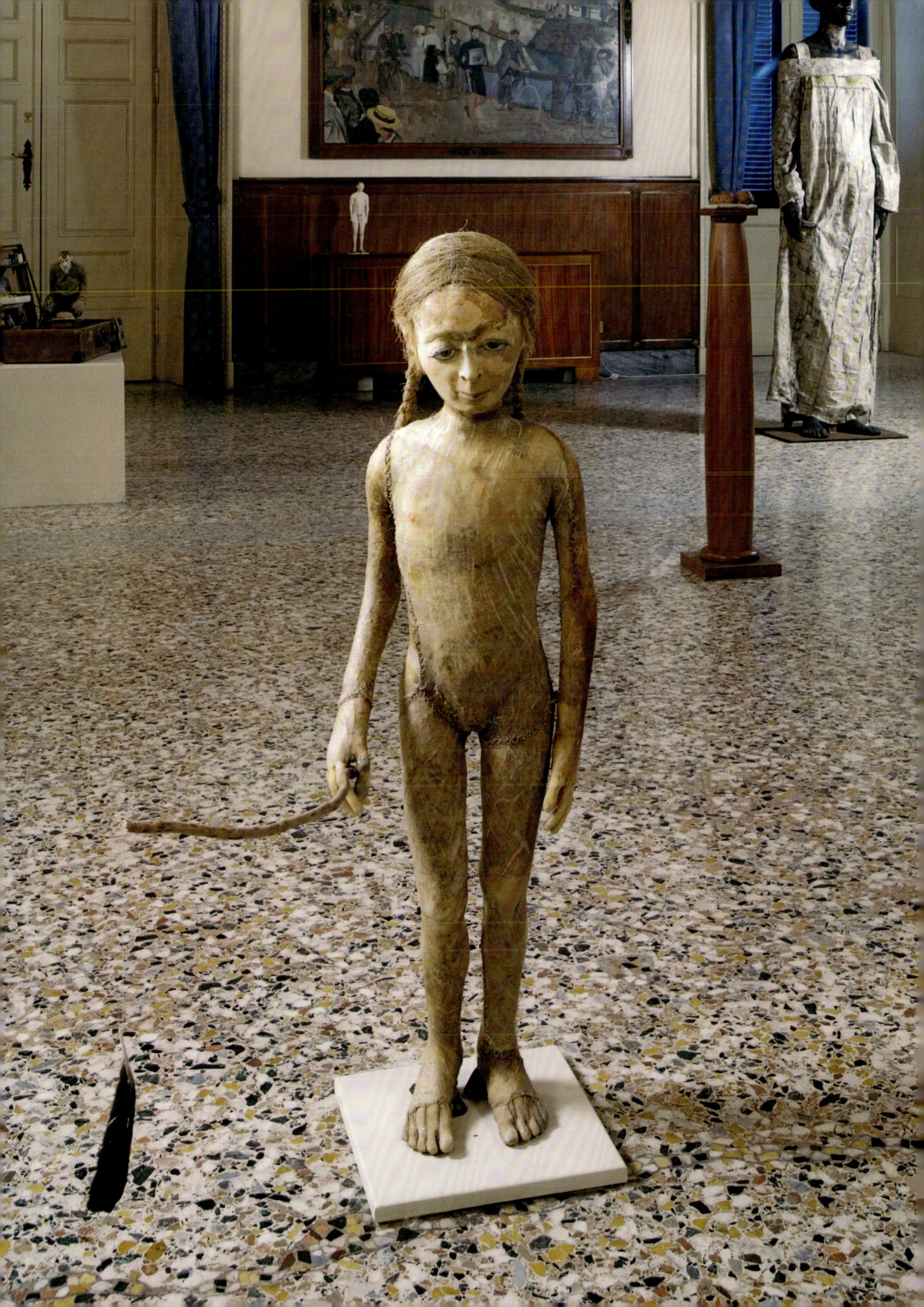

Cecily Brown

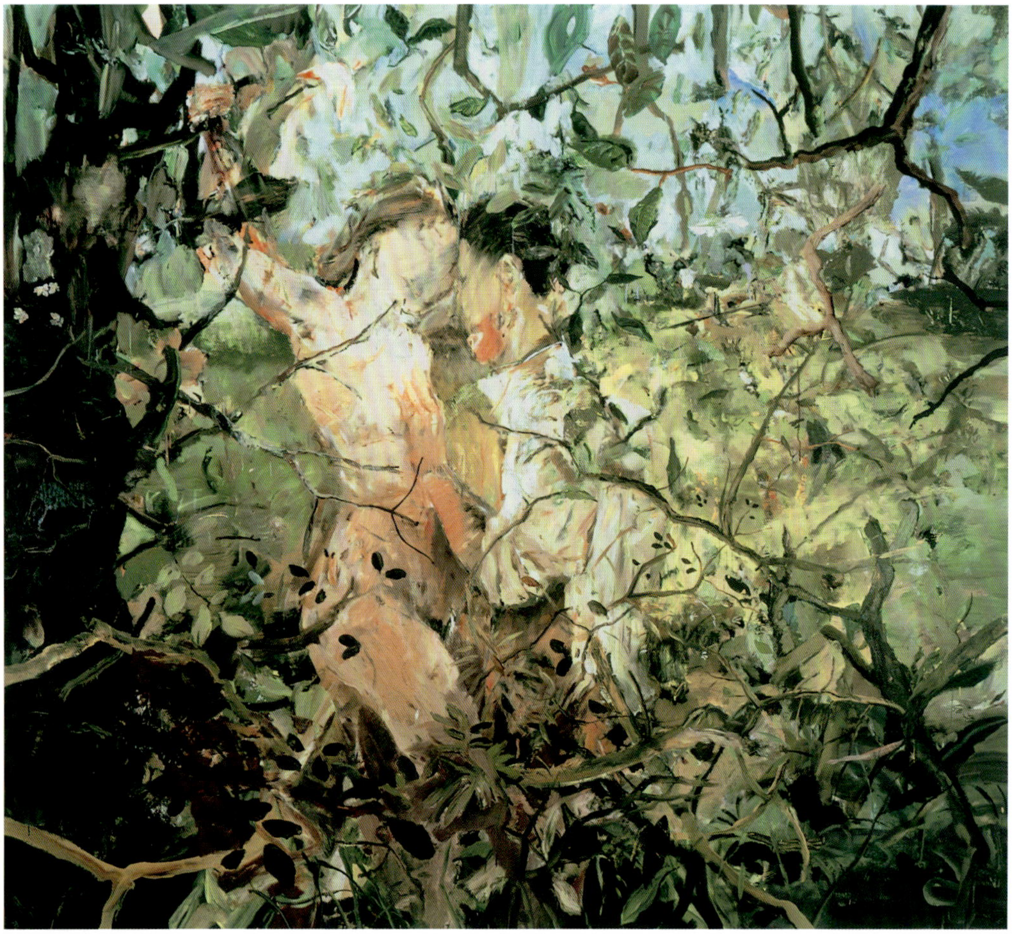

Teenage Wild Life, 2003
Oil on canvas, 203 x 228 cm
London, The Saatchi Collection

Skulldiver III (Flightmask), 2006
Oil on canvas, 216 x 227 cm
Boston, Museum of Fine Arts,
Museum purchase with funds
donated by Ann and Graham Gund

Born in London in 1969. Lives and works in New York.
Cecily Brown has focused primarily on reworking the art of the past in a new and original blend of figurative and abstract painting since the 1990s, when the London art scene was instead concerned above all with installations and dematerialization of the object.
She instead began to revisit the great masters, including Poussin, Hogarth, Rubens, Goya, Velázquez and the Monet of the *Water Lilies*, on large-sized canvases in the light of the work of some of the leading figures in postwar art, especially Francis Bacon and Willem de Kooning.
The focal point of Brown's work is exploration of the human body and sexuality, which is addressed, however, not as a subject but rather as an expedient to transfer the sensuality, carnality and marked erotic content from the scenes depicted into the act of painting itself.
The artist's aim is indeed to develop to the maximum the ability of the pictorial medium to capture physical sensations rather than mental states. The approach of all-over painting borrowed from American Abstract Expressionism is also used by the artist, not so much in order to translate violent and all-encompassing emotions with great immediacy, as to create a sort of bodily connection between herself, the work and the public.
Brown addresses the canvas with dynamic and agitated strokes of the brush or palette knife, shattering the scene represented into an almost kaleidoscopic gestural pattern where bodies in motion, mostly locked in passionate embraces, emerge from the landscape or surrounding environment. The possibility of creating the illusion of dynamism in a static system is one aspect of the potential of painting that Cecily Brown finds most fascinating, which also explains her great admiration not only for the art of the seventeenth and eighteenth centuries – it is impossible not to think of Giambattista Tiepolo, for example, on viewing some of her canvases – but also for the gestural painting of the postwar period.
(*P.V.*)

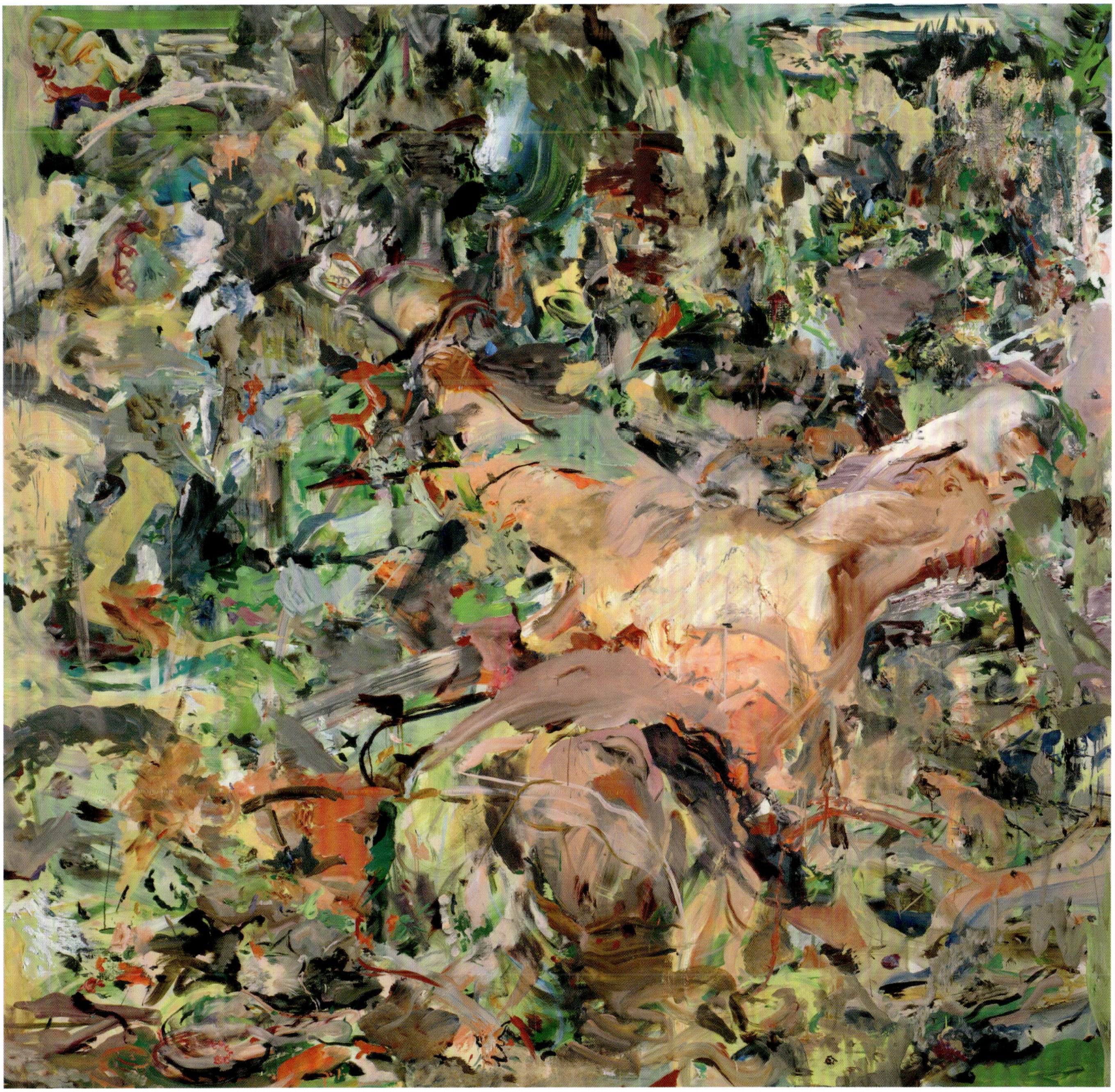

Maurizio Cattelan

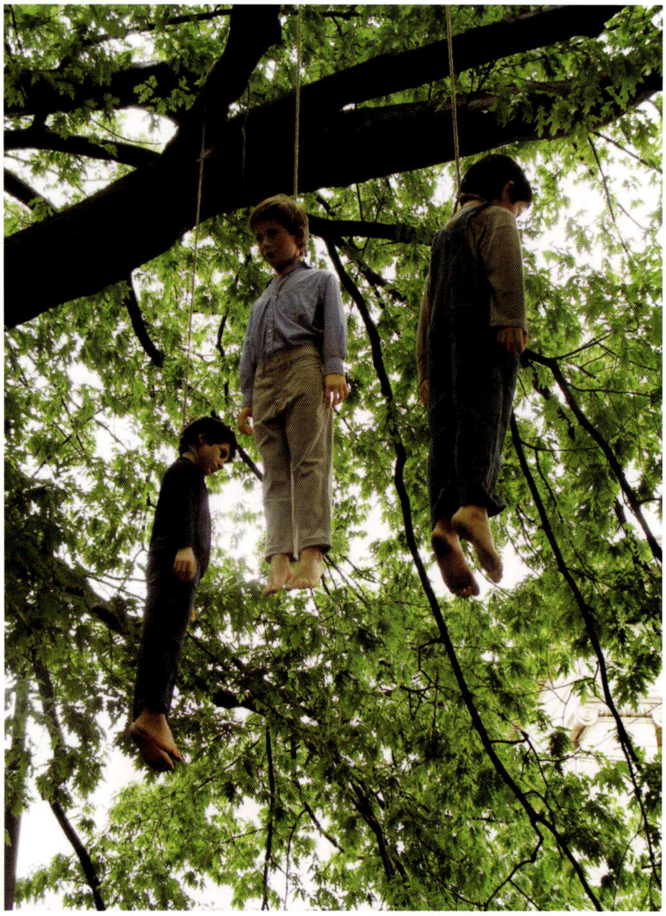

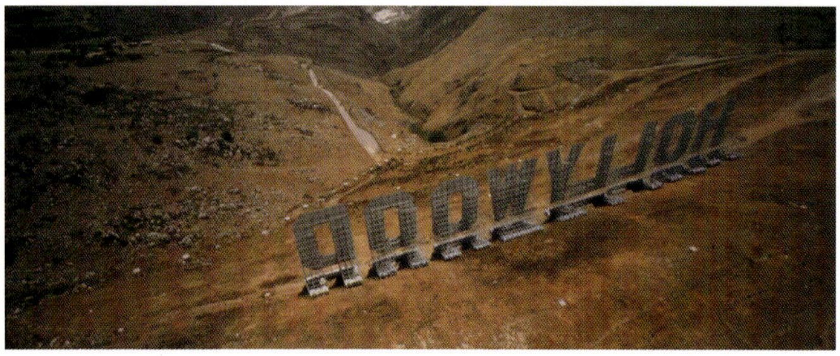

Untitled, 2004
Resin, fiberglass, clothes, hair, 3 mannequins, height 115 cm each
Courtesy Galerie Emmanuel Perrotin, Miami & Paris

Hollywood, 2001
Color photograph, 180 x 400 x 15 cm
Courtesy Galerie Emmanuel Perrotin, Miami & Paris

Safe Fractured, 1996
Safe, 140 x 70 x 90 cm
Courtesy Galerie Emmanuel Perrotin, Miami & Paris

Felix, 2001
Oil on polyvinyl resin and fiberglass, 7.9 x 1.8 x 6.1 m
Chicago, The Museum of Contemporary Art, Chicago, The Edlis/Neeson Art Purchase Fund
Courtesy Galerie Emmanuel Perrotin, Miami & Paris

Born in Padua, Italy, in 1960. Lives and works in New York.

The work of Maurizio Cattelan attained international recognition in the 1990s by virtue of his ability to interpret the spirit of the times with great energy and lucidity. His art is largely based on provocation, shock, disorientation, and manipulation of the flow of information. While these strategies were used in the early phase of his career – some would say too often – in order to investigate and subvert the mechanisms of power within the world of art and the role of the artist in our society, the latest works address the great issues of the present and human life in general: hope, violence, faith, and death. In other words, Cattelan's recent works are revealing the other face of the clown and "court jester", traditional figures often used as points of reference in interpreting his work, not least by Nancy Spector. This sad and contemplative stance contrasts with the vein of irony and self-mockery running through much of his work.

Maurizio Cattelan started out as an artist in the late 1980s after trying his hand at various activities. In fact, art would appear to be a way of avoiding work and the authoritarian structures it involves. It is no coincidence that one of his first works was a medical certificate for sick leave obtained from an obliging doctor (*Certificato medico*, 1989). In the same way, many of his early operations were revealed as attempts to avoid the burden of the expectations generated by a show, both solo and collective. In 1989, for his first solo show at the Galleria Neon in Bologna, Cattelan confined himself to leaving a "back soon" notice on the locked door. His work for a group show at the Castello di Rivara, Turin, in 1992 consisted of a rope of knotted sheets hanging from his bedroom window as though he had just escaped. The gallery was also locked for his first solo show in Milan, at Massimo De Carlo's gallery, but the work was visible in this case through a half-open window: a tightrope-walking teddy bear left free to use the otherwise empty space as he pleased. On being invited to take part in the Venice Biennale the same year, he rented out the space assigned him to an advertising company. Significantly enough, the title of this work was *Lavorare è un brutto mestiere*: Work is a Bad Job. And in 1994, for his first solo show in New York, he simply locked a live donkey in the gallery with some fodder and a deluxe chandelier.

When escape seems impossible, Cattelan launches a direct attack on his "employer" or the context crushing him with its oppressive authority. For a solo show in Paris in 1994, he forced the gallery owner Emmanuel Perrotin to wear a cumbersome rabbit costume whose shape and color also suggested a gigantic penis. He had Massimo De Carlo "crucified" to the wall of his gallery with heavy-duty adhesive tape in 1999. His contribution to the Venice Biennale in 1997 consisted of a flock of stuffed pigeons perched everywhere, even on top of Ettore Spalletti's glacial works. The ostrich with its head hidden in sawdust presented the same year at the *Made in Italy* exhibition at the ICA in London became the emblem of the weak strategies of Italian art as against the aggressiveness of Young British Art. And the *Picasso* that greeted visitors to the New York MoMA in 1998 – an enormous head of papier-mâché looking at carnival masks on one side and Disneyland puppets on the other – proved a thorn in the flesh for the museum's management, who were obliged to reconsider its marketing strategies.

Cattelan alternates between flouting authority and displaying reverential dread, avoiding competition and violating the sanctity of other people's work. His works sometimes seem to present him as a dwarf perched on the shoulders of giants or as fragile and vulnerable with respect to others. In *Mini-Me* (1999), a small puppet bearing his likeness sits on a shelf in the place that should be occupied by the book on the artist published by Phaidon (but reduced to a quarter of the size of the others in the Contemporary Artists series).

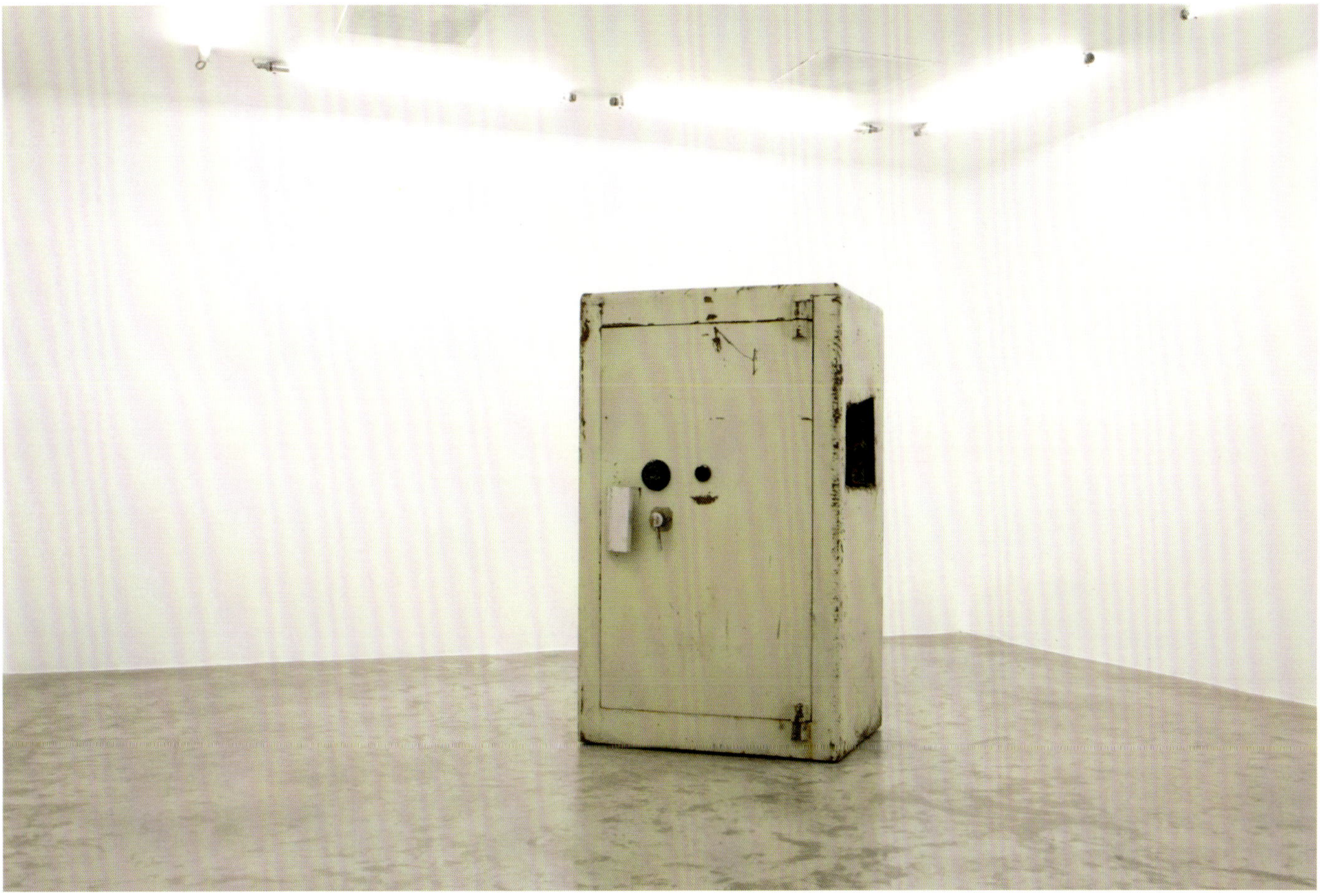

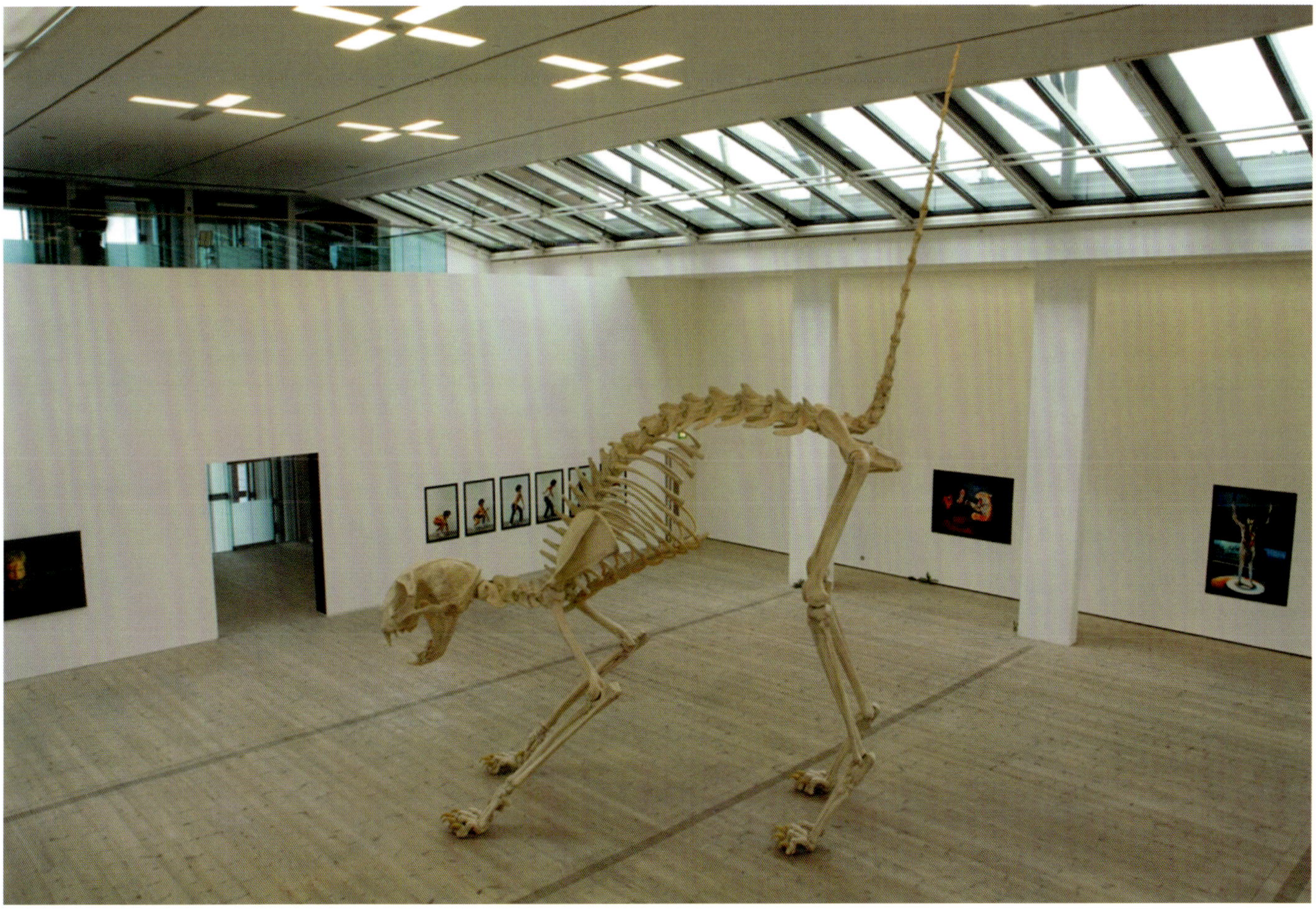

La nona ora, 1999
Polyester resin, hair, dress, shoes, pastoral, stone, carpet, dimensions variable, sculpture Daniel Druet
Courtesy Galerie Emmanuel Perrotin, Miami & Paris

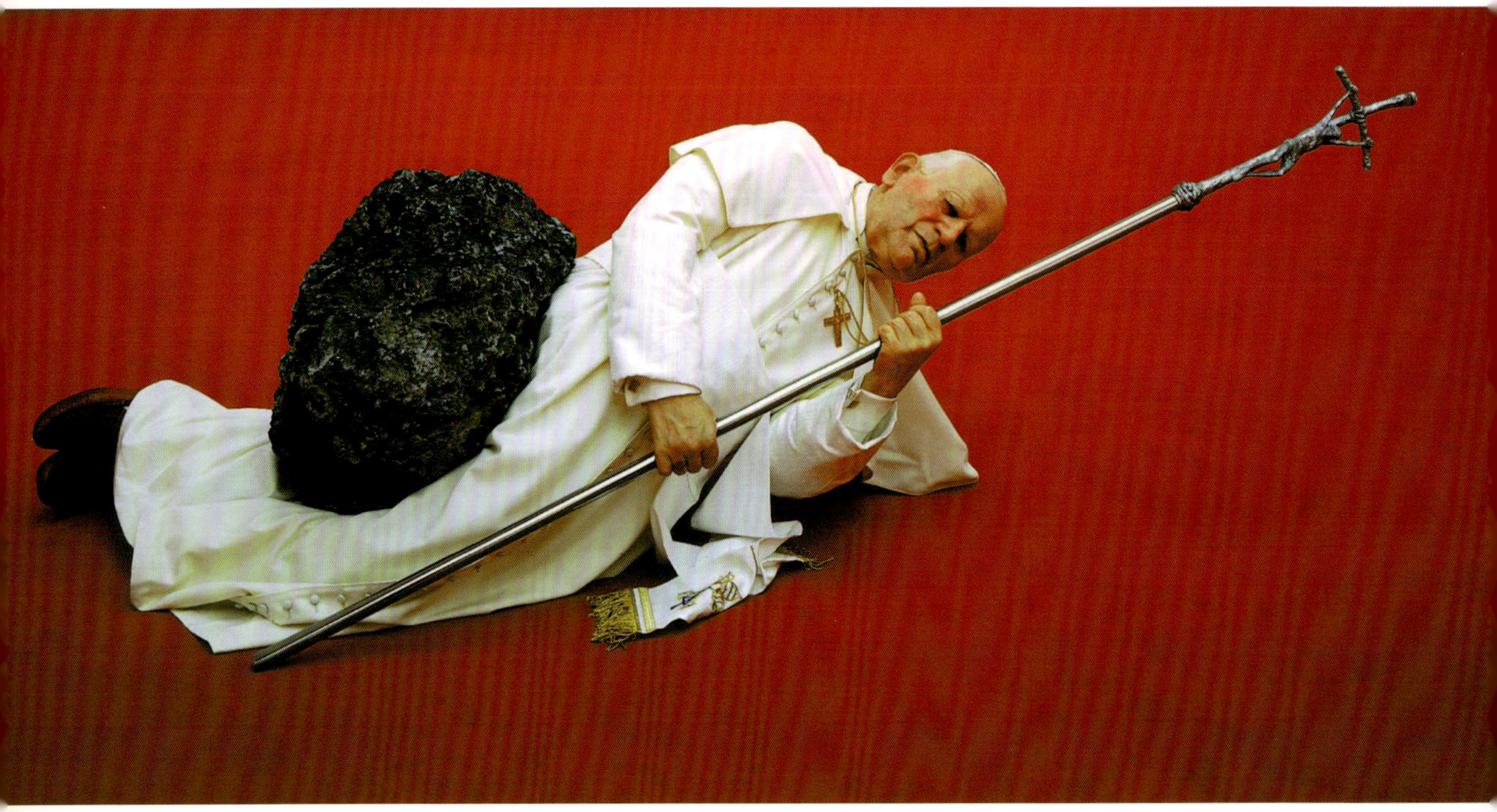

The artist appeared dangling defenseless by the scruff of the neck from a clothes-hanger in *La rivoluzione siamo noi* (2000, We Are the Revolution), peering rapturously at masterpieces of the past from a hole in the floor of a room in the Boijmans Museum the year after, and as a child on a remote-controlled tricycle pestering the line of visitors at the Venice Biennale in *Charlie* (2003).
Even in these works, however, self-referential reflection on the world of art is only one of the components and not necessarily the essential one. Surprise, provocation, and wisecracks are often no more than stratagems employed in order to introduce another theme.
The artist's ambivalent relationship with authority in whatever form it might take sometimes abandons the overtones of farce to turn into tragedy, as in *Charlie Don't Surf* (1997), which shows a child nailed to the Formica top of his school desk with pencils. While the school is attacked as a repressive institution in this case, in *Bidibidobidiboo* (1996) it is probably the family, symbolized by the domestic space of the kitchen, which drives the poor squirrel to the extreme act of suicide. In the same way, *La rivoluzione siamo noi* ironically introduces the subject of history with a capital H, which Cattelan also explores in numerous other works. One example is *Stadium* (1991), which presented two real soccer teams, one made up of Italians and the other of illegal immigrants, playing a match around an oblong table football machine. This work addresses the dramatic condition of a country that has changed from a land of emigration into one of immigration with all the attendant social problems (including racism, as suggested by the word *Raus* on the jerseys of the African team). *Natale 95* (1995) was a neon Christmas star incorporating the symbol of the Red Brigades in a period when terrorism was displaying renewed vitality. Bombs were set off in 1993 near some symbolic cultural venues, including the Uffizi in Florence and the PAC (Padiglione d'Arte Contemporanea) in Milan, where the explosion destroyed part of the building and killed three people. Cattelan bought part of the rubble left and exhibited it in sacks in two installations in London and Paris (*Lullaby*, 1994). Cattelan's extraordinary talent often manifests itself in his ability to encapsulate some great, unresolved issue of our time in a simple image full of compressed energy. It is no coincidence that controversy is still raging over some of his works. Examples include *Mother* (1999), a real fakir buried in the ground with just his joined hands left visible; *Him* (2001), a small Hitler kneeling devoutly in prayer; *Novecento* (1997), a horse hanging from the ceiling with its legs stretched out in an unsuccessful effort to reach the ground; *La nona ora* (1999, The Ninth Hour), which shows Pope John Paul II struck down by a meteorite. The three dummies of children hanged from a tree in a public area in Milan (*Untitled*, 2004) triggered not only heated debate but also acts of vandalism, as citizens found the violence of the image or the accusation implicit in it intolerable. The same ambiguous energy is to be found in the works presented in two exhibitions in 2007, one at the Kunsthaus in Bregenz and the other at the MMK in Frankfurt: works that raise questions about history (Nazism) and the present day, the role of religion in many social dystopias, death, desire, love, and the family. Though born out of the same mechanisms as the previous works, these are austere creations that provide little satisfaction for those in search of the "clown".
The two shows of 2007 came after three years of substantial artistic inactivity spent on other projects. (He also curated the Berlin Biennial together with Massimiliano Gioni and Ali Subotnick.) Cattelan has in any case always been tempted by the demon of idleness. It was in 1992 that he founded the Oblomov Foundation in Milan for the purpose of awarding money to an artist willing to stop work for a year. Once the funds had been raised,

Untitled, 2007
Silicon resin, hair, steel, wooden door, 240 x 130 x 70 cm
Courtesy Galerie Emmanuel Perrotin, Miami & Paris

he used them himself to finance his first trip to New York. The Caribbean Biennial organized with Jens Hoffmann in 1999 in response to the proliferation of biennials was actually a vacation for the two "founders" but also an opportunity to escape from the immense pressure to which artists are subjected by the constant creation of international events. Collaboration is not only a distinguishing characteristic of projects like those cited above (as well as the Wrong Gallery, a gallery of one square meter founded in 2002 with Gioni and Subotnick in New York, and *Permanent Food*, a "magazine of magazines" conceived as a collage of material from other periodicals and edited, together with Paola Manfrin). Cattelan, who speaks mainly in the first-person plural, has frequently stated that he develops his concepts on the telephone and has never laid hands on any of his works. Conceived as "trial runs" that can be reworked in the event of failure, they arise out of prolonged discussions with friends and assistants. The titles often arrive at a later stage and contact with the public remains crucial. On more than one occasion, he has used the work of others through operations of reworking, appropriation or downright plagiarism. This readiness to work with others, operate in different fields, and appropriate other people's creations makes Cattelan an emblematic figure of the present-day world of culture, which is still grappling with the thorny problems of intellectual property, the romantic figure of the "genius," and the new strategies of post-production. (*D.Q.*)

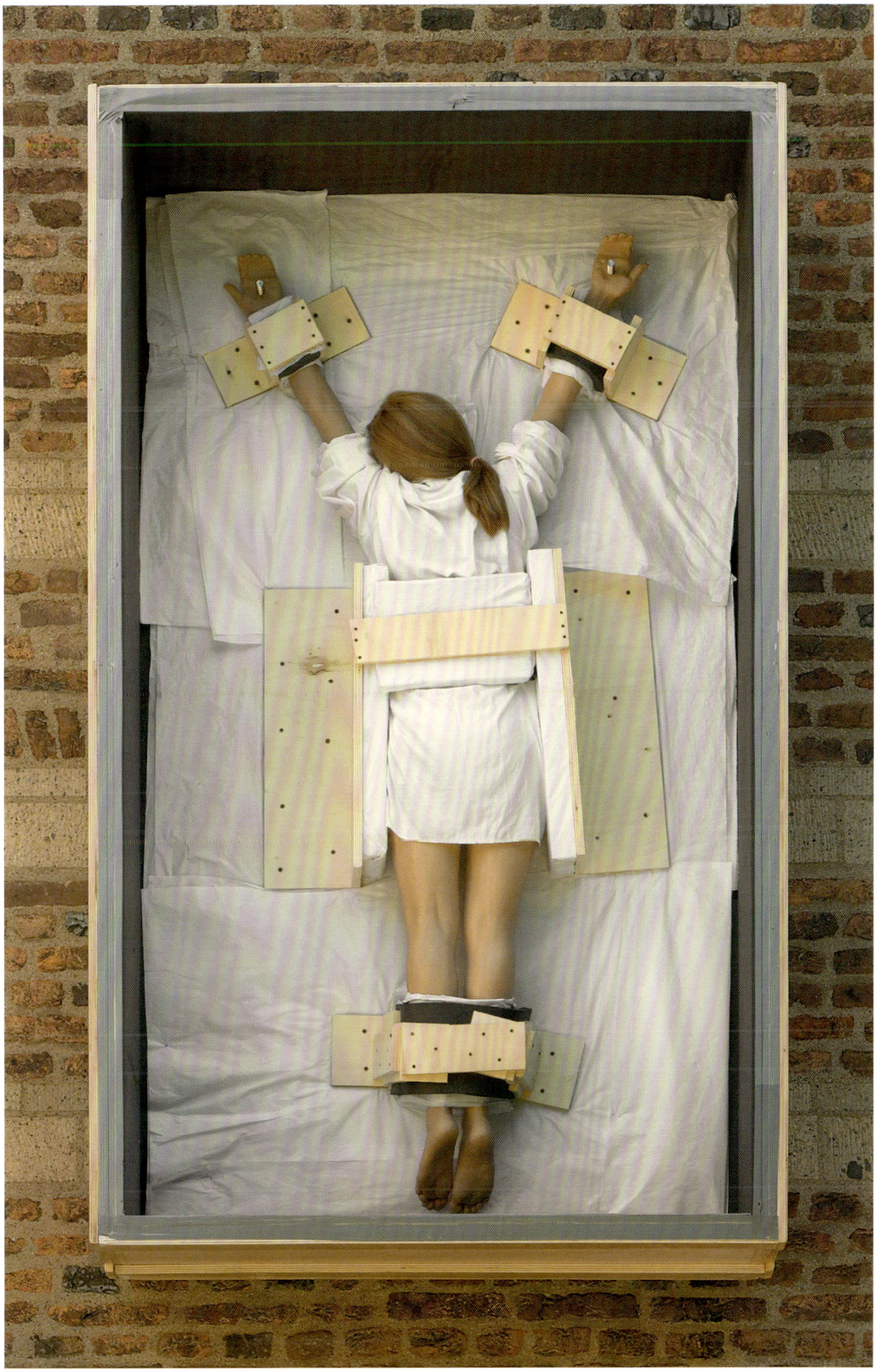

Wim Delvoye

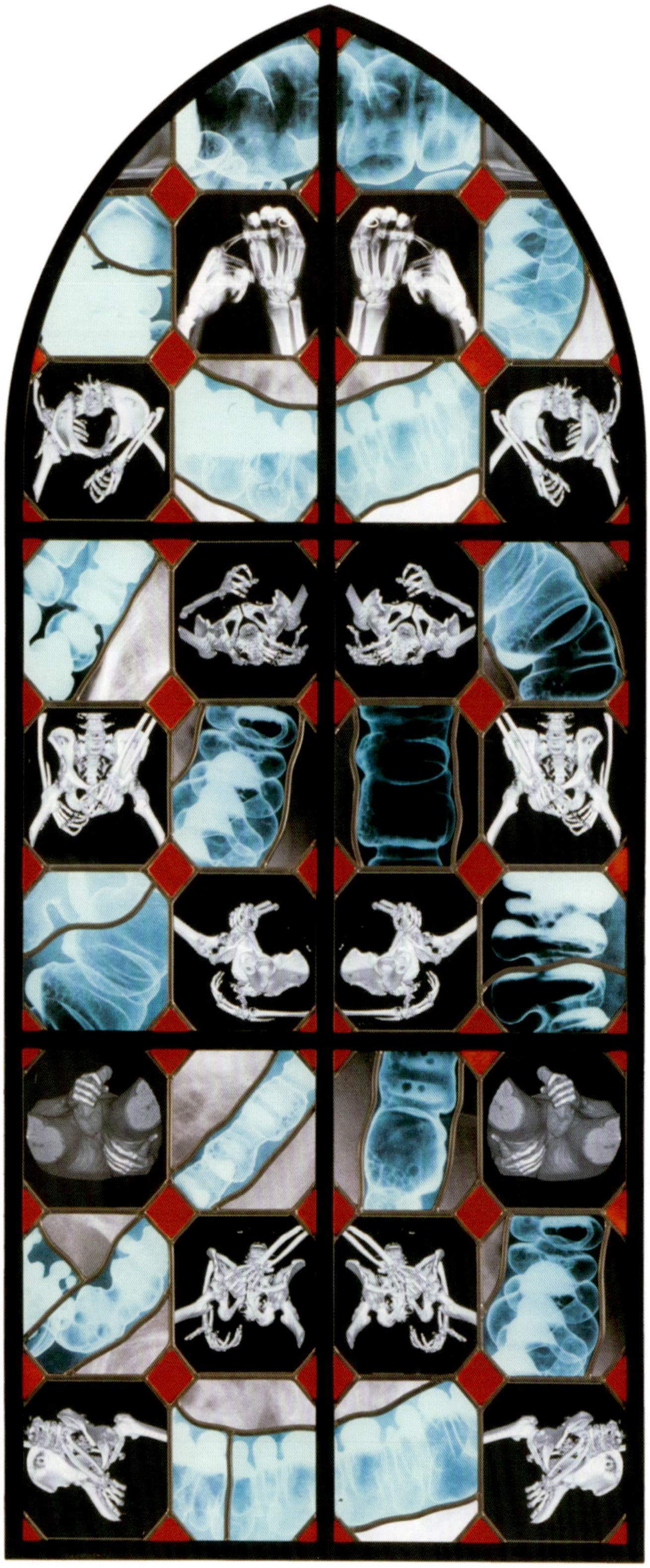

Born in Wervik, Belgium, in 1965. Lives and works in Ghent.
Wim Delvoye's own words are the best introduction to his art: "My works are like a virus inside the art system.... I don't believe in rebellion. I prefer to work my way into the system like cancer and grow inside it like a parasite."
It is not only the art system but also contemporary society in general with its symbols, rituals, and conventions that comes under attack from the corrosive impact of Delvoye's works. The family, work, sport, religion, health, sex, and fashion are areas that the artist contaminates by eliminating the boundaries that traditionally separate them and creating new and paradoxical overlaps. X-rays of parts of the human body become decorative motifs for a faux Gothic stained glass window (*Polymania,* 2003). Other works feature x-rays of people having sex. Trucks and cement mixers become sophisticated "cathedrals of work" in the flowery Gothic or Rococo style (*Cement Truck [Scale Model]*, 2008). The goals on a soccer pitch are blocked with elegant stained glass windows. Simple everyday messages of the kind left on a kitchen table end up (virtually) carved like epigraphs on Mount Rushmore.
The philistine "good taste" that largely governs trends in the consumer society is also exposed to the vitriolic force of Delvoye's works. Suffice it to recall the commonplace spades emblazoned with heraldic coats of arms (*Shovels*, 1990), the saw blades and gas cylinders in blue Delft china exhibited in showcases in place of crockery for special occasions, the floor tiles with their decorative pattern of dog turds (*Mosaics*, 1990), the fake inlaid marble floor made up of slices of sausage and salami (*Marble Floor*, 1999), and the pigs tattooed with "Louis Vuitton" designer motifs or beloved characters of globalized childhood like Disney's Little Mermaid (*Arielle*, 2006).
As is known, advertising logos create brand loyalty and influence consumer choices and habits. The artist's "signature" thus becomes a logo by imitating another with the same initials that is known in every corner of the world, namely the Walt Disney trademark. In the same way, the instantly recognizable Coca-Cola trademark is imitated in the logo of *Cloaca* (2000), the work with which Delvoye launched his attack directly on the heart of the production system. This consists of a perfectly functional machine that mirrors all the phases of digestion including its "end product", which is then offered for consumption in the familiar cans stamped with this logo, thus revisiting Manzoni's "artist's shit" from a new conceptual viewpoint (*Diet Coke Can*, 2002).
(*P.V.*)

Polymania, 2003
Color glass, steel, X–rays,
200 x 80 cm
Courtesy Galerie Emmanuel Perrotin, Miami & Paris

Diet Coke Can, 2002
Color print, 15 x 11.5 cm
Courtesy Galerie Emmanuel Perrotin, Miami & Paris

Arielle, 2006
Stuffed tattooed pig,
70 x 120 x 40 cm
Courtesy Galerie Emmanuel Perrotin, Miami & Paris

Cement Truck (Scale Model), 2008
Cor-Ten steel, 125 x 290 x 90 cm
Courtesy Galerie Emmanuel Perrotin, Miami & Paris

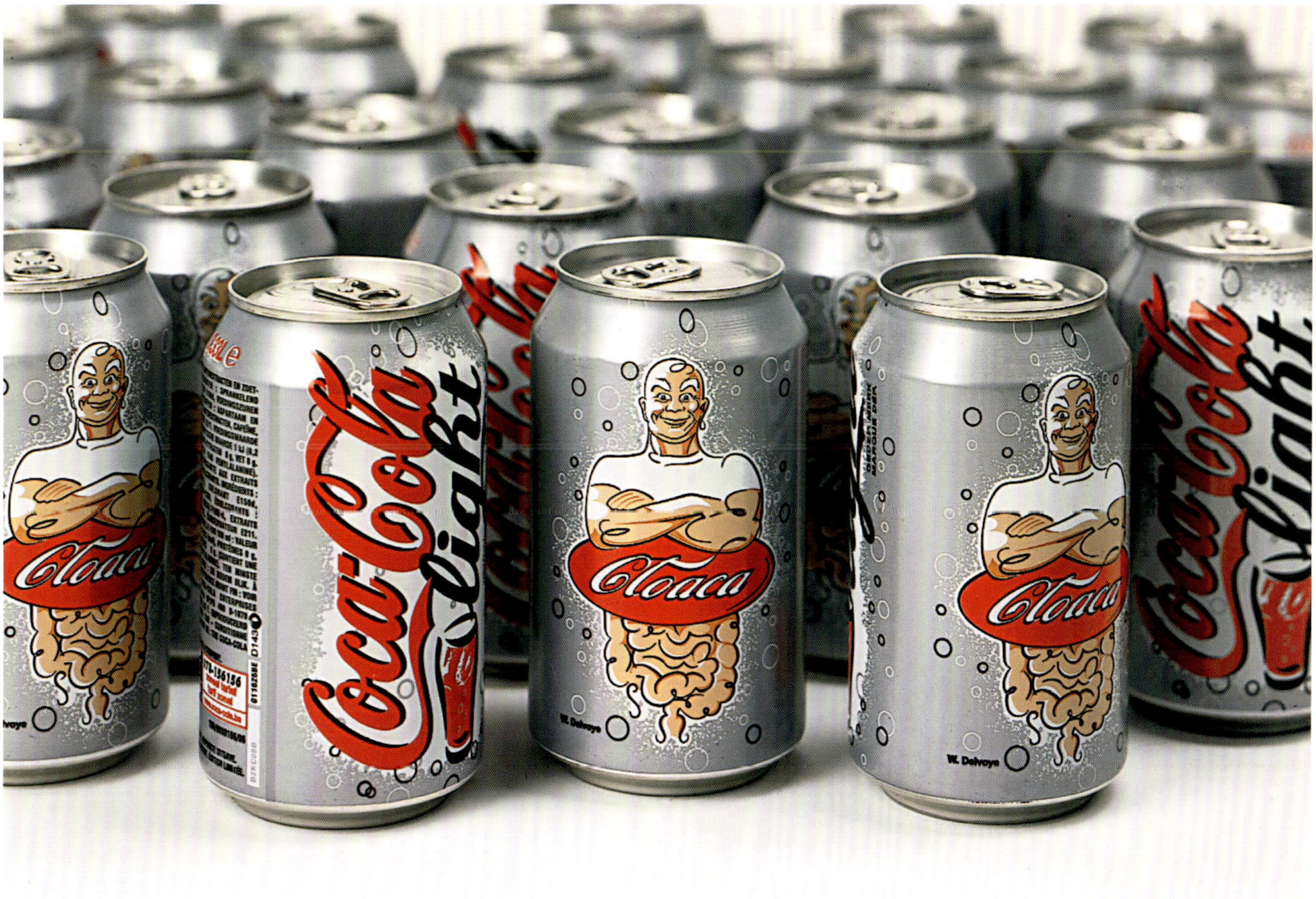
Coca-Cola light
Cloaca
W. Delvoye

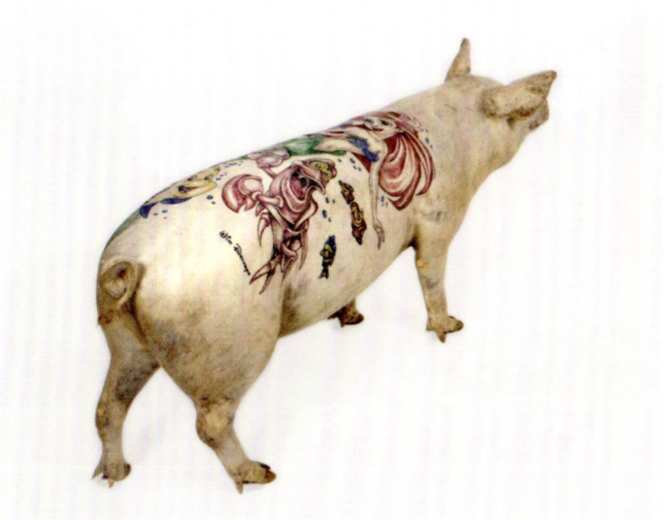

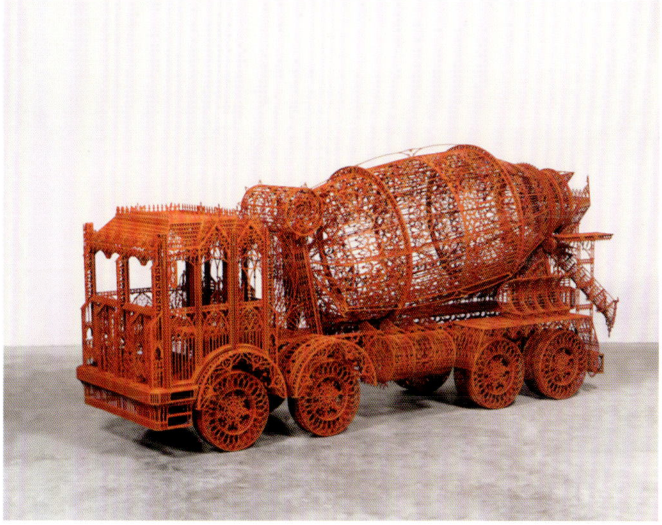

Thomas Demand

Born in Munich, Germany, in 1964. Lives and works in Berlin.
Photography is far from being a faithful mirror of reality, as is well known and amply demonstrated by the work of the artists who addressed this medium in the last century. Thomas Demand provides very effective proof to bear this out, taking photographic images from the mass media as his starting point, faithfully recreating their settings with life-size sculptures and backdrops of painted cardboard, and photographing the ensemble with the utmost attention to lighting and angle. The end result is a print in a format close to the scale of 1:1. The models made for the purpose of taking the photograph are then destroyed and it remains as the sole evidence of the ephemeral reality created by the artist.
His work thus constitutes an essentially conceptual reflection on the various possibilities of the reproduction of reality in its absence and on the habit – an inherent feature of the age we are living in – of experiencing the world above all through its representation, relying on a fragmentary universe of images whose fidelity is not something we should take for granted, as Demand teaches us.
The places that he chooses, reconstructs, and then photographs – thus going from two-dimensional to three-dimensional representation and back again – are in some cases authentic "protagonists" of history or news, just as well-known as their present or past inhabitants, including the hiding place of Saddam Hussein, the home of the Monster of Milwaukee, and the Oval Office in the White House (*Presidency I*, 2008). Sometimes they are apparently anonymous spaces that were actually the scenes of dramatic episodes, like the bathroom of the Swiss hotel in which the member of parliament Uwe Barschel was found dead (*Badezimmer*, 1997) or an office in the secret police headquarters ransacked during the popular uprisings in the German Democratic Republic (*Büro*, 1995).
The total absence of human figures, a constant characteristic of Demand's work, frees his photographs from any didactic component while demonstrating just how effectively images from the mass media succeed in making the public familiar with places of which they often have no direct knowledge. Even those who have never been to Paris – or who preferred to spend their time there visiting the Louvre rather than the Eiffel Tower – have no hesitation in recognizing the shots of an empty underpass in the video loop *Tunnel* (1999) as the place made known all over the world by the accident in which Princess Diana lost her life (*Tunnel*, 1999).
There are sometimes traces of the presence of the missing figures, such as food on the stove, a cupboard door left open or the imprint of L. Ron Hubbard's head on his pillow (*Zimmer*, 1996).
The decision to eliminate the human figure completely also from everyday spaces – another recurrent subject in Demand's work – stems from the desire not to achieve a disturbing, "haunted house" effect but to prompt consideration of our perceptual habits with respect to specific environments and the meta-messages conveyed by certain settings through the information received. News reports thus lead us to interpret a metal detector awaiting passengers ready for boarding in the light of the growing alarm about possible terrorist attacks on aircraft caused by recent events (*Gate*, 2004). Embassy offices bring to mind dangerous diplomatic incidents (*Embassy*). Walls covered with golden discs suggest the glamorous world of showbiz (*Collection*, 2002).
Moreover, by eliminating the human presence, Demand offers us an almost "voyeuristic" representation of anonymous, everyday places. His offices, changing rooms, warehouses, and telephone exchanges are ideally "photographed" at night, when the crowd of employees, attendants, and secretaries who fill them have finished their working day and everything is left in a state of suspended animation, enveloped in a disconcerting silence. Even in

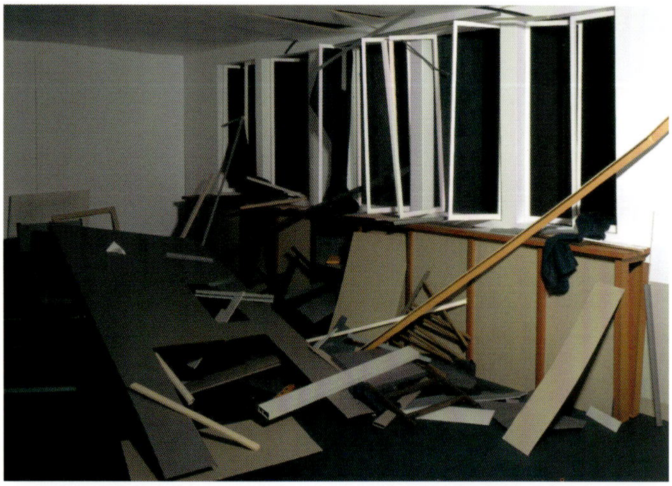

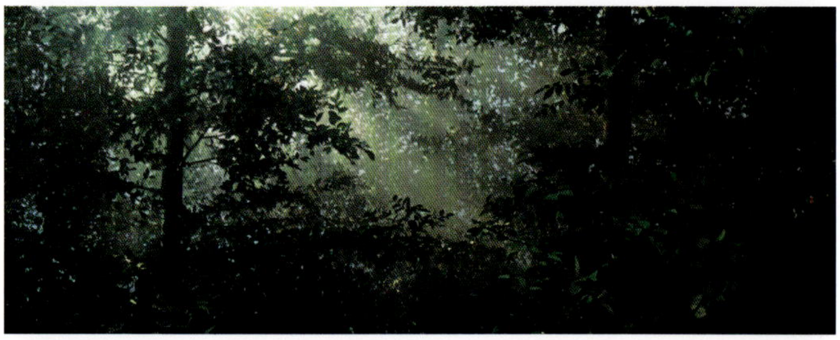

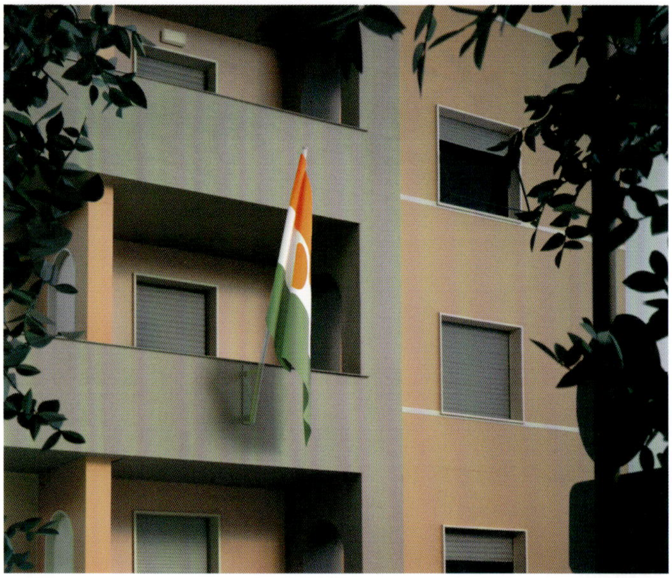

Zimmer, 1996
Color print, 165 x 232 cm
Courtesy 303 Gallery, New York

Clearing, 2003
Color print, 192 x 495 cm
Private collection

Embassy I, 2007
Color print, 204 x 168 cm
Private collection

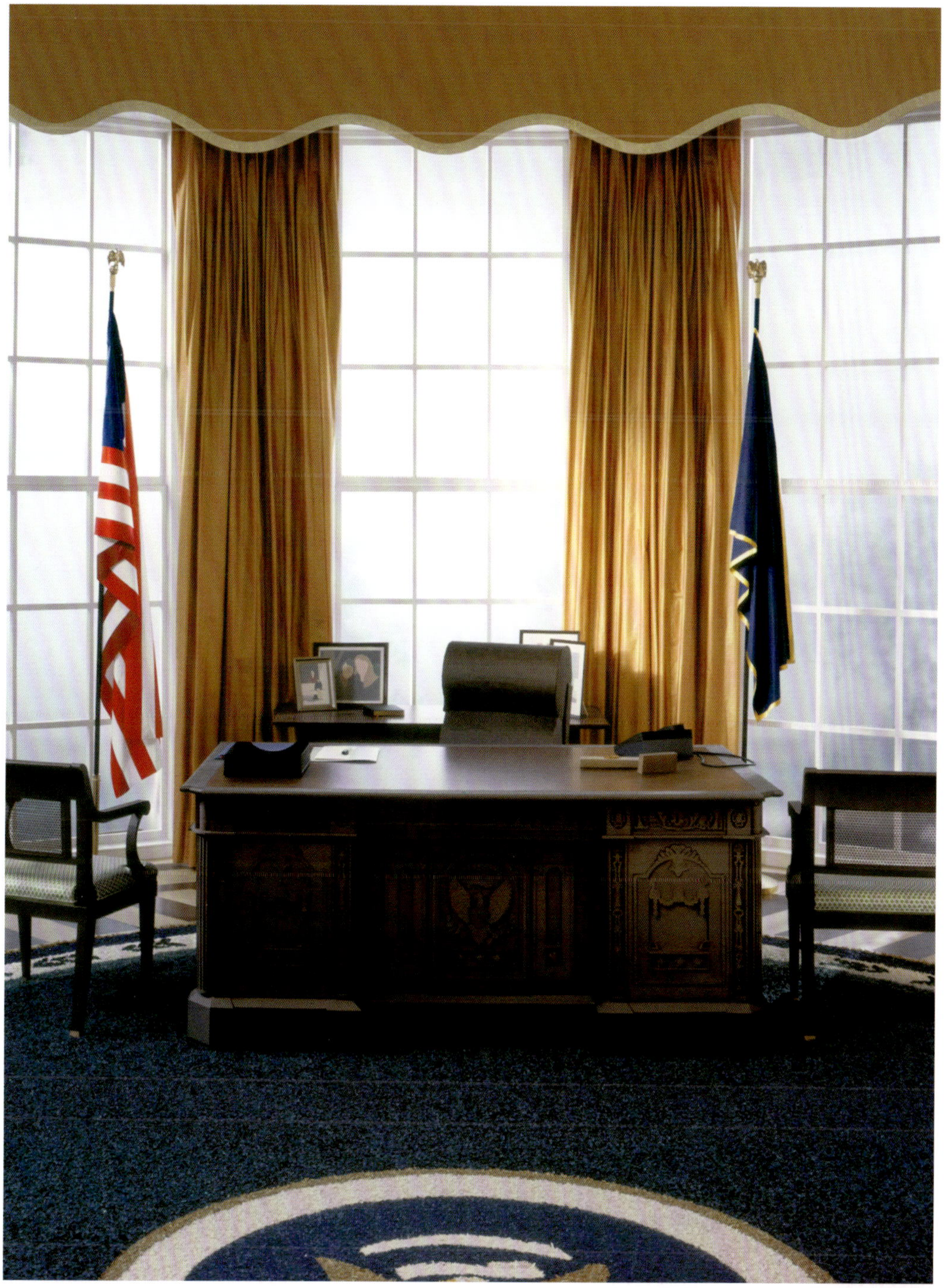

these cases, the environments prove surprisingly familiar.
As Demand explains, his work revolves around the idea of a space that is remembered even though you have never been there: "It is a strange feeling. You find yourself in a time and a place where you could never have really been but where you have already been in your imagination." Nature has also made its appearance recently in Demand's works. The artist tells us that it was the cover of a CD of Beethoven's Eroica symphony that suggested the image of *Clearing* (2003), but in this case it is almost impossible to believe that the effect of the sunbeams filtered through the thick vegetation of a forest was obtained just with thousands of sheets of paper and deft lighting.
(*P.V.*)

Presidency I, 2008
Color print, 223 x 310 cm
Private collection

Mark Dion

Polar Bears and Toucans (from Amazonas to Svalbard), 1991
Stuffed toy polar bear, cassette player, cassette recorded in Venezuela/Amazonas territory, shipping crate, electrical wire, tar, wash tub, 231 x 112 x 75 cm
DuMont Schütte Collection
Courtesy of the artist and Tanya Bonakdar Gallery, New York

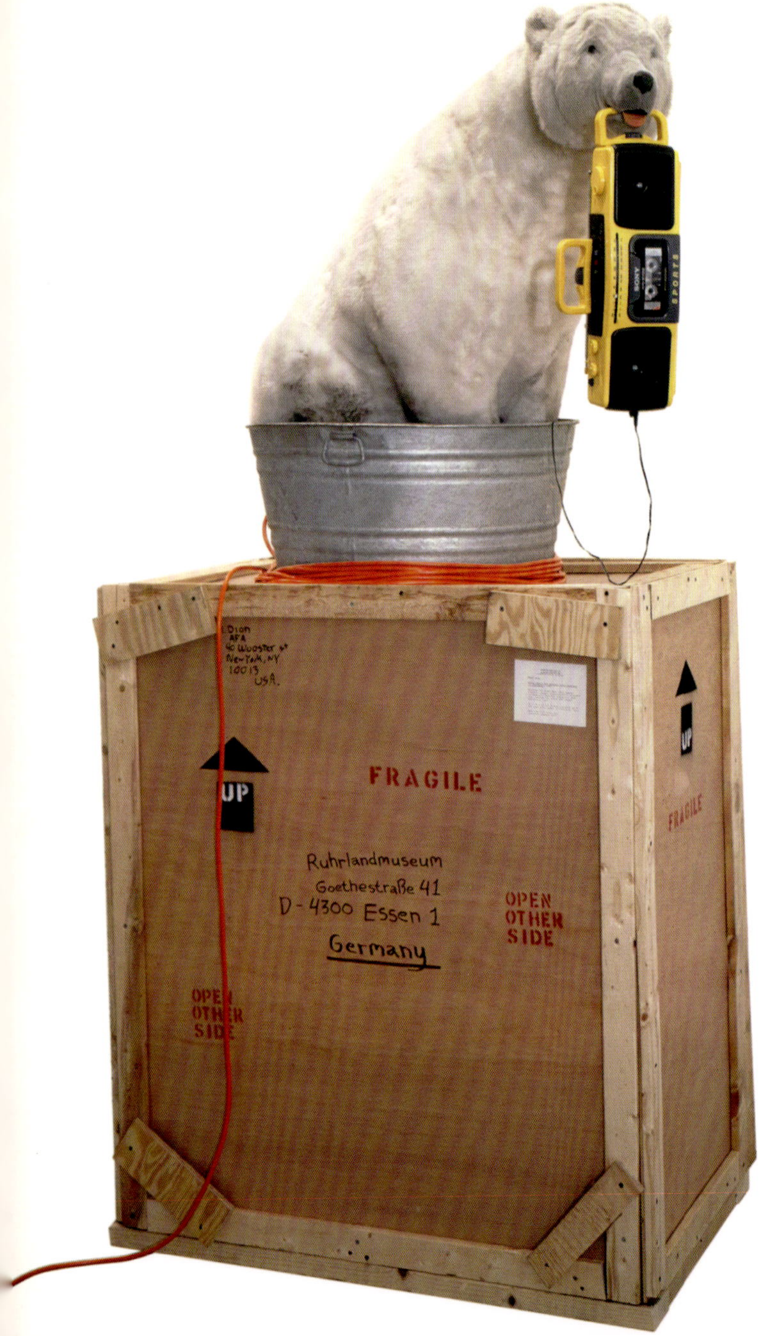

Born in New Bedford, Massachusetts, in 1961. Lives and works in New York and Beach Lake, Pennsylvania.

After finishing his studies and working for some time as an assistant to Ashley Bickerton, Mark Dion started out as an artist in the early 1990s. His work uses installation and the more intimate medium of drawing to address the cultural representation of nature through the ideological filter offered by disciplines like archaeology and zoology, drawing at the same time on the display strategies inherited by museums of science and natural history from the nineteenth-century "cabinet of curiosities" and the still earlier *Wunderkammer*. According to Dion, "Nature is one of the most sophisticated arenas for the production of ideology." Taxonomy as a system of order and control imposed by mankind on nature, the museum ideology and policies of representation, and the contrast both between the subjective and the "scientific" ordering of reality and between nature and culture, these are recurrent themes in complex installations featuring heterogeneous materials accumulated over the years or gathered during his travels and field studies, including stuffed animals, books, notebooks, maps, drawings, and laboratory vessels. Dion is in fact a collector, archivist, explorer, hunter, and biologist, and has often been compared for this reason to figures like Joseph Beuys, Marcel Broodthaers, and Robert Smithson. His attitude toward nature is clearly shown in works like *Library for the Birds of Antwerp* (1993) and *Library for the Birds of Massachusetts* (2005): two trees with various objects hanging from their branches – cages but also bags, photographs, and books – for use by birds. Science and irony, order and surprising association, alternate in a constant subversion of the authoritarian structures of thought. The artist's classificatory rigor can sometimes shift from nature to other territories. *Toys 'R' U.S. (When Dinosaurs Ruled the Earth)*, for example, is an installation of 1994 in which models, gadgets, toys, posters, images, and films connected with the way in which the myth of dinosaurs is cultivated in the world of childhood are reorganized so as to create a child's bedroom. For *Tate Thames Dig*, the project undertaken for the Tate Gallery in 1999, Dion explored the two banks of the Thames in front of Tate Modern with some volunteers in search of material remains of the area's industrial past. The "relics" were then placed in a mahogany display case after the fashion of an ancient cabinet of curiosities, a form of display that remains an essential point of reference for Dion.
(D.Q.)

Library for the Birds of Massachusetts, 2005
Steel, maple tree, plywood, books, and mixed media,
6.1 x 5.5 x 6.1 m
View of the installation realized in 2005 at the Massachusetts Museum of Contemporary Art, North Adams
Courtesy of the artist and Tanya Bonakdar Gallery, New York

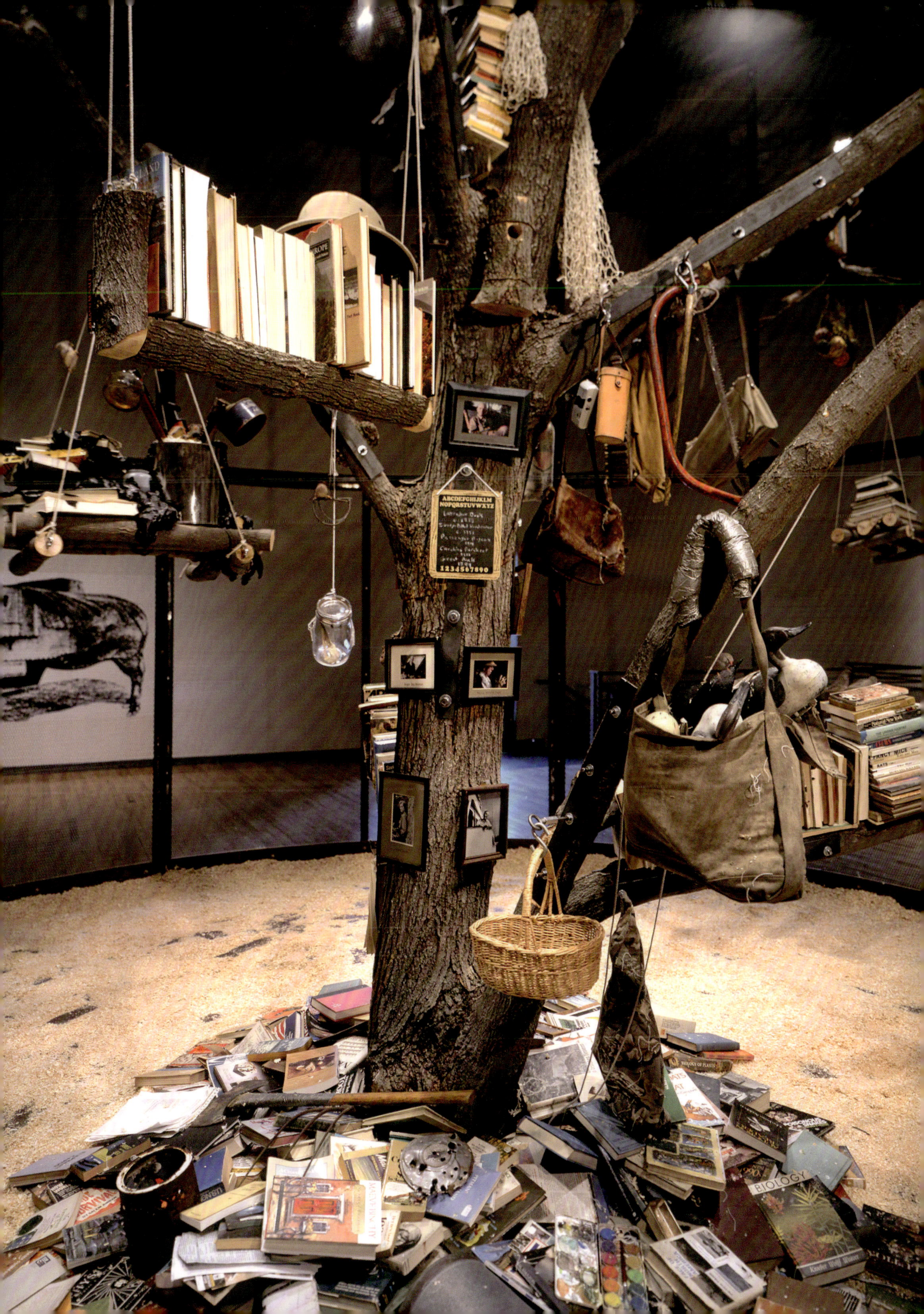
ABCDEFGHIJKLM
NOPQRSTUVWXYZ
1234567890
BIOLOGY

Giovanni Frangi

Born in Milan (Italy) in 1959. Lives and works in Milan.
Inspired by nature, water and the land, important productions in Giovanni Frangi's artistic research are the cycles *La fuga di Renzo* (1996, a prizewinner at the 12th Quadriennale in Rome) and *Il richiamo della foresta* (1999). With *Nobu at Elba* (2003), a monumental project created in the main stables in Villa Menafoglio Litta Panza in Biumo Superiore (Varese), Frangi introduced into his research the theme of a possible coexistence of the sculptural and pictorial media. Ideally conceived as a rustic nocturne, it consists of 4 large black canvases and 20 sculptures of burnt foam rubber, the whole being illuminated at regular intervals until absolute darkness is reached so as to create the illusion of moonlight reflecting on a stream. The work deftly encapsulates the different subjects of Frangi's work: landscape, natural elements, the emotional mimesis between painting and nature, and perception. Alongside his pictorial and sculptural works, Frangi is also interested in photography, which he re-elaborates on emulsioned canvas, and printmaking, in which he uses the carborundum technique to endow the works with greater depth and substance. This process was adopted for the *Pasadena* series of 30 prints exhibited in 2008 at the Galleria d'Arte Moderna in Udine, richly informed by the artist's experience of the Huntington Botanical Gardens in Pasadena. *Pasadena* develops like an emotive journey into the world of nature, emulating the values of the scientific study and catalogue in its serial character while also effectively capturing the encounter between constructed image and natural inspiration.
(*F.T.*)

Nobu at Elba (detail), 2003
Element "C," oil on canvas, 340 x 1550 cm
Courtesy of the artist

Pasadena, 2008
Oil on canvas, 198 x 162 cm
Verona, Galleria dello Scudo

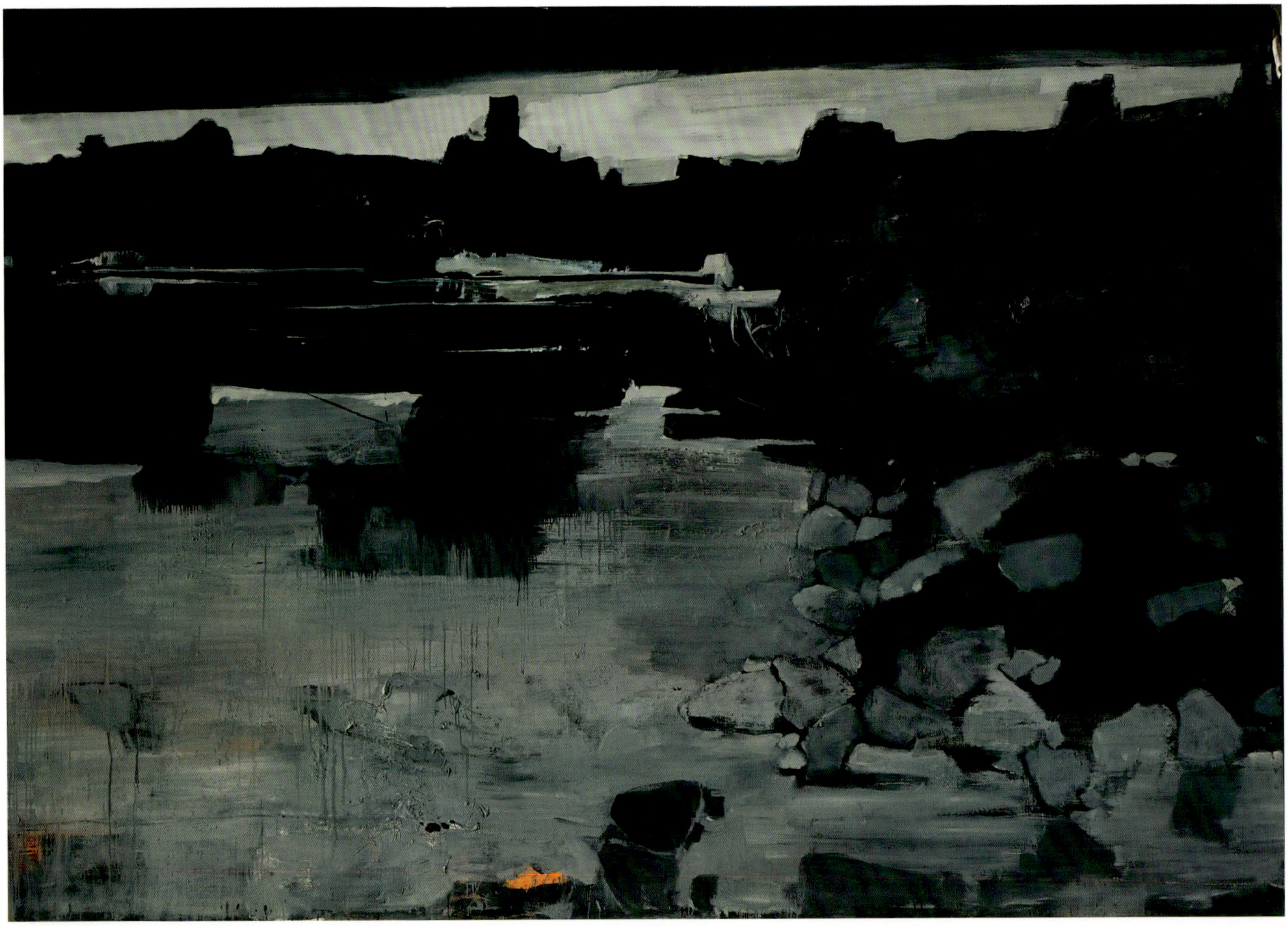

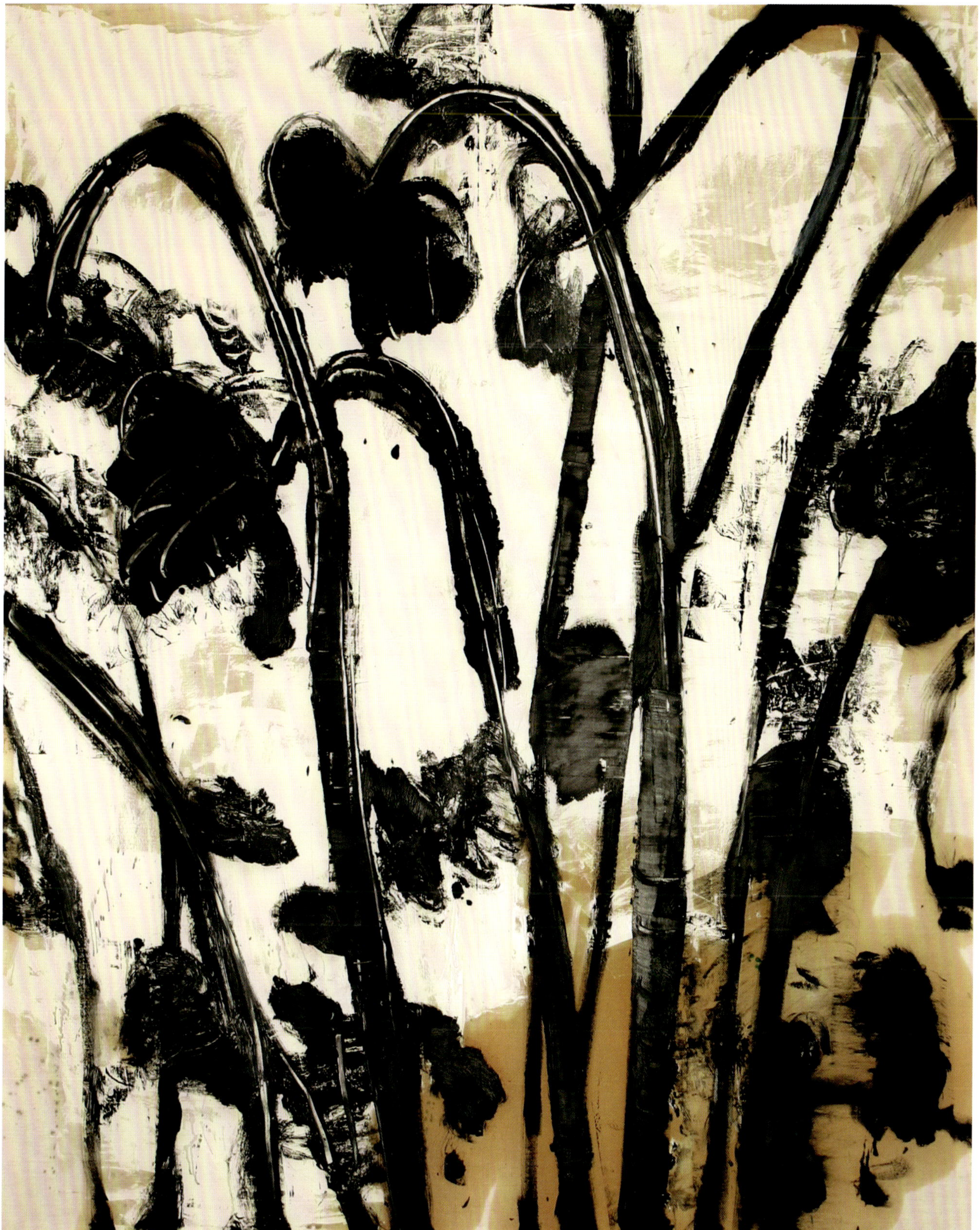

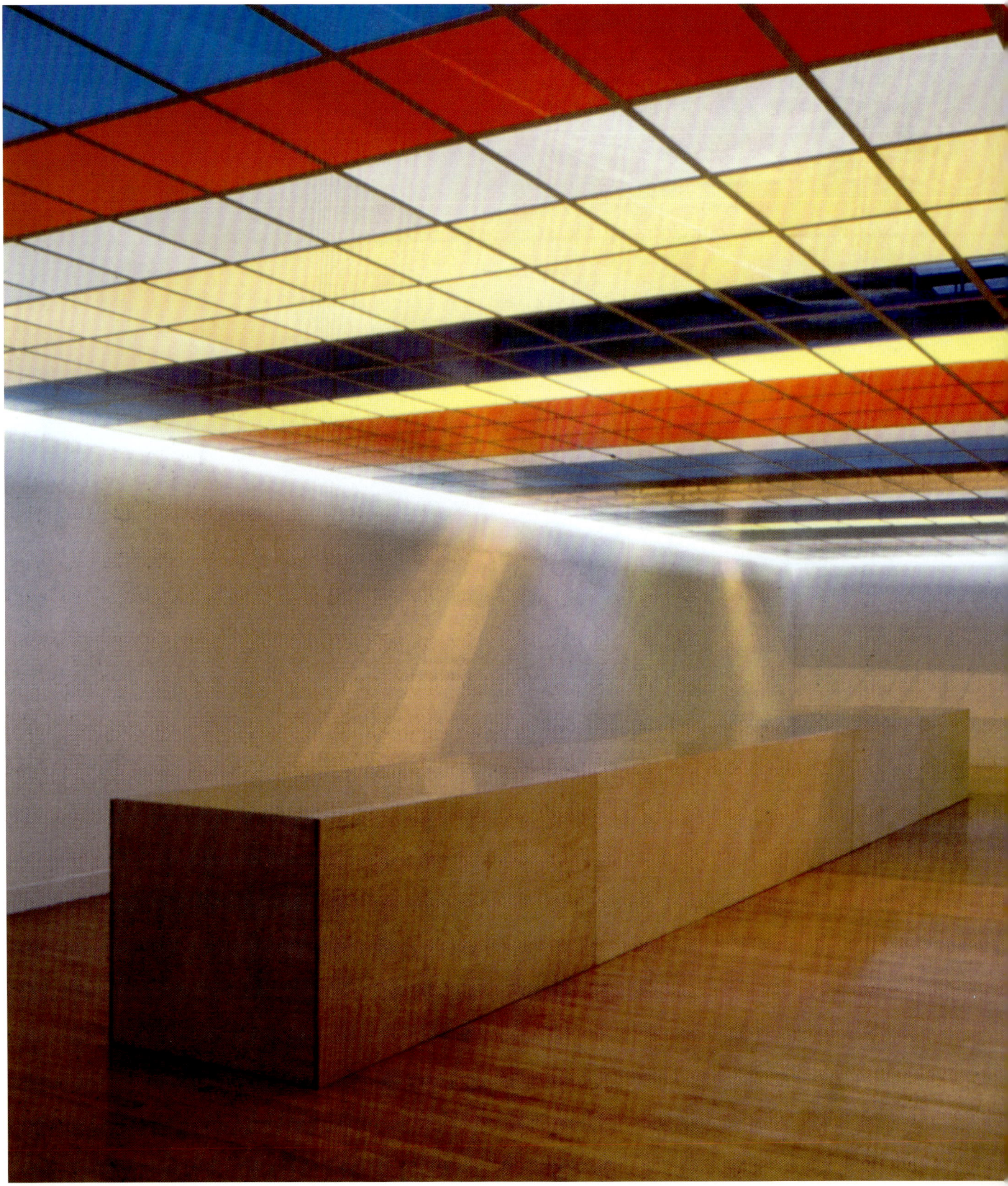

Liam Gillick

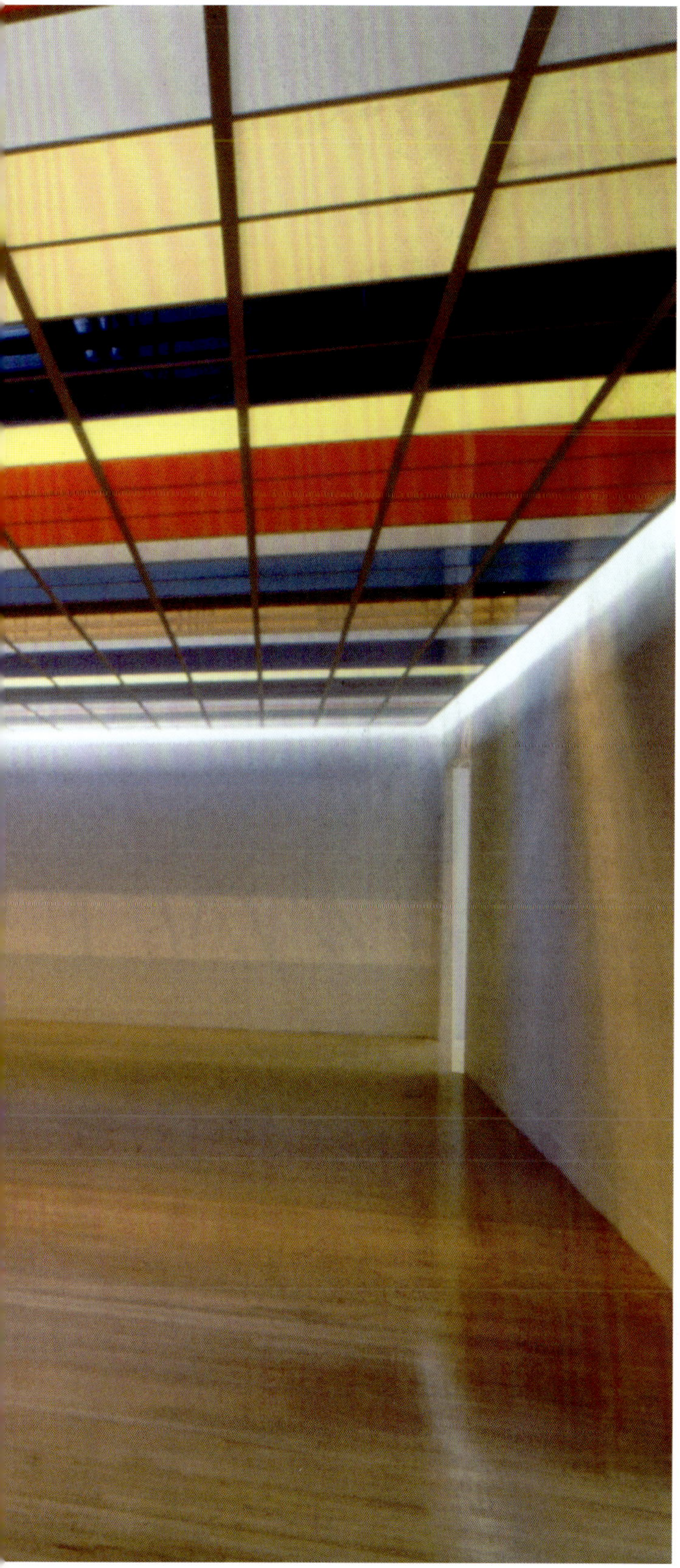

Born in Aylesbury, UK, in 1964. Lives and works in New York and London.

The multifaceted artist Liam Gillick is also active on the contemporary art scene as a designer, critic, curator of events and exhibitions, lecturer and theorist. In many respects, these heterogeneous roles are reflected in the very nature of his works, both those of a relational character and those more directly connected with the dimension of sculpture. The latter, in particular, display the artist's attention to the intrinsic formal and chromatic qualities of materials, the size and positioning of the individual pieces, and the various relations they establish with space, as ascertained also in the light of a deep interest in the semiotics of architecture.

In works like *Coats of Asbestos Spangled with Mica*, which earned him a nomination for the Turner Prize in 2002, and *Returning to an Abandoned Plant* (2007), Gillick uses technical materials like colored Plexiglas and anodized aluminum for the avowed purposes of exploring a borderline territory between sculpture, installation and design, and identifying possible solutions to the problem of revitalizing the architectural vocabulary at the same time.

The "visual pleasure" that the artist seeks to arouse in the spectator through formal rigor and the alternation of colors and opaque, transparent or reflecting surfaces takes on the character of a scathing critique of how the capitalist system has addressed the questions of architecture, turning the modernist project of planning into something utopian and fostering every form of speculation.

Two series of sculptural works of the "screen" and "hanging platform" type initiated in the mid-1990s (*The What If? Scenario* and *Discussion Island/Big Conference Centre*) were exhibited in a solo show at the Whitechapel Art Gallery, London, in 2002.

Significantly enough, Gillick drew upon his experience of Relational Art and work in public places on that occasion and introduced color into the gallery's auditorium and cafeteria so as to makes them more pleasant and thus enhance their function as places to meet and socialize.

(*P.V.*)

Coats of Asbestos Spangled with Mica, 2002
Anodized aluminum framework, Perspex panels
840 x 1680 cm
Courtesy Corvi-Mora Gallery, London

Dominique Gonzalez-Foerster

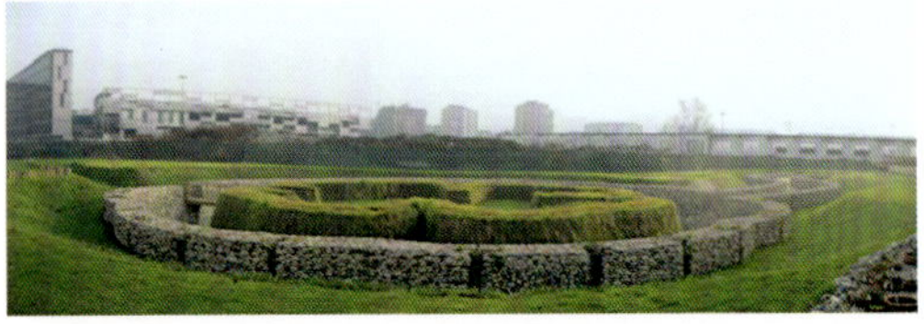

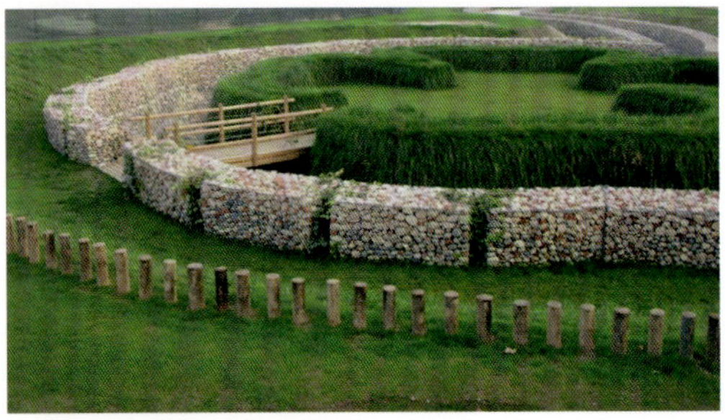

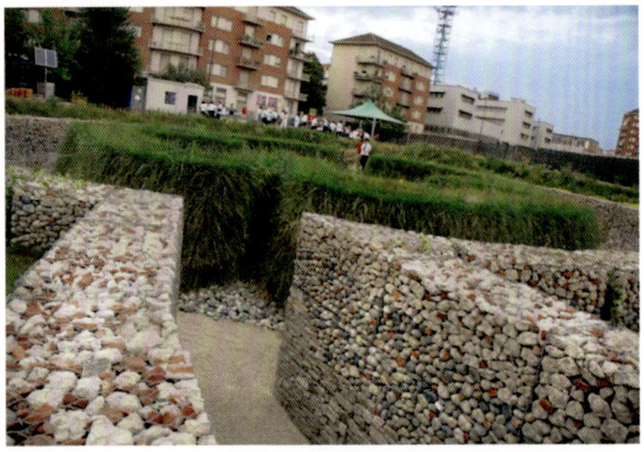

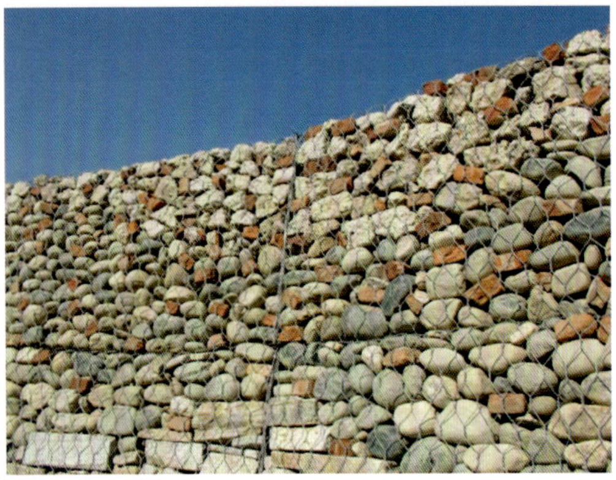

Trèfle, 2006
Stones, metallic net, ø 20 m
Turin, Parco d'Arte Vivente
Courtesy PAV / Città di Torino

Born in Strasbourg in 1965. Lives and works in Rio de Janeiro and Paris.
Dominique Gonzalez-Foerster's art takes space into consideration as part of the work itself in the ideal construction of an artistic and geographic area in which the human being is an integral part of the creative process.
She uses environmental installations as a way to express the role played by the artist and humanity in the process of life, attaching crucial importance in her work to the environment, understood as geographic territory, ecosystem, and cultural and social condition. Site-specific installations are therefore the ideal medium for an artist directly concerned with the role of her work and its relationship with its location. Once example is *Trèfle*, a site-specific installation created in 2006 in the Parco d'Arte Vivente (Park of Living Art) in Turin. It consists of a gigantic four-leaf clover, *trèfle à quatre feuils* in French, made out of soil and elements from the subterranean area of the city. A symbol of good luck, the enormous four-leaf clover with turf is a simultaneously natural and artificial work of landscape architecture that develops spatial and narrative relationships with the park designed by Piero Gilardi and Gianluca Cosmacini.
The key to the interpretation of a large-scale work obviously lies in its relationship with the visitor, above all in settings such as museums.
It is in this light that one should consider the installation *TH2058*, one of the French artist's latest projects, selected in 2008 for the *Unilever Series* in the Turbine Hall of Tate Modern in London.
The work is set 50 years in the future, in 2058, when London has been submerged by flooding and its inhabitants have taken refuge in the exhibition spaces of Tate Modern. The Turbine Hall becomes a dormitory furnished with over 200 bunk beds on which various books are left scattered. The artist thus presents a vision of the shelter, the place inhabited by human beings, through the traces they leave behind them.
The same space also accommodates enlarged reproductions of the spiders of Louise Bourgeois and public works by Alexander Calder, Henry Moore, Claes Oldenburg and Coosje van Bruggen. As in one of the most hackneyed clichés of mid-1960s science fiction movies, the rain has in fact caused the sculptures to grow in size.
(*F.T.*)

TH2058, 2008
Metal beds, books, mixed media
View of the installation realized
in 2008 at Tate Modern, London
for *The Unilever Series*

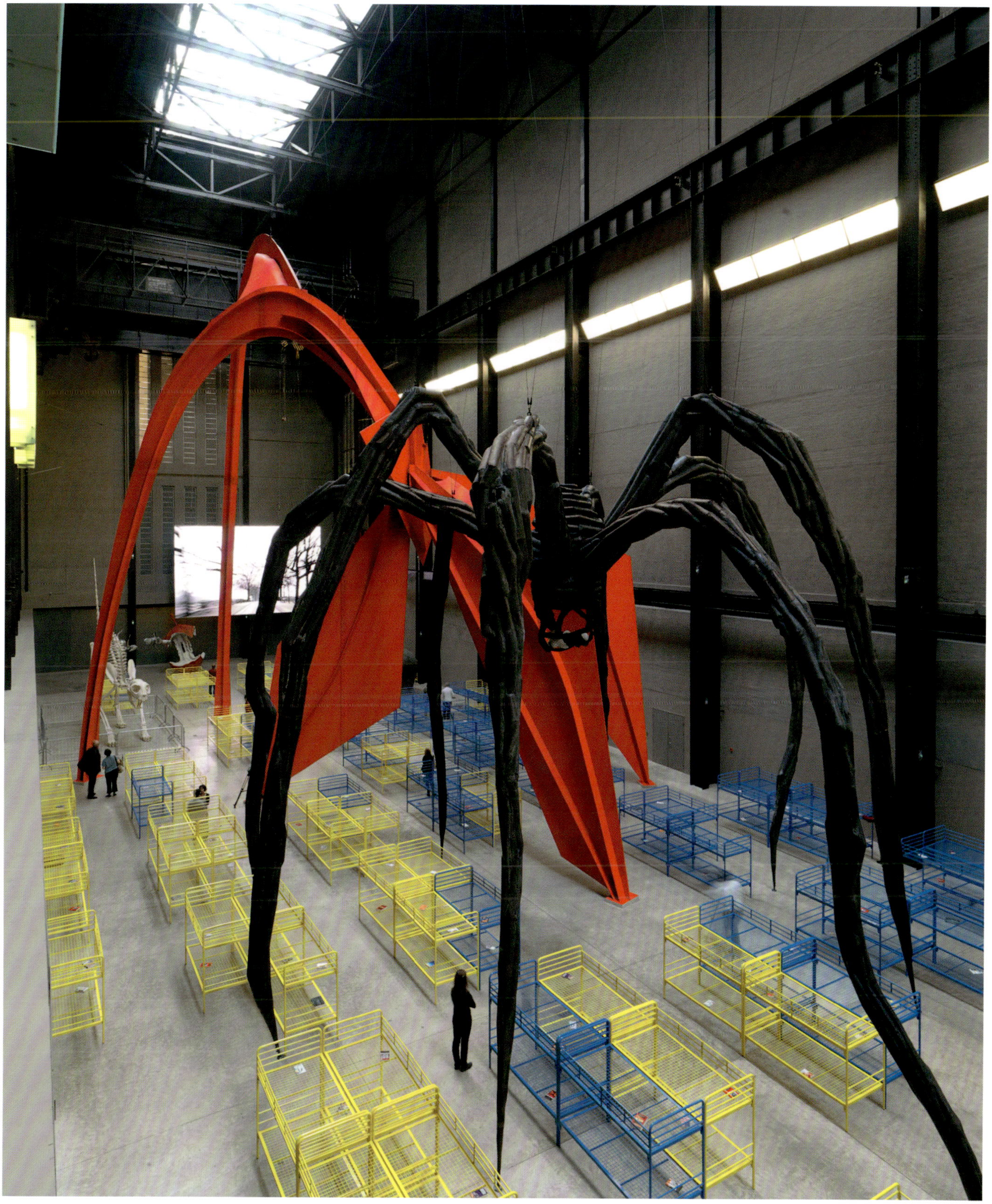

Sarah Lucas

Born in London in 1962. Lives and works in London.
Examination of the sculptural works of Sarah Lucas gives the impression that they can include any object or material whatsoever. The artist is in fact revitalizing assemblage, an art form with almost 100 years of history, with a typically British sense of bitter, sardonic irony that is always underscored in the choice of titles. The dress lying on a chair and clothing no body in *All We Are Saying Is Give Peace A Chance* (2002) is a brilliant way of connecting the tragic events of September 11 and the war in Iraq to the defeat of the ideals that guided the youth movements of the 1970s. The subsequent bomb made out of pizza delivery leaflets in *All We Are Saying Is Give Pizza Chance* (2002) takes up those principles sarcastically to mimic the campaign launched by the British government in support of armed intervention in Afghanistan. The Christ made of cigarettes in *Christ, You Know It Ain't Easy* (2003) is an almost blasphemous imprecation about how hard it is to stop smoking. The spherical steel cage with nylon tights and plaster boots in *Aunty Jam* (2005) is almost a joking tribute to Louise Bourgeois, a sculptor that Lucas deeply admires, not least for their common interest in themes connected with sexuality and gender. Many of her works thus include references to the human body and especially the sexual organs, often suggested by fruit and vegetables or other foodstuffs (*Au Naturel*, 1994). Explicit references to sexuality, eroticism and the stereotypes propagated in the trashy images of a great deal of Britain's sexist subculture are also to be found not only in the sculptures but also in the photographic works, which are often self-portraits in paradoxical and blatantly politically incorrect poses. Sarah Lucas uses herself and her body in these ironic works just like any other object at her disposal, transforming herself in turn into a sort of element of an assemblage. While the artist thus becomes a kind of living sculpture, she does not hide behind a façade of respectability, unlike her renowned predecessors Gilbert & George, but asserts herself as an aggressive and awkward character capable of disorienting the public and causing them to experience the increasingly rare feeling of embarrassment.
(*L.L.*)

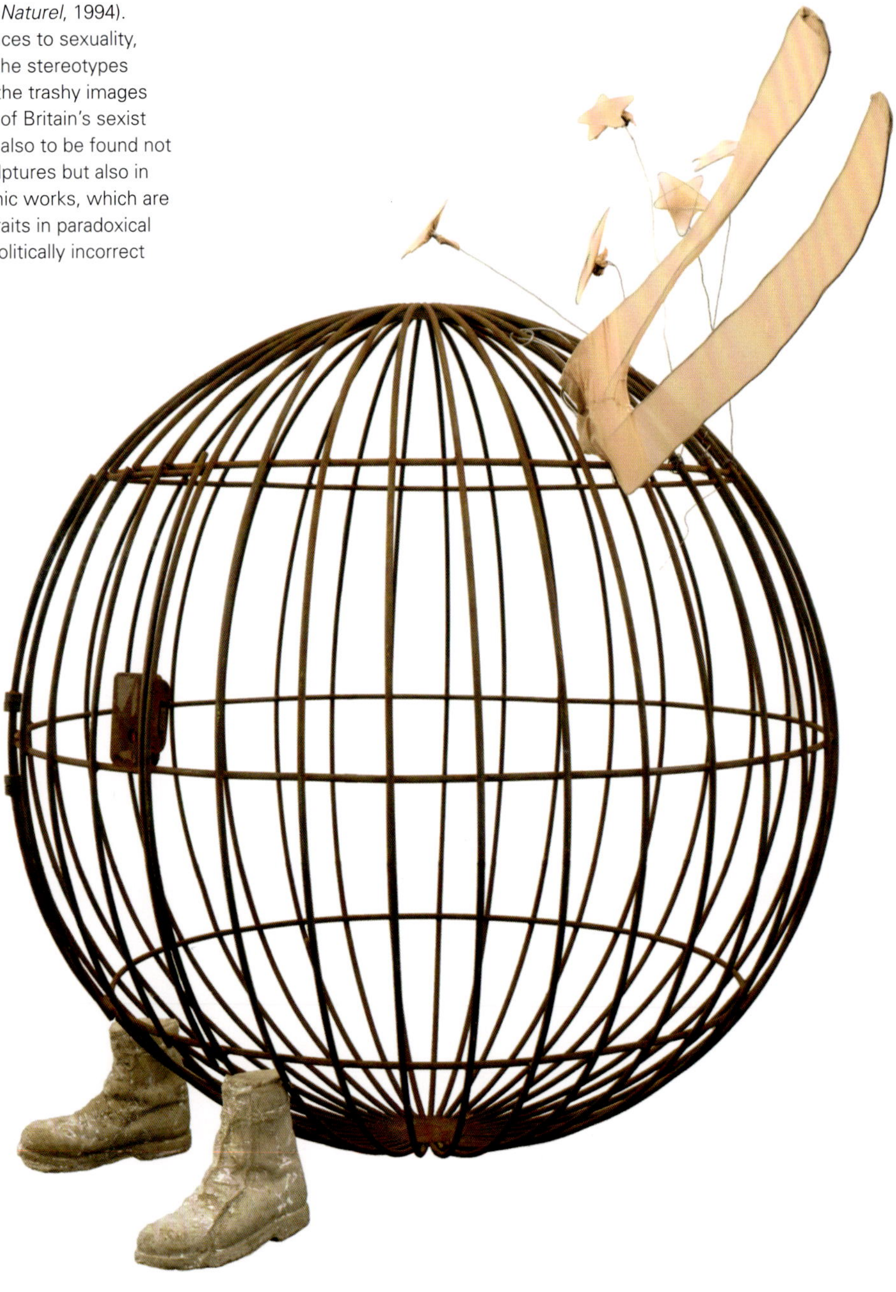

Aunty Jam, 2005
Steel cage, wire, nylon tights, cast concrete 203 x 160 x 239 cm
Courtesy Sadie Coles HQ, London

All We Are Saying Is Give Peace A Chance, 2002
Wooden chair, leather jacket, jeans, boots, braces, pearly buttons, cardboard, 87 x 85 x 110 cm
Courtesy Sadie Coles HQ, London

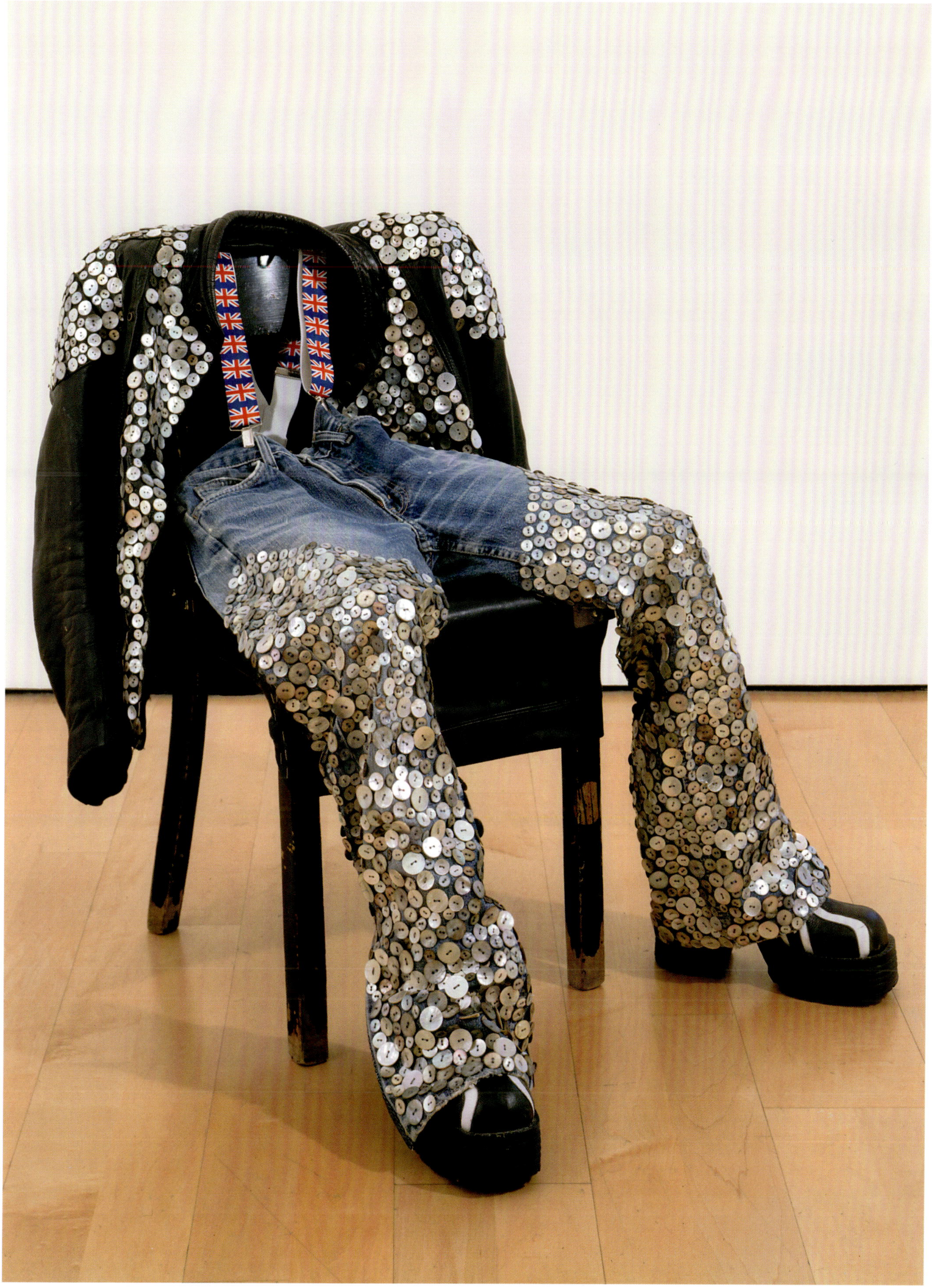

Ron Mueck

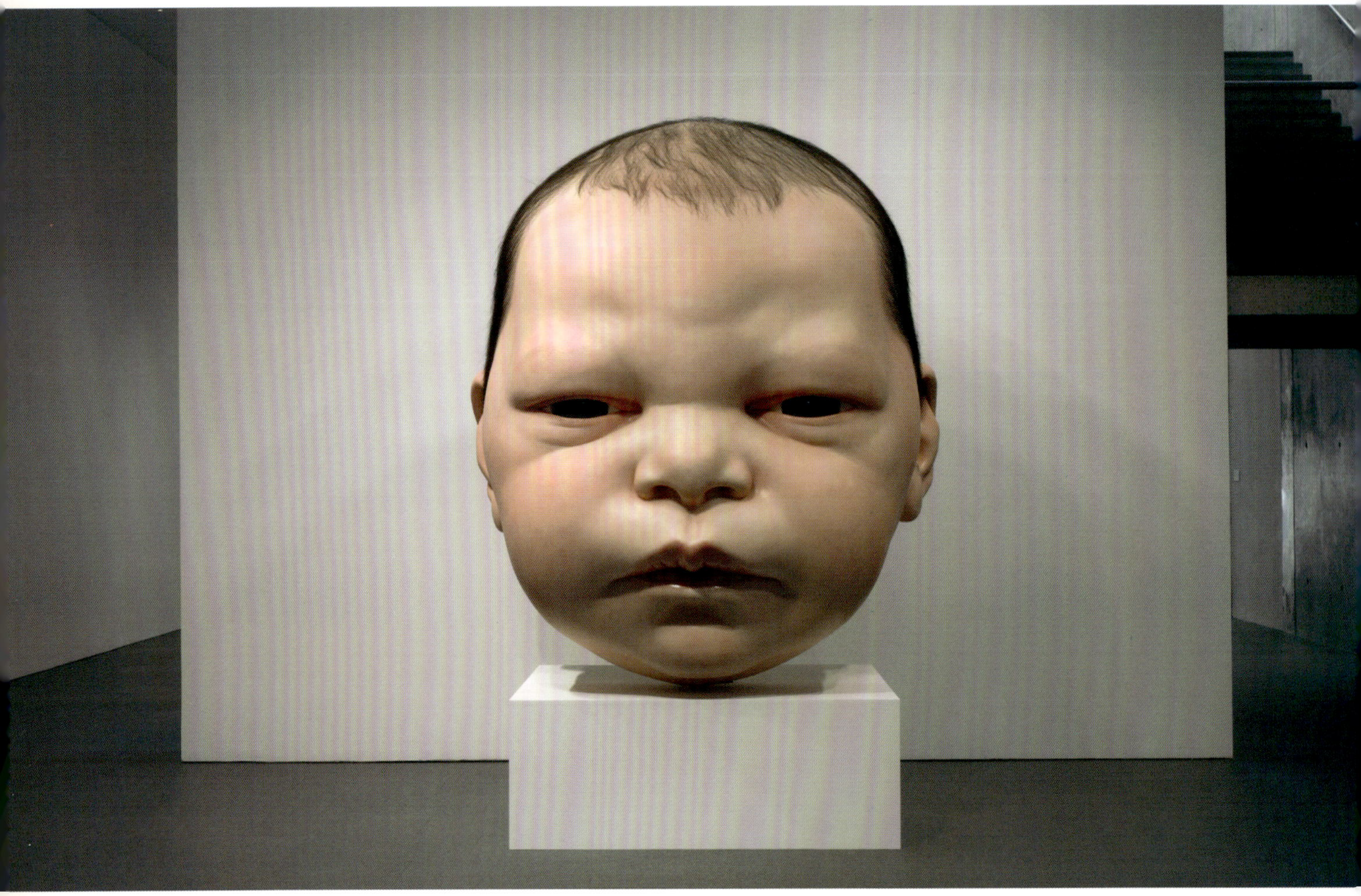

Born in Melbourne, Australia, in 1958. Lives and works in London. It was the decision of Charles Saatchi to include the surprisingly realistic sculpture *Dead Dad* (1996–1997) in the celebrated exhibition *Sensation* at the Royal Academy in London in 1997 that brought Ron Mueck from the dark backstage of cinema, television and advertising into the limelight of the international art scene.
One of the best-known figures in Young British Art, Mueck followed in the footsteps of his German-born parents, who were toy makers, and started out in Australia as a model maker and puppeteer. Having moved to London, he produced special effects for cinema (including the film *Labyrinth*, 1986, starring David Bowie) and set up his own company making dummies for advertising in 1990. Made at first of clay and then of fiberglass and silicone, Mueck's sculptures are extraordinarily realistic reproductions of human figures: men, women and children, naked or dressed in real clothes and accessories, showing veins, wrinkles, moles, hairs and reddened skin. In short, no detail is spared in the almost maniacal pursuit of perfect representation. All this exceptional and intriguing realism is, however, contradicted by the scale of the figures, which are never life-sized. Often monumental, like the gigantic *Boy*, 4.5 meters in height, presented at the 2001 Venice Biennale, they can also be reduced to about half-size, as in the case of *Dead Dad*, a portrait of the artist's deceased father lying naked on his back. At the same time, Mueck's figures are captured in highly expressive attitudes and situations of a disarmingly human nature that involve the spectator emotionally: frightened and defenseless babies, tired and weary women, anxious, melancholy men, unshaven, obese and dead figures. It is in this disturbing and disorienting ambiguity midway between illusion and imitation that the craftsman, the maker of models for television, and the skillful creator of incredible special effects gives way to the artist and the sculptor. Mueck has talked about his efforts to give his sculptures a presence that makes you think they are more than objects, and it is upon this prompting of thought and reflection that the Australian sculptor's artistic credibility rests.
(*L.L.*)

Head of a Baby, 2003
Silicone, resin, and fiberglass, 254 x 219 x 238 cm
Ottawa, The National Gallery of Canada

Seated Woman, 1999
Silicone, acrylic, polyurethane foam, clothes, hair, shoes, bijoux, fabric, 64 x 43 x 42 cm
Fort Worth, Modern Art Museum of Fort Worth

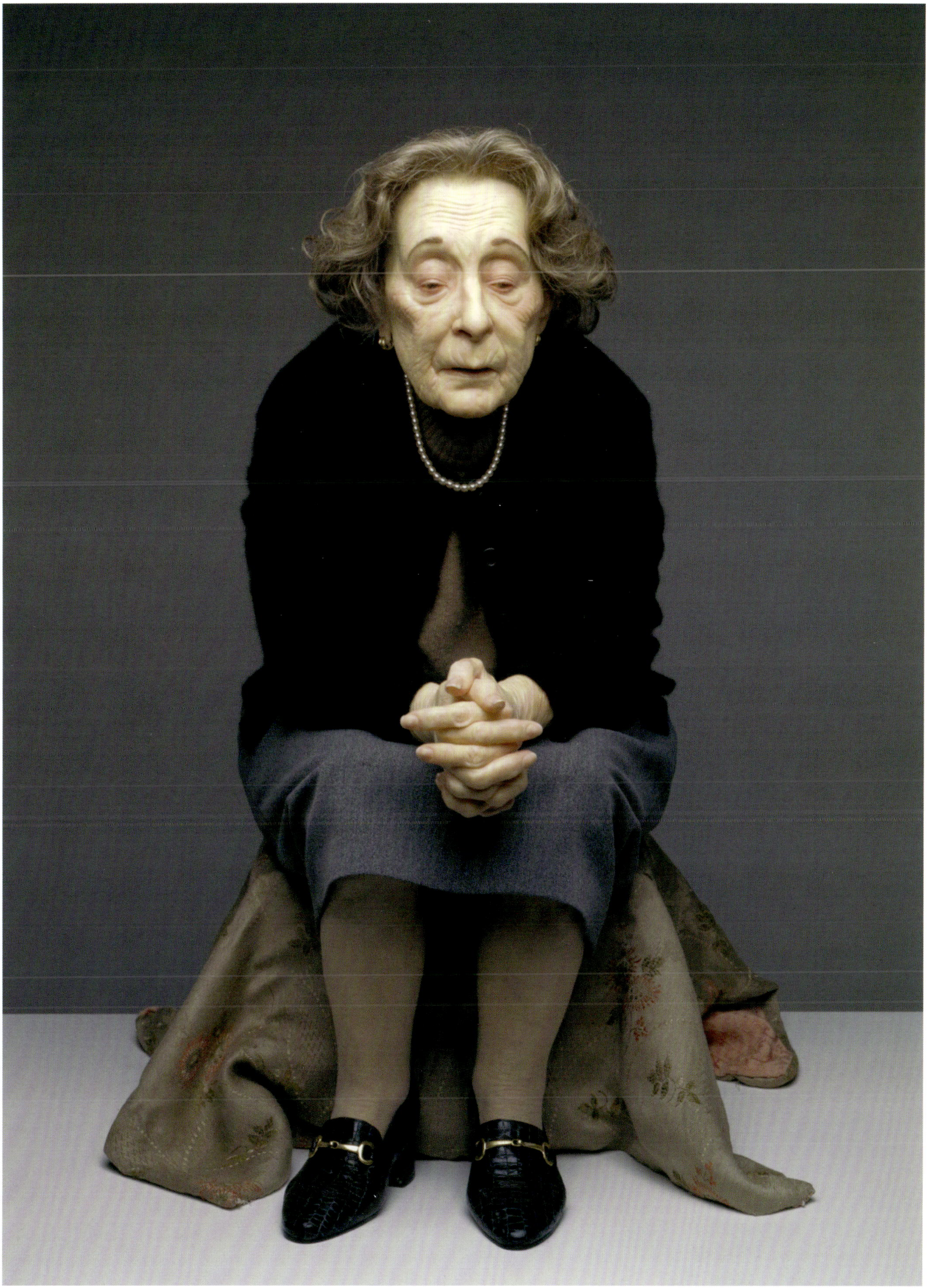

Julian Opie

Radio Wind Tyres, 2000
Color photograph on Perspex,
75 x 112 cm
London, Tate Modern

Escaped Animals, 2002
Powder-coated aluminum, vinyl, metal, and paint, dimensions variable
London, Tate Modern

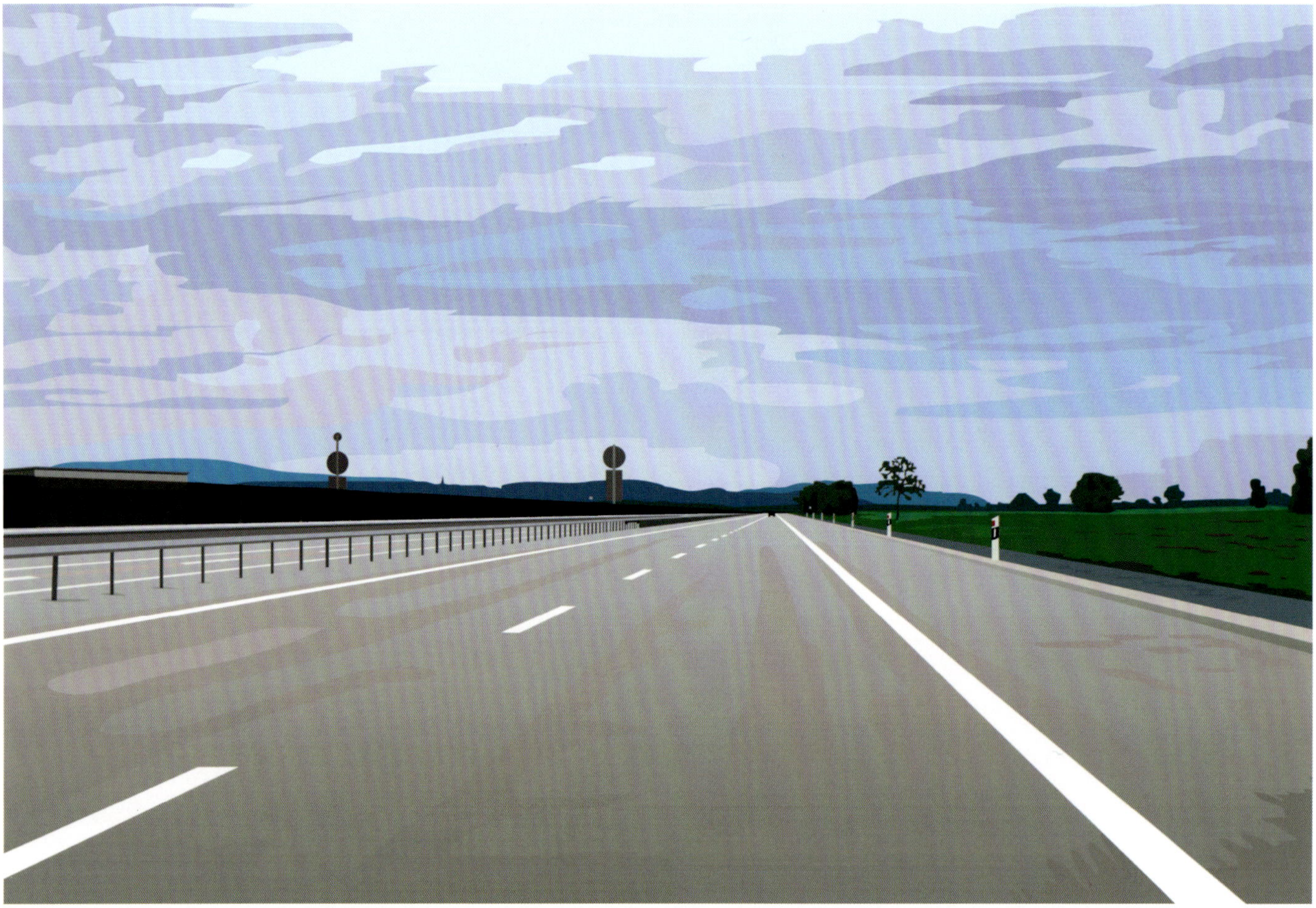

Born in London in 1958. Lives and works in London.
Julian Opie works with painting and sculpture, sometimes combining the two. His early works involve a reversal of the idea of the ready-made, consisting of predominantly metal replicas of everyday objects that were then illusionistically painted (*Making It*, 1983). Closely connected with the American Pop culture from the outset, Opie continued to display its influence also in later decades in his installations as well as his paintings. Similarities with Warhol, Lichtenstein and Oldenburg emerge above all in his interest in linguistic codes and conventional mechanisms of representation, as developed through constant investigation into the power of images and the processes involved in their perception and recognition. His vocabulary reflects the various ways in which we habitually interpret the world around us. His interest is therefore not in reality but rather in the way it reaches us through its representation. For this reason, like the celebrated Pop artists before him, he draws his subjects from the everyday scene and often develops them in series, focusing above all on anti-naturalistic simplification and chromatic alteration to highlight the complexity of the dynamics governing the relations between vision, learning and knowledge.
Opie describes himself as looking for a way to create a reality linked to signs and to what goes beyond them, thus pinpointing at the same time his theoretical intentions and his working methods, which involve the twofold process of iconic reduction and characterization of the subject. In order to reconcile these two antithetical poles of representation, Opie makes use at the same time of faithful photographic reproductions of the reality, constituting the initial starting point, and extremely stylized images connected with it, including comics, cartoons and even road signs (*Escaped Animals*, 2002). These different types of representation of the same subject, superimposed with the aid of digital image-processing programs and manual retouching, result in portraits and landscapes where principles of physiognomic or environmental definition coexist with abstraction to create pictures sharing a common matrix but always remaining different from one another (*Radio Wind Tyres*, from the series *Eight Landscapes*, 2000).
While developing exclusively in the sphere of figuration, Opie's work therefore has an eminently conceptual character that takes shape as reflection on the various types of mediation that stand between contemporary mankind and the real world and systematically replace direct experience with knowledge through images.
(*L.L.*)

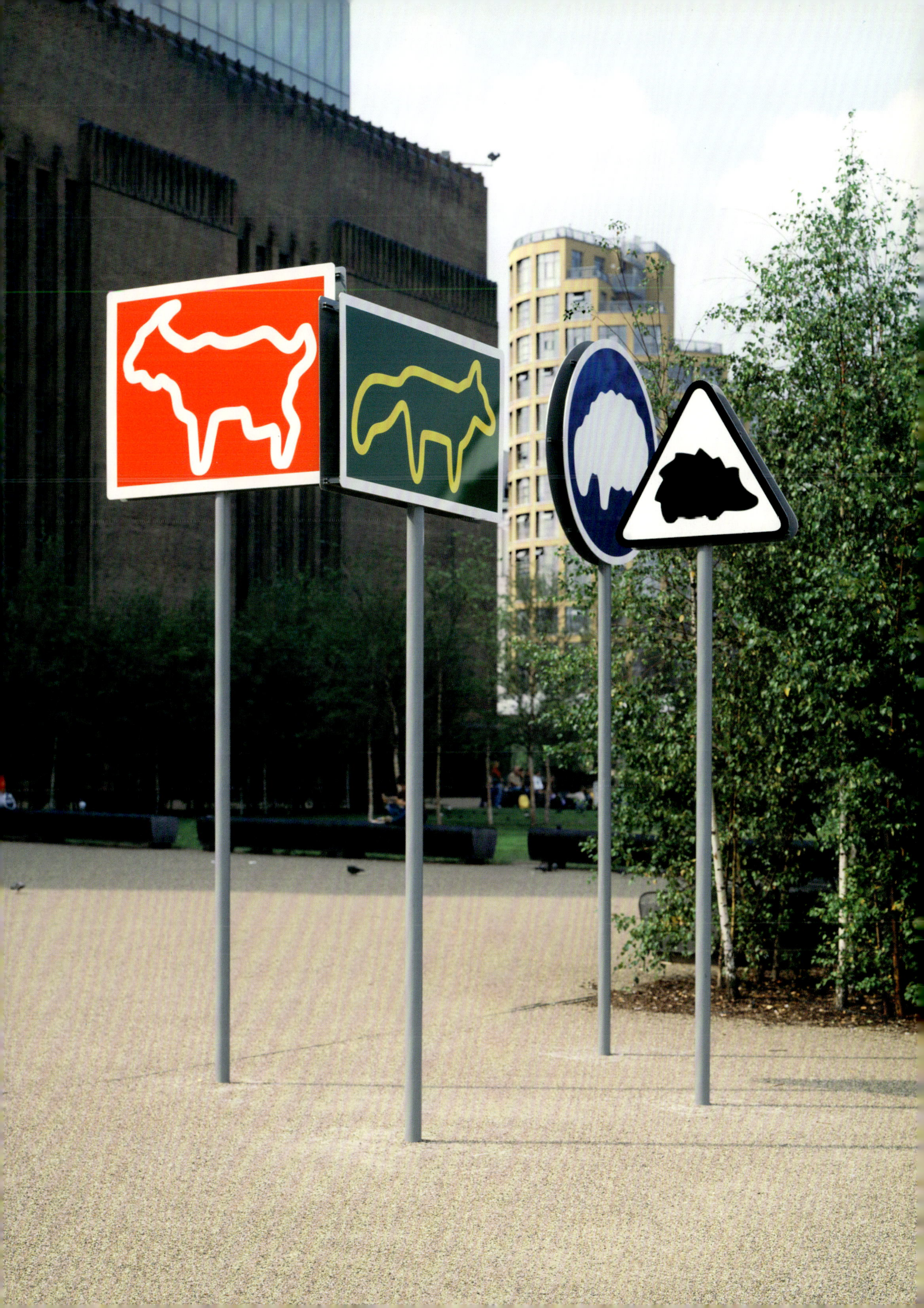

Gabriel Orozco

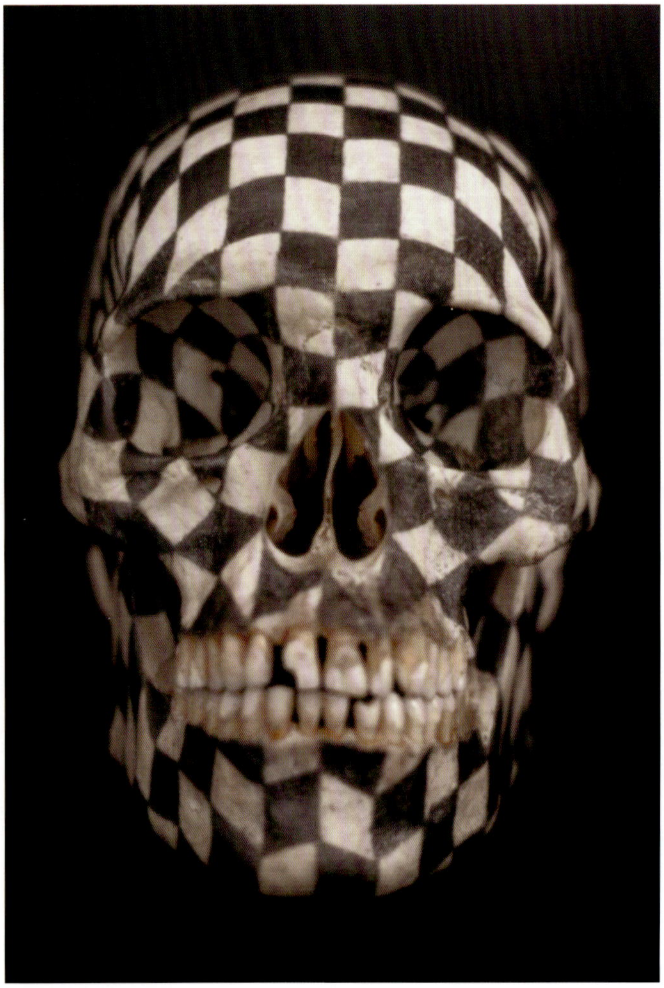

Black Kites, 1997
Graphite on skull,
21.6 x 12.7 x 15.9 cm
London, White Cube

Born in Jalapa, Mexico, in 1962. Lives and works in Paris, New York and Mexico City.
Regarded by critics as among the most influential artists of his generation, Gabriel Orozco is also one of the first examples of a cosmopolitan artist, always on the move and even without a permanent studio. He began to work in the early 1990s, constantly alternating demanding projects that require the involvement of a large and ever-changing team of assistants with minimal operations carried out in the urban space and nearly always documented with photographs. Paradigmatic examples of this include *Extension of Reflexion* (1992), a photographic print that records the tracks left as the artist rode a bicycle in a circle between two puddles, *Pinched Ball* (1993), a worn-out, abandoned soccer ball that become a temporary receptacle for rainwater, and *From Roof to Roof* (1993), a shot immortalizing the circles produced by the artist throwing stones from one roof to another full of water. In 1993, on the occasion of a show at the MoMA in New York, he asked the inhabitants of some apartments facing the museum to display oranges in their windows, thus producing a minimal and at the same time extremely effective work (*Home Run*, 1993).
Certain central features of the artist's work as a whole can be identified in these creations, including the circle, the symbol of infinity and the geometric figure on which the apparent disorder of the world is structured, and an unconventional approach to sculpture, understood essentially as an operation on space. Developed in tactics of "recognition" (of the formal value of an image), the repositioning of an everyday object, painting or authentic reshaping, the artist's "performative" work obliges the viewer to reinterpret the initial object through the artistic act.
La DS (1993) is an automobile icon of the 1960s that Orozco rebuilt after removing its middle section. In *Black Kites* (1997) and later in the spectacular *Dark Waves* (2006), the artist took respectively a human skull and the skeleton of a whale found on a beach in Spain and covered them with a closely worked and orderly geometric pattern in pencil. Designed for the Venice Biennale of 2003, *Shade Between Rings of Air* is a reconstruction in 1:1 scale but rotated by 90 degrees of the canopy built by Carlo Scarpa in the courtyard adjoining the Italian pavilion in 1952.
Orozco initiated a series of apparently "modernistic" paintings called *Samurai Tree* in 2006. Computer designed, they use a limited range of colors and a modular compositional structure based on the rotation of circular shapes around a central axis. Only apparently "abstract" and "two-dimensional", the *Samurai Tree* paintings can be read as a metaphor of perpetual motion and the geometric order underlying reality, which is the primary subject of all the Mexican artist's work.
(D.Q.)

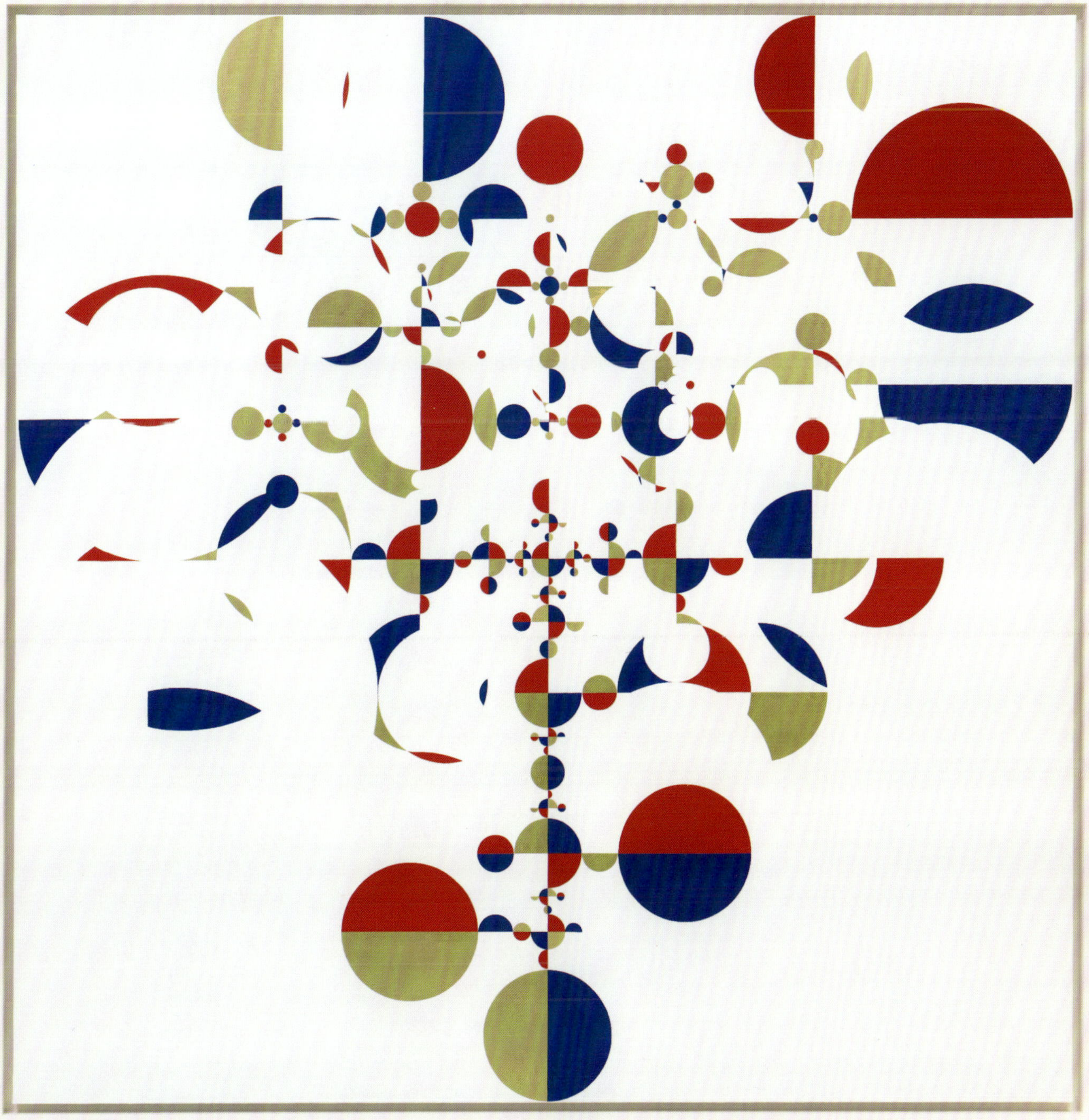

Kytes Tree, 2005
Acrylic on canvas, 200 x 200 cm
New York, The Museum of Modern Art, Purchase and gift of Anna Marie and Robert F. Shapiro and Donald B. Marron

Paola Pivi

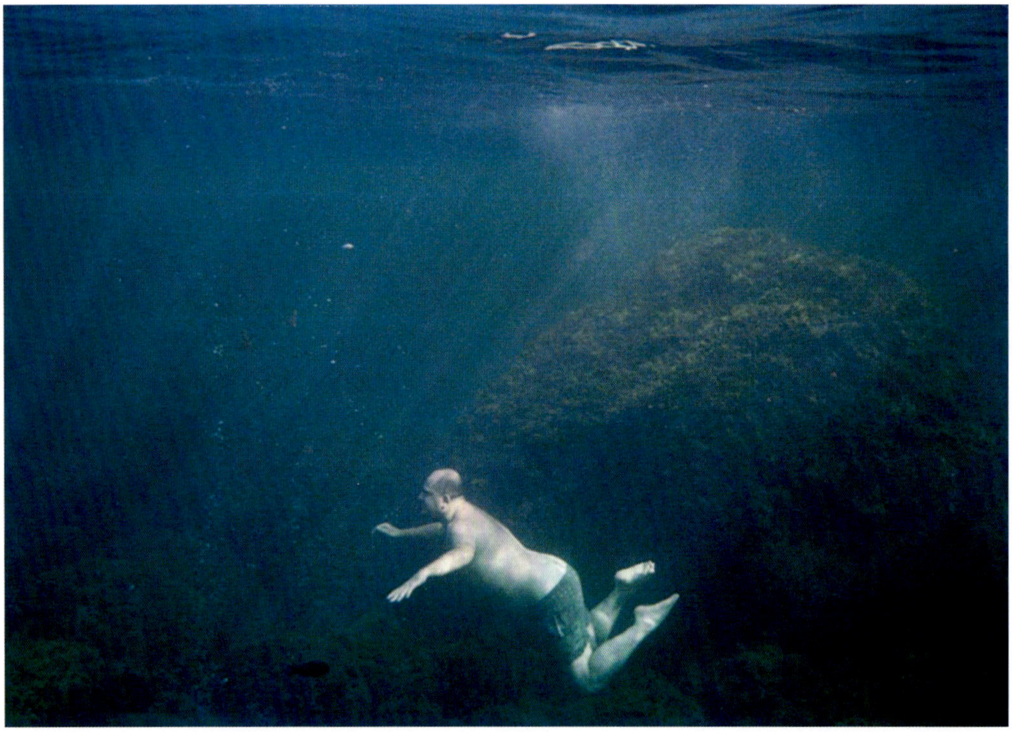

Senza titolo (Massimo), 2003
Color photograph on Dibond,
100 x 150 cm
Rivoli, Castello di Rivoli – Museo d'Arte Contemporanea; Turin, GAM Galleria Civica d'Arte Moderna e Contemporanea,
permanent loan Fondazione CRT Progetto Arte Moderna e Contemporanea

Senza titolo (asino), 2003
Color photograph on Dibond,
180 x 224 cm
Rivoli, Castello di Rivoli – Museo d'Arte Contemporanea; Turin, GAM Galleria Civica d'Arte Moderna e Contemporanea,
permanent loan Fondazione CRT Progetto Arte Moderna e Contemporanea

Born in Milan, Italy, in 1971. Lives and works in Anchorage, Alaska.
The work of the Italian artist Paola Pivi focuses on constructing surrealistic images by placing real objects in disorienting and apparently irreconcilable contexts. She began working in this direction in the late 1990s with a series of installations planned for insertion in different urban environments so as to give rise to visual situations of an absurd character, one example being the FIAT G-91 aircraft exhibited upside-down at the 1999 Venice Biennale.
Pivi works in the fields of sculpture, installation and photography, with a preference for large-scale projects. The last few years before her move to Alaska saw a project for a life-size photograph in 1:1 scale of the island of Alicudi in the Aeolian archipelago, where she lived for some time with the English artist Martin Creed.
The highly evocative power of the realistic quality implicit in photography makes this a particularly suitable medium for the creation of illogical situations.
A surrealistic atmosphere is in fact the dominant element in the images created by Pivi, whose aim is to generate a feeling of disorientation in the viewer, as happens in the series of large-sized photographs of apparently nonsensical subjects taken in 2003. An example is provided by *Senza titolo (asino)*, exhibited at the Venice Biennale in 2003, an untitled large-format photograph of a donkey in a small boat on a calm and apparently boundless expanse of water. The image obviously prompts numerous questions regarding the origin and absurdity of such an event in everyday life.
Forming part of the same series, *Senza titolo (zebre)* gave rise to a great deal of outcry over the ethical issues involved in placing wild animals in an environment completely alien to them – in this case, zebras on top of the Gran Sasso mountain – for artistic purposes.
The human sphere is instead addressed in *Senza titolo (Massimo)*, a photograph of Massimo De Carlo, whose gallery exhibits the artist's work, in the sea at Alicudi. The absence of elements identifying the subject as involved in the art system, the suspension of time and the disregard of the laws of physics shift the snapshot into a dimension beyond the real world.
(*F.T.*)

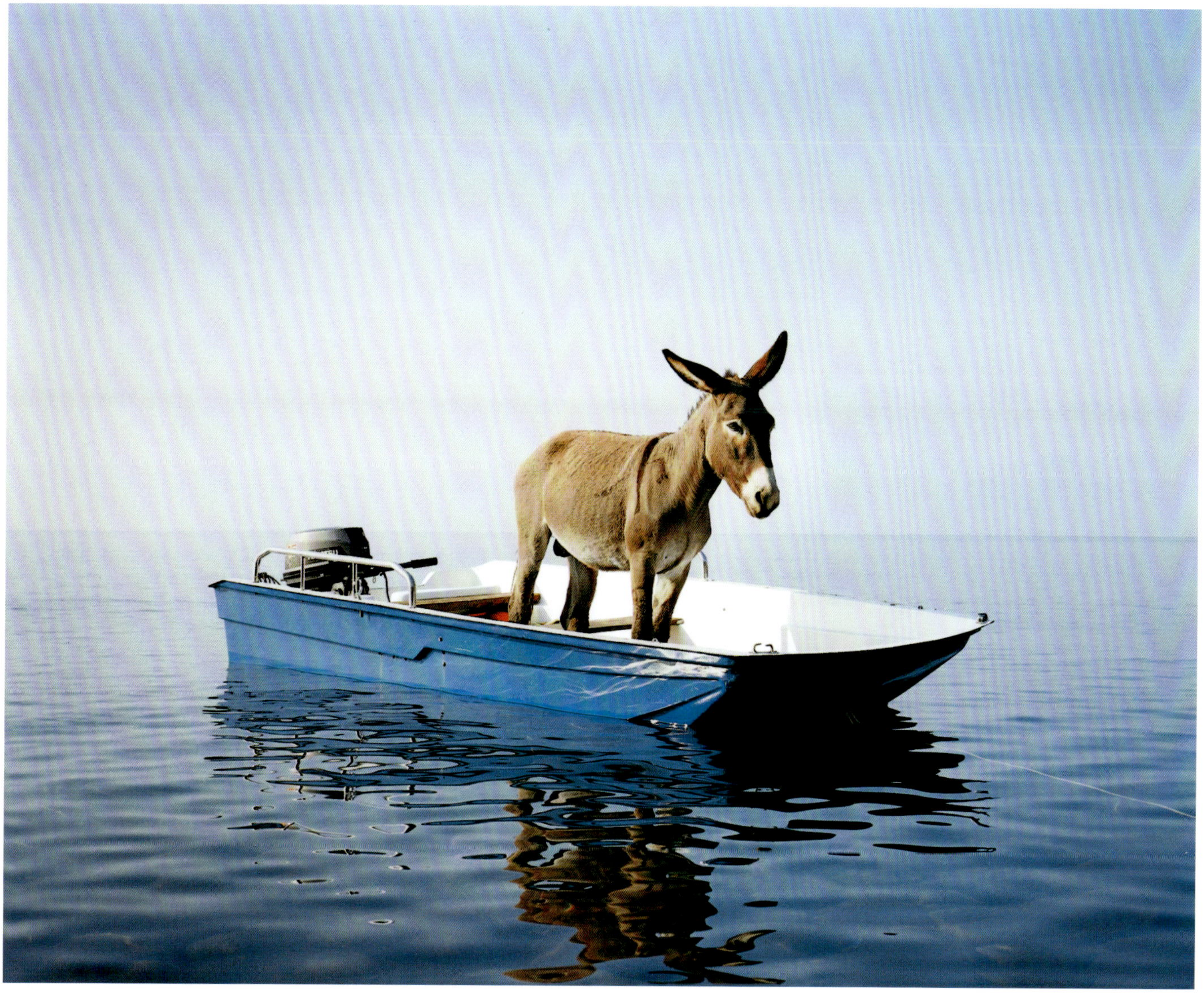

Neo Rauch

Born in Leipzig (Germany) in 1960. Lives and works in Leipzig.
The aim pursued by Rauch is a reinterpretation of the pictorial vocabulary of the twentieth-century European avant-garde, with particular reference to the Metaphysical Art of de Chirico and the Surrealism of Magritte, while maintaining all due detachment. The space investigated is that of domestic interiors and the human figures are avowedly indebted to the portrait painting of German Realism in the second half of the 1920s and '30s. The ambiguous, timeless atmosphere recalls the avant-garde strategy whereby the realistic image masks a rich iconographic subtext.
Among the artist's more recent operations, considerable interest attaches to the *Para* series produced in 2007 for a solo show at the Metropolitan Museum in New York, where the linear narrative component clashes with the equivocal, nostalgic atmosphere of the images, whose interpretive ambivalence endows the works with a degree of richness and complexity recalling the *Magischer Realismus* movement in Germany and coeval developments in Italy. The canvas *Der Nächste Zug* (*The Next Move/The Next Draw*, 2007) clearly exemplifies this. Dominated by two smartly dressed men smoking in the foreground, the scene is the prelude to an interior in which moments of deep intimacy and apparently gelid expectation coexist. The physical characterization of the figures in the middle ground leaves the question of their identification unresolved while suggesting that the possible interpretation of their identity – two women or a couple – is wholly immaterial to the definition of the subject.
The elegance of the dandies' clothes and carefully groomed hair, the interior furnished with a large canopy, and above all the book and the palette speak enigmatically of the past preceding the great revolution in lifestyle brought about by communism in Germany, or perhaps of a timeless *hic et nunc* in which normality and absurdity coexist unreally without jarring.
(F.T.)

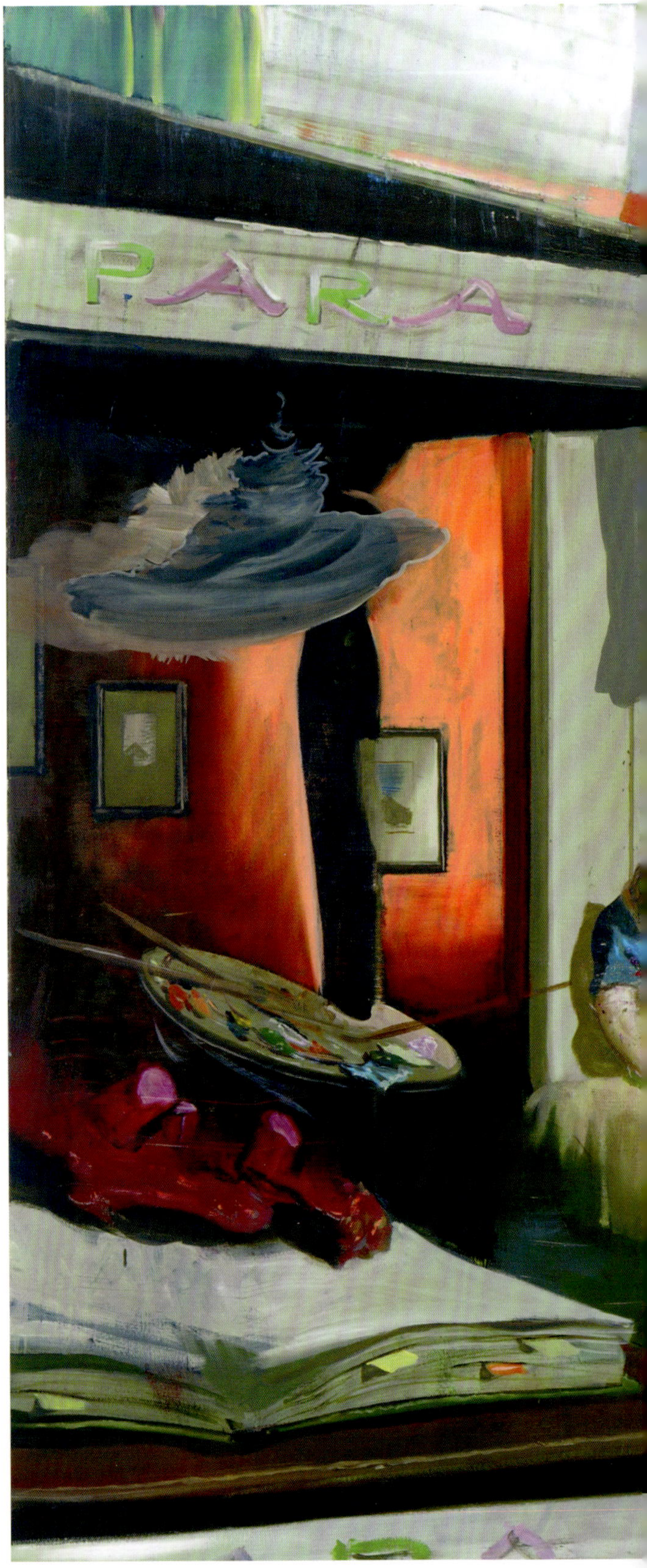

Der Nächste Zug (The Next Move/The Next Draw), 2007
Oil on canvas, 150 x 200 cm
New York, private collection
Courtesy Galerie EIGEN + ART Leipzig/Berlin; David Zwirner, New York

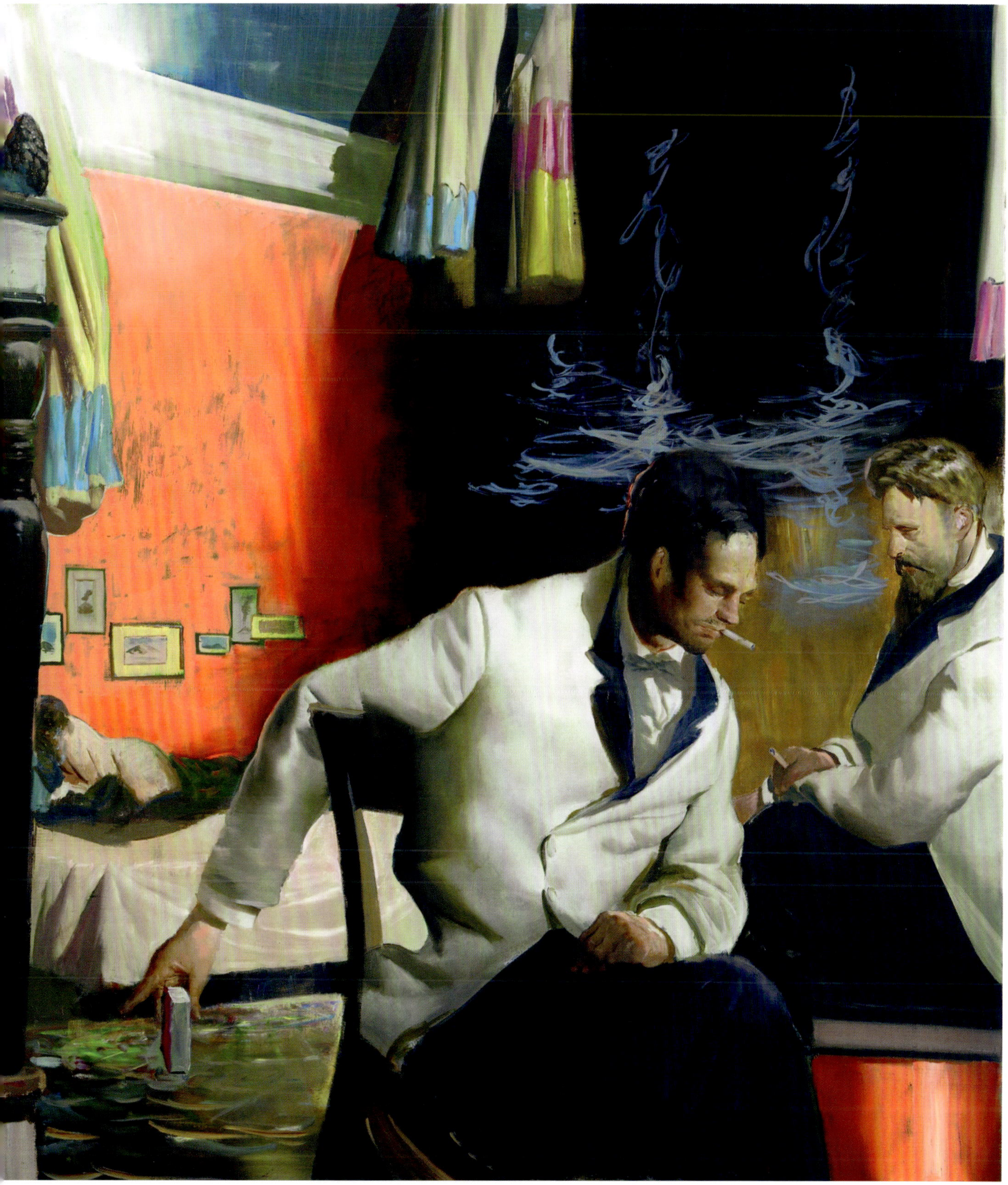

Tobias Rehberger

Born in Esslingen, Germany, in 1966. Lives and works in Frankfurt, Germany.
A pupil of Martin Kippenberger, Tobias Rehberger started out in the early 1990s and became known during that decade through projects that reshape the concept of authoriality by involving various collaborators in the production process, on the one hand, and giving a central role to the viewer and the peculiar way in which he or she looks at and uses the work, on the other. More interested in art as "context" than personal expression, as Martin Pesch wrote in 1996, "Rehberger is heading towards a new definition of what is understood by artistic production. He is not an artist intent on his own particular mode of expression, but rather a person who, through his art, wants to understand more about the structures and relations in which he works." In 1996, for the installation *Fragments of Their Pleasant Spaces (In My Fashionable Version)*, the artist asked some friends about their idea of comfort as a basis for the creation of various "fashionable" interiors. In 1997, for a group show at the ICA in London, Rehberger asked nine friends – including the artists Olafur Eliasson, Jorge Pardo, and Rirkrit Tiravanija – to give him flowers, which he then presented in vases of his own designs as portraits of the people in question. Entitled *Anastasia* and held the same year, his first solo show in New York encompassed the whole range of approaches adopted. The first room of the gallery was redesigned with the aid of three well-known fashion designers, namely Helmut Lang, Martin Margiela, and Walter van Beirendonck. The second was a bedroom with a circular bed and a 36-minute video projection going from one color of the spectrum to another so slowly as to make the change practically imperceptible, thus constituting at the same time a deconstruction of the cinematic medium in an anti-narrative sense and an explicit invitation to sleep and hence to generate a personal narrative by dreaming. In 1999 he commissioned a Thai automobile factory to produce cars on the basis of its interpretation of his own sketches of some celebrated models drawn from memory.
While Jorge Pardo addresses the relationship between art and design, functionality and self-referentiality, Rehberger's concern in this and other works appears to lie more in investigating and recounting the story behind an object. All this is quite evident in *Gu Mo Ni Ma Da* (2006), an installation based on a story told him by his friend the artist Danh Vo. In an effort to escape from the terrible conditions of postwar Vietnam in the 1980s, Vo's father built by himself a sort of ark capable of sailing away with about a hundred people on board. Rehberger took this as an opportunity to reflect on his own history and the figure of his father, the maker of the furniture in the middle of which he grew up. These two personal mythologies gave rise to *Gu Mo Ni Ma Da*, a life-sized reproduction of the boat that is also a reflection on two parallel but very different personal histories, one of a man forced to build a boat in order to escape from an unbearable situation, and the other of someone intent on making a tranquil middle-class home more comfortable.
On Otto, the ambitious new project presented in 2007 at the Prada Foundation in Milan, is an installation made up of various sections that constitute a backward reconstruction – from the poster to the screenplay – of the making of a film that does not exist as such but only through its collateral elements: the poster, the starting point of the entire project; the soundtrack, on which Ennio Morricone collaborated; the actors (including Kim Basinger, Danny DeVito, and Willem Dafoe), who are, however, shot as spectators of another film (*The Lady from Shanghai*, directed by Orson Welles). The result is a fragmentary, spatialized, and disorienting narrative that must once again be reconstructed by the viewer, whose personal vision and understanding take over from a non-existent director.
(*D.Q.*)

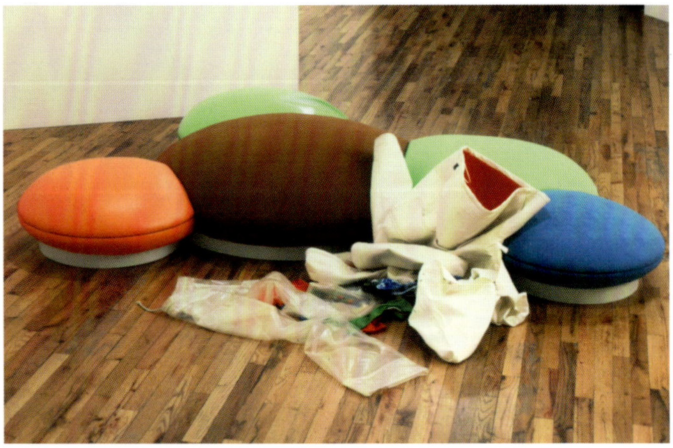

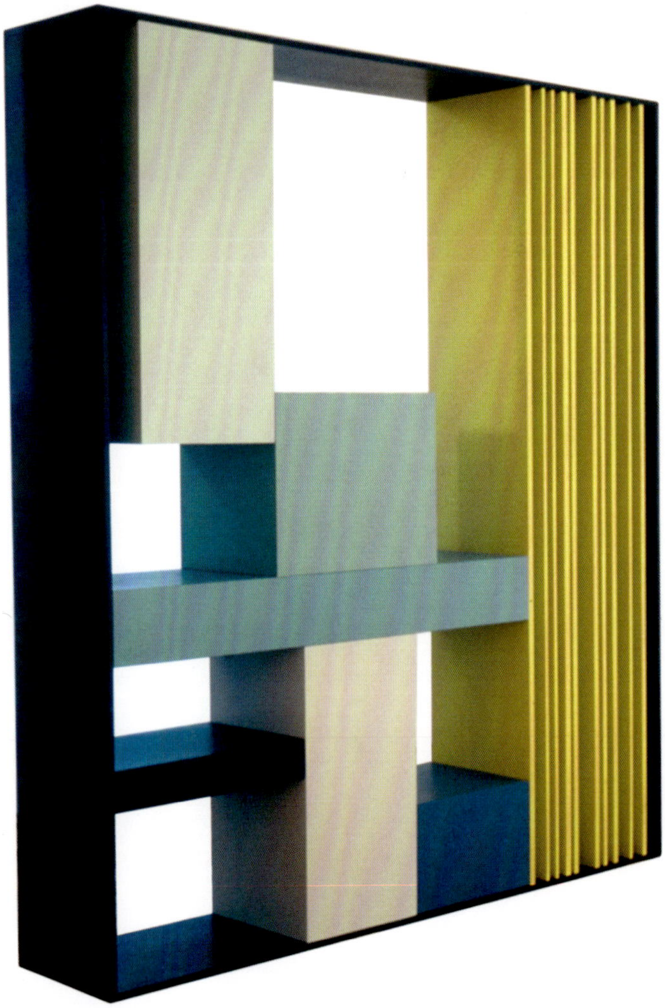

Performance (Frame Two), 1997
Wood, foam, spandex, Walter van Beirendonk, transparent plastic overall, white pants, polyester shirt with printed swan,
243.8 x 243.8 x 35.6 cm circa
Courtesy Friedrich Petzel Gallery, New York

Tom Cruise Jumping Library, 2000
MDF, paint, 3 televisions, 1 VCR,
230 x 210 x 40 cm
Courtesy Friedrich Petzel Gallery, New York

Gu Mo Ni Ma Da, 2006
Mahogany, metal, glass, epoxy, plastic, polyurethane coating,
4.5 x 10.4 x 3.5 m
Courtesy Friedrich Petzel Gallery, New York

Seven Naked Hermann Hesse Fans, 2006
Wall painting, 3.3 x 7 m
Courtesy Haunch of Venison, London

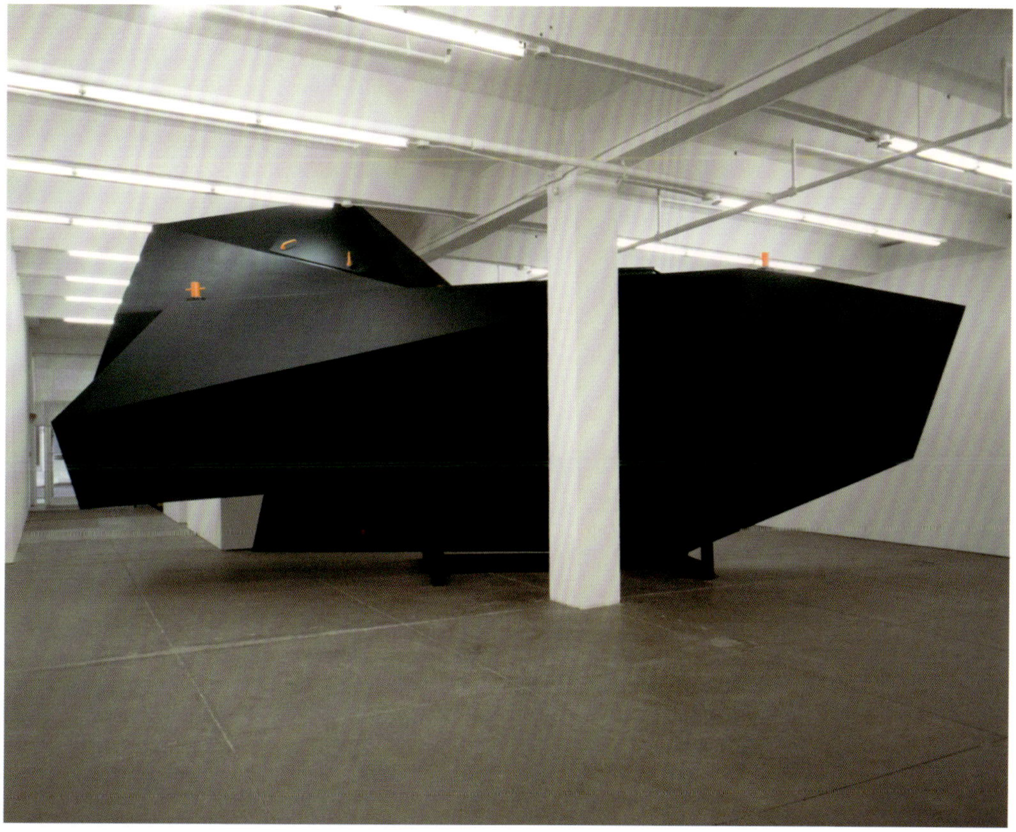

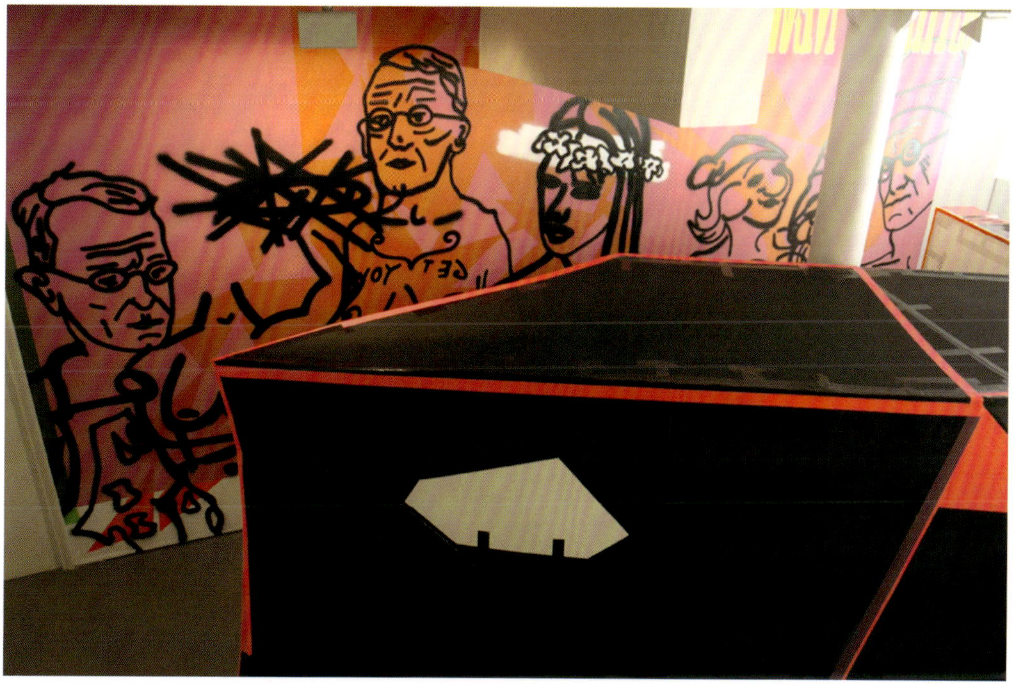

Gregor Schneider

Born in Rheydt, Germany, in 1969. Lives and works in Rheydt.
Gregor Schneider worked obsessively for 12 years, from 1985 to 1997, on transforming the interior of his home at Rheydt in the heart of Germany, knocking down and rebuilding walls, soundproofing rooms, bricking up doors and windows, and creating secret passageways. It became the focal point of his art under the name *Haus Ur*, which was changed into *Totes Haus Ur* for its presentation in the German pavilion at the Venice Biennale in 2001. Schneider was awarded the Golden Lion for the best national participation for having transformed the authoritarian and monumental architectural structure of the pavilion into a haunting maze of rooms that, as the jury put it, "reflects secret conditions of angst but also hope for freedom."
Known as one of the most interesting figures on the German art scene over the last 15 years, Schneider has reconstructed his *Haus Ur* in various exhibition settings, sought out opportunities to work in abandoned buildings or villages (like the town of Garzweiler, 1990–1991), and turned the otherwise austere rooms of galleries and museums all over the world into places steeped in tension and mystery.
Schneider has thus invented a new form of art that can be classified neither as sculpture nor as installation. He creates rooms or rather spaces that are commonplace and terrifying at the same time, capable of suggesting the scenes of violent crimes, torture chambers, cold hospital wards, desolate streets or anonymous rented accommodation. They are environments that establish dialogue with spectators on the basis of personal experiences and subjective inclinations, being read in different ways according to the images with which the individual associates them. According to Schneider, it is not in fact the spaces in themselves that arouse feelings of melancholy, uneasiness, anxiety or fear in the spectator but the imaginative projection of what may have happened there, the acts their inhabitants may have performed. If it is tragic or violent situations that come spontaneously to mind, this is because of the general distrust that human beings feel for their kind and their readiness to believe others capable of any sort of wickedness.
Schneider's work is not, however, confined to the creation of environments with strong evocative potential. It is in fact the echo of Germany's recent history that reverberates in the obsessive transfigurations of his own home (and other buildings) and in particular the rapid postwar reconstruction on a massive scale with which the country attempted to wipe out all trace of the past and give itself a new face. In response to all doomed and disastrous attempts at suppression, Schneider makes the past a "structural" component of the present.
The suffix *Ur* is indeed used in German to indicate an original, pre-existing condition.
This reference to a remote matrix, a sort of fountainhead, makes it impossible to connect Schneider's layered and claustrophobic settings exclusively with his private experience and suggests that they are rather to be seen as reflecting the collective memory of the German people.
In aesthetic terms, Schneider's works can be described as post-Minimalist by virtue of their thorough investigation of the primary values of space and the objects it accommodates, the preference shown for industrially produced materials, and the pictorial qualities given to the surfaces of walls, ceilings and floors through repeated operations of painting, whitewashing and covering.
Cube Hamburg, perhaps Schneider's most controversial work, is also Minimalist in character. It consists of a metal frame and wooden panels covered in velvet to make a black cube measuring 14 x 14 x 14 meters that alludes to the Kaaba in Mecca. Designed to stand in Piazza San Marco during the 2005 Venice Biennale, the work was considered offensive to Muslim culture and its construction was prohibited.
The same thing happened the following year in Berlin. It was not until 2007 that the artist was finally able to carry out his project at the Kunsthalle in Hamburg (*Das Schwarze Quadrad – Hommage an Malewitsch*).
Schneider resumed his work on the transformation of exhibition spaces and the conditioning of individuals in 2008. *Süßer Duft* offered visitors at the MACRO in Rome and the Galerie Maison Rouge in Paris the experience of a solitary "descent into the underworld" through a succession of different rooms (cramped, huge, empty, icy, overheated, flooded with dazzling light, pitch black, wrapped in silence, full of unusual noises).
A form exempting the organizers from all liability in the event of panic attacks had to be signed before entering.
(*P.V.*)

Totes Haus Ur, 2001
Assembly of architecture elements, dimensions variable
View of the installation at the German Pavilion, XLIX Esposizione Internazionale d'Arte, Biennale di Venezia 2001

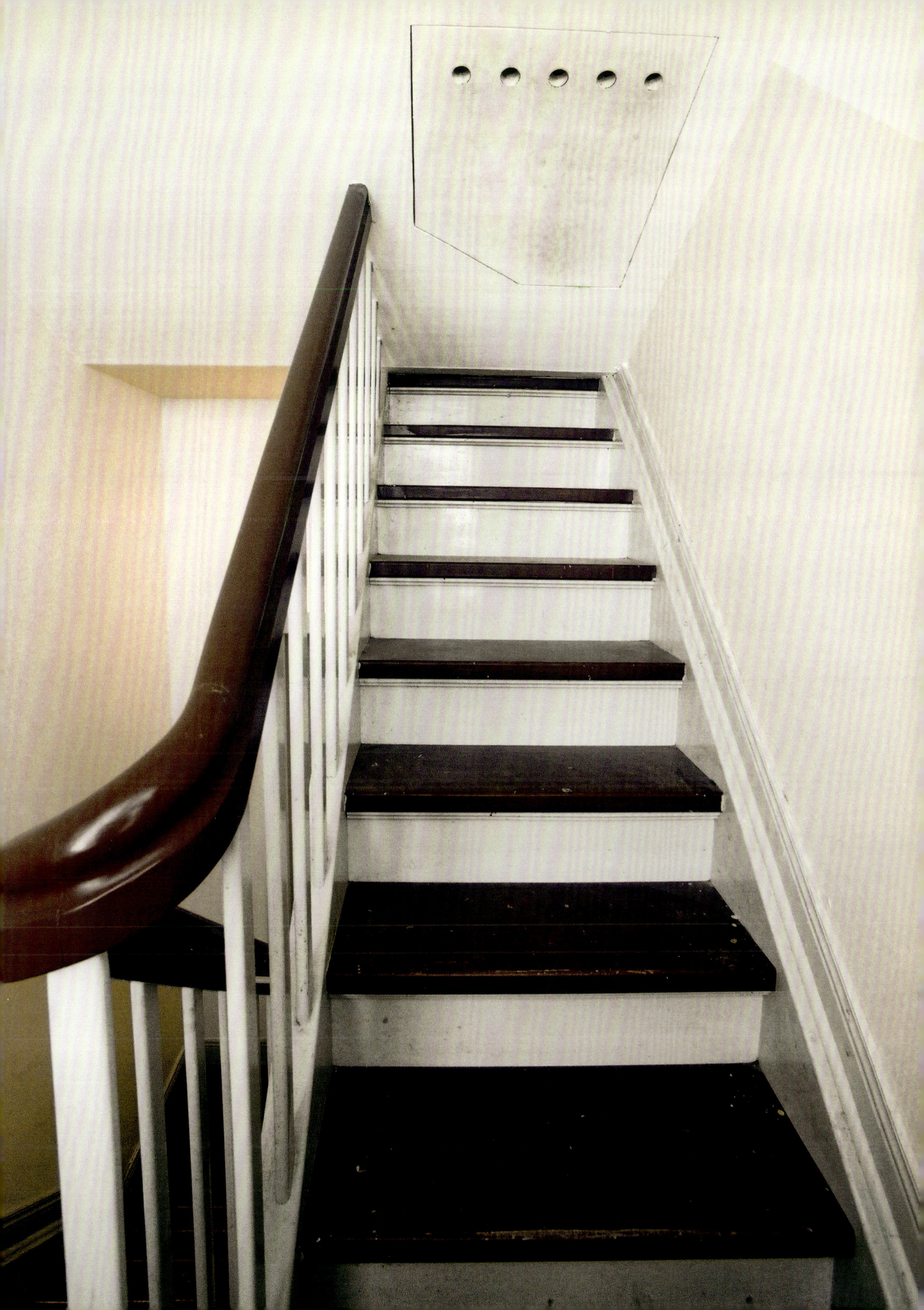

Cube Hamburg, 2005
Metallic structure, wooden panels, velvet, 14 x 14 x 14 m
View of the installation realized in 2007 outside the Hamburger Kunsthalle, Hamburg

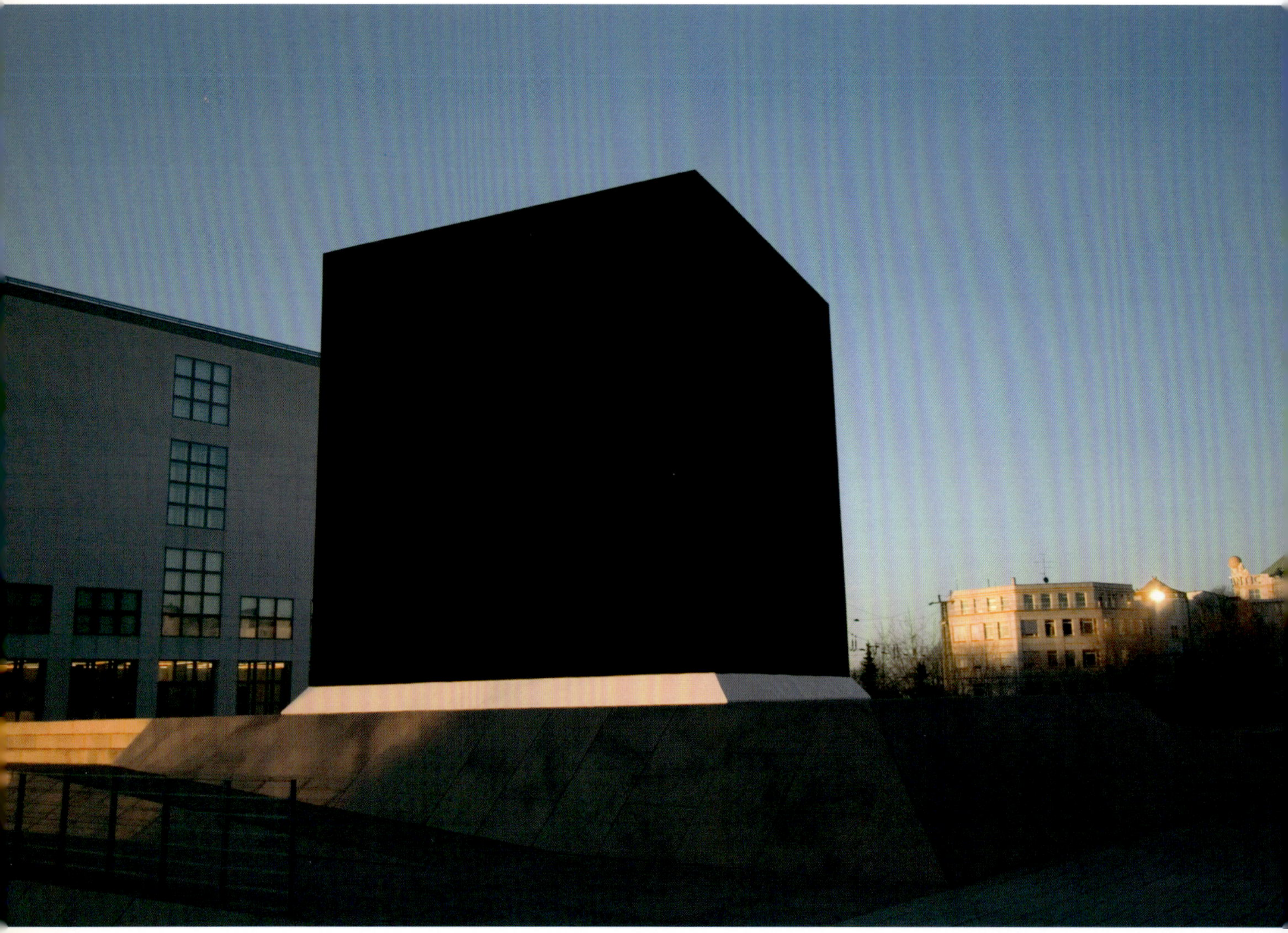

Washing Room (Entrance), 2008
Metal plates, dimensions variable
Detail of the installation *Süßer Duft*
(Sweet Smell) realized in 2008 at
the Galerie La Maison Rouge, Paris

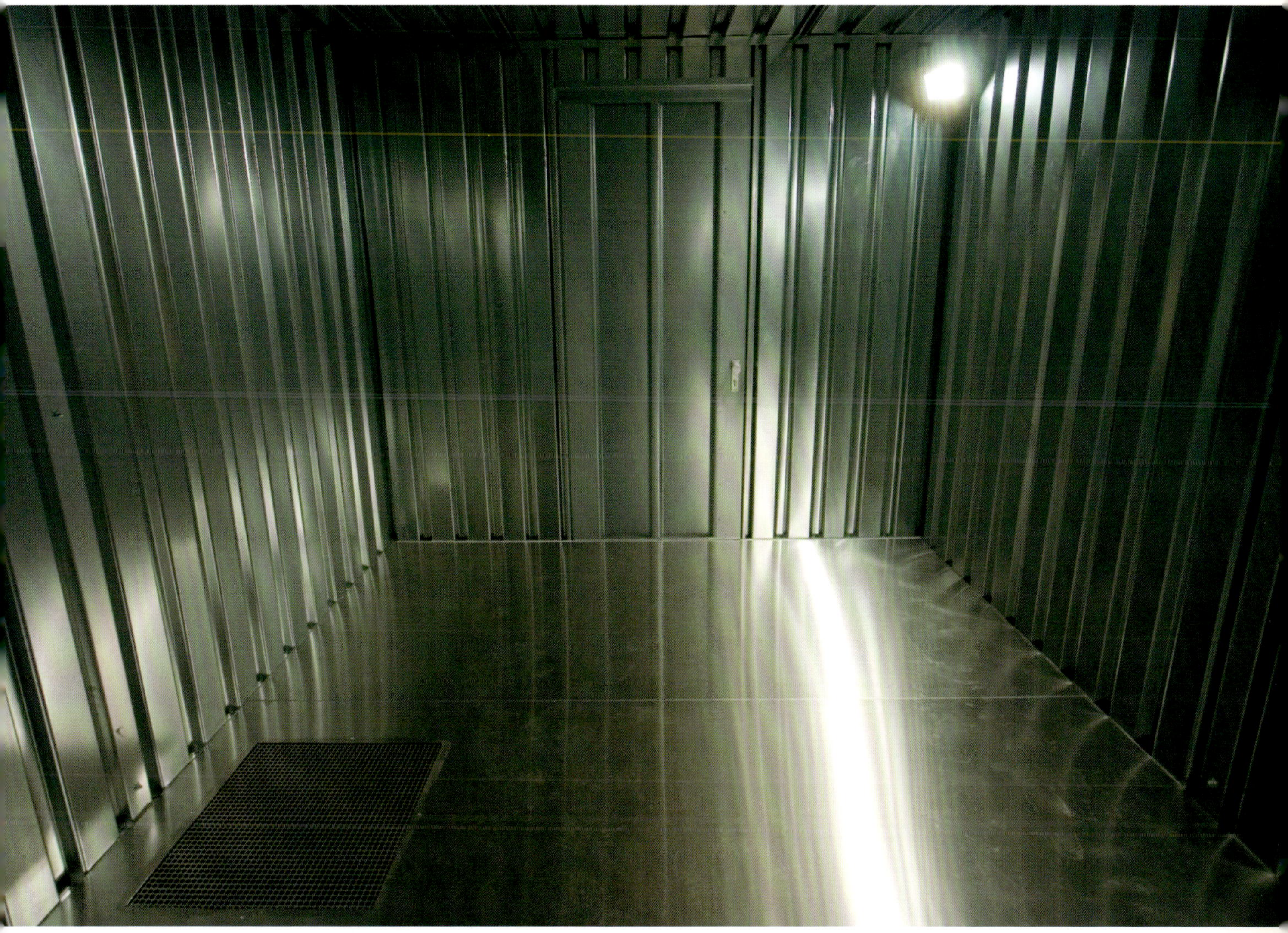

Nedko Solakov

Born in Cherven Briag, Bulgaria, in 1957. Lives and works in Sofia. "Sometimes I feel like a container-creature that verifies and separates different personalities (artist A, artist B, artist C)." It was with these words, written on the wall of the Galleria Minini in Brescia, Italy, that Nedko Solakov presented himself to visitors at his solo show entitled *A Group Show* (2007).
He chose this simultaneously ironic and programmatic title in order to introduce a selection of works produced with a variety of techniques (photography, installation, video, painting and drawing) and to assert the premeditated nature of this operative decision at the same time as a subtle polemical thrust at critics incapable of seeing that the specificity of his art lies precisely in its polysemic character.
The diversification of media is in fact functional to the plurality of subjects that Solakov addresses like a sort of storyteller in his work through a combination of reality and metaphor. These two sides are clearly evident in the works presented by the artist at the main international events. *A Life (Black & White)* involved having the same room painted black and then white in a continuous cycle at the 2001 Venice Biennale. *Discussion (Property)* used video images, words, drawings and a real Kalashnikov hanging on the wall to talk about the arms traffic between the former Soviet Union and Bulgaria, and won him an honorable mention at the 2007 Biennale.
The works exhibited by invitation the same year at Documenta in Kassel were *Fears*, a series of 99 drawings covering a wall of the Fridericianum, and *Top Secret* (1989–1990), a historical work consisting of papers, objects and drawings documenting the artist's collaboration with the Bulgarian secret police up to 1983, which he made known through a voluntary act of self-accusation at a show in Sofia in 1990.
The large-scale installation *I Love Them* (2007) was designed for the lower floor of the Galleria Continua in San Gimignano, a former cinema and theater, where Solakov set up a variety of screens and monitors for the simultaneous but unsynchronized projection of images from seven films including some masterpieces of cinema and television history (*City Lights, The Big Lebowski, Rocco Flickt Rio, Seven Samurai, Fawlty Towers (The Psychiatrist episode), Amadeus, Amarcord*) chosen on the basis of the feelings and emotions they aroused in the artist. The resulting kaleidoscope of lights, colors and images once again suggested a plural subject.
(*P.V.*)

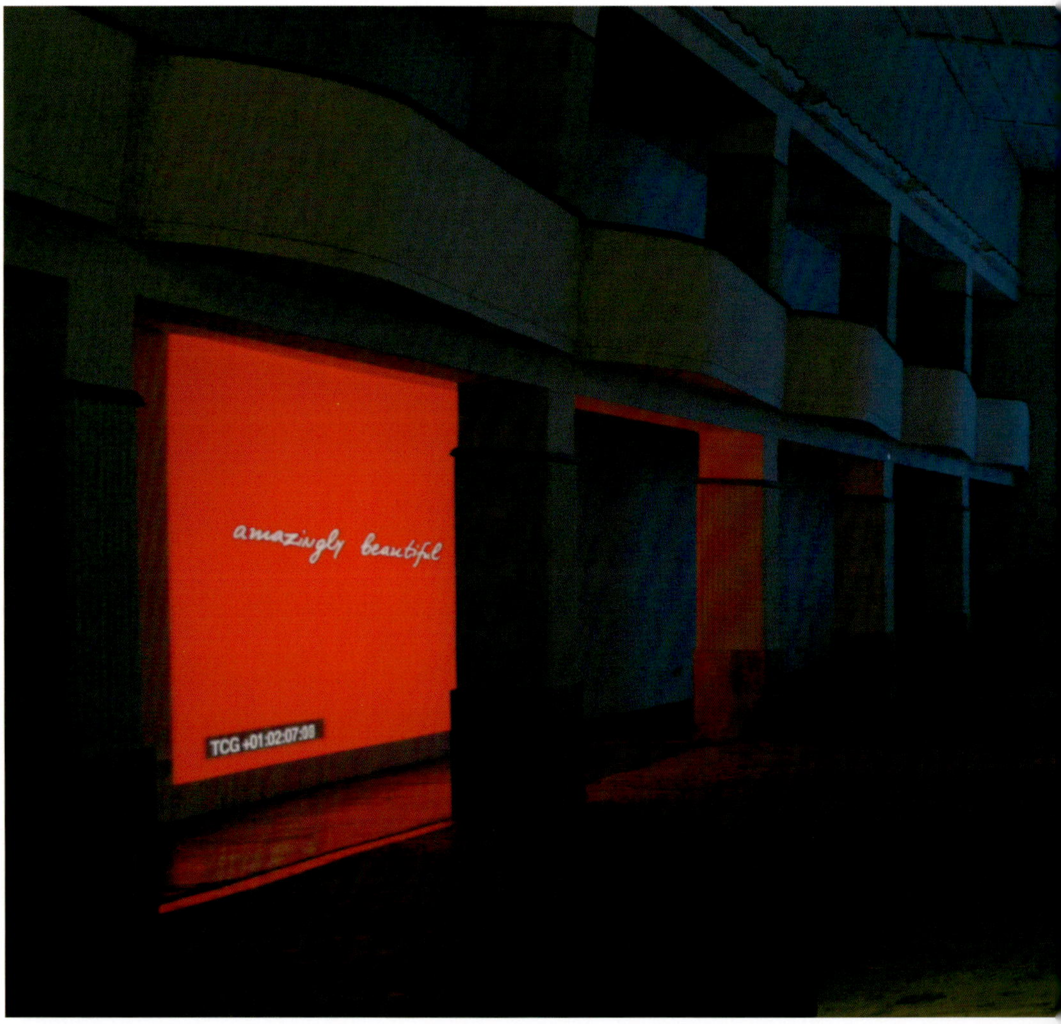

I Love Them, 2007
Seven-channel video installation, silent, duration: *City Lights*, 82'52''; *The Big Lebowsky*, 108'02''; *Seven Samurai*, 189'23''; *Rocco Flickt Rio*, 54'05''; *Fawlty Towers (The Psychiatrist episode)*, 36'32''; *Amadeus*, 153'36''; *Amarcord*, 118'43'', dimensions variable
View of the installation realized in 2007 at the Galleria Continua, San Gimignano
Courtesy Galleria Continua, San Gimignano/Beijing/Le Moulin

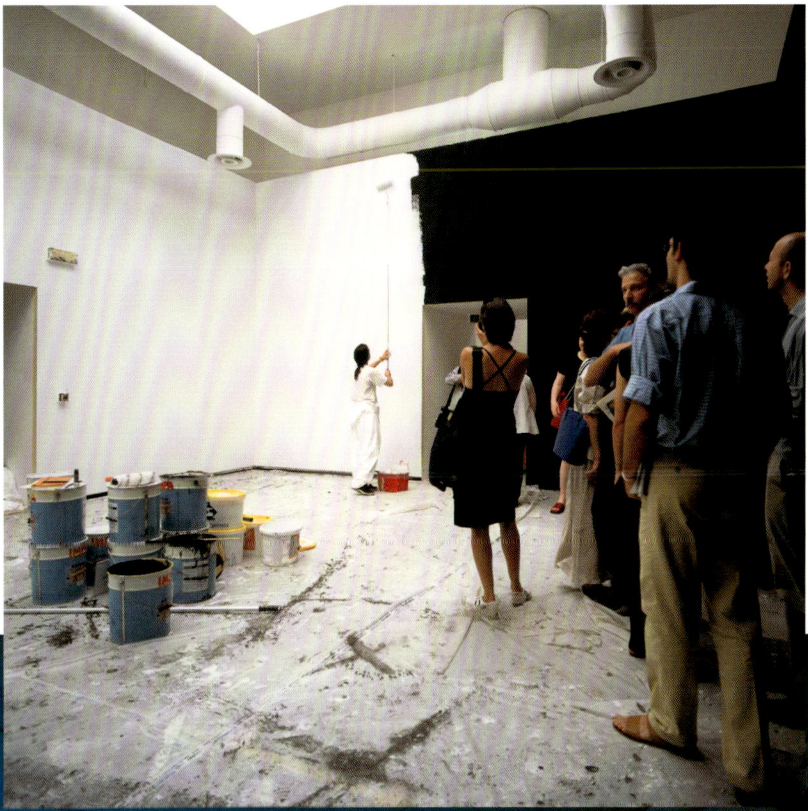

A Life (Black & White), 1998–2001
Black and white paint, dimensions variable
View of the performance at the XLIX Esposizione Internazionale d'Arte, Biennale di Venezia 2001
Courtesy of the artist

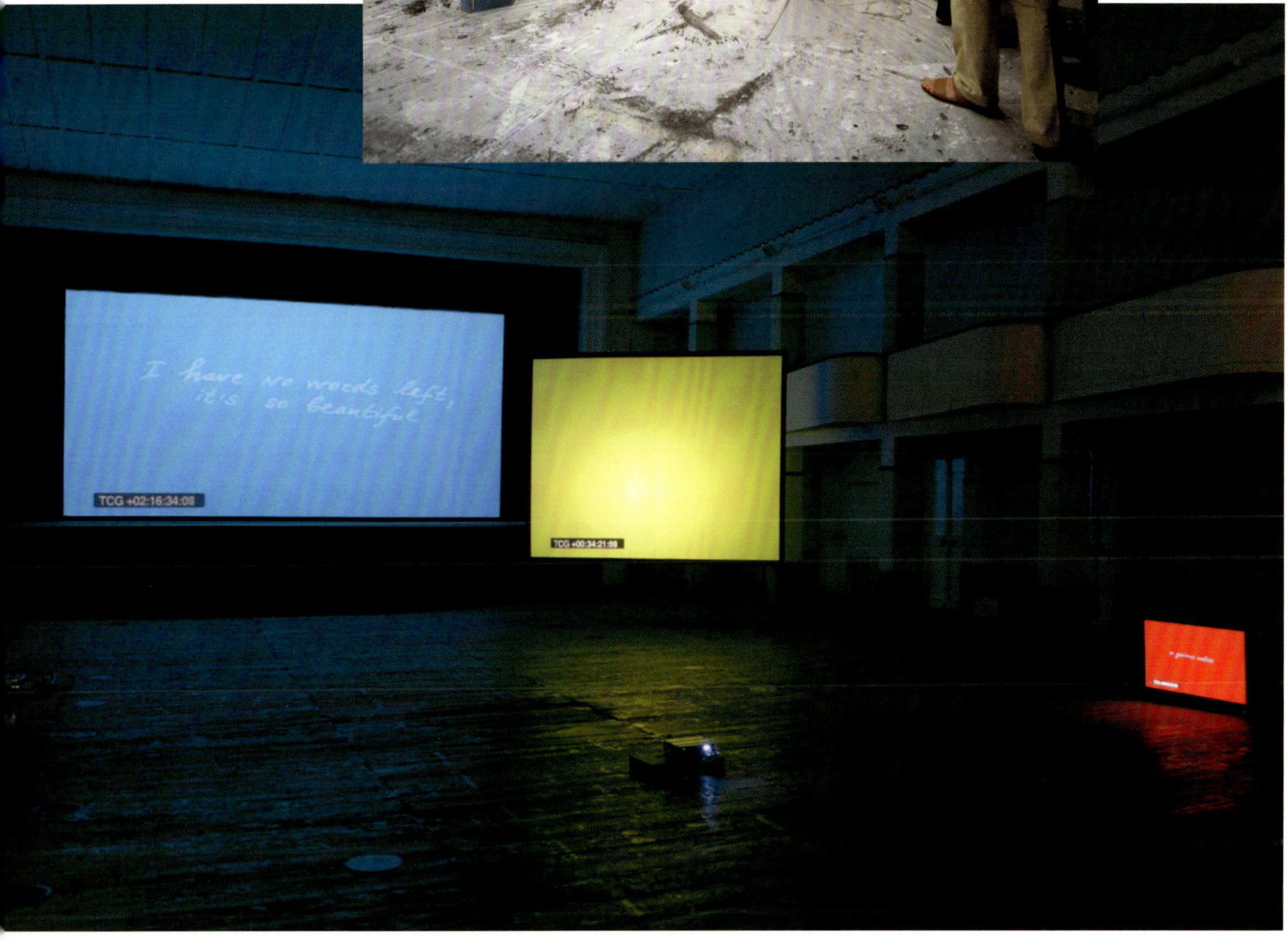

Luc Tuymans

Born in Mortsel, Belgium, in 1958. Lives and works in Antwerp.
Like most contemporary painters addressing the question of a possible role for painting in a society invaded by images created and transmitted through mechanical, technological, and digital media, Luc Tuymans makes his paintings out of "second hand materials" – in his case, news photographs and film stills above all – focusing in particular on subjects laden with tension, violence and political significance.
His technique does not, however, seek to compete with the mass-media image but remains clearly pictorial. This decision stems not from the artist's particular confidence in the communicative qualities of his medium but, on the contrary, from a desire to demonstrate the incapacity of painting to provide any adequate representation of dramatic events such as those that marked the last century and still characterize our everyday life. A particularly eloquent example of this inability is provided by the painting *De Wandeling* (1991, The Walk). In the pictorial translation offered by Tuymans, the photograph of a meeting between Adolf Hitler and Albert Speer loses its dramatic historical connotations to the point where it can be mistaken for an innocent walk at sunset along a mountain path. The inadequacy of painting is therefore closely related to the inadequacy of our memory, our inability to keep mental and visual track of the information and images constantly offered to us by history and the present. This accounts for the almost abstract character of many of the artist's works, their indeterminacy, the appearance of things faded by time. It also explains the wide range of subjects: from episodes connected with the darkest periods of history, like the Holocaust (*Gaskammer*, 1986) and Belgium's colonial policy (*Mwana Kitoko – Beautiful White Man*, 2000), to the simple objects and strangers you come into contact with every day. Whatever the source of inspiration, the artist's representations are always blurred, distant, and nebulous precisely because they are located in the space that separates the image of a given event from the event itself, taking into themselves all the indeterminacy, ambiguity, and incompleteness of a story filtered through time. Even the most innocuous objects and chance encounters are thus transformed into sinister, potentially threatening presences precisely because the mental coordinates needed to establish their correct location have been lost in that in-between space. In effecting the transition from the "second-hand" image to the painting, Tuymans not only blurs its contours (in both the literal and the metaphorical sense) but also deliberately eliminates any supplementary data. The titles therefore often provide crucial indications for our reading of the work, albeit without being exhaustive or unambiguous.
It is the title of *Prisoners of War* (2001) that tells us that what might look like ordinary identity photographs are actually dramatic images of the faces of four prisoners of war. Tuymans knows that painting is incapable of going any further. The prisoners' situation is too dramatic to find any adequate form of representation and any attempt to achieve this by force is doomed to failure. This is the reason for the discreet, humble and almost bashful character of the painting of Luc Tuymans: a pleasant exception to the latest trends in the field of painting.
(L.L.)

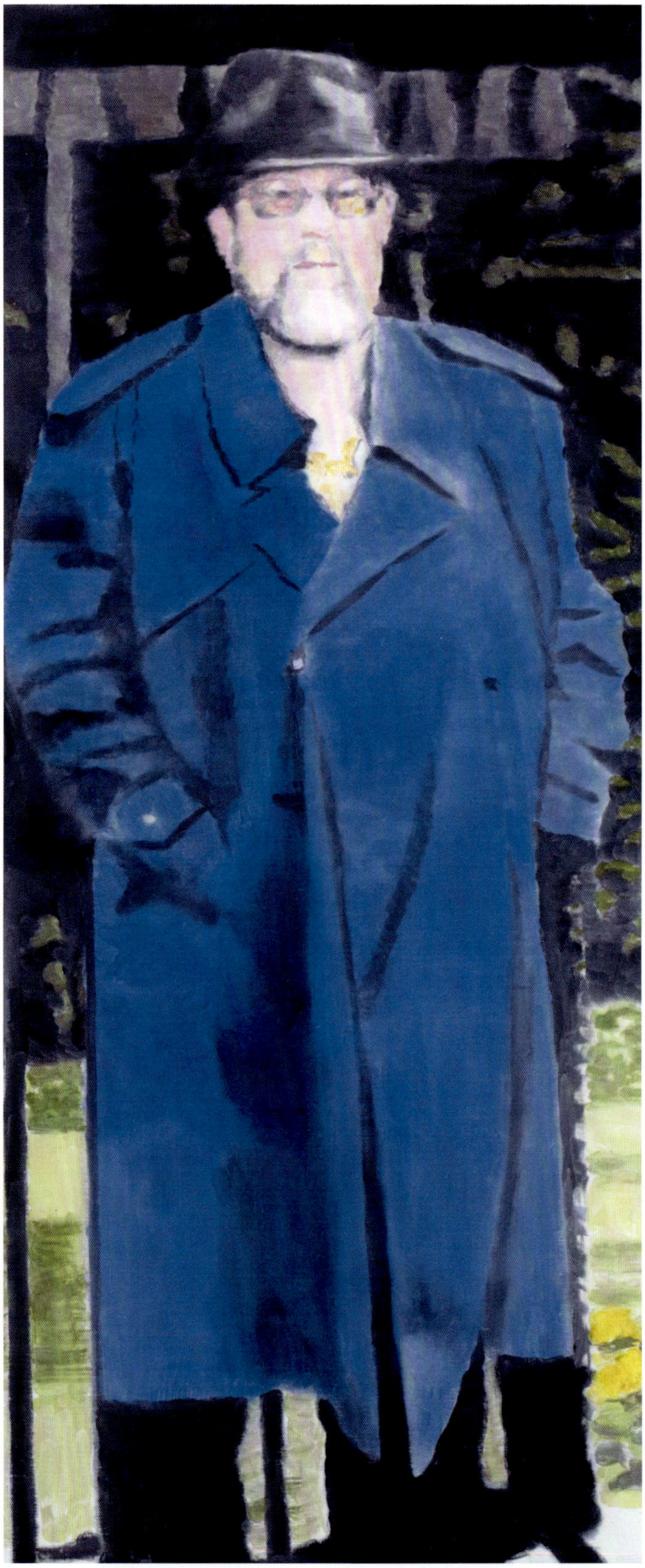

Imperméable, 2006
Oil on canvas, 224 x 94 cm
Private collection

De Wandeling (The Walk), 1991
Oil on canvas, 37 x 48 cm
Tervuren, Belgium, private collection

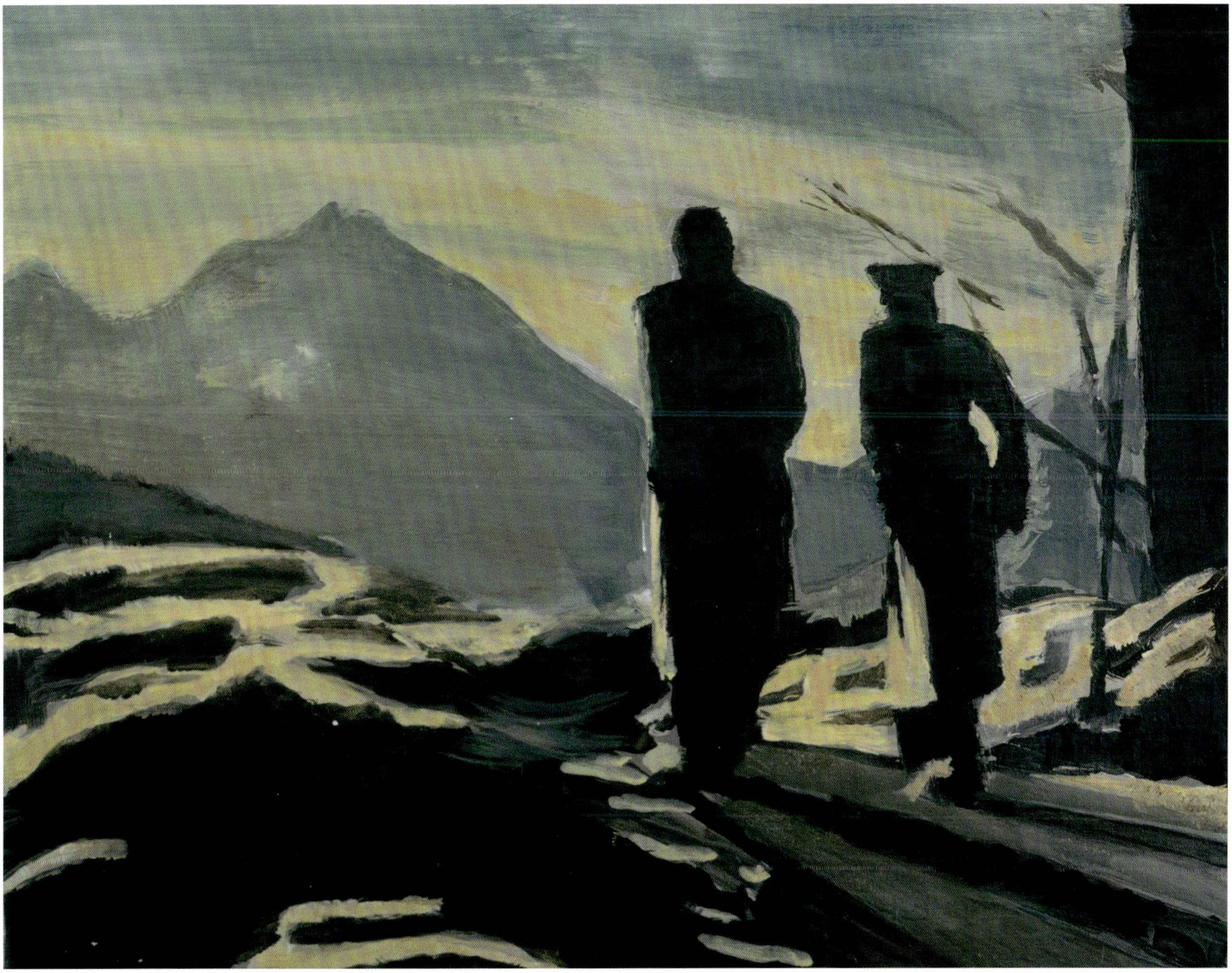

Kara Walker

Born in Stockton, California, in 1969. Lives and works on Rhode Island.
Published in New York in 1994, Kobena Mercer's *Welcome to the Jungle: New Positions in Cultural Studies* introduced the term "stereotypic grotesque" to describe the tendency shared by various American artists since the 1970s – from Betye Saar to Faith Ringgold and David Hammons – to accentuate racial stereotypes in order to heighten the element of protest in their works.
Among the Afro-American artists of the most recent generations, Kara Walker adopts this strategy in an original and effective way, using silhouettes to tell the story of the slavery and discrimination inflicted upon the black population of the United States. Her cutout characters are thus involved in stories of unspeakable cruelty, violence, sexual depravation, and abuse that are, however, presented as caricature. Walker's source of inspiration is in fact the traveling theater and minstrel shows with which, in nineteenth-century America and especially the Antebellum South, the white landowning culture parodied the life of black slaves, portraying them as clownish, backward, thoughtless beings intent on satisfying their primary needs, so as to feel justified in looking down on them. Kara Walker uses the same weapon but takes the stereotype to extremes, thus exposing its underlying mechanism and turning it against all those who still harbor racist ideas today. The world of the silhouettes is not in fact given any precise spatiotemporal location but rather presents a timeless reality that brings spectators face to face with their own hidden wicked thoughts, prejudices, and violent fantasies.
This happens to still greater effect when the figures abandon the dimension of the sheet of paper and present themselves life-sized on the walls of galleries and museums, thus forcing the public to confront their aberrant, violent, appalling stories of rape, torture, sodomy, murder, and cannibalism with no mediation. The added use of light projection or magic lantern effects then makes the spectators an integral part of the work. Transformed in turn into shadows and silhouettes, they enter into the stories, witness those acts of abuses and humiliation, and find themselves forced to take sides, to opt for condemnation, indifference or connivance.
The situation is made still more complicated by Walker's apparent neutrality, her decision to present evil and depravation not as the prerogative of one race – the whites – but as an aberration of human nature. A particularly significant example of this attitude is provided by one of the episodes that did most to bring Kara Walker to the attention of critics and the public at the international level, namely the curtain she designed by invitation of the Vienna Opera House for the 1998–1999 season. Walker covered the immense surface with the story of Orpheus and Eurydice interwoven with episodes of racial violence referring not only to the barbarity of the Nazis but also to the frequent clashes between black and Jewish Americans. The figures involved in these depictions include the "black Jew" of the official Nazi logo for *Entartete Musik*, chosen by the artist to remind two races often involved in episodes of hatred and intolerance of their common history of oppression and the dramatic battles to establish human rights.
(*P.V.*)

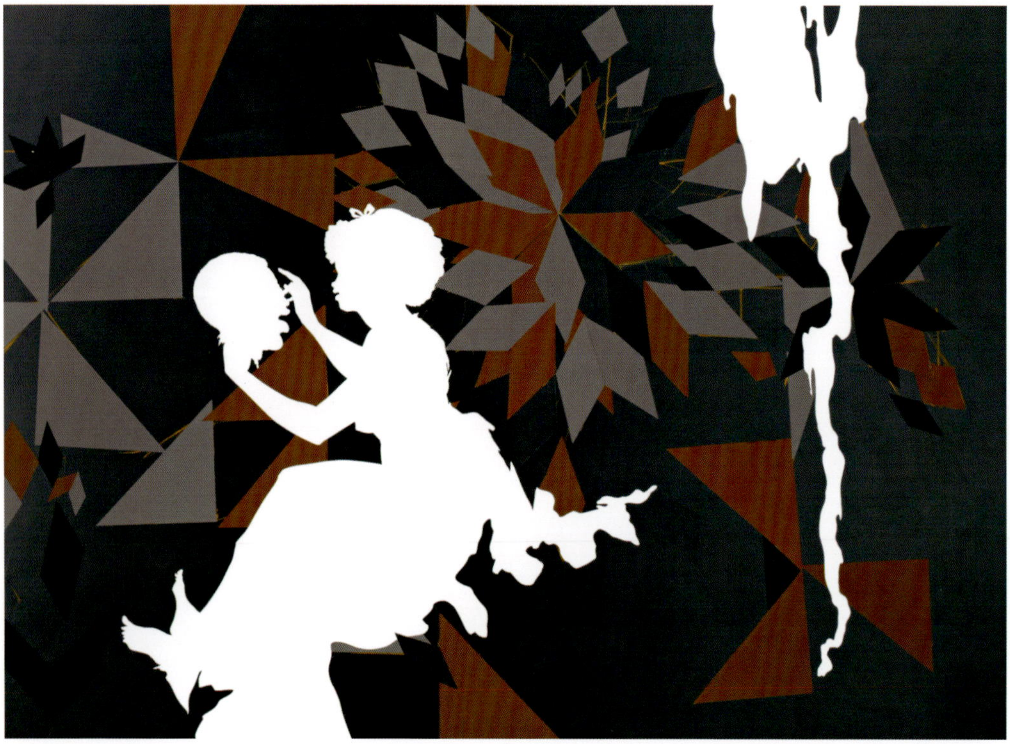

Authenticating the Artifact, 2007
Mixed media, 152.7 x 213.4 x 51 cm
New York, Sikkema Jenkins & Co

Grub for Sharks: A Concession to the Negro Populace, 2004
Paper outlines, dimensions variable
Courtesy of the artist and Sikkema Jenkins & Co, New York

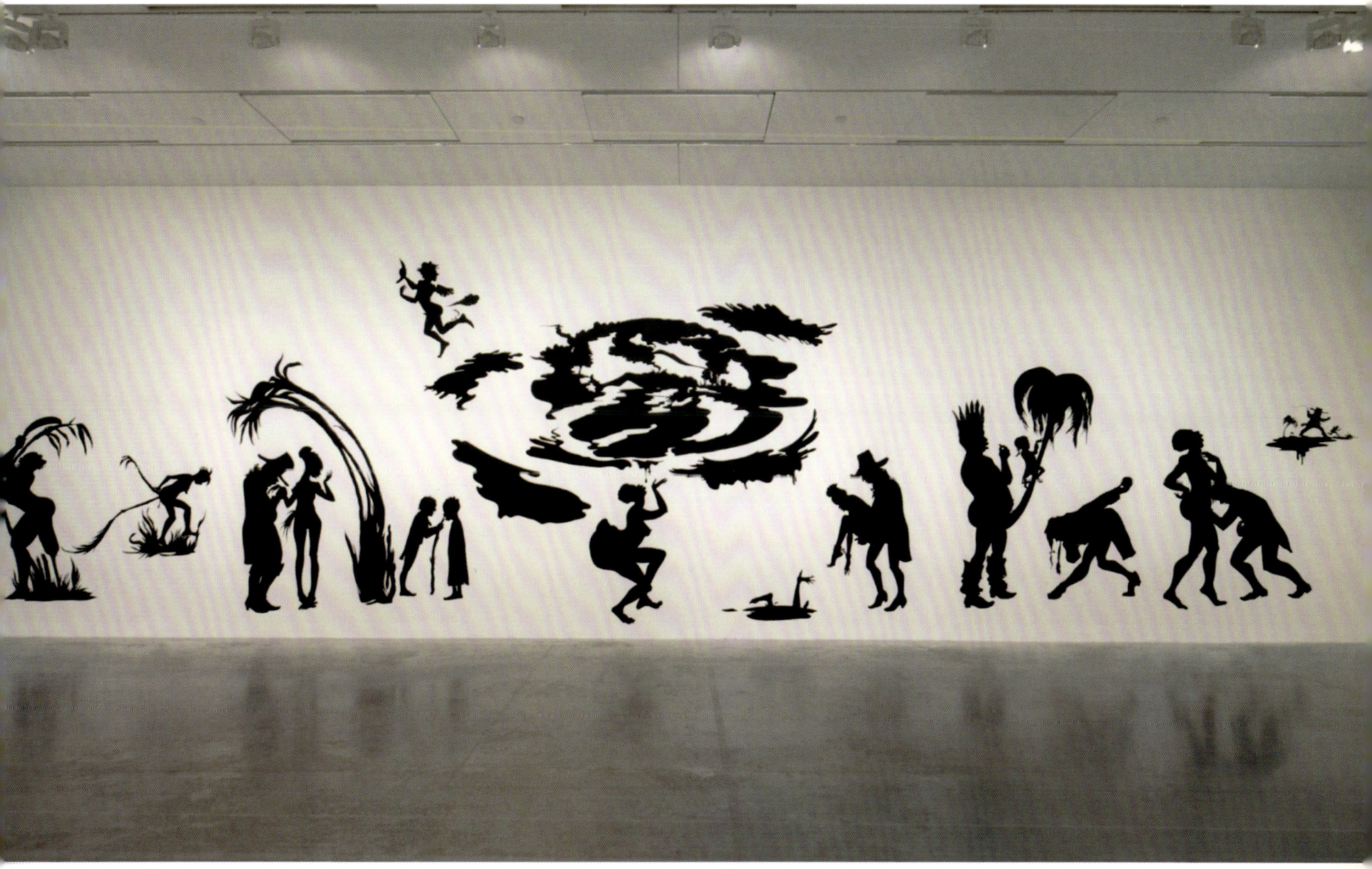

Matthias Weischer

Born in Elte (Germany) in 1973. Lives and works in Leipzig. Considered one of the most promising figures in the New School of Leipzig, Weischer has produced some of the most important work in German painting over the last decade.
The focal point of his canvases is the relationship between the perception of the space and the objects giving it structure, which the artist examines in terms of the role of furnishings, using their weight as objects to create an illusory space characterized by the coexistence of irreconcilable elements.
The accumulation of furniture, mirrors, and decorative elements helps to create the uncanny atmosphere typical of the canvases produced by this German artist, who has also been exploring the vocabulary of graphic art with great interest over the last two years.
The undermining of the spatial and architectural logic of Weischer's environments can be compared in some respects with the works of the Italian Giovanni Battista Piranesi and the illogical, illusory universes created by the Dutch artist M.C. Escher. The three dimensions thus become a method of refuting the practices of spatial cognition.
One example is the canvas *Stellwand* (2005, Folding Screen), where the artist presents the viewer with the interior of a room characterized by the play of light and the shadows cast on the walls and the table. The flat surface provides a basis for traces of human presence, which is conspicuous by its absence: a house of cards constituting an evident metaphor of instability and illusion, some biscuits, and a salt and pepper set.
The window then opens onto a wholly geometric panorama, an orderly repetition of the more fluid patterns created by the light inside.
The evocative power of the presence-absence of human beings is still stronger in the untitled work (*Ohne Titel*) of 2003 where the artist takes up the iconography of the studio with an expressive approach recalling the dummies of de Chirico and Surrealist illusion. Artifice becomes a paradigm of environmental creation.
(*F.T.*)

Stellwand (Folding Screen), 2005
Oil on canvas, 151 x 200 cm
Private collection

Ohne Titel (Untitled), 2003
Oil on canvas, 144 x 105 cm
Bergisch Gladbach, Germany, Hannelore and Peter Molitor Collection

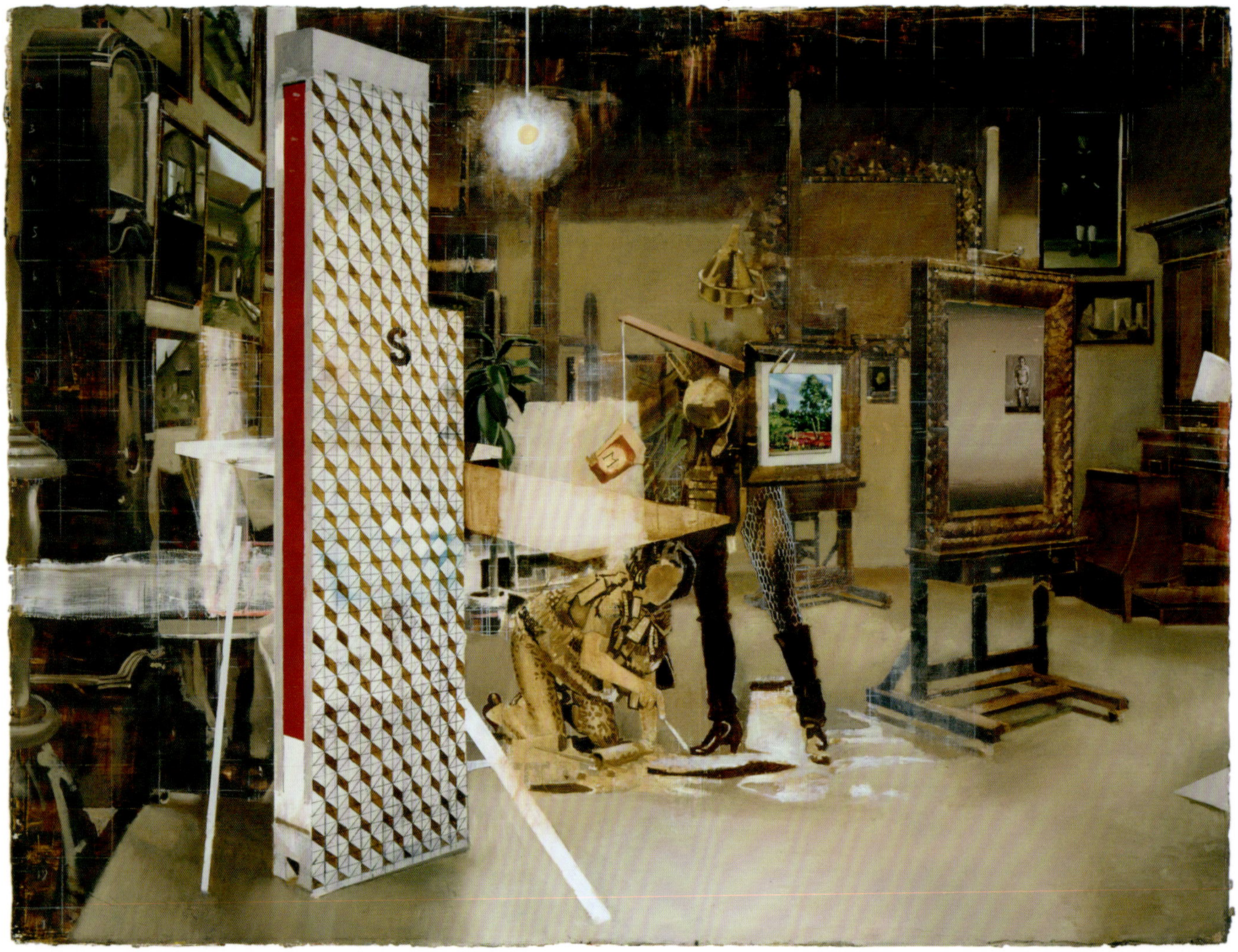

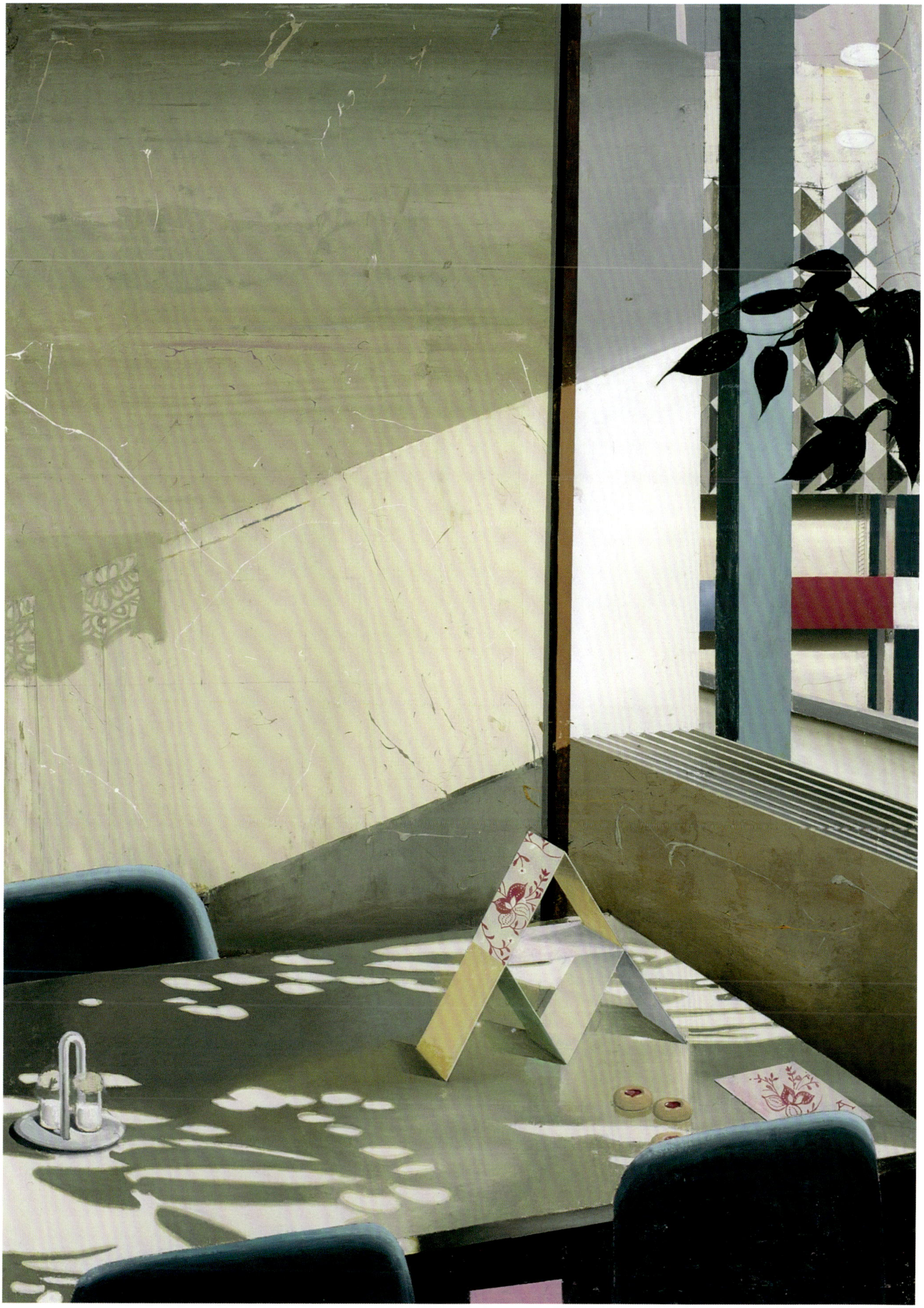

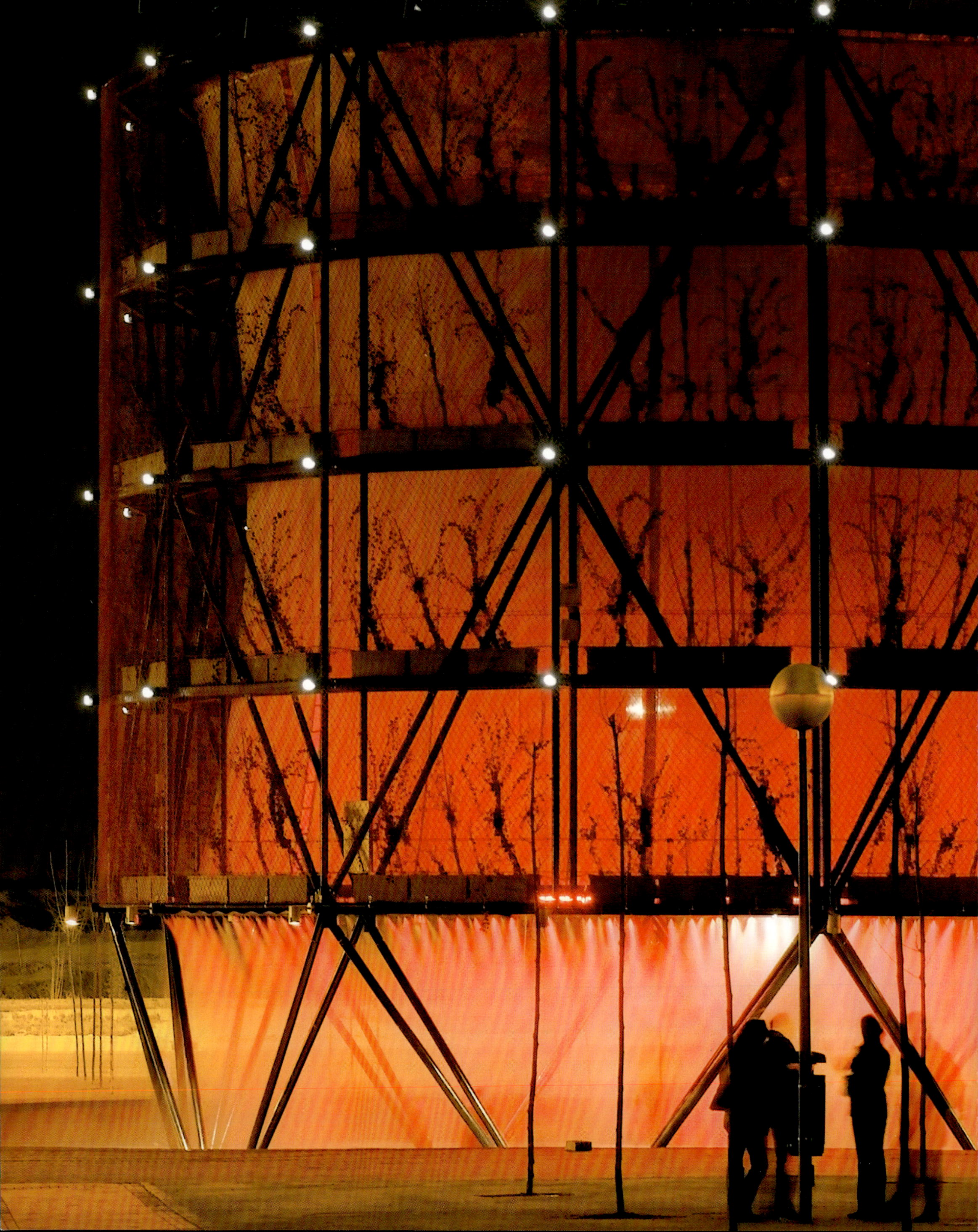

Luca Molinari

New Frontiers Between Arts and Architecture. Projects, Experiences and Research at the Start of the Millennium

Though many foresee the future of architecture as a gradual "return to order" within the mainstream of a discipline that seems impervious to crisis, I believe that nothing has highlighted the need to seek out new approaches and tools to address an ongoing metamorphosis as clearly as the complex relationship between arts[1] and architecture over the last decade.

The relationship between these two disciplines has from the very outset generated theoretical and practical reflections capable at the same time of exploring the conceptual and disciplinary boundaries and of propelling the idea of space and form toward new horizons, thus opening up unprecedented areas of investigation and experimentation.

There remains, however, to take into consideration a basic cultural scenario consolidated in the nineteenth century and much of the twentieth, which saw a sharp division between the two spheres and an idea of art as collaborating with modern architecture in an almost decorative role.

It was not until the 1960s that this crystallized dialogue underwent the first significant changes, leading architects toward a dimension that is both more individualistic and more open to a transversal and problematic relationship with the artistic aspect of their activities, seen no longer as an attack on the moral probity of the work but as a need for expression and investigation.

The relationship between arts and architecture today appears to have broken almost completely free of this burdensome modernist legacy in order to identify new conceptual and practical tools for action on the real world.

Recent years have seen an intensification of this relationship and its differentiation into approaches pursuing different objectives, from the traditional and consolidated practice of the architect who invites an artist to collaborate on a work already underway to the artist who selects the project of real space as an area of investigation and the most evolved forms of collaboration, whereby architect and artist develop a joint project on an equal footing with no restrictions as to tools and ends.

In my view, however, an attempt must be made to identify some common elements in order to develop new maps and keywords capable of putting this increasingly rich and complex situation into a systematic framework.

Despite the different paths taken and aims pursued by all of the various efforts underway, it is in fact possible to recognize some general spheres, scenarios that encapsulate the degrees of continuity with the late 1990s and are at the same time undergoing significant transformations under the pressure of new content.

The city and the metropolitan landscape unquestionably present a framework of continuity in investigations that were underway in the late twentieth century and the dawning twenty-first. This is, I believe, a condition that appears all too obvious in view not only of the centrality assumed by this subject in artistic and architectural explorations from the Modern Movement on but also and above all of the rocketing demographic growth that has led to over 60 percent of the world population being classified today as urban dwellers.

With respect to Modernism, significant shifts in sense can be noted that justify much of the collaboration now underway between art and architecture, whereby the city gradually loses its interest as an aesthetic object to become a political and social stage for action designed to restore civic substance to the disciplines themselves.

It is no coincidence that the period from 1998 to 2006 saw a number of major international exhibitions undertaking a critical appraisal of the global phenomenon of radical transformation of the metropolitan sphere and indirectly raising the question of the operative and cultural tools for the interpretation and planning of reality.

Mutations, organized by Rem Koolhaas in 1998 at Arc-en-Rêve/Bordeaux,[2] *Less Aesthetics, More Ethics*,[3] the 7th edition of the Venice Architecture Biennale, curated in 2000 by Massimiliano Fuksas, *USE. Uncertain States of Europe*, organized by the Multiplicity group at the 2002 Milan Triennial,[4] and finally the 10th Venice Architecture Biennale, *Città. Architettura e società*,[5] curated

Ecosistema Urbano
Ecoboulevard, Madrid, 2007

by Ricky Burdett in 2006: all of these can be read both as an important effort to focus attention on a global, all-encompassing phenomenon and as a critical filter required for a different view of architectural production at the international level.

At the same time, the experiences of some groups of architects and artists in Italy, the United States, the Netherlands, France, and Spain at the turn of the millennium have focused on the participatory political impetus of the project, calling for a different way of reading contemporary reality and influencing its change, and seriously raising the question of the transformation of the disciplinary tools of the architectural and urban project.

In my view, however, the real shift is taking place in more subtle terms from a traditional idea of the city to one of a metropolitan landscape whose characteristics are increasingly indistinct and elusive, and in which the concept of urban architecture is inextricably bound up with those of the community, the body, desire, and nature in a state of radical metamorphosis.

Hovering over the themes is widespread anxiety in search of a way to escape from the architectural aestheticization of a frighteningly complex reality with often dramatic social implications and develop the vision of a once again moral form of planning capable of taking a stance and offering solutions that are useful and essential to improvement. In this connection, architecture has looked to some artistic experiences for a degree of sensitivity, a different response and the capacity to provide the necessary support.

This is an interesting process because it is bound up with another highly significant cultural transition that regards the attack on the very concept of architectural form in its traditional sense of body, space, and recognizable vocabulary.

The underground vein of radical experiences of the 1960s, which aimed at the dematerialization of the modernist architectural machinery in political and linguistic terms, resurfaced in the late 1990s under the pressure of an important series of experimental actions that seemed to undermine the foundations of the tectonic idea of architecture.

The *Blur Building*[6] by Diller + Scofidio for the 2002 Swiss Expo, a powerful and extraordinary cloud/machine constructed in the middle of Lake Neuchâtel, forcefully posed the question of the loss of form of collective space and, at the same time, of the transitory, atmospheric condition of the architectural body in the contemporary world. And this came precisely when dramatic images of the destruction of the Twin Towers on September 11, 2001, and the demolition of the giant Buddha of Bamiyan in Afghanistan were arriving from the real world.

This is a process whereby arts and architecture attack the very idea of the project and physicality at the root, raising structural questions about the vision of space and architecture over the next few years.

At the same time, the tools for theoretical reflection and the dissemination of critical and visual models are undergoing con-

Diller + Scofidio
Blur Building, Swiss Expo, Neuchâtel, 2002

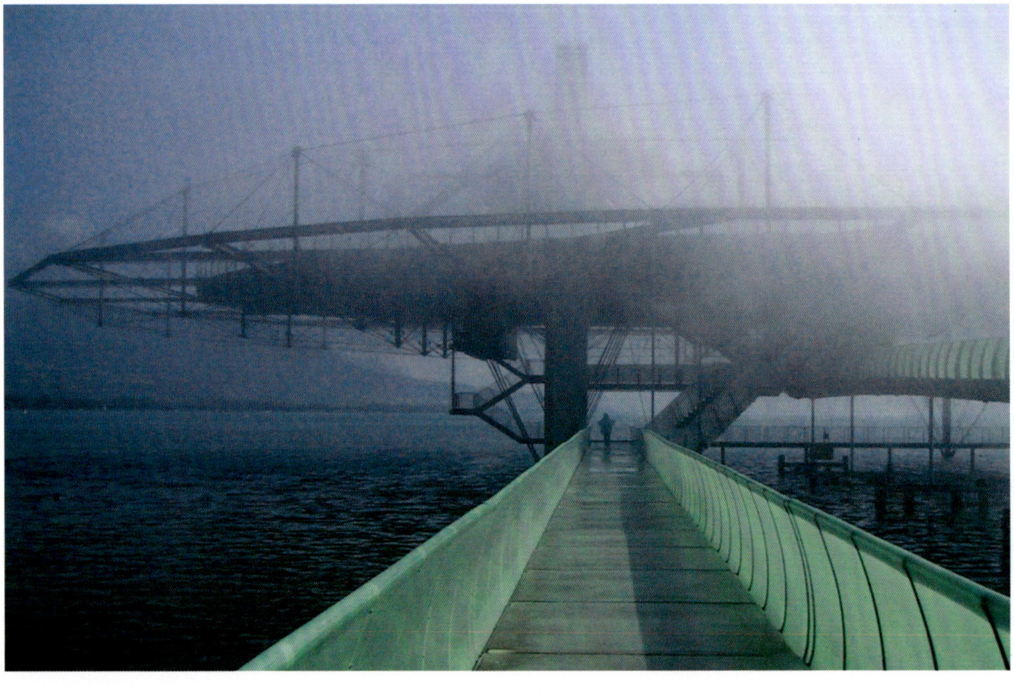

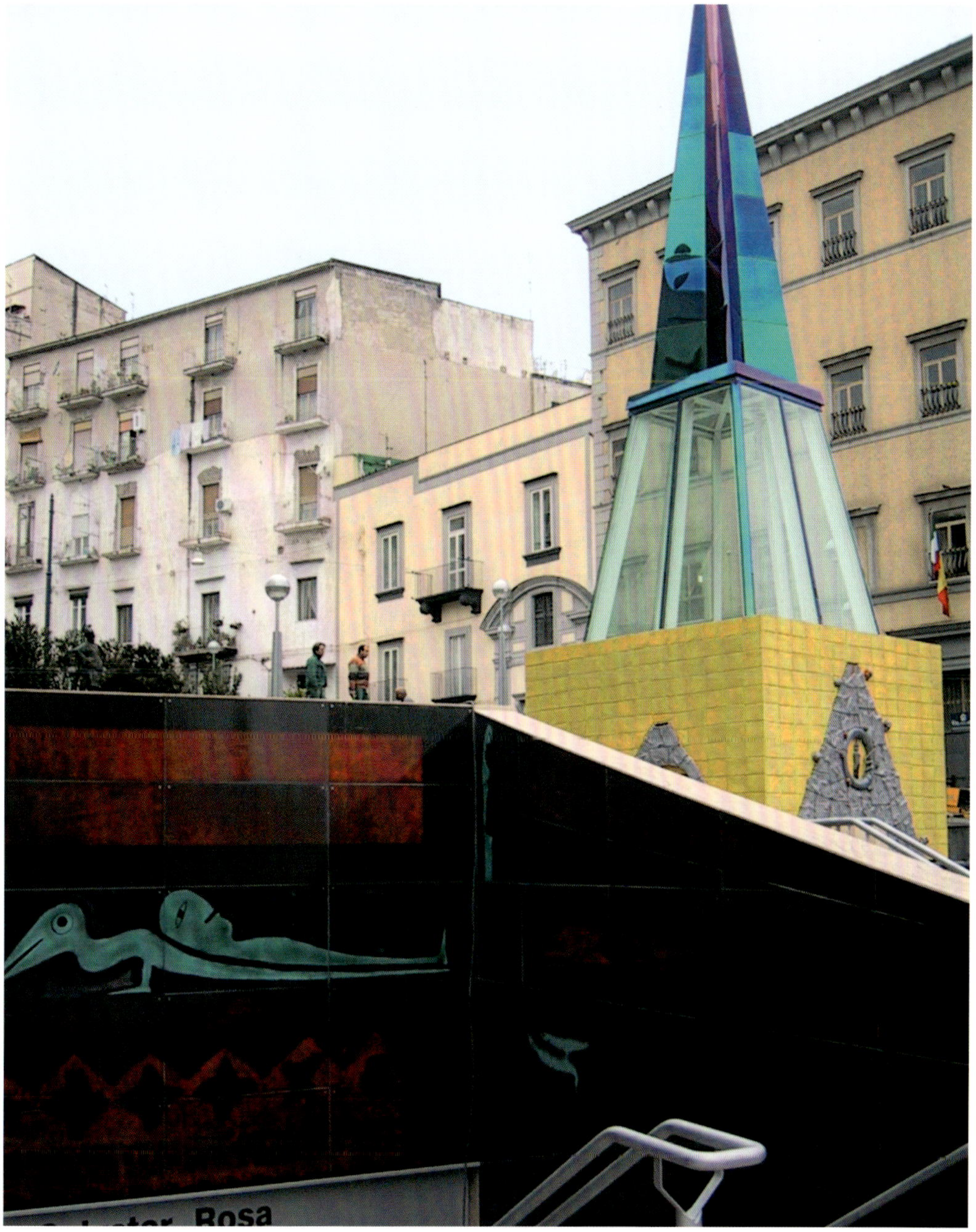

Atelier Mendini with an intervention by Enzo Cucchi
The "Asor Rosa" subway station entrance, Naples

stant, progressive acceleration and attack. The blogs in which different disciplines and new communities exchange views and intermingle, the digitization of every field of knowledge and its widespread, uncontrolled proliferation, the international biennials and countless experimental workshops scattered all over the world in public and private institutions, which stimulate the meeting and mixing of different disciplines: all of these are constructing an unprecedented common ground for the launching of forms of experimentation and investigation whose developments are as yet quite unforeseeable.

The conceptual work of dialogue that Hans Ulrich Obrist has been carrying out over the last two decades (which produced its first important fruit with the publication of his first volume of interviews[7]) has also constructed real and fundamental cultural links between arts and architecture while defining in addition a new way of building up narrative forms on art and memories as accumulated through the history of their protagonists.

It was in 2004 that Germano Celant organized a major exhibition in Genoa devoted to the relationship between art and architecture in the twentieth century,[8] making an attempt to outline this fundamental nexus for the first time and bringing to light the many different sources and drifts that have developed and molded visual thinking on modern space with experimental and visionary power.

Organized along a clear chronological line, the event seemed, however, to peter out

Massimiliano and Doriana Fuksas
Less Aesthetics, More Ethichs
Video installation, 254 x 5 m
View of the installation at the Corderie dell'Arsenale, VII Esposizione Internazionale d'Architettura, Biennale di Venezia, 2000

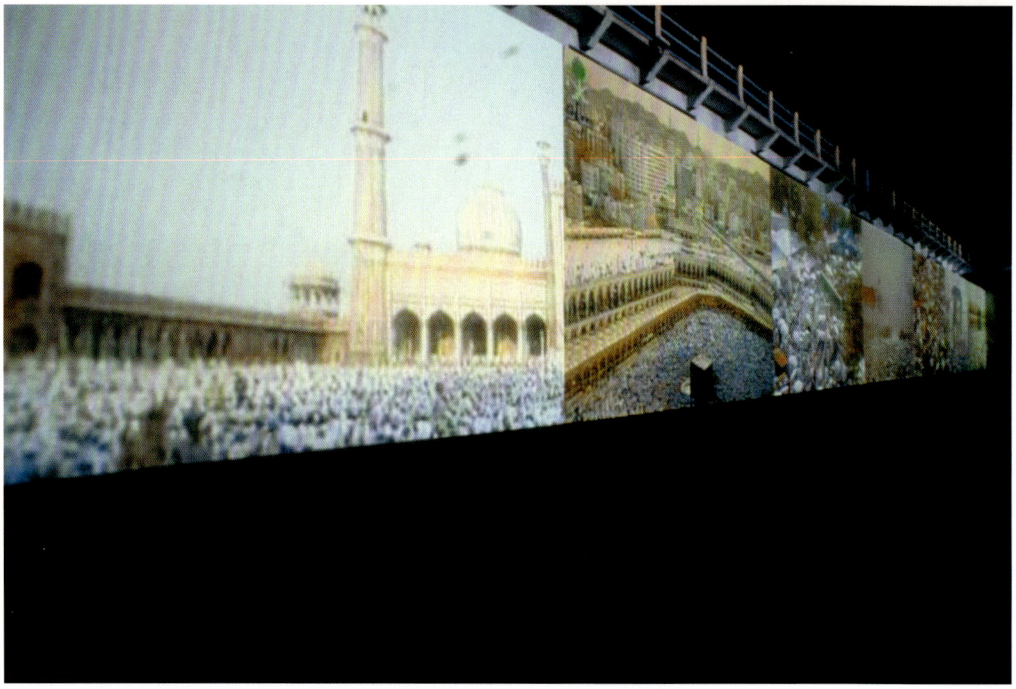

gradually as it drew closer to the present situation, as though losing its way in an unresolved labyrinth of investigations and images that saw architects and artists working in the same spheres and often with the same tools.

This is a condition born out of a contemporary world focused on marked individualism of the signature and the vocabulary used in order to make it recognizable, and one bearing witness at the same time to the increasingly radical blurring of the boundaries and areas marked out in the twentieth century.

We are now living in a consolidated, heterogeneous, and globalized condition of confusion that is perhaps necessary in order to identify paths capable of opening up commonly acceptable areas of investigation and paradigms, as demonstrated for example by the last Venice Architecture Biennale (*Out There. Architecture Beyond Building*, curated by Aaron Betsky[9]), where the impression of confusion and often wishful thinking of the work exhibited showed the limitations of a condition in search of an identity.

While the theoretical principle informing the biennial appeared interesting because of the way it forcefully raised the issue of the contemporary limits of architecture as developed over the last decade, the long series of small units and architectural devices constructed along the Corderie dell'Arsenale instead presented a sort of specious and superficial vanity fair contrasting sharply with another section of the same event housed in the Italian pavilion. Ably curated by Emiliano Gandolfi, *Experimental Architecture*[10] was devoted to emergent approaches in which the anxieties and the keywords launched by dozens of groups and individual figures all over the world posed serious and urgent questions of relationship with collective desires and realities calling for the construction of useful and necessary visions for the near future.

These two events held within a span of five years provide an ideal framework for a rereading of the various forms of relation and collaboration between contemporary architecture and the arts in the last decade along a line marked by the coexistence of very traditional forms of relationship with the development of more problematic and experimental experiences. These are areas of very indistinct character, often the result of occasions that declare no precise ideological choice on the part of the authors but plot the possible coordinates of an important framework for any understanding of the evolution in store for contemporary architecture.

As in the best Western tradition, whereby the artist's action develops within the architect's work, it is also possible to identify important cases of collaboration in recent years, especially on public works.

While the list may appear very long, there are some significant and symbolic partnerships capable of illustrating this scenario very well, starting with one of the most recent and celebrated monuments, namely the Olympic stadium in Beijing by the Basel-based architects Herzog & de Meuron with

Herzog & de Meuron
Olympic Stadium, Beijing, 2008

Junya Ishigami + Associates
Facility-Kanagawa Institute
of Technology, 2008

Ecosistema Urbano
Ecoboulevard, Madrid, 2007

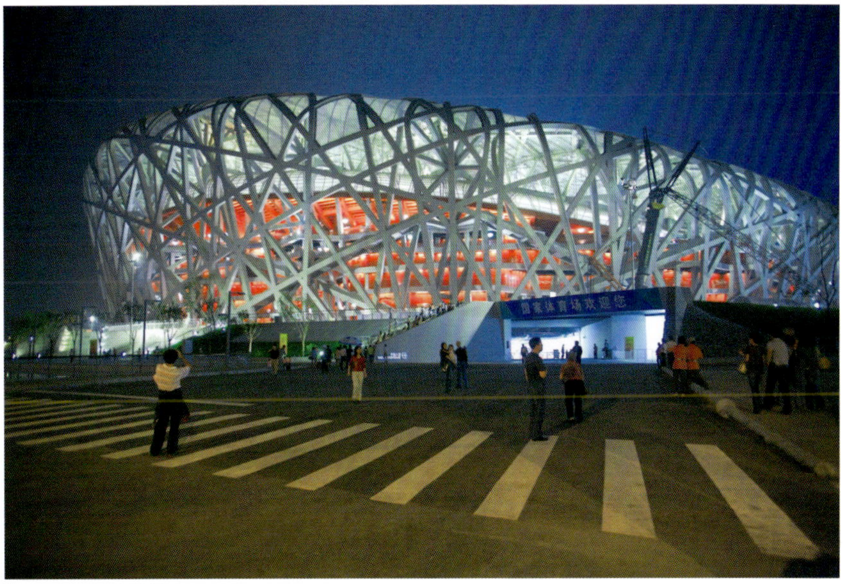

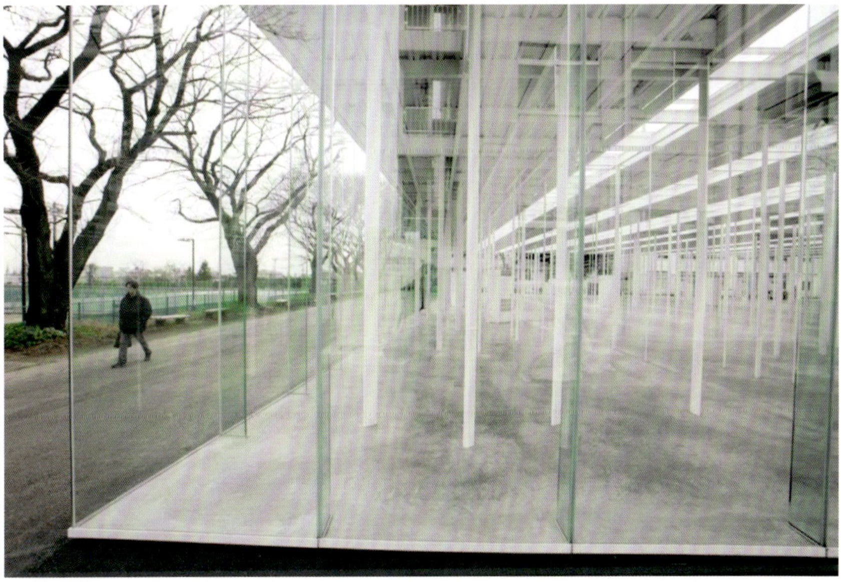

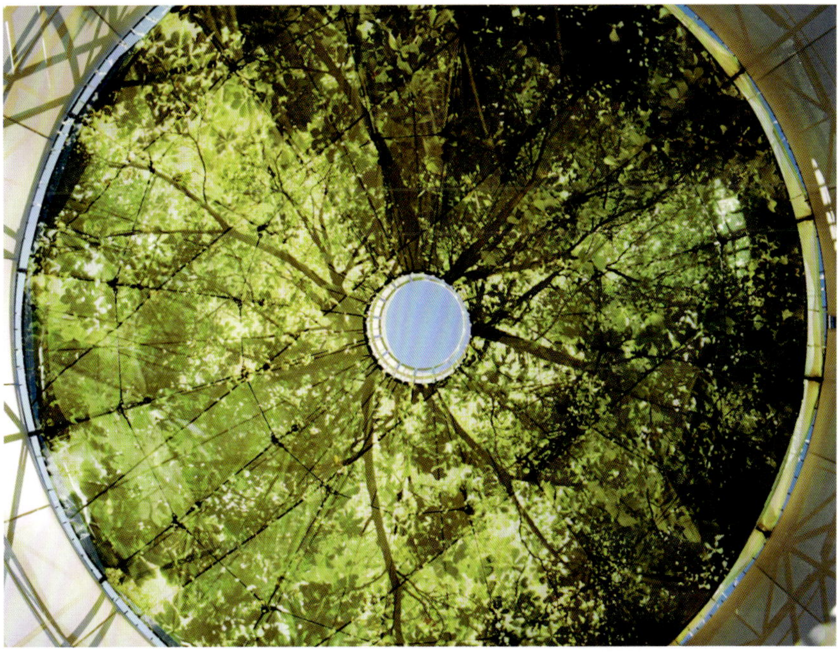

James Turrell
South-west view of Roden Crater,
Painted Desert, Arizona, 2009

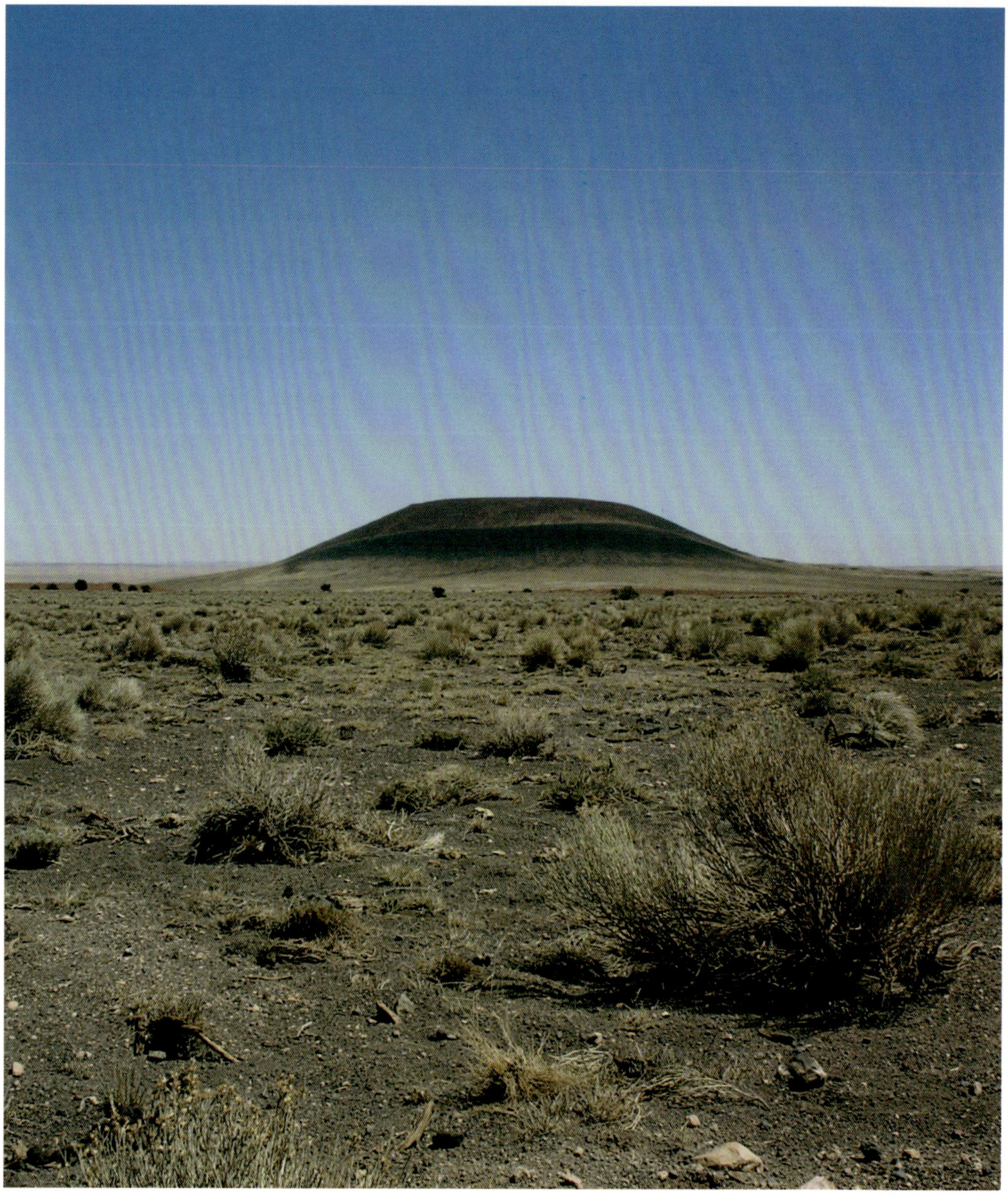

the collaboration of the Chinese artist Ai Weiwei.

Immediately dubbed the "Bird's Nest" by its designers, the work constitutes a major evolutionary step in formal and structural terms with respect to their earlier stadiums in Basel and Munich, where the outer skin covering the shell of the arena was given an all-enveloping translucent surface.[11]

In this case, the stadium's structure of reinforced concrete became a deep, thick array of pillars stretching all the way around to create a strongly defined landmark constituting the symbolic and political fulcrum of the great Chinese Olympics.[12]

The Beijing stadium is unquestionably the most imposing and problematic monument of recent years, involving a constructive relationship between architect and artist, and the role of Ai Weiwei appears more identifiable within the conceptual, ideational dimension of the project than as a site-specific operation, as was instead the case in other projects developed primarily in Europe, Japan, and North America.

One of the urban workshops putting forward a vigorous dialectic between arts and architecture is unquestionably the new subway line in Naples. In a process still underway since the late 1990s, every station is designed by different architects and involves artists in the creation of works that gradually build up a fragmented and polyphonic reading of the city and its many aspects.

The innovation of this operation guided by Achille Bonito Oliva lies in using something as traditional and typically museum-like as the room devoted to an artist in order to construct a complex and challenging urban narrative.

Dozens of works by celebrated artists like Kounellis, Chia, Cucchi, Merz, Richter,

James Turrell
Alpha Tunnel, 2009
Roden Crater, Painted Desert, Arizona

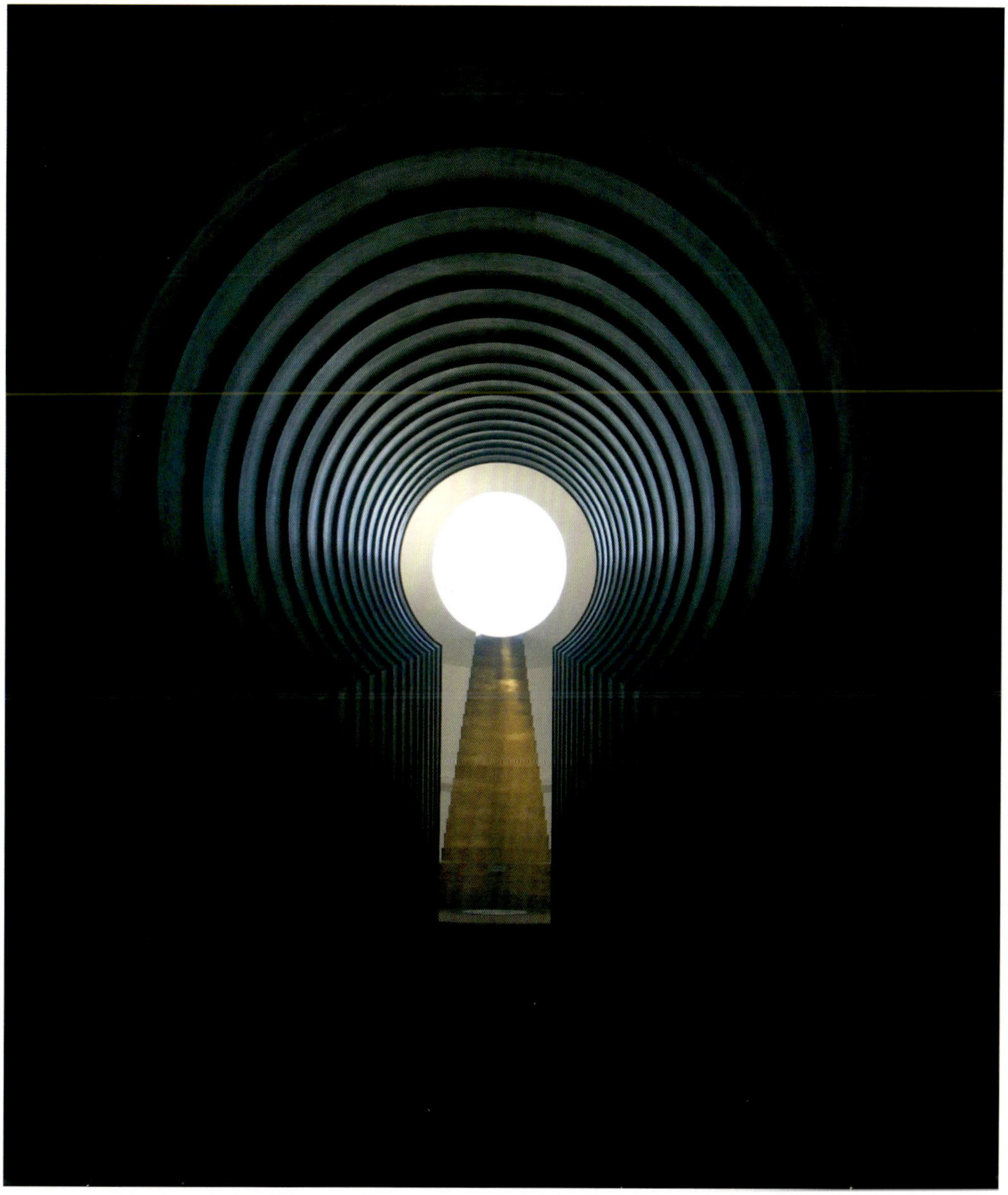

Basilico, Jodice, Paladino, and Sol LeWitt have been assembled and created in the stations designed by Gae Aulenti, Alessandro Mendini, and Alberto & Lorenzo Capobianco alongside works by emerging Neapolitan artists. These not only "decorate" the underground spaces and passageways of the subway but also and above all explode toward the urban areas around the stations so as to contaminate slices of the city in terms of meaning and identity, reconnecting them so as to form a new and unprecedented narrative.[13]

The interwoven relationship between the arts becomes direct collaboration on the actual structure in one of the new stations designed by Future System together with the Anglo-Indian artist Anish Kapoor, where architectural form and work of art combine as a powerful and radical whole.[14]

Kapoor is a key member of the group of artists who have been working for decades on architectural space as the primary area for experimentation and investigation into the absolute concept of form, space, light, and landscape.

This is a stream running parallel to "official" architecture and determining the most immediate degree of disciplinary mimesis.

The works and explorations of Anish Kapoor, Ilya Kabakov, James Turrell, Dan Graham, Vito Acconci, Ai Weiwei, Richard Long, Richard Serra, and Sami Rintala define a "zero degree" of formal but above all conceptual analysis of architectural space by focusing alternatively on the primordial, symbolic, almost natural dimension of the geometric and inhabitable form.

Space becomes an absolute dimension, often isolated in environments untouched by human presence, as though Kubrick's black monolith still possessed the magnetic capacity to take reality back to the condition of an almost mystical *tabula rasa* in which the elementary and often mono-material artifact has the power to restore order in the cosmogonic chaos.

The most extreme experience in this exciting area of investigation is unquestionably the Roden Crater Project developed by James Turrell[15] since halfway through the 1970s, whose first, radical results have, however, only become visible in recent years.

Inside the crater of an extinct volcano in the Painted Desert, Arizona, chosen for its extraordinary physical and climatic characteristics, Turrel has constructed a series of underground chambers connected by tunnels and arranged to receive the desert's light both day and night. This is presented to visitors in ways already tried and tested by the artist in his light installations.

The project that has slowly taken shape over time makes it possible, through the various installations, to observe the constellations and perceive the "sounds" of the universe. The artist's aim and indeed obsession is to induce a radical enhancement of the visitors' sensory organs so as to make them sensitive not only to light from any source – be it the sun, the moon or stars light years away – but also to every sound, both from our terrestrial surroundings and from the immense depths of sidereal space.

In addition to reawakening the ancient and powerful memory of astral machines for talking to the universe and the gods, Turrell's work brings us to another key subject of reflection and investigation that is constantly emerging from the work and collaboration of many artists and architects.

The question of the dialogue to be reestablished with nature and its forms and above all with the idea of a radical metamorphosis of its meaning in the artificial world of today is currently the driving force of many of the most recent and original experimental investigations.

This is perhaps because nature is an essential element for the zero degree that some in the artistic and architectural world are obsessively pursuing, but above all because nature is still capable of offering a way out of the death of contemporary utopia heralded by events in the closing decades of the last century.[16]

This is not a question of simply and superficially adopting the watchwords of environmental compatibility and sustainability as new cultural and linguistic practices serving to renew the array of forms available, but above all of an innovative conceptual attitude that looks to nature as an unstable, almost obscure factor capable of constructing relations with the emotional, bodily, sensory dimension of our reality, as well as generating investigations into space whose contours and results are not susceptible of crystallization.[17]

The explorations of the atmospheric dimension of collective space by Diller & Scofidio, Olafur Eliasson,[18] and Philippe Rahm[19] necessitate reflection on the concept of the body's loss of substance in favor of a different relationship between space, light, and environment.

The massive and aggressive advent of the application of digital technology to architecture and the obsession with the "skin" of the building had already led to talk of the definitive dematerialization of architecture in the late 1990s.

Now that the digital tide has ebbed and the recent works of Kazuko Sejima and Junya Ishigami have silently and radically imposed at the same time a pared-down and almost impalpable dimension of the idea of new collective space, we can see how, within its universe, architecture is constructing roads that lead to a free rereading of the lessons of the twentieth century while silently opening up to a visual and conceptual sphere of far greater density and complexity.

The artificial forest constructed with obsessive lucidity by Ishigami in his projects prompts reflection on the artificial form of nature that enters indirectly into contact with other investigations that draw sustenance from this mother to generate conceptual enzymes and challenging linguistic productions of strong political content with respect to reality. The works of R&SIE(n) & DS,[20] Ecologic Studio,[21] Jakob & MacFarlane,[22] Husos,[23] 2012 Architekten,[24] Coloco,[25] Cloud9[26] and others relate to a widespread and heterogeneous idea of green utopia that goes beyond "green" architecture and instead refers to a superseding of the traditional Western concept of nature.

In these experimental forms, which always and necessarily seek dialogue with other disciplines and arts, we find again the need to develop a new political and social agenda with respect to reality, moving beyond the obsession with language and form as self-representation.

These are experiences that start from open and problematic reflection on the contemporary metropolis and deliberately seek to call into question the tools for monitoring and interpreting the contemporary territory.

Increasingly focused since the second half of the 1990s, the reiterated actions of groups like Stalker,[27] Cliostraat,[28] and Multiplicity[29] have opened up a highly significant viral path for the international architectural culture of the last decade. On the one hand, it is above all the experience of the Milanese group Multiplicity that has enjoyed meaningful cultural and programmatic development with the appointment of Stefano Boeri as editor-in-chief first of *Domus* and then of *Abitare*.

On the other, the collective, communitarian practice of viral action of a political and architectural character in the new metropolitan landscapes is undergoing major growth today because it is leading to important formal and architectural results serving also as a foundation for hypotheses of critical interpretation. The recent works of Ma0,[30] feld72,[31] Didier Fiúza Faustino, Recetas Urbanas,[32] Raumlabor,[33] Map Office,[34] Id-Lab,[35] Eyal Weizman,[36] Estudio Teddy Cruz,[37] Torolab,[38] Elemental, and Ecosistema Urbano[39] – with projects for collective spaces in urban environments and unprecedented forms of collective participation in which social disciplines, architects, and artists shape projects together – open up an interesting path for the construction of the public space of the new generation.

In my view, this is both an important direction for the future of contemporary architecture and an opportunity to declare the end of the disciplinary barricades that led over time to a condition of indefensible cultural asphyxia preventing the development of useful and necessary visions for the near future.

[1] The plural declination of "art" will be used in this essay to assert the degree of richness and complexity of the possible relationships that architecture has built up in recent years with artists now moving uninhibitedly between the most traditional media and photography, video, digital technology, Body Art, and the investigation of sound and the senses.

[2] R. Koolhaas, S. Boeri/Multiplicity, S. Kwinter, N. Tazi, H.U. Obrist (eds.), *Mutations* (Barcelona: Actar, 2000).

[3] M. Fuksas, D. Mandrelli (eds.), *Less Aesthetics, More Ethics* (Venice: Marsilio, 2000).

[4] Multiplicity, *USE. Uncertain States of Europe. A trip through a changing Europe* (Milan: Skira, 2003).

[5] R. Burdett (ed.), *Città, architettura e società* (Venice: Marsilio, 2006).

[6] E. Diller, R. Scofidio, *Blur. The Making of Nothing* (New York: Abrams, 2002). G. Incerti, D. Ricchi, D. Simpson, *Diller + Scofidio (+ Renfro). Architetture in dissolvenza. Opere e progetti 1979-2007* (Milan: Skira, 2007).

[7] H.U. Obrist, *Interviste. Volume 1* (Milan: Charta, 2003).

[8] G. Celant (ed.), *Arti e architettura 1900/1968: scultura, pittura, fotografia, design, cinema e architettura: un secolo di progetti creativi*, exh. cat. (Genoa, Palazzo Ducale, 2004–2005) (Milan: Skira, 2004).

[9] A. Betsky (ed.), *Out There. Architecture Beyond Building* (Venice: Marsilio, 2008), 5 vols.

[10] E. Gandolfi, 'Think Different, Act Different – Architecture Beyond Building,' in A. Betsky, *op. cit.*, III, pp. 18–28.

[11] 'Herzog & de Meuron,' in *El Croquis*, Madrid, nos. 129–130, 2006, pp. 272–299, 348–365.

[12] On the landscape dimension of the Beijing Olympic stadium and the role of Ai Weiwei, also in polemical terms, see L. Poncellini, *Ai Weiwei's Controversy*, in *Yearbook of World Architecture 2008* (Milan: Skira, 2008), pp. 142–143.

[13] For an up-to-date list of stations and involved artists: www. metro.na.it.

[14] E. Cycelin, M. Codognato (eds.), *Anish Kapoor & Future System. Dall'arte all'architettura* (Milan: Electa, 2005).

[15] A. De Rosa (ed.), *James Turrell. Geometrie di Luce. Roden Crater Project* (Milan: Electa, 2006).

[16] G. Clement, *Manifesto del Terzo Paesaggio* (Macerata: Quodlibet, 2005).

[17] See: G. Bruno, *Atlas of Emotions. Journeys in Art Architecture and Film* (London-New York: Verso Book, 2002); G. Bruno, *Public Intimacy. Architecture and Visual Arts* (Cambridge [Mass]: MIT Press, 2007); A. Barbera, A. Perliss, *Architetture invisibili. L'esperienza dei luoghi attraverso gli odori* (Milan: Skira, 2006).

[18] H.U. Obrist, O. Eliasson, *Experiment Marathon* (Cologne: Walter König, 2009); Ph. Ursprung, O. Eliasson, *Studio Olafur Eliasson: an Encyclopedia* (Cologne: Taschen, 2008); O. Eliasson, D. Adjaye, *Your Black Horizon* (Cologne: Walter König, 2008).

[19] Ph. Rahm, *Architecture météorologique* (Paris: Archibooks, 2009). *Gilles Clement, Philippe Rahm: Environ(ne)ment. Approaches for Tomorrow* (Milan: Skira, 2006).

[20] www.new-territories.com.

[21] www.ecologicstudio.com.

[22] www.jakobmacfarlane.com.

[23] www.husos.info.

[24] www.superuse.org.

[25] www.coloco.org.

[26] www.e-cloud9.com.

[27] www.stalkerlab.it.

[28] www.cliostraat.com.

[29] www.multiplicity.it.

[30] www.ma0.it; *Borderlines Ma0* (DD, n. 28) (Seul: DAMDI, 2008).

[31] www.feld72.at.

[32] www.recetasurbanas.net.

[33] www.raumlabor-berlin.de.

[34] www.map-office.com.

[35] www.interactiondesign-lab.com.

[36] http://roundtable.kein.org; E. Weizman, *Hollow Land. Israels Architecture of Occupation* (London: Verso Books, 2007).

[37] www.politicalequator.org.

[38] www.torolab.org.

[39] www.ecosistemaurbano.com.

Banksy

Born in Yate, South Gloucestershire, UK, in 1973. "The thing I hate the most about advertising is that it attracts all the bright, creative and ambitious young people, leaving us mainly with the slow and self-obsessed to become our artists." This remark by Banksy offers an interesting clue for any understanding of his work, which has all the communicative immediacy and capacity for instantaneous imprinting on the observer's memory for advertising. Banksy, whose real identity still remains unknown despite the efforts of the mass media, emerged through Bristol's underground scene of the 1980s with its marked element of punk-anarchist culture. While his graffiti of the 1990s were drawn by hand, the year 2000 saw a switch to stencil, a technique offering greater rapidity of execution and fidelity to the "photocopy aesthetic" that has come to characterize his style. Banksy has been an undisputed legend on the international scene of Street Art ever since. His stencils are to be found on the walls of British cities like Bristol and London but also in Melbourne, New York, Los Angeles, and New Orleans. Situationism, underground culture, appropriationism, and subvertising (the critical subversion of advertising techniques) combine to create images that seldom miss their target. The starting point is often a sign already present on the city walls. An anarchist "A" appears in a banner held by a demonstrating rat. A peace symbol is flanked by the figures of two armed soldiers, one of which is completing it. A stain becomes the urine of one of the Queen's guards and a hole in the wall the place where a maid hides the dirt produced by our society. Banksy's work is not, however, confined to street graffiti. For years now, the artist has been entering celebrated museums like the Louvre, the MoMA, and Tate Britain and illicitly hanging small paintings (often subverted classical images complete with old-style frames and captions), which sometimes remain on view for days before being discovered. While these unauthorized additions are then usually removed, at least one has become part of the permanent collection of the institution in question (the British Museum in London).
Held in Los Angeles in 2002, Banksy's first solo show brought him to the attention of the art market. The auction houses soon followed suit and one of his works fetched £ 102,000 at Sotheby's in 2007. The artist maintains his anonymity, however, handling relations with the market through an agent and above all continuing to create Street Art.
The contradictions of his legend as an outlaw adored by showbiz stars and millionaires as well as kids with spray cans are addressed with postmodern cynicism and shrewdness.
(*D.Q.*)

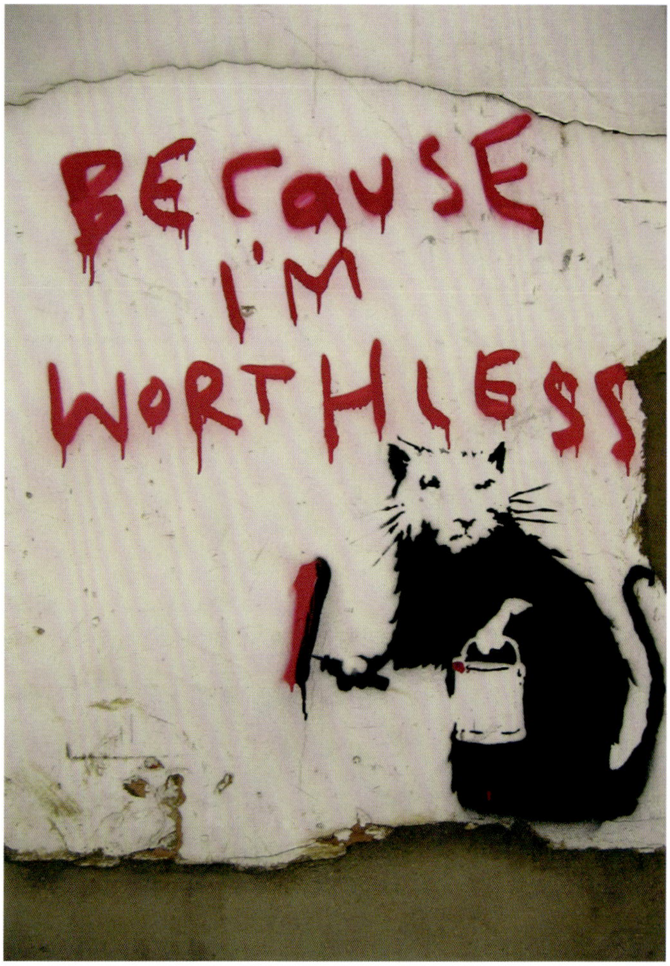

Banksy Rat: Because I'm Worthless, 2004
Wall painting, 210 x 180 cm
London, Farringdon parking lot
(destroyed work)

Window Lovers, 2007–2008
Wall painting, 250 x 115 cm
Bristol, Park Street

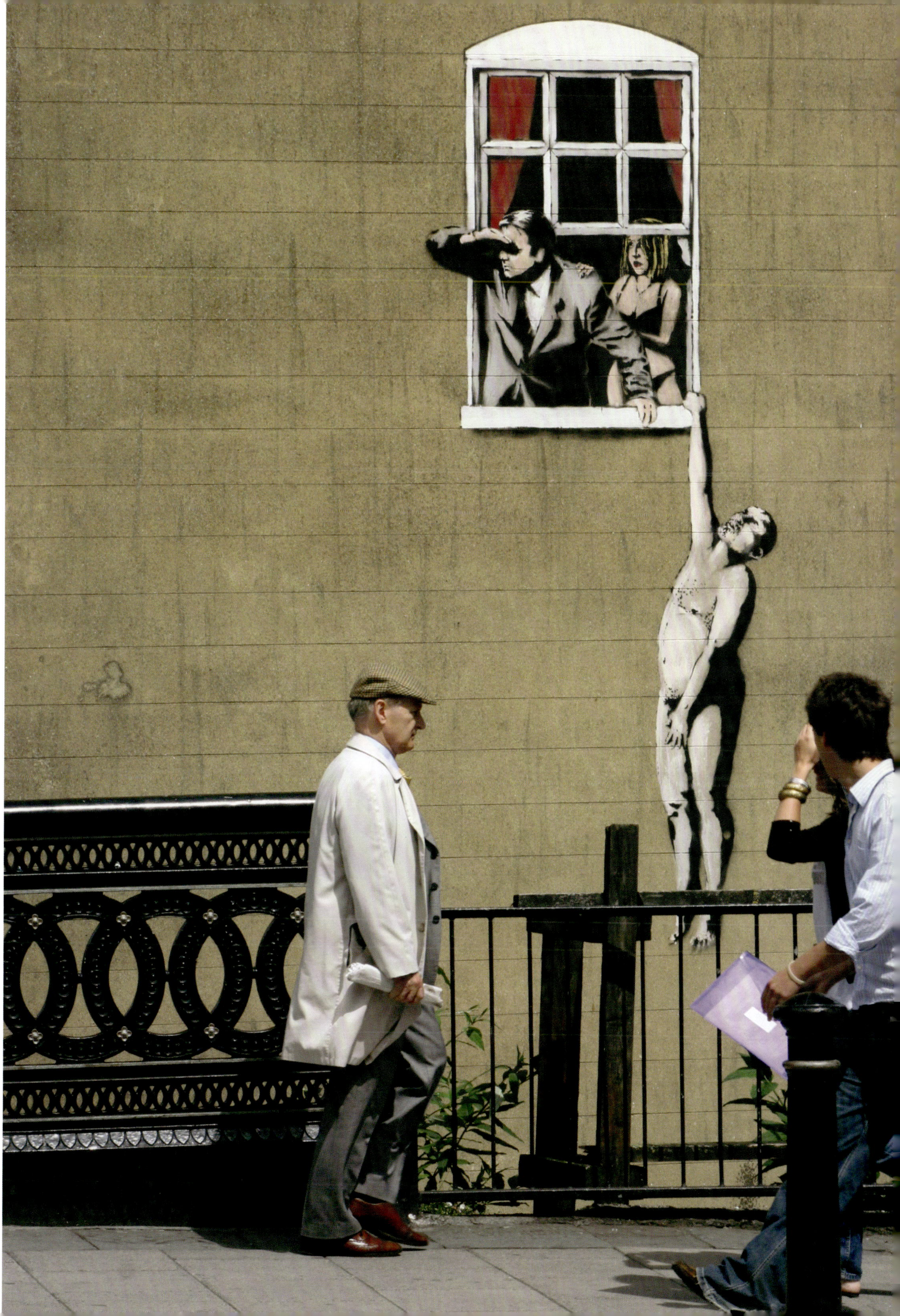

O som Tambem…, 2004
Laser-cut Plexiglas, 4.5 x 9 m
Courtesy Galleria Massimo De Carlo, Milan

25 aprile 1936 (Anche oggi niente), 2008
250 neon lamps, 12 x 22 x 1 m
Courtesy MAXXI_Museo nazionale delle arti del XXI secolo, Rome

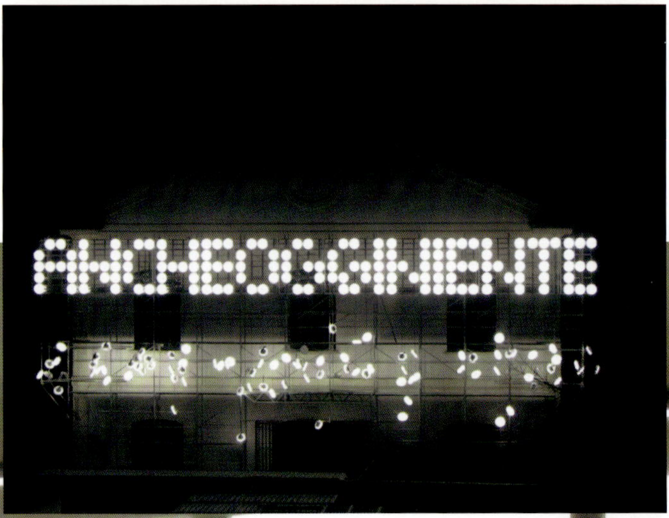

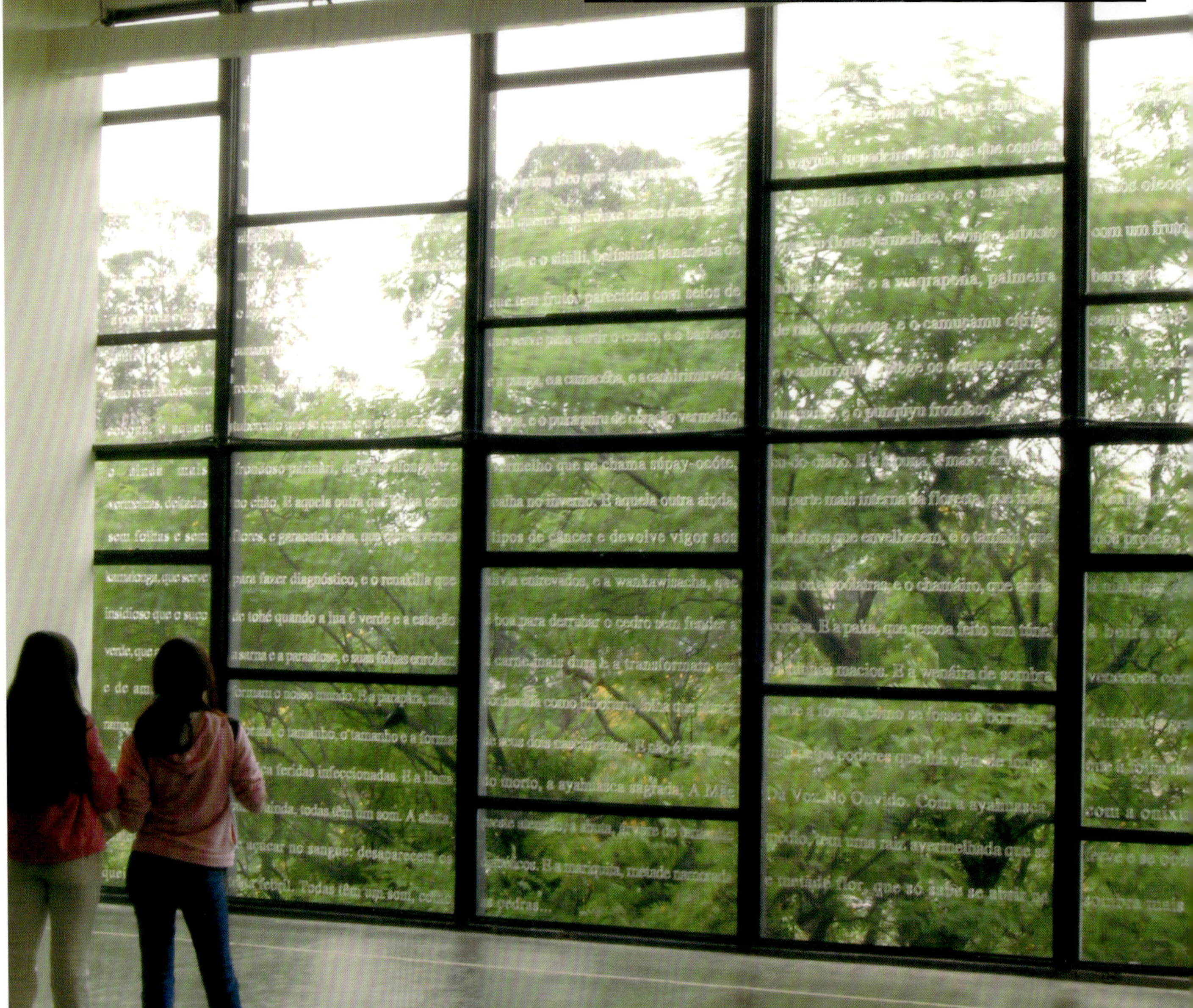

Massimo Bartolini

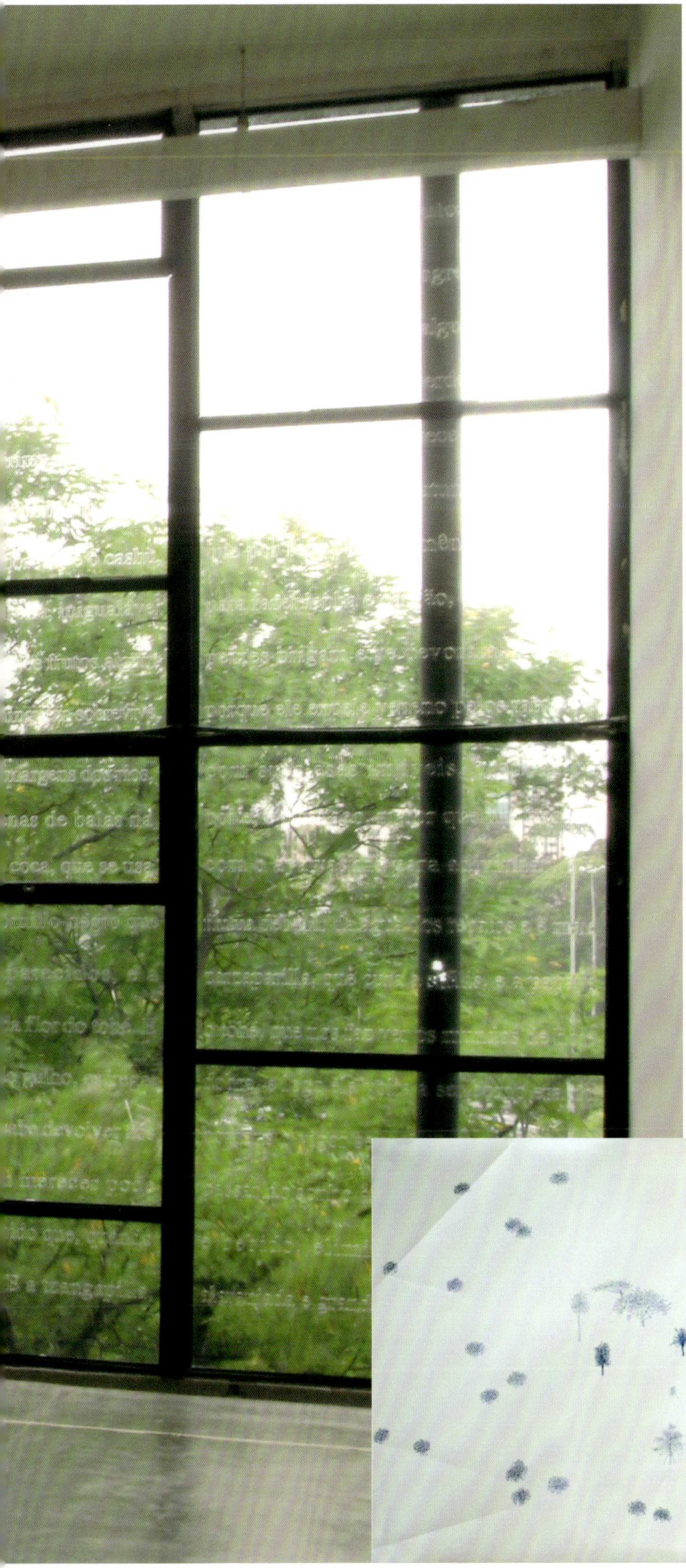

Born in Cecina, Italy, in 1962.
Lives and works in Cecina.
The ultimate goal of Massimo Bartolini is to lead the viewer toward the universe of imagination. All his work strives for the creation of a rarefied, extremely lyrical, and evanescent reality made up of feelings and references to the world of nature and primitive cultures.
The artist's creative process develops through all-enveloping environments and situations so that experience of the artwork is triggered by the multisensory dimension that is a constant point of reference in his installations. The Tuscan artist constructs a cosmos made up of legends and primal memories out of music, light, the natural sounds of atmospheric phenomena, and the ancestral links between the celestial universe and terrestrial world. The work presented by invitation at the 26th Bienal de São Paulo in 2004 was an environmental installation entitled *O som Tambem...*, a citation of the work *Las tres mitades de Ino Moxo* by the Peruvian poet César Calvo, which describes the sounds and properties of the Amazonian flora. Transposed into the Brazilian metropolis, the work produced a semantic shortcircuit between the allusion to the unspoiled environment of the rainforest and the noises of the city, which make their way into the work through letters cut into the Plexiglas of the building designed by Niemeyer. The green of the trees contrasts with the words written on glass, which remain invisible to the viewer until these two elements come into a position of parallel correspondence.
On being invited to take part in a public art project entitled *Dialogues with the City* at the MAXXI, Rome, in 2008, Bartolini presented *25 aprile 1936 (Anche oggi niente)*, an installation of 250 neon lamps on the outer wall of the museum. The phrase written in neon – *Anche oggi niente*: Nothing again today – is based on an entry in Cesare Pavese's diary (originally "*quest'oggi, niente*") referring to the immobility of time and the unchanging present.
(*F.T.*)

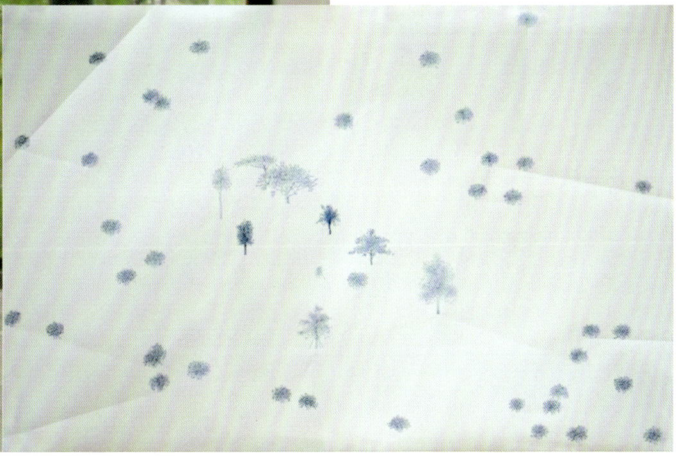

Senza titolo, 2005
Blue ink on paper, 102 x 150 cm
UniCredit Group Collection

Monica Bonvicini

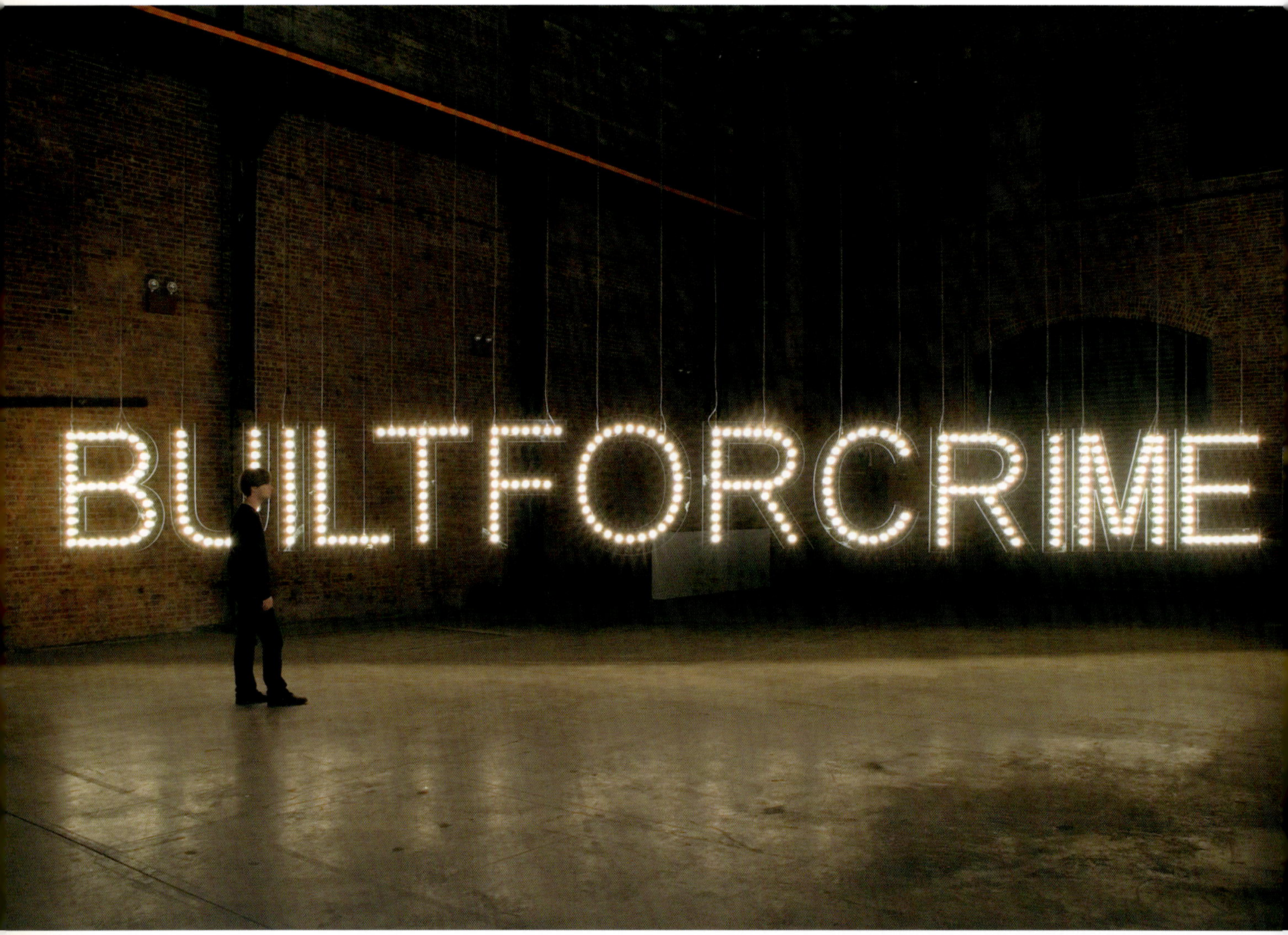

Born in Venice, Italy, in 1965. Lives and works in Berlin.
The relationship between architectural construction and eroticism is the thread running through the works of Monica Bonvicini. The artist has won international recognition over the last decade after embarking in the late 1990s on multidisciplinary work using photography, video, drawing and installations to examine the relations between the structural element and the sphere of intimate life, as in *Don't Miss a Sec*, one of her best-known works. Exhibited in London in 2004, it consists of a steel lavatory encased in two-way mirrored glass placed outside the exhibition venue so that the user can see outside without being seen. An allusion to the voracious appetite of the contemporary world for images and the blurring of the boundary between public and private, the work ironically invites us not to waste time and combine bodily functions with everyday action.
Architectural abstraction and the intimate sphere, especially sexuality, are the primary focus of the work of this Venetian artist, who combines the two elements in a metaphorical identification of eroticism and architectural form. Great importance therefore attaches to the structures and materials used, as they allude to the universe of erotic perversions and fantasies. The chains of *Never Again* thus becomes a metaphor of the affective bond and slavery as well as sexual deviance and constraint at the same time.
This installation of 2005 is a playground for adults based on the sadomasochistic iconography, consisting of a small space crowded with black leather swings on steel chains.
Monica Bonvicini's choice of materials for use in constructing her architectural anomalies also makes constant reference to the modernism of the early twentieth century, as exemplified by her adoption of glass and steel, key materials in the works of Mies van der Rohe and Le Corbusier, for *Built for Crime*.
In this case, the artist uses light and glass to create a large-sized text that presents the two opposite concepts of construction and destruction while applying the same linguistic paradox also in the physical sphere, the supports of the lights and the letters making up the words *Built for Crime* are in fact made of broken safety glass.
(*F.T.*)

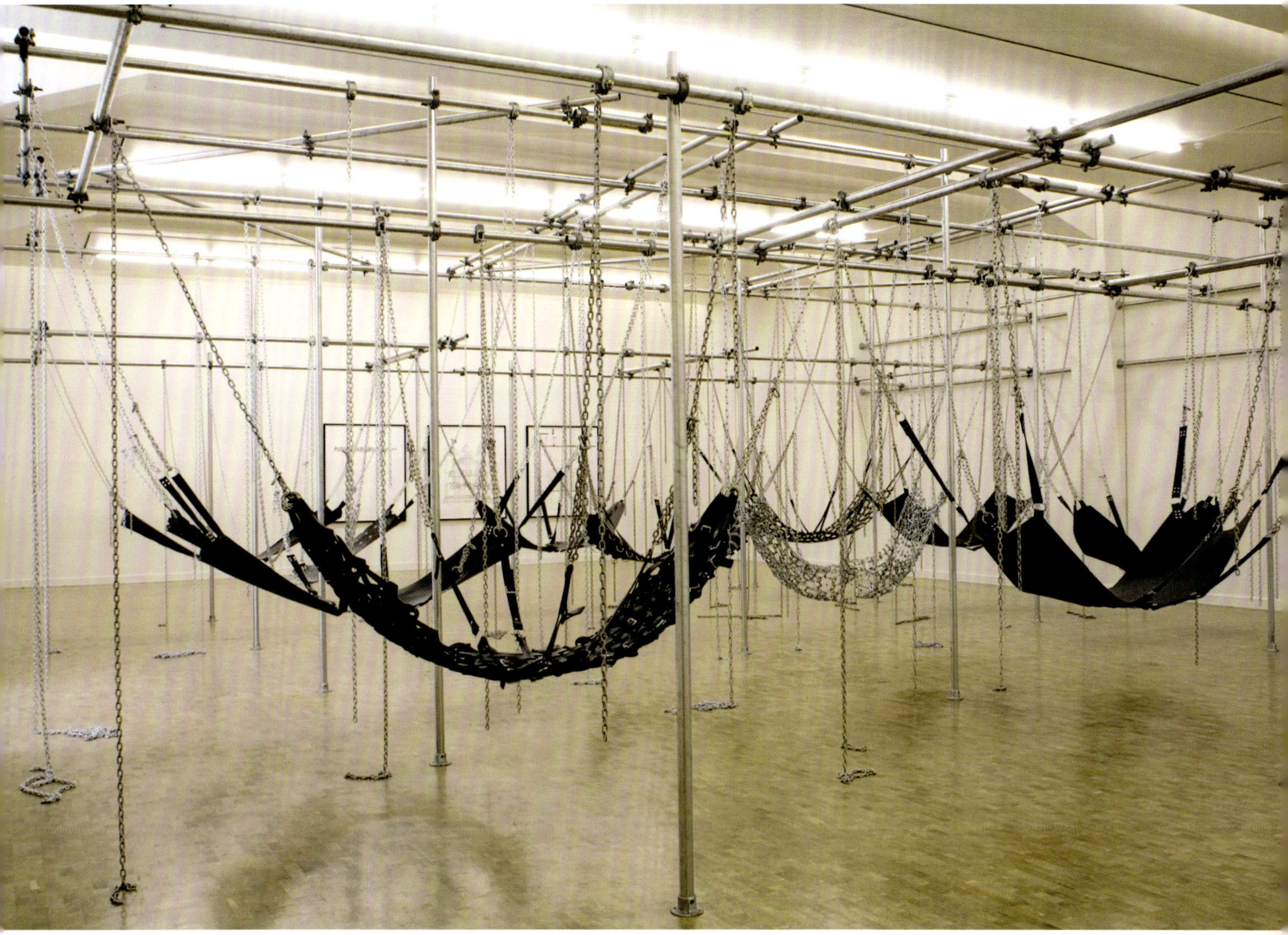

Built for Crime, 2006
Safety glass, light bulbs, 5 dimmers
12.4 x 1.2 m
View of the installation realized
in 2006 at the Sculpture Center,
New York
Courtesy Galleria Emi Fontana,
Milan and West of Rome, Pasadena

Never Again, 2005
Leather, chains, metal rack,
dimensions variable
View of the installation realized
in 2008 at the National Gallery
of Iceland, Reykjavik
Courtesy Galleria Emi Fontana,
Milan and West of Rome, Pasadena

Pedro Cabrita Reis

Born in Lisbon in 1956. Lives and works in Lisbon.
The work of Pedro Cabrita Reis is located in an area where sculpture and architecture intersect. Nearly always conceived as installations, his structures of concrete, brick, steel, aluminum, glass, and neon establish a relationship with the space in which they are set for the purpose of exploring it, transforming it, opening it up to possible new interpretations, and turning it into a territory of thought. While the artist's projects are related to the work of Gordon Matta-Clark, their roots are actually embedded in the Constructivist avant-garde, to which he has devoted in-depth studies. At the same time, they pursue reflection of a more philosophical character aimed at investigating the very concept of space. Cabrita Reis sees this above all as a "territory of perception" in which all subjects enter into relations with elements that are other than themselves and therefore have to develop a "cognitive" strategy in order to address them. The artist is in fact not interested so much in "what" we see on entering an environment inhabited by his works as in "how" we see it, which perceptual mechanisms are triggered and how the materials chosen, the colors, the arrangement of the objects, and their size act upon us. In this sense, his art brings an introspective component into play and establishes coexistence between the more rigorously rational dimension guiding the creation of the work (the measuring of space, building of structures, preference for geometric forms, and choice of materials) and the strictly subjective sphere connected with the feelings, knowledge, recollections and memory of the artist and each viewer.
Philosophical implications are also to be found in the artist's relationship with architecture. Cabrita Reis has often pointed out in interviews and in his writings that he sees architecture not as a source of inspiration but rather as an opportunity to consider the endless complexity of the very act of constructing, an activity that human beings have undertaken since the dawn of history and will continue forever. What fascinates him is the possibility of building and therefore not architecture, which is only one of the many possible manifestations of this action.
This accounts for the apparently unfinished character of many of the artist's works. The columns of bricks held together with cement mortar in *21 Brick Columns* – an installation created in 2005 on the hill beside the Ostia synagogue within the framework of the biennial event *Arte in memoria* – confront visitors with the fact that they exist as such, simply because they have been built, with no need to perform a specific function or take on given form. It is the task of each individual to discern the variety of elements converging in them by means of what the artist describes as "modified" vision, transformed by thought. It is in any case Cabrita Reis himself that leaves the field of exegesis wide open by stating that the structures "may or may not have been part of a building and it is not clear on seeing them whether they were made by a skilled mason and then subjected to some brutal event or simply the wear and tear of time. Fragile in their roughness, these 21 columns may again always have been relics, leaving the hands of their builders on the threshold of life to experience the agony of violence and hope in an attempt to reconstruct a place and reinvent their own memory (the opposite of history)." Like many other works by Cabrita Reis, *21 Brick Columns* is steeped in mystery, silence, fascination, and doubt. Born out of the artist's subjective mental states, it presents itself to the visitors as a mirror in which they can all recognize their own anxieties and expectations.
Describing himself as a "gatherer of memories, mysteries and signs", Cabrita Reis offered an extraordinary effective interpretation of his work in an interview published in the catalogue of the solo show held in 2007 at the MACRO in Rome: "My work is referred to things I've already forgotten and certainly even more to others I haven't found yet. My work is about absence and oblivion but also about a possible humanity. It's about having learnt how to dry mud, to make a brick, and knowing that infinity is the inability to reach the horizon."
(*L.L.*)

Des Dimanches Tristes, 2000
Wood, plastic panels and bottles, two elements, 150 x 180 x 120 cm (lower part); 150 x 130 x 100 cm (upper part)
Collection of the artist

Palais, 1999
Wood, rolled section, plasterboard, enamel on glass, 122 x 120 x 40 cm
Turin, private collection

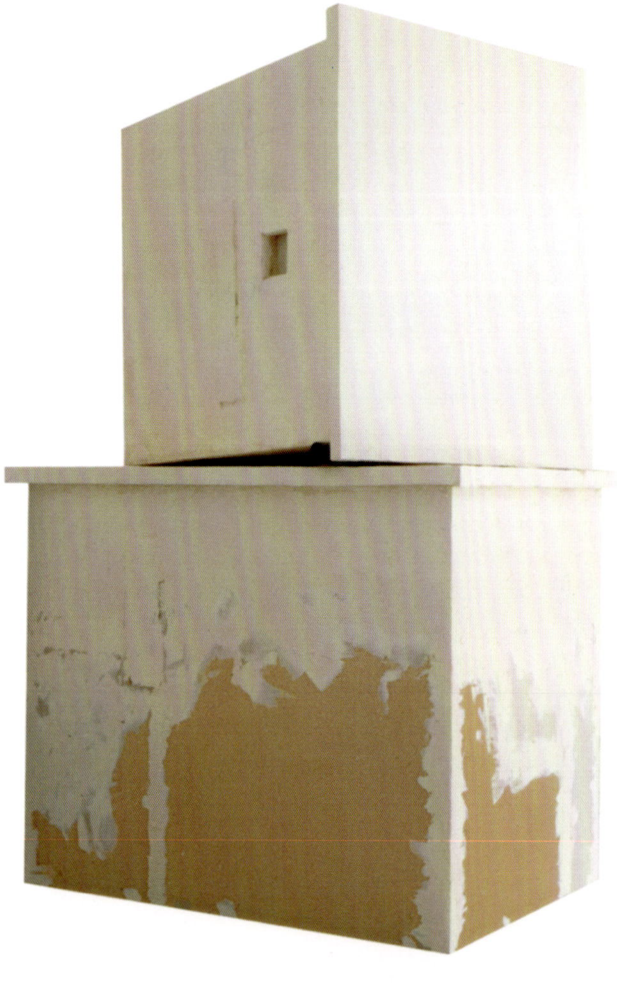

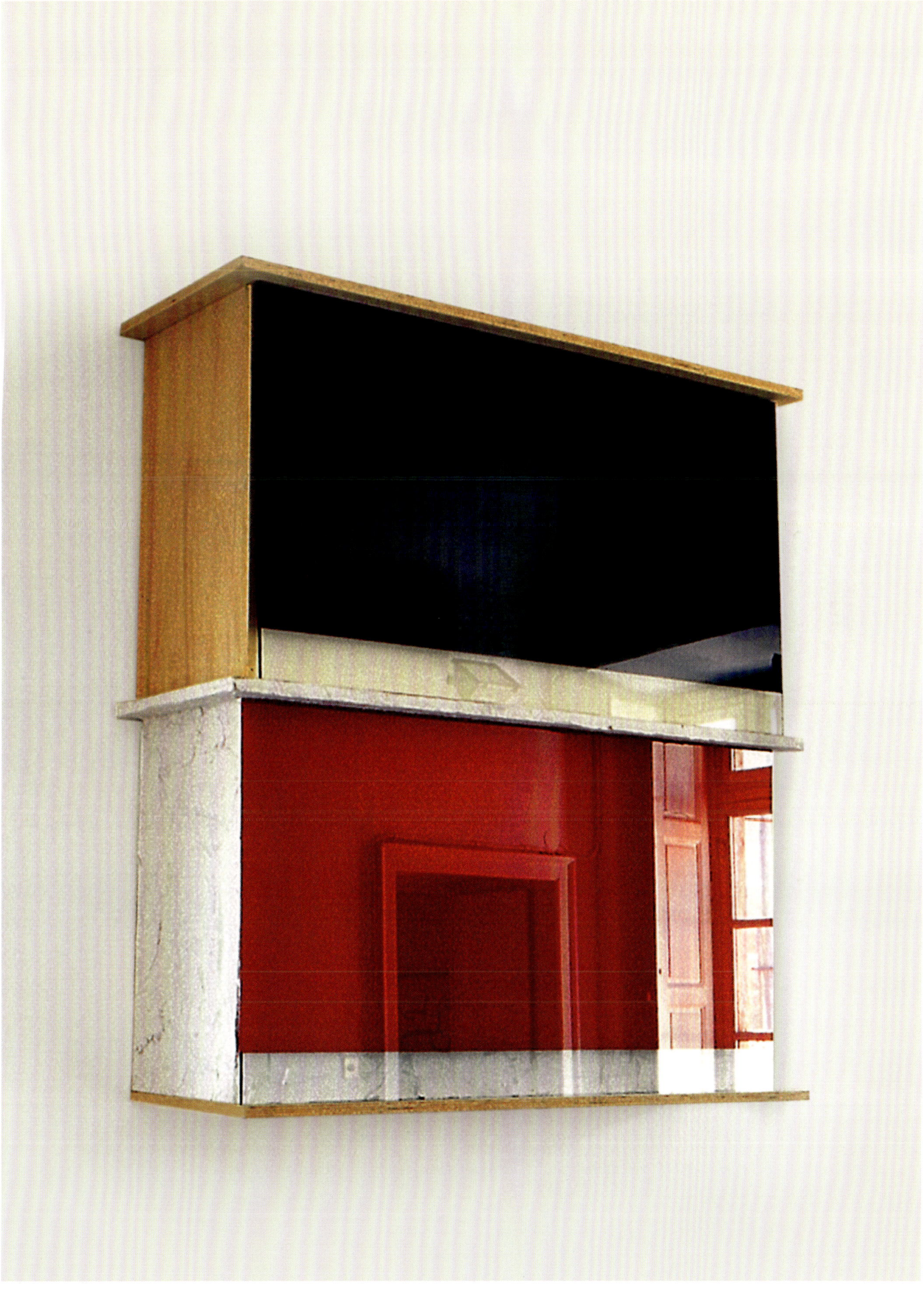

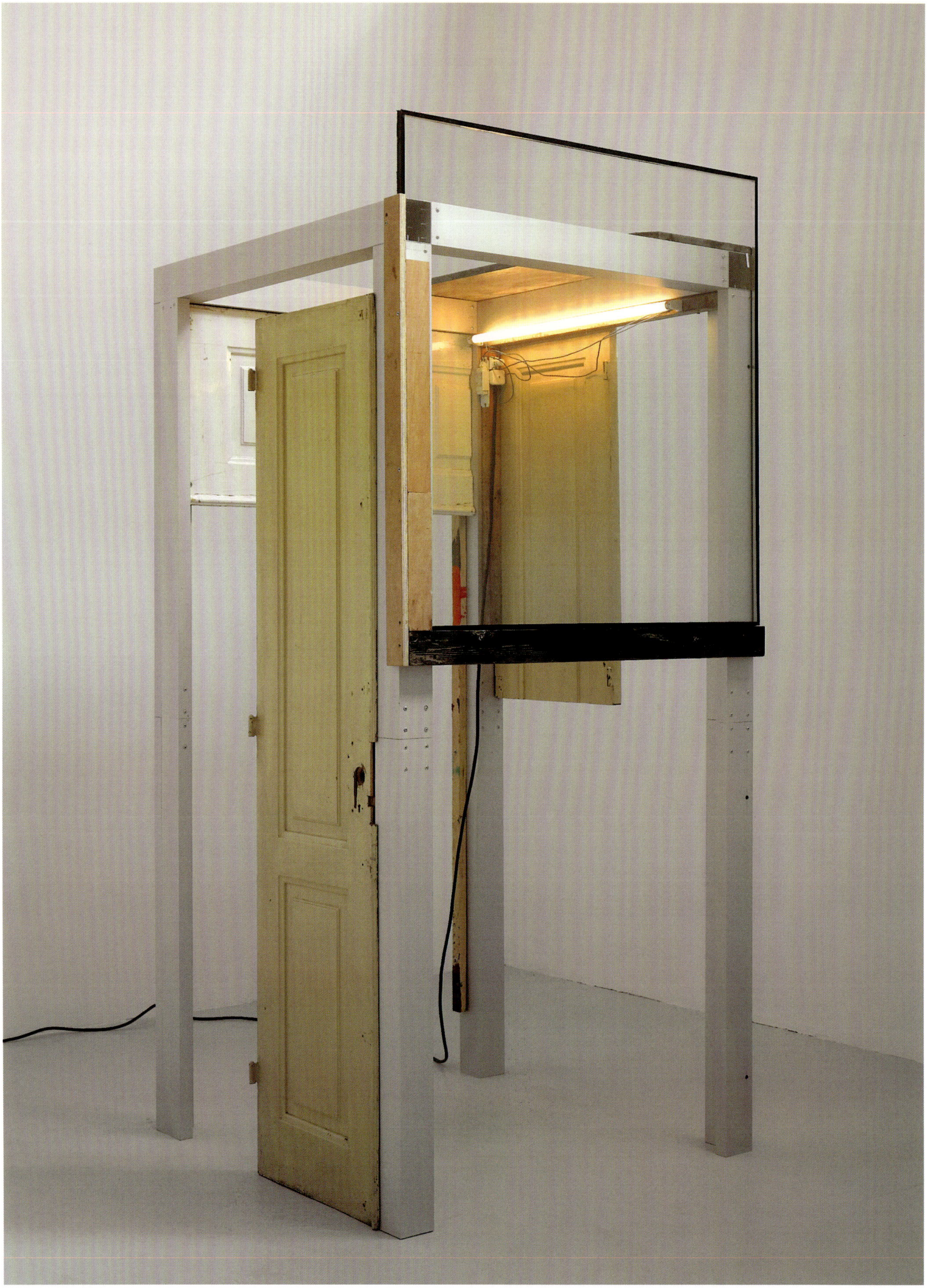

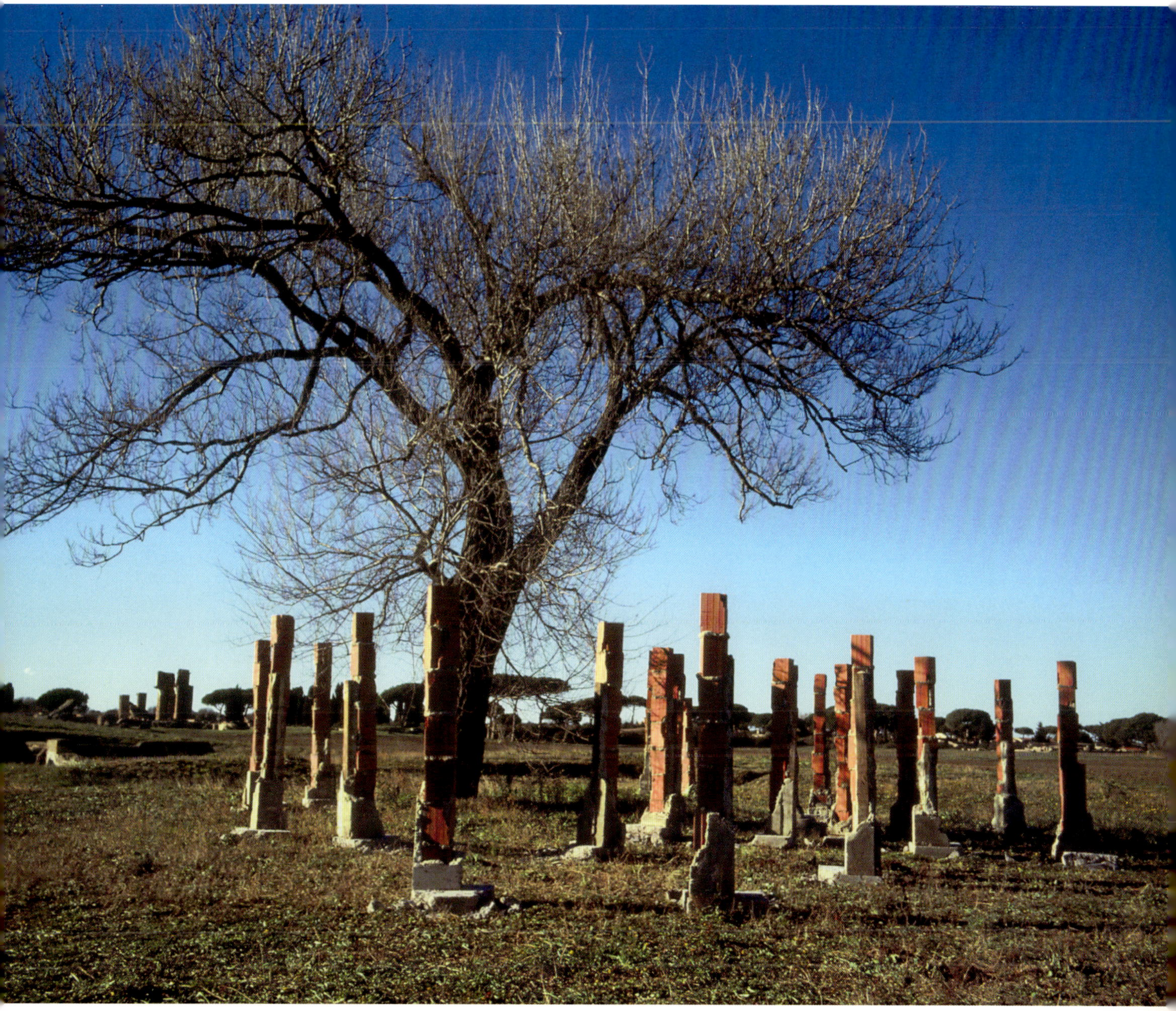

Favorite Places # 1, 2004
Aluminum, wood, glass, hoe, neon,
260 x 120 x 120 cm
Dijon, FRAC – Fonds régional d'art
contemporain de Bourgogne

21 Brick Columns, 2005
Iron structure, bricks, and concrete,
dimensions variable
View of the installation realized
in 2005 at Ostia Antica, Rome

Gianni Caravaggio

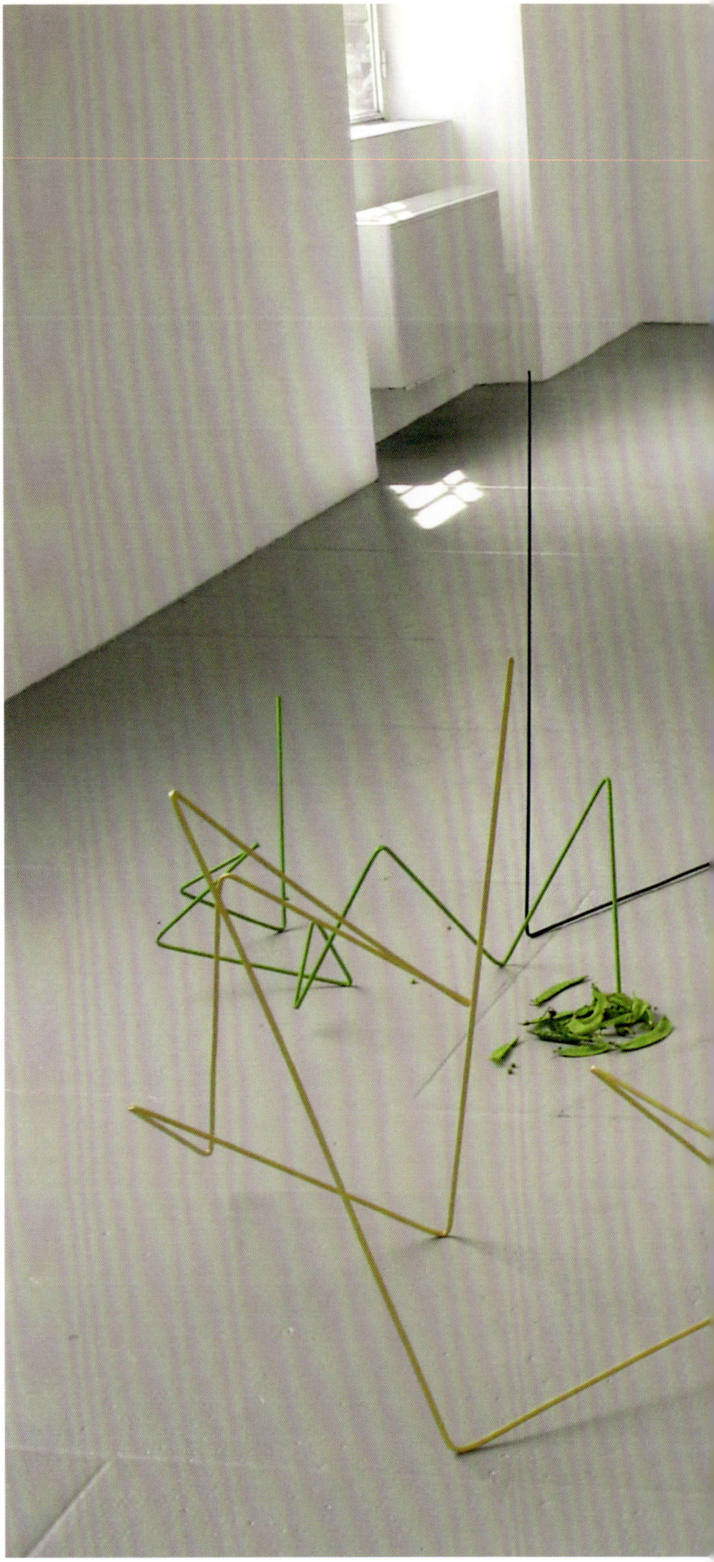

Born in Rocca San Giovanni, near Chieti, Italy, in 1968. Lives and works in Milan.
Gianni Caravaggio's work focuses strongly on the relationship between the entity and its original meaning. His sculptural vocabulary is the physical materialization of the abstract elements of thought, using an extreme synthesis of geometric forms and unified structures to give bodily shape to cognitive concepts and ideas.
The starting point of his work lies in references to pre-Aristotelian philosophical doctrines and knowledge of the laws of physics, both of which can be seen as providing the necessary theoretical framework for any explanation of natural phenomena and interpretation of the universe. Caravaggio's sculptural works thus give shape to these theoretical foundations. Drawing upon the legacy of Arte Povera as channeled through the artist Luciano Fabro, the artist uses a whole range of different materials in an effort to offer his own answers to questions about the origin and meaning of the created universe. In *Crazy Beans*, for example, Caravaggio combines the philosophical idea of the primordial seed with the atomic particle by placing soy, azuki and other beans in space to suggest the expansive, centrifugal motion at the basis of the cosmogonic theory of the Big Bang. The result is complete abstraction of the sculptural object, with broken lines of the same color as the beans indicating the trajectory and evolution of the elementary geometric element of the point, a metaphor of the origin of everything.
The same process of theoretical abstraction underpins the video and five sculptures making up the self-referential installation *Cause*, in that the film heralds the physical presence of the object and recounts its origin through revolving movement. The sculpture is in actual fact the initial moment of a process shown by the video in chronologically reversed time. The sculptural object is tautologically the cause, matrix and starting point, whereas the projection places it in the sphere of the result.
(*F.T.*)

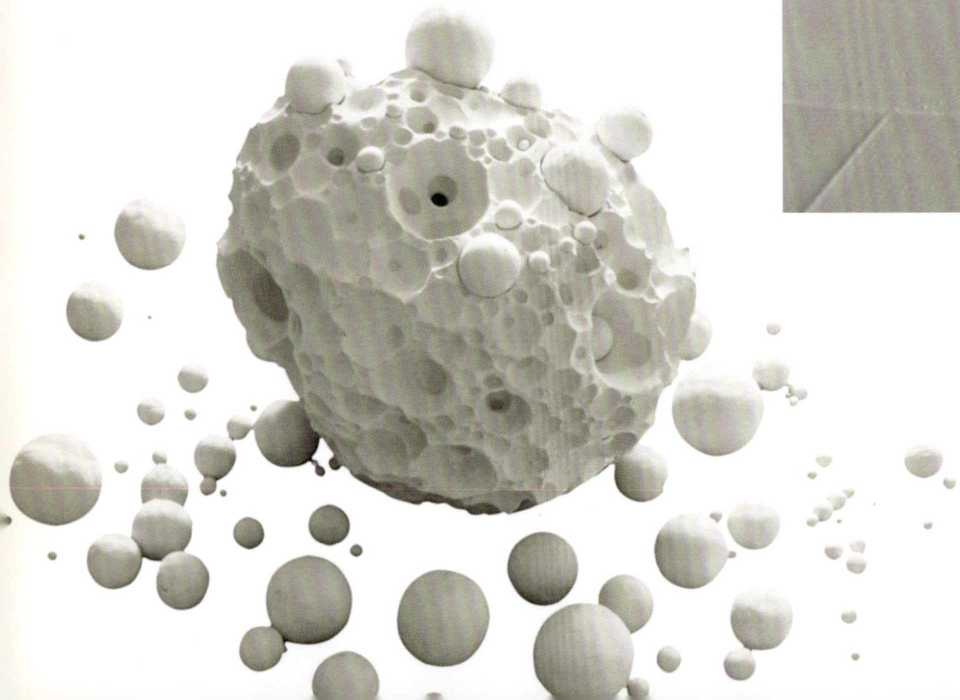

Cause, 2003
Unglazed pottery,
dimensions variable
Courtesy francesca kaufmann

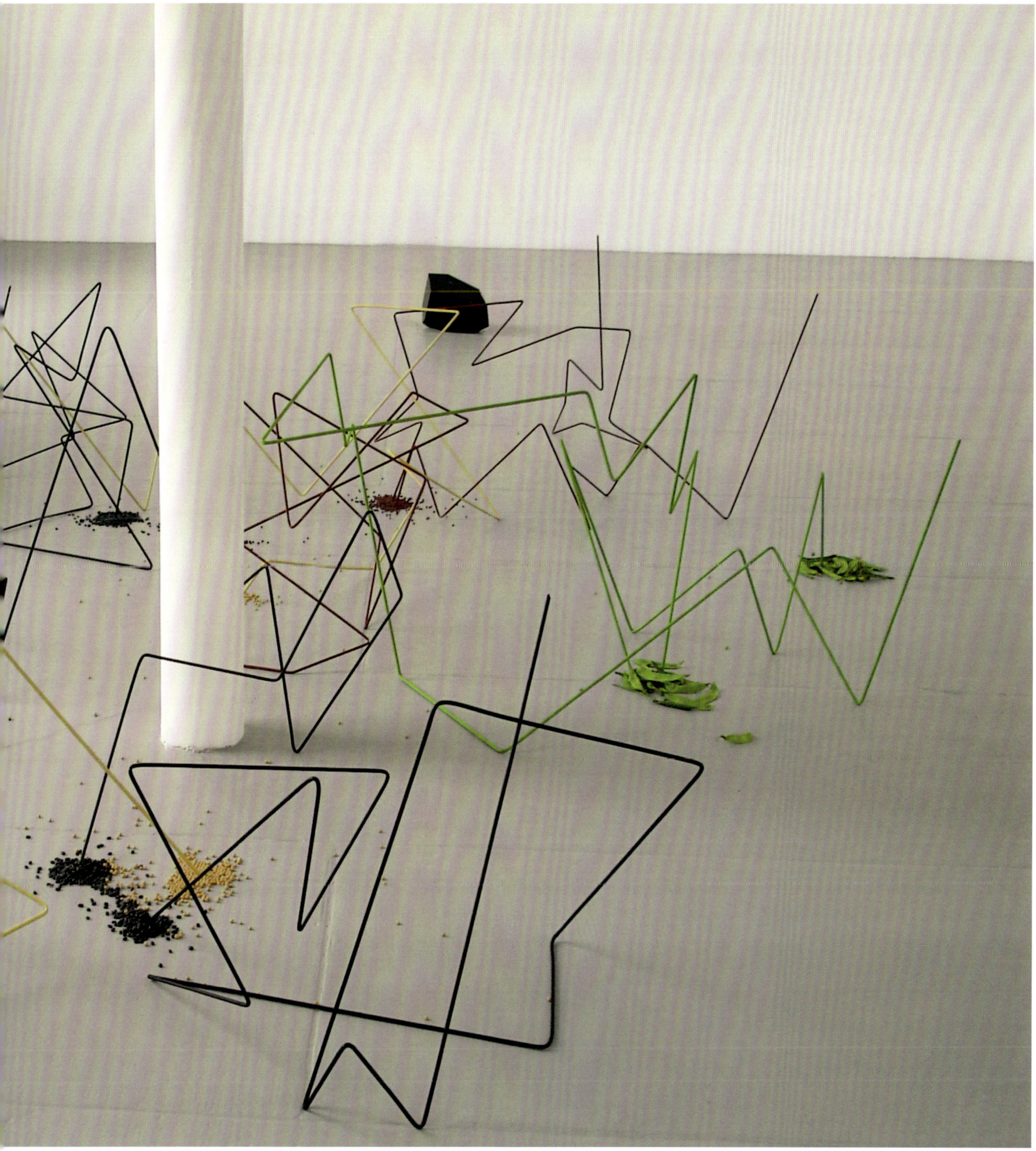

Crazy Beans, 2003
Aluminum, paint, yellow soy beans, red azuki beans, black beans, green peas, dimensions variable
Torre Pellice, Lisa and Tucci Russo Collection

Olafur Eliasson

Erosion, 1997
View of the installation at the
2nd Johannesburg Biennale, 1997

Ice Pavillon, 1998
View of the installation at
Kjarvalstadir, Reykjavik Art Museum,
1998

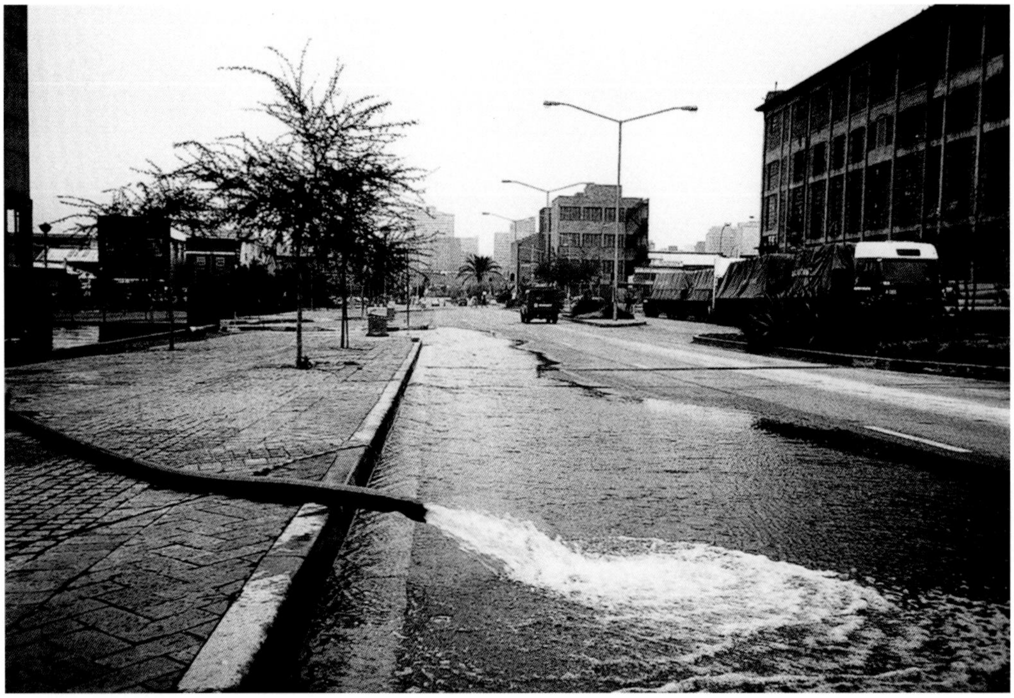

Born in Copenhagen in 1967.
Lives and works in Berlin.
Approximately two million people went to the Turbine Hall of Tate Modern in London between October 2003 and March 2004 to visit a colossal installation by Olafur Eliasson, an artist previously known to few other than insiders. Entitled *The Weather Project*, the work could be described as the simulation of a never-ending sunset. A semicircular disc made up of hundreds of mono-frequency lamps and mounted at one end of the Turbine Hall emitted an intense, all-enveloping yellow light. The already vast exhibition space was dizzyingly doubled by means of a mirror covering the entire surface of the ceiling and the atmosphere was made richer and thicker by the constant use of humidifiers to create mist. The mirror served also to double the luminous semicircle, transforming it into a perfect golden disc, and performed what the artist regarded as the crucial function of reflecting the public.
As Eliasson to explained Hans H. Obrist, the success of *The Weather Project* was probably due to a combination of factors, including the attraction connected with the scale and the unique nature of the event (a mega-project in the mega-museum of one of the world's biggest cities), and the strong media impact developed not only through specialized magazines and art and culture columns, but also through weather forecasts, "the most watched TV programs." And then obviously, there was the universal nature of the subject: who doesn't talk about the weather?
It is, however, hard to imagine that no part was played in this success by a central element of Eliasson's work that he has emphasized repeatedly in numerous interviews, namely his decision to make the public the fulcrum of the work, to use people as a medium and enable them to observe themselves in the act of perception. *Seeing Yourself Sensing* (2001) is not only the title of a work by Eliasson, but the key to his artistic approach as a whole. As Emi Fontana points out, it is no coincidence that the second person singular is often to be found in the titles of his works, from *Come As You Are* (1992), *Your Sun Machine* (1997), and *Your Spiral View* (2002) to *Take Your Time*, the title of the retrospective held in 2007 at the San Francisco Museum of Modern Art. As the artist stated in 1999, "What we have in common is that we are different. This is precisely the huge misunderstanding: that everything is conceived as though we were identical ... To me it is a question of visualizing our senses, and exposing them to ourselves through their instrumental representation." Like all of Eliasson's works, *The Weather Project* makes viewers feel they are the focal point of the work and allows them to concentrate on their senses and bodies, a dimension often neglected by Western art and culture and one that *The Weather Project* succeeds in addressing despite its transformation into a mass experience. People often returned and spent hours lying on the floor of the Turbine Hall. Eliasson's work on the senses makes his art accessible also to those uninterested in understanding its intellectual foundations and motivations.
It is simple and complex at the same time as well as surprisingly political in the final analysis.
As the artist pointed out in 2003, "When the ideology of a display or exhibition is not acknowledged as a part of the exhibition itself, the socializing potential of that exhibition is sacrificed on behalf of formal values. To avoid this situation, any chosen ideological strategy, any marketing choice, any architectural detail, must not only be considered as a condition and part of the project, but must also somehow be revealed to visitors and thus allow for some transparency in the mediation." Equally surprising, however, is the fact that the political nature of the work is channeled through perception and emotion: "Even though I favor political aspects of art, I think that there is a formalizing danger in a programmatic attitude that somehow excludes emotional beliefs. ... By being extremely linear and programmatic...very little space is left for emotions, hence the work becomes formalized in a 'reversed' way." It is on this delicate balance between relational requirements and formal abstraction, between politics and emotion, that the meaning of all of Eliasson's work rests.
Olafur Eliasson graduated from the Royal Danish Academy of Fine Arts in Copenhagen in 1995. His work alternates photography (series of

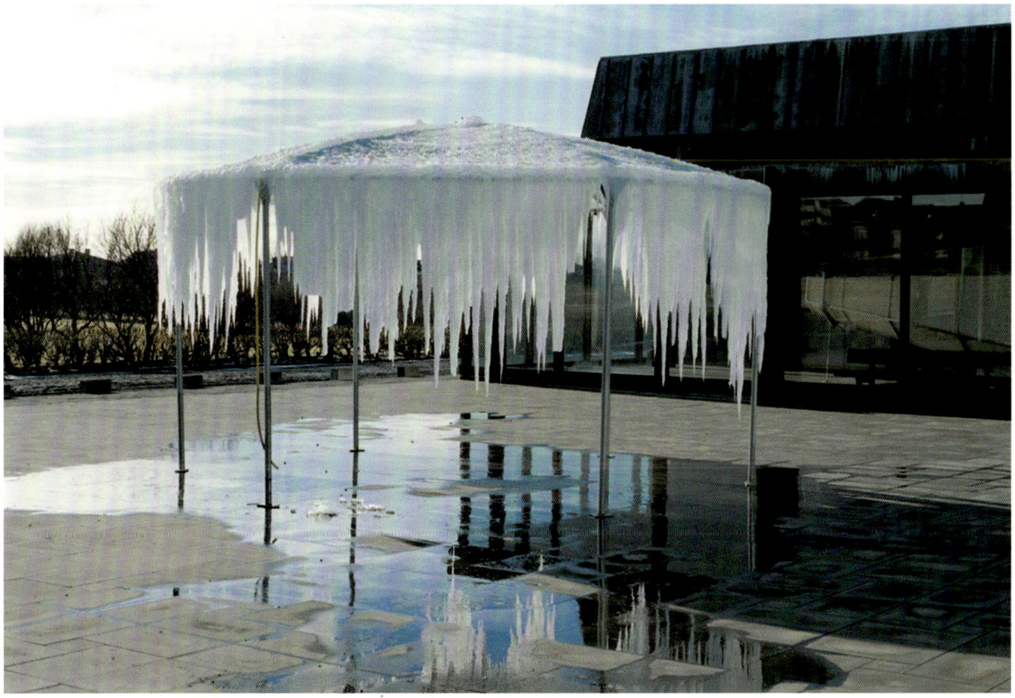

shots of specific details or phenomena of the natural and sometimes urban environment) with environmental installations and models of perceptually unstable settings, often made out of cheap materials like iron and cardboard. Often created in collaboration with the architect Einar Thorsteinn, his environments assign an increasingly important role to intangible factors such as light, sound, and atmospheric humidity. *Your Sun Machine* was created at the Marc Foxx Gallery, Los Angeles, in 1997 by completely emptying the white cube and making a hole in the ceiling to combine the existing source of light with a new and intriguing ray so as to draw the visitor's attention to the movement of the sun and the variability of natural light. The same year also saw *Room for One Color* and *Erosion*. In the first, the ceiling was fitted with lamps emitting light in the yellow area of the visible spectrum in such a way as to filter all the colors in the room through this dominant hue and create a scale ranging from yellow to black. *Erosion* is instead an unauthorized project created for the Johannesburg Biennial, where Eliasson had been invited to exhibit photographs. The artist ran a pipe from an open-air cistern to the street in front and created a river flowing through the city for half a kilometer. The was one of his first improvised public projects, developed outside the institutional framework so as to avoid the constraints inevitably bound up with the "art" label. The artist then used a huge amount of harmless dye to turn the river in Stockholm green the following year. Entitled *Green River*, the operation was to be repeated over the years in various other cities. As he explained some time later, "Working outside with improvised interventions represents a desire to dissolve my work formally and to unmask the formalizing power of institutions – and, of course, to engage the audience." It was, however, above all his spectacular, involvement-generating installations that brought him fame. Created in Reykjavik in 1998, *The Ice Pavilion* is a steel structure with a thick sheet of ice as its roof, alluding at the same time to global warming and the development of new forms of housing. These themes were taken up again with the installation *The Glacierhouse Effect Versus the Greenhouse Effect* in 2005 and in 2007 with *Your Mobile Expectations: BMW H2R Project*, a work on cars commissioned by BMW that simultaneously embodies and attacks the contradictions of today's hyperconsumption of energy.
The Mediated Motion, an exhibition designed for the Kunsthaus Bregenz in collaboration with the landscape architect Günther Vogt in 2001, involved the introduction of natural elements to transform the museum's great orthogonal spaces. One room, to be viewed from a precarious walkway hanging high above, was flooded with fog. Others were filled with water or soil. The US Public Art Fund put up $ 15 million in 2008 for the creation of four artificial waterfalls from the piers of the bridges in New York harbor. The fundamental constant feature of Eliasson's work is, however, above all light: the light of *360 Room for All Colors* (2002), spanning the entire spectrum, inundating the space, and influencing our experience of reality; the light reflected on the inner walls of *Your Spiral View* (2002) and *The Antispective Situation* (2003) with kaleidoscopic effects then developed to extremes in *The Blind Pavilion* at the 2003 Venice Biennale; the light that colored the prismatic walls of *One-Way Colour Tunnel* (2007), the secular cathedral erected on the occasion of the retrospective in the San Francisco Museum of Modern Art.
Having reached full artistic maturity, Olafur Eliasson now has a studio-factory with a team of assistants and prestigious commissions from leading companies like BMW and Louis Vuitton. He has managed in his work to draw upon the legacy of Land Art and Kinetic Art while harnessing the most innovative technologies and the skills of architects and engineers to develop an art intended first and foremost as a personal experience for the viewer.
(D.Q.)

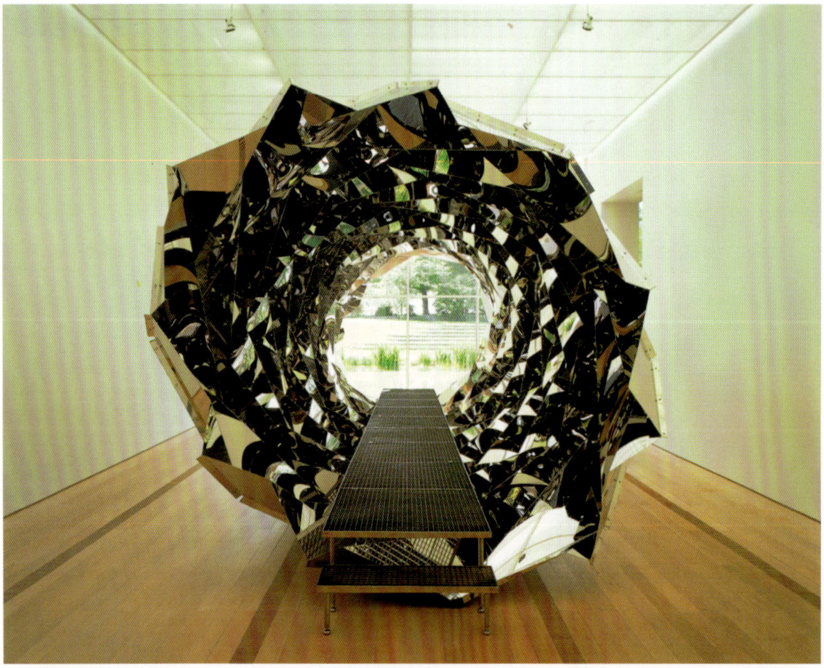

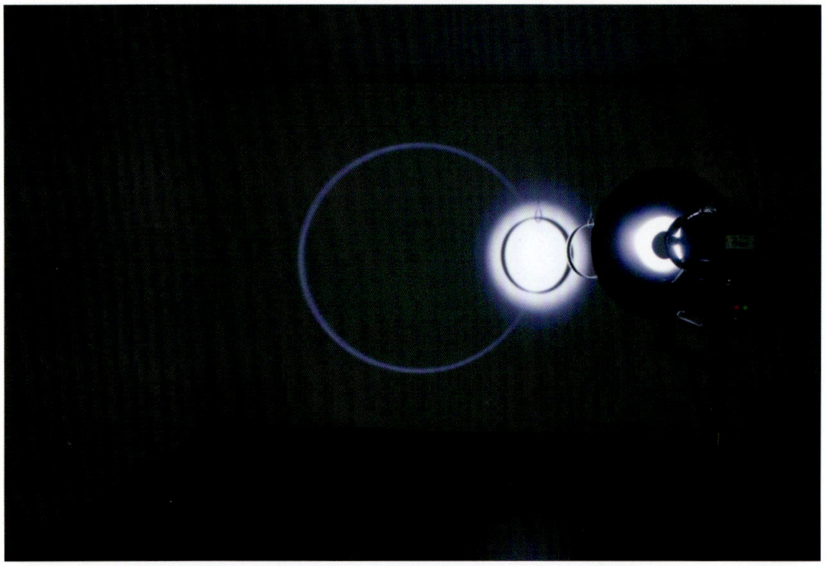

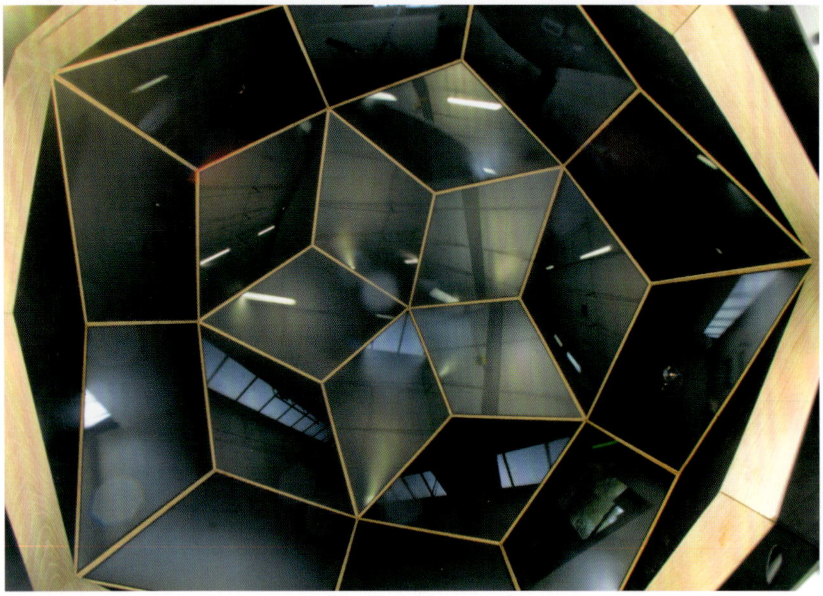

Your Spiral View, 2002
Metal and mirror panels,
dimensions variable
View of the installation realized
in 2002 at the Foundation Beyeler,
Basel

Your Space Embracer, 2004
Lamps and projectors,
dimensions variable
View of the installation in 2004
at Brändstörm & Stene, Stockholm

Polyphonic House, 2007
Metal structure and mirrors,
dimensions variable
View of the installation realized in
2007 at the Studio Olafur Eliasson,
Berlin

The Weather Project, 2003
Lamps and mirrors,
dimensions variable
View of the installation realized
in 2003 at Tate Modern, London
for *The Unilever Series*

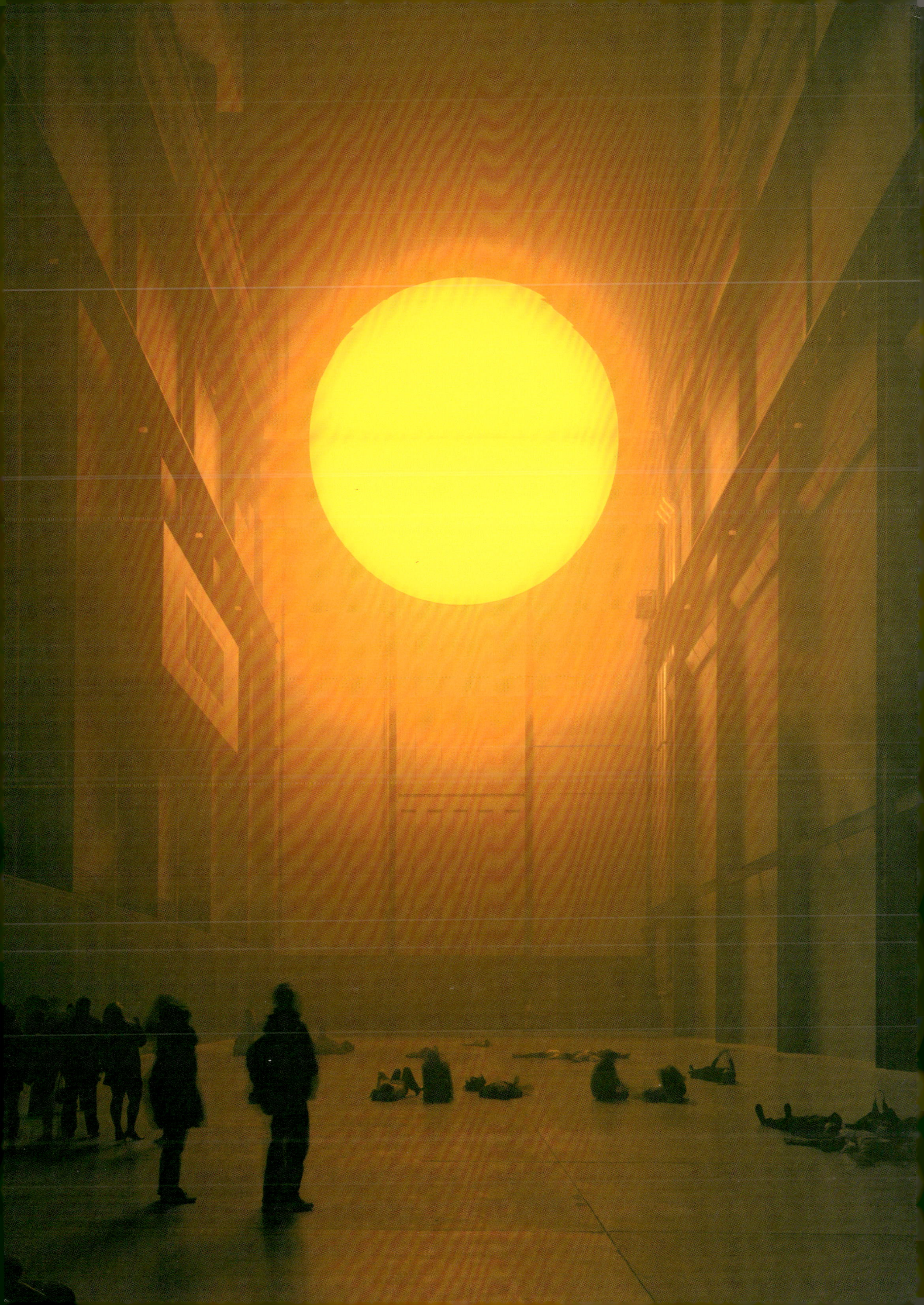

Elmgreen & Dragset

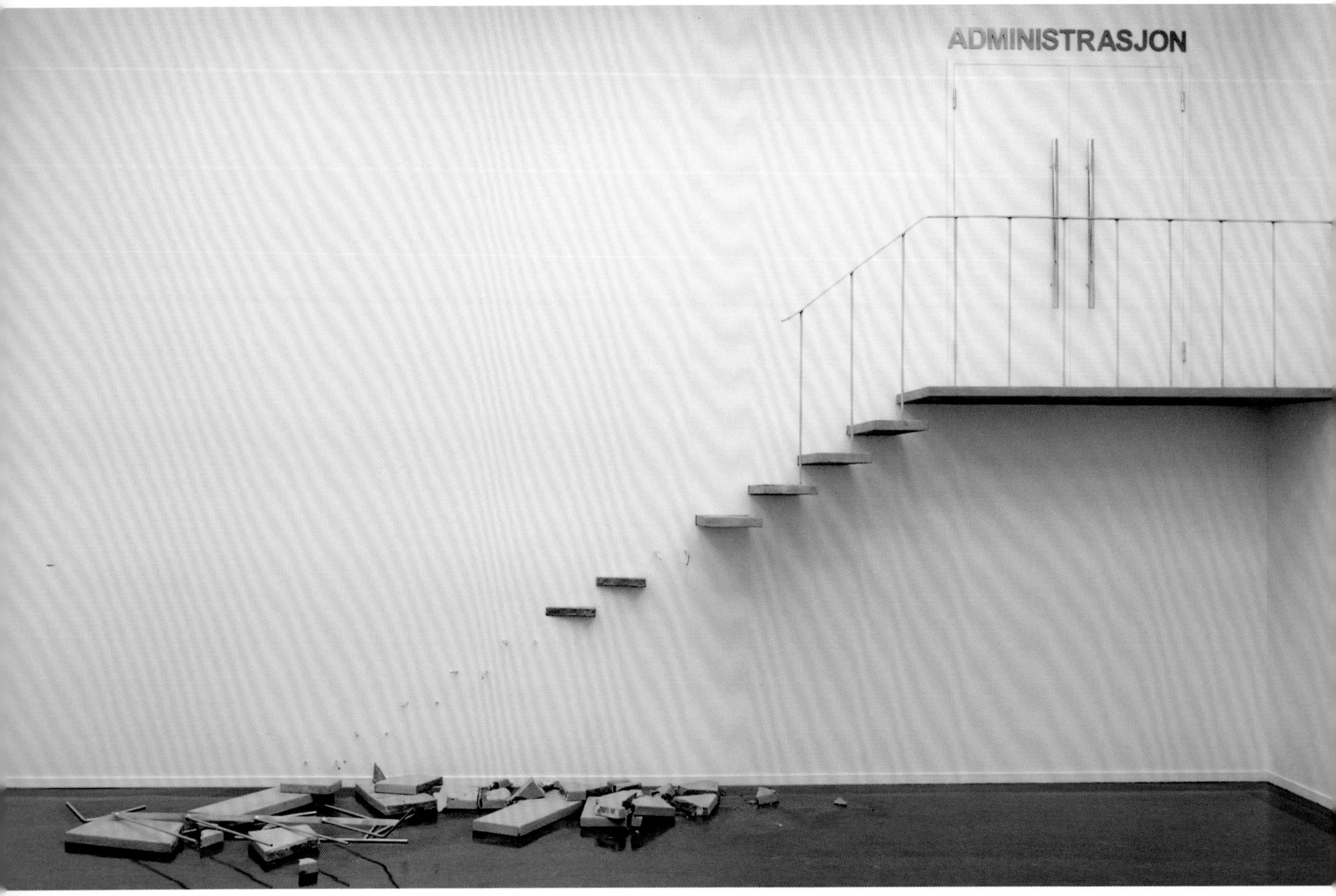

Michael Elmgreen, born in Copenhagen in 1961, and Ingar Dragset, born in Trondheim in 1969, live and work in Berlin.
Michael Elmgreen and Ingar Dragset began working together in 1995 after pursuing separate careers for a short period, respectively in art and theater. Their first works were in the field of performance. *Try* (1997), for example, involved inviting three young people to spend time in the gallery, lying on a carpet, reading and listening to whatever music they liked. The work introduced some themes that were to be developed in the years to come, including the gay identity and its perception in society (the artists are a couple also in their private life), cultural stereotypes, and investigation of the "white cube" of the exhibition venue. Their focus gradually shifted in the late 1990s toward installation, albeit always with a "live" dimension. Under the umbrella title of *Powerless Structures*, nearly all of Elmgreen & Dragset's works have since focused on social space – especially galleries and museums – as a structure of ideological conditioning. A number of works staged between 1997 and 2000 consisted of having the empty space of the venue painted for the entire duration of the exhibition (from twelve hours to several weeks). While intended to call the supposed neutrality of the white cube into question, this operation takes on different connotations each time depending on whether it takes place in a museum, a private space or any one of a variety of cultural settings. In *Elevated Gallery* (2001), a classic white cube is hung at an angle from two helium-filled balloons in a museum room and thus transformed into an object of observation. This deconstructive approach is sometimes applied to particular elements of an exhibition space such as the doors, stairs, floor or ceiling. *Short Cut* (2003) presented a paradoxical image of the contradictions of globalization with the sudden appearance of a car and caravan in the middle of the Galleria Vittorio Emanuele in Milan. *Phone Home* (2003) involved setting up a communication area in a gallery with telephones on a table that visitors were invited to use for private calls, thus bringing their private life into a public space and exposing it to the other visitors. Investigation of the private sphere and how it is influenced by the conventions of design and fashion has remained a key focus of Elmgreen & Dragset's work also in recent years. *Andrea Candela* (2006) involved the use of three identical dummies, dressed in the same way but placed in three domestic environments differing in terms of style and "class", to create an imaginary character. Andrea became "real" through an e-mail address, an account with a gay dating site, and a cell phone number, digital attachments through which his life continues beyond the work.
(*D.Q.*)

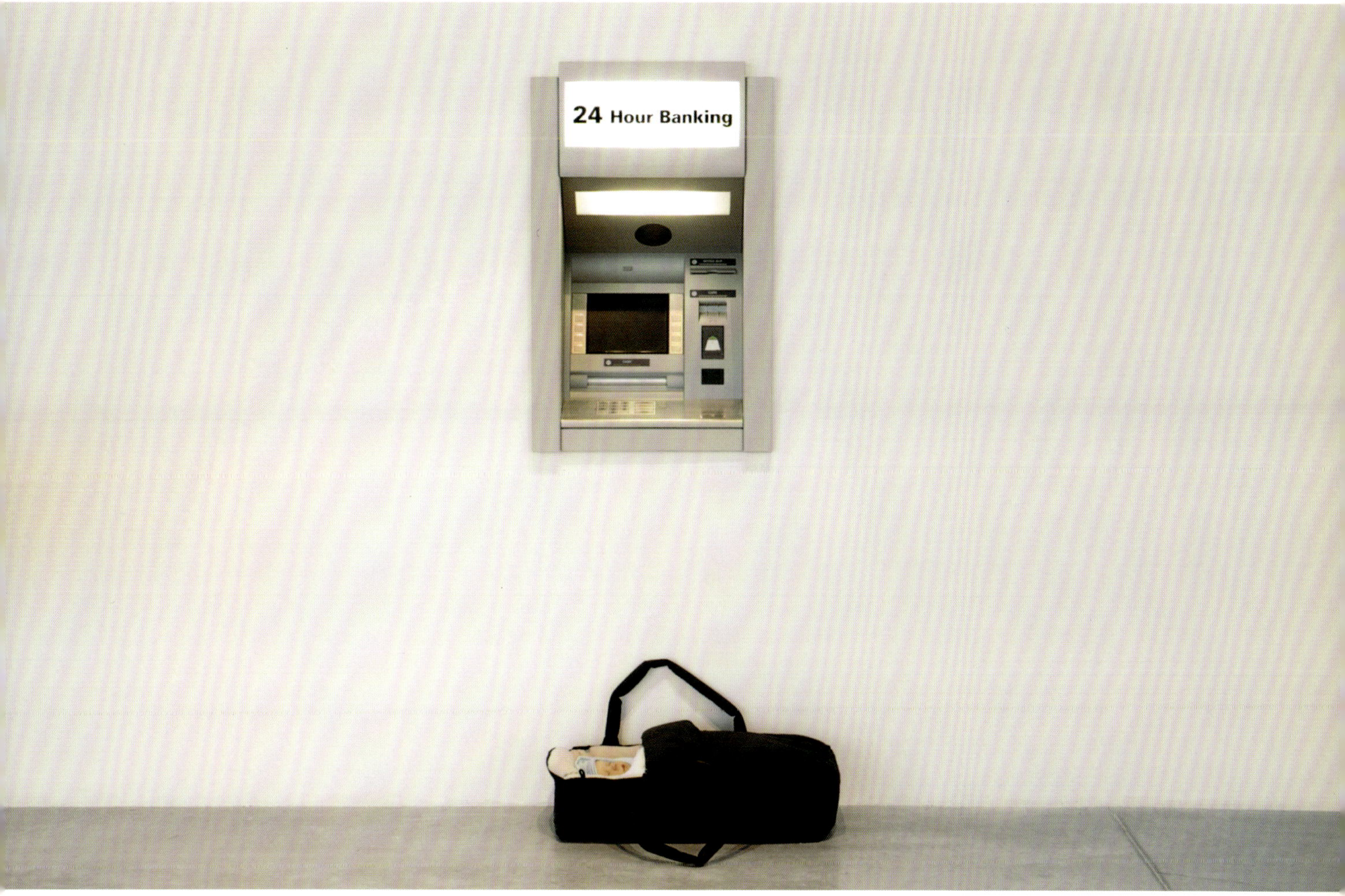

Social Mobility (Emergency Exit), 2006
Aluminum, wood, polystyrene, iron, concrete, 430 x 700 x 200 cm
Courtesy Galleri Nicolai Wallner, Copenhagen; Thyssen-Bornemisza Art Contemporary, Wien

Modern Moses, 2006
Carrycot, bedding, wax figure, baby clothes, stainless steel cash machine, 71 x 37 x 16 cm circa (baby carriage), 94 x 76 cm circa (cash machine front)
Courtesy Galería Helga de Alvear, Madrid; Galleria Massimo de Carlo, Milan

Urs Fischer

Born in Zurich in 1973. Lives and works in Zurich.
Described by critics as a "magician of matter" and "*bricoleur* of chance", Urs Fischer sees sculpture above all as a way of initiating the metamorphosis of materials, objects, and spaces.
His working methods reflect the importance he attaches to transformation and chance: "Every work of mine begins with a drawing, but as soon as I start to work with the materials something goes wrong. The sculptures sometimes won't stand upright and so my frustration turns them into something else. My works are never in the end as I imagined them at the beginning. They are not failures. They just set off in different directions as I work. It is like a two-way street: your thoughts create the images and the images create your thoughts."
His sculptures often originate in the combination of simple everyday objects with fake ready-mades so as to suggest possible new readings. Ordinary wooden chairs can thus be used by a ghost (*Chair for a Ghost*, 2003) or become a set for a comedian (*How to Tell a Joke*, 2007). The object often changes not only in meaning but also in form, as Fischer uses unstable, perishable materials such as glue, wax, bread, and fruit, and leaves the process to follow its natural course once initiated. In *What If The Phone Rings?* (2003) three life-sized female nudes made of wax melted completely during their exhibition at a London gallery.
In *Bread House* (2004) dozens of brightly colored parakeets gradually devoured a fairytale house (5 meters tall and covering a surface area of 20 square meters) built by Fischer with bread rolls instead of bricks.
The artist also investigates the changes brought about by the sculptural work in the space where it is placed. In *Vintage Violence*, a title taken from an album by John Cale, Fischer hung 1700 red raindrops, made of plaster and painted by hand, from the frescoed ceiling of Palazzo Grassi in Venice. *You* (2007) involved the creation of a hole about eight feet deep in the floor of the gallery Gavin Brown's Enterprise in New York. Both installations alter the viewer's perception of the environment by making it unstable and subtly threatening. The space transformed by Fischer reminds us in fact of our own precarious state at the mercy of chance and our ultimate, inescapable destiny.
(*P.V.*)

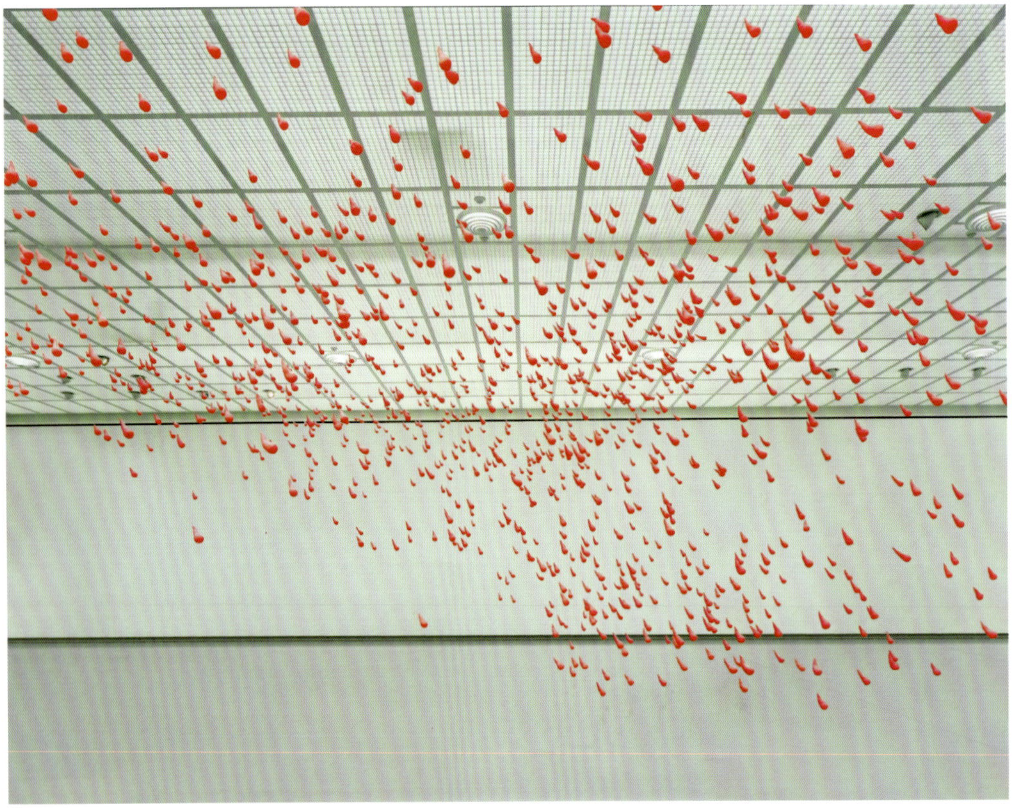

Vintage Violence, 2004–2005
Plaster, resin, pieces of metal, nylon, 1700 rain drops, dimensions variable
Venice, François Pinault Collection

You, 2007
Remains of excavated materials, dimensions variable
Courtesy Galerie Eva Presenhuber, Zurich; Gavin Brown's enterprise, New York

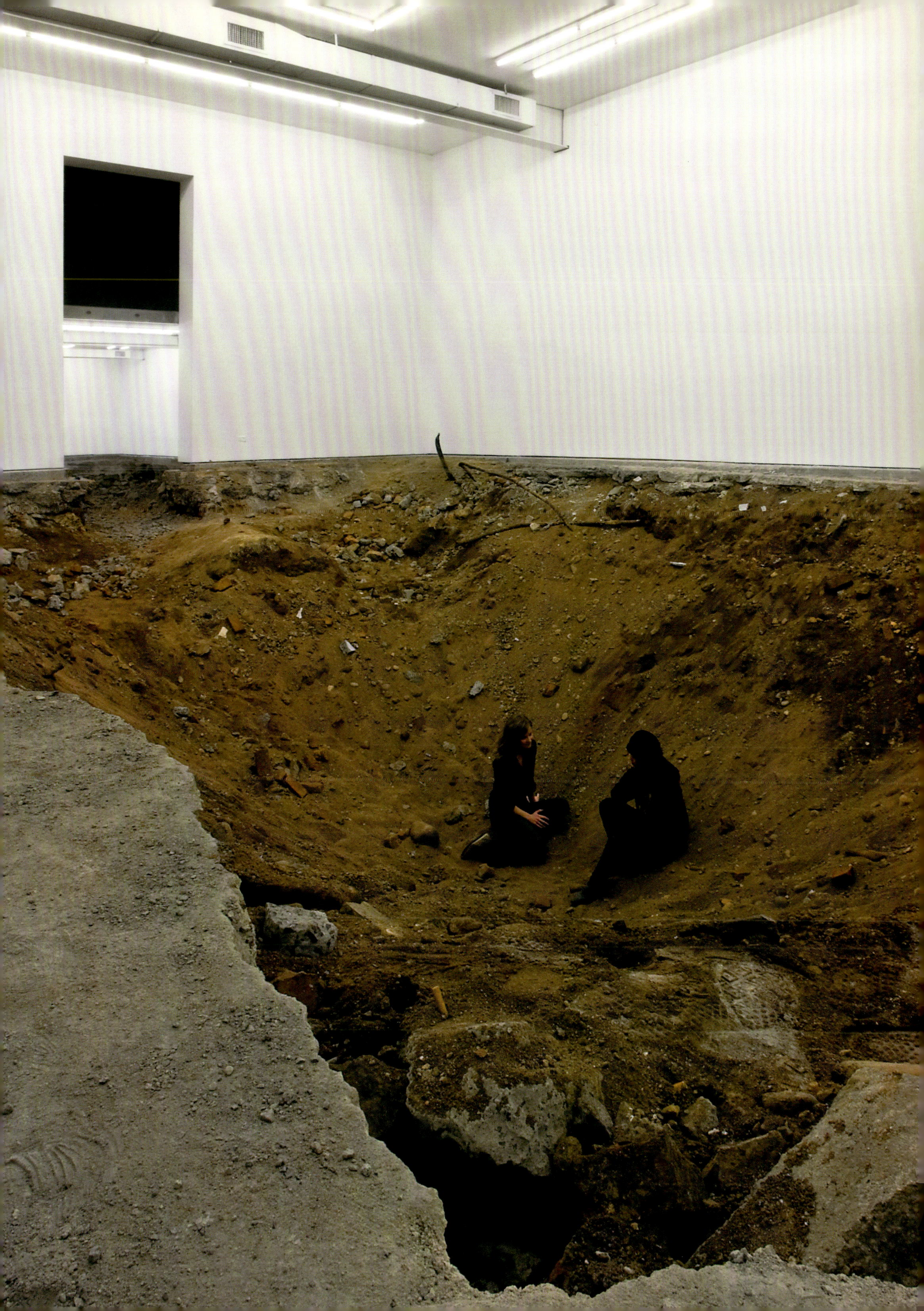

Fischli & Weiss

Peter Fischli, born in Zurich in 1952, and David Weiss, born in Zurich in 1946. They live and work in Zurich. Investigating areas of shadow, revealing the contradictions of a world apparently programmed to work in accordance with set rules, seeking values and meaning in what appears to be commonplace and ordinary, these have been the guiding principles of the Swiss duo Fischli & Weiss for three decades now. Technological media such as photography, video, and light boxes are used by the artists as tools that make it possible to look at the world through different eyes. Their gaze focuses on the little things of everyday life in order to discern their intrinsic qualities or anomalies. In the 16 mm film *Der Lauf der Dinge* (*The Way of Things*, 1986–1987), for example, numerous objects and utensils are involved in a simultaneously exhilarating and disturbing "domino effect" of falls, collisions, small explosions, blasts of air and liquid, jets of steam, and so on for half an hour along a circuit meticulously designed by the two artists through the precise calculation of weights, balances and distances as well as preliminary testing of chemical and physical processes and their effects. An interest in the recontextualization of commonplace objects, evidently influenced by Duchamp, already appeared in *Wurst-Serie* (1979), their first work, where various types of sausage, whole or sliced, are variously disguised and photographed in dramatic situations or arranged so as to suggest bizarre interiors or natural settings.
With a marked sense of irony and a playful, experimental attitude, Fischli & Weiss seek to undermine the habits and expectations that govern our relations with the surrounding world, as is also shown by their work on the materials and colors of everyday objects and creation of "doubles" that trick or disorient the spectator. The series of *Black Sculptures* (1986–1988), for example, transforms a commonplace setting of furniture, trees and utensils into a disquieting black monochrome of rubber. Installations like *Untitled (Rotterdam)* (2000–2004) and *Untitled (Pallets)* (2001–2004) present as ordinary objects sculptural replicas in polyurethane made and painted by the artists with the greatest care to be as lifelike as possible, the aim being precisely to show just how uncertain the boundary between appearance and actuality is. Fischli & Weiss resolve this dualism in some cases through direct intervention in the real world, as happened during the third edition of the Münster Skulptur Projekte in 1997, when they turned a lawn into a simple kitchen garden by planting vegetables, herbs, and flowers with the help of a gardener. The intention to "unveil" the inherent beauty of what is all around us and normally unnoticed informs both the work in Münster and the photographs of the series *Airports* (1988–1997), where Fischli & Weiss seek to counter the general dislike of modern airports, increasingly perceived as "non-places", by focusing on the irresistible fascination of aircraft with their ability to defy gravity and offer mankind the extraordinary experience of flight.
Careful observation of the world also leads the duo to investigate the behavior, habits and dynamics governing social relations.
They were awarded the Golden Lion at the Venice Biennale in 2003 for *Questions* (1980–2003), an installation that combines philosophical questions, existential doubts and mundane

Blumenphoto, 1997–1998
Ink-jet print, 107 x 74 cm
UniCredit Group Collection

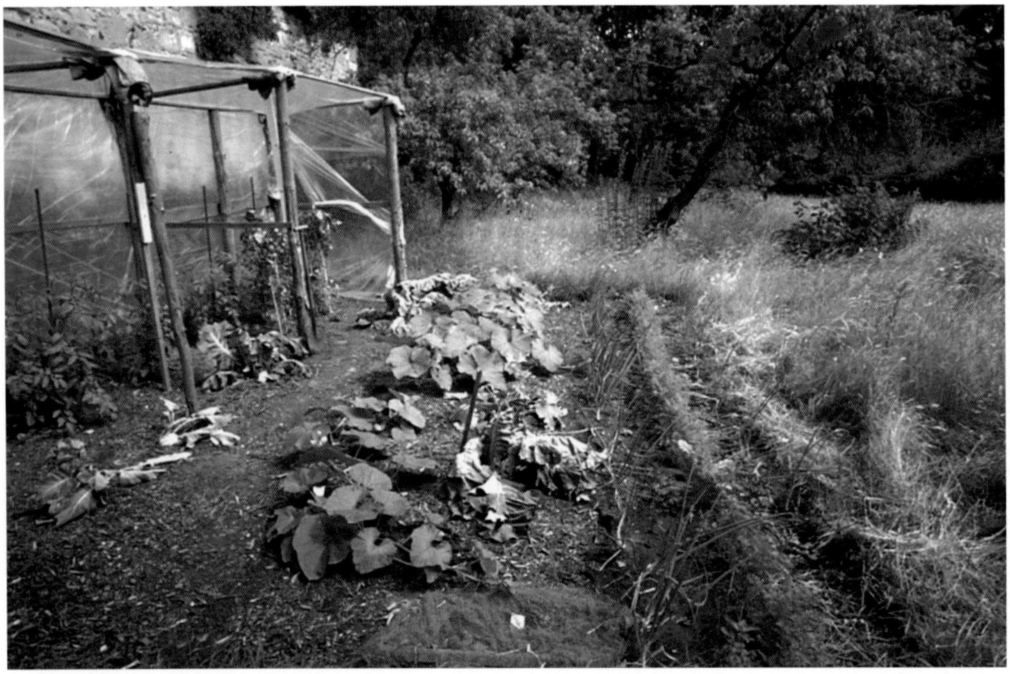

View of the garden conceived for the exhibition *Skulptur Projekte*, Münster, 1997

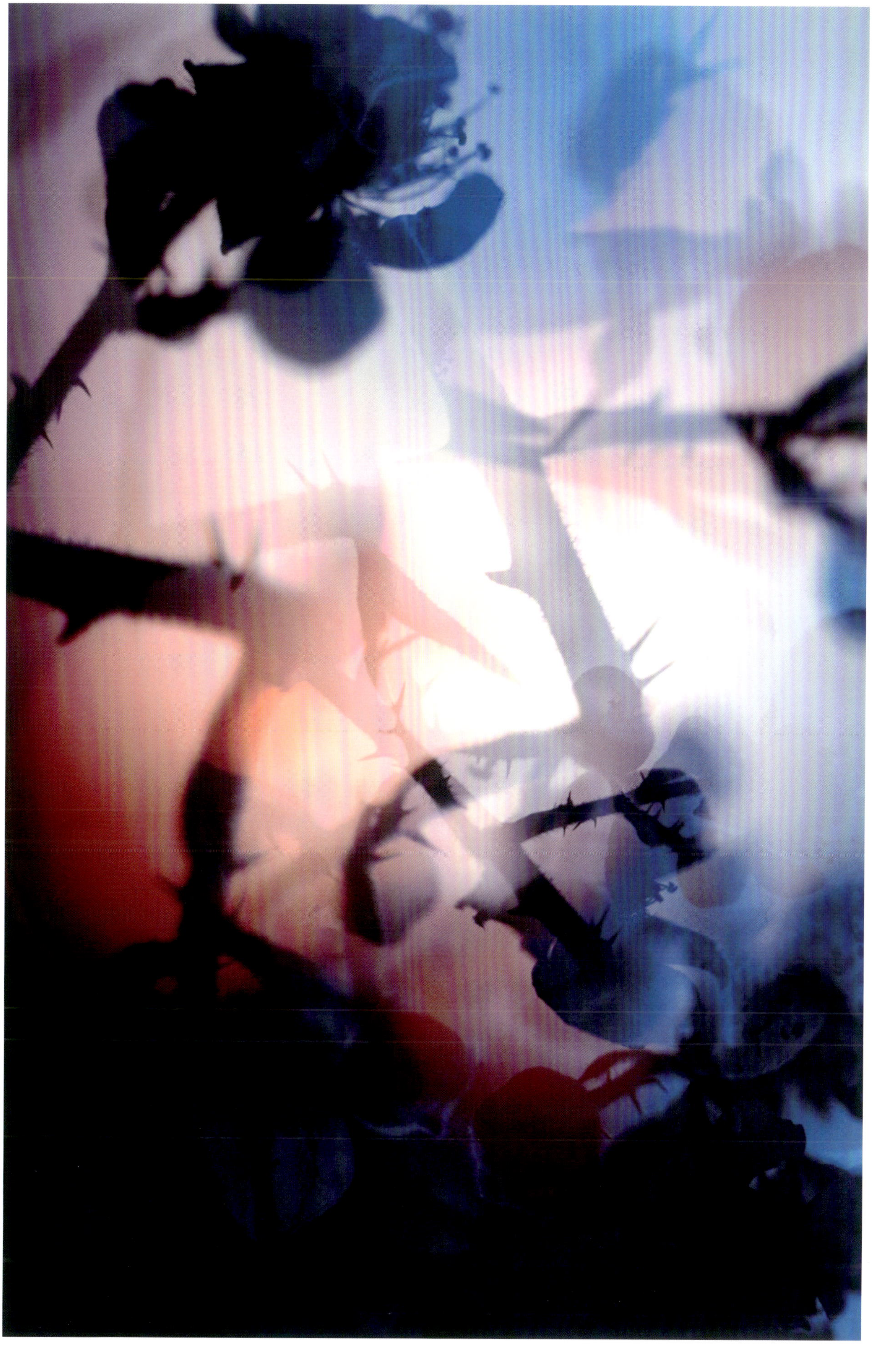

Sonne, Mond und Sterne (Sun, Moon, and Stars), 2008
800 facsimile reprints of advertisement, wooden showcases, glass, and steel, 270 x 72 x 77 cm

Courtesy Sprüth Magers, Berlin/London; Galerie Eva Presenhuber, Zurich; Matthew Marks Gallery, New York

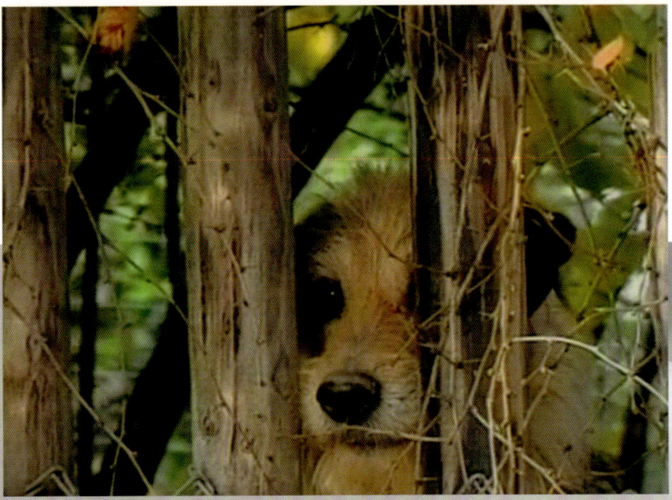

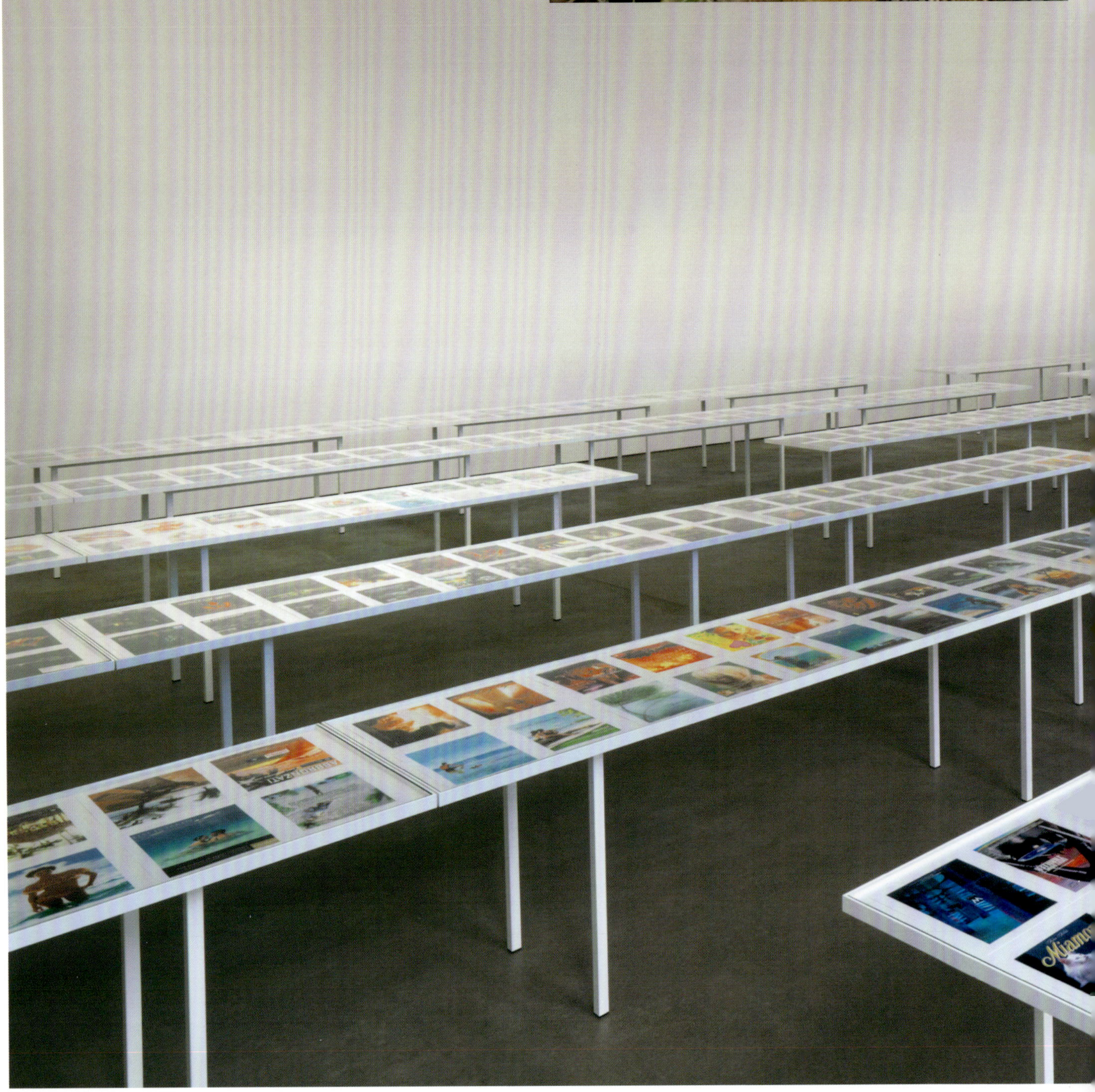

Hunde (Dogs), 2003
Digital video installation,
dimensions variable
Pittsburgh, Carnegie Museum
of Art, Milton Fine Fund

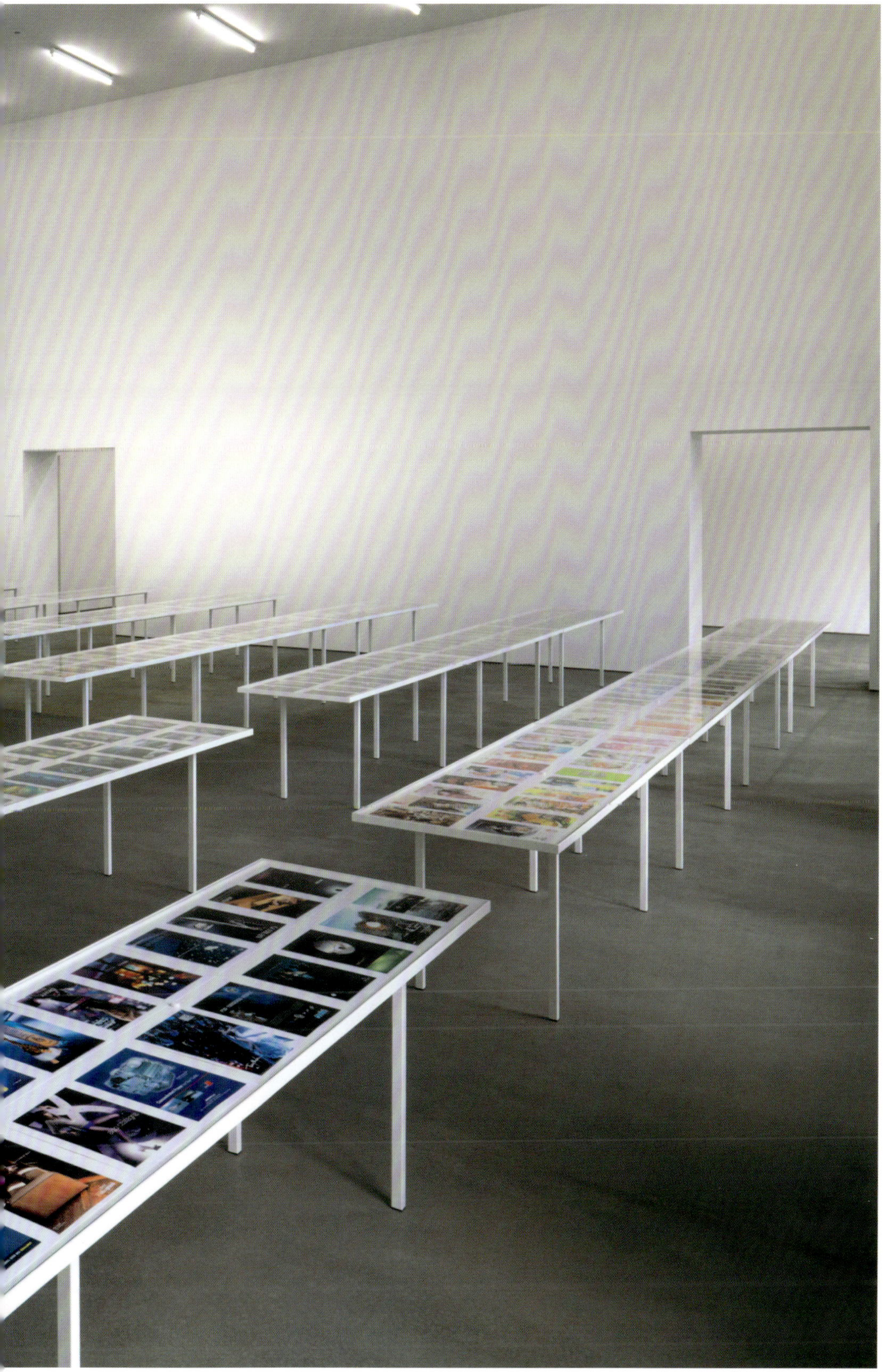

considerations reflecting the multiple facets of human nature. Their attention has also focused on the behavior of animals, understood as a metaphor of human behavior. The video installation and photographic series *Hunde* (2003, Dogs) thus shows three dogs barking and whining in their frustrated desire to get to something on the other side of the fence delimiting their space while images of a cat blissfully drinking milk from a bowl on the opposite wall remind us how pointless and foolish it is to yearn for what is beyond our reach. The criticism of behavior patterns imposed by the consumer society implicit in this and many other works of Fischli & Weiss becomes openly explicit in *Sonne, Mond und Sterne* (2008, Sun, Moon, and Stars), a book in which 800 advertising images are presented in pairs on the basis of specific characteristics of form or content so as to create through association or juxtaposition 400 diptychs that reveal the deep contradictions and ambiguities of mass culture. The advertisements carefully selected by the two artists faithfully represent the lifestyle of present-day human beings while saying nothing about their history and thoughts, thus reflecting the determination of our economic and cultural system that the very concept of contemporaneity should be defined exclusively by goods and services. Midway between the sociological investigation and aesthetic analysis of everyday life, *Sonne, Mond und Sterne* thus becomes a dramatic visual encyclopedia of our age.
(*P.V.*)

Jeppe Hein

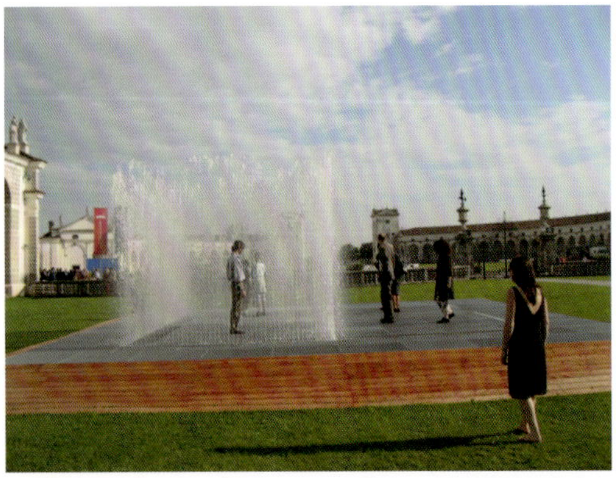

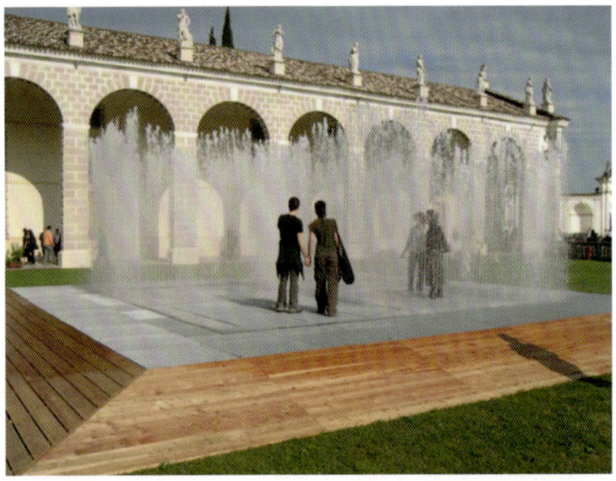

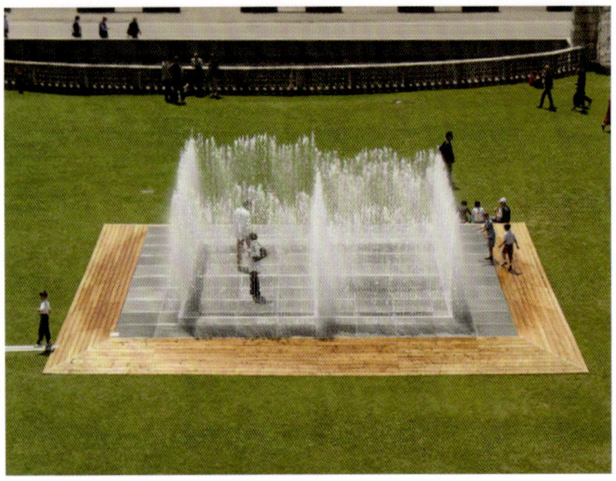

Appearing Rooms, 2004
Water, wood, iron grating, electrical pumps, computer controller,
230 x 700 x 700 cm
View of the installation realized in 2004 at Villa Manin, Passariano, Italy
Courtesy Johann König, Berlin and 303 Gallery, New York

Born in Copenhagen in 1974.
Lives and works in Berlin and Copenhagen.

After a short experience as an assistant in Olafur Eliasson's studio, the Danish artist Jeppe Hein began to attract attention with installations that appear to pay tribute to Minimalism while undermining its lofty, monumental distance from the viewer at the same time: "I want to show that the work isn't anything on its own, it's only what the public informs it with."

The latter's involvement is not only intellectual but also – and often primarily – physical. *Let Me Show You the World* (2000), for example, is simply a small hole in the wall that implicitly invites spectators to look through it. When they do so, a gentle breeze caresses their eyelashes. Hein's works sometimes arouse a feeling of danger. In *Bear the Consequences* (2003), the spectator's entrance into the exhibition space is greeted by a hissing sound and a burst of flame from a hole in the wall. Even though this area is cordoned off, the way the flame gets bigger the closer you approach generates alarm.

In *Continuity Inbetween* (2002) it is instead a jet of water that shoots from a hole in the wall and exits with the greatest precision through another hole in the wall opposite. While the recurrent use of fire and water obviously recalls the work of Eliasson, Hein's interest seems to focus sometimes on the construction or activation of a space and sometimes on developing a dialogue with the spectator based on gestures and emotions. In *Space in Action/Action in Space* (2002) jets of water from a platform create a temporary space. Sensors enable the installation to perceive the approach of a spectator and interrupt the corresponding jets of water temporarily so as to allow him or her into the circumscribed area. Paradoxically enough, this is a fountain designed to keep those experiencing it from getting wet.

In *360° Presence* (2002) it was instead steel balls that took over the floor space of the Galerie König in Berlin, rolling around wildly whenever anyone came in and stopping briefly whenever they collided with something in the empty space, such as a wall, a door or a leg. Water and fire combine in *Arco di fuoco* (2006) to create a simultaneously minimal and spectacular structure with a flame bursting from the point of impact between two jets of water.

(D.Q.)

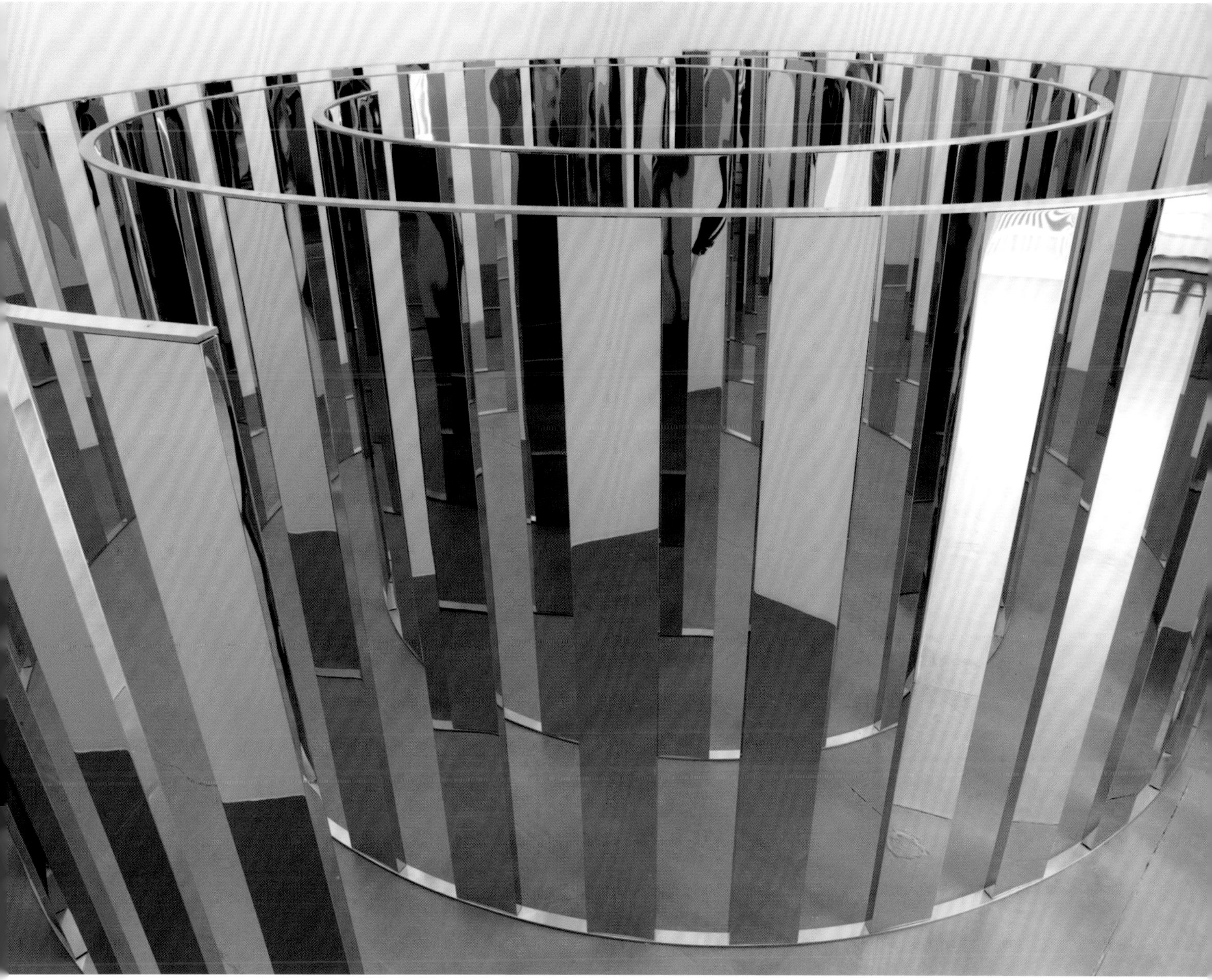

Spiral Labyrinth, 2006
80 high polished mirror plates and
metal frame, 525 x 600 cm;
each plate 230 x 20 x 3.5 cm
(3 versions, each unique)
Copenhagen, Galleri Nicolai Wallner

Thomas Hirschhorn

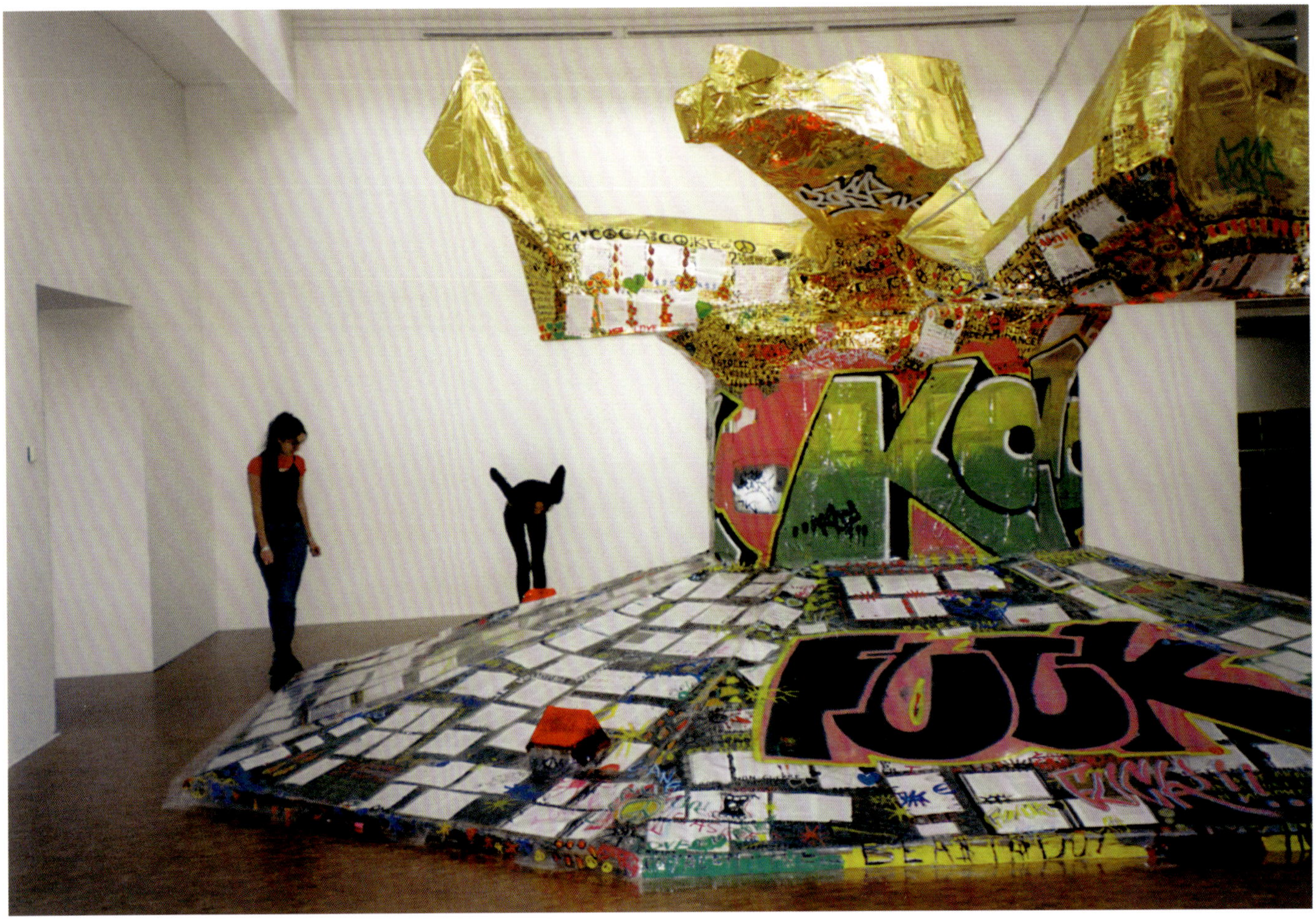

Born in Berne, Switzerland, in 1957. Lives and works in Paris.
Thomas Hirschhorn's sculpture always pursues the precise aim of activating the observer's physical and mental space. Considered one of the leading figures in Relational Art, Hirschhorn plans and creates huge environments that transform exhibition venues, subway corridors, street corners and public gardens into temporary meeting places designed to foster opportunities for social involvement.
Hal Foster has described Hirschhorn's installations as "idea dispensers" halfway between the political agitation kiosks of the Constructivist Gustav Klutsis and the hypertrophic constructions of fragments of memory by Kurt Schwitters. They are designed to inform and educate viewers, prompting reflection and active participation in the debate the artist seeks to develop through them.
In actual fact, Hirschhorn sees art as a political action, a tool to discover the world, confront reality, and develop a critical stance with respect to the age in which we are living. For this reason, his works invade the space hosting them with spray-can graffiti, banners and placards like those carried in protest marches and demonstrations, photographs drawing attention to the endless horrors of our era, symbolic objects (like needles, crutches, chains, and plush toys), books, and photocopies of philosophical, literary, and political texts. They are works already potentially full of voices and designed to acquire a real audio dimension precisely through the comments and observations of the public, who are seen by Hirschhorn as a structural component without which the installation loses its most authentic meaning.
While the subjects that Hirschhorn addresses through his works range from the most atrocious acts of violence to the futile dictates of fashion, they are always of pressing topical relevance, linked to a present that could be different if we were capable of learning from the past. *Chalet Lost History*, the gigantic environment that filled the two floors of Chantal Crousel's Parisian gallery with objects and words in 2004, prompted reflection on the tendency to transform history into an eternal present by constantly repeating its errors and violence. According to Hirschhorn, history is plundered but not understood due to the widespread tendency to appropriate whatever fragments appear necessary, losing both any overall vision and any sense of the real meaning of the

Sculpture Direct, 1999
Cardboard, wood, aluminum foil, gold paper, plastic, tape, light bulbs, 2 videos, and mixed media, dimensions variable
View of the work at the exhibition at the Musée des Beaux-Arts de Nantes, Nantes, 2000

Skulptur-Sortier-Station, Monaco, 1997
Structure in metal and plastic, mixed media, dimensions variable
New York, Barbara Gladstone Gallery

Chalet Lost History, 2004
Cardboard, wood, tape, photographic prints, mixed media, dimensions variable
Paris, Galerie Chantal Crousel

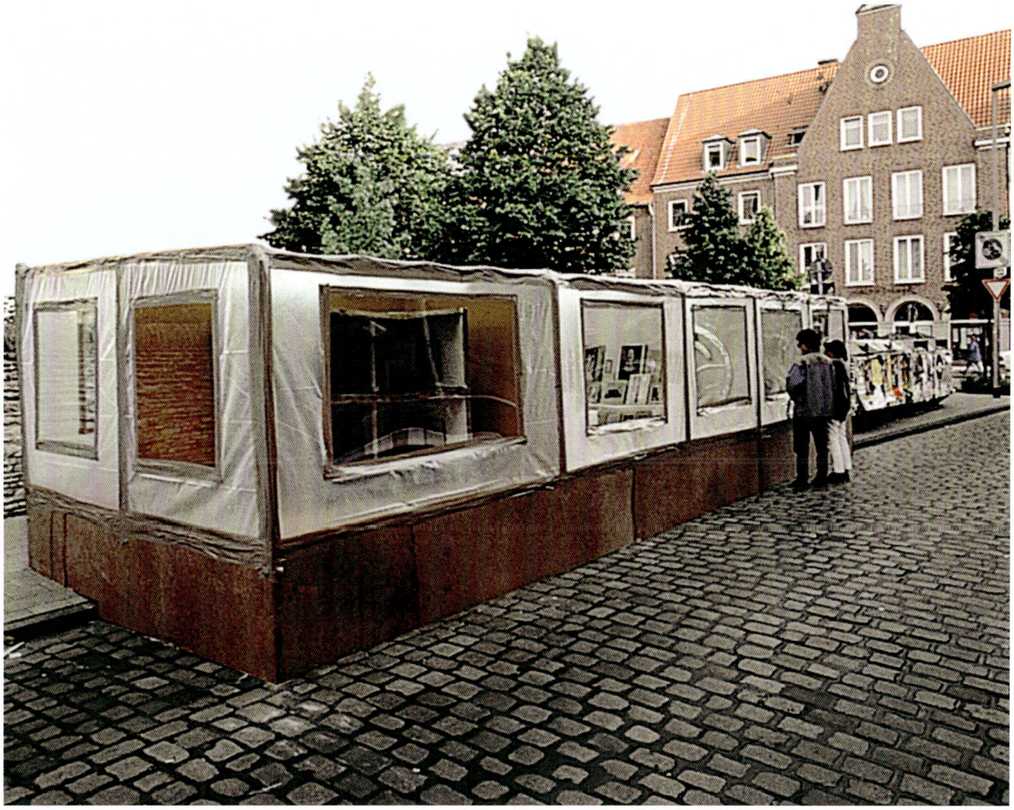

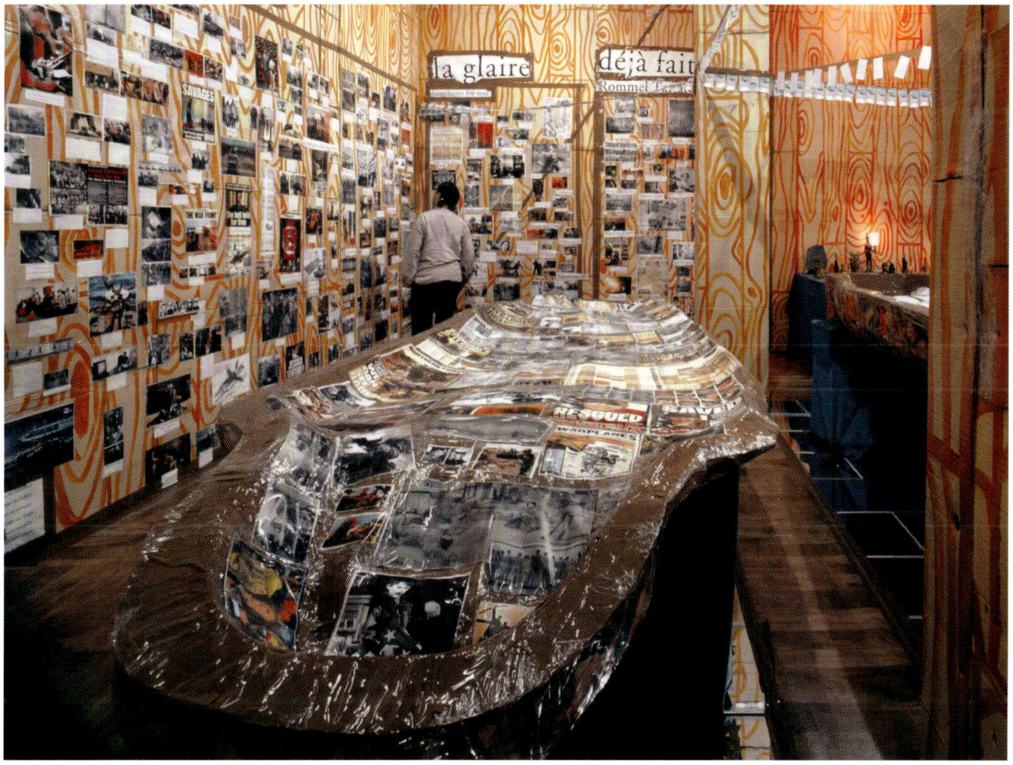

individual events. As he tells us, the inspiration came in this case from images of the pillaging of the Baghdad Archaeological Museum, where the looters drew no distinctions between air conditioners, fans, furniture, plants and objects of inestimable historical and artistic value. The same lack of differentiation between "high" and "low" material is found in Hirschhorn's installation, where books on Middle Eastern art and copies of archaeological artifacts, above all Egyptian, rub shoulders with tacky tourist souvenirs, pyramids made out of packs of cigarettes, and a profusion of pornographic material. The walls are covered with incomplete phrases extrapolated from their context that look like incongruous subtitles for the gory images of the war in Iraq scattered all over the place. Various monitors show video images of archaeological sites, car accidents, and erotic encounters. The entire "chalet" is thus transformed into a chaotic assemblage of contradictory information demonstrating how "history" has now been wiped out by the frenzied and often superficial consumption of objects, images, and words that distinguishes our era. Hirschhorn's art seeks to address this mechanism and act as an antidote against the widespread tendency to give in to globalized communication. It is with educational intentions that the artist uses public places like sidewalks and underpasses to erect temporary "altars" dedicated to artists, writers, and philosophers in order to spread their ideas (*Ingeborg Bachmann Altar*, 1998; *Raymond Carver Altar*, 1999) and creates installations of devastating visual and emotional impact to address issues of urgent social and environmental importance such as the massacre of seals for the fur trade (*Das Auge*, 2008). The same aims also underpin Hirschhorn's examination of current events and the history of our time from unusual angles, as exemplified by the intense metaphor of a tear of blood to commemorate the tragedy of September 11 (*Twin Tear*, 2004). Hirschhorn's decision to build his environments out of cheap and perishable materials like cardboard, papier-mâché, and adhesive tape is linked to the programmatically temporary character of the installations, which thus come in many cases to take on not only the communicative and social functions but also the appearance of carnival floats. Though nearly always devoid of any satirical and sardonic element, Hirschhorn's works can in fact also serve as a way for common people to make their voices heard and protest against the arrogance of the ruling class. (*P.V.*)

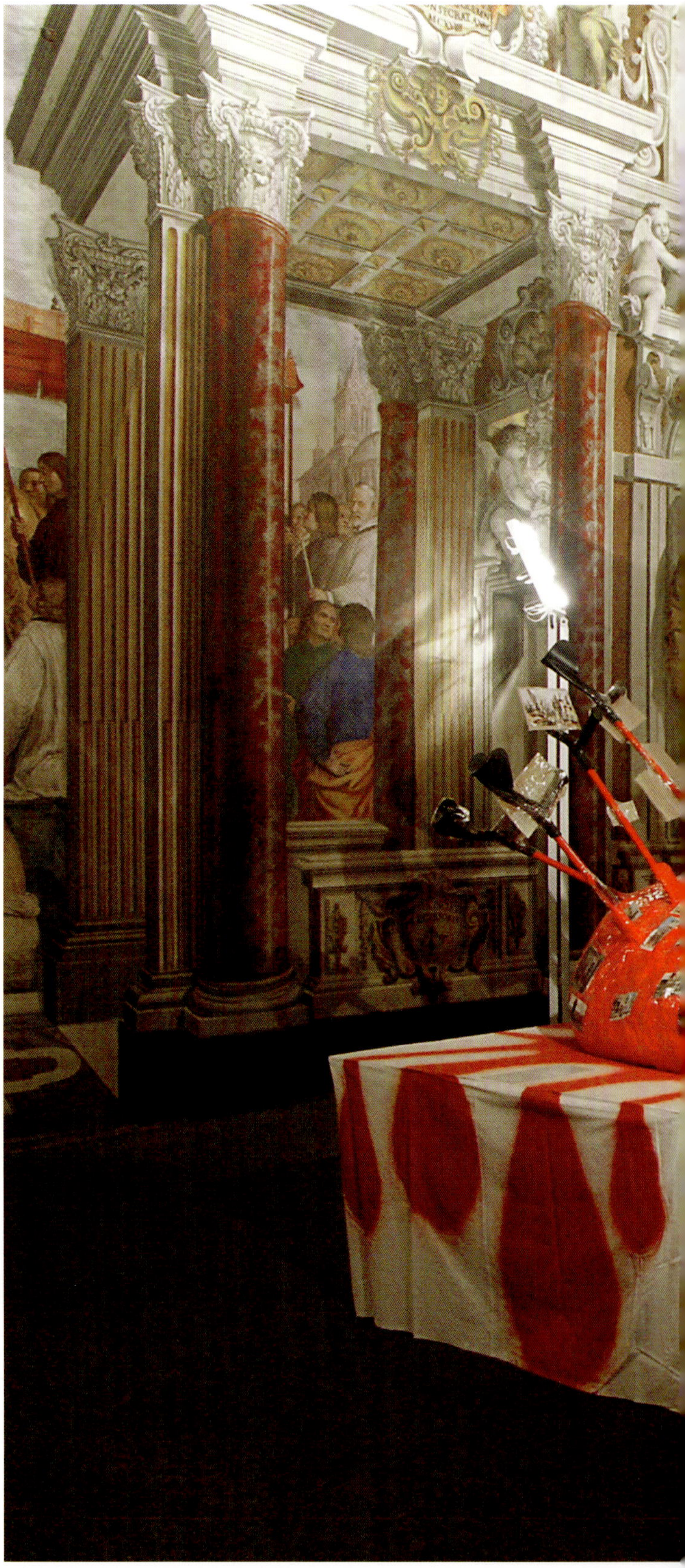

Twin Tear, 2004
Wood, cardboard, screws, adhesive tape, plastic sheet, crutches, prints, fabric, red spray paint, plastic containers,250 x 505 x 245 cm
New York, Barbara Gladstone Gallery

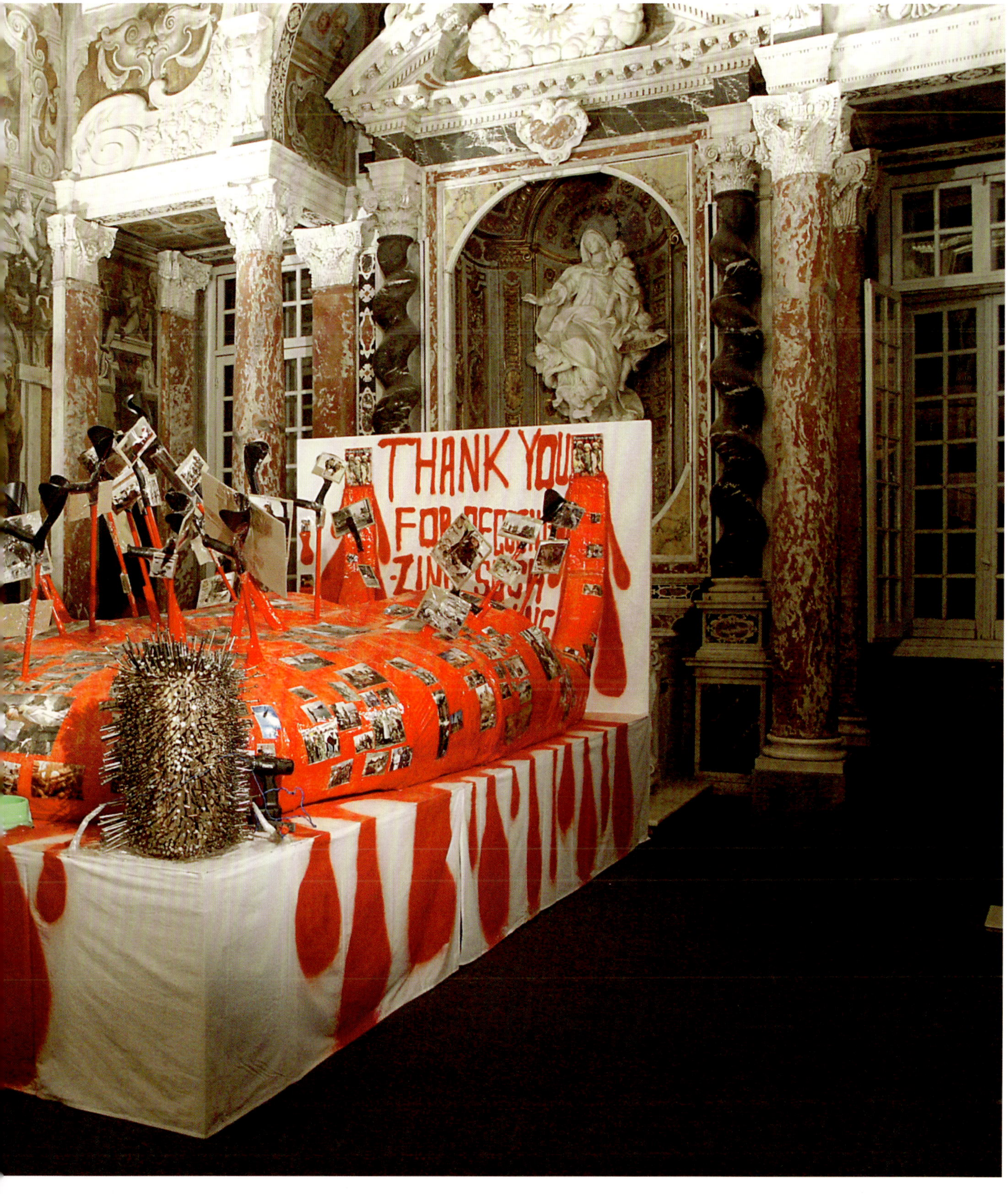

Carsten Höller

Born in Brussels in 1961. Lives and works in Stockholm.
Having taken up art after scientific studies and a doctorate on olfactory communication between insects, Carsten Höller produces what he calls "confusion machines", devices designed to create momentary states of disorientation or slight hallucination in the spectator. It is indeed with the curiosity of an entomologist that Höller studies the physiological sensations experienced by the spectator after interacting with his complex technological contrivances in a sort of scientific laboratory.
Installations that physically involve the spectator or interactive sculptural objects, Höller's works are often playful and irreverent, designed to induce states of excitation, sensory distortion, doubt, and disorientation in psychological temporal, and spatial terms. While making the spectators the object of the artist's investigations, his guinea pigs as it were, these states of confusion also turn them at the same time with their subjective experiences into unique and unrepeatable protagonists of the work.
One example is the gigantic *Spinning Top* (1996) designed to hold one person at a time.
On reaching the maximum speed of rotation, the device can be released from the elastic bands that power it and spin freely in space. During its movement, the occupant can also make coffee with a small machine installed for that purpose.
The artist's work is epitomized by the *Synchro System* project devised in 2000 for the Fondazione Prada: a "village of possibility" made up of psychophysical stimuli and interactive devices; a maze-like pathway along which the spectator is subjected to a series of different stimuli and disorienting situations caused by flashing lights, devices that alter the bodily sensations, dark and confusing places, and environments that produce hallucinatory effects. Visitors lose their way along the 30-meter *Gantenbein Corridor* (2000) as the light gradually dims to the point of total darkness. The title of the work refers to the book *Mein Name sei Gantenbein* by Max Frisch, where the main character pretends to be blind in order to observe the difference between what people say and how they actually act when they think they are not being watched. *Upside Down Mushroom Room* is a room in which huge reproductions of twelve poisonous mushrooms hanging from the ceiling rotate at different speeds to produce hallucinatory effects.
The title *Synchro System* is a

Sliding Doors, 2003
Glass and aluminum,
open 240 x 462 cm, variable length
London, Tate Modern,
Presented by Tate Members 2006

Spinning Top, 1996
Steel, acrylic glass, Lycra, rubber, fiberglass, wood, electric battery, coffee machine, ceramic cups,
150 x 180 x 150 cm
Courtesy of the artist and Esther Schipper, Berlin

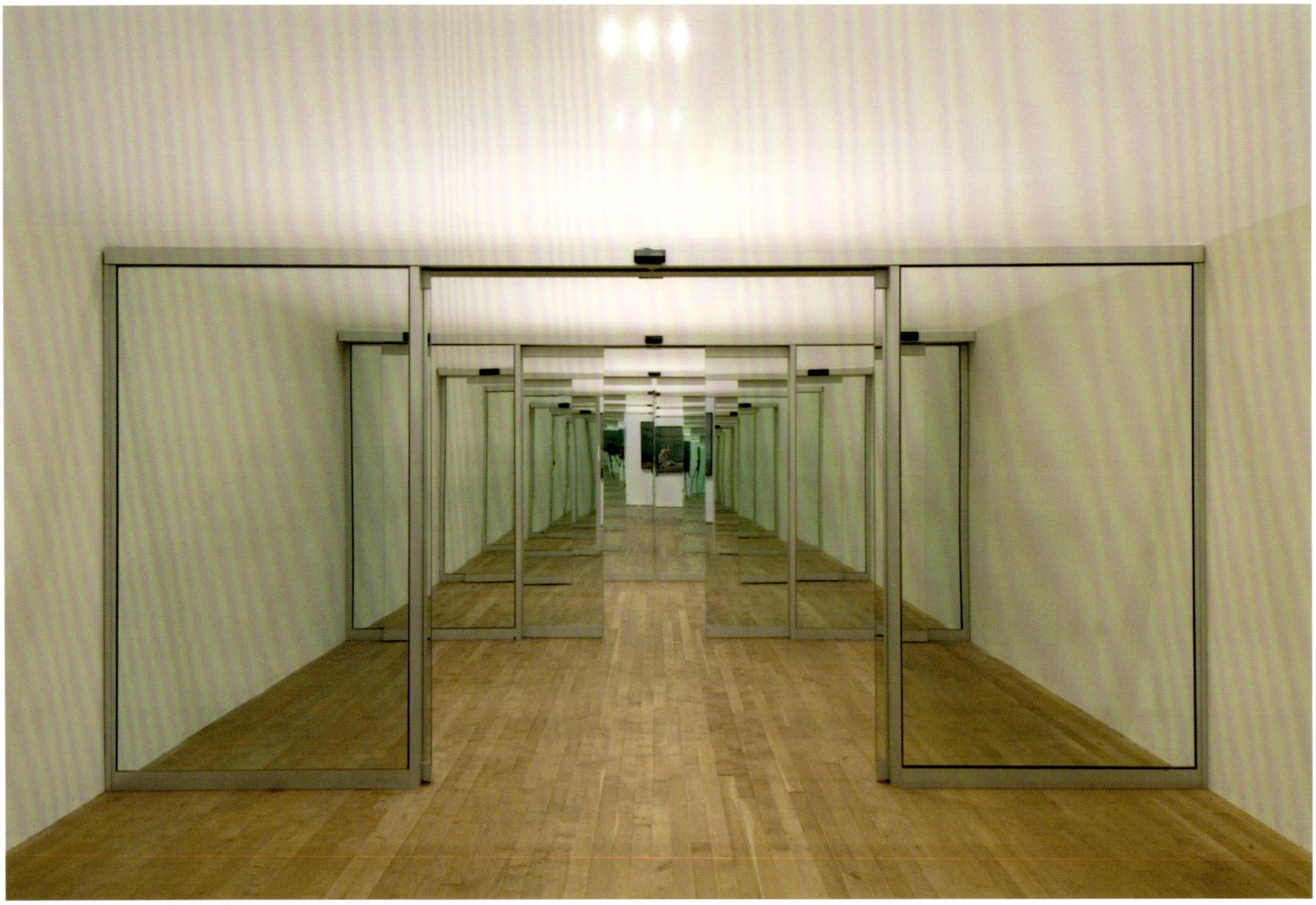

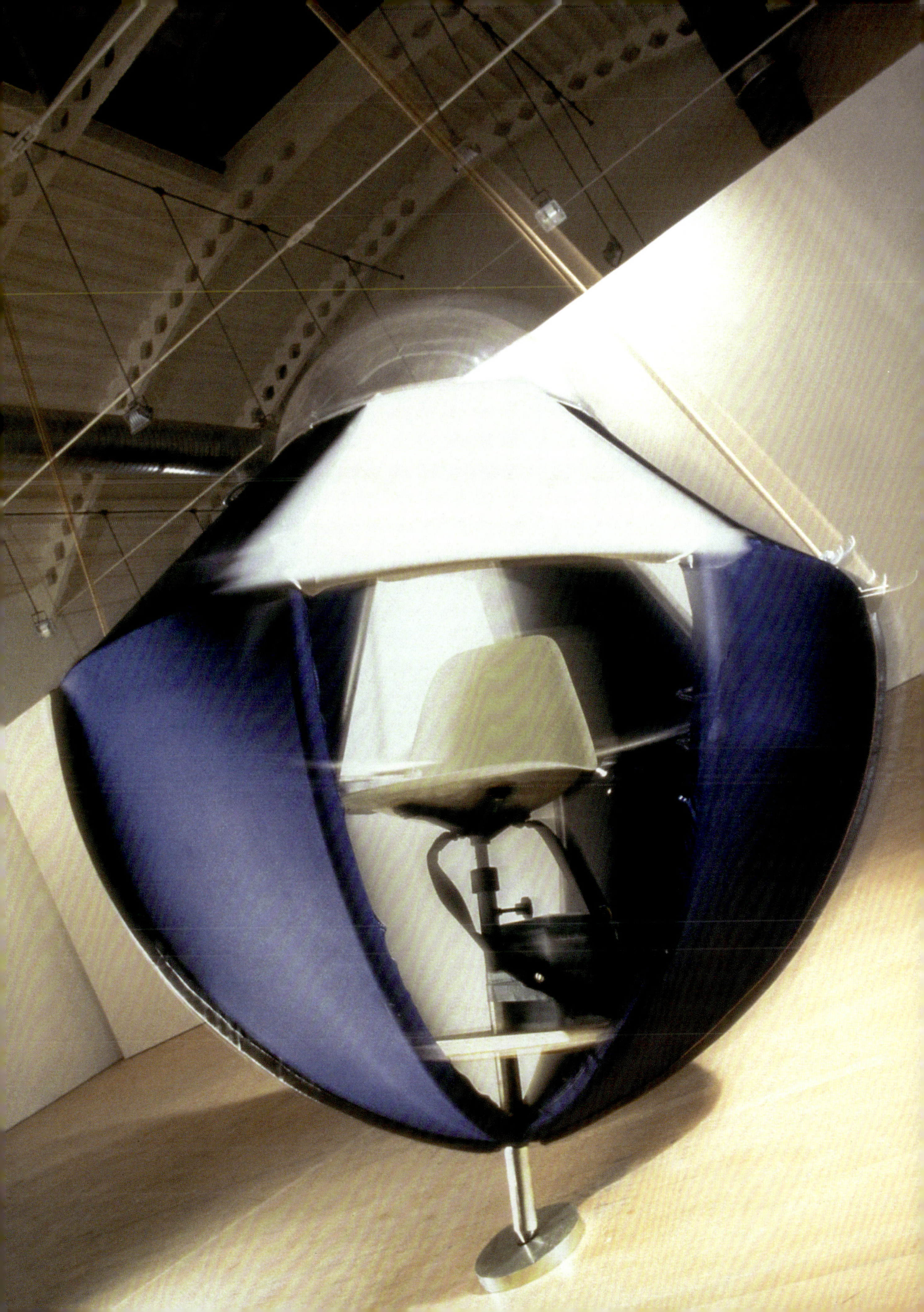

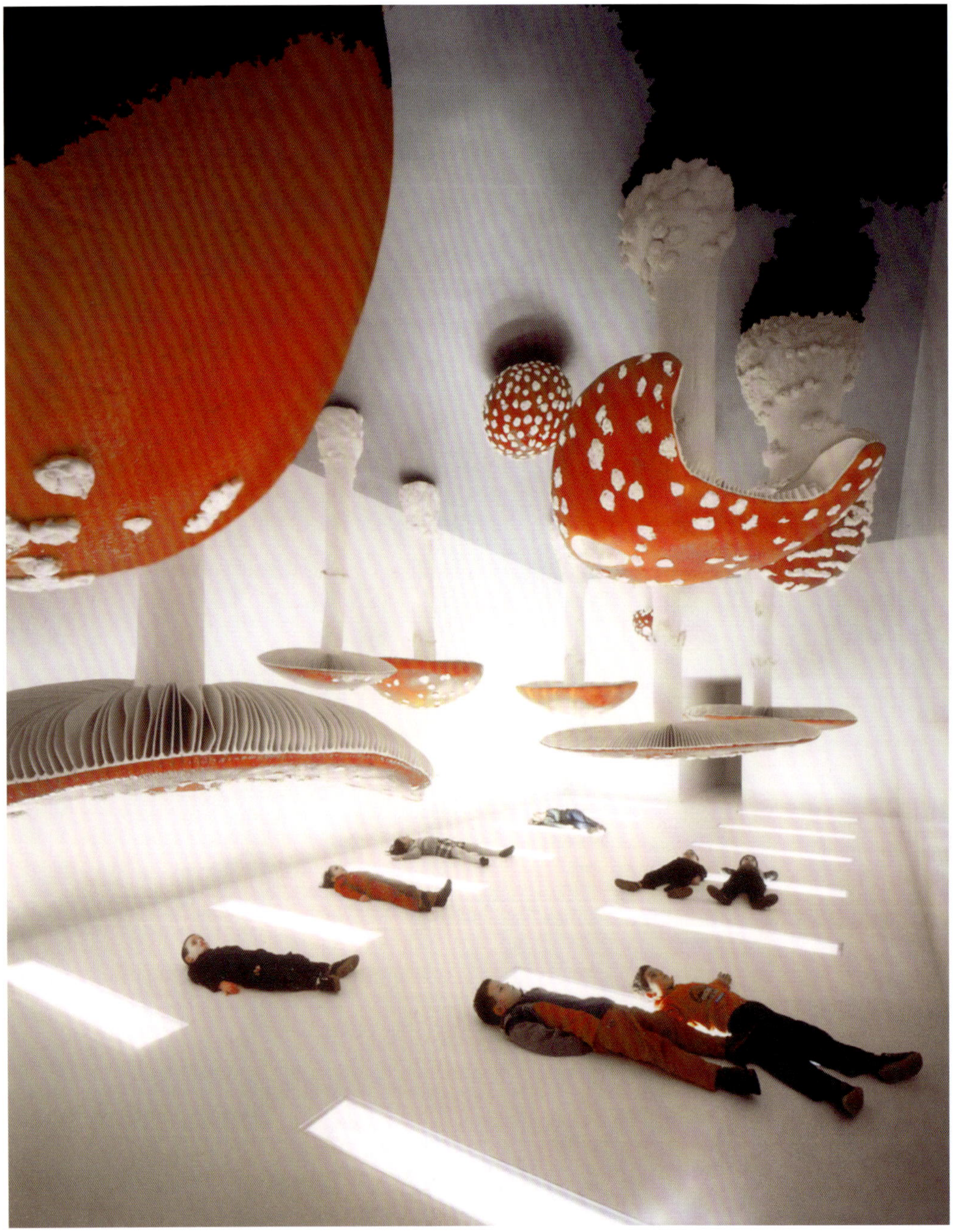

Upside Down Mushroom Room, 2000
Resin, plastic, motors for movement, dimensions variable
View of the installation realized in 2000 at the Fondazione Prada, Milan
Milan, Fondazione Prada

Test Site, 2006
Aluminum, Plexiglas, dimensions variable
View of the installation realized in 2006 at Tate Modern, London for *The Unilever Series*

reference to the synchronization between the visitor and the work, the human being and the "confusion machine". Höller's devices only work if they achieve synchronization with the public.
The artist always adopts the same strategy of defamiliarizing reality and eliminating the natural dimension so as to foster a condition of physical and psychological disorientation in the spectator.
Sliding Doors (2003) is a series of automatic sliding doors with mirror surface that form a long corridor in which the human figure undergoes multiplication leading to the loss of identity.
One of Höller's most sensational and imposing installations, *Test Site* (2006), consists of five tubular slides of aluminum and plexiglas, five "participative" sculptures set up in 2006 in the Turbine Hall of Tate Modern in London. Starting from different levels of the museum, these unusual means of transport enable users to make descents of up to 26 meters, thus altering their relations with the usual categories of space, time and speed.
Höller had already created two giant slides, *Valerio I* and *Valerio II*, in 1998 for the Berlin Biennial, the second of which projected from the façade of the exhibition venue and enabled visitors to get from one floor of the building to another very quickly and experience a state of total spatiotemporal disorientation. As the artist explained in this connection, "I'm interested in the aspect of letting go. Once you let go, you travel without motivation to some specific place. It's a very special state of mind."
An artist-researcher and original leading figure in Relational Art, Höller extends the field of art to include unusual and surprising experiments that prompt rethinking of all preconceived ideas as regards perception of the real world.
(*L.L.*)

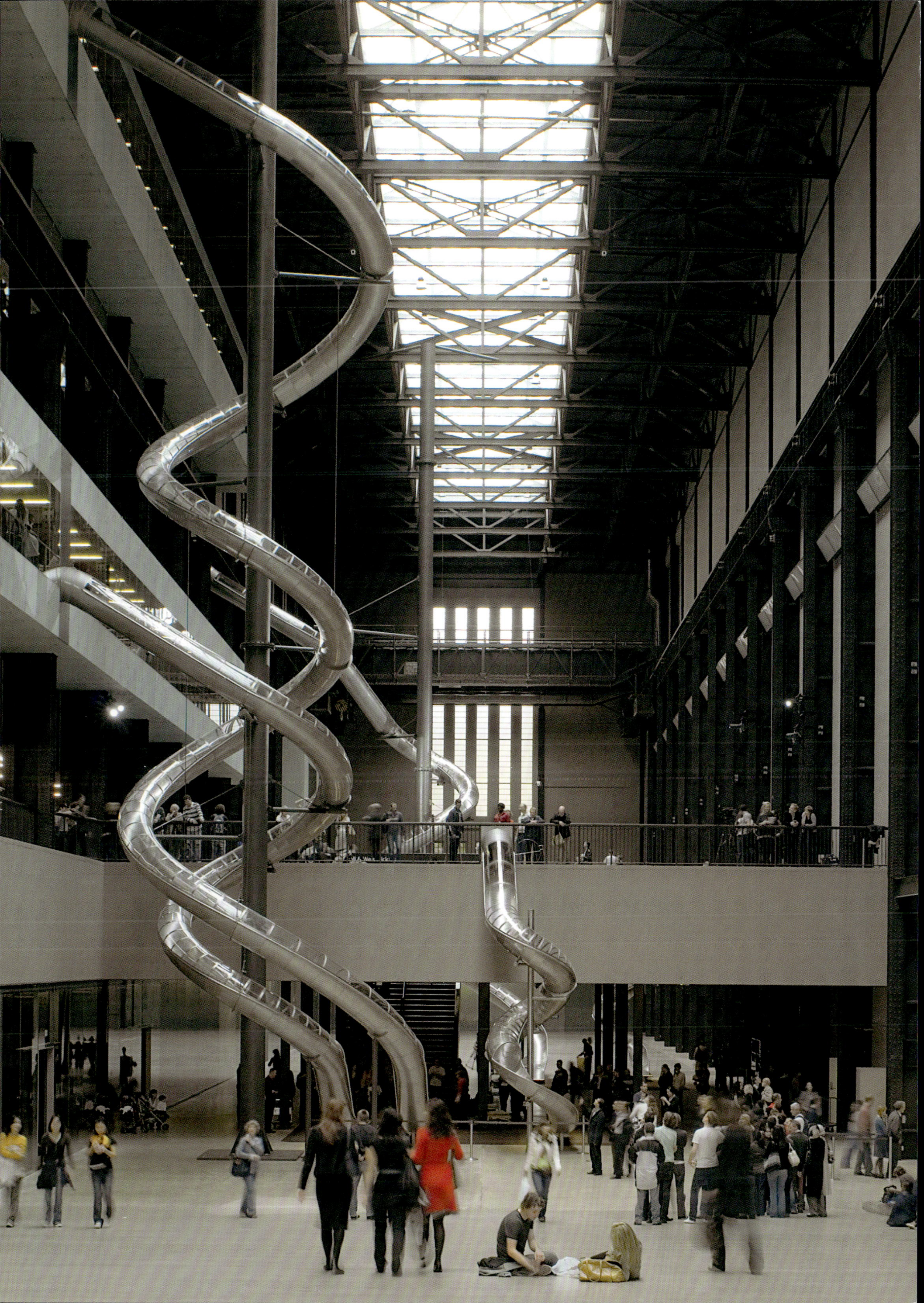

Huang Yong Ping

Born in Xiamen, China, in 1954. Lives and works in Paris.
Since the mid-1980s, when he founded the Xiamen Dada movement in China, Huang Yong Ping has endeavored to forge links between key aspects of Western avant-garde art and Chinese philosophical and cultural traditions.
Influenced above all by Duchamp and Beuys, Huang Yong Ping takes traditional objects and symbolic animals from his native culture and endows them with new and modern significance through obvious references to history, economics and politics.
The disorienting effect of this coexistence of codes belonging to different systems of communication can be seen, for example, in the installation *Intestins de Bouddha* (2006), where four black vultures – real stuffed birds – feed on the intestines of a massive wooden Buddha beneath the gaze of a white vulture to one side.
On the one hand, the work alludes to the tension between China and Tibet. On the other, the subtle parallels drawn between the tortured Buddha and Christ pierced by a spear on the cross recall the common substratum to the two great monotheistic religions.
Resident in Paris since 1989, the year of the dramatic clashes on Tiananmen Square in Beijing, Huang Yong Ping took part the same year in the large-scale exhibition *Magiciens de la Terre* at the Centre Pompidou, the event that opened the debate on post-colonialism and marked the birth of interest in Eastern artists on the part of the Western world of art.
He has since been involved in the major international events and held various solo shows, first in Europe and then in the United States, where he won definitive critical acclaim in 2005 with a retrospective at the Walker Art Center in Minneapolis.
It was also in the United States, at the Gladstone Gallery, New York, that Huang Yong Ping created one of his most impressive works, using the traditional Chinese techniques of pottery and porcelain to construct monumental models of the Coliseum and the Pentagon.
Ambivalent symbols of cultural progress and imperialist violence, both buildings are reinvented by the artist and transformed into harmless nurseries growing plants of various species, thus reflecting hope in the possibility of peaceful coexistence between all the peoples of the world.
(P.V.)

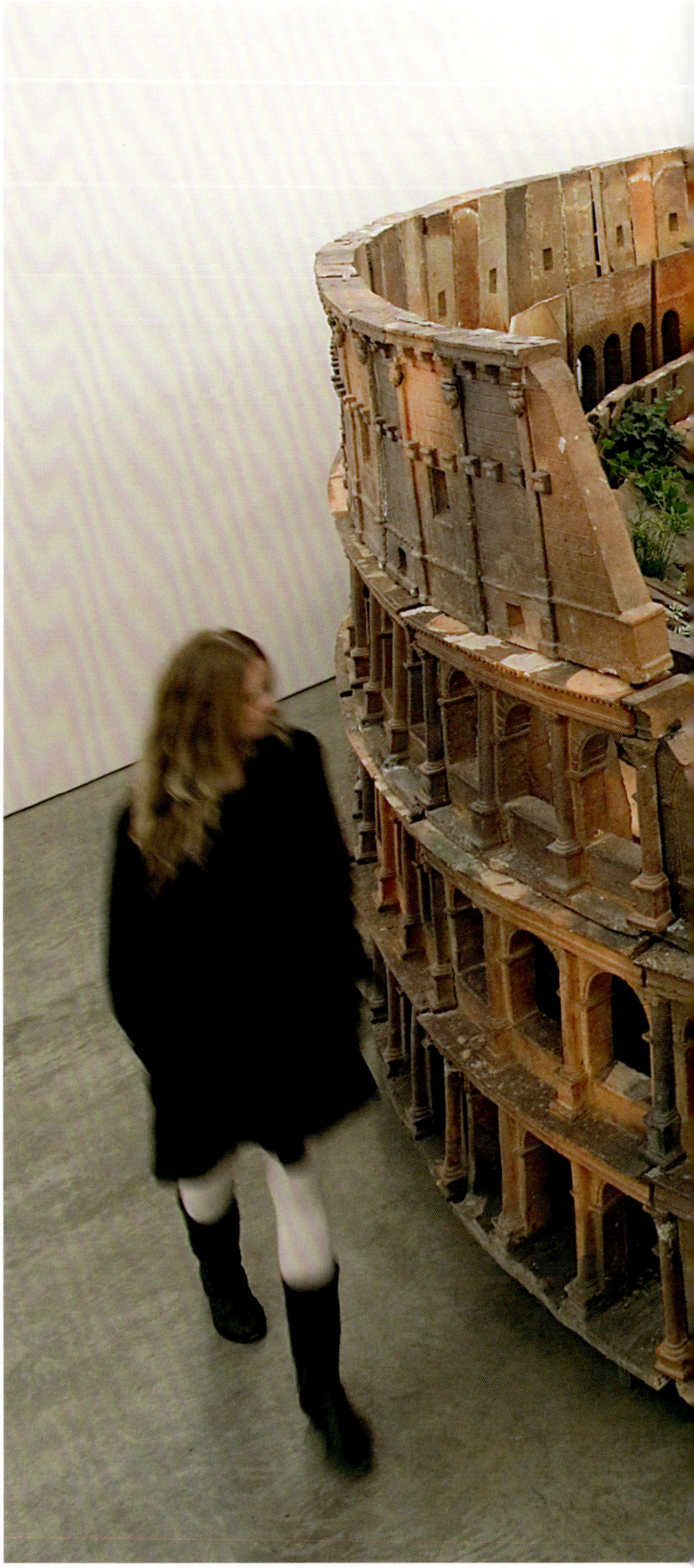

Colosseum, 2007
Ceramic, soil, and plants,
226.1 x 551.2 x 758.2 cm
Courtesy Gladstone Gallery,
New York

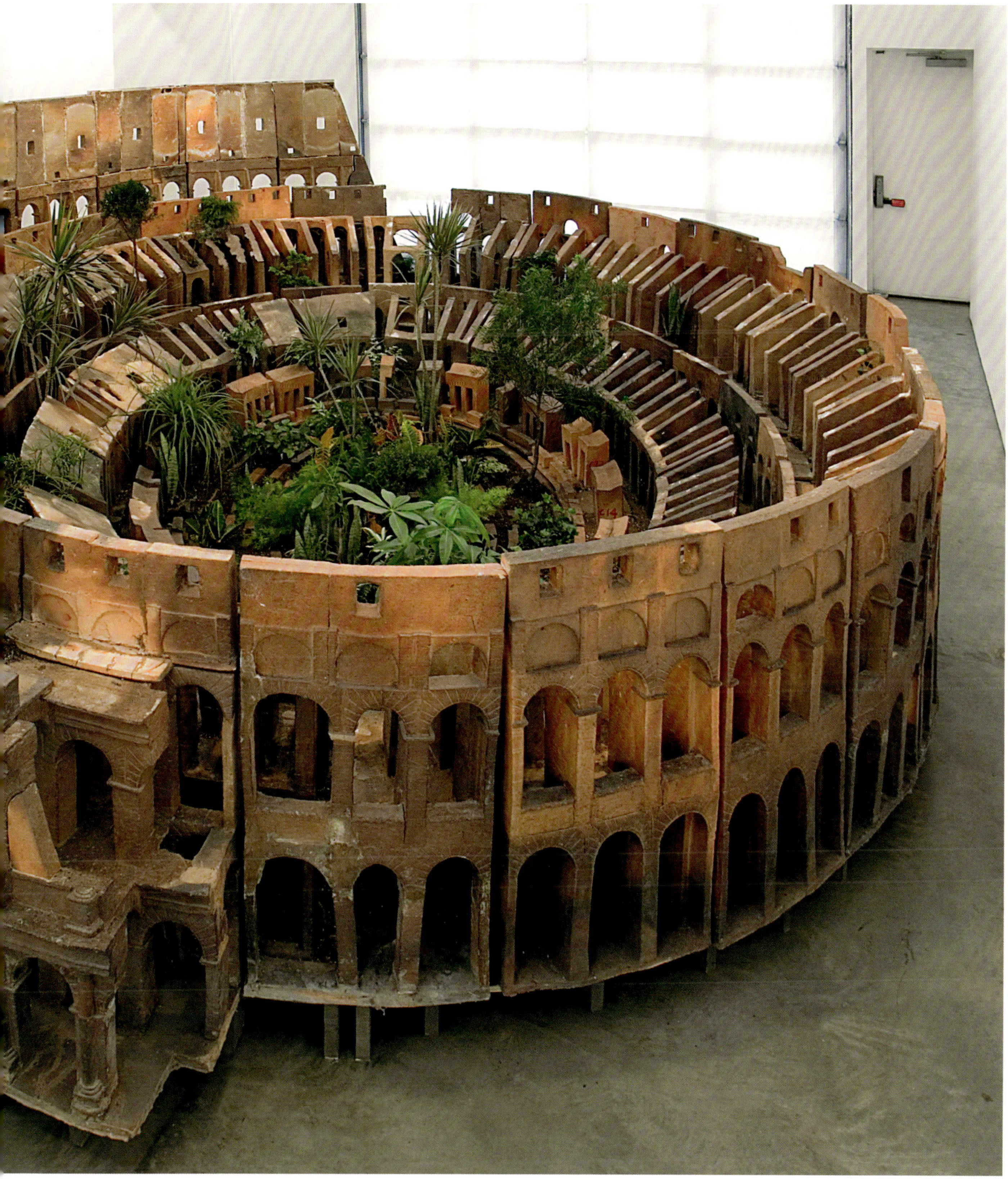

Eva Marisaldi

Born in Bologna in 1966. Lives and works in Bologna.
The multidisciplinary work of this Bolognese artist takes emotional and practical aspects of the human sphere in everyday life as its starting point to address the relationship between the viewer and the work of art. While the results are often wholly unexpected and in no way connected with reality, it is usually aspects of a playful or fairytale nature that come to predominate.
Pixeland, for example, involves colored ceramic objects the same size and shape as normal paper confetti scattered on the ground as though thrown during carnival celebrations. The material paradox of the objects precludes any possibility of functional use as well as simple formal mimesis. The confetti cannot have been thrown, since they would have been shattered, and yet they are placed exactly as though they really had been. Moreover, the very fact of their being small-sized elements so closely linked to a circumscribed and identifiable event rules out any further hypothetical reading to account for their presence.
Absurdity also makes its appearance in the video *Porto fuori* (2007), first and foremost with the explicit play on words in the title, the meaning of which changes with the position of its two component terms. While *fuori* means *outside*, it is above all *porto* that lends itself to misunderstanding in that it means *port* or *harbor* as a noun and *I Bring* or *I Carry* as a verb.
The suggestion of movement is, however, predominant in both terms, just like the idea of going away and the juxtaposition of two environments as different as land and sea. It is on this marked contrast and the presence of a geographical context connecting the two elements that the content of Marisaldi's video plays. It is in fact a sort of window looking onto the harbor in Ravenna, where a self-propelled "marching percussion band" covers the length of the dock before disappearing.
The fact that the object moves at a faster speed than the ship seen in the distance comes to constitute both a physical reference to reality and a disorienting detail of a universe whose laws are turned completely upside-down.
(*F.T.*)

Pixeland, 2005
Porcelain confetti,
dimensions variable
(installation detail)
Brescia, Galleria Massimo Minini

Porto fuori, 2007
Video installation,
dimensions variable
Rome, Galleria SALES

Birthday Party, 2006
Wood, fabric, servo motors,
computers, lights, sound,
70 x 70 x 70 cm
Bologna, MAMbo – Museo d'Arte Moderna di Bologna, UniCredit Group Collection; MAMbo – Museo d'Arte Moderna di Bologna

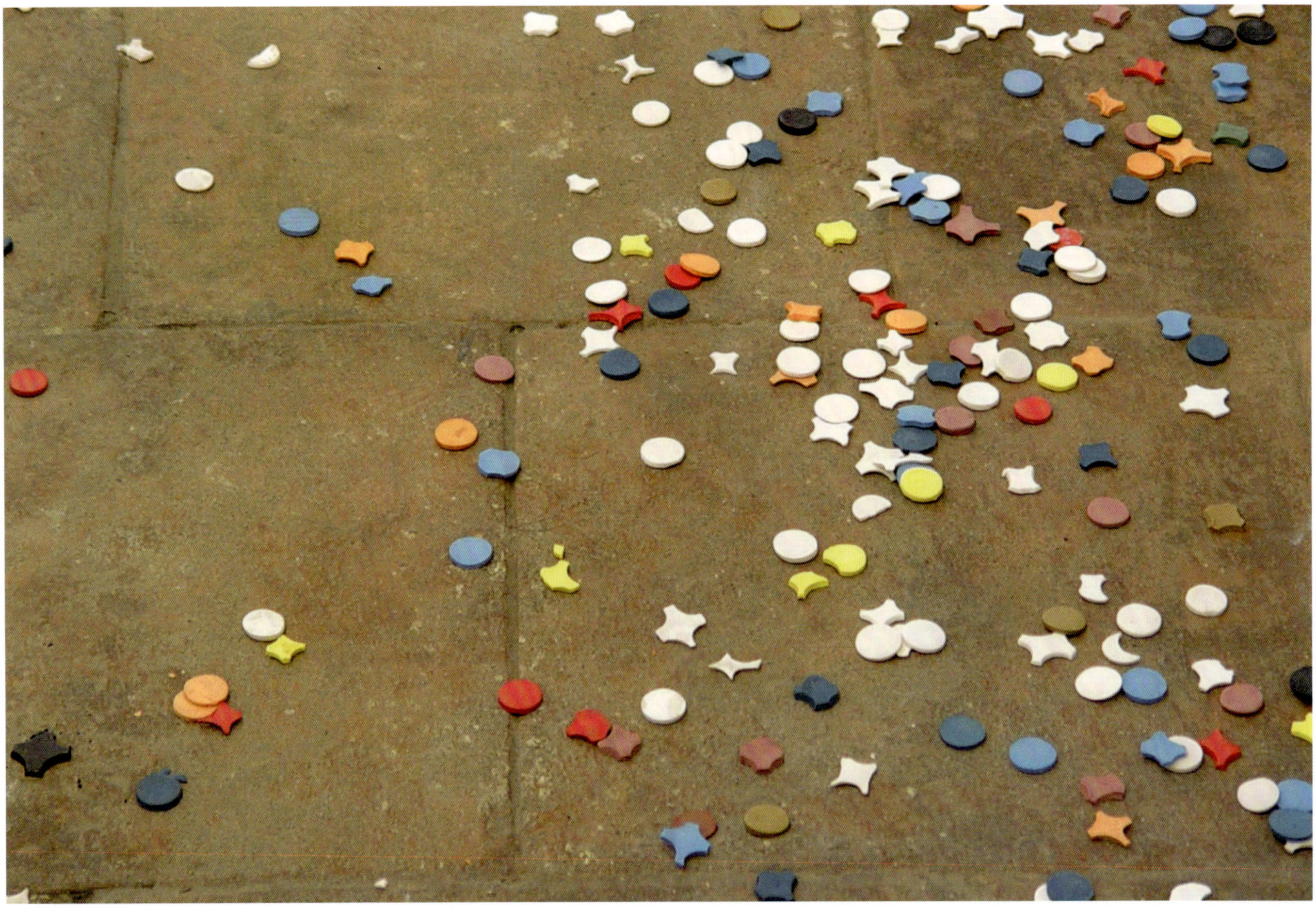

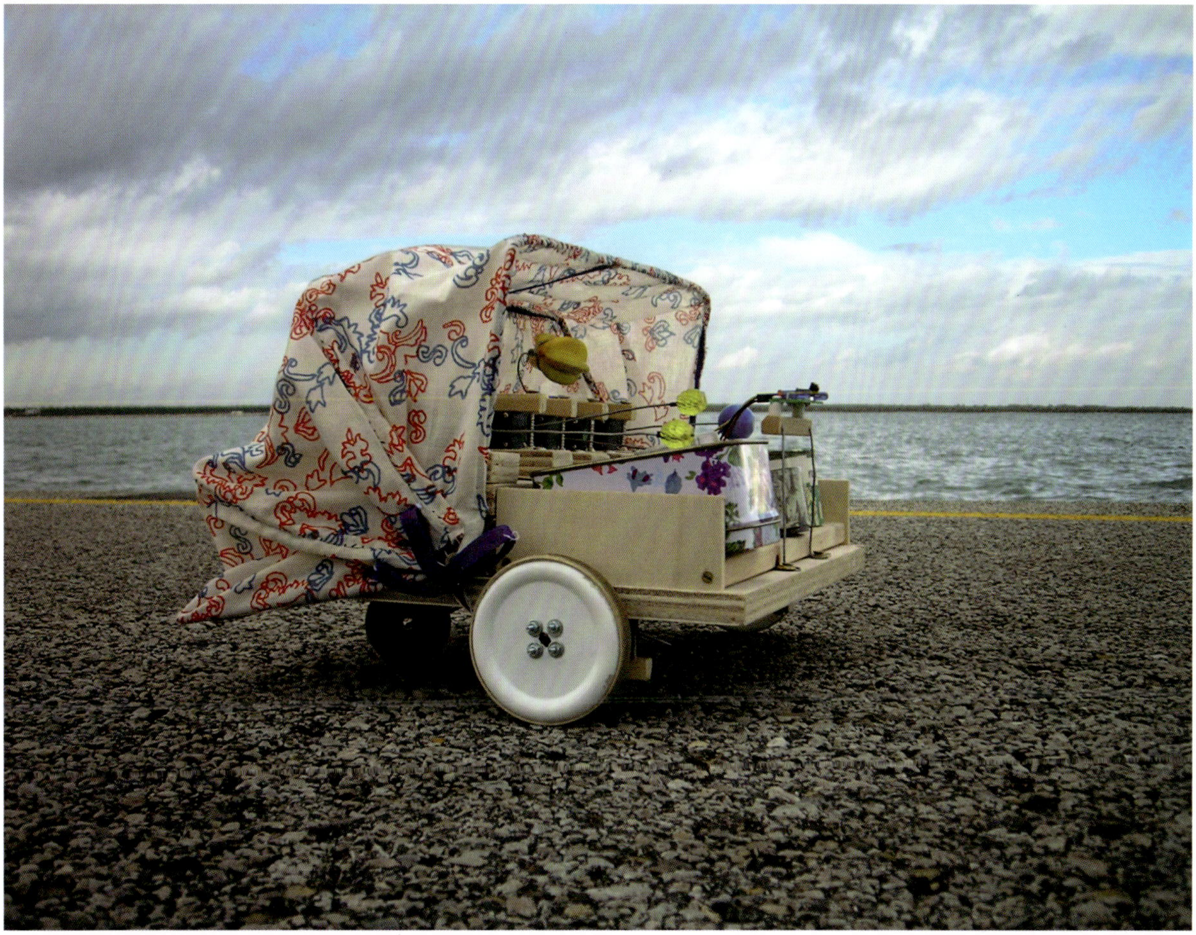

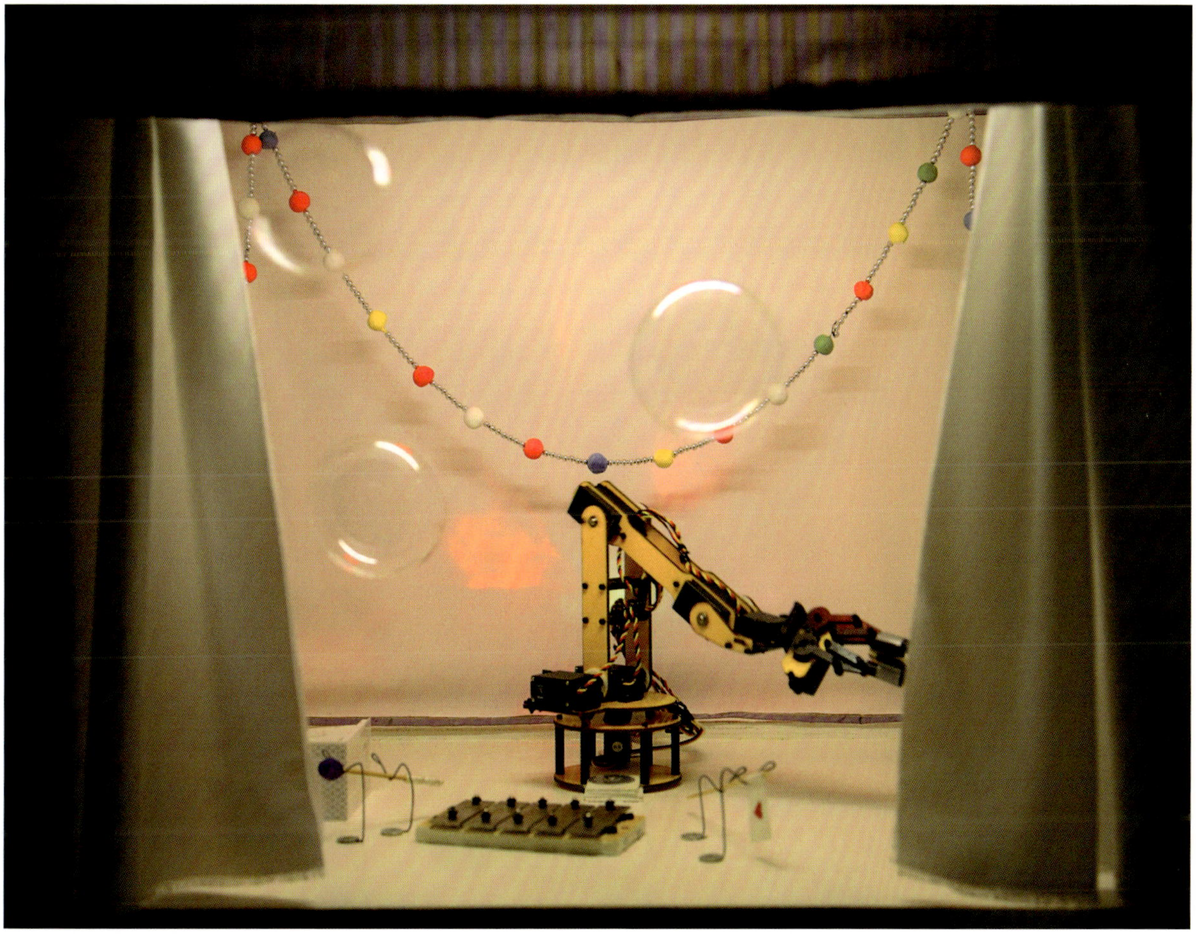

Lucy + Jorge Orta

Born respectively in Sutton Coldfield (UK), in 1966, and Rosario, Argentina, in 1953, Lucy and Jorge Orta have been working together since 1991. They live and work in Paris.

Jorge Orta was already an established artist when he met and married Lucy, a British fashion designer in Paris. Jorge studied art and architecture in Argentina and created various works of public art during the Videla regime aimed at arousing and stimulating a collective voice and transforming society through art. This thrust remains central to his work with Lucy, which took concrete shape in 1991 with the opening of their first joint studio, the Studio-Orta (followed by the Dairy at Marne, La Vallée, in 2002). Knocking down the barriers between art, design, and architecture, Lucy and Jorge create research projects organized in large cycles to experiment with new forms of communal life and management of natural resources. As they stated in an interview, "Together, we would like to become active agents in a world that we are all dreaming of."

This aim is already evident in *Refuge Wear* (1992–1998) and *Body Architecture* (1994–1998), series of garments designed as portable homes and shelters in an effort to reread the basic structure of sociality by addressing the requirements of the most disadvantaged members of the community, namely the homeless. As Jerome Sans points out, "Survival is the new slogan of the decade. By involving individuals in difficulty, whether isolated or as part of a group, and encouraging them to participate in collective actions consisting notably of producing Refuge Wear or Survival Kits, the artist clearly raises the question of the citizen, underlining his role as a part of the whole." The focus of attention shifted with *Nexus Architecture* (1994–2002) to the social dimension, the interdependence of fellow citizens that becomes a physical tie, the creation of a "pack".

While works of this type can be exhibited, they must first be used. It is therefore hardly surprising that urban action and collective performance should be Lucy and Jorge Orta's primary forms of display. The focus on habitation has since broadened to include projects on the responsible use of resources, war and its consequences, and mobility and immigration as key issues of the immediate future. The artists seek to respond to these problems with the visionary ability of the imagination but also in concrete terms. *HortiRecycling* is a recycling program for waste food, which is collected, preserved, and consumed during banquet-performances, and *OrtaWater* a cycle of works involving the purification and manual distribution of water, the management of which is destined to become one of the crucial issues in the near future.

The *Antarctica* project began with the artists' participation on an expedition to this continent, which they see potentially as the country of those with no country, those who have fled from their homeland with no passport, but also in general the solution to a whole series of problems raised by globalization, including migration, climatic change, and the violation of human rights.

(*D.Q.*)

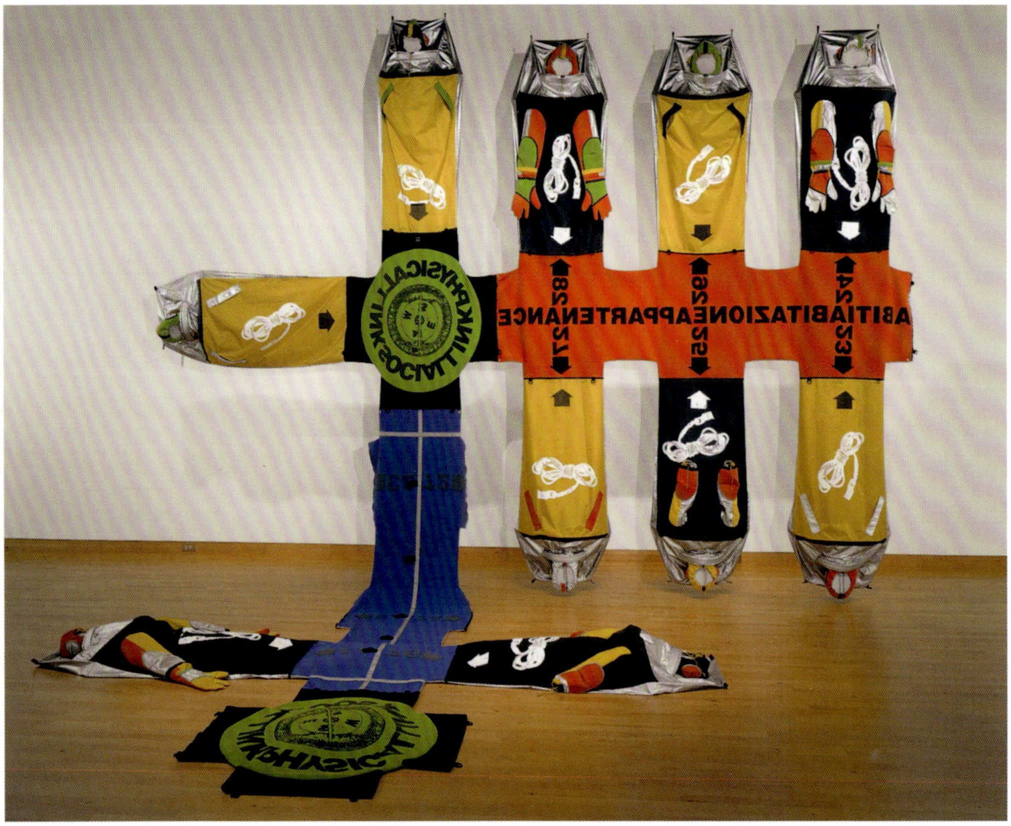

Connector Mobile Village I+II, 2001
Aluminum-coated polyester, reversible Solden Lycra, open cell polyurethane, silkscreen print, zips, 5.7 x 7 m
View of the installation realized in 2001 at the South Florida Contemporary Art Museum, Tampa
Courtesy Galleria Continua, San Gimignano/Beijing/Le Moulin

Fallujah – M.I.U., 2007
Military trailer, epoxy paint, steel, 9 bivouacs, various military surplus objects, 300 x 140 x 189 cm
Courtesy Galleria Continua, San Gimignano/Beijing/Le Moulin

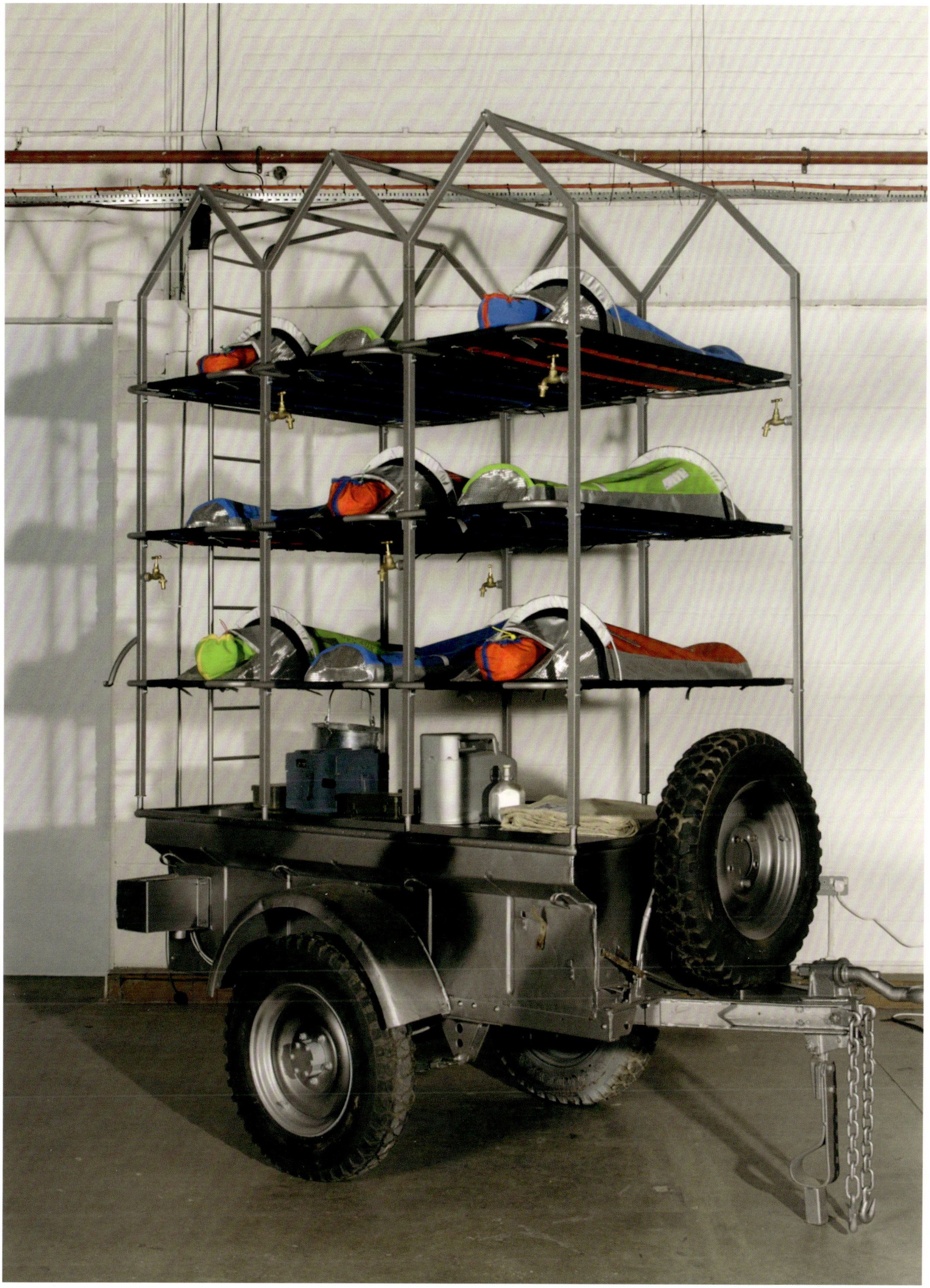

Jorge Pardo

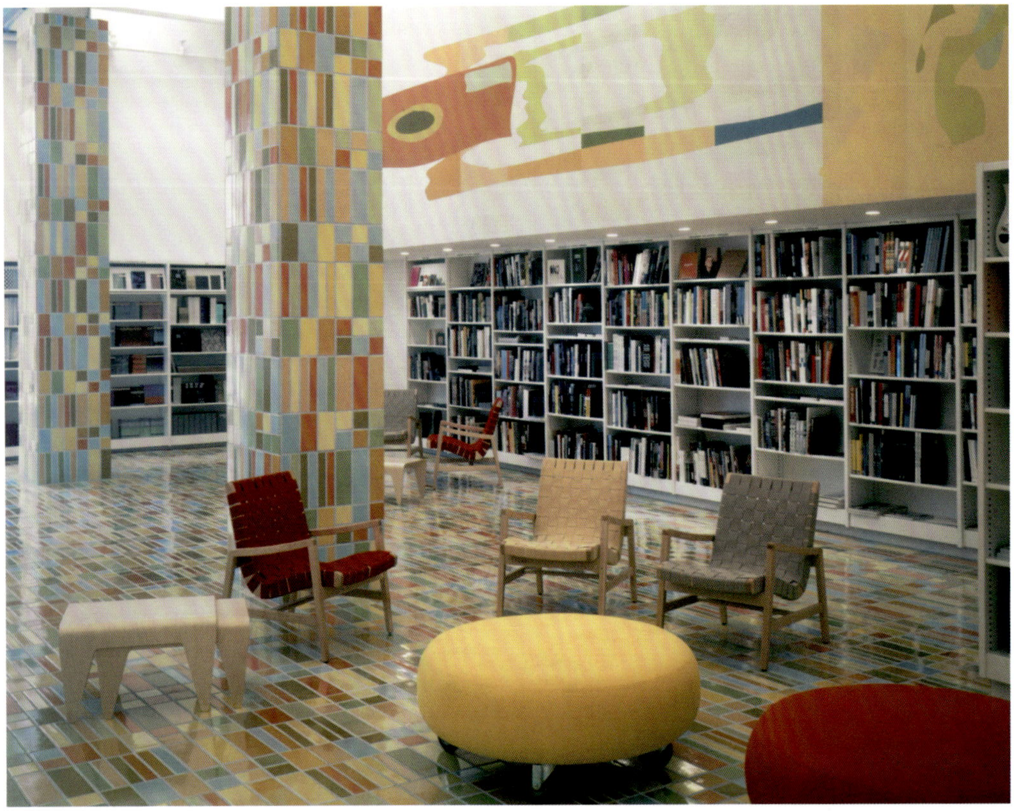

Project, 2000
Furnishings, books, materials divided in 3 different environments: atrium, bookshop, gallery, 33 x 33 m
Courtesy Friedrich Petzel Gallery, New York

Halley's, Ikeya – Seki, Encke's, 1996
9 elements, wood, lacquer, glass, metal, electrical components, dimensions variable
Courtesy Friedrich Petzel Gallery, New York

Born in Havana in 1963. Lives and works in Los Angeles.
The child of Cuban immigrants, Jorge Pardo grew up in Chicago and studied at the Art Center College of Design in Pasadena.
His work is an interesting example of the reappraisal of the forms and ambitions of modernism that played such an important role in the art of the 1990s, even though, as we read in the press release for a show of 1994, Pardo "takes the modernist belief that form follows function to such an extreme that the utopian desire is always in danger of collapse by its own rules." He makes chairs, tables, lamps, wall clocks, and doors, works in interior design and decoration, designs boats and even houses, as on the occasion of his show at the Los Angeles Museum of Contemporary Art in 1998, when he planned and built a house on the sea – *4166 Sea View Lane* – which then became *his* home.
Interweaving art, architecture, and design, Pardo explores the boundaries between the work of art and the everyday object, aesthetics and functionality, exhibition space and recreational space, art and life.
While endowed with immediate aesthetic appeal, his works constitute a meta-reflection on their own identity and the nature of art at the same time. As Kate Bush points out, "Furniture design also supplies Pardo with a useful second language, a readymade vernacular with its own formal values and visual syntax, through which to test the conventional limits of sculpture. Pardo colonises this language as an artist in order to give his audience a familiar way into the work." Much the same could be said of his numerous public projects, which range from urban furnishings (the lighting installed in Liverpool in 2004) to the design of cafés and restaurants and the building of a boat in 1997.
Rather than adopting the syntax of the readymade to introduce the everyday object into the space exhibition, Pardo's work as an artist involves confronting the viewer with the paradox of objects that are art and not art at the same time.
(*D.Q.*)

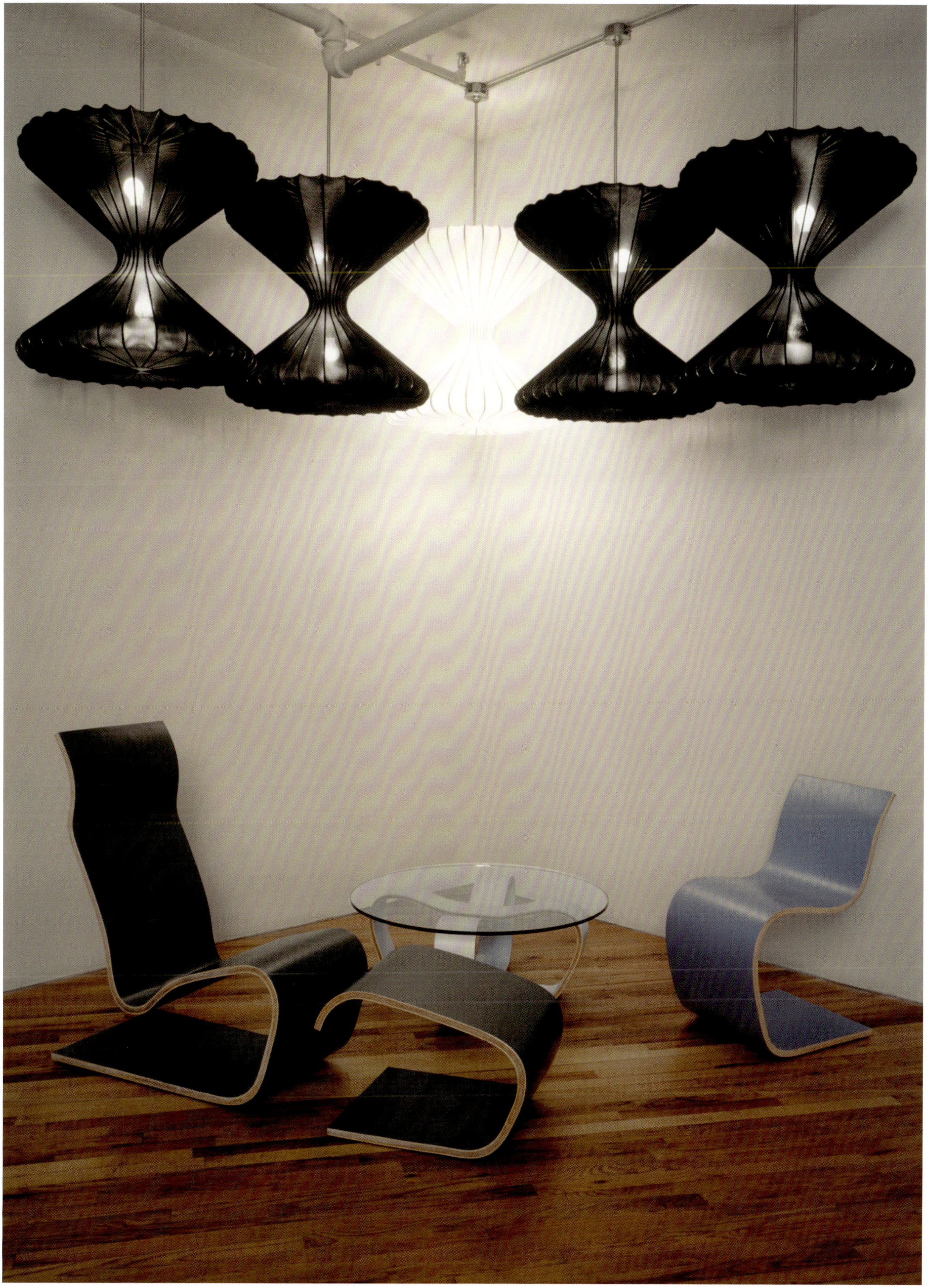

Tomas Saraceno

Cloudy Dunes, 2008
100 meters of electric cables, video projections, dimensions variable
View of the installation realized in 2008 at the Fondazione Edoardo Garrone, Genoa

Biosphere MW32 Air-Port-City, 2007
PVC spheres, ropes, dimensions variable
View of the installation realized in 2007 at Palazzo Ducale, Genoa
Courtesy Galleria Pinksummer, Genoa

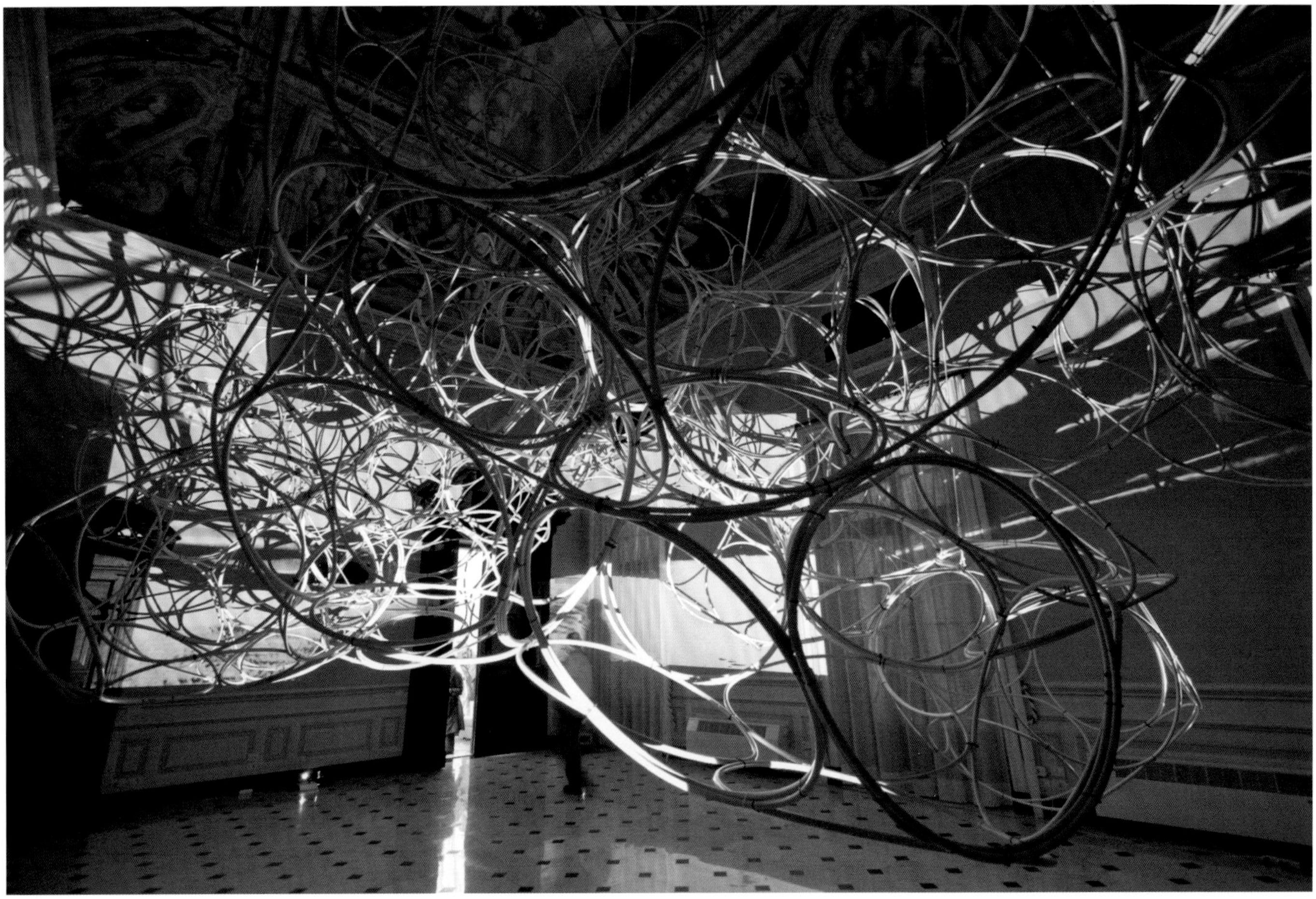

Born in San Miguel de Tucumán, Argentina, in 1973. Lives and works in Germany.
An artist and architect, Tomas Saraceno's work displays an interdisciplinary approach to these two spheres, constantly redefining and reinventing forms of interaction between them and seeking new ways to address his working context. Interested above all in the perceptual processes and critical faculties that guide human beings in their relationship with their surroundings, Saracen endeavors to create "works of synthesis" by bringing scientific, aesthetic, political, and ethical elements together so as to offer the viewer various pathways of knowledge and reflection, above all as regards environmental issues and sustainable development.
His suspended structures and multimedia installations provide an opportunity to consider the conquests of science, the state of the planet, the importance of responsible exploitation of energy, and many other questions of urgent present-day relevance.
A convinced supporter of Buckminster Fuller's view of the world as a system in which every element and living being is connected to every other by an invisible web of relations, Saraceno conceives his works as organisms dependent on the synergy of their component parts. This concept underpins his *Biospheres* and can also be seen, for example, in the installation *Cloudy Dunes*, presented in Genoa in the spring of 2008, where six video projectors transmit images filmed by the artist in the extraordinary natural setting of the Lençóis Maranhenses National Park in the north of Brazil with equipment powered exclusively by clean and renewable energy. The videos are projected onto a gigantic suspended "molecular" structure made out of over 100 meters of tubing for electrical cables and onto the walls of the venue. The work is completed by the spectators, who become an integral part of the installation, interacting with the structure (touching it, moving through it, setting it in motion, casting shadows) and adding the sound of their voices to the background noises of the films shown in the space.
Saraceno's investigations into the possible application of the new technologies for social purposes sometimes overflow into futuristic or utopian dreams, as in the case of the planning of *Air-Port-City*, a nomadic city suspended in mid-air that changes shape and merges with others like a cloud.
(*P.V.*)

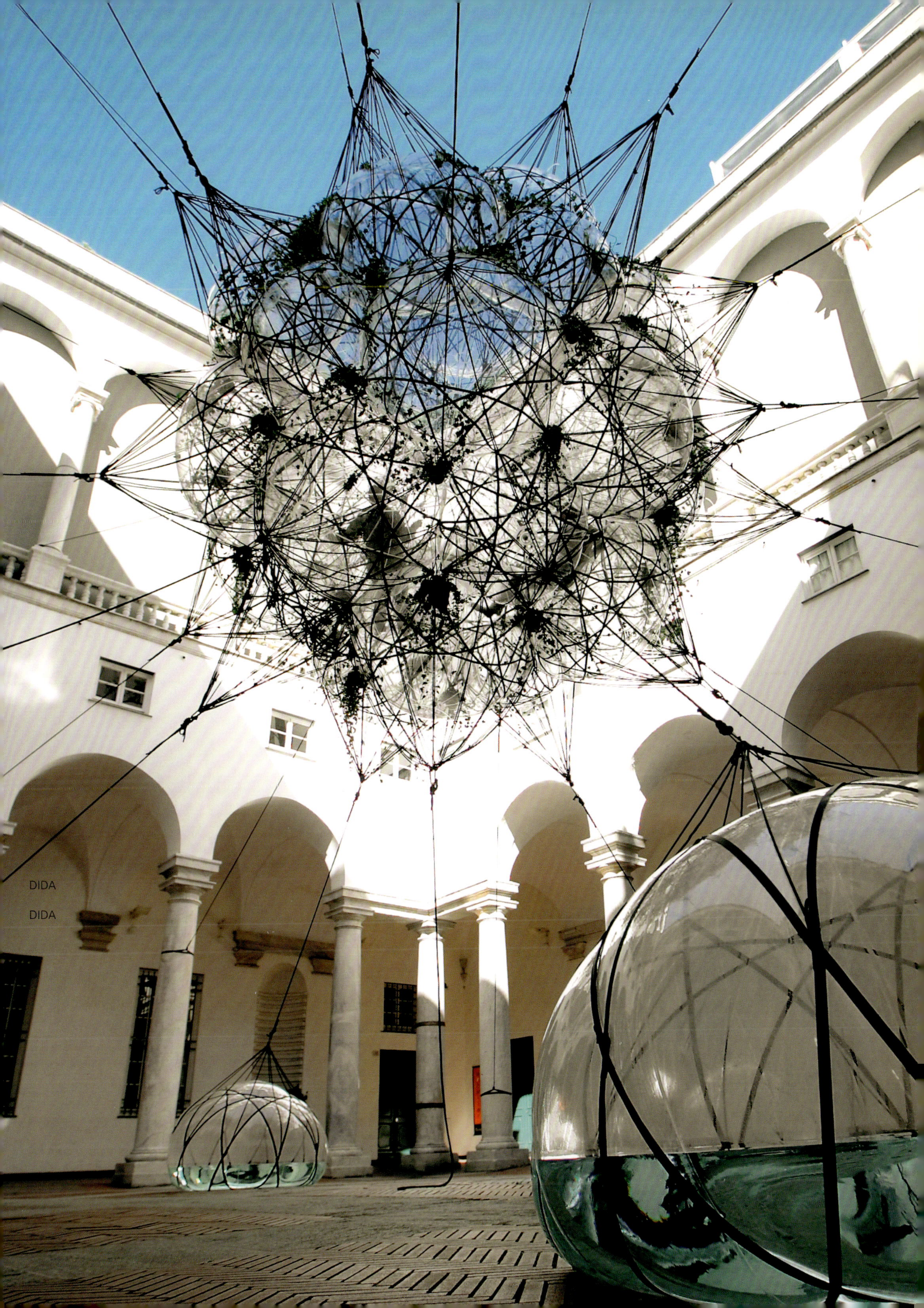

DIDA

DIDA

Arcangelo Sassolino

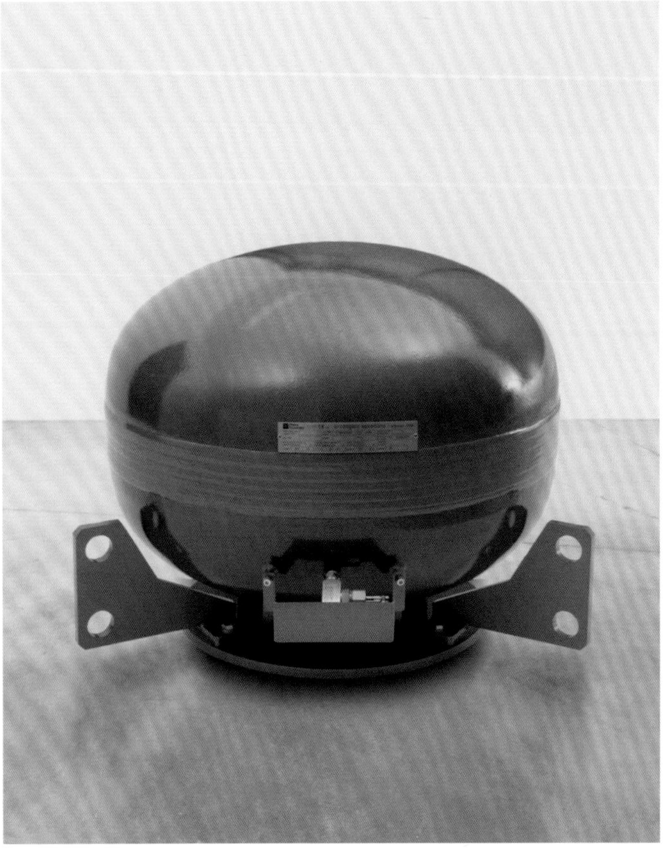

Afasia II, 2008
Steel and 250 bar compressed nitrogen, 53 x 70 x 70 cm
Courtesy Galerie Feinkost, Berlin; Nicola von Senger, Zurich, Galleria Galica, Milan

Afasia I, 2008
Steel, compressed nitrogen, glass, computer, and steel cage, 200 x 500 x 300 cm
Courtesy Galerie Feinkost, Berlin; Nicola von Senger, Zurich, Galleria Galica, Milan

Born in Vicenza (Italy) in 1967. Lives and works in New York and Vicenza.
Constituting a personal synthesis of the artist's experience in engineering and game design, Sassolino's works are installations combining the use of industrial materials, steel, and gas. Presented at *Artissima 12* in the Constellation section for large-sized works conceived for museums and subsequently exhibited at the Palais de Tokyo in the *Superdome* exhibition, *Afasia I* addresses the difficulty of mastering a language and taking advantage of its communicative potential. Based on parallels with the sporting universe of baseball, the installation consists of a huge steel cage containing a nitrogen-powered gun capable of shooting beer bottles at a speed of 600 kph. The noise of the bottle shattering and the deliberately prolonged wait between one "pitch" and another create a suspended atmosphere fraught with expectation.
The artist followed this up immediately with *Afasia II*, using a steel casing and pipes to create a capsule containing nitrogen at a pressure of 250 atmospheres.
As the quantity of the gas is directly proportional to the energy it can release, the object is equivalent to a bomb of great destructive potential or the core of a high-powered engine.
Ideally related to Marcel Duchamp's *Air de Paris* (1919), Sassolino's work places semantics and technology, poetry and the rarefaction of two gases, air and nitrogen, on the same level.
The interest he displays in the relationship between the physical properties of the container and those of the content is part and parcel of an attempt to materialize the state of aphasia, understood as the ability to develop ideas of great complexity but being unable to express them, to free them from the shell in which they were conceived.

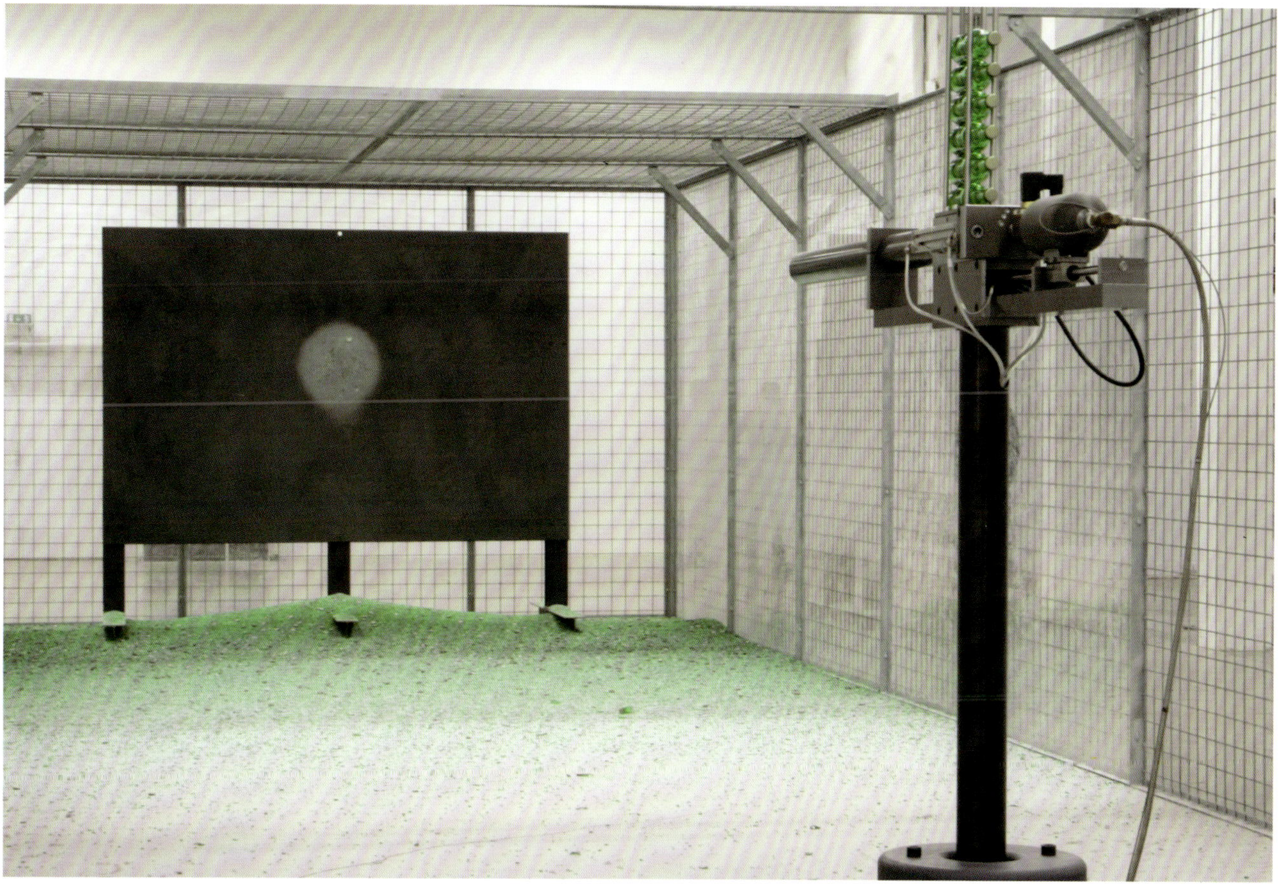

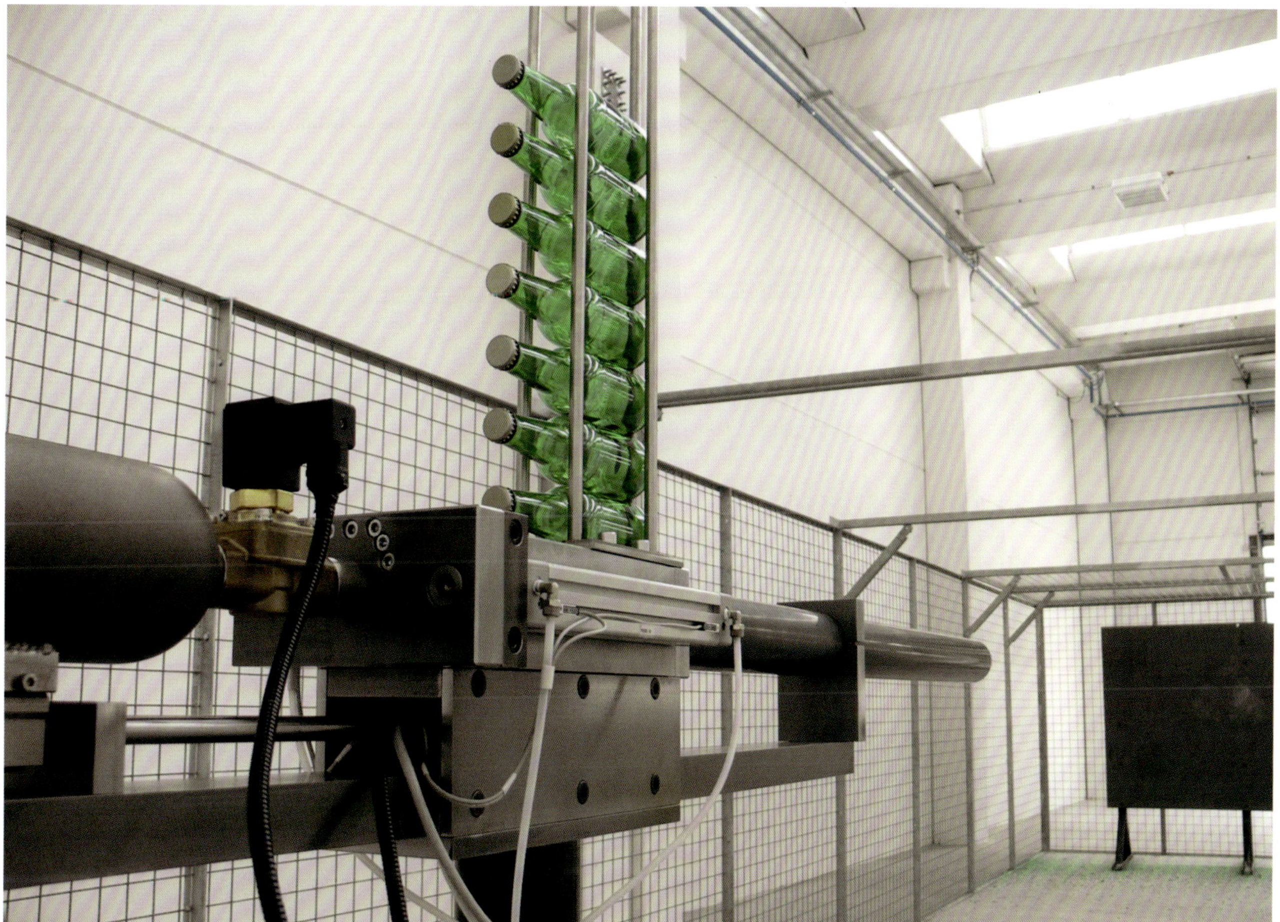

Rachel Whiteread

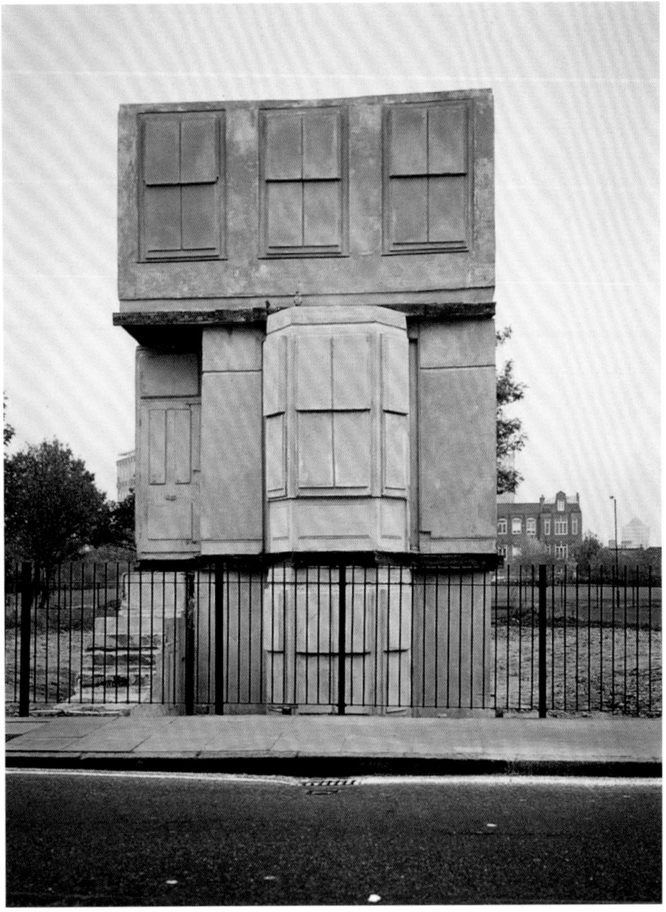

Untitled (House), 1993
Plaster cast of home,
actual dimensions
View of the installation at 193 Grove Road, London (destroyed in 1994)
Courtesy Anthony d'Offay Gallery, London

Twenty-five Spaces, 1995
Cast resin, 25 blocks,
43 x 30 x 30 cm each
Queensland, Queensland Art Gallery

Untitled (Apartment), 2001
White robust plasticized plaster,
2.8 x 11.1 x 6.1 m
New York, Solomon R. Guggenheim Museum, Commissioned by Deutsche Bank AG in consultation with the Solomon R. Guggenheim Foundation for the Deutsche Guggenheim, Berlin

Born in London in 1963. Lives and works in London.
The conception of sculpture in terms of inner space that has guided Rachel Whiteread's work since the late 1980s has led to a particular use of the technique of casts. The artist makes use above all of ductile materials such as plaster, rubber and resin to "solidify" the void that objects form or rather the space they occupy in relation to their own structure and not to their surrounding environment. This approach involves removal of the object of reference, and Whiteread's sculptures are thus transformed into traces of something that is no longer present as a concrete datum but persists nevertheless as a physical entity (through its volume), as a trace of a phenomenal event and, last but not least, as memory.
After applying her particular technique to everyday objects and above all household articles – including chairs, with an explicit reference to Bruce Naumann's cast of the empty space under his chair (1965), tables, bathtubs and washbasins – Whiteread extended her procedure, and above all the philosophical relevance of her operations, to environments and even entire architectural works (*Untitled [Apartment]*, 2001).
The dimension of memory was intimately bound up in the early works with the fact that the initial objects reflect what the critic John Bird has described as the cultural space of the home. It is precisely for this reason that their removal and replacement with their "negative space" arouses an overwhelming sense of melancholy, loss and death in the spectator. These feelings are both subjective, in the sense that they are linked to the personal experience of the individuals involved, and social, since the absence-presence of things that allude symbolically to the home environment as a place of attachments and a stronghold of family values prompts reflection on the drama of homelessness, which has come to affect more and more people for various reasons. It is precisely the urgent nature of this problem that led the artist to create *House* (1993), one of her best known and most controversial works, which resulted in her being the first woman artist to be awarded the illustrious Turner Prize. By a strange twist of fate, it was precisely during the official prize-giving ceremony that the local authorities decided on the demolition of *House*, which actually took place a few months later.
House was a perfect cast of the interior of a Victorian house, already scheduled for demolition within the framework of a redevelopment project for a working-class area in East London. Thus intended as a monument to a type of architecture and a proletarian culture that were both threatened by the speculative plans of high finance, it was instead knocked down by the bulldozers that transformed the area as a whole, which had become suddenly attractive as residential and commercial property. (It was in fact located adjacent to the site of the Canary Wharf redevelopment project.) The artist has since been able, however, to present her idea of the architectural cast as a monument in other contexts with works of great political and moral impact, including the Holocaust Memorial in Vienna (2000).
Rachel Whiteread operated on the monumental scale also on the occasion of the installation *Embankment*, created in 2005 for the Turbine Hall of Tate Modern in London. It consisted of 14,000 polyethylene casts of the insides of boxes stacked up inside the museum so as to suggest various possible architectural or natural scenarios (an ice pack, a marble quarry, a crammed warehouse) but also mental settings for a sense of impermanence and being constantly on the move with no destination, thus establishing a dialogue with the spectators once again on the basis of images and memories, both personal and collective.
(*L.L.*)

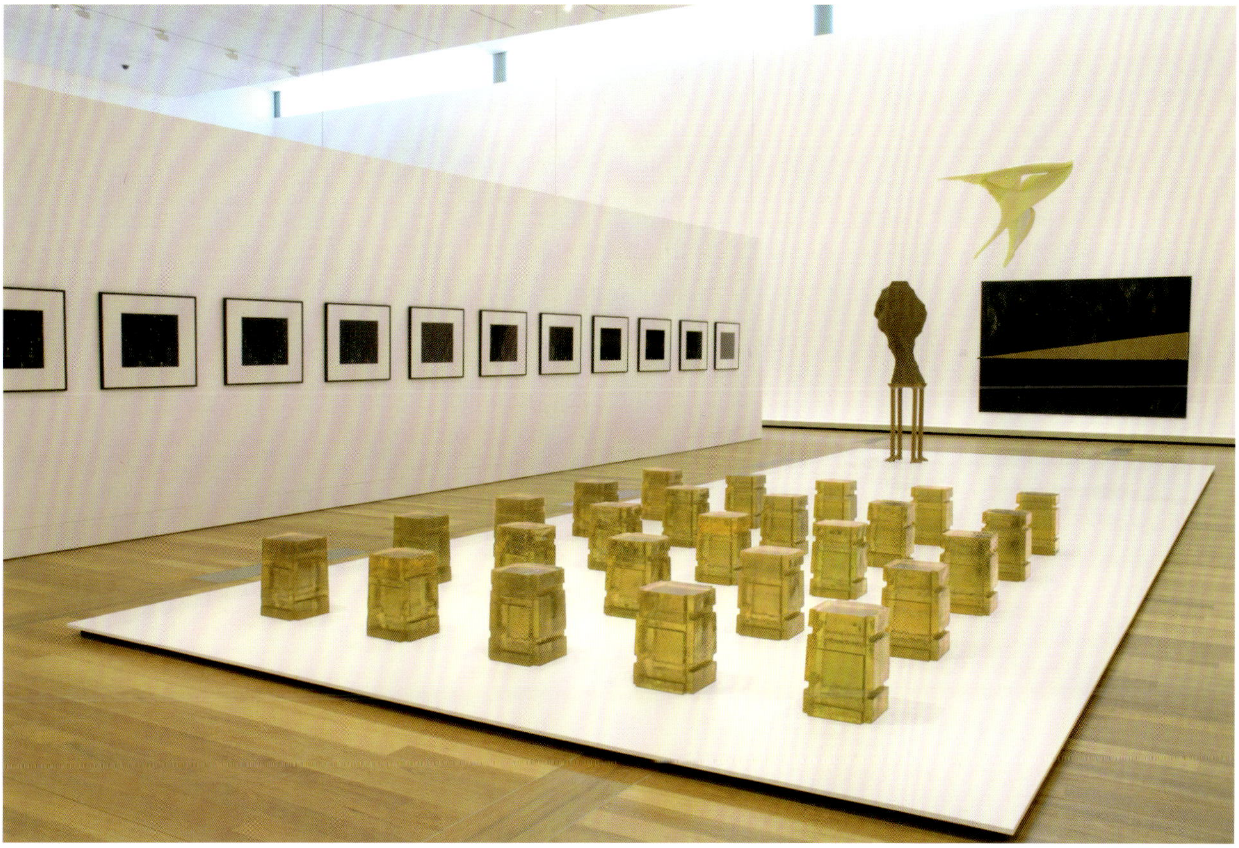

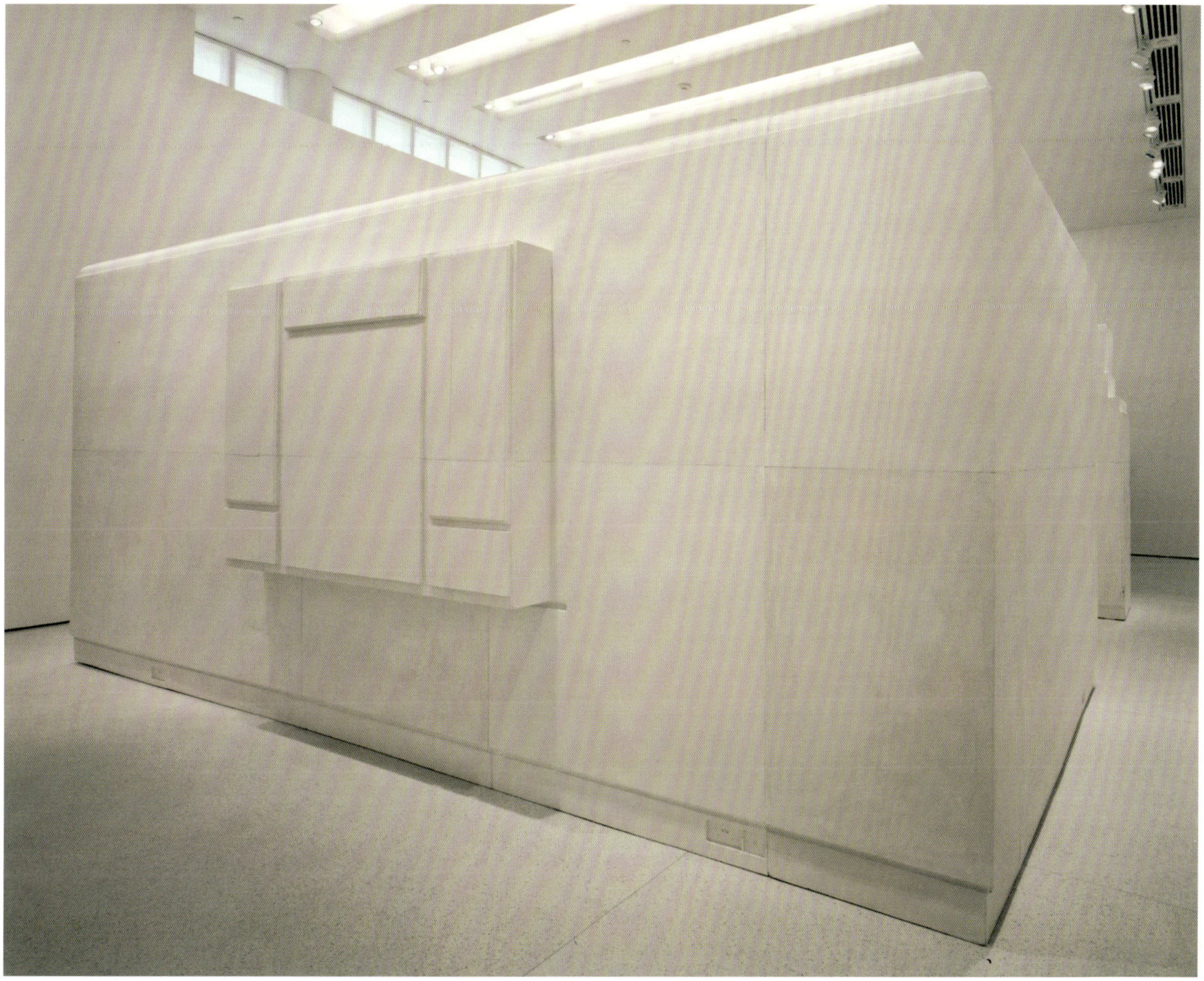

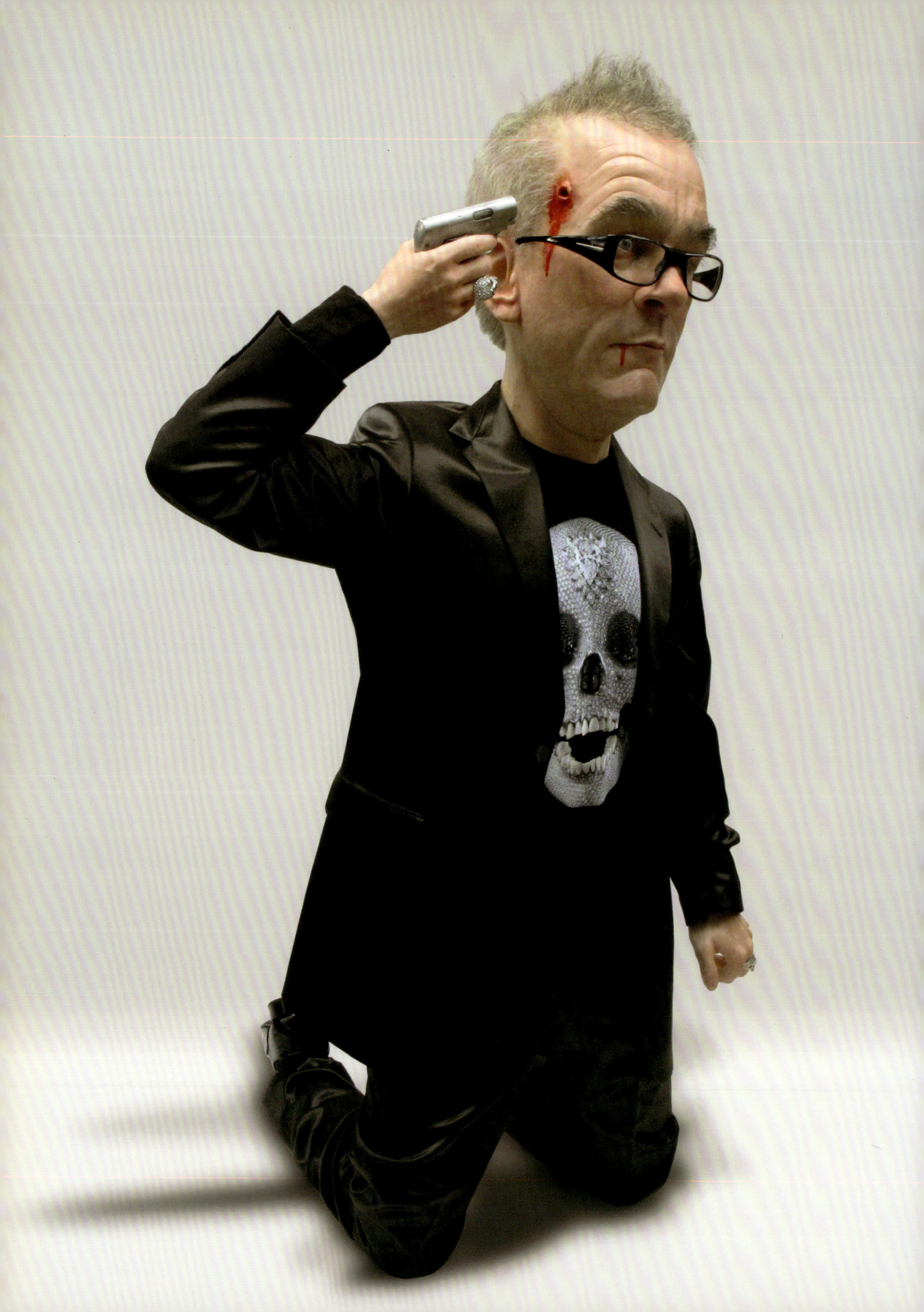

Neo-modernity, Neo-biennalism, Neo-fairism

Complexity and contradiction are the words that best portray art's current situation. A comparison with neo-capitalism's recent debacle may provide some clarification as the art world, even if it is a small one and not so autonomous from the culture market as many an insider would like us to believe, is deeply involved in the formation of value. *Hindenbunny* and *4 the Love of Go(l)d* are symptomatic metaphors. The first image is by Canadian artist Trevor Guthrie, the second one by Spanish artist Eugenio Merino. No comment is needed.

I would like to introduce my topic by highlighting 6 examples of recent[1] contemporary art practice that have had an effect on the economy of art and its rhetoric.

Case 1: Pierre Bergé removes Andy Warhol's portrait of Yves Saint Laurent from the retrospective *Le Grand Monde d'Andy Warhol* at the Grand Palais, Paris, curated by expert Alain Cueff; Bergé, Saint-Laurent's former partner and the owner of the work, claimed it should not hang among Warhol's portraits of other fashion designers, like Armani and Carolina Herrera, but in the room dedicated to artists like Man Ray and Lichtenstein.

Case 2: Coinciding with Art Vienna, an exhibition project titled *curated by_vienna 09* takes place in which international curators Dan Cameron & María de Corral, Matthew Higgs, Gianni Jetzer and Jérôme Sans have been invited to curate a show in 18 galleries divided into four groups of 4–5 galleries each, which will be treated as a single exhibition zone.

Case 3: The exhibition on Indian contemporary art *Indian Highway*, curated by Julia Peyton-Jones and Hans Ulrich Obrist, directors of the Serpentine Gallery, and Gunnar B. Kvaran, director of the Astrup Fearnley Museum, is on an international tour "featuring", according to the Serpentine's press release, "artists who have already made an impact on the international art world alongside less well-established practitioners."

Case 4: Manzoni scholar and senior curator of contemporary art at the Solomon R. Guggenheim Museum, Germano Celant curates *Piero Manzoni: A retrospective* at Gagosian Gallery,[2] New York, featuring important loans from museums and private collections.

Case 5: The exhibition *Hernan Bas: Works from the Rubell Family Collection* at the Brooklyn Museum in New York showcases thirty-eight works in various media by the young Miami-based artist that were collected over the past ten years by the Rubell.

Case 6: The sportlifestyle company PUMA announces the appointment of Mark Coetzee – former director of the Rubell Family Collection and a lecturer in critical theory, art criticism and contemporary art practice at New World School of the Arts (NWSA) – as Program Director of PUMAVision and Chief Curator of puma.creative.

Without imposing or suggesting any interpretation on the reader at this point, I'm sure that what comes to mind when reading these cases is the assertion that contemporary art escapes easy generalization and becomes synonymous with complexity and contradiction.

But let's first look more closely at the formation of value. Value – by which I mean value in formally peaceful ways, not necessarily Karl Marx's concept of surplus value or *Mehrwert* – is still the main objective of (neo-)capitalism. The problem now is that the capitalist system, especially under neo-liberalism, has done precisely the opposite: it has created many interactions that have destroyed value.

Let me explain. Historically, those in power have enriched themselves by ruling over the weak. We can call this, as defined by Spanish economist Josep Burcet, the "parasitism principle".[3] With the advent of the Industrial Revolution and economies based on development, a larger proportion of people gained access to certain levels of wealth and very slowly it opened the door to procedures centered on *win-win* interactions. This can be called the "symbiosis principle". The inexorable increase in sophistication in technology and science during the twentieth century has generated more *win-win* exchanges,

Eugenio Merino
4 the Love of Go(l)d, 2009
Resin, hair, cotton outfit, mixed media, 140 x 73 x 80 cm
Courtesy Galería ADN, Barcelona

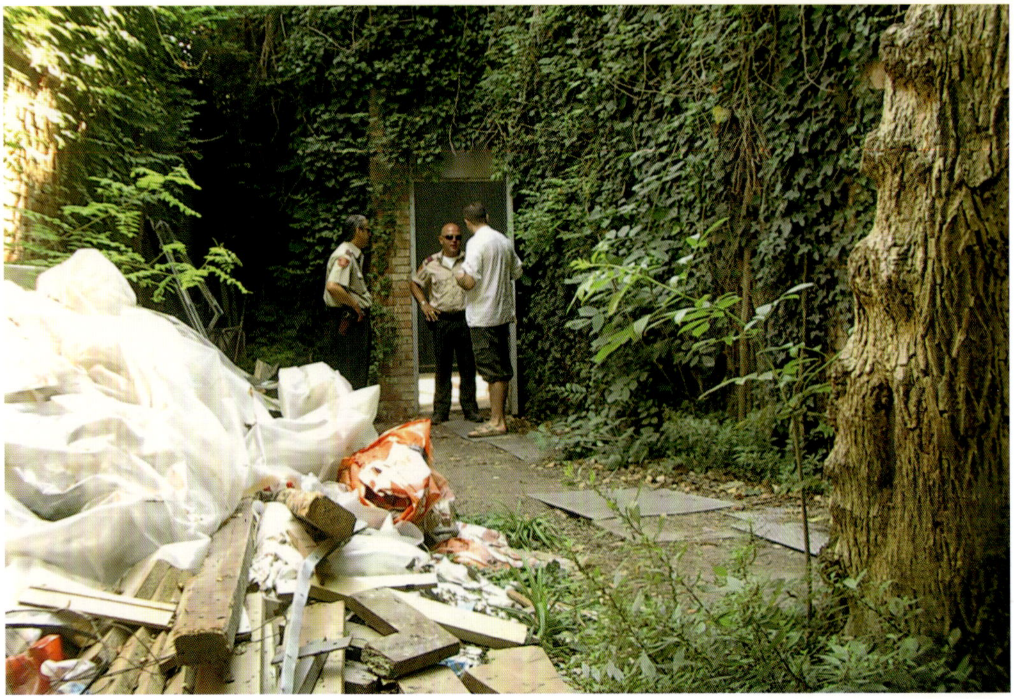

Santiago Sierra
Wall Enclosing a Space, 2003
View of the installation in the Spanish Pavilion, L Esposizione Internazionale d'Arte, Biennale di Venezia 2003
Courtesy prometeogallery di Ida Pisani, Milan/Lucca

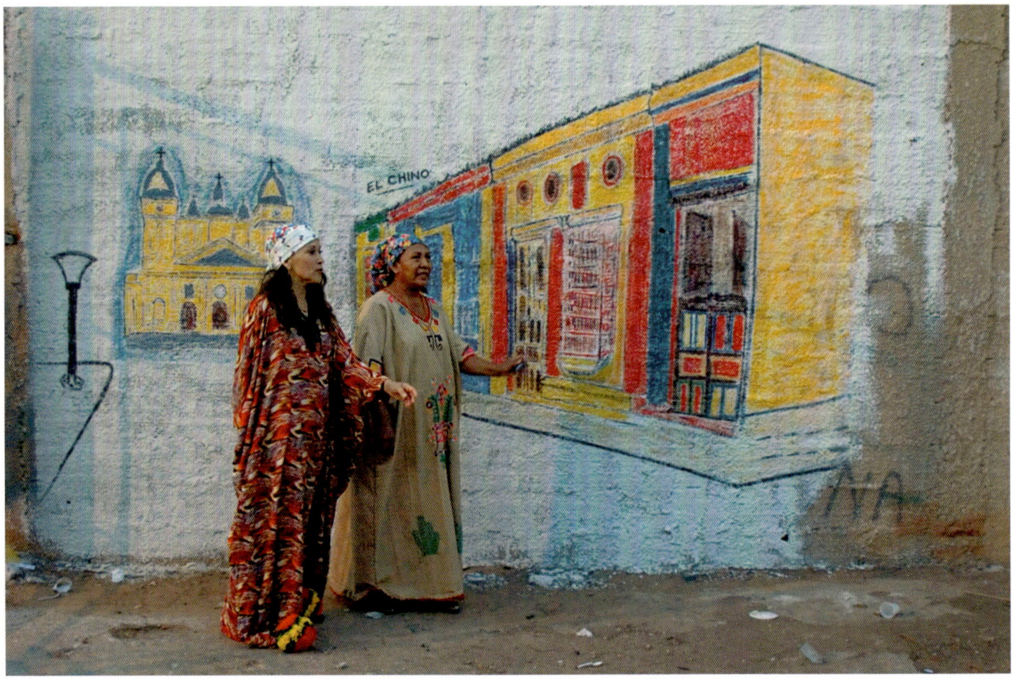

Clemencia Labin, Alba Fernandez
Living Picture Guajiras, 2006
Tableau-vivant, Background wall painting *El chino*, Velada de Santa Lucía, Maracaibo, Venezuela
Courtesy of the artists

which in turn contribute to creating greater value for the society of which they are a part. Periods of expansion are followed by periods of recession, and the crisis is the result of an intensification of *win-lose* interactions. Financial crisis and economic bubbles only indicate that there are still large parts of the economy that pursue wealth in a parasitic way. The challenge for every economy is to have as many *win-win* interactions as possible and to reduce the *win-lose* ones. How does this explain the sub-prime crisis? A world-wide excess of *win-lose* interactions made prices rise artificially but did not create value. Thus, a very small group of speculators won huge amounts of money while a bigger majority lost theirs.

And what does this have to do with the art world? Art's peculiar economy continues insistently and inexplicably to be dominated by these *win-lose* situations. A privileged but small group of dealers, auctioneers, artists, collectors, critics, curators, directors, and advisors establishes hierarchies of power and governs the art world in accordance with their own rules. We can safely use Groys' words: "For the functioning of the art system is based on certain aesthetic value judgments, on certain criteria of choice, rules of inclusion and exclusion, and the like. All these value judgments, criteria, and rules are, of course, not autonomous. Rather, they reflect the dominant social conventions and power structures."[4] Much in the same way as the capitalist system, they know how to reconcile critical or even contradictory elements: the transmutation of the work of art as a symbolic product into merchandise with the same "romantic" demands of authenticity, disinterest, sublimity or humanization.

So, right here we have precisely one of the problems of the art market: its inefficiency, opacity and imperfection. At this point it is impossible to place the dilemma in continuist or rupturist terms. The market is there, and more and newer players are competing in it, and a wider democratization and transparency are not only welcome but highly necessary. We can't blame globalization for the world's problems. Globalization, just like the art market, is neither good nor bad; it simply becomes what we make of it.[5] And speculation has been part of it.

The schizophrenia of the art world and the imperfection of the art system and art market cause disconcerting, not to say farfetched, situations. In the nineteenth century, an artist's life was for the most part deemed "authentic" if it was not compartmentalized: in other words, if he managed to unite all facets of (his) existence to orient it towards both the realization of a work of art and the singularity of the work's creator.[6] In the twenty-first century many members of the art world live compartmentalized lives, and this is what causes hardship when the time comes to create a future project. This actual unstable situation of the artist reminds me of the metaphor of the artist as *Ecce Homo* in the market square, a subject matter very popular between the years 1530 and 1575, for example in Pieter Aertsen's panel *Market with Scenes from the Passion* (circa 1550–1552).[7]

How do we explain that the profession of artist is still in high demand? For Stallabrass it's crystal clear: "The freedom of art is more than an ideal. If, despite the small chance of success, the profession of artist is so popular, it is because it offers the prospect of a labour that is apparently free of narrow specialization, allowing the artist, like heroes in the movies, to endow work and life with their own meanings."[8] Despite this exemplarizing precariousness founded on a romantic idea of art and, secondly, a philosophical conviction that the artist or the writer has a special access to truth, the art world is not willing to admit that without the creation of unique or rare art works by the artist the system would simply collapse.

And what about the other and equally precariously situated members of the art world like art critics, independent curators, dealers and the like? According to Maurizio Lazzarato, globalization has now drastically modified the concepts of art and work through two parallel and complementary trends. "The first", argues Lazzarato, "assimilates artistic and all cultural practices into the capitalist economy by transforming artists into 'workers,' and 'citizens' into various publics. The second turns 'creation' into a process that traverses art, the economy, science, and the social sphere, by transferring the problems, methods, and practices that were thought to be specific to art to other domains."[9] Translated to the art world, this precariousness is the result, on one hand, of a self-imposed and interiorized condition created by ambiguous and contradictory work conditions (discontinuity, flexibility, mobility), and, on the other hand, of the subtle dynamics of capitalism that encourages these insecurely placed individuals to think of themselves as being – just like art – exceptional. Work and leisure are no longer separated, and large amounts of unpaid time are invested in accumulating knowledge that's not only expected of them, but will become absolutely necessary for achieving future projects under these market-driven conditions.

In sum, the spectrum of cases above re-creates new formats of integration between the public and the private sphere; the progressive arrival of the curator in the world of art fairs, and art fairs turned into curatorial platforms; the marketing of cultural difference, but also the need for the inclusion of other modernities in the international art system in a globalized world; private galleries aspiring to rival museums and biennials in artistic legitimization; the centrality of private collectors and their motivations; brands and companies acting more and more as cultural activists and hiring in intellectual capital. There are other interpretations

Marc Bijl
Resist, 2002
View of the installation at Manifesta 4 – European Biennial of Contemporary Art, Frankfurt 2002
Courtesy The Breeder, Athens/Upstream Gallery, Amsterdam

Marc Bijl
Terror, 2002
View of the illegal intervention at *Documenta 11*, Kassel 2002
Courtesy The Breeder, Athens/Upstream Gallery, Amsterdam

possible, but there is no need to elaborate them here now.

Art is a commodity, a very exceptional one that nevertheless functions more and more like the rules of the traditional economy. "Everything that has an everyday value as a commodity," argues Diedrich Diederichsen, "can theoretically also become an object of speculation. But most of the transactions made with commodities in the realm of the visual arts do not (initially) involve speculation, so that they are more comparable with the regular economy of production and consumption, buying and selling."[10]

So we have the "everyday value" and the "speculative value" of the art commodity, both of which express themselves under the notion of price within the art market. Then, in turn, we must distinguish between the art market and the art world embodied by the opposition that exists between the commodity (market) and autonomy (spirituality). Does art hold any power to bridge this everlasting Manichean dialectic? Are we still obliged to choose between the blue and the red pill? Maybe it's all simply a question of a new, if you like, *neo-modern* paradigm.

The advent of neo-modernity

There is an *esprit d'époque* called "neo-modern" which has been manifesting itself in realms as disparate as the visual arts, architecture, religion, economics, politics and philosophy. It's not new, it goes back to the 1980s, and although the concept is not very innovative, its overwhelming presence in very different fields makes its codification inevitable and inalienable. To consider it in more detail.

This return or *ricorso* to the modern invades certain knowledge of our contemporaneity and permits the establishment of more or less probable connections. It overlaps partly with post-modernity, but it lacks a clear starting point, thus it is first necessary to delimit concepts like "modernity" and "modernism".

For many European philosophers and scholars modernity came into being with the Enlightenment and the rule of reason. The Brazilian professor of semiotics, Lucia Santaella, takes as her starting point the argument that "modernity goes back to the Renaissance [...] it began in the age of capitalism, the rise of modern philosophy and science, at the time when painting became portable and music left the churches."[11] Indeed, modernity and its diverse avant-gardes signify a series of European movements, philosophies and cultural changes.

Nowadays, "Issues of modernity are invariably linked to globalization", says Andreas Huyssen, and "the geographic opening of the question of other modernisms and alternative modernities across the world – modernism in other worlds as a mutant global reality rather than something limited to the Northern Transatlantic."[12] Huyssen poses the pertinent question: "what do we make of the return of 'modernity' in contemporary discussions of globalization?"[13]

Already back in 1987 the Brazilian philosopher Sergio Rouanet used the term *neo-modern* in his book *As Razoes do Iluminismo*, in which he states that modernity has led the "neo-modern" project to be defined as "neo-liberal".[14] "What is neo-modern? Neo-modern means searching in the archives of modernity for the authentic sense of modernity; it means contesting the current modernity in the name of virtual modernity; it means requiring from all postmodern visions an inflexibly modern program as the only way to concretize hopes (interrupted partial or betrayed) consolidated on the project of modernity."[15]

All this was confirmed some years later with the defeat of Communism, and the date November 12, 1989 can be cited as the start of a first and *negative neo-modernity* within which neo-conservatism and neo-liberalism prevail as the political and economical philosophies commanded by Margaret Thatcher and Ronald Reagan. This negative neo-modernity, which entails a "negative adaptation" to tradition, coincides with the peak of post-modernity and its predilection for irrationalism, relativism and discontinuity.

In the same year, Habermas developed a new paradigm to re-signify modernity against prevailing conservative post-modern impostures – in particular those of Lyotard – in his *Critical Theory of Modernity*. What led the modernity project to failure was a certain individualist, selfish reasoning that had made the subject dependent on the laws of the capitalist market and State bureaucracy. The communication between the "life world" and the "system world" had to be restored through true reason again.

In turn, sociologist Edward Tiryakian also stressed this neo-modern condition

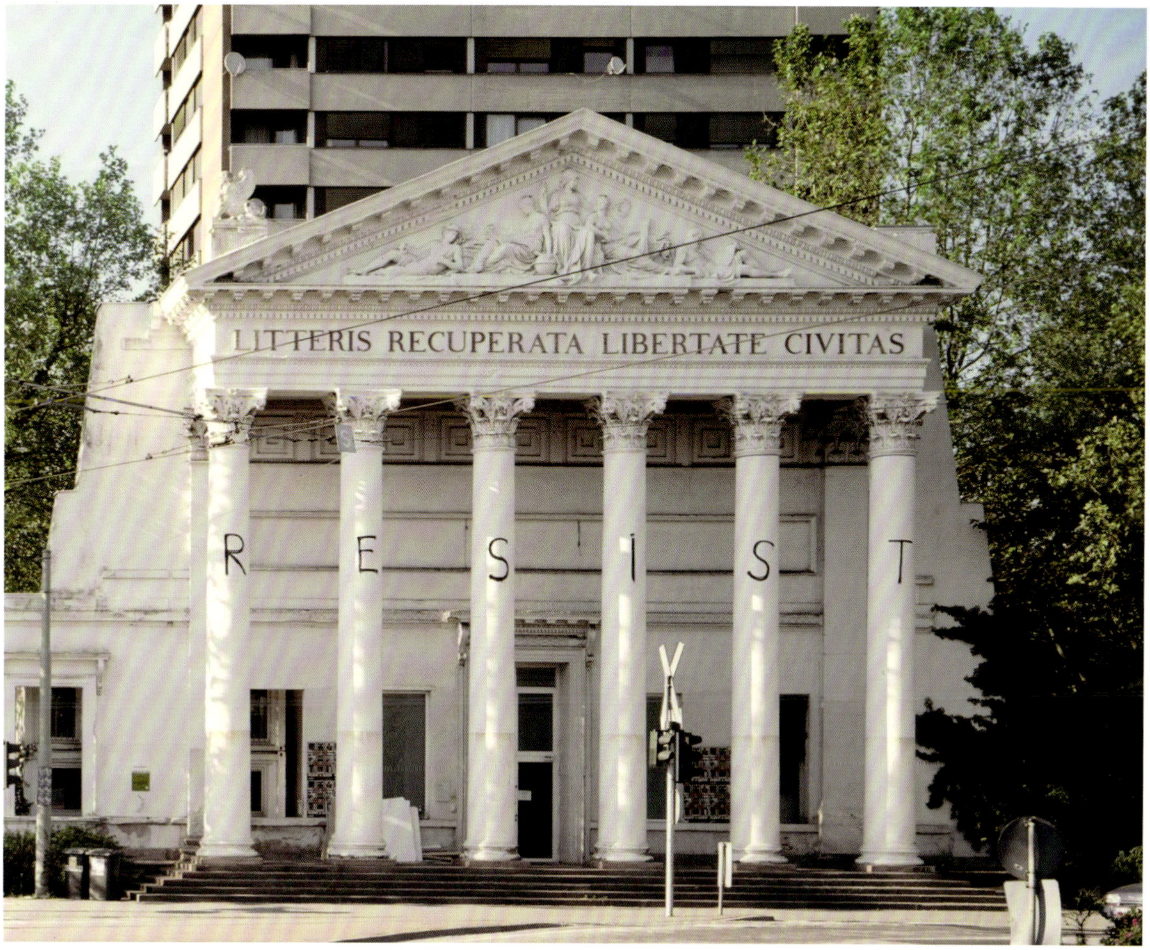
LITTERIS RECUPERATA LIBERTATE CIVITAS
R E S I S T

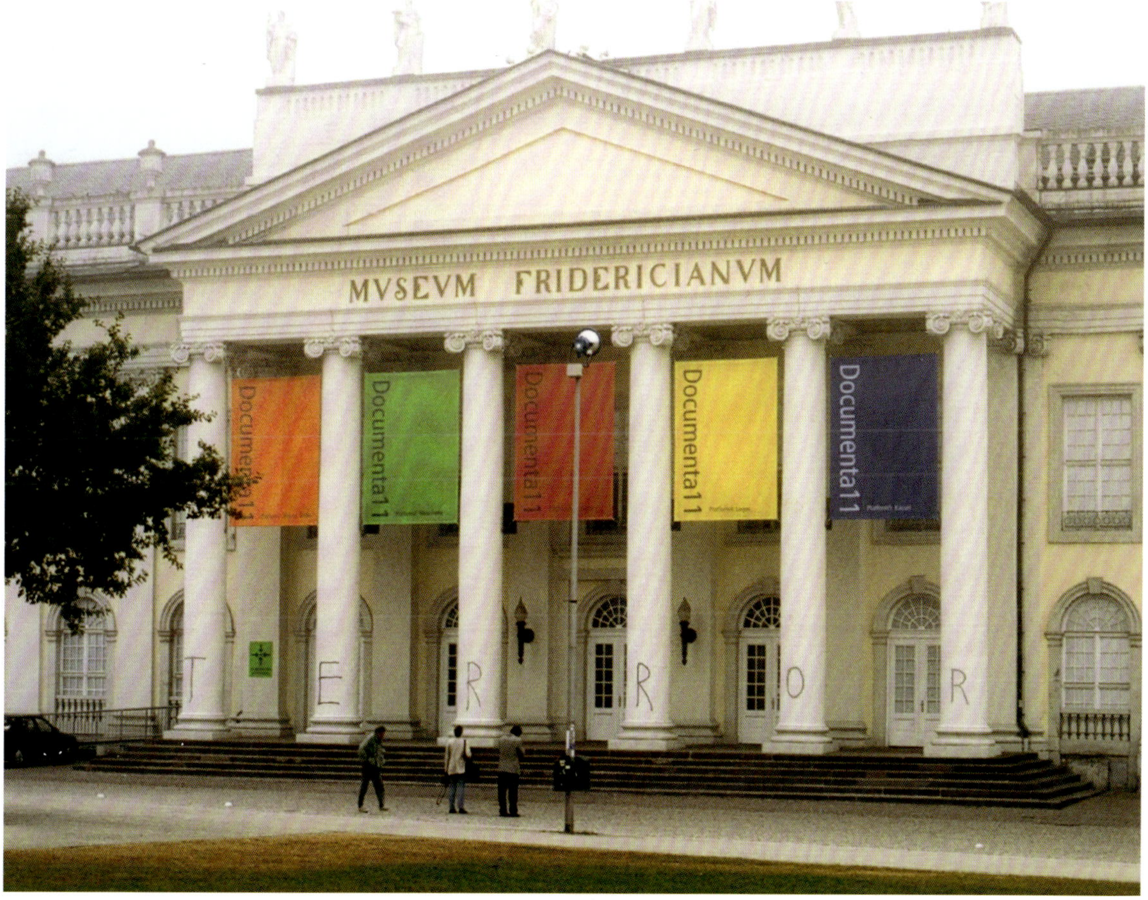
MVSEVM FRIDERICIANVM
Documenta11
Documenta11
Documenta11
Documenta11
Documenta11
T E R R O R

Trevor Guthrie
Hindenbunny (metaphor for 21st century art market hype), 2008
Charcoal on paper, 112 x 95 cm
Courtesy Galerie Römerapotheke, Zürich

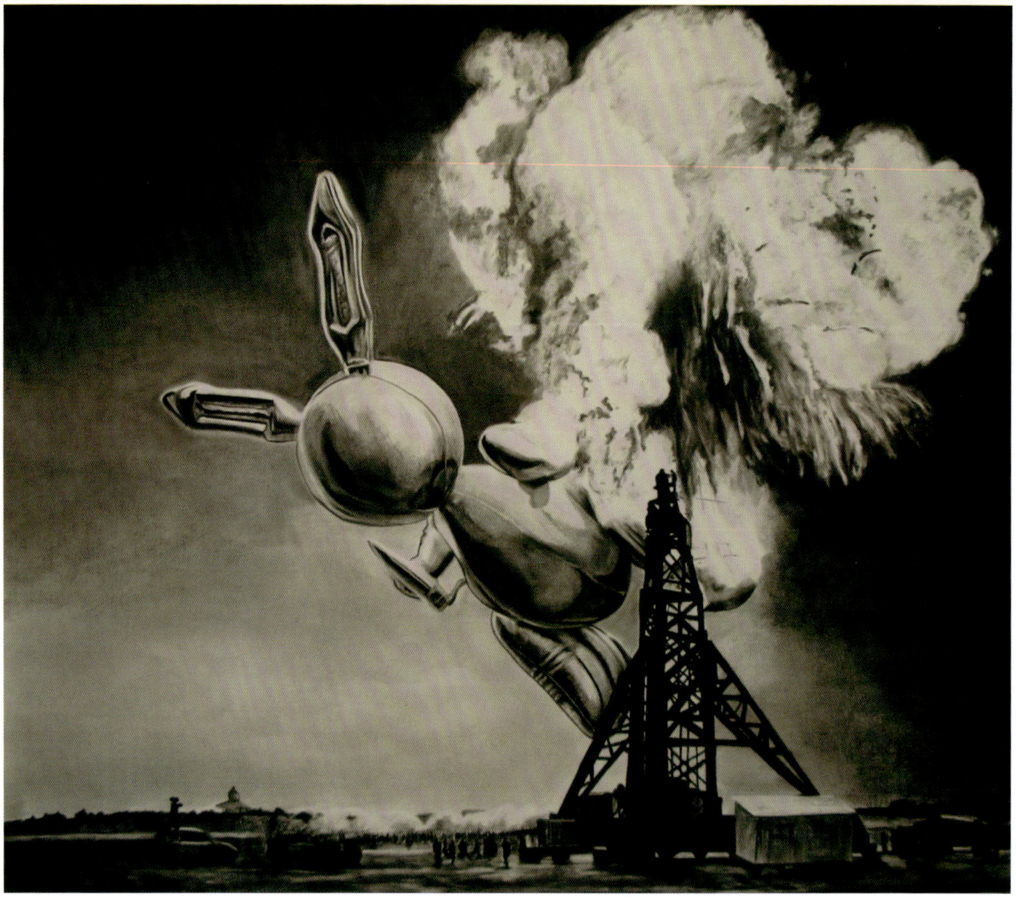

in 1991 in an article titled *Modernization: Exhumetur in pace*: "Neo-modernism will serve as a rough-and-ready characterization of this phase of post-modernization theory until a term appears that represents the new spirit of the times in a more imaginative way."[16]

The most palpable expression of this neo-conservative and neo-liberal failure is the terrorist attack on September 11, 2001, and the bankruptcy of Lehmann Brothers (and subsequent world stock market collapse) on September 14, 2008 owing to toxic assets.

Although the enumeration of dates may seem monotonous, there is no doubt that November 4, 2008 will be less conventional as it represents the election of Barack Obama to the Presidency of the United States, with all its due symbolism. If we proceed with our speculations, we could argue that from this moment the world entered a *positive neo-modernity*, foreshadowing a "positive adaptation" to tradition, which leaves aside post-modernist maxims[17] and regains certain modernist essences like the role of the state, redistribution politics, equality, social care, education and environmental conscience.

"Neo" not only implies a mere repetition, recurrence or recycling of certain modernisms, periods and philosophies from the past, but a revision, revaluation, and, as a result, a critical reformulation of the past looking to the future. This is to a great extent logical as nobody wants to place their faith in the pure future, given that most utopias have shown their complete impracticability. Whereas modernity yearned for the new as a way to utopia, and post-modernity recycled the old in its dystopia, neo-modernity explores new revitalising alternatives conscious of the modernist limitations associated with the demands of the new and the utopian. So, in our analysis neo-modernity embodies an innovation that has shifted from a "negative" to a "positive" adaptation of tradition as seen in diverse models of modernity.

Modernism can be explained as the transition phase of the Western arts and architecture from modernity to post-modernity. Post-modernity involved eclecticism, the looting and mix of past techniques, styles, movements and periods without any order or rank by means of *copy-and-paste* strategies, hyper-texts and hyper-images, and the *everything goes* attitude. Neo-modernity has not only embarked upon a re-reading of modernism, but also of other artistic movements, be it in a literal, formal or conceptual manner. The difference now stems from the fact that only a certain period is being reinterpreted at the time, and not the appropriation of fragments from images or texts from different styles or times, which lead to an artistic practice created from remains or leftovers. In this sense, Eve Sussman's video *89 seconds at Alcazar* (2004) in which she reconstructs the moments prior to the setting of the scene in *Las Meninas*, painted by Velázquez, could be considered symptomatic of this "techno-referential" *esprit d'époque*. Consider Foucault's concept of "a representation of a representation" and the work of art as "*episteme*".

In 1987 Omar Calabrese published his book *L'età neobarocca* (Neo-Baroque: A Sign of the Times) as a cultural phenomenon of the time characterized by a specific internal "form" that evoked the Baroque. More recently, Angela Ndalianis picked up the debate in her book *Neo-Baroque Aesthetics and Contemporary Entertainment* (2004) by referring to the Baroque as a possible frame for apprehending society and contemporary entertainment media. In the field of visual arts, Domus Artium (DA2), Salamanca's Contemporary Art Centre in Spain, opened in October 2005, coinciding with the celebration of the 250th anniversary of the city's Baroque main square, the exhibition *Baroque and Neo-Baroque. The Hell of the Beautiful*. Back in the early 1980s the British music scene was dominated by *New Romantics* like Spandau Ballet and Duran Duran; and, finally, also the Schirn Kunsthalle participated in this "neo" revival in May 2005 with the exhibition *Ideal Worlds – New Romanticism in Contemporary Art*, in which they reflected upon this rebirth of the romantic spirit in contemporary art practices.

In the philosophical field, military neo-liberalism violence and counter-violence – such as the neo-Leninist logic of Al-Qaeda – brings Simon Critchley to propose the term *neo-anarchism* as a new policy of resistance, civil disobedience and non-violence.[18] Neo-modernity manifests itself thus in the formation of a political subjectivity as an appeal to universality, whether a demand for political representation, equality of treatment or anything else. In business we sense a *neo-management* philosophy based on "storytelling" and the attraction of change, as masterly unveiled by Luc Boltanski and Eve Chiapello in *The New Spirit of Capitalism*.[19] Besides, *neo-politics* obliges those who want to achieve power to tell convincing stories about the nation, their problems, and, above all, about themselves, as has been the case with Obama.

To cut this omnipresent, overwhelming but by no means homogenous return to "neo" short, reference could be made to Pope John Paul II's *neo-ecumenism*, taken up by Benedict XVI, and, continuing in the spiritual realm, the *neo-conscience* of spiritual leaders like Eckhart Tolle, Pema Chodron or Acharya Yogeesh and their new interpretation of time and the now.

In brief, it may be affirmed that neo-modernity represents a search for an intermediate space in between modernity's rationalism and post-modernity's relativism. This reinvention of reason connects more with the positive message of Habermas than with the apocalyptic Lyotard and Baudrillard. From a negative neo-modernity we move into a period of positive neo-modernity within which micro-utopias and progress will be possible and desirable, despite the deafening fall of ideologies and grand narratives. It will not entail a full return to them, but it will bring about a curious synthesis of modern assumptions under the conditions of global capitalism.

The art world and the art system, where biennials and art fairs have created over the last years a canon of global homogenization, need to engage as well in the search for a meaningful intermediate space capable of contextualizing as yet unexplored hybrid options.

The "fairization" of biennials and the "biennalization" of art fairs

Art and its institutions cannot escape commodification, especially after the neo-liberalist heyday. The relationship of the museum with consumption has become more than natural. The spaces devoted to shopping are bigger and bigger, and at each visit the visitor has a wider array of articles available: from books, exhibition-related souvenirs to the cafeteria. Some visitors even go straight to the restaurant, which is fine.

Museums are contexts that create signification and recognize artistic value. So do biennials, which tend to act as temporary art museums. Art fairs, like galleries, don't – or at least that is what we tended to believe until Larry Gagosian embarks on an artist he particularly likes![20] Until the 1990s things were very clear and everyone knew his or her place in the art system and in society; now the situation has become much more complex and also much more confusing. Zygmunt Bauman talks about "liquid modernity" and about social forms that as much as they represent structures, institutions and patterns "can no longer (and are not expected) to keep their shape for long, because they decompose and melt faster than the time it takes to cast them."[21] Pine and Gilmore launched the idea of an "economy that stages memorable experiences"[22] for customers eager to live different types of experiences within today's emotional capitalism.

Thus, from the mid '90s on the globalization process, together with low cost travel, new markets (China, India, Russia, Cuba, Puerto Rico, Dubai) and new players – hedge funds, revolving funds, the newly rich – offered to new and not so new audiences a mobile, cosmopolitan, multicultural, and exotic art experience. Temporary events like biennials and art fairs became the driving forces behind the art market.[23] At different levels both developed artistic strategies that reconciled local ambitions and international needs. As was inevitable, globalization brought about homogenization. "You discover sometimes", Robert Storr writes, "that people are overwhelmed by the sense that there is a sameness to international art and that their only choices are to join it or to be left out."[24]

This has had a dual effect: on the audiences and on art production. Many art professionals have started to enjoy a limited tourist/nomadic version of contemporary art, cemented in annual visits to an equally limited group of fairs and biennials. Like the original eighteenth-century concept of the Grand Tour and its pristine effort to "experience in its own flesh" remote places and to "catalogue its reality", the educated traveler today, the same as the anti-hero of yesteryear, aspires to inform himself in his firm desire to be the first one to discover, classify, and collect that "lost work of art". And this is exactly what happened with the other *Grand Tour of the 21st Century*, which, as a result of a once-in-ten-year coincidence (according to the press release[25]) that in turn resulted in a special and practical synergy between the art fair and the biennials, took the sophisticated art crowds in a marathon nonstop tour to Venice-Basel-Kassel-Münster in just 10 days.

The problem now is, and that brings us to the second point, that most of the art is "biennial art" or "art fair art" that responds to a typical globalized canon. It's true that much of this art responds to the nomadic curator's taste or thesis, who in turn interprets local demands, but we will return later to this issue. "Art fair art" has simply to do with hectic production schedules that need to fuel an excessive number of art fairs, especially if the artist is in demand, and with art works that are sexy and arresting, as they are obliged to compete with many others for the attention of a potential collector/client.

Within the actual cultural industry, both the biennale and the art fair have become periodical and long awaited and at the same time foreseeable experiences. I agree with Michele Robecchi when he states that "Comparing fairs and biennials in these terms is superficial but nevertheless useful for understanding two things: first, entertainment is becoming more and more of a decisive factor in this incestuous competition; and second, art fairs have now been unequivocally promoted to 'cultural event' status."[26] The "biennalization" of art fairs and the "fairization" of biennials is not a recent trend, although it seems it has passed its apex. This parasitic or symbiotic behavior often tends to be related to our new world order, but much of its origins can be traced to the historical development of the art market itself.

It all started with the market in early modern Antwerp where the fair, from the ancient usage of the word *jaarmarkt* or annual trade fair, is its iconic metaphor. "This was an age [c. late 1500s]," writes Elizabeth Alice Honig, "when commerce overflowed the boundaries of the marketplace and penetrated all aspects of life: the market, and its pictorial representation, were crucial grounds for testing how ideas could be made to fit into what seemed reasonable patterns of belief and behavior."[27] In the Middle Ages and the Renaissance the *coopman* or trader practiced a "policy of provision", in accordance with which as many goods as possible had to be attracted into towns for the benefit of consumers. The merchants started taking their wares from city to city and from trade fair to trade fair (maybe we

Ibid Projects' director Vita Zaman getting a haircut by Cary Kwok at Herald St., London
Supernova ABMB – Art Basel Miami Beach, 2007
Courtesy Paul Nescio, Amsterdam

Jesús Segura
Reading Zizej for 1 minute, 2008
Video, 1'
View of the performance at Festival Estrella Levante SOS 4.8, Murcia, Spain 2008
Courtesy of the artist and SOS 4.8

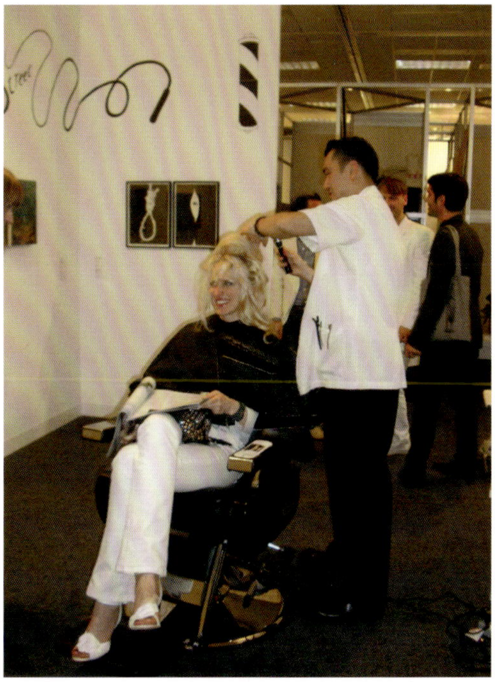

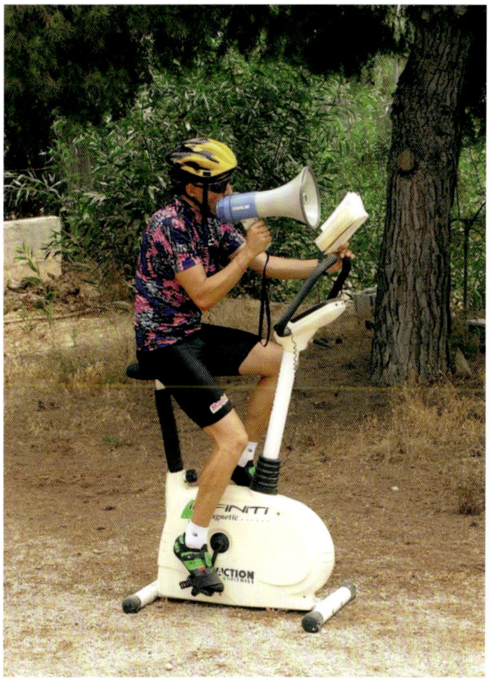

can spot here a comparison with the contemporary gallery owner and his/her participation in art fairs in different cities). In the fifteenth century trade fairs like Antwerp, Bruges and Brabant rose in importance. In the course of the sixteenth century, capitalism emerged as the dominant form of social organization of the economy. Painting and painters interacted with the markets as these were influenced by the changing roles played by merchants, church and city governments, and consumers. Some trade fairs are temporary and others are permanent, but both are awaited with impatience as the marketplace becomes a metaphor for social exchange and acquires its own alternative festive halo. With the unstoppable and constant development of capitalism, in which trade fair becomes synonymous with the dynamism of market commerce, it does not require great imagination to understand the later expansion that has ended up in the current "art fair age".

Biennials, triennials, and other international survey-type exhibitions like Documenta are inspired, on one hand, by the eighteenth-century salon,[28] and on the other, by international trade shows, world fairs, and universal exhibitions that are also called "great exhibitions". These were very large public exhibitions held since the mid-nineteenth century, in which the national pavilions created by the participating countries were the main attractions and used as a way to promote their cultures, resources, industries, and products at that moment in history. The exhibition as such not only had an important informational, but also an educational component from the very beginning, and it was accessible to people of all classes and ages. The *Exposition Nationale des produits de l'industrie agricole et manufacturière*, held in Paris in 1844, in the footsteps of the French tradition of national exhibitions, and the *Great Exhibition of the Works of Industry of All Nations* held in 1851, in the Crystal Palace built in Hyde Park, are clear examples on which many other contemporary international events have based themselves.

"The Venice Biennale," indicates the Biennale's web site, "arose from a resolution passed by the City Council on April 19, 1893, which proposed the founding of a 'biennial national artistic exhibition' to take place the following year to celebrate the silver anniversary of King Umberto and Margherita of Savoy."[29] Thus a political decision underlay its origin as the Biennale represented a sort of acknowledgement to the monarchy for the recent unification of the country. Furthermore, the mayor of the city had other less political and more practical ideas in mind: "When in 1895 the mayor of Venice, Ricardo Selvatico, became involved in planning Venice's first biennial, he was clearly aware of the potential of the idea for a positive promotion of his city. So he considered important the participation of international artists and their presence in order to emphasize international dialogue

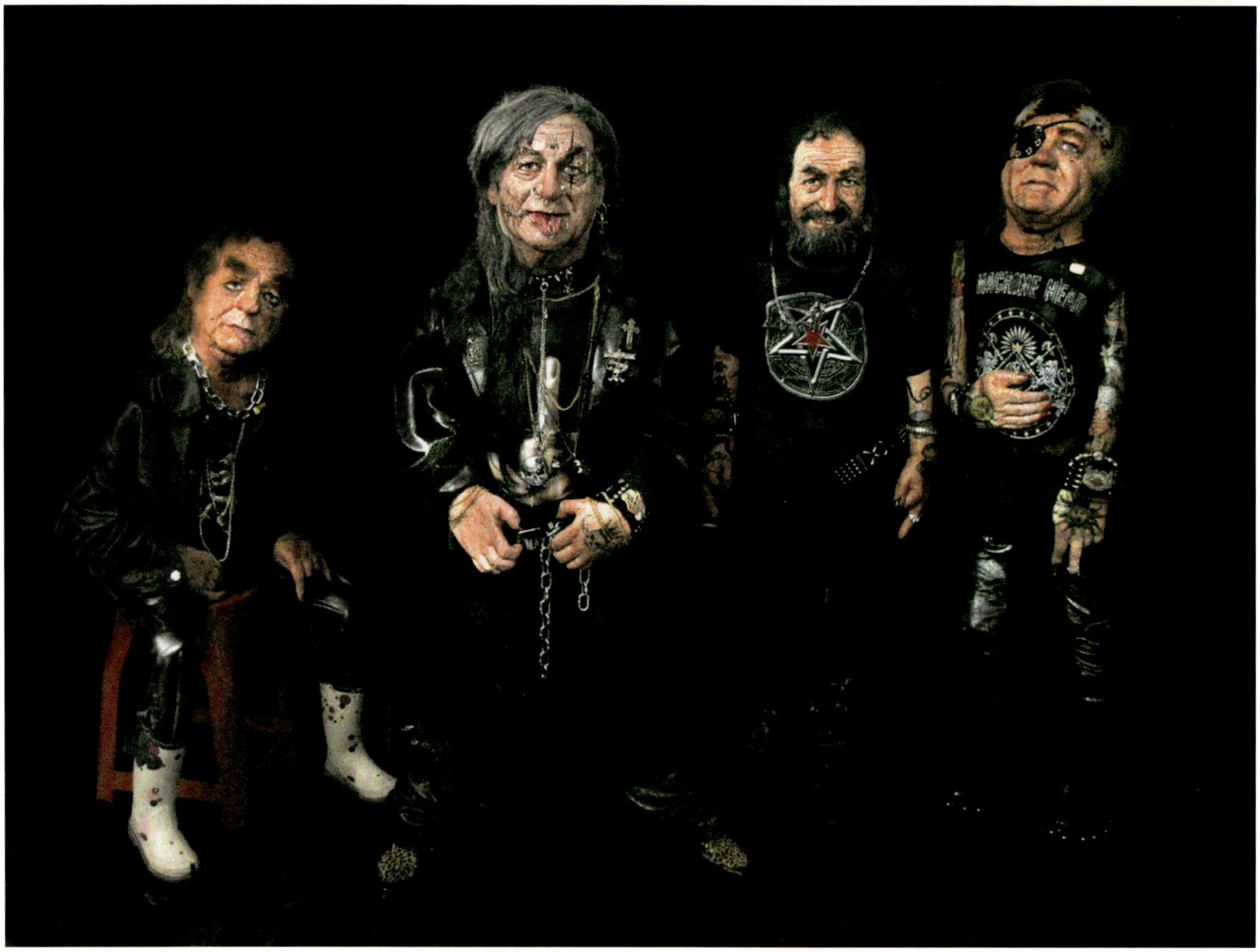
MACHINE HEAD

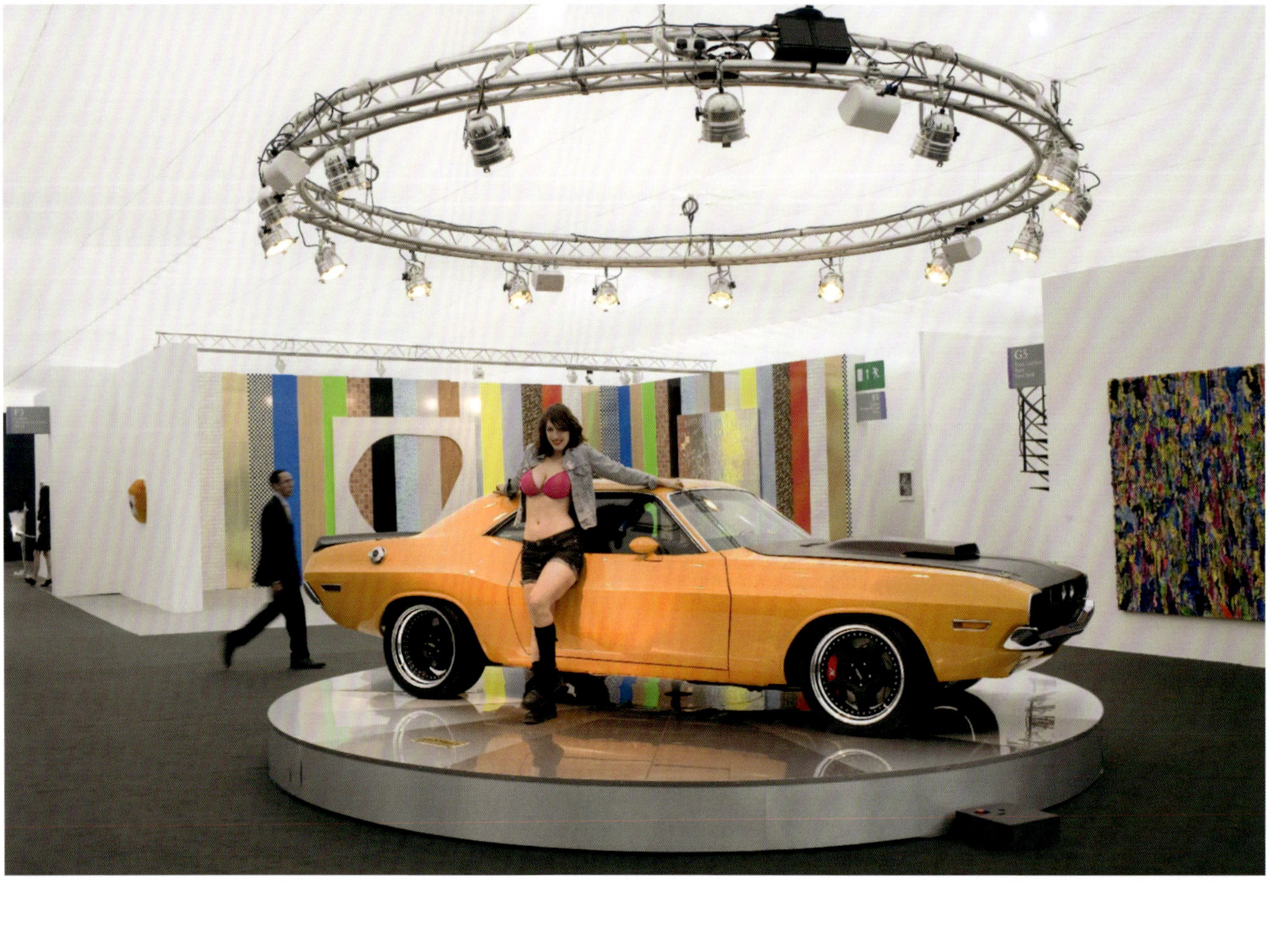
G5

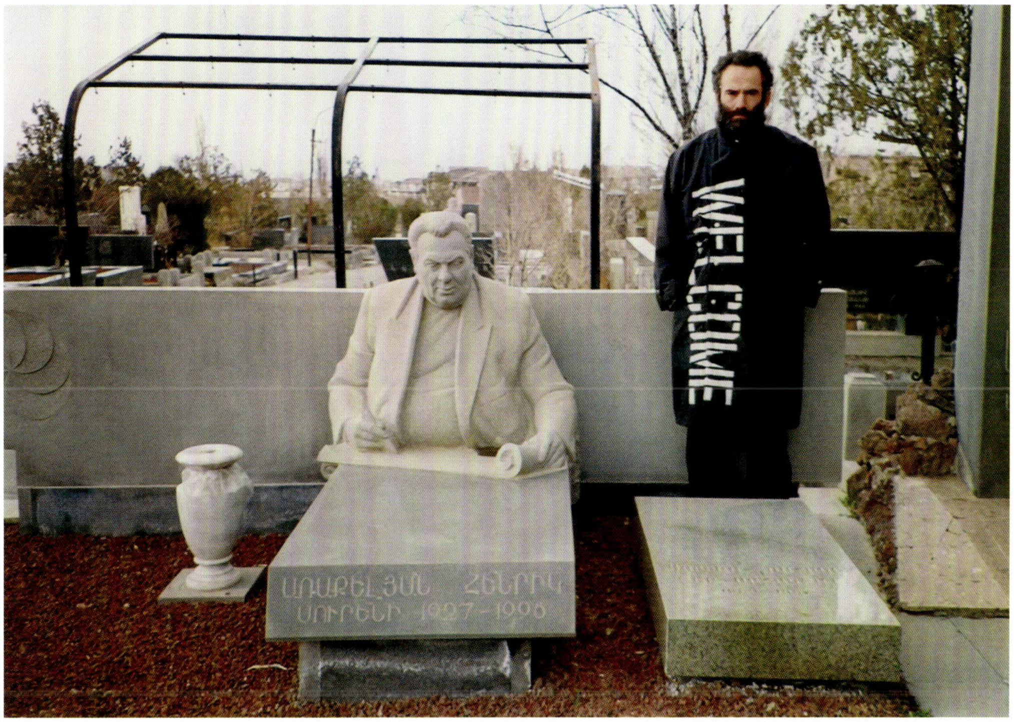

Enrique Marty
The Curatordeus (Szeegyas, Buchlodeus, Behstorr, Bilethoet), 2008
Mixed media, 130 cm each
Courtesy Galería Espacio Mínimo, Madrid

Richard Prince
Untitled, 2007
Automobile, rotating platform, and mixed media, dimensions variable
View of the installation at the Frieze Art Fair, London 2007

Azat Sargsyan
Welcome to Armenia, the Museum under the Heaven, 2008
View of the performance, VI International Biennial of Contemporary Art, Gyumri, Armenia 2008
Courtesy of the artist

and the city as its meeting place," quotes Eivind Furnesvik.[30]

The world's oldest biennale was held on April 30, 1895 and its trademarks of "international dialogue" and "the city as meeting place" heralded the birth of city marketing: it attracted 200,000 visitors! Like the great exhibitions of the century before, Venice started to build the first foreign pavilion in 1907, and since then the number of national pavilions has increased to 29. In 1951 the world's second oldest art biennial, the Bienal de São Paulo, also opted for a mix of international survey and national pavilions.

Documenta is held every 5 years, although until 1972 it was quadrennial. A curious but no less important anecdote is that Kassel had been chosen in 1955 to host the national garden show (BUGA) as "a collective undertaking through which", as the then Federal President Theodor Heuss put it, "a damaged or endangered community can make a recovery".[31] Arnold Bode conceived *European Art of the Twentieth Century* as an exhibition to be integrated within the infrastructure of the garden show. German artists had to recover their contact with contemporary art and the nascent pro-European movement, and "the State of Hessen had to enhance the supra-local significance of the Garden Show in such a way that it not only captured the attention of the experts, but also of those that were interested in culture".[32] For his Documenta, Arnold Bode took the model of The Armory Show of 1913, a commercial show organized by the Association of American Painters and Sculptors. So, Documenta became a mix of tourist, economical, psychological, educational, and artistic elements. The 100 days of Documenta received 130,000 visitors. A little bit more than 50 years later Documenta is considered unanimously the most important international survey on contemporary art in the world.

This brief historical overview is symptomatic of the hybrid origins of and correspondences between art fairs and biennials. If art fairs deal overtly with the market, biennials in turn – especially Documenta and Venice – become a platform for sanctioning art trends and aesthetic attitudes by declaring what is particular, good or relevant art here and now. Whether we like it or not, these power structures, that report to both an international and a local intelligentsia, and in which the curator performs a key role, create their own exhibition requirements and economic efficiency because they are oriented towards an international elite and the construction of value, be it symbolic or real.

To quote Groys: "It can of course be stated that the independent curator, as the museum curator before him, cannot but depend on the art market, even lay the groundwork for it. An art work's value increases when it is presented in a museum, or through its frequent appearance in the diverse temporary exhibitions organized by independent curators."[33]

The curator, whether independent or associated to an institution, has taken on a predominant role in contemporary art in his "profane" activity of detecting, contextualizing and narrativizing works of art. The '90s witnessed the banalization/ biennalization of biennales. This has also resulted, especially in the last 5 years, in a greater presence of the curator at art fairs, which "resort to the curator to act as an enabler or facilitator of a positioning via projects that are specifically created for the fair."[34] Not only as in Art Vienna's case mentioned in the beginning of the essay, but more curators have started to work as artistic directors for art fairs, are conceiving special exhibitions – see Neville Wakefield, who curated the *FRIEZE Projects* – or are finding their ways in to the selection committees. Curators that by definition conceive shows for institutions or biennials have arrived recently in the world of art fairs; although it is maybe more precise to put it the other way around: art fairs have attracted the intellectual capital of curators in a move to distinguish themselves among the mass of art fair proposals. In short, this means that the curator has started to become even more central to contemporary art practices. Here he works directly with/for the market; in the case of biennials it's more elliptical and subtle but still very obvious. It should be seen in a bigger and more structural context: the worldwide shift from a museum-style management centered on the conservation and acquisition of a permanent collection towards a thematic or monographic exhibition policy, which prioritizes objectives of media coverage and increasing visitor numbers, in which the curator becomes a mediator between the institution and the public.

Art fairs and biennials cannot escape contamination, they just reflect the fast advancement of the commodification of culture in a more or less discreet manner. Some more recent examples, by no means exhaustive, will help us to understand this particularly symptomatic moment of crossed relationships.

Ana Somers Cocks wrote an article in 2007 in *The Art Newspaper* titled "Venice Biennale proposes becoming a selling show again". The word 'again' here means that at some point in the past it functioned de facto like an art fair, and that is the case. Ettore Gian Ferrari, the official trader between 1942 and 1968, charged 15% commission for the Biennale and 2% for himself for any art work exhibited at the Biennale that he was commissioned to sell.[35] Davide Croff, the former president of the Biennale Foundation suggested this possibility. This is very comprehensible as the eternal problem with the Venice Biennale is that due to its meager budget it depends too much on the big galleries and big collectors, which happily pay the production, transportation and installation costs, and in return receive a "biennalized" artist. In some cases, this proximity is not only conceptual in nature, but it even becomes geographical, as was the case with the Cornice Art Fair in 2007, which coincided with the preview of the 52nd Biennale and was held only ten minutes away from the Giardini, and whose intention was to be held every 2 years concurrently with La Biennale itself! But also the Docks Art Fair is paired with the Lyon Biennale, and Contemporary Istanbul Art Fair runs parallel to the Istanbul Biennial...

What about ARCO? The Spanish art fair is an interesting case study, especially as from its very beginnings in 1982, due to a disconnection with contemporary art caused by 40 years of dictatorship, the fair turned into a media spectacle with a broad range of cultural experiences – including cocktails, openings, performances, afterhours activities... – and making itself a trendsetter for today's art fairs. And the most surprising facts was the enormous range of conferences that made ARCO function de facto as a quasi-biennial with its "100 speakers": Okwui Enwezor, Hou Hanru, Paulo Herkenhoff, Dan Cameron, Barry Schwabsky, Octavio Zaya to mention just six of practically all the leading thinkers in contemporary art. Furthermore, there is of course FRIEZE. Curated by Neville Wakefield and with a considerable budget, FRIEZE Projects readopted and re-launched the early 1980s idea of the curator as an instigator or initiator of artists' projects.

Another important non-mainstream biennale is the Havana Biennial, which kicked off in 1984. According to Cuban curator Gerardo Mosquera, "It is undeniable that the second Havana Biennial in 1986 was the first truly global exhibition, reuniting 690 artists from 57 countries and taking place 3 years before *Les Magiciens de la Terre*."[36] But even the Havana Biennial, whose 10th show went under the

Pablo Helguera
Artoons, 2008
Courtesy Jorge Pinto Books Inc, New York

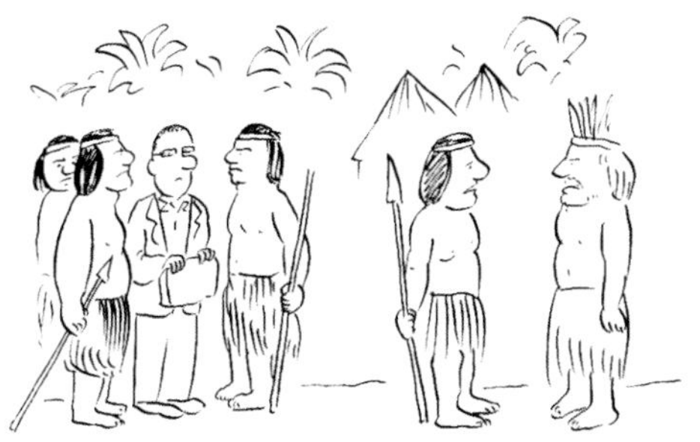

"He says he is curating a biennial and wants to know if anyone here does video."

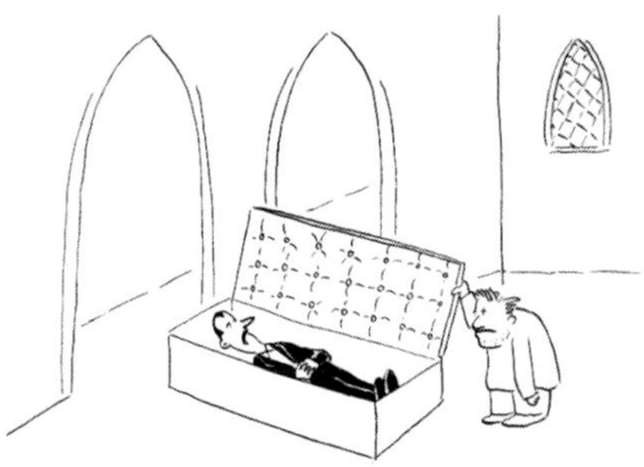

"Just wake me up 'til the next Documenta."

heading "Integration and Resistance in the Global Era", has been subjected to unstoppable fairization as Cuba lost its free oil supply due to the collapse of the Soviet Union in 1989. According to Elvis Fuentes, the Cuban curator of El Museo del Barrio in New York, "In 1991, Mr. Ludwig visited Cuba and started to buy Cuban art. A year later Carlos Aldana was appointed the ideological guardian of sorts at the Ministry of Culture and started to monitor Cuban artists living temporarily outside the island, like José Bedia, Rubén Torres Llorca, and many more, who had been working in Mexico or Europe. Aldana pressed them forcefully to return to Cuba, but most of them decided not to do so, and migrated to the United States or stayed in Mexico and Europe."[37] The result was that the organizers of the 1994 Havana Biennial had few artists to choose from, so they included students in their early 20s from the Instituto Superior de Arte, such as Carlos Garaicoa, Los Carpinteros, Sandra Ramos and Abel Barroso. On the other hand, economic reforms were introduced in 1993, including the de-penalization of hard currency (especially U.S. dollars). Artists started to sell, and, taking advantage of the flow of foreign visitors to the Biennial, many organized small exhibitions in their studios/houses, where they could sell direct. Since then, most Cuban artists have organized studio receptions for foreign visitors that coincide with the event, and this year many collectors from the United States and Europe headed again to Havana – not really because they are interested in the Biennial, but, just as Ludwig did from 1991 on, to visit artists' homes in the hope of buying art at cheaper prices before Cuba collapses. The problem now is that many artists are producing artworks that correspond to the Cuban clichés they think the collectors are interested in.

These extraordinary cross-identifications also concern different aspects of Documenta. According to Antony Hudek, Harald Szeemann's original idea considered the inclusion of artistic actions during the 100 days of Documenta, which was inspired on Szeeman's earlier *Happening & Fluxus* festival that he co-curated with Hanns Sohn in 1970–1971: "Explicitly referencing the art fair – with rows of booths devoted to protagonists of Fluxus and happenings – the *show-like* exhibition was meant to include numerous live performances, many of which ended up censored by local authorities."[38] It's not my intention to split hairs on Okwui's Documenta 11, but his intent to introduce cinema on a large scale in the exhibition spaces reminds us that the premises that cinema originally inhabited were those of the trade fair, within which cinema integrated smoothly in the overall carnivalesque spectacle.[39] Finally, and on a more formal level, the fair-like installation in Buergel's Aue Pavilion helped to stimulate the analogy once more.

Epilogue: on neo-biennalism and neo-fairism

Having arrived at this point, we can now go to the heart of the matter: what should the task of a biennial or an art fair be in the early twenty-first century? In other words: how can we reformulate the functions of biennials and art fairs as institutions and artistic structures?

Before attempting an answer, let me first introduce some brief thoughts about the biennalization of the world. The '90s can be commonly considered "the age of the biennials",[40] and this decade itself as "the age of the art fair", though this, I think, is coming to an end. To a greater or

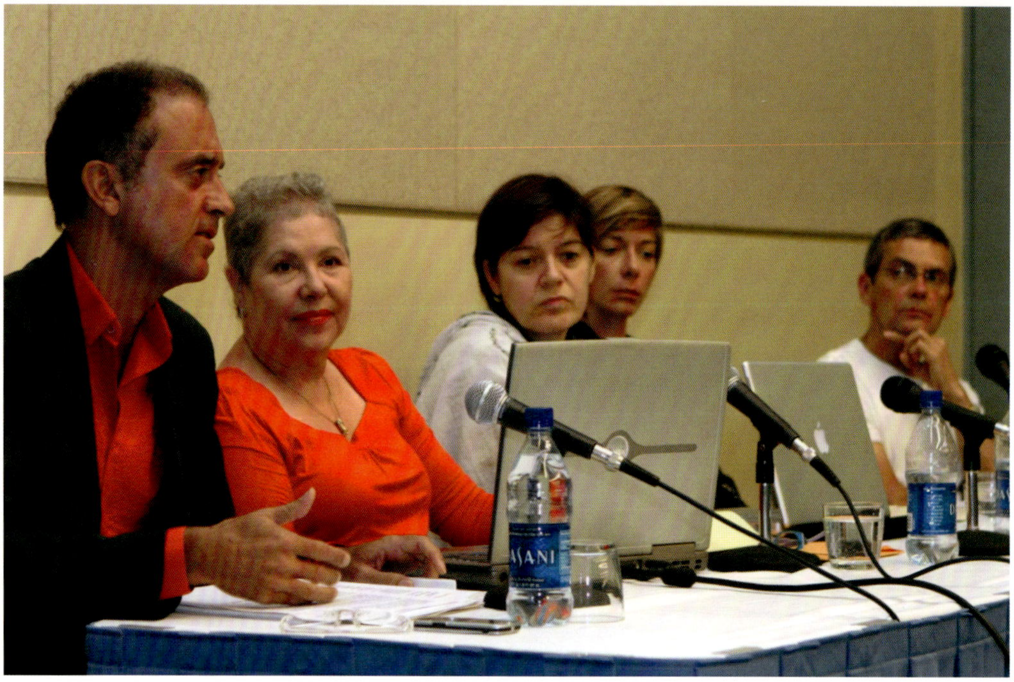

Curator's (on the) Move, photograph taken during the meeting at the Escuela de Artes Plástica of Puerto Rico at III CIRCA – Puerto Rico International Art Fair, Puerto Rico 2008
From left to right: Alexandre Melo, Haydée Venegas, Ute Meta Bauer, Sally Breen, and Michel Blancsubé
Courtesy CIRCA

lesser degree, biennials have lost the significance they once had – that Buergel's Documenta turned into a *Wunderkammer* and Storr's Venice Biennale into a *salon* is a rather conservative and unexpected twist[41] – but even so they keep growing steadily.[42] The reasons are diverse, but we can sum them up as follows: the historical biennial model has recently been into brought question by those cities that started copying it simply because of a search for legitimization from the West, such as the Bienal de São Paulo and Gwangju Biennale, while others questioned the model right from the start and looked for a contextualization – the Mercosur Biennial, Havana Biennial, and The Asia Pacific Triennale. Biennials have been traditionally used as a strategy to put a city on the global map, but at the same time they have been tools in the hands of local politicians with non-cultural agendas, like the Havana Biennial, the Johannesburg Biennale, the Valencia Biennial and the Lima Biennial. Furthermore, the weakness of the biennials lies in the "check-list syndrome", by which the same artists, curators and ideas are repeated over and over, revealing a considerable lack of field work. Lastly, too many biennials are engaged in a dull and repetitive global international discourse without a real connection to local needs and local audiences; examples are the Biennale of Sydney, Shanghai Biennale and Moscow Biennale. This also explains why many biennials like the Valencia Biennial, the Melbourne Biennial and the Johannesburg Biennale have either been discontinued, or just aren't that important anymore, for instance, the Havana Biennial, Bienal de São Paolo, Site Santa Fe, and others.

In contrast, since the advent of Art Basel Miami Beach (ABMB) in 2002, art fairs have experienced a "golden age". Their success can be explained by the fact that they have assumed the status of Urban Entertainment Center (UEC) within the current capitalism of experiences.[43]

Unlike biennials or museums, where the audience is a passive entity, art fairs not only offer a more democratic and less intimidating access to contemporary art, but, and this is really important, they allow the visitor to transcend the mere category of "observer" to become a "role player" through research, bargaining and (though not necessarily) buying a work of art. The 29 art fairs running parallel to ABMB in the 2009 edition give a pretty good idea of the importance of this phenomenon, and thus we cannot simply dispatch it, hoping they will all soon disappear. Art fairs are necessary, and we should not forget that these are structures that in the end support the artist and art production. The market will dictate the continuation or disappearance of many of them.

When I think these days about biennials I can't help but be reminded of Pablo Helguera's *artoon* of the curator visiting a native village: "He says he is curating a biennial and wants to know if anyone here does video." Maybe I would have chosen "installation" instead of "video", as the high-impact spectacular installation has become the commodified medium par excellence that embodies "biennial art" (in the same way that painting as the most saleable art form embodies "art fair art"). Anyway, the parable is poignant, but it reflects the current situation with wit and intelligence.

This brings us to the two basic types of biennial, which represent more or less the majority: 1) the universalist, international, gigantic, authorial, large budget biennial, and 2) the smaller in scale and budget, with a mix of blue-chip international and local artists, more emerging or unstable proposals, centered on local/global discourses. These two types are also applicable to art fairs to a certain extent, where there is also an insistent trend towards "curated sections" and special artists' solo presentations or group exhibitions specifically developed for the fair.

New Institutionalism re-used and renovated the strategies of institutional critique initiated by conceptual art. This allows us to trace an analogy and launch the idea of a "neo-biennalism" and a "neo-fairism": a new way of understanding and reformulating the function of the biennial and the art fair as an institution and artistic structure. Some may argue that it is not appropriate to mix the two concepts as biennials are intellectually legitimated and art fairs are not. I would remind them of Mexican international curator Cuauhtémoc Medina's comments back in 2001: "Curatorship is a creative sublimation of forces such as: the quest for prestige of bourgeois patrons, the tickle of legitimacy and cultural disinfection of state bureaucracies, the search for new hegemonic powers of the old nationalisms, and the ardor of those two omnipresent erotic forces – vanity and greed."[44]

Neo-biennalism and neo-fairism should open the way on the appropriateness of these (mega-)exhibitions and art fairs and tackle necessary questions like: are large, comprehensive ideas that define a certain artistic moment still a biennial's most important mission? Is the authorial biennial curated by a prominent international curator still a valid discourse or shall we make way for less constrained exhibitions in which the experience of the art work becomes a priority and not its description? Should a biennial introduce events also held outside the time of the exhibition, such as lectures, conferences and other pedagogical activities, or should these activities just be limited to the time of the show? Is a biennial still an articulated discourse for the idea of progress and utopia or just a branding tool to bring in high-end tourism? Is it appropriate that art fairs work with curators and are being more and more used as curatorial platforms? Is

Gabriel Sierra
In Living Contact, 2008
Wooden structures,
dimensions variable
View of the installation at the
28ª Bienal de São Paulo,
São Paulo 2008
Courtesy Galería Casas Riegner,
Bogotá

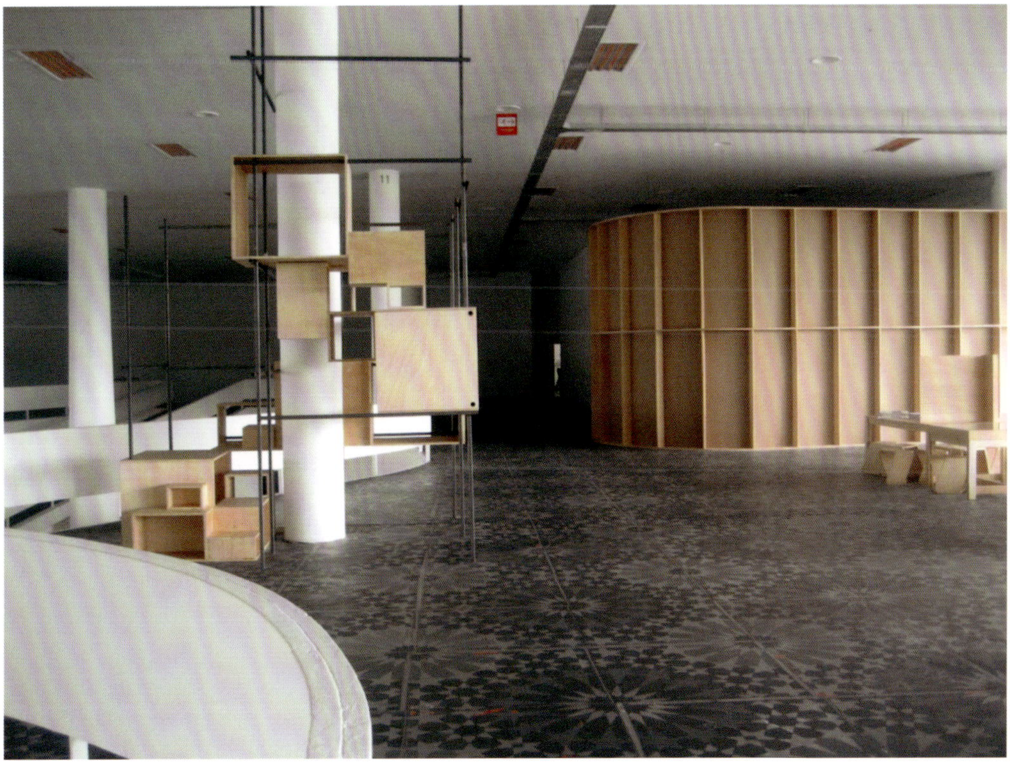

it part of the mission of an art fair to organize conferences and debates? How can an art fair and its dealers make more interesting presentations? Is it appropriate that art fairs take up resources from other artistic institutions? Which brings us to the final and fundamental question: Are we running so short on ideas that we can't come up with other artistic formats?

These are complex questions to which there are no easy answers. Both biennials and art fairs destabilize the traditional limits between the private/market and the public/state. We can either adopt a moralist point of view or turn a blind eye, but that would be like "saying you won't participate in the market", to quote Jerry Saltz, "because you refuse to breathe air that's polluted. Unless you live in a bubble, you may have no choice. Even if you're not making money, that's your relationship to the market."[45]

As we have been speculating on *neo-modernism*, *neo-biennalism*, and *neo-fairism*, let me finish with Neo when he considers turning back, but Trinity forces the moment to its crisis: "You have been down there, Neo. You know that road. You know exactly where it ends, and I know that is not where you want to be." Maybe we should choose the red pill to see how deep the art hole goes....

[1] Maybe we should refer here to the mythical *Freeze* exhibition organized by art students from Goldsmith College back in 1988, amongst whom Damien Hirst, which ushered in a new era in terms of the marketing of an artist.

[2] Harald Szeemann once said that in the '70s it was very normal in Central Europe to have galleries acting like museums or kunsthalles, as there was little else on the contemporary art-scene. Ursula Krinzinger in Graz (Austria) and the Contemporary Art Center in Bellinzona (Switzerland) are two examples.

[3] J. Burcet, *El agujero blanco* (The White Hole), 2003, e-book www.-burcet.net.

[4] B. Groys, *Art Power*, MIT Press, Cambridge(Mass.), p. 13.

[5] A book that highlights the matter very well is *In defense of globalization* (OUP, New York 2004) by Jagdish Bhagwati, Professor of Economics at Columbia University. He reveals the trilogy of dissatisfaction formed by anti-capitalist, anti-globalization and anti-corporate attitudes that deny globalization any beneficial effect on poverty, child labor or women's rights, pp. 87–147.

[6] L. Boltanski and E. Chiapello, *The New Spirit of Capitalism*, trans. G. Elliott, Verso, London 2006.

[7] See P. Barragán, *The Art Fair Age*, Edizioni Charta, Milan 2008, p. 19.

[8] J. Stallabrass, *Art Incorporated*, Oxford University Press, Oxford 2004, p. 3.

[9] M. Lazzarato, "Art and Work", *Parachute*, April–May–June 2006, p. 84.

[10] D. Dierderichsen, *On (Surplus) Value in Art*, Witte de With Publishers and Steinberg Press, Rotterdam and Berlin 2008, p. 32.

[11] E-article http://www.pucsp.br/~lbraga/epap_cult6.htm (Portuguese version in Lucia Santaella, *Cultura das Mídias*, 2004, ed. Sao Paulo: Experimento, Sao Paulo).

[12] A. Huyssen, "Modernity as Antiquity. A Category Mistake", in *Brumaria 9: Modernity? Life!*, autumn 2007, p. 307.

[13] *Ibid.*

[14] S.P. Rouanet,, *As razoes do Iluminismo*, 1987, Companhia das Letras, Sao Paulo, pp. 269–70.

[15] *Ibid.*

[16] E. Tiryankian, *Modernization: Exhumetur in pace*, 1991, *International Sociology* 6, pp. 165–80.

[17] Post-modernist values like pluralism and the respect shown towards others and minorities will be maintained.

[18] S. Critchley, "On Neo-Anarchism" in *Sustainabilities*, 2008, ed. P. Barragán, Edizioni Charta, Milan, pp. 63–67.

[19] Boltanski and Chiapello, *New Spirit...*, op. cit.

[20] In addition to the Manzoni retrospective, Mr. Gagosian has been organizing these monographic exhibitions: *Alighiero e Boetti* (New York, 2001); *Pino Pascali* (New York, 2006); *Mario Merz* (London, 2006), and *Lucio Fontana* (London, 2008). Gagosian has helped foster their market value, but also their international recognition. Does the work become codified within the museum caliber or is it still in the commercial realm?

[21] Z. Bauman, *Liquid Times: Living in an Age of Uncertainty*, 2007, Polity Press, Cambridge, p. 1.

[22] J.B. Pine II and J.H. Gilmore, *The Experience Economy: Work is a Theatre & Every Business a Stage*, 1999, Harvard Business School Press, Boston, p. 95.

[23] Of course we should not forget all those new museums and contemporary art centers that spring up like mushrooms, and the equally excessive and expensive museum enlargements in the name of the democratization of art.

[24] R. Storr, "The Biennale: Art Forum or Global Salon", publication conference held by Robert Storr at Fundación ICO, Madrid, on March 30, 2006, p. 52.

[25] See www.grandtour2007.com.

[26] M. Robecchi, "Let Me Entertain You: The Never-Ending Debate around Art Fairs and Biennials", preface in P. Barragán, *The Art Fair Age*, 2008, Edizioni Charta, Milan, p. 13.

[27] E.A. Honig, *Painting and the Market in Early Modern Antwerp*, 1998, Yale University Press, New Haven, pp. 3–4.

[28] The first salon took already place in 1673 in Paris organized by the French Academy, but they really became common place in the 18th century. See Storr, pp. 10–12.

[29] www.labiennale.org.

[30] E. Furnesvik, "Phantom Pains" in *Verksted #1: New Institutionalism*, 2003, edited by the Office for Contemporary Art (OCA), p. 21, referring to West's 1995 book about the origins of the Venice Biennale.

[31] Quoted by R. Buergel, "The Origins", in *Brumaria 9: Modernity? Life!*, autumn 2007, p. 252.

[32] Arnold Bode quoted in *50 Jahre/Years documenta 1955–2005*, documenta Archiv der Stadt Kassel, Span-

ish translation on occasion of the exhibition at Domus Artium (DA2), Salamanca, 23 June–17 September 2006, pp. 6-7.

[33] B. Groys, *Art Power*, 2008, MIT Press, Cambridge (Mass.), p. 51.

[34] See "The Curated Art Fair and the Art Fair Curator" in P. Barragán *The Art Fair Age*, Edizioni Charta, Milan, pp. 39–58.

[35] A. Somers Cocks, "Venice Biennale proposes to become a selling show again" in *The Art Newspaper* electronic edition http://www.theartnewspaper.com/article01.asp?id=644.

[36] G. Mosquera, "Consolidación y desarrollo", *Exit Express* #37, June-September 2008, p. 11.

[37] Conversation held at El Museo del Barrio in New York on Monday March 16, 2009.

[38] A. Hudek, "El retorno de la exposición" (The Return of the Exhibition), *Exit Express* #37, June–September 2008, p. 13.

[39] There is a wide campaign to confine cinema inside the museum and exhibition walls, but it is condemned to fail as the concepts of immobilization of the image and immobilization of the audience clash completely.

[40] Not only because of their importance to the artistic discourse, but also because of the growing number of biennials in non-mainstream countries during this decade: Sharjah Biennial, United Arab Emirates (1993), Gwangju, South Korea (1995), Johannesburg Biennale (1995), Shanghai Biennale, China (1996), Mercosur Biennial, Porto Alegre, Brazil (1997), Dak'art Biennale, Senegal (1998), Busan Biennale, Korea (1998); and in Europe the Berlin Biennale, Germany (1998).

[41] See for example the interesting articles on this subject by Darío Corbeira "Documenta 12: Aladdin in Kassel" and Carlos Jiménez "Wunderkammer", *Brumaria 9*, Autumn 2007, pp. 365–74.

[42] I have to admit that I am a little bored now by the excess of biennials, especially as they do not add anything to the artistic discourse nor to the city they are held in, like the most recent Brussels Biennial. Now it seems that not only founding biennials, but also setting up conferences about biennials – whether a city has a biennial or not – is the trend. See for example e-flux titled "The Bergen Biennial Conference", from the Kunsthall Bergen, dated February 24, 2009, and also "On biennials/Tutto sulle biennali", dated March 17, 2009, at the Festival of Contemporary Art in Faenza. For both see www.e-flux.com.

[43] For a detailed explanation see Barragán, pp. 25–37.

[44] Cuauhtémoc Medina, "Una teoría sobre la derrota" (A theory about failure), *Lápiz*, no. 169–70, February 2001, p. 34.

[45] Jerry Saltz, "The Zero-Sum Game", *Modern Painters,* February 2007, p. 34.

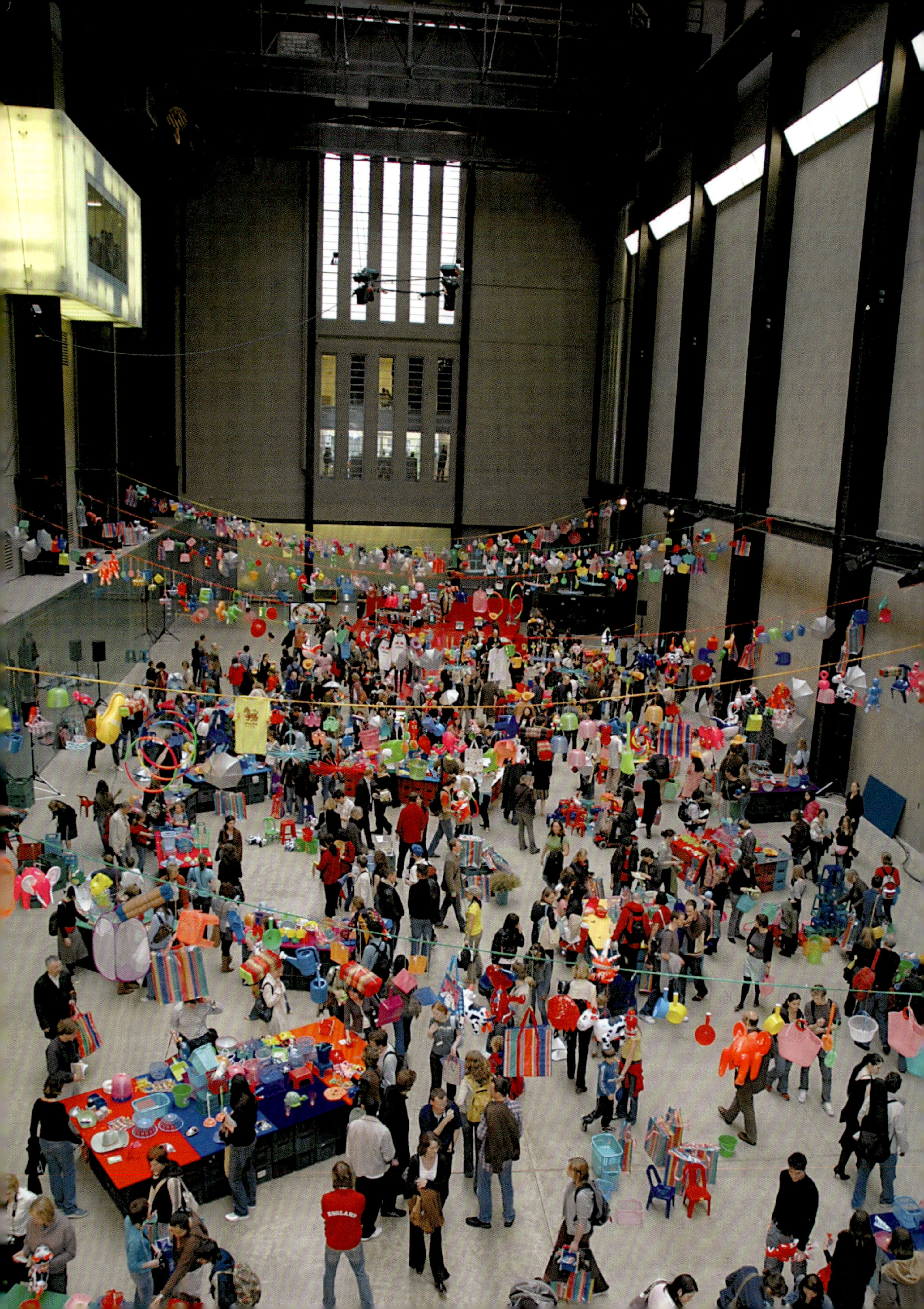
ENGLAND

Walter Guadagnini

The Art Market and New Forms of Art Collecting

"We at Philip Morris think it is appropriate that we participate in bringing these works to the attention of the public, for there is a key element in this 'new art' that has its counterpart in the business world. That element is innovation – without which it would be impossible for progress to be made in any segment of society. ... As businessmen in tune with our times, we at Philip Morris are committed to support the experimental."[1] Long before the processes that were to force the tobacco multinationals to pay out millions in compensation, Philip Morris took pride in its championing of "new" art, asserting a model of artistic patronage that, with rhetorical formulas grounded on an analogous philosophy, can still be found today in the statements of firms financially and organizationally involved in the field of contemporary art.

Forty years ago – the sponsor's statement cited above was published in 1969 – the relationship between business and contemporary culture was already an established fact in the United States and indeed one of the primary factors that had enabled New York to take over from Paris as the art capital after World War II. The alliance between museums and great collections, both private and corporate, paved the way in the 1960s for the worldwide success of Pop Art and Minimalism, the first entirely and inherently American movements in the history of art. This involved essential support from the market and especially the auction circuit, its most effective form in terms of mass-media coverage.

The fame of the American corporate collections crossed the ocean and arrived in Europe, a very different continent both culturally and economically, where government action and private initiative could at most proceed parallel to one another, with mutual distrust, in the almost total absence of any strategic vision of this relationship. With the exception of Japan and South America, areas in any case strongly influenced by the cultural model of the USA, the rest of the world was substantially extraneous for both political and economic reasons to the mechanisms whereby the contemporary art system was constructed.

An epochal watershed in both symbolic and concrete terms came 20 years later, in 1989, with historic events like the fall of the Berlin Wall and the students' rebellion in Beijing – the latter being symptomatic of a radical change underway in Chinese society since the introduction of the first forms of a free market in the late 1970s – and the crucial artistic event of the exhibition *Les Magiciens de la terre* at the Centre Pompidou in Paris, focusing for the first time on artists from non-Western geocultural areas.

The confused and sometimes dramatic transition of the socialist countries of East Europe to the capitalist model and the exponential economic growth of the areas of China, India, Southeast Asia and finally the Gulf led in the following years to a corresponding increase in the number of potential actors in every sector of the art system, from production to dissemination and authentic marketing. The Euro-American cultural duopoly turned into a polycentric system that in any case developed along the lines of the US model, which was in turn adapted to the structures existing in West Europe, where government tended to attach ever greater importance to the involvement of the private sector, not only in the funding but also in the management or joint management – of spaces and projects connected with the creation and dissemination of contemporary art.

This new socioeconomic situation gave rise in the second half of the 1990s and the first decade of the new century to a series of phenomena now known not only to the parties involved but also to the general public, informed by the mass media on a wholly unprecedented scale about developments in the world of contemporary art: the proliferation of biennials and triennials in every corner of the globe; the parallel increase in the number of specialized art fairs; the birth of private foundations and collections of such size and financial power as to challenge the primacy of public initiative in this sphere; the resulting need to build places strongly characterized symbolically in terms of formal recognizability, scale, and fame of the architects involved in order to house

Surasi Kusolwong
One Pound Turbo Market (You'll Have a Good Time), 2006
10,000 different objects, of everyday use from Thailand, sold for one pound each, Perspex box with money, and the artist's performance with music and moving images
View of the performance held on May 26, 2006 for the *Futurist Friday – States of Flux* at Tate Modern, London
Courtesy of the artist

Exterior view of the building designed by Herzog & de Meuron for the Madrid headquarters of the Obra Social Fundaciòn "la Caixa," 2008

Gary Hill
Guilt, 2006
5 telescopes with 5 MDF–board pyramidal mounts, 5 unique gold coins with 5 motorized aluminum stands, 5 Audio Spotlight speakers, 5 DVD players, and 5 DVDs
View of the installation realized in 2006 at Fondation Cartier pour l'art contemporain, Paris

cover the whole range of variants between these two hypothetical extremes.

This applies *a fortiori* to areas like Asia and the Arab world, characterized on the one hand by the assertion of cultural identity grounded on a deeply rooted tradition, and on the other by an equally strong desire to open up to the international contemporary scene. Above all in the case of the Arab countries, it is often precisely in its expressive forms of greatest success, and hence most coveted for reasons of status, that the latter comes into collision with the very elements in which the local culture is rooted.[7]

All this naturally has a crucial impact on the market. The decision to give the collection – including in this case private collections on the scale of those mentioned above – a local or international character, the preference for a particular period, and the choice of one medium rather than another have a direct influence in economic terms independently of the purely speculative aspects. (The latter are not addressed here and are mentioned solely as elements that must be taken into account but require substantially different models of interpretation.) Conversely, the same thing happens when a collection is placed on the market, in that the sale of a part or the whole involves the way in which it is perceived, increasing the economic value with a symbolic added value that may have an effect on the entire system, obviously of a negative character in this case.

The last 15 years have seen a convergence of these economic, social, and cultural factors leading at the same time to the spread of contemporary forms of artistic expression and an increase in the prices of artworks. A few figures regarding auction trends in recent years will suffice to show the scale of this phenomenon. The total annual turnover of auctions went from $ 4.2 billion in 2005 to $ 9.3 billion in 2007. The number of Chinese artists fetching prices in excess of $ 1 million rose from 4 in 2006 to 35 in 2008. Christie's began to operate directly in Dubai in 2006. In 2007, 1254 works fetched prices in excess of $ 1 million. In 2008, the year in which London overtook New York in terms of the volume of transactions, the segment of contemporary art remained the richest in the market but registered a drop of 34.4% with respect to the previous year. In the same year, a work by the artist Iranian Parviz Tanavoli fetched over $ 2 million in Dubai, setting a new record for a contemporary artist from that geographic area.[8]

It is clear that these figures are characterized also by strong speculative components and rest on private collectors of the very latest generation rather than the historical or corporate collections, which are by nature less exposed to the spotlight and more involved in the production phase or support for the activities of galleries. At the same time, there is also a further element prompting reflection on the effective nature of these phenomena, one arising inside the economy generated by auction sales and not out of comparison – useful though this would be – with the entire economy revolving around contemporary art. In 2008, Christie's and Sotheby's generated 73% of the world turnover for auctions but handled only 16% of the works auctioned. If we are to have a clearer idea of the real current situation, it will obviously be essential to examine the movements of the remaining 84%, capable of generating "only" 27% of the proceeds but involving a far greater number of artists and collectors.

Moreover, examination of the data for last year show that an artist like Jeff Wall – a leading figure on the international scene and one who paved the way back in the 1980s for the boom in contemporary photography as regards cultural consideration and the art market – is ranked no higher than 487th in terms of the amount of money generated by his works in auctions. Though surprising at first sight, this is actually due to the fact that only six works came under the hammer. Comparison with the results for the same artist in 2007 reveals, however, that in the space of one year – which significantly included the major anthological exhibition that toured the United States, following the show held in Basel's highly prestigious Schaulager in 2005 – the value of the artist's individual works increased by practically 500%. An evidently extraordinary year for the artist but also a case showing clearly how such data require interpretation on a variety of levels.

This mention of Jeff Wall will enable us to conclude this concise overview with a case study encapsulating all the elements taken into consideration above, namely the creation of the market for photography, which began in the early twentieth century and attained full completion in the 1990s. Attention should be drawn to some key stages in this long and complex process. The first private galleries specializing in

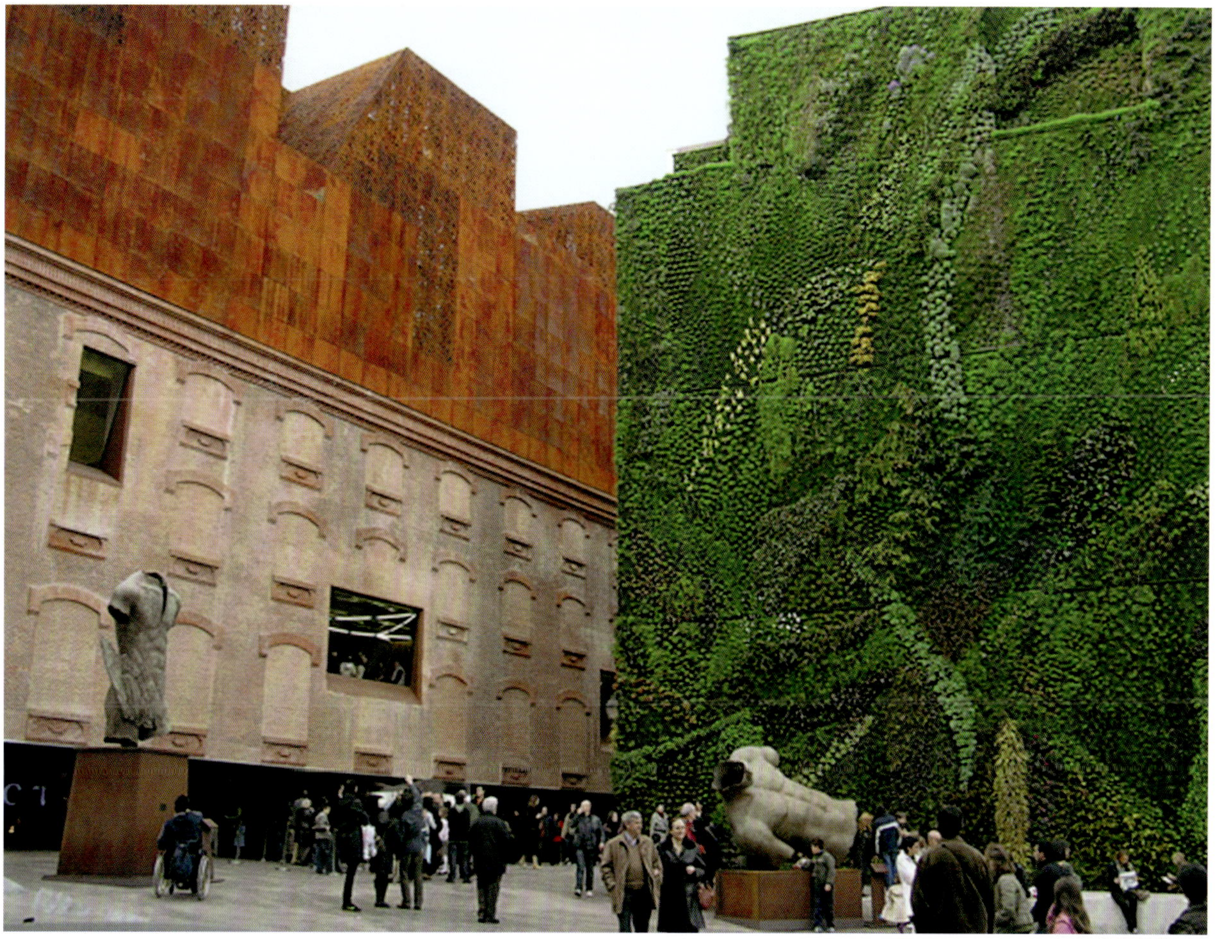

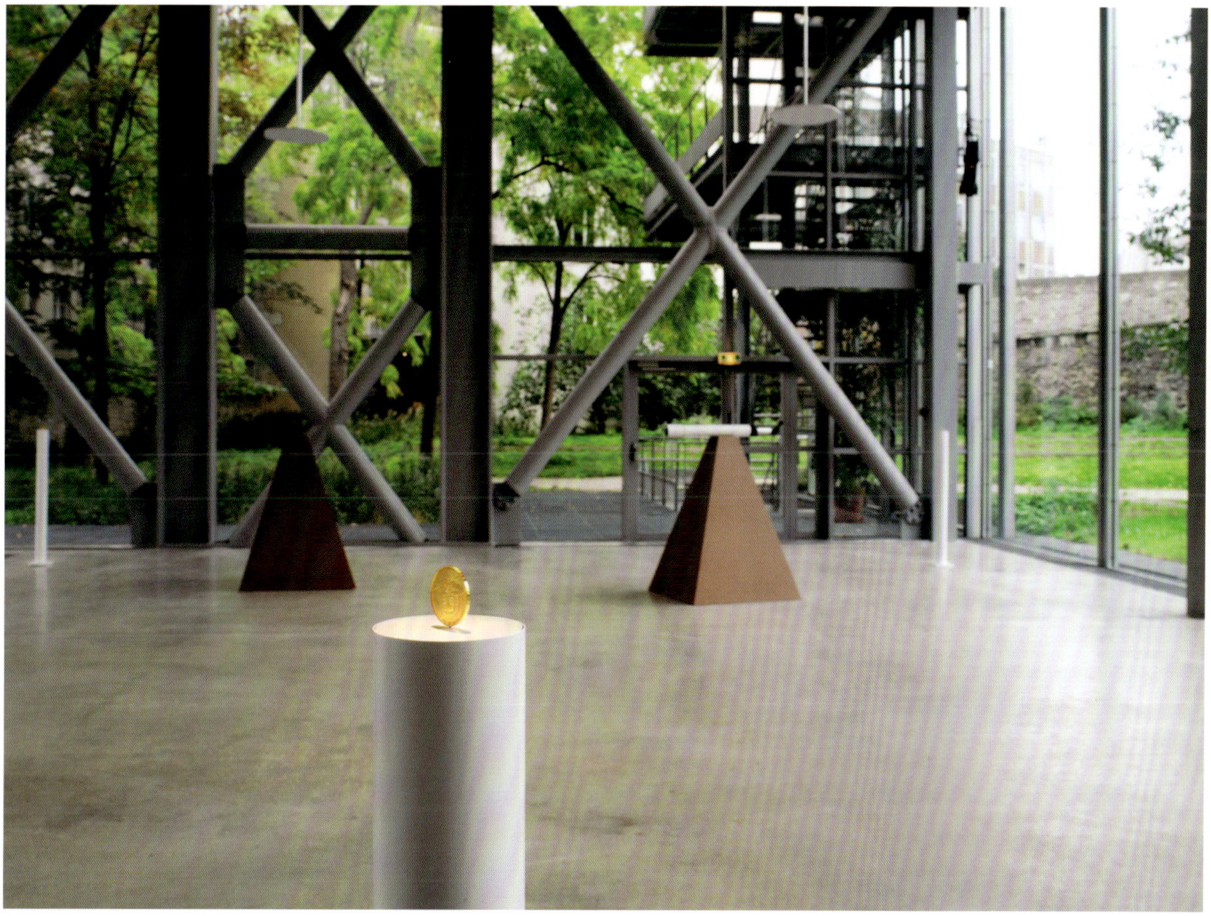

View of the second floor of the Museum Frieder Burda, Baden-Baden, with Richter paintings from the Frieder Burda Collection and the Böckmann Collection

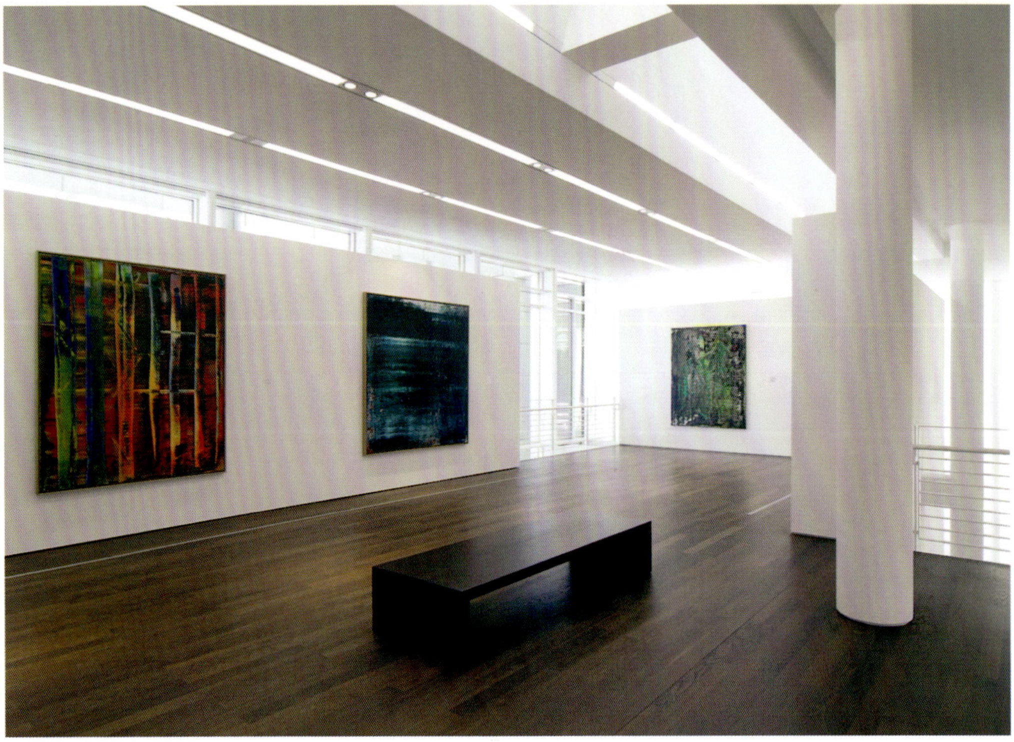

photography opened in the United States and Europe in the late 1960s and early 1970s. In 1967 the Exchange National Bank of Chicago commissioned Nancy and Beaumont Newhall – the latter being the curator of the first photographic department set up by a museum of contemporary art, namely the New York MoMA in 1940 – to create a photographic collection. The ABN AMRO banking group in Europe started work on its own photographic collection in the same year.

The 1970s and 1980s saw the creation of the first public collections, nearly all through sales or donations from private collectors (e.g., the purchase of the Gruber collection to constitute the initial nucleus of the photographic collection of the Ludwig Museum, Cologne, in 1977). At the same time, the consolidation and organization of the photographic market continued through the creation of agreed rules for the evaluation of a product differing in nature from the unique work of art, and through the first auctions devoted exclusively to photographs, like the pioneering sales held by Sotheby's in London and New York in 1975. The 1990s finally marked the definitive crowning of a steadily expanding phenomenon that reached its peak halfway through of the next decade. Paris Photo, the first international trade fair devoted exclusively to photography, opened in 1997.

The items of the Jammes collection were auctioned in 1999 for over € 11 million, € 6 million of which being spent by an emir of Qatar. The annual turnover for this segment of market reached $ 11 million in 2006 and Richard Prince's *Marlboro Man* fetched $ 2.4 million in 2007, breaking the historical record set a few months earlier for Andreas Gursky's *99 Cents*. As regards modern photography, a nude of 1927 by Edward Weston fetched over $1 million in 2008.[9]

The key importance of private and corporate collections in creating cultural and financial prestige, the further guarantee offered by the institution of the museum, the combined action of the art market and auctions, the introduction of new figures in the previously restricted world of art collecting, and the astronomical prices set for contemporary art due to reasons of speculation and taste are all encapsulated in the success of photography, which truly exemplifies the major developments in the art system at the end of the twentieth century and the beginning of the twenty-first.

[1] H. Szeemann (ed.). *When Attitudes Become Form*, exh. cat. (Bern, Kunsthalle, 1969), Bern 1969.
[2] *La grande vague* by Gustave Le Gray was sold on October 27, 1999, during the sale of the Jammes collection in London at Sotheby's. Francis Bacon's *Triptych* was sold on May 14, 2008, again by Sotheby's. A work by Mark Rothko had fetched $45 million at Christie's the day before and a work by Lucian Freud over $30 million, thus showing the existence of a carefully planned media strategy.
[3] As regards the bank sector, attention should be drawn at least to the following: the Deutsche Bank collection, founded in 1979 and turned into a joint venture with the Solomon R. Guggenheim Foundation in 1997; the UBS collection, which owes its present form to the takeover in 2000 of PaineWebber, an American company that had been building up its corporate collection since 1970; the DZ Bank collection, born in the early 1990s; the Dutch ABN AMRO collection, initiated in the early 1980s; the Fundació la Caixa collection, started by the bank of the same name in 1985; the UniCredit Group collection, begun in 2001, which now also includes the collections of Bank Austria and HVB, originating in the early 1980s. As regards companies, attention should be drawn to the Swiss Migros collection, the Fondation Cartier in Paris, and the collection of the Belgian group Lhoist, founded respectively in 1978, 1984, and 1990. For an essential bibliography, see the various books and catalogues published on all of the above, including both the collections as a whole and individual projects.
[4] Attention should be drawn in this connection to the creation in 2005 of the Dutch Association for Corporate Art Collections (VBCN), a model that was then expanded on the international scale in 2006 with the creation of the International Association of Corporate Collections of Contemporary Art (IACCCA), which has a total membership of 21 today.
[5] The private collection of Frieder Burda began in the early 1980s, the Foundation Frieder Burda was created in 1998, and the Frieder Burda Museum in Baden-Baden (designed by Richard Meier) opened in 2004. Founded in the late 1980s, the private collection of José Berardo was originally housed in the Museum of Sintra and was placed on permanent loan to the Portuguese state in 2007. It is now housed in the Center Cultural de Belem in Lisbon, which has been renamed the Museu Colecção Berardo. The Sandretto Re Rebaudengo collection made its first public appearance in an exhibition at the Galleria Civica, Modena, in 1995, the year in which it became a foundation. It opened its own exhibition center in Turin, designed by Claudio Silvestrin, in 2002. Once again, readers are referred to the numerous publications brought out by the bodies in question.
[6] The above-mentioned cases of the Fondation Cartier in Paris and the network of exhibition centers of the Fundació la Caixa provide good examples in this connection. The primary characteristic of these spaces is the presence of strong architectural characterization, as exemplified by the building designed by Jean Nouvel in Paris and the more recent work by Herzog & de Meuron in Madrid.
[7] See the papers delivered and the discussions held at the Global Art Meeting, held in 2007 and 2008 in Dubai and coinciding significantly with the Art Dubai fair: M. Finders (ed.), *Global Art Forum, Transcripts:1*, Art Dubai, Dubai 2008; M. Finders (ed.), *Global Art Forum_2. Transcripts*, Art Dubai, Dubai 2009. Importance also attaches in this connection to the activities of the Cisneros Foundation in Miami, focusing specifically on promoting awareness of the art of Central and South America.
[8] The figures are taken from *Art Market Trends 2008* (www.artprice.com).
[9] A brief but precise reconstruction of these events is to be found in N. Moureau & D. Sagot-Duvauroux, 'La construction du marché des tirages photographiques,' in *Études photographiques*, no. 22, October 2008, pp. 79–99, the notes to which also provide a basic bibliography. The collections of firms often focus on photography, as in the cases of Neuflize Vie of the ABN AMRO group, the French Caisse des dépôts et consignations (CDC), the DZ Bank, the Portuguese Banco Espírito Santo, and the pioneering Austrian Länderbank, then incorporated into Bank Austria, which started its collection back in 1976. It is no coincidence that nearly all of these collections have been entirely or partly taken over by public museums in recent years: the CDC collection by the Centre Pompidou, the DZ Bank collection by the Städel Museum, Frankfurt, and the Bank Austria collection by the Museum der Modern, Salzburg. It is also interesting to note that the venues selected are not museums specifically devoted to photography but institutions whose prestige and visibility rise above the specialist sphere. Once again, readers are referred to the catalogues produced for the exhibitions accompanying the public presentation of the collections on loan.

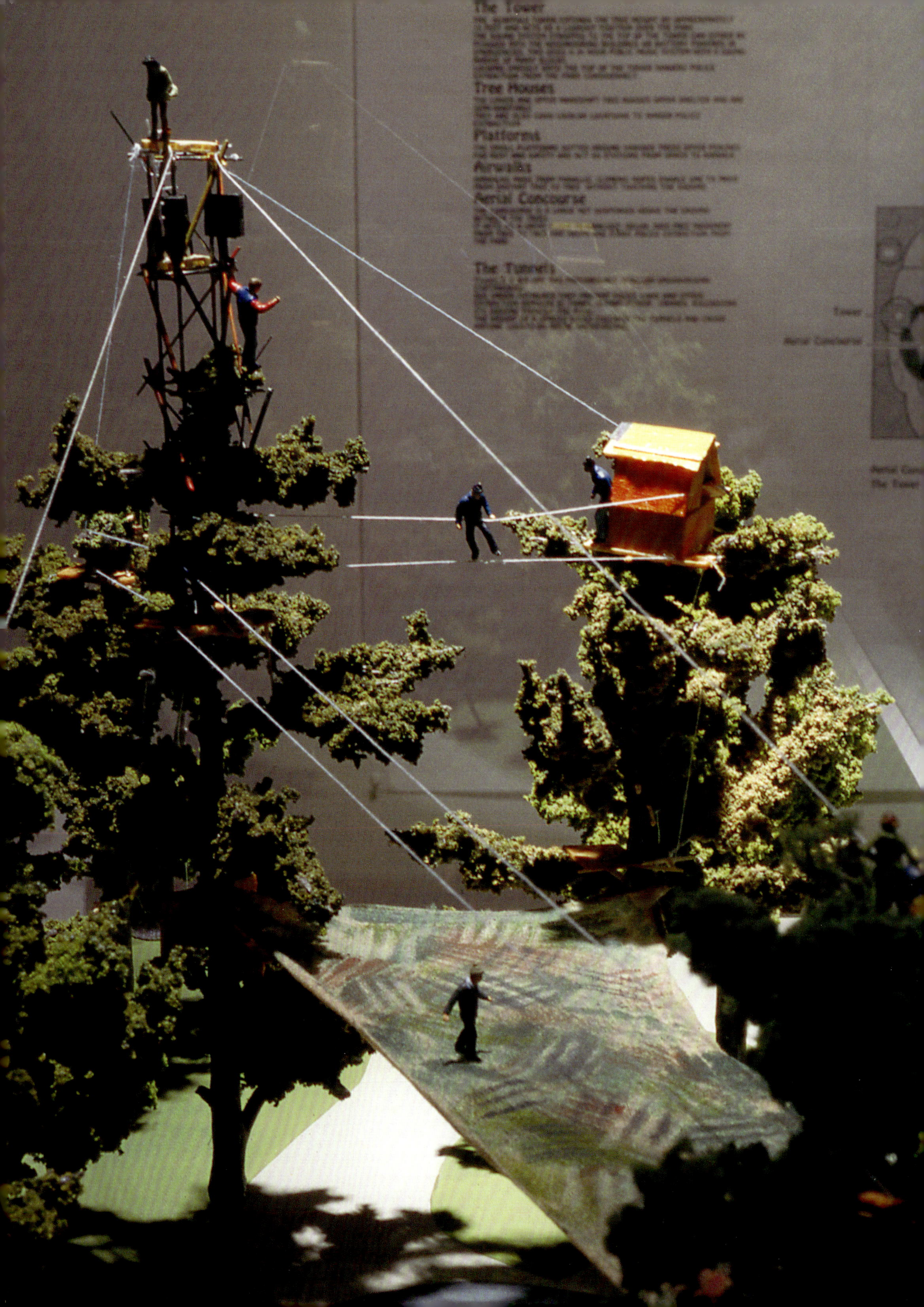
The Tower
Tree Houses
Platforms
Airwalks
Aerial Concourse
The Tunnels

Art and Politics: Defining a Common Space

The politicization of the image does not correspond to – or rather no longer coincides with – its political content. Nor can it any longer be identified with its channels of production or reception, which it transcends. The political status of the image is today something bound up with recognition of the aesthetic character of its manifestation.

Can a freely marketed food product or an urban protest action be exhibited as art? Is there a common link between a process of alternative urban planning or the creation of an independent media network and artistic practice? If the aesthetic and socioeconomic dimensions had something in common, what could it be? And then, where is this bond of belonging to be located? How is it to be described?

The proportion of exhibitions of a political character began to reach significantly high levels halfway through the 1990s. An emerging and constantly expanding art scene started to demand a whole series of social initiatives as its own praxis and to exhibit solo tools and procedures in artistic institutions and at international biennials. Activists, media collectives, and social movements took over the field of exhibitions on a global scale. At the same time, artists got involved, abandoning representation in favor of action. They adopted a pragmatic aesthetic and organized public forums, educational projects, and illegal occupations of urban spaces as well as mechanisms and symbols of protest.

The Danish group Superflex developed the *Biogas* sustainable energy project in Tanzania (1996–1997). Park Fiction initiated a process of participatory planning in 1994 to obstruct a gentrification scheme in a low-income district of Hamburg. The American group Critical Art Ensemble published *Electronic Disturbance* (1994), its first radical contribution to forms of cultural resistance and civil disobedience in digital space. Founded in Buenos Aires in 1997, Etcétera and the Grupo de Arte Callejero originated in the Hijos social movement, a human rights organization formed by the children of *desaparecidos*. The Huit Facettes group of visual artists began to open creativity centers for villagers in the rural areas of Senegal as a possible way of countering Western cultural expropriation in 1996. And this was just the beginning of a whole series of associative and participative practices – what Reinaldo Laddaga describes as "experimental communities" – that were to have a marked impact on the international art scene at the beginning of the new millennium.

The crisis that struck theoretical models of modernist derivation coincided with an art market of ever-growing financial strength, one capable of taking over from the previous twentieth-century debate on the nature of art and reducing all of its possible definitions to interchangeable forms of supply with respect to the variable of demand. The growth and development of this particular economic sector followed the more general trend of the neoliberalist capitalist system and saw its victory confirmed in the late 1980s in concomitance with the collapse of the socialist bloc. The measures to deregulate trade and the financial markets in particular brought all of the world's economies together and made them interdependent, thus showing a new relationship between economy, state, and society. Deregulation policies, the proliferation of multinational corporations, a decrease in political intervention on the market, and the associated dismantling of the welfare state were goals pursued both by local political actors (especially the United States) and by international financial institutions like the World Bank (WB), the International Monetary Fund (IMF), and the World Trade Organization (WTO). If the phenomenon that prevailed in the 1990s under the name of "globalization" resulted – as Alain Touraine claims – in erosion of the public sector and a regime of desocialization, society succeeded on the other hand in reasserting its right to exist by demanding reintegration of the economy in the social sphere. This demand led to the revolt against the 1999 WTO summit meeting in Seattle as the first of an ongoing series of protest struggles. The event in Seattle was to highlight the non-traditional character and origin of the movement of global resistance: web-like, intermittent, non-centralized, kaleidoscopic, multitudinous, and irreducible to unity.

Nils Norman
Tompkins Square Park Monument to Civil Disobedience (detail), 1997
Plastic materials, dimensions variable
View of the model-diagram realized in 1997 at American Fine Arts, New York

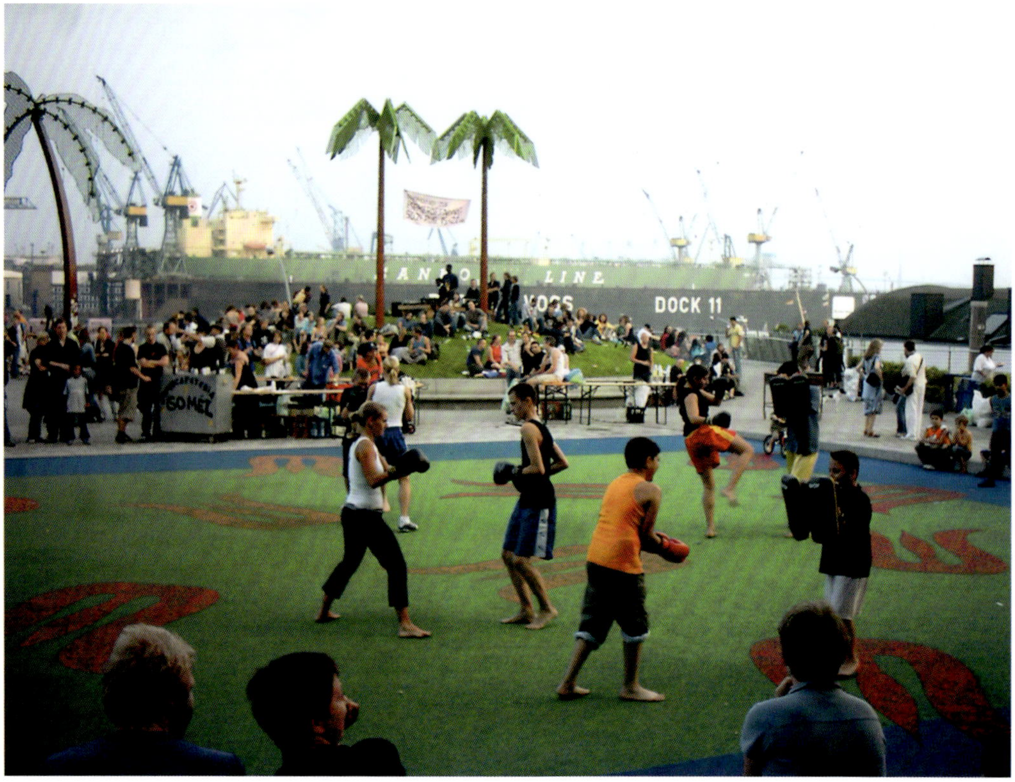

Park Fiction
Kickboxers a St. Pauli, 2005
View of the performance during the inauguration party for the park, permanent picnic against gentrification, on a tulip patterned tartan field

The movement's identification of cultural production and political struggle, creative experimentation in the use of the media, attaching of importance to the creation of individual and group subjectivity as a mechanism of resistance, and demand for autonomous spaces for knowledge and action led to rapid assimilation of these attitudes in the sectors of contemporary aesthetic and artistic debate as well as proposals of structural alliance between art and activism.

The historical phase that saw the parallel if not indeed interwoven development of social movements and artistic practices cannot, however, wholly encompass the implications of the transformation of a sphere such as art in the conditions offered by a state of transition like the one now underway. Something very different is involved and, as many have pointed out, the change is paradigmatic.

If it is possible in examining the immediate premises of the artistic phenomenon to identify connections with the "sociological mappings" suggested by Hal Foster as one of the salient characteristics of the "ethnographic shift" and its representatives (Martha Rosler, Allan Sekula, Mary Kelly, and Lothar Baumgarten), we must instead expel all the criteria of interaction, participation, coexistence, and cohabitation invoked by "relational aesthetics" and its representatives (Pierre Huyghe, Rirkrit Tiravanija, Tobias Rehberger, and Liam Gillick). Despite certain terminological similarities, the literal interactions with the public set in motion by relational aesthetics are completely stripped of the political, economic, and social thrust that lies at the center of the latest practices. As Claire Bishop points out, it is no coincidence that certain artists responded immediately to this idea of free coexistence by rehabilitating the idea of aesthetic boundaries or antagonism (Santiago Sierra and Thomas Hirschhorn).

Despite everything, the type of project we are describing – one that explores new forms of socialization in the correct sense of the term – proves hard to identify in both disciplinary and historical terms, in terms of its antecedents and characteristic discontinuity. What then is its cultural genealogy?

The general impression is that the demands for emancipation and the radical critique arising in the contemporary aesthetic and artistic debate are not really all that "modern" and that they have different points of reference (the "many" instead of the "people"), spaces of intervention (the specific "here and now" with respect to the designated place), and objectives (the end of utopia), as well as the variety of strategies adopted in order to achieve them.

Now that the socialist framework is no more and the production system has been totally transformed with respect to Fordism, can the terms of the question still be those expressed by the political art of the 1970s?

Marjetica Potrč, Liyat Esakov
Dry Toilet, 2003
Building materials and sanitation infrastructure, dimensions variable
Caracas, La Fila, barrio La Vega
Supported by La Vega community, Caracas; *Caracas Case Project* and Federal Cultural Foundation of Germany; Ministry of Environment, Venezuela
Courtesy of the artists

Is there no visible difference between the demonstrations of the Art Workers' Coalition and the protests or *escraches* of the Colectivo Etcétera? Between the strategy of the Material Group's *The People's Choice* (1981) and that of Park Fiction's *Wunscharchiv* (Wish Archives) (1996)? Between Hans Haacke's exposure of the "corporation culture" and the mapping of the hidden links of capitalism developed by the Bureau d'Études? Between the presentation of xenophobia by Adrian Piper and by the Black Audio Film Collective?

In the time of what Maurizio Lazzarato describes as "immaterial labour," it is not only impossible to preserve a rigid division between intellectual production, political action, and culture, but also quite inconceivable to draw any distinction between work and the rest of human activity. Whereas the intellect remained outside the production cycle in the Fordist regime, as Paolo Virno says, work and nonwork develop identical productivity based on the use of general human faculties such as language, feelings, sociality, and aesthetics in the present era of post-Fordism. The differences between the forms of civil disobedience of the 1960s and '70s and the insurgent practices of the present-day art scene thus become immediately comprehensible. Nor is it a coincidence that the forms of contemporary neo-movementism, just like those of present-day artistic activism, are defined precisely on the basis of a common background characterized by the end of "Politics" with a capital P. The real difference between the political art of the 1970s (or the modernist period in general) and the present thus lies in the new relationship with the structure of power and representation. And this is because what has changed is above all the very paradigm of power. The fundamental question posed by the authors of these artistic initiatives is whether it is still possible to locate the forms of contemporary power in the state machinery after Foucault's resolute abandonment of the traditional approach to the problem of power, based on legal-institutional models, for a wholly uninhibited analysis of the concrete ways in which power penetrates the very bodies of the subjects and their forms of life. In short, we should have abandoned a vertical vision of power in favor of a horizontal conception of the same in what the Bureau d'Études describes as a "social system based on information in which every point of society is ideally a producer of information and communication." In this sense, contemporary artistic strategies seek to generate dissent and resistance to the forms of biocapitalism by adopting a transversal approach in such a way as to run all the way through the time of life, since it is a peculiar characteristic of biocapitalism, as Maurizio Lazzarato notes, to shift the exercise of power from the "time of work" to the "time of life" as such.

What characterizes the present situation is thus no longer the need and ambition to take over the state (or component parts of the same, like the museum, the party, the workplace, etc.) but rather a drive to defend and free oneself from it. In this sense, the representation of contemporary dissent manifests itself not only as theoretical criticism or active protest but also and above all as defection, exodus, and flight. As the sociologist Albert Hirschman would have said, "exit" rather than "voice": withdrawal rather than collision, the search for new spaces of intervention, constituent practices, microactions at the local level, forms of self-management, self-organization, and empowerment.

Institutional criticism of the museum is what Broodthaers, Haacke, and other artists of that period have in common. The Art Workers' Coalition expended much of its energy in negotiating with museums and the Material Group endeavored to sabotage the order of the museum and its official role with

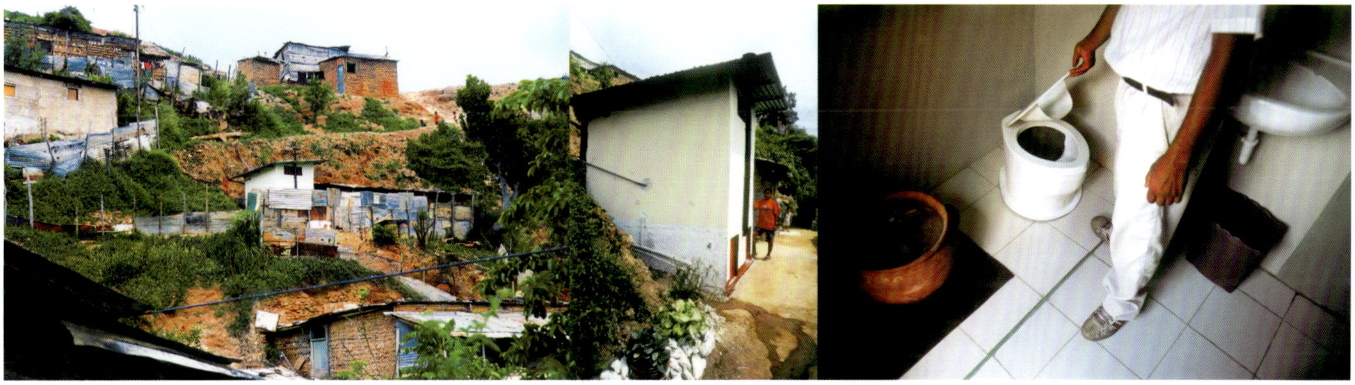

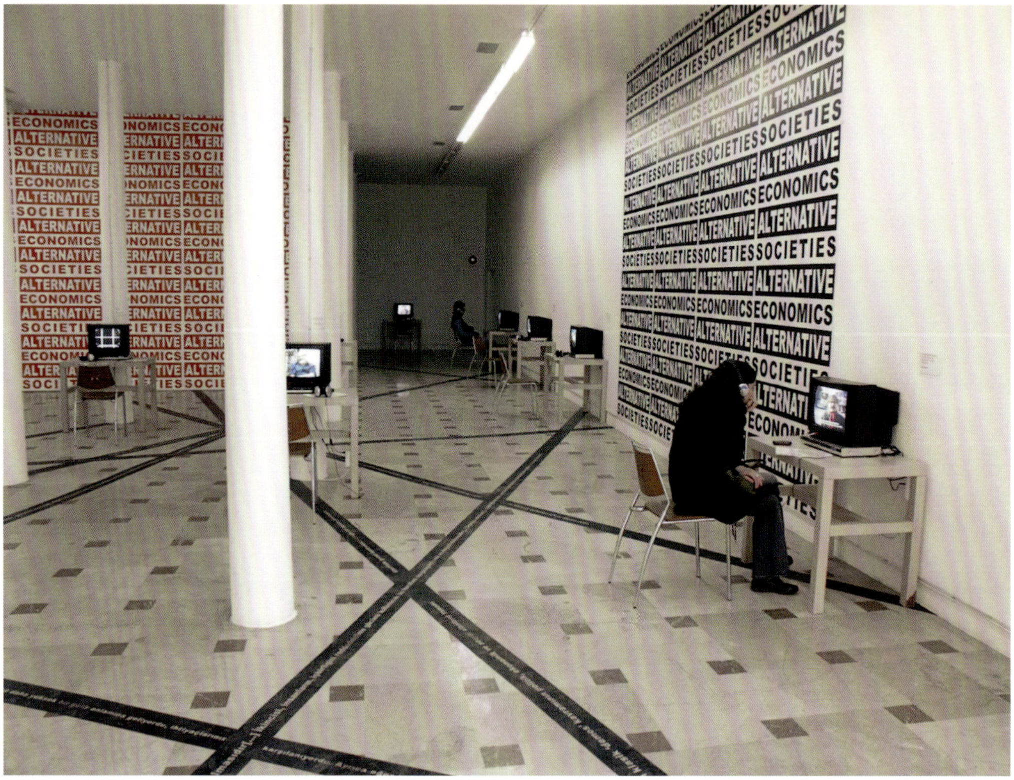

Oliver Ressler
Alternative Economics, Alternative Societies, 2005
Monitor, wooden tables, metal chairs, and plastic materials
View of the installation realized at the Galería Miro Quesada Garland, Lima, during the IX VAE – Festival Internacional de Video/Arte/Electrónica, Lima 2005

the *People's Choice* project. On the contrary, the museum is no longer a possible point of reference for Park Fiction's *Wunscharchiv* and the urban actions of Marjetica Potrč and Nils Norman. And are there many other cases bearing witness to the shift from an unambiguous representation of the role of the author to the mimetic, rhizomatic, and unforeseen forms that this has now come to assume, just as a major change is recorded in the definition of the flexible, open platforms of present-day artistic work teams in which heterogeneous figures meet to discuss, plan, and operate, such as the Danish group Superflex and Chto Delat in Saint Petersburg?

In our view, a radical shift from the aims of modernism has been registered precisely with respect to the relationship between art and politics. We refer not only to the relationship between "pure" art and "politics" that was disintegrated by the historical avant-garde movement but also to the different role of political commitment in art as represented in the theories of Lukacs or Adorno, i.e., in the conception of an organic or a non-organic work of art. Because if the political character of the organic work is based on content, from Adorno's viewpoint the identity between avant-garde and commitment is grounded solely on the structural principle and hence on the formal determination of the artwork. And what we are faced with today is something very different also from the question still addressed by Benjamin, namely the politicization of art as against the aestheticization of politics, where one is in any case subordinated to the other. Regardless of whether we start from the theories of Jacques Rancière or Bernard Stiegler on the question of the sensible world as a meeting point of aesthetics and politics or from a methodological approach belonging to a totally different theoretical tradition and based on transformation of the contemporary production process, such as Italian workerism, the dimension of the relationship now regards the immediate coinciding of work and perception, material and intellectual production, structure and superstructure. Jacques Rancière wrote as follows halfway through the 1990s: "The modern emergence of aesthetics as an autonomous discourse capable of determining an autonomous distinction of the sensible world corresponds to the advent of an appraisal of the sensible world that is separated from any judgment about its use, thus defining a virtual – and claim-asserting – world superimposed on the world of orders and tasks, which assigns to every thing its use." And this virtual world is none other than the one invoked and opened up anew every time by politics. At this point, the fundamental questions seem to be the following. What model of representation of the "many" counters and takes the place of the decline of the unifying images of the modern allegiances of class, people, nation, race, and religion? Is there a substitute for the idea of utopia? Is it possible to establish a relationship between the crisis of political representation and the crisis of aesthetic representation? It is possible to consider a constitutive antagonism of languages against the controlled dimension of the languages themselves? It is still possible to separate the convergent histories of artistic movements from the formation of new social movements? What are their respective places of production? If Zapatism declares that its place is not the factory but the social depths, can artistic practices lay claim to their own place of production and reception? An albeit schematic inventory of these kaleidoscopic initiatives will attempt to supply some answers by guiding us more directly inside the new languages, practices, and relationships of visibility and invisibility generated by the same.

Artistic practices and urban transformation

Underlying the multitude of present-day strategies focusing on urban transformation is the conviction that the city has become one of the major political and social problems of today. The effects of globalization no longer regard the state but the city as the strategic place of economic dynamics, migration, ethnic and cultural change, and the demands of civil society. The question of how to reinvent the way to construct the forms of the city is becoming increasingly urgent, as is the inseparably associated question of rebuilding the democratic power of the city. How then can the territorial, economic, and social transformations be mapped at a time when the techniques of modernist planning have failed and artistic practices seem to be taking on a paramount role in helping to guide a new demand for democracy within the global order? Starting from its own ruins, can the public art of the 1980s still perform some function? It is possible to think of the city as a collective work? And if so, how do artistic practices participate in the invention of new forms of public action when all the classic ties of social belonging have fallen through, as they have today? The contemporary city is a conflictive and non-homogeneous locus of forces in which a progressive emergence of social subjects is established in stable or temporary form in non-official places, in peripheral or in-between spaces, where life develops on the basis of informal economies, alternative models, practices of appropriation and self-organization, which escape all institutional geography. At the same time, the image of neoliberalist urban planning – legitimized as a project of gentrification and spatial policing and subordinated to a new alliance between local urban policies and global capital – has found in groups of artists and activists like Park Fiction and the atelier d'architecture autogérée (a.a.a.) some figures of conflict and resistance in a new configuration. These groups promote processes of autonomous and collective planning for real places and redefine public space in opposition to the dominant systems of urban planning and in accordance with a model that we could describe as "constituent." Examples such as the urban park in the St. Pauli district of Hamburg and the Ecobox project in the La Chapelle district of

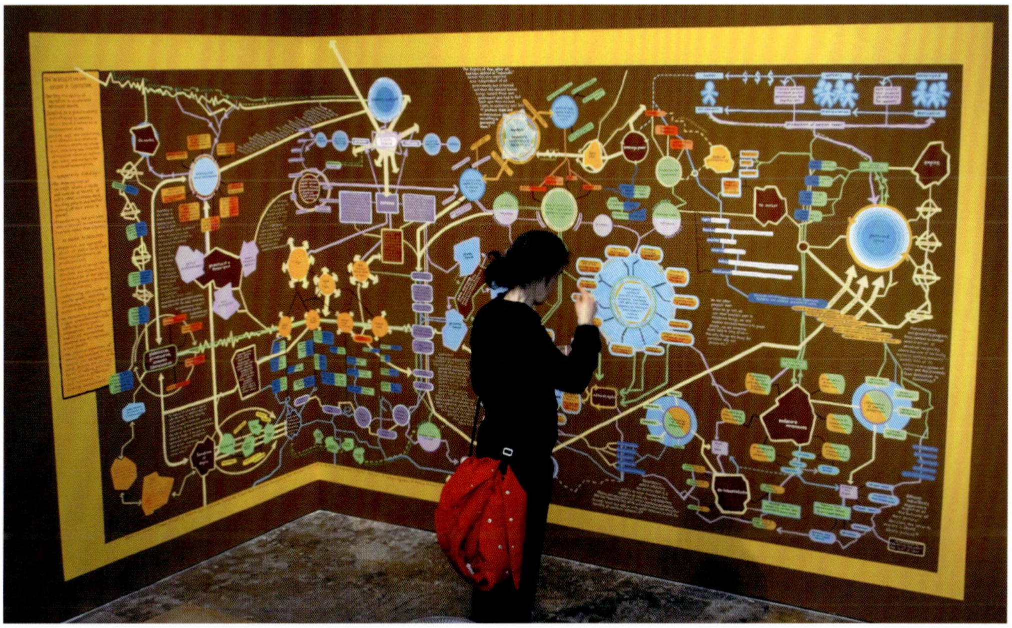

Ashley Hunt
A World Map: In Which We See, 2005
Acrylic on wall, dimensions variable
View of the installation realized in 2005 at the Contemporary Museum, Baltimore

Chto Delat (Nik Oleinikov, Tsaplya and Dmitry Vilensky)
Angry Sandwich People or in a Praise of Dialectic, 2006
Sequence of slides transferred to video, sound, 8'
Courtesy of the artists

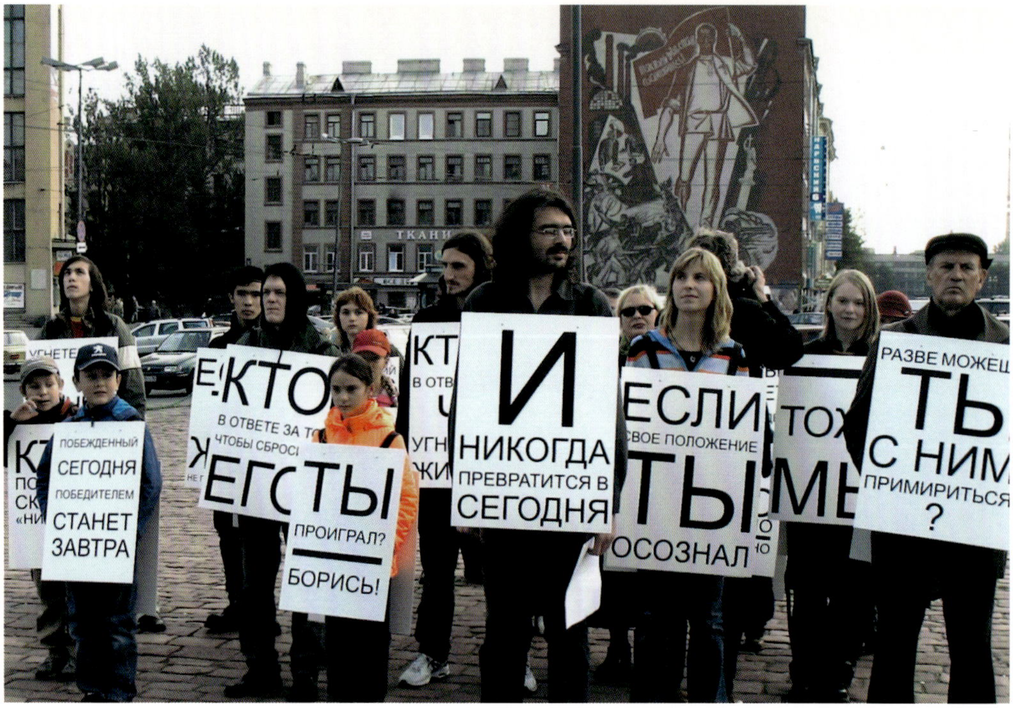

Paris are generators of urban initiatives located outside any antagonism of a dialectical or protest-oriented type in the classic sense and avoiding any trench warfare with the authorities but such as to develop parallel, interdisciplinary universes from an ordinary and "bottom-up" perspective. The democratization of housing policies is a recurrent theme of many of these artistic practices, which participate in forms of resistance and actions making claims at the neighborhood level. Far from reasserting the lost identity of a district or new forms of rootedness, what is demanded is actually a broadening of the subject's capacities or rather transformation of the user from passive consumer to active planner of the city. In this sense, artistic activity plays a key role in translating informal practices into the language of planning. Park Fiction's action for the St. Pauli district of Hamburg thus envisaged the development of a series of tools for use by people, including a wish archives, a container for planning, an office for making plasticine models, a garden library, and a mobile design kit. Rather than following the aims of a specific client, Park Fiction's creation of an urban park developed out of a collective process of Deleuzian and Surrealist derivation with the involvement of artists and social movements to block a property development project in the dock area of Hamburg. Founded in 1994, Park Fiction embarked in 2002, after ten years of democratic urbanization and social battles, on the creation of the park, which is divided into different areas and far away from the idea of "art *as* public space" in Miwon Kwon's sense. Something similar to the activity of Park Fiction is catalyzed around OUT, the "Office for Urban Transformation" that Bert Theis opened in the Isola district of Milan in 2002. OUT itself is based in occupied premises in a centrally located historical area alongside one of Milan's traditionally unresolved urban voids and under threat since the late 1990s from a radical urban renovation project envisaging support for the development of priority sectors of the Milanese economy. In opposition to planning of a top-down nature, OUT seeks to provide an open and operative platform capable of producing images and situations for the neighborhood battle and catalyzing social mobilization and imaginative forces at the grass-roots level, as well as involving the theoretical reflections of experts, remains of the industrial past, and the new immigrants. Intervening in an already very dilapidated area, Bert Theis devised a project of public space for the neighborhood in which the role of the artist is above all that of activating, coordinating, and mediating between different interests rather than acting as a planner or author. The battle for housing is instead the cause that united the Ultra-red group of artists and musicians and the Union de Vecinos organization of public housing tenants when the Los Angeles Housing Authority announced its plans for the demolition of Pico Aliso in East Los Angeles with the eviction of 1200 Latin-American families in 1998. Interpreting the city as a sound map rather than a geometric grid, the militants of Ultra-red have undertaken to produce activist musical projects, radio broadcasts, and other actions to record and preserve the voice of the minorities and the memory of battles for urban rights.

Urban performers and direct justice

Regina José Galindo staged a ritual procession through the streets of Guatemala City on July 23, 2003. *Quien puede borrar las huellas* (Who can wipe out the traces?) immediately became known as an individual act of resistance and collective portrait of a civil society that is always in danger. Walking across Guatemala City from the Constitutional Court to the National Palace and leaving an orderly series of blood-red footprints, the young woman dressed in black made a silent and vigorous protest against the presidential candidacy of General Rios Montt, the country's former bloodthirsty dictator and leader of the Guatemalan Republican Front. The action of walking as ritual and the marks as autographs of a body both individual and universal at the same time transformed the space into a performance setting, allowing the invisible identities of the visible world to emerge and giving voice to what was known but kept silent. An authentic representative of an art "of repetition" in the Deleuzian sense, Regina José Galindo returns to places where the public witnessed the drama of history and uses her body to "repeat" actions. This repetition restores potentiality to what once happened. It does not bring the past back as such but makes it possible again. Galindo enacts not only a protest but also and above all a proposal. Does the street serve here as a space of artistic performance in order to protest or to remember? In point of fact, the action not only protests against the institution for what it keeps hidden but also constitutes an assertion of justice outside the authority of the state. It adds its own memory to the official record. It inaugurates a form of direct justice that accepts no mediation.

In their adhesion to a specific "here" and "now," the performative uniqueness of the action, and the ordinary practices of appropriation, Galindo's actions help to define the emergence of new artistic and social actors. Art and activism do not offer themselves as separate spheres in the urban space of Latin American megalopolises but interact and fuel one another. They form part of the same action. Even though Hannah Arendt once described arts that create no works as having great affinities with politics, the future of a participative and situational rather than representational conception of politics now hinges precisely on the space opened up by performance. Paolo Virno uses the term "virtuosity" for the set of gifts characterizing those who stage performances as creators of unique acts with no end product but necessarily in front of spectators. The category of "virtuosity" succeeds in holding together experiences in the fields of art, language, and work, thus becoming a key word in the post-Fordist vocabulary.

Virtuosity and public space are also at the center of the collective actions of the Grupo de Art Callejero (GAC), who use the deconstruction of urban codes and signs to rewrite a geography of power and repression. On March 24, 2001, a map of Buenos Aires was put up by the group in all the streets of the capital with red squares showing the homes of the perpetrators of mass murder and torture saved from punishment by special measures such as the *ley de obediencia debida* (law of due obedience) but also the secret detention centers. Entitled *Aqui Viven Genocidas* (where genocides live), the map was accompanied by a series of altered street signs placed along the real route through the city. This symbolic protest came into operation on the anniversary of the *coup d'état* of March 1976 and formed a backdrop to public demonstrations and marches. It marked a key stage in the protests held in front of the homes of the murderers, which came to be known as *escraches* (exposures) in the late 1990s. These *escraches* are collective and performative actions that mark a new way of using public space and oppose the inefficiency and complicity of the Argentine justice system with efforts to increase awareness through marches, sound, writing on walls, street theater, photographs, drawings, and posters. These practices take up the legacy of Tucumán Arde, an avant-garde Argentine group that worked in 1968 to transform the artist into a social researcher, and the political legacy of the movements for human rights like the Madres de Plaza de Mayo. Staged every time in a different place, originally the homes of figures involved in the dictatorship but later also the centers of economic, political, and cultural power, an *escrache* consists in exposing the person's identity, face, and past on the spot. Authors of poetic barricades, champions of the right to dream, and trained agitators, the members of the Colectivo Etcétera made the *escrache* the symbolic center of their work between 1998 and 2000, drawing upon the entire arsenal of Surrealism and Dada.

Art as social service

There is a pragmatic project of democracy underlying the refusal of many contemporary artists to represent (in the sense of *in place of* or *for* others) and to separate what-is-done from who-does-it. The creation on the urban scale of spaces of what could be described as "anti-power" (both physical and virtual) is nothing other than the result of this process. Contemporary artists create opportunities for self-empowerment and expansion of the capacity of individuals and communities to plan the basic conditions of their lives. They are above all *toolmakers* and authors of user-friendly interfaces. They supply devices that can be used to make forms of planning and participation in a collective process of construction accessible to all. The idea of tools is a legacy of Conceptual Art that has taken on a completely different character in present-day artistic practice. The services created are not so much instruments ready for use as conditions of social learning (learning by doing). When invited to operate in the Coronation Court tower block on the outskirts of Liverpool in 2000, Superflex produced *Superchannel*, an Internet project for a television channel that involved the block's residents in the creation and development of programs. The project not only gave the tenants an opportunity for self-representation, generating internal communication and external television broadcasts, but also initiated a process of self-management and self-reproduction of the channel itself, which no longer depended on the artists. The devices created by the atelier d'architecture autogérée (a.a.a.) in the La Chapelle district of Paris also pursue this objective.

Ecobox, the garden developed by the French interdisciplinary group on wasteland, was the starting point for the creation of a whole series of services for cultural and social interaction that they call "urban activators": urban cooking, urban radio, etc. Similarly, the work of the British artist and activist Nils Norman involves environmental issues and visionary structures for implementation in the heart of urban centers. On starting out in 1997, Norman designed shelters and walkways suspended between the trees of Tompkins Square Park in New York for people under threat of eviction by the police. *Monument to Civil Disobedience*, one of his first works in model form, was to be followed by projects for vehicles such as *The Gerrard Winstanley Radical Gardening Space Reclamation Mobile Field Center and Weather Station Prototype* (1999) and *Geocruiser* (2001). Produced as an aid for the anarchical movements of squatters and guerrilla gardeners, the first is a bicycle with a trailer carrying a weather station, a library, and a photocopier powered by solar energy. The second is again a mobile library and educational center with books on environmental activism and utopian architecture housed in a bus together with a greenhouse and an organic recycling system. The Spanish artist Santiago Cirugeda instead addresses the theme of the do-it-yourself home and the parasite habitat.

For Marjetica Potrč the informal city represents the point at which the urban dimension begins. It is an observatory and a key laboratory for the production of space, where production is considered as a value of pure use and guaranteed only by forms of continuous appropriation. The survival strategies developed there create a different relationship between temporary and permanent, public and private, individual and collective, every time. It was in the shantytown barrio of La Vega in Caracas in 2003, in collaboration with Israeli architect Liyat Esakov and some members of the local community, that she developed a prototype dry toilet complying fully with the self-organizational and participative logic that informs the construction of the dwelling spaces in that context. One of the most radical interpreters and investigators of the global city and its development, Potrč has worked since the mid-1990s on various case studies in various parts of the world (from reconstruction projects in the Balkans to shantytowns in Africa, the Middle East, and Latin America) where forms of self-organized planning and individual initiatives predominate. Convinced that gated communities and shantytowns are the "most successful" responses to the global city, Potrč focuses on the potential of self-sustainability, an innovative design for survival, and infrastructures. The *Dry Toilet* project carried out in 2003 in the upper section of the La Vega barrio reflects this operative strategy. Given the general lack of drinkable water and the impossibility of access to the municipal water grid, an environmentally safe and immediate solution was developed that required no water and was capable of transforming human waste into fertilizer. The *Dry Toilet* project unquestionably inaugurated a new relationship between architecture and infrastructure in such way

Etcétera
Gente Armada, 2004
Cardboard outlines,
dimensions variable
View of the performance within the project *ExArgentina* realized in 2004 at the Museum Ludwig, Cologne

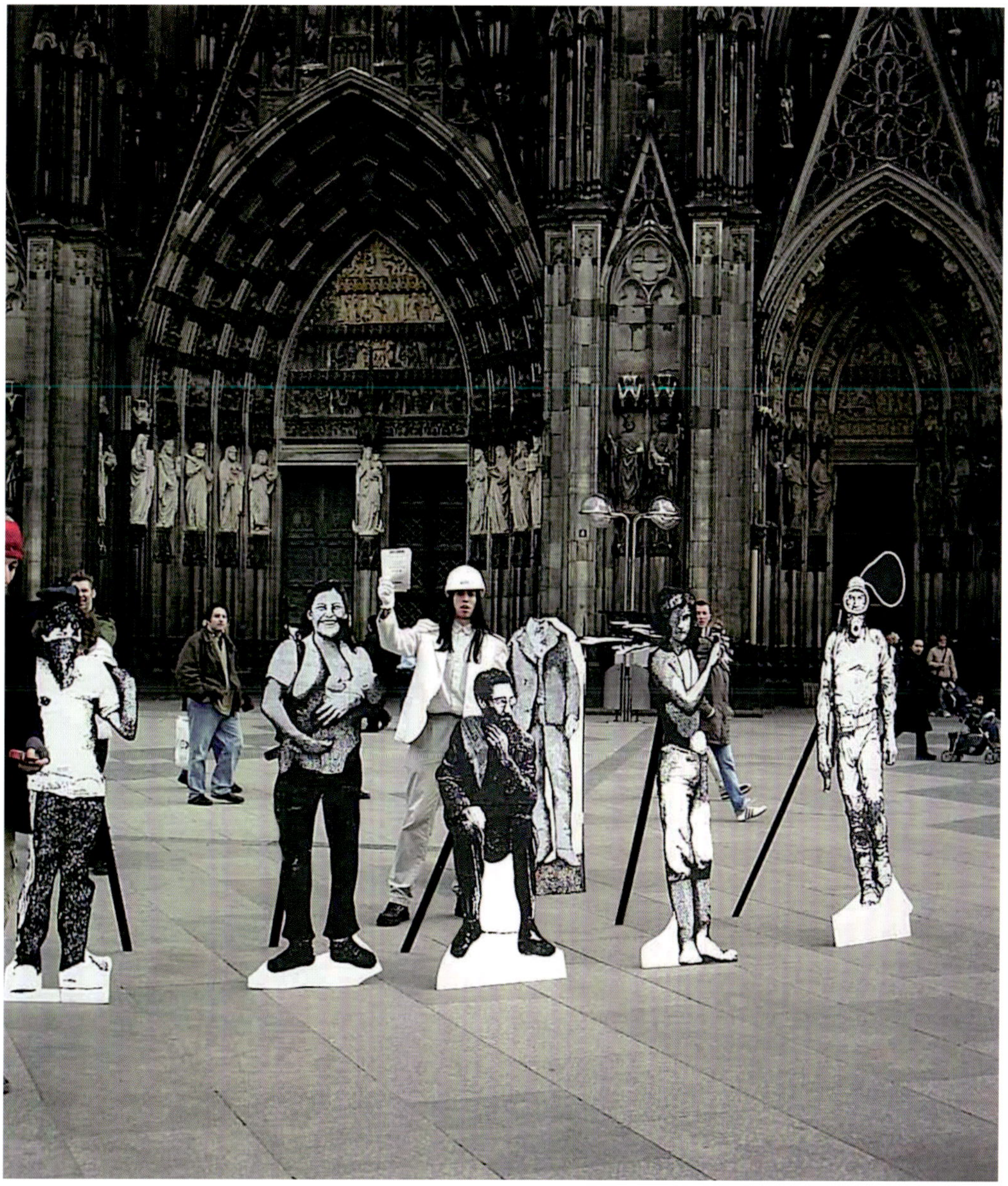

as to shift the capacity for urban production from institutions to individuals.

Art and access to knowledge

Out of all the possible forms of the contemporary power structure, let us take one of those representing science, or rather the part of science that is colonizing organic space and genetic structures. And let us try to understand how this "bioauthority" responds to the ideological needs of capital through the predominant representation of itself in terms of Edenic rhetoric. Here too, as in the mass-media presentation of terrorism and safety, the images we are shown – and indeed are pervasively bombarded with – pursue a strategy of radical concealment. Through presentation as cloning rather than a production process of the food industry, what the Edenic rhetoric makes possible is to shift the focus of discourse from the criticism of production, marketing and value to ethics and morality. But while the industry has succeeded in drawing a veil of silence over the immense output of genetically modified food and thus achieved a high percentage of consolidation, cloning – a biotechnology of which little or practically no use is made – has received great coverage in the media. Faced with this semiotic scenario of reference, which generates widespread feelings of fear and powerlessness in the public, the group of American artists known as the Critical Art Ensemble (CAE) has responded with a constant stream of free information, research on public access to the formulation of communal policies, and socialization of technological knowledge.

The CAE uses forms of tactical media or biopolitical tactics to develop a techno-activist "recombinant theatre" made up of open, mobile laboratories that highlight the

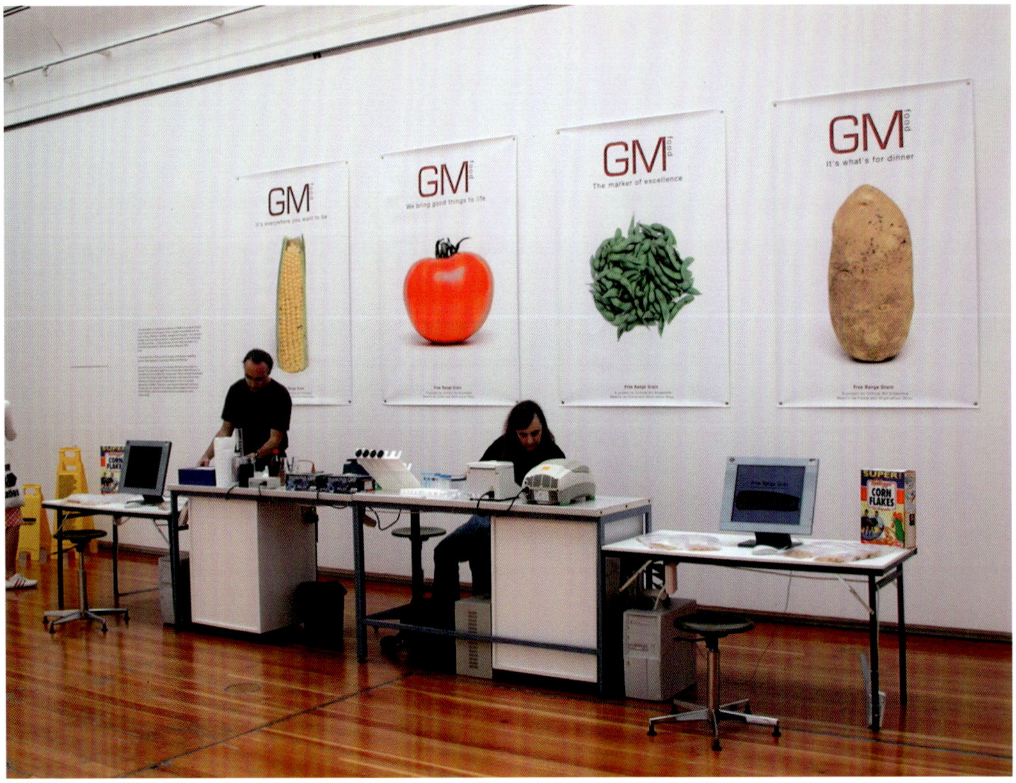

Critical Art Ensemble
Free Range Grain, 2004
Electronic materials and mixed media, dimensions variable
View of the installation realized in 2004 at the Schirn Kunsthalle, Frankfurt

appropriation of resources and profits of the pharmaceutical multinationals and the major chains of food distribution. The aim of the CAE's confrontationist biology in focusing on production processes is not only to reveal the ideological structure of the technology and its representation but also to break down the barriers of specialization and above all the hierarchical divide between scientists and laymen and the rules governing intellectual property so as to open up biotechnology as a field of empowerment.

Oliver Ressler pursues the same aims in his work on environmental subjects such as global warming, where the official image from a popular standpoint is the one presented by Al Gore's film *An Inconvenient Truth* (2006). The phenomenon of global warming, which Ressler rightly addresses in terms of its economic causes, is not regarded by the ruling class as a problem to be solved but rather as way of winning votes in political campaigns. Ressler has also worked for years on deconstructing the machinery of capitalist production and built up an ever-growing video archive of possible economic alternatives in visual and conceptual terms. *Alternative Economics, Alternative Societies*, a project presenting 11 different views through direct interviews, is designed as a representation of the collective redistribution of wealth and a tool for the democratic redistribution of knowledge. The question of knowledge and power has been addressed by many artists directly in the field of teaching and education with radical models of cultural mediation and self-learning. The Copenhagen Free University, Rainer Ganahl, Luca Frei, Université Tangente, Chto Delat, and Oda Projesi are just some of the names that have made teaching methodologies an integral part of their work.

Dataesthetics and critical mapping

As Brian Holmes has observed, the map is perhaps the archetype of the latest artistic practices precisely because it is a tool of political activism. Encompassing a whole variety of viewpoints and media, maps in pdf format, interactive maps on Web supports, diagrams, statistical databases, and eclectic atlases today make up one of the primary fields of the new post-Fordist visual culture. The Bureau d'Études, Raqs Media Collective, Walid Raad and the Atlas Group, Multiplicity, and Ashley Hunt are some of the recurrent names in this sphere. These and many other artists seek to create maps as a sort of cognitive tool for use in the analysis and redefinition of the camouflaged spaces of power. Nor do they stop there. Convinced that the intangible character of data has become a pervasive phenomenon in the transition from the disciplinary society to the regime of biopolitical control, they endeavor to undermine and challenge the power of data through artistic use of the same. Removing data from the jurisdiction of the social sciences and employing them as artistic material, these practices have inherited from Öyvind Fahlström, Mark Lombardi, and Conceptual Art a focus on the autonomous resymbolization and visual presentation of sociopolitical relations, forces, and mechanisms. "Absent from the local landscape, invisible to the naked eye, a maze of laws and regulations gives tangible shape to our existence." This phrase anticipates the legend of the *European Norms of World Production* developed by the Bureau d'Études. Originally conceived for the Florence Social Forum of November 2002, this map of administrative structures formed around the European Commission is one of the many examples of the work developed by the French group since 1998. The phrase is already indicative both of the evidentiary approach that characterizes the anti-geography of the Bureau d'Études and of the aim to transform the European citizen into a public eye capable of coping with the situation. Using distinctively printed synoptic tables, Bureau d'Études maps the financial interconnections of contemporary capitalism and presents the results in large-sized wall charts. The group of French media artists initially alternated the creation of "*zones de gratuité*" – areas of goods and services free from economic constraints – with the founding of proto-political associations such as the Syndicat Potentiel and Université Tangente. Their maps trace the web of property relationships between financial capital, governmental agencies, banks, and firms but also the systems (truth criteria, ideological directives, territorial models, and industrial standards) that make them possible.

The indivisible link between private systems of control and imprisonment on the one hand and the capitalist machinery on the other is the focal point of the maps of the American artist and activist Ashley Hunt. In *A World Map: In Which We See* Hunt examines the way in which the process of economic globalization constructs itself as a transnational system over an erased area, an area of exclusion made up primarily of ever-increasing numbers of prisoners and refugees who are denied all civil rights. He seeks to make this constantly expanding area of invisibility visible in his work by pinpointing relations, dynamics, laws, and concepts rather than geographic situations, places, and data in space. Making use also and indeed above all of video documentation, Hunt focuses all of his process of mapping on bringing to light the prescriptive systems that regulate visibility as a disciplined regime rather than the forms and possibilities of seeing as a physiological faculty, of seeing as such.

Allora & Calzadilla

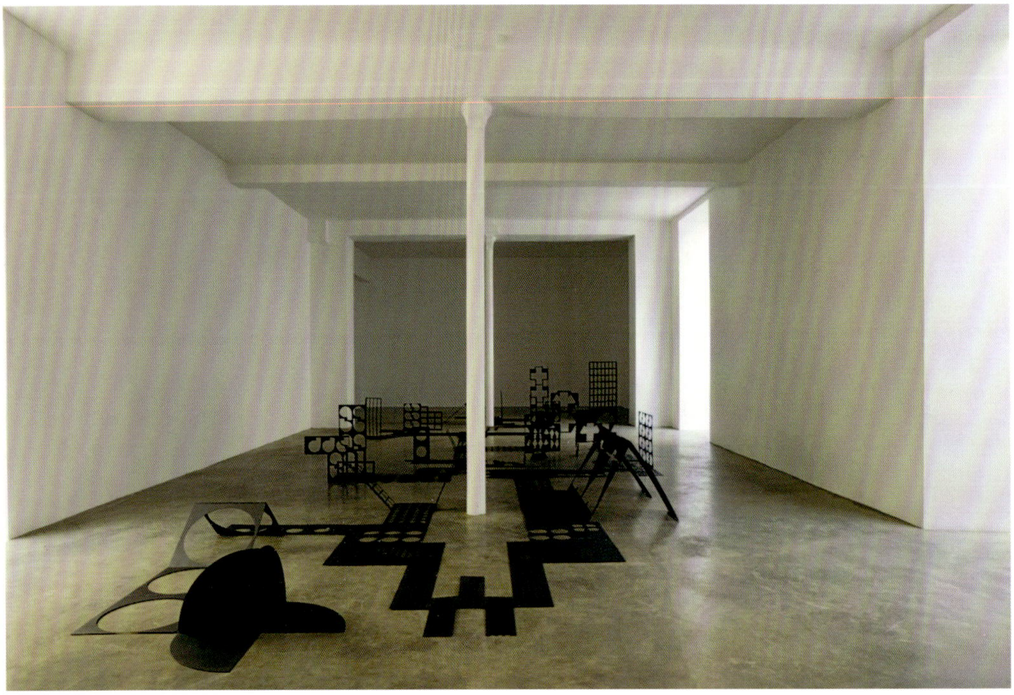

Ruin, 2006
Steel and black paint,
dimensions variable
Paris, Galerie Chantal Crousel

Land Mark (Foot Prints) #1. Set I,
2001–2004
Digital color print, 48.8 x 60.3 cm
Paris, Galerie Chantal Crousel

Jennifer Allora, born in Philadelphia, Pennsylvania, in 1974, and Guillermo Calzadilla, born in Havana in 1971, live and work in San Juan, Puerto Rico.
The works of Jennifer Allora and Guillermo Calzadilla are an intimate and subversive response to the clash between the private, personal sphere and the crushing weight of global action. The two artists focus on the intimacy of the mark, understood as an assertion of mankind's passage through the world. As finalists for the 2006 Hugo Boss Prize, which was then awarded to Tacita Dean, they presented the complete *Landmark* series, created in the area of Vieques beach in Puerto Rico, at the Palais de Tokyo in Paris. The nature of the operation is justified by the historical and political role assumed by the area over the last 60 years as a site for numerous nuclear and technological military experiments carried out by the American government.
The purpose of the action *Landmark* was to highlight the invasive nature of these operations and the demands expressed by the inhabitants to regain possession. In this case, the artistic act involved staking a claim by making marks as ephemeral and non-invasive as footprints in the sand, which were left by the artists and local activists wearing shoes that had messages and drawings cut into the soles. The action of marking the territory involved illegal entry into the areas controlled by military personnel, who constituted not only the adversary but also the intended recipients of the messages.
Coexistence in space is one of the subjects that the works of Allora and Calzadilla address with great insistence in a variety of media. The decision to operate through installation, video, and photography involves a multidisciplinary approach that enables them to explore the idea of form and extend its meanings to different social and human situations. One example is the installation *Ruin* staged in 2006 at the Galerie Chantal Crousel in Paris, which addresses the forms of oppression and democracy, spatial boundaries, and creative and destructive choices in human action. The installation can be altered and modified in accordance with the spectator's wishes.
(*F.T.*)

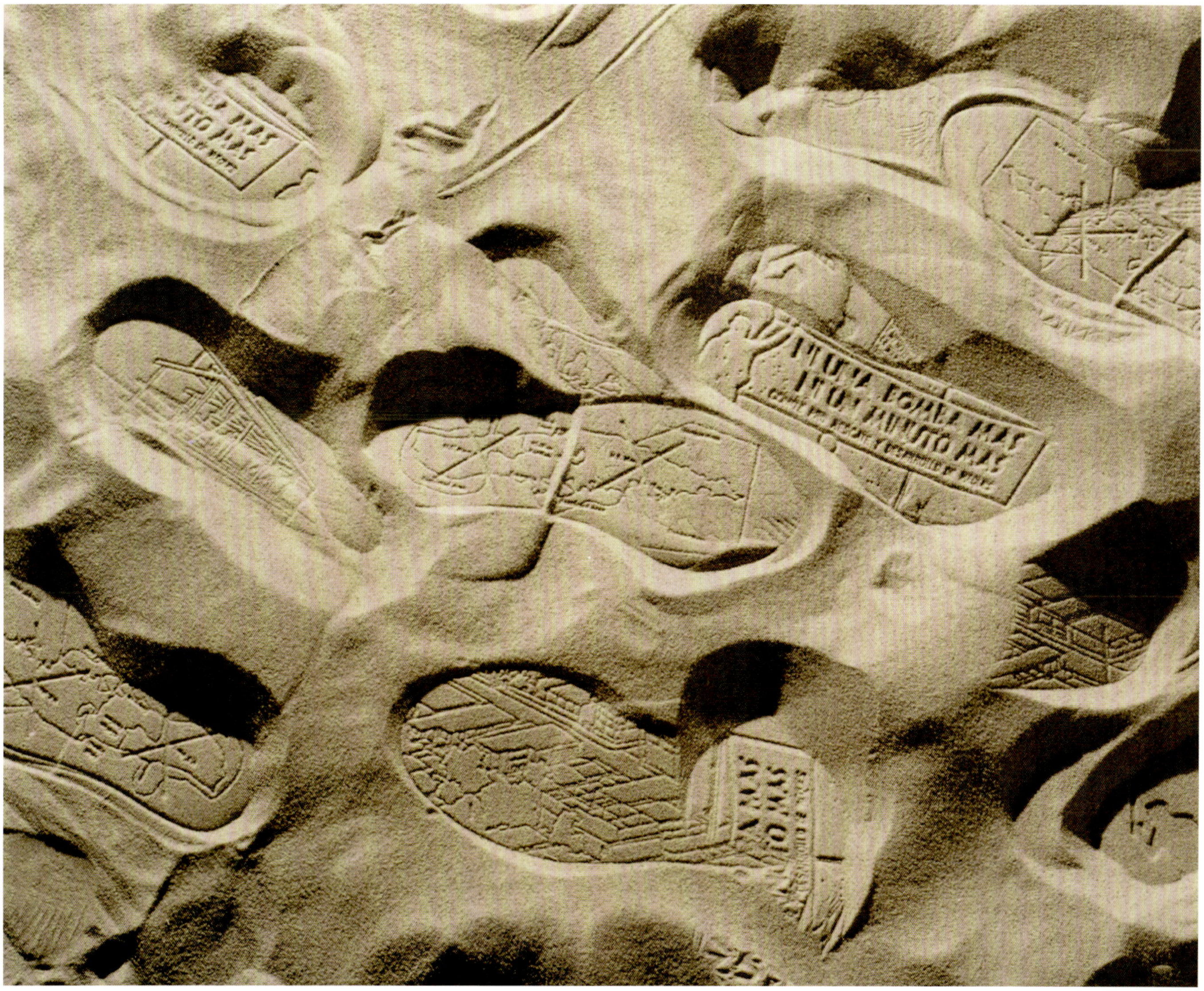
NI UNA BOMBA MAS
NI UN MINUTO MAS

Atelier Van Lieshout

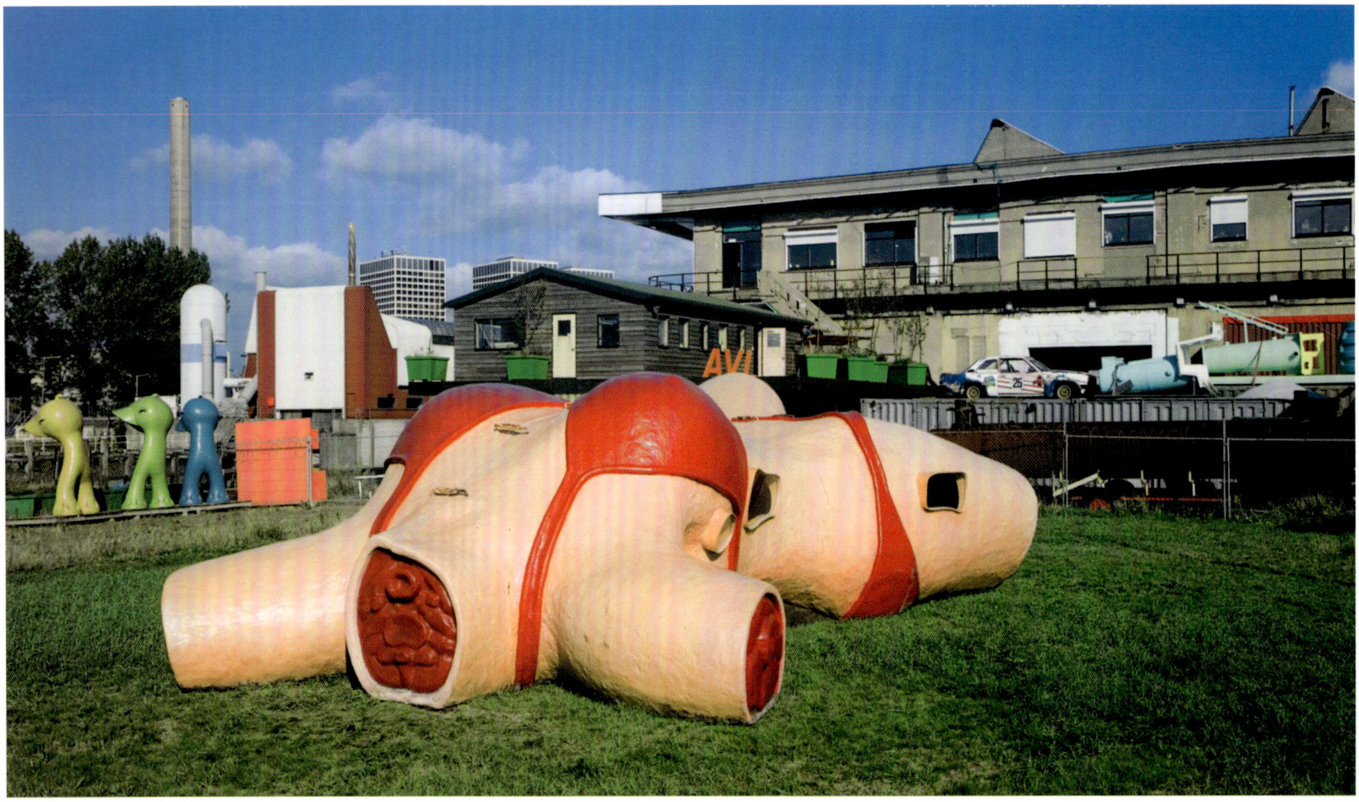

Atelier Van Lieshout, also known by the acronym AVL, is a collective project initiated in Rotterdam halfway through the 1990s that involves artists, architects, and designers under the supervision of Joep van Lieshout. The domestic sphere, human relations, and the social hierarchy are some of the subjects addressed by AVL, whose wholly cosmogonic aim is to give birth to a dystopian universe based on taking some of the values and powers of contemporary society to extremes, a layering of themes regarding the biological, social, and sexual life of the human being understood both as individual and as social animal.
One example of the creative approach of AVL is the *SlaveCity* project: an urbanized area cut off from civilization whose functioning depends on a perfect alliance of autarchic capitalism and ecology. The city's entire economic and organizational system is based on the existence of two rigidly differentiated social classes, the free and the slaves. The division of these classes is not only social but also physical, with the areas of urban space and the services conceived for their survival, feeding and education kept absolutely separate. The ruling class runs and monitors *SlaveCity* from a center called the boardroom and has at its disposal all the emblems of success of contemporary society, including a museum conceived in the form of the digestive apparatus that exhibits the greatest creations of human genius. The slaves live out their existence between work in the fields, power stations, and call centers, and their dormitories, which are rigorously segregated by gender. They are not allowed to reproduce or have families and sex is permitted only in specific locations with a set daily duration. There are no hospitals or cemeteries in the slaves' world, since their destiny, when their productive capacity is exhausted, is to become biogas, the raw material that the city exports and on which its economy is based.
BikiniBar (2006) also bases its allure on the ironic intensity of iconographic choices midway between the grotesque and the delirious as an encounter between architectural structure, artistic creation, and intrusion into the space of the female body.
(*F.T.*)

BikiniBar, 2006
Plastic and color paint, length 14 m
View of the installation for Beaufort 02 – Triënnale voor hedendaagse kunst Beaufort, Belgium 2006

SlaveCity – Board Room, 2007
Wooden table and chairs, painted ceramics, dimensions variable
Courtesy of the artist

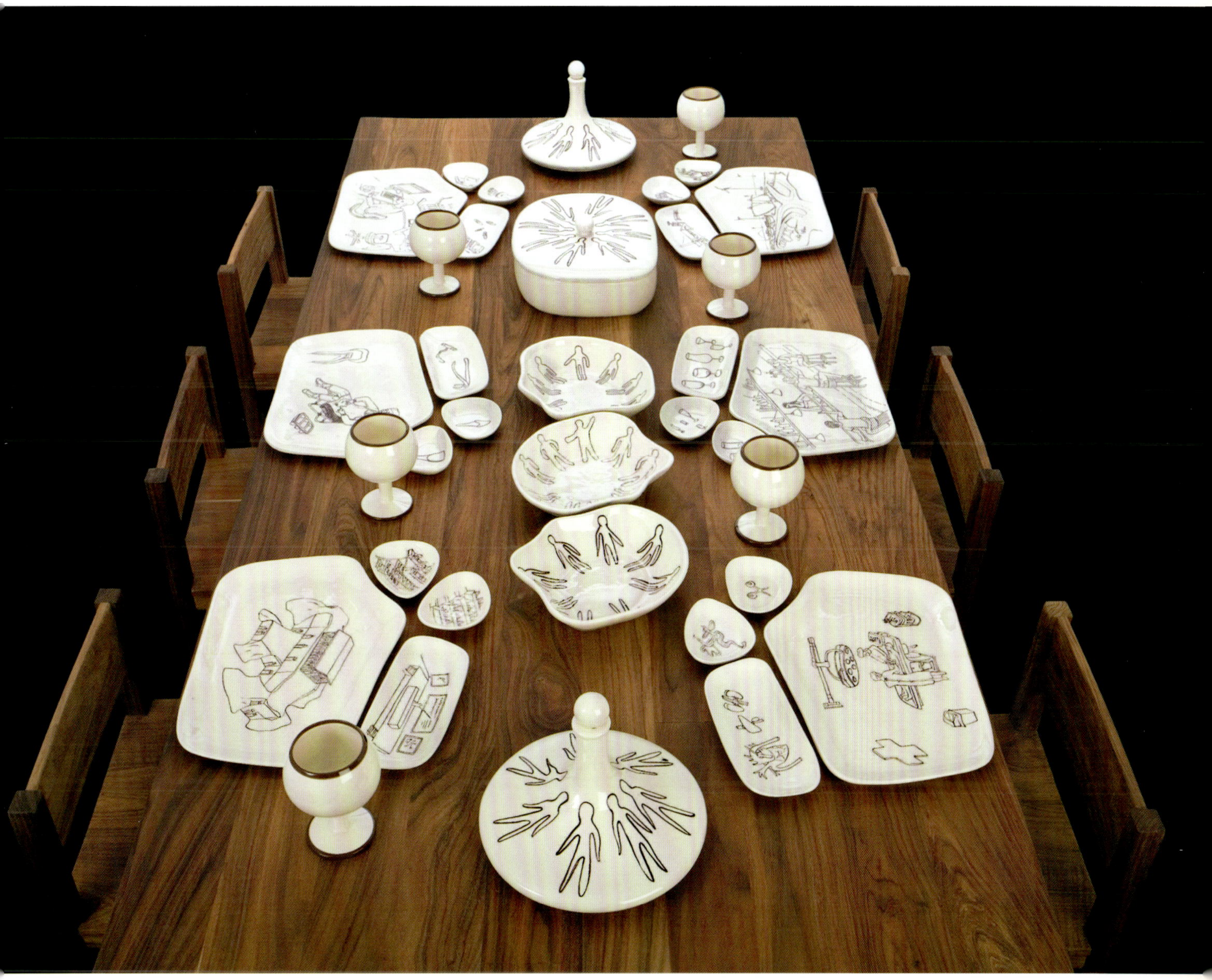

Regina José Galindo

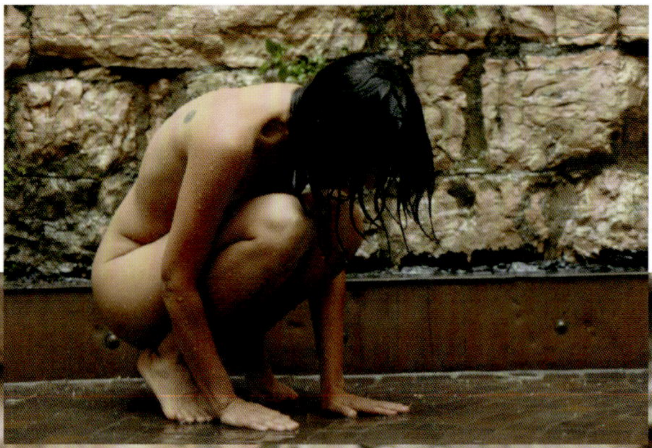

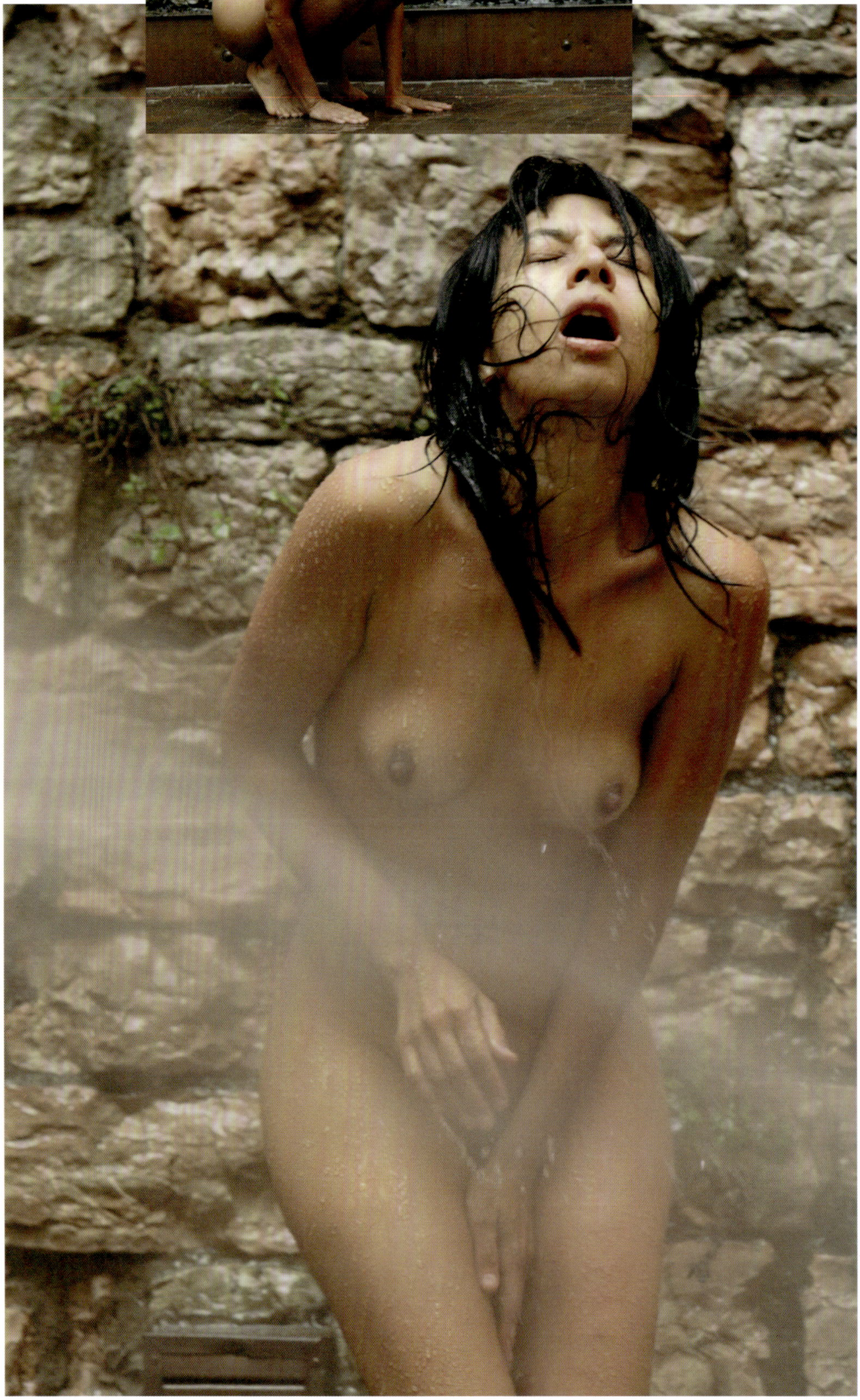

Born in 1974 in Guatemala City. Lives and works in Guatemala City. Invited to participate in the 2005 Venice Biennale, Regina José Galindo presented *Himenoplastia*, a performance featuring the surgical reconstruction of the hymen, an operation restoring the female patient to the physical condition of virginity. The emotional impact of the action, the radical attack on male predominance in the social and cultural sphere, and the highlighting of the divide between conditions and the possibility of medical operations in different situations earned the Guatemalan artist the Golden Lion in the under-35 category.
Galindo's work thus involves the use of her body to focus on the violence inflicted on human beings in general and women in particular, carrying on a tradition initiated in the 1970s and exemplified by the art of Ana Mendieta and Marina Abramovich.
The recent history of the artist's country lies at the heart of *¿Quién puede borrar las huellas?*, a performance of 2003 in which the artist, dressed in black, walked through Guatemala City with her bare feet dipped periodically in a bowl of human blood so as to leave a trail of footprints leading to the Constitutional Court, an emblem of justice in contrast with the bloodstains, a tangible sign of the injustice and violence perpetrated on the population during the civil war.
The violence to which Regina José Galindo exposes her body is exemplified by the performance *Limpieza social*, staged at the Galleria Civica, Trento (Italy), in March 2006, where she was blasted with water from a high-pressure hose as a comment on the tortures inflicted on prisoners of war. The title is also highly significant, as "social cleansing" is a clear reference to ethnic cleaning and annihilation of the uniqueness of the person.
(F.T.)

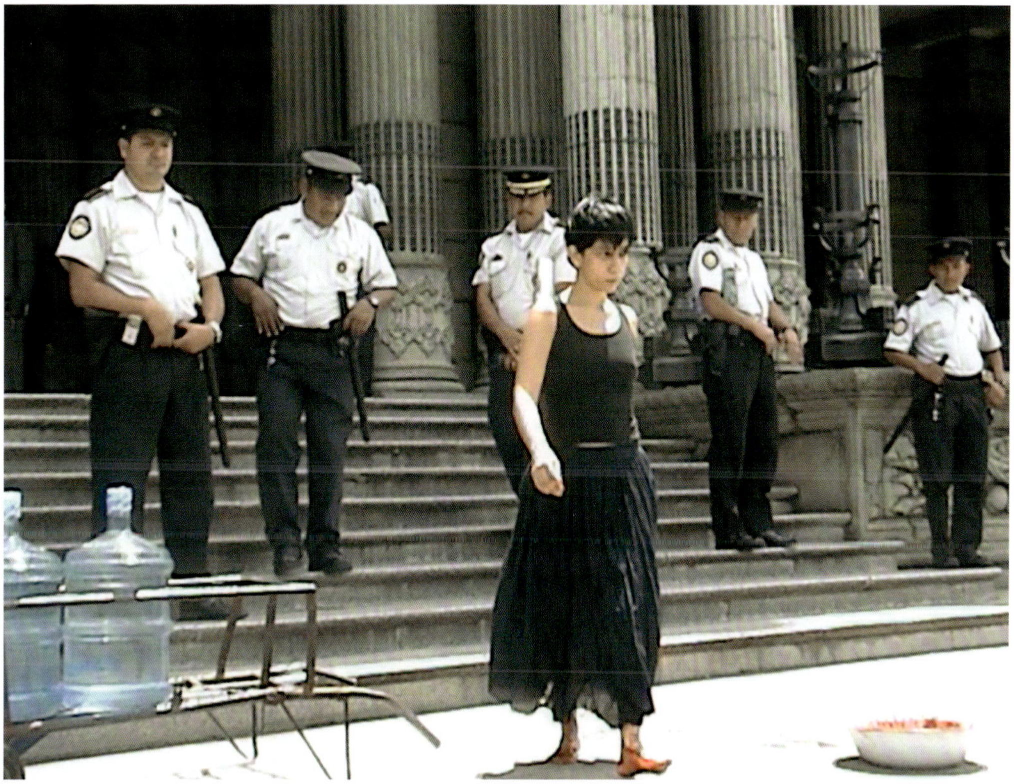

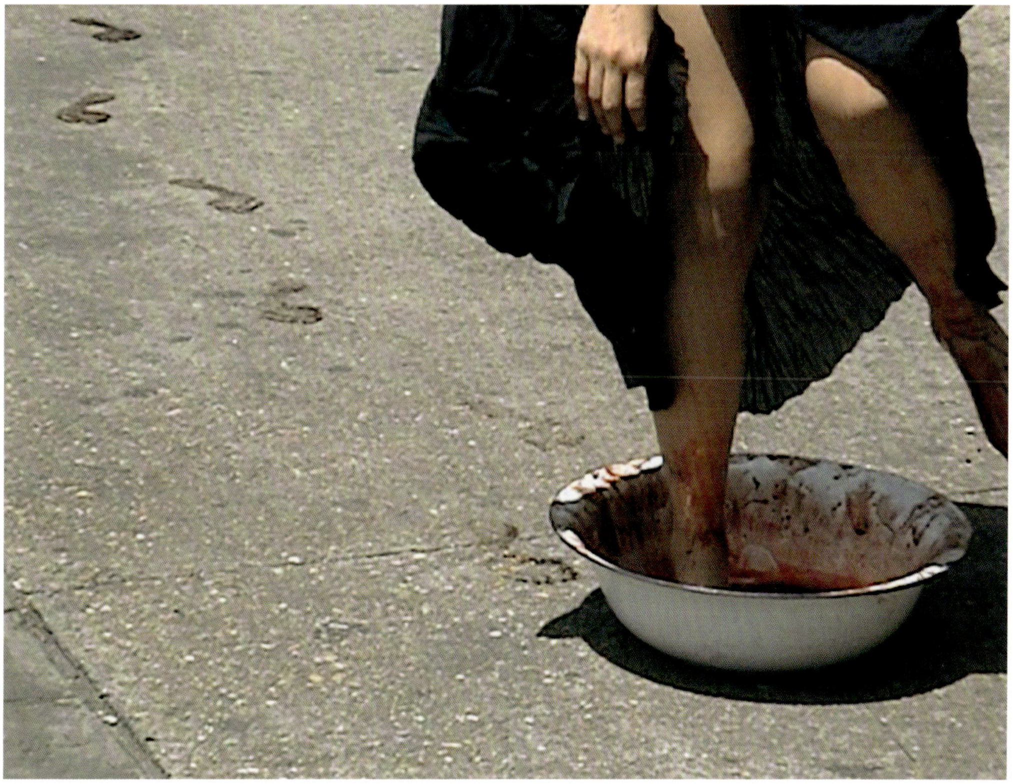

Limpieza social, 2006
Performance held in 2006
at Galleria Civica di Trento
Courtesy prometeogallery di Ida
Pisani, Milan/Lucca

¿Quién puede borrar las huellas?,
2003
Video, 12'
Performance held in 2003 by
walking between the Constitutional
Court and the National Palace,
Guatemala City
Courtesy prometeogallery di Ida
Pisani, Milan/Lucca

William Kentridge

Born in Johannesburg, South Africa, in 1955. Lives and works in Johannesburg.
Kentridge graduated in politics and African studies from the University of the Witwatersrand and obtained a diploma in fine arts from the Johannesburg Art Foundation. It was his passion for cinema and theatre that then drove him to study mime in Paris and to found the Free Filmmakers Cooperative in his native land, where he worked as a film director, writer, set designer, and actor. All of these elements are essential to any understanding of his work, which addresses the history of South Africa, its political tensions, the problem of apartheid and the difficult process of racial reconciliation through drawings and animated films in which marginalization and exploitation become a general condition of downtrodden human dignity. Presented in Kassel at Documenta 11 in 2002, *Confessions of Zeno* is a multimedia theatrical work based on Italo Svevo's *La coscienza di Zeno* that combines puppetry with live singing, acting and video projection to capture the novel's modern vision.
The particular characteristic of Kentridge's videos is the production process, which involves filming a series of large drawings in charcoal and pastel. Each sequence is based on a single drawing, which preserves all the traces of the erasures and changes undergone in the process, every line and every nuance.
This gives the end result a character of wonder and precariousness reminiscent of early twentieth-century cinema and very well suited to what is a poetic system of images, a succession of dreamlike apparitions and figures of great evocative and visionary impact.
Defined by the artist as "a gathering out of chaos to order rather than a reversion from order to a state of dispersal", anti-entropy is the focal point of his three recent videos *Breath*, *Return* and *Dissolve*, all shown in Venice at the exhibition *(Repeat) From the Beginning / Da capo*, which opened at the Bevilacqua La Masa Foundation in November 2008.
(*L.L.*)

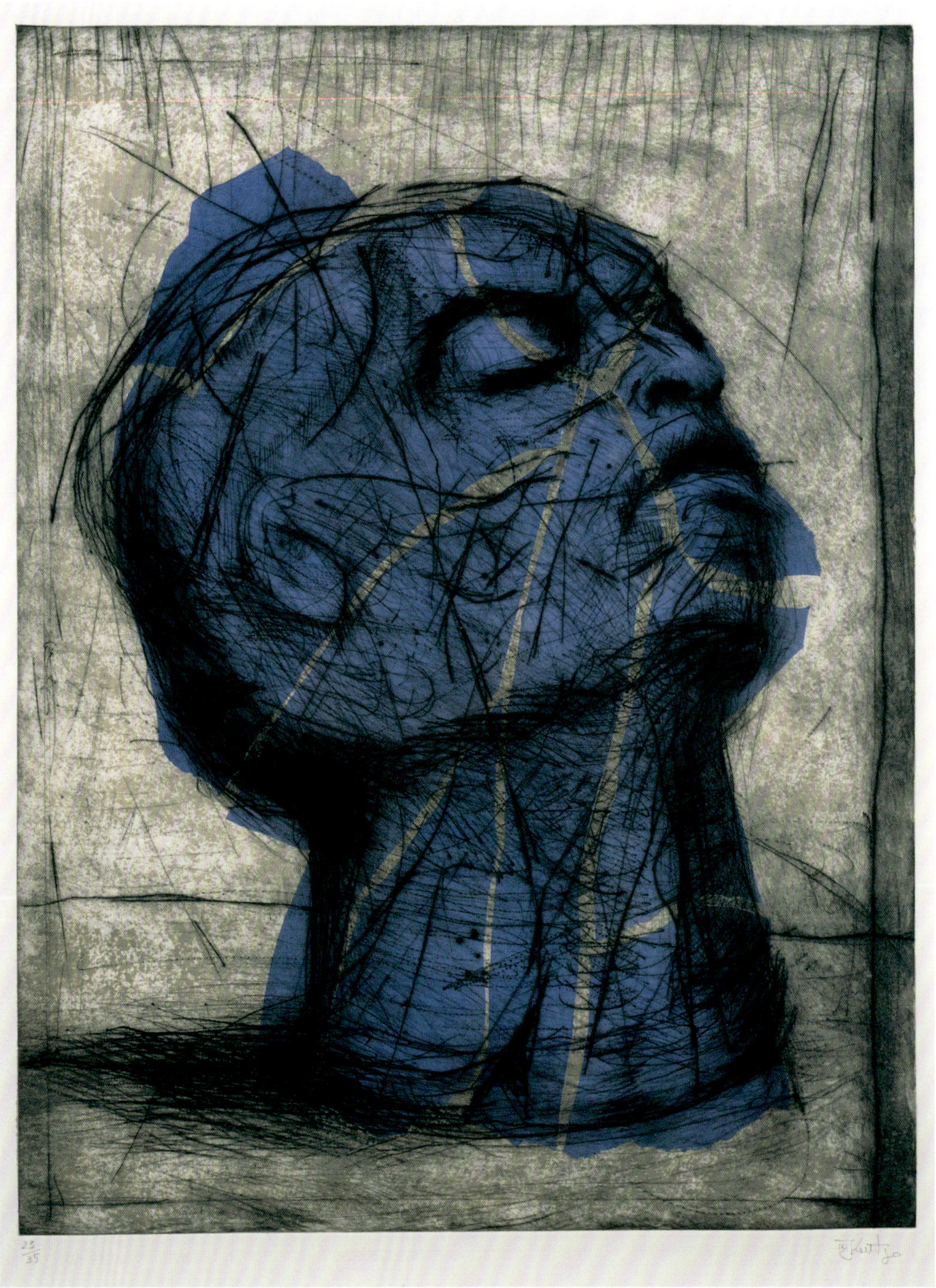

Blue Head, 1993–1998
Aquatint, drypoint, and etching on paper, 102.5 x 78.8 cm
Washington, D.C., Hirshhorn Museum and Sculpture Garden, Smithsonian Institution, Joseph H. Hirshhorn Purchase Fund

The Medicine Chest, 2001
Wood, glass, metal, and DVD,
44.45 x 34.29 x 12.7 cm
Washington, D.C., Hirshhorn Museum and Sculpture Garden, Smithsonian Institution, Gift of Robert Lehrman in honor of James T. Demetrion

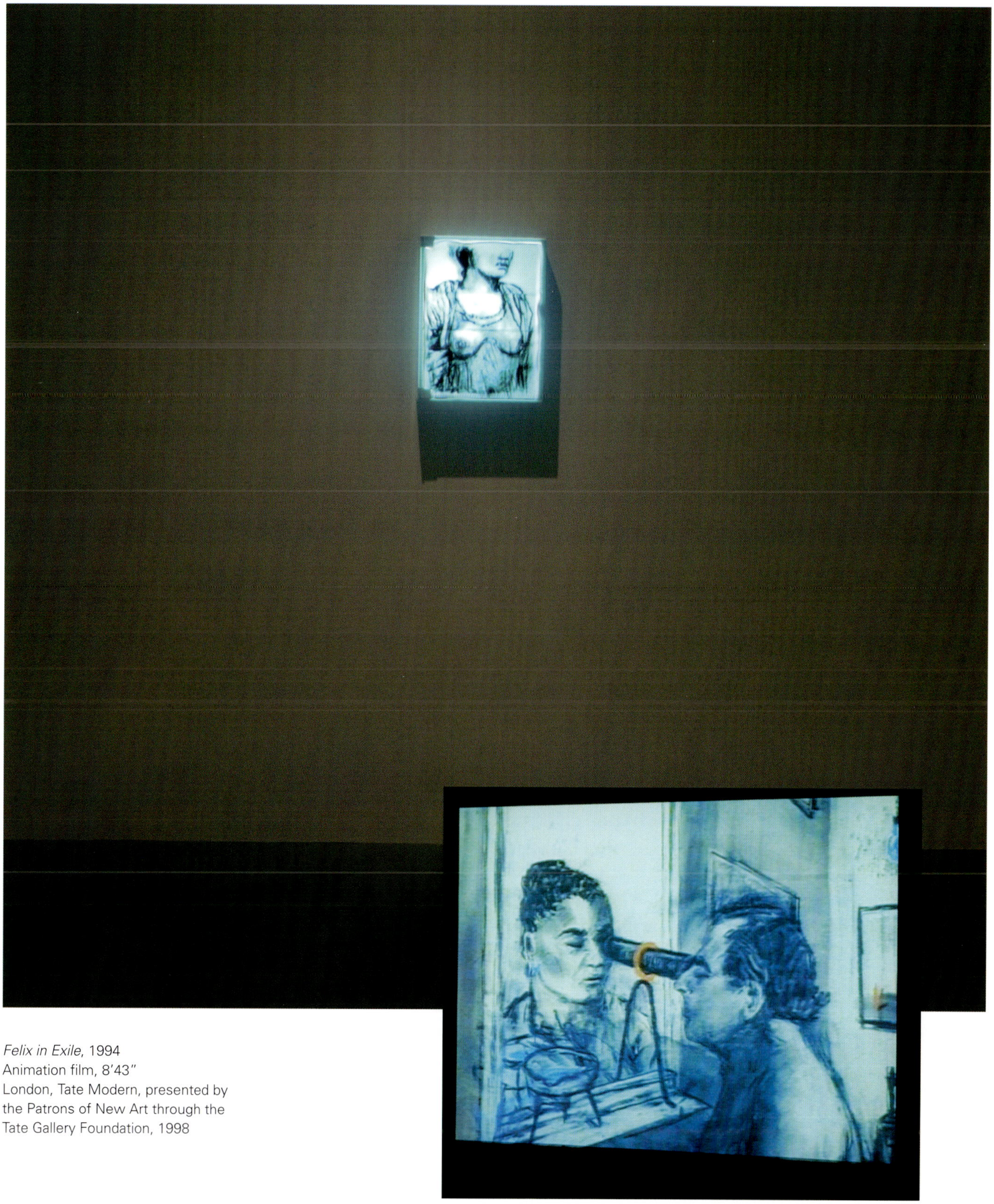

Felix in Exile, 1994
Animation film, 8'43"
London, Tate Modern, presented by the Patrons of New Art through the Tate Gallery Foundation, 1998

Shirin Neshat

Born in Qazvin, Iran, in 1957.
Lives and works in New York.
The Iranian artist Shirin Neshat started out in the 1970s with photographic series of marked visual impact highlighting the paradoxes of Muslim society.
The late 1990s saw a switch to videos in continuing the dialectical operation upon which her work is grounded, namely the construction of an antithetical visual dimension that undermines the superficial meaning of the image. This is exemplified in photographs and videos focusing on the juxtaposition of opposites like black and white, man and woman, individual and collectivity, and East and West.
The artist's geographical and cultural roots emerge in the video *Women Without Men* (2004) based on the novel of the same name by Shahrnush Parsipur. Set during the Iranian coup d'état of 1953, the novel tells the stories of five women who fight against oppression and deprivation of personal freedom, a metaphor of the Iranian nation's struggle for independence. Shirin Neshat drew inspiration from Shahrnush Parsipur's book for a full-length film and a series of video installations focused on the psychology of its main characters, Munis, Mahdokht, Faizeh, Zarrinkolah, and Farrokhlaqa, whose garden provides the refuge from the outside world they are all seeking.
The metaphor of Eden is extended in Shirin Neshat's work to encompass the condition of exile and the need for a safe place not just for women but humanity as a whole. The film focuses far more than the novel on the political situation in Iran, especially in the episode dedicated to Munis, where activism becomes an expression of denied and ideal freedom capable of arousing great hopes and causing great disappointment.
The drama of the conflict in the Middle Eastern countries is the focal point of the video *Passage* (2001), in which Neshat investigates the themes of death and ritual through images of the war between Israelis and Palestinians drawn from the mass media. The video uses the contrast of black and white to highlight the dichotomy of man and woman.
A male procession carries a body wrapped in white cloth. A group of veiled women in black dig a grave with their bare hands sitting in a circle and repeating a litany set to music by Philip Glass. A girl constructs a small circle of stones as a metaphorical pyre for the funeral rites. Gender differences are thus reflected in everyday roles. In this case, the Iranian artist takes up a narrative topos common to Mediterranean cultures all the way back to *The Trojan Women* by Euripides.
The video *The Last Word* (2003) marks a more cinematic approach in the artist's work. It focuses on the interrogation of a woman writer whose words constitute a danger for the system, an allusion to the existential condition of Shahrnush Parsipur. The scene takes place in a neutral room with modern furnishing. Neshat uses light and shadow and the contrast between black and white to subvert the ethical characterization of the characters, making the memories of the woman, in shadow, and the real figures of her questioners, dressed in white, coexist in the same space. The woman's antagonist is the chief interrogator and the two sit on either side of a table entirely covered in books, material evidence of the writer's dangerousness. Inability to relate to expressive and creative freedom is exemplified by the pointless action of moving and rummaging through the books, which are present not only as physical objects but also as a series of deep literary references.
While the atmosphere of the interrogation and the insinuated sense of guilt and blame take us back to Kafka's *Trial*, the role of the female narrator endowed with the power of words conjures up the presence of Scheherazade, the storyteller of the masterpiece of Eastern literature *The Arabian Nights*.
(F.T.)

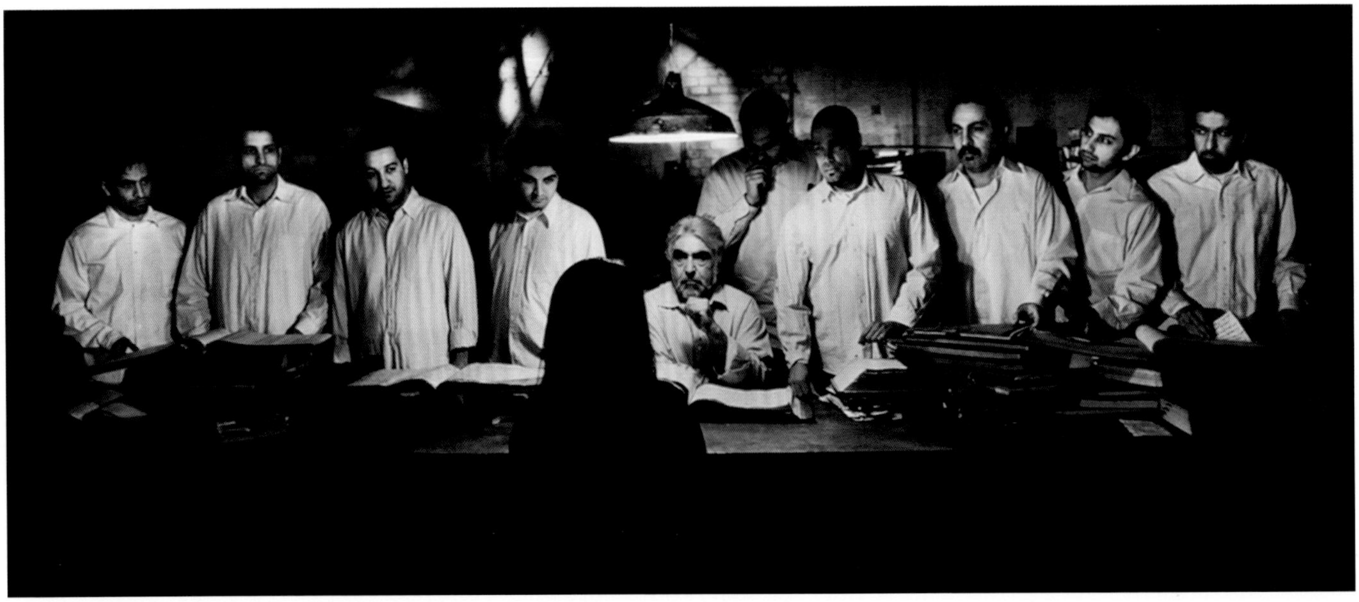

The Last Word, 2003
Gelatin silver print, 40.6 x 76.2 cm
Courtesy Gladstone Gallery,
New York

Women Without Men (Untitled #1),
2004
Color print, 103 x 165 cm
Courtesy Gladstone Gallery,
New York

Munis & Revolutionary Man, 2008
Ink on color print mounted
on aluminum, 124.5 x 230.5 cm
Courtesy Galerie Jérôme
de Noirmont, Paris

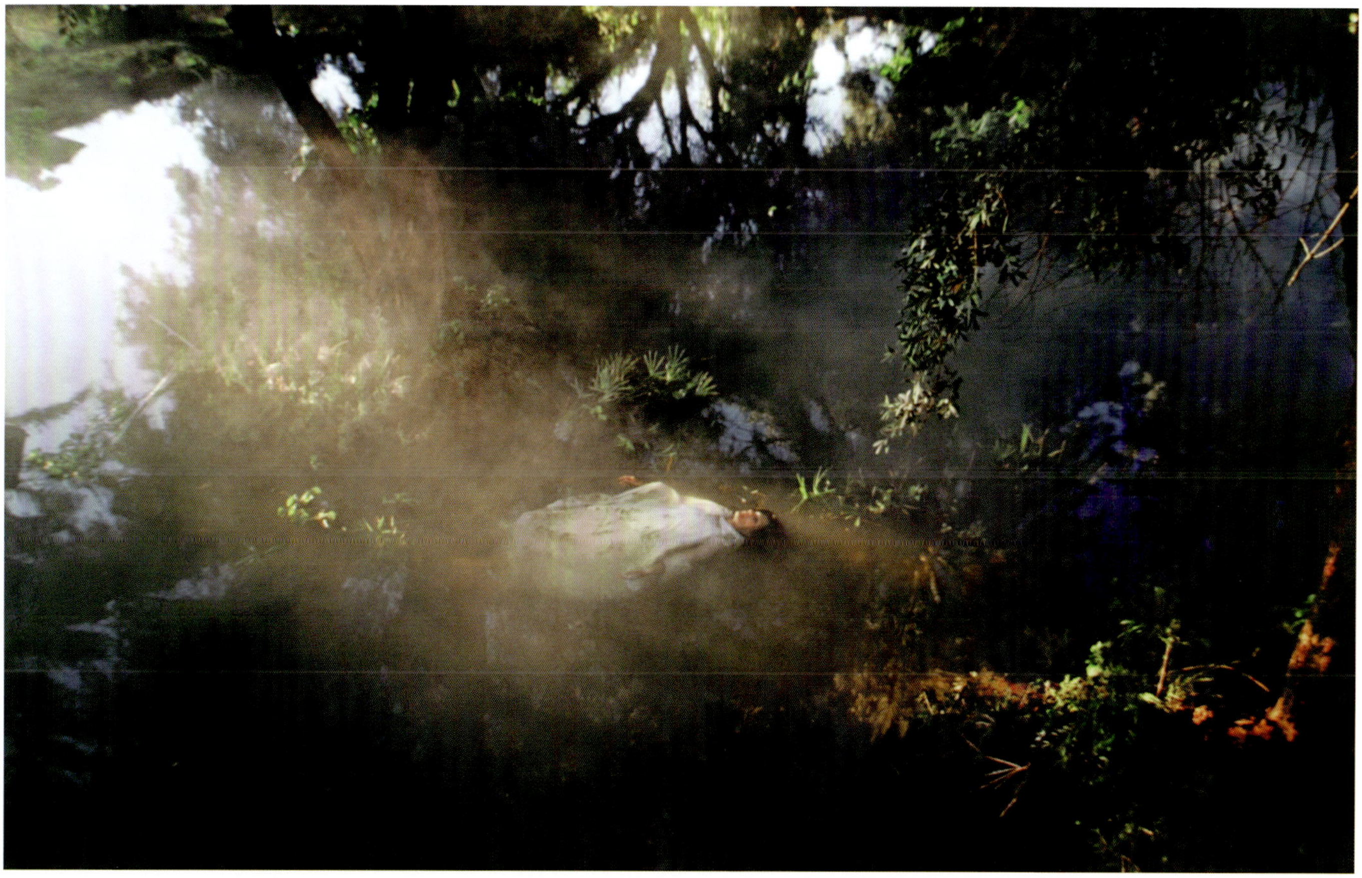

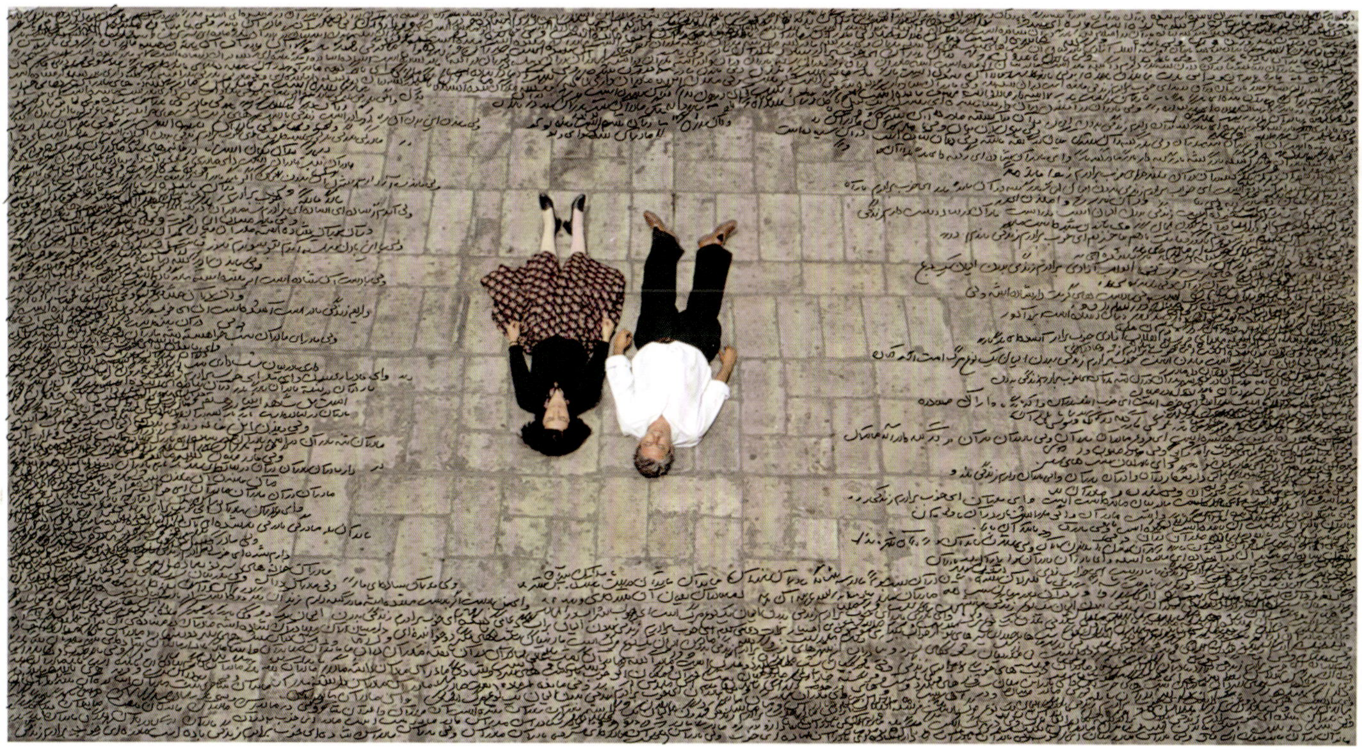

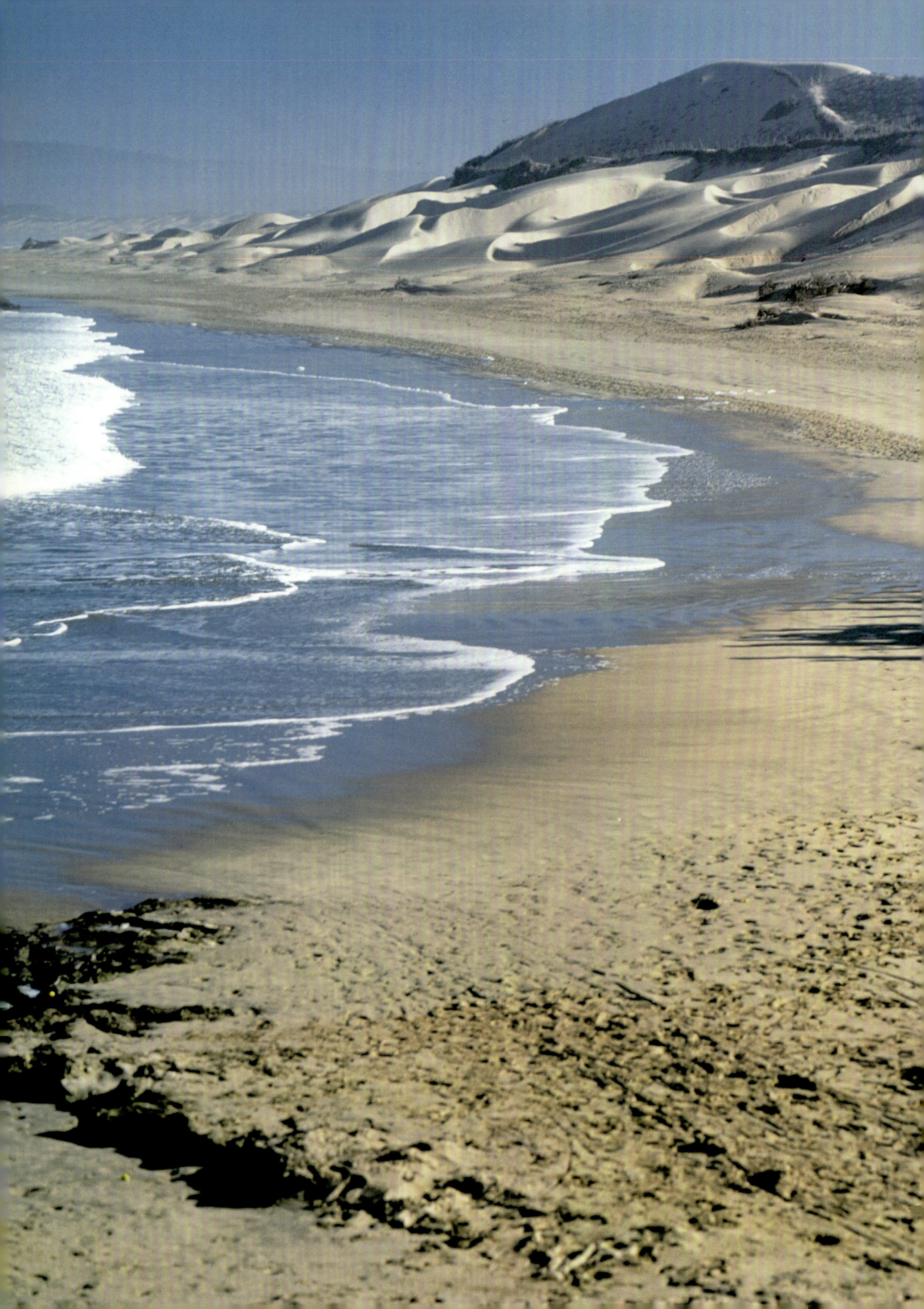

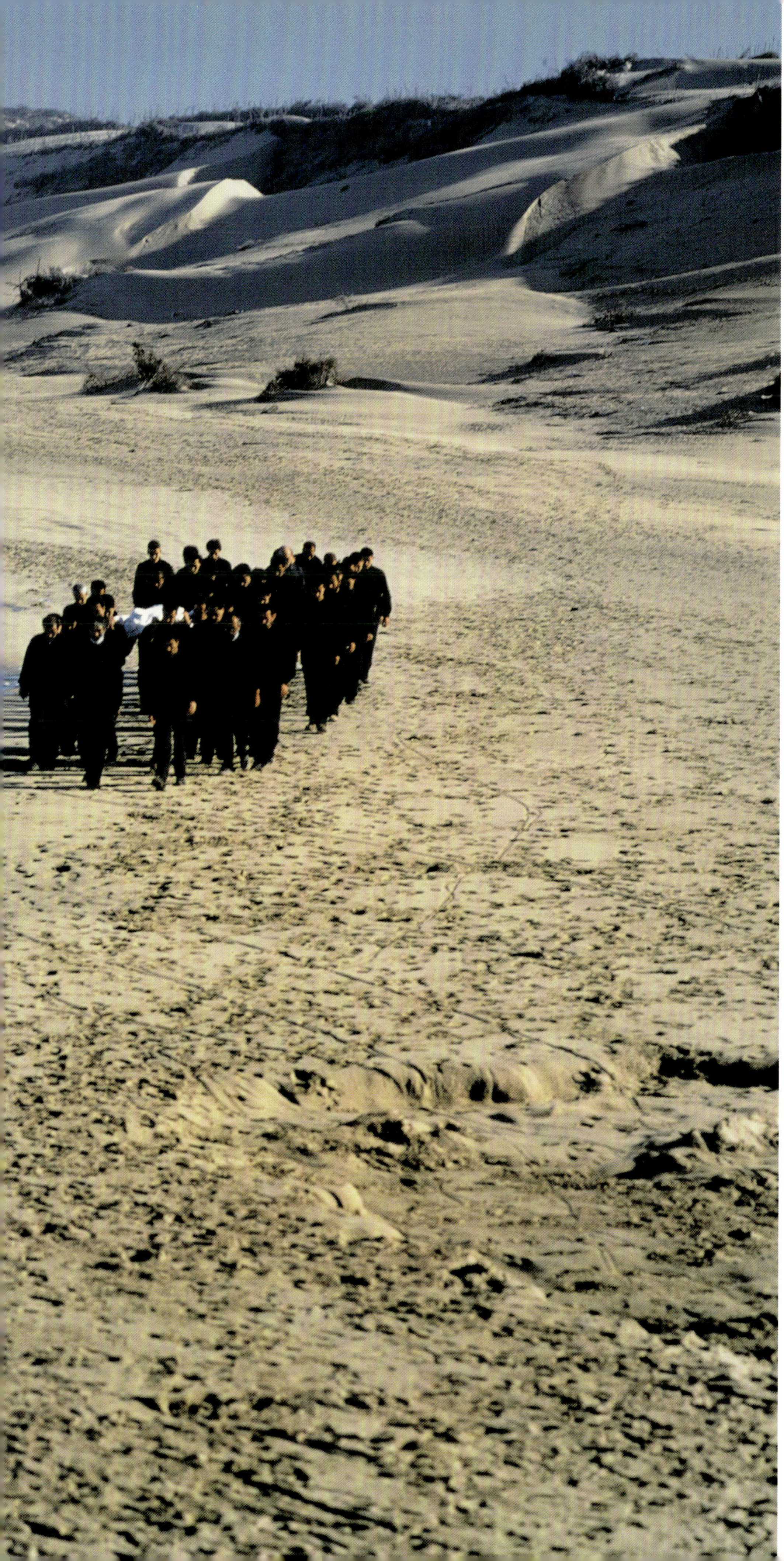

Passage, 2001
Video and sound installation, 11'30'',
dimensions variable
New York, Solomon R. Guggenheim
Museum, Purchased with funds
contributed by Dakis Joannou and
by the International Director's
Council and Executive Committee
members

Doris Salcedo

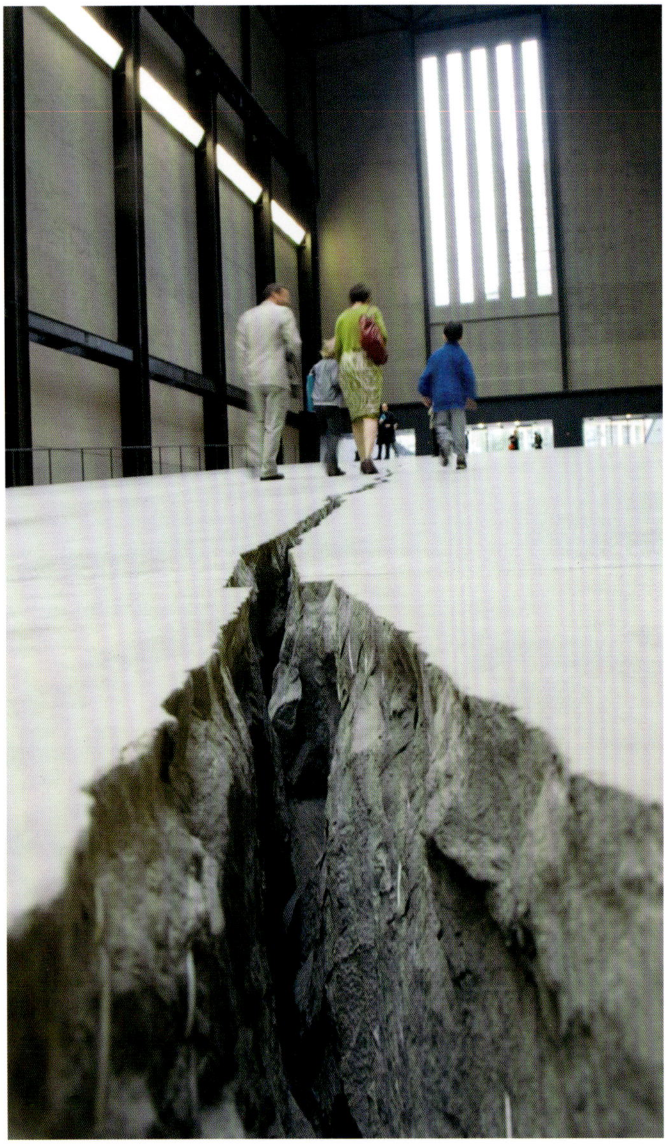

Shibboleth, 2007
Cement and mixed media, length 167 m
View of the installation realized in 2007 at Tate Modern, London for *The Unilever Series*

Abyss, 2005
Bricks, metal, steel, epoxy resin, dimensions variable
View of the installation realized at the Castello di Rivoli – Museo d'Arte Contemporanea
Courtesy Alexander and Bonin, New York and Jay Jopling / White Cube, London

Born in Bogotá in 1958. Lives and works in Bogotá.
On being invited to take part in the first Turin Triennial of Contemporary Art in 2005, Doris Salcedo constructed a room of bricks and cement in the exhibition space of Castello di Rivoli. Devoid of any definite historical connotations but oppressive and claustrophobic, *Abyss* takes the visitor into a sort of huge burial mound situated outside time, a funeral monument haunted by contrition and guilt. Many of her works share the common need to talk about the present through the metaphors of absence, pain, death, and the deprivation of freedom.
The Colombian artist started out in the late 1980s with large-scale installations and sculptures characterized by huge heaps of furniture, old clothes, and rags to be understood as signs of the presence and everyday life of human beings disrupted by the violent action and aggressive invasion of tyranny. Through these enormous installations based on the accumulation of objects and desolating absence of any human figure, Salcedo makes manifest the violent action to which her work bears material witness. One characteristic feature of her art is the tragic immobility of cement with the clothes, traces, and vestiges of the men and women who fell victim to the atrocities of political repression breaking the surface like corpses or ghosts.
The close relationship between presence and absence is clearly evident in *Noviembre 6 y 7*, an installation created in 2002 to commemorate the seventeenth anniversary of the sieges of the Supreme Court in Bogotá.
This involved hanging numerous wooden chairs from the roof of the new Supreme Court building to dangle on the façade for 53 hours like elements emerging from time and being absorbed back into it.
In the same way, the sign of human passage is the dominant feature of the installation presented at the 2003 Istanbul Bienali, a heap of over 1600 wooden chairs piled up in a precarious heap in the space between two buildings as an allusion to the want and destruction caused by war. The accumulation in this case became entropy, an operation of shapelessness proposed by Bataille: "collapse, accumulation but also irretrievable waste".
Deliberately avoiding any distinction between history with either an uppercase or lowercase H, Salcedo proposes a reading of the events of the present by setting them in the context of a past verging on myth. One example is *Shibboleth*, the work created in the Turbine Hall of Tate Modern in London in 2007 as part of the *Unilever Series*.
It consisted of a long crack running across the floor, suggesting a dramatic geologic event or one of the punitive plagues inflicted by God, an expression of the divide between the divine will and human action. It was a fracture that reflects an error, represented in this case by the segregation carried out here through linguistic demarcation.
The Jewish word *shibboleth*, meaning "river", is a term whose specific phonological character made it possible to distinguish the members of different ethnic groups because of the difficulty of pronouncing *sh* and *th*. As we read in the *Book of Judges*, the Ephraimites fleeing for their lives after defeat in battle by the Gileadites were identified through their incorrect pronunciation of the word and put to death. Doris Salcedo's recent work thus focuses on the problem of cultural identity and the consequences of diversity, extending its meaning to every sort of racial distinction and at the same time to the interaction between architecture and installation, the place serving to accommodate art and the significant forms of the creative act.
(*F.T.*)

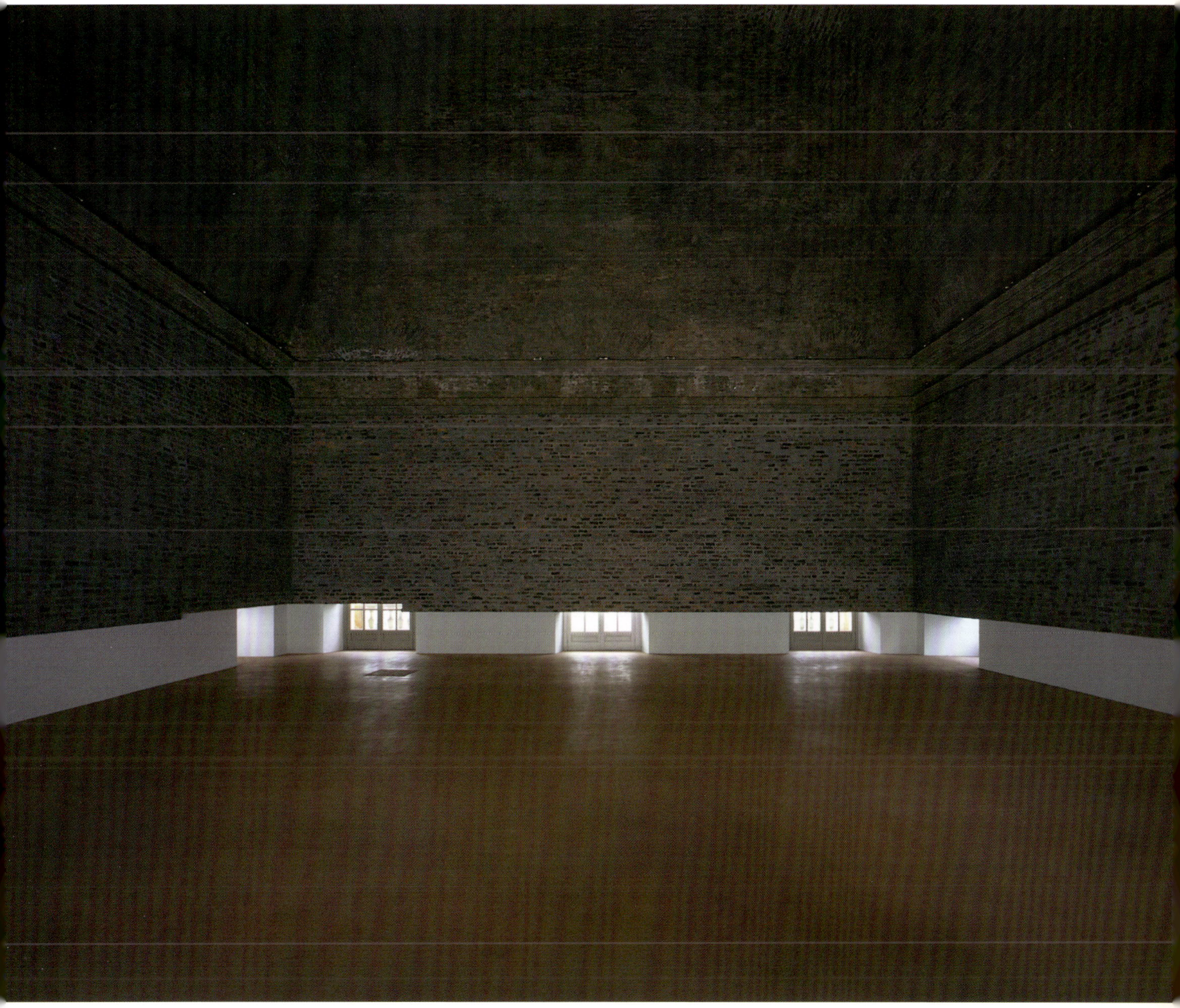

Noviembre 6 y 7, 2002
Video with 280 wooden chairs, 53 hours
Views of the installation realized in 2003
on the Court of Justice façade, Bogotá,
Colombia
Courtesy Jay Jopling / White Cube,
London

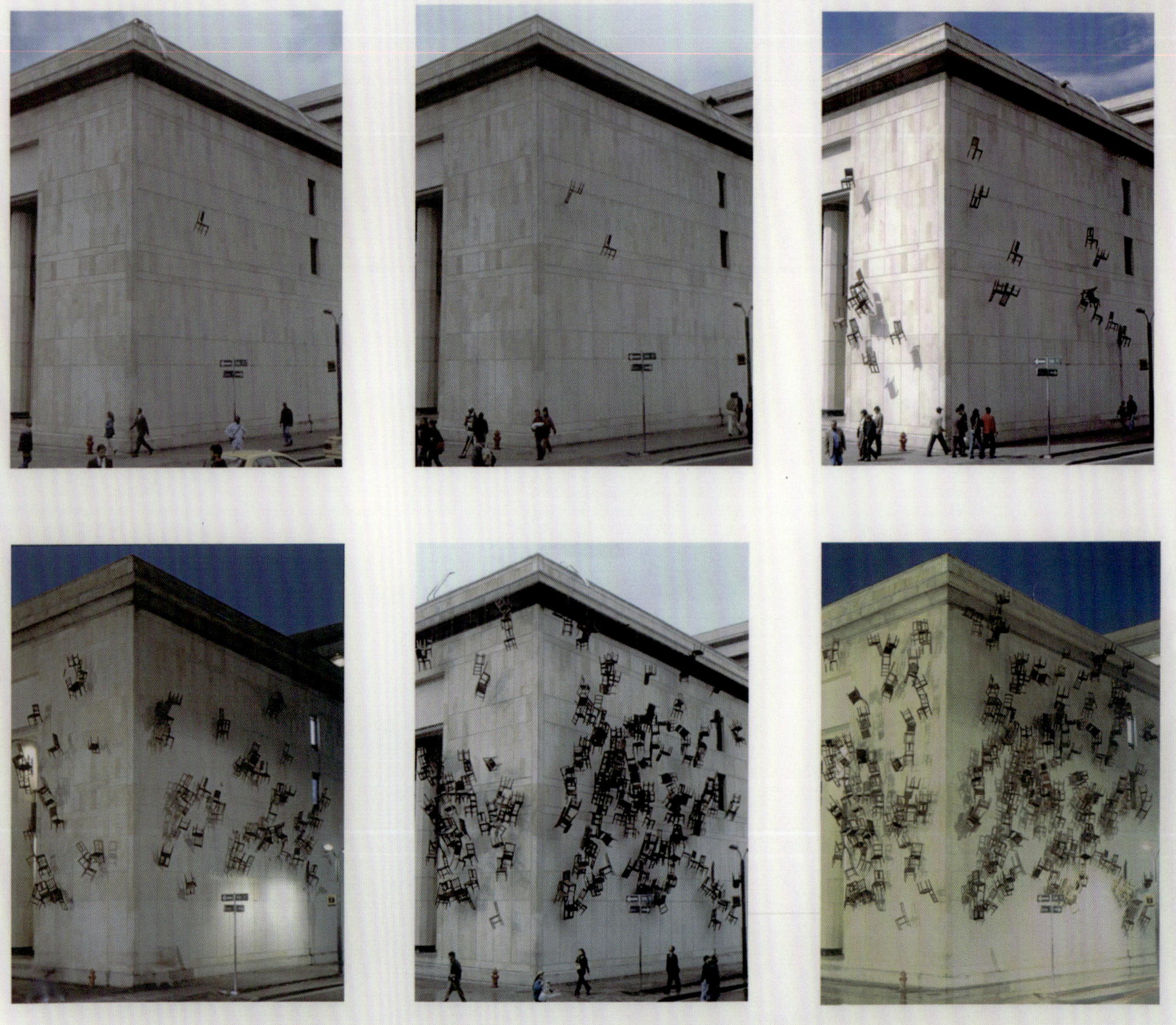

Chairs, 2003
1600 wooden chairs,
dimensions variable
View of the installation for 8.B –
VIII Istanbul Bienali, Istanbul 2003
Courtesy Alexander and Bonin,
New York; White Cube, London

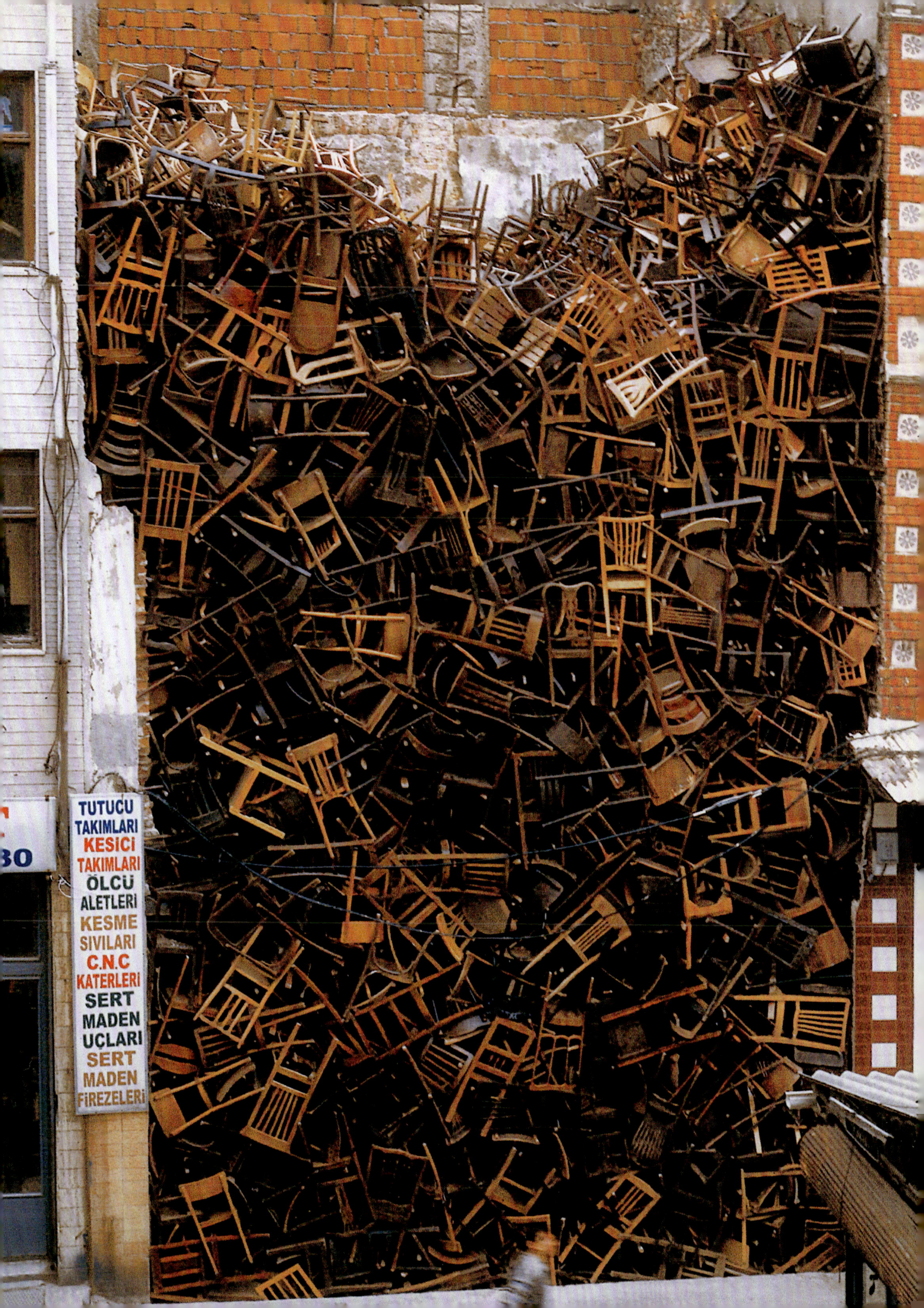
TUTUCU
TAKIMLARI
KESICI
TAKIMLARI
ÖLÇÜ
ALETLERI
KESME
SIVILARI
C.N.C
KATERLERI
SERT
MADEN
UÇLARI
SERT
MADEN
FIREZELERI

Santiago Sierra

Born in Madrid in 1966. Lives and works in Mexico City.
The Spanish artist Santiago Sierra became known in the 1990s with a series of works apparently forming part of the tradition of Minimalism and Land Art. Examples include installing huge industrial containers in various exhibition spaces in 1991, displaying what were literally "twenty one-meter-square pieces of road" in a private gallery in 1992, burning 50 liters of diesel oil to leave a black mark on the ground in a shantytown on the outskirts of Madrid in 1994, hanging scraps from a local market in Mexico where the poor go to pick up substandard but still edible food at the entrance to the subway in 1996, and using diesel oil to set fire to a newly refurbished gallery in 1997. In actual fact, the purpose of these environmental operations is not to obtain formal appreciation but to confront the public with the work needed to produce them, the explicit violation of a place, the desolation of the outskirts, the construction sites, the non-places of a metropolis. The discourse became clearer and more challenging when the focus of attention shifted to the human body. Sierra looked in 1998 for someone with no desire for a tattoo but prepared out of financial necessity to have a 30-centimeter line tattooed on his or her back, an operation expanded in 1999 to involve 6 people, each paid 30 dollars. This was followed by numerous performances consisting essentially of participants selected on criteria such as social condition (*Congregation of Illegal Workers*, 1999), readiness to engage in humiliating actions for a paltry sum of money (*10 People Paid to Masturbate*, 2000) or both.
Two Puerto Rican drug addicts were given a dose of heroin in return for having a 10-inch stripe of their hair shaved off in 2000.
His work for the 2001 Venice Biennale consisted of paying 133 people (mostly immigrants and street sellers) to have their hair dyed blond. In 2002 he hired 18 East European prostitutes in Italy, covered their genitals with polyurethane, and left evidence of this operation in the exhibition space (a deconsecrated church), an action repeated in London with ten Iraqi immigrants in 2004. Sierra responds to those who attack him for this blatant violation of human dignity by stating that this is the society we live in: "Persons are objects of the State and of Capital and are employed as such. This is precisely what I try to show."
His investigations often address subjects such as racism and the protection of boundaries as well as violation of the elitist nature of spaces reserved for art, and hence the contradictions of his own work, which is now exhibited in the most exclusive settings.
(*D.Q.*)

House in Mud, 2005
3 black and white photographs
Serie, 106 x 156 cm each
View of the installation realized in 2005 at the Kestnergesellschaft, Hannover

Polyurethane Sprayed on the Backs of 10 Workers, 2004
Single screen black and white DVD projection, dimensions variable
View of the performance realized in 2004 at the Lisson Gallery, London

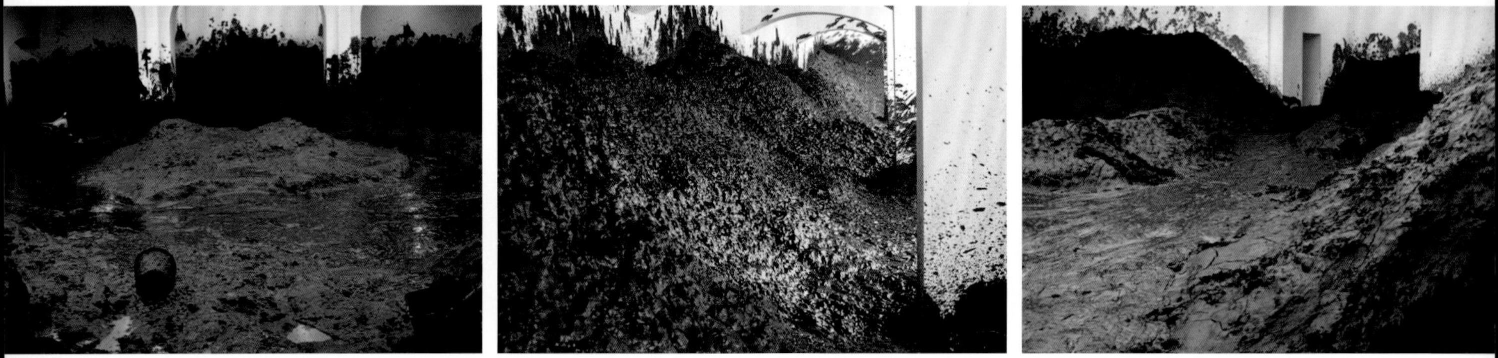

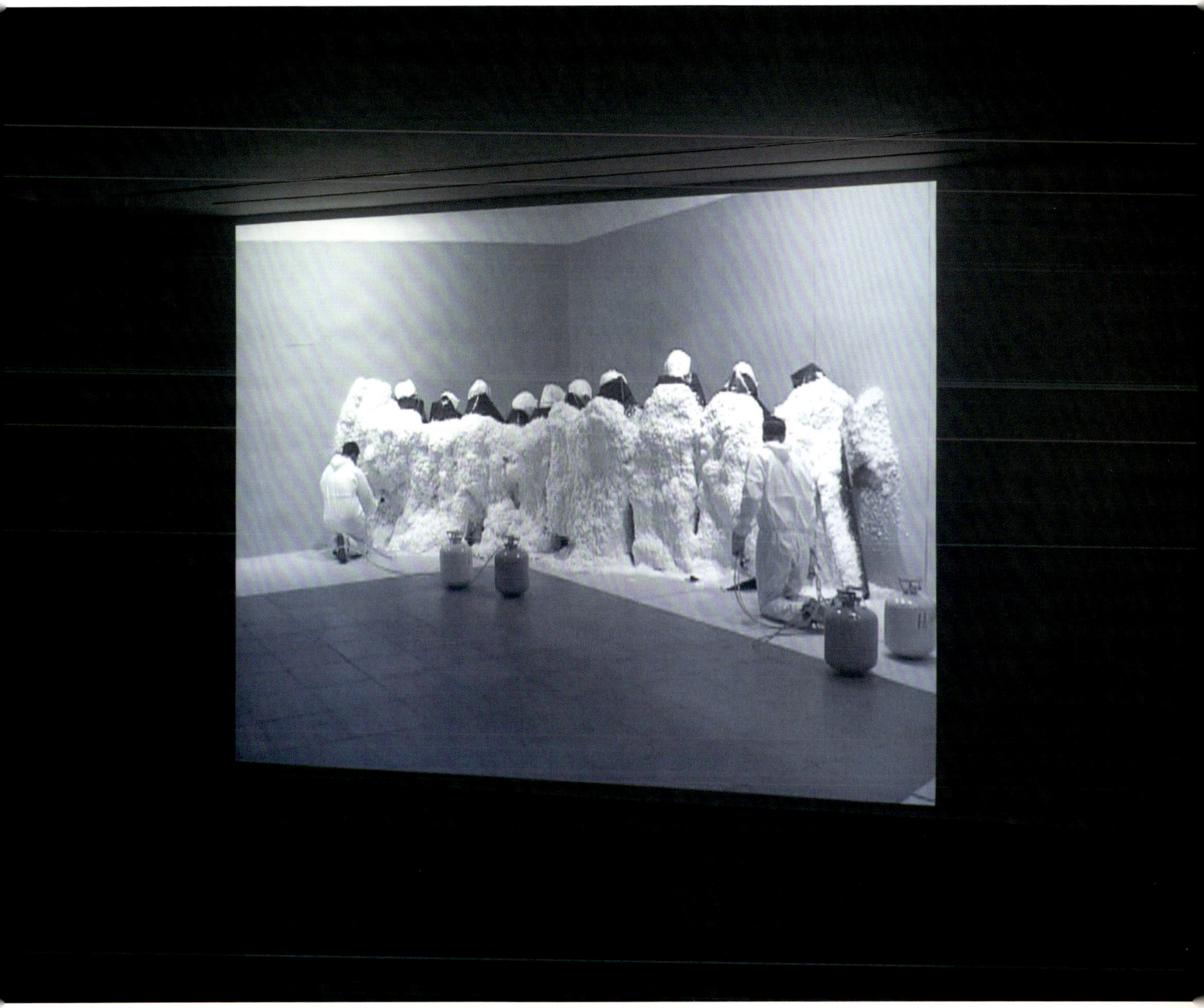

Sislej Xhafa

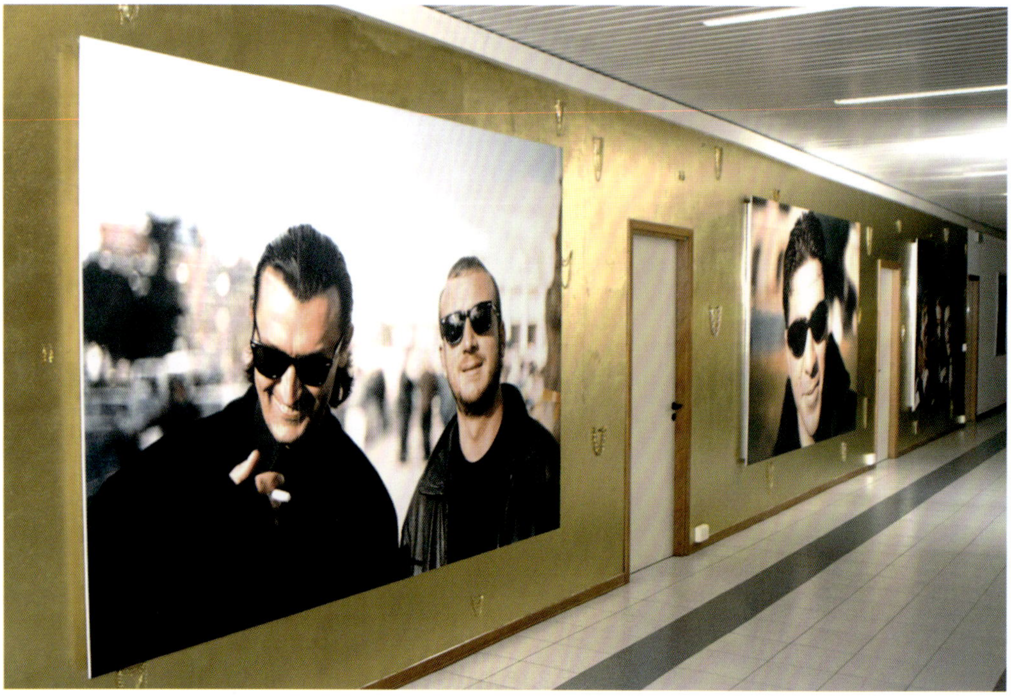

Sweet Invasion, 2000
3 prints, gold walls and jewelry,
200 x 300 cm each print
Courtesy Fondazione Teseco per l'Arte, Pisa

Lapo Cipolla, 2005
Marble, 3 m
View of the installation for *Arte all'Arte X*, Giardino della Madonna, Montalcino
Courtesy Associazione Arte Continua, San Gimignano

Born in Peja, Kosovo, in 1970. Lives and works in New York.
Dressed as a soccer player with an Albanian flag sticking out of his backpack, Sislej Xhafa climbed over the wall of the gardens at the 47th Venice Biennale in 1997 and began to kick a ball around in the area between the French and British pavilions. Entitled *Clandestine Albanian Pavilion*, the performance was his response to the lack of an official space for Albanian artists. The constant kicking of the ball, the location chosen for the performance, and the backpack all refer to the never-ending migration of his people to Europe in search of better living conditions.
The migrant's vision, legality, and the boundary with illegality are the primary themes addressed by Xhafa, who seeks to heighten public awareness of the marginal figures of our society in both social and cultural terms. This is exemplified by *Sweet Invasion* (2000), a series of photographs of smiling, friendly Albanian gangsters with fashionable clothes and accessories. The very fact that the subjects are new contemporary icons, in this case underworld figures, authorizes Xhafa to present their less violent and therefore still more disturbing aspects officially to the world.
The unmistakable vein of irony running through all the Kosovar artist's work is crucial to any understanding of the role of the boundary. Multi-layered and more often blurred than sharply defined, this is investigated by Xhafa through different media with the aim of focusing above all on the differences between contemporary forms of expression and traditional techniques. This is the meaning of *Lapo Cipolla*, a work set in the countryside around Montalcino (Italy), where the artist used marble, a local and historically illustrious material, to create an exact copy of a light three-wheel pickup (the Piaggio Ape) and placed it upside-down against a tree.
The operation related the means of transport to the life and needs of the country, emphasizing the moment at which creative and mechanical technique is literally overturned by the subversive potential of nature, metaphorically represented by the best-known product of the area, namely the wine Brunello di Montalcino. Inebriation, an allusion also to the creative status of the artist, undermines man's ability to act and to handle not only a vehicle but also himself.
(*F.T.*)

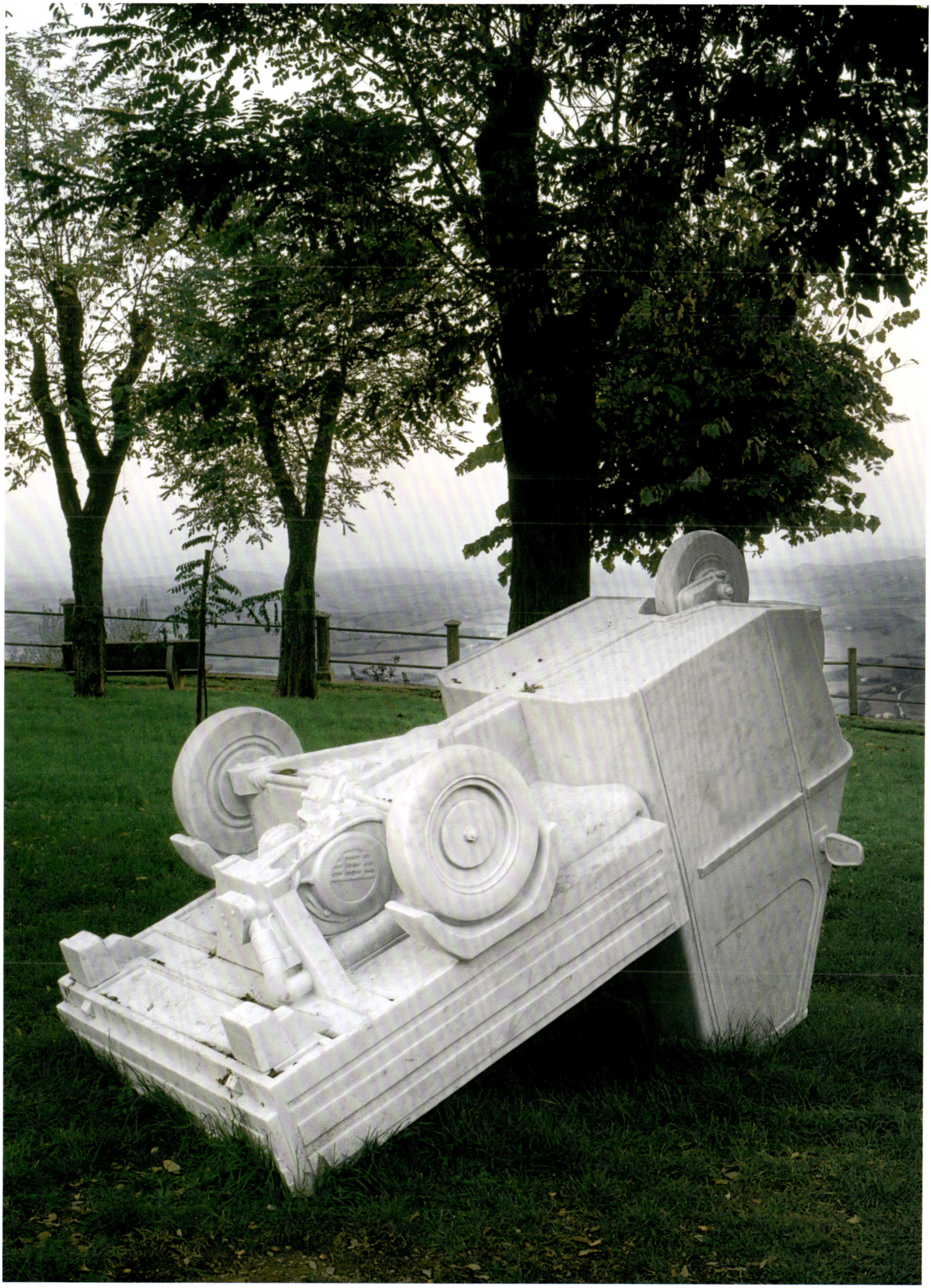

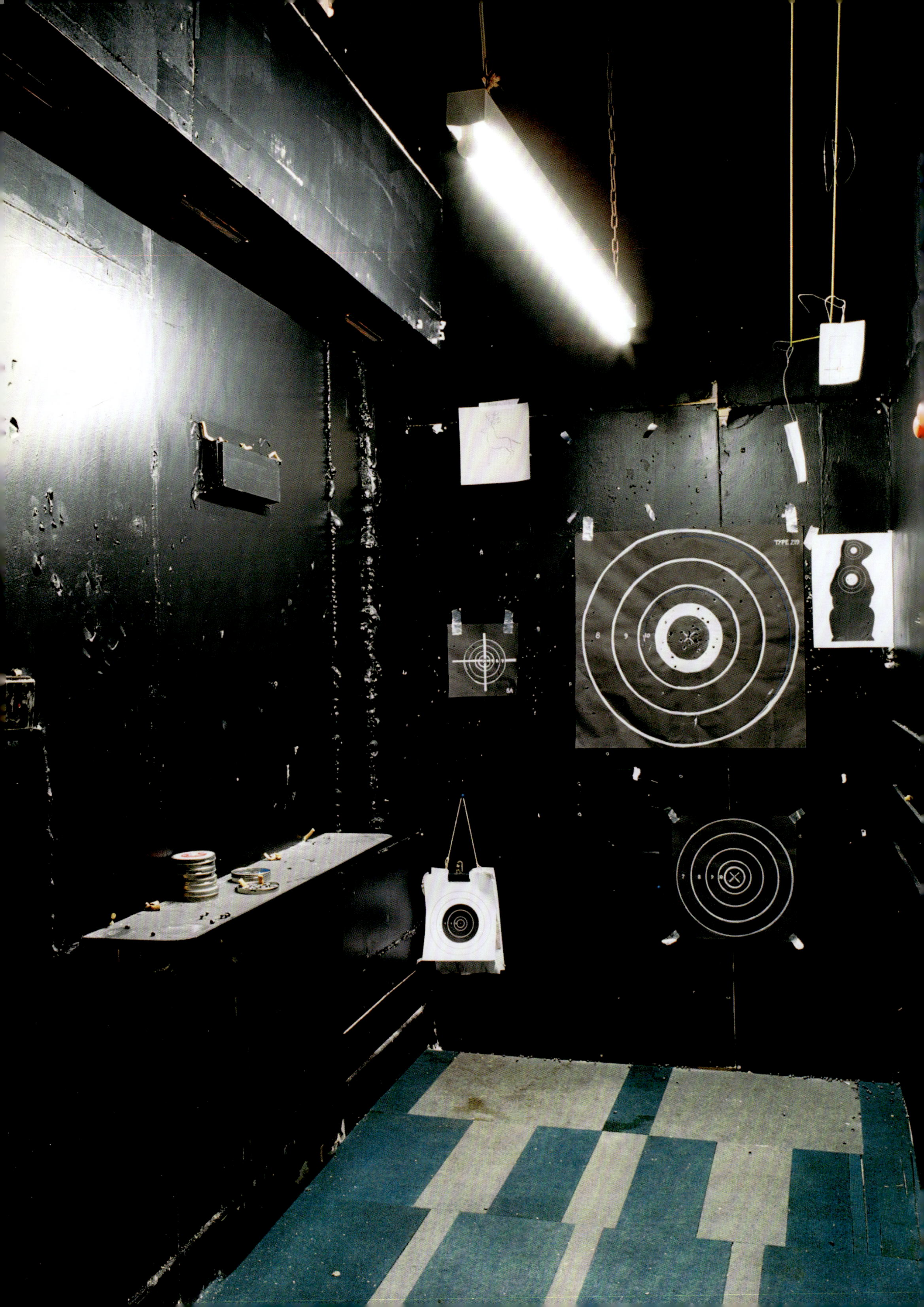
TYPE 219
5A

Contemporary Photography, 2000–2009

When photography made its appearance on the stage of international contemporary art in the mid-1980s, it was greeted as a breath of fresh air in an area that seemed to have been struck by fatigue and a dearth of ideas in recent years. The initial impression was of a flash in the pan, something flaring up suddenly but destined to burn out quickly through lack of fuel. It seemed then that photography still had some thorny internal issues to resolve, tormenting itself about its fate like Schnitzler's Lieutenant Gustl and thus displaying a certain weakness to the outside world. This was not so.

In actual fact, for at least a decade photography had already been incubating the germs of a language that had succeeded since the postwar period in breaking away both from a purely documentary approach and from elementary aesthetic practices. It had thus gradually become a tool for social analysis and criticism primarily with regard to the societies that were taking over in the Western world and imposing styles, customs, and ideologies, first and foremost the United States and Japan.

On looking back, it can be seen that contemporary photography owes a great deal to the American photographers of those years, such as Diane Arbus, William Eggleston, Lee Friedlander, and Robert Adams, and Japanese masters like Shomei Tomatsu and his disciple Daido Moriyama, each with their own peculiarities, pursuing their solitary wanderings through the world with lucidity and stubborn persistence. Then there are some less known and slightly older figures like Ralph Eugene Meatyard and Walter Chappell, who are yet to be fully appreciated for their ability to probe the self and relate it to the surrounding world, something Francesca Woodman and Cindy Sherman splendidly achieved in later decades with these masters as their points of reference.

Working in many cases in close contact with the artists active in those years, photographers did not, however, succeed in emerging except in odd, isolated cases that sometimes led to unexpected but brilliant collaboration. Examples include Robert Frank, who was responsible for the photography of the visionary film *Chappaqua* in 1966, and Gordon Parks, who directed the now classic detective film *Shaft*, one of the first examples of successful blaxploitation, in 1971.

As pointed out above, however, it was not until the following decade that photography found a precise niche of its own, now accepted and appreciated also by the art system for a capacity to capture reality and its multiple facets that painting appeared to be losing at the same time after the boom of new expressionism in the early 1980s. There were also other equally crucial factors involved. In Europe photography found its way into the art schools and received support from both public and private institutions. In a word, they "believed" in it and its physical reality. With the appearance of the first large formats around 1985–86, photography became more tangible and accessible also to those who had previously regarded it as the result of an essentially simple if not indeed banal technological medium, the camera, capable of describing life but not of creating images that could themselves become objects and works of art to grace the lofty walls of museums, as paintings had for centuries and centuries.

Held in Stuttgart to commemorate the 150th anniversary of the birth of photography in 1989, the major exhibition *Photo-Kunst* marked the definitive consecration of this medium. Organized by Jean-François Chevrier, it presented authors and works on the basis of a transversal approach that did not confine itself to "exhibiting" photographs but endeavored to develop a discourse through the experiences of artists with no reference to the hotly debated issue of photography as art. Vito Acconci and Victor Burgin, Hamish Fulton and Sigmar Polke, John Baldessari and Giulio Paolini, Jean-Eugène Atget and Hans Bellmer, Roger Fenton and Alfred Stieglitz, Gustave Le Gray and the Bisson Frères thus found themselves rubbing shoulders. With no defined categories, it was the photographs that spoke, the works of artists and in some cases also of photographers.

In any case, it is no coincidence that this epochal turning point in the history of photography took place precisely in Ger-

Anne Hardy
Close Range, 2006
Diasec mounted c-type print,
190 x 150 cm
Courtesy Maureen Paley, London

Yang Fudong
The Half Hitching Post, 2005
Single channel video, 35 mm, 7′

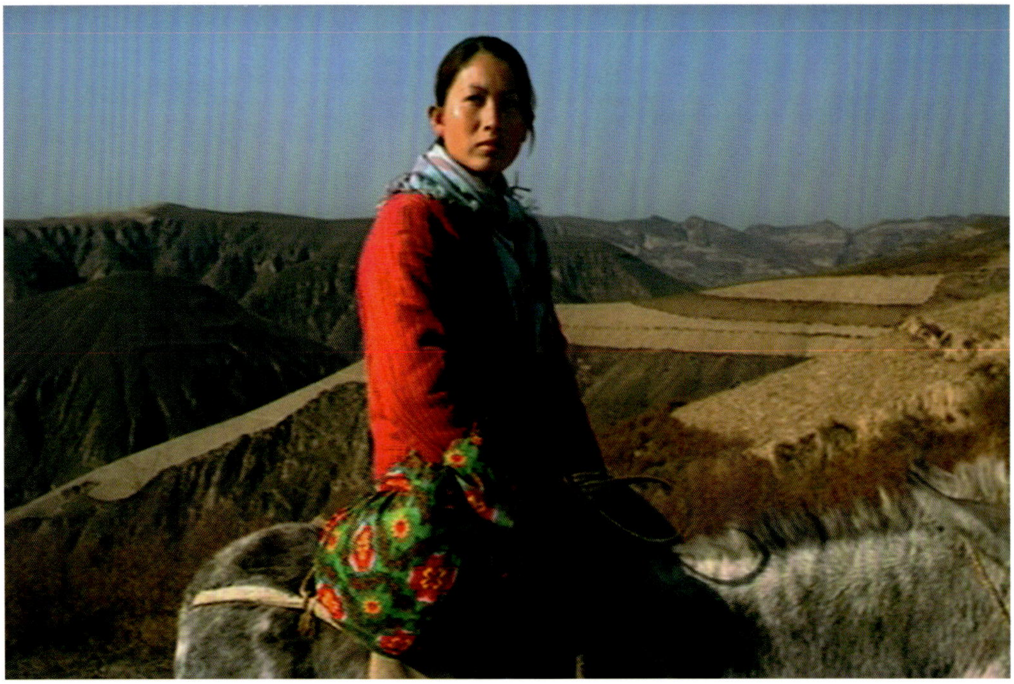

many. It was in fact under the guidance of Bernd Becher that the future protagonists of contemporary photography trained in the first half of the 1980s at the Düsseldorf Academy, including Thomas Struth, Thomas Ruff, Candida Höfer, Axel Hütte, and Andreas Gursky.

The "Düsseldorf School," as it came to be known, dominated the scene in the 1990s and was soon competing with the Americans Richard Prince, Cindy Sherman, and Nan Goldin, the Canadian Jeff Wall, the Japanese Hiroshi Sugimoto and Yasumasa Morimura, and other photographers who then finally emerged to find a fertile terrain and a responsive public. As Thomas Ruff put it, this was a public that had grown up "with the television on": the so-called "generation of images" born around the 1960s and instinctively adopting images as a form of both internal and external communication. At the same time, it was not always adequately served by critics capable of picking up and decoding the countless signals that were beginning to transform the very face of photography, to turn it into an open language susceptible by nature of dilation just as the use of a wide-angle lens expands the view. Distortion of the visual field thus corresponded to the countless forms gradually being taken on by the image, and therefore no longer just the photograph. With the aid of very fast and unstoppable technological progress, the area of investigation broadened every day.

Success on the international scene also enabled photography in that period to widen its horizons of exploration and knowledge considerably to include other places and cultures. This led to the discovery of artists like the Africans Seydou Keita and Malik Sidibé – the latter awarded a Golden Lion for lifetime achievement at the 2007 Venice Biennale – as well as the brilliant and melancholy Ukrainian Boris Michailov. Even the highly controversial Japanese photographer Nobuyoshi Araki was finally granted clearance. Their work mixes past and present, tradition and modernity. They are living witnesses of transformations that have torn apart the societies in which they live as artists.

The decade leading up to the third millennium now saw photography established as a new form of art perfectly capable of representing the ever-changing real world. Both contemporary and historical photographs began to fetch extraordinary prices. Rather than a rediscovery, what was involved in this case was a taking of cognizance, the final recognition of fundamental roots. The advent of digital technology had little effect. Any fears of a drop in quality as a result of transition from analogic to digital and its conceptual implications soon faded as both artists and professionals made deft and uninhibited use of the new software to enhance and underscore the content of their images. Nor did the age-old problem of the reproducibility of the artwork cause many problems. On the contrary, numbered editions made it possible to meet growing demand on the part of collectors. Concerns regarding the preservation of photographs also seem to have been answered both by the progress registered in the materials now commercially available, which are guaranteed to last for decades, and by the fact that the image has become a work of art and as such is perishable, just like a painting or a sculpture.

The protagonists of this happy moment were the non-places and architectural excesses produced by the process of globalization now in full swing on the urban outskirts as in the natural landscape, with differences in approach and nuance from the Alps, as documented in the serial work of Walter Niedermayr from the Alto Adige region in Italy, to China, with the countless new industrial settlements and their dreaming young inhabitants captured by Cao Fei, in the images of the great photographers and in those of the emerging younger generation taking them as points of reference. Among the Europeans, Italians like Gabriele Basilico, Olivo Barbieri, and Francesco Jodice also contributed to a rereading of the urban and metropolitan fabric, connecting photography with architecture and urban planning and providing these with very useful documentation, much as Charles Marville and Jean-Eugène Atget did at the beginning of the twentieth century.

At the same time, attention was focused equally on the new landscape of human beings migrating endlessly from one continent to another in search of better living conditions, carrying remnants and traces of distant cultures with them and struggling for integration into the solidly entrenched Western system.

The traditional photograph came to be accompanied in this area by other uses of the image in videos, art films, and installations. Contemporary artists of the new millennium "adopt" the image also when it does not belong to them directly, assigning it the primary role as narrator of the many events that spread out across the world like a patchwork of unprecedented human and cultural anthropology in which it is not only races and genders that mix but also dreams and desires, illusions and defeats.

Responding with photographs, videos, and films to needs born at the individual level, a new generation of multimedia artists has come to focus on these dissonances. Alienation and loss of identity characterize the social and cultural decline of the Western world (as exemplified in the *Streetwork* series produced in the second half of the 1990s by Philip-Lorca diCorcia) as well as the disappearance of collective memory and the resulting need for recognition – first of all at the political level – for the peoples who look to that part of the planet as a model of well-known advantages and disadvantages, the former outweighing the latter. These are the themes that contemporary photography doggedly examines in depth, often through forms of interpretation that draw upon the sphere of dreams and psychoanalysis, as if our radically transformed world of the last 20 years were no longer enough. And this is precisely the paradox of a reality now literally invaded by images, where everyone has seen everything (*Alle haben Alles gesehen*, the title of a brilliant and premonitory photograph of 1989 by Michael Schuster and Hartmut Skerbisch) and the search for a supposedly different truth becomes a priority.

And if no real and serious risk of implosion – due more to presumable exhaustion than any sudden lack of resources or sources to draw upon – has ever manifested itself, there has been a gradual and inevitable impoverishment of photography and its primal meaning.

Looking to artists as different from one another as Matthew Barney, Peter Fischli and David Weiss, Doug Aitken, Shirin Neshat, and Tacita Dean, to name just a few, the young creators of images now move as though on the flying carpet, stopping every so often to steal a fragment of the quivering life flashing by beneath them and using it as a nucleus to construct their own vision. While the subject matter is firmly established, the stylistic approaches remain very different, regardless of whether the photographs are associated before or after with other forms of image utilization. And even though it is increasingly frequent to see photographs that are really digital stills from videos (a term that cannot fail to recall Steichen's very different and indeed unique still-life work), it is equally true that recent years in particular have seen a vigorous return to black-and-white photography.

The narration of an experience constitutes the basis of the artist's work today, and this takes place in accordance with essentially classical stylistic procedures. Stage photography is still much in vogue in some European countries and the United States, albeit grounded on conceptual rather than emotional constructs. Lavish sets do not, however, always mean major works. This genre has a predilection for atmospheres and settings that are either crepuscular (as in the images of the American Gregory Crewdson) or on the contrary sparkling and fabulous but in any case intentionally ambiguous,

Yang Fudong
The Half Hitching Post, 2005
Single channel video, 35 mm, 7′

Elina Brotherus
Der Wanderer 3, from the cycle
The New Painting, 2004
Color print, 105 x 133 cm
Courtesy of the artist and GB Agency, Paris

where every subject is as though painted in the colorful immobility of lights deftly focused on the contours of things and people (as in some tableaux by Hannah Starkey). The individuals portrayed do not always succeed in entering into a relationship with their surrounding environment and thus creating the tension of an instant or a deep feeling, as the photographer would like. The boundary between ironic and grotesque, inside and outside, pleasure and pain, wavers dangerously and remains indefinite. Too perfect to be authentic, they sometimes give the impression of glossy images produced for glamour magazines. Decidedly more interesting and cultured are instead the works or series of works in which the artist uses the reconstruction of a precise habitat to reveal the history of those who live there – the teenage girls of Sarah Jones – or simply frequent (or frequented) it, in some cases without even showing us the subject investigated. Examples in this connection are provided by the Londoner Anne Hardy, whose richly allusive photographs show us what remains "after" an experience, or the young Swiss artist Bianca Brunner, who leaves it to the viewer's imagination to decide who and what is to animate the space, taking up a position halfway between James Casebere and Thomas Demand. And this is also the *modus operandi* adopted for years now by Miwa Yanagi, who takes a rigorously female viewpoint in giving life and a voice to characters in traditional or high-tech settings, thus respecting the dual culture of the Land of the Rising Sun but offering a new and in some cases disturbing interpretation at the same time. While unquestionably a genetic legacy of Eastern art, the almost maniacal care and sophistication channeled into every work by the Japanese artist serve at the same time to accentuate and highlight the anachronistic conditions in which women are still living today in Japan, as in the celebrated video *Kagome Kagome*.

Another genre that finds a *raison d'être* and logical presence in contemporary photography today is undoubtedly portraiture, which has never disappeared and always succeeded in revitalizing itself. From August Sander up to the present day, skilled photographers have always emerged to offer acute and wholly coherent interpretations. Touched upon by many who have made a field of artistic action out of their own existence, for example Nan Goldin and Wolfgang Tillmans, portraiture has found a superb and penetrating champion in the Czech Jitka Hanzlová. Capable of eliminating the distance between herself and the subject, she astonishes for the freshness of her images and the immediacy of her vision, which does not confine itself to portrayal but tells the tale of the person captured for an instant in the surreptitiously taken photo: a tiny fragment of everyday life stolen on the streets of a great metropolis. The East is also the source of the portraits set in the Russian steppe by Anastasia Khoroshilova, a cross-section of races and professions looking with pride toward the West, and the sad portraits of luckless and forgotten adolescents by the German Ingar Krauss. Something very different is to be found in the self-portraits by Danny Tracey, figures emerging life-sized from the darkness, characters existing only in the artist's imagination, covered in rags found in the street and then assembled, beings with no name and no history, just like the faces again invented, but this time through digital manipulation, by the Pole Aneta Grzeszykowska, close-ups that look back 20 years later on Thomas Ruff's famous series of classmates at the academy, like a sign of time that passes and the technological progress it brings with it.

Videos and photographs suspended in time arrive from Northern Europe to settle on the world's fears and anxieties like a mist whose lightness does not preclude a wealth of content, gazing at the world as into a mirror where the emotions and feelings are reflected to return with greater clarity, purified and freed of all possible dross. In the blinding colors of Annika Larsson's videos, the objects full of life portrayed by Annika von Hausswolff, Torbjørn Rødland's inner landscapes, and Olafur Eliasson's installations, the images arriving from the Nordic countries tell of strong personalities, of artists engaging art and life with lucidity and in silent withdrawal, hermits in search of new balance between being and appearing, capable of astonishing us every time with their linear and fundamental simplicity of approach. Salla Tykka and Elina Brotherus, worthy heirs of the Finnish school, move in diametrically opposite directions. The former probes the spirit, shaking the psyche of her characters until they show themselves naked as they really are. As there is never anything obvious in her videos and images, the spectator becomes involved in the mystery developed on the screen, waiting to discover what is hidden behind the window, at the end of the deep cavern or at the bottom of the pool: the revelation of another possibility, a

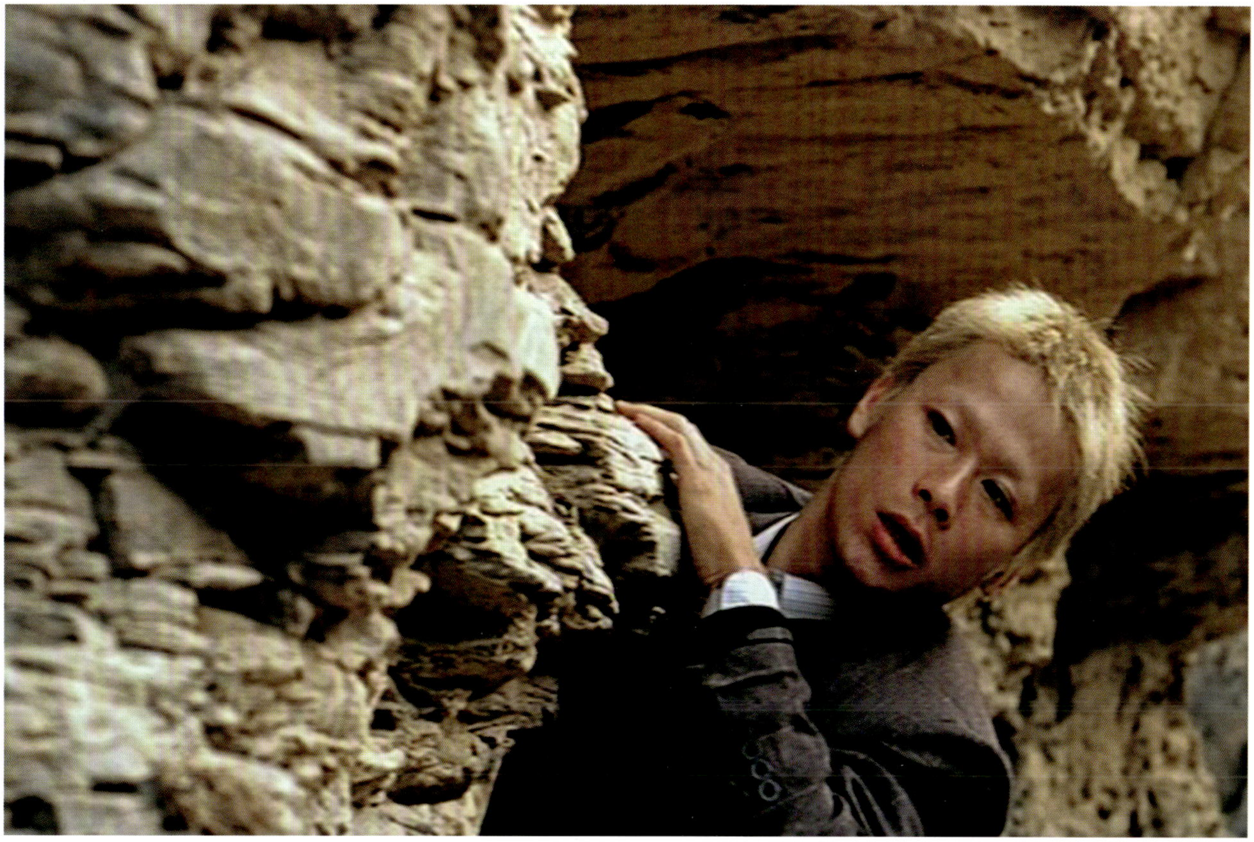

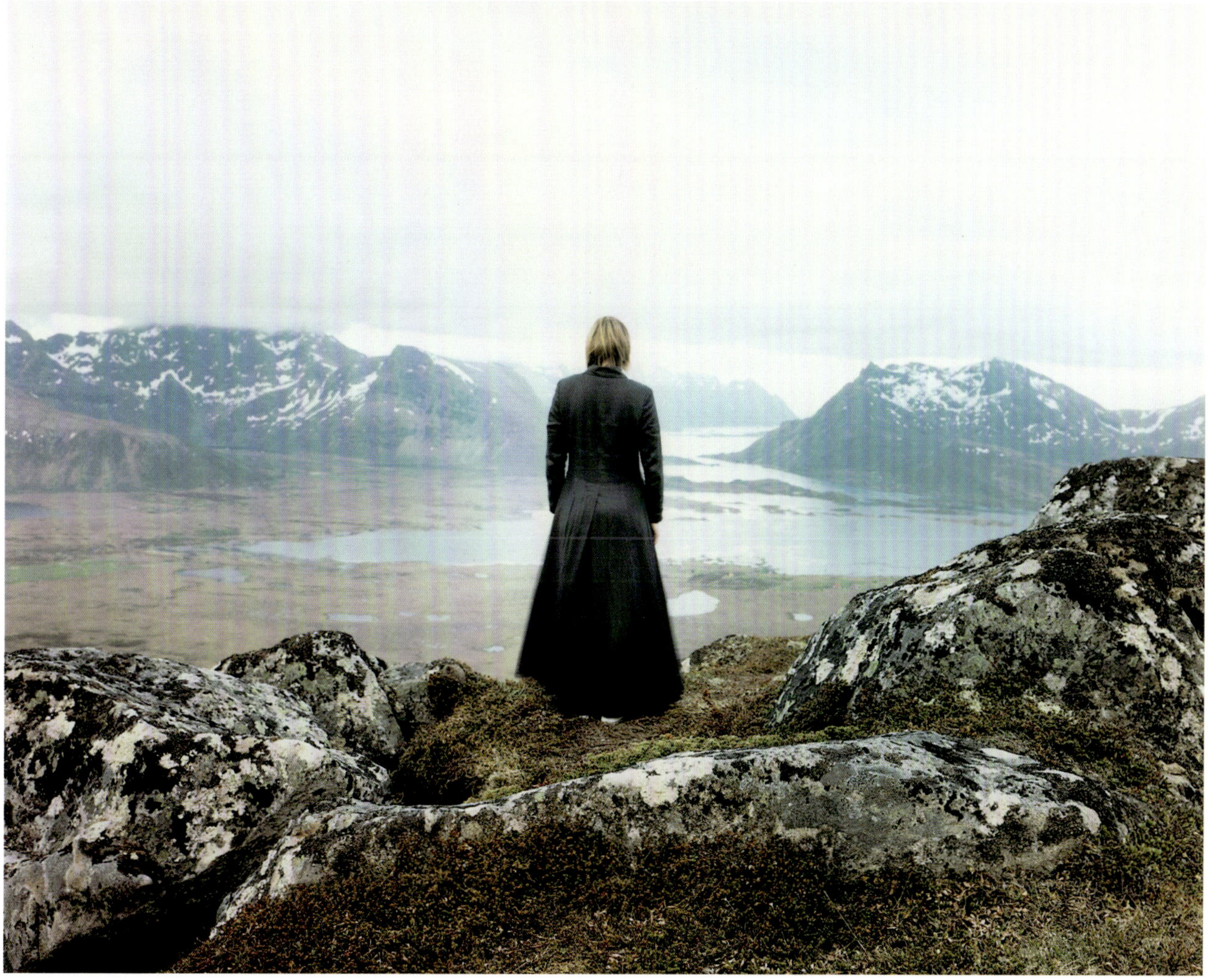

different choice, a world unknown and inaccessible until that moment, and perhaps painful. Elina Brotherus is a gentle and delicate artist who puts herself at the center of the narrative, unashamedly showing her weaknesses and expectations in a play of references involving places and people close and dear to her. There is no mystification. Her photography is made up of direct and genuine images both in vast expanses of Nordic landscape and in the Parisian rooms of the series entitled *This is the first day of the rest of your life*. Sedate only in appearance, her photography invites the viewer to linger and savor in silence, a silence to which we are no longer accustomed and find somewhat frightening for its depth and breadth. A similar but still more vibrant atmosphere emerges from the videos of the Estonian artist Ene-Liis Semper, again both the director and leading character of her works. To a greater extent than Brotherus, she uses the body as an experiential field to create sinuous forms in performances of unique intensity and impact in terms of photography even more than film. It is the light, the camera angles, and the editing as well as the movements and action that specify the content with a rhythm that recalls early twentieth-century Russian cinema and the daring films of Aleksandr Rodchenko.

A strong attachment to memory and the recent past of their countries characterizes many of the recently emerging artists from East Europe, the Middle East, Africa, India, and China. As can be seen on walking through the narrow streets of the artistic districts in Shanghai and Beijing, the future giant of the world economy already possesses a strongly developing home market. Based largely on the combination of different media, Chinese artists' work involves an unprecedented sort of documentary approach that draws upon photography and evolves toward the most disparate forms of expression and representation: from sober black-and-white to large-format digital, from slideshows to video installations, from serial films to interactive installations modeled on Second Life.

Since the fall of the Berlin Wall in 1989, East Europe has gradually come to produce a growing stream of young artists that can already be considered mature if on no other grounds than the quality and authority of their vision. While the Polish contingent is distinguished by the compositional elegance of their works and the cultural background informing their investigation of subjects connected with the human condition (especially Pawel Althamer and Artur Żmijewski), attention should also be drawn to the artists from the Balkans and especially the heterogeneous combination of peoples and traditions in the place once known as Yugoslavia. The memory of the recent wars is necessarily a key point of reference in order not to forget and above all as a warning to a world

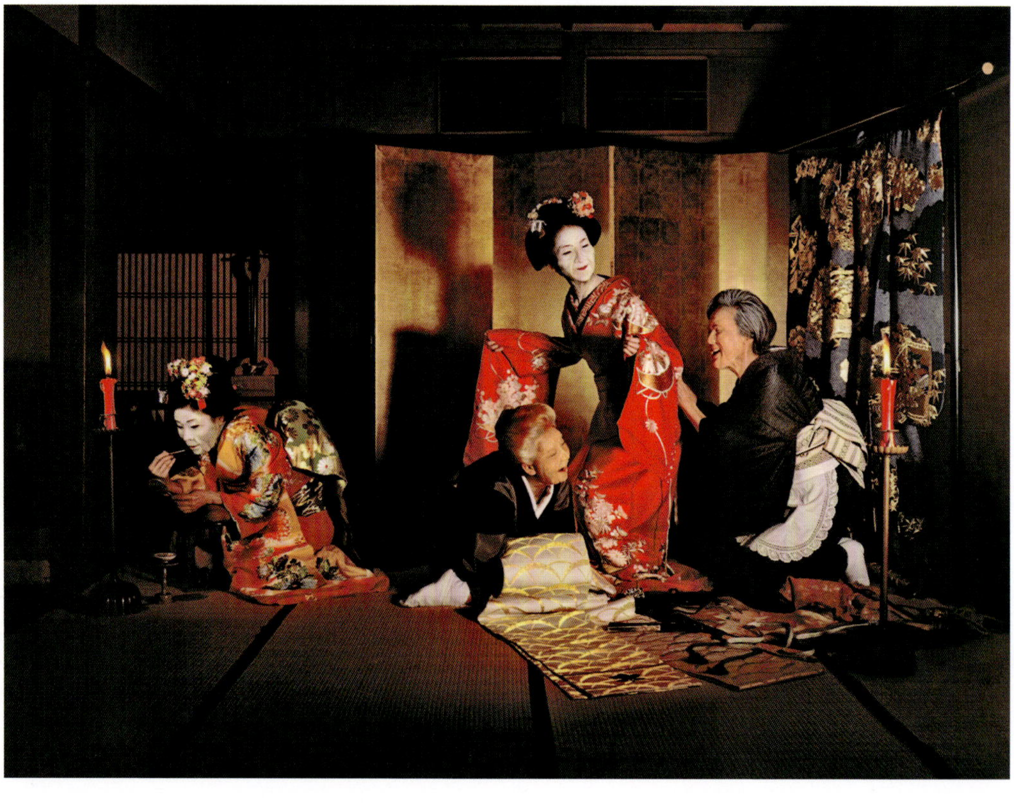

Miwa Yanagi
Geisha (Akiyo, Mai, Hitomi, Noriko), 2002
Color print, 180 x 240 cm
Modena, Collezione di Fotografia Contemporanea della Fondazione Cassa di Risparmio di Modena

that chose to look the other way. This is forcibly asserted by artists like Milica Tomic (whose shocking video *xy ungelost – the reconstruction of the crime* shows the massacre of Albanian demonstrators in 1989, an event soon swallowed up in general oblivion) and Maja Bajevich (whose embarrassing and demoralizing recent video shows the seated artist refusing to respond as she is asked with gradually increasing violence the question that gives the work its title: *How Do You Want to Be Governed?*). The issue of identity and the unavoidable loss of points of reference during the transition from socialism to the Western capitalist model is addressed in various ways in the elegant films of Andreas Fogarasi, who revisits cultural centers in Budapest where the voices of the past still echo from the walls of the large rooms. An ironic approach is instead taken by the Romanian Alexandra Croitoru in a series of self-portraits polemically entitled *Rom*, the term used for the nomadic peoples that camp on the outskirts of the big cities, in which the artist wears a hood in the colors of the Rumanian flag. Nor is there any lack of dawning self-criticism, an inevitable consequence precisely of the Western-style free market. Here too, a sarcastic approach is preferred by artists like the Croatian Renata Poljak (video and photography), whose *Great Expectations* examines the uncontrolled building speculation underway on the Adriatic coast.

Though soberly addressed, the drama of war – and in this case the defense of an identity – is the overriding subject in the works of Middle Eastern artists, as in the series of interiors of homes in the sadly famous Gaza Strip by the Palestinian Taysir Batniji, with family portraits, calendars, school diplomas, notes left on shelves or by clocks, walls with the plaster peeling away but full of what could be thought of as everyday life but for what is happening outside those rooms. Identity plunged into crisis – "the price to be paid by a minority to the majority, perhaps in order to be accepted, perhaps to change its identity, to survive" – is the theme addressed and documented in *Trackers*, a series of black-and-white and color photographs taken by the young Ahlam Shibli in 2005. The work deals with Palestinians of Bedouin descent, full citizens of the state of Israel who serve as volunteers in its army, unlike most other Arab residents of the Jewish state. The *In Between* series of photographs by the artist Hrair Sarkissian, born in Syria, shows us places in Armenia with official buildings and monuments, authentic icons of socialism bearing witness to historical moments that still retain all their relevance with the present conflict between Armenia and Azerbaigian.

Revealed to the world by the great exhibition *In/sight: African Photographers, 1940 to the Present*, organized at the Guggenheim Museum in 1996 by Okwui Enwezor and others, African photography has taken its first significant steps during the last decade after the due recognition granted to figures like Seydou Keita, Malik Sidibé, and Samuel Fosso, as well as the South Africans David Goldblatt and Peter Magubane. While the memory of an entire continent was recorded for years through photojournalism and portraiture (with new discoveries still being made today, like the huge artistic output of the eclectic Senegalese photographer and filmmaker Djibril Diop Mambéty), the same genres are now used to analyze the "normality" of everyday progress that is slower and less sophisticated than in the rest of the world. It is difficult to distinguish distinct schools or styles. African photography is young and hungry, almost ingenuous in its efforts to escape the lure of the West, searching here and there for approaches capable of helping it to establish an identity of its own.

Much the same holds for developments in South Asia, where the influence of polished and perspicacious figures of the recent past and the present, like Raghubir Singh and Dayanita Singh, is still strongly felt. As regards the former, in addition to great skill in geometrically constructing images of street life that nevertheless make few concessions to the exoticism of the places portrayed, attention should also drawn to the influence of Western photographers like Henri Cartier-Bresson, William Gedney, and especially Lee Friedlander. The younger Dayanita Singh instead examines the changes underway in modern Indian society through portraits of whole middle-class families or individuals. Particularly interesting, above all because it appears to sever the umbilical cord still connecting Indian culture with the British style, is the recent work of Vivan Sundaram, whose digital photomontages feature Amrita Sher-Gil, a celebrated cosmopolitan artist of the 1920s and 1930s and greatly renowned in India, who died prematurely at the age of 28. The inclusion of other objects or people (with her father as recurrent figure) offers a perspective completely different from the original and generates a story in which Am-

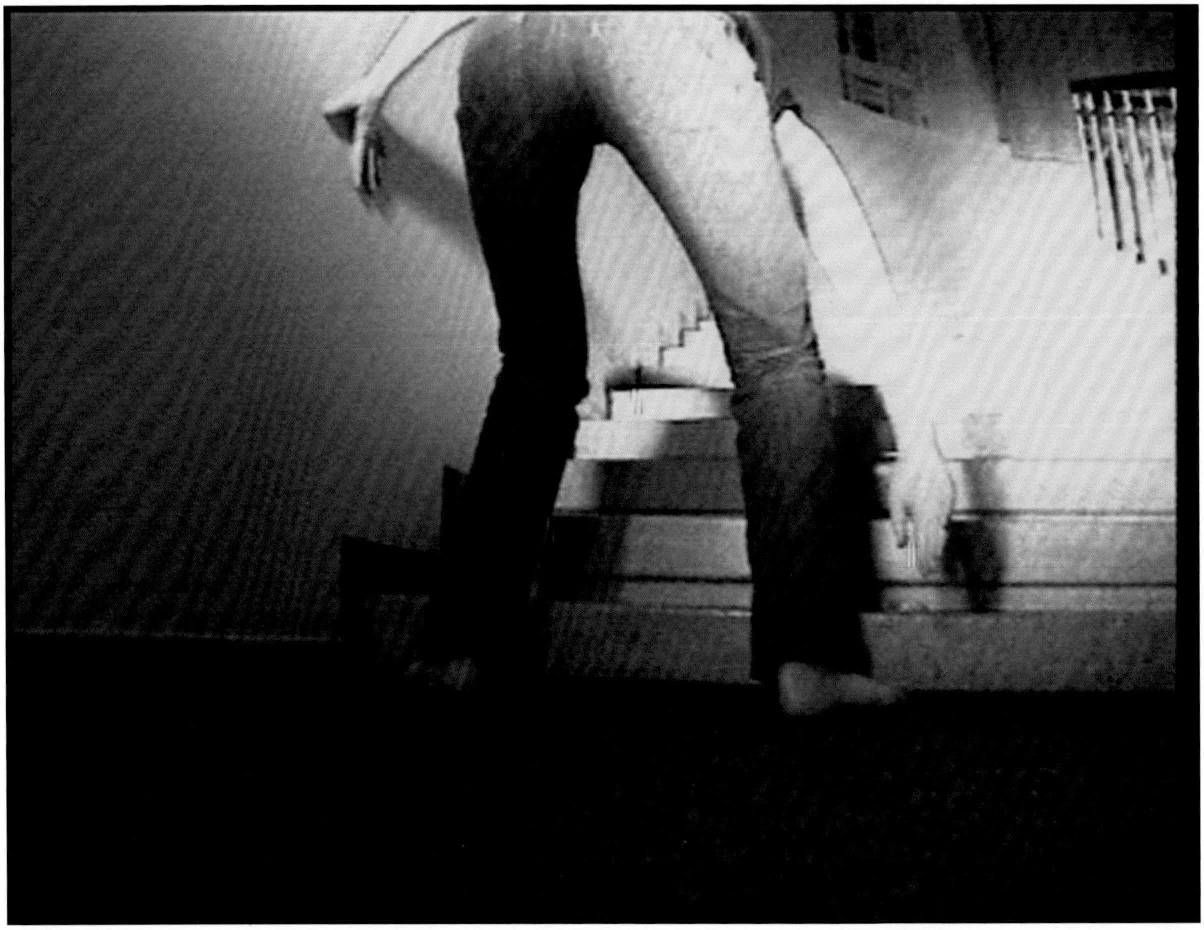

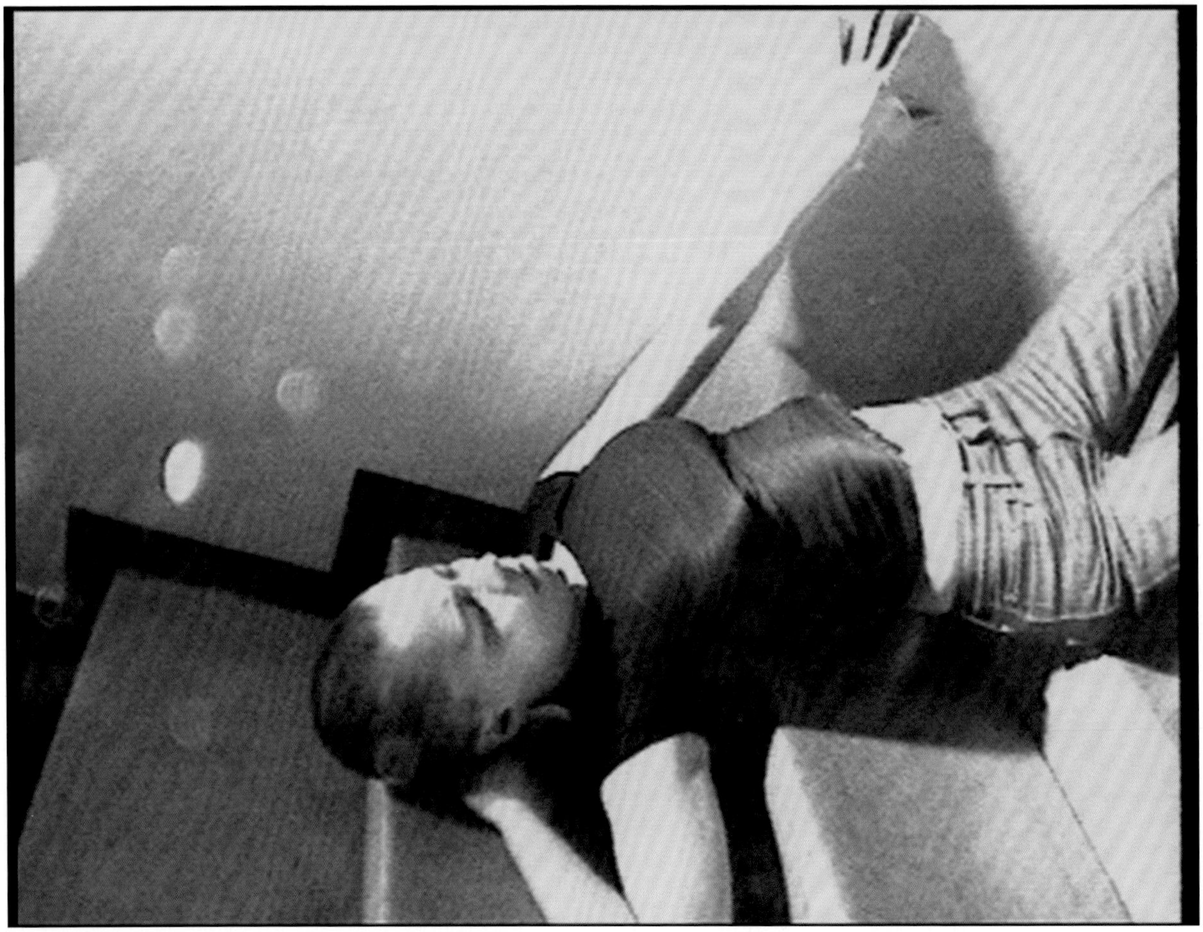

Ene-Liis Semper
Stairs, 2000
Video, 5'
Courtesy Galerie Martin Janda, Wien

rita's identity takes on new meanings susceptible of surprising interpretations.

The Far East confirms in photography what has happened over the last decade in the other fields of art. The deafening noise still encountered today on visiting the studios of Chinese artists do not correspond to an equally valid artistic proposal. To tell the truth, few of the young artists that have emerged have then succeeded in displaying substantial qualities for any length of time despite the support of a rapidly expanding market. The exceptions unquestionably include Yang Fudong and Cao Fei as well as the performer Ma Liuming. The first started out as a photographer and has since produced videos and art films. His point of reference is, however, the most traditional type of studio photography. The camera is in a fixed position, the subject is in the center, and every detail inside the field of vision is organized on the basis of formal rigor leaving little or nothing to chance. The long silences and appropriate use of black-and-white in many of his works give them the character of old-fashioned full-length films, where the sense of the whole seems to develop frame by frame. The other young artists to have distinguished themselves in this area traditionally connected with photography include the Korean Yeondoo Jung, whose manipulated photographs create artificial realities that are so lifelike that this is perceived only through close examination, the Japanese Maiko Haruki, who superimposes in the darkness of her large format works different planes of perspective in which the barely perceptible human figure is certainly not frightened but rather intimately enclosed in its own universe, the Chinese Yang Zhenzhong, whose rudeness in his apparently superficial interviews (in the video *I Know I Will Die*) is matched by a light touch in manipulating the weight and volume of real objects in his images to create an upside-down and perhaps less distasteful world.

Even though the rising Asian tide of the late 1990s led as a direct consequence to a sort of globalization in reverse, an instinctive reaction almost in defense (of leadership and probably also market position) on the part of Western artists, who for some years adopted forms of emphasis similar to those of their Eastern colleagues, and even though cities like London and Berlin were teeming at the dawn of the third millennium with young artists, many of whom have already returned to their places of origin, the present international panorama, though displaying evident and unquestionable heterogeneity due precisely to the many cultural contributions concentrated in just a few places and sharply-defined situations, seems to indicate a dual configuration for contemporary photography in the future. On the one hand, it appears necessary for classical photography to combine with other image-based techniques like video and cinema, in some cases arriving at solutions where the techniques interweave and collaborate to present a true correct and synchronic vision of the reality and its very fast mutations. On the other, we have an imperious return, also in cinema, of black-and-white, long takes and fluctuating images, landscapes and figurative representations – in both natural and metropolitan settings – with metaphysical overtones: human beings who are alienated but aware of the underlying reasons and of their condition. There is thus a decline of ambitious stylistic exercises that seem to be nothing other than narcissistic practices divorced from any time and place: films, videos, and large-sized photographs where everything starts and ends in the presumption of the creative act reproduced through the allure of the places or the perfection of the execution, so far from the real world upon which photography and art in general have finally come to focus once again through the memory and knowledge of the past. At the Yokohama Triennial of 2008, one of the truly useful recent opportunities in the midst of the countless events sprouting every day all over the planet, the return of performance was celebrated as crucial to any understanding of the art of the last few years.

If today more than ever before a certain detachment from the world is necessary in order to arrive at a correct interpretation, it is equally urgent and indispensable to undertake a serious and highly demanding effort of analysis with roots deeply embedded in the knowledge and history that accompany the everyday growth and experience of every single one of us.

Ghada Amer

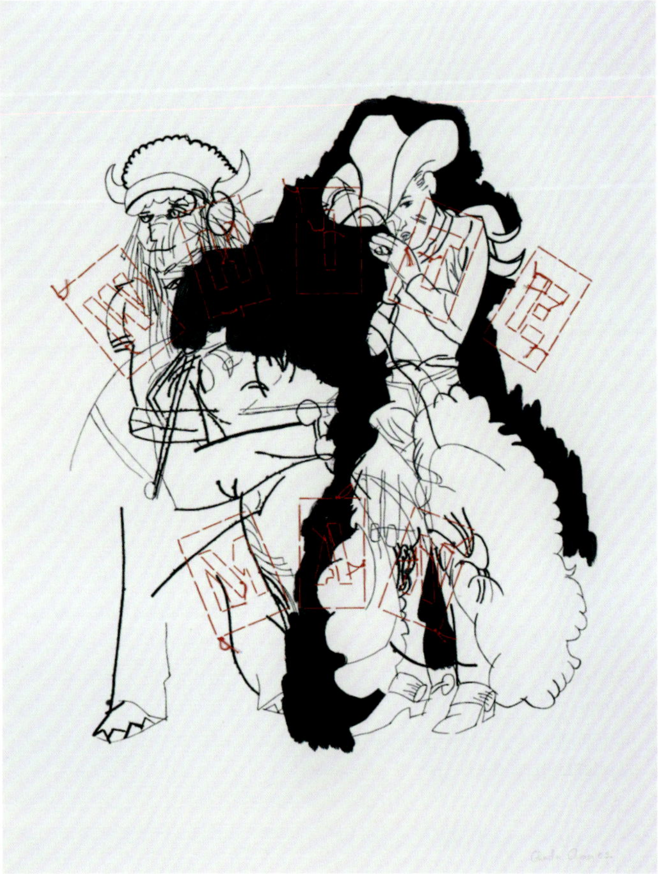

Born in Cairo in 1963. Lives and works in New York.
Ghada Amer's works are characterized by great attention to the meaning of "gender" in contemporary art. The artist focuses in particular on examining the sexual characterization of the expressive medium and the traditional roles connected with its use.
Almost omnipresent in her work, embroidery constitutes a direct expression of this thrust, as the artist channels the creative and productive value of a typically female activity closely connected with her own Middle Eastern origins into the works.
Ghada Amer highlights the male orientation of the contemporary art system and challenges it with ironic iconographic works representing parity between the two genders. On being invited to participate in the section of the 51st Venice Biennale entitled *Always a Little Further*, curated by Rosa Martinez, she exhibited the special project *Yin Yang Garden*, a site-specific installation in the form of an urban flowerbed using the oriental symbol of the Tao (meaning the Way) to deconstruct and criticize the dichotomy of man and woman.
The installation is similar in origin to *Barbie Loves Ken, Ken Loves Barbie*, one of the Egyptian artist's best-known works, consisting of two embroidered cotton overalls reflecting the two physical stereotypes of Western heterosexuality represented by the Barbie and Ken dolls. Like their plastic counterparts, the overalls do not display the sexual characteristics of the bodies. At the same time, the constantly repeated profession of love alludes to the loss of meaning and standardization of the amorous sentiment.
Images of play and fairytale recur in numerous works by Ghada Amer, who uses their communicative potential to unmask pigeonholing in stereotyped sexual roles.
This process underlies *Breathe Into Me* (2003), a series of drawings on paper that harnesses the iconography of cartoon films and comics through more than direct citations of the sexual imagery created by Milo Manara and the standardized iconography of the princess in Disney films.
(*F.T.*)

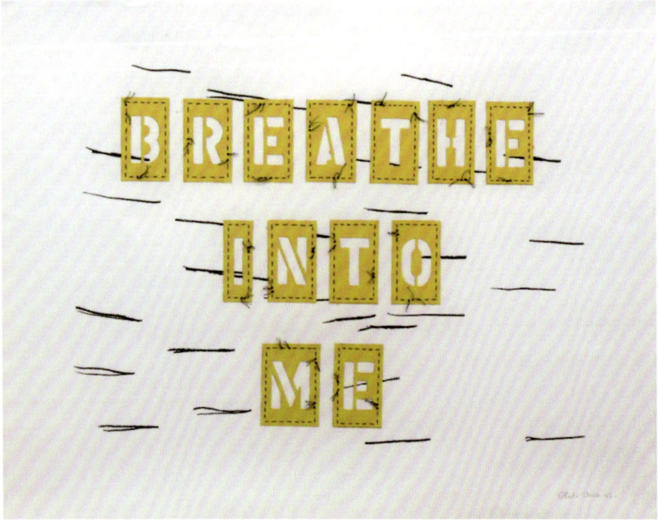

The White Man, 2005
Ink and embroidery on paper, 72.4 x 57.2 cm
New York, Gagosian Gallery

Breathe Into Me, 2003
Acrylic and embroidery on paper, 57.8 x 73 cm
New York, Gagosian Gallery

Barbie Loves Ken, Ken Loves Barbie, 1995–2004
Embroidery on cotton, 180 x 70 x 10 cm
New York, Gagosian Gallery

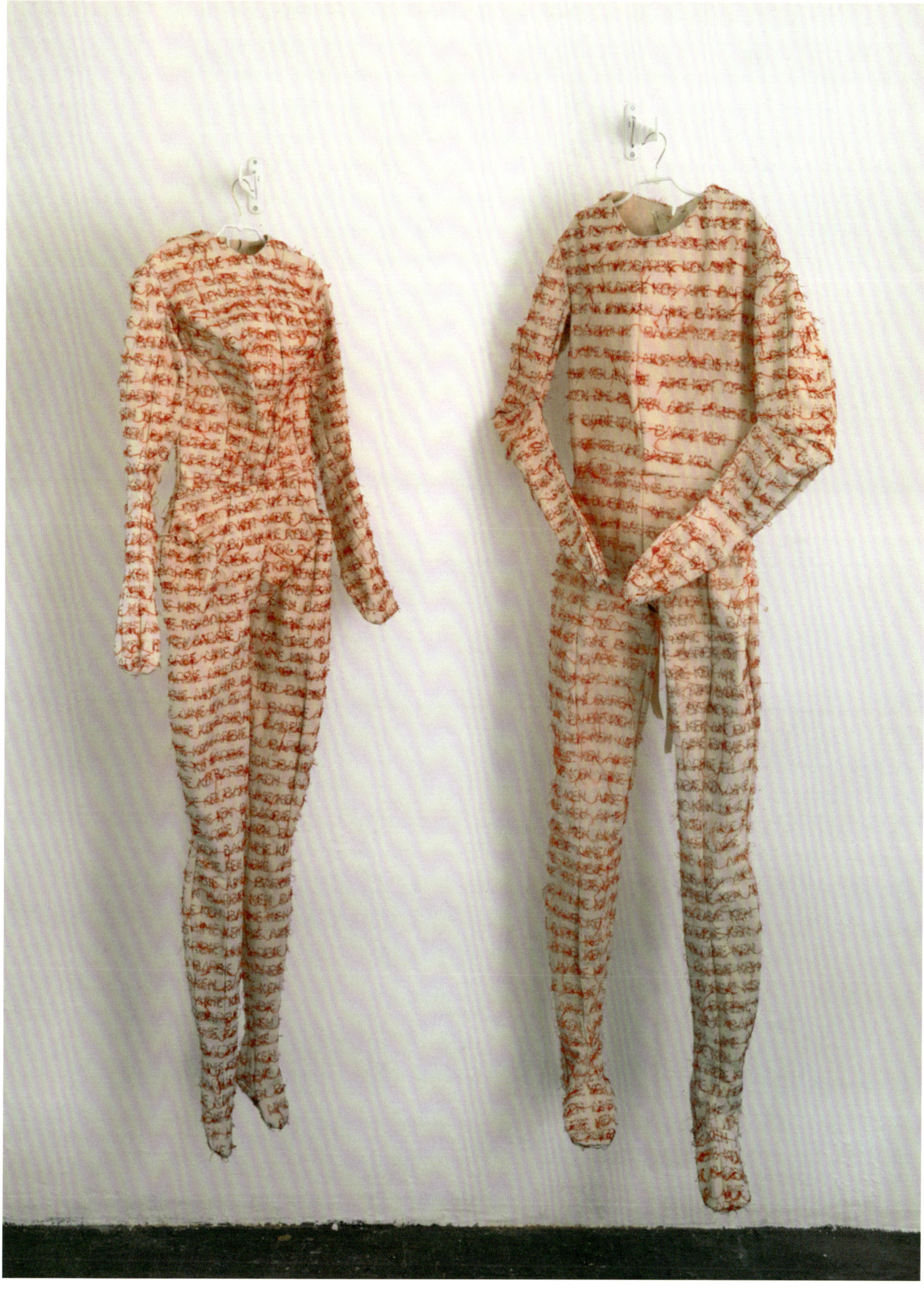

Matthew Barney

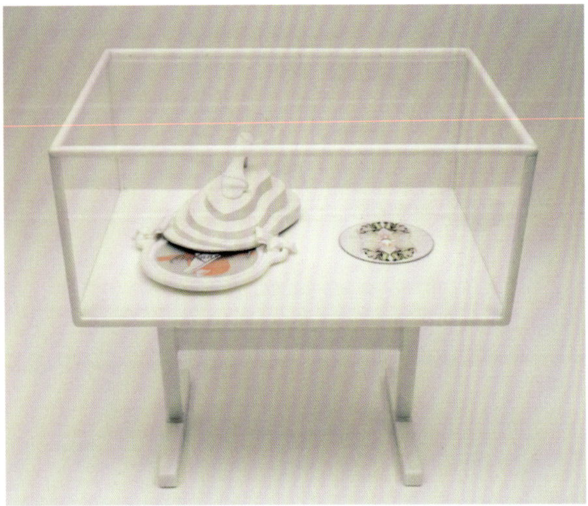

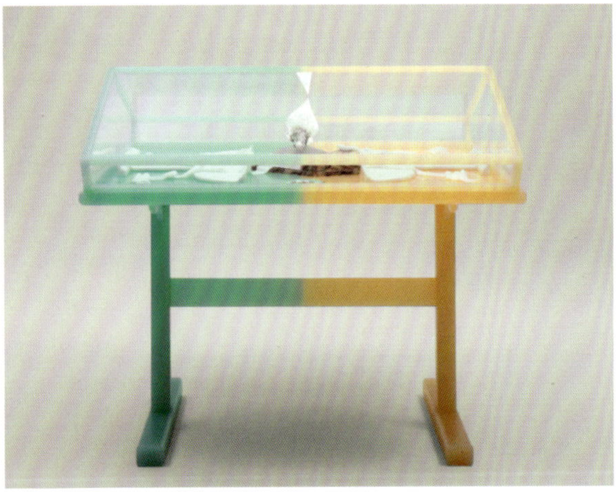

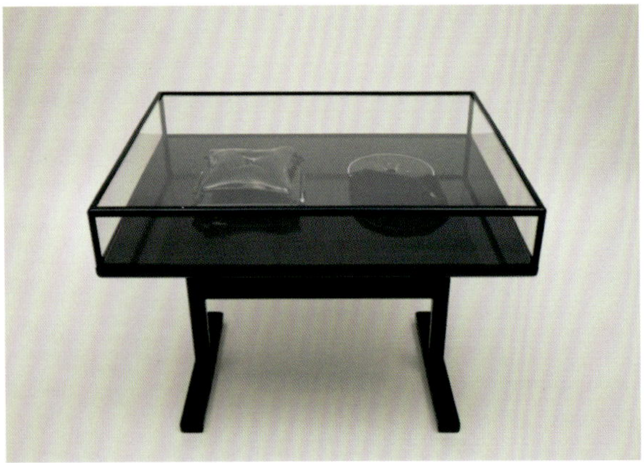

Born in San Francisco, California, in 1967. Lives and works in New York. Matthew Barney's past as a successful athlete, attractive male model, and brilliant student of anatomy and pathology at the Yale school of medicine (soon abandoned in order to take the art course) may help to understand why the body and its transformations, sexuality, stamina, the strengthening of muscles, and every possible form of acrobatic performance are recurrent themes in his work. The *Cremaster* saga (1994–2002) is designed as an allegory of life and its endless potentiality developed around to two primary themes, namely the sexual differentiation of the human embryo and the constant human drive for expression through art, dance, song, architecture, choreography, narrative, mythology, sport, scientific experimentation and, last but not least, violence.
For Barney, all these activities are like extensions of the body – almost artificial limbs – that serve mankind in order to keep the world in a constant state of change. The idea of transformation and metamorphosis is in fact a linchpin of the philosophy of this artist.
The episodes interweave dreams, surrealistic visions, and stories based on real people, like Gary Gilmore, a Mormon from Utah sentenced to death for homicide who chose to be executed by the shedding of blood, and Harry Houdini, the renowned illusionist whose extraordinary control over his body enabled him to perform astonishing feats comparable to real magic. This colossal, highly complex, and multi-layered interdisciplinary work tests the spectator's ability to pick up a whole range of references: Busby Berkeley's musicals and Leni Riefenstahl's film of athletes of the Third Reich (in *Cremaster 1*, 1996); Gothic literature and epic westerns (in *Cremaster 2*, 1999); Celtic mythology and Stanley Kubrick as well as noir, thriller, zombie, and gangster movies in general (in *Cremaster 3*, 2002); Victorian comedy and road movies (in *Cremaster 4*, 1994); Wagner's *Ring* cycle and opera in general (in *Cremaster 5*, 1997). The entire cycle is also crammed with references to the history of Video Art and the early work of Vito Acconci, Marina Abramovich, and Lawrence Wiener. As Nancy Spector observes, it is conceived as a sort of *Gesamtkunstwerk* or total work of art. The decision not to use a linear narrative structure, which is also underscored by the fact that the episodes are not in chronological order and all the stories take place in different geographic settings, suggests the illustrious literary precedent of James Joyce's extraordinary writing. The idea of a *Gesamtkunstwerk* is also borne out by the huge quantity of drawings, sculptures, photographs, and installations that the artist produced in connection with the making of five episodes (shot entirely on high-definition 35 mm film for a total duration of 300 minutes) and then recovered from the sets.
Matthew Barney worked on *The Cremaster Cycle* from 1994 to 2002, and when it was completed many critics and members of the public wondered what the artist would do after the creation of such an exceptional and titanic work.
The answer was soon to come.
Barney returned to the *Drawing Restraint* project, initiated back in 1987 and conceived as a cycle of films linked by the scarlet thread of the relationship between muscular training and creative endeavor, investigated through extreme physical situations that test the bodily endurance of the artist and the athlete to the utmost.
As in *The Cremaster Cycle*, the true protagonist is thus the body undergoing transformation.
(L.L.)

Cremaster 1, 1996
Silkscreened laser disc, cast polyester, prosthetic plastic, and patent vinyl in self-lubricating plastic and acrylic vitrine; with color 35 mm film transferred from video, with sound, 40'30''
New York, Solomon R. Guggenheim Museum, Purchased with funds contributed by International Director's Council

Cremaster 3, 2002
Two silkscreened digital video discs, stainless steel, internally lubricated plastic, marble, and sterling silver in acrylic vitrine, with 35 mm print; color digital video transferred to film with Dolby Digital sound
Vitrine, 110.5 x 119.4 x 101.6 cm
New York, Solomon R. Guggenheim Museum, Purchased with funds contributed by International Director's Council

Cremaster 5, 1997
Silkscreened laser disc, polyester, acrylic, velvet, and sterling silver in acrylic vitrine; with color 35 mm film transferred from video, with sound
Vitrine, 95.9 x 121.3 x 90.8 cm
New York, Solomon R. Guggenheim Museum, Purchased with funds contributed by International Director's Council

Drawing Restraint 9: Shimenawa, 2005
Chromogenic color print in self-lubricating plastic frame, 109.2 x 109.2 cm
New York, The Museum of Modern Art, Gift of Barbara Gladstone

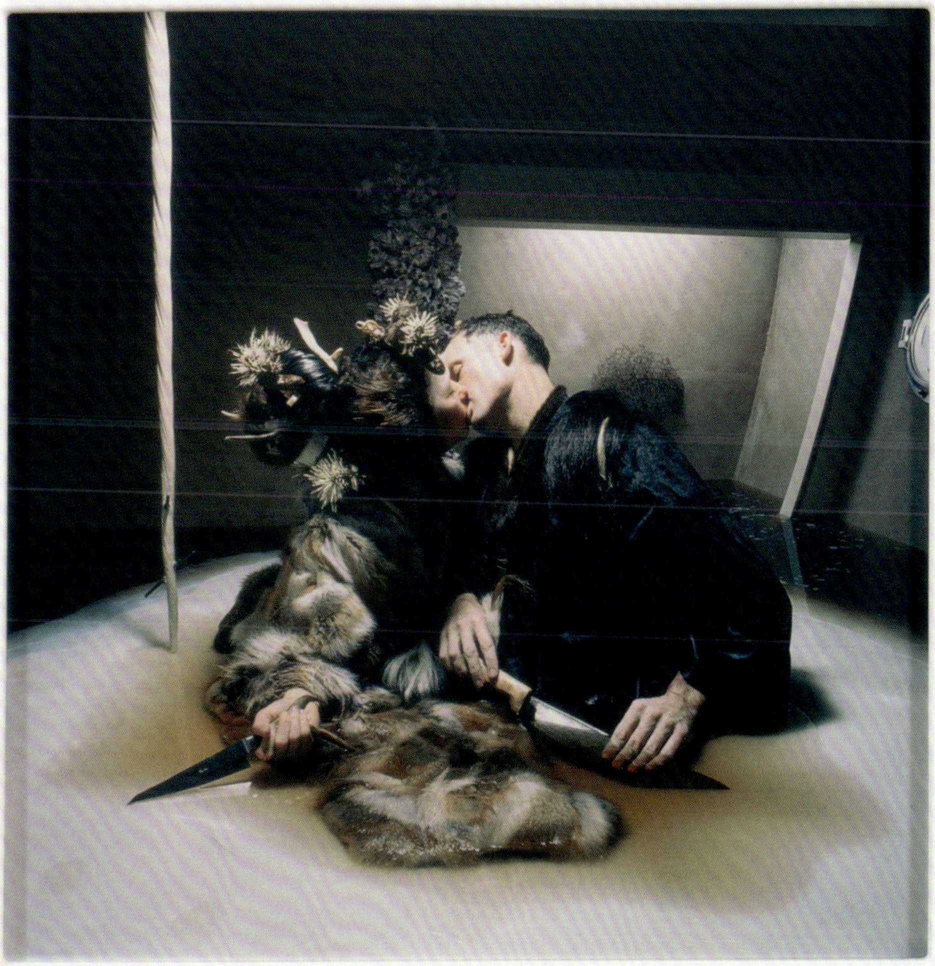

Vanessa Beecroft

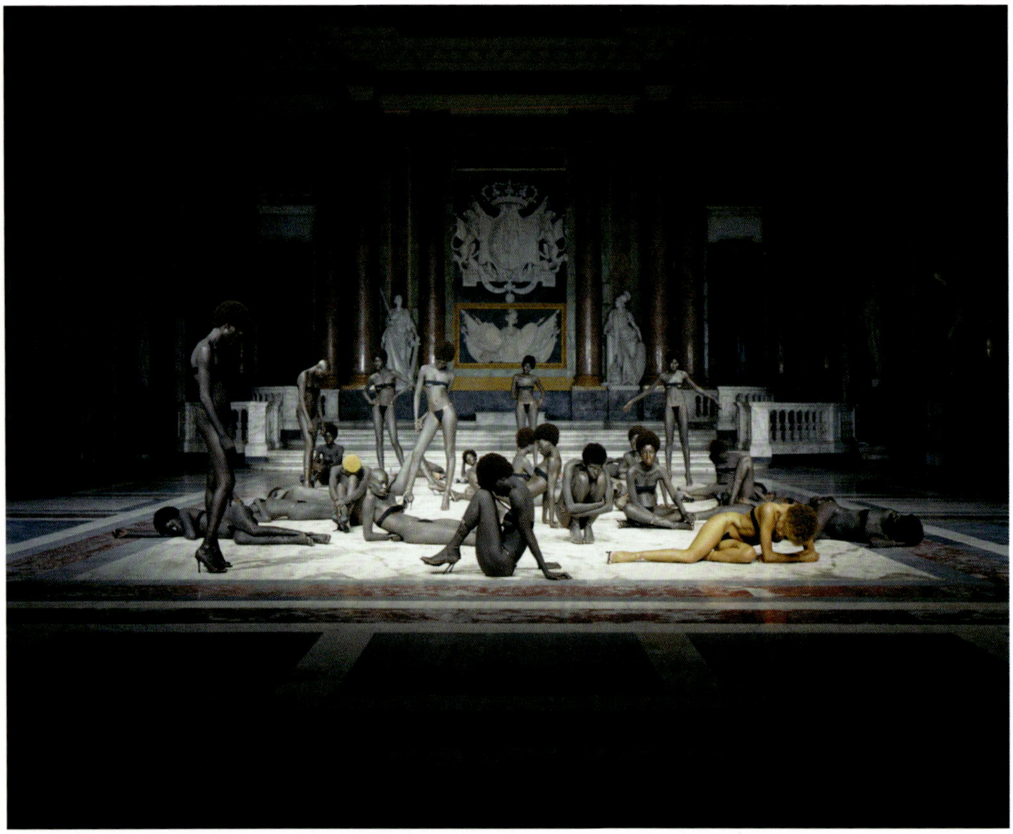

VB48, 2001
Performance at Palazzo Ducale, Genoa, 2001
Courtesy Galleria Massimo Minini, Brescia; Galleria Lia Rumma, Naples/Milan

VB52, 2003
Color print, 230 x 180 cm
Performance at the Castello di Rivoli – Museo d'Arte Contemporanea, October 6, 2003
Courtesy Galleria Lia Rumma, Naples/Milan

Born in Genoa, Italy, in 1969. Lives and works in New York and Los Angeles.

Apparently confined to the sole subject of the body and the sole medium of performance, Vanessa Beecroft's work is actually a complex whole lending itself to a rich variety of readings and also involving photography, video, and drawing. It could indeed be compared to a prism that breaks down and reflects a ray of light in a range of directions, the light in this case being the critical gaze of the public, which focuses on the different works and finds a variety of possible meanings or messages each time. At the same time, the artist tends to step back and behave just like her works, letting herself be observed, examined, and interpreted.

The decision not to make her approach explicit has come over time to constitute practically a hallmark and helped to make Beecroft a figure enveloped in the same icy and mysterious aura as the models used for over 15 years now in a whole variety of prestigious settings to create performances whose meaning has to be sought out, constructed, and imagined anew every time.

It is precisely this similarity between the artist and her models that takes shape at the exegetic level in a dilemma regarding the actual or assumed autobiographical character of her works. For a woman, an obsession with the female body – which Beecroft has displayed since adolescence and expressed during her studies at the Brera Academy in a series of tormented portraits of models from life – is often indicative of a tendency toward compulsive self-observation and comparison with others as well as longing for a different body and aspiring to an ideal of beauty. The ideal in question is one that our society has constructed above all in terms of accentuated slimness, fostering this obsession in the female psyche and especially in young girls deeply scarred by family conflict and the difficulty of feeling accepted and appreciated. While anorexia is a serious, complex problem and not to be treated lightly in any way, it is unquestionably true that the aesthetic and behavioral models proposed, or rather imposed by mass culture, become points of reference for those struggling to establish their identity. The female models that Vanessa Beecroft first paints, then photographs, and finally exhibits in the flesh (and photographs again during the performance) are nearly always perfect embodiments of these aesthetic ideals. The fact that the artist chooses them and gives them a leading role in her works, while showing the greatest reluctance to appear in them herself, suggests a need or desire for identification and hence difficulty in accepting her own body if not indeed a deep form of disturbance in this connection. Beecroft tends to duck questions about the possibility of her personal experience of anorexia, talking vaguely about problems with particular foods like bread and embarrassment when forced to eat in front of other people. At the same time, in a study entitled *Carnal Drawings*, which is devoted to Beecroft's early work but crucial to any understanding of its later developments, the art critic Germano Celant draws upon a conversation with the artist in 2002 to paint the picture of a teenager whose dissatisfaction with her appearance and constant struggle against excess weight involved keeping a cruel "food diary" in which she did not hesitate to insult herself over any extra mouthful swallowed. Beecroft kept this diary obsessively for six years, from September 1987 to October 1993, the year of her first performance with models. A decade later, she took the (her?) problematic relationship with food as the basis for one of her most structured and "narrative" performances, staged on the occasion of a large-scale anthological exhibition held in 2003

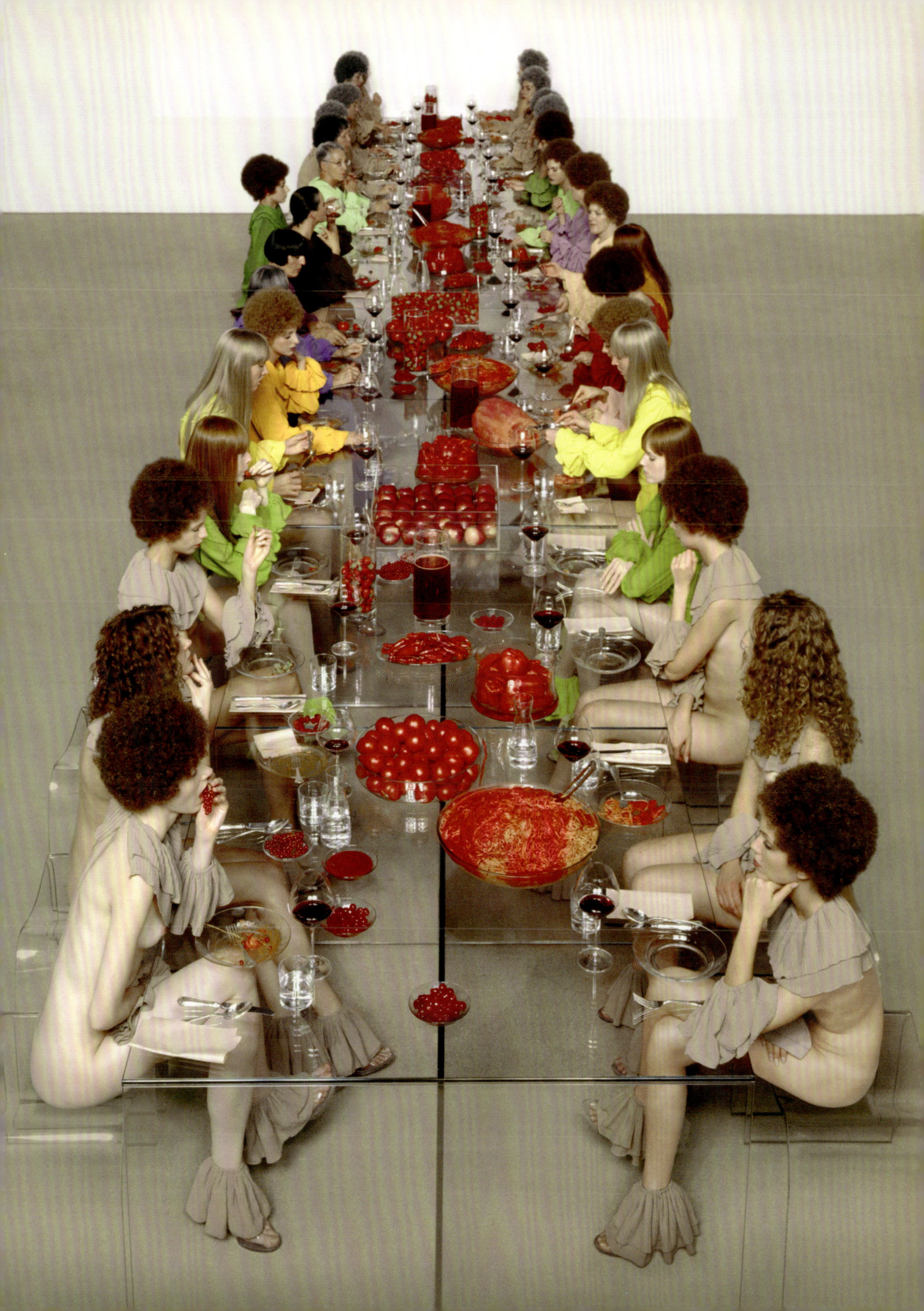

VB61 / Still Death! Darfur Still Deaf?, 2007
Performance at the Pescherie di Rialto, Venice, 2007
Courtesy Galleria Massimo Minini, Brescia; Galleria Lia Rumma, Naples/Milan

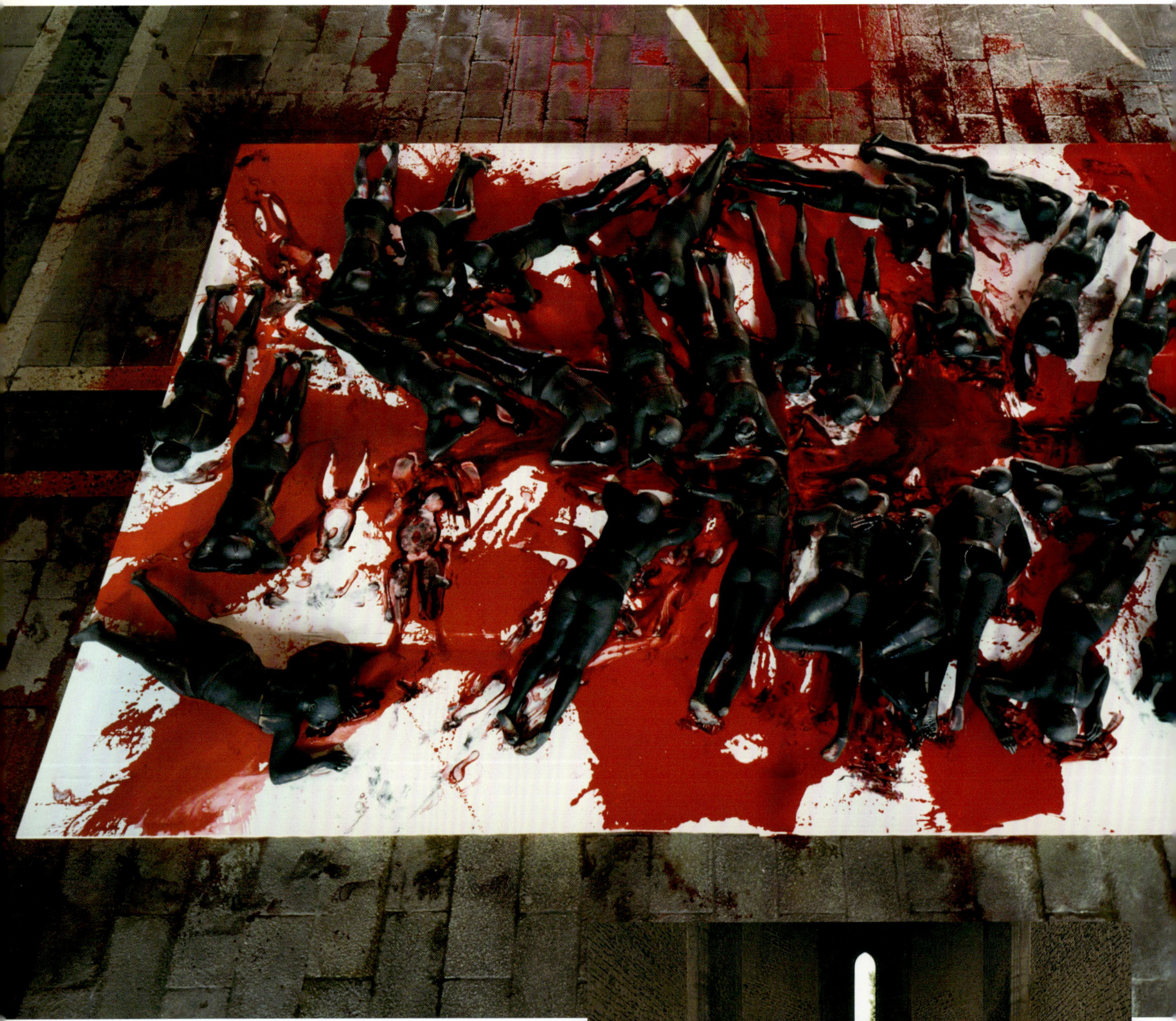

VB62, 2008
Color print, 178 x 226 cm
Performance at the Santa Maria dello Spasimo complex, Palermo, July 12, 2008
Courtesy Fondazione GOCA Palermo; Galleria Lia Rumma Naples/Milan; Galleria Massimo Minini Brescia

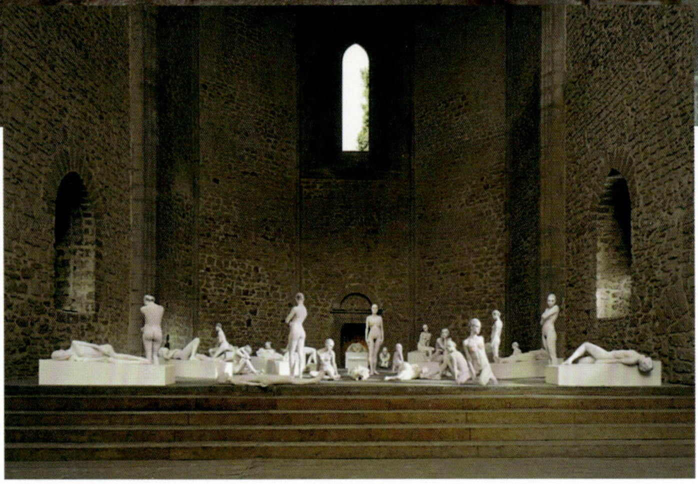

VB58, 2005 (printed 2006)
Color print, 165 x 499 x 2.5 cm
Courtesy Galleria Lia Rumma, Naples/Milan

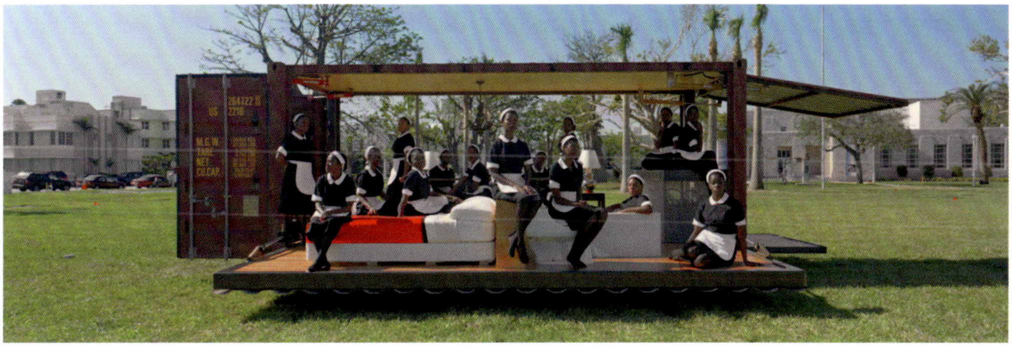

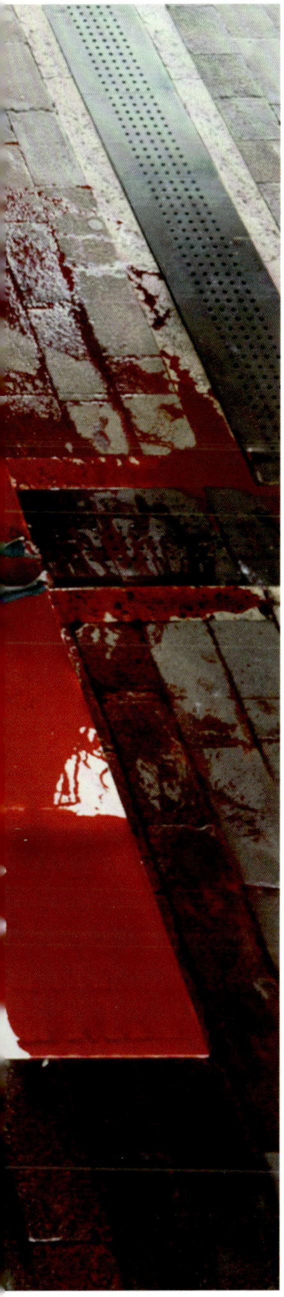

at the Castello di Rivoli - Museo d'Arte Contemporanea. She invited some ladies from Turin's high society to dine together with the customary group of models at a "public meal" – one of her personal taboos, as mentioned above – made up of courses arranged in terms of color, possibly in an attempt to make the "enemy" harmless by transforming it into something abstract that attracts solely by virtue of its chromatic qualities and forms (*VB52*, 2003).
The public and critics also recognize other problems in Beecroft's work, however, including shame and embarrassment, which can be regarded as two-sided in a certain sense: to be experienced both by those who expose their nakedness and by those who find themselves observing naked bodies in public, feeling themselves observed in turn and fearing to be judged for showing too much interest or looking too insistently. The artist, who has often recalled the frustration engendered by her attempts to pinpoint the true nature of people in painted portraits, claims to have found in photography and above all performance the best way to capture the human quality of her subjects. This avowed interest in the emotive dimension of the models is, however, partly refuted by Beecroft's determination to avoid personal relations as much as possible (to the point of systematically ignoring the questionnaires that her assistants require all the girls taking part in the performances to fill in). At the same time, she claims that this detachment is necessary in order to heighten the sense of disorientation and abandonment that the models must feel and transmit to the public.
In this connection, it can also be observed that the decision to use professional models accustomed to exhibiting themselves and being in the spotlight often freezes the emotions and transposes the performance into an almost abstract or metaphysical dimension where the uniformity of the bodies takes on subtly disturbing connotations. This opens up the way to possible new interpretations in which hypotheses of social criticism (an attack on the world of fashion that imposes clichés and leads to depersonalization) alternate with more or less explicit allusions to Beecroft's "connivance" with the glamour system.
At the same time, the object-bodies of the professional models allow the artist to preserve ambiguity also as regards her intention to trigger erotic desires or projective mechanisms in connection with the performances. The models are like ready-mades taken from the most illustrious runways and the trendiest magazines. They can be admired, envied or desired. Once again, it is the public that decides what it wants to find in the work.
The political significance of some recent works by Vanessa Beecroft is also the fruit of a "value added" by critics, which she has skillfully fostered to the point where it has become a further subject within the subject. The centrality of the body remains unchanged and the models can "shoulder" the weight of the political iniquity of the world distribution of wealth or the blood of Darfur (*VB48*, 2001; *VB61*, 2007).
These performances and the photographs documenting them succeed in their aim to communicate above all thanks to Vanessa Beecroft's extraordinary ability to orchestrate every element down to the smallest detail for the purpose of perfect composition in formal and aesthetic terms (*VB62*, 2008). This is a constantly recurring element and one that enables the artist, like the great painters of bygone centuries, to transform even horror into beauty.
(*P.V.*)

John Currin

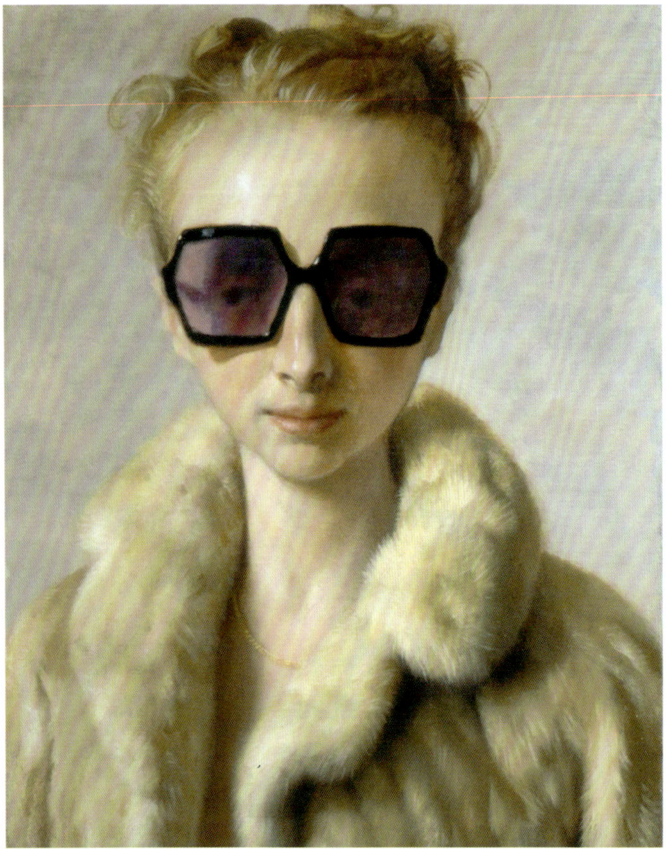

Rachel in Fur, 2002
Oil on canvas, 51 x 41 cm
Courtesy Sadie Coles HQ, London

Thanksgiving, 2003
Ink and gouache on paper,
380 x 460 mm
Courtesy Sadie Coles HQ, London

Born in Boulder, Colorado, in 1962. Lives and works in New York.
One of the best known and most respected painters on the contemporary art scene, John Currin studied at the Yale University school of art and attracted attention in the late 1980s with minute and meticulous oil paintings of a figurative nature displaying an extraordinary mastery of technique.
It is no coincidence that the names of the great masters referred to in connection with his "calligraphic" painting range from Botticelli and Mantegna in the Renaissance to Tiepolo and Fragonard in the eighteenth century and Max Beckmann, Picasso and Balthus in the twentieth. And it is precisely the comparison with Balthus that seems the most apposite, since Currin's formally impeccable work displays an evident streak of perversion.
His female portraits are depictions of deformed beauty. Smartly dressed and evidently rich, often portrayed in the typical settings of high society, the emaciated or Junoesque women in Currin's paintings are actually characterized by obvious flaws such as a hooked nose, an overly prominent bosom or forehead, and even bad teeth. The theme of social satire and caricature underlying these portraits is obvious in a painting such as *Thanksgiving* (2003), where three women of different generations – the model in each case being actually the artist's wife Rachel Feinstein, who is also featured in the disarming *Rachel in Fur* (2002) – prepare to celebrate Thanksgiving in a grotesquely affected manner.
In his most recent paintings of scathing parody, Currin has gone so far as to include explicitly pornographic scenes in which details of sophisticated taste such as necklaces, gloves and fashionable accessories contrast with the prevailing vulgarity of the episodes portrayed.
Currin states that he draws inspiration for his paintings from the images broadcast on television and the photographs published in established magazines of high circulation like *Cosmopolitan* and *Playboy* in an effort to combine cultured art and popular images.
The artist offers this convincing explanation of what he is doing: "One motive of mine is to see if I could make these clearly debased and unbeautiful things become beautiful in a painting."
(*L.L.*)

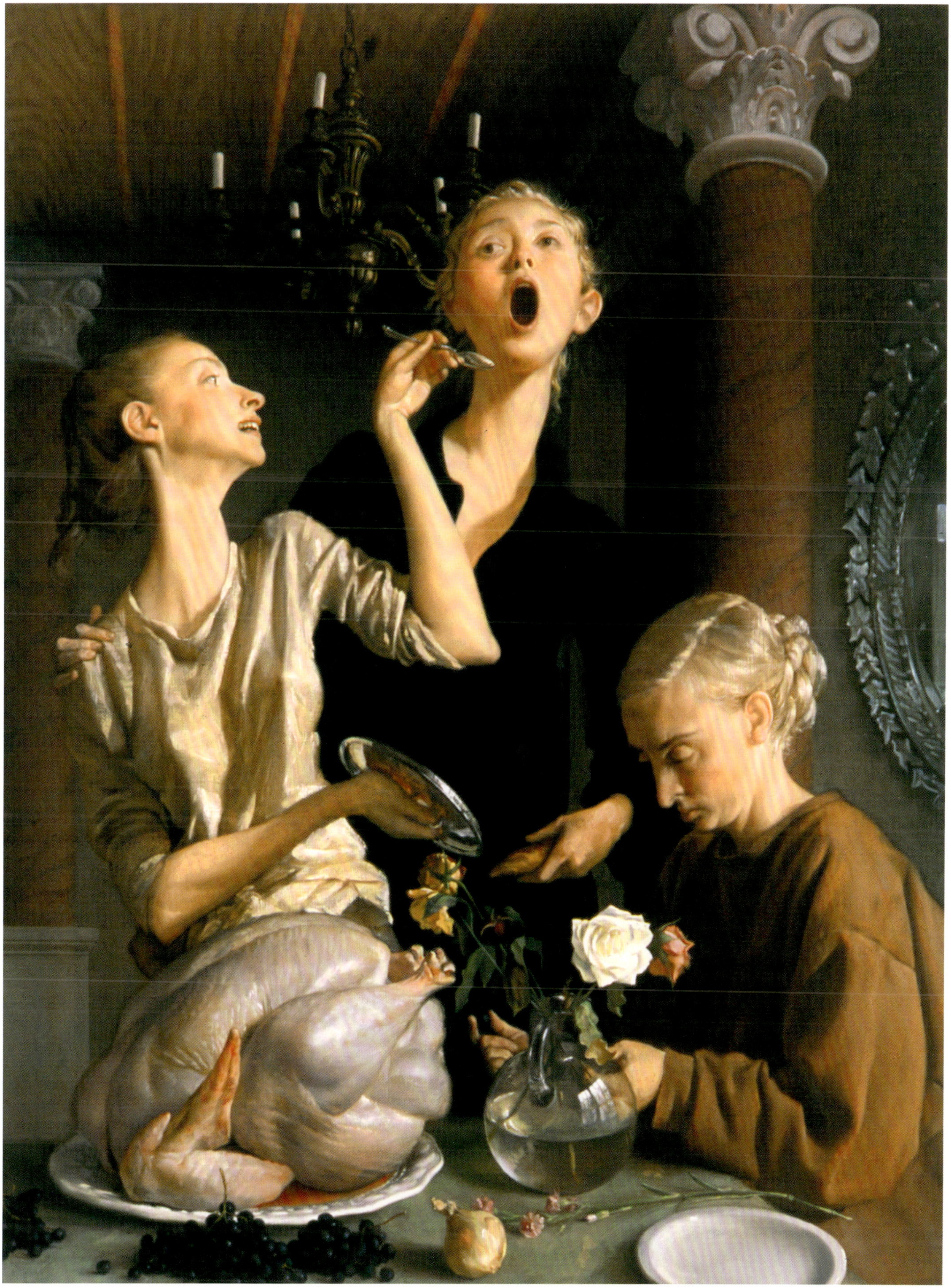

Marlene Dumas

Born in Cape Town, South Africa, in 1953. Lives and works in Amsterdam.
For Whom the Bell Tolls is the title of an extraordinary canvas that Marlene Dumas painted in 2008 with just a tortured and incredulous face in the foreground, whose expressive power is sufficient by itself to make tangible the impending presence of death in the everyday life of every one of us.
In recent years, perhaps since the tragedy of September 11, the representation of death and violence has taken on ever-greater weight and importance in the artist's work, so much so that *Measuring Your Own Grave* (2003), the title of a painting inspired by the Twin Towers, was borrowed for a touring anthological exhibition that recently arrived at the MoMA in New York. This further strengthened the effort she has made from the very outset to give her work a political character, which is no less evident when the dominant theme is sexuality, as explored also in its social and racial implications. Dumas is indeed known for works based on pornographic images that she uses to highlight the vulnerability of the naked body.
The artist's paintings and drawings nearly always originate in photographs taken by herself or others. She works on the initial image by cutting out the subject to be portrayed so as to separate it from the background and thus obtain an almost metaphysical effect of suspension in its pictorial translation. As a result, the violence inherent in the subjects addressed is not illustrated but remains implicit, transformed into a destabilizing force that succeeds through the expressionistic power of the painting or drawing in and disturbing the observer, and often prompting ethical and ideological awareness.
(*P.V.*)

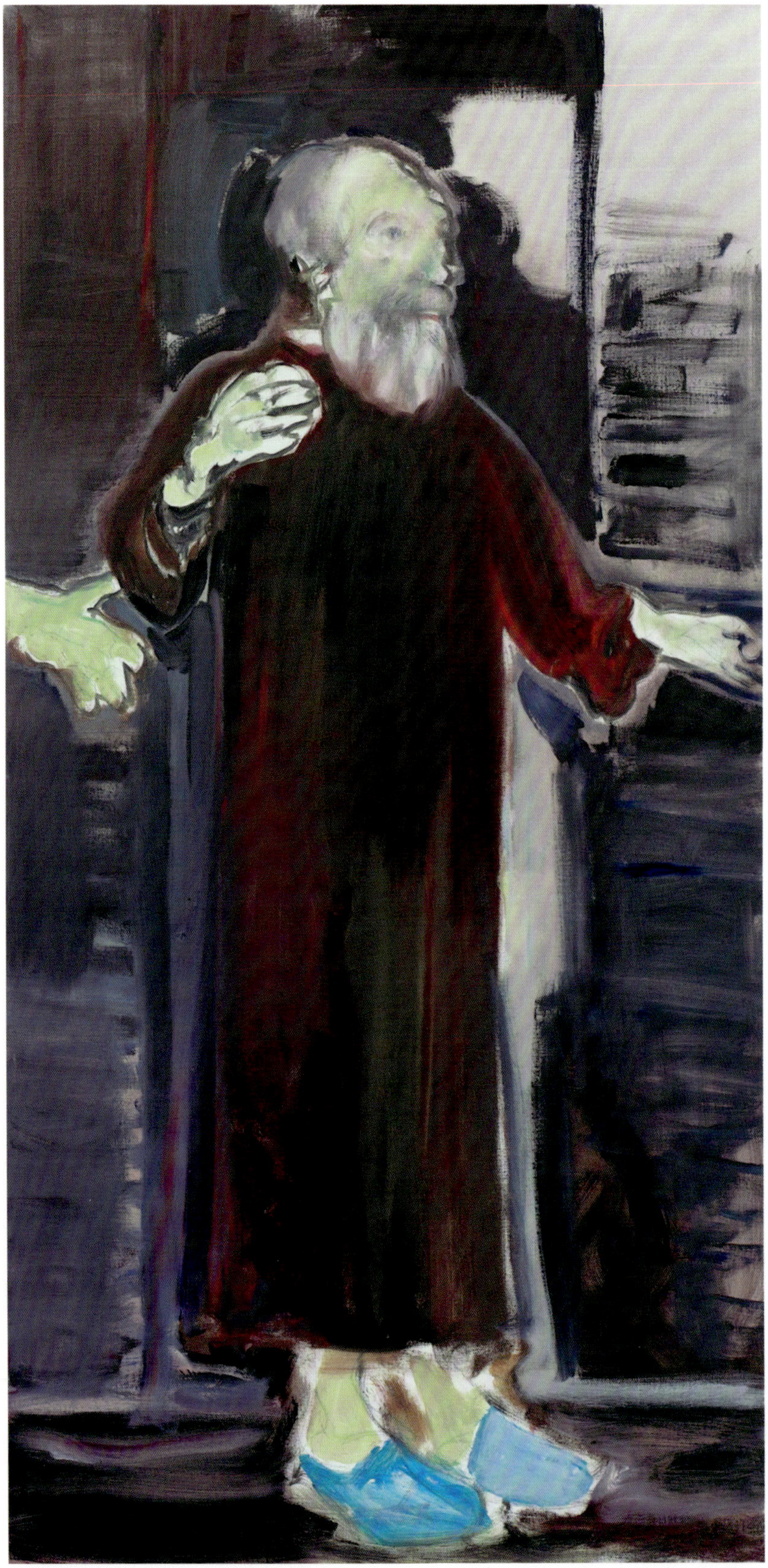

Frisked, 2006
Oil on canvas, 200 x 100 cm
Private collection

For Whom the Bell Tolls, 2008
Oil on canvas, 100 x 90 cm
Dallas, Dallas Museum of Art, The Rachofsky Collection through the DMA/amfAR Benefit Auction Fund

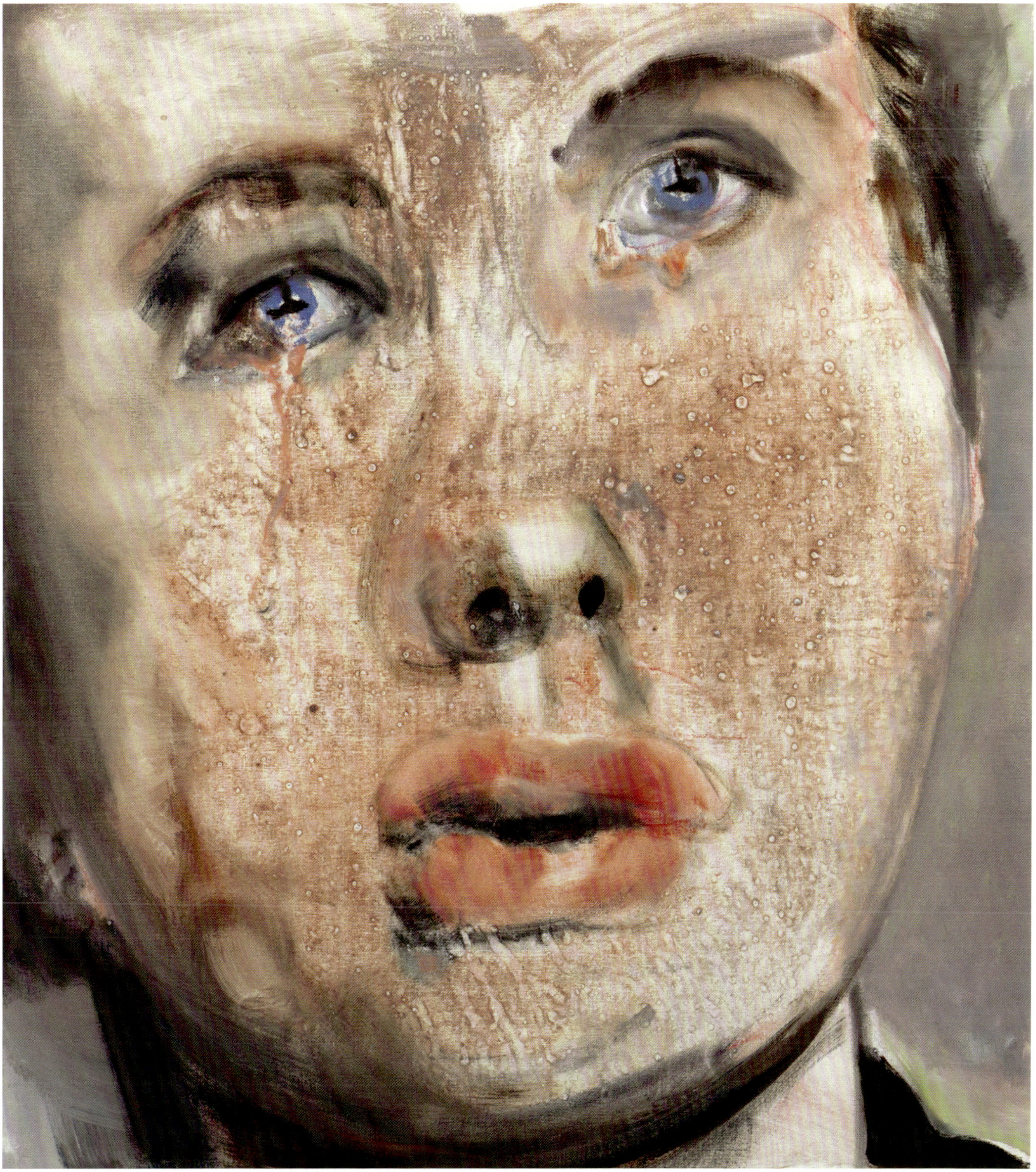

Kiki Smith

Born in Nuremberg, Germany, in 1954. Lives and works in New York. Kiki Smith's work examines the condition of human frailty with particular reference to the female sphere. Drawing and sculpture, techniques she learned from her father, the Minimalist sculptor Tony Smith, are used to probe the concepts of identity and stereotype.

Smith seeks to deconstruct the inherent quality of permanence attached to the female condition and roles by drawing in particular on the images of fairytale and narrative in which these clichés take shape to create visual shortcircuits.

Sleeping Woman with Standing Wolf, part of a cycle created in 2004, exemplifies the artist's artistic vocabulary with its numerous literary references. In addition to the interpretation of the totemic animal derived from the works of Carlos Castaneda, Kiki Smith takes into consideration the hagiographic tradition regarding Saint Genevieve, the patron saint of Paris, and the fairy stories *Sleeping Beauty* and *Little Red Riding Hood* in Perrault's version, the moral of which reveals the model of female behavior inculcated by the society that created these narrative topoi. Woman's role thus consists in waiting for action on the part of man to free her from the ties of childhood and enable her to become an adult conscious of her place in society. The wolf and, by extension, the forest become metaphors of the dangers of an external world unsuitable for female frailty. Kiki Smith's aim is to deactivate the process of identification between woman and her archetype by deconstructing and unmasking the latter.

Kiki Smith presented the installation *Homespun Tales: a Tale of Domestic Occupation*, a reflection on life in a Venetian home, in a solo show held at the Fondazione Querini Stampalia in 2005.

The large-sized work comprised over a hundred elements created with different media that establish narrative links with the architecture of the building and its historical collections, evocatively superimposing the stories of present and past inhabitants in an intimate and emotive narrative captured in the short film *Squatting the Palace* by Vivien Bittencourt and Vincent Katz.

(*F.T.*)

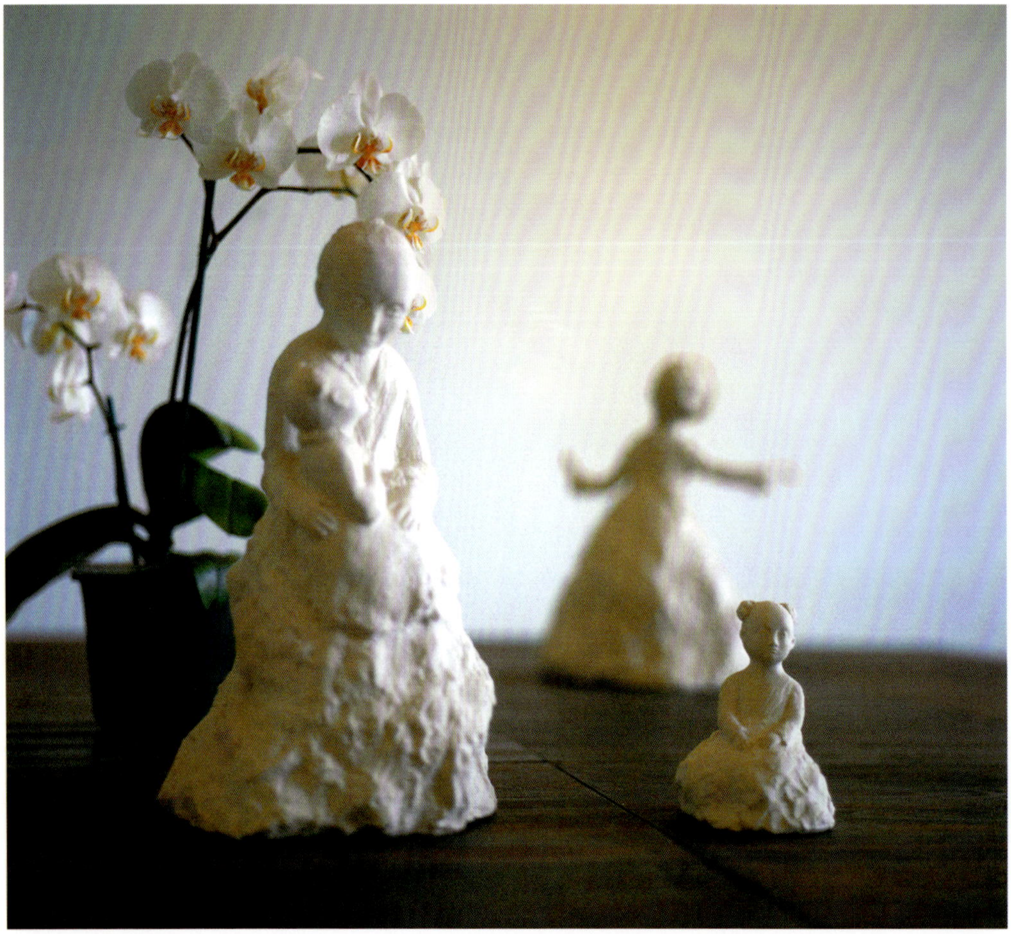

Homespun Tales: A Tale of Domestic Occupation, 2005
Plaster, porcelain, and orchid, dimensions variable
View of the installation realized in 2005 at the Fondazione Querini Stampalia, Venice

Sleeping Woman with Standing Wolf, 2004
Lithography, ink, and collage on paper, 200 x 166 cm
Rovereto, Mart – Museo di Arte Moderna e Contemporanea di Trento e Rovereto, deposit ARLeS

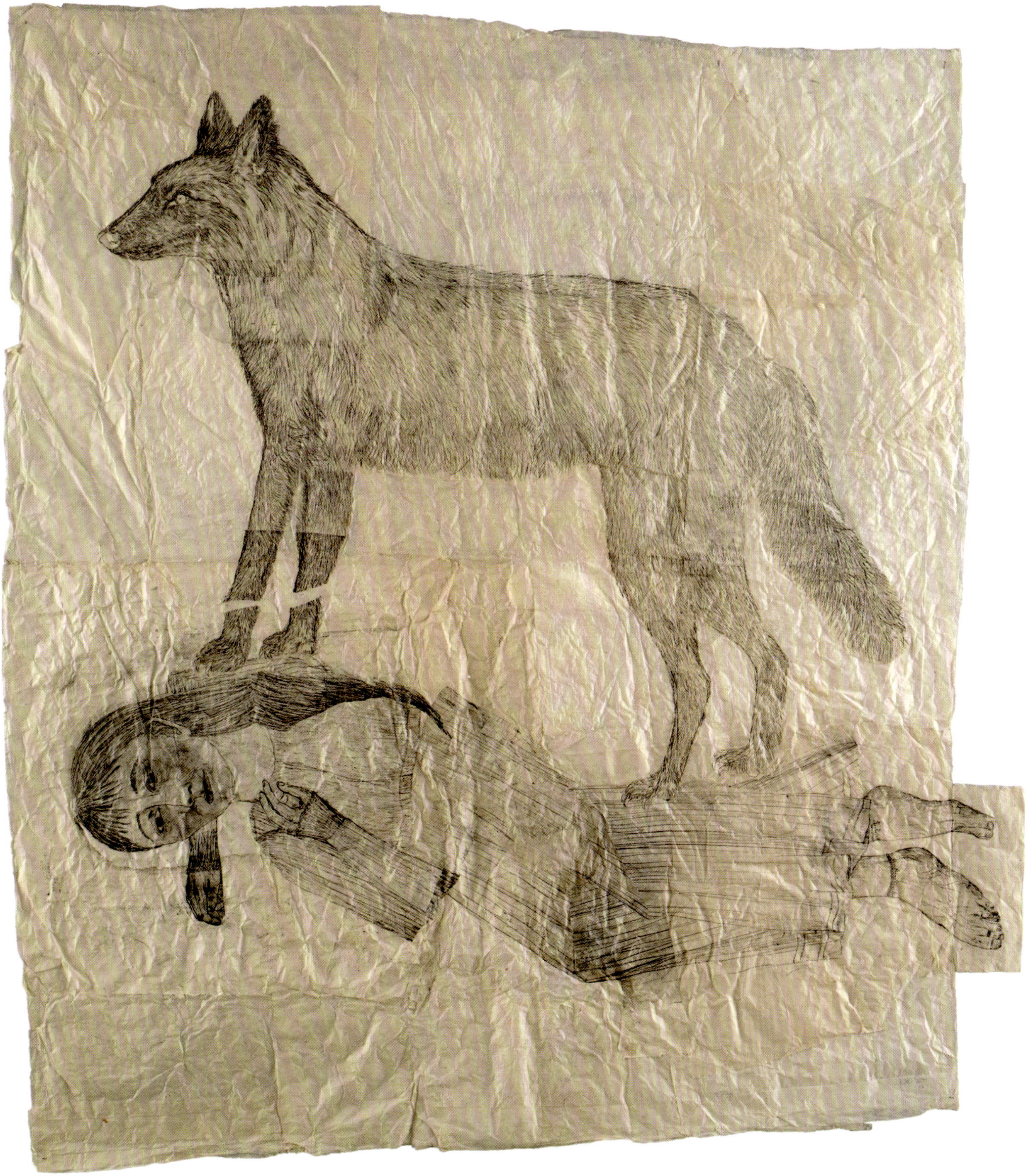

Jeff Wall

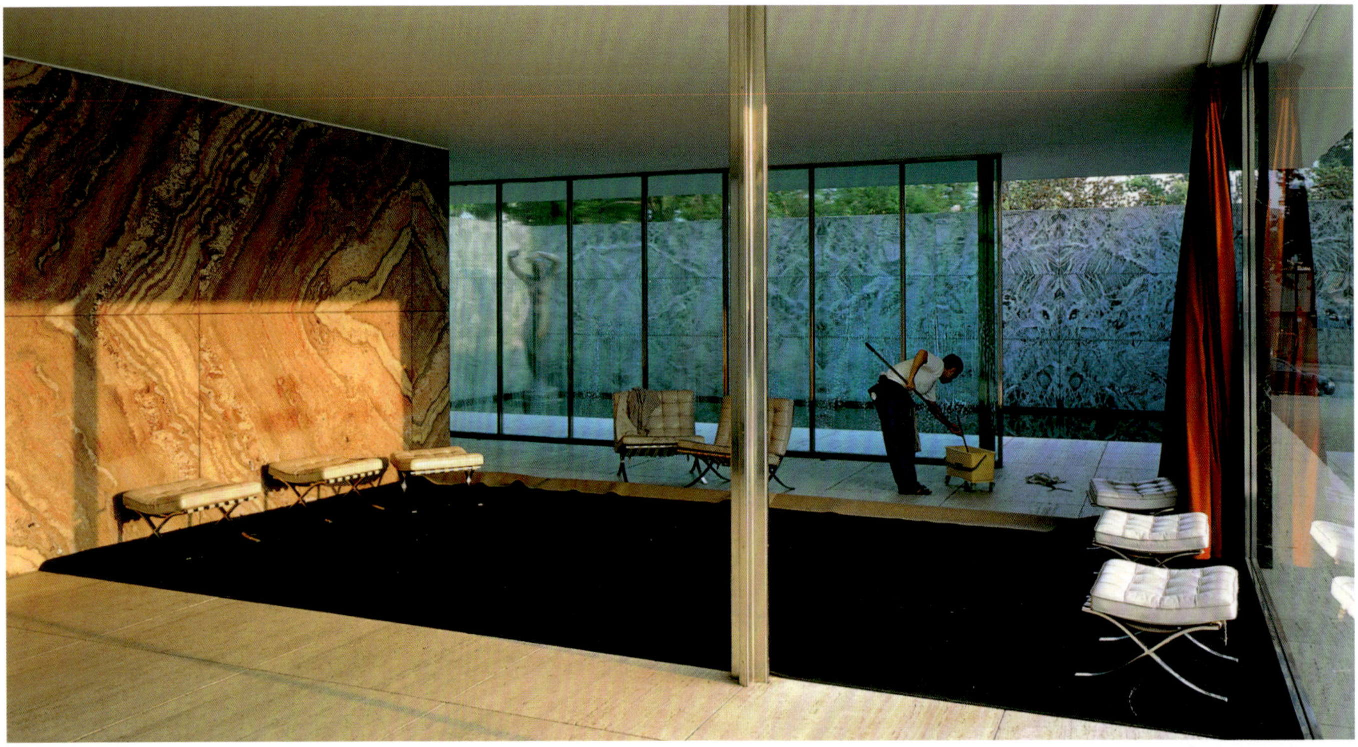

Born in Vancouver in 1946. Lives and works in Vancouver.
Jeff Wall's description of his works as "cinematographic photography" encapsulates a number of its key characteristics, such as the Canadian artist's frequent use of the panoramic format and light-box presentation, precise arrangement of set and meticulous choice of "actors". It is, however, not only the formal and compositional qualities that are "cinematographic" in nature but also the very way in which Wall conceives his photographs. Every image is in fact seen as a moment extrapolated from a story and hence laden with enormous narrative potential capable of prompting the viewer to wonder about what happens before and after that fragment of time and action. In this sense, Wall's photos are something like the images chosen to present a film, torn between the conflicting needs to reveal some details in order to arouse curiosity and to keep the plot a mystery. Even absolutely commonplace situations like someone carrying a covered tray thus become enigmatic in his work. We wonder who the woman is, where she is going, and what the cloth over the tray is hiding.
We realize that what looked like a snapshot at first sight is actually a rigorously planned photograph in terms of formal composition and "screenplay", one in which every element – the woman seen from behind, the otherwise empty streets, the tall hedges, the house buried in vegetation – works to create a sense of timelessness and an aura of mystery.
The stories that Jeff Wall captures in his photographs are nearly always about the everyday life of marginal subjects with a particular focus on their urban or architectural setting. *Morning Cleaning, Mies van der Rohe Foundation, Barcelona* (1999) is wholly emblematic in this sense, as it combines the rigorous elegance of one of the masterpieces of modern architecture, the pavilion built by Mies van der Rohe for the Barcelona International Exposition of 1929, with the work of a cleaner to keep its glass and marble shining every day. Wall's decision to show the man at work in the hours before the building opens to the public is bound up with his desire to draw the viewer's attention to what is normally unnoticed.
(*P.V.*)

Morning Cleaning, Mies van der Rohe Foundation, Barcelona, 1999
Transparency in light box,
180 x 351 x 26 cm
Collection of the artist, on permanent loan to the Museum für Moderne Kunst, Frankfurt

A Woman with a Coverei Tray, 2003
Light box, 164 x 208 x 26 cm
Cologne, Johnen Schöttle

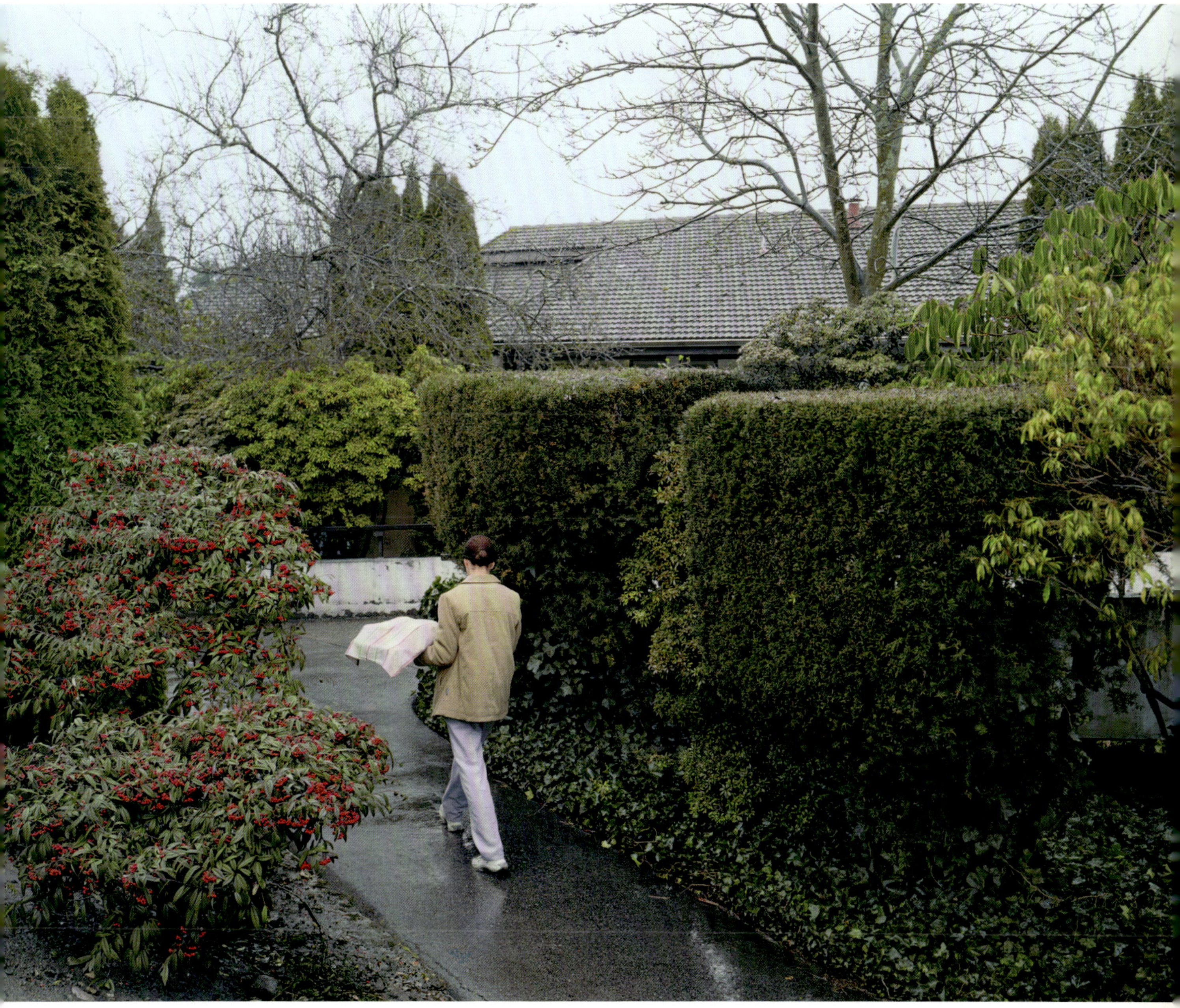

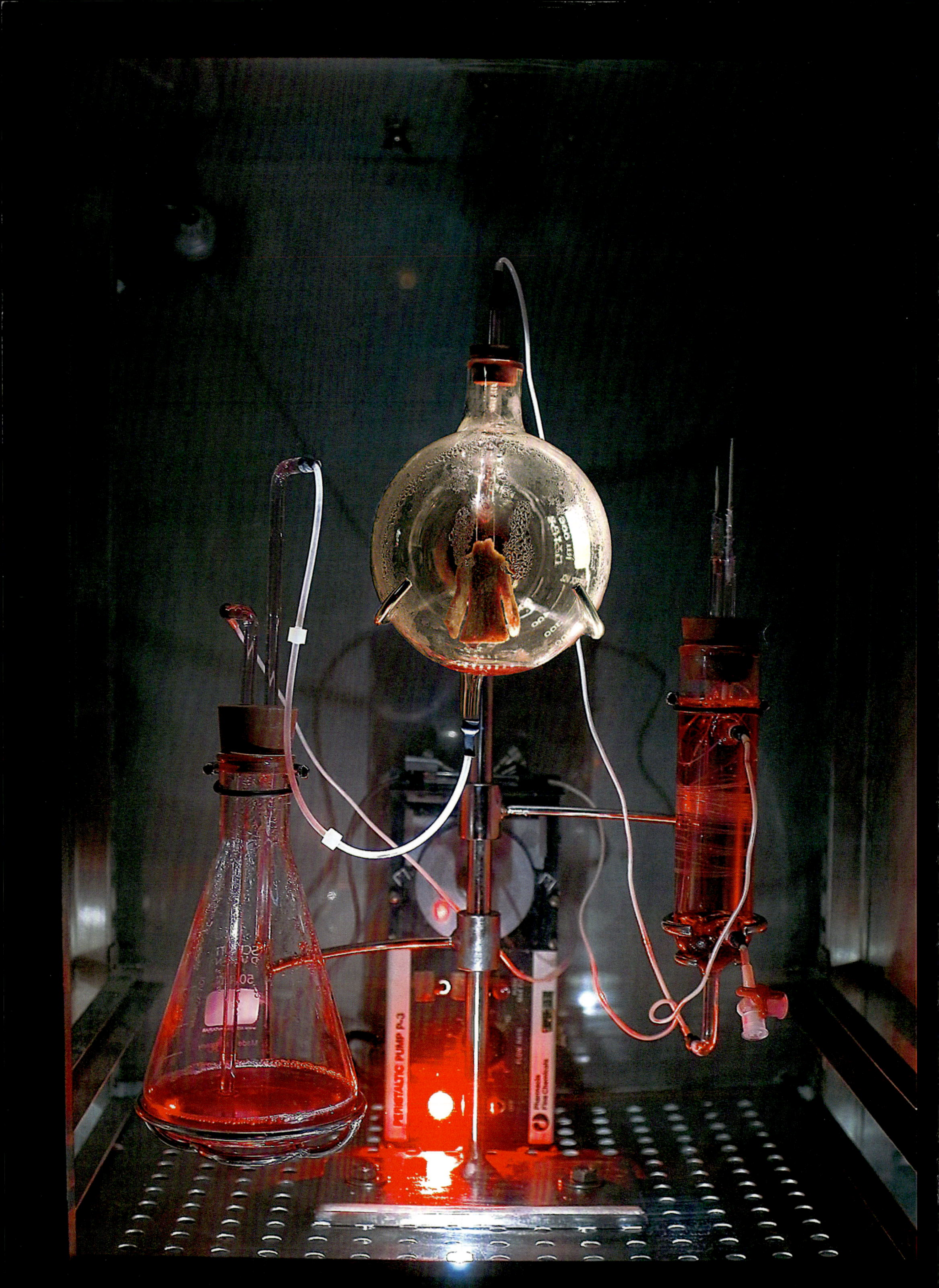
PERISTALTIC PUMP P-3
Pharmacia
Fine Chemicals

Domenico Quaranta

Art and the New Media in the Post-Medium Era

The Tissue Culture & Art Project (Oron Catts & Ionat Zurr) *Victimless Leather – A Prototype of Stitch-less Jacket grown in a Technoscientific "Body"*, 2004 Biodegradable polymeric connective tissue and bone cells, dimensions variable Courtesy of the artist

A technological revolution of enormous proportions has swept through the world in the last 20 years, starting in the capitalist democracies of the West and now gradually reshaping also the developing countries in economic, political, and social terms. Its impact on our everyday life is so self-evident today that any reference to it sounds almost like stating the obvious, as do most of the high-sounding expressions coined just a few years ago, including "information age" (Manuel Castells, 2002),[1] "age of access" (Jeremy Rifkin, 2001),[2] and "being digital" (Nicholas Negroponte, 1996).[3] And yet, our sense of familiarity derives more from the obsessive rhetoric of the mass media than any real cognizance of the changes that have taken place in such a short span of time. That happens because, as Charlie Gere points out, "Almost by definition any radical transformations brought about by the media are impossible to fully grasp at the time they are taking place. This is because how we understand the world is structured by and accessible through our media ... There is not, indeed there cannot be, a point outside of our media from which we can have some kind of privileged... perspective on any aspect of our existence."[4] The "computerization of society" predicted in the 1970s[5] has affected all of the following to the same degree: the production and distribution of goods; the way in which we earn, handle, and use money; the means, the speed, and the frequency with which we travel; how we use our free time; and, last but not least, how we communicate, represent ourselves, and relate to the mass media. Previously crystal-clear distinctions like public and private, property and sharing, free time and work are becoming increasingly blurred as portable computers, satellite navigation systems, cellular telephones, videogames, blogs, social networks, and virtual worlds take on ever-greater importance in our lives. Even phenomena like the economic globalization, the dematerialization of work, international terrorism, and the war in Iraq would prove incomprehensible outside of this horizon.

Culture could hardly remain untouched by a phenomenon that affects the territory of communication first of all. As Gere (2008) observes, "Our culture is becoming so thoroughly digital that the term digital culture risks becoming tautological."[6] Contemporary art is no exception. On the contrary, its peculiar economy – which combines a market of luxury items with a comparatively weak "system" based largely on public and private funding as well as nonprofit initiatives and institutions – has been radically transformed by a revolution in means of communication that greatly reduces the cost of organizing an event or running a magazine. The explosion of low-cost biennials, art publishing, and curatorship owes a great deal to e-mail, the Internet and the digitization of information.[7] The examination of these problems lies, however, beyond the scope of this essay, which addresses the impact of the new technologies on artistic production. As we shall see, this is a highly controversial question and one that it is still very difficult to tackle with fair and balanced judgment.

The Post-Media Condition

Contemporary art has displayed an extraordinary capacity to absorb the new languages and means of communication ever since the 1960s.[8] In particular, the growth of the art market has obliged also the most traditional forms, like painting and sculpture, to update their production systems in the last 20 years so as to meet ever-greater demand through more efficient management of the various stages.

The examples of Jeff Koons and Takashi Murakami are emblematic in this connection. Both create their pictorial works on computers, using software that makes it possible to control every detail of the image, which is then handed over to a host of assistants for scale reproduction in acrylic or oil on canvas. While the use of a post-production program like Adobe Photoshop enables Koons to take to extremes the citationism and assemblage on which most of his work rests, the use of vector graphics programs allows Murakami, as Pamela Lee points out,[9] to employ economies of scale, transposing the same subjects in different shapes and sizes from painting to sculpture, wallpaper, anime, and Louis Vuitton bags.

Above and beyond utilitarian motives or the effective involvement of computers in the production process, however, the traditional arts must necessarily come to terms with a destiny of the image that has altered completely in terms of aesthetics, accessibility, and amount. Thomas Ruff's huge pixels and John Currin's use of pornographic images from the Internet in his paintings are only some of the possible examples.

On another front, the assertion – with support from museums and the "biennial circus" – of an idea of art based more and more on experience and less and less on the object has fostered an increasingly spectacular and technologically mediated development of the installation. The broad range of examples includes Doug Aitken's video installations, which often take over the entire exhibition space and even move outside to address the city (as happened with *Sleepwalkers*, 2007, at the MoMA in New York), the environmental installations of artists like Carsten Höller and Olafur Eliasson, and the works of Mariko Mori, who often works in close contact with the hi-tech companies that supply her with materials.

Discussion of the medium is, however, rigorously avoided both by the artists who use it and by the critics who interpret their work. It would be ingenuous to imagine that this is due to any insufficient familiarity with the new technologies and media on the part of the latter. For example, this is how Francesco Bonami states the question in a recent work: "Let us be clear about this. Photography is no more an art than a paintbrush or the screen of a computer. Those who use the term 'computer art' do not know what they are talking about. They confuse the means with the content, the idea, and the result, mistaking the tool for the work. Art is not like Formula One, where the car is more important than the driver."[10]

Bonami's observation encapsulates a view that has become dominant in the world of art since the 1960s and is discussed by Rosalind Krauss in her book *A Voyage on the North Sea. Art in the Age of the Post-Medium Condition* (1999).[11] As is known, Clement Greenberg's formalist approach had succeeded during the 1950s in establishing the idea that "the unique and proper area of competence of each art coincided with all that was unique in the nature of its medium."[12] According to Krauss, this view was superseded around the 1970s, on the one hand by Marcel Broodthaers with his "eagle principle", which simultaneously shatters the idea of an aesthetic medium from the inside and transforms everything equally into a readymade that eliminates the difference between aesthetics and commercialization,[13] and on the other by video, which shares the "constitutive heterogeneity of television" and thus proclaims the end of the media specificity. As Krauss wrote, in the era of television we are living in a post-medium condition.[14]

From an artistic viewpoint, the installation constitutes the most typical product of the post-medium condition by virtue of its expanded nature and capacity to swallow up and mix all of the media. At the same time, all of the post-Greenberg critics, from Krauss on, were to appear intent on getting rid of the idea of the medium and shifting attention to the content, languages, and dynamics of art. Significance attaches in this connection to the fact that Nicholas Bourriaud, probably the critic who displayed the greatest insight into the impact of the technological revolution on artistic production with his book *Postproduction*,[15] never talks about technologies as media.

There is, however, also something more in this resistance. It is possible to detect a sort of subterranean hostility in Bonami's words, particularly in the vehemence with which the expression "computer art" is attacked. Who is Bonami so angry with?

An art on the edge

In the same period when contemporary art critics were struggling to break free of Greenberg's legacy, another community was intent on taking over the concept of the medium. This included artists, critics, curators, and researchers with a particular interest in the impact of the new technological media (from video to computers) on artistic production. In their language, "medium" was to be understood in terms of the work of Marshall McLuhan, a theorist focusing not on art but on the mass media.[16] Like Greenberg, however, they all believed investigation of the specificity of the medium essential to the development of an art using what were coming to be called "new media": video (for TV transmission or otherwise), satellite communications, radio, fax, computers, the first online networks, cybernetic systems, and all other technological paraphernalia. As David Antin wrote in

Ubermorgen.com
The Agency for Manual Election Recount, 2004
Video, 12'
View of the performance held in 2004 at Kunsthaus Graz, MedienKunstLabor, Graz

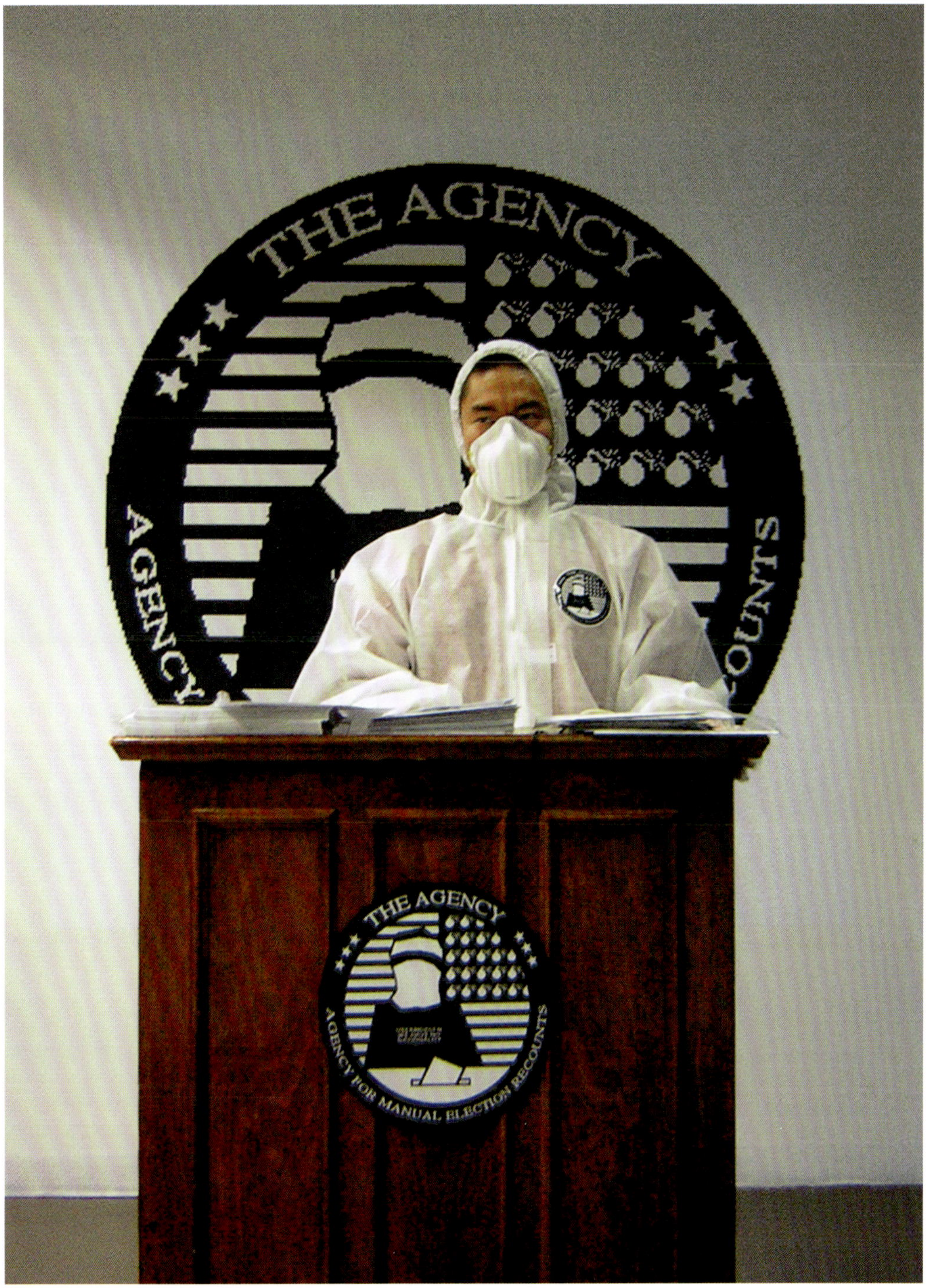

a celebrated essay on Video Art, this community gave rise to two types of critical discourse: "one, a kind of enthusiastic welcoming prose peppered with fragments of communication theory and McLuhanesque media talk; the other, a rather nervous attempt to locate the 'unique properties of the medium.' Discourse 1 could be called 'cyberscat' and Discourse 2, because it engages the issues that pass for 'formalism' in the art world, could be called 'the formalist rap'."[17]

Neither the use of new and barely accessible technologies nor the "formalist rap" did anything to favor the success of this approach, which also came up in the 1970s against the opposition of widespread anti-technological sentiments shared by those who – to some extent rightly – regarded the "scientific and technological system" as involved in the great dramas of the time, from the Cold War to the conflict in Vietnam. Counter-evidence is provided by the growing success of Video Art, above all from the late 1980s on. The only form of Media Art based at the time on comparatively accessible and economical means of production soon broke away from the for-

Eddo Stern
Double Evil, 2007
Shadow sculpture made with kinetic, electronic, and light mixed media, 111.76 x 50.80 x 106.68 cm
Courtesy Postmasters Gallery, New York

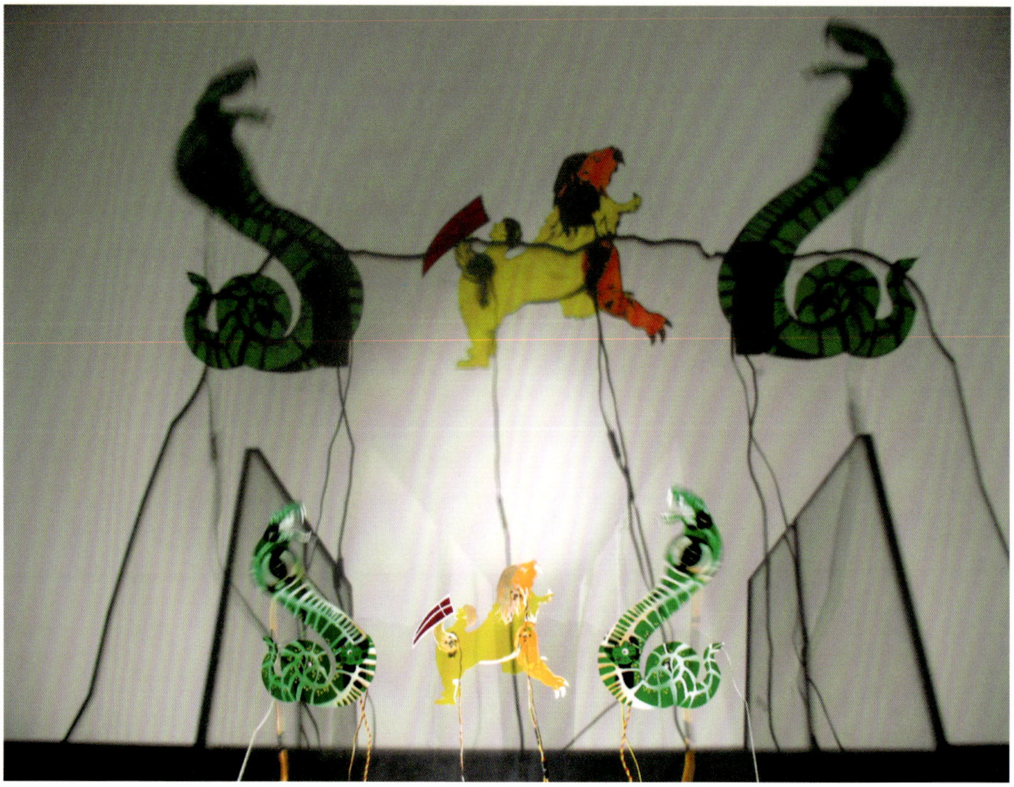

malist approach of its pioneers (like Nam June Paik and the Vasulkas). Taken up by conceptual and performance artists, it prompted readings that have nothing to do either with cyberscat or with formalist rap. (Consider, for example, what Krauss wrote on the aesthetics of narcissism.[18]) Its success was accompanied by gradual abandonment of the term "Video Art," which is only used today by the nostalgic few.[19]

At the same time, the other explorations on the frontiers between art, science, and technology continued to be developed and discussed by a small circle that – as Bonami would say – went on confusing the car with the driver, coining more or less short-lived labels like Digital Art, Multimedia Art, Telecommunication Art, Generative Art, Bio Art, Interactive Art, and New Media Art, the last in a long line. Relegated to the sidelines – apart from rare appearances on the stage of contemporary art, such as the 1986 Venice Biennale[20] – this niche began to develop a distribution system of its own made up of symposia, festivals, and centers of art and new technologies: from SIGGRAPH, a yearly symposium inaugurated in 1974, to the Ars Electronica festival in Linz (Austria), launched in 1979, V2 in Rotterdam, founded in 1981, and the ZKM (Zentrum für Kunst und Medientechnologie) in Karlsruhe (Germany), founded in 1989, to name just a few. Capable of involving a vast public and channeling different interests, this system developed on the frontiers between advanced technological research and experimental music, art and design, academism and DIY. A fully-fledged "world of art" with its own peculiar economy and system of distribution and discussion: the world of New Media Art.

So it was that the younger artists found themselves at a crossroads in the 1990s, when digital technologies gradually became economical, easy to use, and readily accessible to all; when the digital media no longer necessarily required specific skills and became available to artists as one of many possible tools, no longer one path to be followed with total and constant dedication. Were they to continue their work on the stage of contemporary art or New Media Art? Some opted resolutely for the first, including artists from very different backgrounds, such as Carsten Nicolai and Claude Closky, the former developing a rigorous investigation of electronic sound through cold and carefully calibrated installations with marked Minimalist overtones, the latter moving freely between a range of different media, including design, publishing, painting, and the Internet. Others opted equally firmly for the second. Most decided to put off taking any decision, moving to and fro between one world and the other according to circumstances.

There were various reasons for this uncertainty. So far we have described the world of New Media Art from the viewpoint of contemporary art, deliberately adopting a tone of disdain that we do not actually feel. In point of fact, New Media Art has many points to its favor. Why try to conquer a world in which technology is still viewed with distrust when there is already another capable of respecting and appreciating work that makes use of it? At the same time, an economy that disregards the market and is based essentially on public and private funding – or the passionate and disinterested efforts of artists who do other things to make their living – allows a freedom of action unthinkable for any artist involved in the circuit of contemporary art. This freedom is important above all for those opposed to the art system and market for ideological or political reasons or simple aversion.

These advantages are, however, accompanied by some unquestionable disadvantages. First, the work is thus excluded from the traditional channels of the criticism – and history – of contemporary art and tied to a critical discourse that many (like Bonami) regard as bound up with obsolete views.[21] Second, the artist's name is associated with a label (New Media Art) that proves inadequate due to its ambiguous reference to "new" and to its insistence on the idea of the medium. Third, the artist operates on a platform that cultivates "dangerous liaisons" between art and pop entertainment and technological gadgetry.

An ambiguous term

We have endeavored so far to outline the social framework responsible in our view[22] for denying due visibility to an important sector of contemporary art and probably the only one capable of really getting to grips with a key element of present-day life, namely the "computerization of society." The worlds of contemporary art and New Media Art bear equal responsibility in this connection: the first for its distrust of the new technologies and the substantial technological illiteracy of critics clearly afflicted by the "digital divide" between generations; the second for its failure to understand its own transitional nature fully and for having sought to endow an inevitably provisional definition with permanence. Born as an area of freedom, a haven for radical and unfettered experimentation, it has turned into a

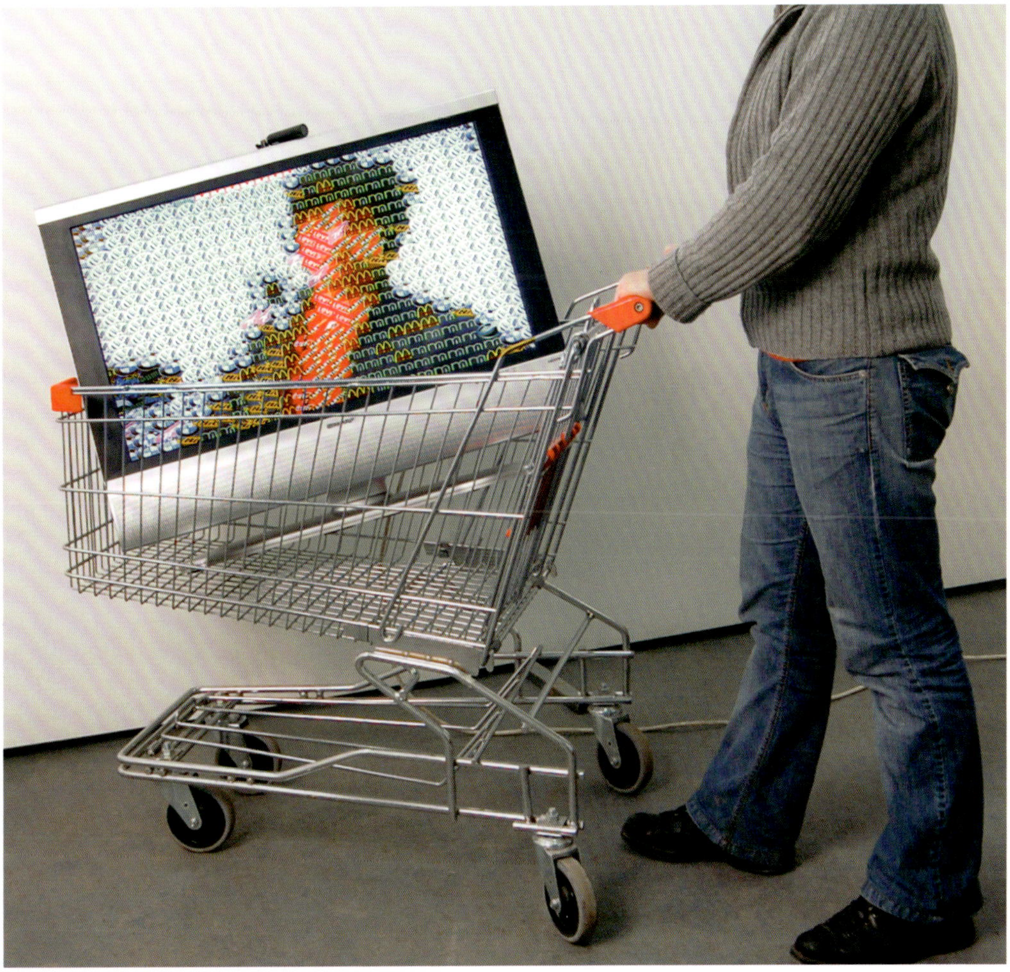

Alexei Shulgin and Aristarkh Chernyshev
Commercial Protest, 2007
LCD TV, supermarket cart, custom electronics, 100 x 95 x 7 cm
Courtesy of the artists and XL Gallery, Moscow

prison and the term "New Media Art" has become an ignominious appellation to be dispensed with as soon as possible.[23]

The inadequacy of the label can be seen in particular in its attempt to act as an umbrella term covering things that have nothing to do with one another. What is there in common between an artist who programs a computer to generate an uninterrupted flow of abstract images and one who uses it to play a hoax on an entire system of politics and the mass media through the creation of a fake website? Nothing, apart from the medium employed. And yet the generative works of Casey Reas and those of the Austrian duo UBERMORGEN.COM – who drove the American media into a frenzy in 2000 by setting up a site that apparently allowed citizens to auction their votes for the presidential elections[24] – come under the same heading and are often found together in the same books and shows. Even though both have contacts with contemporary art, their use of two different platforms and their association with the area of New Media Art continue to limit their visibility. Most people continue to think that the car is being mistaken for the driver here, even though this is absolutely not true.

What future?

A number of questions can be legitimately framed at this point. Does it still make sense to talk about New Media Art in a post-medium era and a historical period in which a "post-medium use" of the new digital media is possible? Above all, does the existence of a circumscribed sphere devoted to the exhibition and discussion of this art still make sense in these circumstances? Should the world of New Media Art not succumb or evolve into something different?[25]

Whether fortunately or unfortunately, there can be no unilateral answer to these questions. Stating that technologies have invaded our society and come into the hands of all and sundry means forgetting the existence of pioneering technological developments and of artists still interested in exploring these new frontiers. This work on the boundaries, temporary hybridization of

Gazira Babeli
"Gaz of the Desert" d'après Delacroix, 2007
Lambda print, 112 x 112 cm
Courtesy Fabio Paris Art Gallery, Brescia

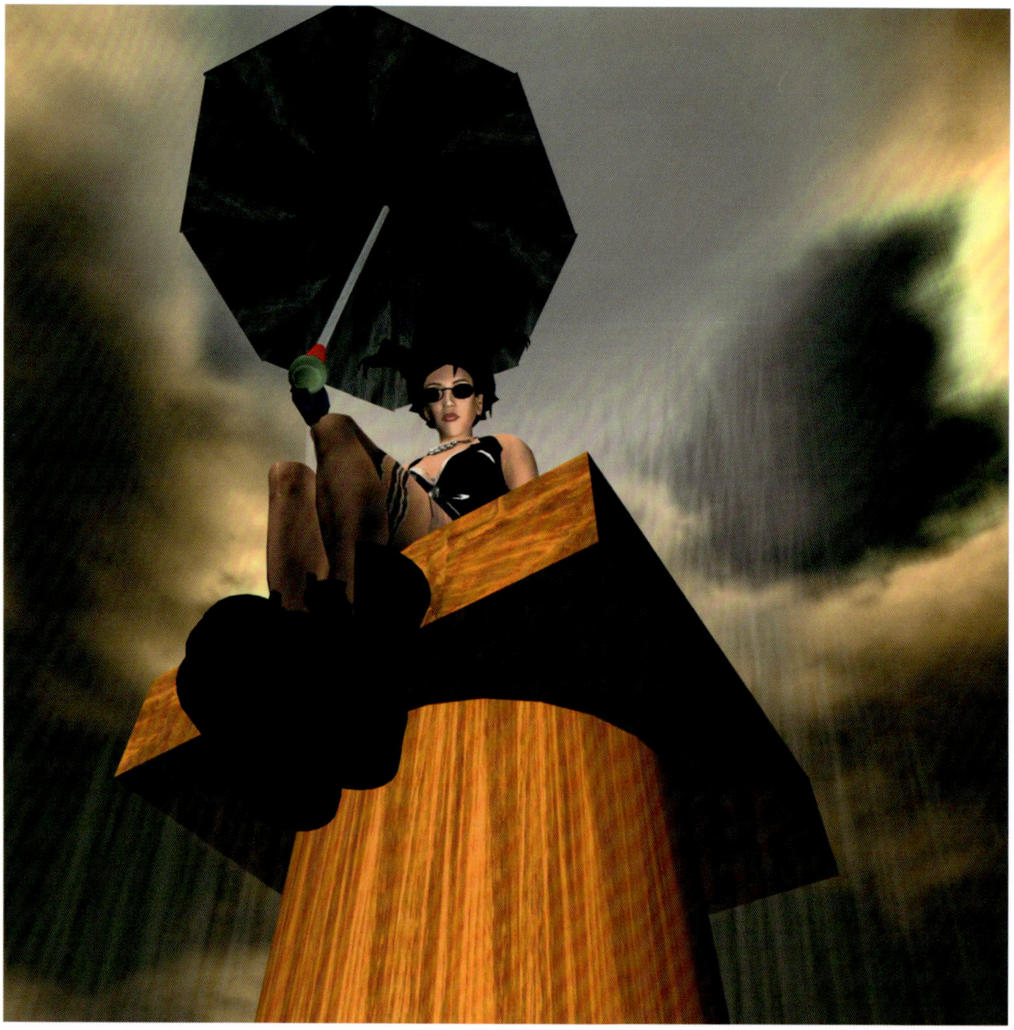

Carsten Nicolai
Wellenwanne, 2001–2003
Aluminum trays, CD player, CD, amplifier, speakers, water, dimensions variable
Courtesy Galerie EIGEN + ART Leipzig/Berlin and PaceWildenstein, New York

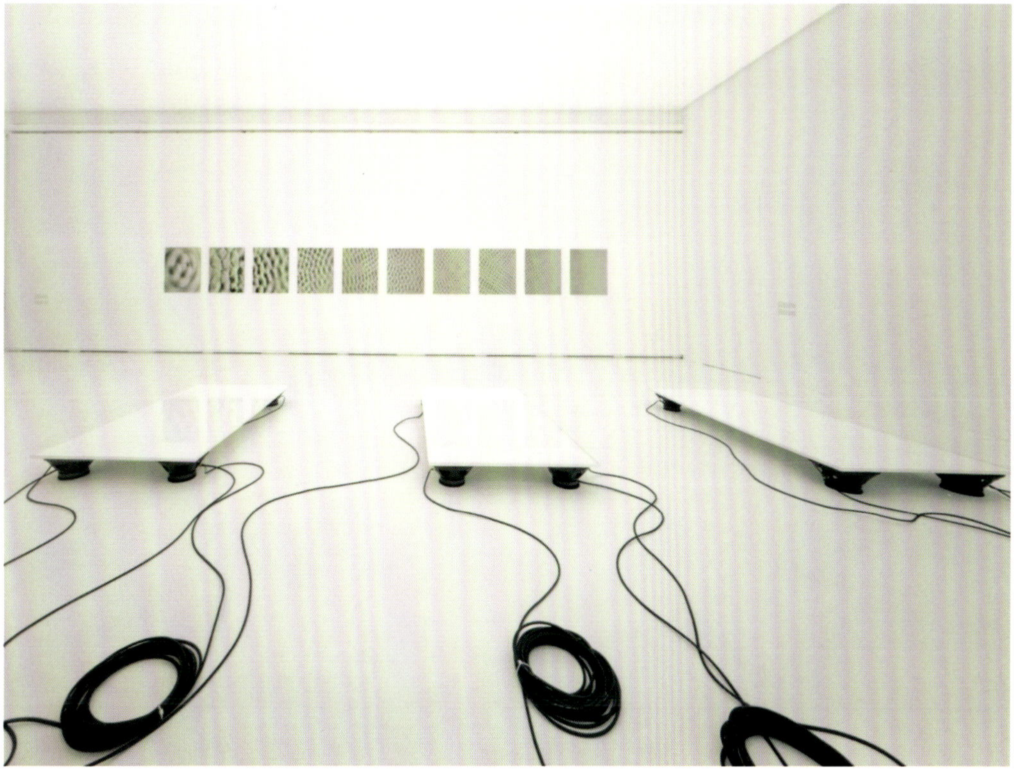

identities, and intermingling with other systems of sense production are precious assets. Innovation in art comes from there. For as long as it is able to fuel this, the world of New Media Art will play an extraordinary role as an "incubator" of innovations capable – as has already happened – of then converging on other systems of production: contemporary art, cinema, music, design, and the mainstream media. The world of New Media Art offers extraordinary places where this can happen, including the MIT Media Lab, the Futurelab of the Ars Electronica Center, and hundreds of other media labs scattered all over the world. A recent example of frontier work is offered by Biotech Art, which came into existence with the opening of biotechnological laboratories to artists.[26] Funded by the University of Western Australia and "dedicated to the research, learning and critique of life sciences,"[27] the Symbiotica laboratory has been operating in Perth since 2000. It offers residencies for artists, who thus find themselves working in close contact with scientists and with the most advanced equipment, something that would be impossible anywhere else.

At the same time, it is precisely Biotech Art that can help us to understand the situation we are going through, a period in which the time between groundbreaking research and its emergence from the laboratories is often so short that the two dimensions can proceed almost synchronically. On the one hand, it is in fact already possible to address biotechnologies with means that are comparatively accessible to non-professionals as regards both cost and specific knowledge. On the other, it is also already possible to make "instrumental" use of these means, utilizing biotechnologies without them necessarily providing the thematic nucleus of the work; in other words, without producing Biotech Art. The best-known example is unquestionably Wim Delvoye's *Cloaca Turbo*, a project launched in 2000 and continued over the years with the creation of increasingly evolved machines employed in the noble mission of producing shit. The project involves exhibition of the apparatus at work, a markedly "Pop" form of communication, but also the conceptual dimension of the sale of the artificial excrement, suitably packaged, as art at an affordable price.

With works like this, we are already so far outside the sphere of investigation into the "specificity of medium" that it would be specious and detrimental to any precise understanding of the nature and meaning of the work to speak about "Biotech Art," even though the term would be perfectly legitimate from a technical point of view.

And so we have finally arrived at the heart of the question. The term "New Media Art" is not in itself harmful, obsolete, stale, and doomed to disappear, "a thing of

Rhizome.org
Rhizome.org homepage

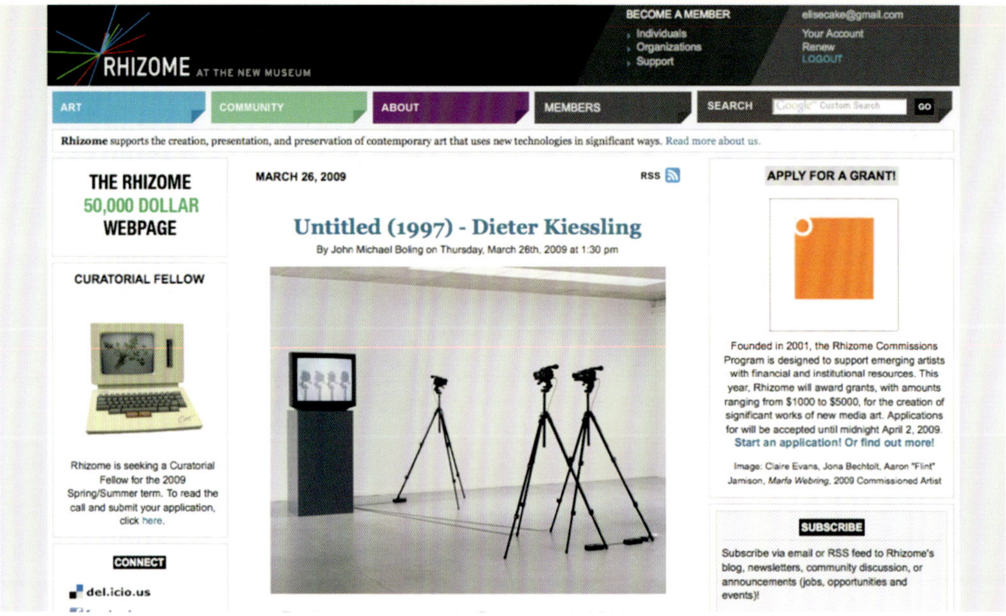

the past," as Andreas Broeckmann wrote. It is instead still useful in order to define the "infancy" of a new art. Its usefulness ceases at the very moment when this art moves past the initial formulation in formalistic terms, which is inevitable in this early phase; when it takes cognizance of the fact that a tool is only a tool; when it joins Eva and Franco Mattes in exclaiming, "the message is the message, who cares about the medium!"[28]; when it finally understands that it is acting in a "post-medium condition." At that point, continuing to talk about New Media Art is not only useless but also in fact dangerous because it prevents awareness of the ripening and the complexity and richness of the work and its meaning. We are all grateful to our parents for our childhood but take offense if they go on treating us as children.

"The art formerly known as new media"[29]
The art formerly known as New Media is one of the possibilities of the art of our time. Sometimes it is better able than more traditional languages to tell us something about the impact of the digital media on our culture, but not necessarily. The Greek artist Miltos Manetas has succeeded in doing this just as well through painting, focusing in particular on videogames and the way in which they have come to change our idea of our subjectivity and how we construct our living space.[30]

Apart from this, however, the move beyond the critical perspective associated with the expression "New Media Art" and its analogues makes a number of interesting discoveries possible. We have already mentioned the work of Casey Reas, an American artist who writes programs that produce specific visual output when executed. Work of this kind is normally described as Software Art or generative art. The starting point for this artist's work is, however, to be found still earlier in Sol LeWitt and his *Wall Drawings*. Like LeWitt, Reas writes instructions for someone else to carry out. Given that the "someone" in this case is a computer, Reas can control and expand the variables so that the work is different every time the program is run. Moreover, the work itself can take on very different forms as an image on a screen, a projection on a wall, an installation, and a print. Like LeWitt, Reas is more interested in the work as concept and process than in the end result. Again like LeWitt, however, he is also making a by no means negligible contribution to the fate of abstraction in contemporary art.[31]

Technically speaking, the works of Gazira Babeli should also be described as Software Art, since she too writes code that triggers events. But Babeli is not interested in the digital generation of images. Operating on the virtual platform of Second Life, a synthetic online world inhabited by millions of users, she ensures that everything she does is translated into a "fact" that has the appearance of reality: earthquakes, storms, tornados, towers that collapse, and characters who become deformed. We are fully in the realm of performance. If we add the fact that Babeli herself is an entirely constructed character, a mask whose real identity is not known, and that all of her work helps to lend substance to her char-

View of the new Ars Electronica Center, 2009
Linz, Austria

Schweger & Partner
View of the ZKM – Zentrum fur Kunst und Medientechnologie, 2000
Karlsruhe, Germany

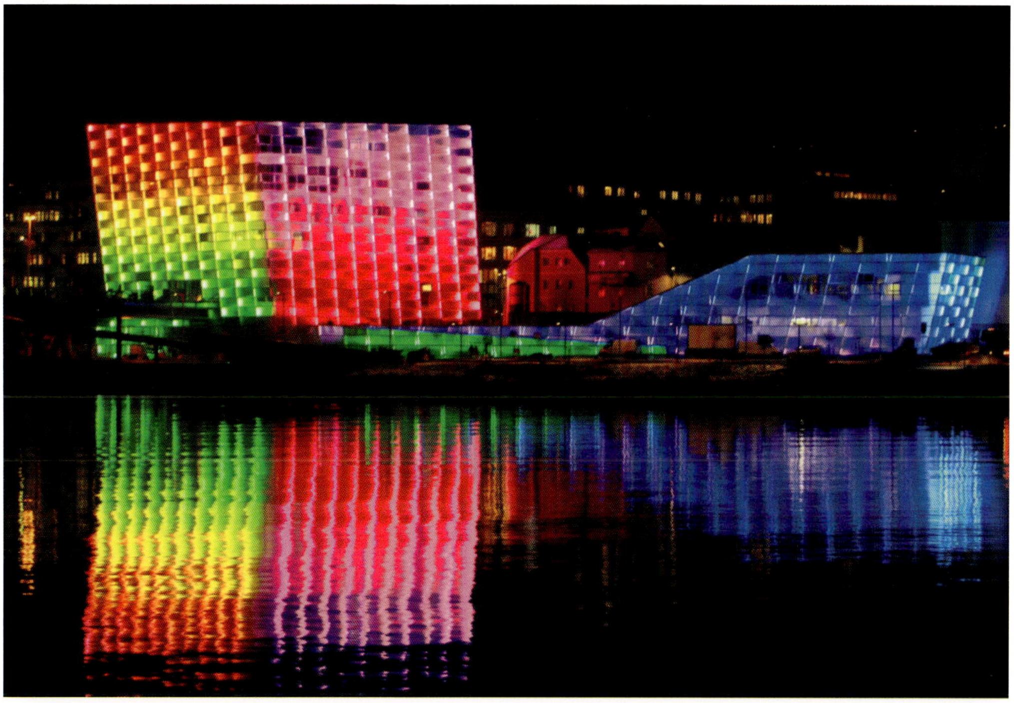

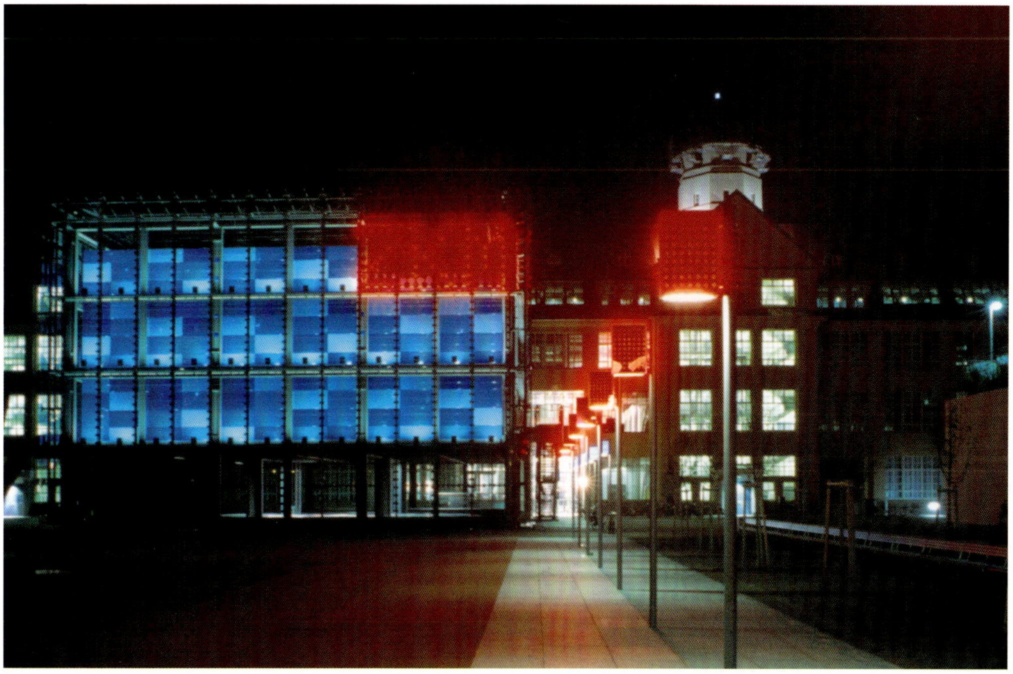

acter, it will be understood that this is not so much an example of New Media Art as a radical work of identity construction and manipulation, taking up the investigations of Cindy Sherman and developing their underlying assumptions in the age of the digital alter ego.[32]

The media as subject

At the same time, I believe that New Media Art – like certain works of Video Art in its day, from Nam June Paik's *McLuhan Caged* (1967) to Dara Birnbaum's *Technology / Transformation: Wonder Woman* (1978) – has brought to light an aspect of formalism that it still makes sense to explore even in a post-medium age. I refer to the possibility of using a medium in order to speak about the medium or media in general; in other words, to transform the medium into subject. The fact is that the media, and the digital media in particular, are not neutral channels for transmitting a message but produce a culture of their own, convey a specific ideology, and condition our life. In one way or another, they interfere with the signal. They are, as we have already pointed out, a constant presence, sometimes so

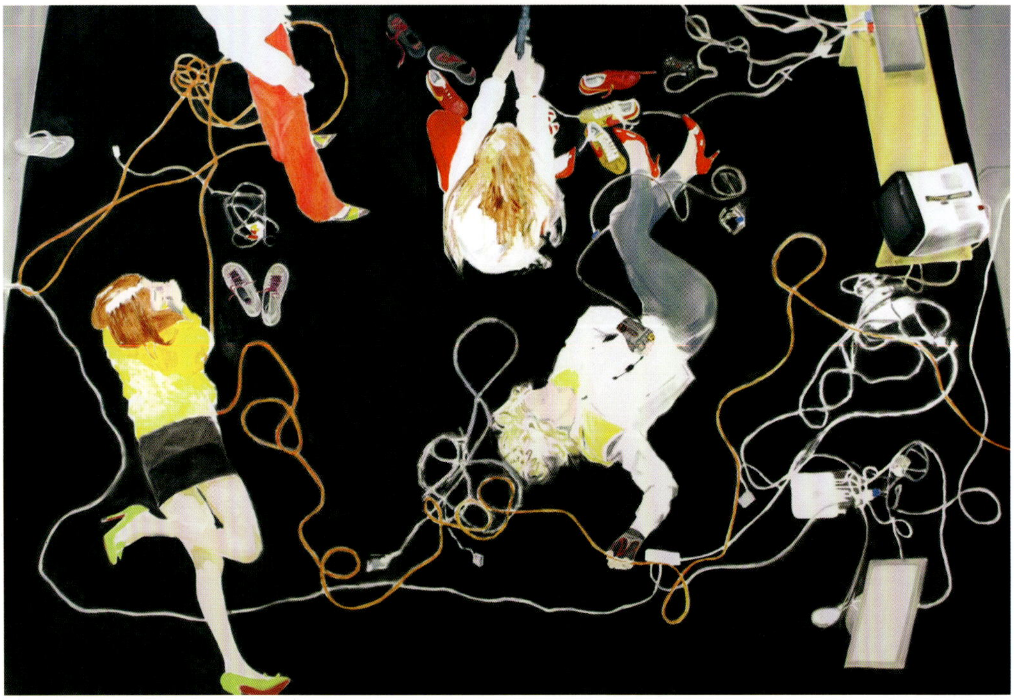

Miltos Manetas
Nikescape, 2005
Oil on canvas, 200 x 300 cm
Dakis Joannou Collection

deeply rooted as to prove invisible. Talking about them and highlighting some of their less known aspects is another way of talking about mankind and our present. And this is destined to become one of the great themes of the art in the near future, unless we fall into a phase of technological regression.

Addressing tools now in everyone's hands, what was formerly known as New Media Art insisted strongly on this approach at the turn of the millennium. A good example is provided by the Jodi duo, who have been developing work of unusual rigor based on subverting the media adopted – from the Internet to e-mail and videogames – since the 1990s. The aim of this subversion is not only to assert a now clearly recognizable abstract aesthetic, but also to strike at the media in their sociopolitical aspects: standardization of the Internet as suppression of its open and democratic nature; the banality of communications; the violence of videogames as a tool of control. In much the same way, the American artist Cory Arcangel often appropriates obsolete technologies and causes them to depart from their conventional functions, thus seeking to "fill a gap in the history of technology and culture"[33] by negatively highlighting the limitations introduced by the commercial standardization of a given device.

If criticism is to follow art along this path, it will in turn clearly have to make up a technological gap that strongly limits its development and improve its understanding of media studies at the same time. In other words, the move beyond the perspective of New Media Art also requires an effort of appropriation on the part of critics of contemporary art that very few have made so far.

[1] M. Castells, *The Information Age: Economy, Society and Culture* (Cambridge [Mass.], Oxford [UK]: Blackwell 1996–98), 3 vols.
[2] J. Rifkin, *The Age of Access: How the Shift from Ownership to Access Is Transforming Capitalism* (New York: Tarcher 2000).
[3] N. Negroponte, *Being Digital* (New York: Vintage 1996).
[4] C. Gere, *Digital Culture* (London: Reaktion Books 2008) p. 9.
[5] In a seminal report to the French president written in 1978 and published in 1980: S. Nora, A. Minc, *Computerization of Society: a Report to the President of France* (Cambridge [Mass.]: MIT Press, 1980).
[6] C. Gere, *op. cit.*, p. 7.
[7] While this subject is still in need of thorough examination, a few interesting observations in this connection are to be found in J. Stallabrass, *Art Incorporated. The Story of Contemporary Art* (Oxford [UK], New York: OUP 2004).
[8] For a historical overview of the artistic use of the new media that is not confined to the digital sphere, see M. Rush, *New Media in Late 20th-Century Art* (London: Thames & Hudson 1999 [2001]). A wealth of information is also provided by E. Shanken, *Art and Electronic Media* (London: Phaidon Press 2009).
[9] P.M. Lee, 'Economies of Scale,' in *Artforum*, XLVI, no. 2 (October 2007), pp. 337–43.
[10] F. Bonami, *Lo potevo fare anch'io. Perché l'arte contemporanea è davvero arte* (Milan: Mondadori 2007), p. 24.
[11] R. Krauss, *A Voyage on the North Sea. Art in the Age of the Post-Medium Condition* (London: Thames & Hudson 1999).

[12] Clement Greenberg, 'Modernist Painting', in *Forum Lectures*, Voice of America, Washington, D.C. 1960; F. Frascina, C. Harrison (eds.), *Modern Art and Modernism: A Critical Anthology* (New York: Harper & Row 1982).

[13] R. Krauss, *A Voyage in the North Sea...* cit., p. 19.

[14] Ibid., p. 32.

[15] N. Bourriaud, *Post Production. La culture comme scénario: comment l'art reprogramme le monde contemporain* (Dijon: Les Presses du Réel 2004).

[16] See M. McLuhan, *Understanding Media* (New York: McGraw Hill 1964).

[17] D. Antin, 'Video: The Distinctive Features of the Medium,' in I. Schneider, B. Korot (eds.), *Video Art* (New York: Harcourt Brace Jovanovich 1976), p. 174.

[18] R. Krauss, 'Video: The Aesthetics of Narcissism,' in *October*, vol. 1 (spring 1976), pp. 50–64.

[19] Cf. D.A. Ross, 'The History Remains Provisional,' in I. Gianelli, M. Beccaria (eds.), *Video Art. The Castello di Rivoli Collection* (Milan: Skira 2005), pp. 1–17.

[20] Cf. *XLII Esposizione Internazionale d'Arte La Biennale di Venezia. Arte e scienza. Biologia / Tecnologia e informatica*, exh. cat. (Milan: Electa 1986).

[21] It should be noted in this connection that no mention of New Media Art is to be found in the recent work H. Foster, R. Krauss, Y.-A. Bois, B.H.D. Buchloh, *Art since 1900. Modernism, Antimodernism, Postmodernism* (London: Thames & Hudson 2004).

[22] We are not alone in this. Andreas Broeckmann, director for many years of Berlin's Trasmedia festival, recently wrote as follows: "For an earlier generation of artists, it was a decisive step to 'go digital', or not. Entire artistic careers were ruined by the stigma of doing 'art with a plug'. (Other careers were made by the exclusivity which that stigma offered in certain circles.)" In A. Broeckmann [ed.], *Deep Screen. Art in Digital Culture*, exh. cat. (Amsterdam, Stedelijk Museum, May 30–September 30, 2008) (Amsterdam: Stedelijk Museum 2008), pp. 154–55.

[23] This dissatisfaction with the term "New Media Art" can be detected among other things in many of the articles in D. Quaranta, Y. Bernard (eds.), *Holy Fire. Art of the Digital Age* (Brescia: FPEditions 2008).

[24] The work in question is *Vote-Auction*, available online at www.vote-auction.net. For further information, see D. Quaranta (ed.), *UBERMORGEN.COM* (Brescia: FPEditions 2009).

[25] The crisis of New Media Art and its fate is discussed at length by Geert Lovink in *Zero Comments, Blogging and Critical Internet Culture* (New York: Routledge 2007).

[26] See J. Hauser (ed.), *L'Art Biotech* (Nantes: Le Lieu Unique 2003).

[27] See http://www.symbiotica.uwa.edu.au/welcome/about_us. Link consulted on April 5, 2009.

[28] In *Portrait of the Artist as a Hard Disk. Data nudism, abstract pornography, online voyeurism. Excerpts from interviews with 0100101110101101.ORG on Life Sharing*, 2000–2003. Available online at http://www.0100101110101101.org/home/life_sharing/interview.html.

[29] I have borrowed for this section the title of an exhibition curated by Sarah Cook and Steve Dietz for the Walter Phillips Gallery September–October 2005. See http://www.banffcentre.ca/wpg/exhibitions/2005/formerly/.

[30] See *Miltos Manetas. Paintings from Contemporary Life* (Milan: Johan & Levi 2008).

[31] On the relationship between Casey Reas and Sol LeWitt, see C. Reas, 'Software and Drawing,' in *Software Structures*, June 2004, available online at http://artport.whitney.org/commissions/softwarestructures/text.html.

[32] See D. Quaranta (ed.), *Gazira Babeli*, FPEditions, Brescia 2008.

[33] D. Birnbaum, C. Arcangel, 'In conversation: Dara Birnbaum and Cory Arcangel,' in *Artforum*, March 2009, pp. 190–99.

Cory Arcangel

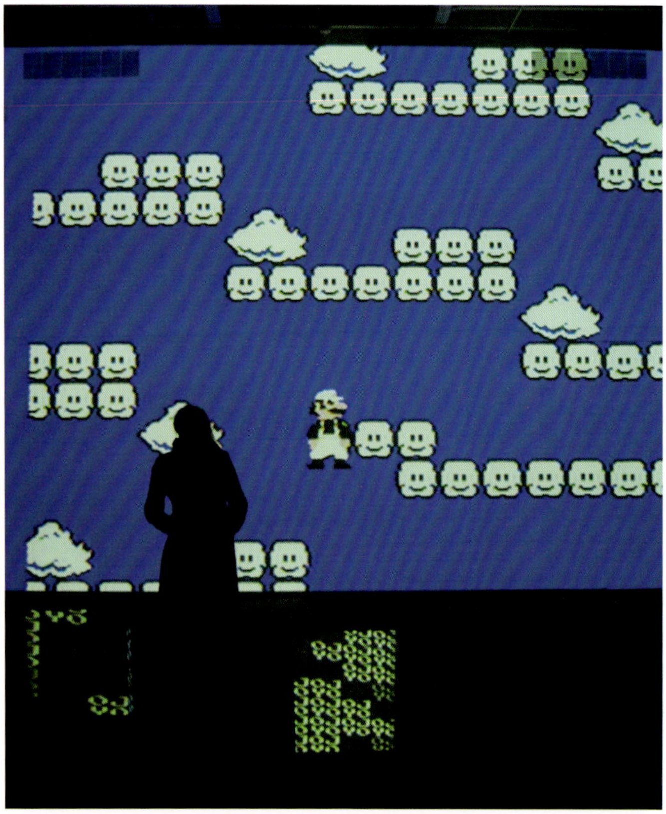

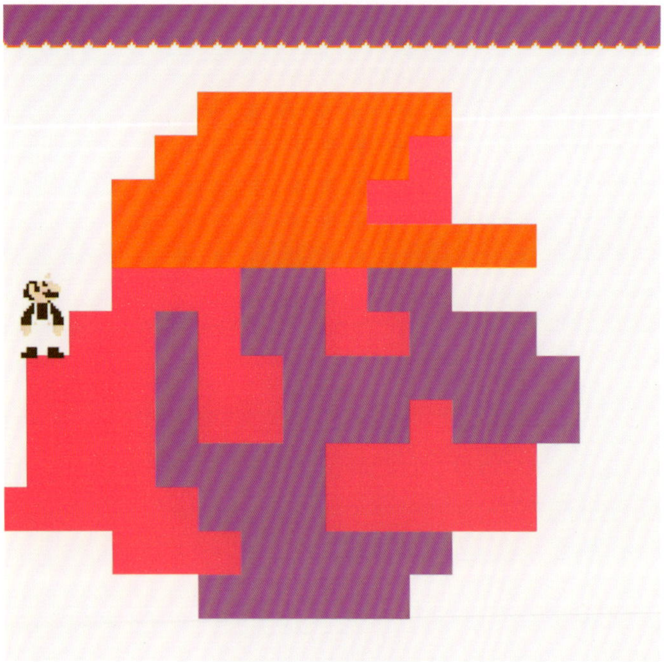

Born in Buffalo, New York, in 1978. Lives and works in New York.
The Deitch Projects gallery in New York presented a show of work by young artists in January 2005. The poster featured a psychedelic reworking of the images contained in a Nintendo cartridge of 1984, including the figure of Super Mario, the legendary plumber that embodied an entire generation's dream of social status and success. The gallery was lined with code print-outs and notes, and the visionary video projected showed Mario plunge into a disintegrating world of alternating fragments of code, brightly colored blocks of pixels, and smiling clouds, all to the accompaniment of a bouncy soundtrack played relentlessly on a Gameboy. The artists were Cory Arcangel, who created the video by reprogramming the game cartridge, and the Paperrad collective, both already cult figures on the Net but as yet unknown to the world of art.
Arcangel is both a musician and a hacker with a passionate interest in programming and obsolete technologies. *Super Mario Movie* (2004) is the result of prolonged work on the manipulation of old videogames and platforms to produce music and videos. *Super Mario Clouds* (2002) is a Mario cartridge from which everything has been erased but the clouds, which drift uninterruptedly from left to right across a blue sky. *I Shot Andy Warhol* (2002) presents Andy Warhol as a target to be shot with a toy gun in a modified version of an old shooting game. *Super Slow Tetris* (2004) is precisely that, a version of the game slowed down so much that it loses any element of play to become a simple object of contemplation. Similarities can be traced here with other celebrated operations of appropriation and post-production, such as Douglas Gordon's *24 Hour Psycho*.
This appropriation of old and new media, making them do things for which they were not designed or eliminating certain elements, has expanded over the years to encompass other objects such as old LPs, video clips, and rock music. *Data Diaries* (2002) is an online work created by tricking Quicktime into thinking that a certain text file is a video. In *Personal Film* (2008) Arcangel transferred onto film a video created simply by using the disturbance filter of a video production program in a sort of ironic remake of Nam June Paik's classic work *Zen For Film* (1964). With irony and a light touch, Arcangel rewrites the destiny of the technologies inhabiting our crowded mass-media panorama and probes the possibilities of their dysfunctional use.
(*D.Q.*)

Super Mario Movie, 2004
with Paper Rad
Handmade "bootleg" Nintendo video game
View of the installation (and still) realized in 2005 at Deitch Projects, New York
Courtesy of the artist and Team Gallery, New York

Colors, 2005
Digital work on Mini-Mac, dimensions variable
Courtesy Team Gallery, New York

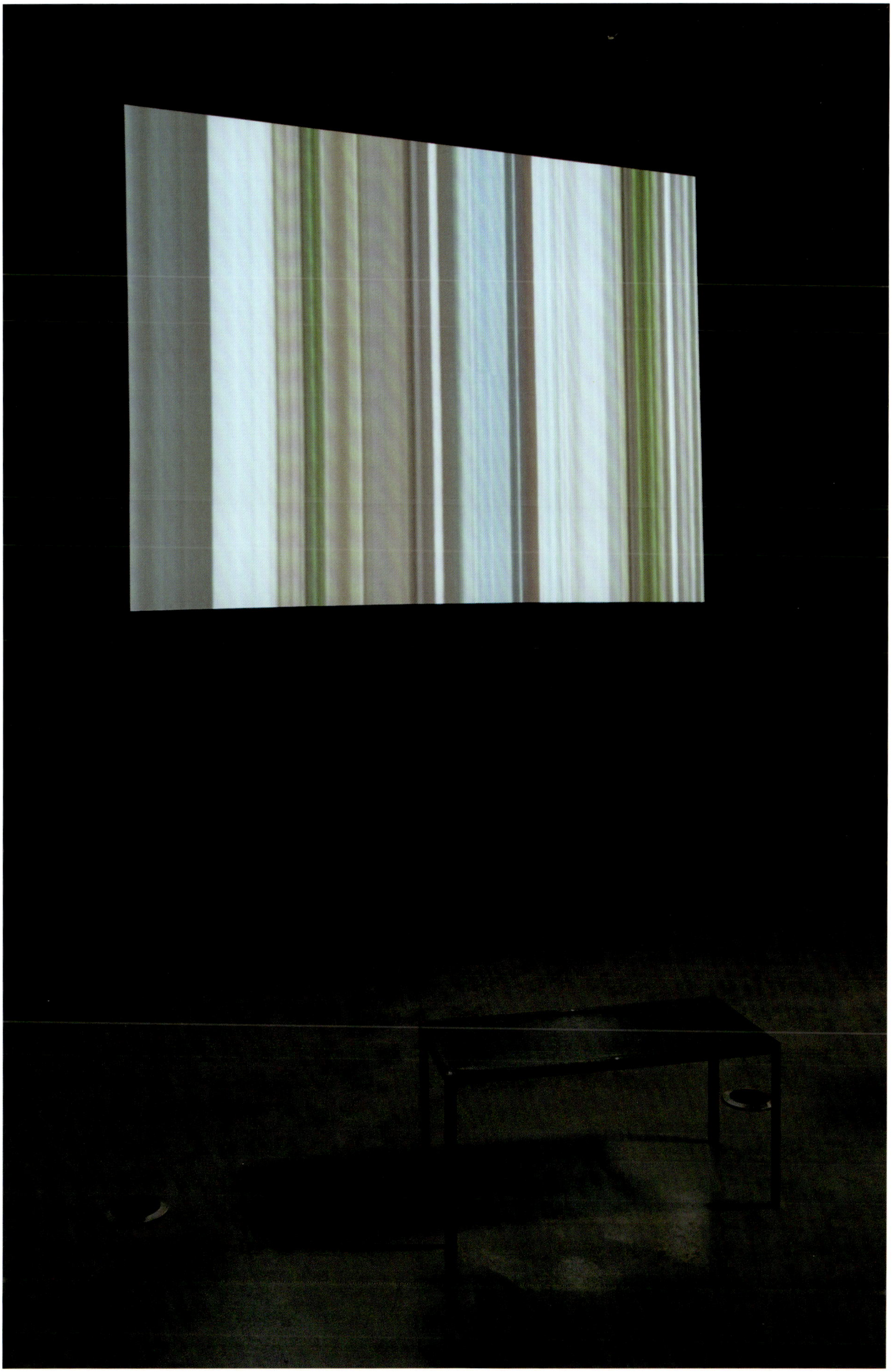

Cao Fei

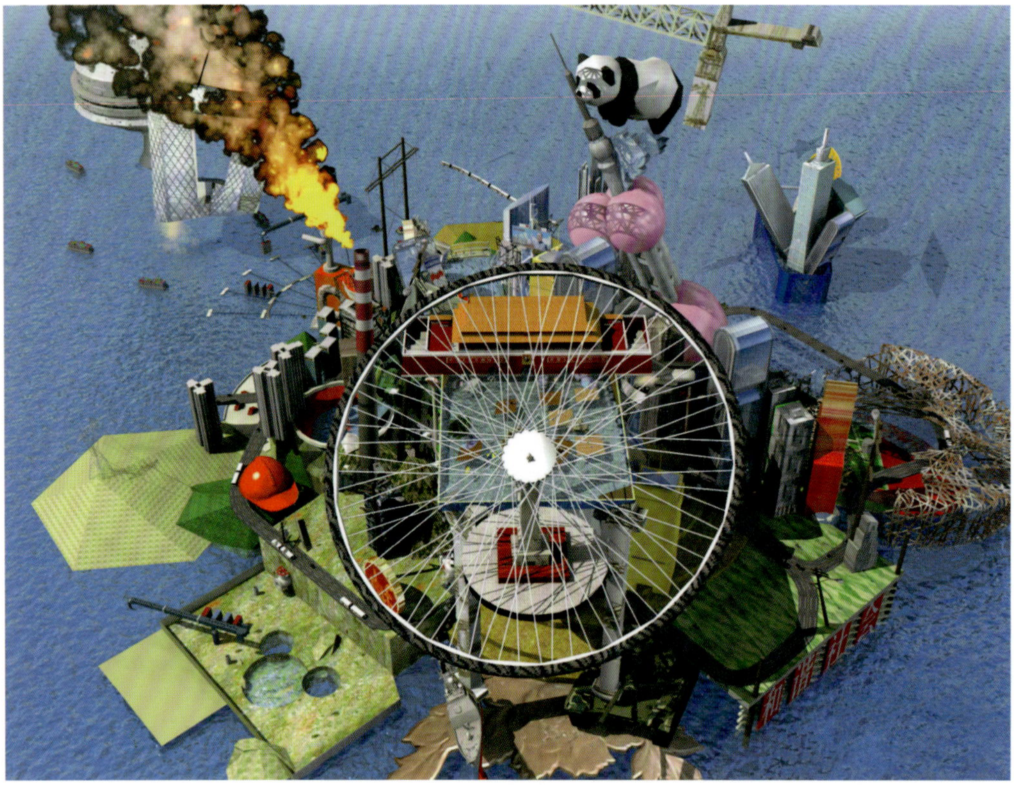

RMB CITY 5, 2007
Digital color print, 120 x 160 cm
Courtesy of the artist and
Lombard-Freid Projects, New York

A Mirage (COSPlayers Series), 2004
Digital color print, 74.3 x 99.7 cm
Courtesy of the artist and
Lombard-Freid Projects, New York

Born in Guangzhou, China, in 1978. Lives and works in Guangzhou.
Cao Fei is one of the most interesting representatives of the new wave of Chinese artists.
As pointed out by the curator Hou Hanru, this is a generation that grew up in a world of electronic advertising and entertainment imported not only from the West but also from nearby countries like Japan and Taiwan. With its kitsch and in some cases practically trash aesthetic, it is this culture that constitutes an essential point of reference for Cao Fei's work, which focuses in particular on the range of juvenile subcultures from hip-hop to cosplay. The artist's purpose is, however, neither to attack nor to celebrate popular culture and tastes in the forms adopted first by Pop Art and later by Jeff Koons and Takashi Murakami. On the contrary, while displaying subtle solidarity with the subcultures, her work seeks to examine the underlying motives, the escapism, and the need to assert themselves socially that drive young people to embrace certain cultural phenomena.
The narrative approach of Cao Fei, who wrote screenplays as a teenager, is expressed primarily through performance and video followed by photography and installation. The video *Rabid Dogs* (2002) shows a group of young Chinese office workers who rebel in ironic and grotesque forms against the poverty and bestiality of a life in which people obey like tame dogs without barking.
COSPlayers (2004), the artist's best-known work, is a project made up of a video and various series of prints. Cosplay, short for costume role-play, involves dressing up as characters from Japanese anime or videogames and using the urban space as a stage to reenact or invent scenes featuring them, a sort of fantasy escapism seen as the only possible form of rebellion.
Cao Fei's video shows the life of a group of Chinese cosplayers, who transform the urban outskirts into unreal scenarios with their performances before returning in costume to their depressing everyday life. In much the same way, Fei addresses hip-hop in various works as the "happiness of the unhappy", "music which humorously expresses negative energy." Presented at the 2007 Venice Biennale, the installation *China Tracy Pavilion* developed at the same time in the real world and the virtual space of Second Life. This celebrated virtual world is for Fei a place for the expansion and enrichment of subjectivity and the construction of an elsewhere in which the contradictions of reality can be overcome or taken to their extreme consequences.
(*D.Q.*)

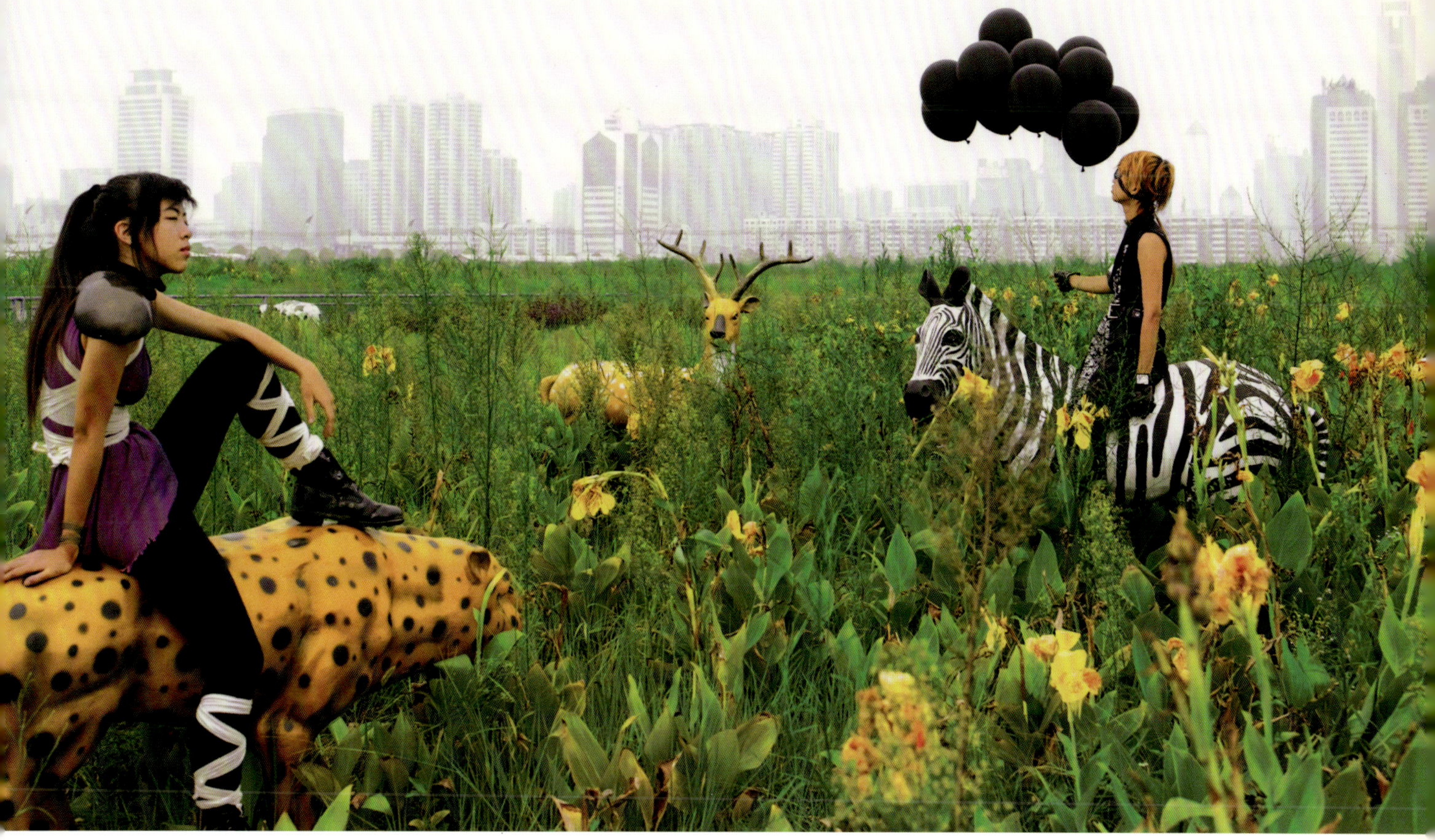

Roberto Cuoghi

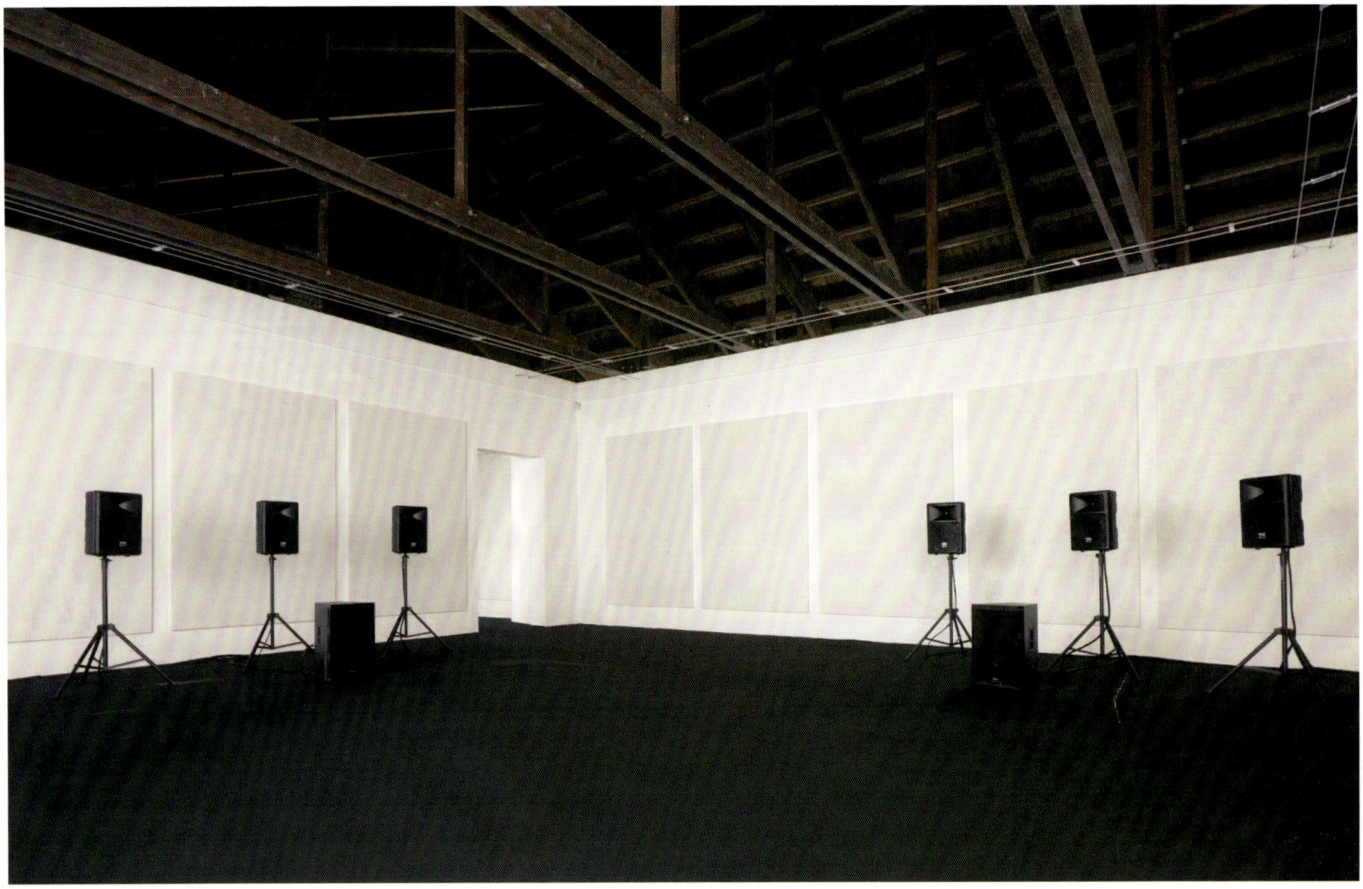

Born in Modena, Italy, in 1973. Lives and works in Milan.
Music and the relations between the worlds of human life and sound are the focal point of the investigations of Roberto Cuoghi. The two solo shows held in 2008 at the Castello di Rivoli and the Institute of Contemporary Arts in London to explore the themes of identity and the inherent meaning of ritual practices both featured *Šuillakku*, a sculptural and sound installation characterized by meticulous scholarly research.
The fulcrum of the work is the demon Pazuzu, a divinity of the Assyrian religion, whose image has been reconstructed on the basis of a statuette in the Louvre. Cuoghi used this to create a large-scale sculpture accompanied by a monumental sound installation reconstructing the ritual lamentations performed by the Assyrian people during religious ceremonies.
The artist studied the language and the instruments of the period in order to achieve an accurate reconstruction of the religious music and hymns. His own voice expresses the entreaties of the believers and his hands crafted the musical instrument capable of summoning up Pazuzu. Attention to historical research and analysis of the role of collective participation and the course of an individual creation are instead the basis of *Mbube*, a piece sung and played by the artist with improvised instruments.
In this case, Cuoghi tells the tale of the song and its fame through its performance. Originally composed by the South African Solomon Linda, it became known throughout the world twenty years later under the title *The Lion Sleeps Tonight*, when the artist had sold the rights for next to nothing.
Cuoghi's work thus addresses the sense of belonging and spread of expressive language through the concepts of freedom and variation, focusing on the human need to rework the creative product for the purposes of appropriation. Like *Mbube*, the lamentation addressed to Pazuzu can in fact manifest itself in the present only through revision prompted by different – but not thereby less significant – motivations.
(*F.T.*)

Šuillakku, 2008
Amplifiers and sound, dimensions variable
Rivoli, Castello di Rivoli – Museo d'Arte Contemporanea, permanent deposit Fondazione CRT Progetto Arte Moderna e Contemporanea

Mbube, 2005
Composition for voice and instruments, 3', dimensions variable
Rivoli, Castello di Rivoli – Museo d'Arte Contemporanea, purchased with contributions by the Compagnia di San Paolo

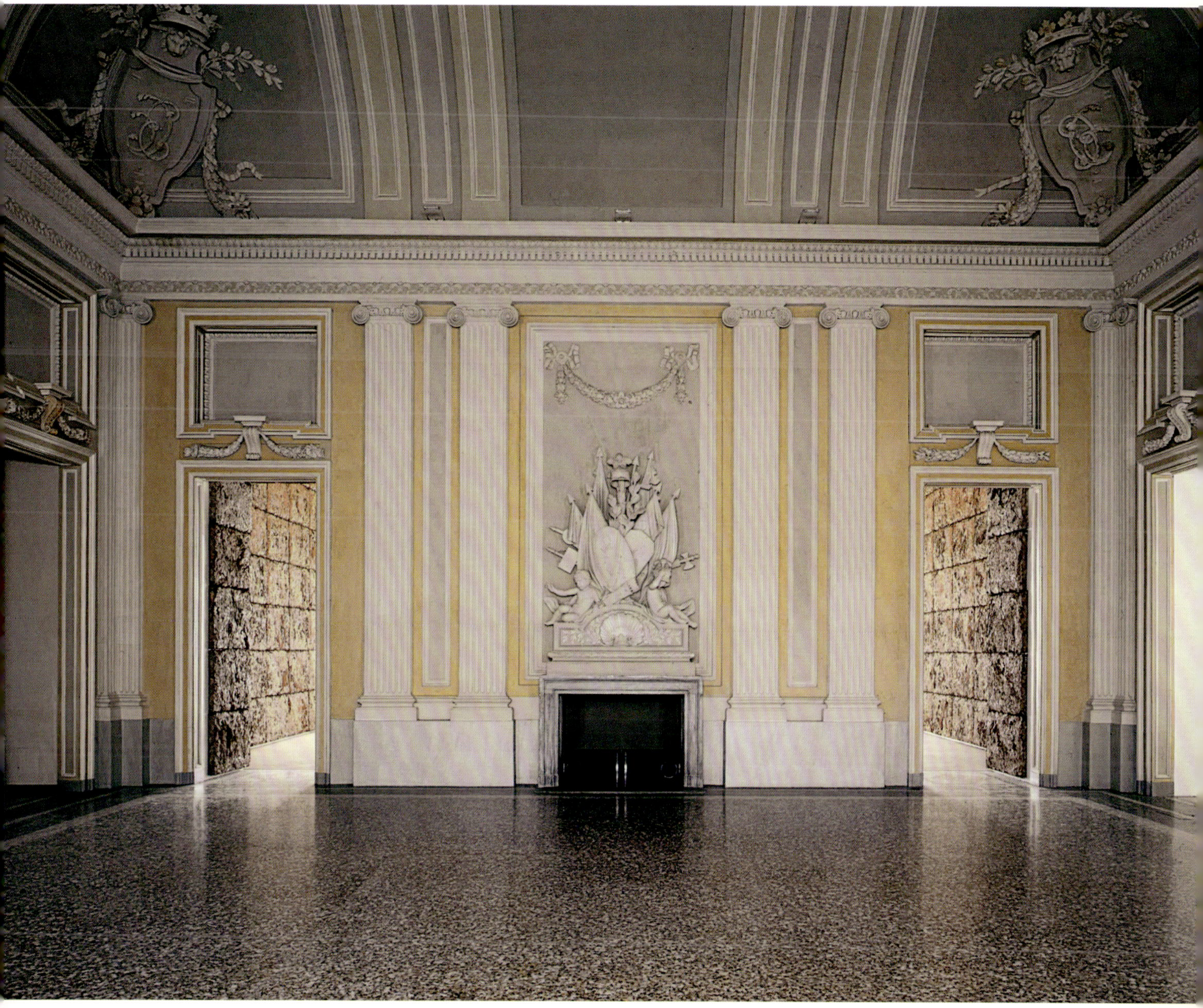

Douglas Gordon

Pretty much every film and video work from about 1992 until now. T o be seen on monitors, some with headphones, others run silently, and all simultaneously, 1992–2006

Televisions and videos, dimensions variable
Courtesy Gagosian Gallery, New York

Born in Glasgow, UK, in 1966. Lives and works in Glasgow and Berlin.
It is precisely the use of words, photographic images, and film sequences, practically all of which are readymade, that distinguishes and defines the work of Douglas Gordon, unquestionably one of the leading figures in the new field of British art involving multimedia technologies.
Gordon is known above all for his 24-hour version of Alfred Hitchcock's masterpiece *Psycho*, a work that the artist described as a "temporal readymade", obtained by applying slow motion to the point of producing a hypnotic effect and disintegrating the storyline to highlight only the film's sophisticated formal qualities (*24-Hour Psycho*, 1993). Gordon never works through direct manipulation – by digital, physical or mechanical alteration of the support – of the images or films used but confines himself rather to sampling in accordance with the readymade philosophy. He does, however, make great use of "special effects" (slow motion, splitting, repetition, and the assemblage of pieces from different films) to transform the images of his video projections into mental visions, elements surfacing in the personal and collective memory. The artist works in fact as a sort of explorer of the psyche, displaying an interest above all in stories featuring characters with split personalities. It is no coincidence that in addition to *Psycho*, the best-known film on schizophrenia, Gordon has worked among other things on films like *Dr Jekyll and Mr Hyde*, projecting sequences respectively in positive and negative on two large screens placed side by side (*Confessions of a Justified Sinner*, 1996) and the celebrated scene from Martin Scorsese's *Taxi Driver* in which Robert De Niro practices in front of a mirror for the showdown with his adversary (*Through a Looking Glass*, 1999). Gordon's predilection for disturbing subjects and existential dichotomies (life and death, good and evil, guilt and innocence) finds its most congenial form of expression in duality (light and darkness, positive and negative,

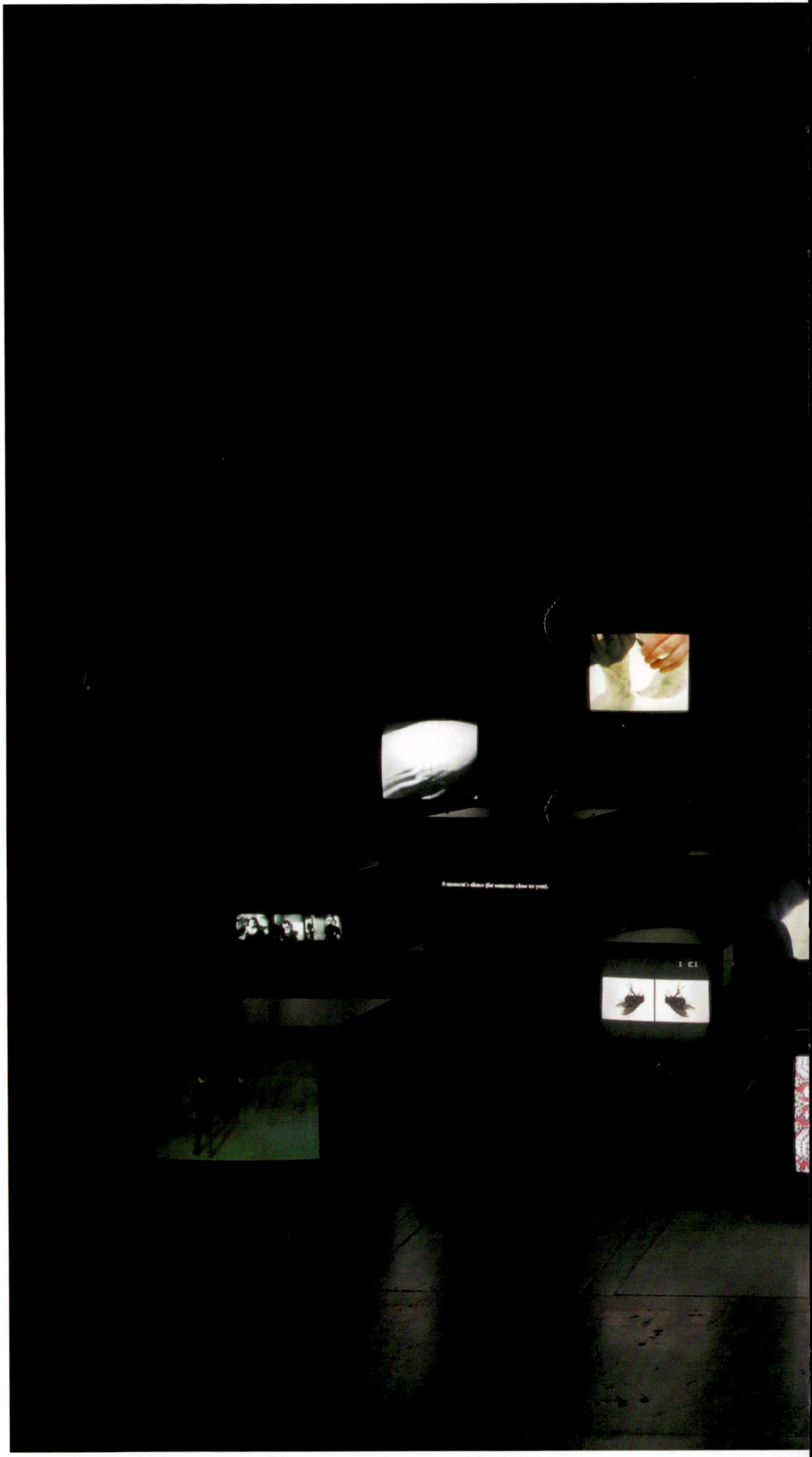

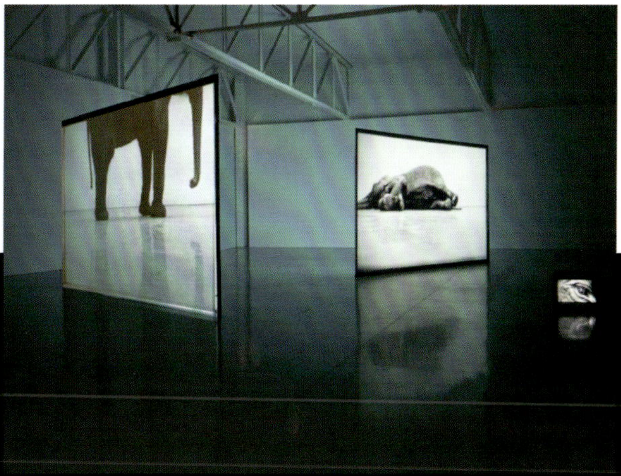

Play Dead Real Time, 2003
Screens, projectors,
dimensions variable
Courtesy Gagosian Gallery,
New York

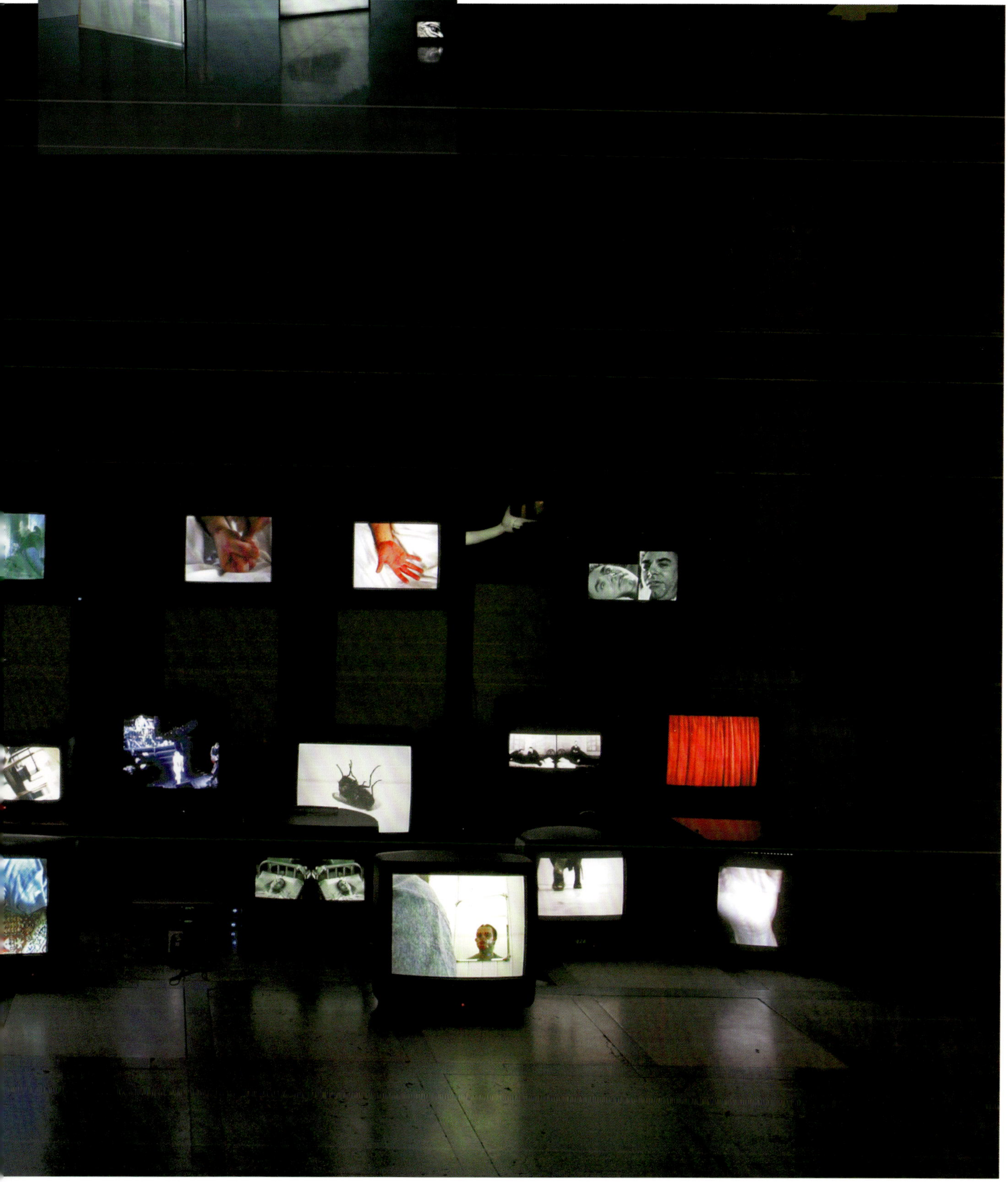

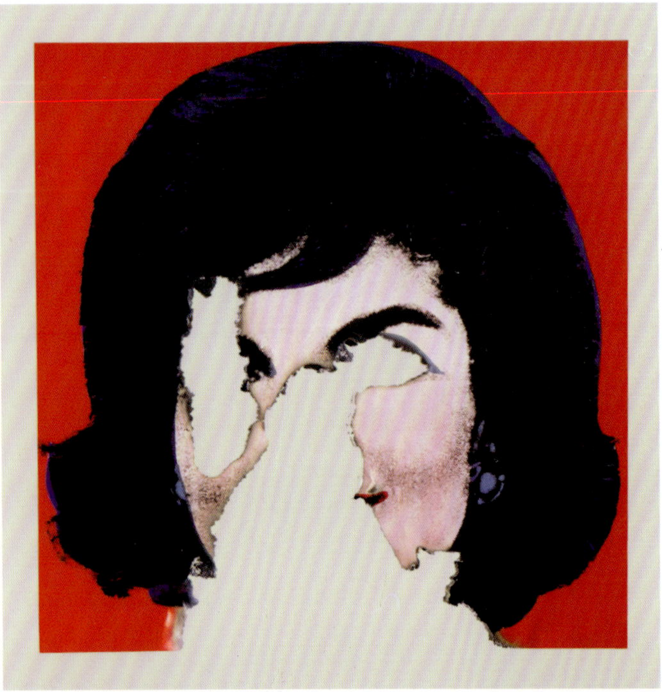

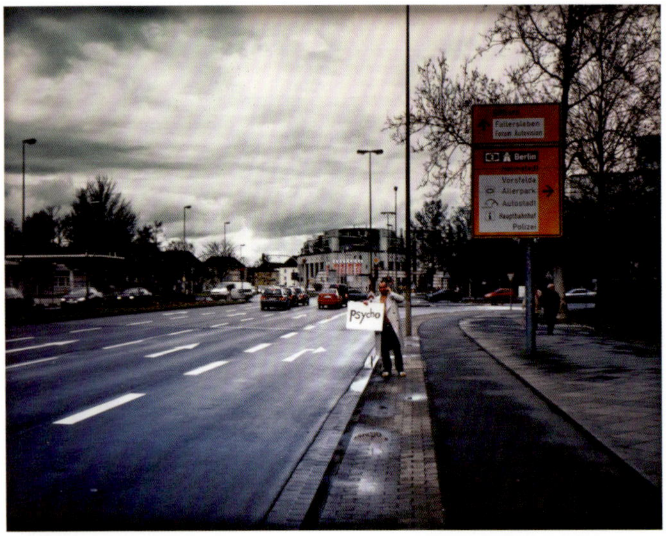

Self-portrait of You + Me (Jackie), 2007
Mixed media, 111.8 x 111.8 cm
Courtesy Gagosian Gallery, New York

Psycho Hitchhiker (Coming or Going), 2007
Lambda print, 46 x 59.6 cm
Courtesy Gagosian Gallery, New York

Prettymucheverywordwritten, spoken, heard, overheard from 1989, 2006
Panels and adhesive letters, dimensions variable
View of the installation realized in 2006 at the Mart – Museo di Arte Moderna e Contemporanea di Trento e Rovereto, Rovereto

reality and fiction) and the formal devices best able to convey the idea of a split personality, such as projection on two screens and mirror images. It is precisely the latter that plays a key part in *Left is Right and Right is Wrong and Left is Wrong and Right is Right* (1999), a two-part video installation where frames from Otto Preminger's film *Whirlpool* are projected side by side in their original orientation and a mirrored version. The title chosen by Gordon is in turn indicative of his interest in another field richly endowed with duality and ambivalence, namely language. In this case the entire sequence of words is based on the two meanings of the term *right*, which can also take on political connotations when combined with *left*. In other cases, Gordon probes the possible rifts between signifier and signified or the capacity of "decontextualized" words to act as authentic Duchampian readymades and confound expectations, as in the performance *Psycho Hitchhiker (Coming or Going)*, created in connection with the anthological exhibition of 2007 in Wolfsburg, Germany, when he transformed himself into a disturbing hitcher bound for the equally disquieting setting of *Psycho*.
Further confirmation of the importance attached to language and written communication in Gordon's work is provided by the installation he created for the solo show of 2006 at the MART in Rovereto, Italy, namely *Prettymucheverywordwritten, spoken, heard...*, which covered the walls of the museum with the Italian translations of just about all the phrases, thoughts, and writings produced by Douglas in the course of his career and presented as autonomous works of art.
The show at the MART also included the two-screen video installation *Play Dead Real Time*, presented for the first time in 2003 at the Gagosian Gallery, New York, a work in which time appears to be slowed down due to the slowness of the movements of a circus elephant playing dead in a completely white space. Gordon filmed the scene with a camera rotating through 360°, thus altering the perception of spatiotemporal relations still further and making the heavy animal appear unusually light and graceful. In this work, however, the elephant also performs a metaphorical function as symbolizing the memory of a condition different from that of captivity. Gordon thus ventures into the territory of other dichotomies such as obedience and free will, rule and instinct, enslavement and freedom.
Dichotomies, splits, allegories, and ambivalence of meaning also characterize the series of *Self-portraits of You and Me*, in which the artist addresses the maxim "We need stars so as to mirror ourselves in them", by printing pieces of images of famous characters in the world of show business on reflecting surfaces so that viewers standing in front of the work will find themselves broken up and merged with pieces of famous faces and bodies (*Self-portrait of You and Me [Elvis]*, 2007). In a certain sense, these self-portraits with no subject – or perhaps with a random and multiple subject – encapsulate the vision informing Gordon's work as a whole, which he summarizes as follows: "My work is more about researching, about memory, about stories that happened, films I saw ... I'm interested in finding out what happens when you look at something so long it disappears. You look at a picture, you start looking through the picture and you get to the other side – and then you go back to the front view."
(*P.V.*)

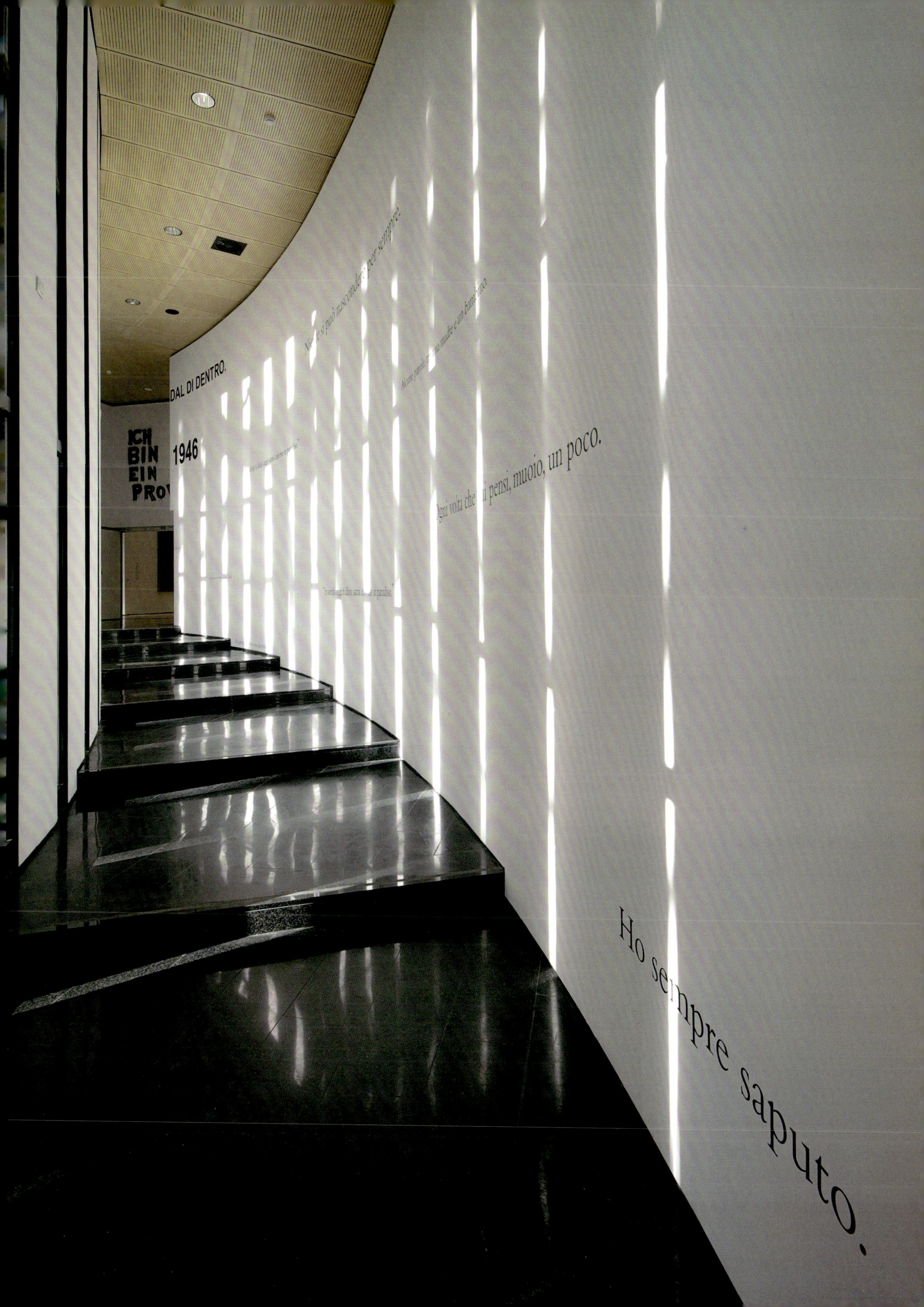

DAL DI DENTRO.
1946
Ogni volta che ci pensi, muoio, un poco.
Ho sempre saputo.

Loris Gréaud

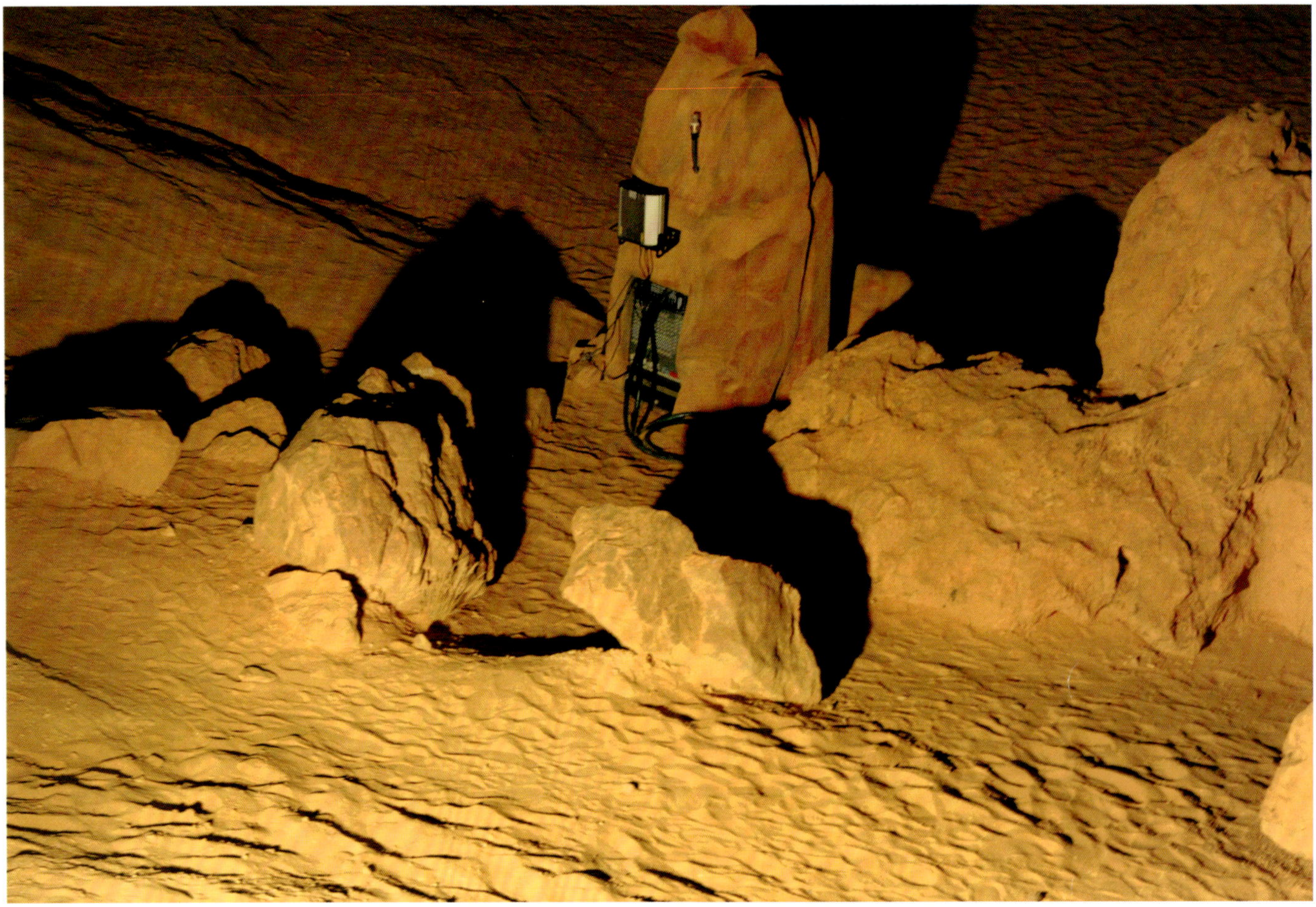

Born in Eaubonne, France, in 1979. Lives and works in Paris.
Most of Gréaud's works show the influence of his multidisciplinary background in a highly creative approach to the vocabularies of the graphic arts, architecture, music, and cinema. The electronic medium is the combinatory module constituting the nucleus of the artist's projects and encapsulating his different forms of creative expression.
This multidisciplinary alliance is exemplified by *Cellar Door*, a project commissioned in 2006 and presented in 2008 at the Palais de Tokyo in Paris and the Institute of Contemporary Arts in London: a space midway between the physical world and the mental sphere; the artist's studio understood as a place of creation but also of obsession.
Cellar Door comprises the creation of an architectural structure, the temporal duration of the exhibition, and the writing of the libretto that constitutes its vital sound element. The artist's intention was to produce a relationship of equivalence between these elements, namely the time of the exhibition, the structure, the musical score, and the text.
The architects Marc Dölger and Damien Ziakovic, the musician Sierra Casady, and the composer Thomas Roussel were involved in the project and the libretto was written by Raimundas Malasauskas and Aaron Schuster.
A relationship of continuity and cosmogonic connection between elements is the focus of *Bucky*, a video shot in 2007 and exhibited in Italy at the Turin Triennale of 2008. This is the transposition onto film of part of a libretto by Gréaud featuring the character Bucky Wonka, an imaginary combination of the architect Buckminster Fuller and the chocolate maker Willy Wonka from the novel by Roald Dahl. The video instead shows the formation of a solid geometric figure out of the union of nine stars bought and identified by the artist on the celestial map. A voice off-camera indicates their location, and the shape generated by drawing lines between the nine stars recalls the American architect's geodetic domes.
(*F.T.*)

Bucky, 2007–2008
16 mm film on hard disk, LCD screen, wood, 111.8 x 111.8 cm
Courtesy Gréaud Studio and Yvon Lambert, Paris

Spore Speakers, 2008
Resin, black silicone, light bulbs, loudspeakers, dimensions variable
Venice, François Pinault Collection
Courtesy Gréaud Studio and Yvon Lambert, Paris

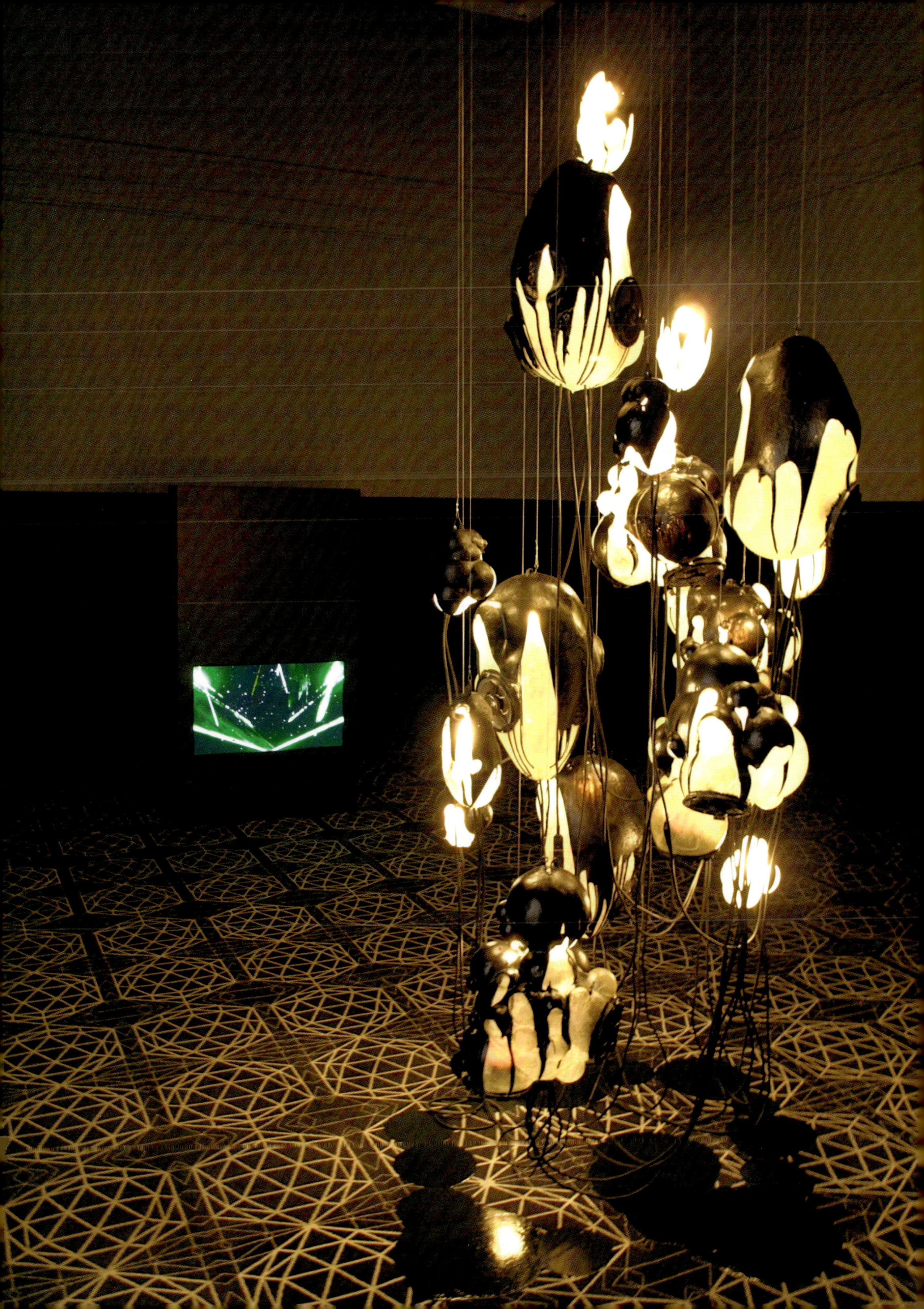

Pierre Huyghe

Born in Paris in 1962. Lives and works in New York and Paris.
Pierre Huyghe has always been interested in investigating the way in which a story takes shape through the person telling it. This is one of the reasons that prompted him to develop the project *No Ghost, Just a Shell* together with Philippe Parreno. The two artists bought a female character by mail order from a specialized Japanese animation company, named her Ann Lee and made her the main character of two different multimedia works, inviting Liam Gillick, Rirkrit Tiravanija, Dominique Gonzalez-Foerster and other colleagues to do likewise at the same time. As Huyghe explained, the initial idea was to liberate a sign (which is exactly what Ann Lee is) from the constraint of copyright and give it the opportunity of coming to life in the stories offered by other people. In the film created by Huyghe, entitled *One Million Kingdoms* (2001) and based on a story drawing freely on Jules Verne's *Journey to the Center of the Earth* and the first moon landings, Ann Lee has the voice of an American girl the artist met and interviewed in Paris. The problem of the rights of the person placing his or her voice at the service of an animated character and thus contributing to the construction of its identity is also addressed by Huyghe in the short film *Blanche Neige Lucie* (1997), the story of the French dubber Lucie Dolène, who filed a suit against the Walt Disney Corporation precisely for its failure to acknowledge her rights for the use of her voice.
Huyghe had already addressed the importance of dubbing as a way of "giving shape" to a story in *Dubbing* (1996), a 120-minute video about a group of dubbers lending their voices to the characters of a film, no image of which is actually seen.
The issues regarding the relationship between the story and the teller and in particular the dualism created between the people involved in real events and those who come for different reasons to perform them, thus transforming them into fiction, return in *The Third Memory* (1999), a complex work about the possible overlapping of true and fictitious stories. Extracts from Sydney Lumet's famous film *Dog Day Afternoon* (1975), inspired by a celebrated bank robbery in Brooklyn by John Wojtowicz, brilliantly played in the film by Al Pacino, are combined with a video in which Wojtowicz gives his own version of the events and accuses the director of "stealing" his story. The problem of "copyright" thus resurfaces, albeit indirectly, interwoven here with the desire to tell the tale shared by the person involved in the real event, the filmmaker who used it as the basis of his story, and the reporters of the time, who were called upon to provide a supposedly objective reconstruction of what happened. The work accordingly includes various documentary materials, both filmed and printed, making it possible to relive the dramatic event through the news reports of the day.
Alongside the question of the manifold relations involved in the act of telling a story, Huyghe is also fascinated by the psychological, social and political relations linking the individual to the natural environment and the constructed space of architecture. The eight-minute video loop *Les Grands Ensembles* (1994–2001) shows two blocks of public housing on the outskirts of Paris that gradually lose their connotations as really existing buildings and turn into abstract objects as the lights in their windows turn rhythmically on and off to the backing of a techno

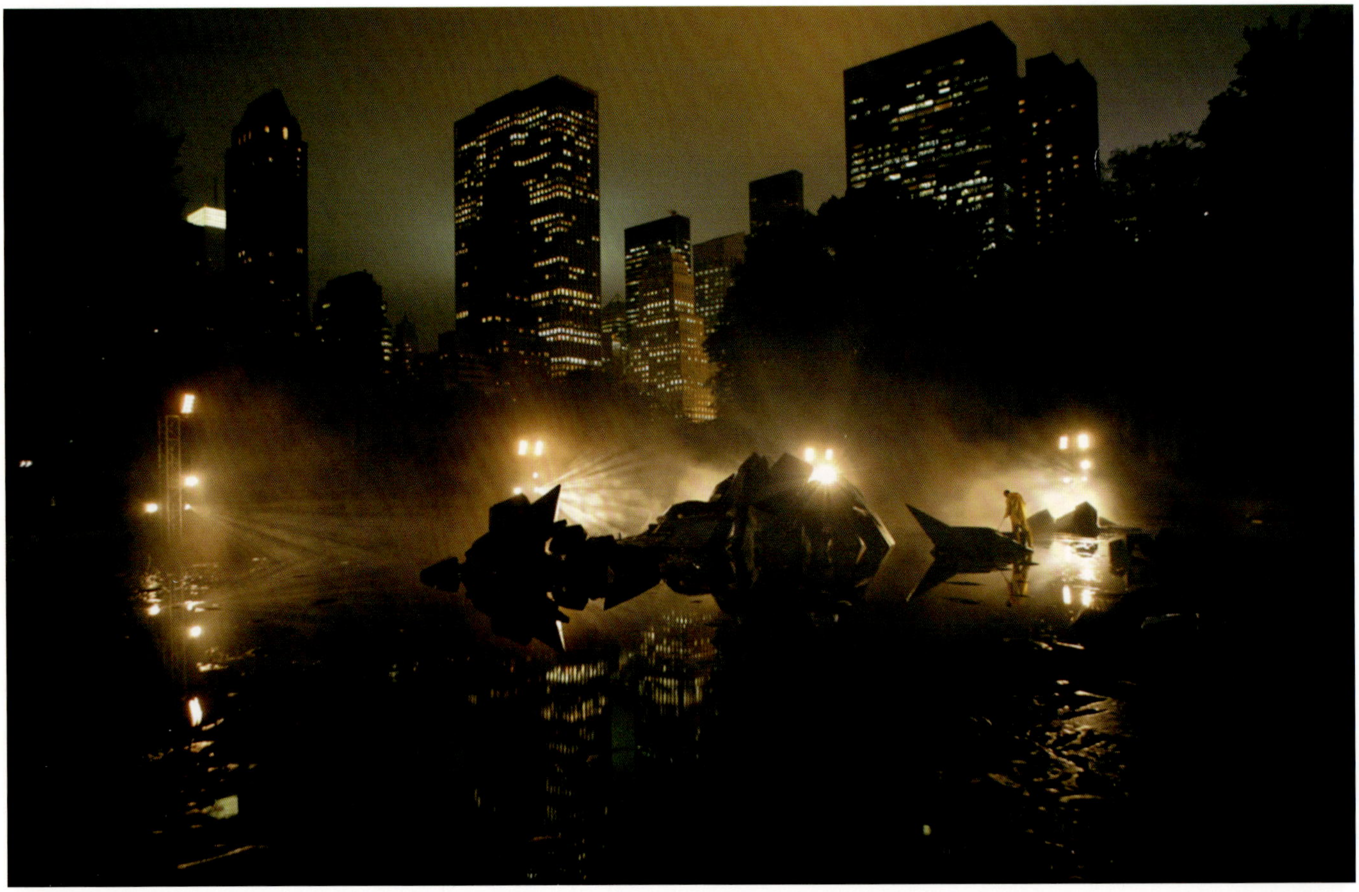

Les Grands Ensembles, 1994–2001
Ink on color ektachrome, Vistavision transferred to Digi Beta and DVD, 8′
Venice, François Pinault Collection
View of the installation, XLIX Esposizione Internazionale d'Arte, Biennale di Venezia 2001

Le Château de Turing, 2001
Vistavision transferred to Digi Beta and DVD, 12′
Venice, François Pinault Collection
View of the installation, XLIX Esposizione Internazionale d'Arte, Biennale di Venezia 2001

Atari Light, 1999–2001
Computer game program, interface, joystick, halogen lamps, dimensions variable
Venice, François Pinault Collection
View of the installation, XLIX Esposizione Internazionale d'Arte, Biennale di Venezia 2001

music soundtrack. Huyghe thus seeks to show the split created between new public housing and the ideas of modern architecture that the two buildings reflect only in formal terms, having betrayed all the philosophical and social assumptions that informed the work of Le Corbusier, for example. At the same time, the artist considers the increasingly dominant role that technology is destined to play in every sector of life, establishing itself as an element able to determine the aesthetics of the contemporary urban landscape and offering itself at the same time as a tool capable of alluring and captivating all those exposed to its constant influence. This is demonstrated by the interactive luminous ceiling of *Atari Light* (1999–2001) – an installation presented in the French pavilion at the 2001 Venice Biennale together with *Les Grands Ensembles* – which can be interpreted precisely as a metaphor of our ambivalent fascination with technology. For that matter, Huyghe's own attitude is also ambivalent, as shown in the recent video *A Journey That Wasn't* (2005), which imagines the existence, perhaps in the heart of Antarctica, of an uncontaminated island where human beings can rediscover contact with nature and live out their own palingenesis.
(*L.L.*)

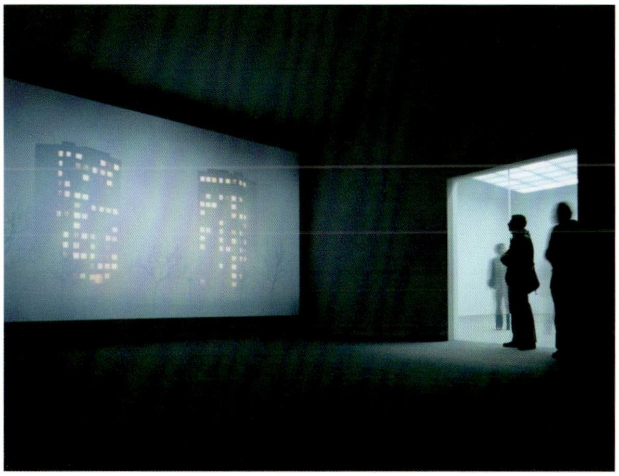

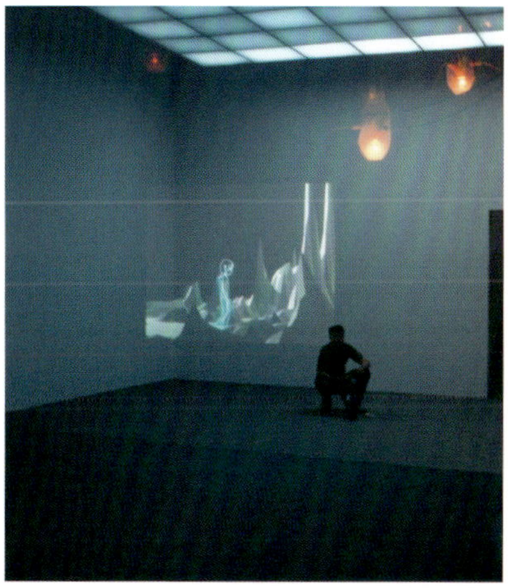

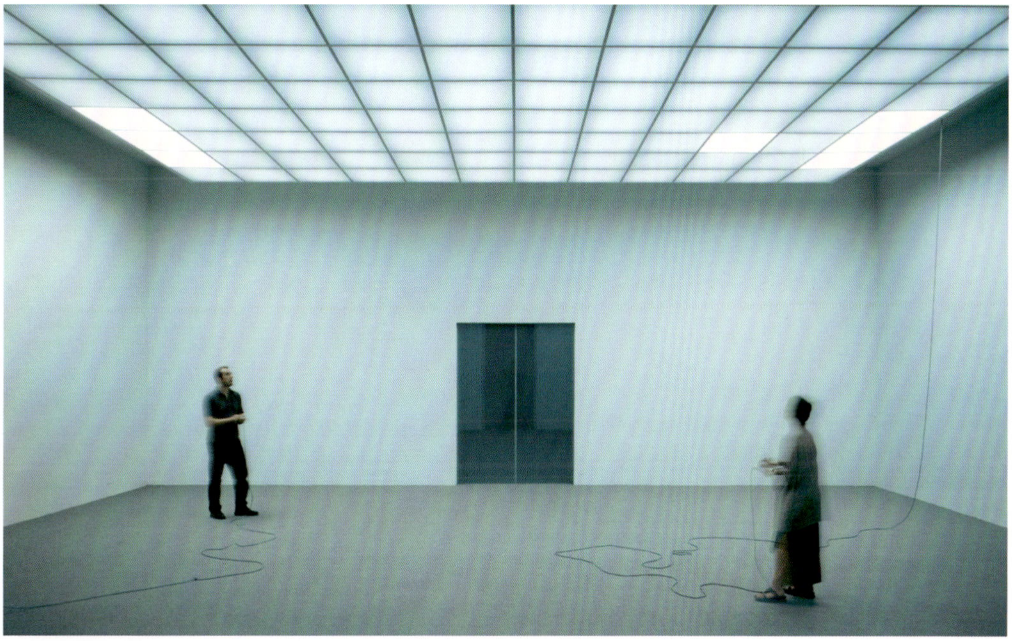

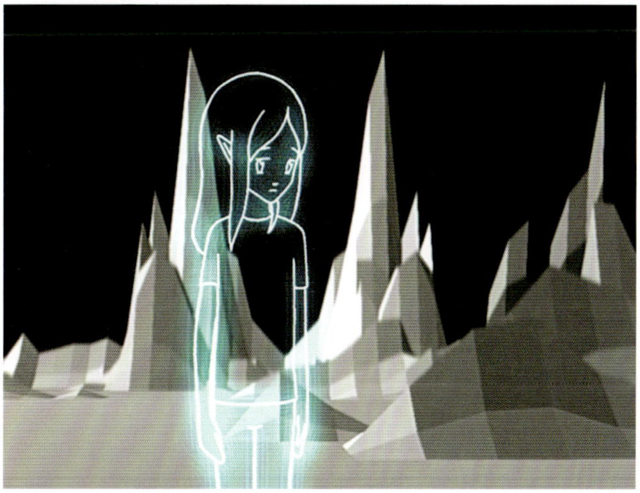

One Million Kingdoms (detail), 2001
Beta digital, 8′
Venice, François Pinault Collection
View of the installation, XLIX Esposizione Internazionale d'Arte, Biennale di Venezia 2001

A Journey That Wasn't, 2005
6 mm film transferred to HD video, sound, 21′41″
Courtesy Marian Goodman Gallery, New York

Eduardo Kac

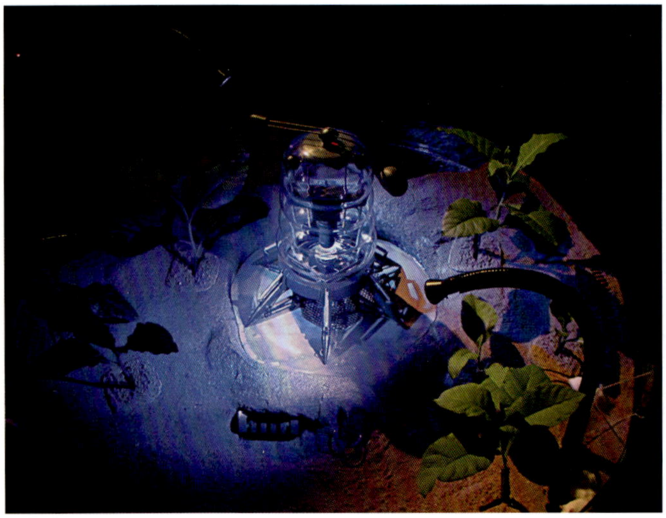

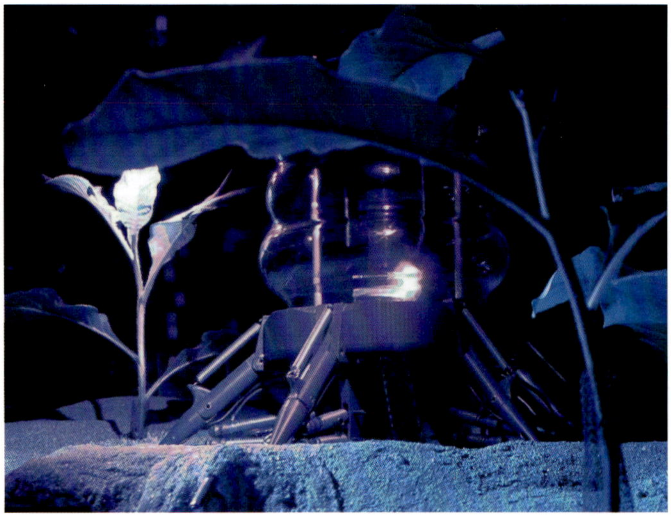

The Eighth Day, 2001 (detail)
Transgenic artwork with biologic robot (biobot), GFP plants, GFP ameba, GFP fish, GFP mice, audio, video, Internet

Born in Rio de Janeiro in 1962. Lives and works in Chicago.
The name of Eduardo Kac is associated in particular with Alba, the fluorescent rabbit he produced in collaboration with a French laboratory in February 2000.
GFP Bunny is an ongoing project intended to trigger public debate on transgenic research by shifting the terms of the issue from the legitimacy of the operation to the problem of the sociall integration of genetically modified individuals.
Kac intended to use the gene GFP, which is normally employed in laboratories as a marker by virtue of its fluorescent nature, as a "social marker" distinguishing the modified being as an "outsider" with which we must become familiar.
But while Kac's intention was to "tame" Alba, the project took an unexpected turn with the laboratory's refusal to release the animal to him, whereupon it became a media campaign for the liberation of an animal held prisoner because of its diversity.
In actual fact, *GFP Bunny* is the culmination of 20 years of rigorous investigation into the social and cultural consequences of new technologies such as telecommunications (fax, Slow Scan TV), telepresence, robotics, and biotechnologies. His *Essay Concerning Human Understanding* (1994), for example, is an installation that establishes an absurd dialogue between a canary and a plant located 600 miles away, thus dramatically highlighting the role of remote communication in human life. While the bird's song reaches the plant over a telephone line, the latter's reaction are picked up by equipment designed to monitor brain waves and translate them into sound. At the same time, the very presence of spectators influences and interferes with the behavior of the bird and the plant.
With *Time Capsule* (1997) Kac became the first artist to have a microchip implanted live on television. The electronic device, which gathers information on the artist, was implanted in his ankle, the part of the body on which slaves were tattooed. Less radical only in appearance, *Genesis* (1999) is a complex installation in which the verse from the Bible giving mankind dominion over nature was first converted into Morse code and then into a genetic sequence implanted in a bacterium kept alive in a Petri capsule. Control over UV lamps that cause mutations in the gene (and hence in the Biblical text) is made available to all visitors on the Internet. In this way, whatever opinions they may have on mankind's right to control nature, spectators find themselves in a contradictory position. If they do not act on the gene, they respect the Biblical text; if they do, they destroy it irrevocably.
Often so accentuated as to cause irritation, the "technological rhetoric" in *Genesis* and the best works by Kac proves perfectly germane to an investigation into the social impact of technology that few other artists have been capable of developing with such energy.
(*D.Q.*)

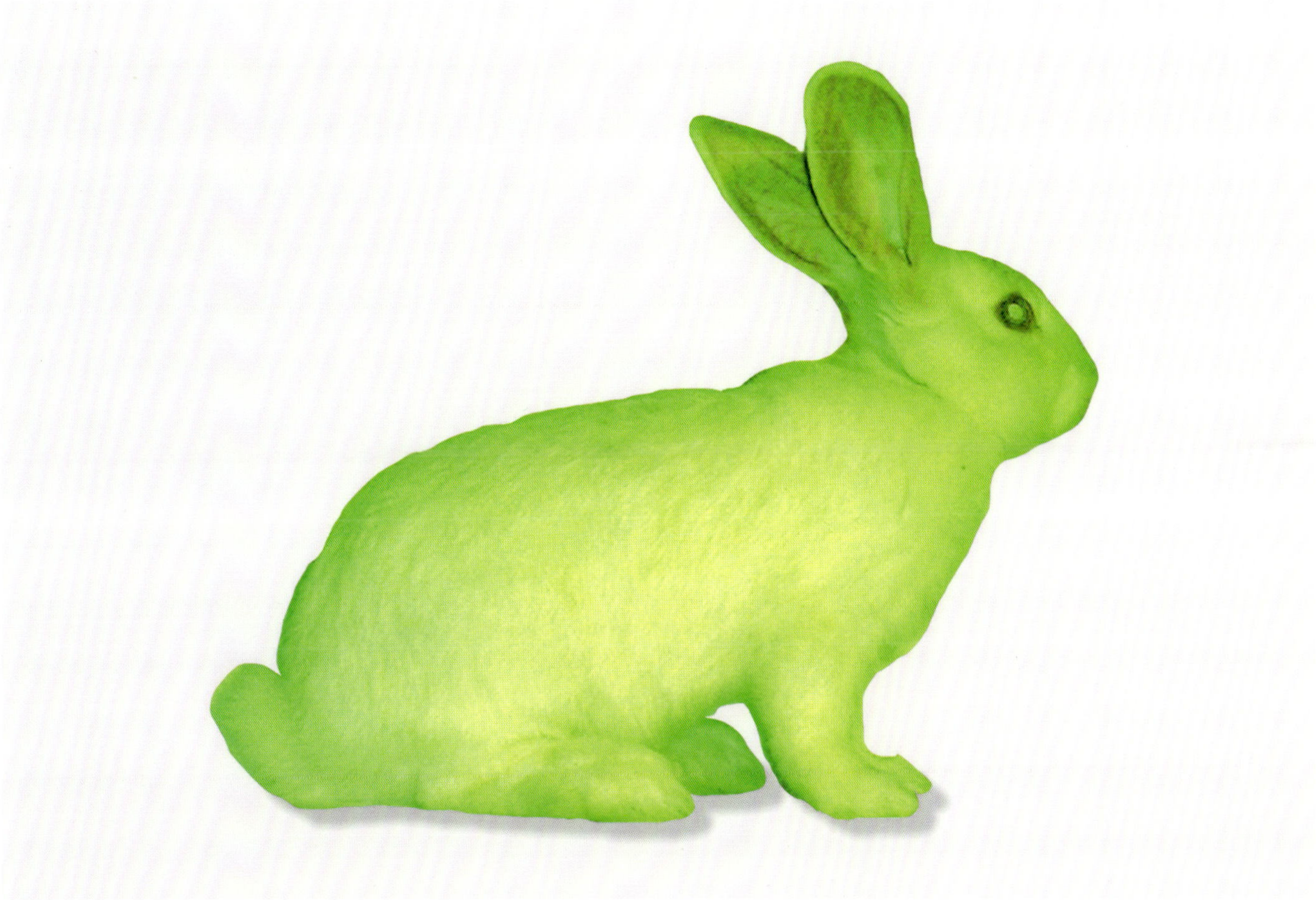

GFP Bunny, 2000
Transgenic artwork, Alba
the fluorescent bunny

Eva and Franco Mattes (0100101110101101.ORG)

Born in Brescia, Italy, in 1976. Have worked together since 1998.
In September 1999 the Italian pavilion at the Venice Biennale presented a tribute to Darko Maver, a mysterious Serbian artist who died in prison in Podgorica a few months earlier. Over the previous two years there had been a great deal of talk about Maver, whose work involved leaving macabre, hyper-realistic mutilated dummies in public places in the Balkans. There was to be still more in 2000, when an official communiqué was received from a mystery group signing itself 0100101110101101.org stating that Darko Maver had never existed: his work was a jumble of images taken from the trash sites that proliferate on the Internet, his biography a story backed up with fake evidence, and his writings a parody of the radical art then in fashion.
In the same period 0100101110101101.org claimed responsibility for a second, colossal hoax: a fake Vatican website that had fooled the faithful for a year with somewhat unorthodox theories combining authentic material – papal speeches and encyclicals as well as Biblical quotations – with fragments of pop culture from sources such as *The Lord of the Rings* and *Star Wars*. These two operations launched 0100101110101101.org on the international scene and encapsulate the primary thrust of their work, namely skillful use of the channels of bottom-up mass communications, especially the Internet, to create collective hallucinations, manipulation of the uncertain boundary between reality and fiction, and the debunking of widely accepted myths.
0100101110101101.org draw on the legacy of American pranksters and media hoaxes as well as the European avant-gardes of the 1980s and the community strategies of Net Art of the 1990s. *Copies* (1999) and *Hybrids* (1998–1999) are respectively clones and collages of websites created by artists and comment on the absurdity of concepts like "unique work of art", "limited access", "original", "intellectual property" and "aura" in the digital era, which eliminates any difference whatsoever between copy and original. Works like *Life Sharing* (2000–2003) and *Vopos* (2002) challenge the obsolete concept of privacy with *glasnost*, total transparency, and the sharing of one's existence. Commissioned by the Walker Art Center of Minneapolis, the former was an online performance in which 0100101110101101.org made accessible through their website the entire content of their computer, including their email and system files. In the second, it was their movements in space that were monitored day after day by means of a GPS system. On being invited to take part in the Venice Biennale in 2001, they released a virus called *Biennial.py* as a comment on the recent mass hysteria generated by the Millennium Bug and the idea of viral infection as a metaphor of art.
The extraordinary attention of the mass media, including the major newspapers, proved unable, however, to penetrate the secret of their identity, which was protected by skillful tactics of dissimulation and constant changes of name. While it soon became clear that there were two people at the heart of the group, many of their projects

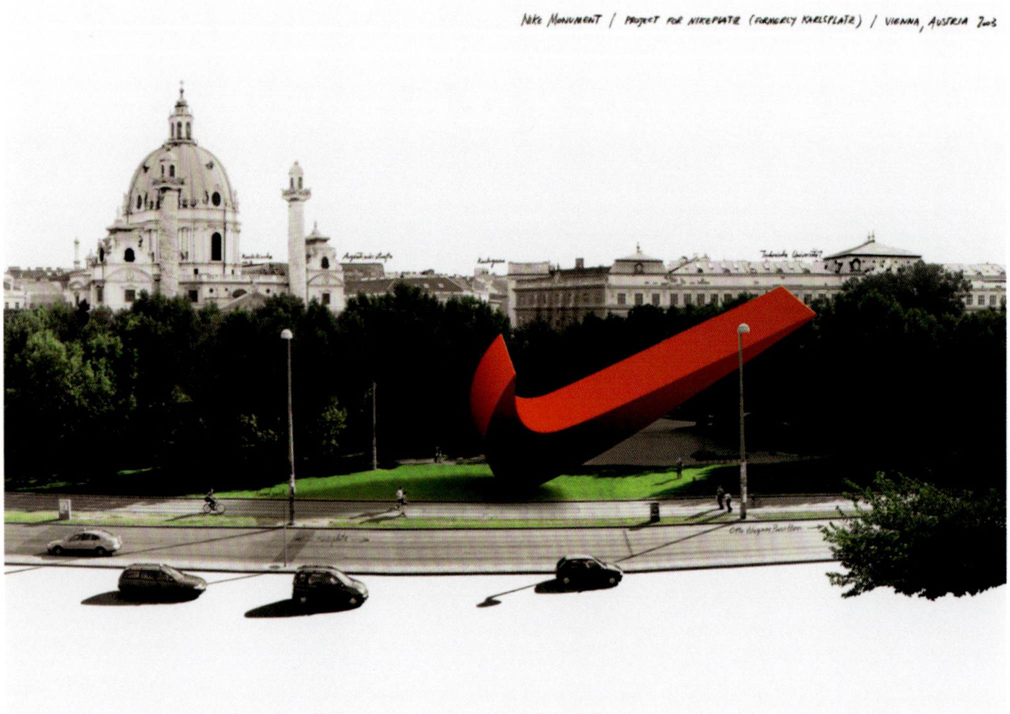

Nike Ground – Project for the fake Nike Monument in Karlsplatz,
2003–2004
Digital color print on canvas,
154 x 108 x 8 cm
Courtesy Fabio Paris Art Gallery

Perpetual Self Dis/Infecting Machine, 2001–2003
Especially made computer, infected with the Biennale.py virus,
70 x 50 x 13 cm
Courtesy Fabio Paris Art Gallery, Brescia

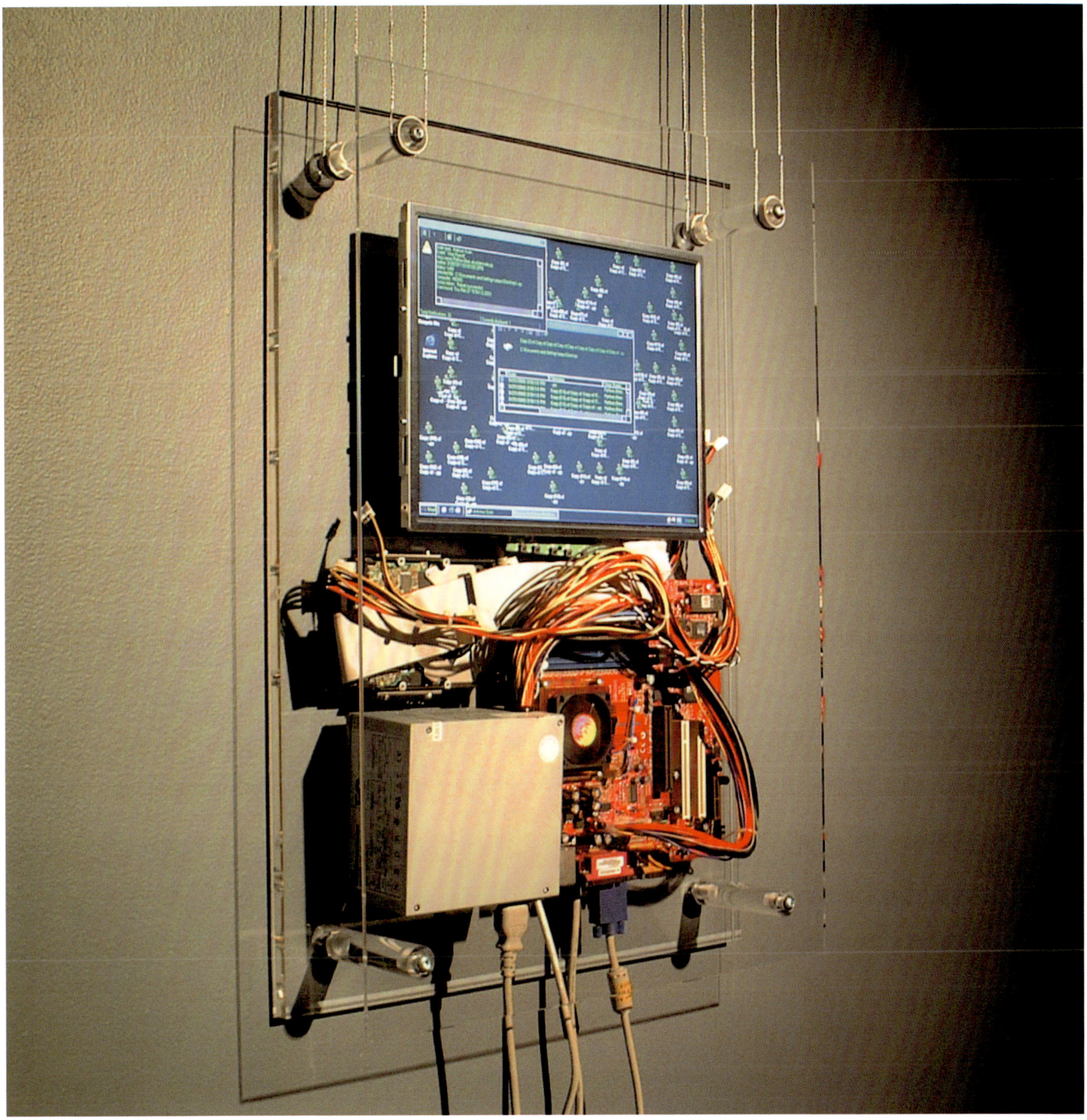

Synthetic Performance in Second Life, 2007
Reconstruction of *Imponderabilia* by Marina Abramovich and Ulay
Courtesy Postmasters Gallery, New York

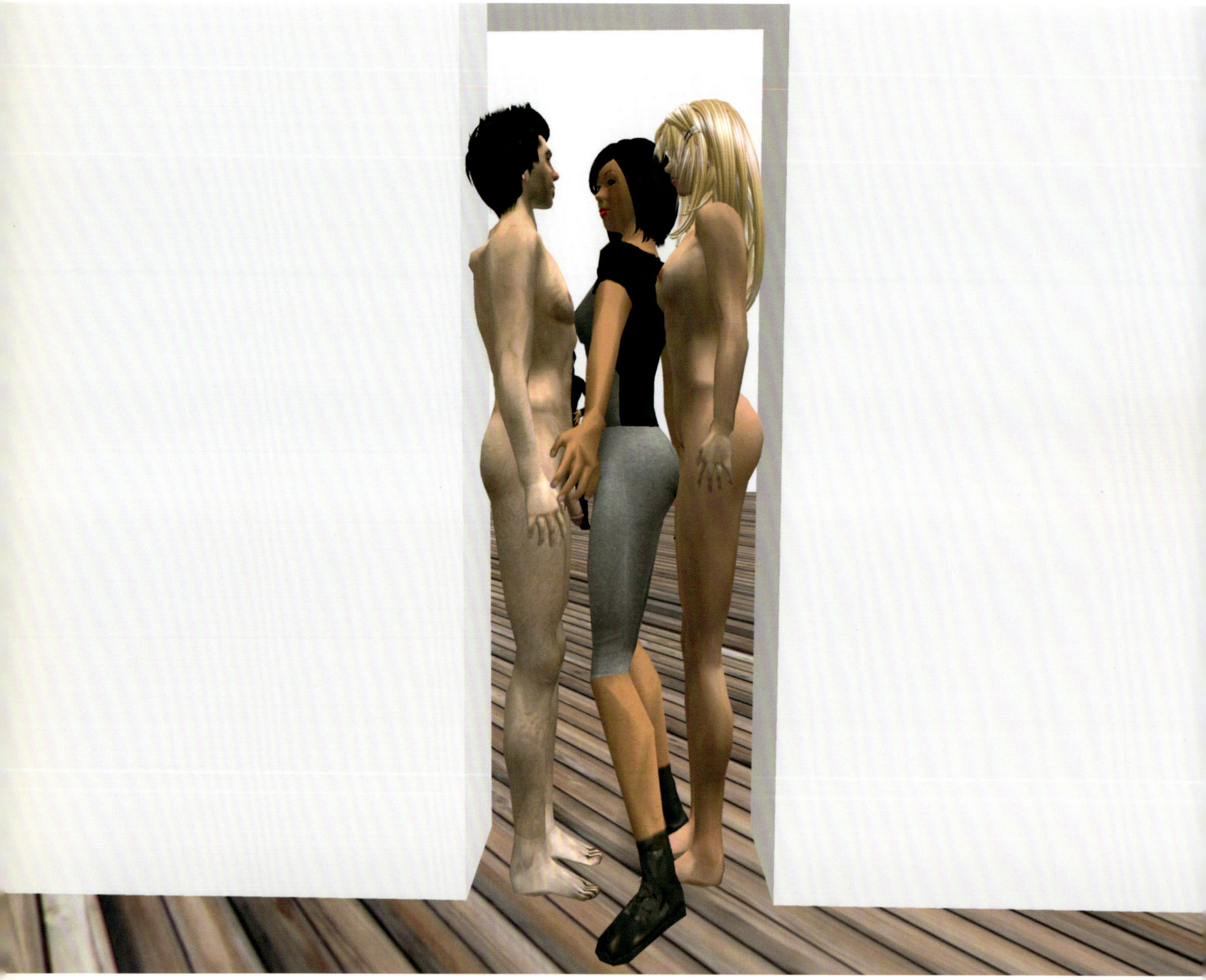

suggested the involvement of a large network of collaborators. One example is *Nike Ground* (2003–2004), in which the duo assumed the identity of the Nike multinational and declared their intention to buy up some famous city squares and turn them into "Nike plazas". The project was developed in the mass media and in the public space of the Karlsplatz in Vienna, where an infobox was installed to provide citizens with information about the project and record their reactions. *United We Stand* (2004), a campaign to promote a nonexistent blockbuster in which the European Union saves the world from nuclear war, was again developed both in the media and on the streets of big cities like New York, Bangalore and Berlin. In both cases, a hallucinatory but plausible reality is deliberately created in order to investigate a specific aspect of the contemporary world: the commercialization of public space, brand ownership, and the lack of a shared idea of Europe. Now known increasingly by the far more pronounceable names of Eva and Franco Mattes, 0100101110101101.org have continued their investigation of the uncertain border between reality and simulation in the virtual worlds, focusing in particular on the construction of identity and the nature of life on screen in projects such as the *Avatar portraits* (2006–2008) and *Synthetic Performances* (2007). The latter repeated some historical actions of the 1960s and 1970s in the synthetic world Second Life, an immaterial space that is nevertheless experienced on a daily basis by millions of people, where concepts like the body, violence, and sexuality take on a new meaning.
(*D.Q.*)

MMMM, 2008
Resin, metal, plastic, colors, and pigments, 90 x 60 x 100 cm
Courtesy of the artists

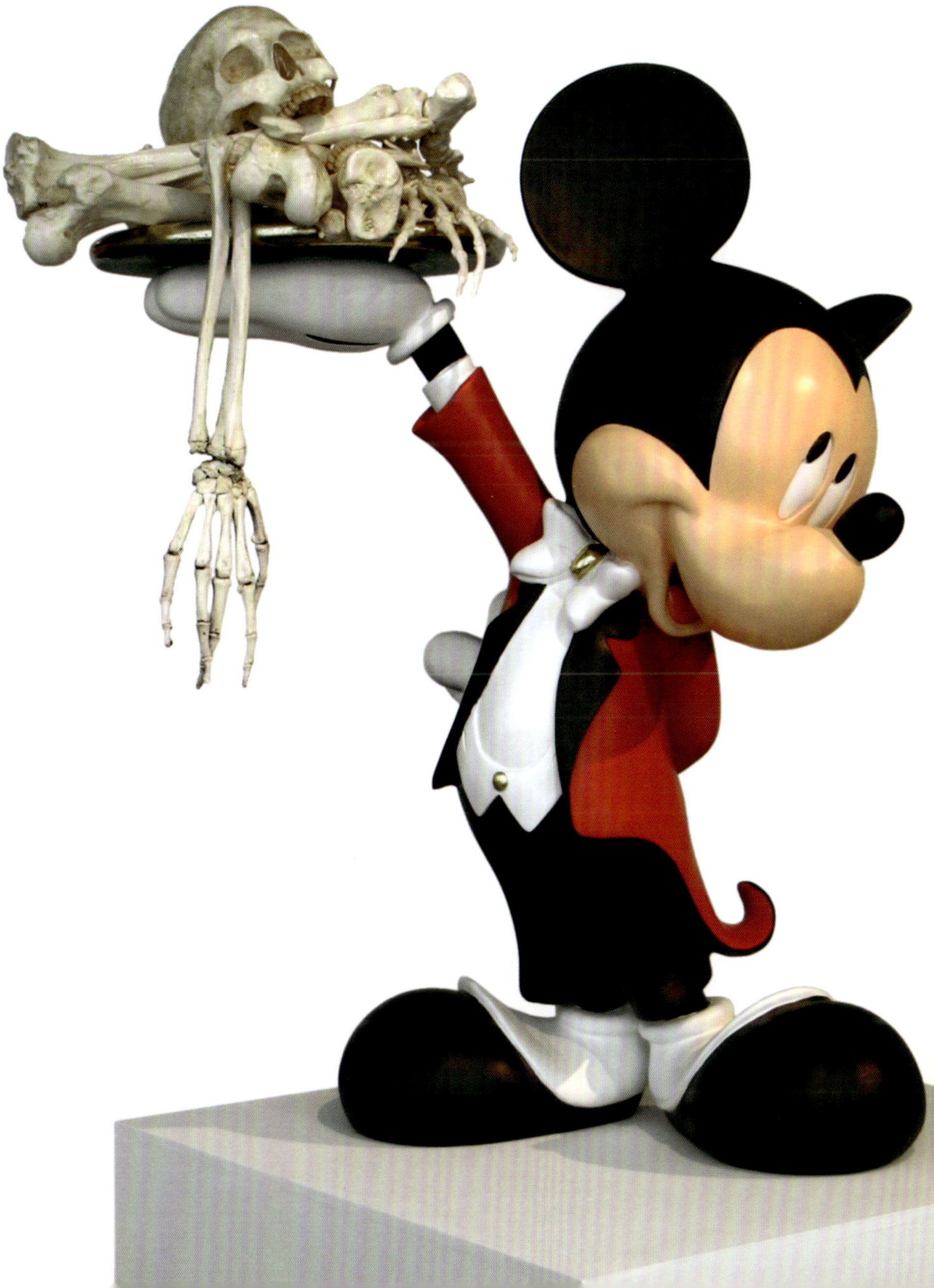

Steve McQueen

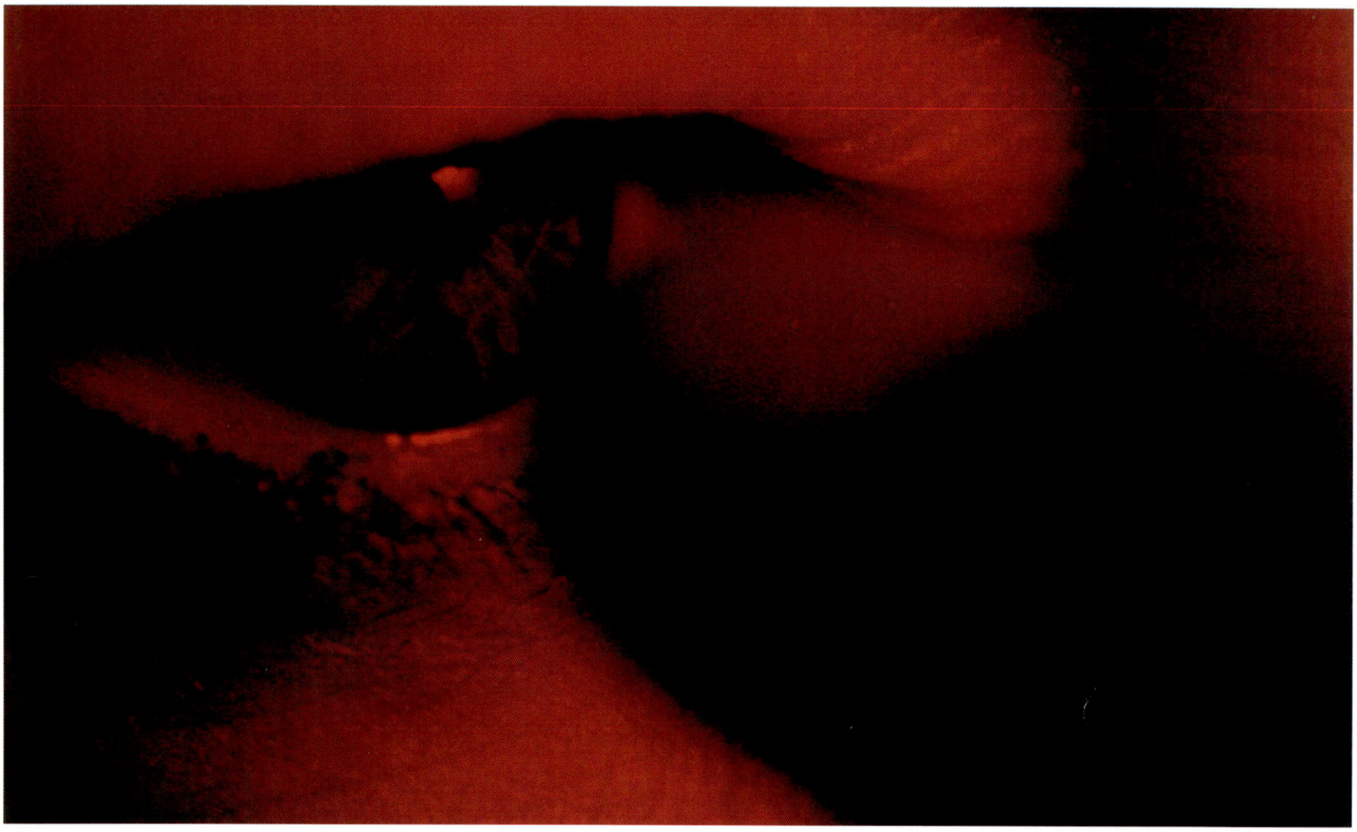

Born in London in 1969. Lives and works in London and Amsterdam. The work of the English artist Steve McQueen constitutes one of the most interesting results of the renewed interest in cinema of art in the 1990s. It was on graduating from Goldsmiths College in London in 1993 that McQueen created *Bear* (1993), which shows two colored men, one being the artist himself, completely naked in a pose ambiguously suggesting something between homoerotic play and a boxing match. Based on the celebrated scene in which the façade of a building collapses on Buster Keaton but leaves him standing unscathed in the space of an open window, *Deadpan* (1997) is turned into something completely different by means of scenic devices that accentuate the threatening solidity of the artist's monumental body and deadpan expression. McQueen draws upon Warhol, the Nouvelle Vague, and the *Cinéma vérité* of the 1970s in work characterized by the use of hand-held cameras, unusual angles, and non-linear narrative. In *Drumroll* (1998), which won him the Turner Prize the following year, three cameras were attached to a barrel that the artist rolled through the streets of New York. The results were then presented as a three-channel installation. The artist claims that unconventional shots make spectators aware of themselves, of their physicality and position in the world. While not neglecting cinema, McQueen then broadened his horizons to take in video, photography, and sculpture, but always with a narrative thrust and strong emotional impact.

Once Upon a Time (2004) is an installation in which a number of slides are projected on a hanging screen in very slow sequence.

The images are from a series taken in the 1970s by NASA and sent into space on the Voyager as a "portrait" of our planet for aliens, presenting the Earth as a Garden of Eden apparently free of all difficulties and contradictions.

Far more dramatic are works like *Running Thunder* (1997), a 16 mm film showing the death of a stallion, and *Gravesend/Unexploded (Handheld)*, shot in the Congo the same year, which pulls no punches in addressing the problems of globalization.

The Hunger, McQueen's first full-length film, was presented in 2008 and won awards in various film festivals, including the Caméra d'Or at Cannes in the section *Un Certain Regard*. It tells the story of Bobby Sands, the young IRA activist who went on hunger strike in prison against the British government's refusal to recognize his status as a political prisoner and starved himself to death. Regardless of its repercussions on McQueen's career, *The Hunger* shows yet again that the boundaries between art and cinema are certainly not clear-cut but rather subject to constant renegotiation.

(*D.Q.*)

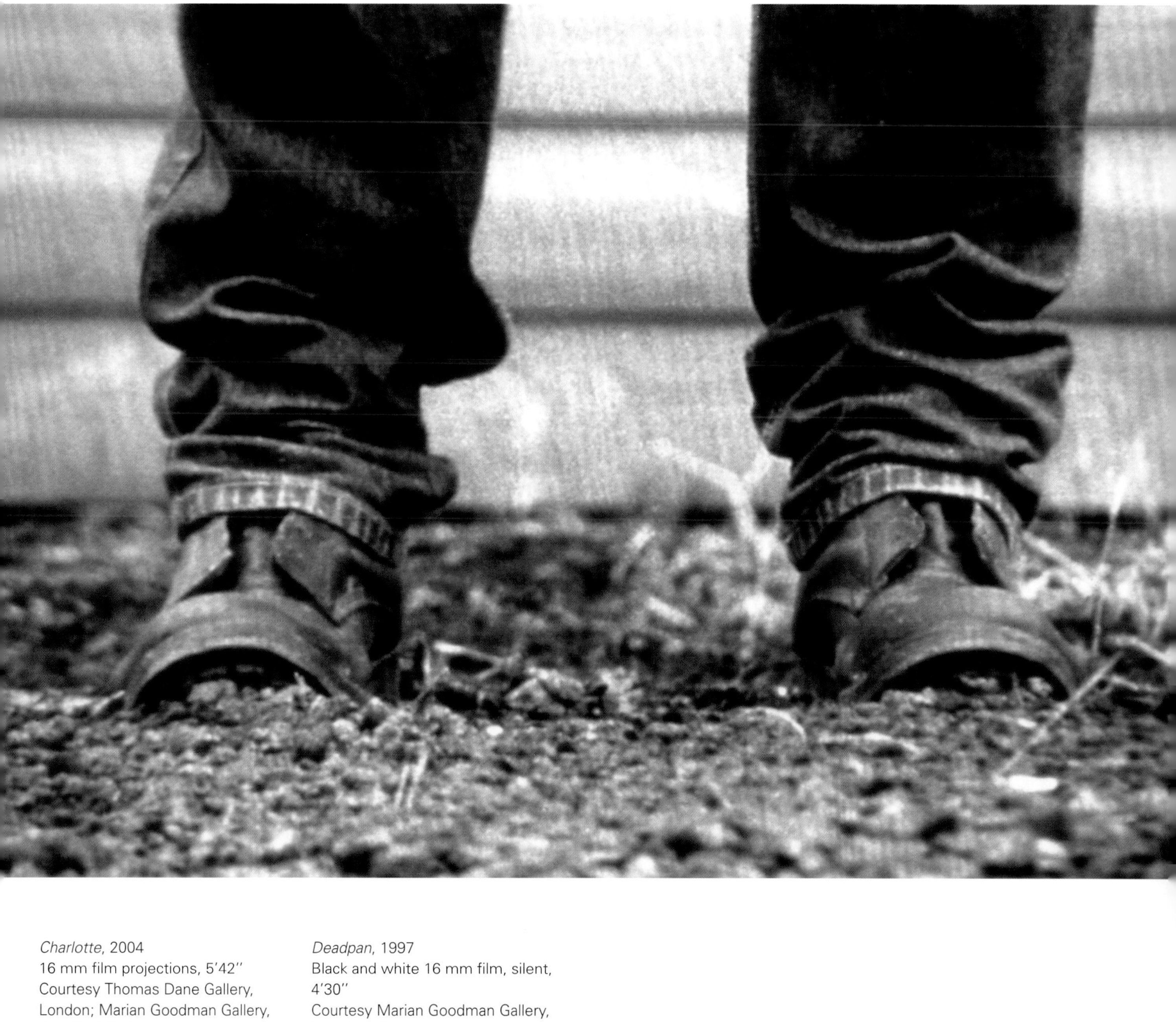

Charlotte, 2004
16 mm film projections, 5'42''
Courtesy Thomas Dane Gallery, London; Marian Goodman Gallery, New York/Paris

Deadpan, 1997
Black and white 16 mm film, silent, 4'30''
Courtesy Marian Goodman Gallery, New York/Paris

Carsten Nicolai

Born in Karl-Marx-Stadt, East Germany, in 1965. Lives and works in Berlin and Chemnitz.
Every work by Carsten Nicolai could be described as a fascinating visual or sound translation of a scientific phenomenon or law. Nicolai, who also works as a musician under the pseudonym Alva Noto (Alva being Edison's middle name), studied architecture and landscape design but was crucially influenced by the techno scene in Berlin, where he moved from East Germany after the fall of the Berlin Wall. He took part in Documenta X in 1997 with a work entitled ∞ (the symbol for infinity) in which 72 audio tracks of 45 seconds each containing sounds normally used to convey specific information were transmitted for a period of 100 days in different contexts and forms (including radio and public places). These minimal operations contaminated the acoustic environment of the city of Kassel by infiltrating everyday life with codes of a not immediately identifiable nature that interfere with it. Nicolai later switched to the medium of installation, characterized by a cold aesthetic of Minimalist origin. Even at its most sculptural, however, his works involve a dialogue, which is not always perceptible, with the public or their context. *Bausatz noto ∞* (1998) consists of four turntables fitted into a tabletop and allows the public to play and interact with an endless series of sound loops. Works like the installation *Frozen water* (2000) and the series of prints entitled *Milch* (2000) focus on capturing sound visually through the effect of its vibrations on a liquid surface. In *Telefunken* (2000) sound becomes visible very simply by connecting the audio signal of a CD player to the video input of a TV set. *Snow Noise* (2002) is a sort of laboratory in which the spectator can initiate and observe the formation of a snowflake, a complex and unrepeatable form that has long fascinated the artist. Nicolai created the two installations *Anti* and *Reflex* for his solo show at the Schim Kunsthalle, Frankfurt, in 2004. The first is a huge black reproduction of the geometric solid in Dürer's *Melancholia I* that reacts to the magnetic fields produced by the spectator. While *Anti* is cryptic and repulsive, *Reflex* is a white dodecahedron of a welcoming character that the visitor can enter and experience as an auditory space.
Enigmatic and intriguing, Nicolai's work highlights the complexity of our perception of the world and fascinates us with its masterly presentation of natural phenomena. (*D.Q.*)

Bausatz noto ∞, 1998
4 record players, vinyl records, console, amplifier, loudspeaker, dimensions variable
Courtesy of the artist

Anti, 2004
Perspex, sound module, Theramin module, signal transducer, amplifier, black paint, 255 x 255 x 300 cm
View of the installation realized in 2005 at the Schirn Kunsthalle, Frankfurt
Courtesy Galerie EIGEN + ART Leipzig/Berlin; PaceWildenstein, New York

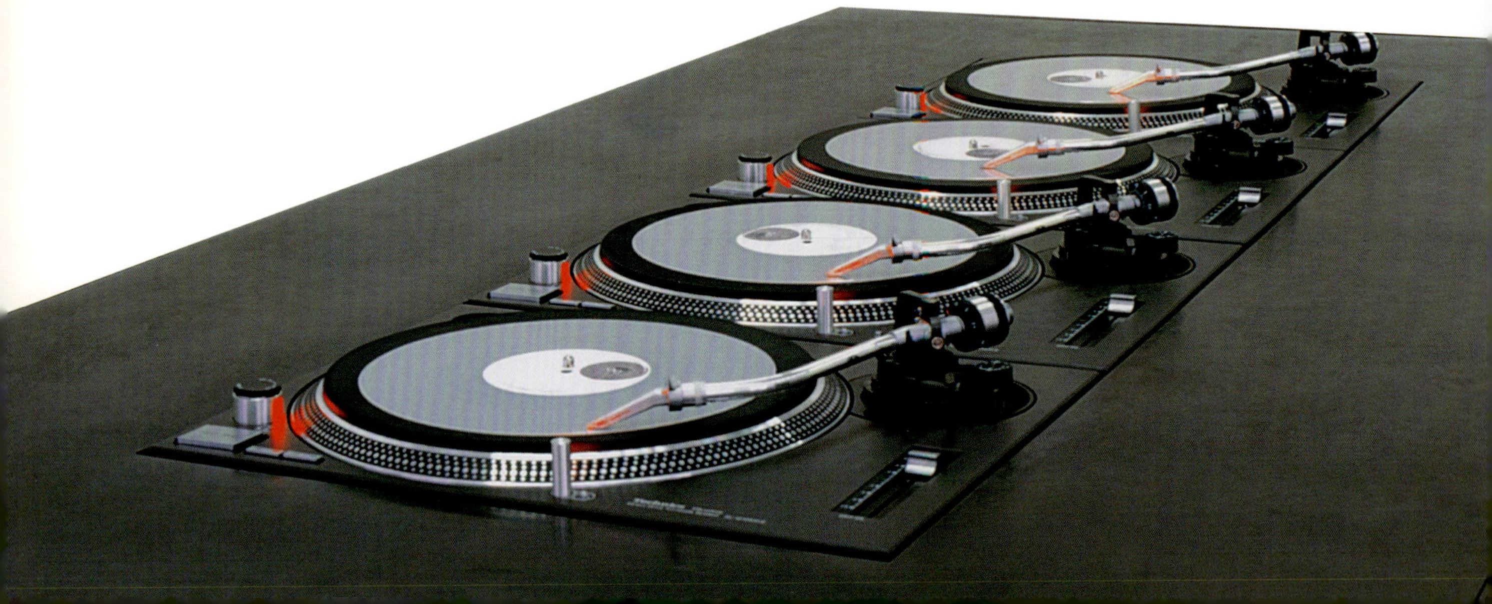

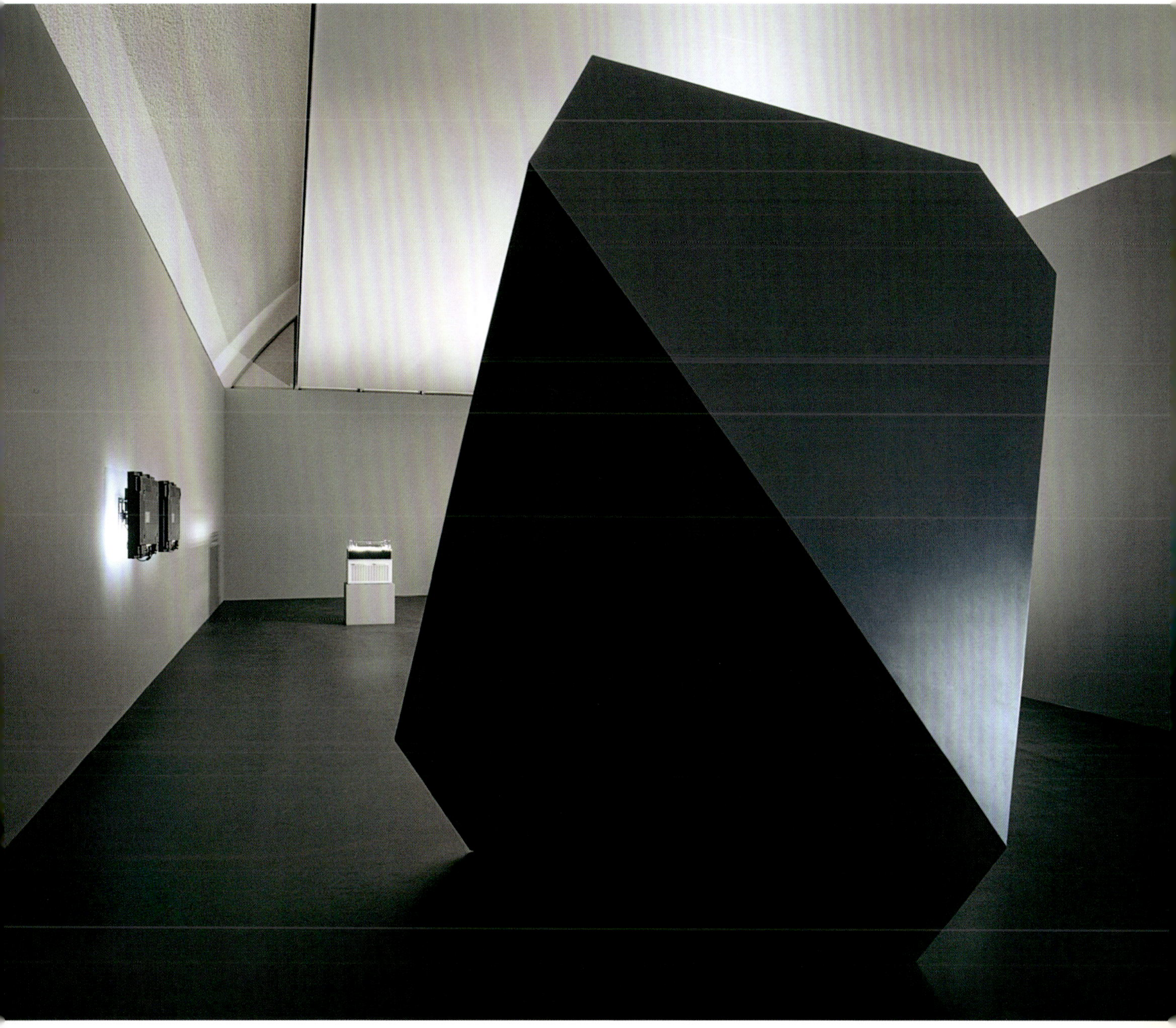

Philippe Parreno

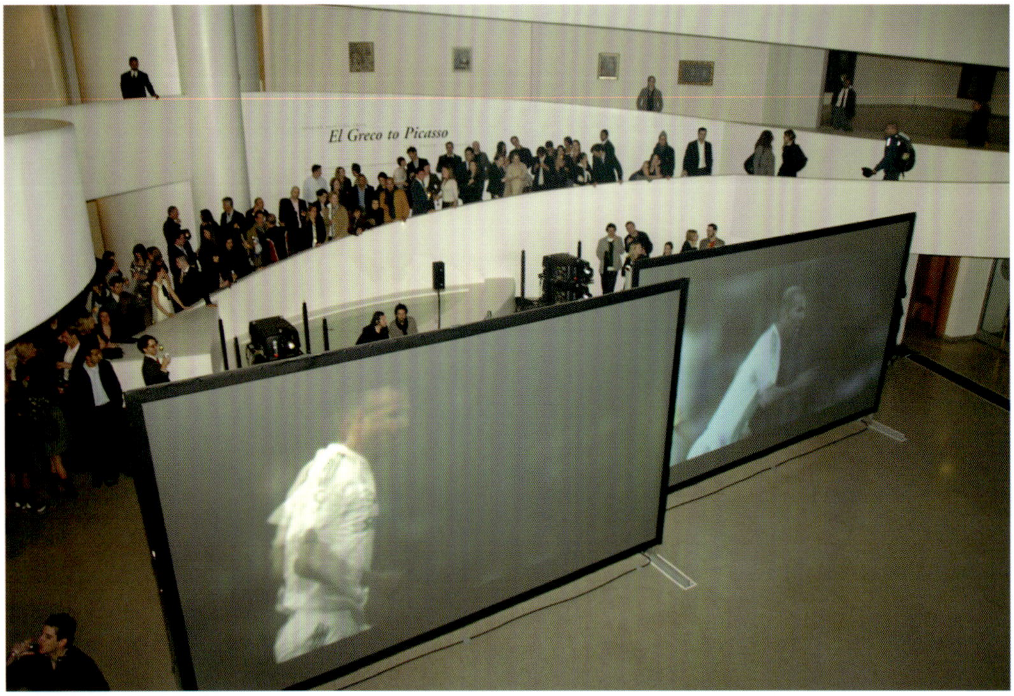

Zidane: un portrait du XXIe siècle, 2006
Two-channel video projection, sound, dimensions variable
New York, Solomon R. Guggenheim Museum, Purchased with funds contributed by the Young Collectors Council, with additional funds contributed by Adidas
(with Douglas Gordon)

El Sueño de una cosa, 2001
Video installation with 35 mm film transferred to HD video, with Dolby stereo, sound, 1'
Courtesy of the artist and Friedrich Petzel Gallery, New York

Born in Oran, Algeria, in 1964. Lives and works in Paris.
Philippe Parreno's works explore a territory halfway between social reality and the world of the mass media, a twofold interest exemplified in what is unquestionably his best-known work, *Zidane: un portrait du XXIe siécle*, created in collaboration with Douglas Gordon. It shows the famous French soccer player Zinédine Zidane filmed all the way through a match with 16 powerful cameras to capture all of his movements and expressions in real time from a whole variety of angles. The two artists then edited the material to create a film lasting 90 minutes (the length of a soccer match) that constitutes a modern celebratory portrait of a contemporary "hero". Initially intended for the cinema circuit, the film was presented at the Cannes Film Festival in 2006, the year it was made, in accordance both with the interest of Gordon and Parreno in cinema as a medium of extraordinary narrative power, and with the French artist's tendency to work outside the traditional exhibition circuits.
Parreno has worked with many other artists, film directors, architects and designers over the last 15 years to explore the possible forms of interaction between different spheres.
The idea of the work as a field open to a variety of contributions has led him to reflect also on the role of the author in relation to the work and its implications at the cultural social and economic level. One result is the project *No Ghost, Just a Shell*, devised together with Pierre Huyghe, which involved 16 artists (including Liam Gillick, Rirkrit Tiravanija, Dominique Gonzalez-Foerster and the M/M team of designers) each creating a story for Ann Lee, a Manga character that Huyghe and Parreno bought by mail order from a Japanese multinational operating in the sector.
Parreno's preference for collaboration also emerges in the work *El Sueño de una cosa* (2001), created by the artist alone but ideally conceived as a joint venture with Robert Rauschenberg and John Cage. Images of the enchanting Norwegian landscape edited by Parreno into a one-minute film with a soundtrack of music by the French composer Edgar Varèse are projected onto five white panels, which are revealed when the lights go on at the end of the projection to be replicas of Rauschenberg's *White Painting* (1951). During the interval of 4 minutes 33 seconds before the film starts again, the spectators could also be said to experience a disembodied and ethereal version of John Cage's famous silent score *4'33"* (1962), a piece inspired in turn by Rauschenberg's white monochrome. *El Sueño de una cosa* is thus a triptych made up of the film, the five white panels onto which the images are projected and the 4 minutes 33 seconds of silence between the end of one projection and the beginning of the next. It is interesting to note that Parreno originally conceived the film, which is exactly the same length as a commercial, for projection in cinemas in the interval between the advertising and the feature film, and that it was shown as such all over Sweden in 2001, manifesting itself on the screen as an alien intrusion into a space reserved for the strategies of commerce and entertainment.
The work then took on its new character by entering the traditional exhibition circuit, thus confirming Parreno's interest in works capable of undergoing transformation in relation to their setting.
(*L.L.*)

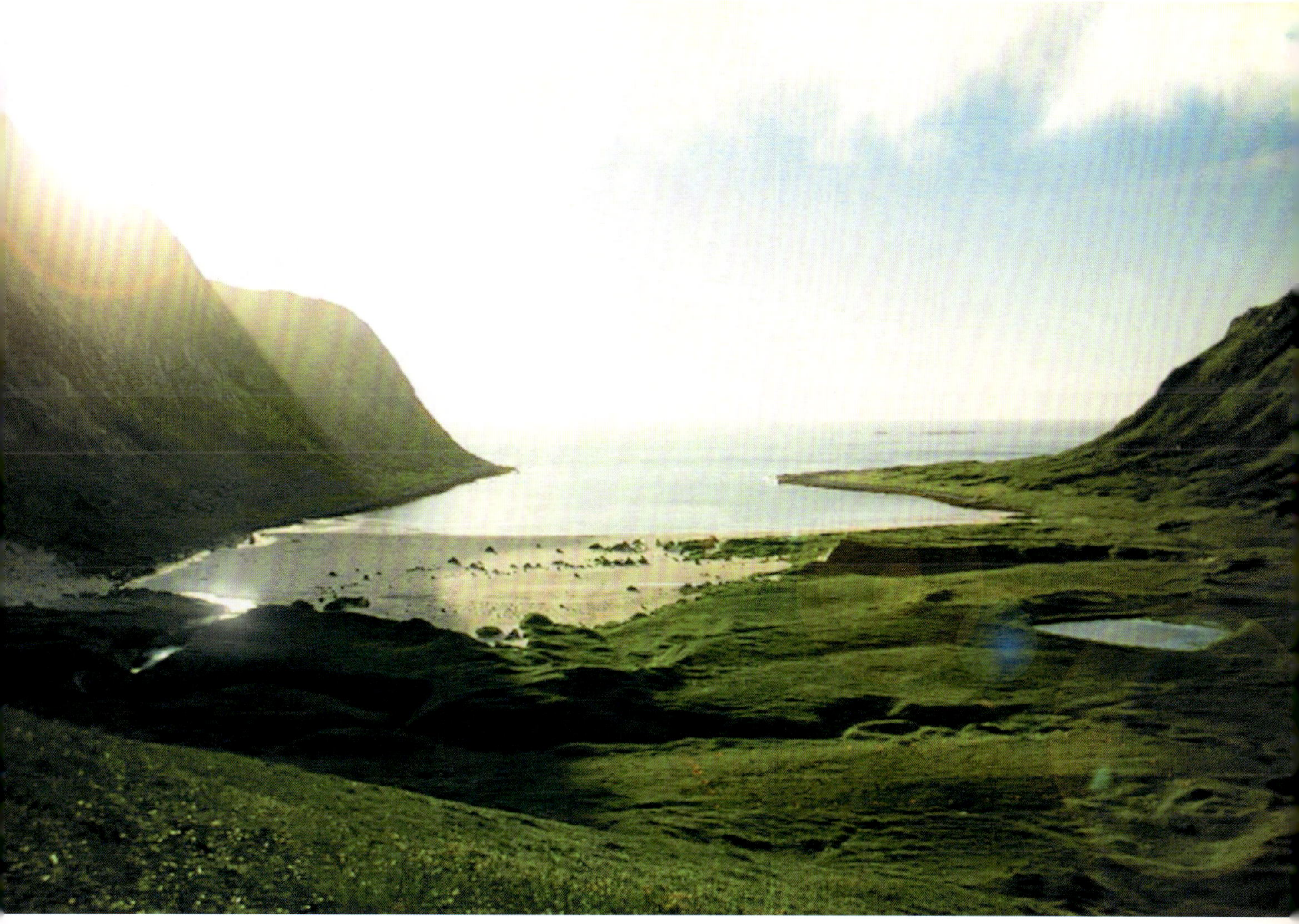

Pipilotti Rist

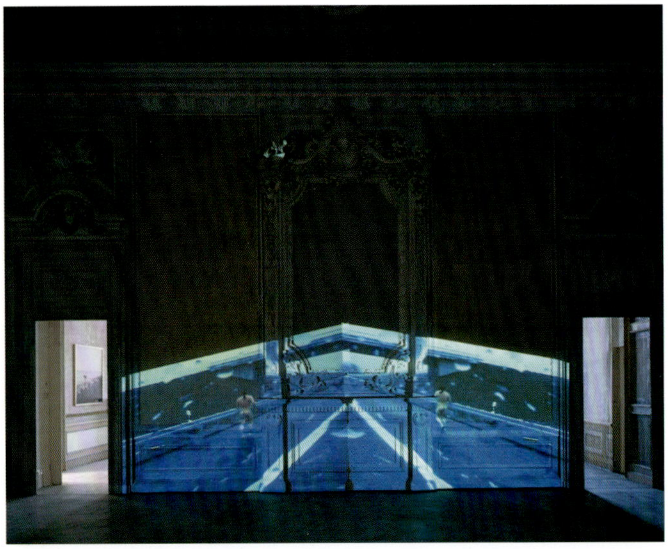

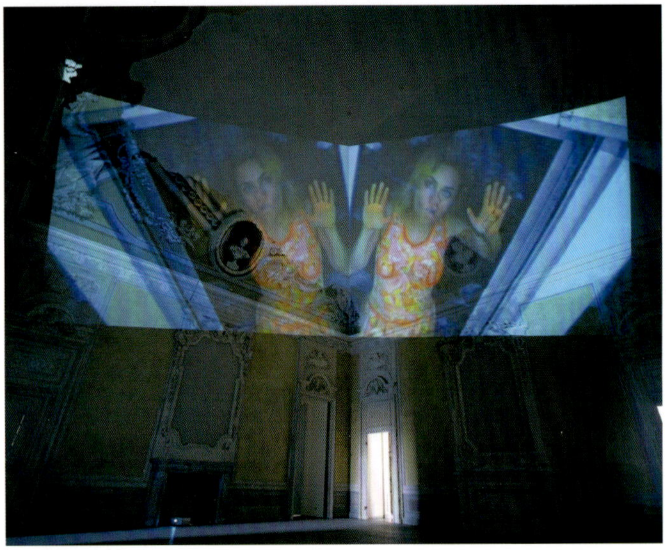

Cinquante Fifty (Installation for a Parking Lot), 2000
Double video projection, color, sound, 4'40'', 2'20''
Rivoli, Castello di Rivoli – Museo d'Arte Contemporanea, permanent deposit
Fondazione CRT Progetto Arte Moderna e Contemporanea

Born in Grabs, Switzerland, in 1962. Lives and works in Los Angeles and Zurich.
The Swiss artist Pipilotti Rist started out in the 1980s with video works focused on the analysis of icons of sexuality and rejection of the female stereotype propagated by the musical and television culture of the period.
The artist has turned her attention to the relationship between video and viewer over the last decade, expanding the sensory approach through the creation of huge site-specific video installations capable of completely enveloping the spectator in surrealistic tales with insidious visual tricks.
Cinquante Fifty (Installation for a Parking Lot) (2000) addresses the urban space and the distance between human beings. The video is set on the outskirts of an unidentified Western urban agglomerate, an allusion to the dehumanizing prototype of the metropolis, and the succession of events devoid of all importance is a metaphor of human solitude and alienation. A woman looking out of a window tries to attract the camera's attention. Another takes a bored look at her surroundings. A naked man, apparently unaware of or indifferent to his condition, walks along the side of a completely deserted freeway.
All this is accompanied by dream-like and disorienting music.
Rist exhibited the video installation *Pour Your Body Out (7354 Cubic Meters)* in the Donald B. and Catherine C. Marron atrium of the MoMA, New York, in 2008.
The huge exhibition area was completely filled with the images projected by the Swiss artist and the sounds from the installation placed in the center. The central element reconstructs the environment of a domestic living room with a large circular sofa, an allusion to the need for exhibition venues to construct a ductile identity for themselves in accordance with the needs expressed by visitors. In this case, there is a reassuring identification between the home and the museum, and in particular between the domestic viewing of the electronic images broadcast by television and those presented by the video artist. The 16 minutes of the video show a natural universe of bright, bold colors accompanied by a hypnotic soundtrack that is shorter than the projection.
The loop highlights the total asynchrony of the two elements, which never coincide in their endless repetition and thus dash any expectation of knowing the work through vision alone. Rist's aim is clearly encapsulated in the meaning of the title of this site-specific installation, in that the viewers are explicitly asked to "pour their bodies out", literally with respect to the domestic context and metaphorically with respect to the passive reception of electronic images. The relationship between cinematographic and real time is shown in *À la belle étoile*, a site-specific video installation designed for the plaza in front of the Centre Pompidou in Paris in 2007. The artist worked on an architectural scale to create a projection of approximately 64 x 36 meters in the cinematic format of 16:9. A relationship is established here between the act of viewing and the passing of time during the day as well as the variations caused by sunlight, which makes the work practically invisible, so that it can be seen only from sunset to dawn.
Large scale is also a feature of the installation *Tyngdkraft, var min vän (Gravity Be My Friend)*, produced in 2007 for Magasin 3 in Stockholm. Viewers are once again offered the opportunity of relating to the work in total freedom, using the space as they please. While the projection of the video on the ceiling requires the audience to lie down, thus eliminating the traditional vertical relationship between observed object and observer, the images introduce them into an aquatic environment where the laws of physics governing gravity are different.
(F.T.)

Put Your Body Out (7354 Cubic Meters), 2008
Multi-channel video (color, sound), projector cages, circular seat element, rug, dimensions variable
New York, The Museum of Modern Art, Commissioned through the generosity of UBS, the Wallis Annenberg Fund for Innovation in Contemporary Art, Pro Helvetia Art Council of Switzerland

À la belle étoile, 2006
Video installation,
dimensions variable
Paris, Musée national d'art moderne – Centre Georges Pompidou

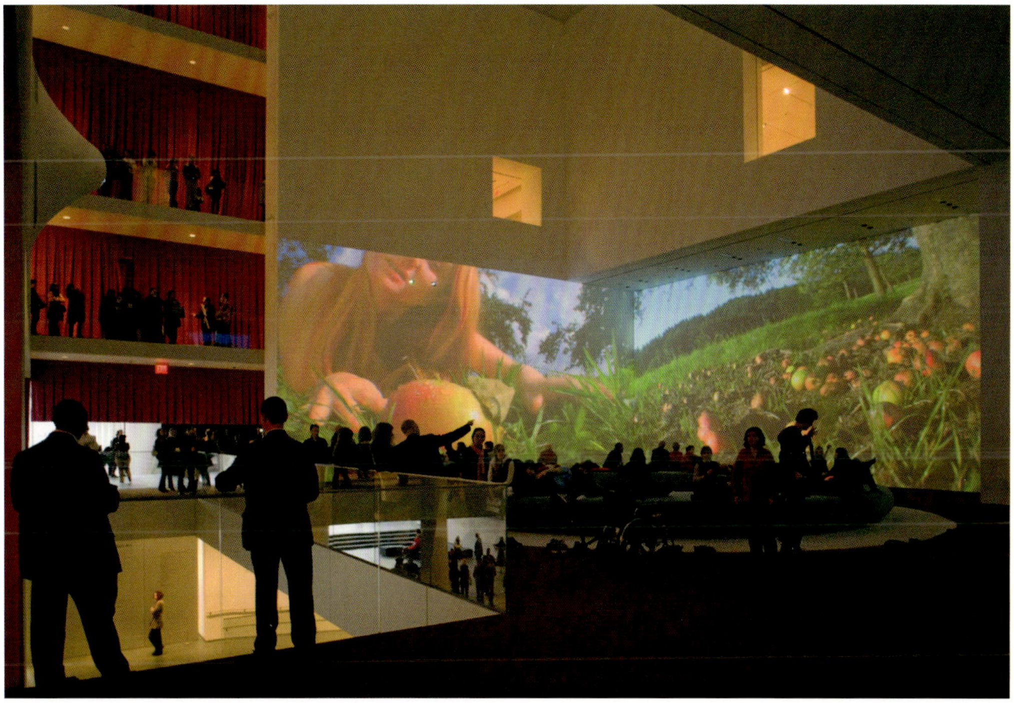

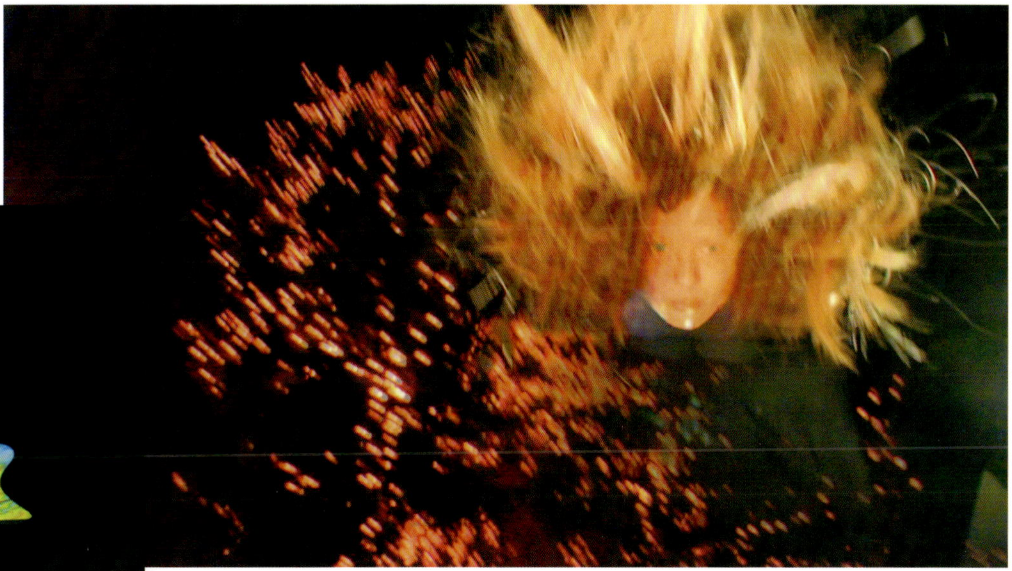

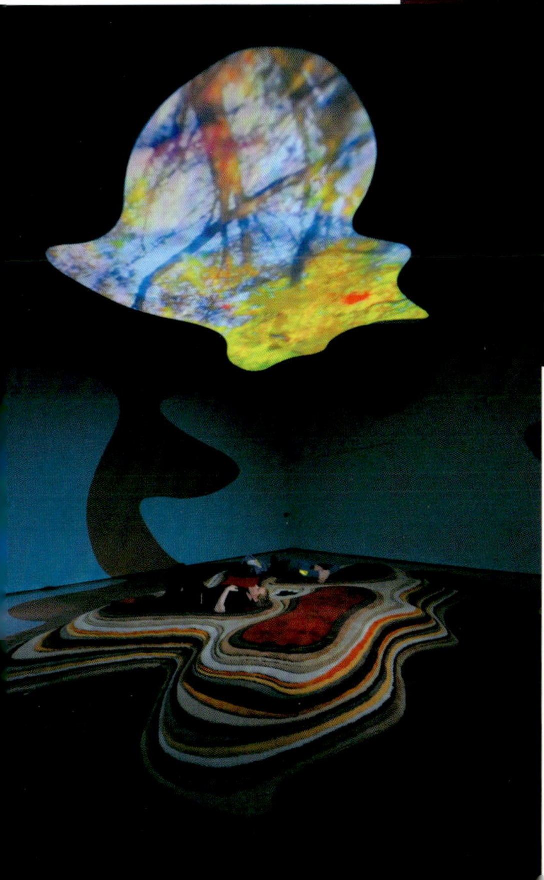

Tyngdkraft, var min vän (Gravity Be My Friend), 2007
Video installation,
dimensions variable
View of the installation realized in 2007 at the FACT Foundation for Art and Creative Technology, Liverpool
Courtesy of the artist and Hauser & Wirth Zürich/London

Piotr Uklanski

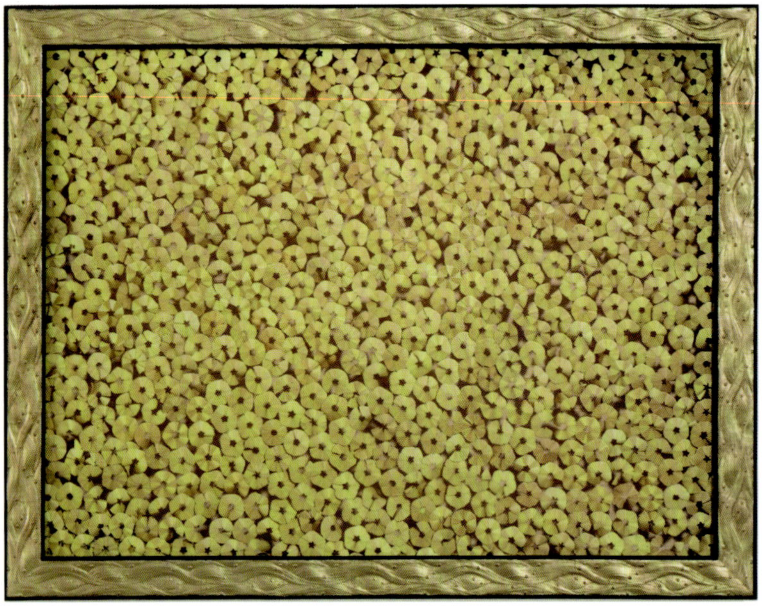

Untitled (Orla), 2005
Sharpened pencils, Plexiglas, 86.5 x 110 x 8.5 cm
Milan, Galleria Massimo De Carlo

Untitled (Dance Floor), 1996
Plexiglas, colored light bulbs, raised structure, dimensions variable
View of the installation realized in 1996 at the Gavin Brown Enterprise, New York
New York, Gagosian Gallery

Born in Warsaw in 1968. Lives and works in New York and Warsaw.
It is not easy to identify a guiding thread in the work of Piotr Uklanski at first sight, not least as the artist avoids giving any explanation when interviewed, often alternating silences with rude or ironic answers. In formal terms, he works with equal mastery in a variety of fields including photography, collage, installation, and sculpture. As he stated in 2003, "I want to be all this: modernist, post-minimalist, Pop-Conceptualist, a photographer, an amateur, the muse of a painter, a political artist like Boltanski, and a director like Polanski." And he is indeed the director of *Summer Love*, described as "the first Polish Western" and presented at the Venice Film Festival in 2006.
Uklanski moves like a tightrope walker along the narrow boundary separating beauty and kitsch, art and mass culture, symbolism and rhetoric, with a neutrality far removed both from pure affirmation and from criticism, which ends up irritating the viewer. He aroused hostile reactions in 1998 with his first presentation of *The Nazis*, a series of photographs showing all the actors that have played the part of Nazi soldiers in the history of cinema. In particular, he was accused of facile generalization and a typically fascist attitude of superficiality in drawing no distinction between films presenting a shallow view of Nazism and those that have contributed to our understanding of history. In actual fact, it is also possible to approach the work at a deeper level, as Bonami did in pointing out that regardless of the intentions of any one film, it is precisely the mystique of cinema that tinges our reading of history with the glamour of the action film and prevents any real understanding of the tragedy.
In the same way, his renowned *Dance Floors*, modular floors emitting colored neon light, are located midway between the radical work of Carl Andre and disco-style aesthetics, generating a joyous, all-enveloping atmosphere that prevents any rational insight into its causes. Mostly included in *The Joy of Photography*, a series underway since 1996, his numerous technically impeccable photographs are often excessively pretty in their painstaking application of the advice imparted in the Kodak manual for amateur photographers of the 1970s from which the title is borrowed. At the same time, however, examination of works like *Untitled (Vesuvius)* (2000) and *Untitled (Island)* (1997) clearly shows that by thrusting their beauty in our faces, Uklanski "creates visual titillation using banal subjects and clichéd techniques" (Alison Gingeras) in order to prompt reflection on the uncertain status of a cultural artifact.
Often striking the pose of a star of the art world, Uklanski also finds opportunities to focus on his own identity (both professional and cultural) and the ambiguities of the system in which he operates. *Untitled (Skull)* (2000) is a soft porn image but also a plagiarism of a work by Dalí, in which the artist's skull is made up of naked male and female bodies with the artist in the middle. He bought three pages of space in *Artforum* in 2003 and used them to present a photograph of a naked female behind and an accompanying text by its owner, his partner Alison Gingeras, curator at the Centre Pompidou and adviser to the great French collector François Pinault. Another recurrent subject is his own national identity, something the world of art exhibits or conceals according to circumstances. In 2004 the artist took an aerial photograph of a group of people arranged so as to create a portrait of Pope John Paul II and then used the image on posters in urban spaces in Poland. The title he gave to his first solo show at the Gagosian, New York, in 2008 was *BIALO-CZERWONA* (white-red), an expression often used to indicate the Polish flag. The show comprised sculptures, photographs, installations, and paintings referring in various ways to Polish nationality and explored national identity as a stereotype: a raised fist against a red and white background; an aerial photograph of a group of people forming the word "*Solidarnosc*" (Solidarity); kitsch installations celebrating vernacular art and local traditions. The allegorical western film *Summer Love*, combining Polish actors and international stars, completed the circle as an emblem of the destiny of the idea of the nation in a globalized culture.
(*D.Q.*)

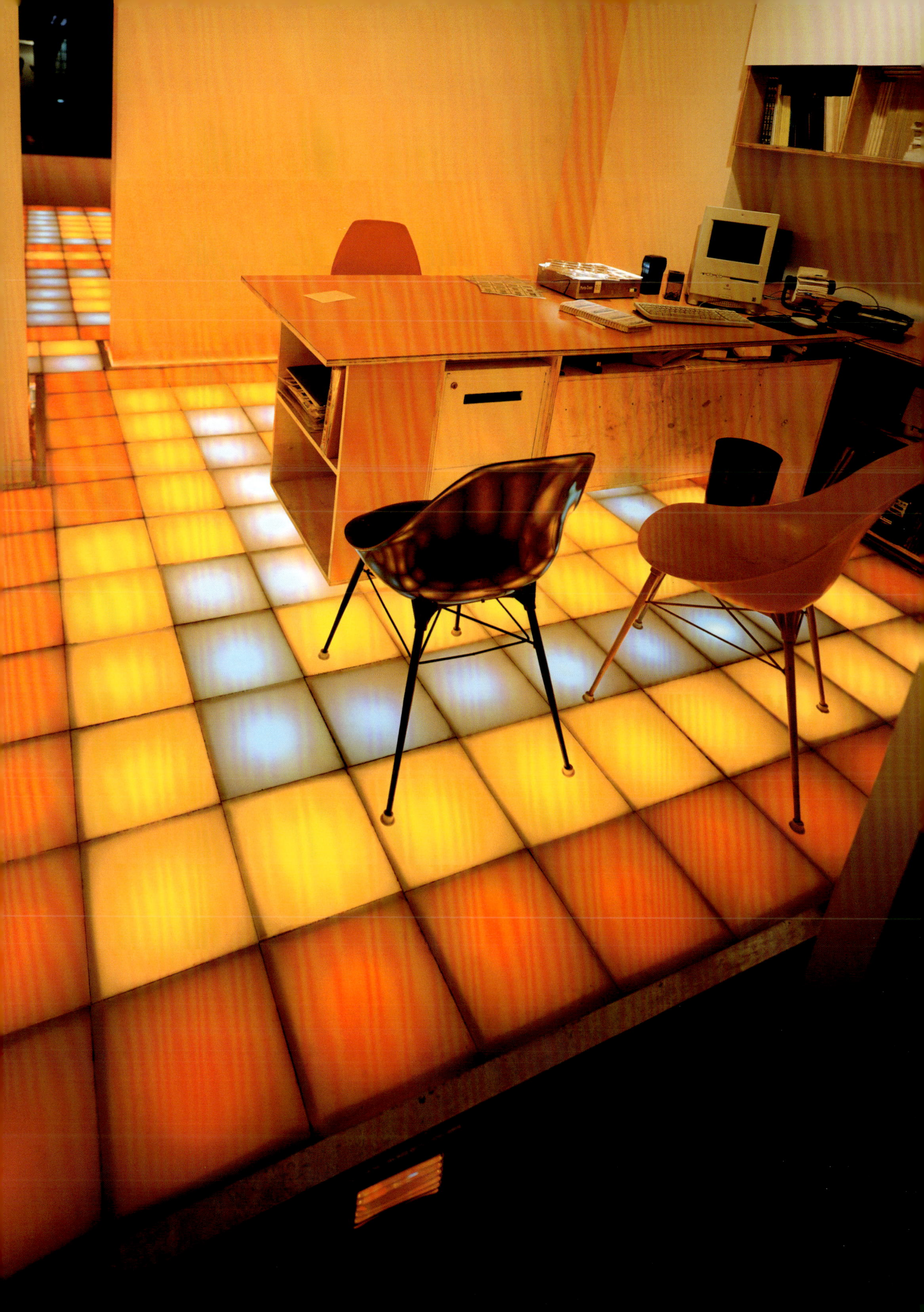

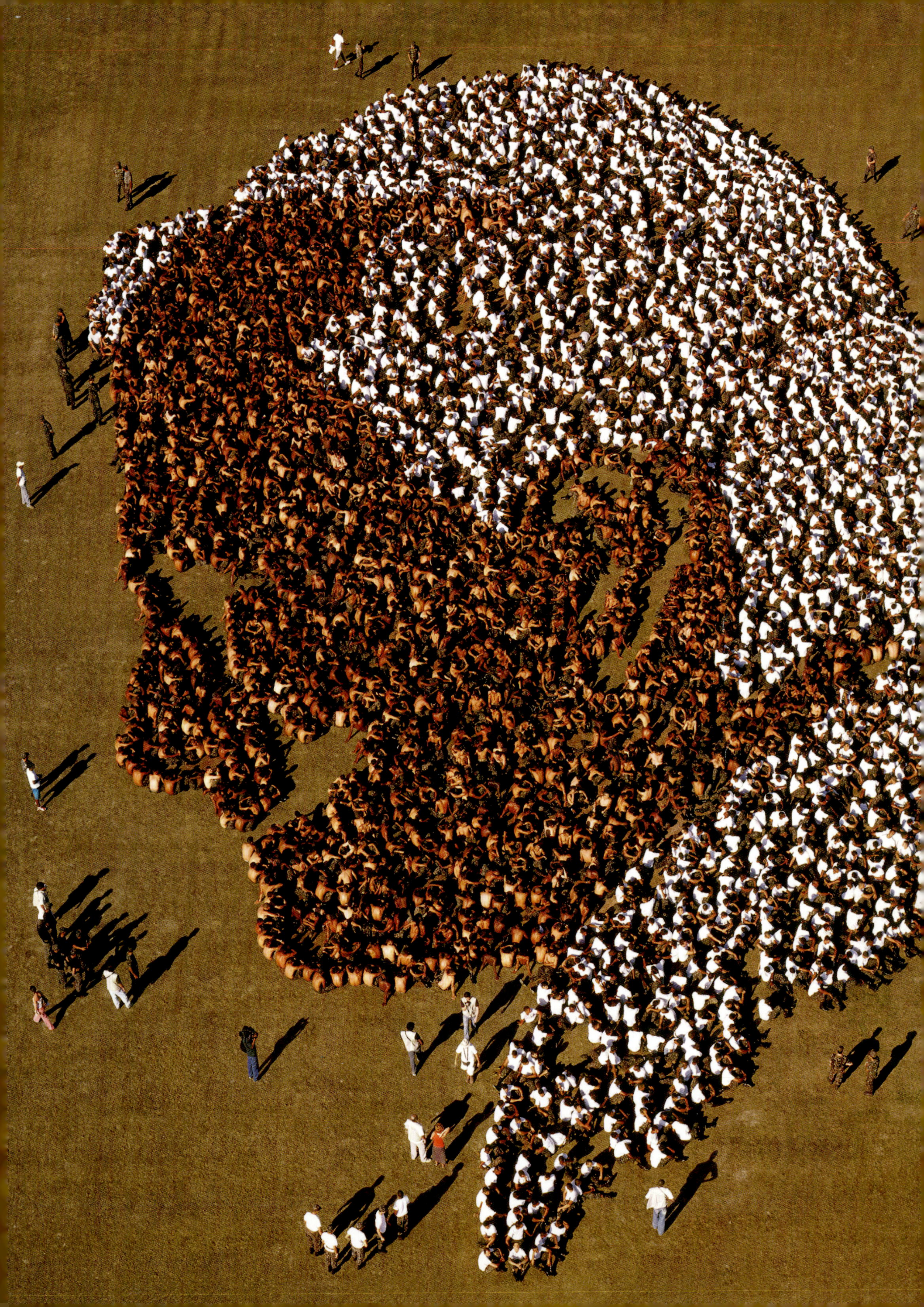

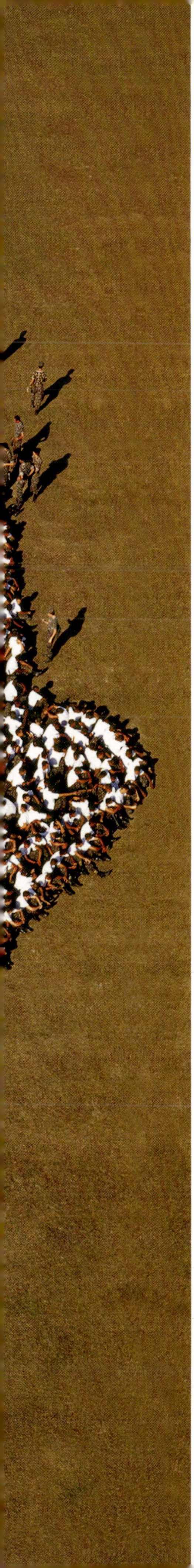

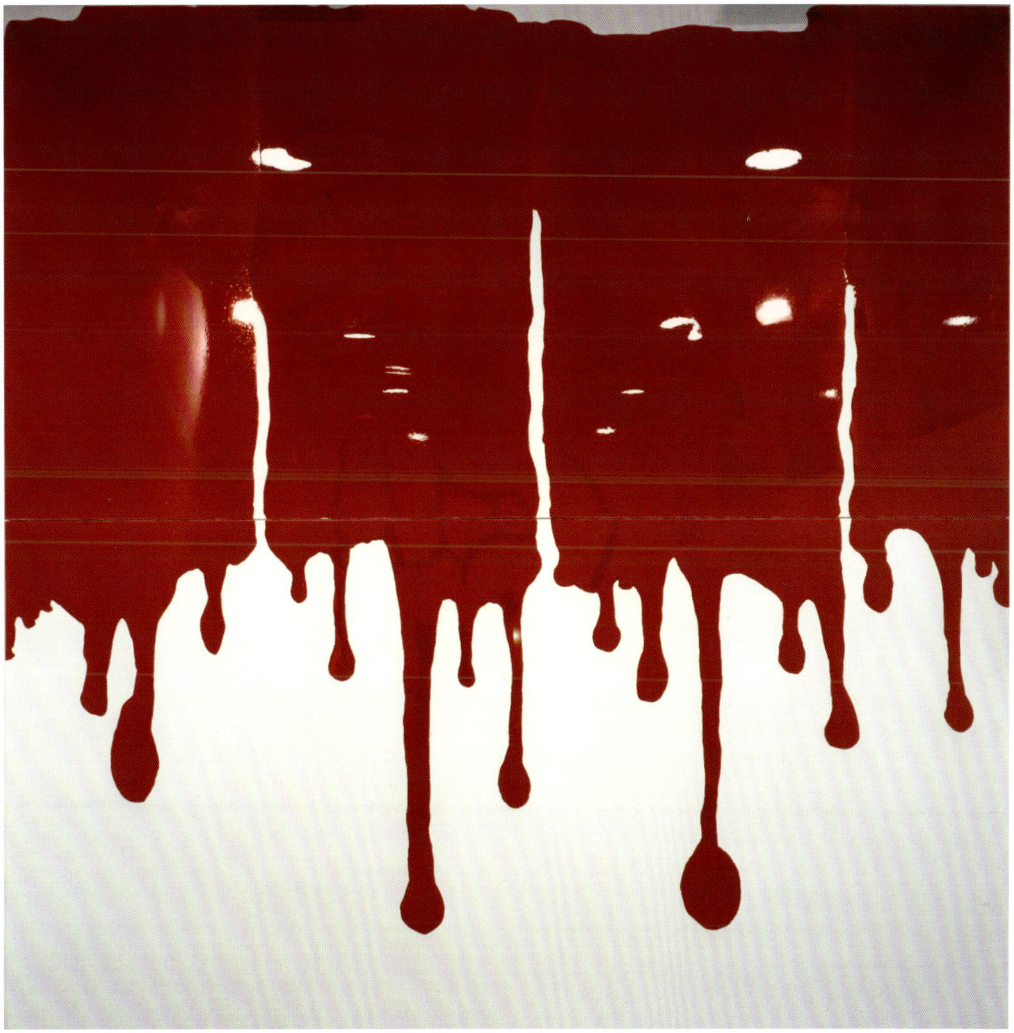

Untitled (Ioannes Paulus PP.II Karol Wojtyla), 2004
Color photograph, 200 x 174.9 cm
New York, Gagosian Gallery

Untitled (Bloody Sunday), 2007
Epoxy resin on canvas,
600 x 600 cm
Milan, Galleria Massimo De Carlo

Nico Vascellari

Born in Vittorio Veneto, Italy in 1976. Lives and works in Milan. Nico Vascellari's work is born out of participation in the activities of *With Love*, a punk noise group from the Bolognese underground scene, and the experience of working from 2000 to 2002 in the design department of Fabrica, a creative workshop set up in 1994 within the framework of Benetton's communication projects.
The artist addresses the relationship between space, sound and perception in installations, performances and videos where the relationship with the public, the emotional and physical action of sound and the assertion of the artist's identity play a fundamental role.
The winner of the 4th Premio Arte Giovane award organized by the DARC and the MAXXI in Italy in 2007, the artist took part in the Venice Biennale with *Revenge*, a performance based on the iconography of punk music and its imagery of extreme acts, which involved the public in a physical and violent way. The room in which Vascellari's action took place was completely lined with amplifiers to intensify the sound as the artist screamed, sang and literally flew over the audience. Including the collateral events of an authentic hardcore concert, such as the distribution of gadgets and T-shirts, the performance was continued throughout the Biennale one with transmission of the Larsen effect of feedback caused by the proximity of microphone and amplifier. Vascellari thus identifies the front-man as the icon of the winner, the idea of vengeance expressed in the title of the performance being a reference to the process whereby the artist's activity achieves recognition and success, as represented by the screaming and the high volume of the music.
Sound is also the essential component of the video *Hymn*, produced in 2008 for the seventh edition of Manifesta and consisting of panoramic views of the countryside projected onto broken mirrors to the accompaniment of a soundtrack of 36 numbers played over home-made amplifiers.
The artist thus examines the link between nature as a source of inspiration and music as a form of human expression.
(*F.T.*)

Revenge, 2007
Video installation
View of the installation at the LII Esposizione Internazionale d'Arte, Biennale di Venezia 2007
Rome, MAXXI_Museo nazionale delle arti del XXI secolo
Courtesy of the artist and DARC

Hymn, 2008
Installation, video projection on broken mirrors and wood, 12 loudspeakers, 36 audio snippets
View of the installation at Manifesta 7 – European Biennial of Contemporary Art, Trentino Alto Adige 2008
Rovereto, private collection
Courtesy of the artist and Monitor, Rome

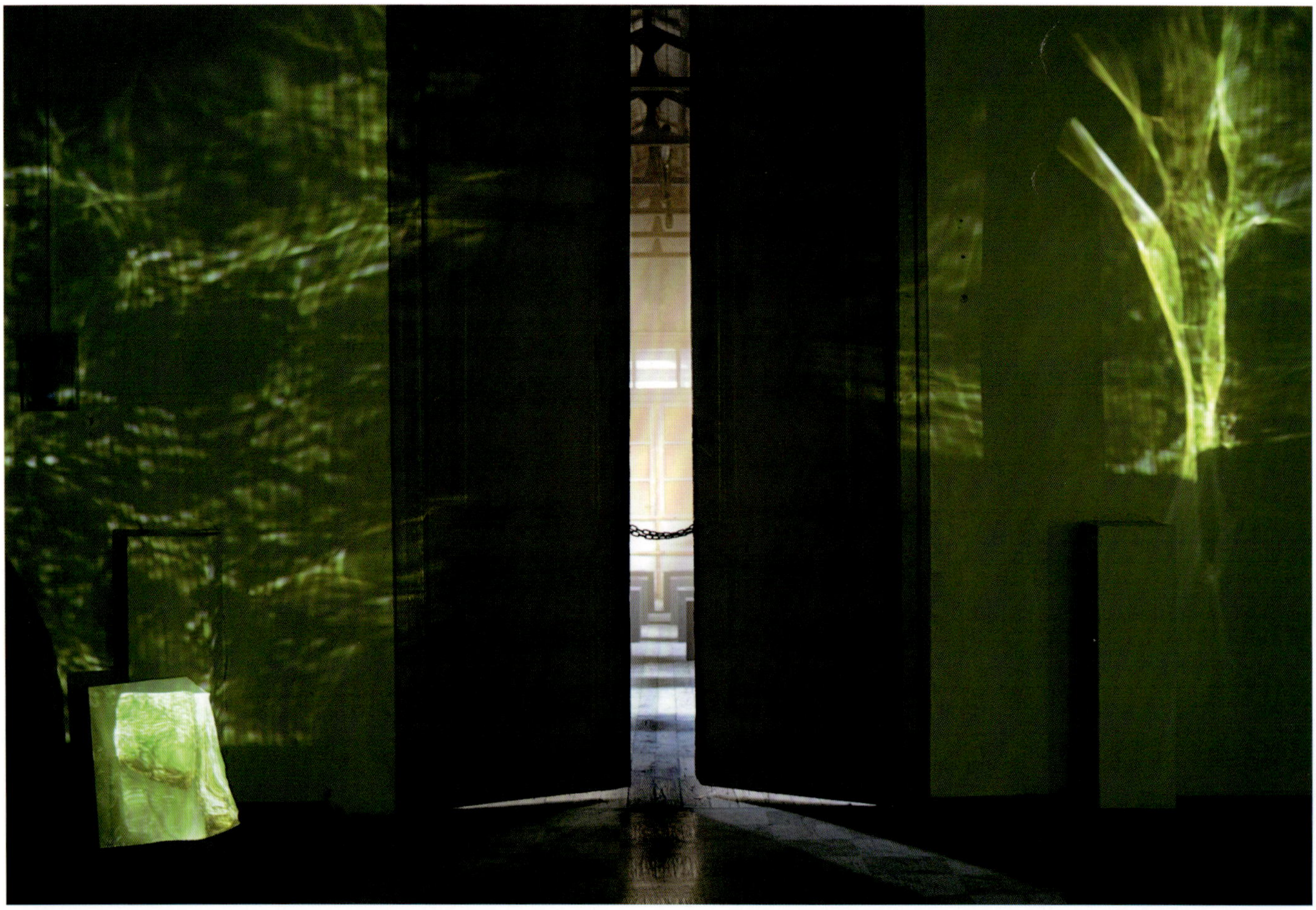

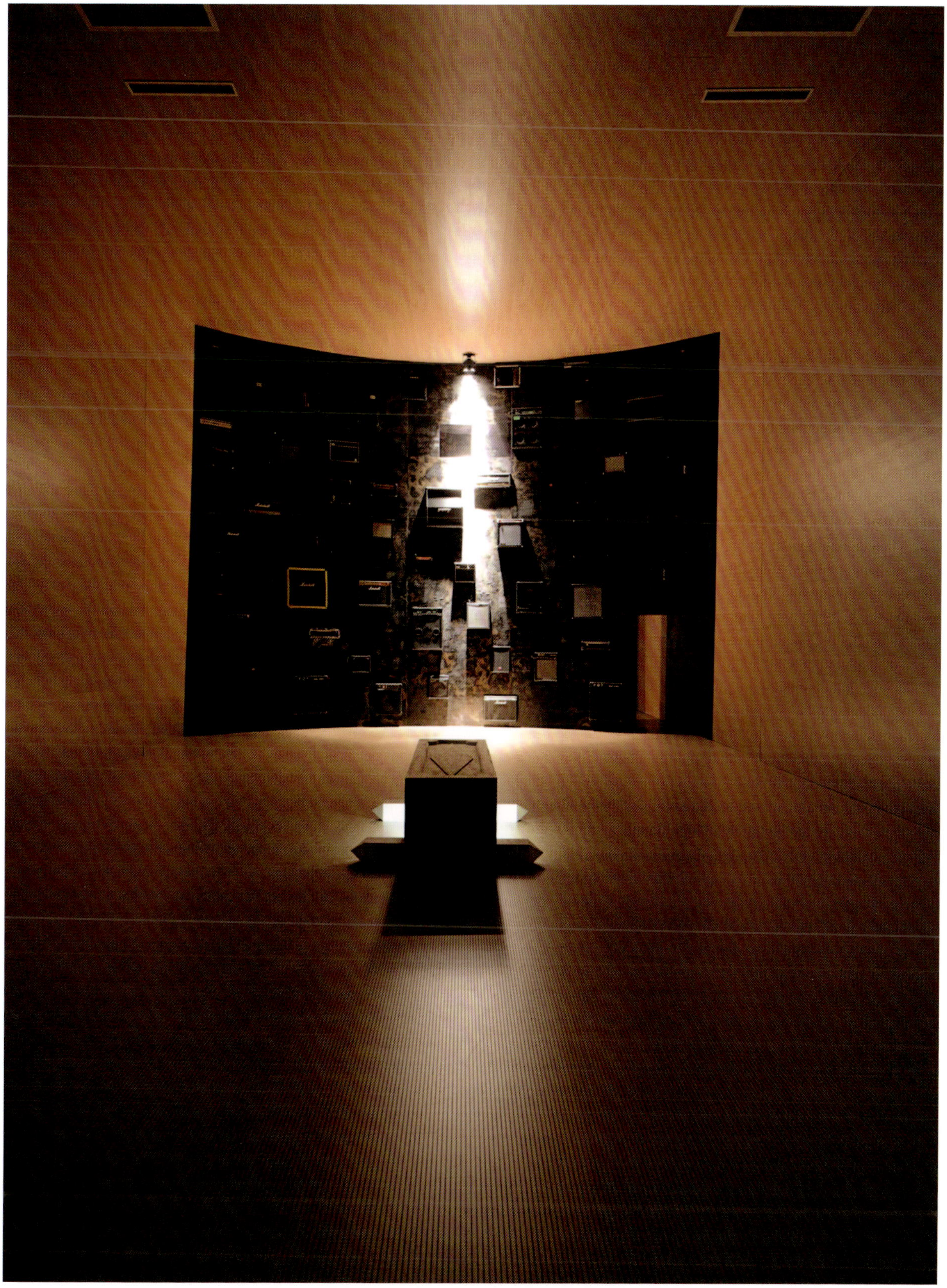

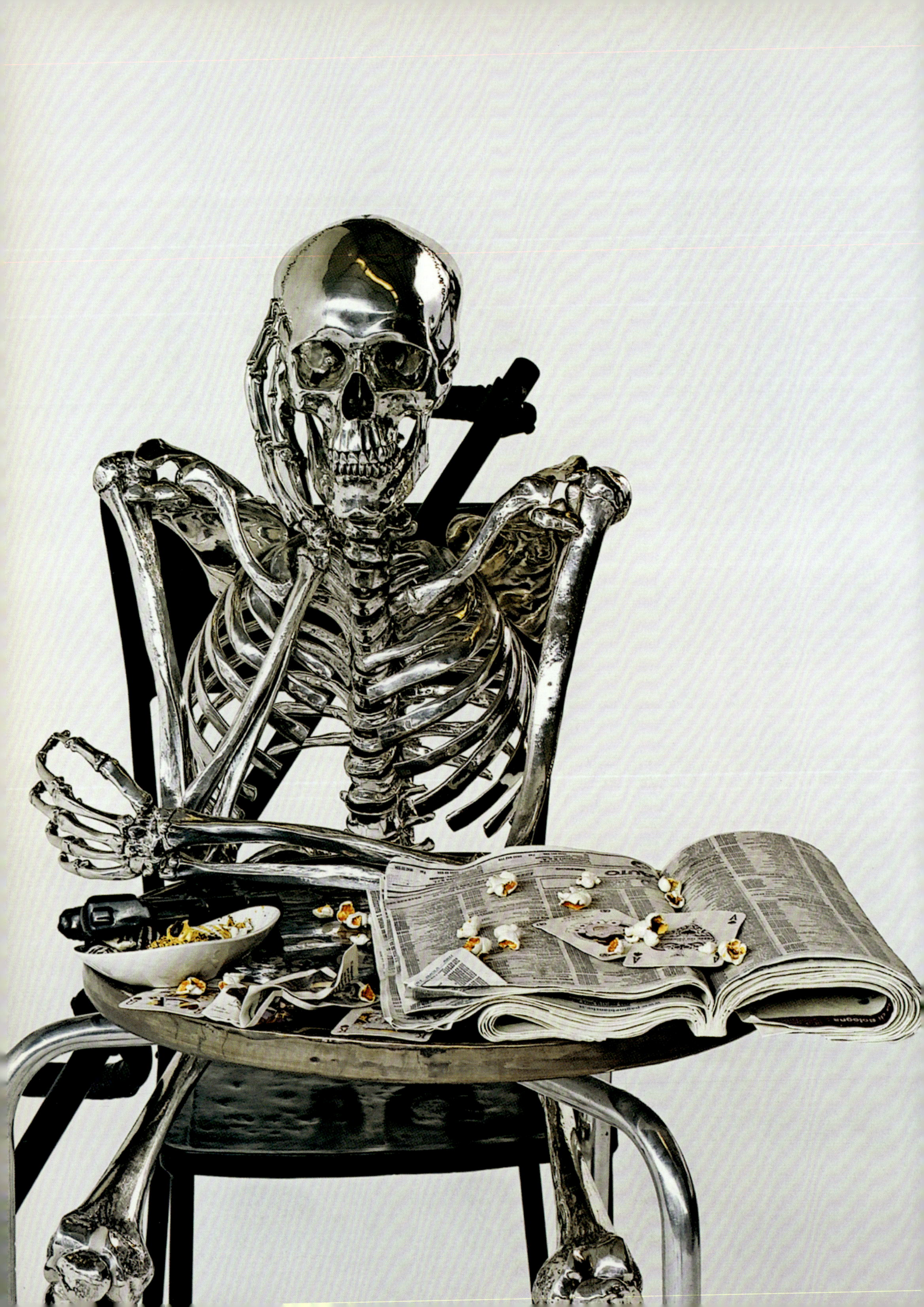

Valerio Terraroli

Contemporary Art and Decorative Arts: Technical Proofs of Connection

Bertozzi & Casoni
Riflessione sulla morte (detail), 2008
Polychrome ceramic, silver, and bronze, 160 x 253 x 128 cm
Private collection

Can the system of the decorative or applied arts present itself as an adversary of the system of contemporary arts? Challengingly formulated by Enzo Biffi Gentili on the occasion of the exhibition held in Turin in 2002 to celebrate the centenary of the city's legendary exhibition of decorative and industrial arts (Esposizione internazionale delle arti decorative e industriali, 1902), this question expands debate about the characteristics and purposes of contemporary art to include the fascinating issue of the relations and/or interference between the forms, techniques, and materials specifically developed for and in the decorative arts and the models and results of a great deal of contemporary art. At the same time, the question is also raised of the decorative value of the art object on the one hand and the conceptual and creative value of the decorative object on the other. In other words, we are asked whether it still makes sense to apply the adjective "decorative" to a form of artistic expression characterized by techniques and materials drawn from the craft tradition.

The existence of synergies – not to mention interrelations and mutual dependencies – between ornamentation and figurative art in the past is an established and evident fact. In the modern era, however, despite the gradually widening gap between the decorative and figurative arts – the former disparagingly defined as minor and the latter therefore necessarily as major – theorized by art historians in the nineteenth century and still widely maintained by art critics and historians in the twentieth, a reuniting of the creative front took place at the turn of the century, when modernism was in full swing.

The modern definition and indeed the very concept of the decorative arts were in fact born around the beginning of the twentieth century, to some degree in connection with the theoretical formulations developed during the long wave of the modernist style and with a need to classify creative dynamics that sought, despite various difficulties, to detach the decorative object as well as decoration *tout court* definitively from their ties with artisanal and exquisitely technical-material creation and yoke them to pure artistic creation. In other words, the European Secessionist movements inflicted a resounding defeat on the academies of fine arts and their monopoly position. Combined with the systematic development of the concept of the *Gesamtkunstwerk* (total work of art), the proliferation of private galleries and clients from the upper and medium bourgeoisie, fully aware of their status and tastes, opened up the way to a violent and decisive wave of forms, themes, and languages that, while looking to classical myth and history, put forward a rereading of the same in the light of the needs, aesthetic dynamics, and expectations of the contemporary world.

Important vehicles for the spread of the new approaches were the views expressed by far-sighted critics like Hermann Bahr in Vienna, who later became one of the theorists of Expressionism, Ludwig Hevesi, again in Vienna, and Julius Meier-Graefe in Berlin, a point of reference for the dissemination in Central Europe not only of the French avant-garde but also of artistic and literary magazines that were new in terms both of content and of graphics, including *Pan* in Berlin (from 1895), *Jugend* in Munich (from 1896), and *Ver Sacrum* in Vienna (from 1898). A part was also played by the direct involvement of Secessionist artists and architects in setting up, organizing, and running workshops of decorative arts of a more or less pre-industrial and artisanal character, like the Vereinigte Werkstätten in Munich and the Wiener Werkstätten in Vienna. Finally, crucial importance attached in the positive appraisal of decoration, both in architecture and in forms of figurative expressions, and of the decorative arts to the reflections, especially in the German area, on pure visibility (*Reine Sichtbarkeit*) and empathy (*Einfühlung*), developed respectively by Adolf Hildebrand and Konrad Fiedler and by Theodor Lipps and August Schmarsow, as well as the systematic historical and critical rereading developed by Alois Riegl and Franz Wickhoff. These leading figures in the "Vienna School" revised the periodic division of the history of art, identifying the numerous connections between figurative and decorative creativity and the central role of the decorative arts in the development of the various civilizations, and ultimately attributing artistic value also

Bertozzi & Casoni
Cestino della discordia, 2007
Polychrome ceramic, 38 x 31 x 30 cm
Private collection

to non-mimetic and purely decorative forms of expression. This concept was taken up the architect and designer August Endell from Munich in a number of articles in specialized journals, where he not only maintained the substantial separation of nature and art but also the need for contemporary art to be characterized by free forms that represent nothing and instead generate intensity and empathy of a rhythmic and musical type. The move toward substantially abstract and rigorously geometric forms inspired by the world of nature, especially plants, but reduced to rhythmically resolved forms of linear expression took concrete shape with the British Arts and Crafts movement and especially in the Glasgow School, where this approach was developed into an authentic vocabulary combining the archaic and the modern, references to the medieval tradition, especially in the employment of traditional materials, and an interest in the industrial production of articles. The dissemination of these inventions took place as from 1893 with *The Studio*, a magazine constituting the manual of the modernist vocabulary in Europe. This was immediately echoed in Germany with the graphic inventions of Herman Obrist in Munich and Otto Eckmann in Berlin, drawing inspiration on the one hand from the most exquisitely Art Nouveau form of biomorphism and, on the other, from the asymmetric spatial rigor of the Japanese graphic arts. At the same time, the Belgian Henry van de Velde developed an approach based on the painting of the French Pointillists and the Nabis group but focusing on forms of a rigorous two-dimensional and, in short, abstract nature. The question of the decorative arts within the sphere of the Secessionist movements thus saw a change in attitude of a kind far less likely to occur in painting or sculpture, namely the total rejection and substantial abandonment of Romanticism and the overturning of an entire formal heritage endorsed by tradition.

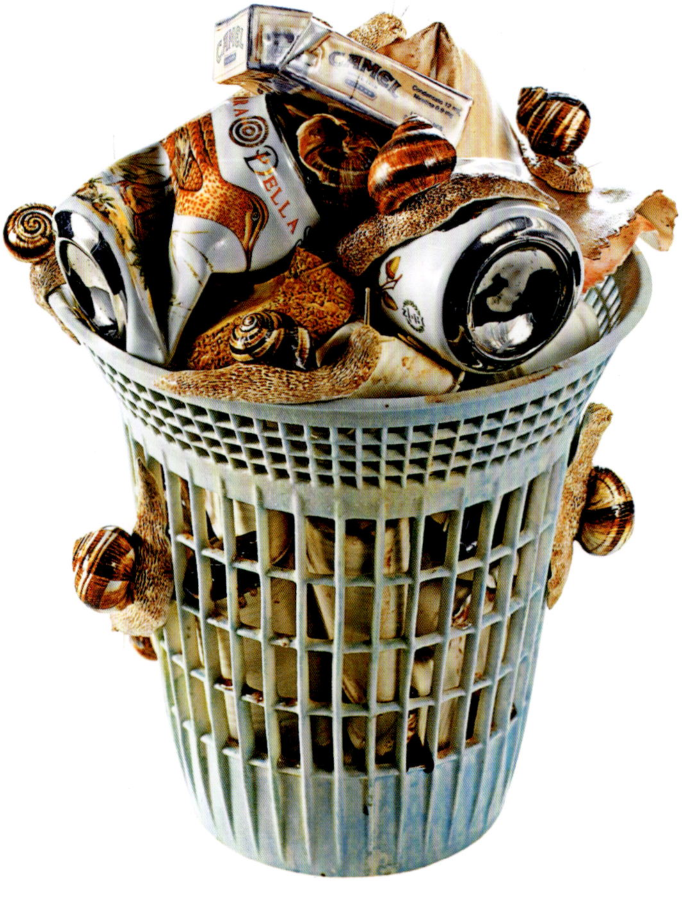

The interchange between the Secessionist artists and the Wiener Werkstätten, founded by Joseph Hoffmann and Koloman Moser in 1903, is fully revealed in a succession of exhibitions that, while predominantly hosting foreign artists such as Munch, Khnopff, the Nabis, van Gogh, Seurat, Ensor, and Segantini, also embraced the decorative arts and the indivisible ties between decoration and figurative art. An example is provided by the exhibition devoted to Beethoven in 1902, where the emblematic fulcrum of the mixed-media sculpture of clearly Symbolist derivation by Max Klinger was surrounded by works of Secessionist artists (Adolf Böhm and Alfred Roller) drawing inspiration from the clear-cut, rhythmic draftsmanship of Ferdinand Hodler and the fabrics of the Wiener Werkstätten, and above all Gustav Klimt's frieze based on the theme of the Ninth Symphony. Painting, combinations of materials (from ceramics to mother-of-pearl and colored glass), gilding, and two-dimensional decoration: all these combined within the setting to create the ideal *Gesamtkunstwerk* aimed at by the Secessionist and avant-garde movements. At the same time, 1902 was the date of the Esposizione internazionale delle arti decorative e industriali organized in Turin, an exhibition establishing the characteristics of European modernism and the Italian variety of Art Nouveau known as Liberty (giving rise to heated debate on modern taste and the values of the new style between figures like Enrico Thovez, Alfredo Melani, Luca Beltrami, and the young Ugo Ojetti). While focusing primarily on the floral and biomorphic line developed in France and Belgium, this also included items inspired to a greater degree by the rigorous, unadorned approach of Austro-German and above all Anglo-Scottish derivation.

The explosion of the artistic avant-gardes in the 1910s does not seem to have directly involved the problem of taste and the decorative arts, except perhaps in the case of Italian Futurism, which set out – at least theoretically – to redefine all the relations between the individual, the city, environments, and objects. While the problems of the reproducibility of forms, the industrial production of articles, and the democratic expansion of the market to include the less affluent remained substantially unresolved, at least as regards critical debate, pragmatic solutions were found in the market, which selected the line most brutally simplified and readily acceptable to the general public from the alternatives available. The need evidently felt by the Futurists was to break away from the constraints of the pictorial and plastic arts – from the "painting" – and initiate an approach of global integration of aesthetic experiences with the individual reality of everyday life in the conviction that communication of the Futurist grammar through the object would alone make it possible to achieve a radical reconstruction of aesthetic perception and hence of the contemporary world.

Gerrit Rietveld's *Red Blue Chair*, designed and produced in the Netherlands between 1917 and 1919, was the prototype of rigorous application of the dictates of rational geometry exemplified in *De Stijl*, the magazine and movement led by Piet Mondrian and Theo van Doesburg. The inclined planes, the sections of the structural elements, and the use of primary colors with evident perceptual and symbolic values all converged in an architectural and exquisitely abstract vision of the article of furniture. Though shattered by the events of the war and the post-war period, Germany too attempted once again, with this project of systematic artistic fusion in the euphoric climate of the nascent Weimar Republic, to embark on the arduous path of the utopia of art for all, and hence of the safeguarding of form within industrial production and the *Gesamtkunstwerk*, the perfect fitting of all the individual parts into a homogeneous whole as regards both form and contents. The Bauhaus was founded in Weimar in April 1919 through the merger of the schools of figurative art and applied art (the latter directed since 1907 by the Belgian Henry van de Velde) under the direction of the young architect Walter Gropius. While the idea of the fusion of the arts had already been addressed by great German masters of the decorative arts like Bruno Paul, Heinrich Tessenow, and Richard Riemerschmid, it was theoretically developed to the full by the architect Otto Bartning in his plan for general reform of the teaching of arts and crafts. This was published in 1918 by the Berlin Art Work Council, made up of avant-garde artists including Gropius, in the days of the November revolution. For all its contradictions, the trajectory of the Bauhaus – from the clashes between Itten and Gropius (1921) to the arrival of Wassili Kandinsky and László Moholy-Nagy (1923), the exhibition organized by Marcel Breuer (1923), and the definitive closing (August 22, 1932) – constituted an extraordinary melting pot of significant ideas and experiments for the future, definitively opening up the way for the relationship between design and industry but also asserting the indivisibility of decorative arts and painting, sculptural form and ornament, in a harmonious, Pandean vision of contemporary artistic practice. These values, which had been the backbone of the modernist utopia, were lost sight of once again, however, during the 1920s and 1930s. This is not because the terms of the question were not known and indeed repeatedly debated, but because the triumph of Art Deco led to a focus on the individuality and sophisticated preciousness of the object, its isolation with respect to a context that it was in harmony with but could easily do without, and ultimately to its absolute gratuitousness, hence increasing the desire for possession out of all proportion. The Art Deco production in the decorative arts – but also in the painting and sculpture of furnishings and ornamentation, which continued substantially unchanged until halfway through the 1930s – was unquestionably for a niche market. It is, however, equally true that the glittering world of sequins and gilding, bewitching boudoirs and sumptuous residences, simultaneously archaic and modern atmospheres – as seen in films and stage plays, on ocean liners, in hotels and cafés – penetrated deeply into the collective consciousness and common feeling, nourishing a desire for identification with this glamorous and exclusive environment that resulted in the production of cheap and tawdry "Twenties-style" objects on an enormous scale. At the same time, Deco became a way for the contemporary world to recover values, both ethical and aesthetic, previously considered lost, such as artisanal traditions and roots at the national and regional level. One example is Italy, where there was an attempt to combine rural culture and metropolitan elegance, pride in national history and responsiveness to an international style. It was the drive to establish Italian artistic production at the European level – to bring its vocabulary up to date and harness its never forgotten relationship with tradition and the close connection between the decorative and the figurative arts – that led to the founding of the ISIA (Istituto Superiore per le Industrie Artistiche) in 1925.

The period of radical detachment if not discontinuity that saw the triumph of the Art Informel vocabulary and the proliferation of Conceptual Art, Pop Art, Land Art, and Body Art, which moreover broke away for obvious reasons from the mechanism of "making" and hence from the pathways of the decorative arts and design, seems to have gone through a moment of rapprochement if not indeed the development of a renewed map of fusion and synergy precisely at the turn of the millennium. The use of techniques and materials more traditionally identified with artistic crafts and the world of the decorative arts became increasingly frequent in the creation of complex installations and works of Land Art. These take on the dual character of conceptual operations presented at the same time with aesthetic-decorative features in virtue of the techniques and materials employed, which are not canonically artistic.

Examples at the international level include the Australian Dale Chihuly. Having started out in the early 1970s with objects of blown glass that constitute authentic sculptures, he progressed to demanding installations and explicit works of Land Art in the 1990s and early 2000s. Emblematic significance attaches in particular to works like the *Cobalt Blue Chandelier* (1994), installed in the Union Station, Tacoma (Washington), and the spectacular *Green Chandelier* placed in the atrium of London's Victoria and Albert Museum, the "temple" of the decorative arts, in 2003. In both cases, the artist reinvents the role of traditional Murano blown glass in his biomorphic reinterpretation of the structure of the classic eighteenth-century Venetian chandelier. The regular polycentric distribution of branches covered in foliage alternating with blossoms, corollas, and stems that conceal the metal structure hanging from the ceiling is replaced with vital stratification, an irrepressible blooming of phytomorphic elements that seem to pour out of the ceiling and fall like a stalactite toward the viewer. Having radically dispensed with any practical function whatsoever, these installations take on the character of signs in space and establish a new and unprecedented relationship with the same that is enhanced by the apparent contradiction between the monumental quality of the object and the extreme fragility of its components. In 2005 and 2006 Chihuly organized in Kew Gardens, just outside London, a series of installations in the open and in the greenhouses that constitute a sort of visual and conceptual pathway through his work (some projects date back to 1991–95) and a new approach to the world of nature: a boat full of

Silvia Zotta
Cerchi al muro ovvero Variations autour de l'ouvrage, 2008
Polychrome majolica,
dimensions variable
Private collection

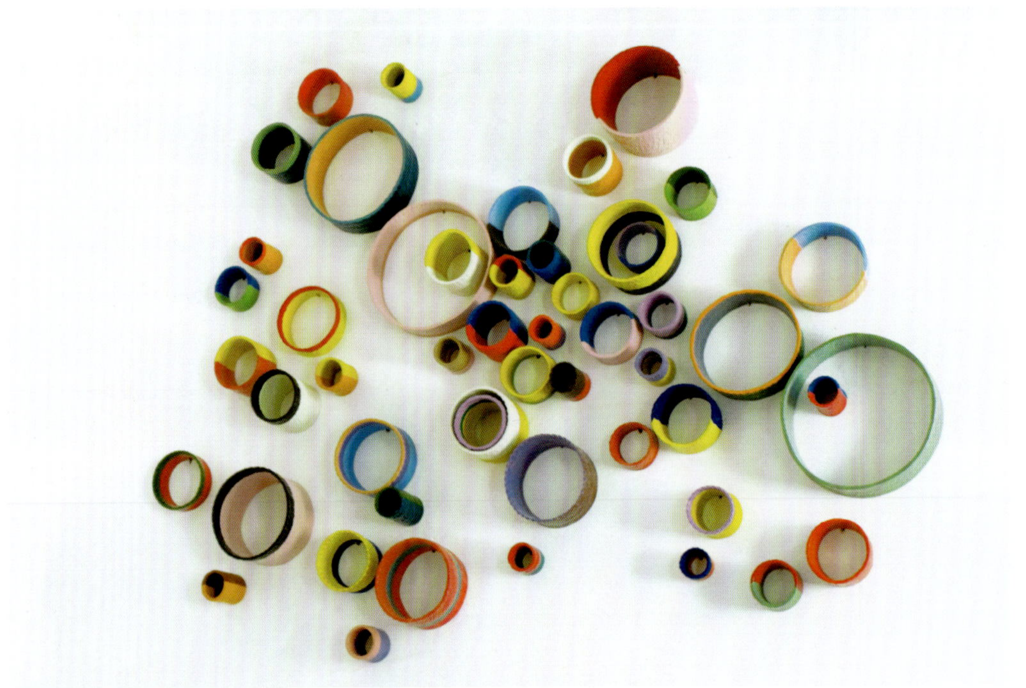

Remo Rachini
Formella, 2009
Nails on poplar wood, 45 x 44 cm
Private collection

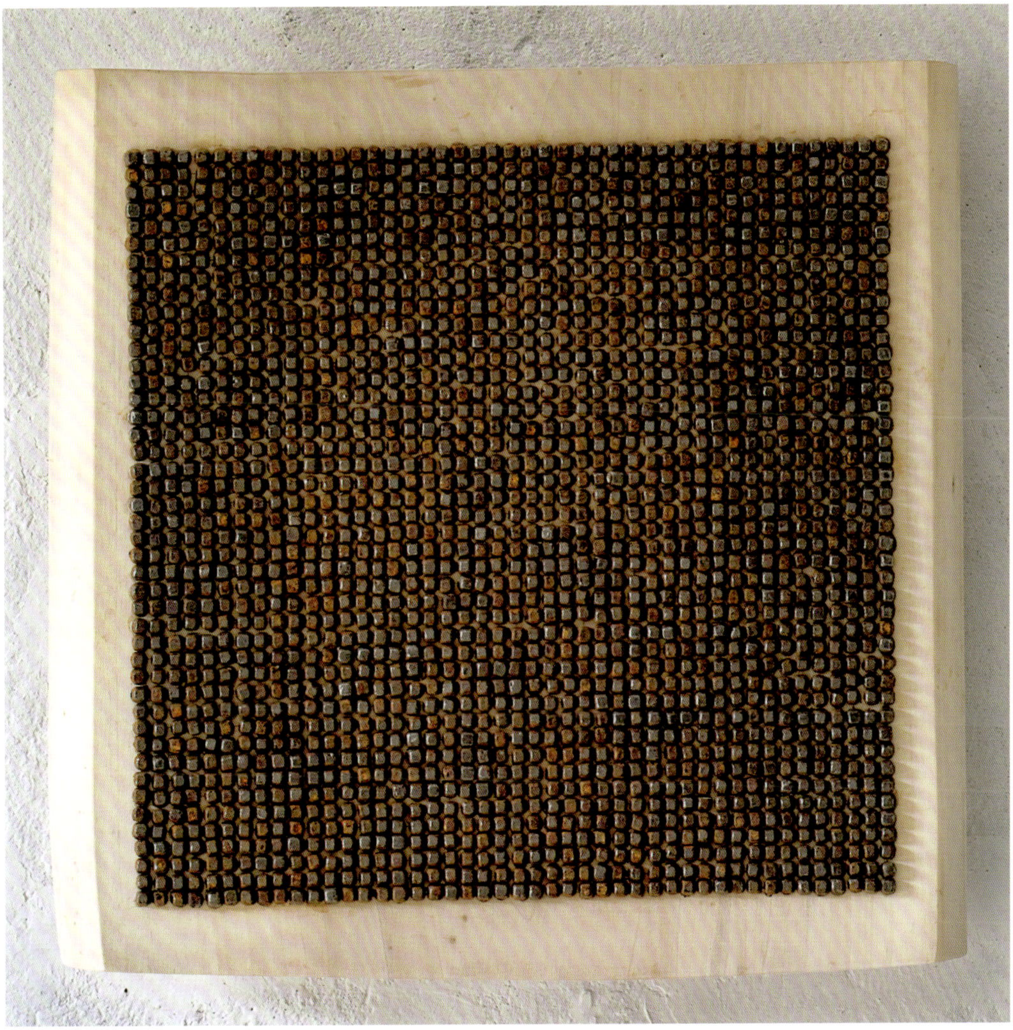

polychromatic glass spheres and flasks anchored in the lake; a gleaming biomorphic pattern created by cobalt blue, ruby red, and ocher yellow chandeliers hanging from posts along the paths; artificial flowers and blossoms grafted onto and intermingled with their natural counterparts in a never-ending interplay of *artificialia* and *naturalia*. Here too, the decorative techniques of blown, ground and zanfirico glass create neither usable objects or exquisitely ornamental works but help with their variegated appearance to make visible an oneiric and cognitive journey between nature and art.

Many examples could be given at the international level of artists who express themselves through the use of the decorative arts, like Arman with his ceramic installations. One particular area is Fiber Art with its constant reutilization of materials like fabric, yarn, natural elements, and wire to create sculptural pseudo-garments or signs and installations: Mona Hatoum's *Keffiah* (1993–99) of cotton embroidered with locks of hair; Ghada Amer's *Index of Pleasures* (2001) and other works of embroidery; Rainer Ganahl's *Afghan Dialog, America Strikes Back* (2002); Eva Marisaldi's "Happy Ending" cushions (*Lieto fine*, 2000); Francesco Vezzoli's *Omaggi a Fortunato Depero* (2003).

Among the Italian artists who have focused on the use of crafts and the great tradition of the decorative arts, attention should be drawn to Luigi Ontani, who has been working with the Ceramica Gatti firm in Faenza since 1980 to develop his creative projects with the employment of majolica and metallic glazes, which give his totem/self-portraits the appearance of precious urns, as in *Canopo Galileo ChiniLei* (2003). And it is ceramics – ranging from painted terracotta to enameled earthenware and majolica – that constitutes the primary medium of a large number of Italian artists, who recognize the great versatility and contemporary power of expression and communication of a material relegated to the manufacture of everyday objects or the preparatory phases of sculptural production. A more explicit and vigorous figurative language, on the almost unbearable boundary of hyperrealism and closely connected with the indistinct atmosphere

Paolo Schmidlin
Eliza-Bette, 2002
Polychrome terracotta, height 90 cm,
base ø 15 cm
Private collection

Livio Scarpella
Baby Reliquiary n. 3, 2007
Baby Fauno Reliquiary, 2007
Gilded bronze, aventurine, embossed
and silver–plated copper, coral,
geodes, 33 x 14 x 14 cm each
Private collection

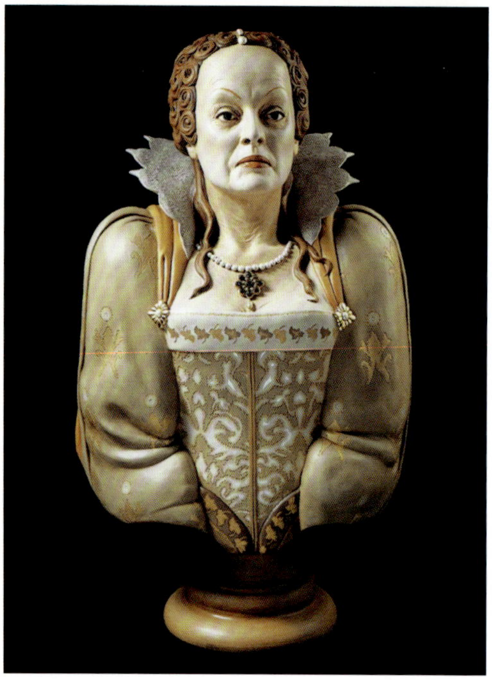

of kitsch, is to be found in the works of Bertozzi & Casoni, Paolo Schmidlin, and Livio Scarpella. It was in Imola in 1980 that Giampaolo Bertozzi and Stefano Dal Monte Casoni founded a partnership now recognized at the international level as a guarantee of sophisticated, intelligent, top-quality production that is often challenging and always highly inventive. Having started with majolica, the duo abandoned artisanal painted ware in 1999–2000 to adopt materials and technologies of industrial derivation, such as porcelain, stoneware, earthenware and semi-refractory clays, with which they obtain unusual "realer than real" effects and complex installations embellished with vitreous pastes. The themes of the *Vanitas* and the *Memento mori* are the primary focus of the two artists' most recent work: from *Minimi avanzi* (2007) to *Vassoio* (2008), from *Cestino della discordia* (2002) to *Intervallo* (2008), authentic masterpieces of still life based on the models of seventeenth-century Dutch and Flemish painters but represented three-dimensionally and with a truly astonishing rendering of the different components. Meditation on death, a sense of the futility of existence, and an ironic game of symbolic and narrative assemblages have given birth to authentic installations: *Composizione 13* (2008), a sarcastic revisitation of Damien Hirst's *Pharmacy* in which domestic first-aid cabinets take the form of a contemporary *Wunderkammer* crammed with remnants and fragments of everyday life in the consumer society; *Madonna scheletrita* (2008), a ceramic skeleton covered in silver pushing a metal lawnmower that cuts down flowers and grass on ground littered with rubbish, all made of polychromatic ceramics; *Riflessione sulla morte* (2008), a mixed-media composition that takes an ironic look at the traditional iconography of scythe-wielding Death, shown here sitting in a bar with popcorn and a pistol as he looks up his next victim in the phone book.

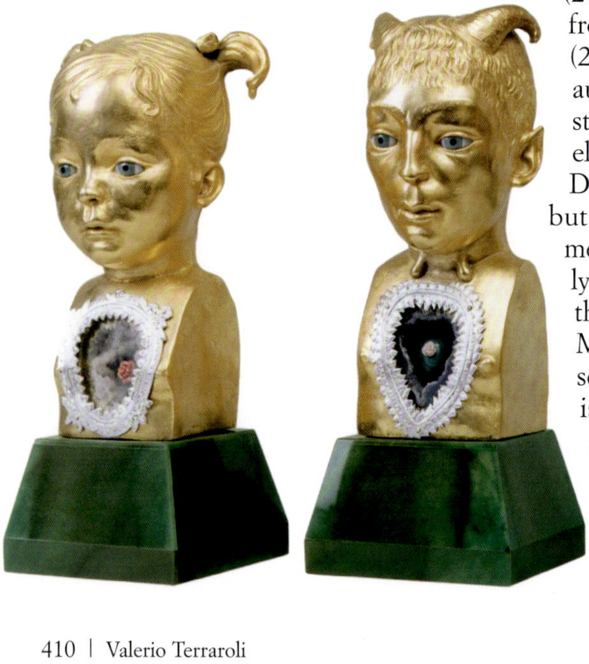

Paolo Schmidlin uses painted terracotta to create his personal vision of contemporary icons: portrait busts or figures cut off at the hips to offer an elegantly distorted rereading of types and characters. From *Eliza-Bette* (2002), the Queen of England halfway between the frowning physiognomy of Bette Davis and a drag queen, to *Miss Kitty* (2009), a violently sarcastic portrait of Pope Benedict XVI, the artist employs the techniques of terracotta and the ancient idea of painted sculpture with mastery and a wholly contemporary compositional approach. Like Schmidlin, Livio Scarpella uses polychromatic terracotta to illustrate his awareness of an indivisible unity of dazzling beauty and existential melancholy, wild strength and total immobility, eroticism (exhibited more than experienced) and gelid detachment with respect to contingent reality, as in *Gas* (2007), *Shunga* (2006), and above all *Senzasangue A* (2008). Finally, attracted by the endless possibilities of the decorative arts, the artist has recently embarked on a sort of revisitation of the reliquary busts of the baroque and late-baroque tradition, employing gilded bronze, malachite, onyx, embossed and silver-plated copper, pearls, coral and geodes to create a collection of *mirabilia* (wonders) with faces of children and fauns.

On the abstract front, in close relation to the idea of redesigning space and endowing the ceramic element with marked and coordinated semantic dignity in both sculptural and pictorial terms, attention should be drawn to Silvia Zotta's *Carta urgente a Buenos Aires* (presented in Turin in 2002), a wall of ceramic panels where writing is grafted onto the polychromatic arrays in a rhythmic, narrative flow of great impact. Zotta's recent work also includes a series of installations based on the repetition of brightly colored solid forms (parallelepipeds, cylinders), which are mounted on the wall in accordance with an almost biomorphic creative design and completely alter our perception of space, as in *Cerchi al muro ovvero Variations autour de l'orange* (2008). This idea of modifying space and creating perceptual-conceptual pathways through the use of ceramics (but also resin, metal, mosaic, enamel and sealing-wax) underpins the work of Remo Rachini, the author of a very recent installation (2009) consisting of approximately rectangular panels mounted on a series of flats arranged so as to create a perspective modulation of architectural space. These panels – of concrete and sealing wax, terracotta and enamel, wood and metal, resin and enamel, cement and mosaic of glass or terracotta, marble, stone, cement and ceramics – are rigorously abstract so as to highlight the physical and chromatic potentialities of the various materials. They constitute a visual-perceptual pathway leading to the rear wall, where a square of Carrara marble with the inscription "O DIO" (O GOD) is set into a cross-shaped arrangement of plates. The evocative and challenging intention is to transform the pathway into a cognitive itinerary developing in both chromatic-formal and existential-conceptual terms. The panels are transmuted into votive offerings, shapeless testimonies densely imbued with existence, flesh and blood, tears and beauty, howling fragments that sometimes display clots, badly stitched cuts and wounds, and old scars, or condense purified visions, fragments of precious spaces, brilliant and bejeweled surfaces. The list of examples could go on with the countless other artists that have in recent years interwoven the work of artistic invention with the technical-material experience of the decorative arts as further proof of a gap that has been bridged, or perhaps of a vision of contemporary art that is no longer idealistic or exquisitely conceptual but on the contrary develops through new investigations carried out with materials and techniques previously harnessed to the full only in the decorative arts.

Livio Scarpella
Senzasangue A (detail), 2008
Polychrome terracotta,
79 x 35 x 18 cm
Private collection

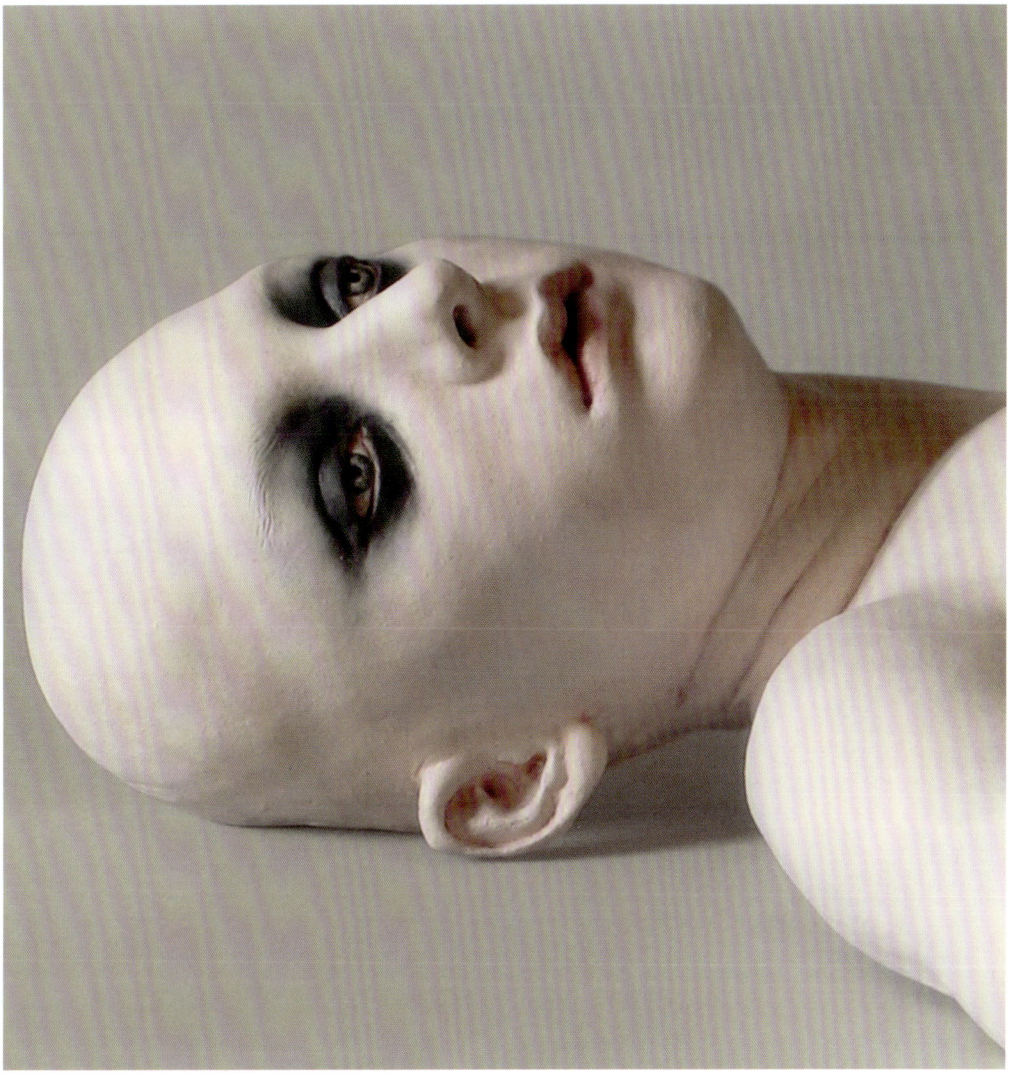

Bibliography

Ahtila, Eija-Liisa

Eija-Liisa Ahtila, exh. cat., ed. by D. Birnbaum (Kassel, Museum Friedericianum, 1998), Museum Fridericianum, Kassel 1998.

Fantasized Persons and Taped Conversations, exh. cat., ed. by M. Hirvi et al. (London, Tate Gallery; Helsinki, Kiasma Museum; Zurich, Kunsthalle, 2002–2003), Ed. Crystal Eye, Helsinki 2002.

E.-L. Ahtila, I. Pohjola (ed. by), *The Cinematic Works,* Ed. Crystal Eye, Helsinki 2004.

Ai Weiwei

C. Merewether, *Ai Weiwei: Works, Beijing 1993–2003*, Timezone 8, Hong Kong 2003.

U. Meile et al., *Ai Weiwei. Works 2004–2007*, JRP Ringier, Zurich 2008.

Aitken, Doug

Doug Aitken, Phaidon, London 2001.

Doug Aitken: New Ocean, exh. cat. (London-Tokyo-Bregenz-Turin, 2001–2003), Walther König, Cologne 2002.

Doug Aitken: Sleepwalkers, exh. cat. (New York, The Museum of Modern Art, Jan. 16–Feb. 12 2007), The Museum of Modern Art, New York 2007.

Allora, Jennifer & Calzadilla, Guillermo

La sindrome di Pantagruel: T1 Turin Triennale Tremusei 2005, exh. cat., ed. by Francesco Bonami, Carolyn Christov-Bakargiev (Turin, T1 Turin Triennale Tremusei, Nov. 9, 2005–Mar. 19, 2006), Skira, Milan 2005.

Allora & Calzadilla, *Land Mark*, exh. cat. (Paris, Palais de Tokyo, June 9–Aug. 27, 2006), Palais de Tokyo, Paris 2006.

Almond, Darren

D. Almond, *Darren Almond. Index*, Walther König, Cologne 2008.

Althamer, Pawel

Pawel Althamer: The Vincent Award 2004, Hatje Cantz, Ostfildern 2005.

Pawel Althamer: Espace 315, Centre Georges Pompidou, Paris 2006.

Amer, Ghada

Ghada Amer, exh. cat., ed. by D. Eccher (Rome, MACRO, May 25–Sep. 30, 2007), Electa, Milan 2007.

Arcangel, Cory

R. Gygax, *Cory Arcangel: Beige*, Museum für Gegenwartskunst, Zurich 2005.

M. Bittanti, D. Quaranta (ed. by), *Gamescenes: Art in the Age of Videogames*, Johan & Levi, Milan 2006.

A New Fiesta in the Making: The Art of Cory Arcangel, exh. cat., ed. by C. Jones (Geneva, Galerie Guy Bärtschi, Mar. 15–May 18, 2007), Galerie Guy Bärtschi, Geneva 2007.

Atelier Van Lieshout

Atelier Van Lieshout, Mondadori Electa, Milan 2007.

Atelier Van Lieshout, NAI Publishers, Rotterdam 2007.

SlaveCity. Joep Van Lieshout, Albion Gallery, London 2008.

Banksy

Banksy, *Wall and Piece*, Random House, London 2005.

S. Wright, *Banksy's Bristol: Home Sweet Home*, Tangent Books, Bristol 2007.

Barney, Matthew

The Cremaster Cycle, exh. cat., ed. by N. Spector (Paris, Musée d'art moderne de la ville de Paris; New York, Solomon R. Guggenheim Foundation, 2003), Hatje Cantz, Ostfildern 2002.

Matthew Barney, Sammlung Goetz, Munich 2008.

Bartolini, Massimo

Massimo Bartolini, exh. cat. (Turin, GAM – Galleria d'Arte Moderna e Contemporanea, 2005), Hopeful Monster, Turin 2005.

Young Italian Artists at the Turn of the Millenium, exh. cat. (Beijing, 2006), Galleria Continua, Beijing 2006.

Beecroft, Vanessa

Vanessa Beecroft: performances 1993-2003, exh. cat., ed. by M. Beccaria (Rivoli, Castello di Rivoli, Museo d'Arte Contemporanea, 2003–2004), Skira, Milan 2003.

Vanessa Beecroft: photographs, films, drawings, exh. cat., ed. by Th. Kellein (Kunsthalle Bielefeld, 2004), Hatje Cantz, Ostfildern 2004.

A. Polier, *Vanessa Beecroft*, Charta, Milan 2007.

Bonvicini, Monica

Monica Bonvicini. Bau, Hopefulmonster, Turin 2000.

Italics, Arte italiana fra tradizione e rivoluzione 1968-2008, exh. cat., ed. by F. Bonami (Venice, Palazzo Grassi, 2008–2009; Chicago, Museum of Contemporary Art, 2009), Electa, Milan 2008.

Brown, Cecily

Cecily Brown, exh. cat., ed. by L. Nochlin, J. Fleming (Des Moines Art Center, 2006), Des Moines Art Center (Iowa) 2006.

Cecily Brown, ed. by D. Ashton, Rizzoli International, New York 2008.

Cabrita Reis, Pedro

Pedro Cabrita Reis. Il silenzio in ascolto, exh. cat. (Turin, GAM – Galleria Civica d'Arte Moderna e Contemporanea, 2001), Hopefulmonster, Turin 2001.

M. Tarantino, A. Searle (ed. by), *Pedro Cabrita Reis*, Hatje Cantz, Ostfildern 2003.

Pedro Cabrita Reis, exh. cat., ed. by C. Gioia, B. Goretti, V. Tieri (Rome, MACRO – Museo d'arte contemporanea, 2006–2007), Electa, Milan 2007.

Calle, Sophie

P. Auster, S. Calle, *Double Game*, Violette, London 1999.

Sophie Calle, M'as-tu Vue ?, exh. cat. (Paris, Centre Georges Pompidou), Prestel, Paris 2003.

S. Calle, *Douleur exquise*, Actes Sud Edition, Arles 2003.

S. Calle, *Take Care of Yourself*, Actes Sud Edition, Arles 2007.

Cao Fei

H.H. Obrist, "First Take. Hans H. Obrist on Cao Fei", in *Artforum*, Jan. 2006, p. 181.

T.J. Carlin, "Cao Fei, RMB City", in *Time Out*, no. 652, Mar.–Apr. 2008, p. 62.

Caravaggio, Gianni

A. Bonito Oliva, *Le Opere e i Giorni*, Skira, Milan 2006.

Gianni Caravaggio, exh. cat., ed. by G. Caravaggio, C. Repetto (Pesaro, Centro Arti Visive Pescheria, Apr. 12–May 25, 2008), Hopefulmonster, Turin 2008.

Cattelan, Maurizio

Maurizio Cattelan, Phaidon, London 2000 [2003].

"Work. Art in Progress", no. 8, Jan.–Mar. 2004 (monographic issue devoted almost entirely to Cattelan's work).

F. Manacorda, *Maurizio Cattelan*, Electa, Milan 2006.

C. Tomkins, *Lives of the Artists*, Henry Holt and Company, New York 2008.

H. Kontova, "Maurizio Cattelan", and U. Kittelmann, "A carte scoperte. Il 'Progetto Cattelan' a Frankfurt", in *Flash Art*, no. 267, Dec. 2007–Jan. 2008.

Closky, Claude

F. Paul, *Claude Closky*, Hazan, Paris 1999.

Claude Closky, Editions Centre Pompidou, Paris, 2006.

Claude Closky, 8002-9891, exh. cat., ed. by J. David (Vitry-sur-Seine, MAC-VAL, Musée d'art contemporain du Val-de-Marne, Mar. 28–June 22, 2008), Editions Mac/Val, Vitry 2008.

Creed, Martin

Martin Creed, exh. cat. (Bern, Kunsthalle, 2004), Kunsthalle, Bern 2004.

Martin Creed: the whole world + the work = the whole world, exh. cat. (Warsaw, Centre for Contemporary Art, Ujazdowski Castle, Apr. 26–June 13, 2006), Centre for Contemporary art Ujazdowski Castle, Warsaw 2004.

Cuoghi, Roberto

Roberto Cuoghi, Skira, Milan 2008.

Currin, John

John Currin, exh. cat., ed. by R. Rosenblum (Chicago, Museum of Contemporary Art, 2003), Museum of Contemporary Art, Chicago 2003.

John Currin, Rizzoli International, New York 2006.

Dean, Tacita

Tacita Dean, exh. cat., ed. by R. Groenenboom (Barcelona, Museu d'Art Contemporani, 2001), Ed. Museu d'Art Contemporani, Barcelona 2000.

E. De Cecco, *Tacita Dean*, Postmedia Books, Milan 2004.

J.-C. Royoux, M. Warner (ed. by), *Tacita Dean*, Phaidon, London 2006.
Tacita Dean: Analogue: Drawings 1991–2006, exh. cat., ed. by T. Vischer, I. Friedli (Basel, Schaulager Basel, 2006), Steidl, Gottingen 2006.
Tacita Dean: Film Works, exh. cat., ed. by B. Fer, R. Carvajal (Miami, 2007), Charta, Milan 2007.

Delvoye, Wim
Wim Delvoye. Cloaca, exh. cat., ed. by A. Dannatt, M. Onfray (Antwerp, Museum van Hedendaagse Kunst Antwerpen), Ludion, Antwerp 2000.
Wim Delvoye. Fabrica, exh. cat., ed. by J.-P. Criqui, D. Soutif et al. (Prato, Centro per l'arte contemporanea Luigi Pecci Prato, 2003), Centro per l'Arte Contemporanea Luigi Pecci, Prato 2003.

Demand, Thomas
Thomas Demand, exh. cat., ed. by M. Beccaria (Rivoli, Castello di Rivoli, Museo d'Arte Contemporanea), Skira, Milan 2002.
Thomas Demand: Phototrophy, exh. cat., ed. by E. Schneider (Kunsthaus Bregenz, 2004), Schirmer/Mosel, Munich 2004.
G. Celant (ed. by), *Thomas Demand: Processo Grottesco / Yellowcake*, Ed. Fondazione Prada, Milan 2007.

Dion, Mark
Mark Dion, Phaidon Press, London 1997.
C.J. Sheehy (ed. by), *Cabinet of Curiosities: Mark Dion and the University as Installation*, University Of Minnesota Press 2006.
D. Buchhart, M. Dion, *Mark Dion: Concerning Hunting*, Hatje Cantz, Ostfildern 2008.

Dumas, Marlene
Marlene Dumas, Phaidon, London 1999.
G. Romano, A. Vettese (ed. by), *Marlene Dumas: Suspect*, Skira, Milan 2003.
I. Bonacossa, *Marlene Dumas*, Mondadori Electa, Milan 2006.
E. Bedford (ed. by), *Marlene Dumas: Intimate Relations*, Jacana Media, Johannesburg 2008.

Durham, Jimmie
L. Mulvey, D. Snauwaert, M. Alice Durant, *Jimmie Durham*, Phaidon, London 1995.
S. Boeri, A. Daneri, *Jimmie Durham*, Charta, Milan 2004.
R. Pinto, *Jimmie Durham. Le ragioni della leggerezza*, Franco Soffiantino arte contemporanea, Turin 2005.

Eliasson, Olafur
Olafur Eliasson. The Weather Project, exh. cat., ed. by Susan May (London, Tate Modern, Oct. 2003–Mar. 2004), Tate Publishing, London 2003.
Olafur Eliasson. Colour Memory and Other Informal Shadows, exh. cat. (Oslo, Astrup Fearnley Museet for Moderne Kunst, Jan. 24–May 2, 2004), Astrup Fearnley Museum of Modern Art, Oslo 2004.
Take your time: Olafur Eliasson, exh. cat., ed. by M. Grynsztejn (San Francisco, San Francisco Museum of Modern Art, Sep. 8, 2007–Mar. 15, 2009), Thames and Hudson, London 2007.
H.U. Obrist, *Olafur Eliasson*, "The Conversation Series", Verlag der Buchhandlung Walther König, Cologne 2008.
A. Engberg-Pedersen, Studio Olafur Eliasson (ed. by), *Studio Olafur Eliasson: An Encyclopedia*, Taschen, Cologne 2008.

Elmgreen & Dragset
Powerless Structures: Works by Michael Elmgreen & Ingar Dragset, n.p., Reykjavík 1998.
Spaced Out. Elmgreen & Dragset, exh. cat., ed. by D. Birnbaum, J. Voltz, Portikus, Frankfurt am Main 2003.
A. Moulton, "Elmgreen & Dragset. How are you today?", in *Flash Art*, no. 259, Aug.–Sep. 2006.
Elmgreen & Dragset: This Is the First Day of My Life, Hatje Cantz, Ostfildern 2009.

Emin, Tracey
N. Brown, *Tracey Emin*, Harry N. Abrams, New York 2006.
Tracey Emin. Works 1963–2006, Rizzoli International, New York 2006.

Fabre, Jan
D. Braeckman, S. Hertmans, R.-H. Marijnissen, *Heaven of Delight*, Mercatorfonds Antwerp 2002.
G. Di Pietrantonio, J. Fabre, *Antropologia di un pianeta*, Galleria d'arte moderna e contemporanea, Bergamo 2007.

Fischer, Urs
Urs Fischer, exh. cat., ed. by A. Gingeras (Paris, Centre Georges Pompidou, 2004), Centre Pompidou, Paris 2004.
Urs Fischer: Kir Royal, exh. cat., ed. by M.Varadinis (Zurich, Kunsthaus, 2004), JRP Ringier Kunstverlag, Zurich 2004.

Fischli & Weiss
B. Soentgen, R. Fleck (ed. by), *Peter Fischli and David Weiss*, Phaidon, London 2005.
Fischli, Weiss: flowers & questions: a retrospective, exh. cat., ed. by B. Curiger (London, Tate Modern; Kunsthaus Zurich, Deichtorhallen Hamburg, 2007–2008), Tate, London 2006.
J. Millar, *Fischli and Weiss. The Way Things Go*, Afterall Books, MIT Press, London 2007.

Frangi, Giovanni
G. Agosti, G. Frangi (eds.), *Giovanni Frangi. Nobu at Elba*, exh. cat. (Villa Menafoglio Litta Panza, Biumo Superiore – Varese), 5 Continents Editions, Milan 2004.
L. Hegyi, D. Paparoni (eds.), *Giovanni Frangi, take-off*, exh. cat. (Galleria dello Scudo, Verona, 2004-2005).
G. Verzotti (ed.), Giovanni Frangi. Pasadena, exh. cat. (Galleria d'Arte Moderna, Udine), Charta, Milan 2008.

Galíndo, Regina José
M. Scotini, V. Siviero, *Regina José Galindo*, Vanilla, Albisola Marina 2006.

Gillick, Liam
Liam Gillick, exh. cat. (Frankfurt, Frankfurter Kunstverein; Westfälischer Kunstverein Münster), Oktagon, Cologne 2000.
Liam Gillick: the Wood Way, exh. cat., ed. by I. Blazwick, D. Birnbaum (London, Whitechapel Art Gallery, 2002), Whitechapel Art Gallery, London 2002.

Gonzalez-Foerster, Dominique
H.U. Obrist, *Dominique Gonzalez-Foerster*, Walther König, Cologne 2008.
Th. 2058: Dominique Gonzalez-Foerster, exh. cat., ed. by J. Morgan (London, Tate Modern, 2008–2009), Tate Publishing, London 2008.

Gordon, Douglas
Douglas Gordon: Timeline, exh. cat., ed. by K.P. Biesenbach (New York, Museum of Modern Art, 2006), Museum of Modern Art, New York 2006.
Douglas Gordon prettymuchverywordwritten, spoken, heard, overhead from 1989…, exh. cat., ed. by M. D'Argenzio, G. Verzotti (Rovereto, Museo d'Arte Moderna e Contemporanea di Trento e Rovereto, 2006), Skira, Milan 2006.
Douglas Gordon: Superhumanatural, exh. cat., ed. by I. Rankin, K. Hartley (Edinburgh, National Galleries of Scotland, 2007), Ed. National Galleries of Scotland, Edinburgh 2007.

Gréaud, Loris
L. Gréaud, R. Malasauskas, A. Schuster, *Cellar Door*, Jrp/Ringier, Zurich 2008.

Gupta, Subodh
51ª Biennale. Sempre un po' più lontano, ed. by R. Martinez, Marsilio, Venice 2005.
P. Nagy, *Start.Stop*, Bodhi Art Gallery editions, Mumbai 2007.
God & Goods. Spirituality and Mass Confusion, exh. cat., ed. by F. Bonami, S. Cosulich Canarutto (Passariano, Villa Manin, 2008), Azienda speciale Villa Manin, Passariano 2008.
Subodh Gupta; Gandhi's Three Monkeys, exh. cat., J. Shainman Gallery, New York 2008.

Hein, Jeppe
S. Boije, *Jeppe Hein*, in *NU-E magazine*, no. 1, Sep. 2003.
K. Bell, *Jeppe Hein*, in *Frieze*, no. 81, Mar. 2004.
J. Hein, F. Bertaux, Ch. Macel, *Jeppe Hein*, Centre Pompidou, Paris 2005.

Hirschhorn, Thomas
Thomas Hirschhorn: Jumbo Spoons and Big Cake…, exh. cat. (Chicago, The Art Institute of Chicago, 2000), The Art Institute of Chicago, Chicago 2000.
A.M. Gingeras, B.H.D. Buchloh (ed. by), *Thomas Hirschhorn*, Phaidon, London 2004.
Thomas Hirschhorn: Utopia, Utopia = One World, One War, One Army, One Dress, exh. cat. (Boston, Institute of Contemporary Art; San Francisco, CCA Wattis Institute for Contemporary Arts, 2005–2006), Institute of Contemporary Art, Boston 2005.

Hirst, Damien
Damien Hirst, exh. cat., ed. by E. Cicelyn, M. Codognato, M. D'Argenzio (Naples, Museo Archeologico Nazionale, 2004–2005), Electa, Naples 2004.
Damien Hirst, The Agony and the Ecstasy. Selected Works from 1989 to 2004, Electa, Milan 2005.
Damien Hirst et al., *I Want to Spend the Rest of My Life Everywhere, with Everyone, One to One, Always, Forever, Now*, Booth-Clibborn Editions, London 2006.
D. Hirst, R. Fuchs et al., *For the Love of God. The Making of the Diamond Skull*, Other Criteria, London 2007.

Höller, Carsten
Carsten Höller. Registro, exh. cat., ed. by G. Celant (Milan, Fondazione Prada, 2000–2001), Fondazione Prada, Milan 2000.
J. Morgan (ed. by), *Carsten Höller. Test Site*, Tate Publishing, London 2006.
F. Bonami, C. Corbetta (ed. by), *Carsten Höller*, Electa, Milan 2007.

Huyghe, Pierre
Pierre Huyghe, exh. cat., ed. by C. Christov-Bakargiev (Rivoli, Castello di Rivoli, Museo d'Arte Contemporanea, 2004), Skira, Milan 2004.
Pierre Huyghe. Celebration Park, exh. cat. (Paris, Musée d'art moderne de la ville de Paris; London, Tate Modern, 2006), Musées de la ville de Paris, Paris 2006.

Jacir, Emily
Emily Jacir. Belongings. Arbeiten-Works 1998-2003, exh. cat. (Linz, O.K. Centrum fur Gegenwartskunst Oberosterreich, 2003–2004), Folio, Vienna 2004.

Kac, Eduardo
The Eighth Day: The Transgenic Art of Eduardo Kac, ed. by B. Sheilah, D. Collins, Institute for Studies in the Arts, Tempe 2003.
E. Kac, *Telepresence and Bio Art – Networking Humans, Rabbits and Robot*, University of Michigan Press, Ann Arbor 2005.
E. Kac, *Signs of Life: Bio Art and Beyond*, MIT Press, Cambridge (Mass.) 2007.

Kentridge, William
C. Christov-Bakargiev (ed. by), *William Kentridge*, Art Data 1999.
F. Pasini (ed. by), *William Kentridge. From the Beginning / Da capo*, Charta, Milan 2008.

Koons, Jeff
The Jeff Koons Handbook, introduction by R. Rosenblum, Anthony d'Offay Gallery, London 1992.
Th. Kellein (ed. by), *Jeff Koons: Pictures 1980-2002*, DAP, New York 2003.
Jeff Koons – Retrospectiv/Retrospective, Astrup Fearnley Museet dor Moderne Kunst, Oslo 2004.
S. Cosulich Canarutto, *Jeff Koons*, Electa, Milan 2006.
C. Tomkins, *Lives of the Artists*, Henry Holt and Company, New York 2008.

Lozano-Hemmer, Rafael
R. Lozano-Hemmer, *Vectorial Elevation: Relational Architecture No. 4*, Conaculta, Mexico City 2000.
Rafael Lozano-Hemmer. Some Things Happen More Often Than All of the Time, exh. cat. (Mexican Pavilion, 52nd Venice Biennale), Turner, Madrid 2007.
Under Scan, exh. cat., ed. by R. Lozano-Hemmer, D. Hill, East Midlands Development Agency, Nottingham 2007.

Lucas, Sarah
Sarah Lucas. Exhibitions and catalogue raisonné 1989-2005, Hatje Cantz, Ostfildern 2005.
M. Robecchi, *Sarah Lucas*, Mondadori Electa, Milan 2007.

Marisaldi, Eva
Eva Marisaldi. Jumps, exh. cat., ed. by R. Daolio (Bologna, MAMBo, Dec. 2, 2007–Feb. 3, 2008), Skira, Milan 2007.

Mattes, Eva and Franco (0100101110101101.ORG)
R. Greene, *Internet Art*, Thames & Hudson, London 2004.
J. Blais, J. Ippolito, *At the Edge of Art*, Thames & Hudson, London 2005.
R. Jana, M. Tribe, *New Media Art*, Taschen, Cologne 2006.
G. Giannachi, *Politics, New Media, Theatre: Performing the Virtual*, Routledge, London, New York 2006.

The Art of Participation: 1950 to Now, ed. by R. Frieling, Thames & Hudson, London 2008.

McQueen, Steve

Ch. Haye, "Motion Pictures – Steve McQueen", in *Frieze*, no. 28, May 1996.

Steve McQueen, exh. cat. (London, ICA, 1999), Institute of Contemporary Arts, London, 1999.

Turner Prize 1999, exh. cat. (London, Tate Gallery, 1999), Tate Gallery, London 1999.

Mehretu, Julie

Julie Mehretu: Drawing Into Painting, exh. cat., ed. by D. Fogle, O. Ilesanmi (Minneapolis, Walker Art Center, 2003; Lake Worth, Florida, Palm Beach Institute of Contemporary Art, 2003; Buffalo, Albright-Knox Art Gallery, 2004), Walker Art Center, Minneapolis 2003.

Julie Mehretu, Back City, exh. cat. (León, MUSAC – Museo de Arte Contemporáneo de Castilla y León, 2006), MUSAC, Léon 2006.

Parkett, Number 76, Parkett Publishers, London 2006.

Mori, Mariko

Mariko Mori, exh. cat. (Chicago, 1998), Museum of Contemporary Art, Chicago 1998.

Mariko Mori: Oneness, exh. cat. (Groeningen, 2007; Aarhus, 2007–2008), Hatje Cantz, Ostfildern 2007.

Mueck, Ron

Ron Mueck, exh. cat., ed. by H. Bastian (Hamburg, Nationalgalerie im Hamburger Bahnhof; Berlin, Museum für Gegenwart, Berlin, 2003), Hatje Cantz, Ostfildern 2005.

Ron Mueck, exh. cat., ed. by K. Hartley (Edinburgh, National Galleries of Scotland, Royal Scottish Academy, 2006), National Galleries of Scotland, Edinburgh 2006.

R. Rosenblum (ed. by), *Ron Mueck*, Thames and Hudson, London 2006.

Murakami, Takashi

Takashi Murakami: The Meaning of the Nonsense of the Meaning, exh. cat. (New York, 1999), Harry N. Abrams, New York 1999.

Superflat (Straight Up Japanese Bad Asses), exh. cat., ed. by Takashi Murakami (Tokyo-Nagoya, 2000; Los Angeles-Minneapolis-Seattle, 2001), Madra, Tokyo 2000.

Little Boy: The Arts of Japan's Exploding Subculture, exh. cat., ed. by Takashi Murakami (New York, Japan Society, 2005), Yale University Press, New Haven-London 2005.

© Murakami, exh. cat. (Los Angeles, 2007–2008; New York, 2008; Frankfurt, 2008; Bilbao, 2009), The Museum of Contemporary Art, Los Angeles & Rizzoli International, New York 2007.

Neshat, Shirin

O. Zaya, H. Dabashi, *Shirin Neshat. La Ultima Palabra / The Last Word*, Charta, Milan 2006.

Shirin Neshat: Women Without Men, Aros Aarhus Kunstmuseum, Aarhus 2008.

Neto, Ernesto

49. Biennale di Venezia 2001: catalogo ragionato, ed. by G. Vallese, Mondadori, Milan 2001.

Ernesto Neto, exh. cat. (Rome, MACRO, Museo d'Arte Contemporanea, May 30, 2008–Feb. 2009), Electa, Milan 2008.

Nicolai, Carsten

Carsten Nicolai – Anti Reflex, exh. cat. (Frankfurt, Schirn Kunsthalle, 2005) Schirn Kunsthalle, Frankfurt; Walther König, Cologne 2005.

Nunzio

G. Drudi, *Nunzio*, Rex Built-In, Pordenone 1996.

Nunzio, ombre, L. Vergine (ed.), Verona, Galleria dello Scudo, 2005.

"Nunzio", in D. Lancioni (ed.), *Italia Contemporanea. Officina San Lorenzo*, exh. cat., Rovereto, Mart, 2009.

Opie, Julian

D. Kurjakovic, *Julian Opie. Portraits*, Codax Publishers, Zurich 2003.

M. Horlock, *Julian Opie*, Tate, London 2004.

L. Grisebach, M. Kliege, *Julian Opie*, Verlag für Moderne Kunst, Nuremberg 2004.

P. Noever, *Julian Opie. Recent Works*, Hatje Cantz, Ostfildern 2008.

Orozco, Gabriel

Textos sobre la obra de Gabriel Orozco, ed. by D. Birnbaum, G. Orozco, Conaculta/Turner Publicaciones S.L., Mexico City 2005.

L. Sabau, G. Orozco: *Samurai's Tree Invariant*, Walther König, Cologne 2006.

S. Cosulich Canarutto, *Gabriel Orozco*, Electa, Milan 2008.

Orta, Lucy + Jorge

Lucy Orta, Phaidon Press, London 2003.

Antarctica, Lucy + Jorge Orta, Electa, Milan 2008.

Paci, Adrian

A. Vettese (ed. by), *Adrian Paci*, Charta, Milan 2006.

Ch. Lange, M. Stanley (ed. by), *Adrian Paci. Per speculum*, Milton Keynes Gallery, Milton Keynes 2007.

Pardo, Jorge

K. Bush, "Design For Life – Jorge Pardo", in *Frieze*, no. 36, Sep.–Oct. 1997.

Jorge Pardo, Haunch of Venison, London 2003.

Jorge Pardo, Phaidon Press, London 2008.

Parreno, Philippe

D. Gordon, Ph. Parreno, *Zidane. Un ritratto del XXI secolo*, DVD with book, Feltrinelli, Milan 2007.

Ph. Parreno, H.-U. Obrist, *Philippe Parreno. The Conversation Series*, Walther König, Cologne 2008.

Ping, Huang Yong

Ph. Vergne, D. Chong, *House of Oracles: A Huang Yong Ping Retrospective*, exh. cat. (Minneapolis, Walker Art Center, 2005–2006; Massachusetts Museum of Contemporary Art, 2006–2007), Ed. Walker Art Center, Minneapolis 2005.

V. Martini, *Huang Yong Ping*, Mondadori Electa, Milan 2008.

Pivi, Paola

L. Cherubini (ed. by), *Paola Pivi*, exh. cat., ed. by L. Cherubini (Rome, MacRo, 2002–2003), Electa, Milan 2003.

Paola Pivi. It just keeps getting better, exh. cat., ed. by A. Szymczyk (Basel, Kunsthalle, Jan. 19–Mar.18, 2007), Walther König, Cologne 2006.

Prince, Richard

B. Hainley (ed. by), *Richard Prince. Paintings, Photographs*, Hatje Cantz, Ostfildern 2002.

M. Collings (ed. by), *Richard Prince. Nurse Paintings*, Barbara Gladstone Gallery, New York 2003.

M. Newman, *Richard Prince, Untitled (Couple)*, Afterall Books, London 2006.

N. Spector, J. Bankowsky (ed. by), *Richard Prince*, Hatje Cantz, Ostfildern 2007.

Neo Rauch

E. Hannemann, G. Tinterow (eds.) *Neo Rauch. Para*, 2007, exh. cat. (New York, Metropolitan Museum of Art), New York 2007

Rehberger, Tobias

Tobias Rehberger, Private Matters, JRP|Ringier / Whitechapel, London 2005.

E. Mitchell, "Tobias Rehberger", in *Interview*, May 2007, pp. 90-94.

D. Baldon, "Tobias Rehberger", in *Artforum*, Sep. 2007, pp. 460-61.

Rist, Pipilotti

P. Phelan, H.U. Obrist, E. Bronfen, *Pipilotti Rist*, Phaidon, London 2001.

Pipilotti Rist – Congratulations!, Lars Müller Publishers, Baden 2007.

Salcedo, Doris

N. Princenthal, C. Basualdo, A. Huyssen, *Doris Salcedo*, Phaidon, London 2000.

La sindrome di Pantagruel. T1 Turin Triennale Tremusei, ed. by F. Bonami, C. Christov-Bakargiev, Skira, Milan 2005.

Doris Salcedo: Shibboleth, exh. cat. (London, Tate Modern, Oct. 9, 2007–Apr. 6, 2008), Tate, London 2007.

Sassolino, Arcangelo

Art12. Looking for something new, Turin 2005.

A. Sassolino, *Arcangelo Sassolino*, JRP Ringier, Zurich 2008.

Schneider, Gregor

Gregor Schneider, exh. cat., ed. by L. Bosse (Paris, Musée d'art moderne de la ville de Paris, 1998), Ed. Paris-Musées, Paris 1998.

P. Schimmel (ed. by), *Gregor Schneider*, Charta, Milan 2004.

G. Schneider (et al.), *Cube Venice 2005. Art in the Age of Global Terrorism*, Charta, Milan 2005.

Gregor Schneider: Die Familie Schneider, exh. cat., ed. by A. O'Hagan (London, 14 & 16 Walden Street), Artangel, London 2006.

Shonibare, Yinka

Yinka Shonibare: Double Dutch, NAI Publishers, Rotterdam 2004.

R. Kent, R. Hobbs, *Yinka Shonibare MBE*, Prestel, Munich 2008.

Sierra, Santiago

Santiago Sierra, exh. cat., ed. by F. Cavallucci, C. Jiménez (Trento, Galleria Civica di Arte Contemporanea, 2005–2006), Silvana Editoriale, Cinisello Balsamo 2005.

Santiago Sierra: 7 trabajos / 7 works, exh. cat. (London, Lisson Gallery, 2007–2008), Lisson Gallery, London 2007.

Slominski, Andreas

Andreas Slominski, exh. cat., ed. by N. Spector (Berlin, Deutsche Guggenheim, 1999), Solomon R. Guggenheim Foundation, New York 1999.

Andreas Slominski, exh. cat., ed. by G. Celant (Milan, Fondazione Prada, 2003), Fondazione Prada, Milan 2006.

Smith, Kiki

Kiki Smith. Homespun Tales. Storie di occupazione domestica, exh. cat., ed. by C. Bertola, V. Katz, B. Tarozzi (Venice, Fondazione Querini Stampalia, June 9–Sep. 11, 2005), Edizioni Fondazione Querini Stampalia, Venice 2005.

Kiki Smith: A Gathering, 1980-2005, exh. cat., ed. by *S. Engberg* (San Francisco Museum of Modern Art, Nov. 19, 2005–Jan. 29, 2006; Minneapolis, Walker Art Center, Feb. 26–May 14, 2006; Houston, Contemporary Arts Museum, July 15–Sep. 24, 2006; New York, Whitney Museum of American Art, Nov. 16, 2006–Feb. 11, 2007), Walker Art Center, Minneapolis 2005.

Solakov, Nedko

Nedko Solakov: Romantic Landscapes with Missing Parts, exh. cat., ed. by A. Tolnay, B. Reinhardt (Berlin, Neuer Berliner Kunstverein, 2002), Hatje Cantz, Ostfildern 2002.

S. Boettger, *Nedko Solakov: 99 Fears*, Phaidon Press, London 2008.

Starling, Simon

Simon Starling, exh. cat., ed. by G. Maraniello (Rome, MACRO, 2003), Electa, Milan 2003.

Struth, Thomas

Thomas Struth, exh. cat., ed. by D. Eklund, A. Goldstein (Dallas, Dallas Museum of Art; New York, Metropolitan Museum of Art, 2002–2003), Dallas Museum of Art, Dallas 2002.

Thomas Struth, exh. cat., ed. by M. Codognato (Naples, MADRE – Museo d'Arte Contemporanea DonnaREgina, 2008), Electa, Milan 2008.

Taylor-Wood, Sam

Sam Taylor-Wood, Steidl, Gottingen 2002.

P. Doroshenko, H. Miller (ed. by), *Sam Taylor-Wood. Still Lives*, Steidl, Gottingen 2006.

Tillmans, Wolfgang

Wolfgang Tillmans: veduta dall'alto, exh. cat., ed. by Z. Felix, G. Verzotti (Rivoli, Castello di Rivoli, Museo d'arte contemporanea, 2001–2002), Charta, Milan 2002.

Wolfgang Tillmans, Yale University Press, New Haven 2006.

W. Tillmans, *Wolfgang Tillmans Manual*, Walther König, Cologne 2007.

J. Jager, *Wolfgang Tillmans. Lighter*, Hatje Cantz, Ostfildern 2008.

Tiravanija, Rirkrit

Rirkrit Tiravanija: Secession, Walther König, Cologne 2003.

Rirkrit Tiravanija: une retrospective (tomorrow is another fine day), Musee d'Art Moderne de la Ville de Paris, Paris 2005.

Trockel, Rosemarie

Rosemarie Trockel, exh. cat., ed. by S. Stich (Boston, Institute of Contemporary Art; Berkeley, University Art Museum), Prestel-Verlag, Munich 1991.

Rosemarie Trockel, bodies of work 1986-1998, exh. cat., ed. by B. Frenssen (Hamburg, Hamburger Kunsthalle; London, Whitechapel Art Gallery; Stuttgart, Staatsgalerie Stuttgart; Marseille, Galeries Contemporaines des Musées de Marseille, 1998–1999), Whitechapel Art Gallery, London 1998.

Rosemarie Trockel. Post-menopause, exh. cat., ed. by B. Engelbach (Cologne, Museum Ludwig; MAXXI, Rome, 2005–2006), Walter König, Cologne 2006.

Tuymans, Luc

J. Vicente Aliaga, N. Spector (ed. by), *Luc Tuymans*, Phaidon, London 1996.

U. Loock, *Luc Tuymans*, Phaidon, London 2003.

E. Dexter, J. Heynen (ed. by), *Luc Tuymans*, Tate, London 2004.

Uklanski, Piotr

Piotr Uklanski. The Joy of Photography, exh. cat. (Strasburg, 2007–2008), Hatje Cantz, Ostfildern 2008.

Piotr Uklanski: Bialo-Czerwona, exh. cat. (New York, Gagosian Gallery, 2008), Gagosian Gallery, New York 2008.

Vascellari, Nico

Nico Vascellari's Taxonomy: Cujo, Edizioni Zero, Milan 2007.

Revenge di Nico Vascellari: Premio per la giovane arte italiana 2006-2007, exh. cat., ed. by P. Colombo, M. Pignatti Morano (Venice, 2007), Electa Mondadori, Milan 2007.

Vezzoli, Francesco

Francesco Vezzoli, exh. cat., ed. by M. Beccaria (Rivoli, Castello di Rivoli, Museo d'arte contemporanea, Jan. 30–May 5, 2002), Skira, Milan 2002.

Francesco Vezzoli. Democrazy, exh. cat., ed. by I. Gianelli (52nd Venice Biennale), Electa, Milan 2007.

Viel, Cesare

Cesare Viel. Mi gioco fino in fondo. Performance e installazioni, exh. cat. (Genoa, Museo d'Arte Contemporanea di Villa Croce, 2008), Ed. Museo di Villa Croce, Genoa 2008.

C. Subrizi, *Cesare Viel. Azioni (1996-2007)*, Silvana Editoriale, Cinisello Balsamo 2008.

Walker, Kara

G. DuBois Shaw, *Seeing the Unspeakable. The Art of Kara Walker*, Duke University Press, Durham-London 2004.

Th. McEvilley, Ph. Vergne (ed. by), *Kara Walker. My Complement, My Enemy, My Oppressor, My Love*, Walker Art Center, Minneapolis 2007.

K. Walker, *Bureau of Refugees*, Charta, Milan 2008.

Matthias Weischer

A. Bonito Oliva, G. Belli (eds.), *Germania contemporanea. Dipingere e narrare: Tim Eitel, Matthias Weischer, David Schnell*, exh. cat. (Rovereto, Museo di Arte Moderna e Contemporanea di Trento e Rovereto, 2008), Skira, Milan 2008.

M. Weischer, *The Garden/Der Garten: Works on Paper/Arbeiten auf Papier*, Museum der Bildenden Künste, Leipzig 2005.

Wall, Jeff

A. Hochdörfer, *Jeff Wall. Photographs*, Walther König, Cologne 2003.

K. Brougher, *Jeff Wall*, Scalo Verlag, Zurich 2004.

C. Burnett, *Jeff Wall*, Tate, London 2005.

Jeff Wall. Selected Essays and Interviews, Museum of Modern Art, New York 2007.

Whiteread, Rachel

Rachel Whiteread. Transient Spaces, Harry N. Abrams, New York 2001.

C. Mullins (ed. by), *Rachel Whiteread*, Tate, London 2004.

C. Townsend, *Rachel Whiteread*, Thames & Hudson, London 2004.

Xhafa, Sislej

Arte all'arte 10. Arte Architettura Paesaggio, Gli Ori, Pistoia 2005.

Sislej Xhafa: See no Evil, Hear no Evil, Speak no Evil, Mazzotta, Milan 2004.

S. Xhafa, *Sislej Xhafa*, Hatje Cantz Publishers, Ostfildern 2006.

Yang Fudong

Yang Fudong, exh. cat., ed. by M. Beccaria (Rivoli, Castello di Rivoli, 2005), Skira, Milan 2006.

Zhang Huan

Zhang Huan: Ash, Haunch of Venison, London 2007.

Zhang Huan Altered States, Charta and Asia Society, New York 2007.

Index of Names, Artists and Works of Art

A

0100101110101101.org *see* Mattes, Eva and Franco: 369n, 386, 387, 388, 389
2012 Architecten: 224
Abitare, magazine: 225
Abakanowicz, Magdalena (Falenty, Poland, 1930): 88
1970–1973, *Abakan Red I*, Zurich, Museum für Gestaltung, Kunstgewerbesammlung: 88, *89*
ABN AMRO: 298, 299n
Abramovich, Marina (Belgrade, 1946) *14*, 15, 88, 316, 344
1976, *Relation in Space* (with Ulay): 88
Abstract Expressionism/ists: 85, 144, 172
Académie française: 290n
Acconci, Vito (New York, 1940): 223, 333, 344
ACT UP (Aids Coalition to Unleash Power), association: 30
action, *Zap*: 30
Action Painting: 62
Adams, Robert (Orange, New Jersey, 1937): 333
Adéagbo, George (Cotonou, Benin, 1942): 37
Adorno, T.W.: 29, 304
Aertsen, Pieter (Amsterdam, 1508 ca – 1575): 277
1550–1552 ca, *Market with Scenes from the Passion*: 277
Ahtila, Eija–Liisa (Hämeenlinna, Finland, 1959): 44, 45
1999, *Consolation Service*: 44
2001, *Lahja (The Present)*, San Francisco Museum of Modern Art: 44, *45*
2002, *The House*: 44, *45*
2006, *The Wind*: 44
Ai Weiwei (Beijing, 1957): 46, 47, 220, 222, 223, 225n
1994, *Han Dynasty Urn with Coca–Cola Logo*: 46, *46*
2007, *Template (Before Collapsing)*: 46, *47*
2007, *Fairytale*: 46
Aitken, Doug (Redondo Beach, California, 1968): 38, 142, 168, 169, 335, 360
1992, *Inflection*: 169
1995, *Monsoon*: 169
1997, *Cathouse*: 169
1997, *Diamond Sea*: 169
1999, *Electric Earth*: 169
2001, *New Ocean*: 169
2002, *Interiors*: *168*, 169
2004, *The Moment Is the Moment*: 169, *169*
2007, *Sleepwalkers*: *168*, 169, 360
Al-Qaeda: 29, 281
Albers, Annie, pseudonym of Annelise Fleischmann (Berlin, 1899 – Orange, Connecticut, 1994): 85
All-over painting: 172
Allora & Calzadilla, collective pseudonym of Jennifer Allora (Philadelphia, 1974) and Guillermo Calzadilla (Havana, 1971): 312, 313
2001–2004, *Land Mark (Foot Prints) #1. Set I*, Paris, Galerie Chantal Crousel: *313*
2006, *Ruin*, Paris, Galerie Chantal Crousel: 312, *312*
Serie *Land Mark*: 312
Almond, Darren (Wigan, United Kingdom, 1971): 48, 49
2003, *If I Had You*: 48, *48*
2008, *Tide*: 48, *49*
Althamer, Pawel (Warsaw, 1967): 41, 170, 338
2000, *Film*: 41
2001, *Weronika*, Switzerland, Lithops Collection: 170, *171*
2007, *Balloon*, view of the installation at Arena Civica of Milan: 170, *170*
Amadeus, film (Miloš Forman, 1984): 208
Amarcord, film (Federico Fellini, 1973): 208
Alÿs, Francis (Antwerp, 1959): 35
Amer, Ghada (Cairo, 1963): 342, 343, 409
1995–2004, *Barbie Loves Ken, Ken Loves Barbie*, New York, Gagosian Gallery: 342, *343*
2001, *Index of Pleasures*: 409
2003, *Breathe Into Me*, New York, Gagosian Gallery: 342, *342*
2005, *The White Man*, New York, Gagosian Gallery: *342*
2007, *Yin Yang Garden*: 342
American Indian Movement: 105
Ando, Tadao (Osaka, 1941): 159, 161, 162, 166, 167
1992, Benesse House, Naoshima, Japan: 166
2004, Full view of the Chichu Art Museum, Naoshima, Japan: *162*, 166, 167
2004, Staircase of Chichu Art Museum, Naoshima, Japan: *161*
Andre, Carl (Quincy, Massachusetts, 1935): 398
Andreolli, G.: 161
Anime, abbreviation of japanese word *animēshon* (cartoon): 116, 117, 372
Antin, D.: 360, 361, 369n
Antoni, Janine (Freeport, Bahamas, 1964): 88
Appadurai, A.: 95, 97n
ARA Associati, architecture studio, Milan: 157
2007 (Aldo Rossi designer), MAMbo, Museo di Arte Moderna, Bologna: 157
Arabian Nights: 320
Araki, Nobuyoshi (Tokyo, 1940): 334
Arbus, Diane (New York, 1923–1971): 333
Arcangel, Cory (Buffalo, New York, 1978): 368, 369n, 370, 371
2002, *Data Diaries*: 370
2002, *I Shot Andy Warhol*: 370
2002, *Super Mario Clouds*: 370
2004, *Super Mario Movie*: 370, *370*
2004, *Super Slow Tetris*: 370
2005, *Colors*: 370, *371*
2008, *Personal Film*: 370
Architects & Associates, architecture studio of Tadao Ando: 166
ARCO – Feria Internacional de Arte Contemporáneo, Madrid: 286
Arendt, H.: 35, 307
Arman, pseudonym of Armand Pierre Fernandez (Nice, 1928 – New York, 2005): 83, 409
1961, *Colère*: 82
Armani, G.: 275
Arnauld, A.: *11*
Ars Electronica Center, Linz: 365, *367*
Ars Electronica Festival, Linz: 362, 367
Art Basel Miami Beach (ABMB), Miami: 288
Art Deco: 407
Art Noveau: 406
Art Vienna: 275, 286
Art Workers' Coalition (collective of artists, film makers, writers and critics founded in New York in 1969): 303
Arte povera: 66, 237
Artforum, magazine: 117, 368n, 398
Artissima 12: 270
Artnews, magazine: 146
Arts & Crafts: 406
Ashton, D.: 145
Asia Pacific Triennial, Brisbane (Australia): 288
Association of American Painters and Sculptors: 285
Ataman, Kutluğ (Istanbul, 1961): 34
2004, *Küba*: 34
Atelier d'architecture autogérée (a.a.a.) (interdisciplinary collective founded in Paris in 2001): 305, 308
Ecobox: 308
Atelier Mendini, architecture studio founded in 1989 by Alessandro Mendini (Milan, 1931) and Francesco Mendini (Milan, 1939): 219
Intervention by Enzo Cucchi, the "Asor Rosa" subway station entrance, Naples: 219, *219*
Atelier Van Lieshout/AVL (collective founded in Rotterdam in 1995 by Joep van Lieshout): 314, 315
Since 2005, *SlaveCity*: 314
2006, *BikiniBar*: *314*
2007, *SlaveCity – Board Room*: 314, *315*
Atget, Jean-Eugène (Libourne, Bordeaux, 1857 – Paris, 1927): 333, 335
Atlas Group, 310
Aulenti, Gae (Palazzolo dello Stella, Udine, 1927): 157, 223
1980–1986, Musée d'Orsay, Paris: 157
Auster, P.: 50, 138
1992, *Leviathan* (novel): 50
Avatar, chosen image for personal

representation inside a virtual community: 389
Ay-O, pseudonym of Takao Iijima (Ibaraki, Japan, 1931): 86

B

Babeli, Gazira (character created in the virtual world of *Second Life*, spring 2006): 364, 366, 367, 369n
2007, *"Gaz of the Desert" d'après Delacroix*: *364*
Bachmann, I.: 138
Bacon, Francis (Dublin 1909 – Madrid, 1992): *11, 172,* 294, 295, 299n
1974–1977, *Triptych*, private collection: 294, *295*, 299n
Bahr, H.: 405
Bajević, Maja (Sarajevo, 1967): 339
2009, *How Do You Want To Be Governed?*: 339
Baldessari, John (National City, California, 1931): 98, 333
Balthus, pseudonym of Balthasar Klossowski de Rola (Paris, 1908 – Rossinière, Switzerland, 2001): 350
Banco Espírito Santo: 299n
Bank Austria: 299n
Banksy, pseudonym of Robin Gunningham (Yate, United Kingdom, 1974): 226
2004, *Banksy Rat: Because I'm Worthless*: *226*
2007–2008, *Window Lovers*: *227*
Barbieri, Olivo (Carpi, Modena, 1954): 335
Barcelona International Exposition: 356
Barney, Matthew (San Francisco, 1967): 20, 21, 38, 92, 335, 344, 345
1994–2002, *The Cremaster Cycle*: 20, 344
1994, *Cremaster 4*: 344
1994, *Cremaster 4: The Loughton Candidate*, New York, private collection: *92*
1995, *Cremaster 1*: 344
1996, *Cremaster 1*, New York, Solomon R. Guggenheim Museum: *344*
1997, *Cremaster 5*, New York, Solomon R. Guggenheim Museum: 344, *344*
1999, *Cremaster 2*: 344
2002, *Cremaster 3*, New York, Solomon R. Guggenheim Museum: 344, *344*
Since 1987, *Drawing Restraint*: 344
2005, *Drawing Restraint 9: Shimenawa*, New York, The Museum of Modern Art: *345*
Barragán, P.: 290n, 291n
Barroso, Abel (Pinar del Río, Cuba, 1971): 287
Bartning, Otto (Karlsruhe, 1883 – Darmstadt, 1959): 407
1918, *Plan for general reform of the teaching of arts and crafts* (plan essay): 407
Bartolini, Massimo (Cecina, Livorno, 1962): 228, 229
2004, *O som Tambem…*: 229, *228–229*
2005, *Senza titolo* (Untitled), UniCredit Group Collection: *229*
2008, *25 aprile 1936 (Anche oggi niente)*: *228*, 229
Basilico, Gabriele (Milan, 1944): 223, 335
Bataille, G., philosopher: 72, 324
Batniji, Taysir (Gaza, Palestine, 1966): 339
Baudelaire, C.: 29
Baudrillard, J.: 281
Bauhaus: 84, 96, 407
Bauman, Z.: 35, 282, 290n
Baumgarten, Lothar (Rheinsberg, Germany, 1944): 302
Beauvoir, S. de: 82
Becher, Bernd, pseudonym of Bernhard Becher (Siegen, 1931 – Rostock, 2007): 333
Beckett, S.B.: 40
Beckmann, Max (Leipzig, 1884 – New York, 1950): 350
Beecroft, Vanessa (Genoa, 1969): 21, 22, 27, 39, 90, 346, 347, 348, 349
1999, *VB39 / U.S. Navy Seal*, San Diego, Museum of Contemporary Art: *26*
2000, *VBGDW*: *26*
2001, *VB48*: *346*, 349
2003, *VB52*: *349*
2003–2004, *VB52*: *347*, 349
2005, *VB58*: *349*
2007, *VB61 / Still Death! Darfur Still Deaf?*: *348*, 349
2008, *VB62*: *348*, 349
Beethoven, L. van: 181, 406
1802–1804, *Eroica symphony*: 181
1824, *Ninth symphony*: 406
Bellmer, Hans (Katowice, 1902 – Paris, 1975): 333
Beltrami, Luca (Milan, 1854 – Rome, 1933): 406
Bene, C.: 15
Benedict XVI, pope: 281, 410
Benetton: 402
Benjamin, W.: 304
Berardo, J.: 295, 299n
Bergé, P.: 275
Bergson, H.: 40
Berkeley, B.: 344
Berlin Biennial: 176, 258, 291n
Berlin Wall: 29, 30, 91, 92, 278, 293, 338, 392
Bernhard, Hans (New Haven, Connecticut, 1973) *see* Ubermoge.com
Bernini, Gian Lorenzo (Naples, 1598 – Rome, 1680): 149
Bertozzi & Casoni, collective pseudonym of company founded in Imola in 1980 by Giampaolo Bertozzi (Borgo Tossignano, Bologna, 1957) and Stefano Dal Monte Casoni (Lugo di Romagna, Ravenna, 1961): 405, 406, 409, 410
2007, *Cestino della discordia*, private collection: *406*, 410
2007, *Minimi avanzi*: 410
2008, *Riflessione sulla morte*, private collection: *404*, 410
2008, *Composizione 13*: 410
2008, *Intervallo*: 410
2008, *Madonna scheletrita*: 410
2008, *Vassoio*: 410
Bertozzi, Giampaolo (Borgo Tossignano, Bologna, 1957): 409
Betsky, A.: 220
Beuys, Joseph (Krefeld, Germany, 1921 – Düsseldorf 1986): 182, 260
Bhabha, H.K.: 95, 97n
Bickerton, Ashley (Barbados, 1959): 182
Bienal de São Paulo, Brazil: 229, 285, 288, 289
Biennale of Sidney: 288
Biffi Gentili, E. : 405
Big Brother: 30
Bijl, Guillaume (Antwerp, 1946): 41
Bijl, Marc (Leerdam, Netherlands, 1970): 278
2002, *Resist*: 278, *279*
2002, *Terror*: 278, *279*
Bio Art: 362
Biotech Art: 365, 369n
Bird, J.: 272
Birnbaum, D.: 122
Birnbaum, Dara (New York, 1946): 367, 369n
1978, *Technology / Transformation: Wonder Woman*: 367
Bishop, C.: 35, 302
Bisson Frères, pseudonym of Louise-Auguste Bisson (Paris, 1814–1876) and Auguste–Rosalie Bisson (Paris, 1826–1900): 333
Bittencourt, V.: 354
Black Audio Film Collective (collective founded in London, from 1982 to 1998, by John Akomfrah, Reece Auguiste, Edward George, Lina Gopaul, Avril Johnson, David Lawson and Trevor Mathison: 303
Black Power: 30
Bloom, H.: 94
BMW: 239
Bo, Jørgen (Copenhagen, 1919–1999): 152
1958–2006, Louisiana Museum of Modern Art, Humlebæk (with Wilhelm Wohlert): 152
Bode, A.: 285, 290n, 291n
Body Art: *11, 14, 20,* 225n, 408
Boeri, S.: 225
Böhm, Adolf (Vienna, 1861 – Klosterneuburg, 1927): 406
Boltanski, Christian (Paris, 1944): 398
Boltanski, L.: 281, 290n
2006, *The New Spirit of Capitalism* (essay, with Eve Chiapello): 281
Bonami, F.: 122, 360, 362, 363, 368n, 398
Bonito Oliva, A.: 105, 222
Bonnet, A.-M.: 149, 149n
Bonvicini, Monica (Venice, 1965): 22, 142, 230, 231
2004, *Don't Miss a Sec*: 230
2005, *Never Again*: 230, *231*
2006, *Built for Crime*: 230, *230*
Book of Judges: 324
Borges, J.L.: 98
Bosch, Hieronymus, Jeroen Anthoniszoon van Aken detto ('s Hertogenbosch, 1450–1516): 108
1504, *The Garden of Earthly Delights*: 108
Botta, Mario (Mendrisio, Switzerland, 1943): 156, 157, 158, 161, 162
1988–2002, Mart – Museo d'Arte Moderna e Contemporanea di Trento e Rovereto, Rovereto: 161, 162, 163
Dome covering of Mart – Museo di Arte Moderna e Contemporanea di Trento e Rovereto: *156*, 157
Covered square of Mart – Museo di Arte Moderna e Contemporanea di Trento e Rovereto: 157, *157*
Ground floor plan of Mart – Museo di Arte Moderna e Contemporanea di Trento e Rovereto: 158, *158*
Dressing of the "Mario Sironi" and "Arturo Martini" rooms at Mart – Museo di Arte Moderna e

Contemporanea di Trento e Rovereto: 159, *159*
Botticelli, Sandro, Alessandro di Mariano di Vanni Filipepi namely (Florence, 1445–1510): 350
Bourgeois, Louise (Paris, 1911): *11, 13, 14, 27n,* 85, 88, 141, 188, 190
1974, *The Destruction of the Father*: *85*
Cells: 14
Spider: 13
Bourriaud, N.: 27n, 360, 369n
Bowie, D.: 192
Braunfels, Stephan (Überlingen, Germany, 1950): 152, 153, 160
1995/1996–2002, Pinakothek der Moderne, Munich: 160
2004, Pinakothek der Moderne, Munich, north view: *152*
2007, Pinakothek der Moderne, Munich, room 24 with works by Arnulf Rainer: *153*
Breuer, Marcel (Pécs, Hungary, 1902 – New York, 1981): 407
Brigate Rosse (Red Brigades): 176
Broeckmann, A.: 366, 369n
Brontë, E.: 130
1847, *Wutherig Heights* (novel): 130
Broodthaers, Marcel (Brussels, 1924 – Cologne, 1976): 37, 98, 182, 303, 360
Brotherus, Elina (Helsinki, 1972): 336, 337, 338
1998, *This Is the First Day of the Rest of Your Life*: 338
2004, *Der Wanderer 3*: 336, *337*
Brown, Cecily (London, 1969): 172, 173
2003, *Teenage Wild Life*, London, The Saatchi Collection: *172*
2006, *Skulldiver III (Flightmask)*, Boston, Museum of Fine Arts: *173*
Bruguera, Tania (Havana, 1968): 16, 22, 93
Bruly Bouabré, Frédéric (Zépréguhe, Ivory Coast, 1921): 94, 97n
Brun, A.: 152
Brunner, Bianca (Switzerland, 1974): 336
Bruno, Andrea (Turin, 1931): 157
1978–1984, restoration of Castello di Rivoli – Museo d'Arte Contemporanea: 157
Brus, Günter (Arning, Austria, 1938): 83
Brussels Biennial: 291n
Bruyckere, Berlinde de (Gand, Belgium, 1964): 22
2003–2004, *Aanéén*, Antoin de Galbert Collection: *22*
Buckminster Fuller, Richard (Milton, 1895 – Los Angeles, 1983): 268, 380
Buergel, R.M.: 287, 288, 290n
Buñuel, L.: 74
1967, *Belle de jour* (film): 74
Burcet, J.: 275, 290n
Burda, F.: 295, 298, *298*, 299n
Burdett, R.: 218
Bureau d'Études (collective founded in Paris in 1998): 303, 310, 311
2000, *European Norms of World-Production*: 311
Burgin, Victor (Sheffield, 1941): 333
Burri, Alberto (Città di Castello, Perugia, 1915 – Nice, 1995): 66, 82
Busan Biennial, South Korea: 291n
Bush, G.W.: 74
Bush, K.: 266
Byrne, Gerard (Dublin, 1969): 42, 43
2001–2008, *Case study (Loch Ness)*: 43
2004, *Homme à femmes (Michel Debraine)*: 43

C

Cabrita Reis, Pedro (Lisbon, 1956): 232, 233, 234, 235
1999, *Palais*, Turin, private collection: *233*
2000, *Des Dimanches Tristes*, collection of the artist: *232*
2004, *Favorite Places # 1*, Dijon, FRAC – Fonds régional d'art contemporain de Bourgogne: *234*
2005, *21 Brick Columns*, installation at Ostia Antica, Rome, 2005: 232, *235*
Cage, John (Los Angeles, 1912 – New York, 1992): 82, 394
1962, *4'33"*: 394
Cahun, Claude, pseudonym of Lucy Renee Mathilde Schwob (Nantes, 1894 – Saint-Hélier, 1954): 83
Cai Guo-Qiang (Quanzhou, China, 1957): 30
Calabrese, O.: 281
1987, *L'età neobarocca* (Neo-Baroque: A sign of the Times) (essay): 281
Calder, Alexander (Philadelphia, 1899 – New York, 1976): 188
Cale, J.: 244
Calle, Sophie (Paris, 1953): 50, 51, 91
1983, *L'Homme au Carnet*: 50
1983, *L'Hotel*: 50
1983, *Suite vénitienne*: 50
1984–2003, *Douleur exquise*: 50
1998, *Des journées entières sous le signe du B, du C, du W. BB*: *50*
1998, *Double Game* (novel): 50
2007, *Prenez soin de vous*, installation at the French Pavilion of Venice Biennale, 2007: 50, *51*
Calvino, I.: 96, 229
1985, *Lezioni americane. Sei proposte per il prossimo millennio* (Six Memos for the Next Millennium): 96
Calvo, C.: 229
1981, *Las tres mitades de Ino Moxo*: 229
Cameron, D.: 114, 275, 286
Campana, D.: 138
Cannes Film Festival: 390, 394
Cao Fei (Guangzhou, China, 1978): 335, 341, 372, 373
2002, *Rabid Dogs*: 372
2004, *A Mirage (COSPlayers Series)*: *373*
2004, Serie *COSplayers*: 372
2007, *RMB CITY 5*: *372*
2007, *China Tracy Pavilion*: 372
Capital, magazine: 83
Capobianco, Alberto and Lorenzo: 223
Caravaggio, Gianni (Rocca San Giovanni, Chieti, 1968): 236, 237
2003, *Cause*: 236, *236*
2003, *Crazy Beans*, Torre Pellice, Lisa and Tucci Russo Collection: 236, *237*
Caribbean Biennial: 177
Carpaccio, Vittore (Venice, 1464 ca – 1526): 22
Carrington, Leonora (Clayten Green, United Kingdom, 1917): 85
Cartier–Bresson, Henri (Chanteloup, Seine-et-Marne, 1908 – L'Île-sur-la-Sorgue, Vaucluse, 2004): 339
Casady, S.: 380
Casebere, James (Lansing, Michigan, 1953): 336
Castaneda, C.: 354
Castells, M.: 359, 368n
Cattelan, Maurizio (Padova, 1960): 13, 22, 25, 27n, 34, 40, 174, 175, 176, 177
1989, *Certificato medico*: 174
1991, *Stadium*: 176
1992, Oblomov Foundation (foundation): 176
1993, *Lavorare è un brutto mestiere* (Work is a Bad Job): 34, 174
1994, *Lullaby*: 176
1995, *Natale 95*: 176
1996, *Safe Fractured*: *175*
1996, *Bidibidobidiboo*: 176
1997, *Charlie Don't Surf*: 176
1997, *Novecento*: 176
1998, *Picasso*: 174
1999, *La nona ora* (The Ninth Hour): 176, *176*
1999, *Mini-me*: 174
1999, *Mother*: 176
2000, *La rivoluzione siamo noi* (We Are the Revolution): 176
2001, *Hollywood*: *174*
2001, *Felix*, Chicago, The Museum of Contemporary Art: *175*
2001, *Him*, François Pinault Collection: *12*, 40, 176
2002, Wrong Gallery (art gallery founded with Gioni and Subotnick): 177
2003, *Charlie*: 176
2004, *Untitled*: *174*, 176
2007, *Untitled*: *177*
Permanent Food (magazine founded with Paola Manfrin): 177
Celant, G.: 219, 275, 346
2003, *Carnal Drawings* (essay): 346
Catts, Oran (Helsinki, 1967) *see* The Tissue Culture and Art Project
Ceramica Gatti: 409
Chappaqua, film (Conrad Rooks, 1966): 333
Chappell, Walter (Portland, Oregon, 1925 – El Rito, New Mexico, 2000): 333
Chen Lingyang (Zhejiang, China, 1975): 19
Chen Zhen (Shanghai, 1955 – Paris, 2000): 18, 25
2000, *Un village sans frontières*: *25*
Chernyshev, Aristarkh (Voroshilovgrad, Russia, 1968) *see* Electoboutique
Chevrier, J.-F.: 333
Chia, Sandro (Florence, 1946): 222
Chiapello, E.: 281, 290n
Chien-Chi-Chang (Taiwan, 1961): 18
Chihuly, Dale (Tacoma, Washington, 1941): 408
1994, *Cobalt Blue Chandelier*: 408
2001, *Green Chandelier*: 408
Chipperfield, David (London, 1953): 159
Chödrön, P.: 281
Christie's, auction hause: 57, 296, 299n
Chto Delat (Nik Oleinikov, Tsaplya and Dmitry Vilensky) (collective founded in Saint Petersburg in 1993 by a group of artists, critics, philosophers and writers): 304, 306, 310, 311
2006, *Angry Sandwich People or in a Praise of Dialectic*: 306, *306*
Cinéma vérité: 390
Cirugeda, Santiago (Seville, 1971): 308
Cisneros Foundation: 299n
Clair, J.: 95

Clark, Lygia (Belo Horizonte, Brazil, 1920 – Rio de Janeiro, 1988): 35, 87
1973, *Baba antropofágica*: 87
Clinton, B.: 74
Cliostraat, architecture and design studio: 225
Closky, Claude (Paris, 1963): 98, 99, 362
1996–1999, *Sans titre (Supermarché)*: *98*
1997, *Do You Want Love or Lust?*: 98
1998, *Magazines*: 98
2004, *Television*: 98
2005, *Journal*: *99*
Cloud9, architecture studio: 224, 225
Coetzee, M.: 275
Coleman, O.: 86
Coloco, architecture studio: 224, 225
Colombo, Gianni (Milan, 1937 – Melzo, 1993): 96
Since 1967, *Spazi elastici*: 96
Conceptual/ists: 66, 100, 308, 408
Constructivism/ists: 144, 232, 252
Contemporary Istanbul Art Fair: 286
Cook, S.: 369n
Copenhagen Free University (collective founded in Copenhagen in 2001): 311
Cornice Art Fair, Venice, 2007: 286
Corral, M. de: 275
Cosmacini, G.: 188
Cosmopolitan, magazine: 350
Cosplaying/yers (putting on a mask of *anime* characters): 372
Cottingham, L.: 30
Crawford, J.: 21
Creed, Martin (Wakefield, United Kingdom, 1968): 41, 100, 101, 102, 103, 198
1995–2004, *Work No. 180: Largo, Larghetto, Adagio, Andante, Moderato, Allegro, Presto, Prestissimo*: 100, *102*
2000, *Work No. 227: The Lights Going On and Off*, installation at Tate Britain, London, 2001: 100, *100–101*
2001, *On/Off*: 41
2004, *Work No. 360: Half the Air in a Given Space*: 102, *103*
2007, *Work No. 790: Everything Is Going To Be Alright*, installation at the Museum of Contemporary Art, Detroit: *100–101*, 102
2008, *Work No. 850*: 41
Crewdson, Gregory (Brooklyn, New York, 1962): 335
Critchley, S.: 281, 290n
Critical Art Ensemble (CAE) (collective founded in Talahasse, Florida, in 1987 by Hope and Steve Kurtz, Steve Barnes, Dorian Burr and Beverly Schlee): 301, 309, 310
1994, *The Electronic Disturbance* (essay): 301, 310
2004, *Free Range Grain*, installation at Schim Kunsthalle, Frankfurt: 310, *310*
Croff, D.: 286
Croitoru, Alexandra (Bucharest, 1975): 339
2004–2006, Serie *Rom*: 339
Crowhurst, D.: 52
Cucchi, Enzo (Morro d'Alba, Ancona, 1949): 219, 222
Cueff, A.: 275
Cui Xiuwen (Heilongjiang, China, 1970): 18
Cunningham, M.: 82
Cuoghi, Roberto (Modena, 1973): 11, 41, 374, 375
2003, *Senza titolo*: *10*
2005, *Mbube*, Rivoli, Castello di Rivoli – Museo d'Arte Contemporanea: 374, *375*
2008, *Šuillakku*, Rivoli, Castello di Rivoli – Museo d'Arte Contemporanea: 374, *374*
Curlet, François (Paris, 1967): 41
Currin, John (Boulder, Colorado, 1962): 350, 351, 360
2002, *Rachel in Fur*: 350, *350*
2003, *Thanksgiving*: 350, *351*

D

Dadaism/ists: 81, 82, 116
Dahl, R.: 380
Dak'art, Dakar (Senegal): 291n
Dal Monte Casoni, Stefano (Lugo di Romagna, Ravenna, 1961): 410
Dalí, Salvador (Figueres, Spain, 1904–1989): 398
Danto, A.C.: 114
David Hammons (Springfield, Illinois, 1943): 212
Davis, B.: 410
De Carlo, M.: 174, 198
de Chirico, Giorgio (Volos, 1888 – Rome, 1978): 200
De Kooning, Willem (Rotterdam, 1904 – New York, 1997): 172
De Maria, Walter (Albany, California, 1935): 166
De Niro, R.: 376
De Stijl, magazine: 407
Dean, Tacita (Canterbury, 1965): 38, 42, 52, 53, 91, 312, 335
1996, *Disappearance at Sea*: 52
1997, *Disappearance at Sea II*: 52
1999, *Bubble House*: 52
2000, *Teignmouth Electron*: 52
2001, *Fernsehturm*: 52, *53*
2002, *Diamond Ring*: *38–39*, 42
2003, *Pie*: 42
2006, *Kodak*: 52, *52*
Debord, G.E.: 34
Déco: 407
Deitch, J.: 31
Delaunay, Sonia (Gradiesk, Ukraine, 1885 – Paris, 1979): 85
Deller, Jeremy (London, 1966): 124
Delvoye, Wim (Wervik, Belgium, 1965): 178, 179, 365
1990, *Mosaics*: 178
1990, *Shovels*: 178
1999, *Marble Floor*: 178
2000, *Cloaca*: 178, 365
2002, *Diet Coke Can*: 178, *179*
2003, *Polymania*: 178, *178*
2006, *Arielle*: 178, *179*
2008, *Cement Truck (Scale Model)*: 178, *179*
Demand, Thomas (Munich, 1964): 180, 181, 336
1995, *Büro*: 180
1996, *Zimmer*: 180, *180*
1997, *Badezimmer*: 180
1999, *Tunnel*: 180
2002, *Collection*: 180
2003, *Clearing*, private collection: *180*, 181
2004, *Gate*: 180
2007, *Embassy I*, private collection: 180, *180*
2008, *Presidency I*, private collection: 180, *181*
Depero, Fortunato (Fondo, Trento, 1892 – Rovereto, 1960): 161
Deutsche Bank: 299n
Dia Art Foundation: 158
Dick, P.K.: 133
1955, *Foster, You're Dead* (novel): 133
Dickinson, E.: 138
diCorcia, Philip-Lorca (Hartford, Connecticut, 1951): 335
1990s, Serie *Streetworks*: 335
Diederichsen, D.: 278, 290n
Dietz, S.: 369n
Digital Art: 362
Dijkstra, Rineke (Sittard, Netherlands, 1959): 91
Diller + Scofidio, architecture studio founded by Elizabeth Diller (Lodz, Poland, 1954) and Ricardo Scofidio (New York, 1935): 218, 224, 225n
2002, *Blur Building*, Swiss Expo, Neuchâtel: 218, *218*
Dion, Mark (New Bedford, Massachusetts, 1961): 182, 183
1991, *Polar Bear and Toucans (from Amazonas to Svalbard)*, DuMont Schütte Collection: *182*
1993, *The Library for the Birds of Antwerp*: 182
1994, *Toys 'R' U.S. (When Dinosaurs Ruled the Earth)*: 182
1999, *Tate Thames Dig*: 182
2005, *Library for the Birds of Massachusetts*, installation at Massachusetts Museum of Contemporary Art, North Adams: 182, *183*
Disney, W.: 40, 342
Djurberg, Nathalie (Lysekil, Sweden, 1978): 88
Docks Art Fair, Lyon: 286
Documenta, Kassel: 35, 44, 46, 208, 283, 285, 287, 288, 318, 392
Dolène, L.: 382
Dölger, M.: 380
Domus, magazine: 225
Donnelly, Trisha (San Francisco, 1974): 38
Dr. Jekyll and Mr. Hyde, film (1941): 376
Dubuffet, Jean (Le Havre, 1901 – Paris, 1985): 82
Duchamp, Marcel (Blainville 1887 – Neuilly-sur-Seine 1968): 81, 114, 143, 246, 260, 270, 378
1919, *Air de Paris*: 270
Dumas, Marlene (Cape Town, South Africa, 1953): 352, 353
2003, *Measuring Your Own Grave*: 352
2006, *Frisked*, private collection: *352*
2008, *For Whom the Bell Tolls*, Dallas, Dallas Museum of Art: 352, *353*
Dürer, Albrecht (Nuremberg, 1471–1528): 392
1514, *Melancholia I*: 392
Durham, Jimmie (Washington, Arkansas, 1940): 37, 104, 105, 106, 107
2000, *The Flower of the Death of Loneliness*, London, The Saatchi Collection: 105, *105*
2003, *The Petrified Forest*, Naples, Maurizio Morra Greco Collection: 106, *106*
2005, *Something (Perhaps a Fugue or an Elegy)*, installation at Venice Biennale, 2005: *104*, 105
2006, *Deposition*: 105, *106–107*

Düsseldorf School: 334
Dutch Association for Corporate Art Collections (VBCN): 299n
DZ Bank: 299n

E
Eckmann, Otto (Hamburg, 1868 – Badenweiler, 1902): 406
Ecologic Studio, architecture studio: 224
Ecosistema Urbano, architecture studio: 217, 221, 225
2007, *Ecoboulevard*, Madrid: 216, *216*, *221*
Eggleston, William (Memphis, Tennessee, 1939): 333
Einfühlung (empaty): 405
Einstein, A.: *19*, 20
Electroboutique (collective founded in Moscow in 2004 by Aristarkh Chernyshev and Alexei Shulgin): 363
2007, *Commercial Protest*: *363*
Elemental, multimedia company: 225
Eliasson, Olafur (Copenhagen, 1967): 38, 202, 224, 225n, 238, 239, 240, 241, 250, 336, 360
1992, *Come as You Are*: 238
1997, *Erosion*, installation at 2nd Johannesburg Biennale, South Africa: *238*, 239
1997, *Room for One Color*: 239
1997, *Your Sun Machine*: 238, 239
1998, *Ice Pavilion*, installation at Kjarvalstadir, Reykjavik Art Museum: 239, *239*
1998–2001, *Green River*: 239
2001, *Seeing Yourself Sensing*: 238
2002, *Your Spiral View*, installation at Foundation Beyeler, Basel: 238, 239, *240*
2002, *360 Room for All Colours*: 239
2003, *The Weather Project*, installation at Turbine Hall, Tate Modern (*The Unilever Series*), London: 238, *241*
2003, *The Antispective Situation*: 239
2003, *The Blind Pavilion*: 239
2004, *Your Space Embracer*, installation at Brändstörm & Stene, Stockholm: *240*
2005, *The Glacierhouse Effect Versus the Greenhouse Effect*: 239
2007, *Polyphonic House*, installation at Studio Olafur Eliasson, Berlin: *240*
2007, *One-Way Colour Tunnel*: 239
2007, *Take Your Time*: 238
2007, *Your Mobile Expectations: BMW H2R Project*: 239
Elmgreen & Dragset, collective pseudonym of Michael Elmgreen (Copenhagen, 1961) and Ingar Dragset (Trondheim, 1969): 42, 242, 243
Serie *Powerless Structures*: 242
1997, *Try*: 242
2001, *Elevated Gallery*: 242
2003, *Phone Home*: 242
2003, *Short Cut*: 242
2006, *Social Mobility (Emergency Exit)*: *242*
2006, *Modern Moses*: *243*
2006, *Andrea Candela*: 242
2007, *Drama Queens*: 42
Emin, Tracey (London, 1963): 54, 55
1997, *Everyone I Have Ever Slept With, 1963–1995*: 55
1998, *My Bed*, London, The Saatchi Collection: 55, *55*
2005, *Woof, The Best Girl Inshow*: *54*
Endell, August (Berlin, 1871–1925): 405
Ensor, James (Ostend, 1860–1949): 406
Entartete Musik (degenerate music): 212
Environment: 252
Enwezor, O.: 286, 287, 339
Enzensberger, H.M.: 17
Ernst, Max (Brühl, 1891 – Paris, 1976): 85
Esakov, Liyat: 303, 309
2003, *Dry Toilet*, Caracas, La Fila, barrio La Vega: *303*, 309
Escher, Maurits Cornelis (Leeuwarden, 1898 – Laren, 1972): 214
Escraches ("unmasking", collective actions): 303, 307
Esposizione internazionale delle arti decorative e industriali, Turin (1902): 405, 406
Estudio Teddy Cruz, architecture studio: 225
Euripides: 320
415 B.C. ca, *The Troian Women* (tragedy): 320
Export, Valie (Linz, 1940): 87
1969, *Action Pants: Genital Panic*: 87
Exposition Nationale des produits de l'industrie agricole et manufacturière, Paris (1844): 283
Exposition Universelle, Paris, 1900: 157
Expressionism: 145, 405
Exter, Alexandra (Bialystok, Poland, 1882 – Fontenay-aux-Roses, France, 1949): 85
Eyre, Janieta (London, 1966): 16, 25
1998, *Two Laundresses by the River Thames*: *24*

F
Fabre, J.-H.: 108
Fabre, Jan (Antwerp, 1958): 11, 27n, 108, 109
2002, *Heaven of Delight*, Brussels, Palais Royal, Salle des Glaces: 108, *108*
2007, *Is the Brain the Most Sexy Part of the Body?*: 108, *108*
2007, *A Medieval Punishment for a Contemporary Artist (Landscape with Self-portrait)*, *109*
Fabrica: 402
Fabro, Luciano (Turin, 1936 – Milan, 2007) : 236
Fahlström, Öyvind (São Paulo, 1928 – Stockholm, 1976): 311
Faithfull, M.: 21
Fautrier, Jean (Paris, 1898 – Châtenay-Malabry, 1964): 82
Fawlty Towers, *sit-com* (1970s): 208
Feinstein, Rachel (Fort Defiance, Arizona, 1971): 350
feld72, collective laboratory for architecture: 225
Fenton, Roger (Crimble Hall, Lancashire, 1819 – London, 1869): 333
Fernandez, A.: 276
Fiber Art: 409
Fiedler, K.: 405
Fischer, Urs (Zurich, 1973): 244, 245
2003, *Chair for a Ghost*: 244
2003, *What If The Phone Rings?*: 244
2004, *Bread House*: 244
2004–2005, *Vintage Violence*, François Pinault Collection: 244, *244*
2007, *How To Tell a Joke*: 244
2007, *You*: 244, *245*
Fischli & Weiss, pseudonym of Peter Fischli (Zurich, 1952) and David Weiss (Zurich, 1946): 246, 247, 248, 249
1979, *Wurst-Serie*: 246
1980–2003, *Questions*: 249
1986–1987, *Der Lauf der Dinge* (The Way of Things): 246
1986–1988, *Black Sculptures*: 246
1988–1997, *Airports*: 246
1997, Garden created for the exhibition *Skulptur Projekte*, Münster, 1997: 246, *246*
1997–1998, *Blumenphoto*, UniCredit Group Collection: *247*
2000–2004, *Untitled (Rotterdam)*: 246
2001–2004, *Untitled (Pallets)*: 246
2003, *Hunde* (Dogs), Pittsburgh, Carnegie Museum of Art: 249, *248*
2008, *Sonne, Mond und Sterne* (Sun, Moon, and Stars): *248–249*, 249
Fischli, Peter *see* Fischli & Weiss: 246, 248, 335
Fiúza Faustino, Didier (Paris, 1968): 225
Flash Art, magazine: 30
Fleurie, Sylvie (Geneva, 1961): 91
Fluxus: 82, 83, 287
Fogarasi, Andreas (Vienna, 1977): 339
Fondation Cartier: 299n
Fondazione Sandretto Re Rebaudengo: 295, 299n
Fontana, E.: 231, 238
Fontana, Lucio (Rosario di Santa Fé, Argentina, 1899 – Comabbio, Varese, 1968): 82, 96
1949, *Ambiente spaziale a luce nera*: 96
Ford, J.: 42
1956, *The Searchers* (film): 42
Fosso, Samuel (Kumba, Cameroon, 1962): 339
Foster, H.: 252, 302
Foucault, P.-M., philosopher: 30, 303
Fragonard, Jean–Honoré (Grasse, 1732 – Paris, 1806): 124, 350
1767, *The Swing*: 124
Frangi, Giovanni (Milan, 1959): 184, 185
1996, *La fuga di Renzo*: 184
1999, *Il richiamo della foresta*: 184
2003, *Nobu at Elba*: 184, *185*
2008, *Pasadena*, Verona, Galleria dello Scudo: 184, *184*
2008, Serie *Pasadena*: 184
Frank, Robert (Zurich, 1924): 333
Frankenthaler, Helen (New York, 1928): 85
Frei, Luca (Lugano, 1976): 311
Freud, Lucian (Berlin, 1922): 141, 143, 299n
1980, *Naked Portrait with Reflection*, private collection: *143*
Freud, S.: 83
Friedlander, Lee (Aberdeen, Washington, 1934): 333, 339
Frieze Art Fair, London: 286
Frisch, M.: 256
1964, *Mein Name sei Gantenbein* (novel): 256
Fuentes, E.: 287
Fuksas, Massimiliano (Rome, 1944): 217, 220
2000, *Less Aesthetics, More Ethichs*, installation at the Corderie dell'Arsenale, Venice Biennale (with Doriana Fuksas): 220, *220*
Fuller, Richard Buckminster (Milton, 1895 – Los Angeles, 1983): 268

Fulton, Hamish (London, 1946): 333
Fundació “la Caixa”: 299n
Future Systems, architecture studio founded by Jan Kaplicky (Prague, 1937) and Amanda Levete (Bridgend, United Kingdom, 1955): 223
Futurelab: 365
Futurism/ists: 82, 154, 161, 407

G
Gagosian, L.: 282, 290n
Galindo, Regina José (Guatemala City, 1974): 16, 22, 93, 307, 316, 317
2003, *¿Quién puede borrar las huellas?*: 307, 316, *317*
2004, *Himenoplastia*: 93, 316
2006, *Limpieza social*: 316, *316*
Gameboy: 370
Ganahl, Rainer (Bludenz, Austria, 1961): 310, 409
2002, *Afghan Dialog, America Strikes Back*: 409
Gandolfi, E.: 220
Garaicoa, Carlos (Havana, 1967): 287
Gedney, William (Greenville, New York, 1932 – New York, 1989): 339
Geerlinks, Margi (Kampen, Netherlands, 1970): 91
2000, *Mothers*: 91
Gehry, Frank O. (Toronto, 1929): 151, 154
1993–1997, Bilbao Guggenheim Museum: 151
Geldzahler, H.: 145
Generative Art: 362, 366
Gere, C.: 359, 368n
Gesamtkunstwerk (Total Art Work): 344, 405, 406
Giacometti, Alberto (Borgonovo di Stampa, Switzerland, 1901 – Chur, 1966): 42
Walking Man: 42
Gian Ferrari, E.: 286
Gilardi, P.: 188
Gilbert & George, collective pseudonym of Gilbert Proesch (San Martino in Badia, Bolzano, 1943) and George Passmore (Plymouth, Devon, 1942): 20, 83, 190
Gillick, Liam (Aylesbury, United Kingdom, 1964): 34, 35, 38, 41, 186, 187, 302, 382, 394
1996, *Ibuka*: 34
1996, *The What if? Scenario*: 187
1997, *Discussion Island/Big Conference Centre*: 187
2002, *Coats of Asbestos Spangled with Mica*, London, Corvi-Mora Gallery: *186–187*, 187
2005, *Texte court sur la possibilité de créer une économie de l’équivalence*: 34
2007, *Returning to an Abandoned Plant*: 187
Gilmore, G.: 344
Gilmore, J.H.: 282, 290n
Gingeras, A.: 398
Ginsberg, A.: 82
Gioni, M.: 176, 177
John Paul II, pope: 176, 281
Glasgow School: 406
Glass, P.: 320
Glimcher, M.: 146
Godard, J.-L.: 41, 102
Godet, R.: 82
Goldberg, R.: 85
Goldblatt, David (Randfontein, South Africa, 1930): 339
Goldin, Nan (Washington, D.C., 1953): 35, 83, 334, 336
Gončarova, Natalja (Tula, Russia, 1881 – Paris, 1962): 85
Gonzalez-Foerster, Dominique (Strasbourg, 1965): 34, 35, 38, 39, 41, 188, 189, 382, 394
1993, *The Daughter of a Taoist*: 34
2001, *Riyo*: 34
2006, *Trèfle*, Turin, Parco d’Arte Vivente: 188, *188*
2008, *TH2058*: 188, *189*
González-Torres, Félix (Guaimaro, Cuba, 1957 – New York, 1996): 29, 30, 31, 39, 83
1992, *Untitled (Petit Palais)*, Philadelphia, The Philadelphia Museum of Art: *28*
Serie *Corner Pieces/Spreads*: 30
Serie *Stacks* (posters): 30, 31
Gordon, Douglas (Glasgow, 1966): 38, 42, 142, 148, 370, 376, 377, 378, 379, 394
Since 1990, *List of Names*: 42
1992–2006, *Pretty much every film and video work from about 1992 until now. To be seen on monitors, some with headphones, others run silently, and all simultaneously*: *376–377*, 378, *379*
1993, *24-Hour Psycho*: 42, 370, 376
1996, *A Divided Self I and II*, Turin, Sandretto Re Rebaudengo Collection: *148*
1996, *Confessions of a Justified Sinner*: 376
1999, *Left Is Right And Right Is Wrong And Left Is Wrong And Right Is Right*: 378
1999, *Through a Looking Glass*: 376
2003, *Play Dead Real Time*: *377*, 378
2006, *Prettymucheverywordwritten, spoken, heard, overheard from 1989*: *379*
2006, *Zidane: un portrait du XXIe siècle* (with Philippe Parreno), New York, Solomon R. Guggenheim Museum: 394, *394*
2007, *Psycho Hitchhiker (Coming or Going)*: 378, *378*
Serie *Self-portraits of You and Me*: 378
2007, *Self-portrait of You and Me (Elvis)*: 378
2007, *Self-portrait of You + Me (Jackie)*: *378*
Gore, A.: 310
2006, *An Inconvenient Truth* (film): 310
Goya y Lucientes, Francisco (Fuendetodos, Saragozza, 1746 – Bordeaux, 1828): 172
Graham, Dan (Urbana, Illinois, 1942): 223
Great Exhibition of the Works of Industry of All Nations: 283
Gréaud, Loris (Eaubonne, France, 1979): 380
2006–2008, *Cellar Door*, 380
2007–2008, *Bucky*: 380, *380*
2008, *Spore Speakers*, François Pinault Collection: *381*
Green, Renée (Cleveland, Ohio, 1959): 93
Greenaway, Peter (Newport, 1942): 21
Greenberg, C.: 29, 85, 144, 145, 149, 360, 369n
Gropius, Walter (Berlin, 1883 – Boston, 1969): 84, 407
Group Material (collective founded in New York in 1979 by Doug Ashford, Julie Ault, Félix González-Torres, Mundy McLaughlin, and Tim Rollins): 303, 304
1981, *The People’s Choice*: 303, 304
Groys, B.: 279, 277, 285, 290n, 291n
Grupo de Arte Callejero (GAC) (collective founded in Buenos Aires in 1997): 301, 307
2001, *Aquí Viven Genocidas*: 307
Grupo Etcétera (collective founded in Buenos Aires in 1997): 301, 303, 307, 308, 309
2004, *Gente Armada*, performance at Museum Ludwig, Cologne: 309, *309*
Grzeszykowska, Aneta (Warsaw, 1974): 336
Guatemalan Republican Front: 307
Star Wars (cinematographic saga): 386
Guerrilla Girls (collective of femminist women artists): 87
Guggenheim, P.: 85
Guggenheim, S.R.: 151
Gupta, Shilpa (Mumbai, India, 1976): 93
Gupta, Subodh (Khagaul, India, 1964): 56, 57
2002, *This Side Is the Other Side*, Rovereto, Mart – Museo d’Arte Moderna e Contemporanea di Trento e Rovereto: *56–57*, 57
2005, *Curry 2 (1)*: *56*, 57
Gursky, Andreas (Leipzig, 1955): 141, 144, 296, 298, 334
1997, *Untitled V*, François Pinault Collection: *144*
2001, *99 cents II*: 298
Gutai Group: 85
Guthrie, Trevor (Dunferline, Scotland, 1964): 275, 280
2008, *Hindenbunny*: 275, 280, *280*
Gwangju Biennial, South Korea: 288, 291n

H
Haacke, Hans (Cologne, 1936): 303
Haaning, Jens (Copenhagen, 1965): 40, 41
1994, *Turkish Jokes*: 40
1996, *Arabic Jokes*: 40
1998, *Superdiscount*: 41
2000, *Untitled (de Appel – de Gelderse Roos)*: 40
Habermas, J.: 278, 281
Hadid, Zaha (Baghdad, 1950): 157, 158, 165, 167
1998/2003–2010, MAXXI_Museo nazionale arti del XXI secolo, Rome: 157, 158
Atrium of the MAXXI_Museo nazionale delle arti del XXI secolo, Rome: 165, *165*
Exterior view of the MAXXI_Museo nazionale delle arti del XXI secolo, Rome: 167, *167*
Hamilton, Ann (Lima, Ohio, 1956): 88
Hammons, David (Springfield, Illinois, 1943): 31, 212
Hanru, H.: 286
Hanzlová, Jitka (Nachod, Czech Republic, 1958): 336

Happening: 82, 87
Happening & Fluxus, festival, 1970–1971: 287
Hardy, Anne (London, 1970): 333, 336
2006, *Close Range*: 333, *332*
Harris, L.A.: 30
Haruki, Maiko (Ibaraki, Japan, 1974): 341
Hassan, S.: 95, 97n
Hatoum, Mona (Beirut, 1952): 16, 22, 88, 90, 409
1993–1999, *Keffiah*: 409
1995, *Hair Necklace*: *16*
1996, *Quarters*: *90*
Hausswolff, Annika von (Göteborg, Sweden, 1967): 336
Havana Biennial, Cuba: 29, 286, 287, 288
Hein, Jeppe (Copenhagen, 1974): 250, 251
2000, *Let Me Show You the World*: 250
2002, *360° Presence*: 250
2002, *Continuity Inbetween*: 250
2003, *Bear the Consequences*: 250
2003, *Space in Action / Action in Space*: 250
2004, *Appearing Rooms*: *250*
2006, *Between Fire and Water*: 250
2006, *Spiral Labyrinth*, Copenhagen, Galleri Nicolai Wallner: *251*
Heiser, J.: 148, 149n
2007, *Plötzlich diese Übersicht* (essay): 148
Helguera, Pablo (Mexico City, 1971): 287, 288, 289
2008, *Artoons*: *287*
Herkenhoff, P.: 286
Herrera, C.: 275
Herzog & de Meuron, architecture studio founded in Basel (1978) by Jacques Herzog (Basel, 1950) and Pierre de Meuron (Basel, 1950): 46, 155, 159, 160, 220, 221, 225n, 296, 299n
1995–2000, Tate Modern, London: 154, 155, 158, 160
1998–1999 (project), 2000–2003 (execution), Schaulager, Basel: 160
2003–2008, Olympic Stadium (*The Nest*), Beijing (with Ai Weiwei): 221, 220, *221*
2008, Exterior view of the building designed for the Fundació "la Caixa", Madrid: *297*
Heuss, T.: 285
Hevesi, L.: 405
Higgins, Dick (Cambridge, 1938 – Québec, 1998): 82
Higgs, M.: 275
Hijos (human rights organisation): 301
Hildebrand, A.: 405
Hill, Christine (Binghamton, New York, 1968): 34
Hill, Gary (Santa Monica, California, 1951), 296
2006, *Guilt*, 296, *297*
Hip-hop: 372
Hirschhorn, Thomas (Berne, 1957): 31, 252, 253, 254, 255, 302
1997, *Skulptur-Sortier-Station, Monaco*, New York, Barbara Gladstone Gallery: *253*
1998, *Ingeborg Bachmann Altar*: 254
1999, *Sculpture Direct*: *252*
1999, *Raymond Carver Altar*: 254
2004, *Chalet Lost History*, Paris, Galerie Chantal Crousel: 252, *253*
2004, *Twin Tear*, New York, Barbara Gladstone Gallery: 254, *254–255*
2006, *The Green Coffin*: *32–33*
2008, *Das Auge*: 254
Hirschman, A.O.: 303
Hirst, Damien (Bristol, 1965): 22, 39, 110, 111, 112, 113, 141, 147, 290n, 410
1991, *The Physical Impossibility of Death in the Mind of Someone Living*: 110
1992, *Pharmacy*, London, Tate Britain: *110*, 410
1996, *Some Comfort Gained from the Acceptance of the Inherent Lies in Everything*, François Pinault Collection: 110, *111*
1997–1998, *The Fragile Truth*: 112
2000–2004, *Where Are We Going? Where Do We Come From? Is There a Reason?*, François Pinault Collection: 112, *112*
2001, *Infinity*, François Pinault Collection: *111*, 112
2004, *Vivisection*, François Pinault Collection: 112, *112*
2007, *For the Love of God*: 112, *113*, 147
2007, *Biopsy Paintings*: 112
2007, *Birth Paintings*: 112
Hitchcock, A.: 42, 376
1960, *Psycho* (film): 42, 376, 378
Hitler, A.: 20, 40, 176, 210
Höch, Hannah (Gotha, Germany, 1889–1978): 83
Hochschule für Bildende Künste: 127
Hodler, Ferdinad (Berne, 1853 – Geneva, 1918): 406
Höfer, Candida (Eberswalde, Germany, 1944): 334
Hoffmann, E.Th.W.: 20
Hoffmann, J.: 177
Hoffmann, Josef (Pirnitz, 1870 – Vienna, 1956): 406
Hogarth, William (London, 1697–1764): 172
Hollein, Hans (Vienna, 1934): 166
1982/1983–1991, Museum für Moderne Kunst, Frankfurt: 166
Höller, Carsten (Brussels, 1961): 34, 38, 39, 96, 256, 257, 258, 259, 360
1994, *Jenny Happy*: 39
1996, *Spinning Top*: 256, *257*
1998, *Valerio I*: 258
1998, *Valerio II*: 258
2000, *Upside Down Mushroom Room*, Milan, Fondazione Prada: 96, 256, *258*
2000, *Gantenbein Corridor*: 256
2000, *Synchro System*: 256
2003, *Sliding Doors*, London, Tate Modern: *256*, 258
2006, *Test Site*: 258, *259*
Confusions Machines: 256
Holmes, B.: 310
Holzer, Jenny (Gallipolis, Ohio, 1956): 16, 88
Honig, E.A.: 282, 290n
Horn, Rebecca (Michelstadt, Germany, 1944): 81, 87
1968, *Arm Extensions*: 87
1970–1972, *Unicorn*, private collection: 80, *81*, 87
Horn, Roni (New York, 1955): 83, 91, 93
2002–2003, *Clownpout (4)*: *93*
Hou Hanru: 372
Houdini, H.: 21, 344
Hu Jieming (Shanghai, China, 1957): 18
2002, *Raft of the Medusa No. 2 Liberty Leading the People*: *18*
Huang Yan (Jilin, China, 1966): 19
Huang Yong Ping (Xiamen, China, 1954): 260, 261
2006, *Intestins de Bouddha*: 260
2007, *Colosseum*: *260–261*
Hubbard, L.R.: 180
Hudek, A.: 287, 291n
Hugo Boss Prize: 58, 132, 312
Huit Facettes (collective founded by Bdoulaye Ndoye, El Hadji Sy, Fodé Camara, Cheikh Niass, Jean Marie Bruce, Muhsana Ali and Kan-si in Senegal in 1995): 301
Hunt, Ashley (Los Angeles, 1970): 305, 310, 311
2005, *A World Map: In Which We See*, installation at Contemporary Museum, Baltimore: *305*, 310, 311
Husos, architecture studio: 224, 225
Hütte, Axel (Essen, Germany, 1951): 334
Huyghe, Pierre (Paris, 1962): 35, 38, 39, 40, 41, 302, 382, 383, 394
1994–2001, *Les Grands Ensembles*, installation at Venice Biennale, 2001: 382, 383, *383*
1994, *Barbés/Rochechouart*: 40
1996, *Anna Sanders Magazine* (with Philippe Parreno): 41
1996, *Dubbing*: 382
1997, *Blanche Niege Lucie*: 382
1999–2001, *Atari Light*, François Pinault Collection: 381, *383*
1999, *The Third Memory*: 382
1999–2003, *No Ghost, Just a Shell* (with Philippe Parreno): 382
2001, *Le Château de Turing*, François Pinault Collection: *383*
2001, *One Million Kingdoms*, François Pinault Collection: 382, *383*
2005, *A Journey That Wasn't*: 40, 383, *382*
Huyssen, A.: 278, 290n
HVB: 299n

I

The Seven Samurai, film (Akira Kurosawa, 1954): 208
Id-Lab, design company: 225
Iglesias, Cristina (San Sebastián, Spain, 1956): 91
Ilya & Emilia Kabakov, collective pseudonym of Ilya Kabakov (Dnipropetrovsk, Ukraine, 1933) and Emilia Kabakov (Dnipropetrovsk, Ukraine, 1945): 223
Informel: 62, 82, 144, 407
Interactive Art: 362
International Association of Corporate Collections of Contemporary Art (IACCCA): 299n
Internationale situationniste, magazine: 34
Irascible Eighteen, group: 82
Irons, J.: 20
Irwin, Robert (Long Beach, California, 1928): 158
1999–2003, Dia:Beacon, Beacon (New York) (OpenOffice): 158
Ishigami, Junya (Kanagawa, Japan, 1974): 221, 224
2008, Facility-Kanagawa Institute of Technology: 221, *221*

ISIA (Istituto Superiore per le Industrie Artistiche): 407
Islam, Runa (Dhaka, Bangladesh, 1970): 94
Istanbul Biennial: 286, 324
Itten, Johannes (Südernlinden, 1888 – Zurich, 1967): 407

J
Jacir, Emily (Bethlehem, Palestine, 1970): 58, 59
2001, *Memorial to 418 Palestinian Villages That Were Destroyed, Depopulated and Occupied by Israel in 1948*, installation at Italian Pavilion at Venice Biennale, 2007: 58, *59*
2004–2007, *Material for a Film*: 58, *58*, 59
Jakob + MacFarlane, architecture studio: 224
Jeong-A, Koo (Seoul, South Korea, 1967): 38
Jetzer, G.: 275
Johannesburg Biennial: 239, 288, 291n
Jodi, artistic duo founded by Joan Heemskerk (Kaatsheuvel, Netherland, 1968) and Dirk Paesmans (Brussels, 1968): 368
Jodice, Francesco (Naples, 1967): 335
Jodice, Mimmo (Naples, 1934): 223
John Paul II, pope: 176, 281
Johns, Jasper (Augusta, Georgia, 1930): 141
Jonas, Joan (New York, 1936): 14, 27n
2007, *The Hand Returns To Its Own Movement…*: 14
Jones, Sarah (London, 1959): 336
Joseph, Pierre (Caen, France, 1965): 38, 39, 41
Joyce, J.: 344
Judd, Donald (Excelsior Springs, Missouri, 1928 – New York, 1994): 136
Jugend, magazine: 405
Jung, C.G.: 83
Juvarra, Filippo (Messina, 1678 – Madrid, 1736): 157
1718 – unfinished, Castello di Rivoli: 157

K
Kabakov, Ilya (Dnipropetrovsk, Ukraine, 1933): 142, 223
Kac, Eduardo (Rio de Janeiro, 1962): 384, 385
1994, *Essay Concerning Human Understanding*: 384
1997, *Time Capsule*: 384
1999, *Genesis*: 384
2000-in progress, *GFP Bunny*: 384, *385*
2000, *Alba* (rabbit: artist creation): 384
2001, *The Eighth Day*: *384*
Kafka, F.: 320
1925, *Der Prozess* (The Trial) (unfinished novel): 320
Kahlo, Frida (Coyoacán, Mexico City, 1907–1954): 85
Kahn, Louis Isidore (Osel, Estonia, 1901 – New York, 1974): 153
1966–1972, Kimbell Art Museum, Fort Worth, Texas: 153
Kandinskij, Vasilij (Moscow, 1866 – Neuilly sur Seine, Paris, 1944): 407
Kant, I.: 145
Kapoor, Anish (Bombay, 1954): 223, 225n
Kaprow, Allan (Atlantic City, New Jersey, 1922 – Encinitas, California, 2006): 82, 97n
1959, *18 Happenings in 6 Parts*: 82
1967, *Fluids*: 82
Katz, V.: 354
Kauffmann, Angelica (Chur, 1741 – Rome, 1807): 85
Kawaii, cuteness: 88, 116, 117
Keita, Seydou (Bamako, Mali, 1921 – Paris, 2001): 334, 339
Kelley, Mike (Detroit, Michigan, 1954): 40
1992, *Heidi* (with Paul McCarthy): 40
Kelly, Mary (Fort Dodge, Iowa, 1941): 91, 302
1975, *Post-Partum Document*: 91
Kentridge, William (Johannesburg, South Africa, 1955): 318, 319
1988, Free Filmmakers Cooperative (association): 318
1993–1998, *Blue Head*, Washington, D.C., Hirshhorn Museum and Sculpture Garden, Smithsonian Institution: *318*
1994, *Felix in Exile*, London, Tate Modern, 1998: *319*
2001, *The Medicine Chest*, Washington, D.C., Hirshhorn Museum and Sculpture Garden, Smithsonian Institution: *319*
2002, *Confession of Zeno*: 318
2008, *Breathe*, *Return*, *Dissolve* (video installations): 318
Kenzo: 95
Kerouac, J.: 82
Khnopff, Fernand (Grembergen-lez-Termonde, 1858 – Brussels, 1921): 406
Khoroshilova, Anastasia (Moscow, 1978): 336
Khurana, Sonia (India, 1968): 93, 94
2004, *Mona's Song*: 94
Kiefer, Alselm (Donaueschingen, 1945): *11*
Kilimnik, Karen (Philadelphia, 1955): 96
Kimsooja (Taegu, South Korea, 1957): 22, 25, 27n
Kinetic art: 239
King, R.: 30
Kippenberger, Martin (Dortmund, 1953 – Vienna, 1997): 202
Klee, Paul (Münchenbuchsee, Berne, 1879 – Muralto, Locarno, 1940): 163, 164, 165
Klein, Yves (Nice, France, 1928 – Paris, 1962): 82
Since 1958, *Antropometrie*: 82
Klimt, Gustav (Vienna, 1862 – Neubau, 1918): 81, 83, 406
Klinger, Max (Leipzig, 1857 – Grossjena, 1920): 406
Klutsis, Gustav (Riga, 1912 – Moscow, 1938): 252
Knapp Dunn, S.: 74
Knapp, G.: 161
Kobro, Katarzyna (Moscow, 1898 – Lódź, 1951): 85
Koester, Joachim (Copenhagen, 1962): 42
2005, *Message from Andrée*: 42
Kokoschka, Oskar (Pöchlarn, Austria, 1886 – Montreux, Switzerland, 1980): 83
Koolhaas, Rem (Rotterdam, Netherlands, 1944): 159, 217
Koons, Jeff (York, Pennsylvania, 1955): 22, 42, 114, 115, 116, 141, 359, 372
1986, *Rabbit*: 42, 114
1988, Serie *Banality*: 114
1989, *Made in Heaven*: 114
1990s, Serie *Celebration*: 114
1992, *Puppy*, New York, Rockefeller Center: 114, *115*, 141
1994–2006, *Hanging Heart*, François Pinault Collection: *140*
1999, *Hair*, private collection: *114*
1999–2001, *Easyfun*: 114
2000, *Split-Rocker*: 114
2001, *Couple*, Santa Monica, The Broad Art Foundation: *114*
2003, Serie *Popeye*: 114
2007–2008, Serie *Hulk Elvis*: 114
Kosuth, Joseph (Toledo, Ohio, 1945): 94
1993, *Zeno at the Edge of the Known World*, Hungarian Pavilion, Venice Biennale: *94*
Kounellis, Jannis (Pireo, Athens, 1936): 222
Krasner, Lee (New York, 1908–1984): 85
Krauss, Ingar (Berlin East, 1965): 336
Krauss, R.: 37, 84, 360, 362
2005, *L'arte nell'era postmediale* (essay): 360
1999, *A Voyage on the North Sea. Art in the Age of the Post–medium condition* (essay): 37, 368n, 369n
2004, *Bachelors* (essays collection): 84
Kruger, Barbara (Newark, New Jersey, 1945): 16
Kubota, Shigeko (Niigata, Japan, 1937): 83, 85
1965, *Vagina Painting*: *83*
Kubrick, S.: 223, 344
Kusama, Yayoi (Nagano, Japan, 1929): 86
1968, *Anti-War Naked Happening*: 87
Kusolwong, Surasi (Ayutthaya, Thailand, 1965): 293
2006, *One Pound Turbo Market (You'll Have a Good Time)*, event/market at Turbine Hall, Tate Modern, London: *292*
Kvaran, G.B.: 275
Kwon, M.: 306

L
La Cecla, F.: 95, 97n
Labin, Clemencia (Maracaibo, Venezuela, 1946), with Alba Fernandez: 276
2006, *Living Picture Guajiras*: 276, *276*
Labyrinth, film (Jim Henson, 1986): 192
LaChapelle, David (Fairfield, Connecticut, 1963): 142
Laddaga, R.: 301
Laloux, Victor (Tours, 1850 – Paris, 1937): 157
1990, Gare d'Orsay: 157
Land Art/ists: 239, 328, 408
Länderbank: 299n
Lang, H.: 202
Larsson, Annika (Stockholm, 1972): 336
Laurette, Matthieu (Villeneuve Saint Georges, France, 1970): 41
1999, *Offshore*: 41
Lazzarato, M.: 277, 303
Le 120 giornate di Sodoma (120 Days of Sodom), film (P.P. Pasolini, 1975): 72
Le Corbusier, pseudonym of Charles-Édouard Jeanneret (La Chaux-de-Fonds 1887 – Roquebrune-Cap Martin 1965: 230, 383

Le Gray, Gustave (Villiers-le-Bel, 1820 – Paris, 1882): 294, 299n, 333
La grande vague: 299n
Lee, P.M.: 117, 359
Lehman Brothers, global financial-services firm: 280
Lemieux, Annette (Norfolk, Virginia, 1957): 16
Leonard, Zoe (Liberty, New York, 1961): 30
Les Magiciens de la Terre, 1989, Paris: 29, 30, 91, 105, 260, 286, 293
Lévi-Strauss, C.: 105
Lévy, B.-H.: 74
LeWitt, Sol (Hartford, Connecticut, 1928 – New York, 2007): 141, 223, 366, 369n
Since 1968, Serie *Wall Drawings*: 141, 366
Lhoist: 299n
Li Shan (Lanxi, China, 1942): 18
Li Wei (Hubei, China, 1970): 18, 19
Libération, newspaper: 50
Liberty: 406
Lichtenstein, Roy (New York, 1923–1997): 194, 275
Lima Biennial: 288
Lin Tianmiao (Taiyuan Shanxi, China, 1961): 18
Linda, S.: 374
Lindbergh, Peter (Lissa, Poland, 1944): 141
1990, *Helena Christensen & Alien*: 147, *147*
Linhart, R.: 31
1978, *L'établi* (essay): 31
Lipps, T.: 405
Lizvlx (Linz, Austria, 1973) *see* Ubermogen.com
Liu Jin (Jiangsu, China, 1971): 19
Liu Xiaodong (Liaoning, China, 1963): 18
Liu Zheng (Hebei, China, 1969): 18, 19
Lockhart, Sharon (Norwood, United Kingdom, 1964): 142
Logan, N.: 133
Lombardi, Mark (Syracuse, New York, 1951 – New York, 2000): 311
Long, Richard (Bristol, 1945): 223
Lorca, F.G.: 91
Los Carpinteros, collective founded by Marco Antonio Castillo Valdés (Camagüey, Cuba, 1971) and Dagoberto Rodríguez Sánchez (Caibarién, Cuba, 1969): 287
Louis Vuitton: 117, 122, 178, 239, 360
Lozano-Hemmer, Rafael (Mexico City, 1967): 60, 61
1999–2000, *Vectorial Elevation*, installation at ARTIUM, Vitoria-Gasteiz, Spain, 2002: 60, *60*
2003, *Amodal Suspension*: 60
2006, *Pulse Room*, installation in Puebla, Mexico, 2006: 60, *61*
2006, *Under Scan*: 60
2008, *Microphones*: 60
Lucas, Sarah (London, 1962): 190, 191
1994, *Au Naturel*: 190
2002, *All We Are Saying Is Give Peace A Chance*: 190, *191*
2002, *All We Are Saying Is Give Pizza Chance*: 190
2003, *Christ, You Know it Aint't Easy*: 190
2005, *Aunty Jam*: 190, *190*
City Lights, film (Charlie Chaplin, 1931): 208
Lukacs, G.: 304
Lumet, S.: 382
1975, *Dog Day Afternoon* (film): 382
Lüthi, Urs (Lucerne, 1947): *14*
Serie *Art Is the Better Life*: *14*
Lynch, D.: 142
Lyon Biennial: 38, 286
Lyotard, J.-F.: 278, 281

M

M/M (collective founded in Paris in 1992 by Michael Amzalag and Mathias Augustyniak): 41, 394
Ma Liuming (Huangshi, China, 1969): 19, 341
Ma0, architecture studio: 225
Madres de Plaza de Mayo: 307
Magischer Realismus: 200
Magubane, Peter (Vrededorp, Johannesburg, 1932): 339
Malani, Nalini (Karachi, Pakistan, 1946): 93
2003, *Unity in Diversity*: 93
Malasauskas, R.: 380
Malraux, A.: 143
Mambéty, Djibril Diop (Dakar, Senegal, 1945 – Paris, 1998): 339
Man Ray, pseudonym of Man Emmanuel Rudzitsky (Philadelphia, 1890 – Paris, 1976): 81, 275
Manara, M.: 342
Manetas, Miltos (Athens, 1964): 366, 368, 369n
2005, *Nikescape*, Dakis Joannou Collection: *368*
Manfrin, P.: 177
Manga, cartoons: 41, 64, 116
Mangano, S.: 72
Manifesta 3, Ljubljana: 41
Manifesta, Biennale di arte contemporanea, Trentino: 402
Mantegna, Andrea (Isola di Carturo, Padua, 1430/1431 – Mantua, 1506): 350
Manzoni, Piero (Soncino, Cremona, 1933 – Milan, 1963): 275, 290n
Mao Zedong: 20
Map office, multi-disciplinary design atelier: 225
Margiela, M.: 202
Margolles, Teresa (Culiacán, Mexico, 1963): 93
Marinetti, Filippo Tommaso (Alexandria, Egipt, 1876 – Bellagio, Como, 1944): 154
Marisaldi, Eva (Bologna, 1966): 262, 263, 409
2000, *Lieto fine*: 409
2005, *Pixeland*, Brescia, Galleria Massimo Minini: 262, *262*
2006, *Birthday Party*, Bologna, Collezione MAMbo – Museo d'Arte Moderna di Bologna, UniCredit Group Collection; MAMbo – Museo d'Arte Moderna di Bologna: *263*
2007, *Porto fuori*, Rome, Galleria SALES: 262, *263*
Machine percussion band (robot): 262
Marras, A.: 95
Martin, J.-H.: 29, 91, 105
Martinez, R.: 342
Marty, Enrique (Salamanca, Spain, 1969): 285
2008, *The Curatordeus*: *284*, 285
Marville, Charles (Paris, 1816–1879): 335
Marx, K.: 275
Theorien Uber den Mehrwert (Concepts of Surplus value): 275
Matta-Clark, Gordon (New York, 1943–1978): 35, 232
Mattes, Eva (Brescia, 1976) and Franco (Brescia, 1976) / 0100101110101101.ORG: 366, 386, 387, 388, 389
1998–1999, *Darko Maver* (character invented): 386
1998–1999, *Hybrids*: 386
1999, *Copies*: 386
2000–2003, *Life Sharing*: 386
2001–2003, *Perpetual Self Dis/Infecting Machine*: *387*
2001, *Biennale.py* (computer virus): 386
2002, *Vopos*: 386
2003–2004, *Nike Ground – Project for the fake Nike Monument in Karlsplatz*: *386*, 389
2004, *United We Stand*: 389
2006–2008, "*avatar portraits*": 389
2007, *Synthetic Performance in Second Life*: *388*
2007, Serie *Synthetic Performances*: 389
2008, *MMMM*: *389*
Maurice E. and Martha Müller Foundation: 164
McCain, J.: 74
McCarthy, Paul (Salt Lake City, Utah, 1945): 40
1991, *Bossy Burger*: 40
1992, *Heidi* (with Mike Kelley): 40
McLuhan, M.: 360, 361, 369n
McQueen, Steve (London, 1969): 30, 31, 390, 391
1993, *Bear*: 390
1997, *Deadpan*: 390, *391*
1997, *Gravesend / Unexploded (Handheld)*: 390
1997, *Running Thunder*: 390
1998, *Drumroll*: 390
2002, *Once Upon a Time*: *31*, 390
2004, *Charlotte*: *390*
2008, *The Hunger*: 390
Meatyard, Ralph Eugene (Normal, Illinois, 1925 – Lexington, Kentucky, 1972): 333
Medeiros, M. de: 34
Media Art: 362
Medina, C.: 289, 291n
Mehretu, Julie (Addis Abeba, Ethiopia, 1970): 62, 63
2002, *Renegade Delirium*: *62*
2006, *Grey Space (Distractor)*: *63*
Meier-Graefe, J.: 405
Meier, R.: 299n
Mekas, J.: 86
Melani, A.: 406
Melbourne Biennial: 288
Mendieta, Ana (Havana, 1948 – New York, 1985): 87, 316
1976, *Siluetas*: 87
1977, *Tree of Life*: 87
Mendini, Alessandro (Milan, 1931): 223
Mercer, K.: 212
1994, *Welcome to the Jungle: New Positions in Cultural Studies* (essay): 212
Mercosur Biennal, Puerto Alegre (Brazil): 288, 291n
Merino, Eugenio (Madrid, 1975): 275
2009, *4 the Love of Go(l)d*: 275, *274*

Merz, Mario (Milan, 1925 – Turin, 2003): 222
Metaphysical Art: 200
Mies van der Rohe, Ludwig (Aachen, 1886 – Chicago, 1969): 230, 356
Migliora, Marzia (Alessandria, 1972): 16, 20, 21
2007, *Bianca e il suo contrario / Bianca and her Opposite*: *20*
2007, *Bianca e il suo contrario / Bianca and her Opposite*: *21*
Migros: 299n
Mikhailov, Boris (Kharkov, Ukraine, 1938): 334
Milan Triennale: 217
Millennium Bug: 386
Minimalism/ists/Minimal Art: 30, 31, 110, 136, 144, 204, 250, 293, 328, 354, 362, 392, 408
MIT Media Lab: 365
Mitchell, Joan (Chicago, 1925 – Paris, 1992): 85
Modern Movement: 217
Modernism: 35, 217, 278, 280, 304, 356, 369n, 406
Moholy-Nagy, László (Bácsborsód, 1895 – Chicago, 1946): 407
Mondrian, Piet (Amersfoort, Utrecht, 1872 – New York, 1944): 407
Monet, Claude (Paris, 1840 – Giverny, 1926): 166, 172
Water Lilies: 172
Montt, R.: 307
Moore, Henry (Castleford, Yorkshire, 1898 – Much Hadham, Hartfordshire, 1986): 188
Moran, J.: 14
Mori, Mariko (Tokyo, 1967): 64, 65, 88, 360
1995, *Birth of a Star 3D*: 64, *64*
1997–1998, *Pure Land*: 64, *65*
1999, *Dream Temple*: 64
2003, *Wave UFO*: 64, *64*
2003, *Oneness*: 64, *65*
2003, *Connected World*: 64
Morimura, Yasumasa (Osaka, Japan, 1951): 19, 20, 334
2007, *A Requiem; Dream of Universe, Albert 2*: *19*
Moriyama, Daido (Ikeda, Osaka, 1938): 333
Moro, Liliana (Milan, 1961): 90
Morricone, E.: 202
Morris, Robert (Kansas City, 1931): 136
Morse, S.: 60, 384
Moscow Biennale: 288
Moser, Koloman (Vienna, 1868–1918): 406
Mosquera, G.: 286, 291n
Mueck, Ron (Melbourne, 1958): 192, 193
1996–1997, *Dead Dad*: 192
1999, *Seated Woman*, Forth Worth, Modern Art Museum of Forth Worth: *193*
2001, *Boy*: 192
2003, *Head of a Baby*, Ottawa, The National Gallery of Canada: *192*
Muehl, Otto (Grodnau, Austria, 1925): 83
Multimedia Art: 362
Multiplicity (investigations agency): 217, 225, 310
Munch, Edvard (Löten, 1863 – Oslo, 1944): 406
Münter, Gabriele (Berlin, 1877–1962): 85
Murakami, Takashi (Tokyo, 1963): 116, 117, 359, 372
1996, *727*: *116*
1996, Hiropon Factory (company): 116, 117
1997, *Miss Ko2*: 116, 117
1997, *Hiropon*: 116, 117
1998–1999, Serie *PO+KU Surrealism*: 117
1998, *Cream*: 117
1998, *My Lonesome Cowboy*: 117
1998, *Spring Liquid*: 117
1999, *Second Mission Project ko² (ga-walk type)*: 117, *117*
1999, *DOB in the Strange Forest*: 117
2000, *Kaikai*: 117
2000, *Kiki*: 117
2001, Kaikai Kiki Co., Ltd. (company): 117
2002, *Homage to Francis Bacon*: 117
2003–2004, *Tongari-kun*: 117
2003, *Superflat Monogram* (image campaign): 116, 117
2004, *Inochi*: 117
2007, *That I May Time Transcend, that a Universe My Heart May Unfold*: *117*
2007, *Oval Buddha*: 117
Mr. DOB (character): 116, 117

N

Nabis: 406
National Exhibition of Industry, Tokyo (1877): 166
Nauman, Bruce (Fort Wayne, Indiana, 1941): 66, 84, 96, 272
1967, *From Hand to Mouth*, Washington, D.C., Hirshhorn Museum and Sculpture Garden: *84*
Ndalianis, A.: 281
2004, *Neo-Baroque Aesthetics and Contemporary Entertainment* (essay): 281
Negroponte, N.: 359, 368n
Neo-biennalism: 275, 277, 279, 281, 282, 283, 285, 286, 287, 289, 290, 291
Neo-fairism: 275, 277, 279, 281, 282, 283, 285, 287, 289, 290, 291
Neo-modernity: 275, 278, 280, 281, 286, 290
Neshat, Shirin (Qazvin, Iran, 1957): 16, 22, 320, 321, 322, 323, 335
2001, *Passage*, New York, Solomon R. Guggenheim Museum: 320, *322–323*
2003, *The Last Word*: 320, *320*
2004, *Women Without Men (Untitled #1)*: 320, *321*
2008, *Munis & Revolutionary Man*: *321*
Net Art: 386
Neto, Ernesto (Rio de Janeiro, 1964): 118, 119
2001, *Walking in Venus Blue Cave*: 118, *118*, 119
2001, *Ô bicho!*: 118,
2008, *While Nothing Happens*: 118, *119*
New Age: 64
New Media Art: 359, 362, 363, 364, 365, 366, 367, 368, 369n
New School of Leipzig: 214
Newhall, N. and B.: 298
Newman, Barnett (New York, 1905–1970): 82
Nicolai, Carsten (Karl-Marx-Stadt, Germany, 1965): 362, 365, 392, 393
1997, ∞: 392
1998, *Bausatz noto ∞*: 392, *392*
2000, *Frozen Water*: 392
2000, *Milch*: 392
2000, *Telefunken*: 392
2001–2003, *Wellenwanne*: *365*
2002, *Snow Noise*: 392
2004, *Anti*: 392, *393*
2004, *Reflex*: 392
Niedermair, Brigitte (Merano, 1971): 27
2008, *Let's Get Married*: *27*
Niedermayr, Walter (Bolzano, 1952): 335
Niemeyer, Oscar (Rio de Janeiro, 1907): 229
Nike: 389
Nintendo: 370
Nishizawa, Ryue (Tokyo, 1966): 166
Noland, Cady (Washington, D.C., 1956): 16
Norman, Nils (Kent, United Kingdom, 1966): 300, 301, 304, 308
1999, *The Gerrard Winstanley Radical Gardening Space Reclamation Mobile Field Center and Weather Station Prototype*: 308
1997, *Tompkins Square Park Monument to Civil Disobedience*: *300*, 308
2001, *Geocruiser*: 308
Noto, Alva, pseudonym of Carsten Nicolai: 392
Nouvel, Jean (Fumel, France, 1945): 154, 299n
2007, Musée du quai Branly, Paris, east view: 154, *154*
Interior view of room painted by the Australian artist Ningura Napurrula, Musée du quai Branly, Paris: 155, *155*
Nouvelle Vague: 390
Nunzio, pseudonym of Nunzio Di Stefano (Cagnano Amiterno, L'Aquila, 1954): 66, 67
1999–2003, *Rovescio (Combustione)*: 66
2003, *Senza titolo*, Unicredit Group Collection: 66, *66*
2006, *Teorema*, Unicredit Group Collection: 66, *67*

O

O'Grady, G.: 96
O'Keeffe, Georgia (Sun Prairie, Wisconsin, 1887 – Santa Fe, New Mexico, 1986): 85
Obama, B.: 74, 81, 280, 281
Obrist, H.U.: 27n, 38, 219, 238, 275
2007, *Postman Time* (Theater production/exhibition with Philippe Parreno): 38
2003, *Interviews (1st volume)*: 219
Obrist, Hermann (Kilchberg, 1862 – Munich, 1927): 406
Oda Projesi (collective founded in Istanbul in 2000 by Özge Açıkkol, Güneş Savaş and Seçil Yersel): 310
Ohanian, Melik (Lyon, 1969): 41
Oiticica, Hélio (Rio de Janeiro, 1937–1980): 35, 87
Ojetti, U.: 406
Olde Wolbers, Saskia (Breda, Netherlands, 1971): 90
Oldenburg, Claes (Stockholm, 1929): 188, 194
Ono, Yoko (Tokyo, 1933): 86
1961, *A Grapefruit* (with David Tudor): 86
1965, *Cut Piece*, performance at Carnegie Recital Hall, New York: 86, *86*

Ontani, Luigi (Grizzana Morandi, Bologna, 1943): 83, 409
2003, *Canopo Galileo ChiniLei*: 409
Op Art: 144
OpenOffice, architecture studio: 158
Opie, Catherine (Sandusky, Ohio, 1961): 91
2004, *Self-Portrait / Nursing*: 91
Opie, Julian (London, 1958): 194, 195
1983, *Making It*: 194
2000, *Radio Wind Tyres* (from Serie *Eight Landscapes*), London, Tate Modern: 194, *194*
2000, Serie *Eight Landscapes*: 194
2002, *Escaped Animals*, London, Tate Modern: 194, *195*
Oppenheim, Meret (Berlin, 1913 – Basel, 1985): 85, 87
Orozco, Gabriel (Jalapa, Mexico, 1962): 35, 196, 197
1992, *Extension of Reflexion*: 196
1992, *Yielding Stone*: 35
1993, *From Roof to Roof*: 196
1993, *Home Run*: 196
1993, *La DS*: 196
1993, *Pinched Ball*: 196
1997, *Black Kites*, London, White Cube: 196, *196*
2003, *Shade Between Rings of Air*: 196
2005, *Kytes Tree*, New York, The Museum of Modern Art: *197*
2006, *Dark Waves*: 196
2006, Serie *Samurai Tree*: 196
Lucy + Jorge Orta, collective pseudonym of Lucy Sutton (Coldfield, United Kingdom, 1966) and Jorge Orta (Rosario, Argentina, 1953): 264, 265
1991, Studio-Orta (the first studio opened): 264
1992–1998, *Refuge Wear*: 264
1994–1998, *Body Architecture*: 264
1994–2002, *Nexus Architecture*: 264
1997–2002, *HortiRecycling*: 264
2001, *Connector Mobile Village I+II*: *264*
2002, *The Dairy* (studio): 264
2005, *OrtaWater*: 264
2007, *Fallujah – M.I.U.*: *265*
2007–2008, *Antarctica*: 264
Otaku (japanese word to mean *manga* or *anime* fan): 116

P
Paci, Adrian (Shkoder, Albania, 1969): 17, 22, 95, 120, 121
2001, *Back Home*: 120, *121*
2004, *Turn on*: *17*
2007, *Centro di Permanenza Temporanea*: 120, *120*
Pacino, A.: 382
Paik, Nam June (Seoul, South Korea, 1932 – Miami, 2006): 142, 362, 367, 370
1964, *Zen For Film*: 370
1967, *McLuhan Caged*: 367
PaineWebber: 299n
Paladino, Domenico, namely Mimmo (Paduli, Benevento, 1948): 223
Pan, magazine: 405
Pane, Gina (Biarritz, 1939 – Paris, 1990): 88
Panofsky, E.: 145
Paolini, Giulio (Genoa, 1940): 333
Papadimitriou, Maria (Athens, 1957): 92
Pape, Lygia (Nova Friburgo, Rio de Janeiro, 1927–2004): 87
Paper Rad, collective founded by Jacob Ciocci (Lexington, Kentucky, 1977), Jessica Ciocci (Lexington, Kentucky, 1976) and Benjamin Jones (Pittsburgh, Pennsylvania, 1977): 370
Pardo, Jorge (Havana, 1963): 202, 266, 267
1996, *Halley's, Ikeya – Seki, Encke's*: *267*
1998, *4166 Sea View Lane*: 266
2000, *Project*: *266*
Park Fiction (collective of artists and musicians founded in Hamburg in 1994): 301, 302, 303, 304, 305, 306
1996, *Wunscharchiv* (Wish Archives): 303, 304
2005, *Kickboxers a St. Pauli*: *302*
Parks, G.: 333
1971, *Shaft* (film): 333
Parreno, Philippe (Oran, Algeria, 1964): 31, 34, 35, 37, 38, 39, 41, 382, 394, 395
1996, *Anna Sanders Magazine* (with Pierre Huyghe): 41
1997, *Ou*: 37
1999–2003, *No Ghost, Just a Shell* (with Pierre Huyghe): 394
2001, *El Sueño de una cosa*: 394, *395*
2006, *Zidane: un portrait du XXIe siècle* (with Douglas Gordon), New York, Solomon R. Guggenheim Museum: 394, *394*
2007, *Postman Time* (Theater production/exhibition with Hans Ulrich Obrist): 38
Parsipur, S.: 320
1990, *Women Without Men* (novel): 320
Pasolini, P.P.: 74
1965, *Comizi d'amore* (documentary): 74
1975, *Le 120 giornate di Sodoma* (120 Days of Sodoma), film: 72
Paul, Bruno (Seifhennersdorf, 1874 – Berlin, 1968): 407
Pavese, C.: 138, 229
Penone, Giuseppe (Garessio, Cuneo, 1947): *11*
Perec, G.: 98
Perrault, C.: 354
1697, *Little Red Riding Hood*: 354
1697, *Sleeping Beauty*: 90, 354
Perrin, Philippe (La Tronche, France, 1964): 38
Perrotin, E.: 174, 176, 177, 178
Pesch, M.: 202
Petri, E.: 58
Petri, J.R.: 384
Peyton-Jones, J.: 275
Peyton, Elizabeth (Danbury, Connecticut, 1965): 96, 141
Philip Morris: 293
Phillips, Richard (Marblehead, Massachusetts, 1962): 41
Piano, Renzo (Genoa, 1934): 153, 163, 164, 165
1971–1977, Centre national d'art et de culture Georges Pompidou (with Richard Rogers): 153, 154
1992–1997, Fondazione Beyeler, Riehen (Basel): 164
1999–2005, Zentrum Paul Klee, Berne: 164, 165
Exterior view of Zentrum Paul Klee, Berne: *163*
Plans of Zentrum Paul Klee, Berne: *163*
2003–2008, Eli Broad Building, Los Angeles County Museum of Art: 164
Picasso, Pablo (Málaga, 1881 – Mougins, 1973): 81, 114, 350
Piccinini, Patricia (Freetown, Sierra Leone, 1965): 91
2005, *Big Mother*: 91
Pinault, F.: 74, 398
Pine, J.B. : 282, 290n
Piper, Adrian (Harlem, New York, 1948): 87, 303
1975, *Light my Fire Sweetie?*: 87
Pirandello, L.: 39
Piranesi, Giovanni Battista (Maiano di Mestre, Venice, 1720 – Rome, 1778): 157, 214
Pirro, U.: 58
Pivi, Paola (Milan, 1971): 13, 22, 198, 199
1998, *100 Cinesi*: *13*
2003, *Senza titolo (Massimo)*, Rivoli, Castello di Rivoli – Museo d'Arte Contemporanea, Turin: 198, *198*
2003, *Senza titolo (asino)*, Rivoli, Castello di Rivoli – Museo d'Arte Contemporanea, Turin: 198, *199*
2003, *Senza titolo (zebre)*: 198
Playboy, magazine: 350
Pointillism/ists: 406
Polanski, R.: 398
Poljak, Renata (Split, Croatia, 1974): 339
2005, *Great Expectations*: 339
Polke, Sigmar (Oels, Germany, 1941): 141, 333
Pollock, Jackson (Cody, 1912 – Long Island, 1956): 39, 82, 85
Pop Art/ists: 34, 39, 40, 72, 114, 116, 144, 145, 146, 194, 293, 372, 408
Popova, Ljubov (Moscow, 1889–1924): 85
Post-Human: 30, 100
Postcolonial Art: 30, 105
Postconceptual: 98
Postminimalism: 204
Postmoderno: 35
Potrč, Marjetica (Ljubljana, Slovenia, 1953): 92, 303, 304, 308, 309
2003, *Caracas Houses Project*: 92
2003, *Dry Toilet*, Caracas, La Fila, barrio La Vega: *303*, 309
Poussin, Nicolas (Les Andelys, 1594 – Rome, 1665): 172
Preminger, O.: 378
1949, *Whirlpool* (film): 378
Prince, Richard (Panama, 1949): 122, 123, 285, 298, 334
1977–1979, *Untitled (Four Women Looking in the Same Direction)*: 122
2000, *Untitled (Cowboy)*: *122*
2001–2002, *Marlboro Man*: 298
2003, *Nurse in Love*: 122, *122*
2003, *Untitled (Publicity)*: 122, *123*
2007, *Untitled*: 284, *284*
Public Art Fund, non-profit organization: 239
Puma: 275

Q
Quaranta, D.: 369n
Queneau, R.: 98

R
R&SIE(n) + DS, architecture studio: 224
Raad, Walid (Chbanieh, Lebanon, 1967): 310
1999, *The Atlas Group* (fictitious archive): 310

Rachini, Remo (Cortona, 1954): 409, 411
2009, *Formella*, private collection: *409*
Rahm, Philippe (Pully, Switzerland, 1967): 224, 225n
Rainer, Arnulf (Baden, Austria, 1929): 96, 153
Rainer, Y.: 86
Ramos, Sandra (Havana, 1969): 287
Rancière, J.: 304
Raqs Media Collective (collective founded by Monica Narula, Jeebesh Bagchi and Shuddhabrata Sengupta in New Delhi in 1991): 310
Rauch, Neo (Leipzig, 1960): 141, 200, 201
2007, *Der Nächste Zug (The Next Move/The Next Draw)*, New York, private collection: 200, *200–201*
2007, Serie *Para*: 200
Raumlabor, collective of architects and designers: 225
Rauschenberg, Robert (Port Arthur, Texas, 1925 – Captiva Island, Florida, 2008): 82, 394
1951, *White Paintings*: 394
Ray, Charles (Chicago, 1953): 96
1990, *Yes*: 96
Reagan, R.: 278
Reas, Casey (Troy, Ohio, 1972): 364, 366, 369n
Recetas Urbanas, architecture studio: 225
Rehberger, Tobias (Esslingen, Germany, 1966): 202, 203, 302
1996, *Fragments of Their Pleasant Spaces (In My Fashionable Version)*: 202
1997, *Performance (Frame Two)*: *202*
2000, *Tom Cruise Jumping Library*: *202*
2006, *Gu Mo Ni Ma Da*: 202, *203*
2006, *Seven Naked Hermann Hesse Fans*: *203*
2007, *On Otto*: 202
Reine Sichtbarkeit (Pure Visibility): 405
Reinhardt, Ad (Buffalo, 1913 – New York, 1967): 143
Relational Art: 34, 187, 252, 258
Rembrandt Harmenszoon van Rijn (Leiden, 1606 – Amsterdam, 1669): 108, 149
Ressler, Oliver (Knittelfeld, Austria, 1970): 304, 310
2005, *Alternative Economics, Alternative Societies*, installation at Galería Miro Quesada Garland, Lima, Peru: *304*, 310
Rhizome.org (web site dedicated to all artistic experiences involving technology): 366
Rhizome.org homepage: *366*
Rhoades, Jason (Newcastle, California, 1965 – Los Angeles, 2006): 37
Richter, Gerhard (Dresden, 1932): 11, 141, 222
Riefenstahl, L.: 344
Riegl, A.: 405
Riemerschmid, Richard (Munich, 1868–1957): 407
Rietveld, Gerrit Thomas (Utrecht, 1888–1964): 407
1917–1918, *Red Blue Chair*: 407
Rifkin, J.: 359, 368n
Ringgold, Faith (Harlem, New York, 1930): 212
Rintala, Sami (Helsinki, 1969): 223
Rist, Pipilotti (Grabs, Switzerland, 1962): 91, 396, 397
2000, *Cinquante Fifty (Installation for a Parking Lot)*, Rivoli, Castello di Rivoli – Museo d'Arte Contemporanea: 396, *396*
2006, *À la belle étoile*, Paris, Musée national d'Art moderne – Centre Georges Pompidou : 396, *397*
2007, *Tyngdkraft, var min vän (Gravity Be My Friend)*: 396, *397*
2008, *Put Your Body Out (7354 Cubic Meters)*, New York, The Museum of Modern Art: 396, *397*
Rivera, Diego (Guanajauto, 1886 – Mexico City, 1957): 85
Robecchi, M.: 282, 290n
Rocco Flickt Rio (film): 208
Rodčenko, Aleksandr (Saint Petersburg, 1891 – Moscow, 1956): 338
Rogers, Richard (Florence, 1933): 153
1971–1977, Centre national d'art et de culture Georges Pompidou (with Renzo Piano): 153, 154
Roller, Alfred (Brünn, 1864 – Vienna, 1935): 406
Rome Quadriennale: 184
Rosenblum, R.: 144
Rosler, Martha (Brooklyn, New York, 1943): 302
Rossetti, Dante Gabriel (London, 1828 – Birchington, 1882): 20
Rossi, Aldo (Milan, 1931–1997): 157
Rothko, Mark (Daugavpils, 1903 – New York, 1970): 299n
Rouanet, S.: 278, 290n
1987, *As razões do Iluminismo* (essay): 278, 290n
Roussel, T.: 380
Rozanova, Olga (Malenki, 1886 – Moscow, 1918): 85
Rødland, Torbjørn (Stavanger, Norway, 1970): 336
Rrose Sélavy, *alter ego* of Marcel Duchamp: 81
Rubens, Pieter Paul (Siegen, 1577 – Antwerp, 1640): 149, 172
Ruff, Thomas (Zell am Harmersbach, Germany, 1958): 334, 336, 360
Russell, K.: 72
1971, *The Devils* (film): 72

S

Saar, Betye Irene (Los Angeles, 1926): 212
Saatchi, C.: 55, 110, 192
Sage, Kay (New York, 1898–1963): 85
Saint Laurent, Y.: 275
Saint Phalle, Niki de (Neuilly-sur-Seine, Paris, 1930 – La Jolla, San Diego, 2002): 83
Sala, Anri (Tirana, 1974): 22, 38
Salcedo, Doris (Bogotá, Colombia, 1958): 94, 324, 325, 326, 327
2002, *Noviembre 6 y 7*, installation on the Court of Justice façade, Bogotá, Colombia: 324, *326*
2003, *Chairs*, installation at VIII Istanbul Bienali: *327*
2005, *Abyss*: 324, *325*
2007, *Shibboleth*: 94, 324, *324*
Salon: 283, 288, 290n
Saltz, J.: 116, 290, 291n
Samba, Chéri (Kinto–Mvuila, Congo, 1956): 94
SANAA, architecture studio of Kazuyo Sejima and Ryue Nishizawa: 166
2004, 21st Century Museum of Contemporary Art, Kanazawa (Japan): 166
Sander, A.: 336
Sands, B.: 390
Sanguineti, E.: 22
Sans, J.: 264, 275
Santaella, L.: 278, 290n
Saraceno, Tomas (San Miguel de Tucumán, Argentina, 1973): 268, 269
2006, *Air-Port-City*: 268
2007, *Biosphere MW32 Air-Port-City*: *269*
2008, *Cloudy Dunes*, installation at Fondazione Edoardo Garrone, Genoa: 268, *268*
Biospheres: 268
Saramago, J.: 105
Sargsyan, Azat (Yerevan, Armenia, 1965): 285
2008, *Welcome to Armenia, the Museum under the Heaven*: 285, *285*
Sarkissian, Hrair (Damascus, Syria, 1973): 339
2006, Serie *InBetween*: 339
Sartre, J.-P.: 42, 82
Sassen, S.: 95, 97n
Sassolino, Arcangelo (Vicenza, 1967): 270, 271
2008, *Afasia I*: 270, *271*
2008, *Afasia II*: 270, *270*
Satie, E.: 14
Satoh, T.: 166
Scanlan, Joe (BirthStoutsville, Ohio, 1961): 41
Scarpa, Carlo (Venice, 1906 – Sendai, Japan, 1978): 155, 157, 196
1957–1964/1974, restoration of Museo di Castelvecchio, Verona: 155
Scarpella, Livio (Ghedi, Brescia, 1969): 409, 410, 411
2006, *Shunga*: 410
2007, *Baby Fauno Reliquiary*, private collection: *410*
2007, *Baby Reliquiary n. 3*, private collection: *410*
2007, *Gas*: 410
2008, *Senzasangue A*, private collection: 410, *411*
Scatter (random composition): 37
Schiele, Egon (Tulln an der Donau, Austria, 1890 – Vienna, 1918): 83
Schindler, Rudolf M. (Vienna, 1887 – Los Angeles, 1953): 132
Schipper, E.: 34
Schmarsow, A.: 405
Schmidlin, Paolo (Milan, 1964): 410
2002, *Eliza-Bette*, private collection: 410, *410*
2009, *Miss Kitty*: 410
Schnabel, Julian (New York, 1951): 142
Schneemann, Carolee (Fox Chase, Pennsylvania, 1939): 83, 84, 87, 97n
1963, *Eye Body*: 87
1964, *Meat Joy*: 87
1975, *Interior Scroll*: 87
Schneider, Gregor (Rheydt, Germany, 1969): 204, 205, 206, 207
1985–1997, *Haus Ur*: 204
1985–2001, *Totes Haus Ur*, installation at German Pavilion, Venice Biennale, 2001: 204, *205*
2005, *Cube Hamburg*, installation at Hamburger Kunsthalle, Hamburg, 2007: 204, *206*

2008, *Washing Room (Entrance)*, installation *Süßer Duft* at the Galerie La Maison Rouge, Paris, 2008: *207*
2008, *Süßer Duft*: 204
Schnitzler, A.: 83, 333
Schuster, A.: 380
Schuster, Michael (Graz, Austria, 1956): 335
1989, *Alle haben Alles gesehen* (with Hartmut Skerbisch): 335
Schwabsky, B.: 286
Schwarzkogler, Rudolf (Vienna, 1940–1969): 83
Schweger & Partner: 367
2000, ZKM – Zentrum fur Kunst und Medientechnologie: *367*
Schwitters, Kurt (Hannover, 1887 – Ambleside, 1948): 252
Scorsese, M.: 376
1976, *Taxi Driver* (film): 376
Scott, Giles Gilbert Sir (London, 1880–1960): 159
Searle, Bernie (Cape Town, South Africa, 1964): 94
2001, *Snow White*: 94
Secessionism/ists: 405,406
Second Life (virtual three-dimensional world launched on 2003, residents users can partecipate, create and trade virtual property and services): 338, 366, 372, 389
Segantini, Giovanni (Arco, Trento, 1858 – sullo Schafberg, Engadin, 1899): 406
Segura, Jesús (Cuenca, Spain, 1967): 283
2008, *Reading Zizej for 1 minute*: *283*
Sehgal, Tino (London, 1976): 38, 39, 41
2002, *This Is Propaganda*: 39
Those Thoughts: 39
Sejima, Kazuyo (Ibaraki, Japan, 1956): 166, 224
Sekula, Allan (Erie, Pensylvania, 1951): 302
Semionaut: 29
Semper, Ene-Liis (Tallinn, Estonia, 1969): 338, 341
2000, *Stairs*: 341, *340*
Serra, Richard (San Francisco, 1939): 223
Seurat, Georges (Paris, 1859–1891): 406
Shanghai Biennale: 288, 291n
Sharjah Biennial, United Arab Emirates: 291n
Sher-Gil, A.: 339, 341
Sherman, Cindy (Glen Ridge, New Jersey, 1954): 16, 141, 333, 334, 367
Shi Xinning (Liaoning, China, 1969): 18
Shibli, Ahlam (Palestine, 1970): 339
Shimabuku (Kobe, Japan, 1969): 42
2000, *Cucumber Journey*: 42
Shōjo bunka (girls culture): 88
Shōjo manga (cartoons for girls aged 10 to 18): 88
Shonibare, Yinka (London, 1962): 95, 124, 125
2001, *The Swing (after Fragonard)*: 124, *124*
2006, *How To Blow up Two Heads at Once*, installation at Venice Biennale, 2007: 124, *124–125*
Shulgin, Alexei (Moscow, 1963) *see* Electoboutique
Sidibé, Malik (Soloba, Mali, 1935/1936): 334, 339
Sierra, Gabriel (San Juan Nepomuceno, Colombia, 1975): 289
2008, *In Living Contact*: *289*
Sierra, Santiago (Madrid, 1966): 16, 22, 25, 27n, 36, 41, 276, 302, 328, 329
1999, *Congregation of Illegal Workers*: 328
1999, *250 cm Line Tattooed on Six Paid Persons*, performance at Espacio Aglutinador, Havana, Cuba: *16*
2000, *10 People Paid to Masturbate*: 328
2000, *68 People Paid to Block a Museum Entrance*: *36*
2000, *Línea de 160 cm tatuada sobre 4 personas*: 41
2000, *One People Paid to Spend 360 Consecutive Hours*: 41
2003, *Wall Enclosing a Space*: 276, *276*
2004, *Polyurethane Sprayed on the Backs of 10 Workers*, performance at Lisson Gallery, London: *329*
2005, *House in Mud*, installation at Kestnergesellschaft, Hannover: *328*
SIGGRAPH: 362
Silvestrin, C.: 299n
Singh, Dayanita (New Delhi, 1961): 339
Singh, Raghubir (Jaipur, India, 1942 – New York, 1999): 339
Situationism/ists: 226
Skerbisch, Hartmut (Ramsau am Dachstein, Germany, 1945): 335
1989, *Alle haben Alles gesehen* (with Michael Schuster): 335
Slominski, Andreas (Meppen, Germany, 1959): 126, 127
1984–1985, *Falle*: 127
1998–1999, *Vogelfangstation* (Bird Trapping Station), New York, Solomon R. Guggenheim Museum: *126–127*, 127
2001–2002, *Trap for Fighting Dogs*: 127
2001, *Van for Mice*: 127
2002, *Double Bass for Mice*: 127
2003, *Sein Leben wegwerfen* (*Throwing Your Life Away*): 127
Smith, Kiki (Nuremberg, Germany, 1954): 14, 16, 90, 354, 355
2001, *Born*: *14*
2004, *Sleeping Woman with Standing Wolf*, Rovereto, Mart – Museo d'Arte Moderna e Contemporanea di Trento e Rovereto, deposit ARLeS: 354, *355*
2005, *Homespun Tales: A Tale of Domestic Occupation*, installation at Fondazione Querini Stampalia, Venice: 354, *354*
2007, *Squatting the Palace* (short film made with Vivien Bittencourt and Vincent Katz): 354
Smith, Tony (South Orange, New Jersey 1912 – New York, 1980): 354
Smithson, Robert (Passaic, New Jersey 1938 – Amarillo, Texas, 1973): 91, 182
1970, *Spiral Jetty*: 91
Software Art: 366
Sohn, H.: 287
Solakov, Nedko (Cherven Briag, Bulgaria 1957): 208, 209
1998–2001, *A Life (Black & White)*, performance at Venice Biennale, 2001: 208, *209*
1989–1990, *Top Secret*: 208
2007, *I Love Them*, installation at the Galleria Continua, San Gimignano, 2007: 208, *208–209*
2007, *Discussion (Property)*: 208
2007, *Fears*: 208
Solomon R. Guggenheim Foundation: 299n
Somers Cocks, A.: 286, 291n
2007, *Venice Biennale proposes becoming a selling show again* (article): 286
Song Yongping (Shanxi, 1961): 19
Sontag, S.: 87
1978, *Illness as a Metaphor* (essay): 87
Sony: 34
Sotheby's, auction hause: 226, 296, 298, 299n
Spalletti, Ettore (Cappelle sul Tavo, 1940): 174
Spector, N.: 174, 344
Speer, A.: 210
Stalin: 20
Stalker, collective: 225
Stallabrass, J.: 277, 290n, 368n
Staller, I.: 114
Starkey, Hannah (Belfast, 1971): 336
Starling, Simon (Epsom, United Kingdom, 1967): 42, 128, 129
2002, *FLAGA (1972–2000)*: 42, *128*, 129
2004, *Tabernas Desert Run*: 42, 129, *129*
Stein, G.: 81
Stepanova, Varvara (Kovno, Lithuania, 1894 – Moscow, 1958): 85
Stern, Eddo (Tel Aviv, 1972): 362
2007, *Double Evil*: *362*
Stiegler, B.: 304
Stieglitz, Alfred (Hoboken, New Jersey 1864 – New York, 1946): 85, 333
Stokker, Lily van der (Den Bosch, Netherlands, 1954): 96
Stone, S.: 74
Storr, R.: 282, 288, 290n
Street Art/ists: 226
Struth, Thomas (Niederrhein, Germany, 1954): 334
Subotnick, A.: 176, 177
Sugimoto, Hiroshi (Tokyo, 1948): 334
Sundaram, Vivan (Simla, India, 1943): 339
Superflex, collective founded in 1993 by Jakob Fenger (Copenhagen, 1968), Bjørnstjerne Reuter Christiansen (Copenhagen, 1969) and Rasmus Nielsen (Copenhagen, 1969): 301, 304, 308
1996–1997, *Biogas*: 301
2000, *Superchannel*: 308
Surrealism/ists: 85, 145, 198, 200
Sussman, Eve (London, 1961): 281
2004, *89 seconds at Alcázar*: 281
Svevo, I.: 318
1923, *La coscienza di Zeno* (novel): 318
Swanson, G.: 21
Sweeney, J.J.: 151
Symbiotica: 365
Symbolism/ists: 406
Syndicat Potentiel (collective founded in Strasbourg in 1992): 311
Szeemann, H.: 17, 18, 287, 290n, 299n

T

Time-Life, magazine: 122
Tanaka, Atsuko (Osaka, 1932 – Nara, 2005): 85
Tanavoli, Parviz (Teheran, Iran, 1937): 296
Tanguy, Yves (Paris, 1900 – Woodbury, Connecticut, 1955): 85
Taniguchi, Yoshio (Tokyo, 1937): 151
2004, Sculpture Garden with the new

exhibition building in the background to the west, New York, Museum of Modern Art: *150*
Tanning, Dorothea (Galesburg, Illinois, 1910): 85
Tàpies, Antoni (Barcelona, 1923): 82
Tate Gallery: 159
Tati, J.: 40
Täuber-Arp, Sophie (Davos, 1889 – Zurich, 1943): 85
Taylor-Wood, Sam (London, 1967): 130, 131
1995–1997, *Five Revolutionary seconds*: 130
1998, *Soliloquy*: 130
2004–2005, Serie *Bram Stoker's Chair*: 130
2004–2005, *Self-Portrait Suspended*: 130
2005, *Bram Stoker's Chair VII*: 130, *130*
2008, *Ghosts X*: *131*
2008, Serie *Ghosts*: 130
Tayou, Pascale Marthine (Yaoundé, Cameroon, 1967): 37
Tessenow, Heinrich (Rostock, 1876 – Berlin, 1950): 407
Tetris: 370
Thatcher, M.: 278
The Armory Show, New York, 1913: 285
The Art Newspaper, magazine: 286, 291n
The Big Lebowski, film (Joel and Ethan Coel, 1998): 208
The Lion Seeps Tonight (song, 1961): 374
The Lord of the Rings, novel: 386
The Seven Samurai, film (Akira Kurosawa, 1954): 208
The Studio, magazine: 406
Theis, Bert (Luxembourg, 1952): 306, 307
2002, OUT (Office for Urban Transformation): 306
The Tissue Culture & Art Project (collective founded in 1996 by Oron Catts and Ionat Zurr): 359
2004, *Victimless Leather – A Prototype of Stitch-less Jacket grown in a Technoscientific "Body"*: *358*
Thorsteinn, Einar (Reykjavik, 1942): 239
Thovez, Enrico (Turin, 1869–1925): 406
Tiepolo, Giambattista (Venice, 1696 – Madrid, 1770): 172, 350
Tillmans, Wolfgang (Remscheid, Germany, 1968): 37, 68, 69, 70, 71, 336
2000, *Irm Hermann*, New York, Solomon R. Guggenheim Museum: *70*
2004, *Anders Pulling Splinter from His Foot*: *68*
2004, *Freischwimmer 40*: *71*
2005, *Truth Study Center*: 68
2006, *Paper Drop (Window)*: *69*
Serie, *Freischwimmer*: 68
Serie *Paper Drop*: 68
Tiqqun, collective: 88, 97n
Tiravanija, Rirkrit (Buenos Aires, 1961): 30, 34, 35, 38, 39, 41, 132, 133, 134, 135, 202, 302, 382, 394
1993, *Live and Eat, Eat and Die*: 132
2002, *Untitled 2002 (He Promised)*, New York, Solomon R. Guggenheim Museum: 132, *132*
2005, *Untitled*: 132, *133*
2005, *Teahouse*: 132, *134–135*
2008, *Foster, You're Dead*: 133, *135*
Tiryakian, E.: 278, 280, 290n
1991, *Modernization: Exhumetur in pace* (magazine article): 280, 290n
Tiziano, Vecellio (Pieve di Cadore, Belluno, 1480/1490 – Venice, 1576): 149
Tolle, E.: 281
Tomatsu, Shomei (Nagoya, Japan, 1930): 333
Tomic' Milica (Belgrade, 1960): 339
1997, *xy ungelost – the reconstruction of the crime*: 339
Tomkins, C.: 114
Torolab, artistic collective: 225
Touraine, A.: 301
Tracey, D.: 336
Turin Triennale of Contemporary Art: 324
Turin Triennale: 380
Trockel, Rosemarie (Schwerte, Germany, 1952): 136, 137
1980s, *Strickbilder* (Knitted Pictures): 136
1992, *The Mistery of Malpica*: 136, *136*
1993, *Parade*: 136
2000, *Untitled*: 136, *137*
2001, *Atlas*, Minneapolis, Walker Art Center: 136, *137*
Troncy, É.: 39
Truffaut, F.: 74
1962, *Jules et Jim* (film): 74
Tucumán Arde (avant-garde group founded in Argentina in 1968): 307
Tudor, David (Philadelphia, 1926 – New York, 1996): 86
1961, *A Grapefruit* (with Yoko Ono): 86
Turner Prize: 48, 52, 55, 100, 124, 129, 187, 272, 390
Turrell, James (Los Angeles, 1943): 96, 166, 222, 223, 224, 225n
Since 1974, Roden Crater Project: 223
2009, *Alpha Tunnel*, Roden Crater, Painted Desert, Arizona: *223*
2009, South-west view of the Roden Crater, Painted Desert, Arizona: 222, *222*
Tuymans, Luc (Mortsel, Belgium, 1958): 210, 211
1986, *Gaskammer*: 210
1991, *De Wandeling* (The Walk), Tervuren, private collection: 210, *211*
2000, *Mwana Kitoko – Beautiful White Man*: 210
2001, *Prisoners of War*: 210
2006, *Imperméable*, private collection: *210*
Twin Towers: 352
Tykkä, Salla (Helsinki, 1973): 336

U

Ubermorgen.com, artistic duo founded in Vienna in 1999 by Lizvlx and Hans Bernhard: 364
2000, *Vote-Auction*: 369n
2004, *The Agency for Manual Election Recount*: 361, *361*
Uklanski, Piotr (Warsaw, 1968): 398, 399, 400, 401
1996, *Untitled (Dance Floor)*, New York, Gagosian Gallery: 398, *399*
1996-in progress, *The Joy of Photography*: 398
1997, *Untitled (Island)*: 398
1998, Serie *The Nazis*: 398
2000, *Untitled (Skull)*: 398
2000, *Untitled (Vesuvio)*: 398
2004, *Untitled (Ioannes Paulus PP.II Karol Wojtyla)*, New York, Gagosian Gallery: 398, *400*
2005, *Untitled (Orla)*, Milan, Galleria Massimo De Carlo: *398*
2006, *Summer Love* (film): 398
2007, *Untitled (Bloody Sunday)*, Milan, Galleria Massimo De Carlo: *401*
Serie *Dance Floors*: 398
Ulay, pseudonym of Frank Uwe Laysiepen (Solingen, Germany, 1943): 88
Ultra-red (collective of artists and musicians founded in Los Angeles in 1994): 307
UniCredit Group: 299n
Université Tangente (collective founded in Strasbourg in 2001): 310, 311

V

V2_Institute for the Unstable Media, Rotterdam: 362
Vaisman, Meyer (Caracas, Venezuela, 1960): 39
Valencia Biennial: 288
Valeri, F.: 21
Van Beirendonck, W.: 202
Van Bruggen, Coosje (Groningen, Netherlands, 1942 – Los Angeles, 2009): 188
Van de Velde, Henry (Antwerp, 1863 – Ober-Ageri, Switzerland, 1957): 406, 407
Van Doesburg, Theo (Utrecht, 1883 – Davos, 1931): 407
Van Gogh, Vincent (Groot Zundert, 1853 – Auvers-sur-Oise, 1890): 406
Van Lieshout, Joep (Ravenstein, Netherlands, 1963): 314
Vaney, A.-L.: 41
Varèse, E.: 394
Vascellari, Nico (Vittorio Veneto, Treviso, 1976): 402, 403
2007, *Revenge*: 402, *402*
2008, *Hymn*, private collection: 402, *403*
Vasulka, Steina, pseudonym of Steinunn Briem Bjarnadottir (Reykjavik, Iceland, 1940): 362
Vasulka, Woody, pseudonym of Bohuslav Peter Vasulka (Brno, Czech Republic, 1937): 362
Velázquez, Diego Rodríguez de Silva y (Seville, 1599 – Madrid, 1660): 172, 281
1656, *Las Meninas*: 281
Venice Architecture Biennale: 217, 220
Venice Biennale: 18, 34, 40, 44, 50, 57, 58, 60, 74, 88, 91, 93, 94, 95, 105, 114, 122, 124, 169, 174, 176, 192, 196, 198, 204, 208, 239, 246, 283, 285, 286, 288, 291, 316, 328, 330, 334, 342, 362, 369n, 372, 383, 386, 402
Ver Sacrum, magazine: 405
Vereinigte Werkstätten, association: 405
Vermeer, Jan (Delft, 1632–1675): 108
Verne, J.: 382
1864, *Journey to the Center of the Earth* (novel): 382
Veronese, Paolo Caliari namely (Verona, 1528 – Venice, 1588): 22
Vezzoli, Francesco (Brescia, 1971): 21, 22, 72, 73, 74, 75, 409
2001, *Self-portrait with Vera*, Verona, Galleria d'Arte Moderna Palazzo Forti, collezione AGI: *73*

2002, *Jean Cocteau Embroidered Tears on the Mask of Berenice*, private collection: *23*
2003, *Omaggi a Fortunato Depero*: 409
2004, *Comizi di Non Amore*: 74, *75*
2005, *La fine di Canterbury*: *72*
2005, *Trailer for a Remake of Gore Vidal's 'Caligula'*, Rivoli, Castello di Rivoli – Museo d'Arte Contemporanea: 72, *74*
2006, *Marlene Redux: A True Hollywood Story*, Venice, François Pinault Collection: 74, *74–75*
2007, *Democrazy*, Unicredit Group Collection: *73*, 74
Vidal, G.: 72, 74
Videla Redondo, J.R.: 264
Videoarte/isti/Video Art: 20, 344, 361, 362, 367, 369n, 396
Viel, Cesare (Chivasso, Turin, 1964): 138, 139
1990, *Noi gestiamo il disordine quotidiano del pensiero*: 138
1992, *Scrivi la tua frase sulla molteplicità*: 138
1994, *Viaggiatori/Viaggiatrici*: 138
1995, *Short Stories*: 138
1997, *Una stanza per sé*: 138
1999–2001, *Lost in Meditation*, Genoa, Sergio Bertola Collection: 138, *138*
Since 2003, *Diario contemporaneo*: 138
2004–2005, *To the Lighthouse. Cesare Viel as Virginia Woolf*: 138
2008, *Mi gioco fino in fondo*, Genoa, Galleria Pinksummer: 138, *139*
Vienna School: 405
Viennese Actionist School: 40
Viola, Bill (New York, 1951): 142, 169
Virno, P., philosopher: 303, 307
Vogue, magazine: 21
Vo, Danh (Saigon, Vietnam, 1975): 202
Vogt, Günther (Liechtenstein, 1957): 239

W
Wagner, R.: 344
1848–1874, *Der Ring des Nibelungen* (Ring Cycle): 344
Wakefield, N.: 286
Walker, Kara (Stockton, California, 1969): 92, 93, 212, 213
2007, *Authenticating the Artifact*, New York, Sikkema Jenkins & Co: *212*
2004, *Grub for Sharks: A Concession to the Negro Populace*: *213*
Wall, Jeff (Vancouver, 1946): 141, 294, 296, 298, 334, 356, 357
1994, *Insomnia*, Hamburg, Hamburger Kunsthalle: *294*
1999, *Morning Cleaning, Mies van der Rohe Foundation, Barcelona*, collection of the artist, permanent loan at Museum für Moderne Kunst, Frankfurt: 356, *356*
2003, *A Woman with a Coverei Tray*, Cologne, Johnen Schöttle: *357*
Walt Disney Company: 178, 382
Wang Guangyi (Harbin, China, 1957): 18
Wang Jianwei (Sichuan, China, 1958): 18
Wang Qingsong (Heilongjiang, China, 1966): 18
Warburg, A.M.: 14
Warhol, Andy, pseudonym of Andrew Warhola (Pittsburgh, Pennsylvania, 1928 – New York, 1987): 41, 72, 116, 144, 194, 275, 370, 390
Watteau, Jean-Antoine (Valenciennes, 1684 – Nogent-sur-Marne, 1721): 21
Weber, S.: 37
Wegman, William (Holyoke, Massachusetts, 1963): 98
Weimar Republic: 407
Weiner, Lawrence (Bronx, New York, 1942): 141, 344
Wall Printings: 141
Weischer, Matthias (Elte, Germany, 1973): 214, 215
2003, *Ohne Titel* (Untitled), Bergisch Gladbach, Germany: 214, *214*
2005, *Stellwand* (Folding Screen), private collection: 214, *215*
Weiss, (Zurich, 1946): 335
Weiss, David *see* Fischli & Weiss: 246, 248
Weizman, E.: 225
Welles, O.: 202
1947, *The Lady from Shanghai* (film): 202
Wenders, W.: 142
West, Franz (Vienna, 1947): 35
Serie *Passtücke*: 35
Weston, Edward (Highland Park, Illinois, 1886 – Carmel, California, 1958): 298
1927, *Nude*: 298
Whiteread, Rachel (London, 1963): 272, 273
1993, *Untitled (House)*: 272, *272*
1995, *Twenty-five Spaces*, Queensland Art Gallery: *273*
2000, *Holocaust Memorial*: 272
2001, *Untitled (Apartment)*, New York, Solomon R. Guggenheim Museum: 272, *273*
2005, *Embankment*: 272
Wickhoff, F.: 405
Wiener Werkstätten: 405, 406
Wilding, Faith (Paraguay, 1943): 87
1971, *Waiting*: 87
Wilke, Hannah (New York, 1940–1993): 87
Williams, Sue (Chicago, 1954): 96
Wilson, E.O.: 108
Wilson, Robert (Waco, Texas, 1941): 21
With Love, punk group: 402
Wohlert, Wilhelm (Denmark, 1920): 152
1958–2006, Louisiana Museum of Modern Art, Humlebæk (with Jørgen Bo): 152
Wojtowicz, J.: 382
Wojtyla, K.: 398
Woodman, Francesca (Denver, 1958 – New York, 1981): 16, 333
Woolf, V.: 138
World Bank (WB): 301
World Trade Organisation (WTO): 301
Wright, Frank Lloyd (Richland Center, Wisconsin, 1867 – Phoenix, Arizona, 1959): 151, 152, 153, 157, 158
1943–1959, Solomon R. Guggenheim Museum, New York: 151, 153, 158
Wunderkammer (Cabinets of Wonder): 108, 182, 288, 291, 410

X
Xhafa, Sislej (Peja, Kosovo, 1970): 22, 330, 331
1997, performance *Clandestine Albanian Pavilon*: 330
2000, *Sweet Invasion*: 330, *330*
2005, *Lapo Cipolla*: 330, *331*
Xiamen Dada: 260

Y
Yanagi, Miwa (Kobe, Japan, 1967): 88, 90, 336, 338
1994, *Kagome Kagome*: 336
2002, *Geisha (Akiyo, Mai, Hitomi, Noriko)*, Modena, Collezione di Fotografia Contemporanea della Fondazione Cassa di Risparmio di Modena: *338*
2004, Serie *Fairy Tale*: 90
Yang Fudong (Beijing, 1971): 18, 76, 77, 334, 336, 341
2001, *Robber South*, Naples, Maurizio Morra Greco Collection: 76, *76*
2005, *The Half Hitching Post*: *334*, *337*
2005, *The Revival of the Snake*, Rivoli, Castello di Rivoli – Museo d'Arte Contemporanea: 76, *76–77*
Yang Zhenzhong (Hangzhou, China, 1968): 341
2000–2005, *I Know I Will Die*: 341
Yeondoo Jung (Jinju, South Korea, 1969): 341
Yogeesh, A.: 281
Yokohama Triennial: 341
Young British Art/ists (YBA): 55, 72, 110, 174, 192
YouTube: 29, 147
Yu Youhan (Shanghai, 1943): 18
Yuskavage, Lisa (Philadelphia, 1962): 90

Z
Żmijewski, Artur (Warsaw, 1966): 338
Zaya, O.: 286
Zhang Huan (An Yang City, China, 1965): 15, 18, 19, 20, 27n, 78, 79
1997, *To Raise the Water Level In A Fish Pond*: 78, *78*
2005, *My Rome*: *15*
2007, *Berlin Buddha*, Switzerland, private collection: 78, *78–79*
Zhang Xiaogang (Kunming, China, 1958): 18
Zhu Ming (Changsha, 1972): 18
Ziakovic, D.: 380
Zidane, Z.: 394
Zittel, Andrea (Escondido, California, 1965): 92
1994, Serie *A-Z Living Units*: 92
ZKM (Zentrum für Kunst und Medientechnologie): 362, *367*
Zotta, Silvia (Buenos Aires, 1969): 408, 410
2002, *Carta urgente a Buenos Aires*: 410
2008, *Cerchi al muro ovvero Variations autour de l'ouvrage*, private collection: *408*, 411
Zuaiter, W.: 58
Zurr, Ionat (England, 1970) *see* The Tissue Culture and Art Project

Photography Credits

Archivio fotografico Mart: pp. 57, 156, 157, 158, 159, 355
© 2005 DigiModern Art, New York / Scala, Firenze: p. 150
© 2008 Photo The Philadelphia Museum of Art / Art Resource: p. 28
© 2009 Photo Scala, Firenze / BPK Bildagentur für Kunst, Kultur und Geschichte, Berlin: pp. 152, 153
Fort Worth Museum, Fort Worth (Texas): p. 192
Franco Soffiantino Arte Contemporanea, Turin, p. 106
Emily Jacir / Photo of the artist: p. 59
Photo Tadao Ando Architect & Associates: p. 162
Photo Antimodular Research: p. 61
Photo Iwan Baan: p. 221
Photo Thierry Bal: p. 265
Photo Bruno Bani: p. 135
Photo © Joséphine de Bère: p. 98
Photo Ela Bialkowska: p. 25, 331
Photo Nicolas Borel / Scala, Firenze: p. 154
Photo Polly Braden: p. 285
Photo Massimiliano Cadamuro: p. 125
Photo Gianni Caravaggio: p. 237
Photo Sergio Clavijo: p. 326
Photo Andre Cypriano: p. 303
Photo Agostino De Rosa © Università Iuav di Venezia: p. 222
Photo Marco de Scalzi: pp. 48, 170
Photo Miryam Devriendt: p. 22
Photo Francesco Di Paolo - Studio dei Barbarico: p. 409
Photo Emilio P. Doiztua: pp. 217, 221
Photo Marco Fedele di Catrano, pp. 106–107
Photo Fotostudio Rapuzzi, Brescia: pp. 410, 411
Photo Barbora Gerny, Zurigo: p. 102
Photo Hugo Glendinning: pp. 49, 103
Photo Gronchi Foto Arte, Pisa: p. 330
Photo Ilmari Kalkkinen: p. 56
Photo © Kleinefenn: p. 253
Photo George Maciunas: p. 83
© Photo Mancia / Bodmer: p. 246
Photo Jason Mandella: p. 231
Photo Attilio Maranzano: p. 13
Photo Dolores Marat / Scala, Firenze: p. 155
Photo Roberto Marossi: p. 171
Photo Andrea Martiradonna: p. 90
Photo Mitsuo Matsuoka: p. 161
Photo Matteo Monti: p. 262
Photo Gianfranco Mura: pp. 20, 21
Photo Museum für Gestaltung Zürich, Kunstgewerbesammlung / Marlen Perez ©ZHdK: p. 89
Photo Volker Naumann, Schönaich: p. 298
Photo Paul Nescio, Amsterdam: p. 283
Photo Minoru Niizuma: p. 86
© Photo Sue Ormerod: p. 272
Photo Ellen Page Wilson: pp. 100–101
Photo Giovanni Pancino: p. 58
Photo Paolo Pellion: pp. 76, 77, 198, 324, 374, 396
Photo Federico Perezzani: p. 271
Photo Massimo Piersanti: p. 235
Photo Prudence Cuming Associates Ltd: p. 113
Photo David Quintas: p. 60
Photo Pamela Radon: p. 271
Photo Antonia Reeve: pp. 376, 378
Photo Rokma: pp. 268, 269
Photo Filippo Romano: p. 221
Photo Roberto Salasso: pp. 165, 167, 228
Photo Javier San Martin: p. 276
Photo Christoph Schaefer: p. 302
Photo Paolo Sfriso: p. 72
Photo Sillani, 2005: p. 134
Photo Brian Slater: p. 397
Photo Seton Smith: p. 354
Photo Lee Stalsworth, p. 319
Photo Andrea Stappert: p. 209
Photo Tate Liverpool 2004: p. 213
Photo Tate Photography: pp. 100-101
Photo Achim Thode: p. 81
Photo Markus Tretter: p. 65
Photo University of South Florida Contemporary Art Museum, Tampa: p. 264
Photo Uwe Walter, Berlin: pp. 270, 365, 393
Photo Stephen White: p. 243
Photo Amos Zampatti: p. 223
Photo Giorgio Zucchiatti: pp. 94, 104
Photo Courtesy Mary Boone Gallery, New York: pp. 46, 47
Photo Courtesy Tommaso Mattina: p. 129
The Bridgeman Art Library / Archivi Alinari: pp. 143, 294, 295